RUGBY LEAGUE 2024-2025
Back to the future

LEAGUE
Publications Ltd

First published in Great Britain in 2024 by
League Publications Ltd, Wellington House, Briggate, Brighouse, West Yorkshire HD6 1DN

Copyright © League Publications Ltd

All rights reserved. No part of this book may be reproduced or transmitted in any form or by any means, electronic or mechanical, including photocopying, recording or by any information storage and retrieval system, without prior permission in writing from the publisher.

A CIP catalogue record for this book is available from the British Library
ISBN 978-1-901347-44-9

Designed and Typeset by League Publications Limited
Printed by TJ Books, Padstow, Cornwall

Contributing Editor
Tim Butcher

Statistics, production and design
Daniel Spencer

Contributors
Thomas Alderson
Peter Bird
Steve Brady
Sam Brocksom
Phil Caplan
Louis Chapman-Coombe
Mark Chestney
Tom Coates
Andrew Cudbertson
John Davidson
Gareth Davies
John Drake
Ian Golden
James Gordon
Michael Hale
Phil Hodgson
Steve Hossack
Stephen Ibbetson
Ellie Indie
Jake Kearnan
Emma Kennedy
David Kuzio
Christian Lee
Callum Linford
Lorraine Marsden
Paddy McAteer
Keith McGhie
Dave Parkinson
Dan Payne
Arindam Rej
Huw Richards
Ian Rigg
Martyn Sadler
Jack Sandler
Kasey Smith
Sebastian Sternik
Mark Taylor
Doug Thomson
Callum Walker
Rob Wallace
Matthew Ward
Jordan Weir
Kai Welch
Gavin Wilson
Ian Wilson
Peter Wilson

Pictures
SWPix
Dean Williams
Craig Hawkhead
NRL Imagery
Simon Hall
James Giblin
Steve Jones (RLPix)
Gareth Lyons
Darren Greenhalgh
Craig Irvine
John Victor
David Greaves
Steve Miller
Alex Boe
Ben Challis
Steve Mower
Bernard Platt
Jonny Tomes-Green
Catalans Dragons
London Broncos
Colin Bradbury
Alex Coleman
Paul Cowan
Thomas Fynn
Jackie Meredith
Dave Murgatroyd
Tom Pearson
Mal Walker

Main cover picture
SWPix

CONTENTS

Acknowledgments	5
Introduction	6

1. The 2024 Season — 9
December 2023 — 10
January — 13
February — 15
March — 22
April — 32
May — 40
June — 48
July — 56
August — 64
September — 75
October — 83
Super League awards — 87

2. Championship & League One 2024 — 89
Championship — 90
League One — 99

3. Women & Wheelchair 2024 — 107
Women — 108
Wheelchair — 116

4. Season Down Under — 121
NRL — 122
State of Origin — 133

5. International Year — 137
England v Samoa Test Series — 138
Other Internationals — 141

6. 2024 Season - In Colour — 145
Personalities of 2024 — 145
Mikey Lewis — 145
Max Jowitt — 146
Junior Nsemba — 147
Sam Burgess — 148
Matt Peet & Bevan French — 149

7. Statistical review 2024 — 161
Super League Players 1996-2024 — 163
Super League XXIX club by club — 193
Super League XXIX round by round — 218
Super League Records 1996-2024 — 234
Championship 2024 club by club — 235
Championship 2024 round by round — 250
League One 2024 club by club — 268
League One 2024 round by round — 278
Challenge Cup 2024 round by round — 288
1895 Cup 2024 round by round — 294
Women's Super League 2024 round by round — 298
Women's Challenge Cup 2024 round by round — 312
2024 Statistical round-up — 315

ACKNOWLEDGEMENTS

The *League Express Yearbook 2024-2025* is the 29th of League Publications Ltd's annual series of Rugby League Yearbooks, which began in the first year of Super League in 1996.

This historical record of the Rugby League year would not be possible without the hard work and dedication of all the contributors to *Rugby Leaguer & Rugby League Express*, *Rugby League World* magazine and the *totalrl.com* website.

We are able to include some wonderful action photography provided by, in particular SWPix, Dean Williams, Craig Hawkhead and NRL Imagery.

Thanks to the Rugby Football League for their help during the year and to the historians and statisticians at clubs who help us resolve any anomalies.

Special thanks to Neil Ormston and the Rugby League Record Keepers' club who have been an invaluable source for the crosschecking of statistics throughout the year.

Acknowledgement also to the series of Rothmans Yearbooks, compiled by our late friend Ray Fletcher, the British Rugby Records Book from London Publications and to the club officials, and some supporters, who helped us verify records.

Special thanks to Doug Thomson for the Championship round-up, to Lorraine Marsden, who wrote the League One and Women's chapters, and to Stephen Ibbetson for his record of the Wheelchair Rugby League season. Stephen also compiled the new statistical section covering the Women's Super League and Challenge Cup.

The amazing statistical review of the Men's game, put together as always with painstaking accuracy, is the work of my colleague Daniel Spencer, who also designed the book.

TIM BUTCHER
Contributing Editor

INTRODUCTION

The Rugby League year of 2024 ended satisfyingly on the first Saturday of November as England wrapped up a 2-0 series win over Samoa. Those convincing England wins certainly whetted the appetite for a home Ashes series that was anticipated for 2025.

So what will we remember from the Rugby League year of 2024, the 29th season of Super League?

The most poignant memory for many came at the start of June, with the passing of Rob Burrow at the age of 41, after his brave fight against Motor Neurone Disease. The Challenge Cup Final the following Saturday provided an emotional day at Wembley. A minute's silence in memory of Rob was observed before both the women's and men's Challenge Cup finals, while Wembley shared in a minute's applause after seven minutes in each of the four finals that day - a tribute also honoured at Twickenham on the same Saturday afternoon at the rugby union Premiership final.

Later in the month at the Rhinos' first home fixture since the death of their legendary player, a packed house was witness to one of the most moving nights in the game's history. The Leeds club paid a brilliant tribute to one of their greatest before and after the match in a wonderful event organised alongside Sky Sports, who presented and televised to the world, as well as those inside Headingley.

There was good news too. At the other side of the globe, Rugby League became the most watched TV sport in Australia, with record attendances across the board, the NRL kicking off its season with two round-one games in Las Vegas.

In the UK, Sky Sports broadcast every Super League fixture, allowing video referees at every game, while the BBC had live coverage of a selection of league games.

When it came to the domestic season, there was only one winner as Wigan swept the board. A World Club Challenge 16-12 home win over Penrith Panthers in February; an 18-8 Challenge Cup Final win over Warrington in June, and the League Leaders' Shield in mid-September. And the Super League title was also retained with a 9-2 Grand Final win over Hull Kingston Rovers.

Superstar Bevan French made history by becoming the first player to win the man of the match award in a Challenge Cup Final and Grand Final - the latter was renamed the Rob Burrow Award - in the same season. And Wigan's prolific production line continued to bear fruit with the emergence of three exciting prospects in Junior Nsemba, Zach Eckersley and Jack Farrimond.

Though Wigan took all the silverware, there were plenty of success stories across the game. Hull KR were certainly one of them. The Robins were contenders right to the end of the season, losing only six league games, with star halfback Mikey Lewis named Steve Prescott Man of Steel at the end of the year and Willie Peters the Coach of the Year. Peters' recruitment proved to be inspired and he got the best out of his squad for most of the year under the on-field leadership of captain Elliot Minchella. The response of the fans was phenomenal.

Robins winger Ryan Hall made history when he scored two tries in Hull KR's 32-6 home victory against Huddersfield Giants on Friday 14th June to become the greatest try-scorer in Super League history, with 248, one more than previous record-holder Danny McGuire.

Wigan only lost one game at home all season as Warrington Wolves, who under new

Introduction

Rob Burrow's children Jackson, Macy and Maya deliver the award named after their late father to the Old Trafford pitch before the Super League Grand Final

coach Sam Burgess were serious challengers all through the year, dominated from start to finish in a 40-4 win in late July. They were edged out in the semi-finals at Hull KR but with Burgess committed to the club until the end of the 2026 season optimism should abound at the Wolves, who in 2024 blooded some very promising youngsters themselves in Leon Hayes, Adam Holroyd and Arron Lindop.

St Helens finished in sixth place, their lowest table finish since 1994. Injuries and suspensions hit them hard but when they mustered their best in the Eliminators, only a George Williams field goal in golden-point extra time could end their season.

Leigh's season was almost a mirror image of Saints'. They got their injuries out of the way early on and just one win from their opening eight games reflected that. They badly missed key players John Asiata and Edwin Ipape but there was no panic as the Leopards re-found their feet, finishing in fifth spot, a 14 per cent rise in attendances reflecting the good feeling around the Leigh Sports Village.

Salford continued to overachieve and were probably the most entertaining team in Super League. They went into the 2024 season having seen the exit of star duo Brodie Croft and Andy Ackers to Leeds and then both wingers Ken Sio and Joe Burgess. They signed an Aussie winger in David Nofoaluma and sent him packing after two games. Then they had the instability mid-season of director of rugby Ian Blease leaving for Leeds and head coach Paul Rowley being linked to both Leeds and Hull FC. That's not forgetting the uncertainty surrounding their tenure at the Salford Community Stadium.

They still finished in fourth spot, guided by brilliant halfback Marc Sneyd and powered by centre Nene Macdonald, both of whom made the Super League Dream Team.

Runners-up in 2023 Catalans didn't make the play-offs for the first time since 2019. Loanee from Hull KR, England stand-off Jordan Abdull played only 15 league games and the Dragons never managed much midfield control without him. They had their own off-field drama in July when star prop Siua Taukeiaho, who hadn't played a game all season, stand-off Jayden Nikorima and fringe prop Damel Diakhate had their contracts terminated for skipping training to go to a pop concert.

Catalans topped the table in April but it was mostly downhill after that, prompting the comeback from retirement of Sam Tomkins.

Leeds Rhinos offloaded coach Rohan Smith as they wallowed in seventh spot in June and former Parramatta coach Brad Arthur replaced him in mid-July. He couldn't work the miracle and the Rhinos finished eighth.

Introduction

Hull FC had the season from hell, made worse for its supporters by the rise of Hull KR. Tony Smith was shown the exit door at the MKM Stadium after a 56-20 home defeat by Huddersfield in March. It was a seventh loss in eight games. But the Airlie Birds only won two more games after that, one of them at home to Champions Wigan. Besides losing the coach, the upheaval included halfback Fa'amanu Brown heading back to Australia in April, Tex Hoy signing for Castleford, and big name signings from the NRL, Franklin Pele and Jayden Okunbor finishing the season playing with Bradford in the Championship. Richie Myler' shock appointment as director of rugby hardly improved matters but the appointment of Brisbane assistant John Cartwright as head coach from 2025 gave something for the fans to look forward to. The youngsters who played alongside a plethora of loan players did the club proud. Forty-five players used over the course of the season, six more than any other Super League club. Fifty points conceded six times and 23 cards (four red and 19 yellow), the most of any side in the top-flight.

Ninth-placed Huddersfield dispensed with their coach Ian Watson in July after a 48-0 hammering at Warrington. Giants captain Luke Yates signed mid-season for the Wolves. Assistant Luke Robinson took over permanently after an interim spell that garnered four wins from 11 games.

Castleford Tigers waited until the season had finished before sacking coach Craig Lingard after a year of mostly struggles illuminated by stellar wins at St Helens and Catalans.

Which left London Broncos propping up the rest at the end of the season. Having been handed a provisional IMG grading at the end of 2023 that left them no hope of making Super League in 2025, the Broncos operated on a mixed full-time part time squad and predictably struggled. They climbed into 11th spot for one week only, on points difference, after their 12-8 round-26 defeat at Catalans. But a 54-0 last-round loss at Warrington handed them the wooden spoon. Wakefield Trinity bounced back into Super League for 2025 to replace the Broncos after winning the Championship.

By the end of the season, Super League expansion was back on the agenda after nine clubs earned Grade A status under the IMG rankings. That would depend on IMG vastly improving the next TV deal - the current contract for 2024-26 was worth just over half of the previous one.

Nothing's ever boring in our sport. It's been another compelling year of Rugby League.

TIM BUTCHER
Contributing Editor

IMG'S REIMAGINING RUGBY LEAGUE STRATEGY FOR 2025

		Score	Grade
1	St Helens	17.02	A
2	Wigan	16.91	A
3	Leeds	16.84	A
4	Warrington	16.27	A
5	Hull KR	15.97	A
6	Catalans	15.52	A
7	Leigh	15.13	A
8	Wakefield	15.09	A
9	Castleford	15.02	A
10	Hull FC	14.51	B
11	Huddersfield	14.48	B
12	Salford	13.97	B
13	Toulouse	13.58	B
14	London	12.65	B
15	York	12.42	B
16	Bradford	12.15	B
17	Barrow	11.22	B
18	Featherstone	10.75	B
19	Keighley	9.02	B
20	Halifax	8.79	B
21	Sheffield	8.77	B
22	Widnes	8.60	B
23	Doncaster	7.52	B
24	Workington	7.26	C
25	Swinton	7.15	C
26	Dewsbury	7.13	C
27	Oldham	7.00	C
28	Hunslet	6.98	C
29	Rochdale	6.47	C
30	Midlands	5.66	C
31	Cornwall	5.29	C
32	Newcastle	5.20	C
33	North Wales	4.72	C

* Batley and Whitehaven's return was incomplete by the RFL deadline.

The 29th League Express Yearbook contains the detailed story of the domestic year, the Australian season and matchfacts for all Super League, Challenge Cup games involving professional teams, Championship and League One games. Matchfacts covering the Women's Super League and Challenge Cup are also included for the first time. Every player who has played Super League is listed along with those players to have made their debuts this year. We have also selected five (six this year) individuals who we judge to have made the biggest impact on Rugby League in 2024.

League Publications publishes the weekly newspaper Rugby Leaguer & Rugby League Express, as well as the monthly glossy magazine Rugby League World and the website 'totalrl.com'.

1
THE 2024 SEASON

DECEMBER 2023
Young Brits in demand

A 3-0 series win by England over Tonga, after three close-fought games, was an excellent way to bring the 2023 season to a close with the performance of some young stars showing real promise for the future. Even if the proposed home series against Samoa at the end of 2024 was cast in almost immediate doubt.

World Cup finalists Samoa were set to follow in the footsteps of Tonga by enjoying a first-ever series in England, until turning down the invitation. They stated a desire to compete in the Pacific Championships instead, alongside the likes of Australia and New Zealand.

That move, which RFL chair Simon Johnson described as 'disappointing', left England without any scheduled fixtures at all in 2024.

Two of the standout stars of the England campaign were promptly tied up by their clubs. Wigan coach Matt Peet said he intended to build his team around halfback Harry Smith after the 23-year-old signed a new four-year deal with the Warriors, keeping him at the club until at least the end of 2027. And Hull KR promptly secured their star halfback Mikey Lewis until the end of 2028.

Smith was named player of the series, earning a place on the four-man shortlist for the International Rugby League Golden Boot, although he missed out to New Zealand prop James Fisher-Harris.

Other young talent had been tempted down under. Wigan's Morgan Smithies, who had been 18th man in the England squad for the third Test, headed to Canberra Raiders, who were reported to have paid a 'significant' transfer fee to Wigan, who also lost second-rower Kai Pearce-Paul to Newcastle Knights.

St Helens said they were thinking of the Super League competition as well as themselves by extending star man Jack Welsby's contract for two years until 2027, amid an increase in long-standing interest from Australian clubs. St George Illawarra Dragons talked openly of their admiration for the 22-year-old who had captained England in the first two Tests in the absence of suspended George Williams.

Utility Joe Shorrocks also left Super League Champions Wigan for Salford in search of more regular rugby. He signed a three-year contract to become the sixth close-season addition to a Red Devils squad shorn of key duo Brodie Croft and Andy Ackers, who had been signed by Leeds. Cade Cust, Wigan's Australian halfback or hooker, also joined Salford. As did ex-Leigh and Leeds outside back Nene Macdonald, Hull KR fullback/winger Ethan Ryan, young Leeds halfback Kai Morgan and St Helens backrower Matty Foster.

After the loss of two of their star players, Salford were expected to struggle on the field and things got worse for them. They were left reeling by the departure of fans favourite and prolific try-scorer Ken Sio on compassionate grounds, barely a month after he had penned a new contract. And they also looked likely to split with winger Joe Burgess, who was under an internal investigation for an unspecified disciplinary matter.

Off the field there was a glimmer of hope for Salford as they signed a year-long extension to the previous lease at the Salford Community Stadium, with the hope that the Salford City Council's deal to become outright owners of the stadium would be finalised by March the following year.

December 2023

St Helens confirmed that new signing Daryl Clark would become only the third player to wear the club's number nine jersey in the Super League era, following in the footsteps of Keiron Cunningham (1996-2010) and James Roby (2011-2023). Saints inducted former captain Roby into their Hall of Fame, waiving a rule that a player should be retired for at least five years before qualifying for the honour.

Head coach Paul Wellens was fined £2,000 for comments about the RFL and match-review panel - more than four months after making them. Wellens said the RFL had failed in its duty to protect its players' following his side's Challenge Cup semi-final defeat to Leigh, during which Saints props Agnatius Paasi and Alex Walmsley suffered serious knee injuries following tackles by Leopards captain John Asiata.

The fine, half of which was suspended until the end of the 2024 season, came little more than a week after the RFL Board approved a change designed to outlaw the kind of tackles. Tackles that make contact on or below the knee could now be considered as dangerous contact, as would hits where the first contact was above the knee but with force applied from the tackler towards the floor.

Leigh owner Derek Beaumont was also hit with a £2,000 fine for his outspoken comments following the Leopards' final game of the regular Super League season. His comments came after Leigh were denied what could have been a decisive try by an obstruction call. Oliver Gildart, the 'scorer' of the disallowed try in question in that game, was also fined £1,000, half of it suspended, for his criticism of match officials in comments to the media in the aftermath.

Magic Weekend was to be held at Elland Road in Leeds in 2024 - a decision met with almost universal condemnation amongst Rugby League supporters. After multiple early stagings at Cardiff's Millennium Stadium and Edinburgh's Murrayfield, Magic had been held for three consecutive years at Manchester's Etihad Stadium. In 2015, it was held for the first time at St James' Park in Newcastle, which had proven a hugely popular location among fans. Magic Weekend would take place on August 17th and 18th, with St James' Park unavailable.

The game's strategic partner IMG had recommended ditching Magic Weekend completely but clubs rejected the proposal.

IMG's provisional gradings at the end of the domestic season also led to much head scratching. Barely a week after winning the Championship Grand Final and with it promotion to the top flight, London Broncos' bubble was burst by a grading which meant they would drop straight out of Super League after one season. They were told to improve 'across the board' after being ranked 24th among professional clubs under the indicative gradings.

Not long after, the Broncos made the decision not to run their highly productive Academy, as this had no impact on their IMG grading.

They were doing their utmost to assemble a squad that could compete at the top level, fullback Josh Rourke following halfback James Meadows, a Broncos product, from Batley. Keighley forward Sadiq Adebiyi and Newcastle winger Gideon Boafo returned to London for second stints. Head coach Mike Eccles also recruited Australian prop Rhys Kennedy from Hull KR and centre Robbie Storey from Keighley.

But London's two star turns from their promotion campaign, Corey Norman and Dean Whare, decided to leave the club.

Another club put in jeopardy by the IMG gradings was Castleford Tigers but they subsequently received a double boost to their hopes of remaining in Super League beyond 2024.

The RFL admitted that their actual 13th-ranked grading score was higher than that published - the Tigers made an error in their data submission - while new investor Martin Jepson injected a seven-figure sum into the club targeted at earning further points. They recognised that Castleford's score would have been higher with the correct data used, increasing from 12.16 to 12.91 points, which would have placed them eleventh in the rankings.

The twelfth highest graded club was Wakefield Trinity, relegated at the end of the 2023 season. They too had received a significant cash injection from a new owner, Matthew Ellis and were building a strong squad for the Championship campaign. They were also poised to open their newly built main stand, which after a fans poll was christened the Neil Fox Stand.

December 2023

Wakefield fielded their new look squad in the Boxing Day Wetherby Whaler Challenge at Headingley and led 22-6 at half-time before Leeds totally dominated the second half to emerge 41-22 winners.

Australian recruit from Newcastle Knights Lachlan Miller was among four fresh faces on display for the Rhinos, who were aiming for a big improvement on an eighth-place finish in 2023.

Coach Rohan Smith also fielded Miller's compatriot Matt Frawley, the former Huddersfield halfback signed from Canberra Raiders, ex-Salford hooker Ackers and French forward Mickael Goudemand, an addition from Catalans Dragons. The Rhinos were still awaiting the arrival from Australia of new signings Croft and centre Paul Momirovski from Penrith.

Jack Welsby was voted Super League's Player of the Year by League Express readers for the second consecutive season.

The St Helens fullback retained the award he first won in 2022, claiming 32 percent of the vote in the annual League Express Readers' Poll to finish ahead of Wigan's Man of Steel winner Bevan French.

Lachlan Lam, whose father Adrian won the Coach of the Year award with 37.6 percent of the vote after the pair helped Leigh win the Challenge Cup, finished third.

French had the consolation of winning the Overseas Player of the Year, with 38.1 percent, although he surprisingly missed out on a place in the Super League Team of the Year, with Hull KR's Mikey Lewis earning the stand-off berth.

Rugby League Commercial was to sell the betting rights to Super League and its other competitions to IMG. Under the terms of the agreement, IMG would have the right to market Rugby League's betting potential to multiple gambling companies over the next three years.

There had recently been an explosion in the value of betting rights. The legalisation of sports betting in dozens of American states in recent years had triggered significant growth in the industry.

In order to take advantage, the NRL was set to open its 2024 season in Las Vegas with a historic double-header.

JANUARY
Safety first

Leeds Rhinos greats Rob Burrow and Kevin Sinfield were awarded CBEs in the New Year Honours List. As part of a planned visit to Headingley stadium, the pair received their honours in person from the Prince of Wales.

The former Leeds and England teammates had inspired the nation with their campaigning since Burrow was diagnosed with motor neurone disease (MND) in 2019. Sinfield was awarded an MBE in 2014 for the achievements of his playing career, before both were honoured for raising MND awareness in 2021 - Sinfield with an OBE, and Burrow an MBE. The CBE was the highest ranking order of the British Empire. More than £15million had been raised for MND through various fundraising initiatives inspired by Burrow. As well as Sinfield's challenges, which had raised over £8m, the inaugural Rob Burrow Leeds Marathon had taken place in 2023.

Also on the New Year Honours list was Ralph Rimmer, the Rugby Football League chief executive for five years between 2018 and 2022. Rimmer, who was chief executive at Huddersfield before a twelve-year career with the governing body, became an OBE for services to Rugby League.

The RFL revealed its strategy for making Rugby League safer for its participants following recent concerns about the long-term effect of concussions for players. There was a threat of legal action from former players who alleged that their declining health was a direct result of injuries suffered during their playing careers. In its most recent published accounts, the RFL revealed that the cost of insurance against its potential liability to compensate former players had doubled within a year.

The recommendations included mandated use of the latest models of instrumented mouthguards for players in the men's and women's Super Leagues and a minimum off-season of four weeks followed by an additional minimum two-week pre-season period without contact training, to reduce cumulative player load. In addition, match limits over a 12-month period would be introduced, with different figures for forwards and backs.

A new ban on above-the-armpit challenges was to come into effect for the forthcoming community-game campaign and at Academy and Reserve level, followed by elite club rugby under RFL auspices from 2025 onwards. Lowering tackle height was trialled in the Academy competition in 2023 and was found to have significantly reduced the amount of head contact.

In the senior game, an 18th player was introduced at the start of 2023 to enable teams to bring on another player if three players had failed head-injury assessments. This was changed so an 18th player could be used after two injuries, be it head injuries or an injury caused by serious foul play for which an opponent has been shown a yellow or red card.

The six-again rule was altered so that penalties were awarded instead of six-agains for infringements by the tackling team within the 40-metre area of the team in possession. There was also an amendment at the scrum, whereby teams awarded penalties could now take the option of resetting the scrum.

Meanwhile, the green card - which sent a player off the field for two minutes if play was stopped for a potential injury - would now only apply to players on the defending team and could not be shown to the ball-carrier. Green cards would only be used in Super League, no longer in the Championship.

January

There was encouraging news from the north-east as Newcastle Thunder, who had withdrawn from the RFL at the end of the 2023 season, were given the green light for a change of ownership from businessman Semore Kurdi and Newcastle Rugby to Thunder chairman Keith Christie.

In Super League there was a major shock when England halfback Jordan Abdull left Hull KR after agreeing a one-season loan deal with Catalans Dragons. The 27-year-old former Hull FC and London Broncos playmaker had had four seasons at Hull KR and was still contracted until 2026 but played just 55 games for the Robins because of a series of injuries. Hull KR said in a statement: 'The loan will see Abdull head to the south of France subject to a medical for the extent of the new season with no recall option.'

The Robins failed in a bid to sign veteran halfback Luke Gale from Championship club Wakefield but they did snap up winger Joe Burgess after he left Salford who, like the player himself, stayed tight-lipped on the exact reasons for the former England winger's departure with two years of his contract remaining.

Warrington Wolves created wiggle room within their squad ahead of Sam Burgess's first campaign as coach by confirming the release of prop Sam Kasiano with a year of his contract still to run.

London Broncos coach Mike Eccles handed Hakim Miloudi a route back into Super League after his time at Barrow in the Championship and more recently in the French Elite. Miloudi previously played in the top flight for Hull FC and Toronto Wolfpack. And the Broncos also signed Jack Campagnolo from Queensland Cup side Souths Logan Magpies. He had featured in the last World Cup, playing in all three of Italy's matches alongside new Broncos teammates Ethan Natoli and Dean Parata.

On the downside, the Broncos' Championship young player of the year, hooker Bill Leyland, suffered an anterior cruciate ligament injury in a 12-12 pre-season draw at Castleford and was out for the year.

Veteran forward Matty Ashurst's Friday-night testimonial game with Wigan was memorable - the match abandoned after 60 minutes due to persistent floodlight failure.

It was Trinity's first game at Belle Vue, now named the DIY Kitchens Stadium with the branding of new club owner Matt Ellis's company, since the completion of redevelopment work including a new main stand. The new floodlights failed first on the stroke of half-time, then multiple times during the break and in the second half.

Referee Chris Kendall made the decision to abandon the game, with Championship favourites Wakefield leading the Super League champions 22-12 at the time.

The BBC were set to show Super League matches live for the first time, meaning Channel 4 would end their deal after two seasons. The free-to-air broadcaster was to screen at least twelve games a season on BBC2 on Saturday evenings for the next three years. Their coverage would run alongside that of main rights holder Sky Sports, who for the first time would show all six matches live each week.

That meant that video referees would be employed at every Super League game.

The BBC had a long association with Rugby League, stretching back to 1948, when the Challenge Cup final, in which Wigan beat Bradford, was screened live for the first time. However league games had not been shown live since the pre-1996 winter era.

FEBRUARY
Crowded house

Round 1

The fans came out in force for the first round of Super League XXIX with a record aggregate attendance of 76,752 – beating the previous record for a six-match opening round by more than ten per cent - despite a wet and cold weekend.

An average crowd of 12,792 was easily the best figure for an opening round in the 29 seasons since Super League was launched in 1996, and one of the best for any round in Super League history.

The figure was impressive because every game was televised by Sky Sports, with the BBC also televising its first ever live Super League game when it covered the clash between Castleford and Wigan on the Saturday evening.

The opening round produced four red and nine yellow cards from the six matches on the back of a refereeing clampdown on head contact, with only the clash between St Helens and London Broncos free of players being forced to leave the field.

There was certainly plenty of card action in the Thursday-night season opener at MKM Stadium as over 20,000 spectators saw Hull KR defeat their nearest rivals 22-0.

The Airlie Birds had two players shown red cards in the derby, with debutant prop Franklin Pele dismissed for a swinging arm on Elliot Minchella and Ligi Sao sent off for striking the head of Matt Parcell with his knee in retaliation to a niggly tackle. A high tackle from another new FC prop, Herman Ese'ese, earned a yellow card.

Rovers coasted to victory without really being tested at all. New half signed from Catalans Tyrone May showed good touches with the ball and showed up especially well in defence on an outstanding Hull KR debut as the Airlie Birds lacked composure and discipline either side of the ball.

The opening try, after six minutes, came from markers not being square as Tom Opacic's offload put Niall Evalds in for a debut try. While Ese'ese was off the pitch, the 4-0 lead became 8-0 as another new signing, Kelepi Tanginoa, ran a strong line to score off a short Mikey Lewis pass following a Minchella offload. And the contest seemed almost over once Lewis had stepped through the line three minutes before half-time and Peta Hiku, another debut, knocked over his only successful goal from five attempts for 14-0.

Rovers were disappointed to only score twice more, on the hour mark from a Matt Parcell crash over and then in the closing seconds through a second Evalds try, both set in motion by the numbers required to stop Ryan Hall on their left edge. In between came a scuffle that saw Parcell shown yellow for a swipe at the face of Sao on the ground in a tackle and Sao retaliating.

Hull FC, who had Jack Walker, Fa'amanu Brown, Smith, Jayden Okunbor and Jack Ashworth on debut as well as Ese'ese and Pele, suffered two injury blows as Joe Cator hobbled off after only six minutes with a hamstring injury and Danny Houghton, re-appointed to the club captaincy, failed a head-injury assessment. Liam Sutcliffe pulled out before kick-off with illness.

Former Wakefield pair Tanginoa and Jai Whitbread, May, Hiku, Evalds and Oliver Gildart debuted for the Robins.

On the Friday night, promoted London Broncos had a daunting return to Super League at

February

St Helens and were 10-0 down after eight minutes before Saints ran out to a 40-4 victory.

Daryl Clark enjoyed a St Helens debut to remember with a try-scoring, man-of-the-match performance. The hooker scored one try and set up another of the eight scored by Saints while fellow debutant Matt Whitley scored two tries on his return to England from Catalans, to the club he supported as a boy. Former Parramatta centre Waqa Blake was Saints' other debutant.

The Broncos were already looking like also rans as pre-season injuries stretched their squad. Prop Lewis Bienek was sidelined with a long-term ankle issue. Star hooker Bill Leyland was out the whole year with a knee injury and Josh Rourke sidelined with a broken leg, an injury sustained in their final pre-season game, an 18-18 draw at third-tier Oldham.

London handed a one-year contract to former Wakefield winger Lee Kershaw after a successful trial and he made his debut along with Robbie Storey, Hakim Miloudi, Rhys Kennedy and Jack Campagnalo. James Meadows and Sadiq Adebiyi made second debuts.

The two other Friday-night games were closer affairs.

At Leigh Sports Village, Huddersfield toughed their way to an opening round 16-8 win, tackling superbly en route to scoring three tries against a Leopards side that was high on effort but low on execution.

Leigh's new halfback Matt Moylan showed rare glimpses of the class that made him a star in the NRL but made Leigh's first try for Josh Charnley with a deft grubber, after Esan Marsters had opened the scoring.

Moylan went off for a head-injury assessment and then Leigh skipper John Asiata was sin-binned for a professional foul after Adam Swift was thrown to the floor in the corner. By the time both returned to the field early in the second half, the Giants were further ahead after Adam Milner squeezed the ball down from a dummy-half scoot and the conversion from Russell moved the Giants eight points ahead.

Huddersfield struck the killer blow with just over 16 minutes remaining as debutant Aussie halfback Adam Clune and Ashton Golding did the running for another debutant, Elliot Wallis to cross in the right corner. Tom Briscoe gave the Leopards a lifeline in the last few minutes, after Moylan, Lachlan Lam and Gareth O'Brien combined, but the Giants held on to navigate their way to victory.

It was a fine win for the Giants who were missing Luke Yates and Tui Lolohea, both suspended from pre-season games. And they had announced that week that England prop Tom Burgess would be joining them for the 2025 season. Adam Swift, Jack Murchie and Hugo Salabio were their other debutants while the Leopards also had Dan Norman on a second debut.

Leeds and Salford put on a highly competitive game at Headingley that the Rhinos edged 22-16, three players, Leeds new centre Paul Momirovski and Salford pair Ryan Brierley and Amir Bourouh all getting yellow cards. Leeds' bench, winning try scorer Sam Lisone in particular, turned matters in their favour, putting them in the lead for the first time in the 69th minute.

While Ash Handley's spectacular opening try, a glorious length of the field effort - turning the Red Devils' defence in and out twice - grabbed the highlight reel, equally important was his try saver to deny Chris Hankinson five minutes from time, the Rhinos only conceding a two-point penalty in the second half.

Ten debutants were on display in total, with one side rebuilding, in part at the expense of the other, and their opponents trying to keep a competitive squad together. Nene Macdonald, who also switched camps the other way and was the subject of an inevitable cacophony of booing every time he touched the ball, never shied away from the task, making ten metres with every carry, the majority post-contact.

Marc Sneyd revelled in dictating the tempo off the prodigious work of Sam Stone, Oli Partington and Shane Wright. After swapping early penalty goals, Cade Cust touched down Sneyd's dink in-goal though within four minutes Handley levelled with his spectacular first try off a lovely long pass from new fullback Lachlan Miller. Partington's drive for the line and Sneyd's goal gave the Red Devils a 14-8 lead at half-time.

The scores were level eight minutes after the break after Miller plucked Chris Atkin's kick and started a fluid counter attack which saw Rhyse Martin grubber into the corner for Handley

February

to grab his second. Martin added his second touchline conversion in an imperious place-kicking display and then swapped penalties again with Sneyd.

And Leeds edged six in front when hardworking Mickael Goudemand drove in hard and low, regaining his feet quickly for Cameron Smith to send Lisone bounding over. It took Handley's late tackle to keep them in front.

David Fusitu'a was a late withdrawal from the Rhinos team with a calf strain and that week underwent knee surgery, keeping the winger out of action for up to eight weeks. Salford had a new recruit on the way in the shape of Wests Tigers winger David Nofoaluma.

New Castleford coach Craig Lingard took plenty of positives from his first Super League game in charge despite a 32-4 opening-round home defeat to Wigan, the Tigers matching the reigning champions until the controversial dismissal of Liam Watts after half an hour.

Between the horribly wet conditions and an energised Jungle crowd, Wigan were in a game and the BBC audience must surely have enjoyed what they saw.

But then it all turned in one moment. Tyler Dupree was struck in the head by the shoulders of both Joe Westerman and Watts, with the latter shown a red card. It was 4-2 to Castleford at the time; two quick tries afterwards, and another three in the second half, saw the Warriors ease home.

After Adam Keighran kicked the subsequent penalty goal to level the scores, the first two tries of the match came in a three-minute burst, with Patrick Mago playing a key role in both. The prop, coming into the campaign in his best-ever shape, first touched down a Kruise Leeming grubber kick which had evaded fullback Luke Hooley.

Then after consecutive penalties - the first for not playing the ball with the foot - Mago made a strong, angled run at the line and flicked a pass away for Man of Steel Bevan French to open his account for the season. Two Harry Smith conversions made it 16-4 and effectively it was game over.

Wigan kept to their task and scored three more tries in the second half. Again, two came in a three-minute burst, including the first of a Liam Marshall double when Jake Wardle expertly played Jai Field's pass on to his winger down the left.

More quick handling on the other edge, from French and Keighran, then allowed Abbas Miski to set up a try for Leeming, with both displaying excellent footballing skills in the process as the winger kicked ahead and the hooker dribbled forward before scoring.

Only with four minutes remaining were Castleford broken again, a right-to-left shift culminating in a great Smith pass to Wardle, who again provided for Marshall in a flash.

Castleford had Hooley, Sam Wood, Innes Senior, Nixon Putt, Elie El-Zakhem and Josh Simm on debut while Keighran, Luke Thompson and Leeming made their's for the Warriors.

Sam Burgess had a baptism of fire on his debut as a Super League coach but played it cool despite his first defeat as Warrington team boss. The Wolves lost 16-10 to Catalans Dragons in a brutal battle at Stade Gilbert Brutus, which saw a sending off (Michael McIlorum) and yellow card (Jordan Crowther) among a series of ferocious tackles and heavy collisions.

Paul Vaughan started from the bench for Warrington after completing a four-match suspension and Burgess gave debuts to Sam Powell, Arron Lindop, Lachlan Fitzgibbon and Zane Musgrove. Club captain Stefan Ratchford was declared fit to play after a calf issue but was not selected, while Catalans handed debuts to Théo Fages, Jordan Abdull, Tariq Sims, Tevita Satae, Jayden Nikorima and Bayley Sironen. Captain Ben Garcia was missing because of a hamstring strain.

Seventeen-year-old winger Lindop scored a spectacular diving corner-flag try on debut to open a 4-0 lead for the Wolves. The Dragons regained the ascendancy after Tariq Sims almost cut George Williams in half with a monster tackle and the hosts led 6-4 at the break thanks to a Jordan Abdull try, improved by Arthur Mourgue.

Mourgue's penalty and self-converted try, following the red card for Michael McIlorum made it 14-4, set the tone for some ferocious French resistance in the second half. But the Wolves bit back with a fast-handling midfield drive which saw Matt Dufty over the line and former Catalans' star Josh Drinkwater converted to make it 14-10 with 15 minutes to play.

February

Abdull missed the chance to extend his side's lead, missing a straightforward penalty shot at goal but the numbers were levelled within the ranks when Crowther was sin-binned for shoulder contact to the head of Romain Navarrete.

Mourgue converted a penalty for another high shot seven minutes from time, and Abdull went close to crossing the line right at the death as the Dragons held on for victory.

McIlorum got a four-match ban, upheld on appeal, forward Paul Seguier two matches for head contact reduced to one match on appeal and Warrington's Crowther one game.

World Club Challenge

Wigan won their record fifth world title with a 16-12 win over NRL Champions Penrith Panthers at a packed out DW Stadium. The official attendance on the Saturday night was 24,091, with all those tickets having been sold weeks in advance.

It was a match full of drama, controversy, skill and defensive steel. Wigan spent much of the game on the back foot, defending their line and clinging on for their lives. They were breached twice in the latter stages of the first half, but no more.

Penrith had all the early pressure but the Warriors defended stoically before, on their first attack, Bevan French cut out three defenders with an outrageous no-look pass that sent Abbas Miski into the right corner.

It took Penrith until the 27th minute to respond. After Isaah Yeo almost broke through on the fourth tackle, Nathan Cleary lofted a kick to their left edge and neither Miski nor Adam Keighran could claim it. Mitch Kenny gratefully did instead, feeding Cleary on his inside to finish what he started and add the conversion for a 6-4 advantage.

But that lead changed hands twice more in an action-packed end to the first half. Six minutes later, Cleary lost possession as Penrith tried to play their way to the try-line. A wonderful move flowed through the hands of Kruise Leeming, French, Keighran and Miski going wide, then back inside through Willie Isa for Leeming to finish.

Smith's goal made it 10-6 to the Super League side but, in the final minute of the half, a Yeo offload went to Dylan Edwards, who spotted Wigan's defenders rushing wide to cover an overlap and stepped inside, finding a gap to surge through.

The boot of Cleary gave Penrith the half-time advantage by two, while the sight of Leeming limping off with an ankle injury was a further blow. But on the ropes, Wigan came out swinging again in a frenetic, dramatic and occasionally mad second half.

The only try of the second half came from Jake Wardle on 53 minutes.

When Wardle squirmed his way towards the try-line, after beating Edwards and Brian To'o to a Jai Field grubber, referee Liam Moore had a good look at the tangle the three men were in before sending the decision to his colleague with an on-field verdict of a try.

With no clear proof the ball had not been grounded, the previous year's Harry Sunderland Trophy winner Wardle turned out to be the match-winner.

Wigan looked to have secured victory with nine minutes remaining after a Penrith knock-on gave them a scrum in the middle of the halfway line. The ball was fed in by Harry Smith, returned to the halfback on the opposite side and he booted straight down the ground. French chased, the ball bounced just right and they had scored under the posts.

Alas, the replay showed French to be marginally in front of the kick and Wigan would have to defend for their lives until the end.

BETFRED WORLD CLUB CHALLENGE

Saturday 24th February 2024

WIGAN WARRIORS 16 PENRITH PANTHERS 12

WARRIORS: 1 Jai Field; 2 Abbas Miski; 3 Adam Keighran; 4 Jake Wardle; 5 Liam Marshall; 6 Bevan French; 7 Harry Smith; 14 Mike Cooper; 9 Brad O'Neill; 10 Liam Byrne; 11 Willie Isa; 12 Liam Farrell (C); 13 Kaide Ellis. Subs (all used): 15 Patrick Mago; 17 Kruise Leeming; 19 Tyler Dupree; 20 Harvie Hill.
Tries: Miski (9), Leeming (33), Wardle (53); **Goals:** Smith 2/3.
PANTHERS: 1 Dylan Edwards; 2 Sunia Turuva; 3 Izack Tago; 4 Taylan May; 5 Brian To'o; 6 Jack Cole; 7 Nathan Cleary (C); 8 Moses Leota; 9 Mitch Kenny; 10 James Fisher-Harris; 11 Luke Garner; 12 Liam Martin; 13 Isaah Yeo. Subs (all used): 14 Tyrone Peachey; 15 Lindsay Smith; 16 Liam Henry; 17 Matt Eisenhuth.
Tries: Cleary (27), Edwards (40); **Goals:** Cleary 2/2.
Rugby Leaguer & League Express Men of the Match:
Warriors: Jai Field; *Panthers:* Isaah Yeo.
Penalty count: 4-5; **Half-time:** 10-12; **Referee:** Liam Moore; **Attendance:** 24,091 *(at DW Stadium).*

February

Wigan's Liam Farrell looks for a way past Penrith's Moses Leota

The deciding moment came as the hooter sounded, as Penrith's Taylan May crossed the try-line while Wigan's Jai Field and Miski tried to stop him grounding.

The video referee could not see conclusive evidence that a try had been scored, so the on-field call of no-try stood and gave Wigan victory.

Round 2

There was controversy the night before the World Club Challenge in Warrington's 36-10 home win over Hull FC, Sam Burgess's first in charge of the Wolves, after the 36th minute dismissal of Airlie Birds new halfback Fa'amanu Brown.

Brown and Warrington's Ben Currie appeared to have an accidental clash of heads, which resulted in a badly bloodied face for Currie, although he wasn't taken off the field for a head-injury assessment. Brown was shown a red card by referee Marcus Griffiths.

Hull were forced into six changes through injury and suspension, with five youngsters coming in. Without 14 first-team players, their bench consisted of three 20-year-olds and one aged 22.

But they put in a supreme effort to restore some pride after a derby bruising in round one, trailing only 8-6 at half-time after winger Lewis Martin's try off a scrum play and delayed Jack Walker pass cancelled out stand-in skipper Danny Walker's dummy-half opener in an early Warrington blitz.

The only Wolves debutant on display was Max Wood, a 19-year-old forward recruited from Wigan in the off-season, who came off the bench to strong effect in the second half and helped turn things in his side's favour, alongside Aussie veteran Paul Vaughan.

February

Hull remained dogged as Walker profited from a deflected kick to reply to a penalty try, awarded after Tex Hoy denied Matty Ashton with a high shot. But from 14-10, Warrington pulled away in the final 25 minutes. Sam Powell darted under the posts from dummy-half for his first Wolves try, then combined beautifully with Lachlan Fitzgibbon to set up a Toby King score.

Two more tries in the final four minutes inflated the score, King and Fitzgibbon leading a break which James Harrison finished off, before Connor Wrench scored in the closing seconds.

Winger Josh Thewlis kicked six goals - having only previously kicked two in his career. He had missed Warrington's season opener at Catalans the previous week after staying in England for the birth of his first child.

There was already growing concern about the RFL's new head-contact framework introduced for 2024 which contributed significantly to four red cards and nine yellow cards being shown in the six round-one games. And as well as greater punishments being handed out on the field, the RFL was also clamping down on foul play through a stricter disciplinary process.

Brown wasn't charged the following Monday and the RFL amended the rules on head-on-head contact. Only in the initial contact could a defending player be sent off for head-to-head contact.

There were considerably fewer charges by the match review panel after the second round of Super League matches, compared to 16 from the first.

Six players were charged including four from Hull, with only Liam Sutcliffe receiving a ban of two matches for contact with a match official.

Leeds' James Donaldson and Sam Lisone were given two and three-game suspensions respectively for head contact in their 22-12 Thursday night defeat at Hull KR. Rovers made it two wins from two, backing up their derby win over Hull FC.

In Tyrone May and Jez Litten, Rovers had two players who helped to dominate the Rhinos, on a heavy ground that cut up atrociously following rainfall over the city in the previous two days.

Rovers coach Willie Peters was forced into two changes after the one-match ban received by Matt Parcell for his sin bin against Hull FC and Dean Hadley was also missing after failing a head-injury assessment the previous week. Jai Whitbread moved up into the front row with Corey Hall coming onto the bench.

Rhinos coach Rohan Smith was forced to make a late change when fullback Lachlan Miller pulled out through illness and was replaced by 19-year old Alfie Edgell. Leeds were also without Mikołaj Olędzki, missing with a shoulder injury, with Justin Sangaré starting alongside Mickaël Goudemand in an all-French front row.

The Rhinos took the lead early on after Peta Hiku was sin-binned for interference in the ruck area. From the penalty, James Bentley got the ball out of a tackle for Brodie Croft to send in Harry Newman for a try on his 100th career appearance. Rhyse Martin, in his 100th Super League game, added the conversion.

With an element of luck Rovers drew level when a Jez Litten kick hit the foot of the post for Sauaso Sue to collect and dive over, with Litten adding the conversion from in front of the posts.

Thirty seconds from the half-time break, the Rhinos were reduced to twelve men when Donaldson was sin-binned and Litten landed the penalty for an 8-6 half-time lead.

With Donaldson still off the field Rovers capitalised to increase their lead with a Ryan Hall try after a video-referee decision. A May kick hit Bentley but came back to May, rebounding off his leg before the ball fell to Oliver Gildart, whose flick pass saw Hall go in at the corner and Litten added a superb touchline conversion.

On the hour the Rhinos replied in fine style and scored a superbly worked try from distance. Croft launched a cross-field kick that landed in Ash Handley's arms and he ran 80 metres all the way to the line, sidestepping Niall Evalds on the way. Martin added the conversion but minutes later the Rhinos were again down to twelve men when Lisone went high on Elliot Minchella for Litten to add the penalty.

Nine minutes from time Rovers scored the try that would seal the win, with May again the instigator when he kicked behind the Rhinos defence. Hiku outpaced Edgell to dive on the ball for

February

the four-pointer with Litten making it five from five with the conversion from close to the posts.

The Rhinos were without young backrower Morgan Gannon. After suffering a head injury in Leeds' pre-season game against Hull KR in early February, Gannon was stood down from action for a three-month period following medical consultation.

The night after, London Broncos attracted a crowd of over five thousand to the Cherry Red Records Stadium at Wimbledon for their opening home game. But despite plenty of effort they fell to a 34-0 defeat to Catalans Dragons.

Théo Fages scored the first try after only 91 seconds and went onto score another as he pulled Catalans' strings efficiently all game.

St Helens continued their perfect start to the season early on Saturday evening with an impressive 28-0 win at Huddersfield.

Matt Whitley and Sione Mata'utia both went over to put Saints 12-0 up at the end of a competitive first half. And the second half started in similar gruelling fashion with both sides trading punches and thrilling line-speed.

The first points of the second half came from Jack Welsby off the back of a third-tackle Daryl Clark grubber in behind the line, allowing Welsby to score under the posts.

In the 62nd minute the Giants finally looked as though they might score, when Esan Marsters, chasing a kick to the line, was seemingly taken out by Clark off the ball and the decision was reviewed by the video referee, who ruled out the possibility of a penalty try but awarded a penalty, resulting in a yellow card for Clark.

Saints finally sealed the game with two tries in the final five minutes.

Some crafty play from Welsby out of dummy-half led to a line-break and the ball went through five sets of hands, ending with Jon Bennison going into the corner.

Shortly afterwards, more broken play saw some Saints off-the-cuff brilliance after Tommy Makinson got an offload away to Welsby, who made a line break and put Morgan Knowles away under the posts.

Round 2 ended on the Sunday afternoon with home side Salford edging a thrilling contest with Castleford by 26-22.

Red Devils centre Nene Macdonald was a constant thorn in Castleford's side and he was rewarded with an excellent try just before half-time, claiming a high Marc Sneyd kick he had no right to take.

Salford looked to be cruising early in the game, thanks to two tries in quick succession from Sam Stone and Amir Bourouh inside the opening twelve minutes but the Tigers hit back through tries from Sam Wood and Jack Broadbent to trail by two points.

They would have been happy to take that to the break following their poor start, but that remarkable try from Macdonald saw the Red Devils extend their advantage to eight.

Salford again took control as they led 24-10 after Stone's second try and looked to be home and dry. But Castleford refused to give in and they eventually reduced the deficit to four points with Joe Westerman and Liam Horne tries to set up a tense finish, but the hosts just held on.

BETFRED SUPER LEAGUE
Sunday 25th February

	P	W	D	L	F	A	D	Pts
St Helens	2	2	0	0	68	4	64	4
Catalans Dragons	2	2	0	0	50	10	40	4
Hull KR	2	2	0	0	44	12	32	4
Wigan Warriors	1	1	0	0	32	4	28	2
Warrington Wolves	2	1	0	1	46	26	20	2
Salford Red Devils	2	1	0	1	42	44	-2	2
Leeds Rhinos	2	1	0	1	34	38	-4	2
Huddersfield Giants	2	1	0	1	16	36	-20	2
Leigh Leopards	1	0	0	1	8	16	-8	0
Castleford Tigers	2	0	0	2	26	58	-32	0
Hull FC	2	0	0	2	10	58	-48	0
London Broncos	2	0	0	2	4	74	-70	0

MARCH
Usual suspects

Round 3

Only two 100 per cent records remained after the first round of March, in the familiar shape of St Helens and Wigan.

Catalans ended their unbeaten start on the Saturday afternoon at a wet Headingley as Leeds emerged 18-10 winners.

The Dragons were disrupted when Mike McMeeken pulled out of the warm-up with a back spasm, allowing Paul Séguier to come in after serving a ban.

Three yellow cards (for Romain Navarrete, Tariq Sims and Jordan Dezaria) proved to be the Dragons' undoing. And they were still missing hooker Michael McIlorum as he continued to serve a four-match suspension following his dismissal in round one against Warrington

With the Rhinos willing to play high-risk football, Ash Handley opened the scoring off a Brodie Croft grubber on four minutes. Harry Newman stepped and powered his way over two minutes later, Sims collecting him high as he went across.

It was a possible eight-point try and although Rhyse Martin missed the conversion from wide out, he slotted over the penalty from in front, as Sims became the first of a quartet to see yellow cards. An Arthur Mourgue penalty just before the break made it 10-2.

Straight after the turnaround, Tevita Satae proved unstoppable off the bench as the Dragons made their size and positional advantage finally pay. On a last-tackle play with his side ranged to the left, Alrix da Costa turned the ball back inside and Satae bludgeoned his way over by the posts. Mourgue's conversion and second penalty tied it at 10-10.

But Handley's second try, improved by Martin, who also kicked his third goal from his second penalty, helped the hosts ease home against 12 men. Navarrete's 74th-minute sin-binning was the fourth yellow card of the afternoon - and third for the Dragons. Leeds' French prop Justin Sangaré was also sin-binned early in the second half.

Hull KR also fell to their first defeat, on the Saturday evening, as Marc Sneyd put on a kicking masterclass to lead Salford to a 17-10 home win.

It took almost an hour - and a yellow card for Deon Cross - for Salford to be broken down. By then, with Sneyd at the helm, they were full value for a 16-0 lead.

The halfback slid a wonderful kick along the wet ground, which held up in the in-goal for Cross to score the opening try after 15 minutes. And four minutes before half-time, Cade Cust's cut-out pass - following a strong run by captain Kallum Watkins - put Chris Hankinson into the corner. Sneyd converted both the tricky conversions and then added two penalties in the first ten minutes of the second half to put the Red Devils well on course.

Only in the final half-hour did the Robins begin to get into gear. It started with the Cross sin bin, for grabbing former teammate Joe Burgess as he attempted a quick restart. Two minutes later, Hull KR were attacking the flank recently vacated by the winger and Peta Hiku dummied his way over for a lifeline.

It was soon a one-score game, as Kelepi Tanginoa ran a great line to break through the defence and sent in Jez Litten, who also added the goal.

All to play for, tensions boiled over bizarrely after Litten objected to a fend by Tim Lafai.

March

Salford got the penalty, came downfield and Sneyd struck the decisive blow with a trademark one-pointer.

Wigan made it two from two on the Friday night with a 30-16 home win over Huddersfield, running away with the game between the twelfth and 22nd minutes, with three quick-fire tries bookended by two from Liam Marshall, who scored a hat-trick overall.

All three came from quick ball handling, the Warriors' well-oiled machine clicking into gear through their trio of talented spine players. At 18-0 by half-time Wigan were virtually out of sight.

The second half was only briefly an affair of any great interest, as twice the Giants got a try to threaten a comeback only for the Warriors to put down their resistance almost instantly on both occasions. Three minutes in, Esan Marsters somehow offloaded the ball when buried by four men in the tackle, allowing Adam Swift to score his first Huddersfield try, which Oliver Russell converted from the touchline.

But another quick, clinical attacking play, through Brad O'Neill, Harry Smith and Jai Field, gave Marshall his hat-trick and a 22-10 lead.

Harry Smith kicked a penalty - after a thrilling break from Jake Wardle and Marshall - twelve minutes from time for a three-score Warriors lead. But the Giants weren't done just yet as Jack Murchie benefited from Adam Keighran missing an Adam Clune kick and Russell goaled to put them back to within eight. But a sloppy Jake Connor pass was then fumbled by Murchie and Wigan marched forward for Tyler Dupree to crash over to erase any doubt.

On the same night, St Helens toughed out a third win of the season with a hard-fought 12-4 home win over Leigh that included a starring role for Matt Whitley.

Much talk pre-match was about how Leigh captain John Asiata would fare in his first game against Saints since his controversial tackling technique came under scrutiny by Paul Wellens after causing two serious injuries in the teams' Challenge Cup semi-final the previous summer.

And within 40 seconds, the row was reignited. Asiata flew in below the knees of Sione Mata'utia in the first set of the game and was sin-binned for the now-banned technique. Having lived up to the role of pantomime villain, there was then little sympathy from the home support when Asiata came off again shortly after returning, in the 15th minute, with a torn calf.

Saints opened a 4-0 half-time lead when Lewis Dodd, James Bell and Whitley all combined brilliantly before Jack Welsby flew over at high speed.

Six minutes after the break, Zak Hardaker replied but five minutes later came the match-winning try. A Konrad Hurrell offload in heavy traffic set Saints in motion again as Dodd broke beyond halfway and Tommy Makinson supported to go over by the posts for a superb try. Mark Percival converted and Saints led 10-4. Saints then took advantage with Leigh offside at the scrum, as Percival goaled from 30 metres and nudged Saints 12-4 to the good after 56 minutes.

Leigh had on-loan Brad Dwyer on debut. The hooker returned to Warrington ahead of the 2024 season from Hull FC but was currently third-choice in his position and had been recruited by the Leopards to cover for long-term injury Edwin Ipape.

Warrington were loaning out players to give them game time and two more, prop Joe Bullock and winger Matty Russell made debuts in Hull FC's last-gasp 28-24 home win over London Broncos.

Morgan Smith was the man who broke London hearts and earned Hull FC their first win of the 2024 season in a nail-biting encounter.

The Broncos had pegged back a twelve-point half-time deficit to take the lead with just minutes remaining before Smith spotted a gap in the Broncos' defence on the last tackle to score next to the posts.

Goal-kicking proved pivotal. Darnell McIntosh converted four of the home tries scored by Nick Staveley, Matty Russell, Lewis Martin, Fa'amanu Brown and Morgan Smith. But Oli Leyland only converted two of the five tries by Hakim Miloudi, two, James Meadows, Lee Kershaw and Robbie Storey.

Warrington made it two wins on the trot with a convincing 30-8 Friday-night home win over Castleford.

The Wolves spent plenty of time attacking Castleford's right edge and Tigers coach Craig

March

Lingard wasn't happy with what he saw defensively as he hooked his right centre Jack Broadbent from the field five minutes into the second half.

The Tigers struck first with an early Josh Simm score. But Warrington replied as a wonderful cut-out pass off a backline spread from Matt Dufty led to some acrobatic brilliance from Matty Ashton in the corner. Another nice backline shift led to some more Ashton acrobatics before Dufty made a break and passed the ball onto Joe Philbin, who scored next to the posts.

The first penalty for a high shot came in the last minute of the first half and Ratchford opted to take the two points from 38 metres out and six metres in from the touchline, with the ball hitting the crossbar and going over for a 16-point margin at half-time.

The momentum stayed with Warrington in the second half after they forced an error in the first two minutes. Dufty crossed shortly afterwards, ignoring an overlap to shimmy his way around three defenders to score under the posts.

The Tigers hit back as a volleyball style tap from Jacob Miller found some space out wide, which resulted in Innes Senior crossing over in the corner. But a Castleford error put the Wolves back on the attack with a backline shift that eventually landed in Josh Thewlis's hands, allowing him to touch down in the corner.

Round 4

Then there was only one perfect record in Super League and that belonged to reigning champions Wigan. St Helens fell to their first defeat of the season with a stunning 24-20 Friday-night reverse at home to Salford.

The Red Devils had last won at St Helens in January 1980 but they were good value for their third consecutive win, with Marc Sneyd having another blinder and continuing his 100 per cent record with conversions from all over the field.

Jack Welsby, Lewis Dodd and Mark Percival scored in the opening 40 minutes, with Deon Cross getting the only first-half try for the visitors. When Dodd's second try put Saints 20-6 ahead just before the hour mark the outcome looked obvious.

But Percival was sent off just after the break for a shoulder charge on Jack Ormondroyd and tries from Nene MacDonald and Chris Atkin closed the gap, before Cross's second score clinched the historic win. Percival was subsequently banned for two games.

That week Salford received £315,000 in immediate financial support from Salford City Council to see them through to the completion of a stadium deal. The Red Devils had experienced well-publicised financial difficulties, raising over £360,000 through a community share scheme and selling three star players for six-figure sums in 2023, while being placed in special measures by the RFL.

Wigan had little difficulty in recording their third win on the Saturday afternoon as they dismantled win-less London Broncos in Wimbledon, scoring ten tries in a 60-22 victory.

Six of the Warriors' side in the capital were Academy products aged 21 or under, including 18-year-old Jack Farrimond, who debuted at halfback alongside the impressive Ryan Hampshire and assisted two tries.

Brad O'Neill, Zach Eckersley and Harvie Hill (twice) were among the try-scorers - the latter two registering for the first time in their Wigan careers - while Tom Forber and Junior Nsemba (returning from injury for a first appearance of the season) came off the bench. Centre Adam Keighran scored his first try for the club in the closing stages. He also kicked ten goals from eleven attempts in the absence of regular kicker Harry Smith.

Lee Kershaw scored a try double for the Broncos, who were running on a mixed part and full-time squad because of their provisional IMG grading and predictably experiencing a torrid start to the season, with on-form Warrington due to visit the following week.

The Wolves edged a good match on the Thursday night as they came away from Hull KR with a 22-20 win.

Willie Peters felt his Robins were the better side in set-for-set rugby. But the Robins threw it away - literally in the case of James Batchelor dropping the ball over the line and Mikey Lewis

March

Salford's Nene Macdonald crashes over against St Helens

failing to put Jez Litten over with a poor pass.

In contrast, the Wolves were clinical, making the most of the momentum they did get sporadically produce to score twice each at the start and end of the first half.

Even so, they trailed with ten minutes to go, until on-form fullback Matt Dufty scored from a scrum play. It came from another error - an Oliver Gildart offload knocked on by Ryan Hall as they sensed an opportunity to break - and a scrum play after Hall knocked down a pass.

The ball was moved left through halfbacks Leon Hayes and George Williams, finding Dufty with the home defence all out of shape. The player of the match proved the match-winner.

The lead had changed hands four times, with both teams suffering from goalkicking problems, to ensure a tight contest. Warrington were 10-0 up in 14 minutes, with Williams and Matty Ashton tries.

Tyrone May, rose high above Dufty to catch Mikey Lewis's kick and the Robins were soon celebrating again as May and Lewis combined to find Oliver Gildart down the left and the centre produced a sweet offload out the back for a Ryan Hall try.

Jez Litten converted both to edge Hull KR in front at 12-10 but a Toby King try snatched that lead away. That was two minutes before half-time and better still was to come, a nice combination down the middle setting fullback Dufty away and his kick behind watched carefully by Connor Wrench before touching down with seconds left on the clock.

The second half was more of the same - another Hull KR fightback, followed by Warrington clinching it late on.

The first 17 minutes brought a rare try-less period, though that shouldn't have been the case. Lewis threw one of the best dummies to leave England captain Williams humiliated. But it was home heads being scratched when the following pass was too far behind the supporting Litten.

Lewis made amends, however, when he sent a wonderful looping pass over the top for Hall, who put Gildart in on his inside. And five minutes later, May played a similar pass down the

March

opposite right edge for Tom Opacic to score, putting Rovers in front by two as Batchelor missed both kicks.

But all Rovers' good work was undone again as the Wolves scored the winner ten minutes from time.

Catalans bounced back from their defeat at Leeds with a 26-12 win over Hull FC in torrential rain in Perpignan.

The pitch held up well and the rain stopped midway through the second half. But by then the damage had been done with handling the first casualty in the heavy downpour followed by a string of players heading to the bench clutching their thighs. Both sides suffered a string of injuries and withdrawals on a slippery pitch.

The Dragons needed head-injury assessments for prop Chris Satae and hooker Alrix Da Costa and they lost fullback Jayden Nikorima in the first half with a thigh strain.

For Hull, winger Matty Russell, fullback Jack Walker and hooker Danny Houghton had to leave the field. And they also lost Jack Ashworth, who was sin-binned for a head clash with Dragons' prop Satae. He was later banned for three matches.

Walker scored a bizarre try when the ball was accidentally knocked forward off the head of centre Carlos Tuimavave. Walker collected and grounded over the line in the right corner and Darnell McIntosh's impressive conversion from the touchline put them within two points. Walker's try celebrations were cut short by a hamstring strain sustained in the act of scoring and Hull missed his energy from fullback for the remainder of the game.

Catalans seized the moment and an interception and 40-metre dash by winger Tom Johnstone put them in position for Arthur Mourgue to force his way over close to the posts. He converted his try to make it 20-12 with 20 minutes to play.

Catalans were in for the kill when winger Tom Davies struck in the right corner in the 70th minute, Morgue converting from the touchline to end it at 26-12.

Leigh Leopards remained pointless as Leeds completed a brilliant comeback victory, scoring 22 unanswered second-half points to shock the home side by 22-16.

The hosts had dominated the opening 40 minutes, scoring three tries through Gareth O'Brien, Kai O'Donnell and Umyla Hanley before they succumbed to a third Super League defeat from their opening three games.

Eight minutes into the half, soft hands from Brodie Croft put a spinning Rhyse Martin through to score and he converted to put the Rhinos on the board at 6-16. It was the start of an inspired second half from the Rhinos' second-rower. Leeds found their groove when Matt Frawley dummied and scythed through from 15 metres. Martin's conversion made it 16-12 and his low kick then unlocked the Leigh defence with Ash Handley touching down after supporting Paul Momirovski. This time Martin couldn't goal but it was now 16-16 with 16 minutes remaining.

Sublime handling and running then paved the way for Croft to hand on for Handley after more Martin trickery in the 69th minute and a third goal from the PNG international handed the Rhinos a six-point advantage.

Leigh's hopes faded when Lachlan Lam was helped from the field with a deep cut to his thigh. Both loose forward John Asiata and winger Tom Briscoe had already been ruled out for at least six weeks after suffering calf tears in the recent defeat at St Helens, while hooker Edwin Ipape was still sidelined with a knee injury.

Castleford were also still chasing a win and on the Friday night they were embarrassed, beaten 50-8 at home by Huddersfield.

Adam Swift, Adam Clune, Sam Halsall and Sam Hewitt all crossed, with Innes Senior responding as the Giants took a 24-4 half-time lead.

Senior's second try against his former side gave Cas slim hope, but Leroy Cudjoe's score sparked a collapse. Swift, Halsall and Cudjoe all claimed second tries, and Kevin Naiqama crossed as Huddersfield scored four late tries.

It was an error-strewn Tigers performance, with Paul McShane, Liam Watts and Danny Richardson absent, but their late collapse - conceding five tries in the final 17 minutes - was witnessed by few remaining supporters.

March

Round 5

Wigan's perfect start to the season continued as they edged their game at Salford, though Warrington leapfrogged them to the top of the table on points difference. The Warriors still had a game in hand on the Wolves.

Wigan's late 22-12 victory at Salford proved their ability to win ugly as they came back from 12-10 down with four minutes left on the Thursday night.

First, Jake Wardle scored from a failed short drop-out by the hosts. And then Bevan French scored an individual try to seal the points, all while Wigan were a man down for the closing period with Harry Smith in the sin bin.

Despite in-form halfback Marc Sneyd causing mayhem with his kicking game in difficult wet conditions, the Warriors limited their opposition to two tries.

The state of the squads was reflected in the changes made from the previous round as while both made five alterations, Wigan recalled five frontline stars in French, Smith, Liam Marshall, Kaide Ellis and Liam Byrne.

The Red Devils' were all forced - Chris Hankinson, Brad Singleton and Ben Hellewell all had long-term injuries, Cade Cust had a head knock, and Jack Ormondroyd was ill (as were several other players who had to battle through). In came two debutants - Aussie winger David Nofoaluma and Matty Foster - and returning loanee from Warrington Gil Dudson.

It wasn't shaping up to be a classic after 39 minutes of rugby with no points, few chances and many errors. Marshall finally broke the deadlock by running onto a sliding kick by Jai Field down the left and things looked more comfortable for the Warriors when 4-0 became 10-0 six minutes into the second half. Two long passes from Smith and French enabled Abbas Miski to cross in the right corner. Smith impressively converted.

Marc Sneyd set up both the comeback tries, first with a grubber for his backrower Sam Stone and then a high bomb which Miski knocked down straight into the grateful arms of Tim Lafai.

The halfback's two conversions edged Salford in front at 12-10 and he looked to have got them another step closer to victory when, with only nine minutes left in the game, his kick for Ryan Brierley saw the fullback taken out by Smith at the cost of a yellow card.

But the cruel twist of fate was to come with Sneyd's fatal decision to kick a GLDO short and hand the game to Wigan.

That week, Wigan head coach Matt Peet and his two assistants, Sean O'Loughlin and Thomas Leuluai, penned new seven-year deals to keep them contracted to the world champions until the end of 2030.

Warrington amassed a 58-4 win at struggling London Broncos. It was no contest once Warrington scored three tries in the first 12 minutes.

Matt Dufty's 64th-minute try to complete his hat-trick took them above Wigan on points difference as they extended their lead to 48 points but also led to their sole failure as Stefan Ratchford, who had equalled the all-time record of kicking 41 consecutive goals, missed breaking the record with a shot he would usually expect to land easily.

St Helens imposed Leeds' first home defeat of the season with an 18-8 win at Headingley.

For the first half-hour, Leeds looked like world-beaters. St Helens' defence, usually so unflustered, was all at sea, gaps opening up everywhere, bodies flying to paper every crack while new ones appeared.

Leading the way was Lachlan Miller, the fullback recruited for his speed and agility and certainly not disappointing in that aspect. Miller made 14 tackle busts and 150 metres.

All that threat and menace had Leeds only 8-0 up, courtesy of a Luis Roberts try and two Rhyse Martin goals. It was as good as they would get, failing to score another point.

By the end of the first half the screw had already begun to turn, helped by the injection of James Bell and Moses Mbye from the bench. The latter put Waqa Blake in for his first St Helens try after Jack Welsby knocked down a Lewis Dodd kick for 8-6 at half-time.

The two match-winning tries in the second half came back-to-back in the middle of it. First Lewis Dodd and Jonny Lomax combined to put Jon Bennison over, following a knock-on by Roberts,

March

Hull KR's Elliot Minchella looks to break free from Huddersfield's Sebastine Ikahihifo

despite a Saints hand seemingly involved. Then Miller kicked the restart out on the full and Mbye used a dummy that had half the Leeds team running into the South Stand to cross unopposed.

Catalans beat Castleford at home by 40-14. But Tigers' Craig Lingard was the happier of the two coaches at the end, which saw bare-chested Yorkshire supporters singing and swinging their shirts in the air at the end while French fans gave a gallic shrug and a polite round of applause for the visitors.

A less than satisfied Steve McNamara paid tribute to his captain Ben Garcia who stood in at hooker, with Michael McIlorum and Alrix Da Costa both missing. Fullback Arthur Mourgue oozed class and collected another 16-point haul.

Giants coach Ian Watson lamented a step back from his Huddersfield team in a 24-12 Saturday home defeat to Hull KR.

Peta Hiku scored two tries early in the second half, the latter coming from a spectacular break by Niall Evalds, who contributed three assists in all. Hiku was at centre after an early season experiment at fullback and looked much more comfortable, as did Evalds, back at fullback.

Rovers were ruthless in the opening half with tries from Joe Burgess and Jez Litten, as the Giants were given little daylight. Hiku's double then took the game away. Ryan Hall added try five before Kevin Naiqama and Adam Swift crossed to end with a scoreline that flattered Huddersfield.

Leigh, shorn of their key players, got their first win in spectacular fashion as they embarrassed a dismal Hull FC side on their home turf by 54-4 on the Saturday.

Ben McNamara had a debut to remember against his old club, partnering the outstanding Matt Moylan in the halves, playing behind a pack that bullied the Black and Whites from start to finish.

The writing was on the wall early as Leigh scored four tries in the opening quarter to effectively end the game as a contest. And it only got worse for Hull, who were left chasing shadows for virtually the whole game.

March

Challenge Cup Round 6

The twelve Super League clubs entered the Challenge Cup at the sixth-round, last-16 phase, along with the four sides from the lower leagues, who were all from the second-tier Championship.

All four Championship sides fell to top-flight opponents. Wigan beat Sheffield Eagles at home 44-18, though the score flattered the hosts. The Eagles put in a sterling performance for the whole 80 minutes and had the Warriors on the ropes several times.

Tries from Bevan French and Liam Marshall put the Warriors 10-0 in front and it looked like they would up the ante. But the Eagles refused to lie down and got back within four points thanks to a try from Matty Marsh.

It seemed likely Wigan would hold a narrow advantage at half-time but a superb passing move saw Matty Dawson-Jones go over in the corner and Cory Aston's touchline conversion saw Sheffield lead for the first time.

A penalty from Harry Smith on the hooter levelled the scores but second-half tries from Jake Wardle and two more from French looked to have decided it, only for a try from Evan Hodgson to keep Sheffield's hopes alive. Late converted tries from Kruise Leeming, Patrick Mago and Marshall finally killed off the Eagles.

Castleford progressed thanks to a 28-14 win at coach Craig Lingard's former club Batley Bulldogs. The Tigers, win-less in Super League, trailed 14-10 with seconds left of a first half which featured a succession of errors as they struggled to adapt to the windy conditions, unique environment and fierce Batley challenge.

But an Innes Senior try on the hooter, plus three further second-half scores going down the infamous Mount Pleasant slope, saw them home.

Holders Leigh had an equally tough game at home to Featherstone before securing a 26-14 win, with Umyla Hanley ending with a hat-trick of tries. And in the only Sunday afternoon Cup game, Catalans were too good for Halifax Panthers, Matt Ikuvalu helping create a hat-trick for winger Tom Davies in the opening 14 minutes of the game. The Dragons ended 40-4 winners.

Hull KR had a surprisingly big win at home to Salford, the 40-0 scoreline reflecting their dominance. The Red Devils had no answers to the ferocity of the Rovers defence and a side even more potent in attack, scoring seven unanswered tries. Kelepi Tanginoa's barnstorming try two minutes from the break, which saw Rovers open up a 22-0 lead going into half-time after Ryan Hall's first-half hat-trick, was the killer.

On the same Friday night, St Helens backed up their league win at Headingley with a 20-6 success over Leeds at the same venue.

Frequent rain showers and a cautious Saints kept the game tight most of the way through but there was no doubting the better side. The only try the Rhinos registered was a 90-metre interception by Harry Newman, which almost gave them the most undeserved of half-time leads.

But Daryl Clark scored a key try on the stroke of half-time for St Helens, running ten metres from dummy-half, before Jon Bennison and Alex Walmsley saw them home in the second half. Lewis Dodd missed the game with an adductor muscle injury, with hooker Moses Mbye's switch to scrum-half proving pivotal.

Struggling Hull FC suffered the biggest defeat of the round, a 50-6 hammering at Huddersfield, winger Adam Swift finishing with four tries against his former club and Wigan junior Sam Halsall with three. Another former Hull man, Jake Connor, was at his inimitable best.

Warrington produced a nine-try performance to power to a 42-0 home win over London. Form fullback Matt Dufty was everywhere with a perfect performance, with Matty Ashton, three tries and Josh Thewlis, two, the major beneficiaries.

Round 6

It was a very good Good Friday for St Helens as they ended Wigan's 16-match winning run with a 12-4 home success and shot to the top of the table in the process. A sell-out crowd witnessed an explosive contest and the game could have gone either way as Saints trailed 4-2 with seven

March

St Helens' Alex Walmsley tackled by Wigan's Kaide Ellis and Brad O'Neill

minutes remaining, following a piece of Bevan French magic for the Warriors.

Liam Byrne's 63rd-minute dismissal for a high tackle on Mark Percival - their second card after Tyler Dupree escaped with a yellow for an elbow to the head of Matty Lees in the first half - was the turning point.

Tommy Makinson leapt into the air to claim a peach of a kick from Lewis Dodd and restore Saints' lead before Konrad Hurrell muscled over to make sure of Saints' fourth consecutive home derby success.

Makinson was a doubt for the derby after missing the previous two games with a hamstring issue, as was Dodd with an adductor injury. But the two combined for the crucial try.

Alex Walmsley delivered another devastating performance, making more metres than any other player on the field and laying the platform for Hurrell's clinching try.

The only points of a ferocious first half came from a 26th-minute Percival penalty. Only with the first period of sustained Wigan pressure did the scoreline turn on its head. In the 56th minute, Hurrell lost possession in costly fashion before French attacked Saints' left edge, sliding a wonderful kick in behind and touching down.

But Byrne's red card gave St Helens a glimmer of opportunity and they took it with both hands. The prop was banned for four games. Dupree got one game and had his appeal rejected. St Helens prop Matty Lees also got two games for head contact.

Saints replaced Warrington at the top, as Catalans joined them, second on points difference, with a 32-24 win over the Wolves at the Halliwell Joes Stadium on the Saturday.

Catalans coach Steve McNamara described Jordan Abdull's latest match-winning performance as a 'masterclass'. The Dragons had no Jayden Nikorima, Arthur Mourgue or Théo Fages through injury, but thanks to Abdull - and the young duo of César Rougé and Ugo Tison (on his fourth Dragons appearance, and limping on one leg in the second half) - there was no problem.

Abdull had a hand - or a foot - in five of the six tries scored by Catalans (and converted four of them), the only exception being the drive by captain Benjamin Garcia that put them 18-0 up after just 13 minutes.

The Wolves conceded three tries and had a player - prop Paul Vaughan - sin-binned in the first 13 minutes but then fought back to 18-12 at half-time, and then from 28-12 to 28-24.

But Catalans' defence turned up when it mattered in the closing stages, withstanding a huge amount of Warrington pressure before going up the other end and wrapping up victory two minutes from time with a try by Abdull. His kick was knocked down in the air by Tom Johnstone and he popped in to seal the Dragons' difficult but ultimately deserved success.

Vaughan was banned for two games for a tip-tackle.

Hull KR kept pace with a comfortable 34-10 home derby win over Hull FC. Before the Good Friday match special tributes were made to former Rovers backrower and club chairman Phil Lowe who had died at the age of 74. It was followed by a dominant Hull KR victory, as they scored six first-half tries for a 28-0 lead.

Rovers were outstanding with the ball and cut Hull to shreds, particularly on the right edge, with Tyrone May tormenting his opponents, allowing Peta Hiku and two-try Joe Burgess to have an absolute field day.

To their credit, Hull rallied in the second half, showing a desire to turn Rovers away from their try line and added two tries of their own from Jayden Okunbor and Cameron Scott. But they were out-classed once again by their near neighbours.

Ryan Brierley enjoyed a busy 300th career appearance, scoring two tries and being sin-binned in the Red Devils' 32-22 home win over Leigh on the Saturday.

Salford were never behind and scored five tries with two each for Brierley and Ethan Ryan and one for Marc Sneyd, who was in the form of his life.

Umyla Hanley scored another hat-trick for the Leopards and Lachlan Lam one try, as they suffered a fourth league loss out of five games.

That week the Leopards were successful in striking off a Grade A dangerous contact charge issued by the RFL disciplinary panel following John Asiata's sin-binning in the first minute of Leigh' 12-4 away loss to St Helens in March. An independent tribunal found Asiata (who was still out with a calf injury) not guilty, and the charge was removed from the player's record.

In the only Sunday game of the 'Rivals Round' Huddersfield claimed a 26-6 win in Wimbledon, to leave London Broncos still pointless.

The Giants led by only 12-6 at half-time. Halfback Oli Leyland opened a 6-0 London lead as he chased his own grubber to the line. Kevin Naiqama made illegal contact while trying to stop him, leading to a penalty try.

But Tui Lolohea's kicking enabled the Giants to score three times in quick succession and secure the lead at the interval. Jake Bibby pounced on his kick, stand-in fullback Esan Marsters powered over before Lolohea's looping pass set up Adam Swift to finish athletically in the corner.

The Giants dominated after the break. Adam Clune forced his way over with Lolohea converting. A Lolohea penalty goal stretched the lead to 14 points in the 51st minute. And Lolohea then did more damage by booting the ball high and across for Sam Halsall to leap, catch and ground.

On the Thursday, Castleford enjoyed one of their best performances to date but still fell to defeat, by 26-6 to Leeds, after dominating the first half but failing to score a try. Castleford forced five goal-line drop-outs in the first half, enjoying set after set on the Leeds line but 0-0 it remained at half-time.

The Rhinos' attack came in for some criticism after the Cup defeat by St Helens and they failed to post any points in the first half at the Jungle. But they turned things around in the second half with Paul Momirovski and compatriot Lachlan Miller both scoring doubles.

Ash Handley celebrated his 200th Leeds appearance, almost ten years on from his debut at the age of 18.

BETFRED SUPER LEAGUE
Sunday 31st March

	P	W	D	L	F	A	D	Pts
St Helens	6	5	0	1	130	44	86	10
Catalans Dragons	6	5	0	1	158	78	80	10
Warrington Wolves	6	4	0	2	180	90	90	8
Wigan Warriors	5	4	0	1	148	66	82	8
Hull KR	6	4	0	2	132	73	59	8
Leeds Rhinos	6	4	0	2	108	88	20	8
Salford Red Devils	6	4	0	2	127	118	9	8
Huddersfield Giants	6	3	0	3	120	104	16	6
Leigh Leopards	5	1	0	4	104	86	18	2
Hull FC	6	1	0	5	64	196	-132	2
Castleford Tigers	6	0	0	6	62	204	-142	0
London Broncos	6	0	0	6	60	246	-186	0

APRIL
Tight at the top

Round 7

The first round of April saw a reshuffle of the top teams with Catalans climbing two points clear at the summit after a 14-8 home Saturday-night win over St Helens, who themselves fell from first to fifth.

A 10,724 crowd (including 1,200 visiting Saints fans) were thrilled by a titanic tussle in Perpignan. Catalans were again missing influential veteran hooker Michael McIlorum, this time with an ankle injury and Saints had to cope without suspended prop Matty Lees, but it was still a compelling battle at the Stade Gilbert Brutus.

Catalans lost stand-off Jordan Abdull to a hamstring strain in the tenth minute and shortly after fullback Jack Welsby split the defence to score from 15 metres out, with captain Jonny Lomax unable to convert from the touchline.

Catalans prop Mike McMeeken hit straight back with a barge between the posts seven minutes from the break, Arthur Mourgue converting for a 6-4 lead. Tommy Makinson then turned the margin around by forcing his way over in the right corner to make it 8-6 to the visitors at the interval.

Early in the second half Catalans suffered a major loss when winger Tom Johnstone caught some friendly fire from teammate Tariq Sims and he left the pitch for concussion assessment, not to return. Saints almost took immediate advantage and Lewis Dodd got the green light from referee Moore when he crossed the line. But video evidence revealed that Mourgue had held him up in-goal with an astonishing defensive effort.

Saints' disappointment was compounded when a fumble from Lomax gifted Catalans field position and centre Matt Ikuvalu scored with 15 minutes left, Mourgue adding the conversion off the post to make it 12-8.

The game had been at boiling point from kick-off but the pressure blew five minutes from the end when a scuffle broke out and Mourgue capitalised with the resulting penalty to stretch the lead to six points and the winning scoreline.

St Helens were only fifth on points difference, level on ten league points with Warrington, Wigan and Hull KR, who all recorded big victories.

Wigan had little trouble in winning the sold-out 'Battle of the Borough' on the Thursday night when they came away from Leigh with a 40-12 win.

The mercurial Bevan French had that week signed a new four-year contract at the Warriors and he went a long way to clinching the game with two pieces of brilliance midway through the first half. For the first, he produced the most unexpected of kicks for a rare try by veteran backrower Willie Isa. Then after Patrick Mago's offload sent Jai Field away, French was in support and sent another intelligently-placed kick towards the try-line. Ricky Leutele should have cleared the danger but didn't and French could celebrate a wonderful score.

The Leopards were doing it tough, having won just one of their opening six Super League games, with central players missing from their pack - Robbie Mulhern pulled out late to join John Asiata, Tom Amone and Edwin Ipape on the sidelines - and it told against Wigan's forwards.

A Matt Parcell hat-trick on his 200th career appearance helped Hull KR to an emphatic

April

Warrington's Jordan Crowther closed down by Leeds' Tom Holroyd and Cameron Smith

50-10 home win over a threadbare London on the Friday night.

London coach Mike Eccles described the first half as the worst 40 minutes of his Rugby League career as Rovers led 40-4 at the break. Five tries in a 15-minute spell midway through the first half took the game away from the Broncos.

Parcell played 80 minutes at dummy-half as Robins coach Willie Peters rested his other hooker Jez Litten and handed halfback Ben Reynolds, signed from Featherstone, a debut off the bench.

Warrington won hands down at Headingley as they emerged with a 34-8 success over the Rhinos.

After going behind to a Harry Newman try, by half-time the Wolves were in complete control, leading 16-4. George Williams was at the heart of everything with a fine individual solo try backed up with involvement in tries for Matty Nicholson and Joe Bullock.

Leeds were disrupted with the losses of Ash Handley and Tom Holroyd early but it was their mounting frustration that cost them, especially after the video referee chalked off a try for Paul Momirovski for a double movement in the 47th minute, with the score at 16-8.

Three Wolves tries in the last 15 minutes blew the score out. Hooker Danny Walker sniped over from dummy-half, before Williams engineered a try for Matt Dufty with a lovely pass and Josh Thewlis ensured a disappointing night for Leeds when picking off Brodie Croft's pass to go over from halfway.

On the same Friday night, Castleford got their first win of the season with a 36-24 home victory over Salford.

The Tigers dedicated their win to prop George Lawler, who that week had been taken to hospital after suffering a seizure at home on Wednesday night, with scans subsequently showing a small bleed on his brain.

The victory came at a cost. Paul McShane pulled out in the warm-up with a hamstring strain while Liam Watts failed a head-injury assessment after being withdrawn in the first half. Josh Simm came off with an arm injury in the final moments. Winger Innes Senior grabbed the headlines with four tries.

April

The Tigers climbed above Hull FC who on the Saturday afternoon fell to another big home defeat, this time by 56-22 to Huddersfield, conceding more than 50 points for the third time in four games as well as picking up three yellow cards - one to Jack Brown and two of them to Ligi Sao.

To make it even worse, the major contribution to Huddersfield's victory was a first-half hat-trick of tries by Adam Swift, a Hull player in 2023. It began right in the first minute after Matty English made a break through the Hull defence. Although he was tackled by Jayden Okunbor, the Giants moved the ball quickly to the left for Jake Connor - another former Hull player - to feed Swift for his first try. Connor converted from the touchline and would go on to land seven out of nine attempts, leaving him just two short of 500 Super League points.

Halfback Jack Charles was one of three teenagers used by coach Tony Smith in the game, with Lewis Martin starting on the left wing and Logan Moy having a bright debut at fullback off the bench.

Smith was sacked the following Wednesday.

Challenge Cup Quarter Finals

Hull KR were through to the Challenge Cup semi-finals for a third season in a row after beating Leigh 26-14 in a Saturday afternoon quarter-final at Craven Park.

Joe Burgess's run in from his own 20-metre line gave KR an early lead before Kai O'Donnell edged the holders ahead. Rovers regained the lead soon after the restart when Burgess crashed over in the corner for his second before Kelepi Tanginoa stretched out the lead.

Umyla Hanley responded as Leigh set up a tense finale but Niall Evalds grabbed a try. Only when skipper Elliot Minchella scored with a mere ten seconds remaining could Craven Park let out a collective sigh of relief.

Leigh were without both Gareth O'Brien and Robbie Mulhern, out for at least the next six weeks with torn calf muscles.

Later that evening, Huddersfield produced a stunning 34-6 win in baking-hot Perpignan after a dominant display over the Super League leaders and a 14-point contribution from star fullback Jake Connor.

Huddersfield were on the front foot from the start and opened the scoring with a dynamic burst from hooker Adam Milner, whose pass through the halves fed Connor for the first try of the game with a powerful short-range burst on the right.

Connor missed his conversion but Milner took the Giants further forward by picking up a ricochet kick from second rower Jack Murchie to ground the ball in the 23rd minute, with Connor on target this time to make it 10-0.

It was all Huddersfield in the first half with the Dragons struggling for territory and possession as tries from Connor, Jack Murchie and in-form winger Adam Swift put the Giants 16-0 ahead at half-time.

Tom Davies bombed a high kick in the opening stages of the second half and prop Sebastine Ikahihifo mopped up the loose ball to stroll over unhindered, with Connor converting again to push the Giants 22-0 ahead and the Giants were effectively through to the semis.

On the Sunday, winger Liam Marshall plundered four tries as Wigan tore apart injury-hit Castleford, leaving the Jungle with a 60-6 victory.

With Wigan surging clear so quickly, it became a question of how many points Matt Peet's men could stack up and it could have been a lot more than 60, especially if Harry Smith had kicked more productively. Smith converted only a half of Wigan's dozen tries as he struggled in sometimes windy conditions.

There were five tries for the Warriors in the first half plus another seven in the second period - and eight different try scorers.

And there was a blow for Wigan as Willie Isa went off midway through the first half with a serious injury to his ankle and lower leg. Tigers PNG prop Sylvester Namo got a five-game ban for dangerous contact.

George Williams underlined his reputation with a masterful performance to help

April

Warrington demolish hosts St Helens 31-8.

In tandem with Williams, Matty Ashton's finishing knew no bounds while Matt Dufty was electric out of the back and James Harrison laid the platform up front.

Ashton produced the finish of a lifetime as his side scored five tries. Holding a 7-6 interval lead, Warrington hit Saints with two early second-half tries, the first of them Ashton's brilliant score in the left corner. The Wolves then ran amok as Connor Wrench, James Harrison and George Williams crossed. Josh Thewlis landed five kicks to add to his first-half try.

Williams also came up with a first-half field goal that gave Warrington their edge at the break.

Saints' first-half points came from a Konrad Hurrell try, improved by Jon Bennison, who scored their only points after the break with a penalty.

Round 8

Having made an early Challenge Cup exit, Hull FC had the Cup weekend off and some time to settle after the departure of head coach Tony Smith and his assistant Stanley Gene.

The new coach was to be sourced by the new Director of Rugby Richie Myler, who had retired from playing (at York) and taken up a three-year contract.

Simon Grix, who joined as an assistant coach over the winter after five years in charge at Championship side Halifax, took over on an interim basis alongside Hull's head of emerging talent, former Bradford and Widnes boss Francis Cummins.

The exodus stretched beyond the coaching staff, with star players Tex Hoy and Fa'amanu Brown both released by the club during a dramatic week. Both players were off-contract at the end of the season but had accelerated their departures, in Hoy's case after being told of his release by Smith before he was sacked.

Fullback Hoy quickly found a new home, at Castleford Tigers, while Brown asked to return down under to be closer to his family, ending a stay of little over three months, and joining St George Illawarra Dragons.

Grix's first match in charge was daunting, a Friday-night trip to St Helens and Saints showed no mercy on their way to a 58-0 thrashing.

Tommy Makinson crossed in the corner after four minutes and Jack Welsby added a tenth try a minute from time with a youthful Hull side conceding regularly in between.

The huge score was enough to improve St Helens' points difference to take them back into second place in the table.

Up the road in Wigan, the Warriors were predicted to enjoy a similar rout as they faced Castleford five days after putting 60 points on them in the Cup. But the Tigers put up sterner resistance before falling to a 36-14 defeat.

Craig Lingard welcomed back Liam Watts in the front row, with Samy Kibula dropping to the bench. Young forward George Hill and winger Louis Senior, on loan for the season from Hull KR, were both handed their debuts, while Rowan Milnes replaced Danny Richardson in the halves.

Bevan French was once again brilliant and he opened the scoring after just seven minutes but then Louis Senior intercepted a pass to run 80 metres and score for Castleford.

Liam Marshall's first try put Wigan back in front but Milnes' penalty on the stroke of half-time made it 12-8.

But Ryan Hampshire scored two tries in four minutes just after half-time as the Warriors then stretched away. Marshall went over in the corner for his second just before the hour mark and opposite wing Abbas Miski grounded a French grubber before Milnes scored a consolation for the Tigers.

The day after on the Saturday, Warrington also recorded a victory but in a much tighter contest at home to Leigh, Matty Nicholson's try ten minutes from time sealing a 16-14 win.

Off-season NRL recruit Lachlan Fitzgibbon scored his first try for the Wolves midway through the first half, after Josh Charnley's try from a lovely team move had given Leigh an

April

Catalans Dragons' Tevita Satae races past Hull KR's Dean Hadley

early 4-0 advantage. Josh Thewlis converted for 6-4 but two tries either side of half-time for the Leopards left Warrington in arrears.

Seven minutes from the break, Zak Hardaker kicked for a Ben McNamara try after Umyla Hanley won a contest for Lachlan Lam's bomb against young halfback Leon Hayes. Matt Moylan converted for 10-6.

The Leopards were full value for their lead and doubled it nine minutes into the second half. After a Matt Dufty error, a wonderful Moylan cut-out ball found Charnley to put his centre Ricky Leutele over.

Up stepped Fitzgibbon again. First his huge shot on Hanley got the crowd off their feet, then moments afterwards Stefan Ratchford forced a Moylan error and the Aussie backrower instigated another try. George Williams found Fitzgibbon running a strong line and, as Ben McNamara clung onto his ankle, he threw a wonderful offload out for Dufty to cross, with Thewlis's goal narrowing Leigh's lead to two.

The winning try came ten minutes from time. Dufty started the move, stretching the Leopards' defence with his wide run and picking out Thewlis on the touchline. Thewlis dashed inside from halfway, breaking clear and, as defenders closed in he had the support of forward Nicholson, who himself had work to do to reach the try-line.

That evening Catalans stayed two points clear of the chasing pack with a convincing 36-6 home win over Hull KR that exorcised the ghost of their Challenge Cup defeat.

Veteran hooker Michael McIlorum returned from injury and took the game by the scruff of the neck, scoring an early try and putting the fire back into the Dragons.

And although the Robins hit straight back with a try from winger Joe Burgess, Catalans dominated a Rovers side badly missing star halfback Mikey Lewis, who missed out on the trip to France with a last-minute hamstring injury. When Théo Fages stepped through a yawning gap in the Robins' defence to put 20 clear points between the sides, the game was already up in the 33rd minute.

Hull KR dropped two points behind the top four and they were joined on ten league points by Huddersfield and Salford.

On the Friday night the Giants imposed a fourth successive home defeat on Leeds with an impressive 30-24 win.

April

The ultimate difference was exemplified by the respective fullbacks. Jake Connor was given more space and time to weave his undoubted magic as the game wore on. He had a part in five of side's six tries in what became an irresistible combination with his left side, exploiting a situation in which Leeds had lost Harry Newman (back) and David Fusitu'a (another knee injury on his seasonal debut).

In contrast, Rhinos fullback Lachlan Miller was the best on the field in the first half but prone to injudicious decisions. His poor kick on the last that led to a seven-tackle set was the precursor to Adam Swift's try just after the hour, which was scored on that seventh play. But his decision to drop out short with the sides tied at 24-all and six minutes remaining was unfathomable. Not sending it ten metres and giving Connor a penalty kick in front of the posts to edge the Giants ahead was ludicrous.

The Rhinos launched one final attack in the Giants' quarter but halfback Adam Clune collected a ball which to the naked eye looked like it had been knocked on and raced clear to settle it.

Salford also had a closer than expected contest in Wimbledon before finishing 12-4 victors over the Broncos.

London were pinned into their own territory most of the game, even during a final quarter when Salford were reduced to twelve men by the dismissal of King Vuniyayawa for a dangerous tackle.

They took the lead after 19 minutes when Iliess Macani scored in the corner before Kallum Watkins replied six minutes later. Deon Cross made it 12-4 to Salford early in the second half before the Broncos' Will Lovell was sin-binned. Vuniyayawa was sent-off for a tip tackle on 55 minutes but on the Monday no further action was taken by the Match Review Panel.

Round 9

St Helens were the only team from the top four in the table to win in round nine and ended up leading the field on points difference after a dramatic 13-12 Thursday-night home win over Huddersfield.

Saints captain Jonny Lomax kicked a field goal with 33 seconds remaining as his team fought back from 12-0 down to end the Giants' five-match winning run. The Saints half coolly struck the match-winning kick perfectly from almost 40 metres out with golden-point looming, the only time in the game that the home team were in front.

It was a cruel way to lose for the Giants, who had led 12-0 thanks to two tries in the first twelve minutes from Kevin Naiqama and Adam Swift, both converted by Jake Connor.

The game turned on a flashpoint just before Saints' second try midway through the second half. Connor, who was otherwise outstanding, clashed with Saints' Morgan Knowles at the play-the-ball and he protested vociferously to referee Liam Moore. As he continued to plead his case to Moore, Saints hooker Daryl Clark spotted that Connor had turned his back and powered through the gap he'd left in the defensive line to touch down.

St Helens were set to be without top prop Alex Walmsley for a significant portion of the season through injury. The England star suffered a hamstring injury in the recent Challenge Cup defeat to Warrington. That issue would keep him out for at least six weeks but the club was also considering putting Walmsley in for knee surgery to fix another problem, ruling him out for much of the summer until the run-in.

Saints were expected to announce the departure of halfback Lewis Dodd from next season. Dodd was reportedly ready to sign a four-year contract for the NRL's bottom club at the time, South Sydney, from 2024.

The night after, Leigh beat Catalans by 30-2, after cutting loose with four unanswered tries in the second half after a first 40 minutes of pure attrition.

Despite early periods of dominant possession, Catalans couldn't score a try, with a solitary penalty goal from Arthur Mourgue their only score.

A long-range try by winger Josh Charnley midway through the first half set up a home

April

6-2 lead, followed by four second-half strikes by the Leopards. Kai O'Donnell and Umyla Hanley crossed in the four minutes after the break and Matt Moylan continued his perfect evening off the tee to put Leigh 18-2 up going into the final quarter. The Leopards fans erupted again moments later when captain John Asiata came off the bench for his first action in eight weeks following a calf injury.

The previous season's runners-up remained try-less and wilted further as O'Donnell crossed again and Moylan sprinted over to take his personal tally to 14 points and cap a memorable win for the hosts.

Wigan were put to the sword at Hull KR, with the final score of 26-10 flattering the Champions.

It was an unexpected mismatch, certainly in the first half. The Robins were physically dominant from the off, as exemplified by Sauaso Sue's opening try when he bulldozed straight through Warriors skipper Liam Farrell. Mikey Lewis converted and Oliver Gildart further extended their advantage with a dummy after nice handling by Lewis and Niall Evalds.

A penalty for an unpacked scrum allowing another Rovers attack and a high shot from Brad O'Neill allowed Lewis to kick for 12-0.

And that was 18-0 shortly after as Peta Hiku broke down the middle from his own half, shrugging off the poor tackle attempts of Farrell and Harry Smith and then combining with Evalds to finish himself.

Only now did the visitors show any signs of life. Abbas Miski scored in the 54th minute off a lovely Bevan French pass over the top. But Hull KR's win was certain just past the hour mark, as Lewis shrugged off French and found Gildart to set up a trademark muscular finish in the corner by Ryan Hall.

There was still time, however, for the most remarkable moment of an unexpected night. When a Jai Field pass missed its target, Adam Keighran, and came off Hall, Kelepi Tanginoa picked up. Everyone - including himself for a time - was waiting for the whistle, and when it didn't come the forward duly hit the accelerator and went on a staggering dash down the field to score.

Farrell crossed, with unusual ease, for the final try in a momentary blip, just about the only thing Hull KR did wrong all night.

On the Saturday, Salford beat Warrington 17-12 at home after a noisy week off the field, in which an approach by Hull FC for head coach Paul Rowley was turned down.

It was a terrific contest that was decided by a penalty try awarded following an off-the-ball tackle on Ryan Brierley by Danny Walker as he attempted to touch down a kick in goal.

Both sides traded first-half tries as efforts from Tim Lafai and Joe Mellor for Salford were cancelled out by James Harrison and George Williams, with Marc Sneyd's field goal giving the hosts a narrow 11-10 half-time lead.

A Stefan Ratchford penalty goal in the 55th minute saw the Wolves hit the front. But a sparkling move down the right ended with Nene Macdonald kicking in-field and Walker conceding the penalty try.

More bad news for the Wolves was the broken ankle suffered by 20-year-old halfback Leon Hayes, who had been keeping Josh Drinkwater out of the side, his season over.

Rowley said after the win that happiness drove him to stay at the club.

Castleford put bottom side London to the sword in emphatic fashion, winning 40-0 on the Friday night at the Jungle. Controlled by Rowan Milnes, the Tigers were red-hot from the first minute as Innes and Louis Senior, alongside new boy Tex Hoy, carved the Broncos apart.

Neither side had broken any pots in 2024 until this game, with Castleford going into the fixture with just one win and the Broncos still stuck on zero.

Craig Lingard welcomed two Castleford debutants in the shape of Hoy and Corey Hall, on loan from Hull KR, whilst another Hull KR loanee, Louis Senior made his first home appearance for the Tigers. Joe Westerman, Paul McShane and Alex Mellor returned too after missing the loss to Wigan.

Innes Senior scored either side of half-time to take his tally of Super League tries this season to nine, one fewer than divisional leader Adam Swift of Huddersfield Giants.

April

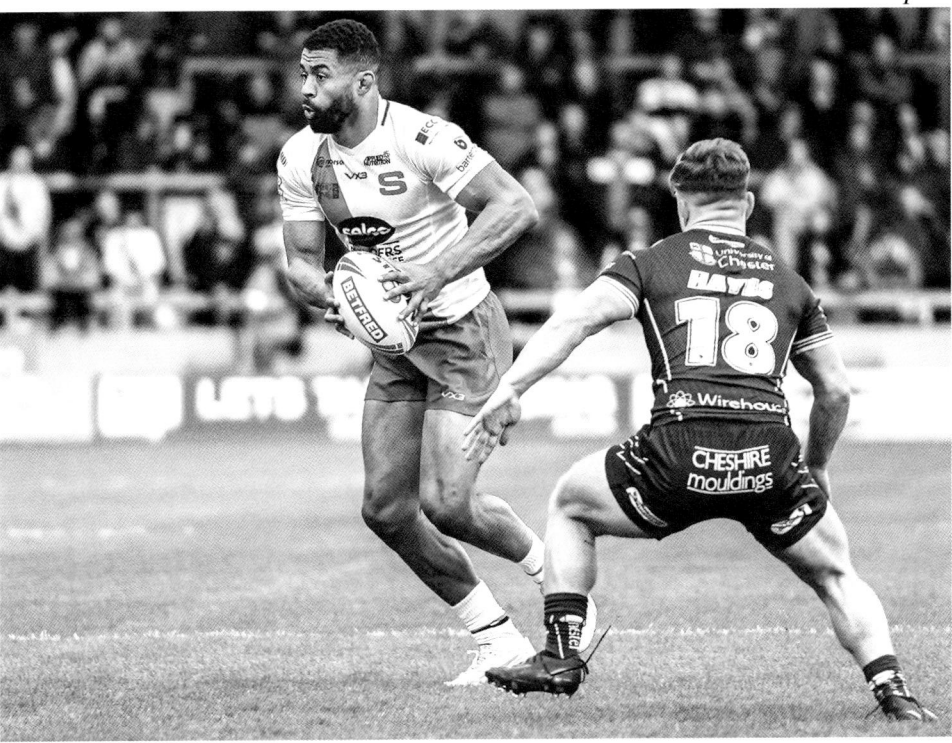

Salford's Kallum Watkins looks for support as Warrington's Leon Hayes moves in

The Tigers were reported to be open to letting Danny Richardson leave on loan after a busy week of deals at the club.

Wigan prop Sam Eseh and Hall and Louis Senior had all joined the Tigers, the latter pair for the rest of the season with Jack Broadbent going in the other direction before moving to the Robins permanently from 2025.

In the only Sunday game, Leeds held their nerve in East Yorkshire to claim a valuable 18-12 win over a stubborn Hull FC side.

It was an end-to-end contest that could have gone either way. Brodie Croft controlled the game well when he needed to, injecting himself at key moments to set up two of the Rhinos' three tries, with Cameron's Smith's second-half score proving to be the difference.

It was certainly a debut to remember for Leeds young winger Riley Lumb, who grabbed a well taken double in an eye-catching first display in Super League.

For Hull, it was a much improved performance, particularly without the ball. After shipping in more than 50 points in four of their last five outings, the home side had more steel in defence but were found lacking with ball in hand and unable to come up with the vital game-levelling score, despite having plenty of field position throughout.

Loanees Ed Chamberlain (from Leigh) and Yusuf Aydin (Hull KR) both made debuts for the Airlie Birds, who had also signed winger Tom Briscoe from Leigh on a permanent deal, with Darnell McIntosh heading the other way.

BETFRED SUPER LEAGUE
Sunday 28th April

	P	W	D	L	F	A	D	Pts
St Helens	9	7	0	2	209	70	139	14
Catalans Dragons	9	7	0	2	210	122	88	14
Wigan Warriors	8	6	0	2	234	118	116	12
Warrington Wolves	9	6	0	3	242	129	113	12
Hull KR	9	6	0	3	214	129	85	12
Salford Red Devils	9	6	0	3	180	170	10	12
Huddersfield Giants	9	5	0	4	218	163	55	10
Leeds Rhinos	9	5	0	4	158	164	-6	10
Leigh Leopards	8	2	0	6	160	144	16	4
Castleford Tigers	9	2	0	7	152	264	-112	4
Hull FC	9	1	0	8	98	328	-230	2
London Broncos	9	0	0	9	74	348	-274	0

MAY
Levelling up

Round 10

The Super League table had a compelling look after the first round of May, as the top-six clubs sat equal on 14 league points.

Wigan went back to top of the table on points difference after a convincing 30-8 home win over Catalans on the first Thursday night of the month.

The Dragons had the better moments of the first half but they only held a two-point advantage at the break. They led 8-0 at one stage with an Arthur Mourgue penalty and a converted Julian Bousquet try but Wigan hit back with Luke Thompson crossing for his first try in cherry and white.

A moment of sheer brilliance from Harry Smith, when he chipped over the top and was on hand to collect his own kick and score, and a try from Adam Keighran saw Wigan take a ten-point lead in the second half. They again had to defend their line heroically before Liam Farrell and Abbas Miski added to the points tally. Form centre Jake Wardle saved two tries in the second half and unselfishly sent Farrell over for his 150th career try.

Catalans remained on 14 league points but sank to fifth on points difference.

Warrington moved into second the following night as winger Josh Thewlis scored a hat-trick of tries in a 24-6 home win over Hull FC.

It was an eventful pre-match, with Warrington having one interchange taken off them following an administrative error that saw Adam Holroyd named in the starting 17 but not the 21-man squad that had been notified to the RFL earlier in the week.

Wolves coach Sam Burgess was furious. Sky Sports cameras showed a very brief altercation post-match between Burgess and newly appointed Hull FC director of rugby Richie Myler, who denied Warrington's request to allow them to play Holroyd without the penalty of an interchange being taken off them.

Despite a ninth defeat in 11 games, Hull FC were cheered by the sight of halfback Jake Trueman making his first appearance of the season. After coming off the bench Trueman provided the cut-out pass that created Tom Briscoe's first try for Hull FC on his return to the club from Leigh.

On the Saturday St Helens missed the chance to go two points clear of the pack as they came out second best at Hull KR, the Robins themselves going joint top on 14 points with a convincing 40-20 win.

Rovers were forced into making a pre-match change as Oliver Gildart pulled up in the warm-up with a knee injury and was replaced by debutant Jack Broadbent five minutes before kick-off. Saints were also forced into changes when winger Tommy Makinson came down with chickenpox in the week, his place taken by Tee Ritson for his first appearance of the season.

Scrum-half Mikey Lewis scored a try, orchestrated three others and kicked superbly to cap a marvellous team effort. Broadbent, who scored a try on debut, and former Wakefield backrower Kelepi Tanginoa also starred in front of another sell-out crowd at Craven Park.

After the game footage emerged on social media of small groups of rival fans clashing and being kept apart by stewards and the RFL promised an investigation.

That came at the end of a week in which St Helens had been fined £1,500, suspended until the end of the 2025 season, for breaches of the RFL Operational Rules relating to stewarding, following an incident after the Super League fixture against Leigh on March 1st. Footage of the incident after the game appeared to show a St Helens fans being attacked by a member of the Leigh staff, with players holding him back.

Salford were in the 14-point brigade too after a Friday-night 18-16 win at Huddersfield.

The game had just about everything - excitement, an almost-remarkable comeback and three cards as Salford held off a desperate Huddersfield final ten-minute onslaught to register their seventh win of the campaign.

The Red Devils had Ryan Brierley and Chris Atkin sin-binned either side of half-time, whilst Elliot Wallis saw red for an alleged headbutt for the Giants, with Ian Watson's men apparently dead and buried as the clock hit 70 minutes. Three tries in the final nine minutes, however, left the visiting supporters biting their fingernails, but Paul Rowley's side did just enough – and deserved to as well.

Nene Macdonald looked to have inspired Salford to a comfortable win, scoring a try in each half and setting up their other score for Ethan Ryan, Marc Sneyd controlling the game as well as converting all three tries for an 18-0 lead.

But the Giants scored three tries in the final ten minutes in a frenetic finale. Adam Swift's 11th try in Super League that season started the comeback, though Jake Connor's unsuccessful conversion attempt proved crucial as further scores from Tui Lolohea and Jake Bibby were not enough to prevent a second consecutive defeat for the Giants.

Leeds were two points behind the leading pack after a comfortable 46-8 home win over off-the-pace London Broncos.

Coach Rohan Smith got what he called a 'professional display', with eight tries – all to different scorers – and the overcoming of further injury disruption to the backs.

Teenager Riley Lumb, looking to continue where he left off on his debut at Hull FC, broke clear on the second tackle after the hosts spread the ball wide in their own half, but pulled a hamstring.

And Brodie Croft, who had terrorised the London defence and picked up his first try in Leeds colours, went off before the half-hour with a groin strain.

Andy Ackers, coming off the bench, created three tries, mesmerising the Broncos' markers, with Lachlan Miller running riot from fullback.

And in the last game of the round on the Saturday evening a hugely entertaining game at Leigh Sports Village ended with the Leopards and Castleford all square at 28-28, with ten minutes of golden point time unable to separate the two.

PNG hooker Edwin Ipape's return off the bench from injury sparked a Leigh Leopards comeback as the Tigers went 10-0 up in the first quarter.

Lachlan Lam's dash in at the corner to stretch the advantage to 28-16 with ten minutes left on the clock looked to have sealed it for Leigh. But Castleford again closed the gap after winning a short kick-off and a batted pass from the outstanding Tex Hoy shipped the ball on for Innes Senior to race over by the left corner flag. Rowan Milnes goaled to close the deficit to six points with seven minutes remaining.

The Tigers were determined and gained a scrum after Josh Charnley nudged the ball forward. From the possession, a wonderful ball from Hoy saw Louis Senior cross in thrilling fashion on the right and Milnes converted superbly from the touchline to level things up at 28-28.

Moylan saw his first attempted field goal go wide in the last seconds of the first period of extra time. Another Moylan attempt rebounded off the upright before Lam saw an effort go agonisingly wide.

There was further late drama when Hoy shot through the centre of the defence and passed wide, only for Umyla Hanley to intercept and Charnley went to ground for the draw.

May
Round 11

After ten consecutive defeats since their elevation to Super League, London Broncos finally got off the mark with a 34-18 home win over Hull FC, bringing them level with the struggling Airlie Birds on league points but with a points difference 32 points worse.

It was an entertaining clash in Wimbledon despite not having the jeopardy of a serious relegation clash. A-rated Hull knew that however poor they were, they were guaranteed a place in Super League under the IMG ratings, while London had no chance of avoiding relegation.

London led 16-12 at the break after a nip and tuck 40 minutes after Herman Ese'ese and Jake Trueman tries against scores from Alex Walker, James Meadows and Robbie Storey.

After the break, Hull prop Yusuf Aydin got the ball down as he was carried over by defenders and Jack Charles' third goal made it 16-18.

But then came the key moment. Jordan Lane was sin-binned for a late tackle and while Oli Leyland hit the post with the penalty, the only one awarded in the second half, London took ruthless advantage of the extra man with tries from Jarred Bassett and Lee Kershaw to lead 28-18 by the time parity was restored.

London put the issue beyond doubt with twelve minutes left when the irrepressible Oli Leyland picked out a loose Hull offload near half way and charged untouched and exultant all the way to the line.

His celebrations before he got there and his somersault on touching down echoed the feelings amongst the Broncos faithful.

The team above the pair on five league points, Castleford Tigers, had been showing some signs of revival but on the Friday night they were humbled by St Helens at the Jungle, a 60-4 defeat coming despite spending almost half of the match with an extra player in a game of two red cards.

Tommy Makinson's dismissal for a late shot on Tex Hoy early in the first half gave underdogs Castleford a leg-up, albeit one they failed to decisively take. Then Liam Horne's red card early in the second half for a tip tackle was fully taken advantage of by St Helens, who went on an absolute rout.

Eight tries in half an hour, three of them by Waqa Blake, left Castleford battered and bruised.

Makinson and Horne got one-match bans which they were able to work off in reserve matches on the following weekend's Challenge Cup semi-finals.

Wigan stayed at the top of the table with a marginally better points difference from Saints, after a Saturday afternoon masterclass at Huddersfield saw them emerge 48-6 victors.

Wigan pulled away brilliantly in the second half after a real tussle at the start - similar to the previous week when they beat Catalans. They were thrown a challenge right from the off when Liam Byrne was shown the yellow card for the first tackle of the game, in which he caught Matty English high with his shoulder. But they led 8-0 by the time Byrne returned to the field - Liam Marshall going the length of the field for the first of his three tries after being handed the ball by the Giants' Sam Halsall, and Harry Smith adding the first two of his eight goals.

From 12-6 ahead at half-time and still only holding a two-score lead past the hour, they ran away in the final quarter. As in the first half, Marshall opened things up after an error from opposing winger Halsall. Following his knock-on, Field sent a cut-out pass to Marshall, who went inside Adam Clune to finish.

The try that ended the contest - and opened the floodgates - came in the 62nd minute. Again French crossed with ease, this time stepping past Tui Lolohea to break the line. Marshall then skipped over for his hat-trick score, provided by Jake Wardle after captain Liam Farrell's break and offload.

Warrington dropped to third despite having on the Thursday won their home game with in-form Hull KR by 20-8.

The Wolves raced into an 18-0 lead through Toby King's double and a penalty try to Matty Ashton, with Josh Thewlis knocking over three goals. Jack Broadbent's score gave Rovers

May

London Broncos' Lee Kershaw celebrates as Robbie Storey crashes over against Hull FC

something to take into the break and the visitors came out transformed as Mikey Lewis's stepping try brought them back within ten points.

But Warrington withstood spells of incessant pressure before a late Thewlis penalty sealed it.

Catalans remained level on league points in fourth after a Saturday-evening 26-0 home win over under-strength Leeds.

The Rhinos, missing Harry Newman, Brodie Croft, Paul Momirovski, James Donaldson, Tom Holroyd, James Bentley, Morgan Gannon and David Fusitu'a, put up some stern resistance in the early stages but couldn't stop Tom Davies opening the scoring on the right wing after Jayden Nikorima and Arthur Mourgue concocted a swift passing movement to the right, Mourgue on target with the conversion to make it 6-0 on 16 minutes.

Mourgue added a penalty and that's how it stayed until half-time at 8-0, with Leeds still in the fight.

A 90-metre breakaway from winger Tom Johnstone and Mourgue's conversion from the touchline put daylight between the sides at 14-0. And it took a flashing 30-metre dash from fullback Mourgue to end the game as a contest with two minutes left and he converted for 20-0. Hooker Alrix Da Costa had the final say with a reach from the tackle for a try just before the hooter, with Mourgue again on target with the kick.

Mike McMeeken pulled a disjointed Dragons side together with another commanding performance as news emerged that he would be leaving the Dragons at the end of the season to join ambitious Championship front-runners Wakefield.

Leigh put days of press speculation and stories about several players' futures behind them with a convincing 40-12 home victory over Salford, with the outstanding Josh Charnley providing the icing on the cake with his 300th career try.

The Leopards scored two tries in the first twelve minutes and, despite a Salford try from Ryan Brierley, they never allowed their opponents back into the game.

Wingers Umyla Hanley and Charnley, who celebrated a new one-year deal, scored twice each.

That week, head coach Adrian Lam ended speculation linking him with a move to the NRL by signing a new deal until the end of 2027.

May

Wigan's Abbas Miski beats Hull KR's Ryan Hall to score in the corner

Challenge Cup Semi-finals

Warrington Wolves and Wigan Warriors earned the right to contest the Challenge Cup Final via two easier than expected semi-finals.

Wigan blitzed Hull KR in the Saturday game at Doncaster, scoring five unanswered tries before half-time and going on to finish 38-6 victors.

The two had met at the same stage 12 months before, when the semi-final was decided by one point in Rovers' favour. But the Warriors - led by the imperious Jake Wardle and Harry Smith - were totally dominant.

After the Warriors were awarded an early penalty for offside, Wigan duly punished Willie Peters' side. The ball was shifted left and Wardle had enough time to crash past Peta Hiku in just the fourth minute. Smith couldn't convert as Wigan led 4-0.

Things got even worse for Rovers as a brilliant set saw Wigan run 80 metres before Bevan French sent up a pinpoint chip to Abbas Miski. The Wigan winger caught superbly and dotted down just before being pushed out of play. This time Smith converted for a 10-0 lead.

Some brilliance from Mikey Lewis almost brought Rovers back into it with his chip and chase just running dead but both sides began to make errors in the Doncaster heat.

On the half hour, Niall Evalds dropped a towering Smith bomb and, in the following set, Smith sent over Junior Nsemba, who had enough power to ride the challenge of Kelepi Tanginoa. Smith was wayward with the conversion attempt though as Wigan were now 14-0 up.

With half-time approaching Joe Burgess couldn't take in a Wardle grubber, as Liam Marshall picked up and fed Miski under the posts. Smith once more couldn't convert but, at 18-0 there was little sign of Rovers inspiring a comeback.

There was still time for Wigan to break down their left once more, Wardle feeding Marshall, before the winger kicked back inside perfectly for Smith to pounce. Adam Keighran added the goal to make it 24-0 at half-time.

Tyler Dupree and Wardle added two more in the second half, after Joe Burgess scored Hull KR's sole try.

The day after, Warrington produced a convincing 46-10 victory against Huddersfield at St Helens, captain George Williams putting on another masterclass,

The Wolves were on top from their superb seventh minute try. A lovely backline shift coming out of their own end resulted in the opener for Josh Drinkwater when Williams threw a

Warrington's Matty Ashton looks to evade Huddersfield's Ashton Golding

lovely two-man cut-out pass to Matty Ashton streaking down the sideline. He found Williams back on the inside in support, he passed to Toby King who then in turn found Drinkwater to finish the job under the posts.

The carnage continued down the same edge moments later as Dufty found some space and delivered a pass to Ashton, who touched down in the ninth minute. Nine minutes later, Danny Walker burrowed his way over, giving Warrington an 18-point lead after as many minutes.

Tui Lolohea started to build some Huddersfield pressure by forcing a goal-line drop-out, and it led to their first points of the day through Adam Swift, who crossed over untouched off the back of a nice backline shift.

However, Williams responded with a brilliant solo try in the 34th minute after Walker busted through some loose Huddersfield defence. Williams showed great footwork to evade both Jake Connor and Adam Clune, who were chasing in cover defence.

A last-second field-goal attempt by Williams on the stroke of half-time hit the upright to conclude the first half of action, with his side 22-4 up.

Early in the second half, Ben Currie charged down a Huddersfield kick and ran 40 metres before he was dragged down by Lolohea. Williams was quick to strike off the back of it and delivered a nice short ball to Matt Dufty, who powered his way over.

Another beautiful backline move then saw Dufty grab his second of the day in the 53rd minute and erase any doubt that the Wolves would be heading to Wembley.

Fireworks erupted in the 58th minute when Jake Connor gave Thewlis a shove over the advertising behind the dead-ball line and in front of the Warrington crowd.

A Warrington error allowed Huddersfield the chance to put some more points on the board through Kevin Naiqama, who struck Sam Powell's arm from first marker, forcing him to drop the ball. Naiqama picked it up and ran it in for a try converted by Connor, who not long after was penalised and yellow carded for an offence on Thewlis, with Warrington electing to take the two points from Thewlis, who also converted six of their eight tries.

Leroy Cudjoe looked to have scored a consolation try off a great put down in the 72nd minute, but it was overruled by the video referee after a desperate tackle by Thewlis.

Instead Warrington finished with a flourish, scoring two more tries in the final four minutes. Sam Powell crashed over next to the posts from an inside ball by Williams and then, after Huddersfield put the kick-off out on the full, Dufty found PNG centre Rodrick Tai out wide, who took on Connor one-on-one and crashed over to score.

May
Round 12

St Helens went back to the top of the table on points difference, leap-frogging Wigan, with Warrington also level on league points as the Challenge Cup finalists continued their brilliant semi-finals form.

The Wolves had the toughest assignment with a Saturday-night meeting with Catalans in Perpignan and they came through with a 16-8 win. Catalans were fully refreshed from a week off for the Cup semis and a third win of the season against the Wolves seemed on the cards at an expectant Stade Gilbert Brutus.

But an inspired decision by coach Sam Burgess to rest and repair his players with a week on the beach at Canet Plage in the build-up paid off.

Mike McMeeken pulled out of Catalans' starting 17 with a hand injury - hooker Michael McIlorum was already missing with a knee issue. Things got worse very quickly when replacement number nine Alrix Da Costa left the field and failed a HIA after just five minutes of the game and they went to crisis level as the Dragons finished the game with spare substitution spots available but no fit players to fill them.

But Warrington's ebullient and energetic approach was the real reason for the result. Former Dragon Josh Drinkwater starred and his relationship with man of the match George Williams in the halves and their seamless link with fullback Matt Dufty was a devastating combination. And the forwards were the foundation, with James Harrison, Paul Vaughan and Ben Currie stand-outs.

The game was played at a ferocious pace throughout with end-to-end action in the warm sunshine. A 2-2 interval scoreline was a fair reflection of a competitive and evenly-balanced opening 40 minutes. But the visitors seized the moment two minutes after the break when Matt Dufty danced through a gap ten metres from the line and George Williams for the first try of the match.

Josh Thewlis put the Wolves two points further ahead with a penalty in the 56th minute as the Dragons started dropping like flies with an alarming series of injuries.and Warrington scored the killer try ten minutes from the end when winger Matty Ashton struck from short range with a dynamic burst to make it 14-2.

Thewlis was unable to convert and Tom Davies then took the game close to the wire with a 30-metre dash to score in the right corner five minutes from time, Mourgue's touchline conversion making it a six-point game.

But it wasn't enough to stop Warrington as Thewlis completed the scoring with a last-gasp penalty.

St Helens coach Paul Wellens was left delighted by the way his team responded to two early injury setbacks during the Friday 40-10 home win over Leeds. Saints lost Joe Batchelor to an ankle injury after just six minutes, while Jonny Lomax also went off just before half-time with a fractured hand.

With winger Matty Russell on debut and making good metres before his injury withdrawal after 25 minutes, the Rhinos opened brightly in what proved to be their best spell. Brodie Croft's delightful early cross-field chip on his own quarter set Ash Handley free on a 70-metre gallop, with Mikołaj Olędzki's fine turn and pass allowing Croft and Rhyse Martin to send Handley over in the corner, with Martin goaling for an early lead.

But Konrad Hurrell positioned James Bell and then sent Sione Mata'utia over to level and it was all Saints from then on. Moses Mbye crashed over on the cusp of half-time and Daryl Clark increased the advantage four minutes after the restart. Luis Roberts cut into the hosts' lead but Jack Welsby's double, either side of Curtis Sironen and Tommy Makinson's scores, helped Saints cruise back to the top spot.

Wigan recorded a 26-6 win at Salford on the Sunday afternoon.

A slow start left Salford with too much to do and, though they were aggrieved by an incident involving Marc Sneyd midway through the first half, they could have no complaints about the final result.

May

Sneyd was forced to the sidelines for two minutes after referee Tom Grant showed him a green card, after he had been felled by an accidental stamp in a tackle and the game was eventually stopped by the referee with Sneyd receiving treatment.

With Sneyd off the field, Wigan forced a repeat set and grabbed a third try to go 18-0 up, amidst apparent confusion on the touchline as Salford sought to clarify the situation.

A bit of late magic from Bevan French added sunshine to the stormy weather, as straight from a scrum he pierced through and slid over in the right corner.

Hull KR went above Catalans into fourth after a Sunday-afternoon 64-14 romp at London. In a brilliant attacking display, Niall Evalds played the key role as, after an evenly-contested opening, Rovers scored four tries in a nine-minute spell during which London hardly touched the ball.

Evalds was in the right place, and provided the perfect delivery, to break London's defence with passes to Jack Broadbent to score out on the far right in the sixth and tenth minutes, then to find Peta Hiku in the twelfth.

And it was only right that Evalds should have administered the coup de grace to a spectacular spell which ended the match as a contest within 15 minutes when he popped up on the end of a dazzling handling move to cross for his 100th career try. With Mikey Lewis landing three goals, Rovers led by 22 points after 15 minutes.

Leigh scraped a 16-10 win at Huddersfield in a frustrating game. No fewer than 22 penalties were awarded by whistle-happy referee James Vella, four of them leading to cards and each of them further disrupting a game that never had any flow.

The Leopards were grateful to have taken the early initiative, tries from Josh Charnley and Edwin Ipape helping them into a 14-0 lead after half an hour.

From there, they withstood going down to eleven players to end the first half, plus a very late scare when Huddersfield closed to within a score as Kevin Naiqama's try gave

BETFRED SUPER LEAGUE
Sunday 26th May

	P	W	D	L	F	A	D	Pts
St Helens	12	9	0	3	329	124	205	18
Wigan Warriors	11	9	0	2	338	138	200	18
Warrington Wolves	12	9	0	3	302	151	151	18
Hull KR	12	8	0	4	326	183	143	16
Catalans Dragons	12	8	0	4	252	168	84	16
Salford Red Devils	12	7	0	5	216	252	-36	14
Leeds Rhinos	12	6	0	6	214	238	-24	12
Huddersfield Giants	12	5	0	7	250	245	5	10
Leigh Leopards	11	4	1	6	244	194	50	9
Castleford Tigers	12	3	1	8	214	374	-160	7
Hull FC	12	1	0	11	144	416	-272	2
London Broncos	12	1	0	11	130	476	-346	2

them a glimmer of hope, to extend their unbeaten run to four matches and crawl slowly towards play-off contention.

On the same Friday night, Castleford put daylight between themselves and Hull FC with a 30-22 win at the Jungle.

Leading 30-10 heading into the final quarter, after five tries all converted by Rowan Milnes, the Tigers conceded two late tries as Hull threatened a remarkable comeback.

As it was, Craig Lingard's men found a defensive steel lacking earlier on in the season to claim two vital points and stretch the gap between themselves and their opponents in the table to five.

Castleford ran into a 12-0 lead inside nine minutes thanks to two fine tries from Liam Horne and Tex Hoy, and ran in three further scores through the excellent Milnes, Jason Qareqare and Corey Hall to ensure a third win in a six-game run which had included just two defeats.

Harvey Barron, Liam Sutcliffe, Tiaki Chan and Jake Trueman all crossed for the Black and Whites but they left the comeback too late.

In the week, Hull FC had named Brisbane assistant John Cartwright as their new head coach from 2025. The Australian hadn't worked as a head coach since his spell of almost eight years as Gold Coast Titans' inaugural NRL coach ended in 2014.

JUNE
The Wembley way

Round 13

Hull KR edged into the top three thanks to four of the top five teams having played each other and completing a 12-0 home win over Leigh on the first Saturday of June.

The Leopards arrived in east Hull on the back of an unbeaten run of four games but ended up being nilled for the first time since August 2021 after a tremendous defensive display from the Robins. And in reply, the potent Rovers attack, which had run riot in London the week before, was stifled by some excellent Leigh defence.

The only try of the first half came when Jai Whitbread went close for Rovers before a quick play-the-ball saw Jez Litten, Tyrone May and Mikey Lewis combine for Tom Opacic to score. It was sent upstairs for video referee Aaron Moore to award the try despite Umyla Hanley's attempted tackle. Mikey Lewis added the conversion via the upright.

Rovers only sealed the game with ten minutes to go with a try to savour. Matt Parcell twice, May and Whitbread were all involved before Niall Evalds ended up going over by the side of the posts, leaving Lewis to add the conversion.

The night before, top side St Helens weren't at their best, particularly in the first half, but they had the class to overcome Catalans by 24-12 on home soil, with a dominant second-half display.

Both sides were missing key personnel but Saints, after the Dragons dominated the first quarter, got on top physically through the middle, lifted by the return of Agnatius Paasi after a ten-month injury lay-off, which ultimately turned the game in their favour, with Jack Welsby able to run riot on the back of it.

The sealing try came when a lovely deft kick into the in-goal from Daryl Clark was dived on by Matty Lees for a simple score under the posts to mount a three-score lead for the home side. Catalans had the final say in the 74th minute, as Julien Bousquet took a short Théo Fages pass to score from close range.

The Dragons were hoping to have long term-absentees Siua Taukeiaho and Tanguy Zenon back for selection in the coming weeks although second-rower Manu Ma'u was still no closer to returning from a foot injury. Prop forward Mike McMeeken had surgery on a broken hand and was forecast be out for ten weeks and hooker Michael McIlorum had medial cartilage knee damage.

Saturday evening had the following weekend's Cup finalists matched up at Halliwell Jones Stadium and while Wigan won the match 19-18 Warrington were the happier party after resting more of their top players.

Sam Burgess overhauled his squad, handing debuts to Cai Taylor-Wray, Jake Thewlis, Nolan Tupaea and Ben Hartill. Wigan also had some faces missing in Jai Field, Jake Wardle, Abbas Miski and Luke Thompson but they relied on Harry Smith and Bevan French steering the ship.

The Warriors fought back from 12-0 down and survived a late rally with 12 men to edge it. They were stunned as a Wolves side featuring 11 changes played with freedom and took control with tries by Arron Lindop and Josh Drinkwater.

But 19-unanswered Wigan points in 17 minutes, with tries from Junior Nsemba, Liam

June

Huddersfield's Luke Yates faces up to Hull FC's Danny Houghton

Marshall and Kruise Leeming, and a Harry Smith field goal on the hooter, turned the game around by the break.

Warrington refused to roll over and set up a grandstand finish when Wigan's Adam Keighran was sent off for a shoulder charge into Lindop's head with just over ten minutes remaining.

Stefan Ratchford crossed for a third Wire try, set up by Drinkwater's kick but Wigan held out for a success which left them second behind Saints in the table on points difference with a game in hand.

The RFL subsequently showed no mercy to Keighran and hit him with a three-match ban. Teammate Tyler Dupree got the same suspension for a head butt on Sam Powell that was unpunished in the game and both missed the Wembley final.

Salford pulled level on points with Catalans on the Sunday afternoon with an eventually comfortable 34-4 home win over London Broncos.

The opening 40 minutes was a slog for both teams. They each saw tries chalked off by the video referee before Salford finally posted some points with five minutes remaining as Sam Stone forced his way over.

Salford improved after the break as London wilted with the home side running in five tries through Deon Cross, Nene Macdonald, Shane Wright and a brace from Tim Lafai.

Marc Sneyd was quiet in the first half, but he came to the party in the second and had a hand in four home tries. On 51 minutes, Macdonald's try following a break from Tim Lafai saw London concede two tries in three minutes and there was no way back.

Huddersfield beat Hull FC by 24-18 on the Friday night to end a sequence of five successive defeats, including their Cup semi-final loss at the hands of Warrington.

The Giants also ended a run of five defeats from as many home Super League matches to open the season. But against a Hull FC side that had lost their last ten games, they were on the ropes at times, and not just in the closing stages when two tries had them clinging on.

June

Herman Ese'ese shook their defence in an immense performance and his try before half-time brought Hull back from 12-0 down after a low-key first half. The visitors then dominated the start and end of the second half - but crucially only registered points at the end.

Oliver Russell converted tries from Jake Bibby and Sebastine Ikahihifo for a 12-0 lead inside half an hour and captain Luke Yates almost added another, stopped only by Yusuf Aydin after rampaging down the middle. Ese'ese gave Hull hope when he charged onto a Ben Reynolds pass and bounced off Leroy Cudjoe and Tui Lolohea to score.

After the break, it was very much against the run of play that Bibby scored his second try and just past the hour, Esan Marsters put Sam Halsall in. And the Giants were 24-6 up with ten minutes remaining when Russell kicked his second penalty of the night.

Then, from nowhere, came a contest. Hull got the ball back from the restart and Ligi Sao offloaded for Logan Moy to score his first professional try. Then Yates spilled a blocked Ben Reynolds kick that rolled around the ground, Jordan Lane picked up and Moy sent Cameron Scott racing towards the corner. Reynolds converted both from out wide, setting up a grandstand finish with two-and-a-half minutes left and six points the difference.

Bibby knocked on a Reynolds kick to really set home nerves jangling but Jake Trueman threw the ball into touch with 30 seconds left and Huddersfield could finally celebrate.

On the Saturday, Leeds comprehensively dispatched Castleford at Headingley by 32-4 to give under-fire coach Rohan Smith some respite.

Playing the entire 80 minutes in the second row, 20-point Rhyse Martin was imperious, making eleven metres per carry and being impeccable with his goalkicking.

The following day, the Rhinos announced the news that many Rugby League supporters had been dreading, even though they recognised that at some point it would be inevitable.

The great Rhinos icon Rob Burrow CBE had finally passed away at the age of 41.

'Rob inspired the entire country with his brave battle against Motor Neurone Disease (MND) since his diagnosis in December 2019. He passed away peacefully at Pinderfields Hospital near his home surrounded by his loving family after becoming ill earlier this week,' said the Leeds media release.

Challenge Cup Final

Wigan Warriors extended their record number of Challenge Cup wins to 21 to mark the centenary of their first win in 1924. By beating Warrington 18-8 at Wembley on Saturday 8th June, Matt Peet's side completed the unique feat of holding all four available trophies at once, alongside the World Club Challenge, Super League title and League Leaders' Shield.

Stand-off Bevan French was awarded the Lance Todd Trophy as man of the match. In the voting by members of the Rugby League Writers and Broadcasters Association the reigning Man of Steel received 25 votes, with Liam Farrell and Harry Smith getting three each, Kaide Ellis getting two votes and Jai Field receiving one vote.

Wigan's star fullback Field suffered a hamstring problem but played the full game to help his side triumph. He was out until round 20.

French created Wigan's first try for 20-year-old Zach Eckersley, who was in for the suspended Adam Keighran, when Wigan took the lead in the 17th minute. His exquisite grubber into the in-goal was expertly weighted for Eckersley to touch it down.

BETFRED CHALLENGE CUP FINAL

Saturday 8th June 2024

WARRINGTON WOLVES 8 WIGAN WARRIORS 18

WOLVES: 1 Matt Dufty; 2 Josh Thewlis; 3 Toby King; 14 Rodrick Tai; 5 Matty Ashton; 6 George Williams (C); 7 Josh Drinkwater; 8 James Harrison; 9 Danny Walker; 10 Paul Vaughan; 13 Matty Nicholson; 12 Lachlan Fitzgibbon; 11 Ben Currie. Subs (all used): 16 Zane Musgrove; 17 Jordan Crowther; 19 Joe Bullock; 32 Sam Powell.
Try: Dufty (64); **Goals:** Josh Thewlis 2/2.
Sin bin: Dufty (4) - high tackle on Marshall.
WARRIORS: 1 Jai Field; 2 Abbas Miski; 26 Zach Eckersley; 4 Jake Wardle; 5 Liam Marshall; 6 Bevan French; 7 Harry Smith; 16 Luke Thompson; 9 Brad O'Neill; 14 Mike Cooper; 21 Junior Nsemba; 12 Liam Farrell (C); 13 Kaide Ellis. Subs (all used): 8 Ethan Havard; 10 Liam Byrne; 15 Patrick Mago; 17 Kruise Leeming.
Tries: Eckersley (17), French (23), Farrell (57); **Goals:** Smith 3/3.
Sin bin: Cooper (2) - high tackle on Josh Thewlis.
Rugby Leaguer & League Express Men of the Match:
Wolves: Sam Powell; *Warriors:* Bevan French.
Penalty count: 9-4; **Half-time:** 2-12; **Referee:** Chris Kendall; **Attendance:** 64,845 *(at Wembley Stadium).*

June

Wigan captain Liam Farrell, flanked by Kruise Leeming and Brad O'Neill, lifts the Challenge Cup

Six minutes later he made his second major contribution to Wigan's victory when he scored a try himself, taking Harry Smith's pass from a scrum move, stepping inside Lachlan Fitzgibbon and taking Paul Vaughan over the line with him.

And he almost scored again just seconds before the interval when he touched the ball down but was adjudged by both the referee Chris Kendall and video referee Liam Moore to have promoted the ball after his arm had touched the ground as he was tackled.

Earlier in the game it had looked as though the final could be ruined by yellow cards when Wigan's Mike Cooper was given ten minutes for a high tackle on Wolves winger Josh Thewlis, who appeared to slip into him, before Warrington fullback Matt Dufty was sin-binned a minute later when he inflicted a high shot on Wigan winger Liam Marshall.

Fortunately there were no more similar incidents and the game settled down when Cooper and Dufty returned to the field, which allowed French to shine as the game's most exciting player, although Harry Smith's superb kicking game would, in other circumstances, have qualified him for the prestigious trophy.

June

Wigan trailed at the end of the twelve-a-side period, with Thewlis knocking over a penalty when their try-line defence was caught offside. But once back to full complements, it was the Warriors who took control.

Smith converted both first-half tries for Wigan to lead 12-2 at the break. The Wolves had one early opening after the restart but Matty Ashton was powered into touch by Eckersley and French, while their pack was stretched as Jordan Crowther hobbled off, following the half-time withdrawal of Lachlan Fitzgibbon.

And the game was up before the hour mark as Liam Farrell stormed over for Wigan's final try. Short passes by Smith and the ever-dangerous Field released the skipper, running a good line, and he slipped past Dufty and held off Matt Nicholson to effectively clinch victory.

Dufty was one of Warrington's stars in 2024 and did well to score as the clock ticked down, stepping through the line on the left for a fine individual try.

But a comeback still seemed unlikely and so it proved, the Wolves not threatening the try-line again as Wigan comfortably held on despite a field-goal attempt being sliced wide by Smith.

It was an emotional day at Wembley. A minute's silence in memory of Rob Burrow was observed before both the women's and men's Challenge Cup finals, while Wembley shared in a minute's applause after seven minutes in each of the four games (the Women's Challenge Cup, the year 7 schools final and the 1895 Cup final). That tribute was also honoured at Twickenham on the same Saturday afternoon at the rugby union Premiership final.

Flowers, shirts, scarves and messages were also laid at the Rugby League statue at Wembley by supporters.

Round 14

Ryan Hall made history as he scored two tries in Hull KR's 32-6 home victory against Huddersfield Giants on Friday 14th June to become the greatest try-scorer in Super League history, with 248, one more than previous record-holder Danny McGuire.

The veteran winger scored the 247th and 248th tries of his Super League career in the space of six minutes late in the game, to equal and then break McGuire's tally.

Hall, who was also England's record try-scorer with 39 in 40 matches, scored 196 of his league tries in twelve seasons with Leeds, the club he was set re-join in 2024 for one final season.

The Giants had Andre Savelio sent off 70 minutes into his debut for an off-the-ball clash with Elliot Minchella before two tries in as many minutes took Hall past McGuire's record and maintained the Robins' third spot in the table.

Huddersfield prop Chris Hill made his 550th career appearance and the following Monday's Match Review Panel decided sending off was sufficient for Savelio.

Warrington slipped two points behind in fourth after a 25-14 home defeat to Salford on the same night.

The Wolves could blame a Wembley hangover but Salford were clinical and led 18-0 after 23 minutes. While Warrington very briefly threatened a second-half comeback, the match was decided in that devastating opening period.

Salford, with forwards Harvey Wilson and Loghan Lewis making debuts off the bench, thought they had a fourth try within three minutes of the restart through Chris Hankinson - excellent as a stand-in fullback - only for an obstruction by Sam Stone to be noticed.

Instead they would have to withstand a minor fightback before finally clinching the win. Two quick tries brought a subdued Halliwell Jones to life, with Rodrick Tai dotting down a Stefan Ratchford kick before Matty Ashton ran in from Toby King's assist after Watkins fumbled Chris Atkin's pass.

The decisive moments came when Danny Walker thought he had kicked a 40/20, only for the officials to spot the ball had been struck just in front of the relevant line. Salford went up the field and Sneyd laid on an exquisite chip for a second Deon Cross try and added the goal.

Cup winners Wigan also struggled on their Friday-night trip to Castleford, sneaking a 10-8 win.

June

The Tigers, buoyed by young hooker Cain Robb and Sylvester Namo's performances, were unlucky not to post their fourth win of the Super League campaign as controversy and stellar Wigan defence kept Craig Lingard's men at bay.

Paul McShane and Joe Westerman dropped out through injury, whilst Matty English made his Castleford debut after joining on a two-week loan from Huddersfield. Ryan Hampshire started at halfback for Wigan and Bevan French was at fullback in the absence of the injured Jai Field.

Liam Marshall went over to send the Warriors ahead, a swift right to left move ending with Jake Wardle sending Marshall over on seven minutes. But the Tigers hit back with six minutes to go until half-time, courtesy of a long-range run-in from Tex Hoy, dummying French to slip over the line.

Rowan Milnes kicked a pair of penalties to give the hosts a four-point lead after an hour but Marshall profited from a deflected offload to pull the teams level before Harry Smith slotted a decisive penalty.

St Helens still topped the table on points difference after their Sunday-afternoon 52-6 win over the Broncos at the Stoop, the Wimbledon pitch undergoing re-seeding.

Saints had conceded the opening score in four of their first five matches and did not start well, losing Tommy Makinson to a foot injury on the first set of six.

London matched them in the first few minutes but once Saints opened the scoring, Waqa Blake taking Moses Mbye's cross-kick to touch down on the right in the seventh minute, they were firmly in control. Hooker Daryl Clark scored a second-half hat-trick within eight minutes.

On the Saturday evening Leigh stunned Catalans in Perpignan, coming home with a 10-2 victory.

The Leopards' win was built on the creativity in attack of captain Lachlan Lam and fullback Matt Moylan, and the belligerent defence of the pack, led by yet another towering performance from prop Tom Amone.

Dragons fullback Arthur Mourgue got the scoreboard clicking with a 17th-minute penalty. Moylan levelled the scores when Dragons' hooker Michael McIlorum was penalised for a high tackle. But Leigh took the lead moments later when Amone forced his way over from short range, with Moylan tagging on the conversion for an 8-2 scoreline at half-time.

Leigh scored the killer points as early as the 54th minute when Dragons' substitute Chris Satae was penalised for obstruction, Moylan converting the penalty to stretch the lead to eight points.

On the Saturday Hull FC ended an eleven-match losing run with an 18-10 victory over Leeds Rhinos at the MKM Stadium, their first win under interim head coach Simon Grix.

It was an emotional afternoon, particularly for the Rhinos, who took to the field for the first time since the passing of club legend Rob Burrow CBE.

Torrential rain led to handling errors in the first period before the home side went over twice in the final minutes of the first half through Lewis Martin and Denive Balmforth to earn a 12-0 lead at the break.

The Airlie Birds picked up where they left off to start the second half, grabbing their third try to put daylight between the sides. Hull kept the ball alive brilliantly, with Cameron Scott taking an offload from Carlos Tuimavave to score on the right.

Leeds' skipper Ash Handley's score got Leeds on the board and Harry Newman grabbed a late consolation effort.

Hull's second win of the season moved them two points clear of bottom club London and they were recruiting heavily for 2025, with Leigh captain John Asiata their highest profile capture.

They also signed incoming head coach John Cartwright's son Jed and Australian fullback Treigh Stewart on immediate contracts. But Hull pulled out on one after being made aware Stewart was allegedly involved in a domestic-violence incident in his home country.

The following Tuesday, Rhinos head coach Rohan Smith left his job, a week after Ian Blease started his new role as Leeds' sporting director. Blease left Salford after eight years as director of rugby at the club he made over 250 appearances for in his playing career.

June
Round 15

On the Friday of the last round before the break to accommodate the France-England game, Leeds beat Leigh 18-10 at Headingley. It was the Rhinos' first home fixture since the death of their legendary player Rob Burrow and a packed house was witness to one of the most moving nights in the game's history.

The Rhinos paid a brilliant tribute to one of their greatest before and after the match, a wonderful event organised alongside Sky Sports, who presented and televised to the world, as well as those inside Headingley.

'It was in the spirit of Rob,' said Chev Walker, taking charge of the team alongside Scott Grix following the departure of coach Rohan Smith earlier in the week.

Leeds followed up a moving build-up with their most determined performance of the year. Brodie Croft shone with his tries - the first stepping inside and riding the challenge of several defenders, the second a length-of-the-field effort after Lachlan Miller picked up Tom Amone's knock-on.

Their final try came, most appropriately, from their number seven, as Matt Frawley finished a break started by Miller and continued through young winger Alfie Edgell.

Leeds had to dig even deeper in the closing stages after Matt Moylan scored from a scrum play and Edwin Ipape charged over to make it 18-10. But they once again rose to the challenge and calmly saw out a victory like no other.

Aaron Pene made his Leigh debut off the bench, barely a week after signing a two-and-a-half-year contract to join from Melbourne Storm and he impressed.

Pressure was mounting on Huddersfield coach Ian Watson following a seventh defeat in eight games on the Saturday night. A second-half fightback in Perpignan from 22-0 down at the interval ended in a 22-18 loss to Catalans.

First-half tries from Tom Davies, Théo Fages, Arthur Romano and Tom Johnstone left the visitors reeling, but second-half strikes from Harry Rushton, Ashton Golding and Luke Yates put the Giants back in the frame, although they couldn't quite finish the job.

Hull KR's match-winning field goal at Castleford on the Thursday night was the first of Jez Litten's 149-game professional career with Hull FC, Doncaster, Hull KR and England - and, as he revealed afterwards, his first at any level. But Litten calmly slotted over from 20 metres out to snatch a 13-12 win for the Robins.

After Sam Wood gave the hosts an early lead, leaping to claim a Rowan Milnes kick, the score was flipped by two defensive lapses in the space of three minutes. First, Mikey Lewis jinked through, with Tom Opacic in support to score. And then Litten sliced between the two markers - Liam Horne and George Griffin - from dummy-half and dashed through the space behind, setting up Elliot Minchella for the try.

But Castleford didn't concede again in the remaining hour, the only other Hull KR point coming from the left boot of Litten after Milnes levelled things up in the second half with a try and conversion.

Litten's winning moment was well executed with five minutes left, carrying towards the posts before Niall Evalds threw the pass back for the hooker in the perfect position. In contrast, Castleford messed up their response when Sylvester Namo knocked on before playing the ball.

Eighteen-year-old halfback Jack Farrimond was handed only his second Super League start for Wigan and managed to steal the headlines away from Bevan French with two tries and six successful conversions in a 36-0 Friday-night home win over London Broncos.

Farrimond lit up renamed The Brick Community Stadium in the first half with two well-taken tries and four conversions – two from the touchline - as he showed no sign of any nerves as the Warriors led 24-0 at the interval.

The youngster, who made his debut against London in March, raced clear in the second half to send Jake Wardle in for Wigan's fifth try. Wardle grabbed his second try with over 20 minutes remaining but the Warriors failed to add any more points.

Warrington coach Sam Burgess admitted his side were fortunate to come away from Hull

June

Fireworks at Headingley to celebrate the life of Leeds legend Rob Burrow

FC with a 24-18 win on the Saturday afternoon.

After taking the early initiative through a Toby King try, Burgess's men were mostly on the back foot against a revitalised Hull FC.

The Wolves' superb defence kept Hull out in the first half but couldn't in the second as an 18-6 lead established by scores against the run of play by Matt Dufty and Danny Walker was wiped out.

Liam Sutcliffe and Tom Briscoe followed Denive Balmforth in scoring for the hosts to level the match going into the final ten minutes.

But with three minutes remaining, a mix-up between Briscoe and Carlos Tuimavave saw the ball knocked on and Warrington were handed the perfect opportunity to win the game. George Williams set up for the match-winning one-pointer, but Brad Fash and Morgan Smith rushed out well to form a barrier and block.

The ball fell to Dufty, an inspired performer on this afternoon and all season. He took the ball left, danced around Ben Reynolds, then bisected Tuimavave and Briscoe for a try worthy of winning any match.

Leaders St Helens dropped two points behind Wigan into second on the Sunday after Salford collected a first league double over St Helens since 1980 with a 20-18 home win.

The hosts lost Tim Lafai in the warm-up resulting in second-rower Sam Stone moving into the left centre. Nene Macdonald, on the other side of the field stepped up superbly.

The deciding try from Chris Hankinson came seven minutes from the end, with mastermind Marc Sneyd nervelessly converting.

BETFRED SUPER LEAGUE
Sunday 23rd June

	P	W	D	L	F	A	D	Pts
Wigan Warriors	14	12	0	2	403	164	239	24
St Helens	15	11	0	4	423	162	261	22
Hull KR	15	11	0	4	383	201	182	22
Warrington Wolves	15	10	0	5	358	213	145	20
Salford Red Devils	15	10	0	5	295	288	7	20
Catalans Dragons	15	9	0	6	288	220	68	18
Leeds Rhinos	15	8	0	7	274	270	4	16
Huddersfield Giants	15	6	0	9	298	317	-19	12
Leigh Leopards	14	5	1	8	264	226	38	11
Castleford Tigers	15	3	1	11	238	429	-191	7
Hull FC	15	2	0	13	198	474	-276	4
London Broncos	15	1	0	14	140	598	-458	2

JULY
Wolves to the Wire

Round 16

Reigning champions Wigan continued their top of the ladder dominance with a tough 24-6 home win over neighbours Leigh.

The 'Battle of the Borough' certainly lived up to its name, with battered and bruised bodies on both sides as Wigan edged out the Leopards.

Wigan lost Mike Cooper inside two minutes with a nasty looking head injury, while the Leopards lost Josh Charnley to a rib injury in a game that was definitely not for the faint-hearted.

Only eight points were scored in the opening 40 minutes, with Bevan French scoring the first of his two tries and Adam Keighran kicking two goals as both teams seemed more interested in coming out on top of the physical battle.

The first points came when Wigan prop Kaide Ellis was hit off the ball by opposite Robbie Mulhern and, after a lengthy stoppage, the Ireland international was sent to the sin bin. Wigan opted to take the points with Adam Keighran putting them 2-0 up.

Wigan ended the half with twelve men themselves as Brad O'Neill lifted Mulhern in the tackle to earn a yellow card, with the Leigh prop going off for a head assessment. It was all Leigh for the next ten minutes but O'Neill - who was banned on the Monday for one game - had returned by the time Brad Dwyer managed to ground the ball under pressure from four Wigan defenders. Matt Moylan converted and Leigh trailed by just two points.

The Warriors hit back almost immediately with Liam Marshall acrobatically getting the ball down in the corner following great work from Jake Wardle. Keighran failed to convert but Wigan now led by six.

They put the game to bed with 20 minutes remaining with a try out of nothing as French took on the Leigh line and kicked ahead before racing past Moylan to touch down. Keighran's conversion made it 18-6.

Leigh pushed Wigan hard in the last ten minutes but the Warriors had the final say as Wardle broke down the left before turning the ball inside for Liam Farrell to score. Keighran made it 24-6 on the hooter.

Wigan's lead in the table was now four points after second-place St Helens were stunned at home on the same Friday night by tenth-placed Castleford, as halfback Rowan Milnes led the Tigers to an 8-6 victory.

Jonny Lomax returned for Saints after five weeks out with a broken hand, but they were still missing Sione Mata'utia, who was withdrawn on the morning of the game with a neck injury, as well as Daryl Clark, Konrad Hurrell, Alex Walmsley, Morgan Knowles, Joe Batchelor, Matt Whitley and Tommy Makinson. Those absences allowed for debuts off the bench for club products Jake Burns and Jonny Vaughan.

Tigers coach Craig Lingard could only name 21 fit players earlier in the week, with his side also injury-ravaged, but he was able to add George Lawler to his side just three months after suffering a seizure and a bleed on the brain. Sam Wood missed out after fracturing his shoulder while making his England debut the week before.

The Tigers ground out the two points, fighting to stay in the contest when Saints could have run away with the game. Missing their influential captain Paul McShane, the Tigers were expertly marshalled by Milnes but he was ably assisted by Tex Hoy, Jacob Miller, Liam Horne and the influential Joe Westerman.

The first half was set to be scoreless but Sam Royle crossed for Saints on the verge of half-time and Mark Percival made it 6-0 after the break with a penalty.

Saints were dominating field position until Waqa Blake dropped a kick under little pressure. The ball rebounded to Lomax, who was adjudged to be offside. Castleford attacked down the left and form young hooker Cain Robb combined with Lawler to find Jacob Miller and his quick hands sent Innes Senior over in the left corner. Milnes missed the touchline conversion attempt.

But the Tigers were level 13 minutes from time after Innes Senior's try and Milnes' penalty after a high tackle by George Delaney on Muizz Mustapha 20 metres out and bang in front of the posts. And with ten minutes remaining Milnes added another penalty to see the Tigers take the lead - a lead they defended until the end.

Warrington moved level with St Helens after putting the cleaners through Huddersfield, with eight tries from eight different players scored in a 48-nil win at Halliwell Jones Stadium.

Fullback Matt Dufty had a field day as the Wolves led 18-0 at the break and Josh Drinkwater's try soon after half-time stretched the lead to 24 points and ensured there was no way back for the visitors.

The Giants, who had been hit by illness in the week, came into the game six points outside the play-off positions but never looked like making ground on the top teams. Owner Ken Davy apologised to fans in the wake of the trouncing coach Ian Watson termed his job one that 'smashes your brain in'.

To add to Huddersfield's troubles, form centre Esan Marsters was out for a lengthy spell due to a knee injury.

Hull KR fell to fourth as a Theo Fages' golden-point field goal gave Catalan Dragons a 15-14 victory at Craven Park on the Saturday evening.

Jez Litten and Jordan Abdull both had failed attempts at one pointers' before the Dragons set up for Abdull again but cleverly switched to their scrum-half to seal the win from 30 metres out.

The first half was dominated by the Dragons, who held a 14-0 half-time lead through tries from Alrix da Costa and Tom Johnstone, a beauty from Fages' midfield break, with Arthur Mourgue converting both as well as a penalty goal. But Rovers came out a seemingly different side in the second half. Two quick Mikey Lewis-converted tries from Jack Broadbent and Joe Burgess put them within striking distance before a late Lewis penalty - after Abdull inexplicably went for a short goal-line dropout that failed to go ten metres - took the game into extra time.

That was a second successive one-point game for the Robins after they defeated Castleford Tigers a fortnight ago.

And it was the second golden-point game of the day after Leeds Rhinos had pipped London Broncos at Headingley by 17-16.

Only misfortune stopped the Broncos, who had fullback Josh Rourke making an impressive debut on his return from a broken leg, registering their first away win of the season.

Leeds may have found a way to win thanks to Brodie Croft's 83rd minute field goal in extra time but the result was an injustice to the Broncos' efforts, all their points coming inside the first 32 minutes.

Rourke crossed for a sixth-minute try that Oli Leyland converted but it was soon 10-6 after Ash Handley and Paul Momirovski tries and a Martin conversion.

But if Leeds thought they were in control, they were in for a shock. Rhys Kennedy spun out of a tackle to score, with Leyland converting to restore London's lead, before Iliess Macani went over in the corner for a half-time lead of 16-10.

So it remained, although on the hour mark Lewis Bienek was adjudged to have not grounded the ball for what would have been a clincher. Instead, Croft's fine pass released Martin on an excellent angled run to the posts, with his goal levelling the scores.

In the only Sunday game, Ryan Brierley marked his return from a three-game injury

July

absence to get Salford over the line with a 22-20 home win over reviving Hull FC to move level on 22 points with Saints, Warrington and Hull KR in second place in the Super League table.

The fullback missed recent wins over London Broncos, Warrington Wolves and St Helens due to a rib problem, but his return helped the Red Devils, missing both first-choice centres Nene Macdonald and Tim Lafai, make it four wins in succession.

The opening half was not a classic but the score was locked at 6-6 at the break with Marc Sneyd slotting over a late penalty after Deon Cross and Ben Reynolds had exchanged tries.

Hull started the second half with 12 men after Tom Briscoe was sent to the sin bin on the stroke of half-time for a professional foul. Salford went 12 points up after the break with Brierley and Chris Hankinson crossing for tries before Denive Balmforth got the visitors within six points with a try.

Sneyd added two more penalties either side of a Jordan Lane try for Hull before Lewis Martin set up a tense finish with a try with three minutes left.

Round 17

Ian Watson, after three-and-a-half seasons at the helm, became the third Super League coach to be sacked in 2024 after the Giants' run of eight defeats from nine games, the last one a 48-0 humiliation at Warrington.

Assistant Luke Robinson held the reins for the daunting trip to Leigh the following Saturday, which ended in a creditable 20-16 defeat.

The Giants looked like a team possessed for the vast majority of the game – at least before Andre Savelio was shown a red card for a shoulder charge on Robbie Mulhern. They had battled to keep the game level at 8-8 despite losing Joe Greenwood and Aidan McGowan to injury. But Savelio's send off was pivotal.

The Leopards couldn't find touch with the penalty as Huddersfield were let off the hook. Adrian Lam's men looked to be self-imploding and a high tackle on Luke Yates handed Jake Connor the opportunity to edge the Giants back in front, despite being down to eleven men - with Chris Hill accompanying Jack Hughes to the sin bin after a scuffle. The fullback duly converted for a 10-8 lead.

But after Connor was caught on the last tackle, Leigh returned fire, Lachlan Lam sending Kai O'Donnell through a huge hole for a great score on 66 minutes. Matt Moylan made it 14-10 with the boot.

Two consecutive penalties handed the Leopards another chance and a flowing move from left to right ended with Zak Hardaker diving over in the corner. Hardaker converted his own try for a 20-10 lead.

The Giants gave themselves a slim chance as time ran down with Sam Halsall's stunning break and kick ahead seeing a penalty try being given after Elliot Wallis was impeded by Hughes on his way to dotting down. Connor converted to reduce the deficit to four at 20-16.

A high tackle on Connor saw the Giants threaten a remarkable win but the attack broke down when the fullback's pass went into touch. Savelio subsequently got a two-game ban.

The major event had happened the day before as first took on second at The Brick Stadium, Wigan edging St Helens 16-12 after a brilliant 80 minutes.

A lot of the talk before the game was about who wasn't playing - the injured Bevan French and suspended Brad O'Neill for Wigan, and the dropped Lewis Dodd for St Helens. But the players who did take to the field put on a magnificent show.

It was uncompromising from the start, when Saints prop Matty Lees was sin-binned after 58 seconds for a high shot on Kaide Ellis, to the end, as Wigan clung on to their four-point lead.

And some of the best performers were those covering the absent stars - 18-year-old Harry Robertson shone on his senior debut when thrust into the fullback role for St Helens and Zach Eckersley did likewise for Wigan as a late replacement in the same, unfamiliar position.

It was Eckersley who scored the winning try twelve minutes from time, when the scores were tied at 12-12 and the tension was at its peak.

July

Saints coach Paul Wellens said after a third defeat in a row that there was still a future for Dodd at the Saints that season. The coach insisted that South Sydney Rabbitohs-bound Dodd was doing all he could to regain his form and get himself back into the side.

Another young English player was NRL bound as Warrington backrower Matty Nicholson was set to join Canberra on a three-year contract.

On the Thursday night Nicholson and his Wolves teammates excelled in a 30-18 home win against Leeds, whose new coach until the end of the season, Brad Arthur, had arrived from Australia that day and watched on.

Arthur can't have been too impressed as the Rhinos went in at half-time trailing by 24-4. Warrington raced into a 12-0 lead in the opening five minutes through tries from Matty Ashton and Matt Dufty. David Fusitu'a got Leeds on the board but Dufty went in again and Rodrick Tai's score on the hooter made it a 20-point gap at the break.

Lachlan Miller crossed for the Rhinos before George Williams was sin-binned for the home side for a high tackle and young centre Ned McCormack further reduced the arrears with his first career try.

Twenty-one-year old prop Tom Whitehead managed to power over from close in for Warrington to quell hopes of a Leeds comeback before Paul Momirovski went over for the Rhinos late on after Ashton was sin-binned for a professional foul.

London Broncos had high hopes going into their game with Castleford in the Kent town of Ebbsfleet - landlords AFC Wimbledon reseeding their home at Plough Lane ahead of the new soccer season. But the Tigers were a much different beast to the one that had struggled in the first part of the season and came away with a comfortable 34-20 victory.

Roared on by their cheerfully ebullient Hawaiian-shirt clad, inflatable-banana waving fans, Castleford took control early on. With Jacob Miller pulling the strings from halfback, they deserved the two points.

Catalans leapfrogged Salford into fifth position in the table on the Saturday night as a 20-0 defeat in Perpignan ended a four-match winning run for the Red Devils. After slipping to an 18-0 half-time deficit at a blazing-hot Stade Gilbert Brutus, the Red Devils stemmed the tide in the second half but couldn't get on the scoreboard.

To Catalans' credit, they continued a three-match winning run on the back of a difficult week in which they sacked three players for attending a pop concert when they should have been training. Siua Taukeiaho, Jayden Nikorima (who the next week signed for Salford) and Damel Diakhate were all dismissed after allegedly feigning illness to avoid training (plus an official club trip to Toulouse for the France-England international) to attend a pop concert.

It was a game littered with stoppages, mistakes and lengthy interventions by the video-referee as the Dragons shut down Salford playmakers Marc Sneyd and Ryan Brierley from start to finish and bossed the forward battle. Arthur Romano went over for two tries and Cesar Rougé got the other, with Arthur Mourgue nailing three first-half conversions and a second-half penalty goal.

Earlier that afternoon, Hull KR sealed a rare treble of derby wins in a single season with a 24-10 away victory.

Hull FC however made the game a far more entertaining derby than most recent clashes between the sides - especially after falling 18 points behind in as many minutes.

Ultimately the Robins' fast start made the difference as three early tries, by Sauaso Sue, Mikey Lewis and Matty Storton, put them on course for a fourth successive victory at the MKM Stadium.

Captains Brad Fash and Elliot Minchella were involved in a number of spats. Referee Chris Kendall had had enough just before half-time and sent both to the bin. In the clash that proved the final straw, Minchella accused Fash of grabbing his testicles. No action was taken against Fash.

Hull began to threaten a little more but it took another yellow card when Joe Burgess foolishly obstructed Tom Briscoe as he attempted a quick restart to change things. Four minutes later, Rovers had conceded not once but twice.

First Lewis Martin crossed in the corner, from Sutcliffe's shift on of a Jake Trueman pass, and then Logan Moy did likewise following an excellent Davy Litten break from his own half.

July

Sutcliffe converted one of the two tries for 10-18 but Hull's momentum slowly dissipated. Burgess restored the visitors' full complement and the comeback was made immensely more difficult by Denive Balmforth being sent to the bin for a shoulder charge on Tyrone May off the ball with ten minutes to go.

Tom Opacic had a try ruled out because Minchella had been tackled before offloading on the ground, but it wouldn't matter as Minchella sealed the result at the death from a Ryan Hall kick inside.

Round 18

Some pundits were predicting that Wigan were unstoppable on their march to a second successive title. But Hull FC demonstrated the conclusion was far from foregone when they beat the Warriors at home by 24-22. It was Hull's third win of the season and Wigan's third defeat.

The league leaders were made to look no better than average as Hull stormed into a 20-point lead thanks to first-half tries from re-called Jack Walker, Liam Sutcliffe and Davy Litten and one from Denive Balmforth three minutes after the break, all converted by young half Jack Charles. Liam Marshall had notched one for Wigan.

Abbas Miski did his best to get Wigan back in the game with an acrobatic effort in the corner but he was denied by an amazing tackle from Walker that effectively won Hull the game. The Warriors made a late fightback though, starting with Brad O'Neill's try and Adam Keighran's conversion which put them 14 points behind with 16 minutes remaining.

Wigan received their first penalty of the game in the 72nd minute when Jack Farrimond was taken high by Litten, which saw the centre miss the rest of the game in the sin bin. From the penalty, the ball went wide and Marshall collected a long pass from Harry Smith to grab his second of the game. Keighran added the goal and Wigan trailed by eight.

Heading into the final five minutes Wigan only trailed by two as a breakaway try from Zach Eckersley set up a tense finish for both sets of supporters.

Warrington and Hull KR were now just two points behind, although Wigan still had a game in hand hanging over from the World Club Challenge.

The night before, the Wolves had to survive with twelve men for an hour as they fought off a St Helens comeback at the Totally Wicked Stadium to win 24-10.

Wolves head coach Sam Burgess was rightly proud of the way his side handled themselves after the dismissal of James Harrison for a high tackle on young opposite prop Noah Stephens. He subsequently received a two-match ban.

Warrington led 12-0 at the time, thanks to tries from Matty Ashton and Matt Dufty and, after Saints pulled the gap back to two points, Adam Holroyd and Matty Nicholson saw the Wire home. Nicholson had also had ten minutes in the sin bin midway through the second half but St Helens couldn't make a two-man advantage count.

A fourth consecutive defeat put more pressure on Saints coach Paul Wellens, whose side ran out of steam after coming back into the contest through Agnatius Paasi and Sam Royle tries.

On the Saturday Hull KR looked on course for defeat at Leeds, in Brad Arthur's first game in charge of the Rhinos. But from a 12-10 deficit going into the last ten minutes of the game, Jai Whitbread and Jez Litten tries grabbed a 20-12 victory for Rovers.

Leeds led 6-0 at half-time with the only points of the first half coming early from Rhyse Martin. He scored inside five minutes after Jack Broadbent - brought in at fullback for the injured Niall Evalds - fumbled a kick by Matt Frawley and converted his own try.

David Fusitu'a threw away the chance to extend the Rhinos' lead early in the second half - quite literally. Some great handling brought the ball to the winger, who stepped around Mikey Lewis, only to lose possession as he went to score.

It proved a turning point as Hull KR struck twice in the following ten minutes, first through old (and future) Headingley favourite Ryan Hall's try off a wide Matt Parcell pass and Lewis's touchline conversion to level. A second Lewis 40/20 didn't bring reward but, shortly afterwards, the halfback's kick was fumbled by Lachlan Miller to concede a drop-out, from which Lewis

July

Castleford's Jason Qareqare looks to fend off Catalans Dragons' Arthur Mourgue

attacked the line and was too strong to be prevented from scoring by Paul Momirovski or Brodie Croft.

Leeds still had the energy to take the game back to the Robins and Martin was held out during a period of pressure that only truly ended with one of the season's more unusual tries. Frawley's high kick bounced off the ground and hit the bottom of the crossbar, bamboozling Broadbent who could only knock the ball into the hands of Miller. Martin's conversion put the Rhinos back ahead at 12-10.

Cue a disastrous final ten minutes for the hosts, who fell behind again when Fusitu'a failed to catch a high Lewis kick, allowing Tyrone May to put Whitbread over via a lengthy video-referee deliberation.

Lewis converted and then Litten, fresh as a late sub, zipped through a sleeping defence to seal Hull KR's victory.

St Helens were now four points off Hull KR and Catalans remained with them after the Sunday game when they fell to a 24-18 defeat at Castleford, as the Liam Horne-inspired Tigers proved too slick and too passionate for their shellshocked French visitors.

Castleford were deserved winners with the PNG international battering anything that moved, whilst the likes of Alex Mellor and Cain Robb stood up against a massive Dragons pack.

Two tries from Horne and another from Jacob Miller put the Tigers 18-0 up but Tom Johnstone pulled one back for the Dragons before the break.

Catalans dominated the second half as Matt Ikuvalu and Arthur Mourgue tries and the latter's third touchline conversion drew them level with eleven minutes to go. But when Dragons winger Tom Davies spilt the ball in his own '20', Rowan Milnes dropped off Tex Hoy and he raced in without a hand laid on him.

Leigh made short work of London Broncos at Leigh Sports Village on the Friday night with a 36-6 win. When Ricky Leutele crossed for the Leopards' third try on seventeen minutes London hopes of a first ever win against Leigh had already evaporated in the 27-degree heat.

Leutele's try was fashioned by a glorious pass from Lachlan Lam, who was near untouchable throughout, running and kicking the Broncos ragged. In contrast, where Lam used guile, Tom Amone – until departing with a head knock due to friendly fire with Matt Davis early in the second half – was a wrecking ball up the middle, and the return of skipper John Asiata perfectly linked the two.

The win kept the Leopards on the fringes of the play-off spots and that was all that concerned their coach Adrian Lam, despite his side dropping their ruthless edge in the second half.

Tries from Darnell McIntosh, Amone, Leutele and Davis put them in charge before half-time. The Broncos improved in the second half as Josh Rourke grabbed a consolation try but scores from

July

Josh Charnley, Gareth O'Brien, Lam and Jack Hughes underlined the Leopards' superiority.

On the same night, Huddersfield pulled off a 16-8 home win over Salford.

After nine defeats in their previous ten games, the match-clinching try at the end from the excellent Adam Milner was greeted by huge celebrations on the field and in the stands.

All five changes for this game were enforced and in the pack, with captain Luke Yates sold to Warrington, Joe Greenwood and Oliver Wilson out with long-term injuries and bans being served by Sam Hewitt and Andre Savelio.

But big efforts from the returning Matty English, fellow middle Harry Rushton and out-of-position Jake Bibby and Ashton Golding made up for all they had lost in the forwards..

Adam Milner clinched the win a minute from time with a drive from dummy-half, Connor adding the final goal while the celebrations began behind him.

Round 19

The last round of July saw a mighty upheaval at the top of Super League, with Warrington and Hull KR ascending to first and second.

Wolves coach Sam Burgess was refusing to allow himself and his team to get carried away after an astounding 40-4 win at previous leaders Wigan. Warrington played a near perfect half as they took advantage of Wigan's errors - a knock-on from Liam Byrne in the first tackle set the tone - to lead 18-4 at the break thanks to tries from Arron Lindop, Adam Holroyd and Matty Ashton.

Wigan were second best for the majority of the game and, after Lindop grabbed his second try just after the half-time break, they were beaten. Further tries from Ashton, Josh Thewlis and Rodrick Tai secured a comfortable win

The victory over Wigan was Warrington's first in the league since beating them at the Magic Weekend in 2021.

Both Jai Field and Bevan French were still out for Wigan and were badly missed, as was centre Adam Keighran, suffering from delayed concussion, with backrower Liam Farrell starting at centre.

Thewlis came back onto the Wolves wing with Lindop moving to centre following a serious facial injury to Stefan Ratchford the previous weekend. James Harrison was suspended and he was replaced in the front row by Luke Yates, who was making his first start since recently joining from Huddersfield Giants.

Yates and Lindop were outstanding, with skipper George Williams at the top of his game. And the Wolves were set to be further boosted by the arrival of England international John Bateman, who had signed for the rest of the season from the NRL Wests Tigers.

Head coach Burgess ended speculation that he was to return to the NRL by signing a new contract to the end of the 2026 season.

A Mikey Lewis hat-trick helped Hull KR to second spot as Wigan went third on points difference - though spirited London Broncos earned many plaudits despite falling to a 40-16 defeat at Craven Park.

Rovers started the game superbly with three tries in the opening 15 minutes but the Broncos slowly got themselves into the game and scored either side of half-time. Ultimately, it took all of Rovers' resolve to finally break the basement side with a three-try final quarter, led by their star halfback Lewis, and secure a seventh win in eight games.

Leigh kept alive their hopes of gate-crashing the play-offs with a staggering 46-4 home win over St Helens

Outclassed and out-enthused, St Helens made it a Super League record of five losses in a row against a brilliant, ruthless Leigh side. Led by the ever-impressive Lachlan Lam as well as the formidable Robbie Mulhern and the flying Josh Charnley, the Leopards never looked like losing – especially as Saints self-imploded with two sin bins, to Mark Percival and Jonny Lomax, either side of half-time.

And things couldn't have started any worse for Saints as Jack Welsby limped off the field with just three minutes gone, clutching his hamstring following a stellar break.

Kai O'Donnell's first-half try was the pick of the Leopards tries, involving half a dozen

Leigh players after Darnell McIntosh's break down the right wing.

On the Monday, Percival was banned for one match for a high tackle, while Lomax was referred to a tribunal, copping a three-match suspension for the same offence.

The night before, visitors Leeds Rhinos comfortably defeated West Yorkshire rivals Huddersfield 34-6. The result put seventh-placed Leeds firmly back in the Super League play-off picture.

There was little to separate the two - converted tries to Ash Handley and Aidan McGowan making it 6-all - until two tries in the final six minutes of the first half.

If the Giants could only blame themselves for the first of those, when fullback Jake Connor spilled an uncontested Matt Frawley kick for Harry Newman to score, they were furious with the officials for the second. Leeds prop Sam Lisone led with his forearm and directly struck Oliver Russell high in a carry, shortly before Rhyse Martin (who converted all their first-half tries) set up Lachlan Miller's break for a Frawley try.

It was only spotted after the try was awarded as Russell bounced back to his feet, and so could only be placed on report - little consolation to the Giants as they went back to the changing rooms 18-6 down. No further action was taken against Lisone by the Match Review Panel.

On the hour, Handley's diving finish in the corner, given the green light by the video referee, gave the Rhinos breathing room.

Two more converted tries from the Rhinos, who welcomed James Bentley back in the second half after almost four months stood down with a head injury, followed in the closing stages. The first came from Brodie Croft, taking on the line and stepping around Matty English to cross following a Jake Bibby error.

Then Connor kicked out on the full to put the visitors back on the attack and Miller went clean through a gap down the middle to complete a first away win in five.

On the Saturday, Salford - with both star centres Nene Macdonald and Tim Lafai back - consolidated their play-off spot with a typically flamboyant 30-22 home win over rejuvenated Castleford.

Despite dominating for most of the game, the Red Devils had to twice come from behind to end a two-match losing run.

Three of their five tries came while the Tigers were down to twelve players, with Liam Horne and Sylvester Namo sin-binned, while Castleford also handed back the lead on the hour via an Ethan Ryan interception try as they proved their own worst enemies. Oliver Partington and Chris Hankinson - a long-range beauty from Ryan Brierley's break - took Salford clear enough to not get too nervous about Luis Roberts' fine individual try that reduced the margin to eight. Horne got a one-match ban for head contact.

Later that night Sam Tomkins came out of retirement to inspire Catalans to a 24-16 win over Hull FC in Perpignan.

Both sides played most of a highly charged game with 12 men, the Dragons' backrower Tariq Sims sent off inside eight minutes for a swinging arm on Ed Chamberlain, Hull's Ligi Sao following him nine minutes later for a high tackle on Tomkins.

Michael McIlorum and Tomkins crossed and Arthur Mourgue booted three goals, with Carlos Tuimavave replying, as Catalans led 14-6 at the break. Jack Walker cut the deficit to two points, but Ben Garcia and Tom Davies secured an important win for Catalans despite Lewis Martin's late score.

Sao got a two-match ban and Sims one game, both for head contact, with Sims also being referred to tribunal for picking up an injured player, eventually suspended for four more games.

BETFRED SUPER LEAGUE
Saturday 27th July

	P	W	D	L	F	A	D	Pts
Warrington Wolves	19	14	0	5	500	245	255	28
Hull KR	19	14	0	5	481	254	227	28
Wigan Warriors	18	14	0	4	469	246	223	28
Catalans Dragons	19	12	0	7	365	274	91	24
Salford Red Devils	19	12	0	7	355	366	-11	24
St Helens	19	11	0	8	455	256	199	22
Leeds Rhinos	19	10	0	9	355	342	13	20
Leigh Leopards	18	8	1	9	372	276	96	17
Huddersfield Giants	19	7	0	12	336	427	-91	14
Castleford Tigers	19	6	1	12	326	503	-177	13
Hull FC	19	3	0	16	268	566	-298	6
London Broncos	19	1	0	18	198	725	-527	2

AUGUST
Robins bobbin'

Round 20

The first Friday night of August saw the top two after round 19 clash and, after a 22-4 victory at Warrington, Hull KR went to the summit for the first ever time in Super League.

Rovers dominated most of the game and were 10-0 up at the break. Prop Suasao Sue touched down next to the posts in the fifth minute as he took Matt Parcell's pass from dummy-half.

Mikey Lewis took to the air with another high kick towards the Warrington line for a charging Tyrone May, who plucked the ball out of the sky brilliantly and touched down to extend their lead to ten points.

Ten minutes after the break, momentum seemed to be turning, Matty Ashton crossing over in the corner untouched off a silky back line spread, with Matt Dufty, who was otherwise kept quiet by a swarming Robins defence, giving the cut-out pass.

Lewis made the most of a Wolves handling error when his own cross-field kick was batted back by Ryan Hall and scooped up by the nifty scrum-half, before storming his way through four defenders to touch down in the 57th minute.

Peta Hiku sealed the win with three minutes to play, beating Arron Lindop on the outside following some crafty May footwork, allowing the red and whites to leapfrog the Wolves, who sank to third, at the top of the table. But they were cheered by the solid debut of John Bateman, who had signed until the end of the season after a fall-out with coach Benji Marshall at NRL Wests Tigers.

Wigan had been temporarily top after their Thursday 28-14 home win over Huddersfield, ending a two-game losing streak, Jai Field making a timely return to action.

Field had been on the sidelines since damaging his hamstring in the Challenge Cup Final win over Warrington and had missed the last six Super League matches. The Australian returned at fullback and played a pivotal role in a strong Wigan comeback, scoring a try before he was rested for the last 15 minutes.

Huddersfield scored first against the run of play when Jake Connor took the line on and sent a ball to Jake Bibby, who tapped the ball on to Sam Halsall with the home fans screaming for a forward pass. Halsall then returned it to Bibby for the try as Connor converted and the Giants led 6-0. Connor slotted over a penalty, after the Warriors were pulled up for offside, for an 8-0 half-time lead.

But Wigan hit back in style with an audacious try spanning the length of the field from Jake Wardle, with Ryan Hampshire crashing down for the hosts' second. Jai Field stepped past two Huddersfield players to score and put Wigan in control as Zach Eckersley sent in another to wrap up the win

Huddersfield managed a late consolation as Halsall out-jumped the Wigan defence to collect an Oliver Russell kick and score in the corner. Connor converted before a penalty on the hooter saw Keighran kick his sixth goal of the evening.

St Helens ended a five-game horror run on the Saturday with a huge 46-6 win at Hull FC, both sides shorn of a raft of star players.

August

London Broncos' Josh Rourke takes on Catalans Dragons' Sam Tomkins

Hull went set for set with them in the opening half hour before Saints got into their groove and ended the first half leading 10-0. After that it was the Saints of old who took the game to the home side, with Hull having little response against a wave of attack. Two tries in the opening nine minutes of the second half saw Saints open up a 22-point lead.

Lewis Dodd was back in the Saints starting line-up after being dropped after the home defeat by Castleford and he scored two tries, as did reserve hooker Jake Burns.

To add to Hull's woes, forwards Jordan Lane and Brad Fash each got a one-match ban for head contact the following Monday.

Also on the Saturday, Salford recorded a telling 22-16 victory at home to Leeds.

It had the feel of a do-or-die game, and it ended with Salford closing in on a play-off spot and Leeds looking almost out of contention, the Red Devils ending six points above seventh-placed Leeds and a further point clear of Leigh, who had a game in hand.

Kallum Watkins led the home side's revival from 16-6 down, scoring two tries in a stirring personal display. Two late Marc Sneyd penalties, the first after a Rhyse Martin high tackle on Loghan Lewis, which home fans felt warranted a yellow card, and the second after a James Bentley high tackle on Jake Shorrocks, which did indeed bring a yellow card stretched the Salford lead to 22-16 and two missed field-goal attempts were inconsequential as they held out for a critical victory.

Leigh's game in hand against Wigan was set for the following Tuesday so they too had a Thursday game and their 20-10 win at Castleford marked a fourth successive victory.

The win was made more impressive by the absence of both Gareth O'Brien (head) and Matt Moylan (rib), which saw Edwin Ipape feature largely as a halfback, plus prop Tom Amone (head). With their other spine players all out injured, Lachlan Lam took full control of Leigh's attack and pulled the strings magnificently, Josh Charnley ending with two tries.

The key moment came when Lam held Tex Hoy up over the line, shortly before Ipape's interception try put the Leopards clear on 46 minutes.

The biggest shock of the weekend came on the Sunday in south London as the Broncos recorded their second win of the season, beating play-off side Catalans 12-10, on their return to Wimbledon after pitch re-seeding.

August

The Broncos edged the first half against a disjointed Dragons and held a 6-0 half-time lead when sub Jacob Jones crashed under the sticks and Oli Leyland converted.

Jarrod Wallace was over for Catalans on 56 minutes in a similar fashion for Arthur Mourgue to level. At the time, London were down to twelve men for the second occasion, with an injured player, Ugo Tison, green-carded for two minutes.

But the outstanding Jarred Bassett quickly restored London's six-point lead on the hour. A series of angle-changing offloads sent Leyland through the cover. He was tackled but not grounded and he found Bassett up in support to cross untouched before he made it 12-6 with the conversion.

London might have finished it but were denied first by Sam Tomkins' superb tackle on Sadiq Adebiyi. Then their choice not to go for a field goal after Leyland's 40/20 almost came back to haunt them. It was a decision they regretted within a minute as Tomkins hoisted a kick which Matthieu Laguerre volley-balled back for Fouad Yaha to cross.

But Mourgue missed the conversion from wide out and London held on for a gloriously unexpected win.

Round 2

Wigan went two points clear at the top of the table again after a 28-6 home win over neighbours Leigh, in the game postponed from February to accommodate the World Club Challenge.

The Warriors raced ahead and led 22-0 to have the game virtually won by half-time. They were helped initially by Jack Hughes' sin-binning for a seventh-minute high tackle on Kruise Leeming, with two tries scored while the Leopards were a player down.

Junior Nsemba got the first in excellent fashion when he recovered a loose pass by Kaide Ellis, darted inside and probed the defensive line until locating a gap to shoot through.

A great team try followed as Wigan reacted to Frankie Halton handing them possession by passing wide from Nsemba, through Zach Eckersley, for Jake Wardle and Liam Marshall to break down the right, centre Jake Wardle receiving the return pass to score.

Two further tries followed in the final six minutes of the first half. Umyla Hanley's dropped ball brought a scrum from which Adam Keighran scored directly through soft defence, then Patrick Mago went through a gap from close range off Leeming's movement from dummy-half.

The Leopards showed their true colours in the second half, after withdrawing fullback Matt Moylan, who was visibly not at full fitness with a rib injury, although they failed to build on Lachlan Lam's try four minutes in, from a Kai O'Donnell break down the middle.

Harvie Hill hit back for the hosts off Leeming's grubber before Leigh spurned several chances to soften the margin of defeat. Lam made a break but sent the final pass to Abbas Miski instead of Josh Charnley, while Darnell McIntosh dived into the corner, only to lose control of the ball before grounding it.

Round 21

Four days later the Warriors were no longer top as they looked short on energy in defeat at Leeds and Hull KR continued their excellent form with a 36-6 win over Castleford at Sewell Group Craven Park, both games played on the Saturday.

Rovers claimed a 16th win in 21 league games as Ryan Hall scored his 331st career try to move into standalone 20th place in the list of all-time scorers in the British game.

It wasn't until late in the game Rovers finally threw off the Tigers' challenge with three tries in the last 16 minutes.

The icing went onto the cake and the Roger Millward MBE trophy was secured with seven minutes to go when a combination of Tyrone May and Mikey Lewis saw the former twist his way over the line. Lewis converted for a fifth win in a row.

Leeds showed signs that new coach Brad Arthur was making an impact with a 30-4 hammering of Wigan at Headingley.

Wigan, with captain Liam Farrell making the 400th appearance of his glorious career were

August

Leeds' Lachlan Miller heads for the Wigan tryline

never really in the contest after conceding a stunning opening try in the 16th minute, undermined by their indiscipline, with Adam Keighran earning a yellow card and, late on, Harry Smith seeing a red card for an elbow to James Bentley when the Leeds man was on the floor.

Smith kicked early to pen Leeds on their own line as the Warriors won the initial territorial battle, but the Leeds break-out was sublime, with stand-in skipper Matt Frawley finding Lachlan Miller, and his delightful pass putting Martin into the clear. Miller backed up on the inside and Harry Newman took the scoring pass despite the attentions of Jai Field. Martin took the lead out to eight points at the break with a penalty goal after a high shot on Bentley and kicked the first points of the second half for an offside offence.

Brodie Croft was twice involved in a flowing move that saw James McDonnell just denied and Smith gave away a seven-tackle set, before Wigan conceded a penalty and Frawley and Brodie Croft sent Miller over for a fine one-handed put down, with Martin landing the touchline conversion.

Keighran was sin-binned for a high tackle, which Martin converted for a three-score lead, and when Liam Marshall failed to take a Junior Nsemba pass in the corner, Miller, David Fusitu'a and Croft countered.

Miller, Newman and Frawley took the move on, and Andy Ackers moved infield and hit McDonnell on his outside for a deserved score.

Bentley then lost possession and gave away a penalty, allowing Smith, Field and Jake Wardle, with a fine flick, to send Marshall over for Wigan's sole points of the afternoon.

Smith's dismissal allowed Leeds a final attack. Frawley chipped for Croft to gather and Miller's delightful cross kick saw Momirovski palm the ball back for Martin to cross and add his seventh goal.

The Warriors remained level at the top with Hull KR but the points difference between the two had grown to 42.

Warrington stayed in third two points behind the leading pair after a Sunday afternoon 36-22 win at London Broncos.

The final scoreline, boosted by Matty Ashton's 100th career try in the final seconds, exaggerated Warrington's superiority. They were always ahead, and there were several points when they threatened to pull away but London kept on coming back at them and were only finally beaten when Rhys Kennedy was sin-binned for a dangerous tackle with nine minutes left.

Rodrick Tai, Ashton, Paul Vaughan and Toby King all crossed for the visitors, with Josh Rourke and Lewis Bienek responding, as Warrington led by 12 at the break.

August

Adam Holroyd put the Wolves further ahead, but Sam Davis and Ugo Tison brought London back within six points before Ashton's try sealed victory.

Moses Mbye struck a golden-point field goal to clinch a 17-16 win for St Helens over Salford.

Tries from Tommy Makinson, Waqa Blake and the back-from-injury Joe Batchelor looked to be taking Saints to victory. But Salford got a foothold in the game with Marc Sneyd's boot and a try from Chris Hankinson. And Nene Macdonald powered over with ten minutes remaining to force extra time before Mbye won it for Saints.

St Helens and Salford were now four points clear in the play-off spots, alongside Catalans who also had the narrowest of wins, a late field goal from Arthur Mourgue earning them a 23-22 victory at Huddersfield.

Days after club owner Bernard Guasch said he was 'ashamed' by their loss at London, a fast start to each half saw the Dragons lead 14-0 and then 22-10, only for quick-fire tries to bring Huddersfield level late on.

The Dragons had scored five tries to four, through Bayley Sironen, Sam Tomkins, Fouad Yaha, Arthur Romano and Matt Ikuvalu but Mourgue's failure to convert all but one looked costly - until the young Frenchman stepped up four minutes from time to slot the winning field goal.

By that time, Tomkins had long departed the field, hobbling off with a hamstring injury early in the second half on only the third appearance of his comeback.

The Giants' tries came from Jake Bibby, Kevin Naiqama, Sam Hewitt and Tui Lolohea

On the Sunday, Leigh returned to winning ways, by 42-12, following a big second half against Hull FC - and their fans had further cause for cheer post-match when Adrian Lam confirmed that his son Lachlan was to stay at the club next season.

Halfback Lam was influential again, displaying the qualities that made him so highly desirable to other clubs, including opponents Hull.

The real hero for the Leopards was Australian second-rower Kai O'Donnell, who scored four of their eight tries in perfect combination with Lam as Leigh eventually finished comfortable winners.

Hull were out-muscled and gave more debuts to props, this time to incoming coach John Cartwright's son Jed and on-loan from Wigan Sam Eseh.

Round 22

With the Magic Weekend moved to mid-August by the RFL, Elland Road Leeds became the controversial venue for the 2024 edition.

The event drew a crowd of 53,103 over the two days, the second-lowest attendance, ahead of only the 2010 weekend in Edinburgh at Murrayfield. And it officially brought the lowest single-day attendance, with only 22,293 heading in through the gates on Sunday. Nevertheless the RFL claimed it as a commercial success.

The first game up had a feeling of unease and uncertainty around the IMG gradings which had been published at the end of the previous season.

London Broncos beat Hull FC hands down, by 29-4 to move level with them at the foot of the table, remaining in bottom spot on a much inferior points difference. It would have been a potentially pivotal victory in any other year when IMG gradings were not deciding who stayed up and who was relegated.

Hull made four changes, with Ligi Sao, Jordan Lane and Brad Fash coming back after suspensions and Ed Chamberlain restored to the starting line-up after an enforced absence through a failed head-injury assessment, while veteran back Tom Briscoe emerged for his 350th Super League appearance. They lost Jack Walker and Carlos Tuimavave to injury during the game but it was a generally lacklustre display from a Hull side made up of inexperience and recently signed players.

Halfback Oli Leyland and fullback Josh Rourke proved to be the Airlie Birds' chief tormentors.

Rourke scored two tries and made another for Jack Campagnolo, while Leyland had a personal tally of 17 points as Broncos recorded only their third win of the season.

August

Lewis Martin had replied to Rourke's opener but Hull FC collapsed as Leyland's boot moved London out of sight and Rourke and Leyland added late tries.

Hull's problems worsened on the Monday as Ligi Sao and Denive Balmforth both were banned for a match for dangerous contact.

Next up, the Wigan-Saints derby saw the Warriors go back to the top of the table, if only for a day, with a 20-0 win over their dearest rivals.

With both sides missing a host of key players - Saints especially depleted - and naming first-time captains in Kaide Ellis and Matty Lees, it was a muted version of the historic rivalry.

Wigan's scratch halfback pairing of Adam Keighran and 18-year-old Jack Farrimond did an effective and decisive job to win a match between what were still two experienced packs.

Saints, meanwhile, were without any of their first-choice spine players, leaving Harry Robertson, Ben Davies, Moses Mbye and James Bell to hold the fort.

Robertson, another 18-year-old, was a big threat from fullback and looked the most likely to break down Wigan, while back-rower Junior Nsemba was a real driving force for Wigan in a game where young talent shone.

Wigan surged in front with back-to-back tries in the space of three first-half minutes, earning twelve of their 20 points.

Keighran's long pass set up Liam Marshall for a 16th-minute opening try. Then Joe Batchelor's tip-tackle put them straight back on the attack and Farrimond scored an excellent try off his own subtle kick in behind the defence.

Keighran converted both efforts, plus a penalty after the half-time hooter awarded for offside as Wigan led 14-0 at the break.

Robertson had two surging runs before that, showing great movement to weave around tackles, but was ultimately stopped right on the line both times.

Ellis was sin-binned for Wigan in the 56th minute for a high tackle on Batchelor (he later got a one-game ban), offering Saints an opportunity to strike back that they threw away - quite literally.

Robertson made a brilliant break and his pass looked to have created a certain try for Matt Whitley, but Jai Field came storming back to make the challenge and force an error with the try-line begging.

After that critical defensive play, Saints hardly threatened again and the Warriors added a third try five minutes from time. Sam Walters was the scorer - his first for the club, in his twelfth appearance - as the backrower touched down a kick from out wide by Abbas Miski.

It was a miserable end for Saints, whose glut of injuries was compounded in the early minutes by Curtis Sironen's exit with a calf complaint.

Saturday's last game saw Warrington maintain their charge towards a top-two place under Sam Burgess with a 24-6 victory over Leeds, after an uncompromising, near watertight performance.

Their commitment to defence was best summed up by the shuddering challenge that set up the opening try after it looked like the sides would go in at half-time with a 2-0 scoreline. Lachlan Miller, clearing his line, was savagely cut down by PNG centre Rodrick Tai and the ball jolted free for George Williams to gather, dummy and sprint clear.

Matt Dufty defied a leg injury to post the points that came off the back of that defensive resolve with a genuine second-half hat-trick.

The Rhinos were in the battle until late but, more than anything in a game where clear-cut chances were few, they missed their leading try-assister Brodie Croft, who was back in Australia on compassionate leave for the funeral of his grandfather.

Sunday's opener was predicted to be a classic but it didn't set alight as Leigh kept the top six in touching distance after a 26-0 win over a Salford side that never recovered from two early yellow cards.

Ethan Ryan and Brad Singleton were both sin-binned for high shots within four minutes of each other in the opening exchanges, whilst Zak Hardaker produced a complete performance at fullback and Kai O'Donnell was his usual rampaging best in the pack.

August

Red Devils coach Paul Rowley welcomed back Tim Lafai from suspension whilst Joe Mellor and Shane Wright replaced Joe Shorrocks and Joe Bullock in the starting line-up.

For Leigh, there was no Matt Moylan and, with Josh Charnley out, Keanan Brand was recalled from his loan spell at Widnes.

Edwin Ipape got Leigh on the board from dummy-half within five minutes and Salford were reduced to 11 soon after. And it didn't exactly help the Red Devils either when Sam Stone went off for a head-injury assessment, which he failed, following a nasty-looking cut.

Umyla Hanley ran in from distance as Leigh made their advantage count before the break.

In the second half, Hardaker went in for Leigh with eight minutes to spare to ensure there was no way back for Salford, before Ricky Leutele dived in to seal the two points.

Lafai and Oliver Partington both got one game bans for dangerous contact.

Hull KR went back to the top and in some style, with a 36-4 win over Catalans, running in eight tries in a sixth straight victory for the Robins.

When the two teams clashed just over a month before, fans were treated to a golden-point thriller as the Dragons came out victorious.

Hull KR went into the break with a 12-4 lead with tries from skipper Elliot Minchella, Peta Hiku and Ryan Hall - all unconverted by Mikey Lewis - against a Bayley Sironen four pointer.

Catalans needed a solid start after the break if they were to mount a comeback, but instead conceded a bizarre try. Barely a minute into the restart, Minchella picked up possession 25 metres out and ran straight past statuesque Dragons prop Julian Bousquet, who had clearly been called as offside at marker by referee Tom Grant, for his second try.

On the 50-minute mark, Rovers were through once again. On this occasion, Lewis unleashed Kelepi Tanginoa who touched down for Hull's fifth try of the match.

Magic Weekend witnessed true wizardry in the 61st minute as Dean Hadley produced an outrageous assist for Hall's second try of the contest. The big second rower pulled out a one-handed no-look pass down the left flank, allowing Hall to make it 26-4.

Tanginoa scored his second before a perfect dink from Tyrone May allowed Niall Evalds to cross the line after he caught it at speed on the full. Lewis, who hit the post three times with his eight conversion attempts, successfully kicked his second of the match.

Huddersfield and Castleford brought the curtain down on Magic Weekend, the Giants taking early dominance before running out 20-12 winners.

The Tigers did threaten a late comeback through two Jason Qareqare tries but they had been woeful for an hour.

Esan Marsters came back in for Huddersfield, with Aidan McGowan left out and Jake Bibby moving to the wing. Kieran Rush and Matty English also made the bench. Paul McShane didn't return in time to replace Cain Robb but Brad Martin and Will Tate returned for Castleford after lengthy spells out. George Lawler and Nixon Putt also dropped out.

It was 12-0 at half-time, Sam Halsall finishing superbly in just the fourth minute, Jake Connor converting superbly from the touchline. And after Huddersfield were awarded a penalty, Leroy Cudjoe scythed through soft defence before sending over Sam Hewitt. Connor converted for a 12-0 lead after 14 minutes.

A towering Olly Russell bomb was dropped by Jason Qareqare into the arms of Lolohea, who couldn't miss Marsters standing on the wing with a well-timed pass. Connor kept up his extraordinary touchline conversion record to make it 18-0.

The Tigers looked lost with ball in hand at times but they finally had some points as the hour approached, with a wonderful looping pass from Tex Hoy sending Qareqare in the corner. Rowan Milnes converted to reduce the deficit to 18-6.

An incredible piece of skill from Liam Horne saw the Tigers back to within six points. A runaround with Rowan Milnes gave the PNG international the space to chip over the top of the Giants' defence for an on-rushing Qareqare to fly in for his second. Milnes' conversion made it 18-12 with ten minutes to go.

But the Giants made sure of victory after Muizz Mustapha caught Andre Savelio high. Connor, who had been impeccable with the boot, duly converted for a 20-12 victory.

August

Hull KR's Joe Burgess celebrates his fourth try against St Helens with Peta Hiku

Round 23

The contest for the League Leaders Shield was turned into a three-horse race as St Helens were taken to the cleaners on their own patch by Hull KR, who stayed top after a 42-6 win on the Saturday afternoon.

While the Robins continued to fly high, injury-hit Saints looked in genuine danger of missing out on the play-offs in a game that was virtually lost from the first minute. George Whitby, the 18-year-old Academy player making his senior debut at scrum-half, and fellow teen Jonny Vaughan collided when they both went to catch the kick-off. Neither claimed it.

Hull KR took full advantage as Joe Burgess scored the first of his four tries in the corner off quick passing, and things only got better for them - and worse for Saints - from there.

Waqa Blake was sin-binned in the eighth minute for a high shot on Jack Broadbent, and by the time he returned St Helens were 16-0 down.

Tommy Makinson was dismissed five minutes from time, for a shoulder to the head of May. He got three matches, reduced to two on appeal.

Wigan stayed level with Hull KR with a tough but important 22-4 home victory over Hull FC. Jai Field was the difference between the two teams as he caused Hull FC problems all afternoon and he had a hand in two of Wigan's tries and could have created more.

The Warriors led 10-4 at the break thanks to scores from winger Jacob Douglas, his first senior try, and Zach Eckersley – with Field providing the final pass for both tries. Hull offered little in the first 28 minutes but managed to score on their first real attack on Wigan's line. Lewis Martin made a break before the ball eventually found Jed Cartwright and he touched down. Jack Charles was off target with the conversion attempt.

Cartwright later left the field for a head assessment with blood pouring from his face, not to return, as his side defended heroically to keep the Warriors out before the break.

Hull improved after the turnaround but two tries in the space of seven minutes from Junior Nsemba and Jack Farrimond saw the Warriors home.

August

Warrington were the third club in the mix after their Friday-night 28-6 win at Castleford.

Star fullback Matt Dufty suffered a knee injury at Magic Weekend that kept him sidelined for a month. But 18-year-old Cai Taylor-Wray shone in Dufty's place, on only his second professional appearance, and lit up an otherwise uninspiring game at Castleford with a brilliant opening try.

He steamed onto a dummy-half pass from Zane Musgrove and into the gap behind the markers, slicing clean through the defensive line, slipped past the fullback Tex Hoy, weaved towards the corner, and held off all other challenges to score his first senior try.

Before that, debutant Tigers halfback Jenson Windley had the home crowd on its feet when he stepped through the line. But Taylor-Wray and Matty Nicholson put him under pressure as he neared the posts and he lost the ball trying to register what would have been a memorable try.

Salford jumped from sixth into fourth in some style with a 60-10 Saturday-evening hammering of Huddersfield, scoring ten tries, including a hat-trick from Ryan Brierley and two from Jayden Nikorima, Marc Sneyd kicking ten goals, as well as scoring a try himself.

The Giants' play-off hopes had long gone, but the two teams above them, Leigh and Leeds did their chances the power of good with wins. Especially so Leeds, who came back to beat Catalans 18-6 at Headingley on the Friday night, meaning the Dragons, along with St Helens, were pulled back to just a point ahead of the seventh-placed Leopards.

The injury-hit Dragons had an all-French spine and led 6-0 at half-time thanks to an Arthur Romano try converted by Arthur Mourgue but, with a twelve-point turnaround in the middle of the second half, the Rhinos were able to overcome them.

Leeds were also extremely well served by their bench to sustain and capitalise on their weight of possession. Jarrod O'Connor's drive and directness out of dummy-half was the key to victory, while James Bentley's work rate in attack and defence was immense. Youngster Tom Nicholson-Watton made almost ten metres a carry and made his presence felt in the tackle.

David Fusitu'a, Matt Frawley and Lachlan Miller tries and three Rhyse Martin goals were reward for Leeds' second-half dominance.

With momentum building, and three home games to come in the last four – including a visit by St Helens – a play-off place looked well within the grasp of Leigh, who on the Sunday recorded their seventh win in eight games, a 32-12 victory at London.

Three tries in the last 15 minutes put the issue beyond doubt after London had competed on equal terms for the first hour, climbing off bottom place for the first time this season when they led between the 14th and 29th minutes.

A tight and intense encounter was in genuine doubt until Kai O'Donnell's clean break, one of not very many on an afternoon when both defensive lines were solid, gave Leigh a two-score lead in the 67th minute.

London's spirit remained unbowed, but the earlier efforts had depleted their energy and further scores from Gareth O'Brien and Aaron Pene, both converted as Zak Hardaker repaired a patchy kicking record, including three first-half misses, gave the final scoreline a lopsided look.

Round 24

The last Friday in August saw Warrington lose ground on the top two as they were defeated 16-12 at Leigh, who climbed into the play-off spots after their eighth win in nine games.

It was a game full of controversy as the Wolves were reduced to twelve men in the eleventh minute after Paul Vaughan was dismissed for a high tackle on Owen Trout.

The decision incensed Wolves boss Sam Burgess. 'I don't think it's right, well I think it's embarrassing. It becomes a theatrical game out there. Numerous players, telling players to stay down. I'm going to ask a couple of questions about what we're going to do to fix this mess, because that was a mess. It spoiled a good game of Rugby League.'

Vaughan was suspended for three games by the RFL Match Review Panel the following Monday.

Leigh made a strong start and had three successive sets on the Warrington line. The

August

Wolves held out with some great defence but on their way out of danger, John Bateman spilled the ball and a quick reaction from Lachlan Lam led to Ricky Leutele racing over. Matt Moylan couldn't goal but Leigh led 4-0.

After Vaughan's red card, Trout left the field for a head-injury assessment, from which he later returned.

Seconds later, the teams came together after a high challenge, and referee Liam Moore spoke with both captains before awarding the Leopards a penalty. This time Moylan kicked the points from 30 metres out to nudge Leigh further in front and it was 6-0.

Warrington created back-to-back sets when George Williams kicked forward and Darnell McIntosh knocked on after Danny Walker's run. They made it count when Williams' fine ball resulted in Matty Ashton going over at the corner. Thewlis converted brilliantly to level the scores going into half-time.

Early errors from Thewlis and King had Leigh on the front foot again and Lachlan Lam's effort was referred to the video-referee, who ruled that he had been held up. Trout then went close before Frankie Halton crashed through on a short pass to regain the advantage for the hosts and Moylan converted.

Another Leigh try followed in the 53rd minute when Josh Charnley took Lam's lofted pass for an unconverted effort in the corner.

The final word went to the Wolves, however, when Ben Currie sent Sam Powell to the line and Thewlis goaled, but it was too late for them to get back into the game.

The same night, Hull KR went four points clear of the Wolves after a 32-12 home win over Salford, the Robins' eighth win in a row.

Confidence was running high at Craven Park as, not for the first time, Mikey Lewis led the effort, constantly searching for openings whether running, passing or kicking.

His try late in the first half was the highlight of the match, running around Salford skipper Kallum Watkins and then bisecting Nene Macdonald and Ethan Ryan to dive joyfully into the corner.

Macdonald's late score was too late for the Red Devils, who finished the weekend in fifth spot.

Bevan French put a spring into the step of Wigan on his return from injury but it was a brutal performance from the Warriors' pack that won the points in Perpignan with a bruising 26-18 win over Catalans.

French and fellow Aussie speedster Jai Field were a constant threat at a steamy Stade Gilbert Brutus but it was the ferocity of props Luke Thompson and Ethan Havard, combined with a belligerent display of controlled aggression from second-rower Junior Nsemba, that wrestled the points from the Dragons.

It was 12-12 at half-time. But Nsemba's 43rd-minute try after breaking free from a tackle to race over from 15 metres was the killer blow for the Catalans.

The hard-earned win kept Wigan level with Hull KR, who had nearly an 84-point superior points difference. Catalans meanwhile were now in seventh, a point behind Leigh.

St Helens looked to have ended a form blip on the Sunday and moved back into the top four, when they won at Huddersfield by 18-10.

The win looked less than likely in the first half as the Giants led 10-6 in the 39th minute when their young prop Fenton Rogers was dismissed by referee Aaron Moore for a high shot on Saints winger Tee Ritson.

The second half saw Saints score twelve unanswered points as they made use of the extra player advantage to secure two vital points heading into the final three games of the season. St Helens did have Noah Stephens sin-binned for a professional foul nine minutes from the end but they were able to hang on to secure the win.

Castleford earned a first win in six games as they won at down-at-heel Hull FC 39-20.

The Tigers stormed into an 18-point lead inside 30 minutes - with teenage halfback and West Hull product Jenson Windley getting his first try in his second appearance - but were pegged back to within just four thanks to two tries either side of half-time from Hull winger Harvey Barron.

August

Rowan Milnes was a constant threat with the boot (seven goals and a field goal) and with ball in hand for the Tigers, with former Hull FC fullback Tex Hoy finishing with two tries.

The saddest sight of all was club great Danny Houghton limping off with a calf injury in the eighth minute of his 450th Hull appearance.

Sunday afternoon, the first day of September, provided one of the most exciting games of the season, as Leeds kept up their play-off push with a 21-20 golden point win at London Broncos.

For the second time in the season, London took the Rhinos to extra time. And once again they emerged pointless as Brodie Croft landed the decisive kick, this time with little more than a minute before the draw was called.

It came after London had had three out of the four shots at goal, including a 40-metre rocket from Jack Campagnolo, whose torpedo-like trajectory took it into a thumping collision with the crossbar.

This was a result Leeds needed. Defeat would have left them with an uphill play-off battle, three points behind Leigh with an inferior points difference.

Papua New Guinea international Rhyse Martin, who had signed for Hull KR for 2025, was instrumental in his side's narrow win, scoring 20 points with three tries and four goals.

London started well, helped by Leeds conceding two penalties in rapid succession and the elusive Campagnolo weaved to the line on the sixth tackle after five minutes for Oli Leyland to convert.

But the lead was short-lived as Croft kicked into the ground and Rhyse Martin claimed the first of his three tries by seizing the ball from Josh Rourke and crossing, adding the points himself to make it 6-6 after ten minutes.

Leeds' expectation of a tight afternoon was made clear in the 23rd minute when they were awarded a penalty ten metres out and took the points, Martin making it 8-6. Leeds threatened for the only time to take control when Frawley's superbly weighted kick sent Martin over, the centre's conversion making the score 14-6 and taking him to 1,000 points for the Rhinos.

Emmanuel Waine was to spend only about 15 minutes on the field, but in that time he claimed the try that, with Leyland's conversion, cut the half-time margin to 14-12. And it looked as if he might have given them the lead immediately after a superb combination with Leyland ended with a review – the first of five in the second half - ruling he had not touched down.

Another saw Rourke's apparent revenge for Martin's first-half larceny ruled out, to the relief of Lachlan Miller, but three minutes later the review favoured London as Lee Kershaw went over in the corner. But their lead was again short-lived, as the magnificent Martin went on a solo run 35 metres to the line, before adding the conversion to make it 20-16.

But London battled on and with five minutes left Kershaw charged down the right and released the ball just as he was tackled into touch. Ethan Natoli picked it up and crossed. A long review confirmed the try and, had Leyland's conversion from the touch-line rebounded in a different direction after striking the post, they might have been spared the golden point and what followed.

'They didn't deserve to lose,' said Leeds coach Brad Arthur. 'We've got the two points but we're not very happy.'

BETFRED SUPER LEAGUE
Sunday 1st September

	P	W	D	L	F	A	D	Pts
Hull KR	24	19	0	5	649	286	363	38
Wigan Warriors	24	19	0	5	597	318	279	38
Warrington Wolves	24	17	0	7	604	317	287	34
St Helens	24	14	0	10	542	350	192	28
Salford Red Devils	24	14	0	10	465	467	-2	28
Leigh Leopards	24	13	1	10	514	350	164	27
Catalans Dragons	24	13	0	11	426	388	38	26
Leeds Rhinos	24	13	0	11	446	418	28	26
Huddersfield Giants	24	8	0	16	412	568	-156	16
Castleford Tigers	24	7	1	16	399	627	-228	15
Hull FC	24	3	0	21	314	744	-430	6
London Broncos	24	3	0	21	293	828	-535	6

SEPTEMBER
Leopards in play-off mix

Round 25

First v second in the table on the first Friday night of September didn't let anyone down as a bumper crowd at The Brick Stadium gathered to see home side Wigan go two points clear with a thrilling 24-20 win over Hull KR.

For large periods the Warriors were behind and looked second best. They were 10-0 down after Matt Parcell and Mikey Lewis tries and then trailed 20-8 when Joe Burgess finished a length-of-the-field move ten minutes into the second half.

Enter Bevan French on 57 minutes. Recovering a scrappy play, the reigning Man of Steel received possession, ran towards the Hull KR line and executed a delightful kick into a pocket of space behind, collecting for a magical try. That only narrowed the deficit, though.

For the Robins, the regret will be two yellow cards - one in the first half to Burgess, and then one on the hour to Jai Whitbread. They conceded two tries in each of the periods when down a man.

Burgess went for a flop on Jai Field after a Jake Wardle break and the Robins were ruthlessly punished, first by Abbas Miski expertly diving into the corner off a Field pass, then by French switching play and putting Junior Nsemba over on the day of his first England squad call-up.

Only Adam Keighran's missed goals kept the Warriors behind at that stage, although two Lewis penalties followed either side of half-time to stretch the lead back out before Burgess's try - as Peta Hiku intercepted a Harry Smith pass and ran the length - appeared to put Hull KR in command.

French's magic touch dispelled that and after prop Whitbread departed for striking the head of Tyler Dupree with his shoulder (Whitbread received a one-match penalty notice the following Monday), Jai Field stretched the visitors' defence with a wide run and sent in Liam Marshall.

Adam Keighran's conversion levelled the scores at 20-20 and five minutes later Marshall put them ahead, a thrilling team try set up by a Patrick Mago runaround with Nsemba, before a Wardle run and perfect pass.

Hull KR's defeat gave third-placed Warrington the chance the following afternoon to make ground on them. They took it, with a hard-fought 16-2 home win over St Helens, who were now in sixth spot and at risk of missing out on the Super League play-offs for the first time in history.

It was a game riddled with errors and cheap penalties on both sides but the final scoreline reflected the fact that St Helens were the guiltiest on both counts.

Saints coach Paul Wellens felt their defence held up well to only concede two tries, scored in the first half by Matty Ashton and Jordan Crowther and both set up by Warrington captain George Williams.

But it was the Wolves defence that really shone, ensuring that an early Jon Bennison penalty provided the only points scored by the visitors.

The early narrative was around cards, as two early incidents set an ill-tempered tone and reignited the current debate on gamesmanship.

September

First Warrington's Lachlan Fitzgibbon was binned for a high tackle on Tee Ritson in the eighth minute (a one-match penalty notice was handed to Fitzgibbon). Then five minutes later Matty Lees of St Helens went off for a late hit on Josh Drinkwater.

In both cases, penalties were not initially awarded and referee Chris Kendall had waved play on. Only after the players in question stayed down for treatment were the respective challenges reviewed and punished.

Lees faced no charge for that offence but was given a one-game ban for contact with the referee, which was reduced to a fine on appeal. Stand-in halfback Moses Mbye however was sidelined for a game for a late tackle.

Later in the day, Salford seriously damaged Catalans' hopes of a play-off spot and boosted their own as they moved up to fourth in the table with a comprehensive 27-12 home win over the Dragons.

Strong early Catalans pressure saw them well on top but they only had an Arthur Mourgue penalty to show for it. They then gifted Salford a try when Tom Davies collided with centre Mathieu Laguerre trying to catch a kick. Quick reactions saw Joe Mellor pick up and Ryan Brierley then linked for Jayden Nikorima to dash under the posts. Marc Sneyd, again at his influential best throughout, added the first two of his eleven-point contribution and the Red Devils led 6-2.

The Dragons were back on terms at 6-6 on 21 minutes when a startling break from recent signing Reimis Smith splintered the home defence and Mourgue supported César Rougé and Théo Fages to scramble over.

But with two minutes remaining of the half, Salford retook the lead when Mellor picked his way over from dummy-half after Brierley's weaving run. Sneyd's second goal made it 12-6 at the break.

The class of Sneyd and Tim Lafai told after the restart, the former helping to tee up the latter for a third score, before Lafai laid on a fourth try with a wonderful pass to Deon Cross.

A spirited late rally by the visitors enabled Bayley Sironen to cross to make it 26-12. But there was still time for Sneyd to slot a mammoth field goal to seal the hosts' 27-12 win.

Leeds and Leigh were now play-off chances after Friday-night wins.

Leigh were in fifth, a point clear of St Helens, after a commanding 34-12 success at Castleford, a six-try win a fifth victory in succession.

Josh Charnley's try in his 300th Super League appearance was part of a procession by the visitors as Tom Amone scored a brace, and Kai O'Donnell, Gareth O'Brien and Ricky Leutele also went over.

The Tigers were unable to send out their club legend Paul McShane, who was playing in his last home game before departing the club, as a winner.

Leeds recorded a third successive win for the first time this season and a record score against the Black and Whites, dispatching woeful Hull FC 68-6 at Headingley.

Hull KR-bound Rhyse Martin signed off with a perfect exhibition from the boot, landing 13 attempts at goal - four from the touchline to tries scored by four-try winger Alfie Edgell - while the last was left to fellow departee James Donaldson, whose successful conversion brought the biggest cheers of the night.

Brodie Croft ran the show with a try double and a hand or foot in most of the others, James Bentley – who also bagged a brace – was again a towering presence off the bench and Lachlan Miller turned the Hull cover inside and out all night.

The Rhinos were now seventh but level on points with St Helens in sixth.

Hull FC very nearly ended the weekend in bottom spot as London almost produced a win at Huddersfield on the Sunday, going down 22-16.

Tui Lolohea scored two tries before half-time to put the hosts 14-6 up, after prop Marcus Stock's try had given the Broncos the advantage. Oli Leyland was instrumental in the Broncos' two-try reply, with grubber kicks from the stand-off setting Hakim Miloudi and Sadiq Adebiyi up for four-pointers that put London ahead 16-14.

Two Olly Russell penalties in quick succession restored the Giants' lead and a late Harry

September

Rushton try, after London captain Will Lovell was shown a yellow card on 75 minutes, saw the Giants home.

The Broncos, already relegated at the start of the season by IMG's controversial gradings, were still level on six points with Hull FC. But their ambition to finish off the bottom spot looked likely to be thwarted with two tough away games - at Catalans and Warrington - to finish the season.

Round 26

Wigan remained two points clear going into the final round of regular-season with a resounding 38-0 home win over Leeds, whose play-off hopes remained in the balance.

Two tries in the space of 60 seconds in the opening ten minutes to Jake Wardle and Bevan French broke Leeds' spirit and they never recovered. With Lachlan Miller out with a hamstring strain their attack never prospered, youngster Alfie Edgell moving to fullback and Riley Lumb outstanding on the wing.

Wigan opened the scoring with a great try in the left corner from a Harry Smith kick, which Liam Marshall did well to collect and release before going into touch. The pass found Wardle and he acrobatically touched down for an unconverted try.

Wigan extended their lead moments later as Kaide Ellis was sent through a massive gap and he kept his composure to send French in under the posts. Adam Keighran made it 10-0 and the Warriors dominated from there.

Prop Ellis's ball-handling skills, hard running and try-scoring exploits set the standard as the Warriors moved one step closer to retaining the League Leaders' Shield for the first time in their history. Further scores from the brilliant French, Marshall, Abbas Miski, Ellis and Keighran followed with Smith's kicking game almost flawless.

Second-placed Hull KR reigned supreme in a 24-0 win at Leigh, with their defence shining through alongside 16 points from Mikey Lewis in a game where the Leopards were looking to confirm a play-off spot.

It was a second successive shut-out forced by Rovers on Leigh in 2024 following their 12-0 win at Craven Park.

Two Lewis kicks and two brilliant chases by Tyrone May led to tries for winger Ryan Hall and Lewis as a breathless first half ended with the visitors 10-0 ahead. Sauaso Sue crashed over for his sixth league try of the season within eight minutes of the restart. And Lewis rounded off a hugely impressive individual and team display, going over from close range after some slick handling and exhibition-like interplay had kept the ball alive on the last tackle.

The only blot for Rovers was a possible suspension for captain Elliot Minchella, who was sin-binned late in the game for a high shot on Matt Moylan. The prop got a two-match ban the following Monday and appealed twice but to no avail.

On the Saturday, Warrington hammered Huddersfield 66-0 at the John Smith's Stadium to stay in third - the points difference boost meaning they could still sneak into the top two should Hull KR slip up in the final round.

Matty Ashton scored three of the dozen tries, including the first two in the opening 14 minutes.

Huddersfield were already being schooled, and an embarrassing evening only got worse and worse.

Ashton was twice denied his hat-trick - he'd have to wait until well into the second half for what felt an inevitable third try - but they did the damage in the middle instead with the help of Ben Currie's class at loose forward. His passes set up tries for both James Harrison - on the back of a Danny Walker 40/20 - and then George Williams.

Two more tries followed on the stroke of half-time as Matty Nicholson's all-too-easy crash-over was followed by a comedy of errors in which Tui Lolohea dropped a Josh Drinkwater kick and Aidan McGowan fumbled around on the ground, allowing bright young fullback Cai Taylor-Wray to pounce.

September

Josh Thewlis converted every one of those tries for a 36-0 half-time lead, plus three of six in the second half including his own score six minutes after the restart, moments after being hit high by Jack Billington in a challenge that earned the young Giants forward a yellow card.

Harvey Livett had a Giants try ruled out for a knock-on before Ashton was on the end of a good shift play to complete his treble just past the hour and reach 20 Super League tries for the season.

It was the first of five tries in just a dozen minutes as Huddersfield utterly capitulated.

A Jon Bennison hat-trick helped St Helens ease past Castleford to all but secure their place in the play-offs with a 40-4 home win, with several key players, Jack Welsby and Lewis Dodd starring, returning to the line-up

Against a Castleford side that had won just once in their last seven, Estonian Akim Matvejev made a debut off the bench for them, Saints played some eye-catching rugby, Jonny Lomax, not long into the second half, putting to bed any sniff of a Castleford comeback.

Hull FC fans could hardly wait for the end of a horrible season and a 58-4 home thrashing by Salford, who secured a play-off place, didn't improve the mood.

Their youngsters, sprinkled with some experience, gave it their all for the full 80 minutes. But they came up against red-hot opponents who dominated every area of the field.

The first of Tim Lafai's two first-half tries gave the Red Devils the early lead, with Deon Cross, Joe Mellor and Brad Singleton also touching down to put Salford 28-0 up at the break. Nene MacDonald, Shane Wright and Kallum Watkins added three more tries before Lafai completed his hat-trick and Salford passed the 50-point mark.

Young backrower Zach Jebson scored his first career try for Hull but Mellor's second try of the evening sent the Black and Whites to bottom spot on points difference - a single point sending London above them.

Just after half-time of the Catalans-London game later on that Saturday evening, it looked highly possible that Hull would a week later finish the season with the wooden spoon.

No-one really expected London to emerge victorious from the home of the Dragons, but they fully deserved their 8-0 lead, before Catalans pipped them 12-8.

From the start, it was clear that this was to be no damage limitation exercise for the visitors, who set about the Dragons with ferocious intent. For long periods in the game London led and looked likely to win.

Jordan Abdull returned after seven weeks out injured to partner Sam Tomkins at six and seven for Catalans but they played second fiddle to Oli Leyland and Jack Campagnolo in the London halves.

The Broncos underlined their recent improvement as Lee Kershaw shocked home fans at the Stade Gilbert Brutus with a first-half try and an Oli Leyland penalty put the Broncos eight points ahead just after the break.

Tries from Jarrod Wallace and Arthur Romano edged the Catalans in front and after that they had to survive with twelve men, Chris Satae sin-binned for a high tackle, and a late flurry of Broncos attacks

The Dragons were faltering but victory at Hull FC next in the final round, and defeats for Leigh and Leeds, would see them sneak into the top six.

Round 27

Wigan won the League Leaders' Shield with a 64-0 hammering of the Salford at The Brick Community Stadium on the Thursday night of the last round.

If the Warriors had stumbled, Hull KR would have overtaken them into top spot. But when Salford released their matchday squad earlier in the week no-one thought that would happen. Eight players made their Red Devils debuts, including brothers Billy and Charlie Glover. Ethan Fitzgerald, Josh Wagstaffe, Charlie McCurrie, Jamie Pye, Leunbou Bardyel-Wells and Jack Gatcliffe were the other debutants.

The game was never really a contest as the Warriors ran in five tries to lead 28-0 at the break. Liam Marshall, Jai Field, Bevan French, Zach Eckersley and Jake Wardle all crossed in the first 40 minutes with Salford barely seeing any of the ball.

September

Field scored twice in the second half to complete a hat-trick, while Kruise Leeming added two tries with Marshall and French both grabbing their second tries.

Salford head coach Paul Rowley stuck by his decision to rest all of his star players despite infuriating supporters of Hull KR. 'The youngsters were fantastic,' said Rowley. "They competed for everything. My objective is to have a fit squad going into the big games, the play-off games. In that respect I was able to utilise the squad and the youngsters and preserve our boys.'

Hull KR sealed second place, securing a week off and a home semi-final but they were made to fight all the way by a Leeds side still harbouring play-off aspirations of their own going into the game.

And, despite missing skipper Elliot Minchella's leadership in the middle of the field after his two-match suspension, Niall Evalds (concussion) and Kelepi Tanginoa, who was still out with a hamstring problem, they still had enough to beat the dogged Rhinos, by 26-16.

The Robins twice went behind to the Rhinos as Rhyse Martin and Alfie Edgell went over but tries from Matt Parcell and Peta Hiku levelled it by half-time. Tom Opacic, Sauaso Sue and Joe Burgess crossed after the break as Leeds could not sustain their strong first-half effort, though they had the consolation of scoring the final try through Andy Ackers.

Rovers hooker Matt Parcell was the star performer after having announced he would be returning home to Australia at the end of the season after five seasons at Rovers and three at Leeds before that.

Rhyse Martin's Leeds career came to a disappointing end at the ground where his next chapter would begin as a Hull KR player. At the weekend he was named in the Super League Dream Team after a stellar season for the Rhinos.

Warrington had to settle for third spot after a dominant 54-0 victory over London Broncos at the Halliwell Jones Stadium on the Friday night.

Coach Sam Burgess welcomed back Matt Dufty, who was electric in his side's performance, winger Matty Ashton scoring a hat-trick for the second week in a row. Canberra-bound backrower Matt Nicholson and 18-year-old Arron Lindop both got try doubles.

The Broncos disappointed on their last game before inevitable relegation and their points difference took enough of a hammering to ensure they finished bottom of the table.

Hull KR's win the same night meant the Wolves, who would be without off-season recruit Lachlan Fitzgibbon for the remainder of the season after shoulder surgery, would have to play an eliminator, with sixth-placed Leigh and fifth-placed St Helens meeting at LSV on the same night.

Defeat for the Leopards would have seen them drop out of the play-off spots to the benefit of Catalans who were expected to beat Hull FC the next day. But they won a red-hot contest 18-12 to leapfrog Saints, who would therefore face a daunting trip to Warrington.

In a game that highlighted the defensive prowess of both sides, Edwin Ipape, back from a shoulder injury, led the Leopards with his line speed and tackling setting the tone.

St Helens roared at the Leopards early on with Jonny Lomax and Jack Welsby combining for Tommy Makinson to dash over in the tenth minute. The decision went upstairs and Sione Mata'utia was adjudged to have obstructed Lachlan Lam in the build-up.

An error from Welsby piled the pressure back on the Saints, and John Asiata charged through the middle to put the Leopards in front after 20 minutes. Matt Moylan goaled and the hosts led 6-0.

With six minutes remaining of the first half, Leigh were up against it as Lomax forced a drop-out. Leigh held firm, then struck with precision on the left as Moylan zipped through to create space and Ricky Leutele strode over and dummied past the last defender. Moylan converted and the hosts led 12-0 at half-time.

After the break, Ricky Leutele shot out of the line and hit Welsby, who was clearly stunned and the Leigh centre was sin-binned for the challenge. Saints, sensing an opportunity, flooded forward. A brilliant pass from Lomax released Makinson to the corner and he was able to ground the ball brilliantly for Saints' first score, with the video-referee reversing the referee's decision. Jon Bennison goaled from the touchline and it was 12-6.

Saints then made it two tries in three minutes when Lomax kicked high and Moylan

September

allowed the ball to bounce. The ball came back inside and Lewis Dodd sent Morgan Knowles hurtling over by the posts for Bennison to draw the sides level.

Mata'utia lost the ball in an Asiata and Amone challenge, handing the Leopards a full set of six on the 20-metre line. Outstanding ball movement out to Charnley then saw him score to give the hosts an advantage in the 68th minute at 16-12.

Into the last eight minutes, Makinson was penalised for passing from the floor after the tackle was completed. Moylan pointed to the posts, and, after winding the clock down, he converted to nudge the Leopards six points clear.

The Leopards earned themselves a crack in the play-offs and would have to travel to Salford for the eliminator.

The curtain came down on Catalans' Super League season before a ball was kicked in their final fixture thanks to Leigh's victory.

Saturday's 24-4 win over second-bottom club Hull FC counted for nothing after the Dragons were edged out of a top-six slot, eventually finishing seventh in the league table just above Leeds on points difference. 'It's simply not good enough,' said coach Steve McNamara after his side missed the play-offs for the first time in five years.

Hull coach Simon Grix once again made changes in giving Ryan Westerman and Callum Kemp their debuts in a side of which nine of the seventeen were Hull-born players.

He also gave club captain Danny Houghton his 451st and final appearance to bring down the curtain on a wonderful 18-year one-club career. It was as well a farewell to Carlos Tuimavave, leaving the club after nine seasons.

Arthur Mourgue's try on the hour, which gave the Dragons a 14-point lead going into the final quarter was the gamebreaker.

Huddersfield ensured their 2024 Super League season ended in victory with a comprehensive 34-10 thrashing of woeful Castleford on the Thursday.

The Giants ran into a 22-0 half-time lead and never looked like relinquishing control as the Tigers saved one of their worst performances of the season for their final game. Backrower Sam Hewitt helped himself to a try-double.

Neither side had anything to play for except pride and the game was very much a damp squib, the Giants being far too clinical for their drab opponents.

Sebastine Ikahihifo, Olly Russell, Chris Hill, Esan Marsters and Adam Milner all made their final appearances for the Giants, as did Paul McShane for the Tigers.

BETFRED SUPER LEAGUE
Final table - Saturday 21st September

	P	W	D	L	F	A	D	Pts
Wigan Warriors	27	22	0	5	723	338	385	44
Hull KR	27	21	0	6	719	326	393	42
Warrington Wolves	27	20	0	7	740	319	421	40
Salford Red Devils	27	16	0	11	550	547	3	32
Leigh Leopards	27	15	1	11	566	398	168	31
St Helens	27	15	0	12	596	388	208	30
Catalans Dragons	27	15	0	12	474	427	47	30
Leeds Rhinos	27	14	0	13	530	488	42	28
Huddersfield Giants	27	10	0	17	468	660	-192	20
Castleford Tigers	27	7	1	19	425	735	-310	15
Hull FC	27	3	0	24	328	894	-566	6
London Broncos	27	3	0	24	317	916	-599	6

The Eliminators

Leigh Leopards won a Super League play-off tie for the first time by overcoming Salford 14-6 in a Friday-night eliminator at a packed-out Salford Community Stadium. The Red Devils smashed their stadium attendance record with a crowd of 10,867 crammed inside.

It was a huge turnaround after Leigh lost six of their first seven games of the season and in early July sat ninth in the table before a run of eleven wins from 13. Injuries to key players had plagued their early season and one of those stars, Papua New Guinea hooker Edwin Ipape, produced back-to-back man-of-the-match performances against St Helens to secure the Leopards' play-off place and then at Salford to reach the semi-finals.

They had to be patient and composed as much of the first half was spent on the back foot and they trailed 2-0 to a Marc Sneyd penalty at the break. But their defensive resolve was rewarded as they turned the contest around from the start of the second half, culminating in

September

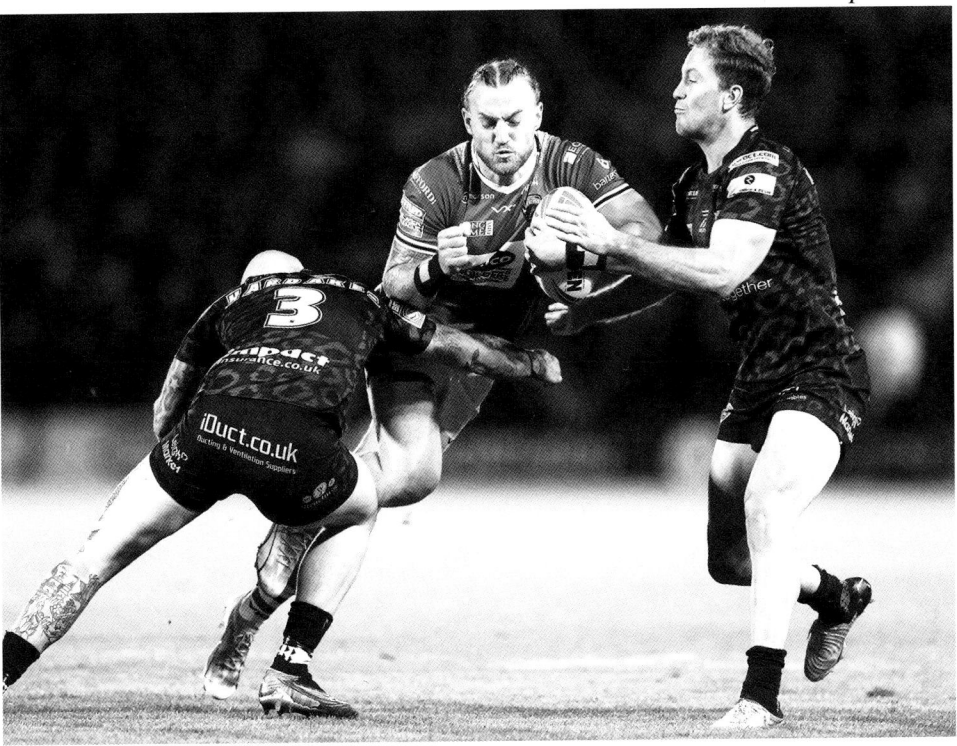

Leigh's Zak Hardaker and Matt Moylan block the path of Salford's Chris Hankinson

three tries in a 13-minute period for Josh Charnley, Gareth O'Brien and the outstanding Ipape.

Only when reduced to twelve men in the final three minutes, by Jack Hughes' yellow card for obstruction, were the Leopards broken down as Ethan Ryan scored - but Sneyd's missed conversion attempt left Salford too far behind and the party could truly begin among more than 4,000 away fans.

The crucial period from the start of the second half saw Leigh build slowly - winning three penalties, forcing two drop-outs and getting another repeat set for a Nene Macdonald knock-down - before one fast play yielded the game's first try in the 53rd minute.

Matt Moylan sprayed a great pass wide close to the line, picking out Ricky Leutele with a two-on-one advantage down the left. Charnley was duly played in and Leigh nudged in front.

The most crucial try was the second. Moments before it, Salford dummy-half Joe Mellor almost broke through, only for Lachlan Lam to grab hold. Then Oliver Partington fatally slipped, Ipape burst through the space left behind and picked out an outrageous pass for the supporting O'Brien to score on his 200th Super League appearance. Ipape then scored Leigh's final try himself, fooling Tim Lafai with a dummy and holding off Chris Hankinson for 2-14 (Moylan could only convert the second try).

After the win, Leigh didn't know if they would have to travel to Wigan or Hull KR the following week but they would have to do without Charnley, who was taken to hospital, later released, with a neck injury. Backrower Frankie Halton failed a head-injury assessment and would have to stand down for eleven days.

As it turned out the Leopards would have to travel to top side Wigan as lowest ranked remaining team, after Warrington won an epic home battle against St Helens on the Saturday. Wolves captain George Williams nailed a one-pointer in golden-point extra time as the Wolves edged the tie 23-22.

It was rated the game of the season. Saints were underdogs after limping into sixth place - their lowest league position of the Super League era - but led 16-4 with an impressive first-half display.

September

George Williams kicks Warrington to play-off victory against St Helens

Then, after the Wolves fought back to lead by six points, Jon Bennison scored a late try and Mark Percival converted from the touchline as the hooter sounded to take the match to golden-point.

The match-winner should really have been no surprise. In a chaotic game, Williams had already provided the classiest moments, with two exceptional assists for Matty Ashton and Toby King tries.

His first assist got Warrington back in the game after a King opener had been responded to by three St Helens tries in a dominant half-hour period.

Williams took the ball into the line and, as he began to fall in the tackle, produced a superb offload to Ashton, who had enough of a gap on the inside to dart over, with Josh Thewlis's conversion cutting their deficit to 10-16 at half-time.

Then, early in the second half, Williams produced the second of two fine cut-out passes - the first was a crisp delivery from dummy-half by Sam Powell - to put King through on his good running line.

Thewlis's boot levelled and the turnaround was complete with 14 minutes remaining. Daryl Clark badly misplaced a pass out of dummy-half as Saints came out their own end and Ashton was free to run in, scoring a second try of the evening.

The Clark error was one of several Saints gifts. Another came right at the start of the tie when Tommy Makinson dropped the kick-off, providing the position for Matt Dufty to put King over.

Makinson himself recovered to score not once but twice. The first was an outstanding finish in the corner, given the benefit of the doubt with replays unable to determine if King had put the diving winger into touch.

The second saw him crash over from a short-side play and, in between, Makinson contributed to their other try of a brilliant spell by forcing a Dufty knock-on in the air, from which the spine of Lewis Dodd, Jonny Lomax and Jack Welsby combined slickly to put Percival over.

Percival converted two of those three tries to put St Helens 16-4 ahead just past the half-hour mark, beyond the hopes of most fans pre-match considering the run of nine defeats in 13 which saw them stumble into the play-offs.

But Williams led the Wolves magnificently and it was fitting he decided the most exciting of elimination games.

OCTOBER
All-four Warriors

Semi-finals

The top two in the Super League table, Wigan and Hull KR, won through to the Grand Final in contrasting styles.

Hull KR were the first team through after edging their home semi with Warrington by 10-8. It wasn't the perfect Rovers performance at a sold-out and bouncing Craven Park. But the core traits of grit, hard work and defensive resilience were in evidence as they built a 10-0 lead in a dominant first half and then just about held on for victory under severe pressure from Warrington in the second half.

It was truly excruciating for Rovers supporters, as the advantage earned by a try from James Batchelor - standing in admirably as captain for the suspended Elliot Minchella - and a very contentious effort by Joe Burgess was so nearly wiped out and, with it, their dreams dashed.

But in the first half they were excellent, winning the all-important forward battle for long periods thanks to the efforts of Sauaso Sue, Jai Whitbread and Dean Hadley to put them on the front foot.

Matt Parcell was held up after crossing early on from dummy-half but Rovers kept the pressure up and made the breakthrough after 17 minutes.

Rodrick Tai obstructed Tyrone May as he chased a Lewis kick, providing a repeat set in the red zone. There May picked out Batchelor, who was touched but not tackled by Josh Drinkwater and Toby King as he stretched out to open the scoring, the try unconverted by Mikey Lewis.

Matt Dufty went over on a rare Warrington attack, only for play to be pulled back for an obstruction by Matty Nicholson which had helped open up a gap.

Hull KR's second try came five minutes before half-time, but not without great controversy.

Centre Peta Hiku was held out five metres from the Wire try-line after a break involving Batchelor and Niall Evalds, and Burgess subsequently darted over from dummy-half.

The on-field decision from referee Liam Moore was 'try' and none of the replays could conclusively prove the ball hadn't been grounded, even if it looked at best unlikely to have been. Jack Smith, on video duty had no option but to confirm the original call and Lewis converted the try for a ten-point half-time lead.

There was less controversy about an otherwise very similar try, five minutes into the second half, which got Warrington back into the game.

It started with Matty Ashton, who so nearly broke free after punching through the middle, and finished with him too via King going close off a Dufty cut-out ball.

Ashton took possession from dummy-half and cleanly dotted down to remove any doubt as the Wolves made the perfect second-half start - or almost perfect, as Josh Thewlis put the kick disappointingly wide of the near post in an ultimately costly miss.

The momentum was with the Wolves, who enjoyed a strong period of pressure before Ashton scored again just before the hour mark.

This was a more trademark finish from the prolific winger on his 100th appearance for the club, diving into the corner on the end of a nice right-to-left shift and assist from Dufty. But again Thewlis couldn't find the target, this time right from the touchline, to keep Hull KR ahead by two points.

October

Hull KR's James Batchelor and Kelepi Tanginoa wrap up Warrington's Toby King

With two points in it, almost all the rest of the game was a Warrington bombardment. But Hull KR's scramble and commitment to defend their line somehow saw them survive.

Warrington's final chance came with just over a minute to go, attacking left through Dufty only for the fullback to lose the ball as Hiku and Burgess tackled him. Toby King subsequently touched down but the try was only ever going to be ruled out by the video referee.

The evening after was a much different affair as a crowd of over 20,000 - the biggest Super League play-off attendance in two decades - witnessed a demonstration of Wigan's sheer class as they hammered Leigh 38-0.

It was barely a contest. Leigh didn't lack for courage and determination but, whether it was the magnitude of the occasion in their first semi-final, the toll of a run of big must-win games or simply the brilliance of Wigan, they looked nothing like the side which won eleven games from 13 to reach this stage, with mistakes aplenty.

Wigan were ruthless in every area of the game. They suffocated the opposition, forced errors and then were utterly clinical with the ball. The stand-out was big second-rower Junior Nsemba, who menaced the Leopards throughout the eighty minutes.

The highlight of the game was the best of the Warriors' six tries on the hour mark from Bevan French who, with the result in no doubt, brought out his box of tricks.

The superstar halfback received the ball from Adam Keighran with his back to the try-line and the defence right on his tail. Yet he jinked this way this and that, elusive as ever, before dabbing a kick past Oliver Holmes.

Nobody could turn and chase, leaving French free to recollect before Zak Hardaker came across, French stepping past the winger before finishing things off with a big dive worthy of the try.

Super League top try-scorer Liam Marshall and second-rower Sam Walters - in for captain Liam Farrell who was struggling to shake off a virus - scored two tries apiece and Jai Field added another brilliant showpiece effort when he outpaced everyone down the left wing.

Walters' second try off a French pass came two minutes after the half-time break and 24-0 down, the Leopards were already beaten.

October

Wigan's Luke Thompson meets Leigh duo John Asiata and Robbie Mulhern head on

Grand Final

Wigan retained the Super League crown and became the first side in the Super League era to win all four trophies in a single season with a 9-2 victory over Hull Kingston Rovers at a cold and damp Old Trafford.

Their victory was built on a determined and superbly organised defence, as it was the year before when they also kept Catalans pointless. They were unyielding down the middle, the likes of Luke Thompson, Kaide Ellis, Ethan Havard and Liam Farrell meeting the challenge of a direct Hull KR head on.

And Harry Smith's pin-point kicking game meant their try-line rarely came under pressure. When it did their defence was simply impregnable.

Bevan French produced the game's only try, a magnificent solo effort as he dummied to beat Mikey Lewis and Matt Parcell, shot through at lightning speed and stepped past fullback Niall Evalds to dive over to the right of the posts.

It was rated the best Grand Final try since Rob Burrow in 2011, making it only more appropriate that French claimed the first Rob Burrow Award (formerly the Harry Sunderland Trophy). French had been the 7/2 favourite to become the first winner of the award and it was deeply moving to see Rob's father Geoff present the trophy to him.

Apart from creating the highlight of the game with that stunning first-half try, French made 31 tackles, ran for 172 metres,

BETFRED SUPER LEAGUE GRAND FINAL

Saturday 12th October 2024

HULL KR 2 WIGAN WARRIORS 9

HULL KR: 2 Niall Evalds; 35 Joe Burgess; 1 Peta Hiku; 36 Jack Broadbent; 5 Ryan Hall; 27 Tyrone May; 7 Mikey Lewis; 8 Sauaso Sue; 14 Matt Parcell; 16 Jai Whitbread; 11 Dean Hadley; 12 James Batchelor; 13 Elliot Minchella (C). Subs (all used): 9 Jez Litten; 15 Sam Luckley; 17 Matty Storton; 20 Kelepi Tanginoa.
Goals: Lewis 1/1.
WARRIORS: 1 Jai Field; 2 Abbas Miski; 3 Adam Keighran; 4 Jake Wardle; 5 Liam Marshall; 6 Bevan French; 7 Harry Smith; 8 Ethan Havard; 17 Kruise Leeming; 16 Luke Thompson; 21 Junior Nsemba; 12 Liam Farrell (C); 13 Kaide Ellis. Subs (all used): 10 Liam Byrne; 15 Patrick Mago; 19 Tyler Dupree; 27 Tom Forber.
Try: French (22); **Goals:** Keighran 2/2; **Field goal:** Smith (40).
Rugby Leaguer & League Express Men of the Match:
Hull KR: Elliot Minchella; *Warriors:* Bevan French.
Penalty count: 4-3; **Half-time:** 0-7; **Referee:** Chris Kendall;
Attendance: 68,173 *(at Old Trafford, Manchester).*

October

Wigan's Bevan French breaks past Hull KR's Kelepi Tanginoa and Elliot Minchella at Old Trafford

including 138 metres across the gain line and 27 metres post-contact. He won 26 of the 32 votes from members of the media, with the other six being split equally between Harry Smith and Luke Thompson.

Hull KR could not be accused of under-performing in the bright lights of their first Grand Final, their hard running pushing Wigan a little further back each time in the early stages, only for Smith to come up with some effective kicks.

Robins halfback Mikey Lewis had developed his kicking game significantly in 2024 but, in the week he was named Man of Steel, he could not rival Smith in those stakes - although he did cross the try-line after eleven minutes.

Following a bright dummy-half run and quick play by Matt Parcell, Lewis kicked to the left corner and Tyrone May rose highest. The ball went down and, via Dean Hadley, into the hands of Lewis to score, but replays confirmed that it had come forward off May.

After Wigan's Junior Nsemba went off - his head hitting the ground hard after a scything tackle by James Batchelor, though he passed the head-injury assessment - Lewis forced a repeat set but Hull KR showed no adventure from it.

In contrast, when Wigan got possession back, they handed it to French and he did the rest in devastating, exhilarating fashion.

October

The try, converted by Adam Keighran, opened up the game and both sides had further chances before half-time.

Liam Marshall ran onto his own kick after a Smith bomb wasn't caught, only for Luke Thompson to be found offside as he also chased it down.

Then came Wigan's best defensive set of the match, after conceding a penalty in possession for crossing. French and Field held Lewis up over the line, Kelepi Tanginoa was prevented from crashing over and then Parcell was tackled on the last play after offloads at the line kept the Warriors on their toes.

Instead the only scoring of the half came from the boot of Smith in its final second, sending a field goal between the posts and into the satisfied sea of Wigan fans behind.

A frantic start to the second half saw Evalds unable to convert a half-chance after a Lewis kick was recycled and Marshall so nearly break away for Wigan. Back came Hull KR and Ryan Hall was blocked from powering into the corner by Abbas Miski, Keighran and French.

With subs adding fresh energy, sets were now going end-to-end. Two Sauaso Sue errors were painful but Rovers held out as hailstones began to fall on Old Trafford.

Hull KR finally got on the scoreboard in the 56th minute through a Lewis penalty, opting to narrow the deficit to one score when Thompson hit Elliot Minchella late.

But from there it all went wrong for the underdogs. They let French make another break off a trademark tricky movement, forcing a drop-out. And then Lewis tipped Farrell over in the tackle and Keighran restored Wigan's seven-point advantage from the tee.

They should have put the contest to bed soon after but Jake Wardle lost the ball as he slid for the line, in a tackle from Hall, after a thrilling run by Jai Field around the defence.

Hull KR were now desperate and piling up what until now had been a modest error count - Wigan were always going to see this out.

Hall, beaten in his seventh Grand Final after six wins with Leeds, came closest but was twice closed down as the champions had an answer for everything.

A season which started with their World Club Challenge glory over Penrith continued with a Challenge Cup triumph against Warrington and moved on to retention of the League Leaders' Shield finished with another trophy for the all-conquering Warriors. Only Wigan's side of 1994 had previously won those four titles in one campaign.

SUPER LEAGUE AWARDS

STEVE PRESCOTT MAN OF STEEL
Mikey Lewis (Hull KR)

YOUNG PLAYER OF THE YEAR
Junior Nsemba (Wigan Warriors)

COACH OF THE YEAR
Willie Peters (Hull KR)

SUPER LEAGUE DREAM TEAM

#	Player	Club	Previous selections
1	Matt Dufty	Warrington Wolves	Debut
2	Matty Ashton	Warrington Wolves	Debut
3	Nene Macdonald	Salford Red Devils	Debut
4	Jake Wardle	Wigan Warriors	2023
5	Liam Marshall	Wigan Warriors	Debut
6	Mikey Lewis	Hull KR	Debut
7	Marc Sneyd	Salford Red Devils	Debut
8	Matty Lees	St Helens	Debut
9	Danny Walker	Warrington Wolves	Debut
10	Luke Thompson	Wigan Warriors	2019
11	Rhyse Martin	Leeds Rhinos	Debut
12	Junior Nsemba	Wigan Warriors	Debut
13	Elliot Minchella	Hull KR	Debut

2 CHAMPIONSHIP & LEAGUE ONE 2024

CHAMPIONSHIP SEASON
Trinity bounce back

What a season for **WAKEFIELD TRINITY**, now under the ownership of ambitious businessman Matt Ellis and with experienced Daryl Powell the coach.

Back in the second tier for the first time since 1998 following a dismal 2023 campaign which ended with relegation from Super League with only four wins, the famous old Yorkshire side romped to 1895 Cup success at Wembley (their first visit since 1979), the Championship Leaders' Shield and Grand Final glory.

The title was won with a highly-convincing showpiece victory over Toulouse, the only team to topple Trinity over the course of 26 league matches (Featherstone managed it in the Challenge Cup).

Long-serving Max Jowitt entered the record books by chalking up 500 points, beating the previous all-time best for a season of 496 by Leeds' Lewis Jones in 1956-57.

Alongside Jowitt, Wakefield had other prolific try-scorers in Derrell Olpherts and Lachlan Walmsley, while success on the field provided the perfect backdrop for forward Matty Ashurst's testimonial and ensured a fitting send-off for retiring duo Luke Gale and Jermaine McGillvary.

It was another season of so near, yet so far for **TOULOUSE OLYMPIQUE**, who after relegation from Super League in 2022, made the play-off final for the second season running - and lost again.

In 2023, it was late-charging London Broncos who put the brakes on the French club's hopes of a top-flight return before the introduction of club grading. And in 2024, Wakefield, having led the way throughout the season, completed the job with their showpiece success at the Yorkshire ground Toulouse's long-serving coach Sylvain Houlès once called home.

Toulouse were the only club to topple Trinity over the regular league season - a convincing 32-4 triumph at their Stade Ernest Wallon in July - but they weren't consistent enough to threaten Wakefield's league leadership.

They had a slow start, with only two wins in their first six outings, and fell to defeat three times running in August.

Australian halfback Ryan Rivett proved a good addition, while Cook Islands international winger Paul Ulberg was again among the tries, with 20 in the league.

There must have been a familiar feel to the season for followers of **BRADFORD BULLS**, for as in 2023, their side finished third and made the play-off semi-finals, where they lost to Toulouse in France, before the coach stepped down.

Twelve months earlier, a change was known about in advance, because with Lee Greenwood in interim charge after Mark Dunning's departure, the Bulls had already announced that Eamon O'Carroll would take the helm for 2024 on a three-year contract, which was later extended through to 2027.

So it was a surprise when former Newcastle coach and Catalans assistant O'Carroll, to whom Greenwood was right-hand man, resigned after the 21-20 play-off loss in Toulouse.

The fact Bradford pushed the home side so close reflected an encouraging campaign during which a host of players were used, including versatile back Tom Holmes, who made a heartening return to action after serious illness. Bradford won 16 and drew two in the league and also reached the semi-finals of the 1895 Cup.

Championship Season

Wakefield's Max Jowitt, Renouf Atoni and Lachlan Walmsley celebrate a try at Featherstone in Round 2

When it comes to instant impacts, that of Mark Applegarth at **YORK KNIGHTS** takes a bit of beating.

Having had a torrid time coaching Wakefield in 2023, when Trinity were relegated from Super League, he rocked up in the north of Yorkshire in June.

Andrew Henderson had taken York to the play-offs in 2023 and his side made it to the 1895 Cup semi-finals in 2024, but in the league, he was struggling for wins.

There had been just three in 10 league matches when Henderson became head of operations and development and rested and refreshed Applegarth, a former York player, took the team reins.

York won 12 of the remaining 16 regular-season games and, having been far too close to the relegation places for comfort, finished fourth to make the play-offs by two points.

They reached the semi-finals, after Applegarth had been nominated for the Championship Coach of the Year award, experienced forward Jordan Thompson for Player of the Year and former Hull KR Academy winger Brad Ward for Young Player of the Year.

As Allan Coleman reviewed his first season as coach of **WIDNES VIKINGS**, he asserted that the fallen giants had 'turned a corner' as they continued to get back on track after falling out of Super League amid severe financial strife in 2018.

The former Swinton boss wasn't universally welcomed on his appointment, but his obvious passion for the job and club, and flying start in the league (six wins in the first seven games) won plenty of supporters over.

Championship Season

Widnes coach Allan Coleman leads the celebrations following victory at York in Round 10

Things weren't seamless, with a run of four straight losses midway through and only one win in the final four regular-season outings as injuries bit.

But with a fifth-placed finish, Coleman became the first coach to take the club to the play-offs since they returned to the Championship.

And although a trip to in-form York for their elimination tie proved a step too far, there seemed to be more optimism in the grand old Rugby League town than has been the case for a while.

Chasing the Super League dream - unsuccessfully - fairly caught up with **FEATHERSTONE ROVERS**, as coach James Ford worked to the much-reduced budget set by long-serving chairman Mark Campbell, who stepped down part way through the year.

By that stage, financial issues had surfaced and while Ford tried to shield his squad from the air of uncertainty around the club, there was a sequence of five straight defeats.

At least Rovers had started the campaign relatively strongly, making the sixth round of the Challenge Cup with the help of a win over neighbours Wakefield well received by the faithful.

And as those behind the scenes worked to create more stability, the team picked up enough victories (there were 14 overall) to squeeze into the play-offs, only to fall disappointingly short at the first hurdle at Bradford.

Winger Connor Wynne enjoyed a fine first season after leaving Hull (19 league tries), while halfback Ben Reynolds, signed from Leigh in October, left for Hull KR in February only to make a Rovers return in July.

Meanwhile popular prop James Lockwood came out of retirement to reinforce the push for the play-offs.

Championship Season

SHEFFIELD EAGLES started the season in fine fettle, with the only defeat in their first 13 matches in all competitions away to Wigan in round six of the Challenge Cup. They went on to become only the second club, after Featherstone, to reach the final of the 1895 Cup twice.

And while the inaugural winners of the competition in 2019 were well beaten by Wakefield at Wembley, they managed 11 wins in their first 14 league games.

At that stage, a second successive play-off appearance by a side boasting plenty of experience looked more than likely.

But from then on there were nine defeats in 12 matches, with the loyal fanbase rocked in July by the revelation with nine games to go that Eagles stalwart and long-serving team chief Mark Aston and physiotherapist Mick Heys had been stood down by the club on a 'no-fault basis' as the RFL announced an investigation into a medical compliance matter.

Assistant coaches Keith Senior and Simon Brown took interim control, with Sheffield missing out on the top six to Featherstone on points difference after a disappointing last-day defeat at relegated Dewsbury.

In October, Aston received an 18-month suspension from coaching from the RFL after being found guilty of breaching the RFL's welfare policy and medical standards, fielding a player against Wigan despite him failing a head injury assessment the round before.

After losing the League One play-off finals of 2021 and 2022, **DONCASTER** finally reclaimed Championship status for the first time since 2015 by beating North Wales Crusaders in the 2023 decider.

It was reward for keeping faith with coach Richard Horne, appointed in mid-2017, and working with chief executive Carl Hall, he set about moulding a squad capable of keeping the Dons in the division.

In came the likes of backs Josh Guzdek (from Sheffield), Luke Briscoe and Craig Hall (both Featherstone) and Reece Lyne (Wakefield) and forwards Suaia Matagi and Alex Sutcliffe (both Castleford), Joe Lovodua (Hull) and Pauli Pauli (York) to join such as skipper and second-rower Sam Smeaton and halfbacks Ben Johnston and Connor Robinson.

The Dons held their own in the section, setting off with a home victory over York and slowly but surely warming to the task and picking up 12 wins and a draw to claim eighth place and lay some foundations.

Highlight for the fans was probably the away success over Featherstone, with Widnes also seen off at the Eco-Power Stadium.

HALIFAX PANTHERS were in a rebuilding phase on and off the pitch after a sluggish season results-wise and the revelation of major financial problems.

The club started September warning that with a tax bill outstanding, they were at 'immediate risk' of folding and admitting they had been unable to fully pay players and staff amid declining sponsorship and decreasing ticket sales.

Halifax survived that scare, albeit while emphasising that there were still significant issues to be addressed, among them the future operation of The Shay, with the local council keen to offload the running of the stadium.

And the Panthers also staved off the threat of relegation with a late run of three wins in four, including a defeat of old rivals Bradford, to take the year's league victory haul to 11.

But they went into the close-season having to replace some key players, such as Joe Keyes and Matty Gee, as well as coach Liam Finn, who moved as assistant to Luke Robinson at Huddersfield. In October, former Saints player Kyle Eastmond was announced as his replacement.

It was a frustrating first season in full control of **BATLEY BULLDOGS** for Mark Moxon. He stepped up after long service as assistant coach to take on the tough task of succeeding Craig Lingard at a club who have become renowned for punching above their weight, making the second-tier Grand Final in 2022.

Championship Season

Ramon Silva held up during Barrow's home win against Sheffield in Round 16

Working to a tight budget and having lost regulars Josh Hodson, James Meadows and Martyn Reilly, both Moxon and prudent chairman Kevin Nicholas were disappointed when before the season started, ex-Whitehaven fullback Josh Rourke activated a Super League release clause in the Batley contract he had recently signed to join London Broncos.

With Lingard coaching at Castleford, a helpful dual-registration deal was struck, enabling popular former fullback Luke Hooley to make appearances.

And versatile former Leeds Academy back Joe Burton proved a useful acquisition from Hunslet as he ran in 18 league tries.

Batley recorded some stirring victories, including a double against Sheffield, but struggled to string together winning sequences and ended up 10th.

After surging to the play-offs back in 2022, **BARROW RAIDERS** finished just a point above the relegation zone the following year, and once again came too close to danger for comfort.

Experienced coach Paul Crarey's charges were in the bottom two at the end of July, but even with injuries causing selection issues, looked to have enough quality to survive.

And thanks to three wins, helpfully against other sides in the lower reaches of the table, plus a draw at Bradford, in their last nine outings, survive they did, finishing 11th and so avoiding the promotion/relegation decider against the League One play-off winners.

Ryan Shaw's effectiveness from the tee and the influence from fullback of Luke Cresswell, proved important to a team who finished with 19 points, taking the scalps of both Featherstone and Sheffield.

Those two victories came at the Northern Competitions Stadium (aka Craven Park) where, as at Featherstone and York, Women's Super League rugby was also played as chairman and former player Steve Neale works to widen the Raiders' reach and appeal.

A season which set off promisingly ended with late drama and the drop for **SWINTON LIONS**.

Coach Alan Kilshaw resigned in the aftermath of defeat at home to League One play-off winners Hunslet, his former club, in a promotion/relegation showdown on a tense Sunday evening in Sale.

The decider was the penultimate match of the 2024 domestic fixtures and part of the process of restructuring to three divisions of 12 by 2026.

Swinton found themselves involved in it after finishing 12th and as they led 20-18, a late Hunslet try ended a two-year second-tier stay.

Kilshaw had come in to replace Widnes-bound Allan Coleman and Swinton won their first four games (two in the 1895 Cup and two in the Challenge Cup).

Championship Season

They were fifth in the table after three victories in their opening six league matches. But 14 defeats in the remaining 20 left them with more work to do.

Centre Jayden Hatton won plenty of plaudits, but the mid-season loss of experienced halfback Dec Patton to Featherstone was a blow.

WHITEHAVEN suffered another year of financial turmoil, and this time were unable to escape the drop.

Amid tax demands, late payments to players, boardroom upheaval and a heap of injuries, Jonty Gorley resigned as coach in mid-August, with the side having slipped into the dreaded bottom two.

They climbed back out after former Super League forward Kyle Amor was persuaded to come to the aid of his hometown and former club by taking charge for the final six fixtures, and won the first of them, relegating Dewsbury in the process.

But it was always going to be an uphill task for the rookie team chief and as selection options dwindled, there were four further defeats, meaning the Cumbrians' fate was confirmed by the time Halifax were beaten in the final round, providing a points tally of 18 from eight wins and two draws. Australian trio Lachlan Hanneghan, Ryan King and Owen McCarron impressed,.

As the dust settled and ex-Workington boss Anthony Murray was installed as coach, Whitehaven revealed a recovery plan based around increased use of locally-sourced players.

There was deja vu for the dedicated followers of promoted **DEWSBURY RAMS**.

The last time they had watched Championship rugby, in 2022, it was a tale of two coaches - Lee Greenwood, then Liam Finn - and not nearly enough wins.

Fast forward to 2024 and the same thing happened, with Paul March succeeding Dale Ferguson, and just two victories, over neighbours Batley and Sheffield, the latter coming five matches after the basement team had fallen through the trapdoor.

Dewsbury started on the back foot, because having replaced Finn, who switched to Halifax after guiding the Rams to the 2023 League One title, former forward Ferguson was struck down by a debilitating illness, missing the first few months of pre-season.

He relinquished the reins six league games in, to focus on playing, with March, who had come in as his assistant, moving up.

The former York, Hunslet and Keighley player-coach was unable to alter the course of the campaign (he was hardly helped by the transfer of prop Jimmy Beckett to Featherstone), but at least promoted a number of players from the amateur ranks as he started preparing for 2025.

CHAMPIONSHIP AWARDS

YOUNG PLAYER OF THE YEAR
Oliver Pratt (Wakefield Trinity)

COACH OF THE YEAR
Daryl Powell (Wakefield Trinity)

PLAYER OF THE YEAR
Max Jowitt (Wakefield Trinity)

Championship Season

Championship Play-offs

There was no feeling of inevitability heading into the top-six play-offs despite the seeming invincibility of Wakefield Trinity.

The first week of eliminators involved four teams who had all recruited handily and were hitting form at the right time.

Third-placed Bradford - on the back of five wins in their last six games - made their home advantage count over lowest-ranked Featherstone as they progressed to the semi-finals with a 25-12 win at Odsal.

Halfback Jordan Lilley claimed 13 points as Featherstone's erratic season petered out long before the final hooter. The Bulls led 7-0 at half-time through a second-minute try from Jayden Myers and two scores from the boot of Lilley, one a field goal five minutes before the break.

A Tom Holmes grubber bounced perfectly for Kieran Gill to stroll in and give Bradford breathing space, with Lilley's conversion making it 13-0 on 50 minutes. Seven minutes later, Myers, Kevin Appo and Gill combined incisively from halfway to send Lilley sliding over (he added the two to take his side further in front) before Mitch Souter put a charging Appo over from close range, with Lilley kicking successfully for 25-0. Josh Hardcastle and Brad Day chased home late consolations, both from kicks and both converted by Ben Reynolds.

Tom Lineham's try hat-trick helped fire York to the semi-finals with a third straight win and eighth in nine matches, the Knights completing a 27-10 win over Widnes at the LNER Stadium.

The tie was still in the balance at the break at 10-10 but three unanswered touchdowns, two of them converted, and a Liam Harris field goal, did the trick for Mark Applegarth's men.

Bradford had to travel to second-placed Toulouse the following week and they made Olympique sweat right to the very end in heatwave conditions, eventually eliminated after a 21-20 defeat.

The Bulls were 12-8 ahead at half-time through Lilley and Franklin Pele tries and two Lilley conversions after Benjamin Laguerre and Paul Ulberg scores gave TO a 8-0 lead. Gill was sin-binned for a high tackle after the half hour and when Myers was shown yellow just before the hour mark it proved very costly as Guy Armitage and Anthony Marion tries put TO eight in front. Lilley kicked a penalty goal to reduce the deficit to six points before Eloi Pelissier potted a field goal with five minutes to go. Appo's try made it a one-point game but the Bulls ran out of time.

In the other semi-final, York gave runaway League Leaders Wakefield their hardest home game of the season before going down fighting by 22-13. With halfback Ata Hingano and prop Jordan Thompson outstanding, the Knights led twice before Trinity edged the closing stages, centre Ian Thornley's try five minutes from time the clincher.

Championship Grand Final

It was pretty much the perfect night for Wakefield. Not only did a dominant 36-0 win over Toulouse deliver the Championship title and complete a treble of trophies, but star fullback Max Jowitt set a new Rugby League record for points in a season by hitting the 500 mark.

It capped a remarkable twelve months since Wakefield were relegated from Super League, with gloom and a losing habit replaced by excitement, passion and a line of great wins since owner Matt Ellis and coach Daryl Powell arrived to transform the club. The capacity crowd of over 8,000 got exactly what they came to see.

Wakefield scored four first-half tries, the first on 16 minutes after Anthony Marion dropped a pass inside his own '20' and a switch play involving Jay Pitts, Luke Gale and Jowitt allowed Derrell Olpherts to score on the left wing.

Then a delayed Luke Gale pass put Matty Ashurst through the space created, and the departing captain exchanged passes with Jowitt to score himself. Another player on his way out, the retiring Jermaine McGillvary, scored Wakefield's third try after the ball went through the hands of Gale, Mason Lino and finally Isaiah Vagana, who offloaded for the ex-England winger.

Championship Season

Wakefield's Derrell Olpherts leaps past Toulouse's Paul Marcon on the way to scoring in the Grand Final

Jowitt converted the first three tries. The first goal put him level with Lewis Jones' 1956-57 record of 496, the second saw him surpass it, and the third struck the 500-point landmark.

He hit the post with the fourth but by then not only was history made, but Trinity had the Grand Final virtually won.

Hooker Thomas Doyle - Liam Hood was taken off with a head knock after ten minutes - sparked that try down the middle with a run from Caleb Uele's ofload, backed up by Ashurst and Jay Pitts before Jowitt was tackled on the next play. With the Toulouse defence at sea, Pitts moved play right, via Gale and Lino, for an Iain Thornley try and a 22-0 half-time lead.

Jowitt's game was ended with a head knock 12 minutes from time after Oliver Pratt had extended the lead. Olpherts grabbed his second - literally, claiming a perfect kick by Gale, who couldn't land the conversion.

And four minutes from time McGillvary also added his second try on the other flank. Lino's ball over the top provided the space, then McGillvary stunned the crowd with a remarkable kick - the second goal of his career, after one for Batley in 2009 - which completed the scoring.

BETFRED CHAMPIONSHIP GRAND FINAL

Saturday 19th October 2024

WAKEFIELD TRINITY 36 TOULOUSE OLYMPIQUE 0

TRINITY: 1 Max Jowitt; 2 Jermaine McGillvary; 4 Iain Thornley; 3 Oliver Pratt; 32 Derrell Olpherts; 6 Luke Gale; 7 Mason Lino; 8 Josh Bowden; 9 Liam Hood; 10 Renouf Atoni; 11 Matty Ashurst; 19 Isaiah Vagana; 13 Jay Pitts. Subs (all used): 5 Lachlan Walmsley; 15 Caleb Uele; 18 Ky Rodwell; 21 Thomas Doyle.
Tries: Olpherts (16, 69), Ashurst (26), McGillvary (33, 76), Thornley (38), Pratt (58);
Goals: Jowitt 3/5, Gale 0/1, McGillvary 1/1.
OLYMPIQUE: 1 Olly Ashall-Bott; 2 Paul Ulberg; 18 Guy Armitage; 5 Paul Marcon; 19 Benjamin Laguerre; 6 Ryan Rivett; 7 Jake Shorrocks; 8 Lambert Belmas; 9 Calum Gahan; 10 Harrison Hansen; 11 Maxime Stefani; 12 Dominique Peyroux; 13 Anthony Marion. Subs (all used): 3 Reubenn Rennie; 14 Eloi Pelissier; 17 James Roumanos; 22 Dimitri Biscarro.
Rugby Leaguer & League Express Men of the Match:
Trinity: Max Jowitt; *Olympique:* Paul Ulberg.
Penalty count: 6-3; **Half-time:** 22-0;
Referee: Aaron Moore; **Attendance:** 8,016.

Championship Season

1895 Cup Final

Wakefield, unbeaten in the Championship at this point, cruised to a 50-6, 1895 Cup Final win against Sheffield Eagles at Wembley.

The match was played following the Challenge Cup Final and an estimated 10,000 Wakefield supporters amassed at one end to witness their side putting on a masterclass that the part-time Eagles, then lying third in the Championship, could not live with.

The competition was split into regional groups for the qualifiers, with Wakefield beating York Knights, Newcastle Thunder (a record win of 110-0), Barrow and Bradford to get to Wembley. The Eagles had accounted for Doncaster, Midlands Hurricanes, Batley Bulldogs and York Knights.

It looked like Sheffield, winners of the inaugural 1895 Cup in 2019, might just continue their love affair with the iconic London ground, having gone ahead through a try from captain and halfback Anthony Thackeray, Cory Aston goaling with just over a quarter of an hour played.

What followed, though, was nine tries and 50-unanswered points for a Wakefield side superbly prepared by coach Daryl Powell. Mark Aston's side set about extending their advantage and looked like they had the numbers down their right edge. But Jack Hansen's pass, hoping to find Ben Jones-Bishop, was plucked out of the air by Lachlan Walmsley. The Australian, the first player to feature in back-to-back 1895 Cup finals after having enjoyed Wembley success with Halifax in 2023, raced the length of the field to level the scores.

Sheffield kicked the restart out on the full and Trinity took no time in punishing the error, with veteran Luke Gale, who later picked up the Ray French Award for player of the match, darting through a gap to slide over. Hooker Thomas Doyle dashed over on the stroke of half-time and the second half was a six-try rout with rookie centre Oliver Pratt and veterans Josh Griffin and Jermaine McGillvary each scoring try-braces, fullback Max Jowitt converting seven tries in total.

AB SUNDECKS 1895 CUP - FINAL

Saturday 8th June 2024

SHEFFIELD EAGLES 6 WAKEFIELD TRINITY 50

EAGLES: 14 Jack Hansen; 2 Ben Jones-Bishop; 3 Kris Welham; 4 James Glover; 5 Matty Dawson-Jones; 6 Cory Aston; 7 Anthony Thackeray; 8 Eddie Battye; 9 Vila Halafihi; 10 Tyler Dickinson; 11 Connor Bower; 12 Joel Farrell; 13 Titus Gwaze. Subs (all used): 22 Kyle Wood; 27 Jesse Sene-Lefao; 18 Aaron Murphy; 17 Mitch Clark. **Try:** Thackeray (16); **Goals:** Aston 1/1.
TRINITY: 1 Max Jowitt; 2 Jermaine McGillvary; 4 Iain Thornley; 3 Oliver Pratt; 5 Lachlan Walmsley; 6 Luke Gale; 7 Mason Lino; 8 Josh Bowden; 9 Liam Hood; 10 Renouf Atoni; 11 Matty Ashurst; 12 Josh Griffin; 13 Jay Pitts. Subs (all used): 14 Liam Kay; 15 Caleb Uele; 18 Ky Rodwell; 21 Thomas Doyle.
Tries: Walmsley (24), Gale (27), Doyle (40), Pratt (43, 53), Griffin (47, 65), McGillvary (62, 74); **Goals:** Jowitt 7/9.
Rugby Leaguer & League Express Men of the Match: *Eagles:* Anthony Thackeray; *Trinity:* Luke Gale.
Penalty count: 6-3; **Half-time:** 6-18; **Referee:** Tom Grant. *(at Wembley Stadium).*

Wakefield coach Daryl Powell shows off the 1895 Cup to Trinity's fans

LEAGUE ONE SEASON
Oldham on the up

As the season was heading towards kick-off, all eyes were on big-spending **OLDHAM** and their team full of former Super League and Championship stars.

Owners Bill Quinn and Mike Ford made no secret of their aim to make it back to the Championship for the first time since 2021 - and the Sean Long-coached side did not disappoint, winning the league at a canter.

They were back at Boundary Park full-time, another signal of their intent, and the local population responded, with over 2,500 in attendance to see them lift the League Leaders' Trophy following a 56-0 win over Workington in the final round of the campaign.

That was the seventh clean sheet kept by the Roughyeds' drum-tight defence in 20 league matches. Of the other 13 games, only Keighley, twice (once in defeat and once in victory) and North Wales Crusaders scored more than ten points against the eventual table-toppers.

In total, the Roughyeds shipped only 144 points - an average of 7.2 per outing - which represented the club's best defensive season since 1910-11.

Their only defeat came in May at the hands of Keighley, who temporarily jumped to the top of the table. But the Roughyeds got back into the winning groove and secured the title, and with it promotion, with a 20-12 revenge win at Cougar Park with two games of the season to spare.

Beating Halifax Panthers in the 1895 Cup at the start of the year filled supporters with confidence that they already had close to a Championship-level squad.

While some experience has been lost with the retirement of Joe Wardle, Adam Sidlow and Jamie Ellis, former Super League stars Adam Milner, Iain Thornley, Matty Ashurst and Gil Dudson lead the way in terms of new recruits.

Oldham celebrate winning the League One title

League One Season

Keighley's Josh Lynam, Mitch Revell and Lachlan Lanskey bring down Midlands Hurricanes' Sam Bowring in Round 18

HUNSLET will join Oldham in the Championship in 2025 after a superb late-season surge saw them earn promotion from a fourth-placed finish.

As the top-two battle was, as expected, between Oldham and Keighley, the bulk of the rest of the league was left fighting for the remaining four play-off spots, with very little between leading chasers, Hunslet and Rochdale, throughout the whole campaign.

But it was in the play-offs that the South Leeds club found a vein of form at just the right time. After finishing one place behind Rochdale, Hunslet travelled to the Hornets in the first round of the play-offs and went down to a 30-18 defeat. Their second chance wasn't one they were going to waste.

The bounced back at home with a narrow victory over Midlands Hurricanes, before travelling to Rochdale once again and extracting their revenge - picking up a 46-26 win to set up a final showdown with Keighley at Cougar Park.

In another battle for bragging rights between George Flanagan Senior and Junior, it was the younger one who was left celebrating as Hunslet emerged 20-6 winners.

In year's gone by, that would have been enough to secure promotion but with a reshuffle of the league structure in 2025, they had to face one final test to make it to the Championship for the first time since 2015.

That was a trip to face former coach Alan Kilshaw's Swinton Lions, who were determined to keep their own place in the game's second tier.

Throughout a tough 80 minutes, the game could have gone either way, but in the end a late try by Hunslet's Jack Render sealed a 22-20 victory and capped a remarkable end to head coach Dean Muir's first season in charge.

What started as a season full of hope and expectation, ultimately ended in disappointment for **KEIGHLEY COUGARS**, who failed to earn the promotion so many had predicted.

The return of star halfback and proven points scorer Jack Miller and the signing of former Bradford fullback Brandon Pickersgill showed intent as coach Matt Foster looked to build on achievements of the previous year. After arriving back at the club in July 2023, Foster led Keighley to 11 wins in 13 games. But it wasn't quite enough and they were relegated from the Championship on points difference.

League One Season

However, that form under the popular former player filled many with optimism that, despite the competition posed by Oldham, the Cougars would bounce straight back up. And they looked on course to do that with just one defeat in their opening 12 games - an 18-26 reverse to Hunslet. But then came a crucial 20-20 draw with Rochdale Hornets. While that result still kept the Cougars a point clear at the top of the table, Oldham still had a game in hand and the club made the shock call to sack Foster - insisting that performances had been dipping over recent weeks.

Director of Rugby and former fans favourite Jake Webster took charge on an interim basis for the final nine games of the season, winning five - the last a 26-22 semi-final victory over Rochdale to leave them just two games away from the Championship return they were aiming for. However Hunslet ended Keighley's season with their Play-off Final victory.

Webster will remain in charge as head coach in 2025 as they mount another promotion push towards the Championship.

ROCHDALE HORNETS' development under the ownership of Andy Mazey and coaching of Gary Thornton continues, with the club enjoying its most successful season yet since the takeover.

A third-place finish shows a marked improvement from seventh a year earlier and Hornets could have gone even further had injuries and suspensions not hit the squad ahead of the Preliminary Final defeat to an in-form Hunslet.

Going into the 2023 season, only nine players from the previous campaign remained and that increased to 12 going into this year. But already the vast majority of the squad have been retained ahead of 2025. Add to that the signings of former Super League forward Josh Johnson and the return of powerful centre Tommy Ashton and it is clear that the Hornets are already hoping for big things ahead of 2025.

Hornets may not have won any of the main silverware but there was still reason to celebrate as halfback Lewis Else beat Oldham duo Danny Craven and Phoenix Laulu-Togaga'e to be named the League One Player of the Year, after an impressive season that saw him score 15 tries in 23 appearances, and have a hand in many more.

Off the field the club is continuing to work with local amateur side Rochdale Mayfield to promote and strengthen the game in the local community.

MIDLANDS HURRICANES proved to be the surprise package of the year after making the play-offs for the first time since their inclusion in the League.

Since starting their semi-professional journey as Coventry Bears in 2015, before rebranding as the Hurricanes ahead of the 2022 season, the club had always prioritised a gradual approach to development as an expansion club.

The club's fifth-placed finish was masterminded by head coach Mark Dunning, who was enjoying his first full year with the club after taking over from Richard Squires the previous May. Dunning's role in the Hurricanes' success this year was rewarded with the Coach of the Year prize.

The Hurricanes had a mixed start to the season, picking up three wins in their opening seven games, before going down to a narrow defeat to Cornwall. They remained in the play-off spots on points difference alone.

But they then started to find their groove and six more wins, with two against eventual top-six challengers North Wales Crusaders and one against Workington Town, coupled with other results on the penultimate weekend, ultimately saw them clinch the historic spot with one game to spare.

The challenge of a debut play-off appearance didn't overawe Dunning's men as they beat Workington 24-22 in that first knock-out game, before going toe-to-toe at eventual promotion winners Hunslet in a narrow 18-14 defeat.

Off the field the club has seen growth recently. 2024 saw them play on the main Alexander Stadium pitch for the first time. And their women's team completed their first competitive season, while work alongside the region's community clubs has continued.

League One Season

WORKINGTON TOWN will undergo something of a turnaround ahead of 2025 with many changes afoot at Derwent Park.

Coach Anthony Murray confirmed before the end of the season that he was to leave for an opportunity elsewhere, which has turned out to be at neighbours Whitehaven after a rumoured moved to Keighley appeared to fall through.

Long-term favourite Carl Forber has hung up his playing boots and he will remain on the backroom staff working alongside new coach Jonty Gorley, who has arrived from Whitehaven. Jason Mossop has also announced his retirement.

With a few other players already following Murray to Haven, Gorley already has work to do to plug some gaps.

Lack of consistency was a big problem throughout the campaign for Murray as injuries hit hard, especially in the middle part of the season. But their largely local squad dug deep and, despite a 56-0 defeat to Oldham on the final day, Town claimed the final play-off spot - setting up a clash with Midlands Hurricanes in a straight knock-out fixture.

The tight clash was ultimately decide by a Jake Sweeting penalty kick eight minutes from time that secured the Hurricanes a 22-20 victory. Throughout that game, as they had all season, Town put in a gritty performance.

Away from the men's team, the ever-improving women's side tasted success, topping League Two and then beating Orrell St James in the final to secure promotion, adding to the League Plate Final victory earlier in the year.

In the three-way tie for the last two play-off spots, **NORTH WALES CRUSADERS** ultimately missed out and had to watch on as other teams' seasons extended past their own.

After the disruption of the previous year where they were effectively nomads, with the majority of home games played away from Stadiwm CSM in Colwyn Bay, it had been hoped that a more settled season would be reflected in on-field results. But the eight wins the Crusaders did manage were not enough to finish in the top six.

Injuries did play a part again but missing out on the play-offs for the first time since 2019 will disappoint the club, which in June was taken over by Elkaleh LLC, a Dubai-based financial company.

The season also signalled the end of head coach and prop Carl Forster's 14-year playing career, which had seen him turn out for St Helens, London and Salford in Super League, as well as Whitehaven, Rochdale and Barrow in the semi-professional ranks.

He has penned a new two-year deal to remain as coach and will be keen to put right some of the wrongs from this year and get the Crusaders back into the play-offs in 2025.

CORNWALL may not have won as many games on the field this year as they did last (three compared to five in 2023) but according to coach Mike Abbott this year's success could be judged on other aspects of the club.

The coach told League Express at the end of the season that more players than ever before had bought into life down in the deep south west, with many now finding their own houses, partners and jobs in the region, indicating their dedication to the cause.

Locals were still buying into the club and seemed to enjoy the rugby on offer, even though they did only witness one win at the Memorial Ground - a 30-6 victory over Newcastle - although they did run others, most notably North Wales Crusaders and Hunslet, close before going down to narrow defeats.

The only other victories enjoyed by Cornwall were on the road against Newcastle Thunder and, impressively, Midlands Hurricane at the Alexander Stadium.

Whether or not the club will be given that chance to further develop itself and the game in the Duchy remains unclear, amid rumours that owner Eric Perez could sell the club, and its RFL place, to Bedford Tigers - one of the three clubs that applied to become the League's 11th club in 2025.

League One Season

Workington's Billy Southward makes a break against North Wales in Round 19

Simply finishing the season and seeing out their 20 league fixtures could be seen as a big success for **NEWCASTLE THUNDER** in 2024.

The North East side once had ambitions to win Super League by 2030 but faced extinction as 2023 came to an end.

Following their relegation from the Championship that year, the club announced it had decided not to participate in League One in 2024.

But then Newcastle earned a reprieve when a change in ownership, led by former managing director and chairman Keith Christie, saw new investment and a new hope that they could compete in the new season after all.

The fixtures were announced in early December with Thunder included for both League One and the 1895 Cup. But they were not formally granted re-admittance until the end of the month, meaning they had just five weeks to build a squad from scratch and prepare for their opening game against York Knights.

It was perhaps no surprise then that that first game ended in a 114-10 thumping, before a similarly heavy 110-0 defeat to eventual winners Wakefield a couple of weeks later.

Coach Chris Thorman spent much of the season utilising loan and dual registration deals with multiple clubs across the leagues, which did add some experience to the side at times, but not enough to stem the flow of heavy defeats.

In May, Thunder moved from Kingston Park back to the Gateshead International Stadium. Performances started to improve although they remained winless.

However, the experience should benefit the young, local players that Thorman and the club are keen to build a team around.

With Dewsbury Rams, Swinton and Whitehaven all relegated from the Championship and **GOOLE VIKINGS** granted a place in League One, there will be some new, and old, faces in the 11-team League One in 2025.

Goole will be the brand new kid on the block, having beaten off competition from Bedford Tigers and Norfolk-based Anglia Vipers to become the latest new club to join the semi-professional ranks.

The Vikings were founded as a community club in 2018 and have most recently been playing in the Yorkshire Men's League, with junior teams playing in the City of Hull and District Competition.

Since the announcement of their inclusion in the league, the Vikings have been busy recruiting a team that they feel can hold their own against some of the big guns in the league.

After signing up former Hull FC and Wigan forward Scott Taylor as coach, player announcements soon followed with Brett Ferres, Jamie Shaul and Thomas Minns among the players adding Super League experience to the fledging side. There is also plenty of Championship and League One knowledge among the recruits, with Tom Holliday, Josh Guzdek, Reece Dean and Jack and Harry Aldous among some of the other players already signed up.

League One Season

LEAGUE ONE AWARDS

PLAYER OF THE YEAR
Lewis Else (Rochdale Hornets)

YOUNG PLAYER OF THE YEAR
Phoenix Laulu-Togaga'e (Oldham)

COACH OF THE YEAR
Mark Dunning (Midlands Hurricanes)

League One Play-offs

Oldham were automatically promoted to the Championship, topping the table by a clear seven points after winning 19 of their 20 matches.

There was a five-team, four-week play-off system as in 2023 to determine the other club to (possibly) be promoted. Because the Championship was reducing in size to 13 in 2025 (then twelve in 2026), the third-tier play-off winners had to face a promotion/relegation play-off the following Sunday against the twelfth-placed (out of 14) Championship club.

At the end of a gruelling process, fourth-placed finishers Hunslet made an incredible return to the Championship as they beat third-from bottom Championship Swinton at a bitterly cold Heywood Road by 22-20.

Hot favourites Swinton - who would now descend to the third tier - led 20-18 with five minutes to go. But Hunslet were on the attack as star halfback Matty Beharrell put a long ball out to Jack Render. The big winger stepped the defender and headed for the corner, ball in right hand and grounded over the line. Although there was no conversion Hunslet led 20-22 in added time.

Swinton tried a short kick-off and regained possession but Hunslet held on and, at the final hooter the Hunslet bench and supporters erupted into scenes of pure joy.

Sixth-placed Workington had been the first team to be eliminated as Midlands Hurricanes edged a competitive and tense contest in Birmingham by 24-22. Five weeks earlier, the sides met at the same venue with Midlands winning 34-22 and Town conceded a glut of penalties as they were beaten again.

Workington scored four tries to Hurricanes' three - fullback Jordan Burns ended with a try-brace - but halfback Jake Sweeting, a Castleford product who had

BETFRED CHAMPIONSHIP PROMOTION/RELEGATION PLAY-OFF

Sunday 13th October 2024

SWINTON LIONS 20 HUNSLET 22

LIONS: 1 Dan Abram; 23 Joe Purcell; 29 Jonny Vaughan; 4 Jayden Hatton; 5 Rhys Williams; 18 Jack Stevens; 7 Jordy Gibson; 10 Gavin Bennion; 14 Josh Eaves; 20 Jack Houghton; 8 Liam Cooper; 12 Mitch Cox; 13 Mikey Wood. Subs (all used): 9 George Roby; 24 Jordan Case; 26 Anthony Walker; 33 Leon Cowen.
Tries: Williams (15), Cox (19), Wood (55), Vaughan (63);
Goals: Abram 2/4.
HUNSLET: 23 George Flanagan; 28 Mackenzie Turner; 5 Alfie Goddard; 4 Jude Ferreira; 31 Jack Render; 13 Michael Knowles; 7 Matty Beharrell; 22 Liam Carr; 15 Ross Whitmore; 32 Matt Fletcher; 11 Josh Jordan-Roberts; 20 Ethan Wood; 16 Jordan Syme. Subs (all used): 8 Harvey Hallas; 17 Lewis Wray; 18 Cam Berry; 26 Ethan O'Hanlon.
Tries: Turner (35), Berry (44), Flanagan (48), Render (75);
Goals: Beharrell 3/4.
Rugby Leaguer & League Express Men of the Match:
Lions: Mitch Cox; *Hunslet:* Harvey Hallas.
Penalty count: 4-4; **Half-time:** 10-6;
Referee: Joe Vella; **Attendance:** 885.

League One Season

Swinton's Jack Stevens closed down by Ethan Wood and Matty Beharrell as Hunslet earn promotion

represented a number of Yorkshire clubs before heading to Birmingham, landed six goals from seven attempts, including a late penalty goal with four minutes remaining.

In the qualifying play-off, Rochdale got the better of Hunslet by 30-18 at their cold and rainy Crown Oil Arena.

Hornets had to overturn a 6-14 deficit after conceding three tries in the first 20 minutes from Jude Ferreira, Alfie Goddard and Render. But they quickly responded with three tries of their own from Lewis Else, Jordan Andrade and Luke Forber and they never lost control from that point on. Else regathered his own cross-field kick that was spilled by Hunslet to seal the match late in the second half.

Hunslet had another chance the following weekend in a sudden-death tie against Midlands at home and they took it in thrilling fashion with an 18-14 win, with Render crossing in the corner in the 79th minute.

The Parksiders looked to be bowing out of the play-offs when the Hurricanes went into the closing stages 14-12 ahead, but a penalty gave the hosts the chance to gain valuable territory – and it wasn't wasted, with Beharrell and George Flanagan Jnr linking to send Render diving in at the corner. The Hurricanes felt that the winger hadn't grounded the ball. Referee Ryan Cox, however, deemed otherwise, the try was given, and Beharrell's touchline conversion saw Hunslet through after the Midlands were unable to make the most of retrieving possession from the restart.

Keighley Cougars became the first team to secure their place in the Play-off Final, following a tight 26-22 victory over Rochdale Hornets.

The Cougars had built up a 22-6 lead heading into the break with tries from Lachlan Lanskey, Josh Lynam, Jack Miller and Mark Ioane. Dean Roberts was the visitors' sole scorer. Rochdale forged an impressive comeback with three tries in the second half, but two Miller penalties saw Keighley edge out the win.

League One Season

George Flanagan Jr meets Ellis Robson and Lachlan Lanskey as Hunslet stun Keighley in the Play-off Final

The following week, Hunslet stunned Rochdale with a 46-26 away success in the Preliminary Final. The two sides were locked 18-18 at half-time but Render starred for Hunslet with two superb tries after the break to put the game out of the Hornets' reach, with further scores from Jude Ferreria, Ethan Wood and Ethan O'Hanlon securing a convincing win.

And the week after, Hunslet were through to the Championship Promotion Final after a 20-6 victory against Keighley Cougars in the League One Play-off Final.

Dean Muir's side went into the game as massive underdogs, having finished fourth and five points behind Keighley. And it was a closely fought contest in the opening quarter before Hunslet took the lead through Wakefield dual reg forward Wood, and former Cougar Beharrell added the extras.

Mackenzie Turner's try in the corner on 30 minutes then increased Hunslet's lead, as the Cougars struggled to find momentum.

George Flanagan Snr did cross the line on the 58th minute to bring the hosts back into the game at 6-12, although then they gave away a costly penalty which allowed Beharrell to edge his side further in front.

Beharrell was once again at the heart of Hunslet's attacks with his vision and deft passes the key to unlocking the Keighley defence and his offload, as he was being wrapped up in front of the posts, led to Render's leaping try in the corner which wrapped up the victory.

BETFRED LEAGUE ONE PLAY-OFF FINAL

Sunday 6th October 2024

KEIGHLEY COUGARS 6 HUNSLET 20

COUGARS: 17 Oscar Thomas; 5 Billy Walkley; 3 Adam Ryder; 11 Ellis Robson; 4 Junior Sa'u; 21 Ben Dean; 7 Jack Miller; 20 Will Maher; 15 Aaron Brown; 30 Mitch Revell; 12 Lachlan Lanskey; 16 Josh Lynam; 13 Dan Parker. Subs (all used): 31 George Flanagan Sr; 10 Mark Ioane; 8 Lewis Hatton; 35 Brad England.
Try: Flanagan Sr (56); **Goals:** Miller 1/1.
Dismissal: Hatton (72) - dissent.
Sin bin: Flanagan Sr (36) - late challenge.
HUNSLET: 23 George Flanagan Jr; 28 Mackenzie Turner; 5 Alfie Goddard; 4 Jude Ferreira; 31 Jack Render; 13 Michael Knowles; 7 Matty Beharrell; 22 Liam Carr; 15 Ross Whitmore; 32 Matt Fletcher; 20 Ethan Wood; 12 Aaron Levy; 16 Jordan Syme. Subs (all used): 18 Cam Berry; 8 Harvey Hallas; 17 Lewis Wray; 26 Ethan O'Hanlon.
Tries: Wood (14), Turner (31), Render (67); **Goals:** Beharrell 4/7.
Rugby Leaguer & League Express Men of the Match: *Cougars:* Jack Miller; *Hunslet:* Matty Beharrell.
Penalty count: 6-10; **Half-time:** 0-12;
Referee: Cameron Worsley; **Attendance:** 1,037.

3
WOMEN
& WHEELCHAIR 2024

WOMEN'S SUPER LEAGUE
Valkyrie ride high

How many times has it been said to 'never write off the Saints'? But judging by results in 2024, you should also never write off **YORK VALKYRIE**.

As far as adversity goes, Lindsay Anfield's side faced more than most as they aimed to become the first side in history to retain a Women's Super League title.

The 2023 Woman of Steel winner Sinead Peach was out of action for the whole season after announcing her pregnancy, while Tara Jane Stanley, the winner of the same individual award in 2022 also found herself in and out of the side all year with various injury concerns, with a knee injury sustained against Leeds at the start of September eventually ruling her out for the remainder of the season.

Kelsey Gentles, Carrie Roberts, Tamzin Renouf, Liv Gale and Rhiannion Marshall also missed long periods of the season, with Gentles putting off much-needed knee surgery until after the end of the campaign in order to help her side battle through adversity the best they could.

Add to all that a sickness bug that swept through the side in the run-up to the Challenge Cup semi-final against Saints and seriously derailed their hopes of getting to Wembley.

All the injuries and unavailabilities meant that barely a week went by where Anfield wasn't having to ask at least one player to play out of position. She also had to call on some of the club's under 19s stars and utilise the dual registration partnership with Sheffield Eagles to fill in some gaps.

That worked out well, with stars like Izzy Brennan, Lisa Parker, Evie Sexton and Lauren Exley being given the chance to prove themselves on the big stage.

With all this adversity, it was perhaps no surprise then that the club were realistically aiming to finish the regular season in the top four. They managed to do that, finishing third behind St Helens and Leeds Rhinos, and ahead of fourth-placed Wigan Warriors.

With injuries still biting hard and second-highest try-scorer Emma Kershaw ruled out with a ruptured spleen, many didn't rate York's chances going into the play-offs.

But a 12-10 semi-final win over Leeds at Headingley set up a visit to Saints' Totally Wicked Stadium and put them 80 minutes away from creating history in the most unlikely of circumstances.

Saints had lost just once all season, they had home advantage and a relatively fit squad, so went into the final as clear favourites.

Despite being written off in some quarters, right from kick-off the Valkyrie dug in, showed resilience and played for each other to come back from a half-time deficit to claim an 18-8 victory.

There were further celebrations for York two days later when Georgie Hetherington, who backed up last year's Grand Final player of the match performance with the same prize this year, became the third York player in as many seasons to claim the coveted Woman of Steel prize.

She also became the first mother to win the individual honour.

Hetherington was a thoroughly deserved winner of the accolade after her efforts, while playing out of position, proved vital for the Valkyrie. The 27-year-old started the year preparing for another season playing on the wing and then filling in at hooker or fullback if and when required. But with how the season went she found her self playing in one of those latter two roles nearly every game and, incredibly, towards the end of the season she was filling both roles within the same fixture.

The hybrid role, a brainchild of Anfield, saw Hetherington at fullback when York were defending, before switching to hooker when on the attack. Whilst not your standard tactic, it was one that proved a revolution for York, and one on which Hetherington thrived.

As if a history-making year on the field wasn't enough, York had already made history off it by handing their entire squad semi-professional contracts ahead of pre-season. The deals include base salaries, a range of performance-related bonuses, maternity leave support and NRLW player options.

York's victory in the Grand Final put an end to **ST HELENS'** hopes of achieving their second treble in four seasons.

Prior to the final, Saints had lost just once all season - which incidentally was against York on the opening day of the league campaign - a winning run that saw them claim both the Challenge Cup for a fourth consecutive year and the League Leaders' Shield, in a season where the club was paying its players for the first time.

Some thought they might struggle after the departures of Eboni Partington to York and Shona Hoyle to Leeds. But the return of Leah Burke after nine months out with an ACL injury, the arrival of young fullback Beri Salihi from Wigan and the return of former Champion Rachael Woosey left Saints as strong as ever.

That strength, and form developed as the season progressed and they all but had the top spot sewn up by the end of July after an important 10-6 win over the Valkyrie. There were still five rounds to be played at that stage but Saints faced bottom four opposition in all of them, while the rest of the top four all still had to play each other, meaning it would take a mighty effort from elsewhere to prevent them from lifting the Shield.

That success was mathematically confirmed with a 92-0 win over Warrington in the penultimate round of the season and Saints were presented with the trophy in front of their own fans a week later following a 68-0 win over Barrow.

That league form, coupled with the win at Wembley earned Matty Smith the Coach of the Year prize, beating Wigan Warriors' Denis Betts and Amanda Wilkinson of Barrow Raiders.

But it already looks as if Saints will be in for a much tougher time of it in 2025, with halfback, and Woman of Steel nominee, Faye Gaskin and international hooker Tara Jones both confirming their retirement from playing.

And both are doing so for very different reasons - Gaskin to begin her IVF journey and start a family and Jones to join the Rugby Football League's full-time match officials squad.

Whilst previously combining her officiating and playing careers, Jones has made history on more than one occasion.

In April this year she became the first woman to referee a full senior professional game in the northern hemisphere when she took charge of the League One game between Oldham and Cornwall at Boundary Park.

That came just nine months after becoming the first female player to score a try at Wembley during St Helens' win over Leeds Rhinos in the 2023 Challenge Cup Final. She also holds the record as the first woman to officiate in Super League when she served as an in-goal judge in March 2018 and also took charge of the Challenge Cup tie between Swinton and West Hull.

Smith has also announced he is to move on for 2025, joining Wigan Warriors as their Academy head coach.

He will be replaced by Derek Hardman, who was in charge during that 2021 treble-winning campaign before handing the reins to Smith ahead of 2023, and former England coach Craig Richards.

The duo have most recently worked together as co-coaches of St Helens' reserve grade team, and will bring with them a vast knowledge of the women's game.

Women's Super League

The losing Super League semi-finalists were second-placed **LEEDS RHINOS** and **WIGAN WARRIORS** who finished fourth.

The off-season signings of Hoyle, as well as York duo Grace Field and Liv Whitehead showed the Rhinos' intent early on, so they will undoubtedly have been left disappointed and a little frustrated at finishing the season empty-handed.

An emotional week following the death of Rob Burrow ended in a trip to Wembley for the Challenge Cup Final. But Leeds struggled to get going and left the capital in despair for a second year in a row.

It was a similar story in the semi-final defeat to York, a slow opening hour from the Rhinos saw them leave themselves too much to do to claw it back in the latter stages.

They also lost their grip on the Nines trophy, losing out to Wigan in what was a repeat of the final of the 2023 competition.

For most of the campaign, Leeds were one of the most potent attacking threats - regularly scoring over 50 points in a game. Only Saints scored more points over the 14-match league campaign. They had the third-best defence in the league too but struggled to get themselves over the line in the games that really mattered.

If that was a mentality issue, coach Lois Forsell will likely look to fix that up when she returns from the maternity leave that saw her miss the last four games of the season, with assistant coach Leon Crick looking after matters in her absence.

A big blow for Leeds came in the summer when prop Zoe Hornby took a step back from the game to focus on her non-playing career, while their 2025 squad has since lost Tara Moxon, who spent time away from the club on loan at Huddersfield this season and Sophie Robinson, who is going travelling. Both Beth Lockwood and captain Hanna Butcher, who in the semi-final against York became the first player to reach 100 appearances for the club, have retired. How the Rhinos replace the experience this quartet of players will take with them will be crucial to their success next season.

Despite the lack of silverware there were positives for Leeds, with young hooker or prop Bella Sykes being named as Young Player of the Year ahead of Wigan duo Isabel Rowe and Eva Hunter, while Lucy Murray was a contender for Woman of Steel after an incredible season on a personal level - often carrying Leeds with such strong and imposing runs down the middle.

Several of the club's academy products enjoyed solid debut seasons in the first team and will have only benefitted for that experience.

It was perhaps Wigan that ended the year the happier of the two clubs and not just for the fact that they finished the year with some silverware.

Signing up club legend Betts as coach proved a masterstroke for the club and, despite his lack of experience in the women's game, he quickly turned his young squad into genuine challengers for the title.

Despite knocking on the door for the last couple of seasons, this is the first time since their Grand Final success of 2018 that big things were expected of the Warriors.

Betts' main aim was to create an environment where his players could be the very best they could be and fulfil their potential.

And in one big week for the club, we saw that starting to come to fruition.

Whilst in previous years they have pushed the top three - St Helens, York and Leeds close, they had never managed to claim victory over any of them. But that all changed on July 20th when a brace from Eva Hunter, plus tries from Ellise Derbyshire and Jenna Foubister helped them to an 18-10 win over the Valkyrie.

That was followed up seven days later by taking the Women's Nines crown from defending champions Leeds.

After conceding just two tries in the group stage wins over York and Huddersfield, Wigan went on to beat Cardiff Demons 40-0 in the semi-final and then picked up a 21-0 victory in the final - the faster pace and more open space of that competition clearly suiting Wigan's youngsters.

The emergence of young talents such as Rowe, Hunter and Foubister will likely be one of Betts' most satisfying aspects of the year. Izzy Rowe has already made her England debut, starting at halfback against France in July. With more years under Betts to come the future stars can certainly lead Wigan to greater success in the future.

Women's Super League

Newly promoted **BARROW RAIDERS** impressed in their debut Super League season, finishing fifth, and leading the pack chasing down the usual suspects in the top four.

Under the guidance of Amanda Wilkinson, who led Wigan to Grand Final success six years before, Barrow were always going to be challenged by the game's very best. But they never panicked, kept their composure and stayed grounded.

Wilkinson largely kept faith in what she already had and the majority of the squad that beat Leigh Leopards in the previous season's Group Two Promotion Final, were back in the club's colours when they kicked off their campaign against Wigan.

That faith more than paid off and while they may not have defeated any of the top four they did run Wigan, York and Leeds close in games throughout the season, which will give them an extra confidence boost going into 2025.

They may still be some way off getting a win over one of the leading sides, but they will continue to snap at their heels in the meantime. And with many members of the squad still relatively new to the game, an extra year's experience in 2024 will like prove invaluable going forward.

They have been hit though by the double retirement of influential halfback Jodie Litherland and outside back Michelle Larkin, who at 45 years old is the oldest player to feature in Super League. How they replace the experienced duo is a big question that Wilkinson will need to find the answer to before next season kicks off.

Despite a heavy recruitment drive that saw the arrival of players such as Sam Hulme from Leeds, former Rhinos forward Ellie Oldroyd and promising duo Grace Ramsden and Kacy Haley from Warrington, **HUDDERSFIELD GIANTS** still found themselves struggling to compete against the teams above them.

The club also tied down stars Amelia Brown and Bethan Oates on contracts, as well as making Lori Halloran the team's first ever professional Women's Rugby League head coach on a two-year deal.

Going into the season hopes were high that the Giants could finally become genuine challengers to the top four. But in each of the games against the sides that finished in the top four they conceded an average of over 59 points, never scoring above 12 of their own.

Unless they can find a way to buck this trend, they may have to wait a little longer to mount any serious play-off charge.

It was a similar story for seventh-placed **WARRINGTON WOLVES** who, like Wigan, welcomed a former player back to the club as coach ahead of the season kicking off.

Fresh from retiring from playing through injury, former captain Armani Sharrock stepped into the role following Lee Westwood's departure and aimed to get her team fitter and stronger.

That meant an earlier than usual start to pre-season and they hit the ground running with strong away performances against Bradford Bulls and London Broncos in the Challenge Cup group stages. That was enough to see them qualify for the quarter-finals but when they needed to step it up against St Helens in the final group game and then Leeds in the knock-out stages they lost 58-6 and 70-10 respectively, showcasing the grim reality of how tough the season ahead would be.

Wins against Featherstone (twice) and Barrow in round three did show some promise. But it is clear there is still some way to go for the Wolves.

And they will have to find their way forward with another new coach at the helm following Sharrock's decision to resign at the end of the campaign, stating that the club's vision for the future of the team did not match her own.

Captain Katie May Williams, Abi Johnston and Louise Fellingham were the first three players to announce their departures from the club and whoever steps in to replace Sharrock must be hoping no more follow through the exit door.

Women's Super League

Unfortunately for **FEATHERSTONE ROVERS**, they couldn't follow in Barrow's footsteps and make an impact in Super League following their automatic promotion from Group Two last season.

In fact their introduction to Super League couldn't have been much tougher and they failed to win a single game during the entire league campaign. They did pick up one win though, a 38-6 victory over Sheffield Eagles in the Challenge Cup group stages.

Rovers finished top of Group Two last season on a dramatic final day which could have seen many different outcomes, with Featherstone, Leigh and Barrow all still in line to go up.

A win over Salford sealed top-spot and many hoped that Featherstone, once a leading light in the women's game, were starting their journey back to the top.

But instead, whether through injury or unavailability, coach Marie Colley struggled for squad consistency throughout the year and they were forced to face a relegation/promotion decider against Leigh to try and retain their position in the league.

LEIGH LEOPARDS, went into the game having been unbeaten all year in the league, finishing top of the table, beating Sheffield to claim the Northern Championship title, and then becoming National Championship winners with victory over London Broncos.

That winning streak continued with a 34-16 win over Featherstone to earn the right to challenge themselves against the game's very best next season.

Tries from Gabi Leigh, Hattie Dogus, Mollie Young and Storm Cobain, plus three Charlotte Melvin goals gave the Leopards a 22-0 half-time lead. And when Becky Greenfield crossed just ten minutes into the second half a Leigh whitewash was on the cards. But tries from Brogan Churm and Alyssa Courtney got Featherstone back into the contest. But late tries from Toryn Blackwood and a second from Young, either side of a Chloe Billington try for Featherstone, stubbed out the threatened comeback and left the Leopards celebrating and planning for life in Super League in 2025.

LONDON BRONCOS were one of the other big winners of the year, retaining their Championship South title with a 28-8 win over Cardiff, before going down 22-18 to Leigh in the National Championship Final.

Super League Play-offs

Defending Champions York Valkyrie had a stronger and more dominant pack to thanks for overcoming Leeds Rhinos 12-10 at Headingley as the play-off got underway at the end of September.

Leeds' already weakened middle unit was further hit by an injury to Bella Sykes after just ten minutes, as Kelsey Gentles and Savannah Andrade gave York serious impetus going forward. And after Lisa Parker had gone close for the Valkyrie before Keara Bennett defused the situation, it was Gentles who finally opened the scoring after 20 minutes - crashing over following a Georgie Hetherington break. The conversion from former Rhinos player Rhiannion Marshall made it 6-0 to the Valkyrie, who remain unbeaten at AMT Headingley.

Hetherington almost doubled York's lead but she lost possession over the line but, despite Leeds going close twice before the break, York held onto their narrow lead.

But it was a lead that was extended just two minutes after the restart when a high kick from Sade Rihari, combined with strong line speed from the outside backs, forced a knock-on from Leeds winger Liv Whitehead. Andrade reacted quickest to the loose ball and raced in to score under the posts. Marshall was again on target with the conversion and York held a two-score advantage.

It was at this point Leeds started to get themselves into the game, creating chances and forcing the Valkyrie to dig in in defence, with Carrie Roberts keeping Sophie Robinson out as the Rhinos looked to mount a comeback.

Leeds finally found a breakthrough with 12 minutes left on the clock when youngster

Ebony Stead, in only her sixth appearance for the club, showed speed and skill to beat the York defence and cross to the left of the posts. Bennett's conversion reduced the deficit to six points and fuelled Leeds' fire.

With York down to 12 men following Tamzin Renouf's sin-binning for a late hit on Ruby Walker, Leeds took full advantage and, when Evie Cousins was tackled just short of gathering Walker's kick into the in-goal, Lucy Murray was there to touch down.

Bennett's conversion would have sent the tie to Golden Point but it fell just short and York held on for the win.

League Leaders St Helens booked their place in the final with a hard-fought 18-4 win over an ever-improving Wigan Warriors.

The competition's leading try scorer Leah Burke added two more to her season tally as they set up a home clash against the reigning champions and put themselves 80 minutes away from claiming the treble.

Despite a positive start from Wigan, as the first half wore on ill-discipline started to cost them and Saints took advantage with Emily Rudge going in off a wonderful Zoe Harris pass in the 14th minute. Faye Gaskin converted for a 6-0 lead.

Wigan were back in it by the break though as their off-the-cuff style paid dividends when Anna Davies broke down the right wing and link up with Georgia Wilson, who put Jenna Foubister over with a brilliant pass. Isabel Rowe missed an apparently straightforward conversion and it remained 6-4 to Saints.

But the hosts piled the pressure on after the break and, when a Rowe kick went out on the full, Saints made them pay as Gaskin's pass found Burke, who pounced for a 10-4 lead.

Minutes later Rachael Woosey crossed out wide out following a break from Katie Mottershead.

The two sides slugged it out for over 20 minutes, with neither finding another breakthrough until Burke finally grabbed her second with just eight minutes to go to seal the win.

Super League Grand Final

York produced the ultimate show of resilience to retain the Women's Super League title and become the first side in the competition's history to go back-to-back.

The Valkyrie and St Helens played a compelling 80 minutes of enthralling Rugby League which saw early chances and great defensive efforts.

But with just over ten minutes on the clock a great tackle from Manuqalo Komaitai temporarily stopped further momentum from Saints, until Jodie Cunningham and Paige Travis linked up to get the ball out to Leah Burke, who showed her finishing prowess from 40 metres for her 28th try of the season and a 4-0 advantage.

York hit straight back though when Beri Salihi couldn't deal with Izzy Brennan's kick and Lacey Owen swept the ball up and dived under the posts. Brennan goaled to put the Valkyrie in front.

However, two penalties for Saints - first for a high shot on Katie Mottershead and then one for a ball steal by Kelsey Gentles - allowed Faye Gaskin two kicks at goals. Both were successful and Saints went in at the break 8-6 up.

Whatever York coach Lindsay Anfield said at half-time certainly seemed to work and it

BETFRED WOMEN'S SUPER LEAGUE GRAND FINAL

Sunday 6th October 2024

ST HELENS 8 YORK VALKYRIE 18

SAINTS: 1 Beri Salihi; 20 Phoebe Hook; 4 Erin Stott; 30 Rachael Woosey; 5 Leah Burke; 6 Zoe Harris; 7 Faye Gaskin; 8 Vicky Whitfield; 9 Tara Jones; 10 Chantelle Crowl; 11 Paige Travis; 12 Emily Rudge; 13 Jodie Cunningham (C). Subs (all used): 14 Naomi Williams; 19 Katie Mottershead; 16 Darcy Stott; 22 Megan Williams.
Try: Burke (11); **Goals:** Gaskin 2/3.
VALKYRIE: 5 Georgie Hetherington; 26 Carrie Roberts; 23 Manuqalo Komaitai; 36 Lisa Parker; 2 Eboni Partington; 6 Sade Rihari (C); 3 Tamzin Renouf; 8 Liv Wood; 29 Izzy Brennan; 10 Jas Bell; 11 Lacey Owen; 12 Savannah Andrade; 33 Megan Pakulis. Subs: 13 Rhiannion Marshall; 15 Kelsey Gentles; 18 Jess Sharp (not used); 28 Remi Wilton (not used).
Tries: Owen (14), Partington (44), Gentles (55);
Goals: Brennan 1/2, Marshall 2/2.
Rugby Leaguer & League Express Women of the Match:
Saints: Paige Travis; *Valkyrie:* Georgie Hetherington.
Penalty count: 3-5; **Half-time:** 8-6;
Referee: Liam Rush; **Attendance:** 4,813.

Women's Super League

Kelsey Gentles leads the York Valkyrie celebration charge following Grand Final victory against St Helens

took just four minutes for her side to regain the lead when a high kick from Marshall caused confusion between Saints' Erin Stott and Phoebe Hook and allowed Saints star Eboni Partington to score in the corner. Marshall converted from the touchline to give York an 12-8 advantage.

Eleven minutes later York had their third and decisive try when Gentles took Georgie Hetherington's pass and ran hard and straight and managed to touch down under the posts, despite the attentions of several Saints players. Marshall's goal after the video referee's deliberations put York ten points ahead.

After Brennan was hit high by Chantelle Crowl, she had the chance to make it a two-score game, but sent the ball wide of the sticks. Crucially though the ball went dead and York were once again able to attack.

Saints never gave up but errors continued to cost them and with York tackling like their lives depended on it, and having used just two of their four named substitutes, they were able to hold on and the Valkyrie were able to celebrate making history.

WOMEN'S AWARDS
WOMAN OF STEEL Georgie Hetherington (York Valkyrie)
YOUNG PLAYER OF THE YEAR Bella Sykes (Leeds Rhinos)
COACH OF THE YEAR Matty Smith (St Helens)

Challenge Cup

Once again the early stages of the Challenge Cup was set to see four groups of four go head to head to determine the eight quarter finalists. But before a ball had even been kicked, struggling one-time runners-up Castleford Tigers decided to withdraw from the competition, stating they were not in a position to compete at that stage of the year.

A 22-16 win for Cardiff Demons over newly-promoted Barrow Raiders was perhaps the only shock of this stage, seeing the Welsh side progress to the knock out stages ahead of the Cumbrians.

They were joined in the quarter finals by the remaining seven Super League sides, with the seeded system meaning St Helens, Leeds, York and Wigan all avoided each other in the first round of knock-out games.

Wins for all four of those sides set up a repeat of the previous year's semi-finals with York

Women's Super League

Faye Gaskin shows her delight at scoring St Helens' opening try against Leeds in the Challenge Cup Final

Valkyrie playing St Helens and Leeds Rhinos facing Wigan Warriors - with both games being played as a double header alongside a men's semi-final.

The clash between defending champions St Helens and York was nowhere near as thrilling as it had been in the same competition the previous season when a late Faye Gaskin field goal sent Saints to Wembley. The reason? A sickness bug that had swept through the York camp in the weeks leading up to game that left them without a number of star players, and others playing while still feeling its effects.

As hard as the depleted York side tried, St Helens raced away to a 32-2 victory to book a second consecutive trip to the National Stadium.

The following day, Leeds also booked their return to Wembley with a 34-20 win over Wigan Warriors, who made the Rhinos work for the entire 80 minutes to claim victory.

That set up a repeat of the previous year's Wembley showdown, with Leeds keen to put on a much stronger performance than they did in the 22-8 defeat in 2023.

But the emotion of the week, which had seen club legend Rob Burrow lose his battle with Motor Neurone Disease, proved too much for Leeds and once again a scoring burst from St Helens broke their resolve and set the holders on a clear path to victory.

The retiring Faye Gaskin and Phoebe Hook scored back-to-back tries to give Saints a 10-0 half time lead, before Luci McColm extended that five minutes into the second half.

Leeds made too many errors and poor decisions to get themselves back into it and with ten minutes remaining Chantelle Crowl forced her way over to seal a 22-0 win, and make it four Challenge Cups in a row for St Helens.

BETFRED WOMEN'S CHALLENGE CUP FINAL

Saturday 8th June 2024

LEEDS RHINOS 0 ST HELENS 22

RHINOS: 1 Ruby Enright; 21 Evie Cousins; 4 Amy Hardcastle; 3 Caitlin Beevers; 18 Liv Whitehead; 6 Hanna Butcher (C); 7 Caitlin Casey; 19 Grace Field; 9 Keara Bennett; 10 Izzy Northrop; 17 Lucy Murray; 11 Shona Hoyle; 12 Bella Sykes. Subs (all used): 2 Sophie Robinson; 8 Zoe Hornby; 13 Bethan Dainton; 25 Ella Donnelly.
SAINTS: 1 Beri Salihi; 20 Phoebe Hook; 4 Erin Stott; 3 Luci McColm; 5 Leah Burke; 6 Zoe Harris; 7 Faye Gaskin; 8 Vicky Whitfield; 9 Tara Jones; 10 Chantelle Crowl; 11 Paige Travis; 12 Emily Rudge; 13 Jodie Cunningham (C). Subs (all used): 14 Naomi Williams; 16 Darcy Stott; 19 Katie Mottershead; 24 Georgia Sutherland.
Tries: Gaskin (25), Hook (30), McColm (45), Crowl (70);
Goals: Gaskin 3/4.
Rugby Leaguer & League Express Women of the Match:
Rhinos: Lucy Murray; *Saints:* Faye Gaskin.
Penalty count: 1-4; **Half-time:** 0-10; **Referee:** Aaron Moore; **Attendance:** 64,845 *(at Wembley Stadium).*

WHEELCHAIR SUPER LEAGUE
Rhinos on a roll

LEEDS RHINOS enjoyed the first perfect league season with their Grand Final triumph over Halifax a tenth win from ten over the regular campaign and play-offs.

On paper, Leeds had the strongest squad in the competition and that came to pass on the pitch with Nathan Collins, Tom Halliwell and Wheels of Steel Josh Butler enjoying fine seasons.

Those stars - and Collins in particular - came to the fore in the play-offs, as Leeds beat Wigan and then Halifax by 20-point margins, albeit both still entertaining and competitive games.

But that's not to say they had it easy by any stretch, with only one of their eight regular-season wins coming by more than 14 points.

So often the Rhinos found a way to win in tight games, solving the puzzles set by the opposition and sometimes their own coach James Simpson.

It proved the perfect preparation for putting to rest two successive years of Grand Final hurt and winning their second Super League title.

WHEELCHAIR AWARDS
WHEELS OF STEEL Josh Butler (Leeds Rhinos)
YOUNG PLAYER OF THE YEAR Rob Hawkins (Halifax Panthers)
COACH OF THE YEAR Wayne Boardman (Halifax Panthers)

Wayne Boardman won the Coach of the Year award in a reflection of **HALIFAX PANTHERS'** achievement to come runners-up in both the regular season and play-offs.

Fourth in 2023, Halifax made strides forward this year with high-scoring early victories away at London and Wigan setting the tone for their campaign.

Ultimately while they were ahead of the rest of the competition, they remained a step behind Leeds, who beat them by twelve points in the opening round and pipped them in the final minute in the reverse fixture.

An impressive semi-final win over London - played at 'home' in Hull due to venue unavailability - set up another clash with the Rhinos but they couldn't keep up a strong first half and had their lead snatched away.

That was despite the best efforts of Rob Hawkins, who was magnificent all season for the Panthers. He won the Young Player of the Year award and can't have been far off scooping the main prize.

It was a third semi-final defeat in three seasons for **LONDON ROOSTERS**, whose wait for a first Grand Final appearance since its founding from the amalgamation of several southern clubs goes on.

This year has to be considered a step backwards for the capital club, who finished joint-top of the regular-season table with eight wins from ten matches in 2023.

Wheelchair Super League

That became just three wins from eight in 2024 as, after getting the better of Wigan in the opening round, the Roosters only gained further points from doing the double over bottom side Hull FC.

Only with their second victory over Hull in the final round was a play-off place secured - otherwise they would have suffered the ignominy of being the one side to miss out altogether.

As it was, they fell to Halifax in the semi-finals, ending a campaign in which the class of Joe Coyd and Lewis King wasn't enough to see them triumph in big games.

Unexpected champions in 2023, **WIGAN WARRIORS** made a good fist of their title defence but ultimately fell short in the key games.

Their campaign started so promisingly, as they reached the Challenge Cup final via impressive victories over both Halifax and Leeds.

They were slain by the superior Catalans in Sheffield, just as they had been in the European Club Championship (played between the English and French champions) at Robin Park a few months earlier, but it still augured well for the league season ahead.

However, they struggled for consistency and won only three of their eight games in the regular season, not helped by the absence of captain Declan Roberts.

A victory over Halifax and two tight tussles with Leeds showed they could still compete with the best on their day, but their campaign came to an end at the semi-final stage as a fourth-placed finish made them face the Rhinos once again and the league leaders gained revenge for last year's Grand Final defeat.

Only one team were going to miss out on the play-offs and, as expected, that team turned out to be **HULL FC**.

That's not to say that this was a year of total failure for the East Yorkshire side, who went into every game as underdogs following the reduction in Super League teams.

Indeed, their fate was only sealed when an under-strength side lost at London in the final round of the season.

They claimed their first point away at Halifax and gained a notable victory at defending champions Wigan, with a two-point defeat to London and twelve-point loss against Leeds in between in a strong middle part of the season.

Ultimately losing every home game at Allam Sports Centre proved costly to their pursuit of a play-off place, but there were still positives for player-coach Mike Swainger to take.

One of those was the form of Tristan Norfolk, who has continued to grow into their key player.

Wheelchair Super League Play-offs

Leeds converted their League Leaders' Shield into a Grand Final place with a 56-36 victory over Wigan, while Halifax saw off London 60-38 in the other play-off semi-final.

Wigan started well and were rewarded with two well-worked tries through Adam Rigby and Nathan Roberts, but Nathan Mulhall replied for Leeds before Josh Butler and Nathan Collins scored two tries each in a devastating spell.

The Warriors also started the second half fast, scoring three tries in 15 minutes from Chris Greenhalgh, Jack Heggie and Toby Burton-Carter to close the gap to two points with a quarter of the game remaining.

But the Rhinos went up another gear as Butler completed the game with four tries while Mulhall and Collins each added another try, the latter taking his total point tally to 32 with a perfect record from the tee.

Wigan scored a late consolation through Heggie, who converted all their tries.

Rob Hawkins starred in the other semi-final with four tries and seven goals, three of the touchdowns coming in an action-packed first half which had a dozen of them in total, with the Panthers holding a 38-28 advantage.

Wheelchair Super League

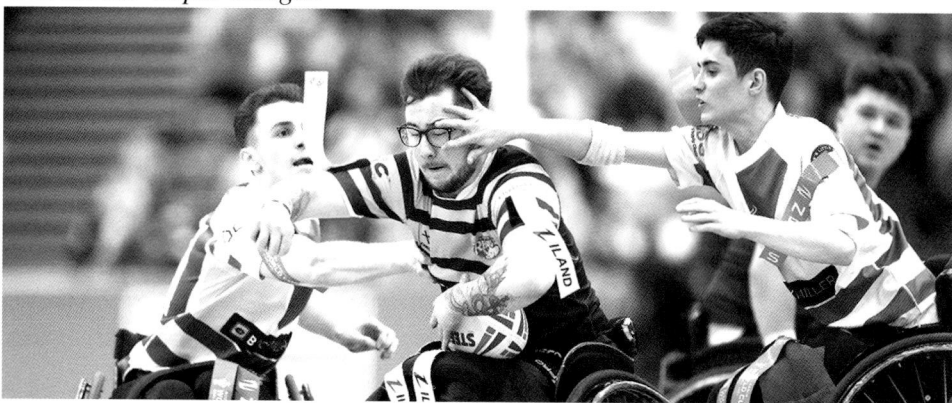

Leeds' Josh Butler takes on Halifax duo Rob Hawkins and Nathaniel Wright during the Super League Grand Final

Nathaniel Wright scored twice while Jérémy Bourson and Nathan Holmes also dotted down in the opening period, responding to early efforts from Jason Owen (who kicked five goals), Jack Linden (twice), Joe Coyd and Lewis King for the Roosters.

Hawkins opened the second half with his fourth try and a strong defensive period helped clinch victory for Halifax (for whom Wayne Boardman also kicked three goals), before King, Bourson, Coyd and Wright scored further tries for their respective sides.

Wheelchair Super League Grand Final

A dominant second-half performance saw Leeds come back from twelve points down to defeat Halifax and reclaim the Super League crown in Hull.

The Rhinos' start couldn't have been better as Nathan Collins scored in the opening minute, yet at the 20-minute mark they were 16-4 down as Rob Hawkins led a Panthers recovery.

He scored two tries, the latter from a deep Wayne Boardman kick, with a Joe Calcott effort in between and a conversion of the last try after Boardman goaled the first.

Leeds halved the deficit when Tom Halliwell stretched out to dot the ball down but it was re-extended through a thrilling Jérémy Bourson sprint after being released by Hawkins, who converted.

However, Collins crashed over too easily from the restart and his two conversions narrowed the Panthers' lead to 22-16 at half-time.

Collins then inspired the turnaround in the first ten minutes of the second half, twice providing brilliant assists with offloads while off-balance - first for Nathan Mulhall, then for Butler, and both converted for 28-22.

Halifax hit back with a world-class try of their own, by Hawkins from another Boardman kick, but Leeds remained on top and, after a period of patient pressure, struck three times in five minutes.

Captain Jodie Boyd-Ward was played in by Collins to regain the lead, then Butler followed in and Halliwell crashed over, with three more Collins conversions making it 46-28. Bourson hit back in the closing stages but Collins played in Butler for his hat-trick try with five minutes to go.

BETFRED WHEELCHAIR SUPER LEAGUE GRAND FINAL

Sunday 13th October 2024

LEEDS RHINOS 52 HALIFAX PANTHERS 32

RHINOS: 1 Nathan Collins; 3 Josh Butler; 4 Nathan Mulhall; 7 Tom Halliwell; 10 Jodie Boyd-Ward. Subs: 5 Becky Wilkinson (not used); 6 Ewan Clibbens; 9 Verity Smith (not used).
Tries: Collins (1, 36), Halliwell (24, 68), Mulhall (44), Butler (49, 64, 76), Boyd-Ward (63); **Goals:** Collins 8/9.
PANTHERS: 1 Wayne Boardman; 2 Rob Hawkins; 6 Nathaniel Wright; 19 Joe Calcott; 24 Jérémy Bourson. Subs: 7 Jordan Holt; 8 Kieron Johnson; 16 Finlay O'Neill (not used).
Tries: Hawkins (7, 16, 52), Calcott (11), Bourson (34, 72); **Goals:** Boardman 1/2, Hawkins 3/4.
Rugby Leaguer & League Express Players of the Match: *Rhinos:* Nathan Collins; *Panthers:* Rob Hawkins.
Penalty count: 7-1; **Half-time:** 16-22;
Referees: Ollie Cruickshank and Jake Brook.
(at Allam Sports Centre, Hull).

Wheelchair Super League

Catalans Dragons celebrate their Challenge Cup Final victory against Wigan

Wheelchair Challenge Cup

Catalans won the Wheelchair Challenge Cup for the first time with a brutally brilliant 81-18 victory over Wigan.

Beaten by Leeds in the final on their first entry into the competition the previous year, the French side were determined to claim the crown in 2024 and nobody could lay a glove on them.

The Dragons won 78-6 at Hull FC and 74-12 at London before the 14-try final success at EIS Sheffield.

Jérémy Bourson scored two and assisted Nicholas Clausells and Arno Vargas as they marched into a 22-0 lead.

Wigan's brief fightback saw Declan Roberts and Adam Rigby dot down, with Roberts converting both.

But a magical kick-and-chase try, with Clausells on the end of a Bourson punt, turned things back in Catalans' favour and a further Bourson score, from his own half, made it 34-12 at half-time.

Gilles Clausells' half-time introduction further lifted the Dragons as he set up two Seb Bechara tries before striking a cheeky field goal.

Vargas scored twice more for a hat-trick, either side of Bourson's fourth, another from a kick.

Two more stunning tries followed, the first a team effort finished Damien Doré, then a Bechara long-range break.

And after Rigby notched a small consolation try with a minute left, converted by Jack Heggie, the French side still managed to have the final say, winning the restart and scoring again through Nicolas Clausells.

Gilles Clausells converted seven of their eight second-half tries, after his nephew knocked over four first-half goals and Bechara one.

Wheelchair European Club Championship

Catalans became the first winners of the European Club Championship, a title contested between the champions of England and France.

BETFRED WHEELCHAIR CHALLENGE CUP FINAL

Saturday 1st June 2024

CATALANS DRAGONS 81 WIGAN WARRIORS 18

DRAGONS: 2 Joël Lacombe, 12 Jérémy Bourson, 13 Nicolas Clausells, 16 Arno Vargas, 28 Damien Doré. Subs (all used): 1 Gilles Clausells, 8 Victor Puly, 10 Seb Bechara.
Tries: Bourson (5, 15, 33, 59), N Clausells (8, 29, 80), Vargas (12, 56, 61), Bechara (41, 50, 72), Doré (63);
Goals: N Clausells 4/5, Bechara 1/1, G Clausells 7/8;
Field goal: G Clausells (53).
WARRIORS: 1 Chris Greenhalgh, 5 Adam Rigby, 6 Jack Heggie, 7 Declan Roberts, 9 Phil Roberts. Subs (all used): 3 Martin Lane, 4 Nathan Roberts, 10 Mark Williams.
Tries: D Roberts (17), Rigby (20, 79);
Goals: D Roberts 2/2, Heggie 1/1.
Rugby Leaguer & League Express Players of the Match: *Dragons:* Jérémy Bourson; *Warriors:* Adam Rigby.
Penalty count: 6-2; **Half-time:** 34-12;
Referees: David Butler and Ollie Cruickshank; **Attendance:** 419.
(at EIS Sheffield).

Wheelchair Super League

Catalans Dragons' Jeremy Bourson in the thick of European Club Championship action against Wigan

Inaugurated in 2023, the first crown was shared between Catalans and Halifax after the pair drew 32-32 on the continent.

There was no doubt about the victor second time around, as Wigan were put to the sword in a 28-68 defeat by the visiting Dragons at Robin Park.

The Warriors only trailed 18-12 after 27 minutes, with two individual Declan Roberts finishes, and in the second half he produced two wonderful assists for Adam Rigby before completing his hat-trick nine minutes from time.

But in a 24-minute period either side of half-time, Catalans scored eight tries, many of them truly exceptional.

The first of this magical spell saw Jérémy Bourson put fist to ball in front of his own posts on the second play of a set. Seb Bechara hared after the kick in behind the Wigan defence and picked it up magnificently at his foot to score.

Arno Vargas followed with a rapid length-of-the-field effort, Damien Doré finished a try involving the whole team, then Bourson scored four in a row, the first a mirror-image of his 17th-minute try off a deep Bechara kick and the second making it 12-46 at half-time.

In total Catalans scored twelve tries, with Doré getting five like Bourson, and Bechara converting ten.

EUROPEAN CLUB CHAMPIONSHIP

Saturday 6th April 2024

WIGAN WARRIORS 28 CATALANS DRAGONS 68

WARRIORS: 1 Chris Greenhalgh, 4 Nathan Roberts, 7 Declan Roberts, 8 Adam Rigby, 9 Phil Roberts. Subs (all used): 3 Martin Lane, 10 Mark Williams, 15 Matt Wooloff.
Tries: D Roberts (7, 21, 71), Rigby (53, 65); **Goals:** D Roberts 4/5.
DRAGONS: 8 Victor Puly, 10 Seb Bechara, 12 Jérémy Bourson, 16 Arno Vargas, 28 Damien Doré. Subs (all used): 1 Gilles Clausells, 2 Joël Lacombe, 9 Jorge Gelade-Panzo.
Tries: Doré (11, 15, 35, 50, 58), Bourson (17, 39, 40, 45, 48), Bechara (26), Vargas (30); **Goals:** Bechara 10/12.
Rugby Leaguer & League Express Players of the Match:
Warriors: Declan Roberts; *Dragons:* Jérémy Bourson.
Penalty count: 5-5; **Half-time:** 12-46;
Referees: David Butler and Djamel Merzouk; **Attendance:** 439.

4
SEASON DOWN UNDER

NRL
Four and counting

Penrith Panthers secured a hard-fought 14-6 win over Melbourne Storm to retain the NRL title and write their names into the record books with a fourth Premiership on the trot.

Ivan Cleary's side became the first since the St George Dragons (1956-1966) and the South Sydney Rabbitohs (1925-1929) to achieve the feat, the first ever since the NRL introduced the salary cap.

There was drama. It came in the 50th minute, with the Panthers leading 10-6, when Storm centre Jack Howarth was denied a try. Referee Ashley Klein said 'no try' and the bunker official Grant Atkins upheld the decision, despite TV replays appearing to show Howarth grounding the ball. Howarth was clearly of the opinion he'd scored.

The NRL later released replays from another angle that only the bunker could see that showed an arm under the ball. If they had shown that on the big screen it would have saved a lot of controversy.

Almost inevitably, the Panthers then scored a third unanswered try when Paul Alamoti dived into the right corner in the 60th minute thanks to a huge play from Liam Martin that clinched him the Clive Churchill Medal.

Martin was magnificent, Nathan Cleary played through the obvious pain barrier to complete a terrific halfback's performance, whilst centres Izaak Tago and Alamoti turned on the style in attack and defence.

In their previous head-to-heads in 2024, the Storm had come out victorious on both occasions, with 24-22 and 8-0 triumphs, Craig Bellamy's side having won the Minor Premiership and enjoying the ascendancy going into the final. Melbourne were aiming for a seventh title – and their first since 2020.

The banned Nelson Asofa-Solomona sat out for the Storm after copping a three-match ban for a high shot on the Roosters' Lindsay Collins in the first tackle of their semi-final.

The Panthers started the brighter of the two sides, Moses Leota's offload almost finding

NRL PREMIERSHIP FINALS SERIES

QUALIFYING FINALS
Friday 13th September 2024
Penrith Panthers 30 .... Sydney Roosters 10
Saturday 14th September 2024
Melbourne Storm 37 .... Cronulla Sharks 10

ELIMINATION FINALS
Saturday 14th September 2024
North Queensland Cowboys 28 .... Newcastle Knights 16
Sunday 15th September 2024
Canterbury Bulldogs 22 .... Manly Sea Eagles 24
(at Accor Stadium, Sydney)

SEMI-FINALS
Friday 20th September 2024
Cronulla Sharks 26 .... North Queensland Cowboys 18
(at Allianz Stadium, Sydney)
Saturday 21st September 2024
Sydney Roosters 40 .... Manly Sea Eagles 16

PRELIMINARY FINALS
Friday 27th September 2024
Melbourne Storm 48 .... Sydney Roosters 18
Saturday 28th September 2024
Penrith Panthers 26 .... Cronulla Sharks 6
(at Accor Stadium, Sydney)

NRL GRAND FINAL

Sunday 6th October 2024

MELBOURNE STORM 6 PENRITH PANTHERS 14

STORM: 1 Ryan Papenhuyzen; 2 Will Warbrick; 3 Jack Howarth; 4 Nick Meaney; 5 Xavier Coates; 6 Cameron Munster; 7 Jahrome Hughes; 8 Tui Kamikamica; 9 Harry Grant (C); 10 Josh King; 11 Shawn Blore; 12 Eliesa Katoa; 13 Trent Loiero. Subs (all used): 14 Tyran Wishart; 15 Christian Welch; 16 Lazarus Vaalepu; 17 Alec MacDonald.
Try: Grant (22); **Goals:** Meaney 1/1.
PANTHERS: 1 Dylan Edwards; 2 Sunia Turuva; 3 Izack Tago; 4 Paul Alamoti; 5 Brian To'o; 6 Jarome Luai; 7 Nathan Cleary (C); 8 Moses Leota; 9 Mitch Kenny; 10 James Fisher-Harris; 12 Liam Martin; 19 Scott Sorensen; 13 Isaah Yeo. Subs (all used): 11 Luke Garner; 14 Brad Schneider; 15 Lindsay Smith; 16 Liam Henry.
Tries: Turuva (27), Martin (40), Alamoti (61); **Goals:** Cleary 1/3.
Rugby Leaguer & League Express Men of the Match:
Storm: Eliesa Katoa; *Panthers:* Liam Martin.
Penalty count: 5-2; **Half-time:** 6-10; **Referee:** Ashley Klein;
Attendance: 80,156 *(at Accor Stadium, Sydney).*

Penrith Panthers celebrate their fourth successive NRL Grand Final triumph

Isaah Yeo but the latter couldn't take it in close to the line.

Meanwhile, Melbourne's early tactic to kick to Penrith's small wingers saw both Will Warbrick and Xavier Coates catch high balls but the pair were easily smothered by terrific Panthers defence.

Bellamy's Melbourne side struck first, in the set after Penrith were found guilty of a ball strip. With Shawn Blore leaving Nathan Cleary on the floor, Harry Grant spotted a gap and ran straight through it, scampering over from dummy-half just after the midway point in the first half.

Nick Meaney converted to make it 6-0 as the Storm drew first blood in a cauldron-like atmosphere.

The reigning champions got the chance to hit back moments later when Warbrick dropped a Cleary bomb – and they weren't going to let the chance go begging.

A superb move saw Alamoti turn and feed Jarome Luai, and he sent Sunia Turuva a perfect pass to fly in at the corner. Melbourne still led 6-4, however, as Cleary sent his conversion wide of the posts.

Inexplicably, Ryan Papenhuyzen sent the resulting kick-off out on the full to invite more Penrith pressure but Turuva knocked on as he chased a Luai grubber under pressure from Eliesa Katoa.

The Panthers had all the momentum by now and Brian To'o went close as an increasingly-tiring Melbourne defence kept firm. But the brick wall yielded on the hooter as a brilliant delayed Cleary pass found the rampaging Martin, who streaked his way to the line through the right channel. Cleary this time converted to send Penrith into a 10-6 half-time lead.

A successful captain's challenge saw Penrith alleviate pressure on their own line at the start of the second half when Coates flew through the air to knock on.

And the Panthers almost made Melbourne pay but Liam Henry was hauled short following a tremendous Turuva catch and pass from a Luai kick.

NRL

Just when the Storm were weathering relentless Penrith charges, they almost levelled proceedings when Coates rose highest to a Cameron Munster chip and fed Howarth who was adjudged to have been held up.

Papenhuyzen and Coates combined down the left to sprint 60 metres as Melbourne began to enjoy some attacking joy, with To'o having to leave the field after struggling with a knee injury.

But when it looked like the Storm would pounce, Martin came up with another magnificent moment on the hour, catching a Cleary bomb before offloading to Leota who, in turn, found Alamoti.

The Penrith centre, who took To'o's place on the wing, then held off three defenders to finish brilliantly in the corner. This time Cleary couldn't convert but Penrith led 14-6.

Cameron Munster was placed on report for an alleged bite on Alamoti. But in the grand scheme of things it mattered little with the Panthers ending the game on the Melbourne line.

It was another season of progress for Rugby League in Australia with average attendances of more than twenty thousand, two of the first round games being staged in Las Vegas and plans in place to expand to 20 clubs by 2032.

Here's how it all went for the 17 clubs in 2024:

PENRITH PANTHERS (Premiers/2nd in table)
Top pointscorer: Nathan Cleary (118); Top tryscorer: Sunia Turuva (17)

When, and how, will it end? Penrith's domination of the NRL ran into a fourth straight Premiership and their hold on the game down under doesn't look like waning any time soon.

Four straight titles in the salary cap era is a truly amazing record. St George and South Sydney achieved it in yesteryear but never had to offload star players to fit under a cap.

This Ivan Cleary-coached side won its first title in 2021 and since then have watched some big-stage players leave. Stephen Crichton, Matt Burton, Api Koroisau, Kurt Capewell, Viliame Kikau, Tyrone May, Spencer Leniu....over half that squad has gone to pastures new. New faces have been brought in but the crucial factor has been the Panthers' ability to produce and develop its own talent that fits into a well-oiled, on-message team.

Liam Martin deserved his Clive Churchill accolade in the Grand Final but without the brilliant Nathan Cleary on the field for Penrith, Melbourne might have reversed the result. As an on-field general, Cleary has no peers.

The Panthers finished second on the ladder, four points behind the Storm. Cleary played only 13 of the 27 matches due to wrist and shoulder injuries - he was seen to be clutching his shoulder in the semi-final win over Cronulla and in the final. Former Hull KR guest Brad Schneider filled his boots admirably.

Lock Isaah Yeo is not far behind Cleary in his importance to the Panthers. Dylan Edwards was brilliant at fullback, regularly making 200 metres per game. Wingers Brian To'o and Sunia Turuva netted 31 tries between them. In the centres, Bulldogs reject Paul Alamoti was a stand-out, brilliant in the Grand Final.

There will be more missing faces in 2025, with three key members of the Grand Final team - Turuva and Jarome Luai both off to Wests Tigers and James Fisher-Harris to the Warriors. Isaiah Papali'i comes in from the Tigers.

A Las Vegas date with the Sharks in round one will probably rule out a chance for the Panthers to avenge their World Club Challenge defeat of 2023. But a fifth NRL Premiership is a distinct possibility.

MELBOURNE STORM (Runners-up/Minor Premiers)
Top pointscorer: Nick Meaney (232); Top tryscorer: Will Warbrick (15)

Nearly but not quite. Melbourne stormed to the 2024 Minor Premiership, finishing four points clear of Penrith, who went on the be their nemesis in a close and hard-fought Grand Final.

The Storm haven't won the title since 2020 but have been consistently in the top echelons, only see the Panthers collect the ultimate prize.

Supercoach Craig Bellamy demands the highest standards and for the bulk of 2024 his side produced the goods. In the Grand Final the Storm scored the first try through captain and dummy-half Harry Grant before going under to the brilliant Panthers.

But what if Jack Howarth's 'try' had been allowed by the video referee and Nick Meaney had converted. A 12-10 lead could well have changed the outcome.

Nelson Asofa-Solomona's suspension from the semi-final hurt the Storm in the Grand Final as the Melbourne pack eventually succumbed to the big Penrith middle.

And Dally M winner Jahrome Hughes didn't reproduce his outstanding form on the big day. The Kiwi halfback was the best player in the NRL, spending most of the year without big-name Cameron Munster and Ryan Papenhuyzen but still guided the ship masterfully.

Fullback Papenhuyzen was one of the positive stories of the year, coming back from some serious injuries to score 13 tries in 20 games. Nick Meaney top-scored in the centres and rookie Howarth made great progress in the other centre. As did wingers Will Warbrick and Xavier Coates, the latter a real star of the final and he also scored the try of the season to win the home game against the Warriors in round two.

Munster came back from a serious groin injury to shine in the finals; back row Eliesa Katoa was named Dally M second-rower of the year in his second Storm season and Tigers recruit Shawn Blore proved a great signing. Christian Welch, Alec MacDonald and Trent Loiero gave great service.

Prop Stefano Utoikamanu arrives from Wests Tigers and should have a huge year in 2025.

The Storm were only defeated five times in 2024, losing by an average margin of just five points. They are unlikely to go away in 2025.

SYDNEY ROOSTERS (3rd)
Top pointscorer Sam Walker (204); Top tryscorer: Daniel Tupou (21)

The Roosters continued to be just behind the eight ball when it came to challenging the hegemony of Penrith and Melbourne. They were good value for their third-placed finish, winning their semi-final against Manly in spectacular style, but losing their other two comfortably to the big two.

A 16-8 win record was registered, as the Roosters top scored with 738 points. But injuries to two members of their spine, halfback Sam Walker and hooker Brandon Smith, hampered them as they marched into the play-offs.

The back three, James Tedesco, Daniel Tupou and Dominic Young, scored almost half the Roosters' tries between them.

Walker was one of the form playmakers in the NRL until he ruptured an ACL early in the 14-12 round 26 defeat to the Raiders. Smith suffered a serious knee injury too, in the second half of the same game (Elliott Whitehead got a three-match suspension for the hip-drop tackle, in the last game of his nine-season Canberra career).

With star players Joseph Sua'ali'i and Joey Manu both off to rugby union, Super League-bound Jared Waerea-Hargreaves (Hull KR) and Luke Keary (Catalans) and Sitili Tupouniua (Bulldogs) exiting too, there are some huge holes for head coach Trent Robinson to fill.

After suffering with mental issues in 2023, Kangaroos backrower Angus Crichton was left out of the Roosters side that travelled to Las Vegas for the season opener against the Broncos. Then the Roosters announced the signing of Gold Coast Titans forward David Fifita. He walked away from that deal and Crichton announced a move to rugby union in France.

But Crichton dominated the State of Origin series, winning the Wally Lewis Medal as NSW clinched the series. The 28-year-old was rewarded with a two-year contract extension at the Roosters. At the end of the year he was named Dally M second rower of the year.

Chad Townsend arrives from the Cowboys to add experience alongside rookie half Sandon Smith, who didn't let anyone down when Walker was crocked.

And James Tedesco remains. After a relatively poor 2023, the 31-year-old scored 17 tries, his best return since the 2019 Premiership winning season.

NRL

CRONULLA SHARKS (4th)
Top pointscorer: Nicho Hynes (131); Top tryscorer: Ronaldo Mulitalo (18)

It didn't end perfectly for the Sharks but there were plenty of positives about their 2024 season.

Let's face it, after losing nine of their previous ten finals games, the Sharks getting to within one win of the Grand Final was progress. As was the top-four finish.

A lightning start to the season, which saw Cronulla win ten of their first eleven games came to a shuddering halt in round 12 when they fell to a 42-0 error-ridden home defeat by the Panthers.

After a mid-season wobble they won five of their last six games to march into the play-offs, getting a hiding at Melbourne before dominating the Cowboys and then bowing out at Penrith.

Nicho Hynes didn't dominate at halfback as he did in 2023 and in the second half of the season Braydon Trindall took control of the attack. He scored 12 tries and laid on 20 in a brilliant season.

The result was seen wide out with wingers Sione Katoa and Ronaldo Mulitalo utilised again as major strike weapons, bagging 35 tries between them. The Sharks pack could challenge any other in the NRL with the likes of Jack Williams, Teig Wilton, cult hero Tom Hazelton, Siosifa Talakai, Cameron McInnes and Toby Rudolf giving coach Craig Fitzgibbon plenty of reward. Briton Nikora was among the best back-rowers in the game. Hooker Blayke Brailey was the only Shark to play all 27 games and made over a thousand tackles.

The retirement of forward leader Dale Finucane on medical advice three games into the season hurt the Sharks and the loss to injury of another prop, Braden Hamlin-Uele restricted him to 12 games. Middle Royce Hunt is leaving for Wests Tigers.

But the arrival of Dally M Prop of the Year Addin Fonua-Blake from the Warriors will give the Sharks more firepower.

NORTH QUEENSLAND COWBOYS (5th)
Top pointscorer: Valentine Holmes (266); Top tryscorer: Kyle Feldt (23)

Eleventh to fifth and progress to week two of the finals was a big, big improvement from the Cowboys.

But their week-two finals defeat by the Sharks was symptomatic of their season as they were poor enough in the first half to trail by 24-0 at half-time before mounting a stirring comeback that fell short with a 26-18 reverse ending their season.

The week before, winger Kyle Feldt inspired the Cowboys to a 28-16 win against the Knights in the first elimination final in Townsville. The veteran winger ran 281 metres, including an intercept try and a long-range break before tapping back the ball from a kick for Reuben Cotter's clinching try.

But after a glittering career at the Cowboys, Feldt is off to St Helens, and centre Valentine Holmes is leaving too, joining St George Illawarra. The pair posted 346 of the Cowboys' 657 points between them. Feldt finished his Cowboys career with an impressive 23 tries, with Holmes not far behind on 16.

Fullback Scott Drinkwater had another great year, with 26 try assists, while winger Murray Taulagi scored eleven tries, in a back three equal to any in the game. Tom Dearden had his best ever season at five-eighth and was named Dally M five-eighth of the year, lock Cotter was a workaholic and hooker Reece Robson a powerhouse in defence.

Chad Townsend is off to the Roosters after falling out of favour. Former Hull FC man Jake Clifford was given the halfback spot late in the season and failed to make much of an impact.

After a bright start the Cowboys lost their way, recording five straight losses from round six before scraping into the finals with three straight wins, including a 38-30 home success over Melbourne.

Karl Lawton from Manly and Leigh's Kai O'Donnell are additions for next year in the pack but coach Todd Payten needs to find some pointscorers in the absence of Feldt and Holmes.

CANTERBURY BULLDOGS (6th)
Top pointscorer: Matt Burton (187); Top tryscorer: Jacob Kiraz (12)

A first finals berth in eight seasons marked great progress for the Bulldogs as they continued their improvement under Cameron Ciraldo, finishing in sixth spot compared to their 15th place finish the year before. With new captain Stephen Crichton leading the way - he was named Dally M Captain of the Year and centre of the year - the Dogs went from wooden spoon contenders to a finals side.

They enjoyed a five-match winning run that began in round 21 with a hammering of Brisbane Broncos at Suncorp and the Bulldogs looked to be heading for the top four. But a 34-22 defeat to Manly was followed by a 44-6 thrashing by the Cowboys in the last two rounds, both on home turf, that slid them to sixth.

They were the best team against the Sea Eagles in the first week of the eliminator but were finally beaten 24-22 by a couple of wonder plays.

Matt Burton was a standout at five-eighth and a Bulldogs threequarter line netted some wonderful tries. Wing, centre and fullback Jacob Kiraz was as dangerous as any outside back in the NRL, playing all 25 games and scoring a team-high 12 tries. Big Viliame Kikau was a menace with his wide running game.

Josh Addo-Carr was dangerous in his 14 games, bagging 11 tries, though his future at the club was uncertain after a positive drugs test.

Hooker Reed Mahoney was great in his second season at the club after joining them from the Eels. Mahoney topped the NRL in defence with 1,240 tackles for the year, including a 70-tackle effort against the Warriors in round 18.

Prop Tom Amone will join after a stellar three years at Leigh along with Sitili Tupouniua from Sydney Roosters.

MANLY SEA EAGLES (7th)
Top pointscorer: Reuben Garrick (202); Top tryscorer: Tommy Talau (18)

In his second season, head coach Anthony Seibold lifted the Sea Eagles from 12th to seventh on the ladder and then into the Semi-finals, where they met their match in the Sydney Roosters.

The week before, the Sea Eagles twice came from ten points down to defeat the Bulldogs 24-22 in an epic sudden-death eliminator. After trailing 16-6 just before half-time and 22-12 with 25 minutes to play, tries to Daly Cherry-Evans and Tolu Koula ensured Manly kept their season alive.

Against the Roosters, lightning centre Koula was concussed in the first tackle of the game and prop Jake Trbojevic followed him in the next hit.

Still, it was a good year to be a Manly fan as some old faces mixed well with a collection of rookies

Club player of the year, Tom Trbojevic didn't have a completely injury-free year, but he still managed 20 games and scored 17 tries. Centre Reuben Garrick won the club's NRL Leading Point Scorer Award for the sixth consecutive year.

Exciting young threequarter Lehi Hopoate had a sensational debut season in the NRL, with nine tries in 12 games.

Ever present Luke Brooks proved a great signing, taking some of the kicking and playmaking pressure off halfback partner Cherry Evans. And the Manly pack proved powerful all year, with Haumole Olakau'atu getting a deserved call-up for NSW in Origin.

NEWCASTLE KNIGHTS (8th)
Top pointscorer: Kalyn Ponga (104); Top tryscorer: Fletcher Sharpe (11)

Newcastle made the finals for the fourth time in five years under Adam O'Brien after squeaking into the top eight, a superior points difference edging them above Canberra. But this year they bowed out in the first week of the play-offs, suffering a 28-16 loss to the Cowboys in Townsville.

NRL

After winning only two of their first seven games, the Knights had to win four of their last five, including a win over the Dolphins in the final round to sneak into the finals places.

They owed much to their brilliant fullback Kalyn Ponga and it is impossible to over-estimate his importance to the Knights attack.

But the big problem in 2024 was their inability to find a settled halfback pairing. The Knights used eleven different combinations, with incumbents Tyson Gamble and Jackson Hastings falling out of favour over the course of the year. Phoenix Crossland and Jack Cogger finished the season in the halves.

The Knights have salary cap issues and were facing losing some talent. How the they balance their books while bringing in players around Ponga is a tricky one.

Bradman Best had another strong year and starred in Origin. Tyson Frizell had a strong season in the back row and London Broncos product Kai Pearce-Paul showed glimpses of what he can do in his first season in the NRL. So did Will Pryce, brilliant in attack but still with work to do on his defence.

CANBERRA RAIDERS (9th)
Top pointscorer: Jamal Fogarty (90); Top tryscorer: Xavier Savage (15)

There was little confidence hanging around Canberra at the start of the campaign but the Raiders only missed out of a play-off berth by a gnat's whisker.

Three straight wins at the end of the campaign saw them finish ninth, on equal points with Newcastle, with a superior for and against getting the Knights over the line.

Their poor points differential was the fifth worst in the NRL. The Raiders had a reputation for hard-fought small victories against top opponents but when they lost, they lost badly. They let in 40 or more points five times.

The back-to-back wins over the Panthers and the Roosters near the end of the season were memorable, the 22-18 home victory over Penrith in round 15 all the more remarkable as it came the week after a 42-4 embarrassment at the hands of the Cowboys in Townsville.

Dally M Prop of the Year Joseph Tapine was excellent for the Raiders and he'll take over as captain from Elliott Whitehead, who will return to Super League and Catalans Dragons. Morgan Smithies had a sound first season after leaving Wigan for the NRL.

The exit of Jack Wighton at the end of 2023 to South Sydney was softened by the emergence of some fine young Raiders, including playmaker Ethan Strange, utility Kaeo Weekes and top try-scorer Xavier Savage.

Halfback Jamal Fogarty's biceps injury suffered in round seven at Brisbane was a handicap and he wasn't back until round 20.

Warrington's Matty Nicholson will join Smithies for 2025 along with youngsters, halfback Ethan Sanders from Parramatta and outside back Savelio Tamale from the Dragons.

Nic Cotric will join Whitehead at Catalans while veteran Jordan Rapana heads for Hull FC.

DOLPHINS (10th)
Top pointscorer: Jamayne Isaako (223); Top tryscorer: Hamiso Tabuai-Fidow (15)

Thirteenth to tenth in the ladder in a second season is progression for Brisbane's second franchise.

For the second season running the Dolphins looked like finals contenders for the first half of the year before injuries hit them hard and they won just four of their last 14 games. Despite that they were still in the hunt until the last game of the regular season, but they lost 14-6 at Newcastle.

The Dolphins were real entertainers with many a length-of-the-field try in 2024. Hamiso Tabuai-Fidow was the standout of an adventurous attacking machine with 15 tries from 16 games and hooker Jeremy Marshall-King was an effective dummy-half until injured in mid-season. Fullback Trai Fuller was one of the NRL's finds of the season.

All the threequarters benefitted from an expansive approach with Jack Bostock, Dally M

Rookie of the Year, opposite winger Jamayne Isaako, Jake Averillo and Dally M centre of the year centre Herbie Farnworth regularly crossing for tries.

In the middles, the Dolphins had bad luck, with new signing Thomas Flegler playing only four games because of nerve damage to his shoulder.

The Bromwich brothers gave great service and Jesse, who is retiring, will be sorely missed.

Life after Wayne Bennett, who will go back to South Sydney a year before he was due to hand over to Kristian Woolf might be tricky. But British fans, especially those from St Helens, will be well aware of Kristian Woolf's capabilities as a head coach.

ST GEORGE ILLAWARRA DRAGONS (11th)
Top pointscorer: Zac Lomax (186); Top tryscorer: Zac Lomax (14)

At the start of the year there wasn't too much optimism knocking around at Kogarah and WIN Stadium - the Dragons entered the 2024 season as joint favourites to lift the wooden spoon. So an improvement of five places on the ladder should be deemed a success.

But it was almost much better as a fade-out in the final weeks of the year saw the Dragons fall just short of a top-eight finish.

Shane Flanagan took over from Anthony Griffin as head coach after a nightmare 2023 and the Dragons were far more competitive, looking well capable of playing finals footy. But after losing their final three games they drifted away.

That dip in form coincided with the Dragons' top try and pointscorer, Zac Lomax, asking for a release. Lomax was chosen in the Dally M Team of the Year on the wing. He's off to Parramatta.

And captain Ben Hunt, who made 34 try assists for the Dragons in 2024, wants a move back to Queensland with his family.

Beating Penrith and Melbourne were the highlights of a mixed bag of a campaign. The 60-18 loss to the Roosters on ANZAC Day was the low.

Hooker Jacob Liddle was excellent from dummy half, while fullback Tyrell Sloan re-found some great attacking form with 13 tries. Jack De Belin and Tom Eisenhuth both played every game and were strong in the middle while back-rower Jaydn Su'a was another who re-found his best under Flanagan.

Incoming is Damien Cook from South Sydney, one of the best dummy-halves in the game, and the Cowboys strong goalkicking centre Valentine Holmes.

BRISBANE BRONCOS (12th)
Top pointscorer: Reece Walsh (92); Top tryscorer: Deine Mariner (17)

The Broncos' fall from a second-placed finish to 12th within the space of one season was hard to fathom. In just under a year they slumped in the table after a nightmare end to the season, losing ten of their last 13 games.

And in an explosive development at the end of September, head coach and long-time servant of the club Kevin Walters stood down - despite being handed a contract extension in March. Then the almost instantaneous appointment of former Wigan coach Michael Maguire raised plenty of eyebrows. The Broncos players took part in an on-line anonymous survey that sealed Walters' fate. Other reports claimed it was a mutual decision, as Walters cited the pressure of coaching for his decision to walk away with two years remaining on his deal.

Either way it was chaotic end to a miserable season in which the Broncos scored some scintillating tries, but also made the most handling errors in the NRL.

Fullback Reece Walsh was brilliant on his day but prone to basic errors. Lock Patrick Carrigan usually led in metres made and tackles while some other stars of 2023 lost their edge.

There were injuries affecting captain Adam Reynolds who only played 13 games and Walsh only managed 14.

NRL

NEW ZEALAND WARRIORS (13th)
Top pointscorer: Shaun Johnson (78); Top tryscorer: Dallin Watene-Zelezniak (15)

A fourth-placed finish in 2023 down to 13th within 12 months can't be cast as anything but a decline for the Warriors.

It was an up and down season after two narrow defeats in the opening rounds to the Sharks and Storm before three wins on the bounce and then a home draw with Manly and four losses on a row. And then they beat the Panthers.

The run-in was disastrous and included a round-16, 66-6 shellacking at the Gold Coast.

After a dream season in 2023, halfback Shaun Johnson experienced a disappointing final year in the NRL.

The return of Roger Tuivasa-Sheck from two years in rugby union didn't have the effect that was expected. He wasn't alone in disappointing. Only winger Dallin Watene-Zelezniak scored more than ten tries. Hooker Wayde Egan was consistently the best for the Warriors all season.

At the start of the year, Addin Fonua-Blake, Dally M prop of the year in 2023, stunned the Warriors when he asked for a release from his contract at the end of the season to move back to Sydney to be closer to his family. He'll be replaced for 2025 by Panthers ferocious prop James Fisher-Harris who himself was persuaded to come home to New Zealand.

On the plus side, the Warriors sold out every game in 2024.

GOLD COAST TITANS (14th)
Top pointscorer: Alofiana Khan-Pereira (96); Top tryscorer: Alofiana Khan-Pereira (24)

The Titans finished fourth last in the ladder, the same position where they ended up 12 months before.

They started the 2024 NRL season poorly, losing their opening six matches. And their season was effectively almost over before it had a chance to get going when captain Tino Fa'asuamaleaui suffered a season-ending ACL rupture in their second game, a 32-0 round three defeat at the Bulldogs.

The run of defeats ended with a 27-24 win at the Warriors and they beat them again, at home in round 16, by 66-6, the club's biggest ever victory. Beating the Dolphins and the Broncos in back-to-back weeks late on was another highlight. The Titans put on a magical attacking display and handed Brisbane a 46-18 loss to all but end their 2024 hopes.

At times, the Gold Coast attack was breathtaking. Winger Alofiana Khan-Pereira scored 24 tries, becoming the first Titan to ever end top try-scorer in the NRL - in a team that finished 14th.

Head coach Des Hasler couldn't improve on the year before as injuries hit his team hard. Key backs Jayden Campbell, AJ Brimson and Harley Smith-Shields missed large slices of the season.

The Titans unearthed one of the best new faces of 2024 in brilliant ball-running fullback Keano Kini, while Brian Kelly enjoyed his best season and veteran Kieran Foran led the team in the absence of Tino. David Fifita, still at times unstoppable while taking a back seat at others. In May, he agreed a move to the Roosters but then apparently changed his mind.

PARRAMATTA EELS (15th)
Top pointscorer: Clint Gutherson (112); Top tryscorer: Maika Sivo (17)

The Eels have fallen from runners-up to 16th in the space of two seasons and only avoided the wooden spoon with a last-day win over Wests Tigers.

They started off well enough with two wins from the first three rounds. But in the second of those key halfback Mitchell Moses suffered a fracture to his left foot, despite playing a starring role through to the end of the 28-24 win. Parramatta lost eight of their next ten games.

Head coach Brad Arthur was unceremoniously sacked in May after almost eleven years at the helm. Assistant Trent Barrett took charge. The Eels sat 14th at the time and the search for a new head coach proved difficult.

Wayne Bennett was approached, Michael Cheika, Michael Maguire, Jason Ryles, Josh Hannay and Brian McDermott were all on the shortlist. Ryles eventually got the job on a four-year contract.

Parramatta lost six straight between rounds 14 and 21, during which time they had no Moses, J'maine Hopgood, Junior Paulo or Maika Sivo. In an injury plagued season, defensively the Eels were the worst team in the competition, missing more tackles at an average of almost 40 per game.

Some of Parra's young stars have left, outside back Blaize Talagi to Penrith, halfback Ethan Sanders the Raiders and dummy-half Matt Arthur to the Knights.

Kangaroos prop Reagan Campbell-Gillard is also leaving and his power in the middle will be hard to replace. But Zac Lomax is arriving after an excellent season for the Dragons..

SOUTH SYDNEY RABBITOHS (16th)
Top pointscorer: Latrell Mitchell (98); Top tryscorer: Jacob Gagai (9)

South Sydney supporters are getting used to missing out on the finals. Once again the Rabbits were predicted to make the top-eight but they failed in even more spectacular style in 2024, finishing next to the bottom of the ladder, only two points above the bottom, with with just seven wins.

The signs weren't good early on. The Bunnies' poor form spilled into 2024 after the dramatic departure of Sam Burgess at the end of the previous season. They got off to a bad start with a 36-24 loss to Manly in Las Vegas and then eight more from their next nine games.

That led to the sacking of head coach Jason Demetriou at the end of April. Assistant coach Ben Hornby took over for the remainder of the 2024 season. Wayne Bennett will return in 2025 on a three-year contract. Bennett coached Souths from 2019-2021 and led them to a grand final in his final season before heading to the new Dolphins franchise.

In the middle of the season the Rabbits won five straight games, two of them against Parramatta, but seven straight defeats in the run-in killed off their season.

Star fullback Latrell Mitchell had a season to forget. Due to injury and suspension, he played in only eleven games. But there was poor form all through the side.

Jack Wighton was one of the highlights in his first season at the club and won the George Piggins Medal as South Sydney's best and fairest.

Hooker Damien Cook is going to the Dragons while Lewis Dodd's arrival from St Helens will be closely watched by British fans. Prop Tom Burgess is taking the return trip to join Huddersfield.

WESTS TIGERS (17th)
Top pointscorer: Apisai Koroisau (106); Top tryscorer: Jahream Bula (10)

Three in a row. Wooden spoons that is. Another tough year for long-suffering Wests Tigers fans saw their side in with a chance of relegating Parramatta to the bottom spot on the last day of the regular season, but they blew it big-style at Campbelltown, conceding 60 points to the Eels.

Early season there was promise with round three and four wins over Cronulla and the Eels. But nine defeats followed before back-to-back wins over the Titans and the Raiders, seven more losses and real hope after wins over South Sydney and Manly before clinching the wooden spoon in style against the Eels.

Rookie coach Benji Marshall said he was optimistic about the club's future. The arrivals of seasoned Premiership winners Jarome Luai and Sunia Turuva from Penrith will add experience, with Luai expected to bring out even more of precocious teenage halfback Lachlan Galvin.

Inexperience was a major factor as Marshall gave NRL debuts to 12 players. There is a nucleus of brilliant young stars, fullback Jahream Bula and Galvin heading the list.

On-field ill-discipline didn't help. The Tigers had 16 players sin-binned and eight suspensions involving six players. Hull FC-bound Aidan Sezer and Justin Olam were suspended twice.

Formidable prop Stefano Utoikamanu is off to Melbourne and he'll be replaced by Cronulla's Royce Hunt. Isaiah Papali'i will leave for the Panthers. John Bateman might also return from his loan spell at Warrington.

NRL

DALLY M AWARDS

Dally M Medal (Player of the Year):
Jahrome Hughes (Melbourne Storm) *(right)*
Provan Summons Medal (True Spirit of the Game):
Tyrone Munro (South Sydney Rabbitohs)
Coach of the Year: Craig Bellamy (Melbourne Storm)
Captain of the Year: Stephen Crichton (Canterbury Bulldogs)
Rookie of the Year: Jack Bostock (Dolphins)

STATE CHAMPIONSHIP *(winners of NSW and Queensland Cups)*
Sunday 6th October 2024
Newtown Jets 18 ....Norths Devils 20
(at Accor Stadium, Sydney)

NRLW GRAND FINAL *(Women's Premiership)*
Sunday 6th October 2024
Cronulla Sharks 28 .... Sydney Roosters 32
(at Accor Stadium, Sydney)

STATE OF ORIGIN - GAME I

Wednesday 5th June 2024

NEW SOUTH WALES 10 QUEENSLAND 38

NEW SOUTH WALES: 1 James Tedesco (Sydney Roosters); 2 Brian To'o (Penrith Panthers); 3 Stephen Crichton (Canterbury Bulldogs); 4 Joseph-Aukuso Suaali'i (Sydney Roosters); 5 Zac Lomax (St George Illawarra Dragons); 6 Jarome Luai (Penrith Panthers); 7 Nicho Hynes (Cronulla Sharks); 8 Jake Trbojevic (Manly Sea Eagles) (C); 9 Reece Robson (North Queensland Cowboys); 10 Payne Haas (Brisbane Broncos); 11 Liam Martin (Penrith Panthers); 12 Angus Crichton (Sydney Roosters); 13 Cameron McInnes (Cronulla Sharks). Subs (all used): 14 Isaah Yeo (Penrith Panthers); 15 Haumole Olakau'atu (Manly Sea Eagles); 16 Spencer Leniu (Sydney Roosters); 17 Hudson Young (Canberra Raiders).
Tries: Tedesco (14), Lomax (44); **Goals:** Hynes 1/2.
Dismissal: Suaali'i (8) - high tackle on Walsh.
QUEENSLAND: 1 Reece Walsh (Brisbane Broncos); 2 Xavier Coates (Melbourne Storm); 3 Valentine Holmes (North Queensland Cowboys); 4 Hamiso Tabuai-Fidow (Dolphins); 5 Murray Taulagi (North Queensland Cowboys); 6 Tom Dearden (North Queensland Cowboys); 7 Daly Cherry-Evans (Manly Sea Eagles) (C); 8 Reuben Cotter (North Queensland Cowboys); 9 Ben Hunt (St George Illawarra Dragons); 10 Lindsay Collins (Sydney Roosters); 11 Jaydn Su'A (St George Illawarra Dragons); 12 Jeremiah Nanai (North Queensland Cowboys); 13 Patrick Carrigan (Brisbane Broncos). Subs (all used): 14 Harry Grant (Melbourne Storm); 15 Moeaki Fotuaika (Gold Coast Titans); 16 J'maine Hopgood (Parramatta Eels); 17 Selwyn Cobbo (Brisbane Broncos). 18th man (used): 18 Felise Kaufusi (Dolphins).
Tries: Hunt (5, 67), Tabuai-Fidow (19, 24, 79), Coates (71);
Goals: Holmes 7/7.
Rugby Leaguer & League Express Men of the Match:
New South Wales: Zac Lomax; *Queensland:* Hamiso Tabuai-Fidow.
Penalty count: 2-2; **Half-time:** 6-20; **Referee:** Ashley Klein;
Attendance: 77,214 *(at Accor Stadium, Sydney)*.

STATE OF ORIGIN - GAME II

Wednesday 26th June 2024

NEW SOUTH WALES 38 QUEENSLAND 18

NEW SOUTH WALES: 1 Dylan Edwards (Penrith Panthers); 2 Brian To'o (Penrith Panthers); 3 Latrell Mitchell (South Sydney Rabbitohs); 4 Stephen Crichton (Canterbury Bulldogs); 5 Zac Lomax (St George Illawarra Dragons); 6 Jarome Luai (Penrith Panthers); 7 Mitchell Moses (Parramatta Eels); 8 Jake Trbojevic (Manly Sea Eagles) (C); 9 Reece Robson (North Queensland Cowboys); 10 Payne Haas (Brisbane Broncos); 11 Liam Martin (Penrith Panthers); 12 Angus Crichton (Sydney Roosters); 13 Cameron Murray (South Sydney Rabbitohs). Subs (all used): 14 Connor Watson (Sydney Roosters); 15 Isaah Yeo (Penrith Panthers); 16 Haumole Olakau'atu (Manly Sea Eagles); 17 Spencer Leniu (Sydney Roosters).
Tries: Martin (11), To'o (18, 27), Lomax (24, 39), Mitchell (33), Edwards (62);
Goals: Lomax 5/7.
Sin bin: Martin (51) - unsporting conduct.
QUEENSLAND: 1 Reece Walsh (Brisbane Broncos); 2 Xavier Coates (Melbourne Storm); 3 Valentine Holmes (North Queensland Cowboys); 4 Hamiso Tabuai-Fidow (Dolphins); 5 Murray Taulagi (North Queensland Cowboys); 6 Tom Dearden (North Queensland Cowboys); 7 Daly Cherry-Evans (Manly Sea Eagles) (C); 8 Reuben Cotter (North Queensland Cowboys); 9 Ben Hunt (St George Illawarra Dragons); 10 Lindsay Collins (Sydney Roosters); 11 Jaydn Su'A (St George Illawarra Dragons); 12 Jeremiah Nanai (North Queensland Cowboys); 13 Patrick Carrigan (Brisbane Broncos). Subs (all used): 14 Harry Grant (Melbourne Storm); 15 Moeaki Fotuaika (Gold Coast Titans); 16 Felise Kaufusi (Dolphins); 17 Kurt Capewell (New Zealand Warriors).
Tries: Nanai (54), Tabuai-Fidow (59), Taulagi (68); **Goals:** Holmes 3/3.
Sin bin: Carrigan (51) - fighting.
Rugby Leaguer & League Express Men of the Match:
New South Wales: Mitchell Moses; *Queensland:* Patrick Carrigan.
Penalty count: 6-9; **Half-time:** 34-0; **Referee:** Ashley Klein;
Attendance: 90,084 *(at Melbourne Cricket Ground)*.

STATE OF ORIGIN - GAME III

Wednesday 17th July 2024

QUEENSLAND 4 NEW SOUTH WALES 14

QUEENSLAND: 1 Reece Walsh (Brisbane Broncos); 2 Selwyn Cobbo (Brisbane Broncos); 3 Dane Gagai (Newcastle Knights); 4 Hamiso Tabuai-Fidow (Dolphins); 5 Valentine Holmes (North Queensland Cowboys); 6 Tom Dearden (North Queensland Cowboys); 7 Daly Cherry-Evans (Manly Sea Eagles) (C); 15 Moeaki Fotuaika (Gold Coast Titans); 14 Harry Grant (Melbourne Storm); 16 Felise Kaufusi (Dolphins); 8 Reuben Cotter (North Queensland Cowboys); 11 Kurt Capewell (New Zealand Warriors); 13 Patrick Carrigan (Brisbane Broncos). Subs (all used): 9 Ben Hunt (St George Illawarra Dragons); 10 Lindsay Collins (Sydney Roosters); 12 Jeremiah Nanai (North Queensland Cowboys); 17 Kalyn Ponga (Newcastle Knights). 18th man (used): 18 Trent Loiero (Melbourne Storm).
Goals: Holmes 2/2.
Sin bin: Nanai (31) - fighting.
NEW SOUTH WALES: 1 Dylan Edwards (Penrith Panthers); 2 Brian To'o (Penrith Panthers); 3 Bradman Best (Newcastle Knights); 4 Stephen Crichton (Canterbury Bulldogs); 5 Zac Lomax (St George Illawarra Dragons); 6 Jarome Luai (Penrith Panthers); 7 Mitchell Moses (Parramatta Eels); 8 Jake Trbojevic (Manly Sea Eagles) (C); 9 Reece Robson (North Queensland Cowboys); 10 Payne Haas (Brisbane Broncos); 11 Liam Martin (Penrith Panthers); 12 Angus Crichton (Sydney Roosters); 13 Cameron Murray (South Sydney Rabbitohs). Subs (all used): 14 Connor Watson (Sydney Roosters); 15 Isaah Yeo (Penrith Panthers); 16 Mitch Barnett (New Zealand Warriors); 17 Spencer Leniu (Sydney Roosters).
Tries: Best (65), Moses (68); **Goals:** Lomax 3/3.
Sin bin: Murray (31) - fighting.
Rugby Leaguer & League Express Men of the Match:
Queensland: Patrick Carrigan; *New South Wales:* Dylan Edwards.
Penalty count: 6-9; **Half-time:** 2-0; **Referee:** Ashley Klein;
Attendance: 52,457 *(at Suncorp Stadium, Brisbane)*.

Wally Lewis Medal (Man of the Series):
Angus Crichton (New South Wales).

STATE OF ORIGIN
Singin' the Blues

Michael Maguire wrested the State of Origin Shield from Billy Slater's grip, overseeing a stirring New South Wales charge in a classic decider on enemy soil.

Prior to the series, the Blues had won just five of 22 game-three deciding matches, including a mere two of 13 in Queensland. But in his first year as Blues coach, Maguire infused his side with a defensive steel that laid the foundation for a breathtaking series turnaround.

Joseph Sua'ali'i's dismissal for a high shot on Reece Walsh just seven minutes into game one set the tone for an explosive campaign. The Maroons eventually strolled to a 38-10 victory in Sydney, but were rattled by the Blues' onslaught three weeks later in Melbourne.

The infusion of halfback Mitchell Moses, fullback Dylan Edwards, centre Latrell Mitchell, lock Cameron Murray and substitute Connor Watson proved the impetus for a stunning reversal and they carried that form north of the border.

Hamiso Tabuai-Fidow's thrilling hat-trick spearheaded Queensland's dramatic 38-10 game-one victory over twelve-man New South Wales at the Accor Stadium in Sydney.

The contest looked to be over inside seven minutes, when Ashley Klein dismissed Joseph Sua'ali'i for a reckless high shot on Reece Walsh, which knocked Walsh out before he hit the ground.

A thrashing loomed when Tabuai-Fidow - who filled Walsh's boots at fullback - scored a quick-fire double. But the gritty Blues worked their way back into the arm-wrestle despite the numerical disadvantage before Ben Hunt completed his brace in the 67th minute to open the floodgates.

Veteran captain Daly Cherry-Evans nabbed the man-of-the-match award for a cool-headed display featuring two try-assists and a vital 40/20.

The 28-point margin was Queensland's biggest ever victory in Sydney.

Despite the lopsided scoreline, new Blues coach Maguire could salvage some positives out of his first game in the interstate arena. Winger Zac Lomax made an impressive Origin debut, claiming a second-half try that had optimistic Blues fans dreaming of a miracle, while hooker Reece Robson and halfback Nicho Hynes vindicated their selection with solid displays and backrowers Angus Crichton and Liam Martin were lion-hearted.

Slater didn't tinker much with the formula that helped him win his first two series at the helm of the sunshine state. Injuries to stand-off Cameron Munster (groin) and enforcer Tino Fa'asuamaleaui (ACL) forced a slight reshuffle, with Cowboy Tom Dearden beating Bronco Ezra Mam to the number six jersey. Snubbing destructive Titans backrower David Fifita for St George Illawarra's Jaydn Su'A was something of a bombshell, although Su'A well and truly justified his selection.

The lightweight bench of hooker Harry Grant, outside back Selwyn Cobbo, prop Moeaki Fotuaika and debutant lock J'maine Hopgood also raised some eyebrows, although Walsh's concussion made Cobbo's inclusion look like a masterstroke.

Maguire, on the other hand, stamped his authority on a new-look teamsheet, entrusting Sharks half Hynes with the playmaking reins in the absence of Nathan Cleary (hamstring), alongside Cowboys hooker Robson, who was favoured over Wests' Api Koroisau.

State of Origin

Maguire also axed captain James Tedesco for Dylan Edwards - until the Penrith fullback succumbed to a late quad injury, awkwardly rushing Tedesco back into a team now skippered by Manly veteran Jake Trbojevic.

Sua'ali'i, Lomax, Cameron McInnes, Haumole Olakau'atu and Spencer Leniu all made their bows for the Blues.

The Maroons struck first on the back of a Jeremiah Nanai charge. Cherry-Evans bamboozled Jarome Luai at marker to hand Hunt the opening points.

Then, from the restart, Sua'ali'i became just the sixth player in Origin history to be sent off.

A ruck infringement by Martin handed Queensland another two points off Valentine Holmes' boot. NSW kept in touch, however, when Luai delivered a deft grubber for Tedesco to score his first Origin try since 2020.

With Tabuai-Fidow shifting to fullback and Cobbo slotting into the centres, the Maroons hammered the edge of the field left undermanned by Sua'ali'i's send-off. That was exactly where the Hammer collected his first two tries, linking up with Cobbo and winger Murray Taulagi in near-identical fashion twice in five minutes.

Finishing the half on the back foot, the Queenslanders seemed content to sit on their 20-6 lead heading into the break, knowing they hadn't forfeited a half-time lead since 2014.

But one man and 14 points down, the Blues refused to give up.

Minutes after the restart, Hynes placed the ball on the head of aerial specialist Zac Lomax, who soared above Cobbo to keep his side in touch.

Then when Martin pulverised Xavier Coates on a kick receipt and a swarm of blue jumpers rattled the ball out of Holmes' grasp, the hosts were on top.

But a Cherry-Evans 40/20 halted their momentum, and it was only a matter of time before the men in maroon broke through.

The Bunker denied try claims to Nanai and Holmes either side of the hour mark, although Hunt eventually put the game beyond doubt. Brian To'o managed to reel in a runaway Coates but the 34-year-old Dragons star Hunt scampered through the fatigued NSW defence to streak 50 metres for the match sealer.

Sniffing blood, Cherry-Evans also grabbed an intercept, snaffling an Isaah Yeo pass then stabbing a well-judged kick inside for Coates to score.

And with just seconds remaining, Tabuai-Fidow connected with Dearden to sprint away for his third try of the evening.

Queensland sat in the box seat to claim their third straight series ahead of game two at the Melbourne Cricket Ground.

New South Wales' new faces spearheaded a record-breaking first-half blitz to send the State of Origin series to a decider, eventually running out 38-18 winners in Melbourne.

Recalled halfback Mitchell Moses set up four tries - including one to debutant fullback Dylan Edwards - while Latrell Mitchell rat riot down the left edge in his first interstate outing since 2021. South Sydney team-mate Cameron Murray got through a mountain of work in the middle.

Wingers Brian To'o and Zac Lomax each bagged a brace as the Blues sprinted to a 34-0 lead after a frightening first 40 minutes, as the masterful kicking game of Moses and halves partner Jarome Luai put their side in complete control.

With Michael Maguire's inclusions leading the way, the men in blue smashed the record half-time advantage (21-0 by Queensland in 1983) to wrap up the win by the break.

Queensland stemmed the bleeding in a spicy second half but the damage was done.

NSW enjoy a good record at the Melbourne Cricket Ground, having won five of their six clashes.

Game one victor Billy Slater made two changes to the line-up that thumped the Blues in Sydney three weeks earlier, replacing injured subs J'maine Hopgood and Selwyn Cobbo with veteran forwards Felise Kaufusi and Kurt Capewell.

Maguire made even deeper cuts in his bid to send the series to a decider. The rookie Origin boss dropped fullback James Tedesco, halfback Nicho Hynes, lock Cameron McInnes and forward Hudson Young, while game one villain Sua'ali'i was suspended, making way for Edwards, Moses, Mitchell, Cameron Murray and Connor Watson, who made his bow off the bench.

After a patient start and a mountain of pressure, the Blues broke through when Moses sent Liam Martin steaming through the Maroons' goal-line defence.

Things got even better for Maguire's men when Mitchell unleashed a back-handed offload to his outside man To'o, who made no mistake in the left corner.

Lomax delivered the moment of the evening when he showed off aerial skills that wouldn't look out of place at an Australian rules football match at the MCG, reeling in a Moses bomb by soaring above opposite man Murray Taulagi.

When a twisting Moses grubber gave To'o his second, the floodgates began to open.

And the points were absolutely flowing once Mitchell marked his interstate return with a four-pointer, after a Stephen Crichton offload released Edwards in the build-up.

Just when Queensland enjoyed a bit of ball at the right end of the field, Stephen Crichton snaffled a stunning intercept to give NSW the ascendancy yet again.

With little over a minute until the half-time siren, Lomax scored his second, taking advantage of some fatigued Maroons defence. The Dragons winger's sideline conversion made the margin 34 points.

Both sides were desperate to seize the momentum heading into the decider in a testy second half.

Referee Ashley Klein sin-binned Martin for rubbing Jaydn Su'A's hair after an error, sparking a melee that also cost Patrick Carrigan 10 minutes on the sideline.

Queensland finally troubled the scorers when Cherry-Evans sent Jeremiah Nanai busting through, then a deft Taulagi kick allowed Tabuai-Fidow to extend his extraordinary try-scoring record in the Origin arena - the Hammer's ninth try in six outings.

The Blues did add a couple of moments to the highlights reel, when Angus Crichton pulverised Val Holmes, then Edwards notched his maiden Origin try on the end of it.

A long Moses ball gave the Penrith fullback plenty of space and the first-gamer beat Tabuai-Fidow and Walsh to the whitewash.

Queensland did claim the final try after Cherry-Evans put Taulagi into the left corner.

It was a classic decider on enemy soil.

Maguire's men dominated the first half with nothing on the scoreboard to show for it, but the dam wall burst deep in the second half, when Bradman Best and Mitchell Moses crossed within three minutes of each other.

Chasing their third consecutive series victory under Slater, the Maroons defended bravely before the blue wave blew them away at the death to secure the series with a 14-4 win.

Referee Ashley Klein sin-binned Jeremiah Nanai and Cameron Murray for their role in a first-half melee.

Blues fullback Dylan Edwards powered through a mountain of work, halves Moses and Jarome Luai split the game open late, and tireless back-rower Angus Crichton claimed the Wally Lewis Medal as man of the series.

NSW steamed into Suncorp Stadium riding a wave of momentum from their thumping Game Two victory in Melbourne, but carrying the baggage of a historically dreadful record in deciders, especially in Brisbane.

Aiming to add 2024 to 1994 and 2005 on that list of rare NSW triumphs in live game threes in hostile territory, Maguire's men patiently outlasted their rivals.

Maguire replaced injured talisman Lachlan Mitchell (foot) with Knights tyro Best, who entered the clash under his own injury cloud (hamstring). Manly forward Haumole Olakau'atu also made way for Mitch Barnett on the bench, handing the 30-year-old Warriors hard man an interstate debut on the biggest of stages.

Slater recalled experienced Newcastle pair Dane Gagai and Kalyn Ponga for their first Origin appearances since the 2022 decider in Brisbane, when Ponga inspired a second-half comeback to clinch victory for the hosts. Incumbent wingers Xavier Coates and Murray Taulagi

State of Origin

New South Wales' Mitchell Moses heads towards the Queensland tryline during Origin III

both succumbed to hamstring injuries, with Selwyn Cobbo returning to favour and Gagai slotting into the centres, shifting Val Holmes to the flank. Dragons backrower Jaydn Su'A dropped out for the X-factor Ponga on the bench, while Slater swung a last-minute surprise, bringing named subs Moeaki Fotuaika, Harry Grant and Felise Kaufusi into the starting line-up for Lindsay Collins, Ben Hunt and Nanai.

A first half of white-knuckle intensity featured as many sin-binnings as it did points.

From the moment Payne Haas took the first hit-up into a wall of maroon jumpers, the Queenslanders defended like men possessed. Daly Cherry-Evans' ankle tap on Best saved a try in the first minute, setting the tone for a desperate 40 minutes without the ball for the hosts.

After the frantic opening simmered into an unflinching arm wrestle, the game exploded again once Cherry-Evans and Luai traded pleasantries. Nanai and Murray ended up in the bin for escalating the all-in melee, which only led to more pressure on the Queensland line.

The Maroons absorbed five penalties, three set restarts, four goal-line drop-outs and 22 play-the-balls inside their 20-metre zone. But they refused to yield.

Instead, they headed to the sheds with a two-point buffer courtesy of Holmes' boot after firebrand Spencer Leniu conceded a penalty for hitting Cherry-Evans late.

The Blues continued their assault following the restart and soon erased their arrears through a Zac Lomax penalty goal resulting from a Patrick Carrigan shot on Moses.

Ponga's injection in the 52nd minute briefly gave Queensland the upper hand. And when Grant caught Reece Robson offside at marker, another Holmes penalty nudged the hosts ahead.

But with 15 minutes remaining, NSW set upon their flagging opponents.

Seconds after coming on, Watson forced an offload that created space for Luai to race into. The stand-off found support in Best, who bounced off club teammates Gagai and Ponga to claim the go-ahead try.

Lomax nailed another clutch shot at goal to stretch the margin to four, soon to be even more once Moses spied an opportunity moments later. Taking the ball 20 metres out, the halfback accelerated between Grant and Hamiso Tabuai-Fidow, then wrong-footed Walsh at the back to complete a superb solo try.

Blues backrower Angus Crichton took home the Wally Lewis Medal as the player of the Origin series. It marked a remarkable comeback for the player who had been playing reserve grade at the start of the year.

5
INTERNATIONAL YEAR

INTERNATIONALS
All good in Wane's world

England completed a 2-0 series victory over Samoa in the autumn to back up their series win over Tonga 12 months before. In the week leading up to the second Test, news broke that Australia would almost certainly tour England in 2025 for a full-blown Ashes series.

Samoa had knocked England out of the World Cup two years before and though they were missing several high-profile stars, their squad was made up of NRL players and provided Shaun Wane's side with two strong challenges in the Tests at Wigan and Leeds.

In the first Test at the Brick Community Stadium in Wigan, England held off a physical Samoa side to claim a hard-fought 34-18 victory.

Shaun Wane's men gave a dominant display, largely bossing the middle of the field, with their captain George Williams a menace to the Samoan defence and his halfback partner Harry Smith constantly causing them problems with a finely judged kicking game.

England 24-man squad *(named 16th October 2024)*: Matty Ashton (Warrington Wolves), John Bateman (Warrington Wolves), Tom Burgess (South Sydney Rabbitohs), Daryl Clark (St Helens), Ben Currie (Warrington Wolves), Herbie Farnworth (Dolphins), Ethan Havard (Wigan Warriors), Chris Hill (Huddersfield Giants), Morgan Knowles (St Helens), Matty Lees (St Helens), Mikey Lewis (Hull KR), Liam Marshall (Wigan Warriors), Mike McMeeken (Catalans Dragons), Harry Newman (Leeds Rhinos), Junior Nsemba (Wigan Warriors), Kai Pearce-Paul (Newcastle Knights), Victor Radley (Sydney Roosters), Harry Smith (Wigan Warriors), Morgan Smithies (Canberra Raiders), Luke Thompson (Wigan Warriors), Danny Walker (Warrington Wolves), Jack Welsby (St Helens), George Williams (Warrington Wolves), Dom Young (Sydney Roosters).
Also in 31-man squad *(named 6th September 2024)*: Tyler Dupree (Wigan Warriors), James Harrison (Warrington Wolves), Tom Johnstone (Catalans Dragons), Jez Litten (Hull KR), Elliot Minchella (Hull KR), Robbie Mulhern (Leigh Leopards), Jake Wardle (Wigan Warriors).

Samoa squad *(named 10th October 2024)*: John Asiata (Leigh Leopards), Shawn Blore (Melbourne Storm), Gordon Chan Kum Tong (Manly Sea Eagles), Luciano Leilua (St George Illawarra Dragons), Ricky Leutele (Leigh Leopards), Jarome Luai (Penrith Panthers), Deine Mariner (Brisbane Broncos), Terrell May (Sydney Roosters), Anthony Milford (Dolphins), Francis Molo (St George Illawarra Dragons), Jeremiah Nanai (North Queensland Cowboys), Josiah Pahulu (Gold Coast Titans), Keenan Palasia (Gold Coast Titans), Junior Pauga (Sydney Roosters), Paul Roache (New Zealand Warriors), Simi Sasagi (Canberra Raiders), Jeral Skelton (Canterbury Bulldogs), Izack Tago (Penrith Panthers), Jake Tago (Parramatta Eels), Blaize Talagi (Parramatta Eels), Jazz Tevaga (New Zealand Warriors), Roger Tuivasa-Sheck (New Zealand Warriors), Lazarus Vaalepu (Melbourne Storm).

Wane had originally selected a 31-man squad for the series and he cut that down to 24 before leaving out five players in order to announce his 19-man squad for the game on the Friday. The five players left out were Danny Walker, Morgan Smithies, Chris Hill, the suspended Luke Thompson and his Wigan teammate Liam Marshall.

In overcast conditions, Samoa captain Jarome Luai laid a shirt in tribute to former Wigan and Samoa star Va'aiga Tuigamala and the men in blue performed a typically intimidating Siva Tau, ending forehead to forehead with the England players on the half-way line, leading to a ferocious first defensive set that was spoiled when Samoa gave away the opening penalty,

The game seemed to be settling into a midfield stalemate before Daryl Clark made a break up the middle that brought a set restart and, on the last, Smith, Victor Radley and Williams sent Herbie Farnworth over, with Smith goaling.

Samoa continued to kick to ever-safe Dom Young, whose catch and instant pass allowed Jack Welsby to make a half break, with Ashton poking his nose through and gaining another penalty. Ethan Havard and Kai Pearce-Paul made ground and Williams again gave the scoring pass for Ashton to step inside and go over, Smith wide with the conversion attempt.

Smith did well to cut off Roger Tuivasa-Sheck's kick and Ashton again elicited a penalty and, with a second set restart, Welsby found Harry Newman back on the inside, his fine ball releasing Williams to pull out of Tuivasa-Sheck's tackle to score the third try.

Clark's pass to Mike McMeeken, which saw him stroll over between the posts, was ruled

Internationals

No way through the Samoa defence for Kai Pearce-Paul

forward, and Deine Mariner then picked off Clark's long ball from half way and raced clear to the posts to cut the deficit to ten points at half-time.

Samoa had been penalised four times and conceded as many set restarts in the opening 40 minutes. But with HIA's to Jazz Tevaga and Jeremiah Nanai reversed at the break, they started the second half brightly.

But the first penalty they conceded in the second half proved to be their undoing, as Radley, Williams and Smith combined, and Farnworth gave a superb flat pass to send Radley over.

As the game opened out, however, Samoa looked increasingly dangerous running on the last tackle, which bore fruit when Luai instigated a move that saw the ball flash through the hands of prop Lazarus Vaalepu, Anthony Milford and Tuivasa-Sheck, with Luai's reverse pass sending Mariner in for his second try.

Williams grubbered for Newman, who found Young, but his pass was forward. McMeeken then gave a midfield offload and Luai got a hand to Clark's pass. Welsby hacked on and regathered and was just brought down by Tuivasa-Sheck, but Ashton again twisted over from a quick play-the-ball.

Then Young was set clear and away, with Mikey Lewis – on around the hour mark at hooker – in support on the inside to touch down.

Samoa refused to throw in the towel as Pearce-Paul, who was otherwise solid, lost possession coming out of his own quarter, with Gordon Chan Kum Tong gathering and holding off Ashton to get the ball down between the posts.

A game that had been played in great spirit otherwise erupted in midfield with Terrell May and Matty Lees coming into contact two minutes before the end.

FIRST TEST

Sunday 27th October 2024

ENGLAND 34 SAMOA 18

ENGLAND: 1 Jack Welsby (St Helens); 2 Dom Young (Sydney Roosters); 3 Harry Newman (Leeds Rhinos); 4 Herbie Farnworth (Dolphins); 5 Matty Ashton (Warrington Wolves); 6 George Williams (Warrington Wolves) (C); 7 Harry Smith (Wigan Warriors); 8 Ethan Havard (Wigan Warriors); 9 Daryl Clark (St Helens); 10 Matty Lees (St Helens); 11 John Bateman (Warrington Wolves); 12 Kai Pearce-Paul (Newcastle Knights); 13 Victor Radley (Sydney Roosters). Subs (all used): 14 Mikey Lewis (Hull KR); 15 Morgan Knowles (St Helens); 16 Mike McMeeken (Catalans Dragons); 17 Tom Burgess (South Sydney Rabbitohs).
Tries: Farnworth (7), Ashton (14, 58), Williams (20), Radley (48), Lewis (71);
Goals: Smith 5/6.
SAMOA: 1 Roger Tuivasa-Sheck (New Zealand Warriors); 2 Jeral Skelton (Canterbury Bulldogs); 3 Izack Tago (Penrith Panthers); 4 Junior Pauga (Sydney Roosters); 5 Deine Mariner (Brisbane Broncos); 6 Anthony Milford (Dolphins); 7 Jarome Luai (Penrith Panthers) (C); 8 Francis Molo (St George Illawarra Dragons); 9 Jazz Tevaga (New Zealand Warriors); 10 Terrell May (Sydney Roosters); 11 Shawn Blore (Melbourne Storm); 12 Jeremiah Nanai (North Queensland Cowboys); 13 John Asiata (Leigh Leopards). Subs (all used): 14 Blaize Talagi (Parramatta Eels); 15 Luciano Leilua (St George Illawarra Dragons); 17 Lazarus Vaalepu (Melbourne Storm); 18 Gordon Chan Kum Tong (Manly Sea Eagles).
Tries: Mariner (33, 51), Chan Kum Tong (75); **Goals:** Pauga 3/3.
Rugby Leaguer & League Express Men of the Match:
England: George Williams; *Samoa:* Jarome Luai.
Penalty count: 6-1; **Half-time:** 16-6; **Referee:** Liam Moore;
Attendance: 15,137 *(at The Brick Community Stadium, Wigan).*

Internationals

Daryl Clark offloads to George Williams as Jarome Luai moves in

England wrapped up the two-match series with a 34-16 win at Headingley after coming back strongly from an early Samoa try, as the tourists looked to have learned the lesson of their slow start at Wigan the week before.

All of England's changes from the first Test were enforced. Tom Burgess was unable to shake off an illness, while Kai Pearce-Paul (calf) and Dom Young (hand) were unavailable because of injuries. That meant England debuts for Wigan pair, Young Player of the Year Junior Nsemba and Super League's top-tryscorer, winger Liam Marshall. Prop Luke Thompson came onto the bench after suspension. Star centre Izack Tago was the biggest omission for Samoa with a shoulder injury and his brother Jake replaced him.

Halfbacks George Williams and Harry Smith were once again pivotal, while Dolphins centre Herbie Farnworth ran riot with two tries and a brilliant break for England's last try.

After Smith's early penalty goal, Samoa took a shock 6-2 lead when Jarome Luai's pin-point dink bounced and was collected by standout backrower Shawn Blore, who crashed through Matty Ashton and Jack Welsby's challenge. Samoa were visibly lifted and Jazz Tevaga was stopped just short of the line two minutes later.

But England kept their composure and were 22-6 to the good by half-time. Marshall cut inside off Williams' long pass for Smith's conversion to retake the lead on 23 minutes. And when centre Junior Pauga was sin-binned two minutes later for a high hit on John Bateman, England were clear with two well-worked tries, Williams scything through the left centre with a two-man overlap and Ashton diving into the right corner from Smith's long bullet pass. Samoa were back to full complement when Farnworth charged through from 30 metres and grounded despite Luai's attempted cover tackle on the line.

SECOND TEST

Saturday 2nd November 2024

ENGLAND 34 SAMOA 16

ENGLAND: 1 Jack Welsby (St Helens); 2 Matty Ashton (Warrington Wolves); 3 Harry Newman (Leeds Rhinos); 4 Herbie Farnworth (Dolphins); 5 Liam Marshall (Wigan Warriors); 6 George Williams (Warrington Wolves) (C); 7 Harry Smith (Wigan Warriors); 8 Ethan Havard (Wigan Warriors); 9 Daryl Clark (St Helens); 10 Matty Lees (St Helens); 11 John Bateman (Warrington Wolves); 12 Junior Nsemba (Wigan Warriors); 13 Victor Radley (Sydney Roosters). Subs (all used): 14 Mikey Lewis (Hull KR); 15 Morgan Knowles (St Helens); 16 Mike McMeeken (Catalans Dragons); 17 Luke Thompson (Wigan Warriors).
Tries: Marshall (22), Williams (26), Ashton (32), Farnworth (37, 54), Welsby (67); **Goals:** Smith 5/7.
SAMOA: 1 Roger Tuivasa-Sheck (New Zealand Warriors); 2 Jeral Skelton (Canterbury Bulldogs); 3 Jake Tago (Parramatta Eels); 4 Junior Pauga (Sydney Roosters); 5 Deine Mariner (Brisbane Broncos); 6 Blaize Talagi (Parramatta Eels); 7 Jarome Luai (Penrith Panthers) (C); 8 Francis Molo (St George Illawarra Dragons); 9 Jazz Tevaga (New Zealand Warriors); 10 Terrell May (Sydney Roosters); 11 Shawn Blore (Melbourne Storm); 12 Jeremiah Nanai (North Queensland Cowboys); 13 Luciano Leilua (St George Illawarra Dragons). Subs (all used): 14 Simi Sasagi (Canberra Raiders); 15 Gordon Chan Kum Tong (Manly Sea Eagles); 16 Keenan Palasia (Gold Coast Titans); 17 Lazarus Vaalepu (Melbourne Storm).
Tries: Blore (13), J Tago (44), Nanai (72); **Goals:** Pauga 2/3.
Sin bin: Pauga (26) - high tackle on Bateman.
Rugby Leaguer & League Express Men of the Match:
England: Herbie Farnworth; *Samoa:* Shawn Blore.
Penalty count: 5-4; **Half-time:** 22-6; **Referee:** Chris Kendall; **Attendance:** 16,068 *(at AMT Headingley, Leeds)*.

Jake Tago was over for Samoa three minutes after the break but the second-half tide was with England, Farnworth charging through for his second and then, on the back of a huge Mike McMeeken drive, bursting though the ruck from 40 metres and sending Welsby under the posts. In between, Thompson was held up over the line and Nsemba was stopped by a wonder tackle from fullback Roger Tuivasa-Sheck, who had a great second half.

Jeremiah Nanai had the last word when he ran on to a Luai grubber in-goal. But it was mission accomplished for Wane and England.

* Wigan winger Anna Davies scored five tries as England Women swept aside Wales in a record 82-0 win in the curtain raiser at Headingley. The margin of victory was ten points better than the 72-0 success over Russia in the 2008 World Cup. Davies' effort saw her eclipse the mark for the most individual tries in a game for the Lionesses, previously shared by Emily Rudge and Leah Burke on four.

A dazzling first-half scoring spree by England's Men lit up an otherwise dismal day for international Rugby League in Toulouse at the end of June, with England emerging 40-8 victors at Stade Ernest Wallon.

A Test match which was intended to be part of the 90th anniversary celebrations for French Rugby League instead got lost in the confusion of a triple-header involving the women's national teams and a Toulouse v Featherstone Championship game, none of which could conjure up a crowd significant enough to create an atmosphere or a sensation of genuine international competition. The mood throughout was as gloomy as the unseasonable cold weather in the Midi.

The game seemed doomed from the start when England coach Shaun Wane was declared unfit to travel to France following ankle surgery. His assistant Andy Last had his flight disrupted and missed training, with former national captain Sam Tomkins helping out at Wane's personal request.

Ten of the starting 13 for France were from the Catalans' ranks and a lack of any NRL-based players in the England ranks, plus debuts for Castleford's Sam Wood, Wigan hooker Brad O'Neill, Hull KR skipper Elliot Minchella and Huddersfield's Oliver Wilson also raised hopes of a French renaissance.

And so it started with stand-off César Rougé rattling Warrington second-rower Matty Nicholson with a huge tackle before fullback Arthur Mourgue kicked low to the left corner for winger Fouad Yaha to collect and cross for a spectacular second-minute try. Mourgue converted, then added a penalty goal for an 8-0 lead.

Jack Welsby charges towards the France tryline

Internationals

The early setback seemed to unsettle England into a series of errors and indecision but, once they clicked into gear a dazzling 10-minute spell put France into a trance with four tries in rapid succession.

Fullback Jack Welsby kicked off the procession with an acrobatic corner-flag finish, then Leeds winger Ash Handley bumped off Mourgue on the opposite flank and backed it up with a second following an incredible midfield burst of pace from his fellow winger Tom Johnstone.

Johnstone then latched on to a terrific floating pass from George Williams to score at the left corner flag and all of a sudden France were ten points behind, only Harry Smith's failure to convert three of the scores keeping the French in the game after half an hour.

England went on with the job after the break, Nicholson picking up a Smith kick for his first England try then Welsby completing his brace, scampering through some weak defence from a quick play-the-ball. Mikey Lewis came off the bench and turned up the heat with a scorching break through the defence to release Williams for a 30-metre canter over the line. And Johnstone wrapped it up at the final hooter, returning a Mourgue drop-out from beneath his own posts with interest.

INTERNATIONAL

Saturday 29th June 2024

FRANCE 8 ENGLAND 40

FRANCE: 1 Arthur Mourgue (Catalans Dragons); 2 Fouad Yaha (Catalans Dragons); 3 Matthieu Laguerre (Catalans Dragons); 4 Enzo Griffier (Sydney Roosters); 5 Hakim Miloudi (London Broncos); 6 Cesar Rouge (Catalans Dragons); 7 Theo Fages (Catalans Dragons); 8 Romain Navarrete (Catalans Dragons); 9 Alrix Da Costa (Catalans Dragons); 10 Julian Bousquet (Catalans Dragons); 11 Mickael Goudemand (Leeds Rhinos); 12 Paul Seguier (Catalans Dragons); 13 Ben Garcia (Catalans Dragons) (C). Subs (all used): 14 Ugo Tison (Catalans Dragons); 15 Tiaki Chan (Wigan Warriors); 16 Franck Maria (Catalans Dragons); 17 Justin Sangare (Leeds Rhinos).
Try: Yaha (2); **Goals:** Mourgue 2/2.
ENGLAND: 1 Jack Welsby (St Helens); 2 Tom Johnstone (Catalans Dragons); 3 Sam Wood (Castleford Tigers); 4 Harry Newman (Leeds Rhinos); 5 Ash Handley (Leeds Rhinos); 6 George Williams (Warrington Wolves) (C); 7 Harry Smith (Wigan Warriors); 8 Luke Thompson (Wigan Warriors); 9 Brad O'Neill (Wigan Warriors); 10 Matty Lees (St Helens); 11 Ben Currie (Warrington Wolves); 12 Matty Nicholson (Warrington Wolves); 13 Elliot Minchella (Hull KR). Subs (all used): 14 Mikey Lewis (Hull KR); 15 James Harrison (Warrington Wolves); 16 Tyler Dupree (Wigan Warriors); 17 Oliver Wilson (Huddersfield Giants).
Tries: Welsby (21, 62), Handley (23, 26), Johnstone (31, 79), Nicholson (57), Williams (72); **Goals:** Smith 4/8.
Rugby Leaguer & League Express Men of the Match:
France: Ben Garcia; *England:* Jack Welsby.
Penalty count: 6-4; **Half-time:** 8-18; **Referee:** Tom Grant.
(at Stade Ernest Wallon, Toulouse).

Women's Test

In the first game of the day, England Women's dominance over France continued with an emphatic 42-0 victory and a promising pointer towards a bright new future built upon youth and experience.

Five debutants all contributed to a comprehensive Test win in Toulouse, the newcomers slotting in seamlessly alongside seasoned internationals and providing head coach Stuart Barrow with a variety of new options as he plotted towards the 2026 World Cup.

Any signs of a closing gap between England and the southern hemisphere nations were difficult to discern from this one-sided

Anna Davies dives over for an England try against France

romp as the French, led by captain Elisa Akpa who had returned from Australia (where she was trialling for Wests Tigers), were completely outplayed in every department. But Barrow was delighted with his side's composure and control.

Captain Jodie Cunningham, her St Helens teammate Emily Rudge and Leeds centre Amy Hardcastle stood tall for England once more. And, with Zoe Harris and Caitlin Beevers also in command, England were never in trouble against a brave but outgunned French team.

The debutants, Georgie Hetherington, Anna Davies, Isabel Rowe, Katie Mottershead and Bella Sykes looked certain to feature in Barrow's World Cup plans.

Internationals

Wheelchair Test

England secured their biggest ever win, by 66-33, over great rivals France at the Robin Park Leisure Centre in October.

Eleven tries - four of them by Rob Hawkins, and all converted by Nathan Collins - saw the world champions score double the points of their opposition in the rout.

It was both their biggest margin of victory over France (surpassing a 56-26 success in Medway in 2016) and the highest number of points scored (beating the previous best of 62 in Manchester two-and-a-half years before).

England's big win was a fair reflection of their dominance against a French side led for the first time by Cyril Torres, who surprisingly left 2023 Golden Boot winner Jérémy Bourson out of his team.

There only looked to be one winner in this tie after an opening ten minutes which brought three England tries. From their first attack, Leeds team-mates Collins, Halliwell and Josh Butler combined beautifully for the latter to score.

Hawkins then added a quick-fire double, with both tries provided by Collins. His perfect kick laid on the first before a Halliwell kick was played on by Collins for the next.

The teams then traded six converted tries before half-time. From 18-0 down, Leo Hivernat hit back by evading a Halliwell tackle to score and goal, but Hawkins' third try - squeezing down the middle after England kept the ball alive from a tap restart - kept the home side comfortable.

Hivernat reduced the arrears to 24-12, only for Seb Bechara to dive over the line in eye-catching fashion after being sent off balance in contact.

Lionel Alazard released fellow substitute Damien Doré as France dialled up the pace, but England won possession back from the restart and Hawkins beat Julien Penella in the corner for his fourth and a 36-18 half-time lead.

By the time Hawkins was withdrawn, England had certainly made sure of victory, with the score extended to 48-18 by two further tries at the start of the second half.

England, who kept the Fassolette-Kielty Trophy contested each time the sides meet, were expecting a tougher challenge in the reverse fixture in Normandy's Saint-Lo on November 23.

World Cup 2026 Qualifiers

France qualified for 2025's qualifying stage for the 10-team Men's World Cup of 2026 with a 48-6 October win over Wales in St Estève.

France progressed to the World Series against Cook Islands, Jamaica and South Africa with the last two places available for the World Cup in Australia. England, New Zealand, Australia, Tonga, Samoa, Papua New Guinea, Lebanon and Fiji were guaranteed entry on the back of the 2021 World Cup (delayed to 2022 because of the Covid pandemic).

The 2025 tournament was to be staged in Australia and also to be delayed by a year after, in 2024, the French Federation pulled out as hosts.

Wales, disrupted by the absence of their coach John Kear, were eliminated. The 69-year-old was unable to travel to France because of illness, with assistant Mark Moxon taking the reins for a difficult challenge against Laurent Frayssinous's side, which was boosted by the late addition of Catalans' César Rougé and Matthieu Laguerre after Nolan Lopez Buttignol and Lucas Albert were called up by their club side Carcassonne for a Super XIII fixture.

Wales were unchanged after the previous week's 48-0 victory over Serbia but could do little to stop France from scoring nine tries in a one-sided romp led by Rougé.

In the women's World Cup, France and Wales won their European qualifiers to join England, Australia, New Zealand and Papua New Guinea in the eight team tournament. The winner of the Asia-Pacific final between Samoa and Fiji will join them, with the eighth team to be decided by a World Series involving the loser of Samoa-Fiji, Ireland, Nigeria and one of Canada, USA or Jamaica.

Internationals

MEN'S WORLD CUP QUALIFIERS

Tuesday 22nd October 2024
Wales 48 Serbia 0
France 74 Ukraine 0
(both at Stade Albert Domec, Carcassonne)
Saturday 26th October 2024
Serbia 50 Ukraine 10
France 48 Wales 6
(both at Stade Municipal, St Esteve)
* France qualify for 2025 World Series
(two will go to World Cup) with Cook Islands,
Jamaica and South Africa

OTHER MEN'S INTERNATIONALS

Wednesday 8th November 2023
South Africa 56 Kenya 12
Saturday 11th November 2023
South Africa 82 Kenya 2
(both at Grizzlies Rugby Park, Pretoria)
Saturday 2nd December 2023
Kenya 6 France 78
(at ASK Showground, Nairobi)
Saturday 2nd December 2023
Jamaica 26 USA 30
(at Mona Bowl, Kingston)
Tuesday 5th December 2023
Kenya 4 France 108
(at ASK Showground, Nairobi)
Sunday 4th February 2024
North Macedonia 22 Chile 36
(at Forshaw Rugby Park, Sylvania Waters)
Saturday 17th February 2024
Montenegro 34 Serbia 52
(at FK Arsenal Stadium, Tivat)
Sunday 18th February 2024
North Macedonia 18 Malta 22
(at Forshaw Rugby Park, Sylvania Waters)
Friday 1st March 2024
USA 16 Canada 16
(at Valley Hill High School, Las Vegas)
Saturday 25th May 2024
Greece 34 Norway 26
(at Agios Dimitrios Municipal Stadium, Athens)
Saturday 14th September 2024
Netherlands 34 Scotland 26
(at RC The Bassets, Sassenheim)
Saturday 21st September 2024
Netherlands 28 Ireland 30
(at Zaandijk RC, Zaandam)
Poland 18 Germany 58
(at Nowe Skalmierzyce)
Saturday 28th September 2024
Italy 0 Malta 42
(at ASD Juvenilia, Bagnaria Arsa)
Serbia 6 Netherlands 52
(at FC Masinac, Nis)
Tuesday 15th October 2024
Wales 22 Jamaica 16
(at The Gnoll, Neath)
Friday 18th October 2024
Czech Republic 0 Ukraine 84
(at City Stadium, Letohrad)
Saturday 19th October 2024
Canada 28 Jamaica 16
(at Lamport Stadium, Toronto)
Czech Republic 34 Poland 24
(at Stadion Romana Sebrleho, Lanskroune)
Sunday 27th October 2024
Ireland 36 Scotland 6
(at Gateshead International Stadium)

MEN'S YOUTH INTERNATIONALS

Under-19 European Championship

Sunday 14th July 2024
Ukraine 24 Serbia 4
Monday 15th July 2024
Scotland 32 USA 10
Wednesday 17th July 2024
Serbia 12 USA 40
England 58 Ukraine 4
France 30 Scotland 18
Saturday 20th July 2024
USA 26 Ukraine 22
Serbia 0 Scotland 56
Final
England 15 France 8
(at Radnicki Stadium, Belgrade)

Academy International

Tuesday 2nd July 2024
England 37 France 40
(at Halliwell Jones Stadium, Warrington)

Under 16 Home Nations Championship

Saturday 1st June 2024
Ireland U16 12 Wales U16 44
(at CYM Rugby Club, Tenenure)
Scotland U16 4 England U16 46
(at Cambuslang Rugby Club)
Saturday 29th June 2024
England U16 44 Ireland U16 10
(at Ince Rose Bridge RLFC)
Sunday 30th June 2024
Wales U16 48 Scotland U16 4
(at Chester RUFC)
Final
Saturday 3rd August 2024
Wales U16 32 England U16 10
(at The Gnoll, Neath)

Other Youth Internationals

Saturday 16th March 2024
Czech Republic U19 16 Norway U19 30
(at RLC Slavia Hradec Králové)
Friday 26th July 2024
France U17 40 England U17 0
Monday 29th July 2024
France U17 42 England U17 8
(both played in Nantes)
Saturday 31st August 2024
Serbia U19 28 Norway U19 22
Serbia U16 24 Norway U16 12
(both at FK Sava 45)

WHEELCHAIR INTERNATIONALS

Celtic Cup

Saturday 8th June 2024
Ireland 68 Scotland 34
Scotland 64 Wales 52
Ireland 68 Wales 32
(all at Kingfisher Sports Centre, Galway)

Friday 2nd February 2024
USA 24 Wales 78
Saturday 3rd February 2024
USA 22 Wales 52
(both at Myrtle Beach Sports Centre)

Saturday 25th November 2023
France 18 England 34
(at Palais Des Sports, Marseille)
Saturday 26th October 2024
England 66 France 33
(at Robin Park Arena, Wigan)

WOMEN'S INTERNATIONALS

World Cup Qualifiers

Saturday 13th April 2024
France 58 Greece 0
(at Stade Georges Dartiailh, Marmande)
Saturday 27th April 2024
Italy 6 Netherlands 56
(at Maurizio Quaggia Stadium, Mogliano)
Wales 28 Ireland 10
(at Cardiff University)
Saturday 18th May 2024
Greece 32 Serbia 4
(at Agios Dimitrios Municipal Stadium, Athens)
Sunday 19th May 2024
Ireland 16 Netherlands 12
(at Donnybrook Stadium, Dublin)
Saturday 22nd June 2024
Serbia 0 France 58
(at Radnicki Stadium, Belgrade)
Netherlands 6 Wales 48
(at RC Waterland, Purmerend)
Thursday 19th September 2024
Kenya 14 Nigeria 22
Sunday 22nd September 2024
Kenya 8 Nigeria 0
(both at NYC Organisation Field, Nairobi)
* Nigeria qualify for 2025 World Series on most conversions
Saturday 12th October 2024
Greece 6 Ireland 42
(at Gkorytsa Stadium, Aspropygos)
Saturday 19th October 2024
Tonga 16 Samoa 30
Saturday 26th October 2024
Fiji 18 Cook Islands 6
(both at National Stadium, Suva)
* France and Wales qualify

Other Women's Internationals

Saturday 11th November 2023
Serbia 4 Greece 8
(in Bojnik)
Saturday 9th December 2023
Greece 0 Netherlands 14
(at Gkorytsa Stadium, Aspropygos, Athens)
Saturday 16th December 2023
Kenya 54 Uganda 0
(at Kisumu Polytechnic Grounds, Kisumu)
Sunday 28th January 2024
Ghana 20 Nigeria 30
(at University of Ghana Stadium, Accra)
Wednesday 15th May 2024
Uganda 16 Kenya 18
Saturday 18th May 2024
Uganda 13 Kenya 12
(both at Elite Stadium Kampala)

Production deadlines prevented coverage of the 2024 Pacific Championships. The tournament will be covered in full in next season's Yearbook.

PERSONALITIES OF 2024
Mikey Lewis
Hull KR & England

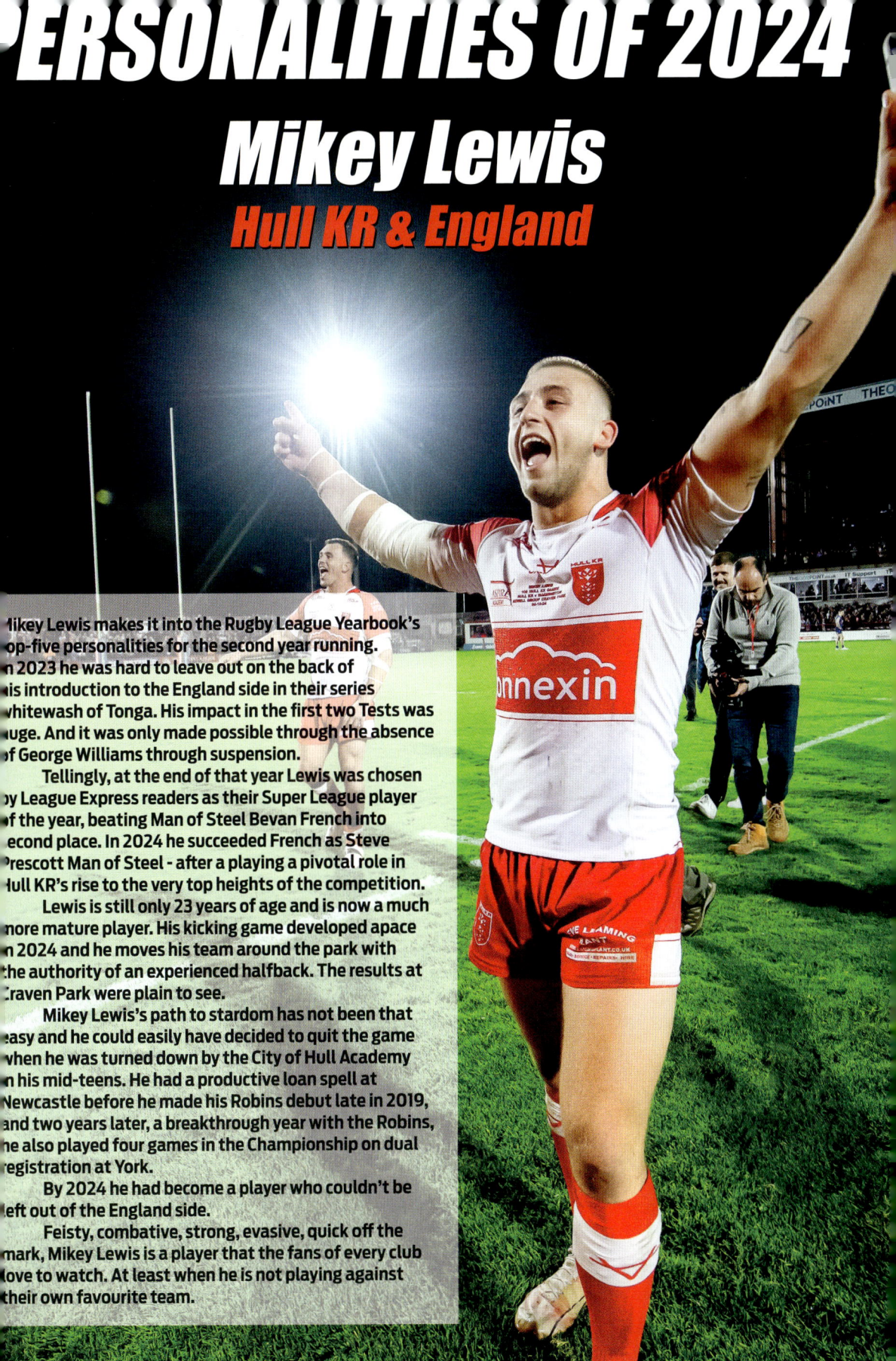

Mikey Lewis makes it into the Rugby League Yearbook's top-five personalities for the second year running. In 2023 he was hard to leave out on the back of his introduction to the England side in their series whitewash of Tonga. His impact in the first two Tests was huge. And it was only made possible through the absence of George Williams through suspension.

Tellingly, at the end of that year Lewis was chosen by League Express readers as their Super League player of the year, beating Man of Steel Bevan French into second place. In 2024 he succeeded French as Steve Prescott Man of Steel - after a playing a pivotal role in Hull KR's rise to the very top heights of the competition.

Lewis is still only 23 years of age and is now a much more mature player. His kicking game developed apace in 2024 and he moves his team around the park with the authority of an experienced halfback. The results at Craven Park were plain to see.

Mikey Lewis's path to stardom has not been that easy and he could easily have decided to quit the game when he was turned down by the City of Hull Academy in his mid-teens. He had a productive loan spell at Newcastle before he made his Robins debut late in 2019, and two years later, a breakthrough year with the Robins, he also played four games in the Championship on dual registration at York.

By 2024 he had become a player who couldn't be left out of the England side.

Feisty, combative, strong, evasive, quick off the mark, Mikey Lewis is a player that the fans of every club love to watch. At least when he is not playing against their own favourite team.

In 2024, Max Jowitt became the first player in British Rugby League to score 500 points in a single season.

The fullback scored 26 tries and kicked 198 goals in 35 games for Wakefield Trinity as they marched to the Championship title, a year after they were demoted from Super League.

Jowitt needed two more points when Wakefield kicked off their Championship Grand Final against Toulouse to equal the previous record of Leeds' great Lewis Jones, whose 496 points scored in the 1956-57 season had stood for over 60 years. That was in the days of the three-point try though that total included representative games.

It took 16 minutes for Jowitt, who was married to his long-term partner Lauren only two days before, to kick the conversion that equalled the record and another seven minutes to surpass it. When Jermaine McGillvary crossed for Wakefield's third try just after the half hour, Jowitt hit the 500-point mark. He didn't score another point and eventually left the field due to a head knock but his landmark added lustre to the finale of a wonderful season for Trinity as they cruised to a 36-0 win over second-placed Toulouse, the only team to have beaten them in the league. Three days later they were confirmed as a Super League side for 2025.

The stars aligned for Trinity during the end of their relegation year in 2023, when they were taken over by millionaire local businessman Matt Ellis and the improvements to Belle Vue, including the re-build of their main stand, headed towards completion.

Max Jowitt made his Wakefield debut on 15th August 2014 and was awarded the Albert Goldthorpe Rookie of the Year Medal in 2016. Injuries limited his progress since then. Like the whole Wakefield club he thrived in the optimism that surrounded Belle Vue in 2024.

Max Jowitt
Wakefield Trinity

To say Junior Nsemba had a breakthrough season in 2024 would be a gross understatement.

The giant back-rower played 28 games for Wigan in their all-conquering season, winning the Challenge Cup, the League Leaders' Shield and the Super League Grand Final. His thunderous late-season form saw him named in the Super League Dream Team, and subsequently as the competition's Young Player of the Year. And he only turned 20 years of age in late June.

Nsemba made his England debut in the second Test against Samoa at Headingley and made an almost impact when he broke for the line in the sixth minute, only denied a debut try in the second half by a wonder Roger Tuivasa-Sheck tackle.

There was little wonder that in September 2024 the Warriors tied Nsemba up contractually until 2030 with, according to club chief executive Kris Radlinski, no clause for an NRL option included in the deal. Nsemba loved it so much at Wigan that the negotiations reportedly took a matter of hours.

Nsemba grew up a stone's throw away from Wigan's ground. Son of parents from Cameroon, his uncle is former Liverpool and Cameroon footballer Rigobert Song, his cousin Alex Song played for Arsenal. His father would have liked Junior to take the same trajectory.

But when at the age of 13 he was asked to make a choice, Rugby League won over the round-ball game. It turned out well, Wigan picking him up from the Wigan St Jude's club and Nsemba making his professional debut at Hull KR in 2022 at the age of 18, alongside six other debutants, including another future star in Zach Eckersley.

He made his way through into the Wigan first team in 2023, making 15 appearances, though he didn't make the side for the Grand Final win over Catalans.

Willie Isa's broken ankle early in the 2024 season gave Nsemba the chance to establish himself and he grew and grew as the season went on. Strong with the ball, strong in defence, not lacking in ball skills and positional awareness, Nsemba is a special talent.

Junior Nsemba
Wigan Warriors & England

At the end of July 2024, Warrington fans got the news they had all been hoping for when the Wolves announced that head coach Sam Burgess had agreed a contract extension until the end of the 2026 season.

Burgess's rookie year as a head coach didn't end perfectly. The Wire finished third in the Super League table following the conclusion of the regular campaign, having won 20 of their 27 regular games. A narrow semi-final defeat at Hull KR followed a thrilling win over St Helens in the first eliminator. And they never hit their straps in the 18-8 Challenge Cup Final loss to Wigan at Wembley in June.

But what an impact Burgess made in his first season. Warrington scored the most points (740) and conceded the least (319) in Super League. And they kept going all year, instead of starting with a bang and then dropping off, as they had done the two seasons before.

There is no doubt that Sam Burgess's ten playing years in Sydney (minus one for his spell in rugby union in 2015) turned him into a huge personality and there has been no shrinkage since his return to England. He's never shy about voicing his opinions on the contentious issue facing the game.

Burgess's coaching achievements have not gone unnoticed in the NRL and he has been open about using Warrington as a stepping stone to secure a head coaching role back in the NRL. He's already rejected offers to return to Australia.

As a player, Burgess guided South Sydney Rabbitohs to a Grand Final win in 2014, memorably playing through the pain of a broken jaw and winning the Clive Churchill Medal as man of the match. In August, he became the first British player to be inducted into the NRL Hall of Fame.

Sam Burgess
Warrington Wolves

Matt Peet & Bevan French
Wigan Warriors

he name of Wigan has long been synonymous with uccess. But the 2024 vintage was something special.

A World Club Challenge win in February, a hallenge Cup in June, the League Leaders' Shield in September, followed by Grand Final glory on the ast day of the domestic season.

The team's response to occasional losses eflected the calm and collected approach of their ead coach Matt Peet. Heavy defeats at home to Varrington and away at Leeds could easily have aused panic.

Peet's thoughtful approach certainly bears ividends. Since he was promoted from assistant on he departure of head coach Adrian Lam in October 021, Wigan had won seven of the ten trophies they ad contested.

The Wigan club certainly knew they were onto good thing. In March they extended the contracts

assistants Sean O'Loughlin and Thomas Leuluai through to the end of 2030.

Mercurial stand-off Bevan French was another to sign a long-term contract, in his case until the end of 2028. And it is impossible to not include him as a personality of the year for the third year running.

There is Rugby League. And there is Bevan French Rugby League. Some fantastic players across Super League, but none quite like French. His off-the-cuff brilliance has played a huge part in Wigan's success story. The eight games he missed through a hamstring injury included those big defeats.

In 2024, Bevan French made history by becoming the first player to be chosen as man of the match in both the Challenge Cup Final and the Grand Final in the same season. The latter made him the first recipient of the Rob Burrow Award, marking the end of the Harry Sunderland Trophy which had been

2024 SEASON IN COLOUR

SEMI-FINAL

LEFT: Wigan's Abbas Miski dives over score against Hull KR

BELOW: Huddersfield's Esan Marsters wrapped up by Warrington's Sam Powell and Zane Musgrove

BETFRED CHALLENGE CUP

QUARTER FINALS

LEFT: Hull KR's Mikey Lewis leads the celebrations following Kelepi Tanginoa's try against Leigh

ROUND

BELOW: Warrington fans show their delight as Connor Wrench crosses against St Helens

RIGHT: St Helens' Daryl Clark skips away from Leeds' James McDonnell

LEFT: Josh Rourke leads the London Broncos celebrations after scoring against Hull FC

BELOW LEFT: Warrington's Matt Dufty heads towards the Leeds tryline despite the challenge of Ash Handley

BELOW: St Helens' Agnatius Paasi can't stop Wigan's Liam Marshall from touching down

BETFRED SUPER LEAGUE
MAGIC WEEKEND

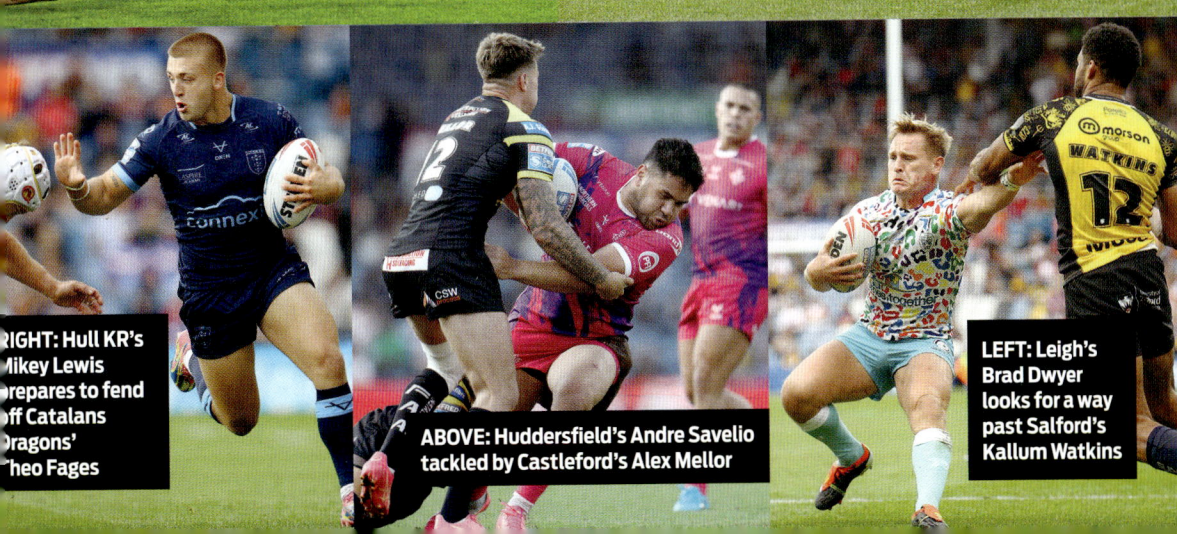

RIGHT: Hull KR's Mikey Lewis prepares to fend off Catalans Dragons' Theo Fages

ABOVE: Huddersfield's Andre Savelio tackled by Castleford's Alex Mellor

LEFT: Leigh's Brad Dwyer looks for a way past Salford's Kallum Watkins

LEFT: Tyler Dupree leads the celebrations as Wigan's victory is confirmed following a last-gasp video referee decision

BELOW: Isaah Yeo wrapped up by Kaide Ellis and Liam Farrell

ABOVE: Liam Marshall claims a high ball

ABOVE: Wigan show off the World Club Challenge trophy

LEFT: Tamzin Renouf, Jasmin Bell, Lacey Owen and Georgie Hetherington mob coach Lindsay Anfield following York's Grand Final win against St Helens

RIGHT: Eboni Partington tackled by Zoe Harris, Emily Rudge and Phoebe Hook

ABOVE: St Helens show off the Challenge Cup after defeating Leeds at Wembley

RIGHT: Hattie Dogus held up by Fran Copley

BELOW: Leigh celebrate after Promotion/Relegation play-off victory against Featherstone

LEFT: Amy Hardcastle looks to make a break as Leah Burke and Luci McColm close in

7
STATISTICAL REVIEW

SUPER LEAGUE PLAYERS
1996-2024

Super League Players 1996-2024

PLAYER	CLUB	YEAR	APP	TRIES	GOALS	FG	PTS
Jordan Abdull	Catalans	2024	15	3	6	0	24
	Hull KR	2020-23	44(6)	11	60	4	168
	London	2019	25(2)	10	1	0	42
	Hull	2014-16, 2018	32(20)	9	7	0	50
Carl Ablett	Leeds	2004, 2006-18	238(37)	63	0	0	252
	London	2005	3(2)	0	0	0	0
Darren Abram	Oldham	1996-97	25(2)	11	0	0	44
Mitch Achurch	Leeds	2013-16	25(50)	14	0	0	56
Andy Ackers	Leeds	2024	19(5)	1	0	0	4
	Salford	2020-23	62(10)	9	0	0	36
	Toronto	2020	5	1	0	0	4
Jamie Acton	Leigh	2017	11(4)	4	0	0	16
Brad Adams	Bradford	2014	1(1)	0	0	0	0
Darren Adams	Paris	1996	9(1)	1	0	0	4
Guy Adams	Huddersfield	1998	1(2)	0	0	0	0
Luke Adamson	Salford	2006-07, 2009-12	73(39)	11	1	0	46
Matt Adamson	Leeds	2002-04	54(8)	9	0	0	36
Phil Adamson	St Helens	1999	(1)	0	0	0	0
Toby Adamson	Salford	2010	(1)	0	0	0	0
Danny Addy	Salford	2021-23	19(20)	0	0	0	0
	Hull KR	2019	9(10)	2	0	0	8
	Bradford	2010-14	49(42)	13	7	0	66
Ade Adebisi	London	2004	(1)	0	0	0	0
Sadiq Adebiyi	London	2019, 2024	24(10)	4	0	0	16
	Wakefield	2022	1(2)	0	0	0	0
Patrick Ah Van	Widnes	2012-18	99	73	56	0	404
	Bradford	2011	26	9	87	0	210
Jamie Ainscough	Wigan	2002-03	30(2)	18	0	0	72
Shaun Ainscough	Bradford	2011-12	27	15	0	0	60
	Wigan	2009-10	12	13	0	0	52
	Castleford	2010	7	4	0	0	16
Glen Air	London	1998-2001	57(13)	27	0	1	109
Guillermo Aispuro-Bichet	Catalans	2024	1(4)	0	0	0	0
Paul Aiton	Catalans	2016-18	30(11)	3	0	0	12
	Leeds	2014-15	36(6)	2	0	0	8
	Wakefield	2012-13	43(2)	7	0	0	28
Makali Aizue	Hull KR	2007-09	18(32)	4	0	0	16
Sitaleki Akauola	Salford	2022	12(7)	2	0	0	8
	Warrington	2018-21	12(48)	6	0	0	24
Darren Albert	St Helens	2002-05	105	77	0	0	308
Lucas Albert	Toulouse	2022	16(5)	1	0	0	4
	Catalans	2015-20	35(10)	7	23	0	74
Wellington Albert	Leeds	2019	2(2)	0	0	0	0
	Widnes	2018	(11)	2	0	0	8
Paul Alcock	Widnes	2003, 2005	1(7)	1	0	0	4
Neil Alexander	Salford	1998	(1)	0	0	0	0
Malcolm Alker	Salford	1997-2002, 2004-07, 2009-10	271(2)	40	0	1	161
Danny Allan	Leeds	2008-09	2(5)	0	0	0	0
Chris Allen	Castleford	1996	(1)	0	0	0	0
Dave Allen	Widnes	2012-14	50(13)	5	0	0	20
	Wigan	2003, 2005	6(15)	2	0	0	8
Gavin Allen	London	1996	10	0	0	0	0
John Allen	Workington	1996	20(1)	6	0	0	24
Ray Allen	London	1996	5(3)	3	0	0	12
Mitch Allgood	Wakefield	2017	6(2)	0	0	0	0
	Hull KR	2015-16	27(2)	5	0	0	20
Richard Allwood	Gateshead	1999	(4)	0	0	0	0
Sean Allwood	Gateshead	1999	3(17)	1	0	0	4
David Alstead	Warrington	2000-02	23(10)	3	0	0	12
Daniel Alvaro	Toulouse	2022	14(1)	1	0	0	4
Luke Ambler	Harlequins	2011	5(17)	1	0	0	4
	Leeds	2010	1(8)	1	0	0	4
Asa Amone	Halifax	1996-97	32(7)	10	0	0	40
Tom Amone	Leigh	2023-24	50(1)	11	0	0	44
Kyle Amor	Warrington	2022	1(3)	0	0	0	0
	St Helens	2014-22	103(87)	18	0	0	72
	Wakefield	2011-13	51(23)	9	0	0	36
	Leeds	2010	(3)	0	0	0	0
Thibaut Ancely	Catalans	2011	(2)	0	0	0	0
Grant Anderson	Castleford	1996-97	15(6)	3	0	0	12
Louis Anderson	Catalans	2012-18	86(41)	32	0	0	128
	Warrington	2008-11	92	18	0	0	72
Paul Anderson	St Helens	2005-06	48(5)	7	1	0	30
	Bradford	1997-2004	74(104)	30	0	0	120
	Halifax	1996	5(1)	1	0	0	4
Paul Anderson	Sheffield	1999	3(7)	1	0	0	4
	St Helens	1996-98	2(28)	4	0	0	18
Scott Anderson	Wakefield	2014-16	25(18)	2	0	0	8
Vinnie Anderson	Salford	2011-12	33(3)	14	0	0	56
	Warrington	2007-10	57(19)	22	0	0	88
	St Helens	2005-06	28(14)	17	0	0	68
Phil Anderton	St Helens	2004	1	0	0	0	0
Chris Annakin	Wakefield	2013-19	7(62)	1	0	0	4
Eric Anselme	Leeds	2008	2(2)	2	0	0	8
	Halifax	1997	(2)	0	0	0	0
Mark Applegarth	Wakefield	2004-07	20(5)	3	0	0	12
Graham Appo	Warrington	2002-05	60(13)	35	80	0	300
	Huddersfield	2001	7	4	0	0	16
Ellis Archer	St Helens	2022	1	0	0	0	0
Guy Armitage	Toulouse	2022	15	7	0	0	28
	London	2019	(2)	0	0	0	0
Anthony Armour	London	2005	11(7)	1	0	0	4
Colin Armstrong	Workington	1996	11(2)	1	0	0	4
Tom Armstrong	Widnes	2017	11	1	0	0	4
	St Helens	2009-11	10(5)	9	0	0	36
Richard Armswood	Workington	1996	5(1)	1	0	0	4
Danny Arnold	Salford	2001-02	26(13)	13	0	0	52
	Huddersfield	1998-2000	55(7)	26	0	0	104
	Castleford	2000	(4)	0	0	0	0
	St Helens	1996-98	40(1)	33	0	0	132
Tinirau Arona	Wakefield	2016-22	110(43)	8	0	0	32
Joe Arundel	Wakefield	2015-21	88(10)	22	4	0	96
	Bradford	2014	9(3)	5	0	0	20
	Hull	2013-14	16	7	1	0	30
	Castleford	2008, 2010-12	35(4)	14	2	0	60
Craig Ashall	St Helens	2006	1	1	0	0	4
Olly Ashall-Bott	Toulouse	2022	24	6	0	0	24
	Huddersfield	2021-22	8(2)	3	0	0	12
	Wakefield	2021	2	1	0	0	4
	Salford	2020	3	1	0	0	4
	Widnes	2018	5	1	0	0	4
Nathan Ashe	St Helens	2011-13	6(4)	0	0	0	0
Chris Ashton	Wigan	2005-07	44(2)	25	2	0	104
Matty Ashton	Warrington	2020-24	84(7)	71	0	0	284
Matty Ashurst	Wakefield	2015-23	177(5)	33	0	0	132
	Salford	2012-14	65(7)	11	0	0	44
	St Helens	2009-11	12(39)	8	0	0	32
Jack Ashworth	Hull	2024	3(11)	0	0	0	0
	Huddersfield	2021-23	7(19)	0	0	0	0
	Leigh	2021	1(4)	0	0	0	0
	St Helens	2015-16, 2018-20	6(37)	4	0	0	16
John Asiata	Leigh	2023-24	37(4)	2	0	0	8
Roy Asotasi	Warrington	2014-15	16(37)	5	1	0	22
Connor Aspey	Salford	2020-21	(2)	0	0	0	0
Peter Aspinall	Huddersfield	2013	1(1)	0	0	0	0
Martin Aspinwall	Hull	2012	12(15)	0	0	0	0
	Castleford	2011	12(6)	2	0	0	8
	Huddersfield	2006-10	72(8)	22	0	0	88
	Wigan	2001-05	85(13)	27	0	0	108
Logan Astley	Wigan	2022	2	0	0	0	0
Cory Aston	Castleford	2019	8	3	0	0	12
Mark Aston	Sheffield	1996-99	67(6)	6	243	6	516
Paul Atcheson	Widnes	2002-04	16(35)	4	0	0	16
	St Helens	1998-2000	58(4)	18	0	0	72
	Oldham	1996-97	40	21	0	0	84
Chris Atkin	Salford	2020-24	50(46)	16	4	1	73
	Hull KR	2018-19	28(19)	7	1	3	33
David Atkins	Huddersfield	2001	26(1)	4	0	0	16
Jordan Atkins	London	2014	13(1)	4	0	0	16
Ryan Atkins	Wakefield	2006-09, 2019-20	90(2)	47	0	0	188
	Warrington	2010-19	235(2)	139	0	0	556
Josh Atkinson	Castleford	2012	2	0	0	0	0
Renouf Atoni	Wakefield	2023	10(11)	1	0	0	4
Brad Attwood	Halifax	2003	(3)	0	0	0	0
Blake Austin	Castleford	2023	5	0	0	1	1
	Leeds	2022-23	39(1)	5	0	1	21
	Warrington	2019-21	57(2)	30	0	6	126
Yusuf Aydin	Hull	2024	16(3)	1	0	0	4
	Hull KR	2023-24	1(6)	0	0	0	0
	Wakefield	2020-22	6(18)	2	0	0	8
	Leeds	2022	(3)	0	0	0	0
Warren Ayres	Salford	1999	2(9)	1	2	0	8
Jerome Azema	Paris	1997	(1)	0	0	0	0
Marcus Bai	Bradford	2006	24	9	0	0	36
	Leeds	2004-05	57	42	0	0	168
David Baildon	Hull	1998-99	26(2)	4	0	0	16
Jean-Philippe Baile	Catalans	2008-14	62(16)	23	0	0	92
Andy Bailey	Hull	2004-05	2(8)	1	0	0	4
Chris Bailey	Huddersfield	2014-15	17(17)	5	0	0	20
	London	2012-13	41	14	0	0	56
	Harlequins	2011	24	3	0	0	12
Connor Bailey	Wakefield	2020	3(2)	0	0	0	0
Julian Bailey	Huddersfield	2003-04	47	13	0	0	52

164

Super League Players 1996-2024

PLAYER	CLUB	YEAR	APP	TRIES	GOALS	FG	PTS
Phil Bailey	Wigan	2007-10	84(4)	13	0	0	52
Ricky Bailey	St Helens	2015, 2017	2	0	0	0	0
Ryan Bailey	Warrington	2016	1(11)	0	0	0	0
	Castleford	2015	3(2)	0	0	0	0
	Hull KR	2015	(1)	1	0	0	4
	Leeds	2002-14	171(102)	17	0	0	68
Jason Baitieri	Catalans	2011-21	136(89)	20	0	0	80
Simon Baldwin	Salford	2004-06	20(29)	3	0	0	12
	Sheffield	1999	7(15)	2	0	0	8
	Halifax	1996-98	41(15)	16	0	1	65
Jordan Baldwinson	Wakefield	2018	(4)	0	0	0	0
	Leeds	2013, 2016-17	4(9)	1	0	0	4
	Bradford	2014	2(4)	0	0	0	0
Rob Ball	Wigan	1998-2000	3(4)	0	0	0	0
Paul Ballard	Celtic	2009	2	0	0	0	0
	Widnes	2005	3(1)	2	0	0	8
Denive Balmforth	Hull	2022, 2024	(19)	5	0	0	20
Darren Bamford	Salford	2005	2(1)	0	0	0	0
Michael Banks	Bradford	1998	(1)	0	0	0	0
Steve Bannister	Harlequins	2007	(6)	0	0	0	0
	St Helens	2006-07	(3)	0	0	0	0
Frederic Banquet	Paris	1996	16(2)	7	4	0	36
Ben Barba	St Helens	2017-18	31	31	0	0	124
Lee Bardauskas	Castleford	1996-97	(2)	0	0	0	0
Harry Bardle	Hull KR	2019	(1)	0	0	0	0
Leunbou Bardyel-Wells	Salford	2024	(1)	0	0	0	0
Craig Barker	Workington	1996	(2)	0	0	0	0
Dwayne Barker	Harlequins	2008	5(5)	1	0	0	4
	London	2004	3	1	0	0	4
	Hull	2003	(1)	0	0	0	0
Connor Barley	Hull KR	2022-23	2(2)	1	0	0	4
Mark Barlow	Wakefield	2002	(1)	0	0	0	0
Danny Barnes	Halifax	1999	2	0	0	0	0
Richie Barnett	Salford	2007	7	4	0	0	16
	Warrington	2006-07	26(10)	15	0	0	60
	Hull	2004-05	21(5)	21	0	0	84
	Widnes	2005	4	2	0	0	8
Richie Barnett	Hull	2003-04	31(1)	17	0	0	68
	London	2001-02	31(4)	13	0	0	52
David Barnhill	Leeds	2000	20(8)	5	0	0	20
Trent Barrett	Wigan	2007-08	53(1)	22	0	4	92
Harvey Barron	Hull	2022-24	18(1)	9	0	0	36
Paul Barrow	Warrington	1996-97	1(10)	1	0	0	4
Scott Barrow	St Helens	1997-2000	9(13)	1	0	0	4
Steve Barrow	London	2000	2	0	0	0	0
	Hull	1998-99	4(17)	1	0	0	4
	Wigan	1996	(8)	3	0	0	12
William Barthau	Catalans	2010, 2012-14	13(3)	2	15	0	38
Ben Barton	Huddersfield	1998	1(6)	1	0	0	4
Danny Barton	Salford	2001	1	0	0	0	0
Wayne Bartrim	Castleford	2002-03	41(2)	9	157	0	350
Greg Barwick	London	1996-97	30(4)	21	110	2	306
Jarred Bassett	London	2024	23(1)	3	0	0	12
David Bastian	Halifax	1996	(2)	0	0	0	0
James Batchelor	Hull KR	2023-24	46	11	0	0	44
	Wakefield	2016-22	60(30)	13	13	0	78
Joe Batchelor	St Helens	2019-24	66(19)	19	0	0	76
Ashley Bateman	Celtic	2009	1	0	0	0	0
John Bateman	Warrington	2024	9(1)	1	0	0	4
	Wigan	2014-18, 2021-22	143(11)	35	0	0	140
	Bradford	2011-13	25(5)	7	0	0	28
David Bates	Castleford	2001-02	(4)	0	0	0	0
	Warrington	2001	1(2)	0	0	0	0
Sam Bates	Bradford	2014	(2)	0	0	0	0
Nathan Batty	Wakefield	2001	1(1)	0	0	0	0
Eddie Battye	Wakefield	2020-23	21(52)	1	0	0	4
	London	2019	19(10)	3	0	0	12
Andreas Bauer	Hull KR	2007	10(2)	5	0	0	20
Russell Bawden	London	1996-97, 2002-04	50(49)	15	0	0	60
Lewis Baxter	Leigh	2024	(2)	0	0	0	0
	St Helens	2022-23	(3)	0	0	0	0
Neil Baxter	Salford	2001	1	0	0	0	0
Neil Baynes	Salford	1999-2002, 2004	84(19)	10	0	0	40
	Wigan	1996-98	(10)	1	0	0	4
Chris Beasley	Celtic	2009	15(5)	2	0	0	8
Chris Beattie	Catalans	2006	22(5)	3	0	0	12
Richard Beaumont	Hull KR	2011-13	1(16)	1	0	0	4
Robbie Beazley	London	1997-99	48(15)	13	0	0	52
Robbie Beckett	Halifax	2002	27	15	0	0	60
Matty Beharrell	Hull KR	2013	1	0	0	0	0
Dean Bell	Leeds	1996	1	1	0	0	4
Ian Bell	Hull	2003	(1)	0	0	0	0
James Bell	St Helens	2022-24	38(30)	8	0	0	32
	Leigh	2021	16(2)	1	0	0	4
Mark Bell	Wigan	1998	22	12	0	0	48
Paul Bell	Leeds	2000	1	0	0	0	0
Steven Bell	Catalans	2009-10	43	14	0	0	56
Troy Bellamy	Paris	1997	5(10)	0	0	0	0
Adrian Belle	Huddersfield	1998	10(2)	0	0	0	0
	Oldham	1996	19	8	0	0	32
Lambert Belmas	Toulouse	2022	2(10)	1	0	0	4
	Catalans	2017-21	3(13)	0	0	0	0
Yacine Ben Abdeslem	Catalans	2024	(1)	0	0	0	0
Jamie Benn	Castleford	1998, 2000	3(8)	1	15	0	34
Andy Bennett	Warrington	1996	6(5)	1	0	0	4
Mike Bennett	St Helens	2000-08	74(70)	15	0	0	60
Gavin Bennion	Salford	2018	1(1)	0	0	0	0
Jon Bennison	St Helens	2021-24	51(2)	20	18	0	116
Andrew Bentley	Catalans	2007-10	9(15)	1	0	0	4
James Bentley	Leeds	2022-24	37(15)	12	0	0	48
	St Helens	2018-21	32(13)	9	0	0	36
John Bentley	Huddersfield	1999	13(4)	3	0	0	12
	Halifax	1996, 1998	22(3)	24	0	0	96
Kane Bentley	Catalans	2007-10	11(19)	5	0	0	20
Ilias Bergal	Toulouse	2022	8	3	0	0	12
Phil Bergman	Paris	1997	20(1)	14	0	0	56
Shaun Berrigan	Hull	2008-10	60(8)	12	0	0	48
Joe Berry	Huddersfield	1998-99	25(14)	3	0	0	12
David Berthezene	Salford	2007	9(1)	0	0	0	0
	Catalans	2006-07	5(14)	0	0	0	0
Colin Best	Hull	2003-04	57	34	0	0	136
Roger Best	London	1997-98	1(5)	1	0	0	4
Bob Beswick	Wigan	2004-05	5(14)	2	0	0	8
Monty Betham	Wakefield	2006	26	2	0	0	8
Mike Bethwaite	Workington	1996	17(3)	1	0	0	4
Denis Betts	Wigan	1998-2001	82(24)	33	0	0	132
Cliff Beverley	Salford	2004-05	47(1)	14	0	0	56
Kyle Bibb	Wakefield	2008-10	1(24)	0	0	0	0
	Harlequins	2010	(2)	0	0	0	0
	Hull KR	2009	(2)	0	0	0	0
Jack Bibby	Huddersfield	2024	(1)	0	0	0	0
	Wigan	2022	(1)	1	0	0	4
Jake Bibby	Huddersfield	2023-24	34(1)	12	0	0	48
	Wigan	2020-22	67	26	0	0	104
	Salford	2016-19	65(3)	32	0	0	128
Adam Bibey	Widnes	2004	(1)	0	0	0	0
Ricky Bibey	Wakefield	2007-09	32(25)	1	0	0	4
	St Helens	2004	4(14)	0	0	0	0
	Wigan	2001-03	5(29)	0	0	0	0
Lewis Bienek	London	2024	5(11)	3	0	0	12
	Castleford	2021	1(5)	0	0	0	0
	Hull	2018, 2020	(8)	0	0	0	0
Jack Billington	Huddersfield	2024	(2)	0	0	0	0
Chris Birchall	Halifax	2002-03	24(22)	4	0	0	16
	Bradford	2000	(1)	0	0	0	0
Deon Bird	Castleford	2006	17(6)	5	0	0	20
	Widnes	2003-04	39(6)	9	0	0	36
	Wakefield	2002	10(1)	1	0	0	4
	Hull	2000-02	37(22)	20	0	0	80
	Gateshead	1999	19(3)	13	0	0	52
	Paris	1996-97	30	12	2	0	52
Greg Bird	Catalans	2009, 2017-19	68(6)	11	3	0	50
Mike Bishay	London	2013-14	7(11)	2	2	0	12
Nathan Blacklock	Hull	2005-06	44(3)	33	0	0	132
Ben Blackmore	Huddersfield	2013-14	3	4	0	0	16
	Castleford	2012	1	0	0	0	0
Richie Blackmore	Leeds	1997-2000	63	25	0	0	100
Anthony Blackwood	Crusaders	2010	1	0	0	0	0
	Celtic	2009	25	5	0	0	20
Jack Blagbrough	Huddersfield	2013	(1)	0	0	0	0
Cheyse Blair	Castleford	2019-22	45(6)	10	0	0	40
Maurice Blair	Hull KR	2015-16, 2018	62(3)	10	1	0	42
Luke Blake	Wakefield	2009	(2)	0	0	0	0
Matthew Blake	Wakefield	2003-04	1(5)	0	0	0	0
Waqa Blake	St Helens	2024	22	11	0	0	44
Steve Blakeley	Salford	1997-2002	103(5)	26	241	2	588
	Warrington	2000	4(3)	1	9	0	22
Richard Blakeway	Castleford	2002-04	1(14)	0	0	0	0
Damien Blanch	Catalans	2011-13	70	42	0	0	168
	Wakefield	2008-10	44(3)	31	0	0	124
	Castleford	2006	3(2)	0	0	0	0
Matt Blaymire	Wakefield	2007-11	96(2)	26	0	1	105
Ian Blease	Salford	1997	(1)	0	0	0	0
Jamie Bloem	Huddersfield	2003	18(4)	3	11	0	34
	Halifax	1998-2002	82(25)	25	100	2	302

Super League Players 1996-2024

PLAYER	CLUB	YEAR	APP	TRIES	GOALS	FG	PTS
Vea Bloomfield	Paris	1996	4(14)	3	0	0	12
Matty Blythe	Warrington	2007-12, 2017	30(28)	12	0	0	48
	Bradford	2013-14	24(6)	8	0	0	32
Gideon Boafo	London	2024	1	0	0	0	0
Ben Bolger	London	2012	2(7)	1	0	0	4
	Harlequins	2010-11	4(15)	0	0	0	0
Pascal Bomati	Paris	1996	17(1)	10	0	0	40
Simon Booth	Hull	1998-99	15(9)	2	0	0	8
	St Helens	1996-97	10(4)	1	0	0	4
Steve Booth	Huddersfield	1998-99	16(4)	2	3	0	14
Alan Boothroyd	Halifax	1997	2(3)	0	0	0	0
Thomas Bosc	Catalans	2006-17	199(21)	48	483	12	1170
John Boslem	Paris	1996	(5)	0	0	0	0
Liam Bostock	St Helens	2004	1	0	0	0	0
Liam Botham	Wigan	2005	5	0	0	0	0
	Leeds	2003-05	2(11)	4	0	0	16
	London	2004	6(2)	3	7	0	26
Frano Botica	Castleford	1996	21	5	84	2	190
Matthew Bottom	Leigh	2005	(1)	0	0	0	0
Hadj Boudebza	Paris	1996	(2)	0	0	0	0
John Boudebza	Hull KR	2015-16	13(17)	2	0	0	8
David Boughton	Huddersfield	1999	26(1)	4	0	0	16
Amir Bourouh	Salford	2022-24	15(15)	1	0	0	4
	Wigan	2019-21	1(8)	0	0	0	0
Julian Bousquet	Catalans	2012-24	131(124)	28	0	0	112
David Bouveng	Halifax	1997-99	66(2)	19	0	0	76
Josh Bowden	Wakefield	2022-23	14(9)	0	0	0	0
	Hull	2012-22	65(100)	13	0	0	52
Matt Bowen	Wigan	2014-15	43	21	31	0	146
Harry Bowes	Wakefield	2020-23	10(16)	0	0	0	0
Tony Bowes	Huddersfield	1998	3(2)	0	0	0	0
Radney Bowker	London	2004	3	1	0	0	4
	St Helens	2001	(1)	0	0	0	0
David Boyle	Bradford	1999-2000	36(13)	15	0	1	61
Ryan Boyle	Castleford	2006, 2008-09, 2013-16	12(60)	5	0	0	20
	Salford	2010-13	57(14)	3	0	0	12
Andy Bracek	Crusaders	2011	(2)	0	0	0	0
	Warrington	2005-08	7(49)	7	0	0	28
	St Helens	2004	(1)	0	0	0	0
David Bradbury	Hudds-Sheff	2000	21(2)	1	0	0	4
	Salford	1997-99	23(10)	6	0	0	24
	Oldham	1996-97	19(6)	9	0	0	36
John Braddish	St Helens	2001-02	1(1)	0	3	0	6
Graeme Bradley	Bradford	1996-98	62(1)	29	0	0	116
Nick Bradley-Qalilawa	Harlequins	2006	27	6	0	0	24
	London	2005	28	19	0	0	76
Darren Bradstreet	London	1999-2000	1(3)	0	0	0	0
Dominic Brambani	Castleford	2004	2(2)	0	0	0	0
Keanan Brand	Leigh	2021, 2024	14	1	0	0	4
	Warrington	2020	3	0	0	0	0
	Widnes	2018	1	0	0	0	0
Joe Bretherton	Toulouse	2022	16(2)	3	0	0	12
	Wigan	2016-17	2(13)	1	0	0	4
Liam Bretherton	Wigan	1999	(5)	2	0	0	8
	Warrington	1997	(2)	0	0	0	0
Johnny Brewer	Halifax	1996	4(2)	2	0	0	8
Chris Bridge	Widnes	2016-17	28(1)	4	11	0	38
	Warrington	2005-15	186(17)	89	248	1	853
	Bradford	2003-04	2(14)	4	6	0	28
Danny Bridge	Bradford	2014	4(4)	0	0	0	0
	Warrington	2013	(2)	0	0	0	0
Ryan Brierley	Salford	2022-24	71(2)	32	9	0	146
	Leigh	2021	17	10	29	0	98
	Hull KR	2020	10	3	8	0	28
	Huddersfield	2016-17	19(1)	6	2	0	28
Lee Briers	Warrington	1997-2013	365(12)	130	810	70	2210
	St Helens	1997	3	0	11	0	22
Carl Briggs	Salford	1999	8(5)	3	0	1	13
	Halifax	1996	5(3)	1	0	0	4
Kyle Briggs	Bradford	2011	6	4	0	0	16
	Harlequins	2011	3	0	0	0	0
Mike Briggs	Widnes	2002	1(2)	1	0	0	4
Kriss Brining	Salford	2017	2(20)	4	0	0	16
Luke Briscoe	Leeds	2014, 2016, 2018-21	47(9)	15	0	0	60
	Wakefield	2014	2	0	0	0	0
Shaun Briscoe	Widnes	2012-13	11(2)	4	0	0	16
	Hull KR	2008-11	92	27	0	0	108
	Hull	2004-07	83(9)	50	0	0	200
	Wigan	2002-03	23(5)	11	0	0	44
Tom Briscoe	Hull	2008-13, 2024	146(3)	85	0	0	340
	Leigh	2023-24	30	15	0	0	60
	Leeds	2014-22	172(2)	66	0	0	264
Darren Britt	St Helens	2002-03	41	3	0	0	12
Gary Broadbent	Salford	1997-2002	117(2)	22	0	0	88
Jack Broadbent	Hull KR	2024	14	7	0	0	28
	Castleford	2023-24	31(2)	7	0	0	28
	Leeds	2020-22	20(1)	9	0	0	36
Paul Broadbent	Wakefield	2002	16(5)	0	0	0	0
	Hull	2000-01	40(9)	3	0	0	12
	Halifax	1999	26(1)	2	0	0	8
	Sheffield	1996-98	63(1)	6	0	0	24
Robin Brochon	Catalans	2018-19, 2021	2(1)	0	0	0	0
Andrew Brocklehurst	Salford	2004-07	34(23)	5	0	0	20
	London	2004	12(6)	2	0	0	8
	Halifax	2001-03	37(8)	2	0	0	8
Louis Brogan	Leigh	2024	(4)	0	0	0	0
Justin Brooker	Wakefield	2001	25	9	0	0	36
	Bradford	2000	17(4)	11	0	0	44
Sam Brooks	Widnes	2016-17	1(3)	1	0	0	4
Danny Brough	Wakefield	2008-10, 2019-20	74(1)	16	247	9	567
	Huddersfield	2010-18	220(4)	45	721	20	1642
	Castleford	2006	10	1	31	2	68
	Hull	2005-06	25(12)	3	85	1	183
Jodie Broughton	Catalans	2016-19	48	34	0	0	136
	Huddersfield	2014-15	30	16	0	0	64
	Salford	2010-13	93	53	0	0	212
	Hull	2008-09	9(3)	6	0	0	24
Alex Brown	Hull KR	2013	16	9	0	0	36
	Huddersfield	2009	1	0	0	0	0
Darren Brown	Salford	1999-2001	47(9)	11	6	0	56
Fa'amanu Brown	Hull	2024	7	3	0	0	12
Gavin Brown	Leeds	1996-97	5(2)	1	2	0	8
Jack Brown	Hull KR	2024	1(8)	0	0	0	0
	Hull	2019-24	12(54)	5	0	0	20
Kevin Brown	Salford	2020-21	18	6	1	0	26
	Warrington	2017-18	41(1)	9	0	0	36
	Widnes	2013-16	80	37	1	1	151
	Huddersfield	2008-12	156	43	0	1	173
	Wigan	2003-06	46(18)	27	0	0	108
Lee Brown	Hull	1999	(1)	0	0	0	0
Michael Brown	Huddersfield	2008	(1)	0	0	0	0
Michael Brown	London	1996	(2)	0	0	0	0
Mitch Brown	Warrington	2018	10(1)	2	0	0	8
	Leigh	2017	21	4	0	0	16
Todd Brown	Paris	1996	8(1)	2	0	0	8
Adrian Brunker	Wakefield	1999	17	6	0	0	24
Lamont Bryan	Harlequins	2008-11	9(22)	2	0	0	8
Justin Bryant	Paris	1996	4(1)	0	0	0	0
	London	1996	7(8)	1	0	0	4
Mark Bryant	London	2012-13	16(36)	3	1	0	14
	Crusaders	2010-11	42(8)	1	0	0	4
	Celtic	2009	23(3)	0	0	0	0
Austin Buchanan	Wakefield	2005-06	6	2	0	0	8
	London	2003	3(1)	2	0	0	8
Jack Buchanan	Widnes	2016-17	29(2)	2	0	0	8
Kieran Buchanan	Hull	2019-20	10(3)	3	0	0	12
McKenzie Buckley	St Helens	2022	(1)	0	0	0	0
Owen Buckley	Widnes	2018	4	3	0	0	12
Danny Buderus	Leeds	2009-11	57(14)	14	0	0	56
Neil Budworth	Celtic	2009	8(19)	0	0	0	0
	Harlequins	2006	2(19)	0	0	0	0
	London	2002-05	59(11)	4	1	0	18
Joe Bullock	Salford	2024	2(6)	0	0	0	0
	Warrington	2022-24	10(36)	1	0	0	4
	Hull	2024	(2)	0	0	0	0
	Wigan	2019-21	27(27)	4	0	0	16
James Bunyan	Huddersfield	1998-99	8(7)	2	0	0	8
Andy Burgess	Salford	1997	3(12)	0	0	0	0
George Burgess	Wigan	2020	2(6)	1	0	0	4
Joe Burgess	Hull KR	2024	20	14	0	0	56
	Salford	2021-23	51	21	0	0	84
	Wigan	2013-15, 2017-20	115	91	0	0	364
Luke Burgess	Salford	2018	3(8)	0	0	0	0
	Catalans	2017	3(2)	0	0	0	0
	Leeds	2008-11	10(63)	6	0	0	24
	Harlequins	2007	(3)	0	0	0	0
Sam Burgess	Bradford	2006-09	46(34)	14	5	0	66
Tom Burgess	Bradford	2011-12	1(41)	3	0	0	12
Greg Burke	Salford	2018-22	34(38)	2	0	0	8
	Widnes	2016-18	22(12)	1	0	0	4
	Wigan	2013-14, 2016	13(26)	1	0	0	4
	Hull KR	2015	9(5)	0	0	0	0
	Bradford	2014	(1)	0	0	0	0
Joe Burke	Crusaders	2011	(1)	0	0	0	0
Mike Burnett	Harlequins	2011	16(4)	1	0	0	4
	Hull	2008-10	13(21)	3	0	0	12

Super League Players 1996-2024

PLAYER	CLUB	YEAR	APP	TRIES	GOALS	FG	PTS
Darren Burns	Warrington	2002-04	66(6)	19	0	0	76
Gary Burns	Oldham	1996	6	1	0	0	4
Jake Burns	St Helens	2024	4(6)	3	0	0	12
Paul Burns	Workington	1996	5(2)	1	0	0	4
Travis Burns	St Helens	2015-16	27(2)	4	28	0	72
	Hull KR	2013-14	46	8	81	2	196
Lachlan Burr	Leigh	2017	5(14)	1	0	0	4
Aidan Burrell	Hull	2021	(1)	0	0	0	0
Luther Burrell	Warrington	2019-20	2(6)	0	0	0	0
Rob Burrow	Leeds	2001-17	313(116)	168	131	5	939
Dean Busby	Warrington	1999-2002	34(34)	7	0	0	28
	Hull	1998	8(6)	0	0	0	0
	St Helens	1996-98	1(7)	0	0	0	0
Tom Bush	Leeds	2010	3(1)	1	0	0	4
Chester Butler	Huddersfield	2019	(1)	0	0	0	0
Rob Butler	London	2019, 2024	31(16)	2	0	0	8
	Wakefield	2022-23	1(11)	0	0	0	0
	Warrington	2021-22	(5)	0	0	0	0
	Leigh	2021	3(3)	0	0	0	0
Ikram Butt	London	1996	5(1)	0	0	0	0
Reiss Butterworth	London	2024	1(2)	0	0	0	0
	Huddersfield	2020	1(1)	0	0	0	0
Robbie Butterworth	Wakefield	2023	1	0	0	0	0
Liam Byrne	Wigan	2019-24	54(59)	2	0	0	8
Shane Byrne	Huddersfield	1998-99	1(5)	0	0	0	0
Todd Byrne	Hull	2008-09	20	4	0	0	16
Didier Cabestany	Paris	1996-97	20(6)	2	0	0	8
Hep Cahill	Widnes	2012-18	106(13)	4	0	0	16
	Crusaders	2011	16	2	0	0	8
Joel Caine	Salford	2004	24	8	13	0	58
	London	2003	6	4	1	0	18
Mark Calderwood	Harlequins	2011	13	2	0	0	8
	Hull	2009-10	23	6	0	0	24
	Wigan	2006-08	64	23	0	0	92
	Leeds	2001-05	117(9)	88	0	0	352
Mike Callan	Warrington	2002	(4)	0	0	0	0
Matt Calland	Huddersfield	2003	2	0	0	0	0
	Hull	1999	1	0	0	0	0
	Bradford	1996-98	44(5)	24	0	0	96
Dean Callaway	London	1999-2000	26(24)	12	0	0	48
Laurent Cambres	Paris	1996	(1)	0	0	0	0
Jack Campagnolo	London	2024	13(1)	2	0	0	8
Chris Campbell	Warrington	2000	7(1)	2	0	0	8
Liam Campbell	Wakefield	2005	(1)	0	0	0	0
Logan Campbell	Hull	1998-99, 2001	70(13)	14	0	0	56
	Castleford	2000	14(2)	3	0	0	12
	Workington	1996	7(1)	1	0	0	4
Terry Campese	Hull KR	2015-16	19(1)	2	4	0	16
Blake Cannova	Widnes	2002	(1)	0	0	0	0
Phil Cantillon	Widnes	2002-03	27(21)	18	0	0	72
	Leeds	1997	(1)	0	0	0	0
Liam Carberry	Widnes	2014-15	2(5)	0	0	0	0
Damien Cardace	Catalans	2012, 2014-15	23	14	0	0	56
Daryl Cardiss	Warrington	2003-04	23(2)	3	4	0	20
	Halifax	1999-2003	91(8)	39	4	0	164
	Wigan	1996-98	12(6)	4	0	0	16
Dale Cardoza	Warrington	2002	5	1	0	0	4
	Halifax	2001	3	1	0	0	4
	Huddersfield	2000-01	20(9)	11	0	0	44
	Sheffield	1998-99	11(7)	3	0	0	12
Paul Carige	Salford	1999	24(1)	7	0	0	28
Dane Carlaw	Catalans	2008-10	58(15)	9	0	0	36
Keal Carlile	Hull KR	2012-15	6(28)	1	0	0	4
	Huddersfield	2009, 2011	2(1)	1	0	0	4
	Bradford	2008	(1)	0	0	0	0
Jim Carlton	Huddersfield	1999	3(11)	2	0	0	8
George Carmont	Wigan	2008-12	136	71	0	0	284
Brian Carney	Warrington	2009	4	2	0	0	8
	Wigan	2001-05	91(10)	42	1	0	170
	Hull	2000	13(3)	7	0	0	28
	Gateshead	1999	3(2)	2	0	0	8
Justin Carney	Hull KR	2018	14	3	0	0	12
	Salford	2016-17	28	12	0	0	48
	Castleford	2013-15	58	56	0	0	224
Martin Carney	Warrington	1997	(1)	0	0	0	0
Todd Carney	Hull KR	2018	(1)	0	0	0	0
	Salford	2017	9(5)	0	7	0	14
	Catalans	2015-16	32	9	4	1	45
Omari Caro	Hull KR	2013-14	21	20	0	0	80
	London	2012	11	4	0	0	16
Paul Carr	Sheffield	1996-98	45(5)	15	0	0	60
Bernard Carroll	London	1996	2(1)	1	0	0	4
Mark Carroll	London	1998	15(3)	1	0	0	4
Tonie Carroll	Leeds	2001-02	42(2)	30	0	0	120
Darius Carter	Huddersfield	2024	1	0	0	0	0
Darren Carter	Workington	1996	10(3)	0	1	0	2
Steve Carter	Widnes	2002	14(7)	4	0	0	16
Jed Cartwright	Hull	2024	5	1	0	0	4
John Cartwright	Salford	1997	9	0	0	0	0
Garreth Carvell	Castleford	2014	1(4)	1	0	0	4
	Hull	2001-08, 2014	75(84)	22	0	0	88
	Warrington	2009-13	77(40)	13	0	0	52
	Leeds	1997-2000	(4)	0	0	0	0
	Gateshead	1999	4(4)	1	0	0	4
Garen Casey	Salford	1999	13(5)	3	23	0	58
Ray Cashmere	Salford	2009-11	63(3)	5	0	0	20
Mick Cassidy	Widnes	2005	24	0	0	0	0
	Wigan	1996-2004	184(36)	30	0	0	120
Loan Castano	Catalans	2022, 2024	(2)	0	0	0	0
Remi Casty	Catalans	2006-13, 2015-20	207(97)	26	0	0	104
Ned Catic	Castleford	2008	7(7)	3	0	0	12
	Wakefield	2006-07	17(29)	4	0	0	16
Mason Caton-Brown	Wakefield	2017-19	34	27	0	0	108
	Salford	2014-16	28	10	0	0	40
	London	2013-14	19	15	0	0	60
Joe Cator	Hull	2020-24	42(13)	1	0	0	4
	Hull KR	2016, 2018	2(3)	0	0	0	0
Chris Causey	Warrington	1997-99	(18)	1	0	0	4
Charlie Cavanaugh	Hull KR	2022	(1)	0	0	0	0
Jason Cayless	St Helens	2006-09	62(9)	7	0	0	28
Arnaud Cervello	Paris	1996	4	4	0	0	16
Marshall Chalk	Celtic	2009	13	4	0	0	16
Ed Chamberlain	Hull	2024	8	0	0	0	0
	Leigh	2023-24	18(4)	4	0	0	16
	Salford	2018-20	10(1)	3	21	0	54
	Widnes	2016-18	16(1)	2	7	0	22
Gary Chambers	Warrington	1996-2000	65(28)	2	0	0	8
Pierre Chamorin	Paris	1996-97	27(3)	8	3	0	38
Alex Chan	Catalans	2006-08	59(19)	11	0	0	44
Jason Chan	Hull KR	2014	5(1)	3	0	0	12
	Huddersfield	2012-14	46(12)	9	0	0	36
	Crusaders	2010-11	48(1)	10	0	0	40
	Celtic	2009	17(6)	3	0	0	12
Joe Chan	Catalans	2021-22	10(16)	9	0	0	36
Tiaki Chan	Hull	2024	1(8)	1	0	0	4
	Wigan	2024	(3)	0	0	0	0
	Catalans	2022-23	1(15)	1	0	0	4
Joe Chandler	Leeds	2008	(1)	0	0	0	0
Michael Channing	Castleford	2013-15	27(2)	8	0	0	32
	London	2012-13	15(3)	2	0	0	8
Jay Chapelhow	Widnes	2016-18	23(15)	4	0	0	16
Ted Chapelhow	Widnes	2016-18	7(13)	0	0	0	0
Chris Chapman	Leeds	1999	(1)	0	0	0	0
Damien Chapman	London	1998	6(2)	3	4	1	21
David Chapman	Castleford	1996-98	24(6)	8	0	0	32
Jaymes Chapman	Halifax	2002-03	5(8)	1	0	0	4
Richard Chapman	Sheffield	1996	1	2	0	0	8
Chris Charles	Salford	2004-06	59(16)	6	140	0	304
	Castleford	2001	1(4)	1	0	0	4
Jack Charles	Hull	2024	14(2)	0	20	0	40
Olivier Charles	Catalans	2007	2	2	0	0	8
Josh Charnley	Leigh	2023-24	51	45	0	0	180
	Warrington	2018-22	94	57	0	0	228
	Wigan	2010-16	151(2)	141	77	0	718
	Hull KR	2010	5	5	0	0	20
Lewis Charnock	St Helens	2013, 2015	4(1)	2	6	0	20
Rangi Chase	Widnes	2017	6	0	0	0	0
	Castleford	2009-13, 2016-17	122(12)	39	0	3	159
	Salford	2014-15	37	10	13	2	68
Andy Cheetham	Huddersfield	1998-99	30	11	0	0	44
Kris Chesney	London	1998	1(2)	0	0	0	0
Chris Chester	Hull KR	2007-08	28(6)	4	0	0	16
	Hull	2002-06	67(25)	13	0	0	52
	Wigan	1999-2001	21(22)	5	0	0	20
	Halifax	1996-99	47(14)	16	15	1	95
Lee Chilton	Workington	1996	10(3)	6	0	0	24
Dane Chisholm	Hull KR	2015	1	0	0	0	0
Gary Christie	Bradford	1996-97	4(7)	1	0	0	4
James Clare	Castleford	2012-15, 2018-22	100(1)	50	0	0	200
Daryl Clark	St Helens	2024	18(4)	7	0	0	28
	Warrington	2015-23	184(30)	47	0	0	188
	Castleford	2011-14	34(51)	31	0	0	124
Dean Clark	Leeds	1996	11(2)	3	0	0	12
Des Clark	St Helens	1999	4	0	0	0	0
	Halifax	1998-99	35(13)	6	0	0	24

167

Super League Players 1996-2024

PLAYER	CLUB	YEAR	APP	TRIES	GOALS	FG	PTS
Jason Clark	Warrington	2019-22	32(45)	2	1	0	10
Mitch Clark	Wigan	2020-21	(16)	2	0	0	8
	Castleford	2018-19	(24)	3	0	0	12
Greg Clarke	Halifax	1997	1(1)	0	0	0	0
John Clarke	Oldham	1996-97	27(4)	5	0	0	20
Jon Clarke	Widnes	2012-14	59(1)	5	0	0	20
	Warrington	2001-11	217(25)	56	2	0	228
	London	2000-01	19(11)	2	0	0	8
	Wigan	1997-99	13(10)	3	0	0	12
Chris Clarkson	Castleford	2019	11(8)	4	0	0	16
	Hull KR	2016, 2018	38(2)	4	0	0	16
	Widnes	2015	17(1)	4	0	0	16
	Leeds	2010-14	16(39)	9	0	0	36
Adam Clay	Salford	2011	2	3	0	0	12
Ryan Clayton	Castleford	2004, 2008-10	36(24)	5	0	0	20
	Salford	2006	3(8)	2	0	0	8
	Huddersfield	2005	4(6)	0	0	0	0
	Halifax	2000, 2002-03	28(12)	6	0	0	24
Jake Clifford	Hull	2023	25	6	50	0	124
Gavin Clinch	Salford	2004	21(1)	1	0	1	5
	Halifax	1998-99, 2001-02	88(2)	26	45	5	199
	Hudds-Sheff	2000	18(2)	5	0	1	21
	Wigan	1999	10(2)	4	12	0	40
Joel Clinton	Hull KR	2010-12	42(14)	2	0	0	8
John Clough	Salford	2004-06	1(16)	0	0	0	0
Paul Clough	Huddersfield	2017-20	35(43)	3	0	0	12
	Widnes	2014	4(8)	1	0	0	4
	St Helens	2005-13	53(113)	16	0	0	64
Tony Clubb	Wigan	2014-21	81(72)	20	0	0	80
	London	2012-13	24(8)	7	0	0	28
	Harlequins	2006-11	100(11)	29	0	0	116
Adam Clune	Huddersfield	2024	23	4	0	0	16
Bradley Clyde	Leeds	2001	7(5)	1	0	0	4
Michael Coady	Leeds	2010	1	0	0	0	0
Evan Cochrane	London	1996	5(1)	1	0	0	4
Ben Cockayne	Hull KR	2007-11, 2014-16	125(30)	38	18	0	188
	Wakefield	2012-13	54	28	2	0	116
Jack Cogger	Huddersfield	2021-22	21(2)	1	0	1	5
Liam Colbon	Hull	2014	8	1	0	0	4
	London	2012-13	22	5	0	0	20
	Hull KR	2009-11	51	20	0	0	80
	Wigan	2004-05, 2007-08	37(14)	15	0	0	60
Anthony Colella	Huddersfield	2003	5(1)	2	0	0	8
Liam Coleman	Leigh	2005	1(4)	0	0	0	0
Andy Coley	Wigan	2008-11	100(10)	8	0	0	32
	Salford	2001-02, 2004-07	112(34)	34	0	0	136
Richard Colley	Bradford	2004	1	0	0	0	0
Steve Collins	Hull	2000	28	17	0	0	68
	Gateshead	1999	20(4)	13	0	0	52
Wayne Collins	Leeds	1997	21	3	0	0	12
Dean Collis	Wakefield	2012-13	64	28	0	0	112
Aurelien Cologni	Catalans	2006	4(1)	3	0	0	12
Nathan Connell	Salford	2024	1(1)	0	0	0	0
Gary Connolly	Widnes	2005	20	4	1	0	18
	Wigan	1996-2002, 2004	168(10)	70	5	0	290
	Leeds	2003-04	27	6	0	0	24
Jake Connor	Huddersfield	2013-16, 2023-24	84(3)	24	65	2	228
	Hull	2017-22	114(13)	34	92	4	324
Nathan Conroy	Bradford	2013-14	(4)	0	0	0	0
Matt Cook	Castleford	2008, 2015-20	22(88)	13	0	0	52
	London	2012-14	50(7)	8	0	0	32
	Hull KR	2010-11	9(16)	7	0	0	28
	Bradford	2005-09	11(52)	4	0	0	16
Mick Cook	Sheffield	1996	9(10)	2	0	0	8
Paul Cook	Huddersfield	1998-99	11(6)	2	13	0	34
	Bradford	1996-97	14(8)	7	38	1	105
Peter Cook	St Helens	2004	(1)	0	0	0	0
Paul Cooke	Wakefield	2010	16(1)	3	36	1	85
	Hull KR	2007-10	54(5)	8	76	2	186
	Hull	1999-2007	177(27)	32	333	4	798
Joseph Coope-Franklin	Salford	2022	1	0	0	0	0
Ben Cooper	Leigh	2005	25(1)	5	0	0	20
	Huddersfield	2000-01, 2003-04	28(12)	3	0	0	12
Mike Cooper	Wigan	2022-24	13(8)	1	0	0	4
	Warrington	2006-13, 2017-22	146(89)	18	0	0	72
	Castleford	2010	1(5)	2	0	0	8
Lachlan Coote	Hull KR	2022-23	26	11	53	1	151
	St Helens	2019-21	58	31	256	1	637
Ged Corcoran	Halifax	2003	1(11)	0	0	0	0
Wayne Corcoran	Halifax	2003	4(2)	0	0	0	0
Jamie Cording	Huddersfield	2011-13	4(21)	5	0	0	20
Josh Cordoba	Hull	2009	8	1	0	0	4
Rio-Osayomwanbo Corkill	St Helens	2022	(1)	0	0	0	0
Mark Corvo	Salford	2002	7(5)	0	0	0	0
Matthew Costello	Salford	2021-23	20(3)	6	0	0	24
	St Helens	2018-20	22(2)	6	0	0	24
Neville Costigan	Hull KR	2014	24	3	0	0	12
Brandon Costin	Huddersfield	2001, 2003-04	69	42	93	3	357
	Bradford	2002	20(1)	8	0	0	32
Wes Cotton	London	1997-98	12	3	0	0	12
Phil Coussons	Salford	1997	7(2)	3	0	0	12
Alex Couttet	Paris	1997	1	0	0	0	0
Nick Couttet	Paris	1997	1	0	0	0	0
Jamie Coventry	Castleford	1996	1	0	0	0	0
Jimmy Cowan	Oldham	1996-97	2(8)	0	0	0	0
Will Cowell	Warrington	1998-2000	6(8)	1	0	0	4
Neil Cowie	Wigan	1996-2001	116(27)	10	0	1	41
Danny Cowling	Wakefield	2012-13	2	0	0	0	0
Jordan Cox	Warrington	2016	(16)	0	0	0	0
	Hull KR	2011-15	17(44)	4	0	0	16
	Huddersfield	2015	(2)	0	0	0	0
Mark Cox	London	2003	(3)	0	0	0	0
James Coyle	Wigan	2005	2(3)	1	0	0	4
Thomas Coyle	Wigan	2008	2(1)	0	0	0	0
Mathieu Cozza	Catalans	2021-22	3(7)	0	0	0	0
Eorl Crabtree	Huddersfield	2001, 2003-16	180(167)	52	0	0	208
Andy Craig	Halifax	1999	13(7)	1	3	0	10
	Wigan	1996	5(5)	2	0	0	8
Owen Craigie	Widnes	2005	15	7	0	2	30
Scott Cram	London	1999-2002	65(7)	4	0	0	16
Danny Craven	Widnes	2012-15, 2017-18	53(17)	13	6	3	67
Steve Craven	Hull	1998-2003	53(42)	4	0	0	16
Nicky Crellin	Workington	1996	(2)	0	0	0	0
Jason Critchley	Wakefield	2000	7(1)	4	0	0	16
	Castleford	1997-98	27(3)	11	0	0	44
Brodie Croft	Leeds	2024	25	8	0	2	34
	Salford	2022-23	32	12	0	0	48
Jack Croft	Wakefield	2019-20, 2022-23	25	2	0	0	8
Jason Croker	Catalans	2007-09	56(2)	11	0	1	45
Martin Crompton	Salford	1998-2000	30(6)	11	6	2	58
	Oldham	1996-97	36(1)	16	0	3	67
Paul Crook	Widnes	2005	2(2)	0	5	1	11
Paul Crook	Oldham	1996	4(9)	0	3	0	6
Jason Crookes	Hull	2013-14	15(1)	5	0	0	20
	Bradford	2009-12	25(1)	7	0	0	28
Ben Crooks	Hull KR	2018-22	69(1)	35	15	0	170
	Leigh	2017	19	6	0	0	24
	Castleford	2016	24(2)	5	1	0	22
	Hull	2012-14	42(3)	30	23	0	166
Lee Crooks	Castleford	1996-97	27(2)	2	14	0	36
Dominic Crosby	Leeds	2018	(2)	0	0	0	0
	Warrington	2017-18	(16)	0	0	0	0
	Wigan	2012-16	57(35)	6	0	0	24
Alan Cross	St Helens	1997	(2)	0	0	0	0
Ben Cross	Widnes	2012-13	27(1)	2	0	0	8
	Wigan	2011	(4)	0	0	0	0
	Leeds	2011	1(9)	0	0	0	0
Deon Cross	Salford	2022-24	81(1)	30	0	0	120
Steve Crossley	Castleford	2015	(6)	0	0	0	0
	Bradford	2010-11	(9)	1	0	0	4
Garret Crossman	Hull KR	2008	8(18)	0	0	0	0
Steve Crouch	Castleford	2004	4(1)	2	0	0	8
Kevin Crouthers	Warrington	2001-03	12(1)	4	0	0	16
	London	2000	6(4)	1	0	0	4
	Wakefield	1999	4(4)	1	0	0	4
	Bradford	1997-98	3(9)	2	0	0	8
Jordan Crowther	Warrington	2023-24	10(17)	1	0	0	4
	Wakefield	2014-19	55(33)	4	0	0	16
Matt Crowther	Hull	2001-03	48	20	166	0	412
	Hudds-Sheff	2000	10(4)	5	22	0	64
	Sheffield	1996-99	43(4)	22	10	0	108
Heath Cruckshank	Halifax	2003	19(1)	0	0	0	0
	St Helens	2001	1(12)	0	0	0	0
Leroy Cudjoe	Huddersfield	2008-24	343(3)	118	57	1	587
Paul Cullen	Warrington	1996	19	3	0	0	12
Francis Cummins	Leeds	1996-2005	217(13)	120	26	2	534

Super League Players 1996-2024

PLAYER	CLUB	YEAR	APP	TRIES	GOALS	FG	PTS
James Cunningham							
	Toulouse	2022	7(5)	1	0	0	4
	Huddersfield	2021	8(1)	0	0	0	0
	Toronto	2020	2(1)	0	0	0	0
	London	2014, 2019	34(8)	3	0	0	12
	Hull	2012, 2014-15	(9)	0	0	0	0
Keiron Cunningham							
	St Helens	1996-2010	357(24)	138	0	0	552
Liam Cunningham	Hull	2010	(1)	0	0	0	0
Ben Currie	Warrington	2012-24	222(32)	78	0	0	312
Andy Currier	Warrington	1996-97	(2)	1	0	0	4
Peter Cusack	Hull	2008-10	34(22)	3	0	0	12
Cade Cust	Salford	2024	10(2)	1	0	0	4
	Wigan	2022-23	27(8)	5	0	0	20
Adam Cuthbertson	Leeds	2015-20	91(39)	30	0	0	120
Alrix Da Costa	Catalans	2016-24	60(53)	6	0	0	24
Will Dagger	Wakefield	2023	14(2)	1	27	1	59
	Hull KR	2018-23	41(4)	3	26	1	65
	Warrington	2017	3	0	0	0	0
Joe Dakuitoga	Sheffield	1996	6(3)	0	0	0	0
Matty Dale	Hull	2006, 2008	(7)	1	0	0	4
	Wakefield	2008	1(1)	0	0	0	0
Brett Dallas	Wigan	2000-06	156	89	0	0	356
Mark Dalle Cort	Celtic	2009	23	4	0	0	16
Myles Dalton-Harrop							
	Salford	2022	1	1	0	0	4
Paul Darbyshire	Warrington	1997	(6)	0	0	0	0
James Davey	Wakefield	2009-11	3(14)	1	0	0	4
Maea David	Hull	1998	1	0	0	0	0
Alex Davidson	Salford	2011, 2013	(3)	0	0	0	0
Paul Davidson	Halifax	2001-03	22(30)	10	0	0	40
	London	2000	6(10)	4	0	0	16
	St Helens	1998-99	27(16)	7	0	0	28
	Oldham	1996-97	17(18)	14	0	1	57
Ben Davies	St Helens	2020-24	31(7)	11	1	0	46
	Salford	2021	2(1)	1	0	0	4
Ben Davies	Castleford	2011, 2013	3(4)	2	0	0	8
	Widnes	2012-13	10(15)	3	0	0	12
	Wigan	2010	(5)	0	0	0	0
Gareth Davies	Warrington	1996-97	1(6)	0	0	0	0
Geraint Davies	Celtic	2009	(7)	0	0	0	0
Henry Davies	Salford	2022	(1)	0	0	0	0
John Davies	Castleford	2010-12	1(6)	1	0	0	4
Jordan Davies	Salford	2013	2(3)	0	0	0	0
Macauley Davies	Wigan	2016	(1)	0	0	0	0
Matthew Davies	London	2019, 2024	1(2)	0	0	0	0
Olly Davies	St Helens	2016	(1)	0	0	0	0
Tom Davies	Catalans	2020-24	102	57	0	0	228
	Wigan	2017-19	57	27	0	0	108
Wes Davies	Wigan	1998-2001	22(22)	11	0	0	44
Brad Davis	Castleford	1997-2000, 2004, 2006	102(3)	31	43	10	220
	Wakefield	2001-03	51(12)	15	22	5	109
Matt Davis	Leigh	2023-24	11(35)	3	0	0	12
	Warrington	2019-22	21(32)	5	0	0	20
	London	2019	4	0	0	0	0
Sam Davis	London	2019, 2024	23(2)	3	0	0	12
Matty Dawson-Jones							
	Hull	2019	1	1	0	0	4
	Leigh	2017	23	12	0	0	48
	St Helens	2014-16	46(1)	15	0	0	60
	Huddersfield	2012-13	4	0	0	0	0
Brad Day	Castleford	2014	(1)	0	0	0	0
Matt Daylight	Hull	2000	17(1)	7	0	0	28
	Gateshead	1999	30	25	0	0	100
Michael De Vere	Huddersfield	2005-06	36	6	74	0	172
Paul Deacon	Wigan	2010-11	32(11)	4	14	0	44
	Bradford	1998-2009	258(43)	72	1029	23	2369
	Oldham	1997	(2)	0	0	0	0
Thomas Deakin	Huddersfield	2024	5(3)	0	0	0	0
Chris Dean	Widnes	2012-18	115(6)	23	0	0	92
	Wakefield	2011	20	8	0	0	32
	St Helens	2007-10	18(3)	9	0	0	36
Craig Dean	Halifax	1996-97	25(11)	12	1	1	51
Gareth Dean	London	2002	(4)	0	0	0	0
Riley Dean	Castleford	2023	4	0	2	0	4
	Warrington	2019-23	8(2)	3	5	0	22
Yacine Dekkiche	Hudds-Sheff	2000	11(3)	3	0	0	12
Brett Delaney	Leeds	2010-18	151(30)	23	0	0	92
George Delaney	St Helens	2022-24	16(28)	1	0	0	4
Jason Demetriou	Wakefield	2004-10	174(3)	50	2	0	204
	Widnes	2002-03	47(1)	15	1	0	62
Martin Dermott	Warrington	1997	1	0	0	0	0
David Despin	Paris	1996	(1)	0	0	0	0
Fabien Devecchi	Paris	1996-97	17(10)	2	0	0	8
Paul Devlin	Widnes	2002-04	32	16	0	0	64

PLAYER	CLUB	YEAR	APP	TRIES	GOALS	FG	PTS
Jordan Dezaria	Catalans	2016-17, 2021-24	18(51)	2	0	0	8
Stuart Dickens	Salford	2005	4(5)	0	4	0	8
Tyler Dickinson	Huddersfield	2016-18	(17)	1	0	0	4
Matt Diskin	Bradford	2011-14	64(16)	11	0	0	44
	Leeds	2001-10	195(37)	40	0	0	160
Andrew Dixon	Salford	2013-14, 2023-24	36(8)	8	0	0	32
	Toulouse	2022	14	0	0	0	0
	Toronto	2020	1(1)	0	0	0	0
	St Helens	2009-12	19(41)	12	0	0	48
Kieran Dixon	London	2012-14, 2019	76(1)	42	77	0	322
	Hull KR	2015-16	23(4)	21	9	0	102
Kirk Dixon	Castleford	2008-14	143(2)	63	267	0	786
	Hull	2004-06	13(4)	7	4	0	36
Paul Dixon	Sheffield	1996-97	5(9)	1	0	0	4
Nabil Djalout	Catalans	2017	1	0	0	0	0
Gareth Dobson	Castleford	1998-2000	(10)	0	0	0	0
Michael Dobson	Salford	2015-17	58(1)	14	77	1	211
	Hull KR	2008-13	142	51	500	11	1215
	Wigan	2006	14	5	61	0	142
	Catalans	2006	10	4	31	1	79
Michael Docherty	Hull	2000-01	(6)	0	0	0	0
Lewis Dodd	St Helens	2020-24	69(10)	27	13	1	135
Mitchell Dodds	Warrington	2016	(2)	0	0	0	0
Erjon Dollapi	London	2013-14	(18)	4	0	0	16
Sid Domic	Hull	2006-07	39(4)	15	0	0	60
	Wakefield	2004-05	48	30	0	0	120
	Warrington	2002-03	41(4)	17	0	0	68
Scott Donald	Leeds	2006-10	131	77	0	0	308
James Donaldson	Leeds	2019-24	23(87)	8	1	0	34
	Hull KR	2015-16, 2018	12(30)	4	0	0	16
	Bradford	2009-14	38(35)	4	0	0	16
Glen Donkin	Hull	2002-03	(10)	1	0	0	4
Stuart Donlan	Castleford	2008	20	8	0	0	32
	Huddersfield	2004-06	59(3)	15	0	0	60
	Halifax	2001-03	65(2)	22	0	0	88
Jason Donohue	Bradford	1996	(4)	0	0	0	0
Jeremy Donougher	Bradford	1996-99	40(21)	13	0	0	52
Justin Dooley	London	2000-01	37(18)	2	0	0	8
Dane Dorahy	Halifax	2003	20	7	45	0	118
	Wakefield	2000-01	16(2)	4	19	1	55
Jamie Doran	Wigan	2014	(2)	0	0	0	0
Luke Dorn	Castleford	2008, 2014-16	78(2)	60	0	0	240
	London	2005, 2012-13	58(8)	42	0	0	168
	Harlequins	2006, 2009-11	83(1)	57	0	0	228
	Salford	2007	19(8)	11	0	0	44
Eribe Doro	Warrington	2020-21	1(3)	1	0	0	4
Brandon Douglas	Castleford	2016	(1)	0	0	0	0
Jacob Douglas	Wigan	2024	2	1	0	0	4
Luke Douglas	St Helens	2017-18	23(32)	5	0	0	20
Ewan Dowes	Hull	2003-11	169(51)	10	0	0	40
	Leeds	2001-03	1(9)	0	0	0	0
Jack Downs	Hull	2015-18	5(15)	1	0	0	4
Adam Doyle	Warrington	1998	9(3)	4	0	0	16
Rod Doyle	Sheffield	1997-99	52(10)	10	0	0	40
Brad Drew	Huddersfield	2005-07, 2010	78(13)	18	13	1	99
	Wakefield	2008-09	27(9)	7	14	1	57
Josh Drinkwater	Warrington	2023-24	47	4	10	0	36
	Catalans	2018, 2020-22	75	15	60	0	180
	Hull KR	2019	29	4	6	0	28
	Leigh	2017	19	1	12	1	29
	London	2014	23(1)	5	54	0	128
Damien Driscoll	Salford	2001	23(1)	1	0	0	4
James Duckworth	London	2014	3	0	0	0	0
	Leeds	2013	2	1	0	0	4
Gil Dudson	Salford	2019-20, 2024	42(14)	2	0	0	8
	Warrington	2023-24	8(7)	0	0	0	0
	Catalans	2021-22	25(10)	5	0	0	20
	Widnes	2015-18	57(11)	1	0	0	4
	Wigan	2012-14	26(16)	2	0	0	8
	Crusaders	2011	3(7)	0	0	0	0
Jason Duffy	Celtic	2009	(1)	0	0	0	0
	Leigh	2005	3(1)	0	0	0	0
John Duffy	Leigh	2005	21	6	0	0	24
	Salford	2000	3(11)	0	1	1	3
	Warrington	1997-99	12(12)	0	0	0	0
Matt Dufty	Warrington	2022-24	56(2)	35	0	0	140
Tony Duggan	Celtic	2009	4	3	0	0	12
Andrew Duncan	London	1997	2(4)	2	0	0	8
	Warrington	1997	(1)	0	0	0	0

169

Super League Players 1996-2024

PLAYER	CLUB	YEAR	APP	TRIES	GOALS	FG	PTS
Andrew Dunemann	Salford	2006	25	1	0	2	6
	Leeds	2003-05	76(4)	11	0	2	46
	Halifax	1999-2002	68	19	0	1	77
Matt Dunford	London	1997-98	18(20)	3	0	1	13
Vincent Duport	Catalans	2007-09, 2011-18	156(16)	75	0	0	300
Tyler Dupree	Wigan	2023-24	11(23)	3	0	0	12
	Salford	2022-23	18(15)	3	0	0	12
Jamie Durbin	Widnes	2005	1	0	0	0	0
	Warrington	2003	(1)	0	0	0	0
Scott Dureau	Catalans	2011-15	88(1)	29	315	10	756
James Durkin	Paris	1997	(5)	0	0	0	0
Bernard Dwyer	Bradford	1996-2000	65(10)	14	0	0	56
Brad Dwyer	Leigh	2024	6(20)	2	0	0	8
	Hull	2023	7(17)	2	0	0	8
	Leeds	2018-22	51(55)	29	0	1	117
	Warrington	2012-17	12(63)	11	0	0	44
	Huddersfield	2013	(6)	0	0	0	0
Luke Dyer	Crusaders	2010	23(1)	5	0	0	20
	Celtic	2009	21	6	0	0	24
	Hull KR	2007	26	13	0	0	52
	Castleford	2006	17(2)	5	0	0	20
Adam Dykes	Hull	2008	12	1	0	2	6
Jim Dymock	London	2001-04	94(1)	15	0	1	61
Leo Dynevor	London	1996	8(11)	5	7	0	34
Jason Eade	Paris	1997	9	4	0	0	16
Michael Eagar	Hull	2004-05	12	4	0	0	16
	Castleford	1999-2003	130(2)	60	0	0	240
	Warrington	1998	21	6	0	0	24
Kyle Eastmond	Leeds	2021	2	0	0	0	0
	St Helens	2007-11	46(20)	35	117	3	377
Greg Eastwood	Leeds	2010	5(12)	1	0	0	4
Barry Eaton	Widnes	2002	25	2	49	4	110
	Castleford	2000	1(4)	0	3	0	6
Josh Eaves	St Helens	2019-21	1(3)	1	0	0	4
	Leigh	2021	4(1)	0	0	0	0
	Wakefield	2021	(3)	0	0	0	0
Greg Ebrill	Salford	2002	15(6)	1	0	0	4
Cliff Eccles	Salford	1997-98	30(5)	1	0	0	4
Chris Eckersley	Warrington	1996	1	0	0	0	0
Zach Eckersley	Wigan	2022, 2024	12(4)	6	0	0	24
Greg Eden	Castleford	2011, 2017-23	116(1)	105	0	0	420
	Hull KR	2013-14	37	23	0	0	92
	Salford	2014	4	1	0	0	4
	Huddersfield	2012	24	8	0	0	32
Alfie Edgell	Leeds	2023-24	12(5)	6	0	0	24
Steve Edmed	Sheffield	1997	15(1)	0	0	0	0
Mark Edmondson	Salford	2007	10(2)	0	0	0	0
	St Helens	1999-2005	27(75)	10	0	0	40
Diccon Edwards	Castleford	1996-97	10(5)	1	0	0	4
Grant Edwards	Castleford	2006	(2)	0	0	0	0
Kenny Edwards	Castleford	2022-23	44(4)	5	0	0	20
	Huddersfield	2020-21	19(7)	2	0	0	8
	Catalans	2018-19	14(18)	10	0	0	40
Max Edwards	Harlequins	2010	1	0	0	0	0
Peter Edwards	Salford	1997-98	35(2)	4	0	0	16
Shaun Edwards	London	1997-2000	32(8)	16	1	0	66
	Bradford	1998	8(2)	4	0	0	16
	Wigan	1996	17(3)	12	1	0	50
Tuoyo Egodo	Castleford	2017-19	10(4)	11	0	0	44
Danny Ekis	Halifax	2001	(1)	0	0	0	0
Abi Ekoku	Bradford	1997-98	21(4)	6	0	0	24
	Halifax	1996	15(1)	5	0	0	20
Shane Elford	Huddersfield	2007-08	26(1)	7	0	0	28
Olivier Elima	Catalans	2008-10, 2013-17	99(35)	34	0	0	136
	Bradford	2011-12	37(3)	12	0	0	48
	Wakefield	2003-07	40(47)	13	0	0	52
	Castleford	2002	(1)	1	0	0	4
Abderazak Elkhalouki	Paris	1997	(1)	0	0	0	0
Brendan Elliot	Leigh	2021	10(1)	3	0	0	12
George Elliott	Leeds	2011	1	0	0	0	0
Andy Ellis	Wakefield	2012	10	0	0	0	0
	Harlequins	2010-11	26(11)	8	0	0	32
Gareth Ellis	Hull	2013-17, 2019-20	96(16)	19	0	0	76
	Leeds	2005-08	109	24	1	0	98
	Wakefield	1999-2004	86(17)	21	2	0	88
Jamie Ellis	Leigh	2021	4(4)	1	1	0	6
	Hull KR	2020	7	1	18	0	40
	Castleford	2012-14, 2018-19	58(8)	12	150	2	350
	Huddersfield	2015-16	37(3)	14	31	3	121
	Hull	2012	4(5)	1	0	0	4
	St Helens	2009	1(2)	0	1	0	2
Kaide Ellis	Wigan	2022-24	51(18)	3	0	0	12
Lennie Ellis	Hull KR	2023	(1)	0	0	0	0
Danny Ellison	Castleford	1998-99	7(16)	6	0	0	24
	Wigan	1996-97	15(1)	13	0	0	52
Elie El-Zakhem	Castleford	2024	25	2	0	0	8
Andrew Emelio	Widnes	2005	22(2)	8	0	0	32
Jake Emmitt	Salford	2013	5(10)	0	0	0	0
	Castleford	2011-13	32(17)	0	0	0	0
	St Helens	2008-10	1(16)	1	0	0	4
Anthony England	Wakefield	2016-19	68(11)	2	0	0	8
	Warrington	2014-15	12(21)	3	0	0	12
Matty English	Huddersfield	2017-24	52(65)	8	0	0	32
	Castleford	2024	(4)	0	0	0	0
Patrick Entat	Paris	1996	22	2	0	0	8
Jason Erba	Sheffield	1997	1(4)	0	0	0	0
Morgan Escare	Salford	2021-22	16(3)	6	3	0	30
	Wakefield	2019, 2022	7	2	0	0	8
	Wigan	2017-19	23(22)	14	39	2	136
	Catalans	2013-16	83	58	1	2	236
Ryan Esders	Harlequins	2009-10	9(11)	3	0	0	12
	Hull KR	2009	(1)	0	0	0	0
Herman Ese'ese	Hull	2024	24	2	0	0	8
Sam Eseh	Hull	2024	1(3)	0	0	0	0
	Leeds	2024	3(2)	0	0	0	0
	Castleford	2024	(1)	0	0	0	0
	Wakefield	2023	(14)	0	0	0	0
Sonny Esslemont	Hull KR	2014-15	(5)	0	0	0	0
Niall Evalds	Hull KR	2024	25	8	0	0	32
	Castleford	2021-23	32	8	0	0	32
	Salford	2013-20	119(11)	88	0	0	352
Ben Evans	Warrington	2014-15	3(16)	2	0	0	8
	Bradford	2013	3(12)	1	0	0	4
James Evans	Castleford	2009-10	26(1)	13	0	0	52
	Bradford	2007-08	43(5)	20	0	0	80
	Wakefield	2006	6	3	0	0	12
	Huddersfield	2004-06	51	22	0	0	88
Kane Evans	Hull	2022-23	14(8)	1	0	0	4
Kyle Evans	Wakefield	2022	3	1	0	0	4
Paul Evans	Paris	1997	18	8	0	0	32
Rhys Evans	Leeds	2020	4(1)	1	0	0	4
	Warrington	2010-17	87(7)	37	0	0	148
Wayne Evans	London	2002	11(6)	2	0	0	8
Toby Everett	London	2014	(2)	0	0	0	0
Richie Eyres	Warrington	1997	2(5)	0	0	0	0
	Sheffield	1997	2(3)	0	0	0	0
Henry Fa'afili	Warrington	2004-07	90(1)	70	0	0	280
David Fa'alogo	Huddersfield	2010-12	38(16)	13	0	0	52
Sala Fa'alogo	Widnes	2004-05	8(15)	2	0	0	8
Richard Fa'aoso	Castleford	2006	10(15)	5	0	0	20
Maurie Fa'asavalu	St Helens	2004-10	5(137)	29	0	0	116
Bolouagi Fagborun	Huddersfield	2004-06	4(2)	1	0	0	4
Theo Fages	Catalans	2024	22	5	0	1	21
	Huddersfield	2022-23	21(1)	3	0	0	12
	St Helens	2016-21	101(25)	34	0	2	138
	Salford	2013-15	57(5)	18	4	0	80
Esene Faimalo	Salford	1997-99	23(25)	2	0	0	8
	Leeds	1996	3(3)	0	0	0	0
Joe Faimalo	Salford	1998-2000	23(47)	7	0	0	28
	Oldham	1996-97	37(5)	7	0	0	28
Jacob Fairbank	Huddersfield	2011-15	12(3)	0	0	0	0
	Wakefield	2014	1(3)	0	0	0	0
	London	2013	4(1)	1	0	0	4
	Bradford	2013	(2)	0	0	0	0
Karl Fairbank	Bradford	1996	17(2)	4	0	0	16
David Fairleigh	St Helens	2001	26(1)	8	0	0	32
David Faiumu	Huddersfield	2008-14	38(108)	13	0	0	52
Jamal Fakir	Bradford	2014	5(8)	1	0	0	4
	Catalans	2006-14	55(100)	13	0	0	52
Jim Fallon	Leeds	1996	10	5	0	0	20
Beau Falloon	Leeds	2016	8(2)	0	0	0	0
Bureta Faraimo	Castleford	2022-23	32(1)	15	0	0	60
	Hull	2018-21	78(1)	37	4	0	156
Owen Farnworth	Widnes	2017-18	1(4)	0	0	0	0
Ben Farrar	London	2014	22	1	0	0	4
	Catalans	2011	13	3	0	0	12
Danny Farrar	Warrington	1998-2000	76	13	0	0	52
Andy Farrell	Wigan	1996-2004	230	77	1026	16	2376
Anthony Farrell	Widnes	2002-03	24(22)	4	1	0	18
	Leeds	1997-2001	99(23)	18	0	0	72
	Sheffield	1996	14(5)	5	0	0	20
Connor Farrell	Widnes	2016	3(9)	3	0	0	12
	Wigan	2014-15	1(8)	1	0	0	4
Craig Farrell	Hull	2000-01	1(3)	0	0	0	0
Izaac Farrell	Huddersfield	2019	2	0	4	0	8
Liam Farrell	Wigan	2010-24	285(50)	127	0	0	508
Jack Farrimond	Wigan	2024	8	4	6	0	28

Super League Players 1996-2024

PLAYER	CLUB	YEAR	APP	TRIES	GOALS	FG	PTS
Brad Fash	Hull	2015, 2017-24	58(102)	6	0	0	24
Abraham Fatnowna							
	London	1997-98	7(2)	2	0	0	8
	Workington	1996	5	2	0	0	8
Sione Faumuina	Castleford	2009	18	1	0	0	4
	Hull	2005	3	1	0	0	4
Vince Fawcett	Wakefield	1999	13(1)	2	0	0	8
	Warrington	1998	4(7)	1	0	0	4
	Oldham	1997	5	3	0	0	12
Danny Fearon	Huddersfield	2001	(1)	0	0	0	0
	Halifax	1999-2000	5(6)	0	0	0	0
Chris Feather	Castleford	2009	1(23)	0	0	0	0
	Bradford	2007-08	7(20)	1	0	0	4
	Leeds	2003-04, 2006	16(35)	6	0	0	24
	Wakefield	2001-02, 2004-05	29(32)	9	0	0	36
Dom Feaunati	Leigh	2005	4	1	0	0	4
	St Helens	2004	10(7)	7	0	0	28
Sosaia Feki	Castleford	2022	(1)	0	0	0	0
Adel Fellous	Hull	2008	1(2)	0	0	0	0
	Catalans	2006-07	16(22)	4	0	0	16
Luke Felsch	Hull	2000-01	46(6)	7	0	0	28
	Gateshead	1999	28(1)	2	0	0	8
Leon Felton	Warrington	2002	4(2)	0	0	0	0
	St Helens	2001	1(1)	0	0	0	0
Dale Ferguson	Huddersfield	2011-13, 2017-19	61(23)	16	0	0	64
	Bradford	2014	3(3)	0	0	0	0
	Hull KR	2013	3(1)	1	0	0	4
	Wakefield	2007-11	40(14)	12	0	0	48
Brett Ferres	Leeds	2016-20	52(16)	11	0	0	44
	Huddersfield	2012-15	72	27	0	0	108
	Castleford	2009-12	78(5)	26	0	0	104
	Wakefield	2007-08	36(2)	6	5	0	34
	Bradford	2005-06	18(17)	11	2	0	48
David Ferriol	Catalans	2007-12	72(55)	8	0	0	32
Jason Ferris	Leigh	2005	4	1	0	0	4
Callum Field	Wigan	2017-18	(8)	0	0	0	0
Jai Field	Wigan	2021-24	72(1)	45	4	0	188
Jamie Field	Wakefield	1999-2006	133(59)	19	0	0	76
	Huddersfield	1998	15(5)	0	0	0	0
	Leeds	1996-97	3(11)	0	0	0	0
Mark Field	Wakefield	2003-07	28(7)	3	0	0	12
Jamie Fielden	London	2003	(1)	0	0	0	0
	Huddersfield	1998-2000	4(8)	0	0	0	0
Stuart Fielden	Huddersfield	2013	8(1)	0	0	0	0
	Wigan	2006-12	105(24)	2	0	0	8
	Bradford	1998-2006	142(78)	41	0	0	164
David Fifita	Wakefield	2016-23	66(79)	25	2	0	104
Lafaele Filipo	Workington	1996	15(4)	3	0	0	12
Salesi Finau	Warrington	1996-97	16(15)	8	0	0	32
Brett Finch	Wigan	2011-12	49(3)	16	0	0	64
Vinny Finigan	Bradford	2010	4(1)	4	0	0	16
Liam Finn	Widnes	2018	1	0	0	0	0
	Wakefield	2004, 2016-18	71(4)	5	220	0	460
	Castleford	2014-15	45(2)	8	5	2	44
	Halifax	2002-03	16(5)	2	30	1	69
Lee Finnerty	Halifax	2003	18(2)	5	2	0	24
Phil Finney	Warrington	1998	1	0	0	0	0
Simon Finnigan	Widnes	2003-05, 2012	56(24)	21	0	0	84
	Huddersfield	2009-10	22(5)	6	0	0	24
	Bradford	2008	14(13)	8	0	0	32
	Salford	2006-07	50	17	0	0	68
Matt Firth	Halifax	2000-01	12(2)	0	0	0	0
Andy Fisher	Wakefield	1999-2000	31(8)	4	0	0	16
Ben Fisher	London	2013	8(12)	1	0	0	4
	Catalans	2012	9(5)	1	0	0	4
	Hull KR	2007-11	78(46)	18	0	0	72
Zach Fishwick	Hull KR	2022	1(6)	1	0	0	4
Ethan Fitzgerald	Salford	2024	1	0	0	0	0
Craig Fitzgibbon	Hull	2010-11	42(1)	9	8	0	52
Lachlan Fitzgibbon							
	Warrington	2024	14	1	0	0	4
Daniel Fitzhenry	Hull KR	2008-09	36(11)	14	0	0	56
Karl Fitzpatrick	Salford	2004-07, 2009-10	89(11)	33	2	0	136
Conor Fitzsimmons							
	Castleford	2016	(2)	0	0	0	0
Mark Flanagan	Salford	2016-20	62(27)	8	0	0	32
	St Helens	2012-15	40(39)	9	0	0	36
	Wigan	2009	3(7)	1	0	0	4
Chris Flannery	St Helens	2007-12	108(11)	32	0	0	128

PLAYER	CLUB	YEAR	APP	TRIES	GOALS	FG	PTS
Darren Fleary	Leigh	2005	24	1	0	0	4
	Huddersfield	2003-04	43(8)	4	0	0	16
	Leeds	1997-2002	98(9)	3	0	0	12
Dan Fleming	Castleford	2013-14, 2020	(16)	1	0	0	4
Greg Fleming	London	1999-2001	64(1)	40	2	0	164
Matty Fleming	Leigh	2019	12(1)	6	0	0	24
	Leigh	2017	5	1	0	0	4
	St Helens	2015-17	17	7	0	0	28
Adam Fletcher	Castleford	2006, 2008	16(7)	11	0	0	44
Bryan Fletcher	Wigan	2006-07	47(2)	14	0	0	56
Richard Fletcher	Castleford	2006	13(5)	3	4	0	20
	Hull	1999-2004	11(56)	5	0	0	20
Greg Florimo	Halifax	2000	26	6	4	0	32
	Wigan	1999	18(2)	7	1	0	30
Ben Flower	Leigh	2021	2(2)	0	0	0	0
	Wigan	2012-20	131(37)	21	0	0	84
	Crusaders	2010-11	10(23)	2	0	0	8
	Celtic	2009	2(15)	0	0	0	0
Jason Flowers	Salford	2004	6(1)	0	0	0	0
	Halifax	2002	24(4)	4	0	0	16
	Castleford	1996-2001	119(19)	33	0	1	133
Stuart Flowers	Castleford	1996	(3)	0	0	0	0
Adrian Flynn	Castleford	1996-97	19(2)	10	0	0	40
Paddy Flynn	Castleford	2016	9(1)	6	0	0	24
	Widnes	2012-15	72	41	0	0	164
Wayne Flynn	Sheffield	1997	3(5)	0	0	0	0
Adam Fogerty	Warrington	1998	4	0	0	0	0
	St Helens	1996	13	1	0	0	4
Israel Folau	Catalans	2020	13	5	0	0	20
Mahe Fonua	Castleford	2022-23	35(1)	5	0	0	20
	Hull	2016-17, 2020-21	78(5)	39	0	0	156
Liam Foran	Salford	2013	10(3)	1	0	0	4
Carl Forber	Leigh	2005	4	1	0	0	4
	St Helens	2004	1(1)	0	6	0	12
Paul Forber	Salford	1997-98	19(12)	4	0	0	16
Tom Forber	Wigan	2022, 2024	(11)	1	0	0	4
	Wakefield	2023	(2)	0	0	0	0
Byron Ford	Hull KR	2007	13	6	0	0	24
James Ford	Castleford	2009	3(5)	1	0	0	4
Mike Ford	Castleford	1997-98	25(12)	5	0	3	23
	Warrington	1996	3	0	0	0	0
Jim Forshaw	Salford	1999	(1)	0	0	0	0
Mike Forshaw	Warrington	2004	20(1)	5	0	0	20
	Bradford	1997-2003	162(7)	32	0	0	128
	Leeds	1996	11(3)	5	0	0	20
Carl Forster	Salford	2015-16	5(7)	1	0	0	4
	St Helens	2011-12, 2014	(4)	0	0	0	0
	London	2014	2(3)	0	0	0	0
Mark Forster	Warrington	1996-2000	102(1)	40	0	0	160
Liam Forsyth	Wigan	2017-18	11(2)	3	0	0	12
Alex Foster	Castleford	2017-21, 2023	41(23)	12	0	0	48
	London	2014	20	3	0	0	12
	Leeds	2013	(8)	1	0	0	4
David Foster	Halifax	2000-01	4(9)	0	0	0	0
Jamie Foster	Huddersfield	2016	3	2	5	0	18
	Bradford	2013-14	32	12	111	0	270
	Hull	2012	9	5	45	0	110
	St Helens	2010-12	44(3)	30	201	0	522
Matty Foster	Salford	2024	(3)	0	0	0	0
	Leigh	2021	4(2)	0	0	0	0
	St Helens	2020	(1)	0	0	0	0
Peter Fox	Wakefield	2007, 2012-14	85	44	0	0	176
	Hull KR	2008-11	95	52	0	0	208
Matty Fozard	London	2019	7(16)	3	0	0	12
	St Helens	2014	1	0	0	0	0
Nick Fozzard	Castleford	2011	7(10)	0	0	0	0
	St Helens	2004-08, 2010	100(25)	7	0	0	28
	Hull KR	2009	18(4)	1	0	0	4
	Warrington	2002-03	43(11)	2	0	0	8
	Huddersfield	1998-2000	24(8)	2	0	0	8
	Leeds	1996-97	6(16)	3	0	0	12
David Fraisse	Workington	1996	8	0	0	0	0
Daniel Frame	Widnes	2002-05	100(6)	24	0	0	96
Romain Franco	Wakefield	2023	4	2	0	0	8
	Catalans	2021-22	6(1)	1	0	0	4
Paul Franze	Castleford	2006	2(1)	0	0	0	0
Matt Frawley	Leeds	2024	25	6	0	0	24
	Huddersfield	2019	19(2)	4	0	0	16
Laurent Frayssinous							
	Catalans	2006	14(2)	3	32	0	76
Bevan French	Wigan	2019-24	95(6)	90	0	0	360
Andrew Frew	Halifax	2003	17	5	0	0	20
	Wakefield	2002	21	8	0	0	32
	Huddersfield	2001	26	15	0	0	60

171

Super League Players 1996-2024

PLAYER	CLUB	YEAR	APP	TRIES	GOALS	FG	PTS
Dale Fritz	Castleford	1999-2003	120(4)	9	0	0	36
Gareth Frodsham	St Helens	2008-09	1(9)	0	0	0	0
Liam Fulton	Huddersfield	2009	12(3)	4	0	0	16
David Furner	Leeds	2003-04	45	8	23	0	78
	Wigan	2001-02	51(2)	21	13	0	110
David Furness	Castleford	1996	(1)	0	0	0	0
David Fusitu'a	Leeds	2022-24	43	18	0	0	72
Matt Gafa	Harlequins	2006-09	81	26	16	0	136
Luke Gale	Wakefield	2023	10	1	2	1	9
	Hull	2022	19	2	38	1	85
	Leeds	2020-21	26	8	16	4	68
	Castleford	2015-18	100	32	402	15	947
	Bradford	2012-14	56(2)	13	108	4	272
	Harlequins	2009-11	56(12)	18	86	3	247
Ben Galea	Hull	2013	12(2)	3	0	0	12
	Hull KR	2008-12	115(2)	33	0	0	132
Danny Galea	Widnes	2014-15	38(4)	5	0	0	20
Tommy Gallagher	Hull KR	2007	1(7)	0	0	0	0
	Widnes	2004	(6)	0	0	0	0
	London	2003	1(9)	1	0	0	4
Keith Galloway	Leeds	2016-17	28(4)	1	0	0	4
Mark Gamson	Sheffield	1996	3	0	0	0	0
Jim Gannon	Hull KR	2007	7(16)	1	0	0	4
	Huddersfield	2003-06	79(14)	11	0	0	44
	Halifax	1999-2002	83(4)	14	0	0	56
Morgan Gannon	Leeds	2021-23	25(21)	7	0	0	28
Josh Ganson	Wigan	2017-18	1(6)	2	0	0	8
Mitch Garbutt	Toulouse	2022	3(5)	1	0	0	4
	Hull KR	2019-20	5(22)	5	0	0	20
	Leeds	2015-18	36(25)	7	0	0	28
Steve Garces	Salford	2001	(1)	0	0	0	0
Ben Garcia	Catalans	2013-24	172(47)	35	0	0	140
Jean-Marc Garcia	Sheffield	1996-97	35(3)	22	0	0	88
Will Gardiner	Hull	2022-24	9(16)	1	0	0	4
Ade Gardner	Hull KR	2014	18	7	0	0	28
	St Helens	2002-13	236(12)	146	0	0	584
Matt Gardner	Harlequins	2009	6(3)	2	0	0	8
	Huddersfield	2006-07	22(3)	7	0	0	28
	Castleford	2004	1	1	0	0	4
Tom Garratt	Hull KR	2022	3(2)	0	0	0	0
Steve Gartland	Oldham	1996	1(1)	0	1	0	2
Daniel Gartner	Bradford	2001-03	74(1)	26	0	0	104
Dean Gaskell	Warrington	2002-05	58(1)	10	0	0	40
Lee Gaskell	Wakefield	2022-23	22	3	2	0	16
	Huddersfield	2017-21	89(1)	24	30	1	157
	Bradford	2014	21	5	0	0	20
	Salford	2013	17	8	2	0	36
	St Helens	2010-13	33(9)	14	12	1	81
Jack Gatcliffe	Salford	2024	(1)	0	0	0	0
George Gatis	Huddersfield	2008	5(5)	1	0	0	4
James Gavet	Huddersfield	2020-21	12(12)	4	0	0	16
Richard Gay	Castleford	1996-2002	94(16)	39	0	0	156
Andrew Gee	Warrington	2000-01	33(1)	4	0	0	16
Matty Gee	Leigh	2021	9(5)	4	0	0	16
	Hull KR	2020	6(5)	0	0	0	0
	London	2019	14(8)	5	0	0	20
	Salford	2015	(2)	0	0	0	0
Anthony Gelling	Leigh	2021	6	2	0	0	8
	Warrington	2020	11	6	0	0	24
	Wigan	2012-17	101(1)	52	0	0	208
Stanley Gene	Hull KR	2007-09	37(17)	9	0	0	36
	Bradford	2006	5(16)	8	0	0	32
	Huddersfield	2001, 2003-05	70(6)	27	0	0	108
	Hull	2000-01	5(23)	6	0	0	24
Steve Georgallis	Warrington	2001	5(1)	2	0	0	8
Luke George	Bradford	2014	9(1)	3	0	0	12
	Huddersfield	2012-13	28(2)	18	0	0	72
	Hull KR	2013	4	2	0	0	8
	Wakefield	2007-11	38(3)	24	0	0	96
Shaun Geritas	Warrington	1997	(5)	1	0	0	4
Alex Gerrard	Salford	2022-23	16(13)	2	0	0	8
	Leigh	2021	5(9)	0	0	0	0
	Widnes	2012-18	48(40)	4	0	0	16
Anthony Gibbons	Leeds	1996	9(4)	2	0	1	9
David Gibbons	Leeds	1996	3(4)	2	0	0	8
Scott Gibbs	St Helens	1996	9	3	0	0	12
Ashley Gibson	Wakefield	2016-17	9	4	0	0	16
	Castleford	2014-15	27	9	0	0	36
	Salford	2010-13	77(4)	41	0	0	164
	Leeds	2005-09	25(7)	13	9	0	70
Damian Gibson	Castleford	2003-04	40(3)	5	0	0	20
	Salford	2002	28	3	0	0	12
	Halifax	1998-2001	104(1)	39	0	0	156
	Leeds	1997	18	3	0	0	12
Kurt Gidley	Warrington	2016-17	44	11	97	0	238
Matt Gidley	St Helens	2007-10	105	40	6	0	172
Tony Gigot	Toulouse	2022	19	2	1	2	12
	Wakefield	2020	6(1)	1	6	0	16
	Toronto	2020	2(1)	0	0	0	0
	Catalans	2010-11, 2015-19	117(13)	43	51	12	286
	London	2014	2	0	4	0	8
Ian Gildart	Oldham	1996-97	31(7)	0	0	0	0
Oliver Gildart	Hull KR	2024	14	2	0	0	8
	Leigh	2023	8	1	0	0	4
	Wigan	2015-21	128(2)	58	0	0	232
	Salford	2015	3	1	0	0	4
Chris Giles	Widnes	2003-04	35	12	0	0	48
	St Helens	2002	(1)	0	0	0	0
Keane Gilford	St Helens	2022	1	0	0	0	0
Kieran Gill	Castleford	2017-18	4	4	0	0	16
Peter Gill	London	1996-99	75(6)	20	0	0	80
Carl Gillespie	Halifax	1996-99	47(36)	13	0	0	52
Michael Gillett	London	2001-02	23(21)	12	2	0	52
Simon Gillies	Warrington	1999	28	6	0	0	24
Tom Gilmore	Salford	2020	2	1	0	0	4
	Widnes	2012-18	38(1)	11	51	3	149
Lee Gilmour	Wakefield	2014	10(3)	2	0	0	8
	Castleford	2013	10(2)	0	0	0	0
	Huddersfield	2010-12	71(1)	17	0	0	68
	St Helens	2004-09	149(3)	41	0	0	164
	Bradford	2001-03	44(31)	20	0	0	80
	Wigan	1997-2000	44(39)	22	0	0	88
Marc Glanville	Leeds	1998-99	43(3)	5	0	0	20
Eddie Glaze	Castleford	1996	1	0	0	0	0
Paul Gleadhill	Leeds	1996	4	0	0	0	0
Ben Gledhill	Salford	2012-13	3(10)	1	0	0	4
	Wakefield	2010-11	(16)	0	0	0	0
Mark Gleeson	Warrington	2000-08	38(102)	12	0	0	48
Martin Gleeson	Salford	2013-14	26(1)	4	0	0	16
	Hull	2011	6	4	0	0	16
	Wigan	2009-11	46(1)	19	0	0	76
	Warrington	2005-09	110(1)	44	0	0	176
	St Helens	2002-04	56(1)	25	0	0	100
	Huddersfield	1999-2001	47(9)	18	0	0	72
Sean Gleeson	Hull KR	2013	6	0	0	0	0
	Salford	2011-12	35	14	0	0	56
	Wakefield	2007-10	67(6)	20	0	0	80
	Wigan	2005-06	3(3)	0	0	0	0
Billy Glover	Salford	2024	1	0	0	0	0
Charlie Glover	Salford	2024	(1)	0	0	0	0
Jon Goddard	Hull KR	2007	20	2	0	0	8
	Castleford	2000-01	(2)	0	0	0	0
Richard Goddard	Castleford	1996-97	11(3)	2	10	0	28
Brad Godden	Leeds	1998-99	47	15	0	0	60
Pita Godinet	Wakefield	2014-15	18(19)	10	0	0	40
Wayne Godwin	Salford	2011-13, 2015	43(8)	6	0	0	24
	Bradford	2008-10	16(44)	9	0	0	36
	Hull	2007	3(13)	1	0	0	4
	Wigan	2005-06	9(38)	6	0	0	24
	Castleford	2001-04	30(33)	18	56	0	184
Jason Golden	London	2012	7(2)	1	0	0	4
	Harlequins	2009-11	34(12)	3	0	0	12
	Wakefield	2007-08	26(5)	1	0	0	4
Marvin Golden	Widnes	2003	4	1	0	0	4
	London	2001	17(2)	1	0	0	4
	Halifax	2000	20(2)	5	0	0	20
	Leeds	1996-99	43(11)	19	0	0	76
Ashton Golding	Huddersfield	2020-24	36(30)	9	0	0	36
	Leeds	2014-18	42(9)	5	14	0	48
Brett Goldspink	Halifax	2000-02	64(5)	2	0	0	8
	Wigan	1999	6(16)	1	0	0	4
	St Helens	1998	19(4)	2	0	0	8
	Oldham	1997	13(2)	0	0	0	0
Lee Gomersall	Hull KR	2008	1	0	0	0	0
Bryson Goodwin	Warrington	2018-19	52	20	29	0	138
Luke Goodwin	London	1998	9(2)	3	1	1	15
	Oldham	1997	16(4)	10	17	2	76
Grant Gore	Widnes	2012-15	6(11)	1	0	0	4
Louix Gorman	Hull KR	2023	1	0	0	0	0
Aaron Gorrell	Catalans	2007-08	23	6	14	0	52
Andy Gorski	Salford	2001-02	(2)	0	0	0	0
Cyrille Gossard	Catalans	2006-12	54(30)	5	0	0	20
Mickael Goudemand	Leeds	2024	10(8)	1	0	0	4
	Catalans	2018-23	26(68)	9	0	0	36
Bobbie Goulding	Salford	2001-02	31(1)	2	56	4	124
	Wakefield	2000	12	3	25	3	65
	Huddersfield	1998-99	27(1)	3	65	4	146
	St Helens	1996-98	42(2)	9	210	4	460
Bobbie Goulding (Jnr)	Wakefield	2013	1(2)	0	1	0	2

Super League Players 1996-2024

PLAYER	CLUB	YEAR	APP	TRIES	GOALS	FG	PTS
Darrell Goulding	Hull KR	2015	8	1	0	0	4
	Wigan	2005-14	129(24)	68	0	0	272
	Salford	2009	9	5	0	0	20
Mick Govin	Leigh	2005	5(6)	4	0	0	16
Craig Gower	London	2012-13	40	7	24	0	76
David Gower	Salford	2006-07	(16)	0	0	0	0
Regan Grace	St Helens	2017-22	128	75	0	0	300
Shane Grady	London	2013	5(4)	1	2	0	8
Brad Graham	Castleford	2020-21	3	1	0	0	4
James Graham	St Helens	2003-11, 2020	143(63)	48	0	0	192
Nathan Graham	Bradford	1996-98	17(28)	4	0	1	17
Nick Graham	Wigan	2003	13(1)	2	0	0	8
Dalton Grant	Crusaders	2011	(1)	0	0	0	0
Jon Grayshon	Harlequins	2007-09	10(32)	4	0	0	16
	Huddersfield	2003-06	7(43)	5	0	0	20
Blake Green	Wigan	2013-14	42(1)	15	0	0	60
	Hull KR	2011-12	35	14	0	0	56
Brett Green	Gateshead	1999	10(2)	0	0	0	0
Chris Green	Wakefield	2019-20	8(19)	1	0	0	4
	Hull	2012-19	33(92)	7	0	0	28
James Green	Castleford	2018	1(3)	0	0	0	0
	Leigh	2017	4(5)	0	0	0	0
	Hull KR	2012-16	8(64)	3	0	0	12
Lucas Green	Warrington	2023-24	(5)	0	0	0	0
Toby Green	Huddersfield	2001	3(1)	1	0	0	4
Craig Greenhill	Castleford	2004	21(4)	1	0	0	4
	Hull	2002-03	56	3	2	0	16
Clint Greenshields	Catalans	2007-12	137	81	0	0	324
Ollie Greensmith	Wakefield	2021	1	0	0	0	0
Brandon Greenwood	Halifax	1996	1	0	0	0	0
Gareth Greenwood	Huddersfield	2003	(1)	0	0	0	0
	Halifax	2002	1	0	0	0	0
James Greenwood	Salford	2015, 2020-23	16(4)	3	0	0	12
	Hull KR	2015-16, 2018-19	29(23)	7	0	0	28
	Wigan	2013, 2015	(2)	0	0	0	0
	London	2014	10(5)	3	0	0	12
Joe Greenwood	Huddersfield	2021-24	32(38)	4	0	0	16
	Wigan	2018-20	23(16)	12	0	0	48
	St Helens	2012-17	40(28)	26	0	0	104
Lee Greenwood	Huddersfield	2005	7	3	0	0	12
	London	2004-05	30(2)	19	0	0	76
	Halifax	2000-03	38(2)	17	0	0	68
	Sheffield	1999	1(1)	0	0	0	0
Nick Gregson	Wigan	2016-17	5(9)	1	0	0	4
James Grehan	Castleford	2012	2(2)	0	0	0	0
Maxime Greseque	Wakefield	2007	2(1)	0	0	0	0
Mathieu Griffi	Catalans	2006-08	1(25)	0	0	0	0
Darrell Griffin	Salford	2013-15	31(27)	1	0	0	4
	Leeds	2012	8(19)	2	0	0	8
	Huddersfield	2007-11	65(60)	13	0	0	52
	Wakefield	2003-06	55(37)	9	3	0	42
George Griffin	Castleford	2020-24	68(13)	5	0	0	20
	Salford	2015-19	69(22)	16	0	0	64
	Wakefield	2015	5	0	0	0	0
	London	2014	(19)	1	0	0	4
	Hull KR	2012-13	11(7)	0	0	0	0
Josh Griffin	Wakefield	2011, 2023	23	7	21	0	70
	Hull	2017-23	119(8)	38	4	0	160
	Salford	2014-16	42	23	77	0	246
	Castleford	2012	20	13	1	0	54
	Huddersfield	2009	2	0	0	0	0
Jonathan Griffiths	Paris	1996	(4)	1	0	0	4
Andrew Grima	Workington	1996	2(9)	2	0	0	8
Tony Grimaldi	Hull	2000-01	56(1)	14	0	0	56
	Gateshead	1999	27(2)	10	0	0	40
Danny Grimley	Sheffield	1996	4(1)	1	0	0	4
Scott Grix	Huddersfield	2010-16, 2019	141(11)	53	32	0	276
	Wakefield	2008-09, 2017-18	81(3)	32	0	0	128
Simon Grix	Warrington	2006-14	133(25)	42	0	0	168
	Halifax	2003	2(4)	0	0	0	0
Brett Grogan	Gateshead	1999	14(7)	3	0	0	12
Brent Grose	Warrington	2003-07	134(5)	55	0	0	220
David Guasch	Catalans	2010	1	0	0	0	0
Joan Guasch	Catalans	2014-16	(6)	0	0	0	0
Renaud Guigue	Catalans	2006	14(4)	3	0	0	12
Jerome Guisset	Catalans	2006-10	102(23)	9	0	0	36
	Wigan	2005	20(2)	3	0	0	12
	Warrington	2000-04	59(65)	21	0	0	84
Awen Guttenbeil	Castleford	2008	19	0	0	0	0
Reece Guy	Oldham	1996	3(4)	0	0	0	0
Josh Guzdek	Hull KR	2013, 2015	2	1	0	0	4
Titus Gwaze	Wakefield	2019-20	(5)	0	0	0	0
Tom Haberecht	Castleford	2008	2(2)	1	0	0	4
Dean Hadley	Hull KR	2019-24	81(15)	6	0	0	24
	Hull	2013-16, 2018-19	55(26)	10	0	0	40
	Wakefield	2017	14(7)	2	0	0	8
Gareth Haggerty	Harlequins	2008-09	8(28)	6	0	0	24
	Salford	2004-07	1(93)	15	0	0	60
	Widnes	2002	1(2)	1	0	0	4
Kurt Haggerty	Widnes	2012	6(8)	2	0	0	8
Andy Haigh	St Helens	1996-98	20(16)	11	0	0	44
Scott Hale	St Helens	2011	(3)	1	0	0	4
Michael Haley	Leeds	2008	(1)	0	0	0	0
Carl Hall	Leeds	1996	7(2)	3	0	0	12
Corey Hall	Castleford	2024	14	2	0	0	8
	Hull KR	2023-24	8(2)	2	0	0	8
	Wakefield	2022-23	27(1)	8	0	0	32
	Leeds	2020-21	1(2)	0	0	0	0
Craig Hall	Hull KR	2011-14, 2018-19	102(3)	51	65	2	336
	Wakefield	2015-16	35	14	30	0	116
	Hull	2007-10	59(9)	39	11	0	178
Glenn Hall	Bradford	2010	7(18)	2	0	0	8
Martin Hall	Halifax	1998	2(10)	0	0	0	0
	Hull	1999	7	0	0	0	0
	Castleford	1998	4	0	0	0	0
	Wigan	1996-97	31(5)	7	6	0	40
Ryan Hall	Hull KR	2021-24	97	58	0	0	232
	Leeds	2007-18	278(3)	196	0	0	784
Sam Hall	Castleford	2020-24	9(26)	2	0	0	8
Steve Hall	Widnes	2004	1	0	0	0	0
	London	2002-03	35(3)	10	0	0	40
	St Helens	1999-2001	36(22)	19	0	0	76
Graeme Hallas	Huddersfield	2001	1	0	0	0	0
	Hull	1998-99	30(10)	6	39	1	103
	Halifax	1996	11(4)	5	0	0	20
Sam Hallas	Leeds	2016	(2)	0	0	0	0
Macauley Hallett	Hull KR	2014	2	3	0	0	12
Dave Halley	Bradford	2007-10	63(12)	20	0	0	80
	Wakefield	2009	5	4	0	0	16
Danny Halliwell	Salford	2007	2(3)	0	0	0	0
	Leigh	2005	5	3	0	0	12
	Halifax	2000-03	17(8)	4	0	0	16
	Warrington	2002	9(1)	8	0	0	32
	Wakefield	2002	3	0	0	0	0
Colum Halpenny	Wakefield	2003-06	103(1)	36	0	0	144
	Halifax	2002	22	12	0	0	48
Sam Halsall	Huddersfield	2023-24	33(1)	16	0	0	64
	Wigan	2020-22	15(1)	7	0	0	28
Frankie Halton	Leigh	2023-24	25(4)	3	0	0	12
	Hull KR	2022-23	20(5)	6	0	0	24
Jon Hamer	Bradford	1996	(1)	0	0	0	0
Andrew Hamilton	London	1997, 2003	1(20)	3	0	0	12
John Hamilton	St Helens	1998	3	0	0	0	0
Gabe Hamlin	Wigan	2018-19	6(18)	3	0	0	12
Karle Hammond	Halifax	2002	10(2)	2	14	0	36
	Salford	2001	2(3)	1	0	0	4
	London	1999-2000	47	23	2	3	99
	St Helens	1996-98	58(8)	28	0	4	116
Ryan Hampshire	Wigan	2013-15, 2023-24	29(6)	12	27	0	102
	Castleford	2016, 2022	24(2)	10	0	0	40
	Wakefield	2018-21	75(6)	22	122	3	355
	Leigh	2017	12(1)	3	0	0	12
Rhys Hanbury	Widnes	2012-18	153	71	99	1	483
	Crusaders	2010-11	26(1)	14	0	0	56
Anthony Hancock	Paris	1997	8(6)	1	0	0	4
Michael Hancock	Salford	2001-02	12(24)	7	0	0	28
Jordan Hand	Wakefield	2015	(2)	0	0	0	0
	St Helens	2013-14	(3)	0	0	0	0
Gareth Handford	Castleford	2001	7(2)	0	0	0	0
	Bradford	2000	1(1)	0	0	0	0
Paul Handforth	Castleford	2006	2(15)	2	1	0	10
	Wakefield	2000-04	17(44)	10	13	0	66
Ash Handley	Leeds	2014-24	191(3)	115	2	0	464
Paddy Handley	Leeds	1996	1(1)	2	0	0	8
Dean Hanger	Warrington	1999	7(11)	3	0	0	12
	Huddersfield	1998	20(1)	5	0	0	20
Chris Hankinson	Salford	2024	14(7)	5	0	0	20
	Toulouse	2022	25	5	64	0	148
	Wigan	2018-20	18(4)	4	19	0	54
Umyla Hanley	Leigh	2023-24	28	10	0	0	40
	Wigan	2020-22	10	4	0	0	16
Josh Hannay	Celtic	2009	17	2	24	0	56

173

Super League Players 1996-2024

PLAYER	CLUB	YEAR	APP	TRIES	GOALS	FG	PTS
Harrison Hansen	Toulouse	2022	1(19)	1	0	0	4
	Widnes	2018	1	1	0	0	4
	Leigh	2017	19(2)	1	0	0	4
	Salford	2014-15	41(2)	7	0	0	28
	Wigan	2004-13	155(62)	39	0	0	156
Lee Hansen	Wigan	1997	10(5)	0	0	0	0
Shontayne Hape	Bradford	2003-08	123(2)	79	0	0	316
Lionel Harbin	Wakefield	2001	(1)	0	0	0	0
Zak Hardaker	Leigh	2023-24	45(3)	9	36	0	108
	Leeds	2011-16, 2022	153	59	55	1	347
	Wigan	2019-22	70(2)	22	195	2	480
	Castleford	2017	28	12	1	0	50
Ian Hardman	Hull KR	2007	18	4	0	0	16
	St Helens	2003-07	32(11)	9	5	0	46
Jeff Hardy	Hudds-Sheff	2000	20(5)	6	0	1	25
	Sheffield	1999	22(4)	7	0	0	28
Spencer Hargrave	Castleford	1996-99	(6)	0	0	0	0
Bryn Hargreaves	Bradford	2011-12	45(5)	1	0	0	4
	St Helens	2007-10	53(44)	7	0	0	28
	Wigan	2004-06	16(12)	1	0	0	4
Lee Harland	Castleford	1996-2004	148(35)	20	0	0	80
Neil Harmon	Halifax	2003	13(3)	0	0	0	0
	Salford	2001	6(5)	0	0	0	0
	Bradford	1998-2000	15(13)	2	0	0	8
	Huddersfield	1998	12	1	0	0	4
	Leeds	1996	10	1	0	0	4
Ben Harris	Bradford	2005-07	70(4)	24	0	0	96
Iestyn Harris	Bradford	2004-08	109(11)	35	87	2	316
	Leeds	1997-2001	111(7)	57	490	6	1214
	Warrington	1996	16	4	63	2	144
Liam Harris	Hull	2018	9(2)	3	0	0	12
Ben Harrison	Wakefield	2016	3	0	0	0	0
	Warrington	2007-15	125(59)	14	0	0	56
James Harrison	Warrington	2022-24	42(11)	11	0	0	44
	Leeds	2020	2(2)	0	0	0	0
Karl Harrison	Hull	1999	26	2	0	0	8
	Halifax	1996-98	60(2)	2	0	0	8
Owen Harrison	Hull KR	2019-20	3(6)	0	0	0	0
Andrew Hart	London	2004	12(1)	2	0	0	8
Ben Hartill	Warrington	2024	(1)	0	0	0	0
Tim Hartley	Harlequins	2006	1	0	0	0	4
	Salford	2004-05	6(7)	5	0	0	20
Carlos Hassan	Bradford	1996	6(4)	2	0	0	8
Phil Hassan	Wakefield	2002	9(1)	0	0	0	0
	Halifax	2000-01	25(4)	3	0	0	12
	Salford	1998	15	2	0	0	8
	Leeds	1996-97	38(4)	12	0	0	48
James Hasson	Wakefield	2017	(4)	0	0	0	0
	Salford	2017	4(1)	0	0	0	0
Jackson Hastings	Wigan	2020-21	42	13	1	3	57
	Salford	2018-19	34	11	4	0	52
Tom Haughey	Castleford	2006	1(3)	1	0	0	4
	London	2003-04	10(8)	1	0	0	4
	Wakefield	2001-02	5(11)	0	0	0	0
Simon Haughton	Wigan	1996-2002	63(46)	32	0	0	128
Solomon Haumono	Harlequins	2006	10(9)	6	0	0	24
	London	2005	24(5)	8	0	0	32
Weller Hauraki	Hull KR	2019-20	34(4)	5	0	0	20
	Widnes	2018	7	0	0	0	0
	Salford	2015-18	45(12)	8	0	0	32
	Castleford	2013-14	50(2)	9	0	0	36
	Leeds	2011-12	18(17)	6	0	0	24
	Crusaders	2010	26(1)	11	0	0	44
Ethan Havard	Wigan	2019-24	38(50)	7	0	0	28
Richie Hawkyard	Bradford	2007	1(2)	1	0	0	4
Andy Hay	Widnes	2003-04	50(2)	7	0	0	28
	Leeds	1997-2002	112(27)	43	0	0	172
	Sheffield	1996-97	17(3)	5	0	0	20
Adam Hayes	Hudds-Sheff	2000	2(1)	0	0	0	0
Joey Hayes	Salford	1999	9	2	0	0	8
	St Helens	1996-98	11(6)	7	0	0	28
Leon Hayes	Warrington	2022-24	10(1)	0	6	0	12
James Haynes	Hull KR	2009	1	0	0	0	0
Callum Hazzard	St Helens	2019	(1)	0	0	0	0
Mathew Head	Hull	2007	9(1)	1	0	1	5
Mitch Healey	Castleford	2001-03	68(1)	10	16	0	72
Daniel Heckenberg	Harlequins	2006-09	31(39)	4	0	0	16
Andrew Heffernan	Hull KR	2018	7	2	0	0	8
Chris Heil	Hull KR	2012-13	4	2	0	0	8
Ben Hellewell	Salford	2022-24	7(18)	4	0	0	16
	Leigh	2021	22	4	0	0	16
	London	2019	2	0	0	0	0
Ricky Helliwell	Salford	1997-99	(2)	0	0	0	0
Tom Hemingway	Huddersfield	2005-09	7(7)	1	17	0	38
Bryan Henare	St Helens	2000-01	4(12)	1	0	0	4

PLAYER	CLUB	YEAR	APP	TRIES	GOALS	FG	PTS
Richard Henare	Warrington	1996-97	28(2)	24	0	0	96
Andrew Henderson	Castleford	2006, 2008	44(11)	4	0	0	16
Ian Henderson	Catalans	2011-15	118(9)	12	0	0	48
	Bradford	2005-07	33(37)	13	0	0	52
Kevin Henderson	Wakefield	2005-11	52(68)	9	0	0	36
	Leigh	2005	(1)	0	0	0	0
Adam Henry	Bradford	2014	23(1)	5	0	0	20
Mark Henry	Salford	2009-11	67	22	0	0	88
Brad Hepi	Castleford	1999, 2001	9(21)	3	0	0	12
	Salford	2000	3(5)	0	0	0	0
	Hull	1998	15(1)	3	0	0	12
Tyla Hepi	Castleford	2020-22	5(17)	0	0	0	0
	Hull KR	2013	(4)	0	0	0	0
Jon Hepworth	Castleford	2003-04	19(23)	7	8	0	44
	Leeds	2003	(1)	0	0	0	0
	London	2002	(2)	0	0	0	0
Marc Herbert	Bradford	2011	20	4	2	0	20
Aaron Heremaia	Widnes	2015-18	44(41)	7	0	0	28
	Hull	2012-14	27(37)	12	0	0	48
Maxime Herold	London	2014	(2)	0	0	0	0
Ian Herron	Hull	2000	9	1	17	0	38
	Gateshead	1999	25	4	105	0	226
Jason Hetherington	London	2001-02	37	9	0	0	36
Gareth Hewitt	Salford	1999	2(1)	0	0	0	0
Sam Hewitt	Huddersfield	2018-24	37(39)	12	0	0	48
	Wakefield	2023	6(1)	0	0	0	0
Andrew Hick	Hull	2000	9(9)	1	0	0	4
	Gateshead	1999	12(5)	2	0	0	8
Jarrad Hickey	Wakefield	2011	(8)	2	0	0	8
Chris Hicks	Warrington	2008-10	72	56	119	0	462
Paul Hicks	Wakefield	1999	(1)	0	0	0	0
Darren Higgins	London	1998	5(6)	2	0	0	8
Iain Higgins	London	1997-98	1(7)	2	0	0	8
Liam Higgins	Wakefield	2011	4(12)	0	0	0	0
	Castleford	2008-10	42(32)	2	0	0	8
	Hull	2003-06	1(34)	0	0	0	0
Jack Higginson	Wigan	2016	2(1)	1	0	0	4
Micky Higham	Leigh	2017	11(1)	2	0	0	8
	Warrington	2009-15	73(78)	34	0	0	136
	Wigan	2006-08	61(28)	13	0	0	52
	St Helens	2001-05	43(56)	32	0	0	128
Chris Highton	Warrington	1997	1(1)	0	0	0	0
David Highton	London	2004-05	21(24)	2	0	0	8
	Salford	2002	4(5)	2	0	0	8
	Warrington	1998-2001	18(14)	2	0	0	8
Paul Highton	Salford	1998-2002, 2004-07	114(80)	14	0	0	56
	Halifax	1996-97	12(18)	2	0	0	8
Adam Higson	Leigh	2017	13	2	0	0	8
Peta Hiku	Hull KR	2024	29	15	1	0	62
	Warrington	2017	4	1	0	0	4
Andy Hill	Huddersfield	1999	(4)	0	0	0	0
Chris Hill	Castleford	1999	4(4)	0	0	0	0
	Huddersfield	2022-24	58	1	0	0	4
	Warrington	2012-21	245(10)	28	0	0	112
	Leigh	2005	(1)	0	0	0	0
Daniel Hill	St Helens	2022	2	0	0	0	0
Danny Hill	Wigan	2006-07	1(10)	0	0	0	0
	Hull KR	2007	2	0	0	0	0
	Hull	2004-06	4(6)	0	0	0	0
George Hill	Castleford	2024	10(3)	0	0	0	0
Harvie Hill	Wigan	2022-24	1(26)	3	0	0	12
Howard Hill	Oldham	1996-97	22(12)	4	0	0	16
John Hill	St Helens	2003	(1)	0	0	0	0
	Halifax	2003	1(2)	0	0	0	0
	Warrington	2001-02	(4)	0	0	0	0
Scott Hill	Harlequins	2007-08	41(2)	13	0	0	52
Mark Hilton	Warrington	1996-2000, 2002-06	141(40)	7	0	0	28
Ryan Hinchcliffe	Huddersfield	2016-18	70(11)	11	0	0	44
Dan Hindmarsh	Castleford	2024	1(6)	0	0	0	0
	London	2019	(6)	0	0	0	0
Ian Hindmarsh	Catalans	2006	25	3	0	0	12
Ata Hingano	Salford	2021	3(2)	1	0	0	4
Keegan Hirst	Wakefield	2017-19	17(44)	1	0	0	4
Jy Hitchcox	Castleford	2016-18	25(1)	21	0	0	84
Brendan Hlad	Castleford	2008	(3)	0	0	0	0
Andy Hobson	Widnes	2004	5(13)	0	0	0	0
	Halifax	1998-2003	51(85)	8	0	0	32
Gareth Hock	Leigh	2017	12(1)	3	0	0	12
	Salford	2014-15	15(1)	4	0	0	16
	Widnes	2013	15(2)	9	1	0	38
	Wigan	2003-09, 2011-12	126(43)	38	0	0	152

Super League Players 1996-2024

PLAYER	CLUB	YEAR	APP	TRIES	GOALS	FG	PTS
Tommy Hodgkinson	St Helens	2006	(1)	0	0	0	0
Andy Hodgson	Wakefield	1999	14(2)	2	1	0	10
	Bradford	1997-98	8(2)	4	0	0	16
Bailey Hodgson	Castleford	2020	1	0	0	0	0
Brett Hodgson	Warrington	2011-13	66	33	268	1	669
	Huddersfield	2009-10	45	13	166	0	384
David Hodgson	Hull KR	2012-14	51	31	0	0	124
	Huddersfield	2008-11	84	59	0	0	236
	Salford	2005-07	81	30	47	0	214
	Wigan	2000-04	90(19)	43	0	0	172
	Halifax	1999	10(3)	5	0	0	20
Elliot Hodgson	Huddersfield	2009	1	0	0	0	0
Josh Hodgson	Hull KR	2010-14	98(29)	35	0	0	140
	Hull	2009	(2)	0	0	0	0
Josh Hodson	Castleford	2024	3	0	0	0	0
Ryan Hoffman	Wigan	2011	28(1)	11	0	0	44
Darren Hogg	London	1996	(1)	0	0	0	0
Michael Hogue	Paris	1997	5(7)	0	0	0	0
Lance Hohaia	St Helens	2012-15	67(9)	21	0	1	85
Chris Holden	Warrington	1996-97	2(1)	0	0	0	0
Daniel Holdsworth	Hull	2013	19	2	28	2	66
	Salford	2010-12	71	18	183	1	439
Stephen Holgate	Halifax	2000	1(10)	0	0	0	0
	Hull	1999	1	0	0	0	0
	Wigan	1997-98	11(26)	2	0	0	8
	Workington	1996	19	3	0	0	12
Stephen Holker	Hull KR	2015-16	(4)	0	0	0	0
Martyn Holland	Wakefield	2000-03	52(3)	6	0	0	24
Oliver Holmes	Leigh	2023-24	15(9)	2	0	0	8
	Warrington	2022	21(2)	3	0	0	12
	Castleford	2010-21	176(35)	42	0	0	168
Tim Holmes	Widnes	2004-05	15(4)	0	0	0	0
Tom Holmes	Huddersfield	2019-20	12(5)	0	0	0	0
	Castleford	2015-17	7(8)	3	0	0	12
Adam Holroyd	Warrington	2022-24	16(7)	5	0	0	20
Graham Holroyd	Huddersfield	2003	3(5)	0	0	0	0
	Salford	2000-02	40(11)	8	75	5	187
	Halifax	1999	24(2)	3	74	5	165
	Leeds	1996-98	40(26)	22	101	8	298
Tom Holroyd	Leeds	2018-21, 2023-24	22(33)	6	0	0	24
Dallas Hood	Wakefield	2003-04	18(9)	1	0	0	4
Liam Hood	Wakefield	2022-23	37(2)	8	0	0	32
	Leigh	2017, 2021	24(8)	7	0	0	28
	Salford	2015	2(15)	0	0	0	0
	Leeds	2012	1(4)	3	0	0	12
Jacob Hookem	Hull	2021-22	1(4)	0	0	0	0
Luke Hooley	Castleford	2024	9(1)	1	3	0	10
	Leeds	2023	8	4	0	0	16
Jason Hooper	St Helens	2003-07	89(6)	35	30	0	200
Will Hope	Salford	2013	1(2)	0	0	0	0
Lee Hopkins	Harlequins	2006-07	44(3)	11	0	0	44
	London	2005	29	6	0	0	24
Sam Hopkins	Leigh	2017	3(17)	6	0	0	24
Will Hopoate	St Helens	2022-23	27	5	0	0	20
Sean Hoppe	St Helens	1999-2002	69(16)	32	0	0	128
Graeme Horne	Hull KR	2012-16	81(18)	21	0	0	84
	Huddersfield	2010-11	23(17)	11	0	0	44
	Hull	2003-09	49(74)	24	0	0	96
Liam Horne	Castleford	2023-24	25(5)	4	0	0	16
Richard Horne	Hull	1999-2014	341(16)	115	12	6	490
Justin Horo	Wakefield	2018-19	22(14)	6	0	0	24
	Catalans	2016-17	34(1)	12	0	0	48
John Hough	Warrington	1996-97	9	2	0	0	8
Danny Houghton	Hull	2007-24	353(57)	49	0	0	196
Sylvain Houles	Wakefield	2003, 2005	8(1)	1	0	0	4
	London	2001-02	17(10)	11	0	0	44
	Hudds-Sheff	2000	5(2)	1	0	0	4
Chris Houston	Widnes	2016-18	58(1)	5	0	0	20
Harvey Howard	Wigan	2001-02	25(27)	1	0	0	4
	Bradford	1998	4(2)	1	0	0	4
	Leeds	1996	8	0	0	0	0
Kim Howard	London	1997	4(5)	0	0	0	0
Stuart Howarth	Wakefield	2011, 2015-16	30(5)	4	0	0	16
	Hull	2015	2(3)	0	0	0	0
	Salford	2012-14	25(12)	1	0	0	4
	St Helens	2013	14(1)	0	0	0	0
Stuart Howarth	Workington	1996	(2)	0	0	0	0
David Howell	London	2012-13	24	5	0	0	20
	Harlequins	2008-11	76	26	0	0	104
Phil Howlett	Bradford	1999	5(1)	2	0	0	8
Tex Hoy	Castleford	2024	17	7	0	0	28
	Hull	2023-24	18(3)	3	2	0	16
Daniel Hoyes	London	2024	(1)	0	0	0	0
Craig Huby	Wakefield	2017-19	25(26)	3	0	0	12
	Huddersfield	2015-16	37(2)	2	0	0	8
	Castleford	2003-04, 2006, 2008-14	130(57)	27	41	0	190
Ryan Hudson	Castleford	2002-04, 2009-12	138(12)	31	0	0	124
	Huddersfield	1998-99, 2007-08	51(22)	10	0	0	40
	Wakefield	2000-01	42(9)	11	0	1	45
Adam Hughes	Widnes	2002-05	89(2)	45	51	0	282
	Halifax	2001	8(8)	8	0	0	32
	Wakefield	1999-2000	43(3)	21	34	0	152
	Leeds	1996-97	4(5)	4	0	0	16
Ian Hughes	Sheffield	1996	9(8)	4	0	0	16
Jack Hughes	Leigh	2023-24	26(18)	3	0	0	12
	Warrington	2016-22	141(2)	19	0	0	76
	Huddersfield	2015	30(1)	5	0	0	20
	Wigan	2011-14	31(33)	9	0	0	36
Jack Hughes	London	2024	(2)	0	0	0	0
Mark Hughes	Catalans	2006	23	9	0	0	36
Steffan Hughes	London	1999-2001	1(13)	1	0	0	4
David Hulme	Salford	1997-99	53(1)	5	0	0	20
	Leeds	1996	8(1)	2	0	0	8
Declan Hulme	Widnes	2013-15	5	2	0	0	8
Paul Hulme	Warrington	1996-97	23(1)	2	0	0	8
Gary Hulse	Widnes	2005	12(5)	2	0	0	8
	Warrington	2001-04	20(28)	8	0	1	33
Alan Hunte	Salford	2002	19(2)	9	0	0	36
	Warrington	1999-2001	83	49	0	0	196
	Hull	1998	21	7	0	0	28
	St Helens	1996-97	30(2)	28	0	0	112
Konrad Hurrell	St Helens	2022-24	55	22	0	0	88
	Leeds	2019-21	47(5)	23	0	0	92
Alex Hurst	London	2013	8(2)	2	0	0	8
Kieran Hyde	Wakefield	2010-11	11	4	4	0	24
Nick Hyde	Paris	1997	5(5)	1	0	0	4
Chaz I'Anson	Hull KR	2007-10	17(13)	3	0	0	12
Sebastine Ikahihifo	Huddersfield	2016-19, 2022-24	54(69)	3	0	0	12
	Salford	2020-21	11(16)	0	0	0	0
Matt Ikuvalu	Catalans	2023-24	33	10	0	0	40
Ryan Ince	Widnes	2016-18	19	11	0	0	44
Greg Inglis	Warrington	2021	2	2	0	0	8
Krisnan Inu	Salford	2019-21	43(3)	20	167	1	415
	Widnes	2018	14	6	21	0	66
	Catalans	2015-17	39	11	3	0	50
Mark Ioane	Leigh	2021	10(5)	2	0	0	8
	London	2019	1(14)	1	0	0	4
Edwin Ipape	Leigh	2023-24	37(7)	14	0	0	56
Andy Ireland	Hull	1998-99	22(15)	0	0	0	0
	Bradford	1996	1	0	0	0	0
Kevin Iro	St Helens	1999-2001	76	39	0	0	156
	Leeds	1996	16	9	0	0	36
Willie Isa	Wigan	2016-24	168(21)	15	0	0	60
	Widnes	2012-15	44(33)	3	0	0	12
	Castleford	2011	7(2)	6	0	0	24
Andrew Isherwood	Wigan	1998-99	(5)	0	0	0	0
Olu Iwenofu	London	2000-01	2(1)	0	0	0	0
Chico Jackson	Hull	1999	(4)	0	0	0	0
Lee Jackson	Hull	2001-02	37(9)	12	1	0	50
	Leeds	1999-2000	28(24)	7	0	0	28
Michael Jackson	Sheffield	1998-99	17(17)	2	0	0	8
	Halifax	1996-97	27(6)	11	0	0	44
Paul Jackson	Castleford	2003-04, 2010-12	44(30)	5	0	0	20
	Huddersfield	1998, 2005-09	50(73)	4	0	0	16
	Wakefield	1999-2002	57(42)	2	0	0	8
Rob Jackson	Leigh	2005	20(3)	5	0	0	20
	London	2002-04	26(14)	9	0	0	36
Wayne Jackson	Halifax	1996-97	17(5)	2	0	0	8
Aled James	Crusaders	2011	1	0	0	0	0
	Celtic	2009	3(3)	0	0	0	0
	Widnes	2003	3	0	0	0	0
Andy James	Halifax	1996	(4)	0	0	0	0
Jordan James	Wigan	2006, 2014	3(18)	4	0	0	16
	Salford	2012-13	1(40)	6	0	0	24
	Crusaders	2010-11	5(24)	3	0	0	12
	Celtic	2009	17(4)	1	0	0	4
Matt James	Wakefield	2012	(4)	0	0	0	0
	Harlequins	2010	(2)	0	0	0	0
	Bradford	2006-09	1(23)	0	0	0	0
Pascal Jampy	Catalans	2006	4(7)	0	0	0	0
	Paris	1996-97	3(2)	0	0	0	0

175

Super League Players 1996-2024

PLAYER	CLUB	YEAR	APP	TRIES	GOALS	FG	PTS
Adam Janowski	Harlequins	2008	(1)	0	0	0	0
Zach Jebson	Hull	2023-24	(11)	1	0	0	4
Ben Jeffries	Bradford	2008-09, 2011-12	76(3)	20	0	0	80
	Wakefield	2003-07, 2010-11	151(10)	70	20	6	326
Mick Jenkins	Hull	2000	24	2	0	0	8
	Gateshead	1999	16	3	0	0	12
Ed Jennings	London	1998-99	1(2)	0	0	0	0
Rod Jensen	Huddersfield	2007-08	26(3)	13	0	0	52
Anthony Jerram	Warrington	2007	(2)	0	0	0	0
Lee Jewitt	Hull KR	2018-19	10(2)	0	0	0	0
	Castleford	2014-16	22(12)	0	0	0	0
	Salford	2007, 2009-13	32(62)	4	0	0	16
	Wigan	2005	(2)	0	0	0	0
Maxime Jobe	Catalans	2022	1	0	0	0	0
Isaac John	Wakefield	2012	13	1	19	0	42
Andrew Johns	Warrington	2005	3	1	12	1	29
Matthew Johns	Wigan	2001	24	3	0	1	13
Andy Johnson	Salford	2004-05	8(26)	7	0	0	28
	Castleford	2002-03	32(16)	11	0	0	44
	London	2000-01	24(21)	12	0	0	48
	Huddersfield	1999	5	1	0	0	4
	Wigan	1996-99	24(20)	19	0	0	76
Bruce Johnson	Widnes	2004-05	(4)	0	0	0	0
Corey Johnson	Leeds	2019, 2021-24	6(22)	1	0	0	4
Dallas Johnson	Catalans	2010	26	1	0	0	4
Greg Johnson	Salford	2014-19	86	36	1	0	146
	Wakefield	2011	11	2	0	0	8
Jack Johnson	Warrington	2015-17, 2019	17	5	0	0	20
	Widnes	2017	3	1	0	0	4
Jason Johnson	St Helens	1997-99	2	0	0	0	0
Josh Johnson	Salford	2019-22	11(16)	1	0	0	4
	Hull KR	2018	2(2)	0	0	0	0
	Huddersfield	2013-16	14(17)	0	0	0	0
Luis Johnson	Castleford	2023-24	3(8)	1	0	0	4
	Hull KR	2019, 2021-23	27(5)	2	0	0	8
	Warrington	2018-20	1(8)	0	0	0	0
Mark Johnson	Salford	1999-2000	22(9)	16	0	0	64
	Hull	1998	10(1)	4	0	0	16
	Workington	1996	12	4	0	0	16
Nick Johnson	Hull KR	2012	1	0	0	0	0
Nick Johnson	London	2003	(1)	0	0	0	0
Paul Johnson	Crusaders	2011	6(4)	0	0	0	0
	Wakefield	2010	12(3)	4	0	0	16
	Warrington	2007-09	37(9)	17	0	0	68
	Bradford	2004-06	46(8)	19	0	0	76
	Wigan	1996-2003	74(46)	54	0	0	216
Paul Johnson	Widnes	2014	5(11)	0	0	0	0
	Hull	2013	3(16)	0	0	0	0
	Wakefield	2011-12	25(21)	6	0	0	24
	St Helens	2010	(2)	0	0	0	0
Richard Johnson	Bradford	2008	(2)	0	0	0	0
Ben Johnston	Castleford	2012	2	0	0	0	0
Jordan Johnstone	Castleford	2023	5(3)	0	0	0	0
	Hull	2020-22	23(27)	1	0	0	4
	Widnes	2016-18	17(13)	1	0	0	4
Tom Johnstone	Catalans	2023-24	45	36	0	0	144
	Wakefield	2015-22	106	81	0	0	324
Ben Jones	Harlequins	2010	(2)	0	0	0	0
Chris Jones	Leigh	2005	1(1)	0	0	0	0
Connor Jones	Salford	2020	7	1	0	0	4
Danny Jones	Halifax	2003	1	0	0	0	0
David Jones	Oldham	1997	14(1)	5	0	0	20
Jacob Jones	London	2024	16(9)	2	0	0	8
Josh Jones	Huddersfield	2021-23	45(1)	8	0	0	32
	Hull	2020	7	0	0	0	0
	Salford	2016-19	92(4)	17	0	0	68
	St Helens	2012-15	88(9)	22	0	0	88
Mark Jones	Warrington	1996	8(11)	2	0	0	8
Phil Jones	Leigh	2005	16	8	31	0	94
	Wigan	1999-2001	14(7)	6	25	0	74
Stacey Jones	Catalans	2006-07	39	11	43	3	133
Stephen Jones	Huddersfield	2005	(1)	0	0	0	0
Stuart Jones	Castleford	2009-12	69(27)	14	0	0	56
	Huddersfield	2004-08	96(22)	17	0	0	68
	St Helens	2003	(18)	2	0	0	8
	Wigan	2002	5(3)	1	0	0	4
Ben Jones-Bishop	Wakefield	2016-20	110	61	0	0	244
	Salford	2015	17	12	0	0	48
	Leeds	2008-09, 2011-14	70(2)	46	0	0	184
	Harlequins	2010	17	10	0	0	40
Jamie Jones-Buchanan	Leeds	1999-2019	293(73)	70	1	0	282
Tim Jonkers	Wigan	2006	3(1)	0	0	0	0
	Salford	2004-06	5(11)	0	0	0	0
	St Helens	1999-2004	41(64)	12	0	0	48
Caelum Jordan	Castleford	2021	1	0	0	0	0
Darren Jordan	Wakefield	2003	(1)	0	0	0	0
Josh Jordan-Roberts	Leeds	2017	(1)	0	0	0	0
Phil Joseph	Salford	2016	(12)	0	0	0	0
	Widnes	2013-15	11(38)	1	0	0	4
	Bradford	2012	(6)	0	0	0	0
	Huddersfield	2004	7(6)	0	0	0	0
Max Jowitt	Wakefield	2014-23	104(2)	32	33	0	194
Warren Jowitt	Hull	2003	(2)	0	0	0	0
	Salford	2001-02	17(4)	2	0	0	8
	Wakefield	2000	19(3)	8	0	0	32
	Bradford	1996-99	13(25)	5	0	0	20
Chris Joynt	St Helens	1996-2004	201(14)	68	0	0	272
Benjamin Jullien	Catalans	2018-22	66(12)	16	0	0	64
	Warrington	2016-17	19(7)	4	0	0	16
Mathieu Jussaume	Toulouse	2022	12	2	0	0	8
Gregory Kacala	Paris	1996	7	1	0	0	4
Andy Kain	Castleford	2004, 2006	9(7)	3	10	0	32
Sam Kasiano	Warrington	2023	6(18)	3	0	0	12
	Catalans	2019-22	3(73)	12	0	0	48
Antonio Kaufusi	Huddersfield	2014	15(2)	1	0	0	4
	Bradford	2014	4	0	0	0	0
	London	2012-13	44(5)	5	0	0	20
Mal Kaufusi	London	2004	1(3)	0	0	0	0
Ben Kavanagh	Hull KR	2018	13(8)	0	0	0	0
	Wakefield	2015	6(3)	0	0	0	0
	Widnes	2012-15	18(33)	0	0	0	0
Liam Kay	Wakefield	2012-13, 2020-23	45(21)	18	0	0	72
	Toronto	2020	6	1	0	0	4
Ben Kaye	Harlequins	2009-10	2(13)	0	0	0	0
	Leeds	2008	2(2)	1	0	0	4
Elliot Kear	Salford	2020-21	12(1)	1	0	0	4
	London	2019	26	3	0	0	12
	Bradford	2012-14	53(2)	17	0	0	68
	Crusaders	2010-11	16(1)	4	0	0	16
	Celtic	2009	3	0	0	0	0
Brett Kearney	Bradford	2010-14	107	55	0	0	220
Stephen Kearney	Hull	2005	22(2)	5	0	0	20
Damon Keating	Wakefield	2002	7(17)	1	0	0	4
Kris Keating	Hull KR	2014	23	5	0	0	20
Shaun Keating	London	1996	1(3)	0	0	0	0
Mark Keenan	Workington	1996	3(4)	1	0	0	4
Adam Keighran	Wigan	2024	26	8	79	0	190
	Catalans	2023	25	13	73	0	198
Jimmy Keinhorst	Hull KR	2019-23	42(21)	13	0	0	52
	Castleford	2021	(2)	1	0	0	4
	Leeds	2012-18	46(23)	25	0	0	100
	Widnes	2018	3	1	0	0	4
	Wakefield	2014	7	1	0	0	4
Albert Kelly	Hull	2017-20	63(2)	39	0	1	157
	Hull KR	2015-16	37	21	3	0	90
Callum Kemp	Hull	2024	1	0	0	0	0
Tony Kemp	Wakefield	1999-2000	15(5)	2	0	1	9
	Leeds	1996-98	23(2)	5	0	2	22
Damien Kennedy	London	2003	5(11)	1	0	0	4
Rhys Kennedy	London	2024	25(1)	1	0	0	4
	Hull KR	2023	16(6)	1	0	0	4
Ian Kenny	St Helens	2004	(1)	0	0	0	0
Sean Kenny	Salford	2016	(4)	0	0	0	0
Shaun Kenny-Dowall	Hull KR	2020-23	83	19	0	0	76
Jason Kent	Leigh	2005	23	1	0	0	4
Liam Kent	Hull	2012-13	1(5)	0	0	0	0
Shane Kenward	Wakefield	1999	28	6	0	0	24
	Salford	1998	1	0	0	0	0
Jason Keough	Paris	1997	2	1	0	0	4
Keiran Kerr	Widnes	2005	6	2	0	0	8
Lee Kershaw	London	2024	25	7	0	0	28
	Wakefield	2019-23	48	17	0	0	68
Martin Ketteridge	Halifax	1996	7(5)	0	0	0	0
Ronnie Kettlewell	Warrington	1996	(1)	0	0	0	0
Joe Keyes	Hull KR	2020-21	5(1)	1	6	0	16
	London	2014	7	5	0	0	20
Younes Khattabi	Catalans	2006-08	24(4)	10	0	0	40
Samy Kibula	Castleford	2024	(5)	0	0	0	0
	Warrington	2020	(2)	0	0	0	0
	Wigan	2018	(1)	0	0	0	0
David Kidwell	Warrington	2001-02	14(12)	9	0	0	36
Ben Kilner	Wigan	2020	(1)	0	0	0	0
Andrew King	London	2003	23(1)	15	0	0	60
Dave King	Huddersfield	1998-99	11(17)	2	0	0	8

Super League Players 1996-2024

PLAYER	CLUB	YEAR	APP	TRIES	GOALS	FG	PTS
George King	Hull KR	2020-24	71(17)	3	0	0	12
	Wakefield	2019-20	8(19)	0	0	0	0
	Warrington	2014-18	12(68)	1	0	0	4
James King	Leigh	2005	5(7)	0	0	0	0
Kevin King	Wakefield	2005	8(1)	2	0	0	8
	Castleford	2004	(1)	0	0	0	0
Matt King	Warrington	2008-11	91	58	0	0	232
Paul King	Wakefield	2010-11	10(19)	0	0	1	1
	Hull	1999-2009	136(93)	20	0	1	81
Toby King	Warrington	2014-22, 2024	140(7)	55	0	0	220
	Wigan	2023	28	11	0	0	44
	Huddersfield	2022	12	2	0	0	8
Jon Luke Kirby	Huddersfield	2019	(3)	0	0	0	0
Will Kirby	Hull	2024	1	0	0	0	0
Andy Kirk	Wakefield	2005	6(3)	1	0	0	4
	Salford	2004	20	5	0	0	20
	Leeds	2001-02	4(4)	0	0	0	0
Ian Kirke	Wakefield	2015	2(2)	1	0	0	4
	Leeds	2006-14	52(132)	10	0	0	40
John Kirkpatrick	London	2004-05	18(1)	5	0	0	20
	St Helens	2001-03	10(11)	10	0	0	40
	Halifax	2003	4	1	0	0	4
Danny Kirmond	Wakefield	2010, 2012-14	147(15)	42	0	0	168
	Huddersfield	2008-11	18(31)	9	0	0	36
Wayne Kitchin	Workington	1996	11(6)	3	17	1	47
Sione Kite	Widnes	2012	6(8)	1	0	0	4
Ian Knott	Leigh	2005	8(1)	2	0	0	8
	Wakefield	2002-03	34(5)	7	79	0	186
	Warrington	1996-2001	68(41)	24	18	0	132
Matt Knowles	Wigan	1996	(3)	0	0	0	0
Michael Knowles	Castleford	2006	(1)	0	0	0	0
Morgan Knowles	St Helens	2016-24	148(48)	28	0	0	112
Phil Knowles	Salford	1997	1	0	0	0	0
Simon Knox	Halifax	1999	(6)	0	0	0	0
	Salford	1998	1(1)	0	0	0	0
	Bradford	1996-98	9(19)	7	0	0	28
Toa Kohe-Love	Warrington	1996-2001, 2005-06	166(3)	90	0	0	360
	Bradford	2004	1(1)	0	0	0	0
	Hull	2002-03	42	19	0	0	76
Paul Koloi	Wigan	1997	1(2)	1	0	0	4
Craig Kopczak	Wakefield	2019-20	25(15)	3	0	0	12
	Salford	2016-18	39(27)	11	0	0	44
	Huddersfield	2013-15	48(37)	6	0	0	24
	Bradford	2006-12	32(83)	10	0	0	40
Michael Korkidas	Wakefield	2003-06, 2009-11	133(36)	15	0	0	60
	Huddersfield	2009	4(1)	1	0	0	4
	Castleford	2008	15(6)	1	0	0	4
	Salford	2007	26(1)	1	0	0	4
Nick Kouparitsas	Harlequins	2011	2(13)	1	0	0	4
Olsi Krasniqi	London	2012-14, 2019	36(35)	3	0	0	12
	Salford	2015-17	8(29)	1	0	0	4
	Harlequins	2010-11	3(20)	1	0	0	4
David Krause	London	1996-97	22(1)	7	0	0	28
Ben Kusto	Huddersfield	2001	21(4)	9	0	1	37
Tim Lafai	Salford	2022-24	64	21	0	0	84
Anthony Laffranchi	St Helens	2012-14	50(18)	19	0	0	76
Ben Laguerre	Toulouse	2022	1	0	0	0	0
Matthieu Laguerre	Catalans	2021-24	36(4)	19	0	0	76
Matty Laidlaw	Hull	2022, 2024	(13)	0	0	0	0
James Laithwaite	Warrington	2013-15	23(22)	1	0	0	4
	Hull KR	2012	1(2)	1	0	0	4
Adrian Lam	Wigan	2001-04	105(2)	40	1	9	171
Lachlan Lam	Leigh	2023-24	56	15	0	0	60
Brock Lamb	London	2019	6	3	0	1	13
Callum Lancaster	Hull	2014-16	7	9	0	0	36
Ben Lane	St Helens	2022	2	0	1	0	2
Jordan Lane	Hull	2018-24	106(32)	15	1	0	62
Mark Lane	Paris	1996	(2)	0	0	0	0
Allan Langer	Warrington	2000-01	47	13	4	0	60
Kevin Langer	London	1996	12(4)	2	0	0	8
Junior Langi	Salford	2005-06	27(7)	7	0	0	28
Samisoni Langi	Wakefield	2023	14	2	0	0	8
	Catalans	2018-22	98(1)	27	0	0	108
	Leigh	2017	3	1	0	0	4
Chris Langley	Huddersfield	2000-01	18(1)	3	0	0	12
Gareth Langley	St Helens	2006	1	1	3	0	10
Jamie Langley	Hull KR	2014	6(5)	1	0	0	4
	Bradford	2002-13	182(57)	36	0	0	144
Ryan Lannon	Salford	2015-22	52(39)	6	0	0	24
	Hull KR	2019	1(5)	1	0	0	4
Kevin Larroyer	Castleford	2017	2(4)	0	0	0	0
	Hull KR	2014-16	34(13)	9	0	0	36
	Catalans	2012-13	9(10)	6	0	0	24
Andy Last	Hull	1999-2005	16(10)	4	0	0	16
Leilani Latu	Warrington	2020	3	1	0	0	4
Sam Latus	Hull KR	2010-13	34(3)	13	0	0	52
Epalahame Lauaki	Wigan	2012-13	14(16)	2	0	0	8
	Hull	2009-11	3(50)	4	0	0	16
Dale Laughton	Warrington	2002	15(1)	0	0	0	0
	Huddersfield	2000-01	36(2)	4	0	0	16
	Sheffield	1996-99	48(22)	5	0	0	20
Ali Lauitiiti	Wakefield	2012-15	46(31)	16	0	0	64
	Leeds	2004-11	64(117)	58	0	0	232
Phoenix Laulu-Toga'e	Hull KR	2022-23	4(4)	0	0	0	0
Quentin Laulu-Toga'e	Castleford	2018	8(1)	6	0	0	24
Jason Laurence	Salford	1997	1	0	0	0	0
Leo Laurent	Catalans	2022	1	0	0	0	0
Graham Law	Wakefield	1999-2002	34(30)	6	40	0	104
Joe Law	Wakefield	2023	(1)	0	0	0	0
Neil Law	Wakefield	1999-2002	83	39	0	0	156
	Sheffield	1998	1(1)	1	0	0	4
Dean Lawford	Widnes	2003-04	17(1)	5	2	4	28
	Halifax	2001	1(1)	0	0	0	0
	Leeds	1997-2000	15(8)	2	3	0	14
	Huddersfield	1999	6(1)	0	6	1	13
	Sheffield	1996	9(5)	2	1	1	11
George Lawler	Castleford	2022-24	46(10)	1	0	0	4
	Hull KR	2016, 2018-21	62(11)	5	0	0	20
Johnny Lawless	Halifax	2001-03	73(1)	10	0	0	40
	Hudds-Sheff	2000	19(6)	3	0	0	12
	Sheffield	1996-99	76(4)	11	0	0	44
Michael Lawrence	Huddersfield	2007-22	235(60)	47	0	0	188
Adam Lawton	Salford	2019	1(1)	0	0	0	0
	Widnes	2013-14	2(10)	5	0	0	20
Corentin Le Cam	Catalans	2021-22	5(6)	0	0	0	0
Charlie Leaeno	Wakefield	2010	7(3)	2	0	0	8
Mark Leafa	Castleford	2008	5(9)	1	0	0	4
	Leigh	2005	28	2	0	0	8
Leroy Leapai	London	1996	2	0	0	0	0
Jim Leatham	Hull	1998-99	20(18)	4	0	0	16
	Leeds	1997	(1)	0	0	0	0
Andy Leathem	Warrington	1999	2(8)	0	0	0	0
	St Helens	1996-98	20(1)	1	0	0	4
Danny Lee	Gateshead	1999	16(2)	0	0	0	0
Jason Lee	Halifax	2001	10(1)	2	0	0	8
Mark Lee	Salford	1997-2000	25(11)	1	0	4	8
Robert Lee	Hull	1999	4(3)	0	0	0	0
Tommy Lee	Hull KR	2018-19	24(6)	2	0	0	8
	St Helens	2017	9(9)	0	0	0	0
	Salford	2014-16	37(5)	4	0	0	16
	London	2013	16(4)	2	0	0	8
	Huddersfield	2012	11(7)	3	0	0	12
	Wakefield	2011	25	6	0	0	24
	Crusaders	2010	3(9)	0	0	0	0
	Hull	2005-09	44(27)	6	0	0	24
Kruise Leeming	Wigan	2024	12(10)	5	0	0	20
	Leeds	2020-23	51(9)	16	0	2	66
	Huddersfield	2013-19	49(67)	15	0	0	60
Matty Lees	St Helens	2017-24	110(41)	6	0	0	24
Matthew Leigh	Salford	2000	(6)	0	0	0	0
Chris Leikvoll	Warrington	2004-07	72(18)	4	0	0	16
Jim Lenihan	Huddersfield	1999	19(1)	10	0	0	40
Mark Lennon	Celtic	2009	10(3)	1	8	0	20
	Hull KR	2007	11(4)	5	7	0	34
	Castleford	2001-03	30(21)	10	21	0	82
Tevita Leo-Latu	Wakefield	2006-10	28(49)	10	0	0	40
Gary Lester	Hull	1998-99	46	17	0	0	68
Stuart Lester	Wigan	1997	1(3)	0	0	0	0
Heath L'Estrange	Bradford	2010-13	56(35)	7	0	0	28
Afi Leuila	Oldham	1996-97	17(3)	2	0	0	8
Kylie Leuluai	Leeds	2007-15	182(45)	20	0	0	80
Macgraff Leuluai	Widnes	2012-18	52(64)	5	0	0	20
Phil Leuluai	Salford	2007, 2009-10	7(47)	3	0	0	12
Thomas Leuluai	Wigan	2007-12, 2017-22	290(3)	64	0	1	257
	Harlequins	2006	15(2)	6	0	0	24
	London	2005	20	13	0	0	52
Ricky Leutele	Leigh	2023-24	47	14	0	0	56
	Huddersfield	2021-22	32	17	0	0	68
	Toronto	2020	6	0	0	0	0
Danny Levi	Huddersfield	2022	19(7)	4	0	0	16
Loghan Lewis	Salford	2024	5(6)	0	0	0	0
Mikey Lewis	Hull KR	2019-24	88(2)	49	82	0	360

Super League Players 1996-2024

PLAYER	CLUB	YEAR	APP	TRIES	GOALS	FG	PTS
Simon Lewis	Castleford	2001	4	3	0	0	12
Oliver Leyland	London	2024	26(1)	3	40	1	93
Paul Leyland	St Helens	2006	1	0	0	0	0
Jon Liddell	Leeds	2001	1	0	0	0	0
Jason Lidden	Castleford	1997	15(1)	7	0	0	28
Jordan Lilley	Leeds	2015-18	21(11)	2	42	0	92
Danny Lima	Wakefield	2007	(3)	0	0	0	0
	Salford	2006	7(2)	0	0	0	0
	Warrington	2004-06	15(47)	9	0	0	36
Jeff Lima	Catalans	2014-15	37(7)	3	1	0	14
	Wigan	2011-12	24(29)	4	0	0	16
Arron Lindop	Warrington	2024	9	6	0	0	24
Tom Lineham	Wakefield	2022-23	19	3	0	0	12
	Warrington	2016-21	115	70	0	0	280
	Hull	2012-15	61(1)	50	0	0	200
Kane Linnett	Hull KR	2019-23	96(1)	35	0	0	140
Mason Lino	Wakefield	2021-23	67	7	132	2	294
Sam Lisone	Leeds	2023-24	9(37)	6	0	0	24
Davy Litten	Hull	2022-24	21(5)	4	0	0	16
Jez Litten	Hull KR	2019-24	50(61)	12	14	1	77
	Hull	2017-19	(17)	1	0	0	4
Harry Little	London	2013	2	0	0	0	0
Jack Littlejohn	Salford	2018	15(3)	3	1	0	14
Craig Littler	St Helens	2006	1	1	0	0	4
Stuart Littler	Salford	1998-2002, 2004-07, 2009-10	217(30)	65	0	0	260
Ben Littlewood	Leeds	2024	(1)	0	0	0	0
Harvey Livett	Huddersfield	2023-24	14(2)	2	0	0	8
	Salford	2021-22	26(1)	8	13	0	58
	Hull KR	2019-20	8(5)	3	0	0	12
	Warrington	2017-19	23(14)	13	21	0	94
Peter Livett	Workington	1996	3(1)	0	0	0	0
Leo Llong	Catalans	2022	(1)	0	0	0	0
Rhodri Lloyd	Wigan	2012-13, 2015	3(4)	0	0	0	0
	Widnes	2014	(4)	0	0	0	0
	London	2013	2	0	0	0	0
Garry Lo	Castleford	2018	1	1	0	0	4
Kevin Locke	Wakefield	2015	3	0	0	0	0
	Salford	2014-15	13	6	11	0	46
Jack Logan	Leigh	2021	5	0	0	0	0
	Hull	2014-16, 2018-19, 2021	37(2)	16	0	0	64
Scott Logan	Wigan	2006	10(11)	0	0	0	0
	Hull	2001-03	27(20)	5	0	0	20
Jamahl Lolesi	Huddersfield	2007-10	75(9)	27	0	0	108
Filimone Lolohea	Harlequins	2006	3(6)	0	0	0	0
	London	2005	8(15)	0	0	0	0
Tui Lolohea	Huddersfield	2022-24	70(5)	18	17	0	106
	Salford	2019-21	50	17	29	1	127
	Leeds	2019	15	2	19	0	46
David Lomax	Huddersfield	2000-01	45(9)	4	0	0	16
	Paris	1997	19(2)	1	0	0	4
Jonny Lomax	St Helens	2009-24	315(2)	128	96	4	708
Dave Long	London	1999	(1)	0	0	0	0
Karl Long	London	2003	(1)	0	0	0	0
	Widnes	2002	4	1	0	0	4
Sean Long	Hull	2010-11	22	6	0	0	24
	St Helens	1997-2009	263(8)	126	826	20	2176
	Wigan	1996-97	1(5)	0	0	0	0
Davide Longo	Bradford	1996	1(3)	0	0	0	0
Ellis Longstaff	Salford	2023	2(3)	2	0	0	8
	Hull	2022	9(1)	6	0	0	24
	Warrington	2020-22	5(9)	0	0	0	0
Gary Lord	Oldham	1996-97	28(12)	3	0	0	12
Paul Loughlin	Huddersfield	1998-99	34(2)	4	4	0	24
	Bradford	1996-97	36(4)	15	8	0	76
Rhys Lovegrove	Hull KR	2007-14	75(74)	19	0	0	76
Karl Lovell	Hudds-Sheff	2000	14	5	0	0	20
	Sheffield	1999	22(4)	8	0	0	32
Will Lovell	London	2012-14, 2019, 2024	53(23)	6	0	0	24
Joe Lovodua	Hull	2022-23	26(16)	6	0	0	24
James Lowes	Bradford	1996-2003	205	84	2	2	342
Laurent Lucchese	Paris	1996	13(5)	2	0	0	8
Sam Luckley	Hull KR	2023-24	5(47)	3	0	0	12
	Salford	2021-22	2(25)	1	0	0	4
Robert Lui	Leeds	2019-21	34	11	0	1	45
	Salford	2016-19	84(3)	26	33	0	170
Zebastian Luisi	Harlequins	2006-07	23(2)	4	0	0	16
	London	2004-05	21(1)	7	0	0	28
Keith Lulia	Bradford	2012-13	50	19	0	0	76
Riley Lumb	Leeds	2024	4	2	0	0	8
Shaun Lunt	Leeds	2012, 2019	15(10)	7	0	0	28
	Hull KR	2015-16, 2018-19	25(18)	11	0	0	44
	Huddersfield	2009-15	73(39)	60	0	0	240

PLAYER	CLUB	YEAR	APP	TRIES	GOALS	FG	PTS
Peter Lupton	Crusaders	2010-11	37(9)	10	0	0	40
	Celtic	2009	16(4)	4	0	0	16
	Castleford	2006, 2008	40	11	0	0	44
	Hull	2003-06	19(26)	10	3	0	46
	London	2000-02	10(15)	2	2	0	12
Darcy Lussick	Salford	2021	(4)	1	0	0	4
Joey Lussick	St Helens	2022-23	9(36)	7	6	0	40
	Salford	2019-20	27(21)	15	4	0	68
Andy Lynch	Castleford	1999-2004, 2014-17	157(54)	17	0	0	68
	Hull	2012-13	39(14)	3	0	0	12
	Bradford	2005-11	159(29)	46	0	0	184
Josh Lynch	Warrington	2022	1	1	0	0	4
Reece Lyne	Wakefield	2013-23	213(1)	60	0	0	240
	Hull	2010-11	11(1)	2	0	0	8
Jamie Lyon	St Helens	2005-06	54(1)	39	172	0	500
Iliess Macani	London	2013-14, 2024	25(4)	9	0	0	36
Nene Macdonald	Salford	2024	25	12	0	0	48
	Leeds	2023	19	2	0	0	8
Duncan MacGillivray	Wakefield	2004-08	75(18)	6	0	0	24
Brad Mackay	Bradford	2000	24(2)	8	0	0	32
Graham Mackay	Hull	2002	27	18	24	0	120
	Bradford	2001	16(3)	12	1	0	50
	Leeds	2000	12(8)	10	2	0	44
Keiron Maddocks	Leigh	2005	1(3)	0	0	0	0
Steve Maden	Leigh	2005	23	9	0	0	36
	Warrington	2002	3	0	0	0	0
Mateaki Mafi	Warrington	1996-97	7(8)	7	0	0	28
Nathan Magee	Castleford	2021	(1)	0	0	0	0
Shaun Magennis	St Helens	2010-12	7(19)	3	0	0	12
Brendan Magnus	London	2000	3	1	0	0	4
Patrick Mago	Wigan	2022-24	4(77)	6	0	0	24
Billy Magoulias	Warrington	2022	5(2)	0	0	0	0
Mark Maguire	London	1996-97	11(4)	7	13	0	54
Adam Maher	Hull	2000-03	88(4)	24	0	0	96
	Gateshead	1999	21(5)	3	0	0	12
Lee Maher	Leeds	1996	4(1)	0	0	0	0
Will Maher	Hull KR	2020-22	21(22)	1	0	0	4
	Castleford	2014-19	5(30)	1	0	0	4
Shaun Mahony	Paris	1997	5	0	0	0	0
Hutch Maiava	Hull	2007	(19)	1	0	0	4
David Maiden	Hull	2000-01	32(10)	11	0	0	44
	Gateshead	1999	5(16)	8	0	0	32
Craig Makin	Salford	1999-2001	24(20)	2	0	0	8
Harvey Makin	London	2024	6	0	0	0	0
Tommy Makinson	St Helens	2011-24	299(5)	191	244	1	1253
Brady Malam	Wigan	2000	5(20)	1	0	0	4
Dominic Maloney	Hull	2009	(7)	0	0	0	0
Francis Maloney	Castleford	1998-99, 2003-04	71(7)	24	33	3	165
	Salford	2001-02	45(1)	26	5	0	114
	Wakefield	2000	11	1	1	0	6
	Oldham	1996-97	39(2)	12	91	2	232
James Maloney	Catalans	2020-21	38	7	169	5	371
Jake Mamo	Castleford	2022-23	17(3)	10	0	0	40
	Warrington	2019-21	42(6)	27	0	0	108
	Huddersfield	2017-18	23	17	0	0	68
Dom Manfredi	Wigan	2013-16, 2018-21	73	55	0	0	220
	Salford	2014	1	2	0	0	8
George Mann	Warrington	1997	14(5)	1	0	0	4
	Leeds	1996	11(4)	2	0	0	8
Dane Manning	Leeds	2009	(1)	0	0	0	0
Josh Mantellato	Hull KR	2015-16	26	16	88	0	240
Misili Manu	Widnes	2005	1	0	0	0	0
Sika Manu	Hull	2016-19	90(4)	10	0	0	40
Willie Manu	St Helens	2013-14	35(11)	9	0	0	36
	Hull	2007-12	133(18)	33	0	0	132
	Castleford	2006	19(4)	9	0	0	36
Manase Manuokafoa	Widnes	2015-17	3(54)	3	0	0	12
	Bradford	2012-14	49(21)	3	0	0	12
Darren Mapp	Celtic	2009	9(2)	1	0	0	4
David March	Wakefield	1999-2007	164(23)	34	126	0	388
Paul March	Wakefield	1999-2001, 2007	42(31)	17	23	0	114
	Huddersfield	2003-06	71(19)	17	36	1	141
Paul Marcon	Toulouse	2022	16	5	0	0	20
Nick Mardon	London	1997-98	14	2	0	0	8
Thibaut Margalet	Catalans	2013-18	1(22)	0	0	0	0
Remy Marginet	Catalans	2011	2	0	9	0	18
Antoni Maria	Catalans	2012-16, 2018-20	10(57)	0	0	0	0
	Hull KR	2019	2(3)	0	0	0	0
	Leigh	2017	2(6)	0	0	0	0

Super League Players 1996-2024

PLAYER	CLUB	YEAR	APP	TRIES	GOALS	FG	PTS
Franck Maria	Catalans	2024	(9)	0	0	0	0
Frankie Mariano	Castleford	2014-16	14(21)	8	0	0	32
	Wakefield	2011-13	41(12)	20	0	0	80
	Hull KR	2010	(3)	0	0	0	0
Anthony Marion	Toulouse	2022	17(3)	1	2	0	8
Oliver Marns	Halifax	1996-2002	54(19)	23	0	0	92
Paul Marquet	Warrington	2002	23(2)	0	0	0	0
Callum Marriott	Salford	2011	(1)	0	0	0	0
Iain Marsh	Salford	1998-2001	1(4)	0	0	0	0
Lee Marsh	Salford	2001-02	3(4)	0	0	0	0
Matty Marsh	Hull KR	2015-16, 2018	18(4)	3	0	0	12
Stefan Marsh	Widnes	2012-18	122	56	21	0	266
	Wigan	2010-11	12	3	0	0	12
Liam Marshall	Wigan	2017-24	166	140	5	0	570
Richard Marshall	Leigh	2005	4(16)	0	0	0	0
	London	2002-03	33(11)	1	0	0	4
	Huddersfield	2000-01	35(14)	1	0	0	4
	Halifax	1996-99	38(34)	2	0	0	8
Esan Marsters	Huddersfield	2023-24	40	9	0	0	36
Brad Martin	Castleford	2020-24	7(29)	2	0	0	8
Charlie Martin	Castleford	2013	(6)	0	0	0	0
Jason Martin	Paris	1997	15(2)	3	0	0	12
Lewis Martin	Hull	2023-24	25	10	0	0	40
Rhyse Martin	Leeds	2019-24	122(3)	36	416	0	976
Scott Martin	Salford	1997-99	32(18)	8	0	0	32
Tony Martin	Hull	2012	10	1	0	0	4
	Crusaders	2010-11	40(1)	14	1	0	58
	Wakefield	2008-09	33	10	33	0	106
	London	1996-97, 2001-03	97(1)	36	170	1	485
Ugo Martin	Catalans	2018	1	0	0	0	0
Mick Martindale	Halifax	1996	(4)	0	0	0	0
Sebastien Martins	Catalans	2006, 2009-11	(21)	2	0	0	8
Shay Martyn	St Helens	2021-22	2	0	4	0	8
Tommy Martyn	St Helens	1996-2003	125(20)	87	63	12	486
Dean Marwood	Workington	1996	9(6)	0	22	0	44
Martin Masella	Warrington	2001	10(14)	5	0	0	20
	Wakefield	2000	14(8)	4	0	0	16
	Leeds	1997-1999	59(5)	1	0	0	4
Colin Maskill	Castleford	1996	8	1	1	0	6
Mose Masoe	Hull KR	2018-19	28(18)	6	0	0	24
	St Helens	2014-15	17(39)	10	0	0	40
Keith Mason	Castleford	2006, 2013	11(6)	0	0	0	0
	Huddersfield	2006-12	118(14)	4	0	0	16
	St Helens	2003-05	33(23)	4	0	0	16
	Wakefield	2000-01	5(17)	0	0	0	0
Nathan Mason	Wakefield	2023	1	0	0	0	0
	Huddersfield	2013, 2015-17, 2022	4(32)	3	0	0	12
	Leigh	2021	4(4)	1	0	0	4
	London	2019	5(10)	1	0	0	4
Willie Mason	Catalans	2016	6(8)	1	0	0	4
	Hull KR	2011	6	1	0	0	4
Samy Masselot	Wakefield	2011	(1)	0	0	0	0
Nathan Massey	Castleford	2008-23	197(81)	10	0	0	40
Suaia Matagi	Castleford	2021-23	12(35)	3	0	0	12
	Huddersfield	2018-20	39(4)	3	0	0	12
Nesiasi Mataitonga	London	2014	11(1)	1	0	0	4
Peter Mata'utia	Warrington	2022-23	50(2)	6	8	0	40
	Castleford	2018-21	63	11	58	1	161
Sione Mata'utia	St Helens	2021-24	64(11)	17	1	0	70
Vila Matautia	St Helens	1996-2001	31(68)	9	0	0	36
Feleti Mateo	London	2005	4(10)	1	0	0	4
Barrie-Jon Mather	Castleford	1998, 2000-02	50(12)	21	0	0	84
Richard Mathers	Wakefield	2012-14	71	24	0	0	96
	Castleford	2011	21(1)	7	0	0	28
	Warrington	2002, 2009-10	42(3)	11	0	0	44
	Wigan	2008-09	23(1)	2	0	0	8
	Leeds	2002-06	85(2)	26	0	0	104
Jamie Mathiou	Leeds	1997-2001	31(82)	3	0	0	12
Masi Matongo	Hull	2015, 2017-20	16(38)	3	0	0	12
Terry Matterson	London	1996-98	46	15	90	6	246
Akim Matvejev	Castleford	2024	1(1)	0	0	0	0
Manu Ma'u	Catalans	2023	4(14)	3	0	0	12
	Hull	2020-22	40	5	0	0	20
Vic Mauro	Salford	2013	1(7)	1	0	0	4
Luke May	Harlequins	2009-10	(3)	0	0	0	0
Tyrone May	Hull KR	2024	28	6	0	0	24
	Catalans	2022-23	36(7)	6	2	0	28
Casey Mayberry	Halifax	2000	1(1)	0	0	0	0
Chris Maye	Halifax	2003	3(4)	0	0	0	0
Judah Mazive	Wakefield	2016	2	1	0	0	4
Joe Mbu	Harlequins	2006-09	33(20)	3	0	0	12
	London	2003-05	29(19)	4	0	0	16
Moses Mbye	St Helens	2023-24	14(19)	5	0	1	21
Danny McAllister	Gateshead	1999	3(3)	1	0	0	4
	Sheffield	1996-97	33(7)	10	0	0	40
John McAtee	St Helens	1996	2(1)	0	0	0	0
Nathan McAvoy	Bradford	1998-2002, 2007	83(31)	46	0	0	184
	Wigan	2006	15(2)	5	0	0	20
	Salford	1997-98, 2004-05	57(4)	18	0	0	72
Tyrone McCarthy	Leigh	2021	8(3)	0	0	0	0
	Salford	2017-20	41(20)	8	2	0	36
	Hull KR	2015	20(1)	4	0	0	16
	Warrington	2009-13	12(24)	2	0	0	8
	Wakefield	2011	2(5)	1	0	0	4
Louie McCarthy-Scarsbrook	St Helens	2011-23	150(189)	59	0	0	236
	Harlequins	2006-10	41(50)	17	0	0	68
Dave McConnell	London	2003	(4)	0	0	0	0
	St Helens	2001-02	3(2)	4	0	0	16
Loui McConnell	Leeds	2020	(2)	0	0	0	0
Ned McCormack	Leeds	2024	2(1)	1	0	0	4
Robbie McCormack	Wigan	1998	24	2	0	0	8
Josh McCrone	Toronto	2020	6	1	0	0	4
Charlie McCurrie	Salford	2024	1	0	0	0	0
Steve McCurrie	Leigh	2005	7(3)	1	0	0	4
	Widnes	2002-04	55(22)	10	0	0	40
	Warrington	1998-2001	69(26)	31	0	0	124
Barrie McDermott	Leeds	1996-2005	163(69)	28	0	0	112
Brian McDermott	Bradford	1996-2002	138(32)	33	0	0	132
Ryan McDonald	Widnes	2002-03	6(4)	0	0	0	0
Wayne McDonald	Huddersfield	2005-06	11(23)	1	0	0	4
	Wigan	2005	(4)	0	0	0	0
	Leeds	2002-05	34(47)	14	0	0	56
	St Helens	2001	7(11)	4	0	0	16
	Hull	2000	5(8)	4	0	0	16
	Wakefield	1999	9(17)	8	0	0	32
James McDonnell	Leeds	2023-24	46(2)	6	0	0	24
	Wigan	2020-22	5(1)	2	0	0	8
Shannon McDonnell	St Helens	2014-16	28	15	0	0	60
	Hull	2013	19	2	0	0	8
	Hull KR	2012	21	6	0	0	24
Craig McDowell	Huddersfield	2003	(1)	0	0	0	0
	Warrington	2002	(1)	0	0	0	0
	Bradford	2000	(1)	0	0	0	0
Wes McGibbon	Halifax	1999	1	0	0	0	0
Jermaine McGillvary	Huddersfield	2010-23	287(1)	196	0	0	784
Dean McGilvray	Salford	2009-10	14	4	0	0	16
	St Helens	2006-08	5(1)	1	0	0	4
Billy McGinty	Workington	1996	1	0	0	0	0
Ryan McGoldrick	Salford	2013	19(1)	3	0	1	13
	Hull	2012	8	1	0	0	4
	Castleford	2006, 2008-12	129(5)	24	11	0	118
Aidan McGowan	Huddersfield	2024	10	2	0	0	8
Kevin McGuinness	Salford	2004-07	63(3)	11	0	0	44
Casey McGuire	Catalans	2007-10	87(4)	27	0	0	108
Danny McGuire	Hull KR	2018-19	36	9	1	3	41
	Leeds	2001-17	331(39)	238	0	6	958
Josh McGuire	Warrington	2023	6	1	0	0	4
Gary McGuirk	Workington	1996	(4)	0	0	0	0
Michael McIlorum	Catalans	2018-24	115(2)	9	0	0	36
	Wigan	2007-17	156(54)	22	0	0	88
Darnell McIntosh	Leigh	2024	14(2)	5	11	0	42
	Hull	2022-24	49(1)	22	16	0	120
	Huddersfield	2017-21	91(1)	43	12	0	196
Richard McKell	Castleford	1997-98	22(7)	2	0	0	8
Chris McKenna	Bradford	2006-07	40(7)	7	0	0	28
	Leeds	2003-05	65(4)	18	0	0	72
Phil McKenzie	Workington	1996	4	0	0	0	0
Chris McKinney	Oldham	1996-97	4(9)	2	0	0	8
Wade McKinnon	Hull	2012	10	4	0	0	16
Callum McLelland	Leeds	2019-21	10(3)	1	0	0	4
Mark McLinden	Harlequins	2006-08	46(1)	20	0	1	81
	London	2005	22(3)	8	0	0	32
Mike McMeeken	Catalans	2021-24	73(1)	16	0	0	64
	Castleford	2015-20	118(13)	30	0	0	120
	London	2012-14	25(9)	5	0	0	20
Shayne McMenemy	Hull	2003-07	80(8)	12	0	0	48
	Halifax	2001-03	63	11	0	0	44
Andy McNally	London	2004	5(3)	0	0	0	0
	Castleford	2001, 2003	2(5)	1	0	0	4

179

Super League Players 1996-2024

PLAYER	CLUB	YEAR	APP	TRIES	GOALS	FG	PTS
Gregg McNally	Leigh	2017	9	3	0	0	12
	Huddersfield	2011	1	0	6	0	12
Ben McNamara	Leigh	2024	6(1)	2	0	0	8
	Hull	2020-23	22(9)	2	16	0	40
Steve McNamara	Huddersfield	2001, 2003	41(9)	3	134	1	281
	Wakefield	2000	15(2)	2	32	0	72
	Bradford	1996-99	90(3)	14	348	7	759
Paul McNicholas	Hull	2004-05	28(12)	4	0	0	16
Neil McPherson	Salford	1997	(1)	0	0	0	0
Shannan McPherson	Salford	2012-14	20(11)	0	0	0	0
Chris McQueen	Huddersfield	2020-23	73(5)	33	0	0	132
Duncan McRae	London	1996	11(2)	3	0	1	13
Paul McShane	Castleford	2015-24	182(26)	25	63	1	227
	Wakefield	2014-15	39(9)	5	0	0	20
	Leeds	2009-13	17(38)	12	0	0	48
	Widnes	2012	6(5)	3	4	0	20
	Hull	2010	(4)	0	0	0	0
Derek McVey	St Helens	1996-97	28(4)	6	1	0	26
Dallas Mead	Warrington	1997	2	0	0	0	0
David Mead	Catalans	2018-20	51	23	0	0	92
James Meadows	London	2019, 2024	16(2)	2	0	0	8
Robbie Mears	Leigh	2005	8(6)	0	0	0	0
	Leeds	2001	23	6	0	0	24
Paul Medley	Bradford	1996-98	6(35)	9	0	0	36
Francis Meli	Salford	2014	16	11	0	0	44
	St Helens	2006-13	194(1)	122	0	0	488
Vince Mellars	Wakefield	2012-13	21(5)	4	0	0	16
	Crusaders	2010-11	46	17	0	0	68
Chris Melling	London	2012-13	25(12)	5	2	0	24
	Harlequins	2007-11	100(11)	33	6	0	144
	Wigan	2004-05	8(2)	1	3	0	10
Alex Mellor	Castleford	2022-24	59(1)	11	0	0	44
	Leeds	2020-22	27(3)	4	0	0	16
	Huddersfield	2017-19	65(10)	19	0	0	76
	Bradford	2013-14	(10)	0	0	0	0
Joe Mellor	Salford	2024	15(6)	7	0	0	28
	Leigh	2021, 2023	21(16)	6	0	0	24
	Toronto	2020	2	0	0	0	0
	Widnes	2012-18	134(1)	46	0	1	185
	Wigan	2012	1(1)	1	0	0	4
	Harlequins	2011	(1)	0	0	0	0
Paul Mellor	Castleford	2003-04	36(3)	18	0	0	72
James Mendeika	London	2013	4(2)	2	0	0	8
Craig Menkins	Paris	1997	4(5)	0	0	0	0
Luke Menzies	Hull KR	2008	(1)	0	0	0	0
Steve Menzies	Catalans	2011-13	61(6)	30	0	0	120
	Bradford	2009-10	52(1)	24	1	0	98
Gary Mercer	Castleford	2002	(1)	0	0	0	0
	Leeds	1996-97, 2001	40(2)	9	0	0	36
	Warrington	2001	18	2	0	0	8
	Halifax	1998-2001	73(2)	16	0	0	64
Trent Merrin	Leeds	2019	27	4	0	0	16
Tony Mestrov	London	1996-97, 2001	59(8)	4	0	0	16
	Wigan	1998-2000	39(39)	3	0	0	12
Keiran Meyer	London	1996	4	1	0	0	4
Brad Meyers	Bradford	2005-06	40(11)	13	0	0	52
Ronan Michael	Huddersfield	2020	(1)	0	0	0	0
Steve Michaels	Hull	2015-17	68(4)	26	0	0	104
Gary Middlehurst	Widnes	2004	(2)	0	0	0	0
Simon Middleton	Castleford	1996-97	19(3)	8	0	0	32
Constantine Mika	Hull KR	2012-13	45(4)	9	0	0	36
Thomas Mikaele	Warrington	2022-23	13(12)	4	0	0	16
Daryl Millard	Catalans	2011-14	91	38	1	0	154
	Wakefield	2010-11	21(1)	11	0	0	44
Shane Millard	Wigan	2007	19(6)	3	0	0	12
	Leeds	2006	6(21)	3	0	0	12
	Widnes	2003-05	69	23	0	0	92
	London	1998-2001	72(14)	11	1	0	46
Jack Miller	Huddersfield	2013	1	0	1	0	2
Jacob Miller	Castleford	2023-24	50	5	0	1	21
	Wakefield	2015-22	177(3)	55	17	9	263
	Hull	2013-14	20	6	9	0	42
Lachlan Miller	Leeds	2024	24	7	0	0	28
Grant Millington	Castleford	2012-21	155(75)	33	0	0	132
David Mills	Harlequins	2006-07, 2010	25(32)	2	0	0	8
	Hull KR	2008-09	20(11)	1	0	0	4
	Widnes	2002-05	17(77)	8	0	0	32
Lewis Mills	Celtic	2009	(4)	0	0	0	0
Adam Milner	Huddersfield	2023-24	30(2)	3	0	0	12
	Castleford	2010-23	177(104)	37	1	0	150
Lee Milner	Halifax	1999	(1)	0	0	0	0

PLAYER	CLUB	YEAR	APP	TRIES	GOALS	FG	PTS
Rowan Milnes	Castleford	2024	22(1)	7	51	1	131
	Hull KR	2020-23	40(3)	6	37	0	98
	Wakefield	2023	1	0	0	0	0
Hakim Miloudi	London	2024	22(1)	5	0	0	20
	Toronto	2020	5(1)	1	0	0	4
	Hull	2018-19	13(2)	5	1	0	22
Elliot Minchella	Hull KR	2020-24	76(13)	15	0	0	60
	Leeds	2013-14	(6)	1	0	0	4
Mark Minichiello	Hull	2015-19	118(4)	20	0	0	80
Greg Minikin	Warrington	2022-23	14(6)	2	0	0	8
	Hull KR	2020-21	23	10	0	0	40
	Castleford	2016-19	89(2)	39	0	0	156
Thomas Minns	Wakefield	2022	4	1	0	0	4
	Hull KR	2016, 2018	24(1)	14	0	0	56
	London	2014	23	6	0	0	24
	Leeds	2013	2(1)	1	0	0	4
John Minto	London	1996	13	4	0	0	16
Abbas Miski	Wigan	2022-24	58	47	0	0	188
Lee Mitchell	Castleford	2012	13(10)	2	0	0	8
	Warrington	2007-11	8(27)	4	0	0	16
	Harlequins	2011	11(1)	1	0	0	4
Sam Moa	Catalans	2017-20	68(6)	6	0	0	24
	Hull	2009-12	29(44)	6	0	0	24
Martin Moana	Salford	2004	6(3)	1	0	0	4
	Halifax	1996-2001, 2003	126(22)	62	0	1	249
	Wakefield	2002	19(2)	10	0	0	40
	Huddersfield	2001	3(3)	2	0	0	8
Adam Mogg	Catalans	2007-10	74	19	0	1	77
Jon Molloy	Wakefield	2013-16	25(18)	5	0	0	20
	Huddersfield	2011-12	2(1)	0	0	0	0
Steve Molloy	Huddersfield	2000-01	26(20)	3	0	0	12
	Sheffield	1998-99	32(17)	3	0	0	12
Chris Molyneux	Huddersfield	2000-01	1(18)	0	0	0	0
	Sheffield	1999	1(2)	0	0	0	0
Paul Momirovski	Leeds	2024	23	7	0	0	28
Joel Monaghan	Castleford	2016-17	29(3)	13	0	0	52
	Warrington	2011-15	127	125	2	0	504
Michael Monaghan	Warrington	2008-14	143(28)	31	0	4	128
Joel Moon	Leeds	2013-18	136(1)	61	0	0	244
	Salford	2012	17	9	0	0	36
Adrian Moore	Huddersfield	1998-99	1(4)	0	0	0	0
Brandon Moore	Huddersfield	2020	4	0	0	0	0
Connor Moore	Hull KR	2022	(3)	0	0	0	0
Danny Moore	London	2000	7	0	0	0	0
	Wigan	1998-99	49(3)	18	0	0	72
Gareth Moore	Wakefield	2011	5	1	14	1	33
Jason Moore	Workington	1996	(5)	0	0	0	0
Richard Moore	Wakefield	2007-10, 2014	52(57)	10	0	0	40
	Leeds	2012-13	3(27)	1	0	0	4
	Crusaders	2011	11(10)	1	0	0	4
	Leigh	2005	2(5)	0	0	0	0
	Bradford	2002-04	1(26)	0	0	0	0
	London	2002, 2004	5(9)	2	0	0	8
Scott Moore	Wakefield	2015-16	12(2)	0	0	0	0
	Castleford	2008, 2015	24(6)	2	0	0	8
	London	2014	26	3	0	0	12
	Huddersfield	2009, 2012	29(7)	9	0	0	36
	Widnes	2012	3(3)	0	0	0	0
	St Helens	2004-07, 2010-11	29(37)	9	0	0	36
Junior Moors	Castleford	2015-20	46(63)	18	0	0	72
Dennis Moran	Wigan	2005-06	39	17	1	1	71
	London	2001-04	107(2)	74	2	5	305
Kieran Moran	Hull KR	2016	(5)	0	0	0	0
Pat Moran	Warrington	2019	(1)	0	0	0	0
Kai Morgan	Salford	2024	1(1)	0	0	0	0
Ryan Morgan	London	2019	21	5	0	0	20
	St Helens	2017-18	46	22	0	0	88
Willie Morganson	Sheffield	1997-98	18(12)	5	3	0	26
Paul Moriarty	Halifax	1996	3(2)	0	0	0	0
Adrian Morley	Salford	2014-15	31(14)	2	0	0	8
	Warrington	2007-13	135(21)	8	0	0	32
	Bradford	2005	2(4)	0	0	0	0
	Leeds	1996-2000	95(14)	25	0	0	100
Chris Morley	Salford	1999	3(5)	0	0	0	0
	Warrington	1998	2(8)	0	0	0	0
	St Helens	1996-97	21(16)	4	0	0	16
Frazer Morris	Wakefield	2016	(1)	0	0	0	0
Glenn Morrison	Wakefield	2010-11	43(1)	9	0	0	36
	Bradford	2007-09	48(2)	19	0	0	76
Iain Morrison	Hull KR	2007	5(6)	1	0	0	4
	Huddersfield	2003-05	11(23)	0	0	0	0
	London	2001	(1)	0	0	0	0

Super League Players 1996-2024

PLAYER	CLUB	YEAR	APP	TRIES	GOALS	FG	PTS
Daniel Mortimer	Leigh	2017	3	0	0	0	0
Dale Morton	Wakefield	2009-11	22(3)	8	5	0	42
Gareth Morton	Hull KR	2007	7(4)	3	23	0	58
	Leeds	2001-02	1(1)	0	0	0	0
Daniel Moss	St Helens	2022	2	0	0	0	0
Kieren Moss	Hull KR	2018	2(1)	4	0	0	16
Lee Mossop	Salford	2017-21	68(3)	6	0	0	24
	Wigan	2008-13, 2015-16	80(65)	11	0	0	44
	Huddersfield	2009	1(4)	1	0	0	4
Aaron Moule	Salford	2006-07	45	17	0	0	68
	Widnes	2004-05	29	12	0	0	48
Bradley Moules	Wakefield	2016	(1)	0	0	0	0
Wilfried Moulinec	Paris	1996	1	0	0	0	0
Gregory Mounis	Catalans	2006-16	149(105)	27	19	0	146
Arthur Mourgue	Catalans	2018-24	66(27)	24	155	1	407
Mark Moxon	Huddersfield	1998-2001	20(5)	1	0	1	5
Logan Moy	Hull	2024	14(2)	3	0	0	12
Matt Moylan	Leigh	2024	24	5	51	0	122
Robbie Mulhern	Leigh	2023-24	48(1)	5	0	0	20
	Warrington	2021-22	20(23)	1	0	0	4
	Hull KR	2016, 2018-20	43(27)	4	0	0	16
	Leeds	2014-15	(5)	0	0	0	0
Anthony Mullally	Toronto	2020	2(4)	0	0	0	0
	Leeds	2016-18	10(48)	9	0	0	36
	Wakefield	2015	(2)	0	0	0	0
	Huddersfield	2013-15	12(24)	5	0	0	20
	Bradford	2014	1(5)	0	0	0	0
	Widnes	2012	(9)	0	0	0	0
Jake Mullaney	Salford	2014	12	2	24	0	56
Craig Mullen	Leigh	2021	9(4)	1	13	0	30
	Wigan	2018	1(1)	0	0	0	0
Brett Mullins	Leeds	2001	5(3)	1	0	0	4
Damian Munro	Widnes	2002	8(2)	1	0	0	4
	Halifax	1996-97	9(6)	8	0	0	32
Matt Munro	Oldham	1996-97	26(5)	8	0	0	32
Jack Murchie	Huddersfield	2024	8	2	0	0	8
Ben Murdoch-Masila	Warrington	2018-20	23(35)	13	0	0	52
	Salford	2016-17	46(1)	15	0	0	60
Craig Murdock	Salford	2000	(2)	0	0	0	0
	Hull	1998-99	21(6)	8	0	2	34
	Wigan	1996-98	18(17)	14	0	0	56
Aaron Murphy	Huddersfield	2012-20	169(6)	71	0	0	284
	Wakefield	2008-11	57(2)	12	0	0	48
Jack Murphy	Wigan	2012, 2014	3	1	0	0	4
	Salford	2013	10	3	1	0	14
Jamie Murphy	Crusaders	2011	(2)	0	0	0	0
Jobe Murphy	Bradford	2013	(4)	0	0	0	0
Justin Murphy	Catalans	2006-08	59	49	0	0	196
	Widnes	2004	5	1	0	0	4
Lewis Murphy	Wakefield	2022-23	22	17	0	0	68
Daniel Murray	Hull KR	2019-20	15(8)	0	0	0	0
	Salford	2017-19	14(14)	2	0	0	8
Doc Murray	Warrington	1997	(2)	0	0	0	0
	Wigan	1997	6(2)	0	0	0	0
Scott Murrell	Hull KR	2007-12	114(24)	24	26	1	149
	Leeds	2005	(1)	0	0	0	0
	London	2004	3(3)	2	0	0	8
Zane Musgrove	Warrington	2024	6(19)	1	0	0	4
Muizz Mustapha	Castleford	2023-24	12(17)	0	0	0	0
	Leeds	2020, 2022	(8)	1	0	0	4
	Hull KR	2021	1(9)	0	0	0	0
David Mycoe	Sheffield	1996-97	12(13)	1	0	0	4
Richie Myler	Leeds	2018-23	113(5)	43	6	1	185
	Catalans	2016-17	40	21	2	0	88
	Warrington	2010-15	127(4)	69	1	1	279
	Salford	2009	18	11	0	0	44
Rob Myler	Oldham	1996-97	19(2)	6	0	0	24
Stephen Myler	Salford	2006	4(8)	1	15	0	34
	Widnes	2003-05	35(14)	8	74	0	180
Vinny Myler	Salford	2004	(4)	0	0	0	0
	Bradford	2003	(1)	0	0	0	0
Matt Nable	London	1997	2(2)	1	0	0	4
Kevin Naiqama	Huddersfield	2023-24	47	21	0	0	84
	St Helens	2019-21	67	36	0	0	144
Brad Nairn	Workington	1996	14	4	0	0	16
Ben Nakubuwai	Leigh	2023-24	2(23)	1	0	0	4
	Salford	2018-19	7(28)	2	0	0	8
Sylvester Namo	Castleford	2024	1(13)	1	0	0	4
Dylan Napa	Catalans	2022	18	0	0	0	0
Frank Napoli	London	2000	14(6)	2	0	0	8
Carlo Napolitano	Salford	2000	(3)	1	0	0	4
Stephen Nash	Castleford	2012	3(4)	0	0	0	0
	Salford	2007, 2009	2(18)	1	0	0	4
	Widnes	2005	4(1)	0	0	0	0
Ethan Natoli	London	2024	13(3)	2	0	0	8
Curtis Naughton	Leigh	2017	5	3	0	0	12
	Hull	2015-16	26	13	1	0	54
	Bradford	2013	1	0	0	0	0
Ratu Naulago	Hull	2019-20	30	20	0	0	80
Romain Navarrete	Catalans	2016-17, 2023-24	47(18)	1	0	0	4
	Toulouse	2022	23	2	0	0	8
	Wakefield	2020	3(7)	0	0	0	0
	Wigan	2017-19	36(20)	0	0	0	0
Jim Naylor	Halifax	2000	7(6)	2	0	0	8
Scott Naylor	Salford	1997-98, 2004	30(1)	9	0	0	36
	Bradford	1999-2003	127(1)	51	0	0	204
Adam Neal	Salford	2010-13	17(28)	0	0	0	0
Mike Neal	Salford	1998	(1)	0	0	0	0
	Oldham	1996-97	6(4)	3	0	0	12
Jonathan Neill	Huddersfield	1998-99	20(11)	0	0	0	0
	St Helens	1996	1	0	0	0	0
Chris Nero	Salford	2011-13	31(16)	7	0	0	28
	Bradford	2008-10	65(5)	24	0	0	96
	Huddersfield	2004-07	97(8)	38	0	0	152
Jason Netherton	Hull KR	2007-14	60(74)	4	0	0	16
	London	2003-04	6	0	0	0	0
	Halifax	2002	2(3)	0	0	0	0
	Leeds	2001	(3)	0	0	0	0
Kirk Netherton	Castleford	2009-10	5(23)	3	0	0	12
	Hull KR	2007-08	9(15)	2	0	0	8
Paul Newlove	Castleford	2004	5	1	0	0	4
	St Helens	1996-2003	162	106	0	0	424
Richard Newlove	Wakefield	2003	17(5)	8	0	0	32
Harry Newman	Leeds	2017-24	91(3)	26	2	0	108
Clint Newton	Hull KR	2008-11	90(3)	37	0	0	148
Terry Newton	Wakefield	2010	(2)	0	0	0	0
	Bradford	2006-09	83(6)	26	0	0	104
	Wigan	2000-05	157(9)	62	0	0	248
	Leeds	1996-1999	55(14)	4	0	0	16
Gene Ngamu	Huddersfield	1999-2000	29(2)	9	67	0	170
Matty Nicholson	Warrington	2022-24	44(3)	16	0	0	64
	Wigan	2022	(1)	2	0	0	8
Tom Nicholson-Watton	Leeds	2023-24	(8)	0	0	0	0
Danny Nicklas	Hull	2010, 2012	2(8)	0	0	0	0
Sonny Nickle	St Helens	1999-2002	86(18)	14	0	0	56
	Bradford	1996-98	25(16)	9	0	0	36
Jason Nicol	Salford	2000-02	52(7)	11	0	0	44
Tawera Nikau	Warrington	2000-01	51	7	0	0	28
Jayden Nikorima	Salford	2024	9	3	0	0	12
	Catalans	2024	3(9)	2	0	0	8
Tom Nisbet	Leigh	2021, 2023	3(1)	0	0	0	0
	St Helens	2020	1	0	0	0	0
David Nofoaluma	Salford	2024	2	0	0	0	0
Rob Nolan	Hull	1998-99	20(11)	6	0	0	24
Paul Noone	Harlequins	2006	5(2)	0	0	0	0
	Warrington	2000-06	60(59)	12	20	0	88
Chris Norman	Halifax	2003	13(3)	2	0	0	8
Corey Norman	Toulouse	2022	11	1	0	0	4
Dan Norman	Leigh	2023-24	3(13)	0	0	0	0
	St Helens	2021-23	2(16)	2	0	0	8
	Salford	2021	(3)	1	0	0	4
	Widnes	2018	(1)	0	0	0	0
Paul Norman	Oldham	1996	(1)	0	0	0	0
Andy Northey	St Helens	1996-97	8(17)	2	0	0	8
Junior Nsemba	Wigan	2022-24	24(15)	7	0	0	28
Danny Nutley	Castleford	2006	28	3	0	0	12
	Warrington	1998-2001	94(1)	3	0	0	12
Tony Nuttall	Oldham	1996-97	1(7)	0	0	0	0
Frank-Paul Nuuausala	Wigan	2016-18	34(8)	2	0	0	8
Levy Nzoungou	Hull	2019	(1)	0	0	0	0
	Salford	2018	(3)	0	0	0	0
Will Oakes	Hull KR	2016, 2018-19	12	5	0	0	20
Adam O'Brien	Huddersfield	2017-23	61(50)	19	0	0	76
	Bradford	2011-14	12(29)	6	0	0	24
Clinton O'Brien	Wakefield	2003	(2)	0	0	0	0
Gareth O'Brien	Leigh	2023-24	46	8	0	3	35
	Castleford	2013, 2020-22	37	6	52	3	131
	Toronto	2020	4	1	2	0	8
	Salford	2016-18	49(3)	12	105	2	260
	Warrington	2011-15	48(3)	16	69	3	205
	St Helens	2013	7	0	25	0	50
	Widnes	2012	4	0	15	0	30
Sam Obst	Hull	2011	17(6)	6	0	0	24
	Wakefield	2005-11	100(28)	40	7	0	174

Super League Players 1996-2024

PLAYER	CLUB	YEAR	APP	TRIES	GOALS	FG	PTS
Jamie O'Callaghan	London	2012-14	44(2)	4	0	0	16
	Harlequins	2008-11	54(3)	12	0	0	48
Eamon O'Carroll	Widnes	2012-17	58(11)	3	0	0	12
	Hull	2012	1(9)	0	0	0	0
	Wigan	2006-11	2(59)	3	0	0	12
Jarrod O'Connor	Leeds	2020-24	55(38)	5	2	0	24
Matt O'Connor	Paris	1997	11(4)	1	26	2	58
Terry O'Connor	Widnes	2005	25	2	0	0	8
	Wigan	1996-2004	177(45)	9	0	0	36
Jarrod O'Doherty	Huddersfield	2003	26	3	0	0	12
David O'Donnell	Paris	1997	21	3	0	0	12
Kai O'Donnell	Leigh	2023-24	47(2)	14	0	0	56
Luke O'Donnell	Huddersfield	2011-13	22(2)	2	0	0	8
Martin Offiah	Salford	2000-01	41	20	0	2	82
	London	1996-99	29(3)	21	0	0	84
	Wigan	1996	8	7	0	0	28
Jacob Ogden	London	2019	2	0	0	0	0
Mark O'Halloran	London	2004-05	34(3)	10	0	0	40
Ryan O'Hara	Hull KR	2012	8(7)	1	0	0	4
	Crusaders	2010-11	41(8)	3	0	0	12
	Celtic	2009	27	3	0	0	12
Hefin O'Hare	Huddersfield	2001, 2003-05	72(10)	27	0	0	108
Edwin Okanga-Ajwang	Salford	2013	2	0	0	0	0
Ben O'Keefe	Wigan	2022	1	1	4	0	12
Hitro Okesene	Hull	1998	21(1)	0	0	0	0
Anderson Okiwe	Sheffield	1997	1	0	0	0	0
Jayden Okunbor	Hull	2024	7	1	0	0	4
Tom Olbison	Toronto	2020	3(3)	0	0	0	0
	Widnes	2017-18	18(22)	4	0	0	16
	Bradford	2009-14	55(26)	11	0	0	44
Michael Oldfield	Catalans	2014-15	41	28	0	0	112
Mikolaj Oledzki	Leeds	2017-24	108(35)	12	0	0	48
Jamie Olejnik	Paris	1997	11	8	0	0	32
Aaron Ollett	Hull KR	2013-15	5(16)	1	0	0	4
Kevin O'Loughlin	Halifax	1997-98	2(4)	0	0	0	0
	St Helens	1997	(3)	0	0	0	0
Sean O'Loughlin	Wigan	2002-20	371(32)	71	3	2	292
Derrell Olpherts	Leeds	2023	12(1)	4	0	0	16
	Castleford	2020-22	59(1)	34	0	0	136
	Salford	2018-19	35	11	0	0	44
Mark O'Meley	Hull	2010-13	70(13)	13	0	0	52
Brad O'Neill	Wigan	2021-24	39(20)	4	0	0	16
Jacques O'Neill	Castleford	2019-21	2(25)	3	0	0	12
Jules O'Neill	Widnes	2003-05	57(3)	14	158	7	379
	Wakefield	2005	10(2)	2	4	0	16
	Wigan	2002-03	29(1)	12	72	0	192
Julian O'Neill	Widnes	2002-05	57(39)	3	0	0	12
	Wakefield	2001	24(1)	2	0	0	8
	St Helens	1997-2000	95(8)	5	0	0	20
Mark O'Neill	Hull KR	2007	17	5	0	0	20
	Leeds	2006	1(8)	0	0	0	0
Steve O'Neill	Gateshead	1999	1(1)	0	0	0	0
Tom Opacic	Hull KR	2023-24	39(2)	14	0	0	56
Tom O'Reilly	Warrington	2001-02	8(6)	1	0	0	4
Matt Orford	Bradford	2010	12	3	31	2	76
Jack Ormondroyd	Salford	2020-24	56(27)	6	0	0	24
	Leeds	2017-18	3(9)	0	0	0	0
Gene Ormsby	Huddersfield	2016-17	8	4	0	0	16
	Warrington	2014-16	37	26	0	0	104
Chris Orr	Huddersfield	1998	19(3)	2	0	0	8
Danny Orr	Castleford	1997-2003, 2011-12	197(23)	75	308	3	919
	Harlequins	2007-10	90(4)	13	96	0	244
	Wigan	2004-06	66(2)	18	12	0	96
Gareth Owen	Salford	2010, 2012-13	4(32)	6	0	0	24
Nick Owen	Leigh	2005	8(1)	1	11	0	26
Richard Owen	Wakefield	2014-15	29(1)	9	0	0	36
	Castleford	2008-14	10(3)	57	0	0	228
Jack Owens	St Helens	2016-17	31	8	14	0	60
	Widnes	2012-15	53(1)	26	103	0	310
Agnatius Paasi	St Helens	2021-24	16(55)	6	0	0	24
Lopini Paea	Wakefield	2015	1(3)	0	0	0	0
	Catalans	2011-14	41(41)	9	0	0	36
Mickey Paea	Hull	2014-15, 2018-19	78(18)	9	0	0	36
	Hull KR	2012-13	34(17)	5	0	0	20
Liam Paisley	Wigan	2018-19	6(2)	2	0	0	8
Mathias Pala	Catalans	2011-15	28(1)	4	0	0	16
Iafeta Palea'aesina	Hull	2014-16	(47)	1	0	0	4
	Salford	2011-12	4(37)	3	0	0	12
	Wigan	2006-10	55(77)	16	0	0	64
Jason Palmada	Workington	1996	12	2	0	0	8
Junior Paramore	Castleford	1996	5(5)	3	0	0	12
Dean Parata	London	2024	8(4)	0	0	0	0
Matt Parcell	Hull KR	2019-24	81(30)	30	0	0	120
	Leeds	2017-19	50(16)	27	0	0	108
Mike Parenti	Catalans	2022	1	0	0	0	0
Paul Parker	Hull	1999-2002	23(18)	9	0	0	36
Rob Parker	Castleford	2011	4(2)	2	0	0	8
	Salford	2009-11	23(14)	4	0	0	16
	Warrington	2006-08	10(56)	6	0	0	24
	Bradford	2000, 2002-05	19(76)	14	0	0	56
	London	2001	9	1	0	0	4
Wayne Parker	Halifax	1996-97	12(1)	0	0	0	0
Ian Parry	Warrington	2001	(1)	0	0	0	0
Jules Parry	Paris	1996	10(2)	0	0	0	0
Oliver Partington	Salford	2023-24	42	3	0	0	12
	Wigan	2018-22	56(30)	5	0	0	20
Regis Pastre-Courtine	Paris	1996	4(3)	4	0	0	16
Cory Paterson	Leigh	2017	13	2	0	0	8
	Salford	2015	14(1)	7	6	0	40
	Hull KR	2013	15	7	0	0	28
Andrew Patmore	Oldham	1996	8(5)	3	0	0	12
Larne Patrick	Castleford	2016-17	14(7)	1	0	0	4
	Huddersfield	2009-14, 2016	30(107)	30	0	0	120
	Wigan	2015	7(20)	4	0	0	16
Luke Patten	Salford	2011-12	53	16	0	0	64
Dec Patton	Salford	2021	6(4)	1	3	0	10
	Warrington	2015-20	69(19)	11	105	6	260
Henry Paul	Harlequins	2006-08	60(1)	8	94	2	222
	Bradford	1999-2001	81(5)	29	350	6	822
	Wigan	1996-98	60	37	23	0	194
Junior Paul	London	1996	3	1	0	0	4
Robbie Paul	Salford	2009	2(24)	2	0	0	8
	Huddersfield	2006-07	44(8)	7	0	0	28
	Bradford	1996-2005	198(31)	121	3	0	490
Pauli Pauli	Salford	2019-21	9(21)	4	0	0	16
	Wakefield	2018-19	14(30)	10	0	0	40
Joseph Paulo	Toulouse	2022	8(4)	0	0	0	0
	St Helens	2019-20	6(25)	1	0	0	4
Jason Payne	Castleford	2006	1(1)	0	0	0	0
Lewis Peachey	Castleford	2019-21	1(10)	0	0	0	0
Danny Peacock	Bradford	1997-99	32(2)	15	0	0	60
Jamie Peacock	Leeds	2006-15	234(16)	24	0	0	96
	Bradford	1999-2005	163(25)	38	0	0	152
Mitchell Pearce	Catalans	2022-23	39	14	0	0	56
Kai Pearce-Paul	Wigan	2020-23	46(13)	7	0	0	28
Martin Pearson	Wakefield	2001	21(1)	3	60	3	135
	Halifax	1997-98, 2000	55(6)	24	181	0	458
	Sheffield	1999	17(6)	9	36	2	110
Nathan Peats	Huddersfield	2021, 2023	27(10)	1	0	0	4
	Toulouse	2022	13	2	0	0	8
	Leigh	2021	2(8)	0	0	0	0
Jacques Pech	Paris	1996	16	0	0	0	0
Mike Pechey	Warrington	1998	6(3)	2	0	0	8
Bill Peden	London	2003	21(3)	7	0	0	28
Adam Peek	Crusaders	2010-11	5(22)	1	0	0	4
	Celtic	2009	5(12)	3	0	0	12
Franklin Pele	Hull	2024	3(5)	1	0	0	4
Eloi Pelissier	Toulouse	2022	2(17)	3	0	1	13
	London	2019	7(6)	1	0	0	4
	Leigh	2017	4(16)	0	0	0	0
	Catalans	2011-16	38(104)	23	0	1	93
Dimitri Pelo	Catalans	2007-10	79	37	0	0	148
Taylor Pemberton	St Helens	2022	(1)	0	0	0	0
Aaron Pene	Leigh	2024	1(14)	1	0	0	4
Sean Penkywicz	Huddersfield	2004-05	21(11)	7	0	0	28
	Halifax	2000-03	29(27)	8	0	0	32
Julian Penni	Salford	1998-99	4	0	0	0	0
Kevin Penny	Warrington	2006-09, 2014-17	83(1)	52	0	0	208
	Wakefield	2011	5	1	0	0	4
	Harlequins	2010	5	3	0	0	12
Lee Penny	Warrington	1996-2003	140(5)	54	0	0	216
Paul Penrice	Workington	1996	11(2)	2	0	0	8
Chris Percival	Widnes	2002-03	26	6	0	0	24
Mark Percival	St Helens	2013-24	219(2)	108	342	0	1116
Apollo Perelini	St Helens	1996-2000	103(16)	27	0	0	108
Ugo Perez	Catalans	2015, 2017-18	2(5)	0	0	0	0
Mark Perrett	Halifax	1996-97	15(4)	4	0	0	16
Josh Perry	St Helens	2011-13	32(9)	2	0	0	8
Shane Perry	Catalans	2009	8(8)	1	0	0	4
Adam Peters	Paris	1997	16(3)	0	0	0	0
Dominic Peters	London	1998-2003	58(11)	12	0	0	48
Mike Peters	Warrington	2000	2(12)	1	0	0	4
	Halifax	2000	1	0	0	0	0

Super League Players 1996-2024

PLAYER	CLUB	YEAR	APP	TRIES	GOALS	FG	PTS
Willie Peters	Widnes	2004	9	3	0	2	14
	Wigan	2000	29	15	5	6	76
	Gateshead	1999	27	11	1	6	52
Dave Petersen	Hull KR	2012	2(2)	1	0	0	4
Matt Petersen	Wakefield	2008-09	14	3	0	0	12
Nathaniel Peteru	Huddersfield	2021	2(12)	3	0	0	12
	Leigh	2021	2(8)	0	0	0	0
	Hull KR	2020	5(3)	0	0	0	0
	Leeds	2018-19	15(6)	0	0	0	0
Adrian Petrie	Workington	1996	(1)	0	0	0	0
Eddy Pettybourne	Wigan	2014	1(15)	0	0	0	0
Dominique Peyroux	Toulouse	2022	15(1)	2	0	0	8
	St Helens	2016-20	88(25)	16	0	0	64
Hugo Pezet	Toulouse	2022	2(1)	0	0	0	0
Cameron Phelps	Widnes	2012-15	66(1)	23	2	0	96
	Hull	2011	19	2	0	0	8
	Wigan	2008-10	43(1)	14	4	0	64
Joe Philbin	Warrington	2014-24	45(140)	13	0	0	52
Rowland Phillips	Workington	1996	22	1	0	0	4
Nathan Picchi	Leeds	1996	(1)	0	0	0	0
Ian Pickavance	Hull	1999	4(2)	2	0	0	8
	Huddersfield	1999	3(14)	0	0	0	0
	St Helens	1996-98	12(44)	6	0	0	24
James Pickering	Castleford	1999	1(19)	0	0	0	0
Steve Pickersgill	Widnes	2012-13	27(8)	1	0	0	4
	Warrington	2005-09	1(36)	0	0	0	0
Nick Pinkney	Salford	2000-02	64	29	0	0	116
	Halifax	1999	26(2)	13	0	0	52
	Sheffield	1997-98	33	10	0	0	40
Mikhail Piskunov	Paris	1996	1(1)	1	0	0	4
Darryl Pitt	London	1996	2(16)	4	0	1	17
Jay Pitts	Wakefield	2008-09, 2020-23	85(9)	11	0	0	44
	London	2019	27	7	0	0	28
	Bradford	2014	15(1)	3	0	0	12
	Hull	2012-14	18(30)	1	0	0	4
	Leeds	2009-10	10(15)	2	0	0	8
Andy Platt	Salford	1997-98	20(3)	1	0	0	4
Michael Platt	Salford	2001-02, 2014	4(1)	1	0	0	4
	Bradford	2007-13	121(6)	44	0	0	176
	Castleford	2006	26	7	0	0	28
Willie Poching	Leeds	2002-06	58(73)	44	0	0	176
	Wakefield	1999-2001	65(4)	20	0	0	80
Ben Pomeroy	Warrington	2017-18	3(7)	1	0	0	4
	Catalans	2014-15	44	10	0	0	40
Quentin Pongia	Wigan	2003-04	15(10)	0	0	0	0
Justin Poore	Hull KR	2014	7	0	0	0	0
	Wakefield	2013	23	1	0	0	4
Dan Potter	Widnes	2002-03	34(2)	6	0	0	24
	London	2001	1(3)	1	0	0	4
Craig Poucher	Hull	1999-2002	31(5)	5	0	0	20
Andy Powell	Wigan	2013	2(3)	1	0	0	4
Bryn Powell	Salford	2004	1(1)	0	0	0	0
Daio Powell	Sheffield	1999	13(1)	2	0	0	8
	Halifax	1997-98	30(3)	17	0	0	68
Daryl Powell	Leeds	1998-2000	49(30)	12	0	2	50
Sam Powell	Warrington	2024	10(19)	2	0	0	8
	Wigan	2012-22	193(57)	40	4	4	172
Karl Pratt	Bradford	2003-05	35(19)	18	0	0	72
	Leeds	1999-2002	62(12)	33	0	0	132
Oliver Pratt	Wakefield	2023	1	0	0	0	0
Paul Prescott	Wigan	2004-13	49(75)	4	0	0	16
Steve Prescott	Hull	1998-99, 2001-03	99	46	191	3	569
	Wakefield	2000	22(1)	3	13	0	38
	St Helens	1996-97	32	15	17	0	94
Lee Prest	Workington	1996	(1)	0	0	0	0
Gareth Price	Salford	2002	(2)	0	0	0	0
	London	2002	2(2)	3	0	0	12
	St Helens	1999	(11)	2	0	0	8
Gary Price	Wakefield	1999-2001	55(13)	11	0	0	44
Richard Price	Sheffield	1996	1(2)	0	0	0	0
Tony Priddle	Paris	1997	11(7)	3	0	0	12
Matt Prior	Leeds	2020-22	52(6)	7	0	0	28
Frank Pritchard	Hull	2016	10(13)	4	0	0	16
Kevin Proctor	Wakefield	2023	12(8)	1	0	0	4
Karl Pryce	Bradford	2003-06, 2012	47(19)	46	1	0	186
	Harlequins	2011	11(7)	12	0	0	48
	Wigan	2009-10	11(2)	12	0	0	48
Leon Pryce	Hull	2015-16	32(2)	8	0	0	32
	Catalans	2012-14	72(2)	15	0	0	60
	St Helens	2006-11	133(3)	64	0	0	256
	Bradford	1998-2005	159(29)	86	0	0	344
Waine Pryce	Wakefield	2007	10(2)	4	0	0	16
	Castleford	2000-06	97(12)	49	0	0	196
Will Pryce	Huddersfield	2021-23	38(6)	17	62	0	192
Maxime Puech	Toulouse	2022	8(9)	0	0	0	0
Tony Puletua	Hull KR	2015	7	0	0	0	0
	Salford	2014	16(9)	3	0	0	12
	St Helens	2009-13	108(18)	39	0	0	156
Andrew Purcell	Castleford	2000	15(5)	3	0	0	12
	Hull	1999	27	4	0	0	16
Rob Purdham	Harlequins	2006-11	112(3)	18	131	1	335
	London	2002-05	53(15)	16	2	1	69
Adrian Purtell	Bradford	2012-14	45(1)	16	0	0	64
Nixon Putt	Castleford	2024	3(4)	0	0	0	0
Jamie Pye	Salford	2024	(1)	0	0	0	0
Jason Qareqare	Castleford	2021-24	33(5)	20	0	0	80
Luke Quigley	Catalans	2007	16(1)	1	0	0	4
Adam Quinlan	Hull KR	2018-21	47	24	0	0	96
	St Helens	2015	11	6	0	0	24
Damien Quinn	Celtic	2009	20(1)	4	12	0	40
Scott Quinnell	Wigan	1996	6(3)	1	0	0	4
Florian Quintilla	Catalans	2008-09	1(4)	0	0	0	0
Lee Radford	Hull	1998, 2006-12	138(30)	23	1	0	94
	Bradford	1999-2005	79(65)	18	12	0	96
Kris Radlinski	Wigan	1996-2006	236(1)	134	1	0	538
Sebastien Raguin	Catalans	2007-12	103(22)	28	0	0	112
Adrian Rainey	Castleford	2002	4(7)	1	0	0	4
Andy Raleigh	Wakefield	2012-14	42(21)	9	0	0	36
	Huddersfield	2006-11	74(46)	13	0	0	52
Jean-Luc Ramondou	Paris	1996	1(1)	1	0	0	4
Chad Randall	London	2012-13	29(9)	4	0	0	16
	Harlequins	2006-11	141(2)	37	0	1	149
Craig Randall	Halifax	1999	8(11)	4	0	0	16
	Salford	1997-98	12(18)	4	0	0	16
Tyler Randell	Wakefield	2017-19	37(8)	9	1	0	38
Jordan Rankin	Castleford	2019-20	29(2)	10	19	0	78
	Huddersfield	2017-18	39	3	9	0	30
	Hull	2014-15	41(6)	20	43	0	166
Scott Ranson	Oldham	1996-97	19(2)	7	0	0	28
Aaron Raper	Castleford	1999-2001	48(4)	4	2	1	21
Sam Rapira	Huddersfield	2016-17	29(19)	3	0	0	12
Steve Rapira	Salford	2014	5(13)	0	0	0	0
Stefan Ratchford	Warrington	2012-24	290(12)	82	601	2	1532
	Salford	2007, 2009-11	65(5)	23	20	0	132
Mike Ratu	Hull KR	2010	5	1	0	0	4
	Leeds	2007, 2009	1(5)	1	0	0	4
Paul Rauhihi	Warrington	2006-09	67(20)	10	0	0	40
Ben Rauter	Wakefield	2001	15(6)	4	0	0	16
Nick Rawsthorne	Hull KR	2020	5	0	0	0	0
	Leigh	2017	1	1	0	0	4
	Hull	2017	3	2	2	0	12
Gareth Raynor	Bradford	2011	18	4	0	0	16
	Crusaders	2010	7	4	0	0	16
	Hull	2001-09	186	102	0	0	408
	Leeds	2000	(3)	0	0	0	0
Tony Rea	London	1996	22	4	0	0	16
Stuart Reardon	Crusaders	2011	25	11	0	0	44
	Bradford	2003-05, 2010	78(11)	37	0	0	148
	Warrington	2006-08	48	12	0	0	48
	Salford	2002	7(1)	3	0	0	12
Mark Reber	Wigan	1999-2000	9(9)	5	0	0	20
Alan Reddicliffe	Warrington	2001	1	0	0	0	0
Tahi Reihana	Bradford	1997-98	17(21)	0	0	0	0
Paul Reilly	Wakefield	2008	5(2)	1	0	0	4
	Huddersfield	1999-2001, 2003-07	150(8)	35	1	0	142
Robert Relf	Widnes	2002-04	68(2)	5	0	0	20
Steve Renouf	Wigan	2000-01	55	40	0	0	160
Steele Retchless	London	1998-2004	177(6)	13	0	0	52
Ben Reynolds	Hull	2024	5	1	14	0	32
	Hull KR	2024	1(1)	0	1	0	2
	Leigh	2017, 2021, 2023	50	14	135	0	326
	Wakefield	2019	5	1	0	0	4
	Castleford	2013-14	1(3)	0	0	0	0
Josh Reynolds	Hull	2021-22	22	7	0	0	28
Scott Rhodes	Hull	2000	2	0	0	0	0
Lucas Ribas	Catalans	2022	(1)	0	0	0	0
Phillipe Ricard	Paris	1996-97	1	0	0	0	0
Andy Rice	Huddersfield	2000-01	2(13)	1	0	0	4
Basil Richards	Huddersfield	1998-99	28(17)	1	0	0	4

183

Super League Players 1996-2024

PLAYER	CLUB	YEAR	APP	TRIES	GOALS	FG	PTS
Craig Richards	Oldham	1996	1	0	0	0	0
Greg Richards	Hull KR	2022	(13)	0	0	0	0
	London	2019	5(15)	0	0	0	0
	Leigh	2017	(1)	0	0	0	0
	St Helens	2013-17	19(49)	1	0	0	4
Pat Richards	Catalans	2016	19	9	69	0	174
	Wigan	2006-13	199	147	759	4	2110
Andy Richardson	Hudds-Sheff	2000	(2)	0	0	0	0
Danny Richardson	Hull KR	2024	1(1)	0	7	0	14
	Castleford	2020-22, 2024	47	5	141	7	309
	St Helens	2017-19	52(2)	9	158	8	360
Sean Richardson	Widnes	2002	2(18)	1	0	0	4
	Wakefield	1999	5(1)	0	0	0	0
	Castleford	1996-97	3(8)	1	0	0	4
Mark Riddell	Wigan	2009-10	45(11)	5	2	0	24
Martyn Ridyard	Huddersfield	2017	7	1	26	0	56
	Leigh	2017	4	0	2	0	4
Neil Rigby	St Helens	2006	(1)	0	0	0	0
Shane Rigon	Bradford	2001	14(11)	12	0	0	48
Craig Rika	Halifax	1996	2	0	0	0	0
Chris Riley	Wakefield	2014-15	44	16	0	0	64
	Warrington	2005-14	146(10)	102	0	0	408
	Harlequins	2011	3	2	0	0	8
Glenn Riley	Warrington	2013-14	(15)	0	0	0	0
Peter Riley	Workington	1996	7(5)	0	0	0	0
Julien Rinaldi	London	2012	4(16)	1	0	0	4
	Wakefield	2002, 2010-11	27(9)	6	0	0	24
	Bradford	2009	(7)	1	0	0	4
	Harlequins	2007-08	4(43)	9	0	0	36
	Catalans	2006	16(6)	3	1	0	14
Dean Ripley	Castleford	2004	3(4)	1	0	0	4
Tee Ritson	St Helens	2023-24	22(1)	3	0	0	12
Leroy Rivett	Warrington	2002	9	1	0	0	4
	Hudds-Sheff	2000	5(1)	1	0	0	4
	Leeds	1996-2000	39(15)	21	0	0	84
Nico Rizzelli	St Helens	2020	1	0	0	0	0
Jason Roach	Warrington	1998-99	29(7)	15	0	0	60
	Castleford	1997	7	4	0	0	16
Ben Roarty	Castleford	2006	11(6)	2	0	0	8
	Huddersfield	2003-05	52	5	0	0	20
Cain Robb	Castleford	2021-24	2(27)	0	0	0	0
Amos Roberts	Wigan	2009-11	47(2)	27	5	0	118
Ben Roberts	Castleford	2015-19	60(15)	20	0	2	82
Luis Roberts	Leeds	2023-24	20(2)	5	0	0	20
	Salford	2020	2	0	0	0	0
Mark Roberts	Wigan	2003	(3)	0	0	0	0
Oliver Roberts	Huddersfield	2016-19, 2022	43(43)	13	0	0	52
	Salford	2020-21	13(7)	1	0	0	4
	Bradford	2013-14	(5)	0	0	0	0
Robert Roberts	Huddersfield	2001	(1)	0	0	0	0
	Halifax	2000	(3)	0	0	0	0
	Hull	1999	24(2)	4	13	4	46
Tyrone Roberts	Warrington	2018	28	5	32	1	85
Harry Robertson	St Helens	2024	9	1	0	0	4
Michael Robertson	London	2012-13	35	17	0	0	68
Stan Robin	Catalans	2015-16	5(2)	1	0	0	4
Chad Robinson	Harlequins	2009	13(1)	2	0	0	8
Connor Robinson	Hull KR	2014-15	(2)	0	0	0	0
Craig Robinson	Wakefield	2005	(1)	0	0	0	0
Jason Robinson	Wigan	1996-2000	126(1)	87	0	1	349
Jeremy Robinson	Paris	1997	10(3)	1	21	0	46
John Robinson	Widnes	2003-04	7	1	0	0	4
Luke Robinson	Huddersfield	2008-15	191(18)	45	4	0	188
	Salford	2005-07	79	28	10	2	134
	Wigan	2002-04	17(25)	9	6	1	49
	Castleford	2004	9	4	3	0	22
Will Robinson	Hull	2000	22	4	0	0	16
	Gateshead	1999	28	9	0	0	36
Ash Robson	Castleford	2015	3	1	0	0	4
Ellis Robson	Toulouse	2022	(2)	0	0	0	0
	Salford	2021	4(3)	1	0	0	4
	Warrington	2020-21	2(3)	0	0	0	0
James Roby	St Helens	2004-23	368(127)	105	1	1	423
Mike Roby	St Helens	2004	(1)	0	0	0	0
Colton Roche	Huddersfield	2018-19	1(7)	0	0	0	0
Carl Roden	Warrington	1997	1	0	0	0	0
Shane Rodney	London	2012-13	28	3	12	0	36
Matt Rodwell	Warrington	2002	10	3	0	0	12
Nathan Roebuck	Warrington	2020	1	1	0	0	4
Darren Rogers	Castleford	1999-2004	162(1)	81	0	0	324
	Salford	1997-98	42	16	0	0	64
Fenton Rogers	Huddersfield	2023-24	(9)	1	0	0	4
	London	2024	2(1)	0	0	0	0
Arthur Romano	Catalans	2017, 2019-20, 2022-24	69(2)	18	0	0	72
Adam Rooks	Hull KR	2019	(4)	0	0	0	0
Fletcher Rooney	Castleford	2023-24	4	2	0	0	8
Jamie Rooney	Wakefield	2003-09	113(7)	60	321	21	903
	Castleford	2001	2(1)	0	6	0	12
Jonathan Roper	Castleford	2001	13	7	12	0	52
	Salford	2000	1(4)	1	3	0	10
	London	2000	4	0	0	0	0
	Warrington	1996-2000	75(8)	33	71	0	274
Scott Roskell	London	1996-97	30(2)	16	0	0	64
Steve Rosolen	London	1996-98	25(9)	10	0	0	40
Adam Ross	London	1996	(1)	0	0	0	0
Cesar Rouge	Catalans	2021-24	21(10)	5	0	0	20
	Hull KR	2023	1	0	0	0	0
Paul Round	Castleford	1996	(3)	0	0	0	0
Josh Rourke	London	2024	12	8	0	0	32
	Salford	2022	1	0	0	0	0
Steve Rowlands	Widnes	2004-05	18(3)	2	15	0	38
	St Helens	2003	(1)	0	0	0	0
Paul Rowley	Leigh	2005	15(7)	3	0	0	12
	Huddersfield	2001	24	3	0	0	12
	Halifax	1996-2000	107(3)	27	1	3	113
Nigel Roy	London	2001-04	100	39	0	0	156
Nicky Royle	Widnes	2004	13	7	0	0	28
Sam Royle	St Helens	2021-24	12(14)	2	0	0	8
	Hull KR	2022	2(1)	1	0	0	4
Shad Royston	Bradford	2011	17(1)	10	0	0	40
Leon Ruan	Hull	2024	1(3)	0	0	0	0
	Leeds	2023-24	(11)	1	0	0	4
Chris Rudd	Warrington	1996-98	31(17)	10	16	0	72
Sean Rudder	Catalans	2006	22(1)	6	0	0	24
	Castleford	2004	9(3)	2	0	0	8
Charly Runciman	Widnes	2016-18	68	9	0	0	36
Kieran Rush	Huddersfield	2023-24	1(6)	0	0	0	0
James Rushforth	Halifax	1997	(4)	0	0	0	0
Harry Rushton	Huddersfield	2023-24	18(15)	3	0	0	12
	Wigan	2020	1	0	0	0	0
Adam Rusling	Castleford	2021	(1)	0	0	0	0
Danny Russell	Huddersfield	1998-2000	50(13)	8	0	0	32
Ian Russell	Oldham	1997	1(3)	1	0	0	4
	Paris	1996	3	0	0	0	0
Matty Russell	Leeds	2024	1	0	0	0	0
	Warrington	2014-18, 2023-24	90(6)	25	0	0	100
	Hull	2012, 2024	8	1	0	0	4
	Toulouse	2022	21	13	0	0	52
	Leigh	2021	12(1)	4	0	0	16
	Toronto	2020	6	2	0	0	8
	Wigan	2012	2	3	0	0	12
Oliver Russell	Huddersfield	2018-24	90(8)	5	194	5	413
Richard Russell	Castleford	1996-98	37(4)	2	0	0	8
Robert Russell	Salford	1998-99	2(1)	0	1	0	2
Sean Rutgerson	Salford	2004-06	60(9)	4	0	0	16
Chris Ryan	London	1998-99	44(3)	17	10	0	88
Ethan Ryan	Salford	2024	21(1)	6	0	0	24
	Hull KR	2020-23	35	17	0	0	68
Matt Ryan	Wakefield	2014-15	28(12)	7	0	0	28
Sean Ryan	Castleford	2004	11(5)	2	0	0	8
	Hull	2002-03	53	8	0	0	32
Justin Ryder	Wakefield	2004	19(3)	11	0	0	44
Jason Ryles	Catalans	2009	19(2)	2	0	0	8
Setaimata Sa	Widnes	2016	7(5)	3	0	0	12
	Hull	2014-15	18(6)	6	0	0	24
	Catalans	2010-12	58(5)	21	0	0	84
Teddy Sadaoui	Catalans	2006	7	0	0	0	0
Jack Sadler	Castleford	2021	1	0	0	0	0
Hugo Salabio	Huddersfield	2024	1(9)	0	0	0	0
	Wakefield	2023	(3)	0	0	0	0
	Catalans	2022	(1)	0	0	0	0
Liam Salter	Hull KR	2012-16, 2018	83(3)	17	0	0	68
Matt Salter	London	1997-99	14(34)	0	0	0	0
Jurnah Sambou	St Helens	2022	1	1	0	0	4
Ben Sammut	Hull	2000	20	4	67	0	150
	Gateshead	1999	26(2)	6	17	0	58
Jarrod Sammut	Wigan	2019	6(6)	2	0	0	8
	Wakefield	2014-15	19(1)	9	52	0	140
	Bradford	2012-13	35(3)	28	47	1	207
	Crusaders	2010-11	17(16)	17	0	0	68
Dean Sampson	Castleford	1996-2003	124(28)	24	0	0	96
Paul Sampson	London	2004	1(2)	1	0	0	4
	Wakefield	2000	17	8	0	0	32
Jack Sanderson	Castleford	2020	3	1	0	0	4
Lee Sanderson	London	2004	1(5)	1	7	0	18
Chris Sandow	Warrington	2015-16	27(1)	11	26	1	97
Jason Sands	Paris	1996-97	28	0	0	0	0
Justin Sangare	Leeds	2023-24	18(22)	2	0	0	8
	Toulouse	2022	5(18)	0	0	0	0

Super League Players 1996-2024

PLAYER	CLUB	YEAR	APP	TRIES	GOALS	FG	PTS
Ligi Sao	Hull	2020-24	84(10)	4	0	0	16
Mitchell Sargent	Castleford	2008-10	37(21)	6	0	0	24
Dan Sarginson	Salford	2020-22	25(1)	4	0	0	16
	Wigan	2014-16, 2018-19	112(2)	30	0	0	120
	London	2012-13	35(1)	10	0	0	40
	Harlequins	2011	8	5	0	0	20
Matt Sarsfield	Salford	2016	2(2)	1	0	0	4
Tevita Satae	Catalans	2024	1(24)	2	0	0	8
	Hull	2019-23	36(52)	14	0	0	56
Junior Sa'u	Leigh	2021	15(1)	3	0	0	12
	Salford	2014-19	115	46	0	0	184
	Wakefield	2019	3	0	0	0	0
Andre Savelio	Huddersfield	2024	4(5)	0	0	0	0
	Hull	2019-23	46(11)	15	0	0	60
	Warrington	2017	3(14)	4	0	0	16
	Castleford	2016	6(1)	1	0	0	4
	St Helens	2014-16	12(25)	2	0	0	8
Lokeni Savelio	Halifax	2000	2(11)	0	0	0	0
	Salford	1997-98	18(20)	0	0	0	0
Tom Saxton	Salford	2007	5	0	0	0	0
	Wakefield	2006	9(6)	2	0	0	8
	Hull	2005	19(8)	3	0	0	12
	Castleford	2002-04	37(12)	11	0	0	44
Jonathan Scales	Halifax	2000	1	0	0	0	0
	Bradford	1996-98	46(4)	24	0	0	96
Latrell Schaumkel	Toulouse	2022	10	4	0	0	16
Andrew Schick	Castleford	1996-98	45(13)	10	0	0	40
Clinton Schifcofske	Crusaders	2010-11	44	5	115	0	250
Brad Schneider	Hull KR	2023	10	3	35	1	83
Garry Schofield	Huddersfield	1998	(2)	0	0	0	0
Jordan Schofield	Wakefield	2023	(1)	0	0	0	0
Gary Schubert	Workington	1996	(1)	0	0	0	0
Matt Schultz	Hull	1998-99	23(9)	2	0	0	8
	Leeds	1996	2(4)	0	0	0	0
John Schuster	Halifax	1996-97	31	9	127	3	293
Bastien Scimone	Catalans	2022-23	1(2)	0	0	0	0
Cameron Scott	Hull	2018-24	60(8)	14	0	0	56
Nick Scruton	Hull KR	2018	7(10)	0	0	0	0
	Wakefield	2014-16	62(3)	9	0	0	36
	Bradford	2009-14	70(27)	5	0	0	20
	Leeds	2002, 2004-08	11(53)	3	0	0	12
	Hull	2004	2(16)	3	0	0	12
Danny Sculthorpe	Huddersfield	2009	5(8)	0	0	0	0
	Wakefield	2007-09	14(28)	1	0	0	4
	Castleford	2006	18(1)	4	0	1	17
	Wigan	2002-05	13(49)	7	0	0	28
Paul Sculthorpe	St Helens	1998-2008	223(4)	94	356	7	1095
	Warrington	1996-97	40	6	0	0	24
Mick Seaby	London	1997	3(2)	1	0	0	4
Danny Seal	Halifax	1996-99	8(17)	3	0	0	12
Matt Seers	Wakefield	2003	11(1)	2	0	0	8
James Segeyaro	Leeds	2016	3	1	0	0	4
Paul Seguier	Catalans	2016-17, 2020-24	45(44)	6	0	0	24
Anthony Seibold	London	1999-2000	33(19)	5	0	0	20
Jesse Sene-Lefao	Castleford	2017-21	72(30)	15	0	0	60
Innes Senior	Castleford	2024	27	14	0	0	56
	Wakefield	2020-21, 2023	30	15	0	0	60
	Huddersfield	2018-19, 2022-23	53	20	0	0	80
Keith Senior	Leeds	1999-2011	319(2)	159	0	0	636
	Sheffield	1996-98	90(2)	40	0	0	160
Louis Senior	Castleford	2024	4	5	0	0	20
	Hull KR	2023-24	16	7	0	0	28
	Huddersfield	2018-22	40	25	0	0	100
Fili Seru	Hull	1998-99	37(1)	13	0	0	52
Ava Seumanufagai	Leigh	2023	1(14)	1	0	0	4
	Leeds	2019-20	26(2)	3	0	0	12
Anthony Seuseu	Halifax	2003	1(11)	1	0	0	4
Jerry Seuseu	Wigan	2005-06	29(9)	1	0	0	4
Charlie Severs	Hull	2022, 2024	(3)	0	0	0	0
Brett Seymour	Hull	2012-13	26(1)	7	0	0	28
Aidan Sezer	Leeds	2022-23	35	3	4	0	20
	Huddersfield	2020-21	22(1)	9	60	2	158
Will Sharp	Hull	2011-12	27(8)	10	0	0	40
	Harlequins	2008-10	65(1)	19	0	0	76
Jamie Shaul	Hull	2013-23	180(3)	88	0	1	353
	Wakefield	2022	5	1	0	0	4
Darren Shaw	Salford	2002	5(9)	1	0	0	4
	London	1996, 2002	22(8)	3	0	0	12
	Castleford	2000-01	50(6)	1	0	0	4
	Sheffield	1998-99	51(1)	3	0	1	13
Isaac Shaw	Hull KR	2023	(1)	0	0	0	0
	Wakefield	2022-23	(6)	0	0	0	0
Mick Shaw	Halifax	1999	5	1	0	0	4
	Leeds	1996	12(2)	7	0	0	28
Ryan Shaw	Hull KR	2016, 2018-19	44(1)	19	125	0	326
	London	2013	2	1	2	0	8
Phil Shead	Paris	1996	3(2)	0	0	0	0
Richard Sheil	St Helens	1997	(1)	0	0	0	0
Kelly Shelford	Warrington	1996-97	25(3)	4	0	2	18
Kyle Shelford	Warrington	2020	(1)	0	0	0	0
	Wigan	2016	(1)	0	0	0	0
Michael Shenton	Castleford	2004, 2006, 2008-10, 2013-21	276(2)	111	0	0	444
	St Helens	2011-12	51	15	0	0	60
Ryan Sheridan	Castleford	2004	2	0	0	0	0
	Widnes	2003	14(3)	2	0	0	8
	Leeds	1997-2002	123(7)	46	0	1	185
	Sheffield	1996	9(3)	5	0	1	21
Louis Sheriff	Hull KR	2011-12	8	3	0	0	12
Rikki Sheriffe	Bradford	2009-10	51	14	0	0	56
	Harlequins	2006-08	35(1)	16	0	0	64
	Halifax	2003	6(1)	3	0	0	12
Ian Sherratt	Oldham	1996	5(3)	1	0	0	4
Brent Sherwin	Catalans	2010	12	1	0	1	5
	Castleford	2008-10	48(1)	4	0	3	19
Peter Shiels	St Helens	2001-02	44(3)	11	0	0	44
Gary Shillabeer	Huddersfield	1999	(2)	0	0	0	0
Mark Shipway	Salford	2004-05	30(12)	3	0	0	12
Jake Shorrocks	Wigan	2016-17, 2019-20	9(19)	2	8	0	24
	Salford	2018	10	0	1	0	2
Joe Shorrocks	Salford	2024	10(16)	0	0	0	0
	Wigan	2019-23	25(40)	3	0	0	12
	Leigh	2023	4	1	0	0	4
Ian Sibbit	Bradford	2011-12	11(7)	0	0	0	0
	Salford	2005-07, 2009-10	64(17)	11	0	0	44
	Warrington	1999-2001, 2003-04	63(18)	24	0	0	96
Mark Sibson	Huddersfield	1999	2	2	0	0	8
Adam Sidlow	Salford	2009-12, 2023-24	37(54)	14	0	0	56
	Leigh	2021	10(1)	6	0	0	24
	Toronto	2020	3(3)	0	0	0	0
	Bradford	2013-14	20(22)	8	0	0	32
Harry Siejka	Wakefield	2014	6(3)	1	0	0	4
Jordan Sigismeau	Catalans	2015-16	11	3	0	0	12
Josh Simm	Castleford	2024	5(1)	4	0	0	16
	St Helens	2019-22	18	7	0	0	28
	Hull	2022	5	2	0	0	8
	Leigh	2021	1	0	0	0	0
Jon Simms	St Helens	2002	(1)	0	0	0	0
Craig Simon	Hull	2000	23(2)	8	0	0	32
	Gateshead	1999	25(4)	6	0	0	24
Mickael Simon	Catalans	2010-14, 2017-20	55(76)	3	0	0	12
	Wakefield	2015-16	15(22)	3	0	0	12
Darren Simpson	Huddersfield	1998-99	17(1)	5	0	0	20
Jamie Simpson	Huddersfield	2011	8(1)	0	0	0	0
Jared Simpson	Huddersfield	2015-18	12	4	0	0	16
Max Simpson	Leeds	2022	4	0	0	0	0
Robbie Simpson	London	1999	6(7)	0	0	0	0
Ashton Sims	Warrington	2015-17	69(11)	5	0	0	20
Korbin Sims	Hull KR	2021-22	12(17)	1	0	0	4
Tariq Sims	Catalans	2024	20(1)	3	0	0	12
Jack Sinfield	Leeds	2022-24	13(2)	2	0	0	8
Kevin Sinfield	Leeds	1997-2015	425(29)	70	1566	31	3443
Matt Sing	Hull	2007-08	41	14	0	0	56
Wayne Sing	Paris	1997	18(1)	2	0	0	8
Brad Singleton	Salford	2023-24	28	1	0	0	4
	Wigan	2020-23	51(8)	5	0	0	20
	Toronto	2020	3(1)	1	0	0	4
	Leeds	2011-19	92(61)	17	0	0	68
	Wakefield	2013	(1)	0	0	0	0
Fata Sini	Salford	1997	22	7	0	0	28
Ken Sio	Salford	2019-23	100(1)	78	13	0	338
	Hull KR	2015-16	42	23	13	0	118
Michael Sio	Wakefield	2015-17	25(14)	6	0	0	24
Bayley Sironen	Catalans	2024	17(4)	3	0	0	12
Curtis Sironen	St Helens	2022-24	49(8)	8	0	0	32
John Skandalis	Huddersfield	2007-08	37(5)	4	0	0	16
Dylan Skee	Harlequins	2008-09	(3)	0	0	0	0
Ben Skerrett	Castleford	2003	1	0	0	0	0
Kelvin Skerrett	Halifax	1997-99	31(6)	2	0	0	8
	Wigan	1996	1(8)	0	0	0	0

Super League Players 1996-2024

PLAYER	CLUB	YEAR	APP	TRIES	GOALS	FG	PTS
Troy Slattery	Wakefield	2002-03	33(5)	4	0	0	16
	Huddersfield	1999	3	1	0	0	4
Mick Slicker	Huddersfield	2001, 2003-05	17(48)	2	0	0	8
	Sheffield	1999	(3)	1	0	0	4
	Halifax	1997	2(5)	0	0	0	0
Nick Slyney	London	2014	20(4)	3	0	0	12
Ian Smales	Castleford	1996-97	10(8)	5	0	0	20
Aaron Smith	Leigh	2023	1	0	0	0	0
	St Helens	2018-21	13(24)	9	0	0	36
	Hull KR	2018	3(1)	0	0	0	0
Aaron Smith	Castleford	2006	(2)	0	0	0	0
	Bradford	2003-04	12(1)	3	0	0	12
Andy Smith	Harlequins	2007	6(3)	3	0	0	12
	Bradford	2004-06	9(9)	4	0	0	16
	Salford	2005	4	1	0	0	4
Byron Smith	Castleford	2004	(9)	0	0	0	0
	Halifax	2003	6(1)	0	0	0	0
Cameron Smith	Leeds	2016-24	91(52)	18	1	0	74
Chris Smith	Hull	2001-02	12	3	0	0	12
	St Helens	1998-2000	62(9)	26	0	0	104
	Castleford	1996-97	36(1)	12	0	0	48
Craig Smith	Wigan	2002-04	77(3)	10	0	0	40
Damien Smith	St Helens	1998	21(1)	8	0	0	32
Daniel Smith	Castleford	2019-23	29(41)	4	0	0	16
	Huddersfield	2015-18	9(38)	5	0	0	20
	Wakefield	2014-15	21(15)	6	0	0	24
Danny Smith	Paris	1996	10(2)	1	15	0	34
	London	1996	2(1)	1	0	0	4
Darren Smith	St Helens	2003	25(1)	14	0	0	56
Gary Smith	Castleford	2001	(1)	0	0	0	0
Harry Smith	Wigan	2019-24	103(14)	18	254	8	588
Harvey Smith	Wakefield	2023	(1)	0	0	0	0
Hudson Smith	Bradford	2000	8(22)	2	0	0	8
	Salford	1999	23(2)	5	0	0	20
James Smith	Salford	2000	23(3)	6	0	0	24
Jamie Smith	Hull	1998-99	24(6)	6	12	0	48
	Workington	1996	5(3)	0	1	0	2
Jason Smith	Hull	2001-04	61(3)	17	0	1	69
Jeremy Smith	Wakefield	2011	9(1)	1	0	0	4
	Salford	2009-10	27(17)	2	0	0	8
Kris Smith	London	2001	(1)	0	0	0	0
	Halifax	2001	(1)	0	0	0	0
Lee Smith	Wakefield	2012-13, 2015	30(4)	16	54	0	174
	Leeds	2005-12	125(10)	60	34	1	309
Leigh Smith	Workington	1996	9	4	0	0	16
Mark Smith	Widnes	2005	12(15)	4	0	0	16
	Wigan	1999-2004	35(77)	8	0	0	32
Martyn Smith	Harlequins	2010	(2)	0	0	0	0
Matty Smith	Warrington	2019	4(1)	0	0	0	0
	Catalans	2019	16	0	0	1	1
	St Helens	2006-08, 2010, 2017-18	38(5)	5	10	4	44
	Wigan	2012-16	122(3)	17	279	25	651
	Salford	2010-12	67(4)	13	6	1	65
	Celtic	2009	15(1)	3	2	1	17
Michael Smith	Hull KR	2007	(3)	1	0	0	4
	Castleford	1998, 2001-04	86(33)	32	0	0	128
	Hull	1999	12(6)	3	0	0	12
Morgan Smith	Hull	2024	22(3)	2	0	0	8
	Wakefield	2023	11(2)	2	0	0	8
	London	2019	15(1)	1	1	2	8
	Warrington	2016-18	(18)	1	1	0	6
Paul Smith	Huddersfield	2004-06	52(17)	13	0	0	52
Paul Smith	Warrington	2001	(1)	0	0	0	0
	Castleford	1997-2000	6(37)	3	0	0	12
Paul Smith	London	1997	7(1)	2	0	0	8
Peter Smith	Oldham	1996	2	0	0	0	0
Reimis Smith	Catalans	2024	5	0	0	0	0
Richard Smith	Wakefield	2001	8(1)	1	0	0	4
	Salford	1997	(1)	1	0	0	4
Tim Smith	Wakefield	2012-15	79	11	0	0	44
	Salford	2014	12	2	7	0	22
	Wigan	2008-09	13(8)	2	0	0	8
Tony Smith	Hull	2001-03	43(5)	26	0	0	104
	Wigan	1997-2000	66(5)	46	0	0	184
	Castleford	1996-97	18(2)	10	0	0	40
Tony Smith	Workington	1996	9	1	0	0	4
Tyrone Smith	Harlequins	2006-07	49(3)	13	0	0	52
	London	2005	20(4)	11	0	0	44
Will Smith	Hull	2022	7	2	0	0	8
Morgan Smithies	Wigan	2019-23	76(29)	2	0	0	8
Rob Smyth	Leigh	2005	15(1)	4	0	0	16
	Warrington	2000-03	65	35	20	0	180
	London	1998-2000	32(2)	9	15	0	66
	Wigan	1996	11(5)	16	0	0	64
Marc Sneyd	Salford	2010-13, 2022-24	112(12)	14	348	13	765
	Hull	2015-21	161	19	558	33	1225
	Castleford	2014	25(1)	6	100	2	226
Steve Snitch	Castleford	2010-12	38(18)	10	0	0	40
	Wakefield	2002-05, 2009	33(55)	9	0	0	36
	Huddersfield	2006-08	24(35)	12	0	0	48
Bright Sodje	Wakefield	2000	15	4	0	0	16
	Sheffield	1996-99	54	34	0	0	136
Iosia Soliola	St Helens	2010-14	83(24)	27	0	0	108
David Solomona	Warrington	2010-12	8(49)	16	1	0	66
	Bradford	2007-09	44(9)	19	0	0	76
	Wakefield	2004-06	73(3)	26	0	0	104
Denny Solomona	Castleford	2015-16	42	58	0	0	232
	London	2014	19(1)	8	0	0	32
Alfred Songoro	Wakefield	1999	8(5)	4	0	0	16
Romain Sort	Paris	1997	(1)	0	0	0	0
Paul Southern	Salford	1997-2002	79(33)	6	13	0	50
	St Helens	2002	1(1)	0	0	0	0
Steve Southern	Wakefield	2012	7(8)	3	0	0	12
Cain Southernwood	Bradford	2010	2	0	0	0	0
Roy Southernwood	Wakefield	1999	1	0	0	0	0
	Halifax	1996	2	0	0	0	0
Jason Southwell	Huddersfield	2004	(1)	0	0	0	0
Waisale Sovatabua	Wakefield	2001-03	44(3)	19	0	0	76
	Hudds-Sheff	2000	23(1)	8	0	0	32
	Sheffield	1996-99	56(17)	19	0	1	77
Jamie Soward	London	2013	6(1)	4	21	0	58
Yusef Sozi	London	2000-01	(5)	0	0	0	0
Scott Spaven	Hull KR	2010	(2)	0	0	0	0
Andy Speak	Castleford	2001	4(4)	0	0	0	0
	Wakefield	2000	6(5)	2	0	0	8
	Leeds	1999	4	1	0	0	4
Dom Speakman	St Helens	2013	(1)	0	0	0	0
Tim Spears	Castleford	2003	(3)	0	0	0	0
Jake Spedding	St Helens	2016-18	3(1)	0	0	0	0
Ady Spencer	London	1996-99	8(36)	5	0	0	20
Jack Spencer	Salford	2009-11	(7)	0	0	0	0
Tom Spencer	Leigh	2021	(1)	0	0	0	0
	Wigan	2012-13	(7)	0	0	0	0
Daniel Spencer-Tonks	Salford	2022	(1)	0	0	0	0
Rob Spicer	Wakefield	2002-05	28(18)	4	0	0	16
Russ Spiers	Wakefield	2011	(2)	0	0	0	0
Gadwin Springer	Toulouse	2022	(5)	0	0	0	0
	Toronto	2020	4(1)	0	0	0	0
	Castleford	2015-18	15(41)	3	0	0	12
	Catalans	2014-15	(3)	1	0	0	4
Stuart Spruce	Widnes	2002-03	45(4)	19	0	0	76
	Bradford	1996-2001	107(2)	57	0	0	228
Lee St Hilaire	Castleford	1997	4(2)	0	0	0	0
Marcus St Hilaire	Bradford	2006-07	34(1)	12	0	0	48
	Huddersfield	2003-05	72(2)	30	0	0	120
	Leeds	1996-2002	59(33)	31	0	0	124
Cyril Stacul	Catalans	2007-12	61(1)	18	0	0	72
Dylan Stainton	Workington	1996	2(3)	0	0	0	0
Mark Stamper	Workington	1996	(1)	0	0	0	0
John Stankevitch	Widnes	2005	17(5)	0	0	0	0
	St Helens	2000-04	74(40)	25	0	0	100
Gareth Stanley	Bradford	2000	1	1	0	0	4
Craig Stapleton	Salford	2009	24	2	0	0	8
	Leigh	2005	27(1)	4	0	0	16
Nick Staveley	Hull	2023-24	4(2)	1	0	0	4
Graham Steadman	Castleford	1996-97	11(17)	5	0	0	20
Jon Steel	Hull KR	2007-08	18	6	0	0	24
Maxime Stefani	Toulouse	2022	13	2	0	0	8
Jamie Stenhouse	Warrington	2000-01	9(3)	3	0	0	12
Gareth Stephens	Sheffield	1997-99	23(6)	2	0	0	8
Noah Stephens	St Helens	2024	(14)	0	0	0	0
David Stephenson	Hull	1998	11(7)	3	0	0	12
	Oldham	1997	10(8)	2	0	0	8
Francis Stephenson	London	2002-05	42(34)	5	0	0	20
	Wigan	2001	2(9)	0	0	0	0
	Wakefield	1999-2000	50(1)	6	0	0	24
Paul Sterling	Leeds	1997-2000	79(12)	50	0	0	200
Jack Stevens	Salford	2022	(1)	0	0	0	0
Paul Stevens	Oldham	1996	2(1)	0	0	0	0
	London	1996	(1)	0	0	0	0
Robson Stevens	Huddersfield	2021	(2)	0	0	0	0

Super League Players 1996-2024

PLAYER	CLUB	YEAR	APP	TRIES	GOALS	FG	PTS
Warren Stevens	Leigh	2005	4(14)	1	0	0	4
	Warrington	1996-99, 2002-05	17(66)	1	0	0	4
	Salford	2001	(8)	0	0	0	0
Anthony Stewart	Harlequins	2006	4	0	0	0	0
	Salford	2004-06	51(2)	15	0	0	60
	St Helens	1997-2003	93(23)	44	0	0	176
Glenn Stewart	Leigh	2017	15	0	0	0	0
	Catalans	2016	28	3	0	0	12
Marcus Stock	London	2024	18(9)	2	0	0	8
Sam Stone	Salford	2023-24	44(1)	10	0	0	40
	Leigh	2021	5	2	0	0	8
Troy Stone	Widnes	2002	18(6)	1	0	0	4
	Huddersfield	2001	12(1)	1	0	0	4
Robbie Storey	London	2024	16	4	0	0	16
Matty Storton	Hull KR	2020-24	38(57)	8	0	0	32
James Stosic	Wakefield	2009	8(10)	1	0	0	4
Lynton Stott	Wakefield	1999	21	4	6	1	29
	Sheffield	1996-98	40(4)	15	0	0	60
Mitchell Stringer	Salford	2005-06	12(4)	0	0	0	0
	London	2004-05	10(19)	0	0	0	0
Graham Strutton	London	1996	9(1)	2	0	0	8
Matt Sturm	Leigh	2005	8(19)	3	0	0	12
	Warrington	2002-04	1(18)	0	0	0	0
	Huddersfield	1998-99	46	8	0	0	32
Sauaso Sue	Hull KR	2023-24	30(13)	8	0	0	32
Anthony Sullivan	St Helens	1996-2001	137(2)	105	0	0	420
Michael Sullivan	Warrington	2006-07	21(16)	8	1	0	34
Phil Sumner	Warrington	1996	(5)	0	0	0	0
Alex Sutcliffe	Castleford	2022-23	16(5)	2	0	0	8
	Leeds	2017, 2019-21	10(5)	2	0	0	8
Liam Sutcliffe	Hull	2023-24	35	11	11	0	66
	Leeds	2013-22	160(32)	62	168	3	587
	Bradford	2014	3(1)	1	0	0	4
Alex Sutton	Wigan	2022	1	0	0	0	0
Ryan Sutton	Wigan	2014-18	38(65)	10	0	0	40
Simon Svabic	Salford	1998-2000	13(5)	3	19	0	50
Luke Swain	Salford	2009-10	54	3	0	0	12
Richard Swain	Hull	2004-07	89	5	0	0	20
Anthony Swann	Warrington	2001	3	1	0	0	4
Logan Swann	Warrington	2005-06	49(1)	17	0	0	68
	Bradford	2004	25	6	0	0	24
Willie Swann	Warrington	1996-97	25(2)	6	0	0	24
Jake Sweeting	Castleford	2021	(1)	1	0	0	4
Adam Swift	Huddersfield	2024	10	11	0	0	44
	Hull	2020-23	58	42	0	0	168
	St Helens	2012-19	120	80	0	0	320
Nathan Sykes	Castleford	1996-2004	158(52)	3	0	0	12
Paul Sykes	Wakefield	2012-14	59(1)	12	135	6	324
	Bradford	1999-2002, 2008-12	99(4)	35	64	2	270
	Harlequins	2006-07	31(2)	15	47	1	155
	London	2001-05	95(1)	26	219	3	545
Wayne Sykes	London	1999	(2)	0	0	0	0
Tom Symonds	Huddersfield	2016-18	6(1)	3	0	0	12
Ukuma Ta'ai	Huddersfield	2013-20	118(63)	43	0	0	172
Semi Tadulala	Wakefield	2004-07, 2011	92	37	0	0	148
	Bradford	2008-09	49	30	0	0	120
Whetu Taewa	Sheffield	1997-98	33(7)	8	0	0	32
Rodrick Tai	Warrington	2024	20	7	0	0	28
Zeb Taia	St Helens	2017-20	96(3)	22	0	0	88
	Catalans	2013-15	75	35	0	0	140
Alan Tait	Leeds	1996	3(3)	1	0	0	4
Brad Takairangi	Hull KR	2021-22	24	4	0	0	16
Fetuli Talanoa	Hull	2014-18	115(1)	54	0	0	216
Willie Talau	Salford	2009-10	22	4	0	0	16
	St Helens	2003-08	130(1)	50	0	0	200
Ian Talbot	Wakefield	1999	9(5)	2	31	0	70
	Wigan	1997	3	1	0	0	4
Albert Talipeau	Wakefield	2004	2(3)	0	0	0	0
Gael Tallec	Halifax	2000	5(19)	3	0	0	12
	Castleford	1998-99	19(21)	3	0	0	12
	Wigan	1996-97	8(12)	3	0	0	12
Joe Tamani	Bradford	1996	11(3)	4	0	0	16
Ryan Tandy	Hull KR	2007	8(4)	2	0	0	8
Adam Tangata	Wakefield	2019-21	2(15)	1	0	0	4
Andrew Tangata-Toa	Huddersfield	1999	15	2	0	0	8
David Tangata-Toa	Celtic	2009	1(18)	4	0	0	16
	Hull KR	2007	(17)	3	0	0	12
Kelepi Tanginoa	Hull KR	2024	10(17)	8	0	0	32
	Wakefield	2019-23	64(18)	21	0	0	84
Jordan Tansey	Huddersfield	2016	2	1	1	0	6
	Wakefield	2015	4	1	0	0	4
	Castleford	2013-15	44(1)	15	0	0	60
	Crusaders	2011	14(4)	5	0	0	20
	Hull	2009-10	30	9	0	0	36
	Leeds	2006-08	18(32)	19	3	0	82
Lama Tasi	Warrington	2019	9(8)	0	0	0	0
	Salford	2014-15, 2017-18	55(26)	4	0	0	16
	St Helens	2016	9(8)	0	0	0	0
Charbel Tasipale	Castleford	2023-24	9	1	0	0	4
Kris Tassell	Wakefield	2002	24	10	0	0	40
	Salford	2000-01	35(10)	12	0	0	48
Will Tate	Castleford	2023-24	8(1)	2	0	0	8
	Hull KR	2020-22	11(5)	4	0	0	16
Shem Tatupu	Wigan	1996	(3)	0	0	0	0
Tony Tatupu	Wakefield	2000-01	20	2	0	0	8
	Warrington	1997	21(1)	6	0	0	24
Jorge Taufua	Wakefield	2022-23	13	1	0	0	4
Sio Siua Taukeiaho	Catalans	2023	3(6)	1	0	0	4
Taulima Tautai	Wigan	2015-19	7(111)	4	0	0	16
	Wakefield	2013-14	6(19)	2	0	0	8
Dave Taylor	Catalans	2016	20(4)	8	0	0	32
Elijah Taylor	Salford	2021-22	34(5)	1	0	0	4
James Taylor	Leigh	2005	(4)	0	0	0	0
Joe Taylor	Paris	1997	9(5)	2	0	0	8
Lawrence Taylor	Sheffield	1996	(1)	0	0	0	0
Scott Taylor	Hull	2016-23	134(31)	20	1	0	82
	Salford	2015	23	5	0	0	20
	Wigan	2013-14	18(29)	6	0	0	24
	Hull KR	2009-12	21(29)	8	0	0	32
Cai Taylor-Wray	Warrington	2024	5(1)	3	0	0	12
Frederic Teixido	Sheffield	1999	(4)	0	0	0	0
	Paris	1996-97	2(3)	1	0	0	4
Lionel Teixido	Catalans	2006-07	11(13)	3	0	0	12
Karl Temata	London	2005, 2012	1(8)	1	0	0	4
	Harlequins	2006-11	94(22)	7	0	0	28
Jason Temu	Hull	1998	13(2)	1	0	0	4
	Oldham	1996-97	25(3)	1	0	0	4
Leo Tennison	Hull KR	2023	(1)	0	0	0	0
Paul Terry	London	1997	(1)	0	0	0	0
Zane Tetevano	Leeds	2021-23	40(6)	3	0	0	12
Anthony Thackeray	Castleford	2008	3(6)	0	0	0	0
	Hull	2007	2	0	0	0	0
Jamie Thackray	Crusaders	2010	1(16)	2	0	0	8
	Hull	2005-06, 2008-09	37(45)	6	0	0	24
	Leeds	2006-07	5(27)	7	0	0	28
	Castleford	2003-04	7(11)	3	0	0	12
	Halifax	2000-02	10(38)	3	0	0	12
Adam Thaler	Castleford	2002	(1)	0	0	0	0
Jake Thewlis	Warrington	2024	1	0	0	0	0
Josh Thewlis	Warrington	2019-24	77(3)	34	70	0	276
Gareth Thomas	Crusaders	2010-11	27(6)	6	0	0	24
Giles Thomas	London	1997-99	1(2)	0	0	0	0
Luke Thomas	Hull KR	2023	(1)	0	0	0	0
	Warrington	2022-23	(6)	1	0	0	4
Oscar Thomas	London	2014	4(2)	0	1	0	2
Rob Thomas	Harlequins	2011	(2)	0	0	0	0
Steve Thomas	London	2004	4(2)	0	0	0	0
	Warrington	2001	2	0	0	0	0
Alex Thompson	Warrington	2009	(1)	1	0	0	4
Alex Thompson	Sheffield	1997	4(11)	0	0	0	0
Bobby Thompson	Salford	1999	28	5	2	0	24
Bodene Thompson	Leeds	2020-22	31(17)	4	0	0	16
	Toronto	2020	4(1)	1	0	0	4
	Warrington	2018	7	0	0	0	0
Corey Thompson	Widnes	2016-17	48	36	9	0	162
David Thompson	Leigh	2017	1	0	0	0	0
	Hull KR	2016	1	0	0	0	0
Joel Thompson	St Helens	2021	13(2)	1	0	0	4
Jordan Thompson	Leigh	2021	13(5)	1	0	0	4
	Hull	2014-17, 2019	27(81)	12	0	0	48
	Leeds	2018	1	0	0	0	0
	Castleford	2009-13	47(24)	25	0	0	100
Luke Thompson	Wigan	2024	27	1	0	0	4
	St Helens	2013-20	100(54)	28	0	0	112
Sam Thompson	Harlequins	2009	(2)	0	0	0	0
	St Helens	2008	(5)	0	0	0	0
Chris Thorman	Hull	2009	19(2)	1	0	0	4
	Huddersfield	2000-01, 2005-08	126(20)	51	320	3	847
	London	2003	26(1)	7	81	1	191
	Sheffield	1999	5(13)	2	8	1	25
Tony Thorniley	Warrington	1997	(5)	0	0	0	0

Super League Players 1996-2024

PLAYER	CLUB	YEAR	APP	TRIES	GOALS	FG	PTS
Andy Thornley	Salford	2009	(1)	1	0	0	4
Iain Thornley	Wigan	2012-14, 2022-23	50	30	0	0	120
	Leigh	2021	19	3	0	0	12
	Catalans	2017-18	31(1)	7	0	0	28
	Hull KR	2016	21	10	0	0	40
Danny Tickle	Hull KR	2018	14(3)	4	20	0	56
	Leigh	2017	10(13)	4	0	0	16
	Castleford	2016	6(3)	0	1	0	2
	Widnes	2014-15	33(1)	3	88	0	188
	Hull	2007-13	159(5)	45	528	1	1237
	Wigan	2002-06	94(36)	34	200	2	538
	Halifax	2000-02	25(17)	10	91	2	224
Kris Tickle	Warrington	2001	(1)	0	0	0	0
Lewis Tierney	Leigh	2021	8	2	0	0	8
	Catalans	2017-20	52	15	0	0	60
	Wigan	2013-17	35	17	0	0	68
James Tilley	St Helens	2013-14	(3)	0	0	0	0
Dane Tilse	Hull KR	2015-16	29(1)	1	0	0	4
John Timu	London	1998-2000	57(3)	11	0	0	44
Liam Tindall	Hull	2024	2	0	0	0	0
	Leeds	2020-23	16(5)	2	0	0	8
Ugo Tison	London	2024	5(14)	1	0	0	4
	Catalans	2022-24	2(2)	0	0	0	0
Kerrod Toby	London	1997	2(2)	0	0	0	0
Tulsen Tollett	London	1996-2001	105(5)	38	49	1	251
Joel Tomkins	Catalans	2020-21	17(6)	5	0	0	20
	Hull KR	2018-19	27	7	0	0	28
	Wigan	2005-11, 2014-18	161(51)	60	0	0	240
Logan Tomkins	Salford	2014-19	85(31)	6	0	0	24
	Wigan	2012-15	9(32)	1	0	0	4
Sam Tomkins	Catalans	2019-24	98(4)	34	135	5	411
	Wigan	2009-13, 2016-18	177(6)	129	125	7	773
Glen Tomlinson	Wakefield	1999-2000	41(5)	8	0	0	32
	Hull	1998	5	1	0	0	4
	Bradford	1996-97	27(13)	12	0	0	48
Willie Tonga	Leigh	2017	3	0	0	0	0
	Catalans	2015	18	6	0	0	24
Ryan Tongia	Wakefield	2011	4	2	0	0	8
Ian Tonks	Castleford	1996-2001	32(50)	11	13	0	70
Tony Tonks	Huddersfield	2012	(1)	0	0	0	0
Motu Tony	Wakefield	2011-12	7(3)	1	0	0	4
	Hull	2005-09	76(20)	25	0	0	100
	Castleford	2004	8(1)	1	0	0	4
Mark Tookey	Harlequins	2006	12(14)	1	0	0	4
	London	2005	13(14)	5	0	0	20
	Castleford	2004	2(8)	1	0	0	4
Clinton Toopi	Leeds	2006-08	40(3)	9	0	0	36
David Tootill	Harlequins	2008	(4)	0	0	0	0
Paul Topping	Oldham	1996-97	23(10)	1	19	0	42
Patrick Torreilles	Paris	1996	9(1)	1	25	0	54
Albert Torrens	Huddersfield	2006	7	5	0	0	20
Mat Toshack	London	1998-2004	120(21)	24	0	0	96
Julien Touxagas	Catalans	2006-11	14(45)	4	0	0	16
Darren Treacy	Salford	2002	24(1)	6	1	0	26
Dean Treister	Hull	2003	16(1)	3	0	0	12
Rocky Trimarchi	Crusaders	2010	16(8)	0	0	0	0
Steve Trindall	London	2003-05	40(20)	3	0	0	12
Shane Tronc	Wakefield	2010	8(3)	2	0	0	8
Kyle Trout	Hull KR	2019-20	1(14)	0	0	0	0
	Wakefield	2012-15	6(17)	3	0	0	12
Owen Trout	Leigh	2024	15(13)	0	0	0	0
	Huddersfield	2020-23	27(23)	9	0	0	36
	Leeds	2019	1(1)	0	0	0	0
George Truelove	Wakefield	2002	2	1	0	0	4
	London	2000	5	1	0	0	4
Jake Trueman	Hull	2023-24	22(2)	4	0	0	16
	Castleford	2017-22	93(2)	28	0	1	113
Billy Tsikrikas	Castleford	2023	(4)	0	0	0	0
Va'aiga Tuigamala	Wigan	1996	21	10	3	0	46
Fereti Tuilagi	St Helens	1999-2000	43(15)	21	0	0	84
	Halifax	1996-98	55(3)	27	0	0	108
Carlos Tuimavave	Hull	2016-24	159(6)	50	0	0	200
Evarn Tuimavave	Hull KR	2013	11(12)	2	0	0	8
Sateki Tuipulotu	Leeds	1996	6(3)	1	2	0	8
Nolan Tupaea	Warrington	2024	1	0	0	0	0
Anthony Tupou	Wakefield	2016	12(9)	4	0	0	16
Bill Tupou	Wakefield	2015-21	109(3)	38	0	0	152
Tame Tupou	Bradford	2007-08	10(7)	8	0	0	32
Jansin Turgut	Salford	2019	8(2)	1	0	0	4
	Hull	2015-18	10(18)	3	0	0	12
Neil Turley	Leigh	2005	6(3)	2	20	1	49
Calum Turner	Castleford	2018-20	7(6)	4	10	0	36
Darren Turner	Huddersfield	2000-01, 2003-04	42(13)	13	0	0	52
	Sheffield	1996-99	41(29)	15	0	0	60
Ian Turner	Paris	1996	1(1)	1	0	0	4
Jordan Turner	Castleford	2021-23	39(4)	17	0	1	69
	Huddersfield	2017-20	66(2)	10	0	1	41
	St Helens	2013-16	106(4)	44	13	3	205
	Hull	2010-12	62(5)	28	0	0	112
	Salford	2006-07, 2009	22(10)	4	1	0	18
Chris Tuson	Hull	2014	10(1)	0	0	0	0
	Wigan	2008, 2010-13	24(49)	13	0	0	52
	Castleford	2010	3(5)	0	0	0	0
Gregory Tutard	Paris	1996	1(1)	0	0	0	0
Brendon Tuuta	Warrington	1998	18(2)	4	0	0	16
	Castleford	1996-97	41(1)	3	0	0	12
Steve Tyrer	Salford	2010	20	6	9	0	42
	Celtic	2009	8	2	5	0	18
	St Helens	2006-08	17(3)	12	42	0	132
Bobby Tyson-Wilson	Hull	2015	(1)	0	0	0	0
Harry Tyson-Wilson	Hull	2014	(1)	0	0	0	0
Akuila Uate	Huddersfield	2019	12	5	0	0	20
Wayne Ulugia	Hull KR	2014	3	1	0	0	4
Mike Umaga	Halifax	1996-97	38(1)	16	5	0	74
Kava Utoikamanu	Paris	1996	6(3)	0	0	0	0
Frederic Vaccari	Catalans	2010-11, 2013-14	50	26	0	0	104
David Vaealiki	Wigan	2005-07	67(1)	17	0	0	68
Joe Vagana	Bradford	2001-08	176(44)	17	0	0	68
Nigel Vagana	Warrington	1997	20	17	0	0	68
Tevita Vaikona	Bradford	1998-2004	145(2)	89	0	0	356
Lesley Vainikolo	Bradford	2002-07	132(4)	136	1	0	546
Junior Vaivai	Toulouse	2022	5	2	0	0	8
	Hull KR	2018-19	22(1)	8	0	0	32
Eric Van Brussell	Paris	1996	2	0	0	0	0
Jace Van Dijk	Celtic	2009	19	1	1	0	6
Richard Varkulis	Warrington	2004	4(1)	3	0	0	12
Marcus Vassilakopoulos	Sheffield	1997-99	15(11)	3	10	2	34
	Leeds	1996-97	1(3)	0	0	0	0
Manu Vatuvei	Salford	2017	7	5	0	0	20
Jonny Vaughan	St Helens	2024	2(6)	0	0	0	0
Paul Vaughan	Warrington	2023-24	45(4)	8	0	0	32
Atelea Vea	Leigh	2017	19(1)	5	0	0	20
	St Helens	2015-16	19(17)	10	0	0	40
	London	2014	19(3)	2	0	0	8
Josh Veivers	Salford	2012	5	2	0	0	8
	Wakefield	2011	10(2)	2	22	0	52
Phil Veivers	Huddersfield	1998	7(6)	1	0	0	4
	St Helens	1996	(1)	1	0	0	4
Michael Vella	Hull KR	2007-11	111(5)	13	0	0	52
Bruno Verges	Catalans	2006	25	6	0	0	24
Eric Vergniol	Paris	1996	14(1)	6	0	0	24
Albert Vete	Castleford	2023-24	3(6)	0	0	0	0
	Hull KR	2021-22	11(20)	7	0	0	28
Gray Viane	Salford	2007	9	2	0	0	8
	Castleford	2006	20(7)	14	0	0	56
	Widnes	2005	20	13	0	0	52
	St Helens	2004	4	1	0	0	4
Joe Vickery	Leeds	2013	9	1	0	0	4
Daniel Vidot	Salford	2016	5(1)	5	0	0	20
Adrian Vowles	Castleford	1997-2001, 2003	125(1)	29	1	1	119
	Wakefield	2002-03	24(3)	6	1	0	26
	Leeds	2002	14(3)	2	0	0	8
Mitieli Vulikijapani	Hull	2021-23	17(5)	7	0	0	28
King Vuniyayawa	Hull	2024	(2)	0	0	0	0
	Salford	2022-24	27(26)	4	0	0	16
	Leeds	2021	3(12)	1	0	0	4
Josh Wagstaffe	Salford	2024	1	0	0	0	0
Emmanuel Waine	London	2024	(9)	1	0	0	4
Michael Wainwright	Castleford	2008-10	70	22	0	0	88
	Wakefield	2004-05	21(10)	8	0	0	32
Mike Wainwright	Salford	2000-02, 2007	75(3)	9	0	0	36
	Warrington	1996-99, 2003-07	168(14)	23	0	0	92
Shannon Wakeman	Huddersfield	2017-18	16(13)	3	0	0	12
Adam Walker	Salford	2019	9(14)	4	0	0	16
	Wakefield	2017	5(1)	0	0	0	0
	St Helens	2017	(9)	1	0	0	4
	Hull KR	2013-16	60(27)	6	0	0	24
	Huddersfield	2010-12	1(5)	0	0	0	0

Super League Players 1996-2024

PLAYER	CLUB	YEAR	APP	TRIES	GOALS	FG	PTS
Alex Walker	London	2014, 2019, 2024	39(1)	8	0	0	32
	Wakefield	2020-21	8	1	0	0	4
Anthony Walker	Wakefield	2015-17	1(11)	1	0	0	4
	St Helens	2013-14	9(7)	2	0	0	8
Ben Walker	Leeds	2002	23(1)	8	100	0	232
Brad Walker	Wakefield	2020-22	17(8)	0	3	0	6
	Widnes	2016-18	3(5)	0	0	0	0
Chev Walker	Bradford	2011-14	44(22)	5	0	0	20
	Hull KR	2008-09	24(7)	5	0	0	20
	Leeds	1999-2006	142(19)	77	0	0	308
Chris Walker	Catalans	2010	11	6	2	0	28
Danny Walker	Warrington	2019-24	58(59)	14	0	0	56
	Widnes	2017-18	3(16)	2	0	0	8
Jack Walker	Hull	2022, 2024	20	7	0	0	28
	Hull KR	2023	10	5	0	0	20
	Leeds	2017-20, 2022	60(4)	18	0	0	72
Jonathan Walker	Hull KR	2014	2(6)	0	0	0	0
	Castleford	2010-13	17(31)	4	0	0	16
Jonny Walker	Wigan	2010	(1)	0	0	0	0
Marcus Walker	Hull	2021	1	0	0	0	0
Matt Walker	Huddersfield	2001	3(6)	0	0	0	0
Anthony Wall	Paris	1997	9	3	3	0	18
Blake Wallace	Leigh	2021	2	0	0	0	0
	Toronto	2020	5(1)	0	7	0	14
Jarrod Wallace	Catalans	2024	(7)	2	0	0	8
Jon Wallace	London	2014	4(12)	0	0	0	0
Mark Wallace	Workington	1996	14(1)	3	0	0	12
Elliot Wallis	Huddersfield	2024	15	7	0	0	28
	Castleford	2023	13	4	0	0	16
	Hull KR	2018	4	2	0	0	8
Alex Walmsley	St Helens	2013-24	179(79)	49	0	0	196
Adam Walne	Huddersfield	2018-20	4(9)	0	0	0	0
	Salford	2012-17	15(50)	2	0	0	8
Jordan Walne	Hull KR	2018	(6)	0	0	0	0
	Salford	2013-17	20(32)	3	0	0	12
Joe Walsh	Huddersfield	2009	1(1)	1	0	0	4
	Harlequins	2007-08	1(4)	0	0	0	0
Liam Walsh	Widnes	2017	(1)	0	0	0	0
Luke Walsh	Catalans	2017-18	23	2	71	4	154
	St Helens	2014-16	56(2)	14	188	9	441
Lucas Walshaw	Wakefield	2011-14	15(6)	3	0	0	12
Josh Walters	Leeds	2014-18	15(36)	9	0	0	36
Kerrod Walters	Gateshead	1999	10(12)	2	1	0	10
Kevin Walters	Warrington	2001	1	0	0	0	0
Sam Walters	Wigan	2024	7(7)	3	0	0	12
	Leeds	2020-23	24(17)	9	0	0	36
Jason Walton	Wakefield	2016	7(8)	0	0	0	0
	Salford	2009, 2014-15	7(19)	1	0	0	4
Barry Ward	St Helens	2002-03	20(30)	4	0	0	16
Danny Ward	Harlequins	2008-11	89(7)	4	0	0	16
	Hull KR	2007	11(9)	0	0	0	0
	Castleford	2006	18(7)	2	0	0	8
	Leeds	1999-2005	70(48)	9	0	1	37
Robbie Ward	Leeds	2014-15	5(3)	1	0	0	4
Stevie Ward	Leeds	2012-20	86(29)	19	0	0	76
Joe Wardill	Hull KR	2016, 2018	6(2)	1	0	0	4
Jake Wardle	Wigan	2023-24	56	24	0	0	96
	Warrington	2022	11	6	0	0	24
	Huddersfield	2018-22	62	22	6	0	100
Joe Wardle	Leigh	2023	5(6)	1	0	0	4
	Huddersfield	2011-16, 2019-21	152(1)	65	0	0	260
	Castleford	2018	15(2)	1	0	0	4
	Bradford	2010	1(1)	0	0	0	0
Phil Waring	Salford	1997-99	6(8)	2	0	0	8
Brett Warton	London	1999-2001	49(7)	14	133	0	322
Kyle Warren	Castleford	2002	13(14)	3	0	0	12
Danny Washbrook	Hull	2005-11, 2016-19	136(71)	19	0	0	76
	Wakefield	2012-15	93(8)	12	0	0	48
Adam Watene	Wakefield	2006-08	45(8)	5	0	0	20
	Bradford	2006	(4)	0	0	0	0
Frank Watene	Wakefield	1999-2001	24(37)	6	0	0	24
Trent Waterhouse	Warrington	2012-14	65(5)	15	0	0	60
Luke Waterworth	Wigan	2016	1	0	0	0	0
Kallum Watkins	Salford	2020-24	81(1)	23	0	0	92
	Leeds	2008-19	215(7)	110	85	0	610
Dave Watson	Sheffield	1998-99	41(4)	4	0	0	16
Ian Watson	Salford	1997, 2002	24(17)	8	3	5	43
	Workington	1996	4(1)	1	15	0	34
Kris Watson	Warrington	1996	11(2)	2	0	0	8
Anthony Watts	Widnes	2012	(1)	0	0	0	0
Brad Watts	Widnes	2005	6	3	0	0	12
Liam Watts	Castleford	2018-24	98(38)	9	0	0	36
	Hull	2012-18	116(19)	9	0	0	36
	Hull KR	2008, 2010-12	31(26)	6	0	0	24
Michael Watts	Warrington	2002	3	0	0	0	0
Brent Webb	Catalans	2013-14	10	2	0	0	8
	Leeds	2007-12	137(1)	73	0	0	292
Jason Webber	Salford	2000	25(1)	10	0	0	40
Ian Webster	St Helens	2006	1	0	0	0	0
Jake Webster	Castleford	2013-18	103(12)	45	0	0	180
	Hull KR	2008-12	95(1)	34	7	0	150
James Webster	Hull	2008	1	0	0	0	0
	Hull KR	2007-08	36	2	0	2	10
Pat Weisner	Hull KR	2007	(2)	0	0	0	0
	Harlequins	2006	10(6)	3	0	0	12
Taylor Welch	Warrington	2008	1	0	0	0	0
Kris Welham	Salford	2017-20	85(1)	27	0	0	108
	Hull KR	2007-15	164(2)	90	1	0	362
Paul Wellens	St Helens	1998-2015	399(40)	199	34	1	865
Calvin Wellington	St Helens	2016	1	0	0	0	0
Jack Wells	Salford	2021-22	6(6)	1	0	0	4
	Wigan	2016-17, 2020	5(12)	1	0	0	4
	Toronto	2020	(2)	1	0	0	4
Jon Wells	Harlequins	2006-09	66	10	0	0	40
	London	2004-05	42(2)	19	0	0	76
	Wakefield	2003	22(1)	1	0	0	4
	Castleford	1996-2002	114(14)	49	0	0	196
Jack Welsby	St Helens	2018-24	117(10)	61	0	3	247
Dwayne West	St Helens	2000-02	8(16)	6	0	0	24
	Wigan	1999	1(1)	0	0	0	0
Joe Westerman	Castleford	2008-10, 2022-24	141(7)	34	151	0	438
	Wakefield	2020-21	31	6	0	0	24
	Hull	2011-15, 2018-19	135(13)	36	52	1	249
	Warrington	2016-17	45(1)	12	0	0	48
Ryan Westerman	Hull	2024	1	0	0	0	0
Craig Weston	Widnes	2002, 2004	23(9)	2	1	2	12
	Huddersfield	1998-99	46(1)	15	15	0	90
Dayne Weston	Leigh	2017	6(5)	1	0	0	4
Ben Westwood	Warrington	2002-19	363(29)	112	64	0	576
	Wakefield	1999-2002	31(7)	8	1	0	34
Michael Weyman	Hull KR	2014	22(1)	7	0	0	28
Andrew Whalley	Workington	1996	(2)	0	0	0	0
Dean Whare	Catalans	2021-22	36	6	0	0	24
Paul Whatuira	Huddersfield	2008-10	59	23	0	0	92
Scott Wheeldon	Castleford	2014-15	14(23)	5	0	0	20
	London	2012-13	27(4)	3	0	0	12
	Hull KR	2009-12	30(42)	4	0	0	16
	Hull	2006-08	2(60)	4	0	0	16
Gary Wheeler	Toronto	2020	(2)	2	0	0	8
	Warrington	2015-16	6(4)	4	0	0	16
	St Helens	2008-14	48(10)	17	13	0	94
Matt Whitaker	Castleford	2006	8(2)	0	0	0	0
	Widnes	2004-05	10(20)	9	0	0	36
	Huddersfield	2003-04	3(14)	0	0	0	0
Jai Whitbread	Hull KR	2024	24(3)	3	0	0	12
	Wakefield	2022-23	29(8)	4	0	0	16
	Leigh	2021	2(2)	1	0	0	4
George Whitby	St Helens	2024	1	1	1	0	6
Ben White	Leeds	2014	1	0	0	0	0
David White	Wakefield	2000	(1)	0	0	0	0
Josh White	Salford	1998	18(3)	5	5	1	31
	London	1997	14(2)	8	0	1	33
Lloyd White	Toulouse	2022	5	0	0	0	0
	Widnes	2012-18	72(43)	27	24	1	157
	Crusaders	2010-11	13(11)	8	0	0	32
	Celtic	2009	6	1	0	0	4
Paul White	Salford	2009	1	1	0	0	4
	Wakefield	2006-07	24(12)	12	0	0	48
	Huddersfield	2003-05	11(32)	17	16	0	100
Elliott Whitehead	Catalans	2013-15	64(1)	30	0	0	120
	Bradford	2009-13	90(10)	30	0	0	120
Tom Whitehead	Warrington	2022-24	2(6)	1	0	0	4
Harvey Whiteley	Leeds	2017, 2020	(3)	0	0	0	0
Richard Whiting	Hull	2004-15	163(72)	69	19	2	316
Matt Whitley	St Helens	2024	19(1)	4	0	0	16
	Catalans	2019-23	93(4)	31	0	0	124
	Widnes	2015-18	50(27)	13	0	0	52
Emmerson Whittel	Bradford	2014	(1)	0	0	0	0
Danny Whittle	Warrington	1998	(2)	0	0	0	0
David Whittle	St Helens	2002	1(2)	0	0	0	0
	Warrington	2001	1(2)	0	0	0	0
Jon Whittle	Wakefield	2006	8(2)	3	0	0	12
	Widnes	2005	13	2	0	0	8
	Wigan	2003	1	0	0	0	0

189

Super League Players 1996-2024

PLAYER	CLUB	YEAR	APP	TRIES	GOALS	FG	PTS
Joel Wicks	London	2013-14	3(10)	0	0	0	0
Dean Widders	Castleford	2009-11	25(32)	23	0	0	92
Gareth Widdop	Castleford	2023	21	1	37	1	79
	Warrington	2020-22	45	20	36	1	153
Stephen Wild	Salford	2011-13	71	4	0	0	16
	Huddersfield	2006-10	116(2)	33	0	0	132
	Wigan	2001-05	67(20)	24	0	0	96
Nathan Wilde	Leigh	2023	(8)	0	0	0	0
Sam Wilde	Widnes	2017-18	14(7)	2	0	0	8
	Warrington	2015-17	3(15)	1	0	0	4
Matty Wildie	Leigh	2021	2(9)	0	0	0	0
	Wakefield	2010-14	13(26)	3	0	0	12
Brayden Wiliame	Catalans	2017-19	64	25	0	0	100
Oliver Wilkes	Wakefield	2008-09, 2012-13	55(47)	10	0	0	40
	Harlequins	2010-11	39(13)	4	0	0	16
	Wigan	2006	1(5)	0	0	0	0
	Leigh	2005	13(1)	1	0	0	4
	Huddersfield	2000-01	1(6)	0	0	0	0
	Sheffield	1998	(1)	0	0	0	0
Jon Wilkin	Toronto	2020	5	1	0	0	4
	St Helens	2003-18	350(30)	78	0	2	314
Alex Wilkinson	Hull	2003-04	11(4)	1	0	0	4
	Huddersfield	2003	8	4	0	0	16
	London	2002	5(1)	0	0	0	0
	Bradford	2000-01	3(3)	1	0	0	4
Bart Williams	London	1998	5(3)	1	0	0	4
Connor Williams	Salford	2016	(1)	0	0	0	0
Daley Williams	Salford	2006-07	9(2)	4	0	0	16
Danny Williams	Harlequins	2006	9(13)	4	0	0	16
	London	2005	1(6)	0	0	0	0
Danny Williams	Bradford	2014	7	2	0	0	8
	Salford	2011-14	54	31	0	0	124
	Leeds	2006, 2008	13(2)	7	0	0	28
	Hull	2008	3	0	0	0	0
Dave Williams	Harlequins	2008-11	1(17)	0	0	0	0
Desi Williams	Wigan	2004	2	0	0	0	0
George Williams	Warrington	2021-24	76	30	0	5	125
	Wigan	2013-19	149(13)	55	56	1	333
Jonny Williams	London	2004	(4)	0	0	0	0
Jordan Williams	London	2024	(12)	1	0	0	4
Lee Williams	Crusaders	2011	1(7)	0	0	0	0
Rhys Williams	Salford	2013, 2020-23	55	18	0	0	72
	London	2019	29	13	0	0	52
	Warrington	2010-13	23(1)	15	0	0	60
	Castleford	2012	8	4	0	0	16
	Crusaders	2011	6	3	0	0	12
Sam Williams	Wakefield	2017	17(5)	4	26	0	68
	Catalans	2014	11(1)	4	21	0	58
Sonny Bill Williams	Toronto	2020	4(1)	0	0	0	0
Luke Williamson	Harlequins	2009-10	39	6	0	0	24
Aaron Willis	Castleford	2023	(1)	0	0	0	0
John Wilshere	Salford	2006-07, 2009	72(2)	32	142	0	412
	Leigh	2005	26	8	6	0	44
	Warrington	2004	5	2	0	0	8
Craig Wilson	Hull	2000	2(16)	1	0	1	5
	Gateshead	1999	17(11)	5	0	1	21
George Wilson	Paris	1996	7(2)	3	0	0	12
Harvey Wilson	Salford	2024	1(4)	1	0	0	4
John Wilson	Catalans	2006-08	69	23	0	0	92
Oliver Wilson	Huddersfield	2019-24	44(43)	0	0	0	0
Richard Wilson	Hull	1998-99	(13)	0	0	0	0
Scott Wilson	Warrington	1998-99	23(2)	6	0	0	24
Jenson Windley	Castleford	2024	3(2)	1	0	0	4
Johan Windley	Hull	1999	2(2)	1	0	0	4
Jake Wingfield	St Helens	2020-24	7(36)	0	0	0	0
Paul Wingfield	Warrington	1997	5(3)	6	1	0	26
Frank Winterstein	Widnes	2012-13	37(9)	16	0	0	64
	Crusaders	2010-11	26(19)	4	0	0	16
	Wakefield	2009	(5)	0	0	0	0
Lincoln Withers	Hull KR	2012-13	18(22)	10	0	0	40
	Crusaders	2010-11	47	4	0	0	16
	Celtic	2009	21	6	0	0	24
Michael Withers	Wigan	2007	6(1)	1	0	0	4
	Bradford	1999-2006	156(6)	94	15	4	410
Michael Witt	London	2012-13	37	10	89	1	219
	Crusaders	2010-11	39	13	47	4	150
Jeff Wittenberg	Huddersfield	1998	18(1)	1	0	0	4
	Bradford	1997	8(9)	4	0	0	16
Josh Wood	Wakefield	2020-21	7(6)	1	0	0	4
	Salford	2015-19	19(17)	2	0	0	8
Kyle Wood	Wakefield	2012-13, 2017-21	62(93)	26	0	0	104
	Huddersfield	2011, 2013-16	39(33)	7	0	0	28
	Castleford	2010	1(4)	0	0	0	0
Martin Wood	Sheffield	1997-98	24(11)	4	18	2	54
Max Wood	Warrington	2024	1(10)	0	0	0	0
Mikey Wood	Huddersfield	2016-17	1(1)	0	0	0	0
Nathan Wood	Warrington	2002-05	90	38	0	3	155
	Wakefield	2002	11	2	0	0	8
Paul Wood	Warrington	2000-14	138(171)	40	0	0	160
Phil Wood	Widnes	2004	2(1)	0	0	0	0
Sam Wood	Bradford	2013-14	7(1)	0	0	0	0
Sam Wood	Castleford	2024	15	3	0	0	12
	Hull KR	2022-23	26(4)	8	2	0	36
	Huddersfield	2016-18, 2020-21	39(9)	13	4	0	60
James Woodburn-Hall	London	2013-14	9(4)	2	0	0	8
Darren Woods	Widnes	2005	(1)	0	0	0	0
David Woods	Halifax	2002	18(2)	8	0	0	32
Josh Woods	Wigan	2017-18	10(1)	1	4	1	13
Simon Worrall	Leeds	2008-09	5(16)	1	0	0	4
Michael Worrincy	Bradford	2009-10	12(34)	12	0	0	48
	Harlequins	2006-08	20(12)	10	0	0	40
Rob Worrincy	Castleford	2004	1	0	0	0	0
Greg Worthington	Toronto	2020	(1)	0	0	0	0
James Worthington	Wigan	2017	1	2	0	0	8
Troy Wozniak	Widnes	2004	13(7)	1	0	0	4
Matthew Wray	Wakefield	2002-03	13(3)	2	0	0	8
Connor Wrench	Warrington	2020-24	35(2)	15	0	0	60
David Wrench	Wakefield	2002-06	28(52)	6	0	0	24
	Leeds	1999-2001	7(17)	0	0	0	0
Callum Wright	Wigan	2014	(2)	0	0	0	0
Craig Wright	Castleford	2000	1(9)	0	0	0	0
Nigel Wright	Huddersfield	1999	4(6)	1	0	0	4
	Wigan	1996-97	5(5)	2	0	1	9
Ricky Wright	Sheffield	1997-99	2(13)	0	0	0	0
Shane Wright	Salford	2022-24	27(23)	8	0	0	32
Vincent Wulf	Paris	1996	13(4)	4	0	0	16
Connor Wynne	Hull	2019-22	29(4)	11	0	0	44
Andrew Wynyard	London	1999-2000	34(6)	4	0	0	16
Bagdad Yaha	Paris	1996	4(4)	2	4	0	16
Fouad Yaha	Catalans	2015-24	142	91	0	0	364
	Hull KR	2023	2	0	0	0	0
Malakai Yasa	Sheffield	1996	1(3)	0	0	0	0
Andy Yates	Wakefield	2016	(7)	0	0	0	0
	Leeds	2015	(9)	1	0	0	4
Luke Yates	Warrington	2024	10(1)	0	0	0	0
	Huddersfield	2021-24	75(5)	11	0	0	44
	Salford	2020	12(5)	3	0	0	12
	London	2019	28	2	0	0	8
Kirk Yeaman	Hull	2001-16, 2018	322(18)	159	0	0	636
Dominic Young	Huddersfield	2019-20	2	0	0	0	0
Grant Young	London	1998-99	22(2)	2	0	0	8
Nick Youngquest	Castleford	2011-12	37	28	0	0	112
	Crusaders	2010	26(1)	9	0	0	36
Ronel Zenon	Paris	1996	(4)	0	0	0	0
Tanguy Zenon	Hull KR	2023	2	0	0	0	0
	Catalans	2022-23	2(2)	1	0	0	4
Nick Zisti	Bradford	1999	6(1)	0	0	0	0
Freddie Zitter	Catalans	2006	1	0	0	0	0

All totals in 'Super League Players 1996-2024' include play-off games & Super League Super 8s from 2015-2018. Super 8s (Qualifiers) not included.

Toronto Wolfpack games from 2020 season also included.

Super League Players 1996-2024

NEW FACES - Players making their Super League debuts in 2024

PLAYER	CLUB	DEBUT vs	ROUND	DATE
Guillermo Aispuro-Bichet	Catalans	Castleford (a)	18	21/7/24
Leunbou Bardyel-Wells	Salford	Wigan (a)	27	19/9/24
Jarred Bassett	London	Catalans (h)	2	23/2/24
(club debut: Batley (h), Ch1, 5/2/23)				
Yacine Ben Abdeslem	Catalans	Leeds (a)	23	23/8/24
Jack Billington	Huddersfield	Warrington (a)	16	5/7/24
Waqa Blake	St Helens	London (h)	1	16/2/24
Gideon Boafo	London	Hull KR (a)	7	5/4/24
(club debuts: Warrington (a) (D2), CC6, 23/3/24; Keighley (h), CC1, 20/3/21)				
Louis Brogan	Leigh	Castleford (h)	10	4/5/24
Fa'amanu Brown	Hull FC	Hull KR (h)	1	15/2/24
Jake Burns	St Helens	Castleford (h)	16	5/7/24
Jack Campagnolo	London	St Helens (a)	1	16/2/24
Darius Carter	Huddersfield	Warrington (h)	26	14/9/24
Jed Cartwright	Hull FC	Leigh (a)	21	11/8/24
Jack Charles	Hull FC	London (h)	3	3/3/24
Adam Clune	Huddersfield	Leigh (a)	1	16/2/24
Nathan Connell	Salford	London (h)	13	2/6/24
Thomas Deakin	Huddersfield	London (a)	6	31/3/24
Jacob Douglas	Wigan	Warrington (a)	13	1/6/24
Elie El-Zakhem	Castleford	Wigan (h)	1	17/2/24
Herman Ese'ese	Hull FC	Hull KR (h)	1	15/2/24
Jack Farrimond	Wigan	London (a)	4	9/3/24
Ethan Fitzgerald	Salford	Wigan (a)	27	19/9/24
Lachlan Fitzgibbon	Warrington	Catalans (a)	1	17/2/24
Jack Gatcliffe	Salford	Wigan (a)	27	19/9/24
Billy Glover	Salford	Wigan (a)	27	19/9/24
Charlie Glover	Salford	Wigan (a)	27	19/9/24
Ben Hartill	Warrington	Wigan (h)	13	1/6/24
George Hill	Castleford	Wigan (a)	8	19/4/24
Josh Hodson	Castleford	Leeds (h)	6	28/3/24
(club debut: Batley (a), CC6, 23/3/24)				
Daniel Hoyes	London	Hull KR (a)	7	5/4/24
(club debut: York (a), Ch14, 5/6/22)				
Jack Hughes	London	Hull KR (a)	7	5/4/24
(club debut: Warrington (a), CC6, 23/3/24)				
Jacob Jones	London	Catalans (h)	2	23/2/24
(club debuts: Newcastle (a) (D2), Ch6, 18/3/23; Keighley (h), CC1, 20/3/21)				
Callum Kemp	Hull FC	Catalans (h)	27	21/9/24
Will Kirby	Hull FC	Salford (a)	16	7/7/24
Loghan Lewis	Salford	Warrington (a)	14	14/6/24
Oliver Leyland	London	St Helens (a)	1	16/2/24
(club debut: York (h), CC2, 28/1/24)				
Arron Lindop	Warrington	Catalans (a)	1	17/2/24
Ben Littlewood	Leeds	Wigan (h)	21	10/8/24
Riley Lumb	Leeds	Hull FC (h)	9	28/4/24
Harvey Makin	London	Huddersfield (h) (D2)	6	31/3/24
(club debut: Batley (a), Ch16, 25/6/23)				
Franck Maria	Catalans	Hull FC (h)	4	9/3/24

PLAYER	CLUB	DEBUT vs	ROUND	DATE
Akim Matvejev	Castleford	St Helens (a)	26	13/9/24
Ned McCormack	Leeds	Warrington (h)	7	5/4/24
Charlie McCurrie	Salford	Wigan (a)	27	19/9/24
Aidan McGowan	Huddersfield	Warrington (a)	16	5/7/24
Lachlan Miller	Leeds	Salford (h)	1	16/2/24
Paul Momirovski	Leeds	Salford (h)	1	16/2/24
Kai Morgan	Salford	Hull KR (h)	3	2/3/24
Logan Moy	Hull FC	Huddersfield (h)	7	6/4/24
Matt Moylan	Leigh	Huddersfield (h)	1	16/2/24
Jack Murchie	Huddersfield	Leigh (a)	1	16/2/24
Zane Musgrove	Warrington	Catalans (a)	1	17/2/24
Sylvester Namo	Castleford	Huddersfield (a)	4	8/3/24
Ethan Natoli	London	Leeds (a)	10	3/5/24
(club debut: Batley (h), Ch1, 5/2/23)				
Jayden Nikorima	Catalans	Warrington (h)	1	17/2/24
David Nofoaluma	Salford	Wigan (h)	5	14/3/24
Jayden Okunbor	Hull FC	Hull KR (h)	1	15/2/24
Dean Parata	London	St Helens (a)	1	16/2/24
(club debut: Widnes (h), Ch1, 30/1/22)				
Franklin Pele	Hull FC	Hull KR (h)	1	15/2/24
Aaron Pene	Leigh	Leeds (a)	15	21/6/24
Nixon Putt	Castleford	Wigan (h)	1	17/2/24
Jamie Pye	Salford	Wigan (a)	27	19/9/24
Harry Robertson	St Helens	Wigan (a)	17	12/7/24
Tariq Sims	Catalans	Warrington (h)	1	17/2/24
Bayley Sironen	Catalans	Warrington (h)	1	17/2/24
Reimis Smith	Catalans	Hull KR (MW)	22	18/8/24
Noah Stephens	St Helens	Castleford (a)	11	10/5/24
Marcus Stock	London	St Helens (a)	1	16/2/24
(club debut: Batley (h), Ch1, 5/2/23)				
Robbie Storey	London	St Helens (a)	1	16/2/24
Rodrick Tai	Warrington	Catalans (h)	6	30/3/24
(club debut: London (h), CC6, 23/3/24)				
Cai Taylor-Wray	Warrington	Wigan (h)	13	1/6/24
Jake Thewlis	Warrington	Wigan (h)	13	1/6/24
Nolan Tupaea	Warrington	Wigan (h)	13	1/6/24
Jonny Vaughan	St Helens	Castleford (h)	16	5/7/24
Josh Wagstaffe	Salford	Wigan (a)	27	19/9/24
Emmanuel Waine	London	St Helens (a)	1	16/2/24
(club debut: Newcastle (a), Ch6, 18/3/23)				
Jarrod Wallace	Catalans	Hull FC (h)	19	27/7/24
Ryan Westerman	Hull FC	Catalans (h)	27	21/9/24
George Whitby	St Helens	Hull KR (h)	23	24/8/24
Jordan Williams	London	St Helens (a)	1	16/2/24
(club debut: Whitehaven (h), Ch2, 9/2/20)				
Harvey Wilson	Salford	Warrington (a)	14	14/6/24
Jenson Windley	Castleford	Warrington (a)	23	23/8/24
Max Wood	Warrington	Hull FC (h)	2	23/2/24

Players making their club debuts in other competitions in 2024

PLAYER	CLUB	DEBUT vs	ROUND	DATE
Joe Stocks	London	Warrington (a)	CC6	23/3/24

Super League Players 1996-2024

OLD FACES - Players making their Super League debuts for new clubs in 2024

PLAYER	CLUB	DEBUT vs	ROUND	DATE	PLAYER	CLUB	DEBUT vs	ROUND	DATE
Jordan Abdull	Catalans	Warrington (h)	1	17/2/24	Lee Kershaw	London	St Helens (a)	1	16/2/24
Andy Ackers	Leeds	Salford (h)	1	16/2/24	Samy Kibula	Castleford	Salford (a)	2	25/2/24
Sadiq Adebiyi	London	St Helens (a) (D2)	1	16/2/24	Kruise Leeming	Wigan	Castleford (a)	1	17/2/24
Jack Ashworth	Hull FC	Hull KR (h)	1	15/2/24	Nene Macdonald	Salford	Leeds (a)	1	16/2/24
Yusuf Aydin	Hull FC	Leeds (h)	9	28/4/24	Tyrone May	Hull KR	Hull FC (a)	1	15/2/24
John Bateman	Warrington	Hull KR (h)	20	2/8/24	Darnell McIntosh	Leigh	Huddersfield (a)	12	24/5/24
Lewis Baxter	Leigh	Salford (a)	6	30/3/24	Ben McNamara	Leigh	Hull FC (a)	5	16/3/24
Jack Bibby	Huddersfield	Warrington (h)	26	14/9/24	James Meadows	London	St Helens (a) (D2)	1	16/2/24
Lewis Bienek	London	Hull FC (h)	11	12/5/24	Joe Mellor	Salford	Leigh (h)	6	30/3/24
	(club debuts: Widnes (h) (D2), Ch1, 30/1/22; Batley (h), S8Q2, 14/8/16)				Rowan Milnes	Castleford	Salford (a)	2	25/2/24
Tom Briscoe	Hull FC	Warrington (a) (D2)	10	3/5/24	Hakim Miloudi	London	St Helens (a)	1	16/2/24
Jack Broadbent	Hull KR	St Helens (h)	10	4/5/24	Jayden Nikorima	Salford	Castleford (h)	19	27/7/24
Jack Brown	Hull KR	Warrington (a)	11	9/5/24	Dan Norman	Leigh	Huddersfield (h) (D3)	1	1/3/24
Joe Bullock	Salford	Huddersfield (a)	18	19/7/24	Sam Powell	Warrington	Catalans (a)	1	17/2/24
Joe Bullock	Hull FC	London (h)	3	3/3/24	Ben Reynolds	Hull FC	Castleford (a)	12	24/5/24
Joe Burgess	Hull KR	Salford (a)	3	2/3/24	Ben Reynolds	Hull KR	London (h)	7	5/4/24
Reiss Butterworth	London	Wigan (h)	4	9/3/24	Danny Richardson	Hull KR	London (a)	12	26/5/24
Ed Chamberlain	Hull FC	Leeds (h)	9	28/4/24	Fenton Rogers	London	Hull FC (a)	3	3/3/24
Tiaki Chan	Hull FC	London (a)	11	12/5/24	Josh Rourke	London	Leeds (a)	16	6/7/24
Tiaki Chan	Wigan	Huddersfield (h)	3	3/3/24	Leon Ruan	Hull FC	St Helens (h)	20	3/8/24
Daryl Clark	St Helens	London (h)	1	16/2/24	Matty Russell	Leeds	St Helens (a)	12	24/5/24
Brodie Croft	Leeds	Salford (h)	1	16/2/24	Matty Russell	Hull FC	London (h) (D2)	3	3/3/24
Cade Cust	Salford	Leeds (a)	1	16/2/24	Ethan Ryan	Salford	Wigan (h)	5	14/3/24
Gil Dudson	Salford	Wigan (h) (D2)	5	14/3/24	Hugo Salabio	Huddersfield	Leigh (a)	1	16/2/24
Brad Dwyer	Leigh	St Helens (a)	3	1/3/24	Tevita Satae	Catalans	Warrington (h)	1	17/2/24
Matty English	Castleford	Wigan (h)	14	14/6/24	Andre Savelio	Huddersfield	Hull KR (a)	14	14/6/24
Sam Eseh	Hull FC	Leigh (a)	21	11/8/24	Innes Senior	Castleford	Wigan (h)	1	17/2/24
Sam Eseh	Leeds	Leigh (h)	15	21/6/24	Louis Senior	Castleford	Wigan (a)	8	19/4/24
Sam Eseh	Castleford	St Helens (h)	11	10/5/24	Joe Shorrocks	Salford	Leeds (a)	1	16/2/24
Niall Evalds	Hull KR	Hull FC (a)	1	15/2/24	Josh Simm	Castleford	Wigan (h)	1	17/2/24
Theo Fages	Catalans	Warrington (h)	1	17/2/24	Morgan Smith	Hull FC	Hull KR (h)	1	15/2/24
Matty Foster	Salford	Wigan (h)	5	14/3/24	Adam Swift	Huddersfield	Leigh (a)	1	16/2/24
Matt Frawley	Leeds	Salford (h)	1	16/2/24	Kelepi Tanginoa	Hull KR	Hull FC (a)	1	15/2/24
Oliver Gildart	Hull KR	Hull FC (a)	1	15/2/24	Luke Thompson	Wigan	Castleford (a)	1	17/2/24
Mickael Goudemand	Leeds	Salford (h)	1	16/2/24	Liam Tindall	Hull FC	Leigh (h)	5	16/3/24
Corey Hall	Castleford	London (h)	9	26/4/24	Ugo Tison	London	Salford (h)	8	20/4/24
Chris Hankinson	Salford	Leeds (a)	1	16/2/24	Owen Trout	Leigh	St Helens (a)	3	1/3/24
Peta Hiku	Hull KR	Hull FC (a)	1	15/2/24	King Vuniyayawa	Hull FC	Wigan (h)	18	20/7/24
Dan Hindmarsh	Castleford	Wigan (a)	8	19/4/24	Jack Walker	Hull FC	Hull KR (h) (D2)	1	15/2/24
	(club debut: Wigan (h), CCQF, 14/4/24)				Elliot Wallis	Huddersfield	Leigh (a)	1	16/2/24
Luke Hooley	Castleford	Wigan (h)	1	17/2/24	Sam Walters	Wigan	Warrington (a)	13	1/6/24
Tex Hoy	Castleford	London (h)	9	26/4/24		(club debut: Hull KR, CCSF, 18/5/24)			
Luis Johnson	Castleford	Warrington (a) (D2)	3	1/3/24	Jai Whitbread	Hull KR	Hull FC (a)	1	15/2/24
Adam Keighran	Wigan	Castleford (a)	1	17/2/24	Matt Whitley	St Helens	London (h)	1	16/2/24
Rhys Kennedy	London	St Helens (a)	1	16/2/24	Sam Wood	Castleford	Wigan (h)	1	17/2/24
					Luke Yates	Warrington	St Helens (a)	18	19/7/24

SUPER LEAGUE XXIX
Club by Club

Super League XXIX - Club by Club

KEY DATES

12th December 2023 - threequarter Fletcher Rooney signs full-time contract to end of 2026.

18th December 2023 - backrower Luis Johnson joins from Hull KR one one-year contract after trial.

20th December 2023 - Papua New Guinea second-row Emmanuel Waine signs one-year contract extension.

22nd December 2023 - prop Muizz Mustapha extends contract until end of 2027 season.

5th February 2024 - ex-London Broncos prop Daniel Hindmarsh-Takyi signs from Queensland Cup side Northern Pride on one-year contract.

17th February 2024 - Liam Watts sent off in 32-4 round-one home defeat to Wigan.

20th February 2024 - Liam Watts banned for four games for head contact. Appeal fails. Charbel Tasipale one-match ban reduced to £250 fine.

25th February 2024 - 26-22 round-two defeat at Salford.

1st March 2024 - 30-8 defeat at Warrington.

8th March 2024 - 50-8 home defeat to Huddersfield.

16th March 2024 - 40-14 defeat at Catalans.

23rd March 2024 - Innes Senior try double in 28-14 Challenge Cup round-six win at Batley.

28th March 2024 - 26-6 home Easter Thursday defeat to Leeds.

3rd April 2024 - prop George Lawler suffers seizure at home from small bleed on brain.

5th April 2024 - 36-24 round-7 home win over Salford is first of season.

14th April 2024 - 60-6 home defeat to Wigan in Challenge Cup quarter-final.

16th April 2024 - Hull KR winger Louis Senior joins on rolling loan deal.

17th April 2024 - prop Sylvester Namo gets five-game ban for dangerous contact against Wigan. Appeal fails.

19th April 2024 - 36-14 league defeat at Wigan.

22nd April 2024 - released Hull FC fullback Tex Hoy signed until end of season.

23rd April 2024 - centre Corey Hall joins from Hull KR until end of season.

23rd April 2024 - Jack Broadbent signs for Hull KR for season, prior to permanent three-year deal from 2025.

26th April 2024 - Tex Hoy and Corey Hall make debuts in 40-0 home win over London Broncos.

4th May 2024 - Louis Senior scores two tries in 28-all draw at Leigh after golden-point time.

9th May 2024 - halfback Danny Richardson joins Hull KR on season-long loan.

10th May 2024 - 60-4 hammering at home by St Helens.

13th May 2024 - Liam Horne given one-match ban for dangerous throw.

16th May 2024 - teenage forward George Hill signs three-year contract extension, with club option for further year.

17th May 2024 - Fijian international winger Jason Qareqare signs new two-year contract.

20th May 2024 - backrower Alex Mellor and hooker Cain Robb sign new two-year contracts.

22nd May 2024 - on-loan wingers Innes and Lewis Senior sign two-year contracts.

24th May 2024 - 30-22 home win over Hull FC puts Tigers five points clear of bottom two.

30th May 2024 - hooker Liam Horne has one-year extension clause activated to end of 2026.

1st June 2024 - 32-4 defeat at Leeds.

11th June 2024 - Tex Hoy signs two-year contract to end of 2026.

12th June 2024 - Huddersfield Giants prop Matty English joins on rolling loan.

14th June 2024 - 10-8 home defeat to Wigan.

20th June 2024 - late Jez Litten field goal means 13-12 home defeat to Hull KR.

5th July 2024 - George Lawler returns as Rowan Milnes penalty earns stunning 8-6 win at St Helens.

12th July 2024 - Innes Senior and Alex Mellor score doubles in 34-20 win over London in Ebbsfleet.

21st July 2024 - 24-18 home win over Catalans.

27th July 2024 - Liam Horne and Sylvester Namo sin-binned in 30-22 defeat at Salford.

29h July 2024 - Liam Horne banned for one game for high tackle.

1st August 2024 - 20-10 home defeat to Leigh.

9th August 2024 - 36-6 defeat at Hull KR.

18th August 2024 - 20-12 defeat by Huddersfield in Magic Weekend at Elland Road, Leeds.

21st August 2024 - Parramatta Eels back Zac Cini signs two-year deal.

23rd August 2024 - 28-6 home defeat by Warrington.

31st August 2024 - Tex Hoy scores try double in commanding 39-20 win at Hull FC, despite second-half sin-binnings of prop Sylvester Namo and hooker Liam Horne.

2nd September 2024 - Sylvester Namo gets two-match suspension for late tackle. Liam Horne banned for one match for head contact.

5th September 2024 - captain Paul McShane to retire from full-time rugby at end of 2024 season.

6th September 2024 - 34-12 home defeat to Leigh.

13th September 2024 - Akim Matvejev debuts in 40-4 defeat at St Helens.

19th September 2024 - 34-10 defeat at Huddersfield ends season in 10th spot.

24th September 2024 - 24-year-old halfback Daejarn Asi signs from Parramatta for 2025.

7th October 2024 - Jacob Miller, Elie El Zakhem, Brad Martin, Samy Kibula, Nixon Putt, Daniel Hindmarsh, Luis Johnson and Corey Hall all leave.

CLUB RECORDS

Highest score:
106-0 v Rochdale, 9/9/2007
Highest score against:
12-76 v Leeds, 14/8/2009
Record attendance:
25,449 v Hunslet, 9/3/35

MATCH RECORDS

Tries:
5 Derek Foster v Hunslet, 10/11/72
John Joyner v Millom, 16/9/73
Steve Fenton v Dewsbury, 27/1/78
Ian French v Hunslet, 9/2/86
St John Ellis v Whitehaven, 10/12/89
Greg Eden v Warrington, 11/6/2017
Goals: 17 Sammy Lloyd v Millom, 16/9/73
Points: 43 Sammy Lloyd v Millom, 16/9/73

SEASON RECORDS

Tries: 42 Denny Solomona 2016
Goals: 158 Sammy Lloyd 1976-77
Points: 355 Luke Gale 2017

CAREER RECORDS

Tries: 206 Alan Hardisty 1958-71
Goals: 875 Albert Lunn 1951-63
Points: 1,870 Albert Lunn 1951-63
Appearances: 613 John Joyner 1973-92

Super League XXIX - Club by Club

CASTLEFORD TIGERS

DATE	FIXTURE	RESULT	SCORERS	LGE	ATT
17/2/24	Wigan (h)	L4-32	g:Richardson(2)	11th	10,117
25/2/24	Salford (a)	L26-22	t:Wood,Broadbent,Westerman,Horne g:Richardson,Hooley(2)	10th	4,770
1/3/24	Warrington (a)	L30-8	t:Simm,I Senior	11th	8,483
8/3/24	Huddersfield (h)	L8-50	t:I Senior(2)	11th	7,040
16/3/24	Catalans Dragons (a)	L40-14	t:Westerman,Simm(2) g:Milnes	11th	8,159
23/3/24	Batley (a) (CCR6)	W14-28	t:Simm,Milnes,I Senior(2),McShane,Miller g:McShane(2)	N/A	2,015
28/3/24	Leeds (h)	L6-26	t:Simm g:Richardson	11th	9,026
5/4/24	Salford (h)	W36-24	t:I Senior(4),S Hall,Martin g:Richardson(6)	10th	7,967
14/4/24	Wigan (h) (CCQF)	L6-60	t:I Senior g:Richardson	N/A	4,097
19/4/24	Wigan (a)	L36-14	t:L Senior,Milnes g:Milnes(3)	10th	13,029
26/4/24	London Broncos (h)	W40-0	t:Miller,Milnes,McShane,Mellor,I Senior(2),L Senior g:Milnes(6)	10th	6,996
4/5/24	Leigh (a)	D28-28 (aet)	t:L Senior(2),Hoy,Wood,I Senior g:Milnes(4)	10th	8,035
10/5/24	St Helens (h)	L4-60	t:L Senior	10th	7,869
24/5/24	Hull FC (h)	W30-22	t:Horne,Hoy,Milnes,Qareqare,C Hall g:Milnes(5)	10th	8,269
1/6/24	Leeds (a)	L32-4	t:El-Zakhem	10th	14,529
14/6/24	Wigan (h)	L8-10	t:Hoy g:Milnes(2)	10th	6,965
20/6/24	Hull KR (h)	L12-13	t:Wood,Milnes g:Milnes(2)	10th	7,897
5/7/24	St Helens (a)	W6-8	t:I Senior g:Milnes(2)	10th	9,808
12/7/24	London Broncos (a) ●	W20-34	t:Hoy,I Senior(2),Mellor(2),Milnes g:Milnes(5)	10th	2,050
21/7/24	Catalans Dragons (h)	W24-18	t:Horne(2),Miller,Hoy g:Milnes(4)	10th	7,331
27/7/24	Salford (a)	L30-22	t:Qareqare(2),El-Zakhem,Johnson g:Milnes(3)	10th	3,146
1/8/24	Leigh (h)	L10-20	t:Rooney,Westerman g:Milnes	10th	7,247
9/8/24	Hull KR (a)	L36-6	t:Mellor g:Milnes	10th	9,585
18/8/24	Huddersfield (MW) ●●	L12-20	t:Qareqare(2) g:Milnes(2)	10th	N/A
23/8/24	Warrington (h)	L6-28	t:Hooley g:Hooley	10th	7,449
31/8/24	Hull FC (a)	W20-39	t:I Senior,Milnes,Windley,Hoy(2),Namo g:Milnes(7) fg:Milnes	10th	10,271
6/9/24	Leigh (h)	L12-34	t:C Hall,Milnes g:Milnes(2)	10th	9,053
13/9/24	St Helens (a)	L40-4	t:Rooney	10th	12,058
19/9/24	Huddersfield (a)	L34-10	t:Qareqare,Mellor g:Milnes	10th	4,138

● Played at Kuflink Stadium, Ebbsfleet
●● Played at Elland Road, Leeds

Innes Senior

		APP		TRIES		GOALS		FG		PTS	
	D.O.B.	ALL	SL	ALL	SL	ALL	SL	ALL	SL	ALL	SL
Jack Broadbent	1/11/01	9(1)	7(1)	1	1	0	0	0	0	4	4
Elie El-Zakhem	17/4/98	26	25	2	2	0	0	0	0	8	8
Matty English	14/11/97	(4)	(4)	0	0	0	0	0	0	0	0
Sam Eseh	30/6/03	(1)	(1)	0	0	0	0	0	0	0	0
George Griffin	26/6/92	8(1)	8(1)	0	0	0	0	0	0	0	0
Corey Hall	7/8/02	14	14	2	2	0	0	0	0	8	8
Sam Hall	8/5/02	6(9)	5(9)	1	1	0	0	0	0	4	4
George Hill	29/7/04	10(3)	10(3)	0	0	0	0	0	0	0	0
Dan Hindmarsh	8/10/98	1(7)	1(6)	0	0	0	0	0	0	0	0
Josh Hodson	15/6/00	5	3	0	0	0	0	0	0	0	0
Luke Hooley	1/8/98	9(2)	9(1)	1	1	3	3	0	0	10	10
Liam Horne	3/2/98	23(4)	21(4)	4	4	0	0	0	0	16	16
Tex Hoy	4/11/99	17	17	7	7	0	0	0	0	28	28
Luis Johnson	20/2/99	5(5)	3(5)	1	1	0	0	0	0	4	4
Samy Kibula	7/8/99	1(5)	(5)	0	0	0	0	0	0	0	0
George Lawler	1/9/95	13(2)	13(2)	0	0	0	0	0	0	0	0
Brad Martin	6/2/01	2(8)	1(7)	1	1	0	0	0	0	4	4
Akim Matvejev	29/6/06	1(1)	1(1)	0	0	0	0	0	0	0	0
Paul McShane	19/11/89	9(2)	8(2)	2	1	2	0	0	0	12	4
Alex Mellor	24/9/94	26	24	5	5	0	0	0	0	20	20
Jacob Miller	22/8/92	26	24	3	2	0	0	0	0	12	8
Rowan Milnes	1/9/97	23(1)	22(1)	8	7	51	51	1	1	135	131
Muizz Mustapha	3/4/00	9(5)	9(5)	0	0	0	0	0	0	0	0
Sylvester Namo	26/8/00	1(14)	1(13)	1	1	0	0	0	0	4	4
Nixon Putt	3/3/95	3(4)	3(4)	0	0	0	0	0	0	0	0
Jason Qareqare	26/1/04	17	17	6	6	0	0	0	0	24	24
Danny Richardson	2/9/96	5	4	0	0	11	10	0	0	22	20
Cain Robb	5/1/03	(18)	(16)	0	0	0	0	0	0	0	0
Fletcher Rooney	12/1/06	3	3	2	2	0	0	0	0	8	8
Innes Senior	30/5/00	29	27	17	14	0	0	0	0	68	56
Louis Senior	30/5/00	4	4	5	5	0	0	0	0	20	20
Josh Simm	27/2/01	6(1)	5(1)	5	4	0	0	0	0	20	16
Charbel Tasipale	24/2/00	6	5	0	0	0	0	0	0	0	0
Will Tate	20/12/01	3	3	0	0	0	0	0	0	0	0
Albert Vete	24/1/93	(4)	(3)	0	0	0	0	0	0	0	0
Liam Watts	8/7/90	12(10)	12(9)	0	0	0	0	0	0	0	0
Joe Westerman	15/11/89	26	24	3	3	0	0	0	0	12	12
Jenson Windley	18/8/06	3(2)	3(2)	1	1	0	0	0	0	4	4
Sam Wood	11/6/97	16	15	3	3	0	0	0	0	12	12

'SL' totals include Super League games only; 'All' totals also include Challenge Cup

LEAGUE RECORD
P27-W7-D1-L19
(10th)
F425, A735, Diff-310
15 points.

CHALLENGE CUP
Quarter Finalists

ATTENDANCES
Best - v Wigan (SL - 10,117)
Worst - v Wigan (CC - 4,097)
Total (SL only) - 103,226
Average (SL only) - 7,940
(Up by 754 on 2023)

Super League XXIX - Club by Club

KEY DATES

5th January 2024 - England halfback Jordan Abdull joins from Hull KR on season-loan.

17th February 2024 - Michael McIlorum sent off in 16-10 home round-one win over Warrington.

20th February 2024 - Michael McIlorum banned for four matches for head contact. Paul Seguier two-game ban reduced to one game on appeal.

22nd February 2024 - head coach Steve McNamara signs new two-year contract extension.

23rd February 2024 - Tariq Sims and Theo Fages both score doubles in 34-0 win at London.

26th February 2024 - captain Benjamin Garcia signs new two-year contract.

2nd March 2024 - 18-10 defeat at Leeds ends winning start.

9th March 2024 - 26-12 rainy home win over Hull FC.

16th March 2024 - 40-14 home win over Castleford.

24th March 2024 - Tom Davies scores hat-trick in 40-4 Challenge Cup round-six win at Halifax.

27th March 2024 - prop Damel Diakhate signs one-season contract following release by Hull FC.

30th March 2024 - Jordan Abdull stars in 32-24 win at Warrington.

7th April 2024 - 14-8 home win over St Helens.

13th April 2024 - Jordan Abdull injures hamstring in 34-6 Challenge Cup quarter-final home defeat by Huddersfield. Bayley Sironen charged with head contact but cleared on appeal.

16th April 2024 - Ugo Tison goes to London Broncos on loan.

20th April 2024 - dominant seven-try 36-6 home win over Hull KR. Michael McIlorum gets two-game ban for tripping and dangerous contact. Mike McMeeken suspended for one game for dangerous contact.

26th April 2024 - 30-2 defeat at Leigh

2nd May 2024 - 30-8 defeat at Wigan.

3rd May 2024 - Mike McMeeken to join Wakefield at end of season.

16th May 2024 - prop Romain Navarrete signs two-year contract to end of 2026 season.

16th May 2024 - winger Tom Johnstone to leave for Wakefield at end of season.

25th May 2024 - 16-8 home defeat to Warrington.

31st May 2024 - 24-12 defeat at St Helens.

3rd June 2024 - prop Jordan Dezaria signs two-year contract extension to end of 2026 season.

4th June 2024 - Mike McMeeken out for three months after surgery on broken thumb.

5th June 2024 - on-loan from Hull KR Jordan Abdull signs for Hull FC from 2025.

5th June 2024 - winger Tom Davies to join Hull KR at end of season.

9th June 2024 - forward Paul Seguier signs one-year contract extension.

12th June 2024 - St Helens and England winger Tommy Makinson signs from 2025 on two-year contract.

15th June 2024 - 10-2 home defeat by Leigh.

22nd June 2024 - 22-18 home win over Huddersfield. Arthur Romano and Michael McIlorum banned for one game for dangerous contact. Romano's ban doubled on frivolous appeal.

26th June 2024 - Canberra Raiders winger Nick Cotric signs three-year contract from 2025.

28th June 2024 - Salford prop Oliver Partington signs two-year contract from 2025.

1st July 2024 - halfback César Rougé signs two-year contract extension to end 2026.

6th July 2024 - Théo Fages golden-point field goal earns 15-14 win at Hull KR.

11th July 2024 - England forward Elliott Whitehead re-joins from Canberra Raiders for 2025 season.

12th July 2024 - Sydney Roosters halfback Luke Keary signs two-year contract from 2025.

12th July 2024 - prop Siua Taukeiaho, stand-off Jayden Nikorima and prop Damel Diakhate have contracts terminated for breach of club discipline.

13th July 2024 - Arthur Romano scores double in 20-0 home win over Salford.

18th July 2024 - hooker Michael McIlorum to join Hull KR for 2025 season.

19th July 2024 - Sam Tomkins comes out of retirement and signs for rest of season.

20th July 2024 - Dolphins prop Jarrod Wallace signs with immediate effect until end of season.

21st July 2024 - Tom Johnstone breaks fibula in 24-18 defeat at Castleford.

27th July 2024 - Sam Tomkins returns and Jarrod Wallace makes debut in 24-16 home win over Hull FC. Tariq Sims sent off for high tackle on seven minutes.

29th July 2024 - Tariq Sims gets one match for head contact and four further matches for lifting injured player.

1st August 2024 - Melbourne centre Reimis Smith signs with immediate effect to end of season.

4th August 2024 - shock 12-10 defeat at London Broncos

7th August 2024 - Tongan prop Tevita Pangai Jr signs from NRL Dolphins for 2025 season.

8th August 2024 - New Zealand rugby union winger Ben Lam signs from Montpellier on trial till December.

9th August 2024 - late Arthur Mourgue field goal secures 23-22 win at Huddersfield. Sam Tomkins suffers hamstring injury.

18th August 2024 - Reimis Smith makes debut in 36-4 defeat by Hull KR in Magic Weekend at Elland Road, Leeds.

23rd August 2024 - 18-6 defeat at Leeds.

31st August 2024 - 26-18 home defeat to Wigan sees Dragons drop out of top six.

7th September 2024 - 27-12 defeat at Salford sees Dragons drop to eighth spot.

13th September 2024 - centre Matt Ikuvalu to leave at end of season.

14th September 2024 - Jordan Abdull returns for nervy 12-8 home win over London Broncos.

21st September 2024 - 24-4 final-round win at Hull FC means seventh-place finish.

4th October 2024 - Sam Tomkins signs contract for 2025.

CLUB RECORDS

Highest score: 92-8 v York, 12/5/2013
Highest score against:
0-62 v Hull FC, 12/5/2017
Record attendance: 31,555 v Wigan, 18/5/2019 *(Barcelona)*
11,856 v Wigan, 2/7/2016 *(Stade Gilbert Brutus)*

MATCH RECORDS

Tries:
4 Justin Murphy v Warrington, 13/9/2008
Damien Cardace v Widnes, 31/3/2012
Kevin Larroyer v York, 12/5/2013
Jodie Broughton v St Helens, 14/4/2016
Fouad Yaha v Salford, 21/7/2018
David Mead v Huddersfield, 29/9/2019
Fouad Yaha v Leeds, 23/3/2019
Brayden Wiliame v Doncaster, 11/5/2019
Goals:
11 Thomas Bosc v Featherstone, 31/3/2007
Thomas Bosc v Batley, 29/5/2010
Scott Dureau v Widnes, 31/3/2012
Points:
30 Adam Keighran v Leeds, 16/9/2023

SEASON RECORDS

Tries: 29 Morgan Escare 2014
Goals: 134 Scott Dureau 2012
Points: 319 Scott Dureau 2012

CAREER RECORDS

Tries: 104 Fouad Yaha 2015-2024
Goals:
579 *(inc 14fg)* Thomas Bosc 2006-2017
Points: 1,380 Thomas Bosc 2006-2017
Appearances:
337 Remi Casty 2006-2013; 2015-2020

Super League XXIX - Club by Club

CATALANS DRAGONS

DATE	FIXTURE	RESULT	SCORERS	LGE	ATT
17/2/24	Warrington (h)	W16-10	t:Abdull,Mourgue g:Mourgue(4)	6th	8,876
23/2/24	London Broncos (a)	W0-34	t:Fages(2),Sims(2),Nikorima,Bousquet g:Mourgue(5)	2nd	5,102
2/3/24	Leeds (a)	L18-10	t:Satae g:Mourgue(3)	4th	14,168
9/3/24	Hull FC (h)	W26-12	t:Nikorima,Laguerre,Mourgue,Davies g:Abdull(2),Mourgue(3)	3rd	9,140
16/3/24	Castleford (h)	W40-14	t:Mourgue,Abdull,Johnstone,Laguerre,Davies,Ikuvalu,Rouge g:Mourgue(6)	4th	8,159
24/3/24	Halifax (a) (CCR6)	W4-40	t:Davies(3),Seguier,Romano,Rouge,Satae g:Abdull(6)	N/A	1,811
30/3/24	Warrington (a)	W24-32	t:Davies,Johnstone(2),Garcia,Rouge,Abdull g:Abdull(4)	2nd	11,240
6/4/24	St Helens (h)	W14-8	t:McMeeken,Ikuvalu g:Mourgue(3)	1st	10,724
13/4/24	Huddersfield (h) (CCQF)	L6-34	t:Ikuvalu g:Mourgue	N/A	5,892
20/4/24	Hull KR (h)	W36-6	t:McIlorrum,Ikuvalu,Davies,Dezaria,Fages,Johnstone,Sims g:Mourgue(4)	1st	8,783
26/4/24	Leigh (a)	L30-2	g:Mourgue	2nd	7,321
2/5/24	Wigan (a)	L30-8	t:Bousquet g:Mourgue(2)	5th	14,481
11/5/24	Leeds (h)	W26-0	t:Davies,Johnstone,Mourgue,Da Costa g:Mourgue(5)	4th	9,546
25/5/24	Warrington (h)	L8-16	t:Davies g:Mourgue(2)	5th	9,440
31/5/24	St Helens (a)	L24-12	t:Johnstone,Bousquet g:Mourgue(2)	5th	11,088
15/6/24	Leigh (h)	L2-10	g:Mourgue	6th	9,480
22/6/24	Huddersfield (h)	W22-18	t:Davies,Fages,Romano,Johnstone g:Mourgue(3)	6th	8,254
6/7/24	Hull KR (a)	W14-15 (aet)	t:Da Costa,Johnstone g:Mourgue(3) fg:Fages	6th	9,579
13/7/24	Salford (h)	W20-0	t:Rouge,Romano(2) g:Mourgue(4)	5th	7,750
21/7/24	Castleford (a)	L24-18	t:Johnstone,Ikuvalu,Mourgue g:Mourgue(3)	5th	7,331
27/7/24	Hull FC (h)	W24-16	t:McIlorrum,Tomkins,Garcia,Davies g:Mourgue(4)	4th	9,214
4/8/24	London Broncos (a)	L12-10	t:Wallace,Yaha g:Mourgue	6th	1,900
9/8/24	Huddersfield (a)	W22-23	t:Sironen,Tomkins,Yaha,Romano,Ikuvalu g:Mourgue fg:Mourgue	5th	3,330
18/8/24	Hull KR (MW) ●	L4-36	t:Sironen	5th	N/A
23/8/24	Leeds (a)	L18-6	t:Romano g:Mourgue	6th	13,050
31/8/24	Wigan (h)	L18-26	t:Yaha,Fages,Romano g:Mourgue(3)	7th	11,038
7/9/24	Salford (a)	L27-12	t:Mourgue,Sironen g:Mourgue(2)	8th	4,910
14/9/24	London Broncos (h)	W12-8	t:Wallace,Romano g:Mourgue(2)	8th	8,855
21/9/24	Hull FC (a)	W4-24	t:Satae,Laguerre,Mourgue,Davies g:Mourgue(4)	7th	9,384

● *Played at Elland Road, Leeds*

		APP		TRIES		GOALS		FG		PTS	
	D.O.B.	ALL	SL	ALL	SL	ALL	SL	ALL	SL	ALL	SL
Jordan Abdull	5/2/96	16	15	3	3	12	6	0	0	36	24
Guillermo Aispuro-Bichet	12/7/05	1(4)	1(4)	0	0	0	0	0	0	0	0
Yacine Ben Abdeslem	19/11/03	(1)	(1)	0	0	0	0	0	0	0	0
Julian Bousquet	18/7/91	24(3)	23(2)	3	3	0	0	0	0	12	12
Loan Castano	24/2/02	(1)	(1)	0	0	0	0	0	0	0	0
Alrix Da Costa	2/10/97	16(5)	15(4)	2	2	0	0	0	0	8	8
Tom Davies	11/1/97	26	24	12	9	0	0	0	0	48	36
Jordan Dezaria	6/11/96	4(20)	4(19)	1	1	0	0	0	0	4	4
Theo Fages	23/8/94	24	22	5	5	0	0	1	1	21	21
Ben Garcia	5/4/93	27	25	2	2	0	0	0	0	8	8
Matt Ikuvalu	9/11/93	22	20	6	5	0	0	0	0	24	20
Tom Johnstone	13/8/95	17	17	9	9	0	0	0	0	36	36
Matthieu Laguerre	3/2/99	11(3)	9(3)	3	3	0	0	0	0	12	12
Franck Maria	31/7/97	(9)	(9)	0	0	0	0	0	0	0	0
Michael McIlorrum	10/1/88	10	9	2	2	0	0	0	0	8	8
Mike McMeeken	10/5/94	14(1)	12(1)	1	1	0	0	0	0	4	4
Arthur Mourgue	2/5/99	26(1)	25(1)	7	7	73	72	1	1	175	173
Romain Navarrete	30/6/94	28(1)	26(1)	0	0	0	0	0	0	0	0
Jayden Nikorima	5/10/96	4(9)	3(9)	2	2	0	0	0	0	8	8
Arthur Romano	17/8/97	22(1)	21	8	7	0	0	0	0	32	28
Cesar Rouge	3/10/02	12(9)	11(8)	4	3	0	0	0	0	16	12
Tevita Satae	22/10/92	1(26)	1(24)	3	2	0	0	0	0	12	8
Paul Seguier	8/9/97	11(10)	9(10)	1	0	0	0	0	0	4	0
Tariq Sims	9/2/90	21(1)	20(1)	3	3	0	0	0	0	12	12
Bayley Sironen	23/12/96	17(5)	17(4)	3	3	0	0	0	0	12	12
Reimis Smith	13/5/97	5	5	0	0	0	0	0	0	0	0
Ugo Tison	7/7/01	1	1	0	0	0	0	0	0	0	0
Sam Tomkins	23/3/89	5(1)	5(1)	2	2	0	0	0	0	8	8
Jarrod Wallace	23/7/91	(7)	(7)	2	2	0	0	0	0	8	8
Fouad Yaha	19/8/96	12	11	3	3	0	0	0	0	12	12

'SL' totals include Super League games only; 'All' totals also include Challenge Cup

Arthur Mourgue

LEAGUE RECORD
P27-W15-D0-L12
(7th)
F474, A427, Diff+47
30 points.

CHALLENGE CUP
Quarter Finalists

ATTENDANCES
Best - v Wigan (SL - 11,038)
Worst - v Huddersfield (CC - 5,892)
Total (SL only) - 119,259
Average (SL only) - 9,174
(Down by 65 on 2023)

Super League XXIX - Club by Club

KEY DATES

4th February 2024 - Luke Yates suspended for three matches for dangerous contact in 20-14 pre-season defeat at Castleford. Tui Lolohea, two, and Leroy Cudjoe, one, use reserve game to reduce bans.

6th February 2024 - England prop Tom Burgess signs from South Sydney on three-year deal from 2025.

16th February 2024 - Elliot Wallis, Adam Swift, Adam Clune, Jack Murchie and Hugo Salabio make debuts in 16-8 round-one win at Leigh. Jake Connor fails HIA.

24th February 2024 - 28-0 home defeat to St Helens in round two.

27th February 2024 - young forward Fenton Rogers goes on loan to London Broncos.

1st March 2024 - 30-16 round-three defeat at Wigan.

4th March 2024 - hooker Adam Milner banned for one match for head contact.

8th March 2024 - Adam Swift, Sam Halsall, Leroy Cudjoe all score doubles in 50-8 win at Castleford.

16th March 2024 - 24-12 home defeat to Hull KR.

23rd March 2024 - Adam Swift scores four tries in 50-6 home Challenge Cup round-six win over Hull FC.

31st March 2024 - 26-6 win at London Broncos.

2nd April 2024 - Harry Rushton signs new three-year contract to end of 2027.

6th April 2024 - Adam Swift scores hat-trick in 56-20 win at Hull FC.

13th April 2024 - 34-6 Challenge Cup quarter-final win at Catalans.

19th April 2024 - 30-24 comeback victory at Leeds is fifth straight win.

22nd April 2024 - outside back Sam Halsall signs new contract to end of 2027 season.

25th April 2024 - last-minute Jonny Lomax field goal means 13-12 defeat at St Helens.

3rd May 2024 - Elliot Wallis sent off for alleged head butt as late comeback falls short in 18-16 home defeat by Salford.

6th May 2024 - Elliot Wallis not charged.

8th May 2024 - backrower Sam Hewitt signs new contract until 2027.

11th May 2024 - 48-6 home defeat by Wigan.

19th May 2024 - 46-10 Challenge Cup semi-final defeat by Warrington at St Helens.

22nd May 2024 - stand-off Tui Lolohea signs new two-year contract. Winger Innes Senior to turn season-loan at Castleford into permanent deal.

24th May 2024 - Jack Murchie suffers knee injury in 16-10 home defeat to Leigh.

27th May 2024 - captain prop Luke Yates to join Warrington at end of season. Centre Esan Marsters to join Salford.

31st May 2024 - 24-18 home win over Hull FC ends five-match losing run.

12th June 2024 - prop Matty English joins Castleford on loan.

14th June 2024 - 32-6 defeat at Hull KR.

22nd June 2024 - 22-18 defeat at Catalans. Esan Masters out for two months with knee injury.

28th June 2024 - halfback Oliver Russell to join Wakefield for 2025.

4th July 2024 - Jack Murchie undergoes season-ending knee surgery.

5th July 2024 - chairman Ken Davy apologises to fans after 48-0 defeat at Warrington.

12th July 2024 - head coach Ian Watson sacked. Assistant Luke Robinson takes interim charge.

13th July 2024 - Andre Savelio sent off in 58th minute of 20-16 defeat at Leigh. Prop Joe Greenwood suffers shoulder injury.

15th July 2024 - Andre Savelio gets two matches for high tackle; Sam Hewitt two matches for punching.

15th July 2024 - transfer fee paid by Warrington for captain and prop Luke Yates to move immediately.

19th July 2024 - 16-8 home win over Salford ends four-match losing run.

25th July 2024 - 34-6 home defeat by Leeds.

31st July 2024 - Adam Swift season ended after surgery on groin injured in Cup semi-final defeat to Warrington.

1st August 2024 - 28-14 defeat at Wigan after leading 8-0 at half-time.

9th August 2024 - late Arthur Mourgue field goal means 23-22 home defeat to Catalans.

16th August 2024 - Leroy Cudjoe signs contract extension to end of 2025.

18th August 2024 - 20-12 win over Castleford in Magic Weekend at Elland Road, Leeds.

24th August 2024 - 60-10 hammering at Salford.

1st September 2024 - prop Fenton Rogers sent off in 39th-minute of 18-10 home defeat to St Helens.

2nd September 2024 - Fenton Rogers gets three-match ban for head contact and one more game for dangerous contact. Sam Hewitt gets one game for dangerous contact.

4th September 2024 - Luke Robinson appointed head coach on three-year contract.

8th September 2024 - 22-16 home win over London Broncos.

11th September 2024 - hooker Zac Woolford signs from Canberra Raiders on one-year deal for 2025.

14th September 2024 - 66-0 home defeat by Warrington.

19th September 2024 - 34-10 home win over Castleford ends season in 9th spot.

26th September 2024 - Hull FC centre Liam Sutcliffe signs on three-year deal.

CLUB RECORDS

Highest score:
142-4 v Blackpool, 26/11/94
Highest score against:
12-94 v Castleford, 18/9/88
Record attendance:
32,912 v Wigan, 4/3/50 *(Fartown)*
15,629 v Leeds, 10/2/2008
(McAlpine/Galpharm/John Smith's Stadium)

MATCH RECORDS

Tries:
10 Lionel Cooper v Keighley, 17/11/51
Goals: 18 Major Holland
v Swinton Park, 28/2/1914
Points: 39 Major Holland
v Swinton Park, 28/2/1914

SEASON RECORDS

Tries: 80 Albert Rosenfeld 1913-14
Goals: 156 *(inc 2fg)* Danny Brough 2013
Points: 346 Danny Brough 2013

CAREER RECORDS

Tries: 420 Lionel Cooper 1947-55
Goals: 958 Frank Dyson 1949-63
Points: 2,072 Frank Dyson 1949-63
Appearances: 485 Douglas Clark 1909-29

Super League XXIX - Club by Club

HUDDERSFIELD GIANTS

DATE	FIXTURE	RESULT	SCORERS	LGE	ATT
16/2/24	Leigh (a)	W8-16	t:Marsters,Milner,Wallis g:Russell(2)	4th	8,508
24/2/24	St Helens (h)	L0-28		8th	6,812
1/3/24	Wigan (a)	L30-16	t:Wallis,Swift,Murchie g:Russell(2)	8th	15,357
8/3/24	Castleford (a)	W8-50	t:Swift(2),Clune,Halsall(2),Hewitt,Cudjoe(2),Naiqama g:Russell(7)	8th	7,040
16/3/24	Hull KR (h)	L12-24	t:Naiqama,Swift g:Connor(2)	8th	5,428
23/3/24	Hull FC (h) (CCR6)	W50-6	t:Halsall(3),Naiqama(2),Swift(4),Livett g:Connor(2),Lolohea(3)	N/A	1,673
31/3/24	London Broncos (a)	W6-26	t:Jake Bibby,Marsters,Swift,Clune,Halsall g:Lolohea(3)	8th	2,300
6/4/24	Hull FC (a)	W22-56	t:Swift(3),Murchie,Marsters,Yates,Naiqama,Lolohea(2),Jake Bibby g:Connor(7),Lolohea	6th	9,631
13/4/24	Catalans Dragons (a) (CCQF)	W6-34	t:Connor,Milner,Swift,Ikahihifo,Marsters,Naiqama g:Connor(5)	N/A	5,892
19/4/24	Leeds (a)	W24-30	t:Marsters,Wallis,Swift,Livett,Naiqama,Clune g:Connor(3)	6th	13,128
25/4/24	St Helens (h)	L13-12	t:Naiqama,Swift g:Connor(2)	7th	9,888
3/5/24	Salford (h)	L16-18	t:Swift,Lolohea,Jake Bibby g:Connor(2)	8th	4,833
11/5/24	Wigan (h)	L6-48	t:Wallis g:Connor	8th	5,334
19/5/24	Warrington (CCSF) ●	L10-46	t:Swift,Naiqama g:Connor	N/A	9,253
24/5/24	Leigh (h)	L10-16	t:Hewitt,Naiqama g:Russell	8th	4,385
31/5/24	Hull FC (h)	W24-18	t:Jake Bibby(2),Ikahihifo,Halsall g:Russell(4)	8th	4,102
14/6/24	Hull KR (a)	L32-6	t:Marsters g:Russell	8th	9,304
22/6/24	Catalans Dragons (a)	L22-18	t:Rushton,Golding,Yates g:Russell(3)	8th	8,254
5/7/24	Warrington (a)	L48-0		8th	9,760
13/7/24	Leigh (a)	L20-16	t:Wallis(2),Connor g:Connor(2)	9th	7,160
19/7/24	Salford (h)	W16-8	t:Halsall,Milner g:Connor(4)	9th	4,119
25/7/24	Leeds (h)	L6-34	t:McGowan g:Connor	9th	4,923
1/8/24	Wigan (a)	L28-14	t:Jake Bibby,Halsall g:Connor(3)	9th	11,660
9/8/24	Catalans Dragons (h)	L22-23	t:Jake Bibby,Naiqama,Hewitt,Lolohea g:Connor(3)	9th	3,330
18/8/24	Castleford (MW) ●●	W12-20	t:Halsall,Hewitt,Marsters g:Connor(4)	9th	N/A
24/8/24	Salford (a)	L60-10	t:Hewitt,Rogers g:Russell	9th	3,319
1/9/24	St Helens (h)	L10-18	t:Wallis,Jake Bibby g:Russell	9th	3,877
8/9/24	London Broncos (h)	W22-16	t:Lolohea(2),Rushton g:Russell(5)	9th	3,439
14/9/24	Warrington (h)	L0-66		9th	4,181
19/9/24	Castleford (h)	W34-10	t:Hewitt(2),Rushton,McGowan,Lolohea,Clune g:Russell(5)	9th	4,138

● Played at Totally Wicked Stadium, St Helens
●● Played at Elland Road, Leeds

Adam Swift

		APP		TRIES		GOALS		FG		PTS	
	D.O.B.	ALL	SL	ALL	SL	ALL	SL	ALL	SL	ALL	SL
Jack Bibby	14/10/01	(1)	(1)	0	0	0	0	0	0	0	0
Jake Bibby	17/6/96	17(1)	17(1)	8	8	0	0	0	0	32	32
Jack Billington	24/10/04	(2)	(2)	0	0	0	0	0	0	0	0
Darius Carter	25/11/04	1	1	0	0	0	0	0	0	0	0
Adam Clune	8/6/95	26	23	4	4	0	0	0	0	16	16
Jake Connor	18/10/94	20(1)	17(1)	2	1	42	34	0	0	92	72
Leroy Cudjoe	7/4/88	24	21	2	2	0	0	0	0	8	8
Thomas Deakin	16/2/02	5(3)	5(3)	0	0	0	0	0	0	0	0
Matty English	14/11/97	9(8)	6(8)	0	0	0	0	0	0	0	0
Ashton Golding	4/9/96	3(19)	3(16)	1	1	0	0	0	0	4	4
Joe Greenwood	2/4/93	11(4)	10(3)	0	0	0	0	0	0	0	0
Sam Halsall	18/8/01	18(1)	17(1)	10	7	0	0	0	0	40	28
Sam Hewitt	29/4/99	16(1)	16(1)	7	7	0	0	0	0	28	28
Chris Hill	3/11/87	19	19	0	0	0	0	0	0	0	0
Sebastine Ikahihifo	27/1/91	6(21)	6(18)	2	1	0	0	0	0	8	4
Harvey Livett	4/1/97	7(2)	6(2)	2	1	0	0	0	0	8	4
Tui Lolohea	23/1/95	26(2)	23(2)	7	7	7	4	0	0	42	36
Esan Marsters	17/8/96	22	19	7	6	0	0	0	0	28	24
Aidan McGowan	12/3/02	10	10	2	2	0	0	0	0	8	8
Adam Milner	19/12/91	22	19	3	2	0	0	0	0	12	8
Jack Murchie	26/6/97	11	8	2	2	0	0	0	0	8	8
Kevin Naiqama	4/2/89	26	23	11	7	0	0	0	0	44	28
Fenton Rogers	4/8/03	(8)	(8)	1	1	0	0	0	0	4	4
Kieran Rush	3/9/02	(6)	(6)	0	0	0	0	0	0	0	0
Harry Rushton	13/11/01	17(8)	17(5)	3	3	0	0	0	0	12	12
Oliver Russell	21/9/98	17(2)	17(2)	0	0	32	32	0	0	64	64
Hugo Salabio	27/7/00	1(11)	1(9)	0	0	0	0	0	0	0	0
Andre Savelio	21/3/95	4(5)	4(5)	0	0	0	0	0	0	0	0
Adam Swift	20/2/93	13	10	17	11	0	0	0	0	68	44
Elliot Wallis	10/5/00	17	15	7	7	0	0	0	0	28	28
Oliver Wilson	22/3/99	8(13)	6(13)	2	2	0	0	0	0	0	0
Luke Yates	6/3/95	14(2)	12(2)	2	2	0	0	0	0	8	8

'SL' totals include Super League games only; 'All' totals also include Challenge Cup

LEAGUE RECORD
P27-W10-D0-L17
(9th)
F468, A660, Diff-192
20 points.

CHALLENGE CUP
Semi-Finalists

ATTENDANCES
Best - v St Helens (SL - 6,812)
Worst - v Hull FC (CC - 1,673)
Total (SL only) - 58,901
Average (SL only) - 4,531
(Down by 713 on 2023)

Super League XXIX - Club by Club

HULL F.C.

KEY DATES

26th October 2023 - Fijian international threequarter Mitieli Vulikijapani signs one-year contract extension.

15th February 2024 - props Franklin Pele and Ligi Sao sent off in 22-0 home round one defeat to Hull KR. Joe Cator (hamstring), Danny Houghton (HIA) and Cameron Scott (calf) injured.

20th February 2024 - Franklin Pele gets four-game ban for head contact. Ligi Sao gets three games for flailing legs after foul tackle. Herman Ese'ese gets two matches for head contact

22nd February 2024 - Franklin Pele ban reduced to three games and Ligi Sao to one game after successful appeals.

23rd February 2024 - Fa'amanu Brown sent off after accidental head contact in 36-10 defeat at Warrington. Nine Academy graduates feature.

26th February 2024 - Fa'amanu Brown found not guilty as RFL amend head-on-head contact framework. Liam Sutcliffe gets two-match penalty notice for 'contact with a match official'.

27th February 2024 - winger Matty Russell and prop Joe Bullock join on loan from Warrington

3rd March 2024 - last-minute Morgan Smith try snatches 28-24 home win over London Broncos. Jack Brown banned for one game for dangerous throw.

9th March 2024 - Jack Ashworth sin-binned in 26-12 rainy defeat at Catalans and suspended for three games for late tackle.

2nd April 2024 - young prop Nick Staveley out for season after rupturing ACL in training.

6th April 2024 - Logan Moy makes debut in 56-22 home defeat by Huddersfield. Ligi Sao and Jack Brown get one-match bans.

11th April 2024 - head coach Tony Smith sacked. Assistant Simon Grix takes interim charge.

12th April 2024 - halfback Fa'amanu Brown and fullback Tex Hoy leave the club.

15th April 2024 - Richie Myler appointed director of rugby.

23rd April 2024 - approach for Salford head coach Paul Rowley turned down.

23rd April 2024 - winger Tom Briscoe signs on 18-month deal from Leigh, winger Darnell McIntosh moving the other way. Centre Ed Chamberlain joins on loan from Leigh.

24th April 2024 - prop Yusuf Aydin joins on loan from Hull KR.

1st May 2024 - Leigh loose forward John Asiata signs three-year contract from 2025 season.

3rd May 2024 - Jake Trueman plays first game of season in 24-6 defeat at Warrington.

7th May 2024 - prop Yusuf Aydin signs immediately from Hull KR on two-and-a-half year deal. Jack Brown goes the other way. Wigan prop Tiaki Chan arrives on loan.

12th May 2024 - 34-18 defeat at winless London Broncos. Herman Ese'ese charged with verbal abuse.

22nd May 2024 - Brisbane assistant John Cartwright announced as head coach on three-year contract from 2025 season.

24th May 2024 - teenage fullback Logan Moy signs new three-year contract.

28th May 2024 - Herman Ese'ese verbal abuse charges dropped.

30th May 2024 - youngsters Harvey Barron, Zach Jebson, and Matty Laidlaw have options taken up for 2025.

5th June 2024 - Jordan Abdull to return from Hull KR via loan with Catalans, on three-year contract for 2025.

6th June 2024 - Newcastle second-rower Jed Cartwright and Brisbane Tigers fullback Treigh Stewart sign with immediate effect pending visa clearance.

10th June 2024 - threequarter Davy Litten signs new two-year contract.

10th June 2024 - contract offer to fullback Treigh Stewart withdrawn after accusations in Australia of domestic violence incident.

11th June 2024 - winger Lewis Martin and 18-year-old halfback Jack Charles sign new two-year contracts to end of 2026 season

15th June 2024 - 18-10 home win over Leeds ends run of 11 successive defeats in league and cup.

19th June 2024 - prop Franklin Pele released and joins Championship Bradford Bulls.

24th June 2024 - hooker Amir Bourouh signs for 2025 from Salford on three-year contract

25th June 2024 - centre/backrower Cameron Scott to join Wakefield at end of season.

27th June 2024 - hooker Denive Balmforth signs one-year contract extension for 2025.

4th July 2024 - halfback Cade Cust signs from Salford from 2025 season.

5th July 2024 - Jayden Okunbor signs for Bradford with immediate effect.

7th July 2024 - 22-20 defeat at Salford despite scoring four tries to three. Backrower Will Kirby makes debut.

8th July 2024 - on-loan from Hull KR Ben Reynolds takes option to re-join Featherstone on permanent basis.

8th July 2024 - Leigh centre Zak Hardaker and backrower Oliver Holmes sign two-year contracts from 2025; centre Ed Chamberlain three years.

17th July 2024 - Ed Chamberlain joins on loan for season. Prop King Vuniyayava signs on loan from Salford.

20th July 2024 - 24-22 home victory over Wigan ends league leaders eight-match winning run.

27th July 2024 - Ligi Sao sent off in 16th minute of 24-16 defeat at Catalans and gets two-match ban for head contact.

31st July 2024 - utility forward Joe Cator released and joins Toulouse.

31st July 2024 - Leeds prop Leon Ruan joins on loan. Wigan prop Sam Eseh joins on loan to end of season.

3rd August 2024 - 46-6 home hammering by St Helens. Backrower Jordan Lane banned for one game for head contact. Prop Brad Fash one game for dangerous contact.

11th August 2024 - prop Jed Cartwright makes debut in 42-12 defeat at Leigh.

17th August 2024 - 29-4 defeat by London in Magic Weekend at Elland Road, Leeds.

28th August 2024 - halfback Jake Trueman released from rest of contract to sign for Wakefield.

30th August 2024 - hooker Danny Houghton to retire at end of season.

10th September 2024 - centre Carlos Tuimavave to leave at end of season.

11th September 2024 - Canberra Raiders utility back Jordan Rapana signs from 2025 on two-year contract.

12th September 2024 - halfback Aidan Sezer signs from Wests Tigers for 2025 on two-year contract.

14th September 2024 - 58-4 home hammering by Salford sends FC to bottom of table on points difference for a week.

21st September 2024 - 24-4 final round home defeat by Catalans.

CLUB RECORDS

Highest score: 88-0 v Sheffield, 2/3/2003
Highest score against:
10-80 v Warrington, 30/8/2018
Record attendance:
28,798 v Leeds, 7/3/36 (The Boulevard)
23,004 v Hull KR, 2/9/2007
(KC/KCOM/MKM Stadium)

MATCH RECORDS

Tries: 7 Clive Sullivan v Doncaster, 15/4/68
Goals:
14 Jim Kennedy v Rochdale, 7/4/1921
Sammy Lloyd v Oldham, 10/9/78
Matt Crowther v Sheffield, 2/3/2003
Points:
36 Jim Kennedy v Keighley, 29/1/1921

SEASON RECORDS

Tries: 52 Jack Harrison 1914-15
Goals: 170 Sammy Lloyd 1978-79
Points: 369 Sammy Lloyd 1978-79

CAREER RECORDS

Tries: 250 Clive Sullivan 1961-74; 1981-85
Goals: 687 Joe Oliver 1928-37; 1943-45
Points: 1,842 Joe Oliver 1928-37; 1943-45
Appearances: 500 Edward Rogers 1906-25

Super League XXIX - Club by Club

HULL F.C.

DATE	FIXTURE	RESULT	SCORERS	LGE	ATT
15/2/24	Hull KR (h)	L0-22		10th	20,014
23/2/24	Warrington (a)	L36-10	t:Martin,Walker g:McIntosh	11th	9,431
3/3/24	London Broncos (h)	W28-24	t:Staveley,Russell,Martin,F Brown,Smith g:McIntosh(4)	9th	10,066
9/3/24	Catalans Dragons (a)	L26-12	t:F Brown,Walker g:McIntosh(2)	9th	9,140
16/3/24	Leigh (h)	L4-54	t:Hoy	10th	10,227
23/3/24	Huddersfield (h) (CCR6)	L50-6	t:Lane g:Charles	N/A	1,673
29/3/24	Hull KR (a)	L34-10	t:Okunbor,Scott g:McIntosh	10th	11,050
6/4/24	Huddersfield (h)	L22-56	t:Sutcliffe(2),F Brown,Pele g:Charles(3)	11th	9,631
19/4/24	St Helens (a)	L58-0		11th	10,488
28/4/24	Leeds (h)	L12-18	t:Smith,Martin g:Charles(2)	11th	10,505
3/5/24	Warrington (a)	L24-6	t:Briscoe g:Charles	11th	8,680
12/5/24	London Broncos (a)	L34-18	t:Ese'ese,Trueman,Aydin g:Charles(3)	11th	3,225
24/5/24	Castleford (a)	L30-22	t:Barron,Sutcliffe,Chan,Trueman g:Reynolds(3)	11th	8,269
31/5/24	Huddersfield (a)	L24-18	t:Ese'ese,Moy,Scott g:Reynolds(3)	11th	4,102
15/6/24	Leeds (h)	W18-10	t:Martin,Balmforth,Scott g:Reynolds(3)	11th	12,166
22/6/24	Warrington (h)	L18-24	t:Balmforth,Sutcliffe,Briscoe g:Reynolds(3)	11th	10,083
7/7/24	Salford (a)	L22-20	t:Reynolds,Balmforth,Lane,Martin g:Reynolds(2)	11th	3,910
13/7/24	Hull KR (h)	L10-24	t:Martin,Moy g:Sutcliffe	11th	15,392
20/7/24	Wigan (h)	W24-22	t:Walker,Sutcliffe,Litten,Balmforth g:Charles(4)	11th	9,771
27/7/24	Catalans Dragons (a)	L24-16	t:Tuimavave,Walker,Martin g:Charles(2)	11th	9,214
3/8/24	St Helens (h)	L6-46	t:Walker g:Lane	11th	9,885
11/8/24	Leigh (a)	L42-12	t:Moy,Barron g:Charles(2)	11th	8,400
17/8/24	London Broncos (MW) ●	L4-29	t:Martin	11th	N/A
25/8/24	Wigan (a)	L22-4	t:Cartwright	11th	12,347
31/8/24	Castleford (h)	L20-39	t:Sao,Barron(2),Tuimavave g:Charles(2)	11th	10,271
6/9/24	Leeds (a)	L68-6	t:Barron g:Charles	11th	14,105
14/9/24	Salford (h)	L4-58	t:Jebson	12th	9,274
21/9/24	Catalans Dragons (h)	L4-24	t:Martin	11th	9,384

● Played at Elland Road, Leeds

		APP		TRIES		GOALS		FG		PTS	
	D.O.B.	ALL	SL	ALL	SL	ALL	SL	ALL	SL	ALL	SL
Jack Ashworth	3/7/95	3(11)	3(11)	0	0	0	0	0	0	0	0
Yusuf Aydin	13/9/00	16(3)	16(3)	1	1	0	0	0	0	4	4
Denive Balmforth	1/10/03	(15)	(15)	4	4	0	0	0	0	16	16
Harvey Barron	13/5/03	12	12	5	5	0	0	0	0	20	20
Tom Briscoe	19/3/90	15	15	2	2	0	0	0	0	8	8
Fa'amanu Brown	24/12/94	8	7	3	3	0	0	0	0	12	12
Jack Brown	25/6/00	2(7)	2(6)	0	0	0	0	0	0	0	0
Joe Bullock	27/11/92	(2)	(2)	0	0	0	0	0	0	0	0
Jed Cartwright	24/10/96	5	5	1	1	0	0	0	0	4	4
Joe Cator	15/6/98	5(1)	5(1)	0	0	0	0	0	0	0	0
Ed Chamberlain	8/2/96	8	8	0	0	0	0	0	0	0	0
Tiaki Chan	15/6/00	1(8)	1(8)	1	1	0	0	0	0	4	4
Jack Charles	30/1/06	15(2)	14(2)	0	0	21	20	0	0	42	40
Herman Ese'ese	7/4/94	25	24	2	2	0	0	0	0	8	8
Sam Eseh	30/6/03	1(3)	1(3)	0	0	0	0	0	0	0	0
Brad Fash	24/1/96	4(8)	4(8)	0	0	0	0	0	0	0	0
Will Gardiner	21/5/01	7(11)	7(10)	0	0	0	0	0	0	0	0
Danny Houghton	25/9/88	14(1)	14	0	0	0	0	0	0	0	0
Tex Hoy	4/11/99	5(2)	4(2)	1	1	0	0	0	0	4	4
Zach Jebson	9/5/04	(10)	(10)	1	1	0	0	0	0	4	4
Callum Kemp	18/9/06	1	1	0	0	0	0	0	0	0	0
Will Kirby	22/2/06	1	1	0	0	0	0	0	0	0	0
Matty Laidlaw	22/1/04	(5)	(5)	0	0	0	0	0	0	0	0
Jordan Lane	20/10/97	26(1)	25(1)	2	1	1	1	0	0	10	6
Davy Litten	3/5/03	4(3)	4(3)	1	1	0	0	0	0	4	4
Lewis Martin	19/8/04	25	24	9	9	0	0	0	0	36	36
Darnell McIntosh	5/7/97	9	8	0	0	8	8	0	0	16	16
Logan Moy	10/8/05	14(2)	14(2)	3	3	0	0	0	0	12	12
Jayden Okunbor	2/3/97	7(1)	7	1	1	0	0	0	0	4	4
Franklin Pele	18/12/00	3(5)	3(5)	1	1	0	0	0	0	4	4
Ben Reynolds	15/1/94	5	5	1	1	14	14	0	0	32	32
Leon Ruan	14/5/03	1(3)	1(3)	0	0	0	0	0	0	0	0
Matty Russell	6/6/93	2	2	1	1	0	0	0	0	4	4
Ligi Sao	11/10/92	21	20	1	1	0	0	0	0	4	4
Cameron Scott	7/10/99	11(1)	10(1)	3	3	0	0	0	0	12	12
Charlie Severs	1/10/03	(1)	(1)	0	0	0	0	0	0	0	0
Morgan Smith	30/4/98	23(3)	22(3)	2	2	0	0	0	0	8	8
Nick Staveley	19/1/04	5	4	1	1	0	0	0	0	4	4
Liam Sutcliffe	25/11/94	17	16	5	5	1	1	0	0	22	22
Liam Tindall	27/9/01	3	2	0	0	0	0	0	0	0	0
Jake Trueman	16/2/99	10(1)	10(1)	2	2	0	0	0	0	8	8
Carlos Tuimavave	10/1/92	15	15	2	2	0	0	0	0	8	8
King Vuniyayawa	13/3/95	(2)	(2)	0	0	0	0	0	0	0	0
Jack Walker	8/8/99	14	14	5	5	0	0	0	0	20	20
Ryan Westerman	15/1/06	1	1	0	0	0	0	0	0	0	0

'SL' totals include Super League games only; 'All' totals also include Challenge Cup

Herman Ese'ese

LEAGUE RECORD
P27-W3-D0-L24
(11th)
F328, A894, Diff-566
6 points.

CHALLENGE CUP
Round Six

ATTENDANCES
Best - v Hull KR (SL - 20,014)
Worst - v Salford (SL - 9,274)
Total (SL only) - 146,669
Average (SL only) - 11,282
(Down by 1,073 on 2023)

Super League XXIX - Club by Club

HULL KR

KEY DATES

1st November 2023 - Danny Ward joins as assistant coach on two-year contract.

6th November 2023 - second rower Kane Linnett announces retirement. Kelepi Tanginoa signs from Wakefield on three-year contract.

17th November 2023 - halfback Mikey Lewis signs new contract to end of 2028.

22nd December 2023 - Elliot Minchella announced as new captain.

5th January 2024 - halfback Jordan Abdull joins Catalans Dragons on season-loan.

10th January 2024 - winger Joe Burgess signs one-year contract after release by Salford.

15th February 2024 - 22-0 round-one win at Hull FC.

15th February 2024 - prop Sam Luckley signs three-year contract extension to end of 2027 season.

22nd February 2024 - one-year deal with Sydney Roosters prop Jared Waerea-Hargreaves announced for 2025 season.

22nd February 2024 - 22-12 home win over Leeds.

23rd February 2024 - Ben Reynolds signs from Championship club Featherstone on two-year contract.

2nd March 2024 - 17-10 defeat at Salford ends winning start.

7th March 2024 - late Matt Dufty try means 22-20 home defeat to Warrington.

16th March 2024 - 24-12 win at Huddersfield ends two-match losing run.

23rd March 2024 - Ryan Hall scores double in 40-0 home, round six thrashing of Salford.

28th March 2024 - young forward Leo Tennison signs new two-year deal to end of 2026 season.

29th March 2024 - 34-10 Good Friday win over Hull FC.

13th April 2024 - 26-14 home Challenge Cup win over Leigh.

16th April 2024 - winger Louis Senior joins Castleford on loan.

20th April 2024 - Mikey Lewis misses 36-6 defeat at Catalans.

23rd April 2024 - utility back Jack Broadbent signs from Castleford for 2024, prior to permanent three-year deal next season. Winger Ryan Hall to join Leeds at end of season.

24th April 2024 - winger Joe Burgess signs two-year contract extension to end of 2026.

26th April 2024 - Yusuf Aydin joins Hull FC on loan.

26th April 2024 - Mikey Lewis returns in commanding 26-10 home win over Wigan.

4th May 2024 - Jack Broadbent makes try-scoring debut in 40-20 home win over St Helens.

7th May 2024 - Hull FC prop Jack Brown signs immediate two-and-a-half year deal. Yusuf Aydin goes other way.

9th May 2024 - Castleford halfback Danny Richardson joins on season-long loan. Ben Reynolds goes to Hull FC on loan.

9th May 2024 - 20-8 defeat at Warrington.

13th May 2024 - head coach Willie Peters signs new four-year contract to end of 2028 season.

18th May 2024 - 38-6 Challenge Cup semi-final defeat by Wigan at Doncaster.

23rd May 2024 - utility back Louix Gorman signs new three-year contract.

5th June 2024 - Jordan Abdull signs for Hull FC from 2025 after season-loan with Catalans.

5th June 2024 - winger Tom Davies signs for 2025 on three-year contract from Catalans.

14th June 2024 - winger Ryan Hall becomes Super League all-time record try-scorer with two late tries in 32-6 home win over Huddersfield.

20th June 2024 - late Jez Litten field goal earns 13-12 win at Castleford.

27th June 2024 - prop forward, Eribe Doro signs for 2025 on two-year deal from Bradford.

6th July 2024 - golden-point field goal from Theo Fages means 15-14 home defeat by Catalans.

8th July 2024 - halfback Ben Reynolds, currently on loan at Hull FC, released to join Featherstone on permanent basis.

13th July 2024 - 24-10 win at Hull FC.

15th July 2024 - London Broncos hooker Bill Leyland signs two-year contract fro 2025 season.

18th July 2024 - Catalans Dragons' hooker Michael McIlorum signs one-year deal for 2025 season.

26th July 2024 - Mikey Lewis scores hat-trick as 40-16 home win over London moves Robins into second spot. Matty Storton gets one match ban for 'other contrary behaviour'.

2nd August 2024 - 22-4 win at Warrington sends Robins to top of table.

9th August 2024 - Joe Burgess scores try-double in 36-6 home win over Castleford.

18th August 2024 - Elliot Minchella, Ryan Hall and Kelepi Tanginoa all score doubles in 36-4 win over Catalans in Magic Weekend at Elland Road, Leeds.

18th August 2024 - centre Tom Opacic to leave at end of season.

23rd August 2024 - Castleford halfback Danny Richardson signs two-year contract from 2025.

24th August 2024 - Joe Burgess scores four tries as 42-6 win at St Helens maintains lead at top of Super League.

28th August 2024 - Leeds Rhinos PNG forward Rhyse Martin joins on two-year deal from 2025 season.

30th August 2024 - 32-12 home win over Salford maintains top spot.

6th September 2024 - Joe Burgess and Jai Whitbread sin-binned as 24-20 defeat at Wigan leaves Robins two points behind the top-of-the-table Warriors.

9th September 2024 - Jai Whitbread suspended for one game for head contact.

13th September 2024 - Mikey Lewis scores try-double in 24-0 win at Leigh.

15th September 2024 - Elliot Minchella banned for two games for head contact.

18th September 2024 - hooker Matt Parcell and prop George King to leave at end of season.

20th September 2024 - 26-16 final-round home win over Leeds means second-placed finish.

27th September 2024 - captain Elliot Minchella to miss play-off semi-final after two appeals against two-match ban fail.

4th October 2024 - 10-8 home semi-final win over Warrington.

8th October 2024 - halfback Mikey Lewis named 2024 Steve Prescott MBE Man of Steel. Willie Peters named Coach of the Year.

12th October 2024 - 9-2 defeat to Wigan in close Grand Final.

CLUB RECORDS

Highest score:
100-6 v Nottingham City, 19/8/90
Highest score against:
6-84 v Wigan, 1/4/2013
Record attendance:
27,670 v Hull FC, 3/4/53 *(Boothferry Park)*
12,100 v Hull FC, 1/2/2019 *(Craven Park)*

MATCH RECORDS

Tries: 11 George West
v Brooklands Rovers, 4/3/1905
Goals:
14 Alf Carmichael v Merthyr, 8/10/1910
Mike Fletcher v Whitehaven, 18/3/90
Colin Armstrong v Nottingham City, 19/8/90
Damien Couturier v Halifax, 23/4/2006
Points: 53 George West
v Brooklands Rovers, 4/3/1905

SEASON RECORDS

Tries: 45 Gary Prohm 1984-85
Goals: 199 Mike Fletcher 1989-90
Points: 450 Mike Fletcher 1989-90

CAREER RECORDS

Tries: 207 Roger Millward 1966-80
Goals: 1,268 Mike Fletcher 1987-98
Points: 2,760 Mike Fletcher 1987-98
Appearances: 489 Mike Smith 1975-91

Super League XXIX - Club by Club

HULL KR

DATE	FIXTURE	RESULT	SCORERS	LGE	ATT
15/2/24	Hull FC (a)	W0-22	t:Evalds(2),Tanginoa,Lewis,Parcell g:Hiku	3rd	20,014
22/2/24	Leeds (h)	W22-12	t:Sue,R Hall,Hiku g:Litten(5)	3rd	9,879
2/3/24	Salford (a)	L17-10	t:Hiku,Litten g:Litten	5th	5,036
7/3/24	Warrington (h)	L20-22	t:May,R Hall,Gildart,Opacic g:Litten(2)	7th	9,524
16/3/24	Huddersfield (a)	W12-24	t:Burgess,Litten,Hiku(2),R Hall g:Litten(2)	5th	5,428
22/3/24	Salford (h) (CCR6)	W40-0	t:R Hall(2),Burgess,Tanginoa,Hiku,Storton,Evalds g:Litten(5),Batchelor	N/A	5,636
29/3/24	Hull FC (h)	W34-10	t:Evalds,Burgess(2),Lewis,Batchelor,Hiku,Tanginoa g:Litten(2),Lewis	5th	11,050
5/4/24	London Broncos (h)	W50-10	t:Parcell(3),Batchelor(2),Tanginoa,R Hall,Lewis,Hiku g:Lewis(7)	4th	10,201
13/4/24	Leigh (h) (CCQF)	W26-14	t:Burgess(2),Tanginoa,Evalds,Minchella g:Lewis(3)	N/A	7,363
20/4/24	Catalans Dragons (a)	L36-6	t:Burgess g:Reynolds	5th	8,783
26/4/24	Wigan (h)	W26-10	t:Sue,Gildart,Hiku,R Hall,Tanginoa g:Lewis(3)	5th	9,945
4/5/24	St Helens (h)	W40-20	t:May,Lewis,Broadbent,Hiku,Litten,Hadley,R Hall g:Lewis(6)	4th	10,171
9/5/24	Warrington (a)	L20-8	t:Broadbent,Lewis	5th	8,578
18/5/24	Wigan (CCSF) ●	L6-38	t:Burgess g:Lewis	N/A	11,163
26/5/24	London Broncos (a)	W14-64	t:Broadbent(2),Hiku,Evalds(2),Parcell,Hadley,Luckley(2),Lewis(2) g:Lewis(9),Richardson	4th	3,750
1/6/24	Leigh (h)	W12-0	t:Opacic,Evalds g:Lewis(2)	3rd	9,899
14/6/24	Huddersfield (h)	W32-6	t:Hiku(2),May,Parcell,R Hall(2) g:Lewis(4)	3rd	9,304
20/6/24	Castleford (a)	W12-13	t:Opacic,Minchella g:Lewis(2) fg:Litten	3rd	7,897
6/7/24	Catalans Dragons (h) (aet)	L14-15	t:Broadbent,Burgess g:Lewis(3)	4th	9,579
13/7/24	Hull FC (a)	W10-24	t:Sue,Lewis,Storton,Minchella g:Lewis(4)	3rd	15,392
20/7/24	Leeds (a)	W12-20	t:R Hall,Lewis,Whitbread,Litten g:Lewis(2)	3rd	14,555
26/7/24	London Broncos (h)	W40-16	t:Sue,R Hall,Lewis(3),Parcell,Tanginoa g:Richardson(6)	2nd	9,346
2/8/24	Warrington (a)	W4-22	t:Sue,May,Lewis,Hiku g:Lewis,Litten(2)	1st	12,102
9/8/24	Castleford (h)	W36-6	t:Hiku,Burgess(2),Lewis,R Hall,Evalds,May g:Lewis(4)	1st	9,585
18/8/24	Catalans Dragons (MW) ●●	W4-36	t:Minchella(2),Hiku,R Hall(2),Tanginoa(2),Evalds g:Lewis(2)	1st	N/A
24/8/24	St Helens (a)	W6-42	t:Burgess(4),Lewis,May,Tanginoa,Whitbread g:Lewis(5)	1st	13,588
30/8/24	Salford (h)	W32-12	t:Broadbent(2),Whitbread,Lewis,Opacic,Litten g:Lewis(4)	1st	9,694
6/9/24	Wigan (a)	L24-20	t:Parcell,Lewis,Burgess g:Lewis(4)	2nd	16,719
13/9/24	Leigh (a)	W0-24	t:R Hall,Lewis(2),Sue g:Lewis(4)	2nd	8,412
20/9/24	Leeds (h)	W26-16	t:Parcell,Hiku,Opacic,Sue,Burgess g:Lewis(3)	2nd	11,200
4/10/24	Warrington (h) (SF)	W10-8	t:Batchelor,Burgess g:Lewis	N/A	11,200
12/10/24	Wigan (GF) ●●●	L2-9	g:Lewis	N/A	68,173

● Played at Eco-Power Stadium, Doncaster
●● Played at Elland Road, Leeds
●●● Played at Old Trafford, Manchester

		APP		TRIES		GOALS		FG		PTS	
	D.O.B.	ALL	SL	ALL	SL	ALL	SL	ALL	SL	ALL	SL
Yusuf Aydin	13/9/00	(2)	(2)	0	0	0	0	0	0	0	0
James Batchelor	9/4/98	27	24	4	4	1	0	0	0	18	16
Jack Broadbent	1/11/01	14	14	7	7	0	0	0	0	28	28
Jack Brown	25/6/00	1(8)	1(8)	0	0	0	0	0	0	0	0
Joe Burgess	14/10/94	23	20	18	14	0	0	0	0	72	56
Niall Evalds	26/8/93	28	25	10	8	0	0	0	0	40	32
Oliver Gildart	6/8/96	15	14	2	2	0	0	0	0	8	8
Dean Hadley	5/8/92	30	27	2	2	0	0	0	0	8	8
Corey Hall	7/8/02	(2)	(2)	0	0	0	0	0	0	0	0
Ryan Hall	27/11/87	32	29	16	14	0	0	0	0	64	56
Peta Hiku	4/12/92	32	29	16	15	1	1	0	0	66	62
George King	24/2/95	3(10)	3(9)	0	0	0	0	0	0	0	0
Mikey Lewis	4/7/01	30	28	19	19	76	72	0	0	228	220
Jez Litten	10/3/98	18(12)	15(12)	5	5	19	14	1	1	59	49
Sam Luckley	29/11/95	1(26)	1(24)	2	2	0	0	0	0	8	8
Tyrone May	21/6/96	31	28	6	6	0	0	0	0	24	24
Elliot Minchella	28/1/96	27(1)	24(1)	5	4	0	0	0	0	20	16
Tom Opacic	7/9/94	15(3)	13(2)	5	5	0	0	0	0	20	20
Matt Parcell	30/10/92	15(15)	14(13)	9	9	0	0	0	0	36	36
Ben Reynolds	15/1/94	1(1)	1(1)	0	0	1	1	0	0	2	2
Danny Richardson	2/9/96	1(1)	1(1)	0	0	7	7	0	0	14	14
Louis Senior	30/5/00	1	1	0	0	0	0	0	0	0	0
Matty Storton	10/3/99	7(18)	7(16)	2	1	0	0	0	0	8	4
Sauaso Sue	20/4/92	27(4)	24(4)	7	7	0	0	0	0	28	28
Kelepi Tanginoa	1/3/94	10(20)	10(17)	10	8	0	0	0	0	40	32
Jai Whitbread	16/1/98	27(3)	24(3)	3	3	0	0	0	0	12	12

'SL' totals include regular season & play-offs; 'All' totals also include Challenge Cup

Ryan Hall

LEAGUE RECORD
P27-W21-D0-L6
(2nd/Grand Final Runners-up)
F719, A326, Diff+393
42 points.

CHALLENGE CUP
Semi-Finalists

ATTENDANCES
Best - v Leeds (SL - 11,200)
v Warrington (SF - 11,200)
Worst - v Salford (CC - 5,636)
Total (SL, inc play-offs) - 140,577
Average (SL, inc play-offs) - 10,041
(Up by 1,233 on 2023)

Super League XXIX - Club by Club

KEY DATES

7th November 2023 - prop Kieran Hudson joins on one-year contract from Castleford Tigers. Richie Myler leaves for York.

30th November 2023 - Cameron Smith named new captain.

26th December 2023 - 41-22 win over Wakefield in Wetherby Whaler Challenge.

12th January 2024 - backrower James McDonnell extends contract until end of 2025.

4th February 2024 - Morgan Gannon faces three-month lay-off after head injury in 26-18 home win over Hull KR in James Donaldson Testimonial match.

6th February 2024 - England centre Harry Newman signs new two-year contract to end of 2026 season.

16th February 2024 - Ash Handley scores double as late Sam Lisone try seals 22-16 home round-one win over Salford.

22nd February 2024 - Lachlan Miller misses 22-12 defeat at Hull KR through illness. Prop Sam Lisone, three games, and James Donaldson, two, both sin-binned for head contact. Lisone appeal fails.

29th February 2024 - hooker Corey Johnson joins Bradford on loan.

2nd March 2024 - two tries from Ash Handley in 18-10 home win over Catalans. James Bentley gets one-match suspension for striking out at Dragons forward Tariq Sims.

8th March 2024 - Ash Handley scores double in 22-16 win at Leigh after trailing 16-0 at half-time.

11th March 2024 - winger Derrell Olpherts leaves for Wakefield.

15th March 2024 - 18-8 defeat to St Helens.

22nd March 2024 - 20-6 home Challenge Cup round-six defeat to St Helens.

27th March 2024 - forward Leon Ruan goes on loan to Doncaster.

28th March 2024 - James Bentley suffers concussion in 26-6 Easter Thursday win at Castleford. Justin Sangaré banned for one game for head contact. Cameron Smith has one-match ban for dangerous contact downgraded to fine.

5th April 2024 - winger Ned McCormack makes debut as Ash Handley suffers rib injury in 34-8 round seven home defeat to Warrington.

19th April 2024 - David Fusitua returns for 30-24 home defeat to Huddersfield and injures other knee, Harry Newman suffers back spasms.

22nd April 2024 - former winger Ryan Hall signs one-year contract for 2025 season.

28th April 2024 - two tries from debutant teenage winger Riley Lumb in 18-12 win at Hull FC.

3rd May 2024 - Riley Lumb pulls hamstring in 46-8 home win over London Broncos.

11th May 2024 - 26-0 defeat at Catalans.

16th May 2024 - winger Matty Russell joins from Warrington on loan.

20th May 2024 - Morgan Gannon ruled out for 2024 season to recover from concussion.

24th May 2024 - Matty Russell plays his only game in 40-10 defeat at St Helens.

1st June 2024 - 32-4 home win over Castleford.

2nd June 2024 - Rhinos great Rob Burrow passes away after long fight with MND.

9th June 2024 - Salford director of rugby Ian Blease appointed new sporting director of Rhinos.

15th June 2024 - 18-10 defeat at Hull FC.

19th June 2024 - head coach Rohan Smith leaves by mutual consent. Assistant coaches Chev Walker and Scott Grix take interim charge.

19th June 2024 - Wigan prop Sam Eseh joins on loan. Harry Newman, Ash Handley, Tom Holroyd and Sam Lisone stood down under concussion protocols.

21st June 2024 - Brodie Croft scores try-double in 18-10 home win over Leigh as capacity crowd celebrates the life of Rob Burrow.

6th July 2024 - Brodie Croft golden-point field goal secures 17-16 home win over London Broncos.

10th July 2024 - Brad Arthur, sacked by Parramatta, appointed head coach to end of season.

11th July 2024 - Brad Arthur arrives to watch 30-18 defeat at at Warrington.

20th July 2024 - 20-12 home defeat to Hull KR in Brad Arthur's first game in charge.

25th July 2024 - Ash Handey scores try double in 34-6 win at Huddersfield.

30th July 2024 - backrower Rhys Martin turns down contract offer and will leave at end of season.

3rd August 2024 - 22-16 defeat at Salford after leading 12-0.

5th August 2024 - Cameron Smith banned for one game for late tackle.

10th August 2024 - 30-4 home win over leaders Wigan.

17th August 2024 - 24-6 defeat by Warrington in Magic Weekend at Elland Road, Leeds.

22nd August 2024 - head coach Brad Arthur extends contract to end of 2025 season.

23rd August 2024 - second-half comeback to keep play-off hopes alive with 18-6 home win over Catalans.

28th August 2024 - forward Rhyse Martin to join Hull KR at end of season.

1st September 2024 - Brodie Croft kicks golden-point field goal to secure 21-20 win at London Broncos.

5th September 2024 - wingers David Fusitu'a and Luis Roberts and hooker Corey Johnson to leave at end of season.

6th September 2024 - young winger Alfie Edgell scores four tries in 68-6 hammering of Hull FC at Headingley.

13th September 2024 - 38-0 defeat at Wigan leaves Rhinos one point from play-off places.

20th September 2024 - 26-16 final round defeat at Hull KR ends play-off hopes with eighth-placed finish.

5th October 2024 - Samoa forward Keenan Palasia signs from Gold Coast Titans and front-rower Cooper Jenkins from Norths Devils on two-year deals.

9th October 2024 - fullback Jake Connor signs from Huddersfield Giants on two-year contract.

CLUB RECORDS

Highest score:
106-10 v Swinton, 11/2/2001
Highest score against:
6-74 v Wigan, 20/5/92
Record attendance:
40,175 v Bradford, 21/5/47

MATCH RECORDS

Tries:
8 Fred Webster v Coventry, 12/4/1913
Eric Harris v Bradford, 14/9/31
Goals:
17 Iestyn Harris v Swinton, 11/2/2001
Points:
42 Iestyn Harris v Huddersfield, 16/7/99

SEASON RECORDS

Tries: 63 Eric Harris 1935-36
Goals: 173 *(inc 5fg)* Kevin Sinfield 2012
Points: 431 Lewis Jones 1956-57

CAREER RECORDS

Tries: 391 Eric Harris 1930-39
Goals:
1,831 *(inc 39fg)* Kevin Sinfield 1997-2015
Points: 3,967 Kevin Sinfield 1997-2015
Appearances: 625 John Holmes 1968-89

Super League XXIX - Club by Club

LEEDS RHINOS

DATE	FIXTURE	RESULT	SCORERS	LGE	ATT
16/2/24	Salford (h)	W22-16	t:Handley(2),Lisone g:Martin(5)	5th	15,126
22/2/24	Hull KR (a)	L22-12	t:Newman,Handley g:Martin(2)	7th	9,879
2/3/24	Catalans Dragons (h)	W18-10	t:Handley(2),Newman g:Martin(3)	7th	14,168
8/3/24	Leigh (a)	W16-22	t:Martin,Frawley,Handley(2) g:Martin(3)	5th	8,100
15/3/24	St Helens (h)	L8-18	t:Roberts g:Martin(2)	6th	15,284
22/3/24	St Helens (h) (CCR6)	L6-20	t:Newman g:Martin	N/A	7,108
28/3/24	Castleford (a)	W6-26	t:Momirovski(2),Miller(2) g:Martin(5)	6th	9,026
5/4/24	Warrington (h)	L8-34	t:Newman,Roberts	8th	12,297
19/4/24	Huddersfield (h)	L24-30	t:Momirovski(2),Fusitu'a,O'Connor g:Martin(4)	8th	13,128
28/4/24	Hull FC (a)	W12-18	t:Lumb(2),Smith g:Martin(3)	8th	10,505
3/5/24	London Broncos (h)	W46-8	t:Croft,Handley,McDonnell,Roberts,Goudemand,Sinfield,Lisone,Sangare g:Martin(7)	7th	13,259
11/5/24	Catalans Dragons (a)	L26-0		7th	9,546
24/5/24	St Helens (a)	L40-10	t:Handley,Roberts g:Martin	7th	11,367
1/6/24	Castleford (h)	W32-4	t:Handley,Croft,Frawley,Martin(2) g:Martin(6)	7th	14,529
15/6/24	Hull FC (h)	L18-10	t:Handley,Newman g:Martin	7th	12,166
21/6/24	Leigh (h)	W18-10	t:Croft(2),Frawley g:Martin(3)	7th	17,535
6/7/24	London Broncos (h)	W17-16 (aet)	t:Handley,Momirovski,Martin g:Martin(2) fg:Croft	7th	12,958
11/7/24	Warrington (a)	L30-18	t:Fusitu'a,Miller,McCormack,Momirovski g:Martin	7th	8,471
20/7/24	Hull KR (h)	L12-20	t:Martin,Miller g:Martin(2)	7th	14,555
25/7/24	Huddersfield (a)	W6-34	t:Handley(2),Newman,Frawley,Croft,Miller g:Martin(5)	7th	4,923
3/8/24	Salford (a)	L22-16	t:Frawley,Edgell,Croft g:Martin(2)	7th	4,473
10/8/24	Wigan (h)	W30-4	t:Newman,Miller,McDonnell,Martin g:Martin(7)	7th	12,459
17/8/24	Warrington (MW) ●	L6-24	t:Momirovski g:Martin	8th	N/A
23/8/24	Catalans Dragons (h)	W18-6	t:Fusitu'a,Frawley,Miller g:Martin(3)	8th	13,050
1/9/24	London Broncos (a)	W20-21 (aet)	t:Martin(3) g:Martin(4) fg:Croft	8th	4,403
6/9/24	Hull FC (h)	W68-6	t:Newman,Smith,Edgell(4),Bentley(2),Croft(2) g:Martin(13),Donaldson	7th	14,105
13/9/24	Wigan (a)	L38-0		7th	15,146
20/9/24	Hull KR (a)	L26-16	t:Martin,Edgell,Ackers g:Martin(2)	8th	11,200

● *Played at Elland Road, Leeds*

		APP		TRIES		GOALS		FG		PTS	
	D.O.B.	ALL	SL	ALL	SL	ALL	SL	ALL	SL	ALL	SL
Andy Ackers	25/12/93	20(5)	19(5)	1	1	0	0	0	0	4	4
James Bentley	19/10/97	5(10)	4(10)	2	2	0	0	0	0	8	8
Brodie Croft	14/7/97	26	25	8	8	0	0	2	2	34	34
James Donaldson	14/9/91	1(10)	1(10)	0	0	1	1	0	0	2	2
Alfie Edgell	25/7/04	12(4)	12(4)	6	6	0	0	0	0	24	24
Sam Eseh	30/6/03	3(2)	3(2)	0	0	0	0	0	0	0	0
Matt Frawley	24/12/94	26	25	6	6	0	0	0	0	24	24
David Fusitu'a	16/10/94	12	12	3	3	0	0	0	0	12	12
Mickael Goudemand	9/3/96	10(8)	10(8)	1	1	0	0	0	0	4	4
Ash Handley	16/2/96	19	18	14	14	0	0	0	0	56	56
Tom Holroyd	9/2/01	1(5)	1(4)	0	0	0	0	0	0	0	0
Corey Johnson	16/11/00	(4)	(4)	0	0	0	0	0	0	0	0
Sam Lisone	19/2/94	4(20)	4(19)	2	2	0	0	0	0	8	8
Ben Littlewood	20/1/05	(1)	(1)	0	0	0	0	0	0	0	0
Riley Lumb	18/12/04	4	4	2	2	0	0	0	0	8	8
Rhyse Martin	1/3/93	28	27	10	10	88	87	0	0	216	214
Ned McCormack	8/2/05	2(1)	2(1)	1	1	0	0	0	0	4	4
James McDonnell	12/1/00	24(2)	23(2)	2	2	0	0	0	0	8	8
Lachlan Miller	14/8/94	25	24	7	7	0	0	0	0	28	28
Paul Momirovski	13/7/96	24	23	7	7	0	0	0	0	28	28
Harry Newman	19/2/00	23	22	8	7	0	0	0	0	32	28
Tom Nicholson-Watton	13/12/02	(7)	(7)	0	0	0	0	0	0	0	0
Jarrod O'Connor	20/7/01	9(19)	9(18)	1	1	0	0	0	0	4	4
Mikolaj Oledzki	8/11/98	22	21	0	0	0	0	0	0	0	0
Luis Roberts	24/3/02	13	13	4	4	0	0	0	0	16	16
Leon Ruan	14/5/03	(6)	(6)	0	0	0	0	0	0	0	0
Matty Russell	6/6/93	1	1	0	0	0	0	0	0	0	0
Justin Sangare	7/3/98	19(5)	18(5)	1	1	0	0	0	0	4	4
Jack Sinfield	21/9/04	4	4	1	1	0	0	0	0	4	4
Cameron Smith	7/11/98	27	26	2	2	0	0	0	0	8	8

'SL' totals include Super League games only; 'All' totals also include Challenge Cup

Jarrod O'Connor

LEAGUE RECORD
P27-W14-D0-L13
(8th)
F530, A488, Diff+42
28 points.

CHALLENGE CUP
Round Six

ATTENDANCES
Best - v Leigh (SL - 17,535)
Worst - v St Helens (CC - 7,108)
Total (SL only) - 182,453
Average (SL only) - 14,035
(Up by 230 on 2023)

Super League XXIX - Club by Club

KEY DATES

7th November 2023 - England prop Robbie Mulhern signs new contract to end of 2026.

20th November 2023 - released Cronulla Sharks halfback Matt Moylan signs on two-year contract.

23rd January 2024 - Aaron Smith leaves for Barrow Raiders.

3rd February 2024 - 28-12 win at Warrington in pre-season warm-up.

16th February 2024 - hooker Edwin Ipape suffers knee injury early in 16-8 round-one home defeat to Huddersfield.

20th February 2024 - young threequarter Jacob Jones joins London Broncos on loan.

26th February 2024 - Brad Dwyer joins on initial two-week loan from Warrington.

27th February 2024 - Tom Amone has two-match ban for head contact reduced to one match on appeal. Ricky Leutele found not guilty on appeal after one-match suspension for head contact. Jack Hughes found not guilty of dangerous contact charge.

29th February 2024 - centre Keanan Brand joins Bradford on loan.

1st March 2024 - Brad Dwyer stars and gets late yellow card in 12-4 defeat at St Helens. John Asiata sin-binned after 40 seconds and injures calf. Tom Briscoe suffers calf injury.

4th March 2024 - captain John Asiata avoids suspension.

8th March 2024 - Lachlan Lam suffers knee injury in 22-16 home defeat by Leeds.

16th March 2024 - Matt Moylan stars in 54-4 win at Hull FC.

23rd March 2024 - Umyla Hanley hat-trick seals 26-14 home Challenge Cup sixth round win over Featherstone.

27th March 2024 - dangerous contact charge after John Asiata's sin-binning in the first minute of Leigh's 12-4 away loss to St Helens in March is dropped on appeal.

30th March 2024 - Umyla Hanley's scores hat-trick in 32-22 defeat at Salford.

4th April 2024 - 40-12 home defeat to Wigan in front of sell-out crowd.

9th April 2024 - on-loan Warrington hooker Brad Dwyer signs on two-year deal.

13th April 2024 - 26-14 Challenge Cup quarter-final defeat at Hull KR.

20th April 2024 - late Matty Nicholson try means 16-14 defeat at Warrington.

23rd April 2024 - Hull FC winger Darnell McIntosh signs on two-and-a-half year contract. Tom Briscoe moves the other way.

23rd April 2024 - Ed Chamberlain moves to Hull FC on loan.

26th April 2024 - John Asiata returns off bench in commanding 30-2 home win over leaders Catalans.

1st May 2024 - John Asiata to join Hull FC at end of season.

3rd May 2024 - winger Umyla Hanley signs new two-year contract.

4th May 2024 - Edwin Ipape returns from injury in 28-all home draw with Castleford after golden-point time.

10th May 2024 - Josh Charnley and Umyla Hanley score braces in 40-12 home win over Salford.

15th May 2024 - forward Matt Davis signs two-year contract extension, fullback Gareth O'Brien and Josh Charnley sign one-year deals.

17th May 2024 - head coach Adrian Lam signs three-year contract extension.

24th May 2024 - 16-10 win at Huddersfield stretches unbeaten run to four games.

25th May 2024 - Melbourne Storm release prop forward Aaron Pene as he joins Leigh on two-and-half-year contract ending in November 2026. Ben Nakubuwai released immediately.

29th May 2024 - Ben Nakubuwai joins Featherstone on loan. Nathan Wilde joins Doncaster on loan.

1st June 2024 - 12-0 defeat at Hull KR.

16th June 2024 - prop Tom Amone scores game's only try in 10-2 win at Catalans.

19th June 2024 - backrower Louis Brogan, on loan at Widnes, signs new three-year contract to end of 2027.

22nd June 2024 - 18-10 defeat at Leeds as capacity crowd gathers to remember Rob Burrow. Aaron Pene makes impressive debut off bench.

26th June 2024 - Newcastle Knights fullback David Armstrong joins on three-year contract from 2025 season.

5th July 2024 - 24-6 defeat at Wigan.

8th July 2024 - centre Zak Hardaker signs for Hull FC from 2025.

9th July 2024 - centre Ed Chamberlain and backrower Oliver Holmes to join Hull FC at end of season.

13th July 2024 - Edwin Ipape gets one-match ban for dangerous contact in 20-16 home win over Huddersfield.

19th July 2024 - 36-6 home win over London Broncos.

25th July 2024 - former Castleford junior, fullback Bayley Hodgson signs until end of 2026 season on return from Australia.

26th July 2024 - 46-4 home win over St Helens.

1st August 2024 - Josh Charnley scores try double in 20-10 win at Castleford.

6th August 2024 - 28-6 Tuesday-night defeat at Wigan.

11th August 2024 - Kai O'Donnell scores four tries in 42-12 home win over Hull FC. Josh Charnley gets one-match ban for kicking out while grounded.

18th August 2024 - 26-0 win over Salford in Magic Weekend at Elland Road, Leeds.

25th August 2024 - 32-12 win at London maintains play-off push.

30th August 2024 - 16-12 home win over Warrington.

6th September 2024 - 34-12 win at Castleford moves Leopards up to fourth in Super League table.

13th September 2024 - 24-0 home defeat by Hull KR drops Leopards to sixth.

20th September 2024 - 18-12 final round home win over St Helens earn fifth-place finish.

27th September 2024 - 14-6 win at Salford in eliminator play-off.

5th October 2024 - 38-0 semi-final defeat at Wigan.

9th October 2024 - Gold Coast Titans prop forward Isaac Liu signs on two-year deal.

11th October 2024 - Australian backrower Ben Condon signs two-year deal from Manly Sea Eagles.

12th October 2024 - Tonga International utility back Fanitesi (Tesi) Niu signs on three-year contract.

CLUB RECORDS

Highest score: 100-4 v York, 21/8/2022
Highest score against:
4-94 v Workington, 26/2/95
Record attendance:
31,326 v St Helens, 14/3/53 *(Hilton Park)*
10,556 v Batley, 17/9/2016
(Leigh Sports Village)

MATCH RECORDS

Tries: 6 Jack Wood v York, 4/10/47
Neil Turley v Workington, 31/1/2001
Goals: 16 Krisnan Inu v York, 21/8/2022
Points: 42 Neil Turley v Chorley, 4/4/2004

SEASON RECORDS

Tries: 55 Neil Turley 2001
Goals: 187 Neil Turley 2004
Points: 468 Neil Turley 2004

CAREER RECORDS

Tries: 189 Mick Martyn 1954-67
Goals: 1,043 Jimmy Ledgard 1948-58
Points:
2,492 John Woods 1976-85; 1990-92
Appearances: 503 Albert Worrall 1920-38

Super League XXIX - Club by Club

LEIGH LEOPARDS

DATE	FIXTURE	RESULT	SCORERS	LGE	ATT
16/2/24	Huddersfield (h)	L8-16	t:Charnley,Briscoe	9th	8,508
1/3/24	St Helens (a)	L12-4	t:Hardaker	10th	13,028
8/3/24	Leeds (h)	L16-22	t:O'Brien,O'Donnell,Hanley g:Moylan(2)	10th	8,100
16/3/24	Hull FC (a)	W4-54	t:Hanley,Charnley,Leutele(2),Mulhern,McNamara,Holmes(2),Moylan g:Moylan(9)	9th	10,227
23/3/24	Featherstone (h) (CCR6)	W26-14	t:Hanley(3),Charnley,Moylan g:Moylan(3)	N/A	4,287
30/3/24	Salford (a)	L32-22	t:Hanley(3),Lam g:Moylan(3)	9th	6,177
4/4/24	Wigan (h)	L12-40	t:Leutele,Charnley g:Moylan(2)	9th	10,308
13/4/24	Hull KR (a) (CCQF)	L26-14	t:O'Donnell,Hanley g:Moylan(3)	N/A	7,363
20/4/24	Warrington (a)	L16-14	t:Charnley,McNamara,Leutele g:Moylan	9th	10,443
26/4/24	Catalans Dragons (h)	W30-2	t:Charnley,O'Donnell(2),Hanley,Moylan g:Moylan(5)	9th	7,321
4/5/24	Castleford (h)	D28-28 (aet)	t:Moylan,Ipape,Charnley,Leutele,Lam g:Moylan(4)	9th	8,035
10/5/24	Salford (h)	W40-12	t:Hanley(2),Charnley(2),Davis,Dwyer,Lam g:Moylan(2),Hardaker(4)	9th	8,103
24/5/24	Huddersfield (a)	W10-16	t:Charnley,Ipape g:Moylan(4)	9th	4,385
1/6/24	Hull KR (a)	L12-0		9th	9,899
15/6/24	Catalans Dragons (a)	W2-10	t:Amone g:Moylan(3)	9th	9,480
21/6/24	Leeds (h)	L18-10	t:Moylan,Ipape g:Moylan	9th	17,535
5/7/24	Wigan (a)	L24-6	t:Dwyer g:Moylan	9th	16,053
13/7/24	Huddersfield (h)	W20-16	t:McIntosh,O'Donnell,Hardaker g:Moylan(3),Hardaker	8th	7,160
19/7/24	London Broncos (a)	W36-6	t:McIntosh,Amone,Leutele,Davis,Charnley,Lam,Hughes g:Hardaker(4)	8th	6,677
26/7/24	St Helens (h)	W46-4	t:Hanley,Amone,McIntosh,O'Donnell,Charnley(2),Lam,Moylan g:McIntosh(7)	8th	8,021
1/8/24	Castleford (a)	W10-20	t:Hardaker,Charnley(2),Ipape g:Hardaker(2)	8th	7,247
6/8/24	Wigan (a)	L28-6	t:Lam g:McIntosh	8th	13,249
11/8/24	Hull FC (h)	W42-12	t:O'Donnell(4),Halton,Hardaker(2),McIntosh g:McIntosh(3),Hardaker(2)	8th	8,400
18/8/24	Salford (MW) ●	W26-0	t:Ipape,Hanley,Hardaker,Leutele g:Hardaker(5)	7th	N/A
25/8/24	London Broncos (a)	W12-32	t:McIntosh,Halton,Leutele,O'Donnell,O'Brien,Pene g:Hardaker(4)	7th	1,950
30/8/24	Warrington (h)	W16-12	t:Leutele,Halton,Charnley g:Moylan(2)	6th	9,434
6/9/24	Castleford (a)	W12-34	t:O'Donnell,Charnley,Amone(2),O'Brien,Leutele g:Moylan(5)	5th	9,053
13/9/24	Hull KR (h)	L0-24		6th	8,412
20/9/24	St Helens (h)	W18-12	t:Asiata,Leutele,Charnley g:Moylan(3)	5th	9,899
27/9/24	Salford (a) (E)	W6-14	t:Charnley,O'Brien,Ipape g:Moylan	N/A	10,867
5/10/24	Wigan (a) (SF)	L38-0		N/A	20,511

● Played at Elland Road, Leeds

		APP		TRIES		GOALS		FG		PTS	
	D.O.B.	ALL	SL	ALL	SL	ALL	SL	ALL	SL	ALL	SL
Tom Amone	19/12/96	24	23	5	5	0	0	0	0	20	20
John Asiata	19/4/93	14(3)	14(3)	1	1	0	0	0	0	4	4
Lewis Baxter	1/6/02	(2)	(2)	0	0	0	0	0	0	0	0
Keanan Brand	8/1/99	3	2	0	0	0	0	0	0	0	0
Tom Briscoe	19/3/90	2	2	1	1	0	0	0	0	4	4
Louis Brogan	6/5/00	(4)	(4)	0	0	0	0	0	0	0	0
Ed Chamberlain	8/2/96	5(3)	5(3)	0	0	0	0	0	0	0	0
Josh Charnley	26/6/91	27	25	19	18	0	0	0	0	76	72
Matt Davis	5/7/96	6(16)	5(15)	2	2	0	0	0	0	8	8
Brad Dwyer	28/4/93	7(20)	6(20)	2	2	0	0	0	0	8	8
Frankie Halton	18/6/96	27(1)	25(1)	3	3	0	0	0	0	12	12
Umyla Hanley	5/3/02	29	27	14	10	0	0	0	0	56	40
Zak Hardaker	17/10/91	24(3)	22(3)	6	6	22	22	0	0	68	68
Oliver Holmes	7/8/92	1(5)	1(4)	2	2	0	0	0	0	8	8
Jack Hughes	4/1/92	18(13)	16(13)	1	1	0	0	0	0	4	4
Edwin Ipape	2/2/99	17(2)	17(2)	6	6	0	0	0	0	24	24
Lachlan Lam	25/3/98	29(1)	28	6	6	0	0	0	0	24	24
Ricky Leutele	10/4/90	30	28	11	11	0	0	0	0	44	44
Darnell McIntosh	5/7/97	14(2)	14(2)	5	5	11	11	0	0	42	42
Ben McNamara	18/12/01	8(1)	6(1)	2	2	0	0	0	0	8	8
Matt Moylan	16/6/91	26	24	6	5	57	51	0	0	138	122
Robbie Mulhern	18/10/94	23	22	1	1	0	0	0	0	4	4
Ben Nakubuwai	15/3/96	(8)	(6)	0	0	0	0	0	0	0	0
Dan Norman	8/9/97	4(11)	3(10)	0	0	0	0	0	0	0	0
Gareth O'Brien	31/10/91	19	19	4	4	0	0	0	0	16	16
Kai O'Donnell	21/2/99	29	27	12	11	0	0	0	0	48	44
Aaron Pene	26/9/95	1(14)	1(14)	1	1	0	0	0	0	4	4
Owen Trout	15/10/99	16(14)	15(13)	0	0	0	0	0	0	0	0

'SL' totals include regular season & play-offs; 'All' totals also include Challenge Cup

Ricky Leutele

LEAGUE RECORD
P27-W15-D1-L11
(5th/Semi-Final)
F566, A398, Diff+168
31 points.

CHALLENGE CUP
Quarter Finalists

ATTENDANCES
Best - v Wigan (SL - 10,308)
Worst - v Featherstone (CC - 4,287)
Total (SL only) - 108,378
Average (SL only) - 8,337
(Up by 1,083 on 2023)

Super League XXIX - Club by Club

LONDON BRONCOS

7th November 2023 - stand-off Oli Leyland and front rower Jordan Williams sign new contracts.

10th November 2023 - released Hull Kingston Rovers prop Rhys Kennedy signs one-year contract. Winger Gideon Boafo and halfback James Meadows return from Newcastle and Batley respectively.

14th November 2023 - fullback Alex Walker signs new one-year contract. Hooker Sam Davis extends for a year.

20th November 2023 - Papua New Guinea second-row Emmanuel Waine and prop Rob Butler sign one-year contract extensions.

21st November 2023 - Ryan Sheridan joins as assistant coach.

22nd November 2023 - Championship player of the year hooker Dean Parata extends contract for 2024 season. Centre Dean Whare, at end of contract, leaves.

11th December 2023 - former Salford and Whitehaven fullback Josh Rourke signs for 2024 season.

3rd January 2024 - threequarter Hakim Miloudi signs one-year contract.

9th January 2024 - Wakefield winger Lee Kershaw joins on one-month's trial.

16th January 2024 - Italy international halfback Jack Campagnolo signs from Queensland Cup side South Logan Magpies.

21st January 2024 - hooker Bill Leyland suffers season-ending anterior cruciate ligament injury in 12-12 pre-season draw at Castleford.

4th February 2024 - Josh Rourke breaks leg in 18-18 pre-season draw at Oldham.

6th February 2024 - former Wakefield winger Lee Kershaw signs for 2024 season after successful trial.

16th February 2024 - 40-4 round-one defeat at St Helens.

20th February 2024 - young threequarter Jacob Jones joins from Leigh on loan.

24th February 2024 - crowd of over five thousand attends for 34-0 home defeat by Catalans.

27th February 2024 - young forward Fenton Rogers joins on loan from Huddersfield.

1st March 2024 - Brewdog announced as new shirt sponsors.

3rd March 2024 - last-minute try from Morgan Smith snatches 28-24 home win for Hull FC.

7th March 2024 - Hull KR hooker Reiss Butterworth joins on loan.

9th March 2024 - 60-22 home defeat to Wigan.

17th March 2024 - 58-4 home defeat by Warrington.

KEY DATES

23rd March 2024 - 42-0 Challenge Cup round-six defeat at Warrington.

26th March 2024 - Wigan prop Harvey Makin joins on initial month's loan.

31st March 2024 - 26-6 home defeat to Huddersfield.

5th April 2024 - 50-10 defeat at Hull KR.

16th April 2024 - Catalans utility Ugo Tison joins on loan.

20th April 2024 - 12-4 home defeat by Salford.

26th April 2024 - 40-0 defeat at Castleford.

3rd May 2024 - 46-8 defeat at Leeds.

12th May 2024 - 34-18 home win over Hull FC ends ten-match losing run.

23rd May 2024 - on-loan French international halfback Ugo Tison signs till end of season from Catalans on permanent contract. Second-rower Jacob Jones's loan deal from Leigh extended to end of season.

27th May 2024 - 64-14 home defeat to Hull KR.

2nd June 2024 - 34-14 defeat at Salford after trailing only 6-0 at half-time.

16th June 2024 - 52-6 defeat to St Helens at the Stoop. Ethan Natoli and Rhys Kennedy receive one-match dangerous contact bans.

21st June 2024 - 36-0 defeat at Wigan.

6th July 2024 - Brodie Croft gold-point field goal means 17-16 defeat at Leeds. Josh Rourke makes impressive delayed debut.

12th July 2024 - 34-20 defeat by Castleford in Ebbsfleet.

15th July 2024 - Hull KR sign sidelined for season hooker Bill Leyland.

19th July 2024 - 36-6 defeat at Leigh.

26th July 2024 - 40-16 defeat at Hull KR.

4th August 2024 - 12-10 home win over Catalans on return to Wimbledon.

6th August 2024 - back-rower Ethan Natoli to leave for French club Pia at end of season.

11th August 2024 - 36-22 home defeat by Warrington.

17th August 2024 - 29-4 win over Hull FC in Magic Weekend at Elland Road, Leeds.

25th August 2024 - 32-12 home defeat by Leigh.

1st September 2024 - Brodie Croft golden-point field goal means 21-20 defeat at home to Leeds.

8th September 2024 - Will Lovell sin-binned five minutes from end of 22-16 defeat at Huddersfield.

14th September 2024 - 12-8 defeat at Catalans but Broncos climb above Hull FC on one-point difference.

20th September 2024 - 54-0 final round defeat at Warrington means bottom place finish.

23rd September 2024 - Broncos owner David Hughes puts club up for sale after 27 years at helm.

4th October 2024 - Oli Leyland signs for Warrington. Centre Jarred Bassett returns to Australia. Josh Rourke signs for Wakefield.

CLUB RECORDS

Highest score: 82-0 v Highfield, 12/11/95
82-2 v Barrow, 20/5/2006
Highest score against:
6-82 v Warrington, 20/3/2011
10-82 v Warrington, 8/6/2013
Record attendance:
15,013 v Wakefield, 15/2/81
(Craven Cottage)
5,102 v Catalans Dragons, 23/2/2024
(Cherry Red Records Stadium)

MATCH RECORDS

Tries:
5 Martin Offiah v Whitehaven, 14/3/99
Sean Morris v Batley, 13/9/2015
Goals:
13 Rob Purdham v Barrow, 20/5/2006
Points:
34 Rob Purdham v Barrow, 20/5/2006
Jarrod Sammut v Sheffield, 13/5/2018

SEASON RECORDS

Tries: 43 Mark Johnson 1993-94
Goals: 159 John Gallagher 1993-94
Points: 384 John Gallagher 1993-94

CAREER RECORDS

Tries:
109 Luke Dorn 2005-2006; 2009-2013
Goals: 309 Steve Diamond 1981-84
Points: 772 Paul Sykes 2001-2007
Appearances:
202 Steele Retchless 1998-2004

Super League XXIX - Club by Club

LONDON BRONCOS

DATE	FIXTURE	RESULT	SCORERS	LGE	ATT
16/2/24	St Helens (a)	L40-4	t:Storey	12th	14,058
23/2/24	Catalans Dragons (h)	L0-34		12th	5,102
3/3/24	Hull FC (a)	L28-24	t:Meadows,Kershaw,Miloudi(2),Storey g:O Leyland(2)	12th	10,066
9/3/24	Wigan (h)	L22-60	t:Jones,Kershaw(2),Williams g:O Leyland(3)	12th	4,116
17/3/24	Warrington (h)	L4-58	t:Miloudi	12th	3,324
23/3/24	Warrington (a) (CCR6)	L42-0		N/A	3,416
31/3/24	Huddersfield (h)	L6-26	t:O Leyland g:O Leyland	12th	2,300
5/4/24	Hull KR (a)	L50-10	t:Davis,Macani g:O Leyland	12th	10,201
20/4/24	Salford (h)	L4-12	t:Macani	12th	2,450
26/4/24	Castleford (a)	L40-0		12th	6,996
3/5/24	Leeds (a)	L46-8	t:Natoli,Storey	12th	13,259
12/5/24	Hull FC (h)	W34-18	t:Walker,Meadows,Storey,Bassett,Kershaw,O Leyland g:O Leyland(5)	12th	3,225
26/5/24	Hull KR (h)	L14-64	t:Walker,Macani,Bassett g:O Leyland	12th	3,750
2/6/24	Salford (a)	L34-4	t:Miloudi	12th	2,843
16/6/24	St Helens (h) ●	L6-52	t:Kershaw g:O Leyland	12th	4,600
21/6/24	Wigan (a)	L36-0		12th	14,280
6/7/24	Leeds (a)	L17-16 (aet)	t:Rourke,Kennedy,Macani g:O Leyland(2)	12th	12,958
12/7/24	Castleford (h) ●●	L20-34	t:Rourke,Lovell,Stock,Bienek g:O Leyland(2)	12th	2,050
19/7/24	Leigh (a)	L36-6	t:Rourke g:O Leyland	12th	6,677
26/7/24	Hull KR (a)	L40-16	t:Bienek,Rourke,Macani g:O Leyland(2)	12th	9,346
4/8/24	Catalans Dragons (h)	W12-10	t:Jones,Bassett g:O Leyland(2)	12th	1,900
11/8/24	Warrington (h)	L22-36	t:Rourke,Bienek,Davis,Tison g:O Leyland(3)	12th	2,150
17/8/24	Hull FC (MW) ●●●	W4-29	t:Rourke(2),Campagnolo,O Leyland g:O Leyland(6) fg:O Leyland	12th	N/A
25/8/24	Leigh (a)	L12-32	t:Davis,Rourke g:O Leyland(2)	12th	1,950
1/9/24	Leeds (h)	L20-21 (aet)	t:Campagnolo,Waine,Kershaw,Natoli g:O Leyland(2)	12th	4,403
8/9/24	Huddersfield (a)	L22-16	t:Stock,Miloudi,Adebiyi g:O Leyland(2)	12th	3,439
14/9/24	Catalans Dragons (a)	L12-8	t:Kershaw g:O Leyland(2)	11th	8,855
20/9/24	Warrington (a)	L54-0		12th	10,192

● *Played at Twickenham Stoop*
●● *Played at Kuflink Stadium, Ebbsfleet*
●●● *Played at Elland Road, Leeds*

		APP		TRIES		GOALS		FG		PTS	
	D.O.B.	ALL	SL	ALL	SL	ALL	SL	ALL	SL	ALL	SL
Sadiq Adebiyi	8/1/97	18(3)	18(3)	1	1	0	0	0	0	4	4
Jarred Bassett	23/11/91	24(1)	23(1)	3	3	0	0	0	0	12	12
Lewis Bienek	11/4/98	5(11)	5(11)	3	3	0	0	0	0	12	12
Gideon Boafo	10/2/99	2	1	0	0	0	0	0	0	0	0
Rob Butler	15/5/98	14(10)	14(9)	0	0	0	0	0	0	0	0
Reiss Butterworth	7/12/98	1(2)	1(2)	0	0	0	0	0	0	0	0
Jack Campagnolo	15/6/98	13(1)	13(1)	2	2	0	0	0	0	8	8
Matthew Davies	9/4/98	1(1)	1(1)	0	0	0	0	0	0	0	0
Sam Davis	11/11/98	22(1)	21(1)	3	3	0	0	0	0	12	12
Daniel Hoyes	12/12/03	(1)	(1)	0	0	0	0	0	0	0	0
Jack Hughes	15/11/00	(3)	(2)	0	0	0	0	0	0	0	0
Jacob Jones	15/2/99	16(9)	16(9)	2	2	0	0	0	0	8	8
Rhys Kennedy	11/10/94	26(1)	25(1)	1	1	0	0	0	0	4	4
Lee Kershaw	2/5/97	26	25	7	7	0	0	0	0	28	28
Oliver Leyland	17/5/01	27(1)	26(1)	3	3	40	40	1	1	93	93
Will Lovell	10/5/93	27	27	1	1	0	0	0	0	4	4
Iliess Macani	6/12/93	13(1)	13(1)	5	5	0	0	0	0	20	20
Harvey Makin	17/11/03	(6)	(6)	0	0	0	0	0	0	0	0
James Meadows	15/6/99	16(2)	15(2)	2	2	0	0	0	0	8	8
Hakim Miloudi	26/6/93	23(1)	22(1)	5	5	0	0	0	0	20	20
Jensen Monk	31/12/03	(1)	0	0	0	0	0	0	0	0	0
Ethan Natoli	5/4/95	13(3)	13(3)	2	2	0	0	0	0	8	8
Dean Parata	4/10/91	9(4)	8(4)	0	0	0	0	0	0	0	0
Fenton Rogers	4/8/03	2(1)	2(1)	0	0	0	0	0	0	0	0
Josh Rourke	27/10/99	12	12	8	8	0	0	0	0	32	32
Marcus Stock	1/5/96	19(9)	18(9)	2	2	0	0	0	0	8	8
Joe Stocks	1/9/04	(1)	0	0	0	0	0	0	0	0	0
Robbie Storey	21/10/99	17	16	4	4	0	0	0	0	16	16
Ugo Tison	7/7/01	5(14)	5(14)	1	1	0	0	0	0	4	4
Emmanuel Waine	6/10/96	(9)	(9)	1	1	0	0	0	0	4	4
Alex Walker	4/9/95	12(1)	11(1)	2	2	0	0	0	0	8	8
Jordan Williams	4/6/97	1(12)	(12)	1	1	0	0	0	0	4	4

'SL' totals include Super League games only; 'All' totals also include Challenge Cup

Oliver Leyland

LEAGUE RECORD
P27-W3-D0-L24
(12th)
F317, A916, Diff-599
6 points.

CHALLENGE CUP
Round Six

ATTENDANCES
Best - v Catalans Dragons (SL - 5,102)
Worst - v Catalans Dragons
(SL - 1,900)
Total (SL only) - 41,320
Average (SL only) - 3,178
(Up by 2,159 on 2023, Championship)

Super League XXIX - Club by Club

KEY DATES

7th November 2023 - halfback Cade Cust signs from Wigan on one-year contract.

20th November 2023 - utility Joe Shorrocks signs from Wigan on three-year deal.

5th December 2023 - winger Ken Sio released on compassionate grounds.

8th December 2023 - centre Chris Hankinson signs from Featherstone on two-year deal.

15th December 2023 - halfback Joe Mellor signs from Leigh on two-year contract.

21st December 2023 - Red Devils sign 12-month extension to tenancy agreement.

10th January 2024 - winger Joe Burgess released for 'failing to meet club standards'.

3rd February 2024 - prop Alex Gerrard confirmed as leaving the club.

4th February 2024 - 52-10 defeat at St Helens in pre-season friendly. King Vuniyayawa gets one-match ban for late tackle.

14th February 2024 - winger David Nofoaluma signs one-year contract following off-season release by Wests Tigers.

16th February 2024 - Ryan Brierley sin-binned in 22-16 round-one defeat at Leeds.

22nd February 2024 - Ryan Brierley wins appeal as charge downgraded.

25th February 2024 - centre Nene Macdonald stars in 26-22 home round-two win over Castleford.

2nd March 2024 - 17-10 home win over unbeaten Hull KR.

8th March 2024 - Deon Cross scores late try to secure 24-20 win at St Helens.

13th March 2024 - Wales prop Gil Dudson signs on season-loan from Warrington.

14th March 2024 - two Wigan tries in last four minutes mean 22-12 home defeat. David Nofoaluma debuts.

23rd March 2024 - 40-0 Challenge Cup round six defeat at Hull KR.

31st March 2024 - Ryan Brierley scores twice on 300th career appearance in 32-22 home Easter win over Leigh. Joe Mellor makes debut.

3rd April 2024 - Kai Morgan joins Rochdale on loan.

5th April 2024 - 36-24 round seven defeat at winless Castleford. Amir Bourouh gets one-game ban for dangerous throw. David Nofoaluma plays last game.

20th April 2024 - prop King Vuniyayawa sent off for dangerous tackle in 56th minute of 12-4 win at London. No further action taken by MRP.

23rd April 2024 - Hull FC approach for head coach Paul Rowley turned down.

25th April 2024 - Matt Foster joins Swinton on loan.

27th April 2024 - 17-12 home win over Warrington.

1st May 2024 - Marc Sneyd signs new two-year contract.

3rd May 2024 - Nene Macdonald stars with two tries in 18-16 win at Huddersfield. Joe Mellor suffers broken hand.

10th May 2024 - Jack Ormondroyd suffers rib Injury in 40-12 defeat at Leigh.

13th May 2024 - David Nofoaluma released for disciplinary reasons.

20th May 2024 - prop Harvey Wilson signs from Wigan on contract to end of 2025.

25th May 2024 - Huddersfield centre Esan Marsters signs three-year contract from 2025 season.

26th May 2024 - 26-6 home defeat by Wigan.

30th May 2024 - forward Loghan Lewis signs from Canberra Raiders for rest of season, with option for further year.

2nd June 2024 - Red Devils back in the top six after 34-4 home victory over London Broncos.

10th June 2024 - director of rugby Ian Blease leaves for Leeds Rhinos as sporting director.

11th June 2024 - backrower Sam Stone signs new two-year deal to end of 2026.

14th June 2024 - Loghan Lewis and Harvey Wilson make debuts in 25-14 win at Warrington. Deon Cross scores double.

23rd June 2024 - Deon Cross scores double in 20-18 home win over St Helens. Tim Lafai injured in warm-up.

28th June 2024 - prop Oliver Partington to join Catalans Dragons from 2025 season,

4th July 2024 - halfback Cade Cust signs for Hull FC.

7th July 2024 - Marc Sneyd's five goals key to 22-20 home win over Hull FC.

13th July 2024 - 20-0 defeat at Catalans.

16th July 2024 - Warrington prop Joe Bullock joins on loan to end of season.

18th July 2024 - halfback Jayden Nikorima, sacked by Catalans, signs until end of 2025 season. Prop King Vuniyayawa goes to Hull FC on loan.

19th July 2024 - 16-8 defeat at Huddersfield.

24th July 2024 - utility Ben Hellewell signs one-year contract extension

27th July 2024 - halfback Jayden Nikorima makes debut in 30-22 home win over Castleford.

3rd August 2024 - 22-16 home win over Leeds after trailing 12-0 during Tim Lafai sin bin.

5th August 2024 - Tim Lafai banned for one game for head contact.

8th August 2024 - Moses Mbye golden-point field goal means 17-16 defeat at St Helens.

18th August 2024 - 26-0 defeat by Leigh in Magic Weekend at Elland Road, Leeds.

24th August 2024 - Ryan Brierley scores hat-trick, Marc Sneyd kicks ten goals and scores try in 60-10 home romp over Huddersfield.

30th August 2024 - 32-12 defeat at Hull KR.

7th September 2024 - 27-12 home win over Catalans moves Red Devils up to fourth in the table.

14th September 2024 - Tim Lafai scores hat-trick as 58-4 win at Hull FC confirms play-off spot.

18th September 2024 - virtual reserve side suffers 64-0 thrashing at Wigan.

26th September 2024 - forward Loghan Lewis signs new one-year contract.

27th September 2024 - 14-6 home defeat by Leigh ends season.

9th October 2024 - London Broncos hooker Sam Davis signs on two-year deal.

CLUB RECORDS

Highest score:
100-12 v Gateshead, 23/3/2003
Highest score against:
16-96 v Bradford, 25/6/2000
Record attendance:
26,470 v Warrington, 13/2/37
(The Willows)
10,867 v Leigh, 27/9/2024
(Salford Community Stadium)

MATCH RECORDS

Tries:
6 Frank Miles v Lees, 5/3/1898
Ernest Bone v Goole, 29/3/1902
Jack Hilton v Leigh, 7/10/39
Goals:
14 Steve Blakeley v Gateshead, 23/3/2003
Points:
39 Jim Lomas v Liverpool City, 2/2/1907

SEASON RECORDS

Tries: 46 Keith Fielding 1973-74
Goals: 221 David Watkins 1972-73
Points: 493 David Watkins 1972-73

CAREER RECORDS

Tries: 297 Maurice Richards 1969-83
Goals: 1,241 David Watkins 1967-79
Points: 2,907 David Watkins 1967-79
Appearances:
498 Maurice Richards 1969-83

Super League XXIX - Club by Club

SALFORD RED DEVILS

DATE	FIXTURE	RESULT	SCORERS	LGE	ATT
16/2/24	Leeds (a)	L22-16	t:Cust,Partington g:Sneyd(4)	7th	15,126
25/2/24	Castleford (h)	W26-22	t:Stone(2),Bourouh,Macdonald g:Sneyd(5)	6th	4,770
2/3/24	Hull KR (h)	W17-10	t:Cross,Hankinson g:Sneyd(4) fg:Sneyd	6th	5,036
8/3/24	St Helens (a)	W20-24	t:Cross(2),Macdonald,Atkin g:Sneyd(4)	6th	11,548
14/3/24	Wigan (h)	L12-22	t:Stone,Lafai g:Sneyd(2)	7th	6,087
22/3/24	Hull KR (a) (CCR6)	L40-0		N/A	5,636
30/3/24	Leigh (h)	W32-22	t:Brierley(2),Ryan(2),Sneyd g:Sneyd(6)	7th	6,177
5/4/24	Castleford (a)	L36-24	t:Brierley(2),Lafai,Macdonald g:Sneyd(4)	7th	7,967
20/4/24	London Broncos (a)	W4-12	t:Watkins,Cross g:Sneyd(2)	7th	2,450
27/4/24	Warrington (h)	W17-12	t:Lafai,Mellor,Brierley g:Sneyd(2) fg:Sneyd	6th	5,910
3/5/24	Huddersfield (a)	W16-18	t:Macdonald(2),Ryan g:Sneyd(3)	6th	4,833
10/5/24	Leigh (a)	L40-12	t:Brierley,Lafai g:Sneyd(2)	6th	8,103
26/5/24	Wigan (h)	L6-26	t:Partington g:Sneyd	6th	4,087
2/6/24	London Broncos (h)	W34-4	t:Stone,Cross,Macdonald,Lafai(2),Wright g:Sneyd(5)	6th	2,843
14/6/24	Warrington (a)	W14-25	t:Macdonald,Cross(2),Sneyd g:Sneyd(4) fg:Sneyd	5th	9,257
23/6/24	St Helens (h)	W20-18	t:Cross(2),Watkins,Hankinson g:Sneyd(2)	5th	5,724
7/7/24	Hull FC (h)	W22-20	t:Cross,Brierley,Hankinson g:Sneyd(5)	5th	3,910
13/7/24	Catalans Dragons (a)	L20-0		6th	7,750
19/7/24	Huddersfield (a)	L16-8	t:Mellor g:Sneyd(2)	6th	4,119
27/7/24	Castleford (h)	W30-22	t:Macdonald,Brierley,Ryan,Partington,Hankinson g:Sneyd(5)	5th	3,146
3/8/24	Leeds (h)	W22-16	t:Watkins(2),Mellor g:Sneyd(5)	4th	4,473
8/8/24	St Helens (a)	L17-16 (aet)	t:Hankinson,Macdonald g:Sneyd(4)	6th	11,050
18/8/24	Leigh (MW) ●	L26-0		6th	N/A
24/8/24	Huddersfield (h)	W60-10	t:Atkin,Brierley(3),Nikorima(2),Ryan,Wilson,Macdonald,Sneyd g:Sneyd(10)	4th	3,319
30/8/24	Hull KR (a)	L32-12	t:Mellor,Macdonald g:Sneyd(2)	5th	9,694
7/9/24	Catalans Dragons (h)	W27-12	t:Nikorima,Mellor,Lafai,Cross g:Sneyd(5) fg:Sneyd	4th	4,910
14/9/24	Hull FC (a)	W4-58	t:Lafai(3),Cross,Mellor(2),Singleton,Macdonald,Wright,Watkins g:Sneyd(9)	4th	9,274
19/9/24	Wigan (a)	L64-0		4th	15,589
27/9/24	Leigh (h) (E)	L6-14	t:Ryan g:Sneyd	N/A	10,867

● *Played at Elland Road, Leeds*

		APP		TRIES		GOALS		FG		PTS	
	D.O.B.	ALL	SL	ALL	SL	ALL	SL	ALL	SL	ALL	SL
Chris Atkin	7/2/93	13(9)	13(8)	2	2	0	0	0	0	8	8
Leunbou Bardyel-Wells	26/10/03	(1)	(1)	0	0	0	0	0	0	0	0
Amir Bourouh	5/1/01	8(5)	7(5)	1	1	0	0	0	0	4	4
Ryan Brierley	12/3/92	22(1)	21(1)	11	11	0	0	0	0	44	44
Joe Bullock	27/11/92	2(6)	2(6)	0	0	0	0	0	0	0	0
Nathan Connell	5/1/03	1(1)	1(1)	0	0	0	0	0	0	0	0
Deon Cross	30/7/96	28	27	12	12	0	0	0	0	48	48
Cade Cust	14/9/98	11(2)	10(2)	1	1	0	0	0	0	4	4
Andrew Dixon	28/2/90	1(2)	1(2)	0	0	0	0	0	0	0	0
Gil Dudson	16/6/90	4(12)	3(12)	0	0	0	0	0	0	0	0
Ethan Fitzgerald	4/10/03	1	1	0	0	0	0	0	0	0	0
Matty Foster	25/6/01	(3)	(3)	0	0	0	0	0	0	0	0
Jack Gatcliffe	5/10/98	(1)	(1)	0	0	0	0	0	0	0	0
Billy Glover	9/8/01	1	1	0	0	0	0	0	0	0	0
Charlie Glover	9/3/05	(1)	(1)	0	0	0	0	0	0	0	0
Chris Hankinson	30/11/93	14(7)	14(7)	5	5	0	0	0	0	20	20
Ben Hellewell	30/1/92	1(5)	1(5)	0	0	0	0	0	0	0	0
Tim Lafai	27/5/91	22	21	10	10	0	0	0	0	40	40
Loghan Lewis	23/11/02	5(6)	5(6)	0	0	0	0	0	0	0	0
Nene Macdonald	11/5/94	26	25	12	12	0	0	0	0	48	48
Charlie McCurrie	16/5/02	1	1	0	0	0	0	0	0	0	0
Joe Mellor	28/11/90	15(6)	15(6)	7	7	0	0	0	0	28	28
Kai Morgan	13/4/04	1(1)	1(1)	0	0	0	0	0	0	0	0
Jayden Nikorima	5/10/96	9	9	3	3	0	0	0	0	12	12
David Nofoaluma	28/11/93	2	2	0	0	0	0	0	0	0	0
Jack Ormondroyd	7/11/91	12(1)	11(1)	0	0	0	0	0	0	0	0
Oliver Partington	3/9/98	22(1)	22	3	3	0	0	0	0	12	12
Jamie Pye	17/8/02	(1)	(1)	0	0	0	0	0	0	0	0
Ethan Ryan	12/5/96	22(1)	21(1)	6	6	0	0	0	0	24	24
Joe Shorrocks	25/11/99	11(16)	10(16)	0	0	0	0	0	0	0	0
Adam Sidlow	25/10/87	1	1	0	0	0	0	0	0	0	0
Brad Singleton	29/10/92	22	22	1	1	0	0	0	0	4	4
Marc Sneyd	9/2/91	28	27	3	3	98	98	4	4	212	212
Sam Stone	4/8/97	23	22	4	4	0	0	0	0	16	16
King Vuniyayawa	13/3/95	3(10)	3(9)	0	0	0	0	0	0	0	0
Josh Wagstaffe	27/7/04	1	1	0	0	0	0	0	0	0	0
Kallum Watkins	12/3/91	28	27	5	5	0	0	0	0	20	20
Harvey Wilson	31/1/04	1(4)	1(4)	1	1	0	0	0	0	4	4
Shane Wright	13/3/96	15(12)	15(11)	2	2	0	0	0	0	8	8

'SL' totals include regular season & play-offs; 'All' totals also include Challenge Cup

Nene Macdonald

LEAGUE RECORD
P27-W16-D0-L11
(4th/Eliminator)
F550, A547, Diff+3
32 points.

CHALLENGE CUP
Round Six

ATTENDANCES
Best - v Leigh (SL-E - 10,867)
Worst - v London Broncos (SL - 2,843)
Total (SL, inc play-offs) - 71,259
Average (SL, inc play-offs) - 5,090
(Down by 203 on 2023)

Super League XXIX - Club by Club

KEY DATES

5th December 2023 - coach Paul Wellens fined £2,000 by RFL for breach of operational rules after Challenge Cup semi-final defeat by Leigh in July.

20th December 2023 - fullback Jack Welsby signs new contract to end of 2027 season.

12th January 2024 - Fiji international centre Waqa Blake signs one-year contract after release by Parramatta.

26th January 2024 - Jonny Lomax named captain and signs contract extension to end of 2026.

4th February 2024 - 52-10 pre-season home win over Salford.

14th February 2024 - centre Mark Percival signs two-year contract extension to end of 2026 season.

16th February 2024 - Matt Whitley scores two tries on debut in 40-4 round-one home win over London.

24th February 2024 - 28-0 win at Huddersfield in round two. Matty Lees leaves field after coughing blood but cleared by hospital.

1st March 2024 - 12-4 home win over Leigh. Konrad Hurrell gets one-match ban for head contact.

8th March 2024 - late Deon Cross try means 24-20 home defeat to Salford. Mark Percival sent off in 43rd minute.

11th March 2024 - Mark Percival suspended for two games for shoulder charge.

15th March 2024 - 18-8 win at Leeds.

22nd March 2024 - 20-6 Challenge Cup round-six win at Leeds. James Bell appeal against one-game ban for dangerous contact fails.

29th March 2024 - late Tommy Makinson and Konrad Hurrell tries edge 12-4 Good Friday home win over Wigan. Matty Lees gets two-match penalty notice for head contact.

6th April 2024 - 14-8 defeat at Catalans.

12th April 2024 - prop Alex Walmsley signs new two-year deal to end of 2026 season.

14th April 2024 - Alex Walmsley injures hamstring in 31-8 home Challenge Cup quarter-final defeat to Warrington.

19th April 2024 - Waqa Blake scores twice in 58-0 home win over Hull FC.

25th April 2024 - last-minute Jonny Lomax field goal secures 13-12 home win over Huddersfield.

26th April 2024 - prop Alex Walmsley to undergo knee surgery while sidelined with hamstring injury.

1st May 2024 - Lewis Dodd to leave for South Sydney at end of season.

4th May 2024 - 40-20 defeat at Hull KR.

10th May 2024 - Tommy Makinson sent off in 13th minute of 60-4 win at Castleford and gets one-game ban for head contact.

20th May 2024 - Tommy Makinson to leave for Catalans at end of season.

24th May 2024 - Jonny Lomax suffers broken hand in 40-10 home defeat of Leeds.

31st May 2024 - Agnatius Paasi plays first game of season in 24-12 home win over Catalans.

16th June 2024 - Daryl Clark scores eight-minute hat-trick in 52-6 win over London at the Stoop.

23rd June 2024 - 20-18 defeat at Salford. Sione Mata'utia gets one-match penalty for head contact.

5th July 2024 - shock 8-6 home defeat to Castleford. Hooker Jake Burns and threequarter Jonny Vaughan make debuts.

12th July 2024 - fullback, 18-year-old Harry Robertson makes impressive debut in 16-12 defeat at Wigan.

19th July 2024 - 24-10 home defeat to Warrington despite prop James Harrison 20th-minute send off.

26th July 2024 - Mark Percival and Jonny Lomax sin-binned in 46-4 defeat at Leigh. Jack Welsby suffers hamstring injury, out for eight weeks.

29th July 2024 - Mark Percival banned for one match for high tackle. Jonny Lomax referred to tribunal.

31st July 2024 - Jonny Lomax gets three-game ban for high tackle.

3rd August 2024 - 46-6 win at Hull FC ends record Super League losing run at five games.

7th August 2024 - utility back Tristan Sailor signs from Brisbane on two-year contract from 2025.

8th August 2024 - Moses Mbye golden-point field goal secures 17-16 home victory over Salford. Alex Walmsley and Joe Batchelor return from injury. Lewis Dodd (elbow) and Daryl Clark (foot) pick up injuries.

12th August 2024 - Morgan Knowles gets two-match ban for head contact.

14th August 2024 - head coach Paul Wellens signs new contract to end of 2025.

17th August 2024 - depleted side beaten 20-0 by Wigan in Magic Weekend at Elland Road, Leeds.

22nd August 2024 - North Queensland Cowboys winger Kyle Feldt signs on two-year contract from 2025.

24th August 2024 - patched up side suffers 42-6 home defeat to Hull KR. Halfback George Whitby makes debut. Tommy Makinson sent off near end for high tackle on Tyrone May. Waqa Blake sin-binned for high tackle in first half.

26th August 2024 - Tommy Makinson gets three-match ban for head contact.

1st September 2024 - 18-10 win at Huddersfield takes Saints back into top four.

2nd September 2024 - former Wakefield winger Lewis Murphy signs from Sydney Roosters on two-year contract from 2025 season.

6th September 2024 - Lee Briers to join first-team coaching staff from 2025 on two-year contract.

7th September 2024 - 16-2 defeat at Warrington sees Saints drop to sixth in table.

9th September 2024 - prop Matty Lees gets one-game ban for contact with referee, but wins appeal. Moses Mbye gets one game for late tackle.

11th September 2024 - backrowers Sione Mata'utia and Sam Royle to leave at end of season.

13th September 2024 - Jon Bennison scores hat-trick in 40-4 home win over Castleford.

20th September 2024 - 18-12 final round defeat at Leigh means sixth-place finish.

28th September 2024 - George Williams golden-point field goal means away eliminator defeat at Warrington.

2nd October 2024 - centre Waqa Blake released at end of one-year contract.

CLUB RECORDS

Highest score:
112-0 v Carlisle, 14/9/86
Highest score against:
6-78 v Warrington, 12/4/1909
Record attendance:
35,695 v Wigan, 26/12/49 *(Knowsley Road)*
17,980 v Wigan, 6/4/2012
v Wigan, 18/4/2014
v South Sydney, 22/2/2015
v Wigan, 30/3/2018
v Wigan, 15/4/2022
v Wigan, 29/3/2024
(Langtree Park/Totally Wicked Stadium)

MATCH RECORDS

Tries: 6 Alf Ellaby v Barrow, 5/3/32
Steve Llewellyn v Castleford, 3/3/56
Steve Llewellyn v Liverpool, 20/8/56
Tom van Vollenhoven v Wakefield, 21/12/57
Tom van Vollenhoven v Blackpool, 23/4/62
Frank Myler v Maryport, 1/9/69
Shane Cooper v Hull, 17/2/88
Goals: 16 Paul Loughlin v Carlisle, 14/9/86
Points:
40 Paul Loughlin v Carlisle, 14/9/86

SEASON RECORDS

Tries: 62 Tom van Vollenhoven 1958-59
Goals: 214 Kel Coslett 1971-72
Points: 452 Kel Coslett 1971-72

CAREER RECORDS

Tries: 392 Tom van Vollenhoven 1957-68
Goals: 1,639 Kel Coslett 1962-76
Points: 3,413 Kel Coslett 1962-76
Appearances: 551 James Roby 2004-2023

Super League XXIX - Club by Club

ST HELENS

DATE	FIXTURE	RESULT	SCORERS	LGE	ATT
16/2/24	London Broncos (h)	W40-4	t:Dodd,Welsby,Walmsley,Makinson,Clark,Whitley(2),Lomax g:Percival(3),Makinson	1st	14,058
24/2/24	Huddersfield (a)	W0-28	t:Whitley,Mata'utia,Welsby,Bennison,Knowles g:Percival(3),Makinson	1st	6,812
1/3/24	Leigh (h)	W12-4	t:Welsby,Makinson g:Percival(2)	1st	13,028
8/3/24	Salford (h)	L20-24	t:Welsby,Dodd(2),Percival g:Percival,Dodd	2nd	11,548
15/3/24	Leeds (a)	W8-18	t:Blake,Bennison,Mbye g:Lomax(3)	3rd	15,284
22/3/24	Leeds (a) (CCR6)	W6-20	t:Clark,Bennison,Walmsley g:Lomax(4)	N/A	7,108
29/3/24	Wigan (h)	W12-4	t:Makinson,Hurrell g:Percival,Lomax	1st	17,980
6/4/24	Catalans Dragons (a)	L14-8	t:Welsby,Makinson	5th	10,724
14/4/24	Warrington (h) (CCQF)	L8-31	t:Hurrell g:Bennison(2)	N/A	11,280
19/4/24	Hull FC (h)	W58-0	t:Makinson,Lomax,Blake(2),Bell,Batchelor,Percival,Hurrell,Sironen,Welsby g:Percival(6),Bennison(3)	2nd	10,488
25/4/24	Huddersfield (h)	W13-12	t:Makinson,Clark g:Percival(2) fg:Lomax	1st	9,888
4/5/24	Hull KR (a)	L40-20	t:Welsby,Blake,Hurrell(2) g:Percival(2)	3rd	10,171
10/5/24	Castleford (a)	W4-60	t:Mata'utia,Lomax,Welsby(2),Percival,Blake(3),Bell,Dodd g:Percival(8)	2nd	7,869
24/5/24	Leeds (h)	W40-10	t:Mata'utia,Mbye,Clark,Welsby(2),Sironen,Makinson g:Percival(6)	1st	11,367
31/5/24	Catalans Dragons (h)	W24-12	t:Hurrell,Mata'utia,Makinson,Lees g:Percival(4)	1st	11,088
16/6/24	London Broncos (a) ●	W6-52	t:Blake(2),Dodd,Mbye,Clark(3),Hurrell,Percival g:Percival(8)	1st	4,600
23/6/24	Salford (a)	L20-18	t:Bell,Sironen,Percival g:Percival(3)	2nd	5,724
5/7/24	Castleford (h)	L6-8	t:Royle g:Percival	2nd	9,808
12/7/24	Wigan (a)	L16-12	t:Welsby,Blake g:Percival(2)	4th	20,152
19/7/24	Warrington (h)	L10-24	t:Paasi,Royle g:Percival	4th	13,135
26/7/24	Leigh (a)	L46-4	t:Davies	6th	8,021
3/8/24	Hull FC (h)	W6-46	t:Dodd(2),Makinson,Clark,Whitley,Burns(2),Paasi g:Makinson(7)	5th	9,885
8/8/24	Salford (h) (aet)	W17-16	t:Makinson,Blake,Batchelor g:Percival(2) fg:Mbye	4th	11,050
17/8/24	Wigan (MW) ●●	L0-20		4th	N/A
24/8/24	Hull KR (h)	L6-42	t:Whitby g:Whitby	5th	13,588
1/9/24	Huddersfield (a)	W10-18	t:Lomax,Mata'utia,Robertson g:Bennison(3)	4th	3,877
7/9/24	Warrington (a)	L16-2	g:Bennison	6th	12,015
13/9/24	Castleford (h)	W40-4	t:Burns,Bennison(3),Lomax,Paasi,Makinson,Delaney g:Bennison(3),Mata'utia	5th	12,058
20/9/24	Leigh (a)	L18-12	t:Makinson,Knowles g:Bennison(2)	6th	9,899
28/9/24	Warrington (a) (E)	L23-22 (aet)	t:Makinson(2),Percival,Bennison g:Percival(3)	N/A	12,111

● Played at Twickenham Stoop
●● Played at Elland Road, Leeds

		APP		TRIES		GOALS		FG		PTS	
	D.O.B.	ALL	SL	ALL	SL	ALL	SL	ALL	SL	ALL	SL
Joe Batchelor	28/10/94	14(5)	13(4)	2	2	0	0	0	0	8	8
James Bell	2/5/94	11(15)	11(13)	4	4	0	0	0	0	16	16
Jon Bennison	1/12/02	16(1)	14(1)	7	6	14	12	0	0	56	48
Waqa Blake	26/10/94	24	22	11	11	0	0	0	0	44	44
Jake Burns	23/6/00	4(6)	4(6)	3	3	0	0	0	0	12	12
Daryl Clark	10/2/93	20(4)	18(4)	8	7	0	0	0	0	32	28
Ben Davies	21/4/00	5(6)	5(6)	1	1	0	0	0	0	4	4
George Delaney	4/2/04	11(15)	10(14)	1	1	0	0	0	0	4	4
Lewis Dodd	27/1/02	20(1)	19(1)	7	7	1	1	0	0	30	30
Konrad Hurrell	5/8/91	15	13	7	6	0	0	0	0	28	24
Morgan Knowles	5/11/96	18	16	2	2	0	0	0	0	8	8
Matty Lees	4/2/98	26	25	1	1	0	0	0	0	4	4
Jonny Lomax	4/9/90	24	22	5	5	8	4	1	1	37	29
Tommy Makinson	10/10/91	21	20	14	14	9	9	0	0	74	74
Sione Mata'utia	25/6/96	19(4)	18(3)	5	5	1	1	0	0	22	22
Moses Mbye	13/8/93	15(9)	14(8)	3	3	0	0	1	1	13	13
Agnatius Paasi	30/11/91	6(10)	6(10)	3	3	0	0	0	0	12	12
Mark Percival	29/4/94	21	21	6	6	58	58	0	0	140	140
Tee Ritson	7/1/96	10	10	0	0	0	0	0	0	0	0
Harry Robertson	21/12/05	9	9	1	1	0	0	0	0	4	4
Sam Royle	12/2/00	1(5)	1(5)	2	2	0	0	0	0	8	8
Curtis Sironen	31/7/93	20(3)	18(3)	3	3	0	0	0	0	12	12
Noah Stephens	3/10/04	(14)	(14)	0	0	0	0	0	0	0	0
Jonny Vaughan	12/2/04	2(6)	2(6)	0	0	0	0	0	0	0	0
Alex Walmsley	10/4/90	13(2)	11(2)	2	1	0	0	0	0	8	4
Jack Welsby	17/3/01	24(1)	22(1)	12	12	0	0	0	0	48	48
George Whitby	17/5/06	1	1	1	1	1	1	0	0	6	6
Matt Whitley	20/1/96	20(2)	19(1)	4	4	0	0	0	0	16	16
Jake Wingfield	1/8/01	(9)	(8)	0	0	0	0	0	0	0	0

'SL' totals include regular season & play-offs; 'All' totals also include Challenge Cup

Tommy Makinson

LEAGUE RECORD
P27-W15-D0-L12
(6th/Eliminator)
F596, A388, Diff+208
30 points.

CHALLENGE CUP
Quarter Finalists

ATTENDANCES
Best - v Wigan (SL - 17,980)
Worst - v Castleford (SL - 9,808)
Total (SL only) - 159,084
Average (SL only) - 12,237
(Down by 619 on 2023)

Super League XXIX - Club by Club

KEY DATES

1st November 2023 - stand-off Riley Dean leaves the club and joins Queensland Cup side Mackay Cutters.

10th November 2023 - Sam Powell joins from Wigan on two-year contract.

11th November 2023 - prop Sam Kasiano released from contract.

19th January 2024 - teenage prop Max Wood, released by Wigan, signs one-year deal for 2024, with option of further year in club's favour.

31st January 2024 - prop Joe Philbin signs new contract until end of 2026 season.

3rd February 2024 - 28-12 home defeat by Leigh in Joe Philbin Testimonial match. Young prop Luke Thomas suffers season-ending knee injury.

6th February 2024 - prop James Harrison signs contract extension to end of 2026 season.

17th February 2024 - 17-year-old Arron Lindop scores first try on debut in 16-10 round-one defeat at Catalans.

20th February 2024 - Jordan Crowther gets one-match ban for 'other contrary behaviour'.

23rd February 2024 - prop Max Wood makes debut in 36-10 round-two home win over Hull FC.

26th February 2024 - hooker Brad Dwyer joins Leigh on loan.

27th February 2024 - winger Matty Russell and prop Joe Bullock join Hull FC on loan.

1st March 2024 - Matty Ashton scores try-double in 30-8 home win over Castleford.

7th March 2024 - late Matt Dufty try grabs 22-20 win at Hull KR.

17th March 2024 - Stefan Ratchford equals consecutive goal record of 41 in 58-4 win at London.

20th March 2024 - fullback Matt Dufty signs new contract to end of 2026.

23rd March 2024 - Matty Ashton hat-trick in 42-0 home Challenge Cup round-six win over London. Rodrick Tai scores on debut.

30th March 2024 - 32-24 home defeat to Catalans.

4th April 2024 - 20-year-old prop Dan Okoro signs from Bradford.

5th April 2024 - 34-8 win at Leeds.

9th April 2024 - hooker Brad Dwyer signs for Leigh.

10th April 2024 - prop Joe Bullock signs two-year contract extension to end of 2026.

14th April 2024 - 31-8 Challenge Cup quarter-final win at St Helens.

20th April 2024 - late Matty Nicholson try edges 16-14 home win over Leigh.

27th April 2024 - young halfback Leon Hayes breaks ankle and ends season in 17-12 defeat at Salford.

2nd May 2024 - youngsters Leon Hayes and Adam Holroyd sign new contracts to end of 2027 season.

3rd May 2024 - Josh Thewlis hat-trick in 24-6 win over Hull FC. Administrative error when naming squad sees Wolves field 16-man team.

9th May 2024 - Toby King scores try-brace in 20-8 home win over Hull KR.

16th May 2024 - winger Matty Russell joins Leeds on loan.

19th May 2024 - 46-10 Challenge Cup semi-final win over Huddersfield at St Helens.

25th May 2024 - hard-fought 16-8 win at Catalans. Joe Philbin has adductor surgery.

27th May 2024 - prop Luke Yates signs from Huddersfield on two-year deal from 2025.

1st June 2024 - Cai Taylor-Wray, Jake Thewlis, Nolan Tupaea and Ben Hartill all make debuts in 19-18 home defeat by Wigan.

8th June 2024 - 18-8 Challenge Cup final defeat by Wigan.

14th June 2024 - 25-14 home defeat by Salford.

22nd June 2024 - late Matt Dufty try earns 24-18 win at Hull FC.

5th July 2024 - 48-0 home win over Huddersfield. Connor Wrench suffers season-ending ACL injury.

11th July 2024 - Matt Dufty scores try-double in 30-18 home win over Leeds.

12th July 2024 - backrower Matty Nicholson to join NRL side Canberra Raiders at end of season on three-year contract, for 'significant' transfer fee.

12th July 2024 - winger Matty Ashton signs new contract to end of 2028 season.

15th July 2024 - transfer fee paid to Huddersfield for prop Luke Yates to sign immediately.

16th July 2024 - captain Stefan Ratchford signs new contract to end of 2025.

19th July 2024 - 24-10 win at St Helens despite James Harrison 20th-minute send off.

22nd July 2024 - James Harrison banned for two matches for head contact.

26th July 2024 - John Bateman signs from NRL side Wests Tigers on loan for remainder of season.

26th July 2024 - Arron Lindop and Matty Ashton score doubles in 40-4 win at Wigan as Wolves go top.

2nd August 2024 - 22-4 home defeat to Hull KR.

11th August 2024 - 36-22 win at London Broncos.

17th August 2024 - Matt Dufty scores hat-trick in 24-6 win over Leeds in Magic Weekend at Elland Road, Leeds.

22nd August 2024 - Matt Dufty out for up to six weeks after surgery on knee problem.

23rd August 2024 - 28-6 win at Castleford.

30th August 2024 - prop Paul Vaughan sent off in 16-12 defeat at Leigh for high shot on Owen Trout.

2nd September 2024 - Paul Vaughan to miss final three matches of regular season on back of three-match ban for head contact.

7th September 2024 - four Josh Thewlis goals key in 16-2 home win over St Helens.

9th September 2024 - Lachlan Fitzgibbon banned for one game for head contact.

14th September 2024 - Matty Ashton scores hat-trick in 66-0 win at Huddersfield.

20th September 2024 - Matty Ashton scores hat-trick as 54-0 final round thrashing of London means third-placed finish.

21st September 2024 - young props Max Wood (three years) and Tom Whitehead (two years with an extra year option) sign new contracts.

28th September 2024 - George Williams golden-point field goal earns 23-22 home eliminator win over St Helens.

4th October 2024 - 10-8 semi-final defeat at Hull KR.

8th October 2024 - London Broncos halfback Oli Leyland and St George Illawarra Dragons second row Dan Russell sign on two-year contracts.

CLUB RECORDS

Highest score:
112-0 v Swinton, 20/5/2011
Highest score against:
12-84 v Bradford, 9/9/2001
Record attendance:
34,404 v Wigan, 22/1/49 *(Wilderspool)*
15,026 v Wigan, 14/4/2023
(Halliwell Jones Stadium)

MATCH RECORDS

Tries:
7 Brian Bevan v Leigh, 29/3/48
Brian Bevan v Bramley, 22/4/53
Goals:
16 Lee Briers v Swinton, 20/5/2011
Points:
44 Lee Briers v Swinton, 20/5/2011

SEASON RECORDS

Tries: 66 Brian Bevan 1952-53
Goals: 170 Steve Hesford 1978-79
Points: 363 Harry Bath 1952-53

CAREER RECORDS

Tries: 740 Brian Bevan 1945-62
Goals: 1,159 Steve Hesford 1975-85
Points: 2,586 Lee Briers 1997-2013
Appearances: 620 Brian Bevan 1945-62

Super League XXIX - Club by Club

WARRINGTON WOLVES

DATE	FIXTURE	RESULT	SCORERS	LGE	ATT
17/2/24	Catalans Dragons (a)	L16-10	t:Lindop,Dufty g:Drinkwater	8th	8,876
23/2/24	Hull FC (h)	W36-10	t:Walker,Ashton,Powell,King,Harrison,Wrench g:Josh Thewlis(6)	5th	9,431
1/3/24	Castleford (h)	W30-8	t:Ashton(2),Philbin,Dufty,Josh Thewlis g:Ratchford(5)	3rd	8,483
7/3/24	Hull KR (a)	W20-22	t:Williams,Ashton,King,Wrench,Dufty g:Josh Thewlis	4th	9,524
17/3/24	London Broncos (a)	W4-58	t:Holroyd(2),Josh Thewlis(3),Dufty(3),Harrison,Ratchford g:Ratchford(9)	1st	3,324
23/3/24	London Broncos (h) (CCR6)	W42-0	t:Josh Thewlis(2),Crowther,Tai,King,Ashton(3),Nicholson g:Ratchford(3)	N/A	3,416
30/3/24	Catalans Dragons (h)	L24-32	t:Musgrove,King,Harrison,Williams g:Josh Thewlis(4)	3rd	11,240
5/4/24	Leeds (a)	W8-34	t:Nicholson,Williams,Bullock,Walker,Dufty,Josh Thewlis g:Ratchford(5)	2nd	12,297
14/4/24	St Helens (a) (CCQF)	W8-31	t:Josh Thewlis,Ashton,Wrench,Harrison,Williams g:Josh Thewlis(5) fg:Williams	N/A	11,280
20/4/24	Leigh (h)	W16-14	t:Fitzgibbon,Dufty,Nicholson g:Josh Thewlis(2)	4th	10,443
27/4/24	Salford (a)	L17-12	t:Harrison,Williams g:Ratchford(2)	4th	5,910
3/5/24	Hull FC (h)	W24-6	t:Josh Thewlis(3),Williams g:Josh Thewlis(4)	2nd	8,680
9/5/24	Hull KR (h)	W20-8	t:King(2),Ashton g:Josh Thewlis(4)	3rd	8,578
19/5/24	Huddersfield (CCSF) ●	W10-46	t:Drinkwater,Ashton,Walker,Williams,Dufty(2),Powell,Tai g:Josh Thewlis(7)	N/A	9,253
25/5/24	Catalans Dragons (a)	W8-16	t:Williams,Ashton g:Josh Thewlis(4)	3rd	9,440
1/6/24	Wigan (h)	L18-19	t:Lindop,Drinkwater,Ratchford g:Ratchford(3)	4th	12,181
8/6/24	Wigan (CCF) ●●	L8-18	t:Dufty g:Josh Thewlis(2)	N/A	64,845
14/6/24	Salford (h)	L14-25	t:Tai(2),Ashton g:Drinkwater	4th	9,257
22/6/24	Hull FC (a)	W18-24	t:King,Dufty(2),Walker g:Josh Thewlis(4)	4th	10,083
5/7/24	Huddersfield (h)	W48-0	t:Vaughan,King,Wrench,Drinkwater,Nicholson,Dufty,Ratchford,Tai g:Ratchford(8)	3rd	9,760
11/7/24	Leeds (h)	W30-18	t:Ashton,Dufty(2),Tai,Whitehead g:Ratchford(5)	2nd	8,471
19/7/24	St Helens (a)	W10-24	t:Ashton,Dufty,Holroyd,Nicholson g:Ratchford(2),Drinkwater(2)	2nd	13,135
26/7/24	Wigan (a)	W4-40	t:Lindop(2),Holroyd,Ashton(2),Josh Thewlis,Tai g:Josh Thewlis(6)	1st	15,764
2/8/24	Hull KR (a)	L4-22	t:Ashton	3rd	12,102
11/8/24	London Broncos (a)	W22-36	t:Tai,Ashton(2),Vaughan,King,Holroyd g:Drinkwater(6)	3rd	2,150
17/8/24	Leeds (MW) ●●●	W6-24	t:Williams,Dufty(3) g:Josh Thewlis(4)	3rd	N/A
23/8/24	Castleford (a)	W6-28	t:Taylor-Wray,Bateman,Nicholson,Ashton,Josh Thewlis g:Josh Thewlis(4)	3rd	7,449
30/8/24	Leigh (h)	L16-12	t:Ashton,Powell g:Josh Thewlis(2)	3rd	9,434
7/9/24	St Helens (h)	W16-2	t:Ashton,Crowther g:Josh Thewlis(4)	3rd	12,015
14/9/24	Huddersfield (a)	W0-66	t:Ashton(3),Harrison,Williams,Nicholson(2),Taylor-Wray(2),Josh Thewlis,King,Tai g:Josh Thewlis(9)	3rd	4,181
20/9/24	London Broncos (h)	W54-0	t:Ashton(3),Nicholson(2),Lindop(2),Harrison,Josh Thewlis,Currie g:Josh Thewlis(7)	3rd	10,192
28/9/24	St Helens (h) (E)	W23-22 (aet)	t:King(2),Ashton(2) g:Josh Thewlis(3) fg:Williams	N/A	12,111
4/10/24	Hull KR (a) (SF)	L10-8	t:Ashton(2)	N/A	11,200

● Played at Totally Wicked Stadium, St Helens ●● Played at Wembley Stadium ●●● Played at Elland Road, Leeds

Matt Dufty

	D.O.B.	APP ALL	APP SL	TRIES ALL	TRIES SL	GOALS ALL	GOALS SL	FG ALL	FG SL	PTS ALL	PTS SL
Matty Ashton	28/7/98	29	25	32	27	0	0	0	0	128	108
John Bateman	30/9/93	9(1)	9(1)	1	1	0	0	0	0	4	4
Joe Bullock	27/11/92	1(8)	1(6)	1	1	0	0	0	0	4	4
Jordan Crowther	19/2/97	7(16)	5(14)	2	1	0	0	0	0	8	4
Ben Currie	15/7/94	27	25	1	1	0	0	0	0	4	4
Josh Drinkwater	15/6/92	25	23	3	2	10	10	0	0	32	28
Gil Dudson	16/6/90	(1)	(1)	0	0	0	0	0	0	0	0
Matt Dufty	10/1/96	28	24	20	17	0	0	0	0	80	68
Lachlan Fitzgibbon	5/1/94	17	14	1	1	0	0	0	0	4	4
Lucas Green	11/9/04	(1)	(1)	0	0	0	0	0	0	0	0
James Harrison	15/6/96	21(6)	17(6)	7	6	0	0	0	0	28	24
Ben Hartill	25/8/05	(1)	(1)	0	0	0	0	0	0	0	0
Leon Hayes	4/3/04	10	8	0	0	0	0	0	0	0	0
Adam Holroyd	5/9/04	14(4)	13(3)	5	5	0	0	0	0	20	20
Toby King	9/7/96	27	23	12	11	0	0	0	0	48	44
Arron Lindop	17/3/06	9	9	6	6	0	0	0	0	24	24
Zane Musgrove	26/3/96	6(22)	6(19)	1	1	0	0	0	0	4	4
Matty Nicholson	18/7/03	22(4)	19(3)	10	9	0	0	0	0	40	36
Joe Philbin	16/11/94	5(15)	3(14)	1	1	0	0	0	0	4	4
Sam Powell	3/7/92	10(23)	10(19)	3	2	0	0	0	0	12	8
Stefan Ratchford	19/7/88	10(1)	9(1)	3	3	42	39	0	0	96	90
Matty Russell	6/6/93	1	1	0	0	0	0	0	0	0	0
Rodrick Tai	21/12/98	23	20	9	7	0	0	0	0	36	28
Cai Taylor-Wray	24/2/06	5(1)	5(1)	3	3	0	0	0	0	12	12
Jake Thewlis	24/5/05	1	1	0	0	0	0	0	0	0	0
Josh Thewlis	30/4/02	26	22	15	12	82	68	0	0	224	184
Nolan Tupaea	19/6/05	1	1	0	0	0	0	0	0	0	0
Paul Vaughan	23/4/91	23(4)	20(4)	2	2	0	0	0	0	8	8
Danny Walker	29/6/99	24(7)	20(7)	4	3	0	0	0	0	16	12
Tom Whitehead	7/11/02	1(4)	1(4)	1	1	0	0	0	0	4	4
George Williams	31/10/94	26	23	10	8	0	0	2	1	42	33
Max Wood	28/6/04	1(11)	1(10)	0	0	0	0	0	0	0	0
Connor Wrench	4/10/01	10	9	4	3	0	0	0	0	16	12
Luke Yates	6/3/95	10(1)	10(1)	0	0	0	0	0	0	0	0

'SL' totals include regular season & play-offs; 'All' totals also include Challenge Cup

LEAGUE RECORD
P27-W20-D0-L7
(3rd/Semi-Final)
F740, A319, Diff+421
40 points.

CHALLENGE CUP
Runners-up

ATTENDANCES
Best - v Wigan (SL - 12,181)
Worst - v London Broncos (CC - 3,416)
Total (SL, inc play-offs) - 142,944
Average (SL, inc play-offs) - 10,210
(Down by 684 on 2023)

Super League XXIX - Club by Club

KEY DATES

10th November 2023 - hooker Sam Powell signs for Salford.

20th November 2023 - utility Joe Shorrocks signs for Salford.

5th December 2023 - halfback Harry Smith signs new four-year contract to end of 2027 season.

11th December 2023 - halfback Ryan Hampshire signs new one-year contract.

12th January 2024 - fullback Jai Field signs new four-year contract to end of 2027 season.

13th January 2024 - winger Abbas Miski signs new four-year contract to end of 2027 season.

4th February 2024 - 40-0 win at Hull FC in pre-season warm-up.

17th February 2024 - Liam Marshall scores try double in 32-4 round-one win at Castleford. Luke Thompson fails HIA.

24th February 2024 - 16-12 home win over Penrith Panthers secures record World Club title.

1st March 2024 - Liam Marshall scores hat-trick as Tiaki Chan makes debut in 30-16 home win over Huddersfield.

9th March 2024 - halfback Jack Farrimond makes debut in 60-22 win at London.

14th March 2024 - tries in last four minutes to Jake Wardle and Bevan French, with Harry Smith in sin bin, earns 22-12 win at Salford.

20th March 2024 - coaching team Matt Peet, Sean O'Loughlin and Thomas Leuluai extend contracts to 2030.

22nd March 2024 - Bevan French scores hat-trick in 44-18 home Challenge Cup round-six win over Sheffield.

26th March 2024 - centre Jake Wardle signs new five-year contract to end of 2029.

29th March 2024 - 12-4 Good Friday defeat at St Helens.

2nd April 2024 - Bevan French signs new four-year contract to end of 2028.

2nd April 2024 - Liam Byrne suspended for four matches for head contact. Tyler Dupree gets one game for same offence and appeal fails.

4th April 2024 - 40-12 win at Leigh.

14th April 2024 - Liam Marshall scores four tries in 60-6 Challenge Cup quarter-final win at Castleford.

19th April 2024 - Liam Marshall and Ryan Hampshire score twice in 36-14 home league win over Castleford.

23rd April 2024 - Sam Eseh joins Castleford on loan.

26th April 2024 - 26-10 defeat at Hull KR.

2nd May 2024 - Liam Farrell scores 150th career try in 30-8 home win over Catalans.

11th May 2024 - Liam Marshall scores hat-trick as Bevan French stars in 48-6 win at Huddersfield. Liam Byrne sin-binned in first minute.

13th May 2024 - Liam Byrne gets two-game ban for head contact.

18th May 2024 - 38-6 Challenge Cup semi-final win over Hull KR at Doncaster.

20th May 2024 - young prop Harvey Wilson signs for Salford.

26th May 2024 - 26-6 win at Salford.

1st June 2024 - Adam Keighran sent off after 70 minutes of 19-18 win at Warrington. Threequarter Jacob Douglas makes debut.

1st June 2024 - Adam Keighran (reckless shoulder charge) and Tyler Dupree (head butt) to miss Challenge Cup Final after being given three-game bans.

8th June 2024 - Bevan French wins Lance Todd Trophy in 18-8 Challenge Cup final win over Warrington.

14th June 2024 - Jai Field missing with pulled hamstring as Liam Marshall scores two tries and Harry Smith kicks decisive penalty goal in 10-8 win at Castleford.

19th June 2024 - Sam Eseh joins Leeds on loan.

21st June 2024 - Jack Farrimond scores two tries and kicks six from six goals in 36-0 home win over London.

5th July 2024 - Bevan French scores double in 24-6 home win over Leigh.

12th July 2024 - rookie fullback Zach Eckersley scores winning try in ferocious 16-12 home win over St Helens. Adam Keighran gets one match for dangerous throw.

20th July 2024 - 24-22 defeat at Hull FC ends eight-match winning league run.

26th July 2024 - 40-4 home defeat by Warrington is first home loss since May 2023. Brad O'Neill suffers ACL injury.

1st August 2024 - Jai Field back from injury for 28-14 home win over Huddersfield after trailing 8-0 at half-time.

2nd August 2024 - winger Liam Marshall signs new four-year deal to end of 2028.

6th August 2024 - 28-6 Tuesday-night home win over Leigh in game re-arranged to accommodate World Club Challenge takes Warriors clear at top of table.

10th August 2024 - Harry Smith sent off in 30-4 defeat at Leeds.

13th August 2024 - halfback Harry Smith suspended for three games for deliberate elbow into the face of Leeds' James Bentley.

17th August 2024 - Liam Farrell injured in warm-up as depleted side beats St Helens 20-0 in Magic Weekend at Elland Road, Leeds.

25th August 2024 - academy graduates Jacob Douglas, Zach Eckersley, Junior Nsemba and Jack Farrimond score all four tries in 22-4 home win over Hull FC.

31st August 2024 - 26-18 win at Catalans.

6th September 2024 - Liam Marshall scores two tries as 24-20 home win over Hull KR moves Warriors two points clear in top spot.

13th September 2024 - Bevan French scores double in 38-0 home win over Leeds.

18th September 2024 - 64-0 home thrashing of Salford secures consecutive League Leaders Shield.

25th September 2024 - 20-year-old centre Zach Eckersley signs new four-year contract.

25th September 2024 - forward Junior Nsemba signs new six-year contract.

26th September 2024 - prop Mike Cooper retires on medical advice after suffering concussion in July.

4th October 2024 - forward Willie Isa signs one-year contract extension. Ryan Hampshire to leave at end of season.

5th October 2024 - 38-0 semi-final home win over Leigh.

8th October 2024 - 20-year-old backrower Junior Nsemba named Super League Young Player of the Year.

12th October 2024 - Rob Burrow Award winner as man of the match Bevan French scores only try of 9-2 Grand Final victory over Hull KR.

CLUB RECORDS

Highest score:
116-0 v Flimby & Fothergill, 14/2/25
Highest score against:
0-75 v St Helens, 26/6/2005
Record attendance:
47,747 v St Helens, 27/3/59 (Central Park)
25,004 v St Helens, 25/3/2005
(JJB/DW/Brick Community Stadium)

MATCH RECORDS

Tries: 10 Martin Offiah v Leeds, 10/5/92
Shaun Edwards v Swinton, 29/9/92
Goals: 22 Jim Sullivan
v Flimby & Fothergill, 14/2/25
Points: 44 Jim Sullivan
v Flimby & Fothergill, 14/2/25

SEASON RECORDS

Tries: 62 Johnny Ring 1925-26
Goals: 186 Frano Botica 1994-95
Points: 462 Pat Richards 2010

CAREER RECORDS

Tries: 478 Billy Boston 1953-68
Goals: 2,317 Jim Sullivan 1921-46
Points: 4,883 Jim Sullivan 1921-46
Appearances: 774 Jim Sullivan 1921-46

Super League XXIX - Club by Club

WIGAN WARRIORS

DATE	FIXTURE	RESULT	SCORERS	LGE	ATT
17/2/24	Castleford (a)	W4-32	t:Mago,French,Marshall(2),Leeming g:Smith(5),Keighran	2nd	10,117
24/2/24	Penrith Panthers (h) (WCC)	W16-12	t:Miski,Leeming,Wardle g:Smith(2)	N/A	24,091
1/3/24	Huddersfield (h)	W30-16	t:Marshall(3),French,Dupree g:Smith(5)	2nd	15,357
9/3/24	London Broncos (a)	W22-60	t:Wardle,Miski,Dupree,Hill(2),O'Neill,Mago,Eckersley,Hampshire,Keighran g:Keighran(10)	1st	4,116
14/3/24	Salford (a)	W12-22	t:Marshall,Miski,Wardle,French g:Smith,Keighran(2)	2nd	6,087
22/3/24	Sheffield (h) (CCR6)	W44-18	t:French(3),Marshall(2),Wardle,Leeming,Mago g:Smith(6)	N/A	5,733
29/3/24	St Helens (a)	L12-4	t:French	4th	17,980
4/4/24	Leigh (a)	W12-40	t:Miski,Isa,French,Smith,Field,Keighran,Nsemba,Marshall g:Smith(4)	3rd	10,308
14/4/24	Castleford (a) (CCQF)	W6-60	t:Marshall(4),O'Neill,French,Keighran,Miski(2),Leeming,Wardle,Dupree g:Smith(6)	N/A	4,097
19/4/24	Castleford (h)	W36-14	t:French,Marshall(2),Hampshire(2),Miski g:Keighran(2),Smith(4)	3rd	13,029
26/4/24	Hull KR (a)	L26-10	t:Miski,Farrell g:Keighran	3rd	9,945
2/5/24	Catalans Dragons (h)	W30-8	t:Thompson,Smith,Keighran,Farrell,Miski g:Smith(5)	1st	14,481
11/5/24	Huddersfield (a)	W6-48	t:Marshall(3),French(2),Leeming,Miski(2) g:Smith(8)	1st	5,334
18/5/24	Hull KR (CCSF) ●	W6-38	t:Wardle(2),Miski(2),Nsemba,Smith,Dupree g:Smith(2),Keighran(3)	N/A	11,163
26/5/24	Salford (a)	W6-26	t:Keighran,Nsemba,O'Neill,French g:Keighran(5)	2nd	4,087
1/6/24	Warrington (a)	W18-19	t:Nsemba,Marshall,Leeming g:Keighran(3) fg:Smith	2nd	12,181
8/6/24	Warrington (CCF) ●●	W8-18	t:Eckersley,French,Farrell g:Smith(3)	N/A	64,845
14/6/24	Castleford (h)	W8-10	t:Marshall(2) g:Smith	2nd	6,965
21/6/24	London Broncos (h)	W36-0	t:Farrimond(2),Marshall,Miski,Wardle(2) g:Farrimond(6)	1st	14,280
5/7/24	Leigh (h)	W24-6	t:French(2),Marshall,Farrell g:Keighran(4)	1st	16,053
12/7/24	St Helens (h)	W16-12	t:Wardle,Keighran,Eckersley g:Smith(2)	1st	20,152
20/7/24	Hull FC (a)	L24-22	t:Marshall(2),O'Neill,Eckersley g:Keighran(3)	1st	9,771
26/7/24	Warrington (h)	L4-40	t:Marshall	3rd	15,764
1/8/24	Huddersfield (h)	W28-14	t:Wardle,Hampshire,Field,Eckersley g:Keighran(6)	2nd	11,660
6/8/24	Leigh (h)	W28-6	t:Nsemba,Wardle,Keighran,Mago,Hill g:Keighran(4)	1st	13,249
10/8/24	Leeds (a)	L30-4	t:Marshall	2nd	12,459
17/8/24	St Helens (MW) ●●●	W0-20	t:Marshall,Farrimond,Walters g:Keighran(4)	2nd	N/A
25/8/24	Hull FC (h)	W22-4	t:Douglas,Eckersley,Nsemba,Farrimond g:Keighran(3)	2nd	12,347
31/8/24	Catalans Dragons (a)	W18-26	t:Field,Forber,Nsemba,Keighran g:Keighran(5)	2nd	11,038
6/9/24	Hull KR (h)	W24-20	t:Miski,Nsemba,French,Marshall(2) g:Keighran(2)	1st	16,719
13/9/24	Leeds (h)	W38-0	t:Wardle,French(2),Marshall,Ellis,Miski,Keighran g:Keighran(5)	1st	15,146
19/9/24	Salford (h)	W64-0	t:Marshall(2),Field(3),French(2),Eckersley,Wardle,Leeming(2) g:Keighran(10)	1st	15,589
5/10/24	Leigh (h) (SF)	W38-0	t:Marshall(2),Walters(2),French,Field g:Keighran(7)	N/A	20,511
12/10/24	Hull KR (GF) ●●●●	W2-9	t:French g:Keighran(2) fg:Smith	N/A	68,173

● Played at Eco-Power Stadium, Doncaster   ●● Played at Wembley Stadium   ●●● Played at Elland Road, Leeds   ●●●● Played at Old Trafford, Manchester

		APP		TRIES		GOALS		FG		PTS	
	D.O.B.	ALL	SL	ALL	SL	ALL	SL	ALL	SL	ALL	SL
Liam Byrne	18/8/99	10(12)	8(11)	0	0	0	0	0	0	0	0
Tiaki Chan	15/6/00	(3)	(3)	0	0	0	0	0	0	0	0
Mike Cooper	15/9/88	5(3)	3(3)	0	0	0	0	0	0	0	0
Jacob Douglas	3/3/04	2	2	1	1	0	0	0	0	4	4
Tyler Dupree	8/2/00	6(23)	5(20)	4	2	0	0	0	0	16	8
Zach Eckersley	10/11/03	13(3)	12(3)	7	6	0	0	0	0	28	24
Kaide Ellis	4/8/96	31	26	1	1	0	0	0	0	4	4
Liam Farrell	2/7/90	29	24	4	3	0	0	0	0	16	12
Jack Farrimond	26/10/05	8	8	4	4	6	6	0	0	28	28
Jai Field	6/9/97	24	20	7	7	0	0	0	0	28	28
Tom Forber	22/5/03	(10)	(10)	1	1	0	0	0	0	4	4
Bevan French	4/1/96	25	20	23	18	0	0	0	0	92	72
Ryan Hampshire	29/12/94	9	8	4	4	0	0	0	0	16	16
Ethan Havard	26/10/00	16(7)	15(6)	0	0	0	0	0	0	0	0
Harvie Hill	3/9/03	1(15)	1(12)	3	3	0	0	0	0	12	12
Willie Isa	1/1/89	8	6	1	1	0	0	0	0	4	4
Adam Keighran	24/4/97	30	26	9	8	82	79	0	0	200	190
Kruise Leeming	7/9/95	12(15)	12(10)	8	5	0	0	0	0	32	20
Patrick Mago	4/12/94	3(31)	3(26)	4	3	0	0	0	0	16	12
Liam Marshall	9/5/96	33	28	35	29	0	0	0	0	140	116
Abbas Miski	25/7/95	31	26	16	11	0	0	0	0	64	44
Junior Nsemba	27/6/04	25(3)	22(2)	8	7	0	0	0	0	32	28
Brad O'Neill	22/7/02	21	16	4	3	0	0	0	0	16	12
Harry Smith	25/1/00	29	24	3	2	54	35	2	2	122	80
Luke Thompson	27/4/95	31	27	1	1	0	0	0	0	4	4
Sam Walters	25/12/00	7(8)	7(7)	3	3	0	0	0	0	12	12
Jake Wardle	18/11/98	33	28	14	9	0	0	0	0	56	36

'SL' totals include regular season & play-offs; 'All' totals also include Challenge Cup & World Club Challenge

Liam Marshall

LEAGUE RECORD
P27-W22-D0-L5
(1st/Grand Final Winners, Champions)
F723, A338, Diff+385
44 points.

CHALLENGE CUP
Winners

ATTENDANCES
Best - v Penrith Panthers (WCC - 24,091)
Worst - v Sheffield (CC - 5,733)
Total (SL, inc play-offs) - 214,337
Average (SL, inc play-offs) - 15,310
(Up by 1,694 on 2023)

SUPER LEAGUE XXIX
Round by Round

ROUND 1

Thursday 15th February 2024

HULL FC 0 HULL KR 22

HULL FC: 31 Jack Walker (D2); 26 Lewis Martin; 23 Davy Litten; 17 Cameron Scott; 5 Darnell McIntosh; 19 Morgan Smith (D); 7 Fa'amanu Brown (D); 8 Herman Ese'ese (D); 9 Danny Houghton (C); 10 Franklin Pele (D); 11 Jayden Okunbor (D); 12 Ligi Sao; 14 Joe Cator. Subs (all used): 1 Tex Hoy; 15 Jordan Lane; 16 Jack Ashworth (D); 20 Jack Brown.
Dismissal: Pele (40) - swinging arm on Minchella; Sao (74) - use of the knee on Parcell.
Sin bin: Ese'ese (12) - high tackle on Tanginoa.
HULL KR: 1 Peta Hiku (D); 2 Niall Evalds (D); 3 Tom Opacic; 4 Oliver Gildart (D); 5 Ryan Hall; 27 Tyrone May (D); 7 Mikey Lewis; 11 Dean Hadley; 9 Jez Litten; 16 Jai Whitbread (D); 20 Kelepi Tanginoa (D); 12 James Batchelor; 13 Elliot Minchella (C). Subs (all used): 8 Sauaso Sue; 10 George King; 14 Matt Parcell; 19 Yusuf Aydin.
Tries: Evalds (6, 80), Tanginoa (18), Lewis (37), Parcell (59); **Goals:** Hiku 1/5, Batchelor 0/1.
Sin bin: Parcell (74) - contact with the head of Sao.
Rugby Leaguer & League Express Men of the Match: *Hull FC:* Jayden Okunbor; *Hull KR:* Tyrone May.
Penalty count: 4-8; **Half-time:** 0-14;
Referee: Liam Moore; **Attendance:** 20,014.

Friday 16th February 2024

LEEDS RHINOS 22 SALFORD RED DEVILS 16

RHINOS: 1 Lachlan Miller (D); 24 Luis Roberts; 3 Harry Newman; 4 Paul Momirovski (D); 5 Ash Handley; 6 Brodie Croft (D); 7 Matt Frawley (D); 25 James Donaldson; 9 Andy Ackers (D); 8 Mikolaj Oledzki; 18 Mickael Goudemand (D); 12 Rhyse Martin; 13 Cameron Smith (C). Subs (all used): 11 James Bentley; 14 Jarrod O'Connor; 15 Sam Lisone; 17 Justin Sangare.
Tries: Handley (23, 48), Lisone (69); **Goals:** Martin 5/5.
Sin bin: Momirovski (57) - shoulder charge on Atkin.
RED DEVILS: 1 Ryan Brierley; 23 Chris Hankinson (D); 3 Nene Macdonald (D); 4 Tim Lafai; 5 Deon Cross; 6 Cade Cust (D); 7 Marc Sneyd; 8 Brad Singleton; 9 Amir Bourouh; 17 Jack Ormondroyd; 11 Sam Stone; 12 Kallum Watkins (C); 13 Oliver Partington. Subs (all used): 14 Chris Atkin; 15 Shane Wright; 16 Joe Shorrocks (D); 18 Ben Hellewell.
Tries: Cust (18), Partington (33); **Goals:** Sneyd 4/4.
Sin bin: Brierley (13) - high tackle on Croft; Bourouh (65) - professional foul.
Rugby Leaguer & League Express Men of the Match: *Rhinos:* Ash Handley; *Red Devils:* Nene Macdonald.
Penalty count: 11-7; **Half-time:** 8-14;
Referee: Aaron Moore; **Attendance:** 15,126.

LEIGH LEOPARDS 8 HUDDERSFIELD GIANTS 16

LEOPARDS: 1 Gareth O'Brien; 2 Tom Briscoe; 3 Zak Hardaker; 4 Ricky Leutele; 5 Josh Charnley; 6 Matt Moylan (D); 7 Lachlan Lam; 8 Tom Amone; 9 Edwin Ipape; 10 Robbie Mulhern; 11 Kai O'Donnell; 12 Jack Hughes; 13 John Asiata (C). Subs (all used): 14 Dan Norman (D3); 15 Matt Davis; 16 Frankie Halton; 18 Ben Nakubuwai.
Tries: Charnley (22), Briscoe (73); **Goals:** Hardaker 0/2.
Sin bin: Asiata (33) - professional foul; Leutele (44) - high tackle on Connor.
GIANTS: 1 Jake Connor; 2 Adam Swift (D); 3 Esan Marsters; 4 Kevin Naiqama; 20 Elliot Wallis (D); 7 Adam Clune (D); 23 Oliver Russell; 8 Chris Hill (C); 9 Adam Milner; 18 Sebastine Ikahihifo; 11 Jack Murchie (D); 12 Sam Hewitt; 21 Leroy Cudjoe. Subs (all used): 14 Ashton Golding; 15 Matty English; 17 Oliver Wilson; 26 Hugo Salabio (D).
Tries: Marsters (10), Milner (33), Wallis (64);
Goals: Russell 2/3.
Rugby Leaguer & League Express Men of the Match: *Leopards:* Lachlan Lam; *Giants:* Leroy Cudjoe.
Penalty count: 10-6; **Half-time:** 4-12;
Referee: Jack Smith; **Attendance:** 8,508.

ST HELENS 40 LONDON BRONCOS 4

SAINTS: 1 Jack Welsby; 2 Tommy Makinson; 23 Konrad Hurrell; 4 Mark Percival; 3 Waqa Blake (D); 6 Jonny Lomax (C); 7 Lewis Dodd; 8 Alex Walmsley; 9 Daryl Clark (D); 10 Matty Lees; 19 Matt Whitley (D); 16 Curtis Sironen; 15 James Bell. Subs (all used): 11 Sione Mata'utia; 18 Jake Wingfield; 20 George Delaney; 21 Ben Davies.
Tries: Dodd (5), Welsby (8), Walmsley (24), Makinson (37), Clark (49), Whitley (67, 75), Lomax (70);
Goals: Percival 3/5, Makinson 1/3.
BRONCOS: 20 Oliver Leyland; 2 Lee Kershaw (D); 21 Robbie Storey (D); 4 Hakim Miloudi (D); 5 Iliess Macani; 6 Jack Campagnolo (D); 7 James Meadows (D2); 8 Rob Butler; 9 Sam Davis; 19 Rhys Kennedy (D); 11 Will Lovell (C); 17 Sadiq Adebiyi (D2); 13 Dean Parata. Subs (all used): 15 Marcus Stock; 16 Jordan Williams; 18 Emmanuel Waine; 24 Matthew Davies.
Try: Storey (44); **Goals:** Campagnolo 0/1.
Rugby Leaguer & League Express Men of the Match: *Saints:* Daryl Clark; *Broncos:* Oliver Leyland.
Penalty count: 6-6; **Half-time:** 20-0;
Referee: James Vella; **Attendance:** 14,058.

Saturday 17th February 2024

CASTLEFORD TIGERS 4 WIGAN WARRIORS 32

TIGERS: 1 Luke Hooley (D); 23 Jason Qareqare; 3 Jack Broadbent; 4 Sam Wood (D); 5 Innes Senior (D); 6 Danny Richardson; 7 Jacob Miller; 10 George Lawler; 14 Liam Horne; 17 Nixon Putt (D); 11 Elie El-Zakhem (D); 22 Charbel Tasipale; 13 Joe Westerman (C). Subs (all used): 2 Josh Simm (D); 8 Liam Watts; 19 Sam Hall; 20 Muizz Mustapha.
Goals: Richardson 2/2.
Dismissal: Watts (29) - shoulder charge on Dupree.
WARRIORS: 1 Jai Field; 2 Abbas Miski; 3 Adam Keighran (D); 4 Jake Wardle; 5 Liam Marshall; 6 Bevan French; 7 Harry Smith; 16 Luke Thompson (D); 9 Brad O'Neill; 10 Liam Byrne; 11 Willie Isa; 12 Liam Farrell (C); 13 Kaide Ellis. Subs (all used): 14 Mike Cooper; 15 Patrick Mago; 17 Kruise Leeming (D); 19 Tyler Dupree.
Tries: Mago (35), French (38), Marshall (51, 76), Leeming (54); **Goals:** Smith 5/6, Keighran 1/1.
Sin bin: Smith (21) - dangerous challenge on Hooley.
Rugby Leaguer & League Express Men of the Match: *Tigers:* Liam Horne; *Warriors:* Patrick Mago.
Penalty count: 11-8; **Half-time:** 4-16;
Referee: Tom Grant; **Attendance:** 10,117.

CATALANS DRAGONS 16 WARRINGTON WOLVES 10

DRAGONS: 1 Arthur Mourgue; 2 Tom Davies; 3 Arthur Romano; 21 Matt Ikuvalu; 24 Tom Johnstone; 27 Jordan Abdull (D); 7 Theo Fages (D); 16 Romain Navarrete; 9 Michael McIlorum (C); 10 Julian Bousquet; 11 Tariq Sims (D); 12 Paul Seguier; 8 Mike McMeeken. Subs (all used): 6 Jayden Nikorima (D); 15 Bayley Sironen (D); 20 Tevita Satae (D); 23 Jordan Dezaria.
Tries: Abdull (38), Mourgue (49);
Goals: Mourgue 4/5, Abdull 0/1.
Dismissal: McIlorum (41) - high tackle on Philbin.
WOLVES: 1 Matt Dufty; 33 Arron Lindop (D); 3 Toby King; 20 Connor Wrench; 5 Matty Ashton; 6 George Williams (C); 7 Josh Drinkwater; 8 James Harrison; 9 Danny Walker; 16 Zane Musgrove (D); 11 Ben Currie; 12 Lachlan Fitzgibbon (D); 17 Jordan Crowther. Subs (all used): 10 Paul Vaughan; 15 Joe Philbin; 22 Gil Dudson; 32 Sam Powell (D).
Tries: Lindop (16), Dufty (61); **Goals:** Drinkwater 1/2.
Sin bin: Crowther (68) - shoulder charge on Navarrete.
Rugby Leaguer & League Express Men of the Match: *Dragons:* Theo Fages; *Wolves:* George Williams.
Penalty count: 7-5; **Half-time:** 6-4;
Referee: Chris Kendall; **Attendance:** 8,876.

ROUND 2

Thursday 22nd February 2024

HULL KR 22 LEEDS RHINOS 12

HULL KR: 1 Peta Hiku; 2 Niall Evalds; 3 Tom Opacic; 4 Oliver Gildart; 5 Ryan Hall; 7 Mikey Lewis; 27 Tyrone May; 16 Jai Whitbread; 9 Jez Litten; 10 George King; 20 Kelepi Tanginoa; 12 James Batchelor; 13 Elliot Minchella (C). Subs (all used): 8 Sauaso Sue; 17 Matty Storton; 19 Yusuf Aydin; 21 Corey Hall.
Tries: Sue (33), R Hall (46), Hiku (71); **Goals:** Litten 5/5.
Sin bin: Hiku (6) - interference.
RHINOS: 29 Alfie Edgell; 24 Luis Roberts; 3 Harry Newman; 4 Paul Momirovski; 5 Ash Handley; 6 Brodie Croft; 7 Matt Frawley; 17 Justin Sangare; 9 Andy Ackers; 18 Mickael Goudemand; 11 James Bentley; 12 Rhyse Martin; 13 Cameron Smith (C). Subs (all used): 14 Jarrod O'Connor; 15 Sam Lisone; 23 Leon Ruan; 25 James Donaldson.
Tries: Newman (11), Handley (60); **Goals:** Martin 2/2.
Sin bin: Donaldson (40) - high tackle; Lisone (66) - high tackle.
Rugby Leaguer & League Express Men of the Match: *Hull KR:* Jez Litten; *Rhinos:* Andy Ackers.
Penalty count: 11-3; **Half-time:** 8-6;
Referee: Jack Smith; **Attendance:** 9,879.

Friday 23rd February 2024

LONDON BRONCOS 0 CATALANS DRAGONS 34

BRONCOS: 20 Oliver Leyland; 2 Lee Kershaw; 21 Robbie Storey; 4 Hakim Miloudi; 5 Iliess Macani; 6 Jack Campagnolo; 7 James Meadows; 8 Rob Butler; 9 Sam Davis; 19 Rhys Kennedy; 11 Will Lovell (C); 17 Sadiq Adebiyi; 13 Dean Parata. Subs (all used): 3 Jarred Bassett; 15 Marcus Stock; 16 Jordan Williams; 29 Jacob Jones (D3).
DRAGONS: 1 Arthur Mourgue; 24 Tom Johnstone; 3 Arthur Romano; 21 Matt Ikuvalu; 5 Fouad Yaha; 27 Jordan Abdull; 7 Theo Fages; 16 Romain Navarrete; 14 Alrix Da Costa; 10 Julian Bousquet; 11 Tariq Sims; 15 Bayley Sironen; 13 Ben Garcia (C). Subs (all used): 6 Jayden Nikorima; 8 Mike McMeeken; 20 Tevita Satae; 23 Jordan Dezaria.
Tries: Fages (2, 22), Sims (11, 47), Nikorima (56), Bousquet (70); **Goals:** Mourgue 5/6.
Rugby Leaguer & League Express Men of the Match: *Broncos:* Sadiq Adebiyi; *Dragons:* Theo Fages.
Penalty count: 5-6; **Half-time:** 0-16;
Referee: Tom Grant; **Attendance:** 5,102.

WARRINGTON WOLVES 36 HULL FC 10

WOLVES: 1 Matt Dufty; 2 Josh Thewlis; 3 Toby King; 20 Connor Wrench; 5 Matty Ashton; 18 Leon Hayes; 7 Josh Drinkwater; 8 James Harrison; 9 Danny Walker (C); 10 Paul Vaughan; 28 Adam Holroyd; 12 Lachlan Fitzgibbon; 11 Ben Currie. Subs (all used): 15 Joe Philbin; 16 Zane Musgrove; 32 Sam Powell; 34 Max Wood (D).
Tries: Walker (5), Ashton (42, pen), Powell (55), King (63), Harrison (76), Wrench (80); **Goals:** Josh Thewlis 6/8.
Sin bin: Powell (65) - high tackle on Walker.
HULL FC: 31 Jack Walker; 25 Harvey Barron; 4 Liam Sutcliffe; 5 Darnell McIntosh; 26 Lewis Martin; 1 Tex Hoy; 19 Morgan Smith; 16 Jack Ashworth; 7 Fa'amanu Brown (C); 20 Jack Brown; 11 Jayden Okunbor; 24 Nick Staveley; 15 Jordan Lane. Subs (all used): 21 Will Gardiner; 23 Davy Litten; 28 Denive Balmforth; 29 Charlie Severs.
Tries: Martin (21), Walker (50); **Goals:** McIntosh 1/2.
Dismissal: F Brown (36) - contact with the head of Currie.
Rugby Leaguer & League Express Men of the Match: *Wolves:* Paul Vaughan; *Hull FC:* Nick Staveley.
Penalty count: 11-10; **Half-time:** 8-6;
Referee: Marcus Griffiths; **Attendance:** 9,431.

Saturday 24th February 2024

HUDDERSFIELD GIANTS 0 ST HELENS 28

GIANTS: 6 Tui Lolohea; 2 Adam Swift; 3 Esan Marsters; 4 Kevin Naiqama; 20 Elliot Wallis; 7 Adam Clune; 23 Oliver Russell; 8 Chris Hill (C); 9 Adam Milner; 18 Sebastine Ikahihifo; 11 Jack Murchie; 12 Sam Hewitt; 21 Leroy Cudjoe. Subs (all used): 14 Ashton Golding; 15 Matty English; 17 Oliver Wilson; 26 Hugo Salabio.
SAINTS: 1 Jack Welsby; 2 Tommy Makinson; 3 Waqa Blake; 4 Mark Percival; 5 Jon Bennison; 6 Jonny Lomax (C); 7 Lewis Dodd; 8 Alex Walmsley; 9 Daryl Clark; 10 Matty Lees; 19 Matt Whitley; 16 Curtis Sironen; 13 Morgan Knowles. Subs (all used): 11 Sione Mata'utia; 15 James Bell; 18 Jake Wingfield; 20 George Delaney.
Tries: Whitley (9), Mata'utia (38), Welsby (50), Bennison (75), Knowles (77);
Goals: Percival 3/4, Makinson 1/2.
Sin bin: Clark (62) - professional foul.
Rugby Leaguer & League Express Men of the Match: *Giants:* Adam Clune; *Saints:* Alex Walmsley.
Penalty count: 7-4; **Half-time:** 0-12;
Referee: Aaron Moore; **Attendance:** 6,812.

Sunday 25th February 2024

SALFORD RED DEVILS 26 CASTLEFORD TIGERS 22

RED DEVILS: 1 Ryan Brierley; 23 Chris Hankinson; 3 Nene Macdonald; 4 Tim Lafai; 5 Deon Cross; 6 Cade Cust; 7 Marc Sneyd; 8 Brad Singleton; 9 Amir Bourouh; 17 Jack Ormondroyd; 11 Sam Stone; 12 Kallum Watkins (C); 16 Joe Shorrocks. Subs (all used): 10 King Vuniyayawa; 14 Chris Atkin; 15 Shane Wright; 18 Ben Hellewell.
Tries: Stone (10, 49), Bourouh (12), Macdonald (39);
Goals: Sneyd 5/5.
Sin bin: Ormondroyd (65) - late challenge on Miller; Watkins (79) - holding down.
TIGERS: 1 Luke Hooley; 23 Jason Qareqare; 3 Jack Broadbent; 4 Sam Wood; 5 Innes Senior; 6 Danny Richardson; 7 Jacob Miller; 10 George Lawler; 14 Liam Horne; 17 Nixon Putt; 11 Elie El-Zakhem; 22 Charbel Tasipale; 13 Joe Westerman (C). Subs (all used): 16 Rowan Milnes (D); 19 Sam Hall; 20 Muizz Mustapha; 26 Samy Kibula (D).
Tries: Wood (24), Broadbent (32), Westerman (56), Horne (79); **Goals:** Richardson 1/2, Hooley 2/2.
Rugby Leaguer & League Express Men of the Match: *Red Devils:* Nene Macdonald; *Tigers:* Joe Westerman.
Penalty count: 6-9; **Half-time:** 18-10;
Referee: James Vella; **Attendance:** 4,770.

ROUND 3

Friday 1st March 2024

ST HELENS 12 LEIGH LEOPARDS 4

SAINTS: 1 Jack Welsby; 2 Tommy Makinson; 23 Konrad

Hurrell; 4 Mark Percival; 5 Jon Bennison; 6 Jonny Lomax (C); 7 Lewis Dodd; 8 Alex Walmsley; 9 Daryl Clark; 11 Sione Mata'utia; 19 Matt Whitley; 16 Curtis Sironen; 13 Morgan Knowles. Subs (all used): 14 Moses Mbye; 15 James Bell; 18 Jake Wingfield; 20 George Delaney.
Tries: Welsby (30), Makinson (51); **Goals:** Percival 2/3.
LEOPARDS: 1 Gareth O'Brien; 2 Tom Briscoe; 3 Zak Hardaker; 4 Ricky Leutele; 5 Josh Charnley; 6 Matt Moylan; 7 Lachlan Lam; 12 Jack Hughes; 33 Brad Dwyer (D); 10 Robbie Mulhern; 11 Kai O'Donnell; 16 Frankie Halton; 13 John Asiata (C). Subs (all used): 14 Dan Norman; 15 Matt Davis; 17 Owen Trout (D); 18 Ben Nakubuwai.
Try: Hardaker (46); **Goals:** Hardaker 0/1.
Sin bin: Asiata (1) - dangerous challenge on Mata'utia; Dwyer (75) - holding down.
Rugby Leaguer & League Express Men of the Match: *Saints:* Matt Whitley; *Leopards:* Matt Moylan.
Penalty count: 9-5; **Half-time:** 4-0;
Referee: Liam Moore; **Attendance:** 13,028.

WARRINGTON WOLVES 30 CASTLEFORD TIGERS 8

WOLVES: 1 Matt Dufty; 2 Josh Thewlis; 3 Toby King; 4 Stefan Ratchford (C); 5 Matty Ashton; 18 Leon Hayes; 7 Josh Drinkwater; 8 James Harrison; 9 Danny Walker; 10 Paul Vaughan; 28 Adam Holroyd; 12 Lachlan Fitzgibbon; 11 Ben Currie. Subs (all used): 15 Joe Philbin; 16 Zane Musgrove; 32 Sam Powell; 34 Max Wood.
Tries: Ashton (23, 29), Philbin (34), Dufty (43), Josh Thewlis (75); **Goals:** Ratchford 5/5, Josh Thewlis 0/1.
TIGERS: 1 Luke Hooley; 2 Josh Simm; 3 Jack Broadbent; 4 Sam Wood; 5 Innes Senior; 16 Rowan Milnes; 7 Jacob Miller; 10 George Lawler; 14 Liam Horne; 20 Muizz Mustapha; 11 Elie El-Zakhem; 12 Alex Mellor; 13 Joe Westerman (C). Subs (all used): 17 Nixon Putt; 19 Sam Hall; 30 Luis Johnson (D2); 26 Samy Kibula.
Tries: Simm (10), I Senior (50); **Goals:** Milnes 0/2.
Rugby Leaguer & League Express Men of the Match: *Wolves:* Leon Hayes; *Tigers:* Jacob Miller.
Penalty count: 5-4; **Half-time:** 20-4;
Referee: Aaron Moore; **Attendance:** 8,483.

WIGAN WARRIORS 30 HUDDERSFIELD GIANTS 16

WARRIORS: 1 Jai Field; 2 Abbas Miski; 3 Adam Keighran; 4 Jake Wardle; 5 Liam Marshall; 6 Bevan French; 7 Harry Smith; 16 Luke Thompson; 9 Brad O'Neill; 19 Tyler Dupree; 11 Willie Isa; 12 Liam Farrell (C); 13 Kaide Ellis. Subs (all used): 15 Patrick Mago; 20 Harvie Hill; 24 Tiaki Chan (D); 27 Tom Forber.
Tries: Marshall (12, 22, 46), French (16), Dupree (75); **Goals:** Smith 5/6.
Sin bin: Keighran (40) - delaying restart.
GIANTS: 1 Jake Connor; 2 Adam Swift; 3 Esan Marsters; 4 Kevin Naiqama; 20 Elliot Wallis; 23 Oliver Russell; 7 Adam Clune; 8 Chris Hill (C); 9 Adam Milner; 18 Sebastine Ikahihifo; 11 Jack Murchie; 12 Sam Hewitt; 21 Leroy Cudjoe. Subs (all used): 14 Ashton Golding; 15 Matty English; 17 Oliver Wilson; 26 Hugo Salabio.
Tries: Wallis (32), Swift (43), Murchie (71); **Goals:** Russell 2/3.
Sin bin: Milner (19) - contact with the head of Dupree.
Rugby Leaguer & League Express Men of the Match: *Warriors:* Liam Marshall; *Giants:* Esan Marsters.
Penalty count: 7-11; **Half-time:** 18-4;
Referee: Jack Smith; **Attendance:** 15,357.

Saturday 2nd March 2024

LEEDS RHINOS 18 CATALANS DRAGONS 10

RHINOS: 1 Lachlan Miller; 24 Luis Roberts; 3 Harry Newman; 4 Paul Momirovski; 5 Ash Handley; 6 Brodie Croft; 7 Matt Frawley; 17 Justin Sangare; 9 Andy Ackers; 18 Mickael Goudemand; 11 James Bentley; 12 Rhyse Martin; 13 Cameron Smith (C). Subs (all used): 16 James McDonnell; 10 Tom Holroyd; 14 Jarrod O'Connor; 23 Leon Ruan.
Tries: Handley (26, 65), Newman (28); **Goals:** Martin 3/5.
Sin bin: Sangare (52) - high tackle on Da Costa.
DRAGONS: 1 Arthur Mourgue; 24 Tom Johnstone; 3 Arthur Romano; 21 Matt Ikuvalu; 5 Fouad Yaha; 27 Jordan Abdull; 7 Theo Fages; 10 Julian Bousquet; 14 Alrix Da Costa; 16 Romain Navarrete; 11 Tariq Sims; 15 Bayley Sironen; 13 Ben Garcia (C). Subs (all used): 6 Jayden Nikorima; 12 Paul Seguier; 20 Tevita Satae; 23 Jordan Dezaria.
Try: Satae (45); **Goals:** Mourgue 3/3.
Sin bin: Sims (29) - high tackle on Newman; Dezaria (58) - high tackle on Croft; Navarrete (73) - professional foul.
Rugby Leaguer & League Express Men of the Match: *Rhinos:* Brodie Croft; *Dragons:* Tevita Satae.
Penalty count: 7-4; **Half-time:** 10-2;
Referee: Chris Kendall; **Attendance:** 14,168.

SALFORD RED DEVILS 17 HULL KR 10

RED DEVILS: 14 Chris Atkin; 23 Chris Hankinson; 3 Nene Macdonald; 4 Tim Lafai; 5 Deon Cross; 6 Cade Cust; 7 Marc Sneyd; 17 Jack Ormondroyd; 9 Amir Bourouh; 8 Brad Singleton; 11 Sam Stone; 12 Kallum Watkins (C); 16 Joe Shorrocks. Subs (all used): 10 King Vuniyayawa; 15 Shane Wright; 18 Ben Hellewell; 22 Kai Morgan (D).
Tries: Cross (15), Hankinson (36); **Goals:** Sneyd 4/4;
Field goal: Sneyd (71).
Sin bin: Cross (53) - professional foul.
HULL KR: 1 Peta Hiku; 35 Joe Burgess (D); 3 Tom Opacic; 4 Oliver Gildart; 5 Ryan Hall; 27 Tyrone May; 7 Mikey Lewis; 11 Dean Hadley; 9 Jez Litten; 16 Jai Whitbread; 20 Kelepi Tanginoa; 12 James Batchelor; 13 Elliot Minchella (C). Subs (all used): 8 Sauaso Sue; 10 George King; 14 Matt Parcell; 15 Sam Luckley.
Tries: Hiku (55), Litten (65); **Goals:** Batchelor 0/1, Litten 1/1.
Sin bin: Hiku (63) - dissent.
Rugby Leaguer & League Express Men of the Match: *Red Devils:* Marc Sneyd; *Hull KR:* Dean Hadley.
Penalty count: 8-5; **Half-time:** 12-0;
Referee: Tom Grant; **Attendance:** 5,036.

Sunday 3rd March 2024

HULL FC 28 LONDON BRONCOS 24

HULL FC: 31 Jack Walker; 41 Matty Russell (D2); 5 Darnell McIntosh; 3 Carlos Tuimavave; 26 Lewis Martin; 19 Morgan Smith; 7 Fa'amanu Brown; 16 Jack Ashworth; 9 Danny Houghton (C); 12 Ligi Sao; 11 Jayden Okunbor; 24 Nick Staveley; 15 Jordan Lane. Subs: 20 Jack Brown; 29 Charlie Severs (not used); 40 Jack Charles (D); 42 Joe Bullock (D).
Tries: Staveley (18), Russell (30), Martin (38), F Brown (56), Smith (79); **Goals:** McIntosh 4/5.
Sin bin: Russell (34) - high tackle on O Leyland.
BRONCOS: 20 Oliver Leyland; 2 Lee Kershaw; 21 Robbie Storey; 3 Jarred Bassett; 4 Hakim Miloudi; 6 Jack Campagnolo; 7 James Meadows; 8 Rob Butler; 9 Sam Davis; 19 Rhys Kennedy; 11 Will Lovell (C); 29 Jacob Jones; 13 Dean Parata. Subs (all used): 5 Iliess Macani; 15 Marcus Stock; 16 Jordan Williams; 30 Fenton Rogers (D).
Tries: Meadows (14), Kershaw (42), Miloudi (52, 61), Storey (75); **Goals:** O Leyland 2/5.
Rugby Leaguer & League Express Men of the Match: *Hull FC:* Matty Russell; *Broncos:* James Meadows.
Penalty count: 8-9; **Half-time:** 16-4;
Referee: James Vella; **Attendance:** 10,066.

ROUND 4

Thursday 7th March 2024

HULL KR 20 WARRINGTON WOLVES 22

HULL KR: 1 Peta Hiku; 2 Niall Evalds; 3 Tom Opacic; 4 Oliver Gildart; 5 Ryan Hall; 27 Tyrone May; 7 Mikey Lewis; 11 Dean Hadley; 9 Jez Litten; 16 Jai Whitbread; 20 Kelepi Tanginoa; 12 James Batchelor; 13 Elliot Minchella (C). Subs (all used): 8 Sauaso Sue; 10 George King; 14 Matt Parcell; 15 Sam Luckley.
Tries: May (17), R Hall (25), Gildart (57), Opacic (62); **Goals:** Litten 2/2, Batchelor 0/2.
WOLVES: 1 Matt Dufty; 2 Josh Thewlis; 3 Toby King; 20 Connor Wrench; 5 Matty Ashton; 6 George Williams (C); 18 Leon Hayes; 8 James Harrison; 9 Danny Walker; 10 Paul Vaughan; 28 Adam Holroyd; 12 Lachlan Fitzgibbon; 11 Ben Currie. Subs (all used): 15 Joe Philbin; 16 Zane Musgrove; 17 Jordan Crowther; 32 Sam Powell.
Tries: Williams (8), Ashton (14), King (38), Wrench (40), Dufty (70); **Goals:** Josh Thewlis 1/3, Hayes 0/2.
Rugby Leaguer & League Express Men of the Match: *Hull KR:* Mikey Lewis; *Wolves:* Matt Dufty.
Penalty count: 2-2; **Half-time:** 12-18;
Referee: Aaron Moore; **Attendance:** 9,524.

Friday 8th March 2024

CASTLEFORD TIGERS 8 HUDDERSFIELD GIANTS 50

TIGERS: 1 Luke Hooley; 2 Josh Simm; 12 Alex Mellor; 4 Sam Wood; 5 Innes Senior; 16 Rowan Milnes; 7 Jacob Miller; 10 George Lawler; 14 Liam Horne; 21 Sylvester Namo (D); 30 Luis Johnson; 22 Charbel Tasipale; 13 Joe Westerman (C). Subs (all used): 3 Jack Broadbent; 17 Nixon Putt; 19 Sam Hall; 27 Albert Vete.
Tries: I Senior (23, 49); **Goals:** Hooley 0/2.
GIANTS: 1 Jake Connor; 24 Sam Halsall; 3 Esan Marsters; 4 Kevin Naiqama; 2 Adam Swift; 23 Oliver Russell; 7 Adam Clune; 8 Chris Hill; 14 Ashton Golding; 18 Sebastine Ikahihifo; 11 Jack Murchie; 12 Sam Hewitt; 21 Leroy Cudjoe. Subs (all used): 6 Tui Lolohea; 13 Luke Yates (C); 17 Oliver Wilson; 26 Hugo Salabio.
Tries: Swift (6, 69), Clune (14), Halsall (32, 73), Hewitt (40), Cudjoe (63, 78), Naiqama (80); **Goals:** Russell 7/10.
Rugby Leaguer & League Express Men of the Match: *Tigers:* Innes Senior; *Giants:* Leroy Cudjoe.
Penalty count: 4-3; **Half-time:** 4-24;
Referee: Liam Moore; **Attendance:** 7,040.

LEIGH LEOPARDS 16 LEEDS RHINOS 22

LEOPARDS: 1 Gareth O'Brien; 24 Umyla Hanley; 3 Zak Hardaker; 4 Ricky Leutele; 5 Josh Charnley; 6 Matt Moylan; 7 Lachlan Lam (C); 12 Jack Hughes; 33 Brad Dwyer; 10 Robbie Mulhern; 11 Kai O'Donnell; 16 Frankie Halton; 8 Tom Amone. Subs (all used): 14 Dan Norman; 15 Matt Davis; 17 Owen Trout; 18 Ben Nakubuwai.
Tries: O'Brien (14), O'Donnell (21), Hanley (26); **Goals:** Moylan 2/4.
Sin bin: O'Brien (52) - holding down.
RHINOS: 1 Lachlan Miller; 24 Luis Roberts; 3 Harry Newman; 4 Paul Momirovski; 5 Ash Handley; 6 Brodie Croft; 7 Matt Frawley; 8 Mikolaj Oledzki; 9 Andy Ackers; 18 Mickael Goudemand; 16 James McDonnell; 12 Rhyse Martin; 13 Cameron Smith (C). Subs (all used): 10 Tom Holroyd; 14 Jarrod O'Connor; 17 Justin Sangare; 23 Leon Ruan.
Tries: Martin (49), Frawley (61), Handley (63, 69); **Goals:** Martin 3/4.
Sin bin: Sangare (76) - late challenge on Amone.
Rugby Leaguer & League Express Men of the Match: *Leopards:* Tom Amone; *Rhinos:* Rhyse Martin.
Penalty count: 12-5; **Half-time:** 16-0;
Referee: Chris Kendall; **Attendance:** 8,100.

ST HELENS 20 SALFORD RED DEVILS 24

SAINTS: 1 Jack Welsby; 2 Tommy Makinson; 3 Waqa Blake; 4 Mark Percival; 5 Jon Bennison; 6 Jonny Lomax (C); 7 Lewis Dodd; 8 Alex Walmsley; 9 Daryl Clark; 11 Sione Mata'utia; 19 Matt Whitley; 16 Curtis Sironen; 13 Morgan Knowles. Subs (all used): 14 Moses Mbye; 15 James Bell; 18 Jake Wingfield; 20 George Delaney.
Tries: Welsby (12), Dodd (19, 59), Percival (35); **Goals:** Percival 1/3, Dodd 1/1.
Dismissal: Percival (44) - shoulder charge on Ormondroyd.
RED DEVILS: 1 Ryan Brierley; 23 Chris Hankinson; 3 Nene Macdonald; 4 Tim Lafai; 5 Deon Cross; 6 Cade Cust; 7 Marc Sneyd; 17 Jack Ormondroyd; 9 Amir Bourouh; 8 Brad Singleton; 11 Sam Stone; 12 Kallum Watkins (C); 16 Joe Shorrocks. Subs (all used): 10 King Vuniyayawa; 14 Chris Atkin; 15 Shane Wright; 18 Ben Hellewell.
Tries: Cross (25, 76), Macdonald (64), Atkin (70); **Goals:** Sneyd 4/4.
Rugby Leaguer & League Express Men of the Match: *Saints:* Lewis Dodd; *Red Devils:* Marc Sneyd.
Penalty count: 7-6; **Half-time:** 14-6;
Referee: Tom Grant; **Attendance:** 11,548.

Saturday 9th March 2024

LONDON BRONCOS 22 WIGAN WARRIORS 60

BRONCOS: 4 Hakim Miloudi; 2 Lee Kershaw; 21 Robbie Storey; 3 Jarred Bassett; 5 Iliess Macani; 20 Oliver Leyland; 7 James Meadows; 19 Rhys Kennedy; 9 Sam Davis; 30 Fenton Rogers; 11 Will Lovell (C); 29 Jacob Jones; 15 Marcus Stock. Subs (all used): 1 Alex Walker; 8 Rob Butler; 16 Jordan Williams; 31 Reiss Butterworth (D).
Tries: Jones (15), Kershaw (38, 70), Williams (42); **Goals:** O Leyland 3/4.
Sin bin: Butler (47) - dangerous challenge.
WARRIORS: 1 Jai Field; 2 Abbas Miski; 3 Adam Keighran; 4 Jake Wardle; 26 Zach Eckersley; 23 Ryan Hampshire; 30 Jack Farrimond (D); 16 Luke Thompson; 9 Brad O'Neill; 19 Tyler Dupree; 11 Willie Isa; 12 Liam Farrell (C); 15 Patrick Mago. Subs (all used): 20 Harvie Hill; 21 Junior Nsemba; 24 Tiaki Chan; 27 Tom Forber.
Tries: Wardle (5), Miski (10), Dupree (18), Hill (28, 72), O'Neill (50), Mago (55), Eckersley (60), Hampshire (65), Keighran (78); **Goals:** Keighran 10/11.
Rugby Leaguer & League Express Men of the Match: *Broncos:* Lee Kershaw; *Warriors:* Tyler Dupree.
Penalty count: 11-5; **Half-time:** 10-22;
Referee: James Vella; **Attendance:** 4,116.

CATALANS DRAGONS 26 HULL FC 12

DRAGONS: 6 Jayden Nikorima; 2 Tom Davies; 21 Matt Ikuvalu; 4 Matthieu Laguerre; 24 Tom Johnstone; 27 Jordan Abdull; 7 Theo Fages; 16 Romain Navarrete; 14 Alrix Da Costa; 10 Julian Bousquet; 11 Tariq Sims; 8 Mike McMeeken; 13 Ben Garcia (C). Subs (all used): 1 Arthur Mourgue; 12 Paul Seguier; 20 Tevita Satae; 23 Jordan Dezaria. 18th man (used): 28 Franck Maria (D).
Tries: Nikorima (1), Laguerre (11), Mourgue (57), Davies (71); **Goals:** Abdull 2/3, Mourgue 3/3.
HULL FC: 31 Jack Walker; 26 Lewis Martin; 5 Darnell McIntosh; 3 Carlos Tuimavave; 41 Matty Russell; 19 Morgan Smith; 7 Fa'amanu Brown; 8 Herman Ese'ese; 9 Danny Houghton (C); 12 Ligi Sao; 11 Jayden Okunbor; 24 Nick Staveley; 15 Jordan Lane. Subs (all used): 1 Tex Hoy; 16 Jack Ashworth; 21 Will Gardiner; 42 Joe Bullock.

Tries: F Brown (17), Walker (47); **Goals:** McIntosh 2/3.
Sin bin: Ashworth (35) - high tackle on Satae.
Rugby Leaguer & League Express Men of the Match:
Dragons: Ben Garcia; *Hull FC:* Fa'amanu Brown.
Penalty count: 8-5; **Half-time:** 14-6;
Referee: Jack Smith; **Attendance:** 9,140.

ROUND 5

Thursday 14th March 2024

SALFORD RED DEVILS 12 WIGAN WARRIORS 22

RED DEVILS: 1 Ryan Brierley; 26 David Nofoaluma (D); 3 Nene Macdonald; 4 Tim Lafai; 5 Deon Cross; 14 Chris Atkin; 7 Marc Sneyd; 20 Andrew Dixon; 9 Amir Bourouh; 10 King Vuniyayawa; 11 Sam Stone; 12 Kallum Watkins (C); 16 Joe Shorrocks. Subs (all used): 2 Ethan Ryan (D); 15 Shane Wright; 21 Matty Foster (D); 27 Gil Dudson (D2).
Tries: Stone (51), Lafai (63); **Goals:** Sneyd 2/2.
WARRIORS: 1 Jai Field; 2 Abbas Miski; 3 Adam Keighran; 4 Jake Wardle; 5 Liam Marshall; 6 Bevan French; 7 Harry Smith; 16 Luke Thompson; 9 Brad O'Neill; 10 Liam Byrne; 11 Willie Isa; 12 Liam Farrell (C); 13 Kaide Ellis. Subs: 15 Patrick Mago; 19 Tyler Dupree; 20 Harvie Hill; 27 Tom Forber (not used).
Tries: Marshall (40), Miski (46), Wardle (76), French (79);
Goals: Smith 1/2, Keighran 2/2.
Sin bin: Smith (71) - obstruction.
Rugby Leaguer & League Express Men of the Match:
Red Devils: Tim Lafai; *Warriors:* Liam Farrell.
Penalty count: 6-7; **Half-time:** 0-4;
Referee: Chris Kendall; **Attendance:** 6,087.

Friday 15th March 2024

LEEDS RHINOS 8 ST HELENS 18

RHINOS: 1 Lachlan Miller; 24 Luis Roberts; 3 Harry Newman; 12 Rhyse Martin; 5 Ash Handley; 6 Brodie Croft; 7 Matt Frawley; 17 Justin Sangare; 9 Andy Ackers; 8 Mikolaj Oledzki; 11 James Bentley; 16 James McDonnell; 13 Cameron Smith (C). Subs (all used): 10 Tom Holroyd; 14 Jarrod O'Connor; 18 Mickael Goudemand; 29 Alfie Edgell.
Try: Roberts (10); **Goals:** Martin 2/2.
SAINTS: 1 Jack Welsby; 3 Waqa Blake; 19 Matt Whitley; 23 Konrad Hurrell; 5 Jon Bennison; 6 Jonny Lomax (C); 7 Lewis Dodd; 8 Alex Walmsley; 9 Daryl Clark; 10 Matty Lees; 11 Sione Mata'utia; 12 Joe Batchelor; 13 Morgan Knowles. Subs (all used): 14 Moses Mbye; 15 James Bell; 18 Jake Wingfield; 20 George Delaney.
Tries: Blake (34), Bennison (57), Mbye (61);
Goals: Lomax 3/3.
Rugby Leaguer & League Express Men of the Match:
Rhinos: Lachlan Miller; *Saints:* James Bell.
Penalty count: 8-4; **Half-time:** 8-6;
Referee: Jack Smith; **Attendance:** 15,284.

Saturday 16th March 2024

HUDDERSFIELD GIANTS 12 HULL KR 24

GIANTS: 1 Jake Connor; 2 Adam Swift; 3 Esan Marsters; 4 Kevin Naiqama; 24 Sam Halsall; 23 Oliver Russell; 7 Adam Clune; 8 Chris Hill; 9 Adam Milner; 18 Sebastine Ikahihifo; 11 Jack Murchie; 12 Sam Hewitt; 21 Leroy Cudjoe. Subs (all used): 6 Tui Lolohea; 13 Luke Yates (C); 16 Harry Rushton; 17 Oliver Wilson.
Tries: Naiqama (66), Swift (76); **Goals:** Connor 2/2.
HULL KR: 2 Niall Evalds; 35 Joe Burgess; 1 Peta Hiku; 4 Oliver Gildart; 5 Ryan Hall; 27 Tyrone May; 7 Mikey Lewis; 8 Sauaso Sue; 9 Jez Litten; 16 Jai Whitbread; 11 Dean Hadley; 12 James Batchelor; 13 Elliot Minchella (C). Subs (all used): 10 George King; 14 Matt Parcell; 15 Sam Luckley; 20 Kelepi Tanginoa.
Tries: Burgess (3), Litten (22), Hiku (44, 53), R Hall (61);
Goals: Litten 2/5, Batchelor 0/1.
Rugby Leaguer & League Express Men of the Match:
Giants: Esan Marsters; *Hull KR:* Niall Evalds.
Penalty count: 4-7; **Half-time:** 0-8;
Referee: Tom Grant; **Attendance:** 5,428.

HULL FC 4 LEIGH LEOPARDS 54

HULL FC: 1 Tex Hoy; 5 Darnell McIntosh; 3 Carlos Tuimavave; 4 Liam Sutcliffe; 2 Liam Tindall (D); 19 Morgan Smith; 7 Fa'amanu Brown; 8 Herman Ese'ese; 9 Danny Houghton (C); 12 Ligi Sao; 11 Jayden Okunbor; 24 Nick Staveley; 15 Jordan Lane. Subs (all used): 10 Franklin Pele; 17 Cameron Scott; 20 Jack Brown; 21 Will Gardiner.
Try: Hoy (11); **Goals:** Hoy 0/1.
Sin bin: Pele (40) - late challenge.
LEOPARDS: 1 Gareth O'Brien; 24 Umyla Hanley; 3 Zak Hardaker; 4 Ricky Leutele; 5 Josh Charnley; 6 Matt Moylan; 21 Ben McNamara (D); 14 Dan Norman; 33 Brad Dwyer; 10 Robbie Mulhern (C); 11 Kai O'Donnell; 16 Frankie Halton; 12 Jack Hughes. Subs (all used): 15 Matt Davis; 17 Owen Trout; 18 Ben Nakubuwai; 20 Oliver Holmes.
Tries: Hanley (4), Charnley (8), Leutele (15, 75), Mulhern (18), McNamara (29), Holmes (49, 53), Moylan (65); **Goals:** Moylan 9/10.
Rugby Leaguer & League Express Men of the Match:
Hull FC: Tex Hoy; *Leopards:* Matt Moylan.
Penalty count: 1-4; **Half-time:** 4-30;
Referee: Aaron Moore; **Attendance:** 10,227.

CATALANS DRAGONS 40 CASTLEFORD TIGERS 14

DRAGONS: 1 Arthur Mourgue; 2 Tom Davies; 21 Matt Ikuvalu; 4 Matthieu Laguerre; 24 Tom Johnstone; 27 Jordan Abdull; 7 Theo Fages; 8 Mike McMeeken; 13 Ben Garcia (C); 16 Romain Navarrete; 11 Tariq Sims; 12 Paul Seguier; 15 Bayley Sironen. Subs (all used): 10 Julian Bousquet; 17 Cesar Rouge; 23 Jordan Dezaria; 28 Franck Maria.
Tries: Mourgue (15), Abdull (20), Johnstone (36), Laguerre (43), Davies (49), Ikuvalu (64), Rouge (68);
Goals: Mourgue 6/7.
TIGERS: 3 Jack Broadbent; 2 Josh Simm; 22 Charbel Tasipale; 4 Sam Wood; 5 Innes Senior; 16 Rowan Milnes; 7 Jacob Miller; 19 Sam Hall; 14 Liam Horne; 10 George Lawler; 25 Brad Martin; 12 Alex Mellor; 13 Joe Westerman (C). Subs (all used): 1 Luke Hooley; 24 Cain Robb; 26 Samy Kibula; 27 Albert Vete.
Tries: Westerman (33), Simm (53, 77); **Goals:** Milnes 1/3.
Rugby Leaguer & League Express Men of the Match:
Dragons: Arthur Mourgue; *Tigers:* Joe Westerman.
Penalty count: 5-4; **Half-time:** 16-6;
Referee: James Vella; **Attendance:** 8,159.

Sunday 17th March 2024

LONDON BRONCOS 4 WARRINGTON WOLVES 58

BRONCOS: 1 Alex Walker; 2 Lee Kershaw; 3 Jarred Bassett; 4 Hakim Miloudi; 5 Iliess Macani; 6 Jack Campagnolo; 7 James Meadows; 8 Rob Butler; 31 Reiss Butterworth; 29 Jacob Jones; 11 Will Lovell (C); 30 Fenton Rogers; 13 Dean Parata. Subs (all used): 19 Rhys Kennedy; 15 Marcus Stock; 16 Jordan Williams; 20 Oliver Leyland.
Try: Miloudi (23); **Goals:** Miloudi 0/1.
WOLVES: 1 Matt Dufty; 2 Josh Thewlis; 3 Toby King; 20 Connor Wrench; 5 Matty Ashton; 4 Stefan Ratchford (C); 18 Leon Hayes; 8 James Harrison; 32 Sam Powell; 10 Paul Vaughan; 28 Adam Holroyd; 15 Joe Philbin; 17 Jordan Crowther. Subs (all used): 16 Zane Musgrove; 19 Joe Bullock; 29 Tom Whitehead; 34 Max Wood.
Tries: Holroyd (5, 12), Josh Thewlis (7, 41, 51), Dufty (30, 45, 64), Harrison (60), Ratchford (71);
Goals: Ratchford 9/10.
Rugby Leaguer & League Express Men of the Match:
Broncos: Hakim Miloudi; *Wolves:* Stefan Ratchford.
Penalty count: 3-2; **Half-time:** 4-24;
Referee: Liam Rush; **Attendance:** 3,324.

ROUND 6

Thursday 28th March 2024

CASTLEFORD TIGERS 6 LEEDS RHINOS 26

TIGERS: 3 Jack Broadbent; 2 Josh Simm; 18 Josh Hodson; 4 Sam Wood; 5 Innes Senior; 6 Danny Richardson; 7 Jacob Miller; 10 George Lawler; 9 Paul McShane; 8 Liam Watts; 11 Elie El-Zakhem; 12 Alex Mellor; 13 Joe Westerman (C). Subs: 14 Liam Horne; 19 Sam Hall; 27 Albert Vete; 30 Luis Johnson (not used).
Try: Simm (71); **Goals:** Richardson 1/2.
RHINOS: 1 Lachlan Miller; 24 Luis Roberts; 3 Harry Newman; 4 Paul Momirovski; 5 Ash Handley; 6 Brodie Croft; 7 Matt Frawley; 8 Mikolaj Oledzki; 9 Andy Ackers; 17 Justin Sangare; 11 James Bentley; 12 Rhyse Martin; 13 Cameron Smith (C). Subs (all used): 14 Jarrod O'Connor; 15 Sam Lisone; 16 James McDonnell; 18 Mickael Goudemand.
Tries: Momirovski (42, 52), Miller (66, 74);
Goals: Martin 5/5.
Rugby Leaguer & League Express Men of the Match:
Tigers: Joe Westerman; *Rhinos:* Lachlan Miller.
Penalty count: 4-6; **Half-time:** 0-0;
Referee: Aaron Moore; **Attendance:** 9,026.

Friday 29th March 2024

HULL KR 34 HULL FC 10

HULL KR: 2 Niall Evalds; 35 Joe Burgess; 1 Peta Hiku; 3 Tom Opacic; 5 Ryan Hall; 27 Tyrone May; 7 Mikey Lewis; 8 Sauaso Sue; 9 Jez Litten; 16 Jai Whitbread; 11 Dean Hadley; 12 James Batchelor; 13 Elliot Minchella (C). Subs (all used): 14 Matt Parcell; 15 Sam Luckley; 17 Matty Storton; 20 Kelepi Tanginoa.
Tries: Evalds (13), Burgess (16, 40), Lewis (20), Batchelor (28), Hiku (36), Tanginoa (70);
Goals: Litten 2/6, Lewis 1/1.
HULL FC: 1 Tex Hoy; 5 Darnell McIntosh; 17 Cameron Scott; 4 Liam Sutcliffe; 26 Lewis Martin; 19 Morgan Smith; 7 Fa'amanu Brown; 8 Herman Ese'ese; 9 Danny Houghton (C); 16 Jack Ashworth; 11 Jayden Okunbor; 12 Ligi Sao; 15 Jordan Lane. Subs (all used): 10 Franklin Pele; 20 Jack Brown; 21 Will Gardiner; 40 Jack Charles.
Tries: Okunbor (50), Scott (53); **Goals:** McIntosh 1/2.
Rugby Leaguer & League Express Men of the Match:
Hull KR: Tyrone May; *Hull FC:* Ligi Sao.
Penalty count: 6-2; **Half-time:** 28-0;
Referee: Liam Moore; **Attendance:** 11,050.

ST HELENS 12 WIGAN WARRIORS 4

SAINTS: 1 Jack Welsby; 2 Tommy Makinson; 23 Konrad Hurrell; 4 Mark Percival; 5 Jon Bennison; 6 Jonny Lomax (C); 7 Lewis Dodd; 8 Alex Walmsley; 9 Daryl Clark; 10 Matty Lees; 19 Matt Whitley; 16 Curtis Sironen; 13 Morgan Knowles. Subs (all used): 11 Sione Mata'utia; 12 Joe Batchelor; 14 Moses Mbye; 18 Jake Wingfield.
Tries: Makinson (73), Hurrell (79);
Goals: Percival 1/1, Lomax 1/2.
WARRIORS: 1 Jai Field; 2 Abbas Miski; 3 Adam Keighran; 4 Jake Wardle; 5 Liam Marshall; 6 Bevan French; 7 Harry Smith; 10 Liam Byrne; 9 Brad O'Neill; 16 Luke Thompson; 11 Willie Isa; 12 Liam Farrell (C); 13 Kaide Ellis. Subs: 15 Patrick Mago; 17 Kruise Leeming; 19 Tyler Dupree; 21 Junior Nsemba (not used).
Try: French (56); **Goals:** Smith 0/1.
Dismissal: Byrne (63) - high tackle on Percival.
Sin bin: Dupree (29) - use of the elbow on Lees.
Rugby Leaguer & League Express Men of the Match:
Saints: Alex Walmsley; *Warriors:* Brad O'Neill.
Penalty count: 8-5; **Half-time:** 2-0;
Referee: Chris Kendall; **Attendance:** 17,980.

Saturday 30th March 2024

WARRINGTON WOLVES 24 CATALANS DRAGONS 32

WOLVES: 1 Matt Dufty; 2 Josh Thewlis; 3 Toby King; 14 Rodrick Tai; 5 Matty Ashton; 6 George Williams (C); 18 Leon Hayes; 8 James Harrison; 9 Danny Walker; 10 Paul Vaughan; 28 Adam Holroyd; 12 Lachlan Fitzgibbon; 11 Ben Currie. Subs (all used): 15 Joe Philbin; 16 Zane Musgrove; 17 Jordan Crowther; 32 Sam Powell. 18th man (used): 13 Matty Nicholson.
Tries: Musgrove (27), King (33), Harrison (53), Williams (58); **Goals:** Josh Thewlis 4/4.
Sin bin: Vaughan (11) - dangerous challenge on Rouge.
DRAGONS: 17 Cesar Rouge; 2 Tom Davies; 3 Arthur Romano; 21 Matt Ikuvalu; 24 Tom Johnstone; 27 Jordan Abdull; 18 Ugo Tison; 16 Romain Navarrete; 9 Michael McIlorum; 10 Julian Bousquet; 11 Tariq Sims; 8 Mike McMeeken; 13 Ben Garcia (C). Subs (all used): 12 Paul Seguier; 15 Bayley Sironen; 20 Tevita Satae; 23 Jordan Dezaria.
Tries: Davies (4), Johnstone (7, 50), Garcia (12), Rouge (45), Abdull (79); **Goals:** Abdull 4/6.
Rugby Leaguer & League Express Men of the Match:
Wolves: George Williams; *Dragons:* Jordan Abdull.
Penalty count: 6-5; **Half-time:** 12-18;
Referee: Jack Smith; **Attendance:** 11,240.

SALFORD RED DEVILS 32 LEIGH LEOPARDS 22

RED DEVILS: 1 Ryan Brierley; 2 Ethan Ryan; 3 Nene Macdonald; 4 Tim Lafai; 5 Deon Cross; 6 Cade Cust; 7 Marc Sneyd; 17 Jack Ormondroyd; 24 Joe Mellor (D); 15 Shane Wright; 11 Sam Stone; 12 Kallum Watkins (C); 13 Oliver Partington. Subs (all used): 9 Amir Bourouh; 10 King Vuniyayawa; 14 Chris Atkin; 16 Joe Shorrocks.
Tries: Brierley (13, 32), Ryan (36, 74), Sneyd (56);
Goals: Sneyd 6/6.
Sin bin: Brierley (39) - obstruction.
LEOPARDS: 1 Gareth O'Brien; 24 Umyla Hanley; 3 Zak Hardaker; 19 Ed Chamberlain; 5 Josh Charnley; 6 Matt Moylan; 7 Lachlan Lam; 14 Dan Norman; 33 Brad Dwyer; 10 Robbie Mulhern (C); 11 Kai O'Donnell; 12 Jack Hughes; 17 Owen Trout. Subs (all used): 15 Matt Davis; 18 Ben Nakubuwai; 21 Ben McNamara; 29 Lewis Baxter (D).
Tries: Hanley (28, 69, 76), Lam (61); **Goals:** Moylan 3/5.
Sin bin: Lam (7) - obstruction.
Rugby Leaguer & League Express Men of the Match:
Red Devils: Marc Sneyd; *Leopards:* Umyla Hanley.
Penalty count: 5-4; **Half-time:** 20-6;
Referee: James Vella; **Attendance:** 6,177.

Sunday 31st March 2024

LONDON BRONCOS 6 HUDDERSFIELD GIANTS 26

BRONCOS: 1 Alex Walker; 2 Lee Kershaw; 21 Robbie Storey; 3 Jarred Bassett; 5 Iliess Macani; 20 Oliver Leyland; 7 James Meadows; 19 Rhys Kennedy; 9 Sam Davis; 15 Marcus Stock; 11 Will Lovell (C); 29 Jacob Jones; 13 Dean Parata. Subs (all used): 8 Rob Butler; 16 Jordan Williams; 31 Reiss Butterworth; 33 Harvey Makin (D2).
Try: O Leyland (11, pen); **Goals:** O Leyland 1/1.

GIANTS: 3 Esan Marsters; 24 Sam Halsall; 5 Jake Bibby; 4 Kevin Naiqama; 2 Adam Swift; 6 Tui Lolohea; 7 Adam Clune; 13 Luke Yates (C); 19 Thomas Deakin (D); 17 Oliver Wilson; 11 Jack Murchie; 22 Harvey Livett; 21 Leroy Cudjoe. Subs (all used): 10 Joe Greenwood; 14 Ashton Golding; 16 Harry Rushton; 18 Sebastine Ikahihifo.
Tries: Jake Bibby (23), Marsters (28), Swift (36), Clune (45), Halsall (61); **Goals:** Livett 0/3, Lolohea 3/3.
Rugby Leaguer & League Express Men of the Match: *Broncos:* Lee Kershaw; *Giants:* Tui Lolohea.
Penalty count: 6-9; **Half-time:** 6-12;
Referee: Tom Grant; **Attendance:** 2,300.

ROUND 7

Thursday 4th April 2024

LEIGH LEOPARDS 12 WIGAN WARRIORS 40

LEOPARDS: 1 Gareth O'Brien; 24 Umyla Hanley; 3 Zak Hardaker; 4 Ricky Leutele; 5 Josh Charnley; 6 Matt Moylan; 7 Lachlan Lam (C); 14 Dan Norman; 21 Ben McNamara; 17 Owen Trout; 11 Kai O'Donnell; 16 Frankie Halton; 12 Jack Hughes. Subs (all used): 15 Matt Davis; 18 Ben Nakubuwai; 19 Ed Chamberlain; 33 Brad Dwyer.
Tries: Leutele (33), Charnley (61); **Goals:** Moylan 2/3.
Sin bin: Moylan (12) - high tackle.
WARRIORS: 1 Jai Field; 2 Abbas Miski; 3 Adam Keighran; 4 Jake Wardle; 5 Liam Marshall; 6 Bevan French; 7 Harry Smith; 16 Luke Thompson; 9 Brad O'Neill; 20 Harvie Hill; 11 Willie Isa; 12 Liam Farrell (C); 13 Kaide Ellis. Subs (all used): 15 Patrick Mago; 17 Kruise Leeming; 21 Junior Nsemba; 24 Tiaki Chan.
Tries: Miski (7), Isa (17), French (26), Smith (29), Field (46), Keighran (52), Nsemba (57), Marshall (66);
Goals: Smith 4/8.
Rugby Leaguer & League Express Men of the Match: *Leopards:* Josh Charnley; *Warriors:* Bevan French.
Penalty count: 7-4; **Half-time:** 6-20;
Referee: Jack Smith; **Attendance:** 10,308.

Friday 5th April 2024

CASTLEFORD TIGERS 36 SALFORD RED DEVILS 24

TIGERS: 3 Jack Broadbent; 2 Josh Simm; 18 Josh Hodson; 4 Sam Wood; 5 Innes Senior; 6 Danny Richardson; 7 Jacob Miller; 19 Sam Hall; 14 Liam Horne; 8 Liam Watts; 12 Alex Mellor; 11 Elie El-Zakhem; 13 Joe Westerman (C). Subs (all used): 21 Sylvester Namo; 24 Cain Robb; 25 Brad Martin; 26 Samy Kibula.
Tries: I Senior (15, 31, 57, 77), S Hall (25), Martin (60);
Goals: Richardson 6/7.
RED DEVILS: 1 Ryan Brierley; 26 David Nofoaluma; 3 Nene Macdonald; 4 Tim Lafai; 5 Deon Cross; 6 Cade Cust; 7 Marc Sneyd; 17 Jack Ormondroyd; 9 Amir Bourouh; 15 Shane Wright; 11 Sam Stone; 12 Kallum Watkins (C); 13 Oliver Partington. Subs (all used): 10 King Vuniyayawa; 14 Chris Atkin; 16 Joe Shorrocks; 24 Joe Mellor.
Tries: Brierley (11, 48), Lafai (38), Macdonald (44);
Goals: Sneyd 4/5.
Sin bin: Bourouh (23) - dangerous challenge on Mellor.
Rugby Leaguer & League Express Men of the Match: *Tigers:* Innes Senior; *Red Devils:* Tim Lafai.
Penalty count: 7-6; **Half-time:** 18-14;
Referee: Chris Kendall; **Attendance:** 7,967.

HULL KR 50 LONDON BRONCOS 10

HULL KR: 2 Niall Evalds; 23 Louis Senior; 1 Peta Hiku; 3 Tom Opacic; 5 Ryan Hall; 7 Mikey Lewis; 27 Tyrone May; 8 Sauaso Sue; 14 Matt Parcell; 15 Sam Luckley; 20 Kelepi Tanginoa; 12 James Batchelor; 13 Elliot Minchella (C). Subs (all used): 16 Jai Whitbread; 17 Matty Storton; 18 Ben Reynolds (D); 21 Corey Hall.
Tries: Parcell (8, 34, 78), Batchelor (19, 51), Tanginoa (24), R Hall (30), Lewis (32), Hiku (38); **Goals:** Lewis 7/9.
Sin bin: Luckley (2) - dangerous challenge.
BRONCOS: 1 Alex Walker; 22 Gideon Boafo; 21 Robbie Storey; 4 Hakim Miloudi; 5 Iliess Macani; 20 Oliver Leyland; 7 James Meadows; 19 Rhys Kennedy; 9 Sam Davis; 15 Marcus Stock; 11 Will Lovell (C); 29 Jacob Jones; 13 Dean Parata. Subs (all used): 8 Rob Butler; 27 Daniel Hoyes; 28 Jack Hughes; 33 Harvey Makin.
Tries: Davis (5), Macani (59); **Goals:** O Leyland 1/2.
Rugby Leaguer & League Express Men of the Match: *Hull KR:* Matt Parcell; *Broncos:* Sam Davis.
Penalty count: 0-3; **Half-time:** 40-4;
Referee: Liam Rush; **Attendance:** 10,201.

LEEDS RHINOS 8 WARRINGTON WOLVES 34

RHINOS: 1 Lachlan Miller; 24 Luis Roberts; 3 Harry Newman; 4 Paul Momirovski; 5 Ash Handley; 6 Brodie Croft; 7 Matt Frawley; 8 Mikolaj Oledzki; 9 Andy Ackers; 10 Tom Holroyd; 16 James McDonnell; 12 Rhyse Martin; 13 Cameron Smith (C). Subs (all used): 14 Jarrod O'Connor; 15 Sam Lisone; 18 Mickael Goudemand; 31 Ned McCormack (D).
Tries: Newman (9), Roberts (42);
Goals: Martin 0/1, Miller 0/1.
WOLVES: 1 Matt Dufty; 2 Josh Thewlis; 20 Connor Wrench; 4 Stefan Ratchford (C); 5 Matty Ashton; 6 George Williams; 18 Leon Hayes; 8 James Harrison; 9 Danny Walker; 17 Jordan Crowther; 13 Matty Nicholson; 12 Lachlan Fitzgibbon; 11 Ben Currie. Subs (all used): 19 Joe Bullock; 28 Adam Holroyd; 32 Sam Powell; 34 Max Wood.
Tries: Nicholson (18), Williams (30), Bullock (37), Walker (65), Dufty (75), Josh Thewlis (77);
Goals: Ratchford 5/6.
Rugby Leaguer & League Express Men of the Match: *Rhinos:* Mikolaj Oledzki; *Wolves:* Ben Currie.
Penalty count: 4-4; **Half-time:** 4-16;
Referee: Aaron Moore; **Attendance:** 12,297.

Saturday 6th April 2024

HULL FC 22 HUDDERSFIELD GIANTS 56

HULL FC: 1 Tex Hoy; 5 Darnell McIntosh; 17 Cameron Scott; 4 Liam Sutcliffe; 26 Lewis Martin; 40 Jack Charles; 19 Morgan Smith; 8 Herman Ese'ese; 7 Fa'amanu Brown; 10 Franklin Pele; 11 Jayden Okunbor; 12 Ligi Sao; 15 Jordan Lane (C). Subs (all used): 14 Joe Cator; 20 Jack Brown; 30 Matty Laidlaw; 37 Logan Moy (D).
Tries: Sutcliffe (9, 24), F Brown (46), Pele (74);
Goals: Charles 3/4.
Sin bin: J Brown (38) - dangerous challenge; Sao (60) - late challenge, (78) - high tackle.
GIANTS: 1 Jake Connor; 5 Jake Bibby; 3 Esan Marsters; 4 Kevin Naiqama; 2 Adam Swift; 6 Tui Lolohea; 7 Adam Clune; 15 Matty English; 9 Adam Milner; 17 Oliver Wilson; 11 Jack Murchie; 21 Leroy Cudjoe; 13 Luke Yates (C). Subs (all used): 14 Ashton Golding; 16 Harry Rushton; 18 Sebastine Ikahihifo; 26 Hugo Salabio.
Tries: Swift (1, 15, 32), Murchie (20), Marsters (29), Yates (36), Naiqama (39), Lolohea (49, 64), Jake Bibby (79); **Goals:** Connor 7/9, Lolohea 1/1.
Rugby Leaguer & League Express Men of the Match: *Hull FC:* Jack Charles; *Giants:* Adam Swift.
Penalty count: 4-7; **Half-time:** 10-40;
Referee: Tom Grant; **Attendance:** 9,631.

CATALANS DRAGONS 14 ST HELENS 8

DRAGONS: 1 Arthur Mourgue; 2 Tom Davies; 3 Arthur Romano; 21 Matt Ikuvalu; 24 Tom Johnstone; 27 Jordan Abdull; 7 Theo Fages; 8 Mike McMeeken; 14 Alrix Da Costa; 16 Romain Navarrete; 11 Tariq Sims; 12 Paul Seguier; 13 Ben Garcia (C). Subs (all used): 4 Matthieu Laguerre; 17 Cesar Rouge; 20 Tevita Satae; 28 Franck Maria.
Tries: McMeeken (31), Ikuvalu (65); **Goals:** Mourgue 3/3.
SAINTS: 1 Jack Welsby; 2 Tommy Makinson; 11 Sione Mata'utia; 23 Konrad Hurrell; 5 Jon Bennison; 6 Jonny Lomax (C); 7 Lewis Dodd; 8 Alex Walmsley; 9 Daryl Clark; 20 George Delaney; 19 Matt Whitley; 16 Curtis Sironen; 13 Morgan Knowles. Subs (all used): 12 Joe Batchelor; 14 Moses Mbye; 15 James Bell; 18 Jake Wingfield.
Tries: Welsby (19), Makinson (38); **Goals:** Lomax 0/2.
Rugby Leaguer & League Express Men of the Match: *Dragons:* Ben Garcia; *Saints:* Lewis Dodd.
Penalty count: 6-3; **Half-time:** 6-8;
Referee: Liam Moore; **Attendance:** 10,724.

ROUND 8

Friday 19th April 2024

LEEDS RHINOS 24 HUDDERSFIELD GIANTS 30

RHINOS: 1 Lachlan Miller; 2 David Fusitu'a; 3 Harry Newman; 4 Paul Momirovski; 24 Luis Roberts; 6 Brodie Croft; 7 Matt Frawley; 8 Mikolaj Oledzki; 9 Andy Ackers; 17 Justin Sangare; 16 James McDonnell; 12 Rhyse Martin; 13 Cameron Smith (C). Subs (all used): 14 Jarrod O'Connor; 15 Sam Lisone; 18 Mickael Goudemand; 30 Tom Nicholson-Watton.
Tries: Momirovski (16, 51), Fusitu'a (31), O'Connor (55);
Goals: Martin 4/4.
Sin bin: Miller (79) - dissent.
GIANTS: 1 Jake Connor; 2 Adam Swift; 3 Esan Marsters; 4 Kevin Naiqama; 20 Elliot Wallis; 6 Tui Lolohea; 7 Adam Clune; 15 Matty English; 9 Adam Milner; 10 Joe Greenwood; 21 Leroy Cudjoe; 22 Harvey Livett; 13 Luke Yates (C). Subs (all used): 14 Ashton Golding; 16 Harry Rushton; 17 Oliver Wilson; 18 Sebastine Ikahihifo.
Tries: Marsters (45), Wallis (47), Swift (64), Livett (66), Naiqama (70), Clune (77); **Goals:** Connor 3/8.
Sin bin: Yates (29) - high tackle on Roberts.
Rugby Leaguer & League Express Men of the Match: *Rhinos:* Rhyse Martin; *Giants:* Esan Marsters.
Penalty count: 4-5; **Half-time:** 12-2;
Referee: Chris Kendall; **Attendance:** 13,128.

ST HELENS 58 HULL FC 0

SAINTS: 5 Jon Bennison; 2 Tommy Makinson; 23 Konrad Hurrell; 4 Mark Percival; 3 Waqa Blake; 1 Jack Welsby; 6 Jonny Lomax (C); 11 Sione Mata'utia; 14 Moses Mbye; 10 Matty Lees; 19 Matt Whitley; 12 Joe Batchelor; 13 Morgan Knowles. Subs (all used): 15 James Bell; 16 Curtis Sironen; 20 George Delaney; 21 Ben Davies.
Tries: Makinson (4), Lomax (15), Blake (27, 68), Bell (33), Batchelor (43), Percival (48), Hurrell (52), Sironen (58), Welsby (79); **Goals:** Percival 6/7, Bennison 3/3.
HULL FC: 37 Logan Moy; 5 Darnell McIntosh; 23 Davy Litten; 4 Liam Sutcliffe; 26 Lewis Martin; 40 Jack Charles; 19 Morgan Smith; 8 Herman Ese'ese; 9 Danny Houghton (C); 10 Franklin Pele; 15 Jordan Lane; 17 Cameron Scott; 14 Joe Cator. Subs (all used): 21 Will Gardiner; 27 Zach Jebson; 28 Denive Balmforth; 30 Matty Laidlaw.
Rugby Leaguer & League Express Men of the Match: *Saints:* Jonny Lomax; *Hull FC:* Logan Moy.
Penalty count: 8-2; **Half-time:** 24-0;
Referee: Tom Grant; **Attendance:** 10,488.

WIGAN WARRIORS 36 CASTLEFORD TIGERS 14

WARRIORS: 6 Bevan French; 2 Abbas Miski; 3 Adam Keighran; 4 Jake Wardle; 5 Liam Marshall; 23 Ryan Hampshire; 7 Harry Smith; 16 Luke Thompson; 17 Kruise Leeming; 19 Tyler Dupree; 21 Junior Nsemba; 12 Liam Farrell (C); 13 Kaide Ellis. Subs (all used): 14 Mike Cooper; 15 Patrick Mago; 20 Harvie Hill; 26 Zach Eckersley.
Tries: French (8), Marshall (35, 58), Hampshire (44, 49), Miski (73); **Goals:** Keighran 2/2, Smith 4/4.
TIGERS: 3 Jack Broadbent; 33 Louis Senior (D); 18 Josh Hodson; 4 Sam Wood; 5 Innes Senior; 16 Rowan Milnes; 7 Jacob Miller; 8 Liam Watts (C); 14 Liam Horne; 19 Sam Hall; 22 Charbel Tasipale; 11 Elie El-Zakhem; 29 George Hill (D). Subs (all used): 24 Cain Robb; 25 Brad Martin; 26 Samy Kibula; 32 Dan Hindmarsh.
Tries: L Senior (19), Milnes (79); **Goals:** Milnes 3/3.
Rugby Leaguer & League Express Men of the Match: *Warriors:* Bevan French; *Tigers:* Rowan Milnes.
Penalty count: 7-4; **Half-time:** 12-8;
Referee: James Vella; **Attendance:** 13,029.

Saturday 20th April 2024

LONDON BRONCOS 4 SALFORD RED DEVILS 12

BRONCOS: 1 Alex Walker; 2 Lee Kershaw; 21 Robbie Storey; 4 Hakim Miloudi; 5 Iliess Macani; 20 Oliver Leyland; 7 James Meadows; 8 Rob Butler; 9 Sam Davis; 19 Rhys Kennedy; 11 Will Lovell (C); 29 Jacob Jones; 15 Marcus Stock. Subs (all used): 13 Dean Parata; 16 Jordan Williams; 33 Harvey Makin; 34 Ugo Tison (D).
Try: Macani (19); **Goals:** O Leyland 0/1.
Sin bin: Lovell (49) - dangerous challenge on Lafai.
RED DEVILS: 1 Ryan Brierley; 2 Ethan Ryan; 3 Nene Macdonald; 4 Tim Lafai; 5 Deon Cross; 6 Cade Cust; 7 Marc Sneyd; 17 Jack Ormondroyd; 24 Joe Mellor; 10 King Vuniyawa; 15 Shane Wright; 12 Kallum Watkins (C); 13 Oliver Partington. Subs (all used): 14 Chris Atkin; 16 Joe Shorrocks; 20 Andrew Dixon; 27 Gil Dudson.
Tries: Watkins (25), Cross (43); **Goals:** Sneyd 2/2.
Dismissal:
Vuniyayawa (56) - dangerous challenge on Stock.
Rugby Leaguer & League Express Men of the Match: *Broncos:* Marcus Stock; *Red Devils:* Ryan Brierley.
Penalty count: 7-5; **Half-time:** 4-6;
Referee: Aaron Moore; **Attendance:** 2,450.

WARRINGTON WOLVES 16 LEIGH LEOPARDS 14

WOLVES: 1 Matt Dufty; 2 Josh Thewlis; 20 Connor Wrench; 3 Toby King; 5 Matty Ashton; 6 George Williams; 18 Leon Hayes; 8 James Harrison; 9 Danny Walker; 15 Joe Philbin; 13 Matty Nicholson; 12 Lachlan Fitzgibbon; 17 Jordan Crowther. Subs (all used): 4 Stefan Ratchford (C); 10 Paul Vaughan; 19 Joe Bullock; 32 Sam Powell.
Tries: Fitzgibbon (20), Dufty (64), Nicholson (70);
Goals: Josh Thewlis 2/3.
LEOPARDS: 6 Matt Moylan; 24 Umyla Hanley; 3 Zak Hardaker; 4 Ricky Leutele; 5 Josh Charnley; 21 Ben McNamara; 7 Lachlan Lam (C); 8 Tom Amone; 15 Matt Davis; 10 Robbie Mulhern; 16 Frankie Halton; 11 Kai O'Donnell; 17 Owen Trout. Subs (all used): 12 Jack Hughes; 14 Dan Norman; 20 Oliver Holmes; 33 Brad Dwyer.
Tries: Charnley (3), McNamara (33), Leutele (49);
Goals: Moylan 1/3.
Rugby Leaguer & League Express Men of the Match: *Wolves:* Lachlan Fitzgibbon; *Leopards:* Tom Amone.
Penalty count: 5-3; **Half-time:** 6-10;
Referee: Liam Moore; **Attendance:** 10,443.

CATALANS DRAGONS 36 HULL KR 6

DRAGONS: 1 Arthur Mourgue; 2 Tom Davies; 3 Arthur Romano; 21 Matt Ikuvalu; 24 Tom Johnstone; 17 Cesar Rouge; 7 Theo Fages; 16 Romain Navarrete; 9 Michael McIlorum; 10 Julian Bousquet; 11 Tariq Sims; 8 Mike McMeeken; 13 Ben Garcia (C). Subs (all used): 6 Jayden Nikorima; 15 Bayley Sironen; 20 Tevita Satae; 23 Jordan Dezaria.
Tries: McIlorum (7), Ikuvalu (18), Davies (26), Dezaria (31), Fages (33), Johnstone (70), Sims (76); **Goals:** Mourgue 4/7.
HULL KR: 2 Niall Evalds; 35 Joe Burgess; 3 Tom Opacic; 1 Peta Hiku; 5 Ryan Hall; 27 Tyrone May; 18 Ben Reynolds; 16 Jai Whitbread; 9 Jez Litten; 10 George King; 11 Dean Hadley; 12 James Batchelor; 13 Elliot Minchella (C). Subs (all used): 14 Matt Parcell; 15 Sam Luckley; 17 Matty Storton; 20 Kelepi Tanginoa.
Try: Burgess (11); **Goals:** Reynolds 1/1.
Sin bin: Storton (56) - dangerous challenge.
Rugby Leaguer & League Express Men of the Match: *Dragons:* Michael McIlorum; *Hull KR:* Ben Reynolds.
Penalty count: 6-6; **Half-time:** 26-6;
Referee: Jack Smith; **Attendance:** 8,783.

ROUND 9

Thursday 25th April 2024

ST HELENS 13 HUDDERSFIELD GIANTS 12

SAINTS: 5 Jon Bennison; 2 Tommy Makinson; 23 Konrad Hurrell; 4 Mark Percival; 3 Waqa Blake; 1 Jack Welsby; 6 Jonny Lomax (C); 11 Sione Mata'utia; 14 Moses Mbye; 10 Matty Lees; 19 Matt Whitley; 12 Joe Batchelor; 13 Morgan Knowles. Subs (all used): 9 Daryl Clark; 15 James Bell; 16 Curtis Sironen; 20 George Delaney.
Tries: Makinson (27), Clark (62); **Goals:** Percival 2/2; **Field goal:** Lomax (80).
GIANTS: 1 Jake Connor; 2 Adam Swift; 5 Jake Bibby; 4 Kevin Naiqama; 20 Elliot Wallis; 6 Tui Lolohea; 7 Adam Clune; 17 Oliver Wilson; 9 Adam Milner; 10 Joe Greenwood; 16 Harry Rushton; 21 Leroy Cudjoe; 13 Luke Yates (C). Subs (all used): 14 Ashton Golding; 15 Matty English; 18 Sebastine Ikahihifo; 24 Sam Halsall.
Tries: Naiqama (5), Swift (12); **Goals:** Connor 2/2.
Rugby Leaguer & League Express Men of the Match: *Saints:* Daryl Clark; *Giants:* Adam Swift.
Penalty count: 3-4; **Half-time:** 6-12;
Referee: Liam Moore; **Attendance:** 9,888.

Friday 26th April 2024

CASTLEFORD TIGERS 40 LONDON BRONCOS 0

TIGERS: 34 Tex Hoy (D); 33 Louis Senior; 35 Corey Hall (D); 4 Sam Wood; 5 Innes Senior; 16 Rowan Milnes; 7 Jacob Miller; 8 Liam Watts; 9 Paul McShane (C); 13 Joe Westerman; 12 Alex Mellor; 11 Elie El-Zakhem; 29 George Hill. Subs (all used): 14 Liam Horne; 19 Sam Hall; 24 Cain Robb; 25 Brad Martin.
Tries: Miller (2), Milnes (25), McShane (28), Mellor (31), I Senior (36, 43), L Senior (50); **Goals:** Milnes 6/7.
BRONCOS: 1 Alex Walker; 2 Lee Kershaw; 21 Robbie Storey; 3 Jarred Bassett; 4 Hakim Miloudi; 20 Oliver Leyland; 7 James Meadows; 19 Rhys Kennedy; 9 Sam Davis; 15 Marcus Stock; 11 Will Lovell (C); 29 Jacob Jones; 13 Dean Parata. Subs (all used): 16 Jordan Williams; 17 Sadiq Adebiyi; 33 Harvey Makin; 34 Ugo Tison.
Rugby Leaguer & League Express Men of the Match: *Tigers:* Rowan Milnes; *Broncos:* Oliver Leyland.
Penalty count: 5-6; **Half-time:** 30-0;
Referee: Jack Smith; **Attendance:** 6,996.

HULL KR 26 WIGAN WARRIORS 10

HULL KR: 2 Niall Evalds; 35 Joe Burgess; 1 Peta Hiku; 4 Oliver Gildart; 5 Ryan Hall; 27 Tyrone May; 7 Mikey Lewis; 8 Sauaso Sue; 9 Jez Litten; 16 Jai Whitbread; 11 Dean Hadley; 12 James Batchelor; 13 Elliot Minchella (C). Subs (all used): 14 Matt Parcell; 15 Sam Luckley; 17 Matty Storton; 20 Kelepi Tanginoa.
Tries: Sue (6), Gildart (12), Hiku (30), R Hall (61), Tanginoa (69); **Goals:** Lewis 3/6.
WARRIORS: 1 Jai Field; 2 Abbas Miski; 3 Adam Keighran; 4 Jake Wardle; 5 Liam Marshall; 6 Bevan French; 7 Harry Smith; 16 Luke Thompson; 9 Brad O'Neill; 19 Tyler Dupree; 21 Junior Nsemba; 12 Liam Farrell (C); 13 Kaide Ellis. Subs (all used): 8 Ethan Havard; 14 Mike Cooper; 15 Patrick Mago; 17 Kruise Leeming.
Tries: Miski (54), Farrell (76); **Goals:** Keighran 1/2.
Rugby Leaguer & League Express Men of the Match: *Hull KR:* Kelepi Tanginoa; *Warriors:* Kruise Leeming.
Penalty count: 4-3; **Half-time:** 18-0;
Referee: Tom Grant; **Attendance:** 9,945.

LEIGH LEOPARDS 30 CATALANS DRAGONS 2

LEOPARDS: 6 Matt Moylan; 24 Umyla Hanley; 3 Zak Hardaker; 4 Ricky Leutele; 5 Josh Charnley; 21 Ben McNamara; 7 Lachlan Lam; 8 Tom Amone; 15 Matt Davis; 17 Owen Trout; 11 Kai O'Donnell; 16 Frankie Halton; 12 Jack Hughes. Subs (all used): 13 John Asiata (C); 14 Dan Norman; 20 Oliver Holmes; 33 Brad Dwyer.
Tries: Charnley (26), O'Donnell (46, 64), Hanley (50), Moylan (73); **Goals:** Moylan 5/5.
DRAGONS: 1 Arthur Mourgue; 2 Tom Davies; 21 Matt Ikuvalu; 3 Arthur Romano; 24 Tom Johnstone; 17 Cesar Rouge; 7 Theo Fages; 12 Paul Seguier; 14 Alrix Da Costa; 16 Romain Navarrete; 11 Tariq Sims; 15 Bayley Sironen; 13 Ben Garcia (C). Subs (all used): 4 Matthieu Laguerre; 6 Jayden Nikorima; 20 Tevita Satae; 28 Franck Maria.
Goals: Mourgue 1/1.
Rugby Leaguer & League Express Men of the Match: *Leopards:* Tom Amone; *Dragons:* Tevita Satae.
Penalty count: 3-7; **Half-time:** 6-2;
Referee: Aaron Moore; **Attendance:** 7,321.

Saturday 27th April 2024

SALFORD RED DEVILS 17 WARRINGTON WOLVES 12

RED DEVILS: 1 Ryan Brierley; 2 Ethan Ryan; 3 Nene Macdonald; 4 Tim Lafai; 5 Deon Cross; 14 Chris Atkin; 7 Marc Sneyd; 17 Jack Ormondroyd; 24 Joe Mellor; 10 King Vuniyayawa; 15 Shane Wright; 12 Kallum Watkins (C); 13 Oliver Partington. Subs (all used): 6 Cade Cust; 16 Joe Shorrocks; 20 Andrew Dixon; 27 Gil Dudson.
Tries: Lafai (10), Mellor (30), Brierley (72); **Goals:** Sneyd 2/4; **Field goal:** Sneyd (39).
WOLVES: 1 Matt Dufty; 2 Josh Thewlis; 4 Stefan Ratchford (C); 3 Toby King; 24 Matty Russell; 6 George Williams; 18 Leon Hayes; 8 James Harrison; 9 Danny Walker; 10 Paul Vaughan; 12 Lachlan Fitzgibbon; 13 Matty Nicholson; 11 Ben Currie. Subs (all used): 15 Joe Philbin; 17 Jordan Crowther; 19 Joe Bullock; 32 Sam Powell.
Tries: Harrison (16), Williams (27); **Goals:** Ratchford 2/3.
Rugby Leaguer & League Express Men of the Match: *Red Devils:* Ryan Brierley; *Wolves:* Danny Walker.
Penalty count: 7-7; **Half-time:** 11-10;
Referee: James Vella; **Attendance:** 5,910.

Sunday 28th April 2024

HULL FC 12 LEEDS RHINOS 18

HULL FC: 31 Jack Walker; 26 Lewis Martin; 43 Ed Chamberlain (D); 4 Liam Sutcliffe; 2 Liam Tindall; 19 Morgan Smith; 40 Jack Charles; 8 Herman Ese'ese; 9 Danny Houghton (C); 20 Jack Brown; 15 Jordan Lane; 12 Ligi Sao; 14 Joe Cator. Subs (all used): 10 Franklin Pele; 21 Will Gardiner; 37 Logan Moy; 45 Yusuf Aydin (D).
Tries: Smith (7), Martin (54); **Goals:** Charles 2/2.
RHINOS: 1 Lachlan Miller; 33 Riley Lumb (D); 4 Paul Momirovski; 12 Rhyse Martin; 24 Luis Roberts; 6 Brodie Croft; 7 Matt Frawley; 8 Mikolaj Oledzki; 9 Andy Ackers; 17 Justin Sangare; 16 James McDonnell; 18 Mickael Goudemand; 13 Cameron Smith (C). Subs (all used): 14 Jarrod O'Connor; 15 Sam Lisone; 23 Leon Ruan; 29 Alfie Edgell.
Tries: Lumb (12, 35), Smith (52); **Goals:** Martin 3/3.
Rugby Leaguer & League Express Men of the Match: *Hull FC:* Herman Ese'ese; *Rhinos:* Brodie Croft.
Penalty count: 7-1; **Half-time:** 6-12;
Referee: Liam Rush; **Attendance:** 10,505.

ROUND 10

Thursday 2nd May 2024

WIGAN WARRIORS 30 CATALANS DRAGONS 8

WARRIORS: 1 Jai Field; 2 Abbas Miski; 3 Adam Keighran; 4 Jake Wardle; 5 Liam Marshall; 6 Bevan French; 7 Harry Smith; 16 Luke Thompson; 9 Brad O'Neill; 10 Liam Byrne; 21 Junior Nsemba; 12 Liam Farrell (C); 13 Kaide Ellis. Subs (all used): 8 Ethan Havard; 15 Patrick Mago; 17 Kruise Leeming; 19 Tyler Dupree.
Tries: Thompson (27), Smith (46), Keighran (49), Farrell (65), Miski (80); **Goals:** Smith 5/5.
DRAGONS: 1 Arthur Mourgue; 24 Tom Johnstone; 3 Arthur Romano; 4 Matthieu Laguerre; 5 Fouad Yaha; 6 Jayden Nikorima; 27 Jordan Abdull; 16 Romain Navarrete; 14 Alrix Da Costa; 10 Julian Bousquet; 11 Tariq Sims; 8 Mike McMeeken; 13 Ben Garcia (C). Subs (all used): 12 Paul Seguier; 15 Bayley Sironen; 17 Cesar Rouge; 20 Tevita Satae.
Try: Bousquet (22); **Goals:** Mourgue 2/2.
Rugby Leaguer & League Express Men of the Match: *Warriors:* Jake Wardle; *Dragons:* Mike McMeeken.
Penalty count: 7-7; **Half-time:** 6-8;
Referee: Jack Smith; **Attendance:** 14,481.

Friday 3rd May 2024

HUDDERSFIELD GIANTS 16 SALFORD RED DEVILS 18

GIANTS: 1 Jake Connor; 2 Adam Swift; 3 Esan Marsters; 4 Kevin Naiqama; 20 Elliot Wallis; 6 Tui Lolohea; 7 Adam Clune; 17 Oliver Wilson; 9 Adam Milner; 10 Joe Greenwood; 16 Harry Rushton; 24 Sam Halsall; 13 Luke Yates (C). Subs (all used): 5 Jake Bibby; 14 Ashton Golding; 18 Sebastine Ikahihifo; 26 Hugo Salabio.
Tries: Swift (71), Lolohea (75), Jake Bibby (78); **Goals:** Connor 2/3.
Dismissal: Wallis (60) - headbutt on Lafai.
RED DEVILS: 1 Ryan Brierley; 2 Ethan Ryan; 3 Nene Macdonald; 4 Tim Lafai; 5 Deon Cross; 14 Chris Atkin; 7 Marc Sneyd; 8 Brad Singleton; 24 Joe Mellor; 17 Jack Ormondroyd; 11 Sam Stone; 12 Kallum Watkins (C); 13 Oliver Partington. Subs (all used): 6 Cade Cust; 15 Shane Wright; 16 Joe Shorrocks; 27 Gil Dudson.
Tries: Macdonald (8, 48), Ryan (20); **Goals:** Sneyd 3/3.
Sin bin: Brierley (39) - high tackle on Marsters; Atkin (64) - obstruction.
Rugby Leaguer & League Express Men of the Match: *Giants:* Sebastine Ikahihifo; *Red Devils:* Marc Sneyd.
Penalty count: 10-5; **Half-time:** 0-12;
Referee: Tom Grant; **Attendance:** 4,833.

LEEDS RHINOS 46 LONDON BRONCOS 8

RHINOS: 1 Lachlan Miller; 5 Ash Handley; 24 Luis Roberts; 12 Rhyse Martin; 33 Riley Lumb; 6 Brodie Croft; 21 Jack Sinfield; 17 Justin Sangare; 14 Jarrod O'Connor; 8 Mikolaj Oledzki; 16 James McDonnell; 18 Mickael Goudemand; 13 Cameron Smith (C). Subs (all used): 9 Andy Ackers; 15 Sam Lisone; 23 Leon Ruan; 29 Alfie Edgell.
Tries: Croft (2), Handley (15), McDonnell (32), Roberts (38), Goudemand (42), Sinfield (47), Lisone (58), Sangare (69); **Goals:** Martin 7/8.
BRONCOS: 1 Alex Walker; 2 Lee Kershaw; 21 Robbie Storey; 3 Jarred Bassett; 4 Hakim Miloudi; 20 Oliver Leyland; 34 Ugo Tison; 19 Rhys Kennedy; 9 Sam Davis; 17 Sadiq Adebiyi; 11 Will Lovell (C); 29 Jacob Jones; 15 Marcus Stock. Subs (all used): 7 James Meadows; 8 Rob Butler; 12 Ethan Natoli; 33 Harvey Makin.
Tries: Natoli (27), Storey (55); **Goals:** O Leyland 0/2.
Rugby Leaguer & League Express Men of the Match: *Rhinos:* Lachlan Miller; *Broncos:* Will Lovell.
Penalty count: 2-2; **Half-time:** 22-4;
Referee: Aaron Moore; **Attendance:** 13,259.

WARRINGTON WOLVES 24 HULL FC 6

WOLVES: 1 Matt Dufty; 2 Josh Thewlis; 3 Toby King; 14 Rodrick Tai; 33 Arron Lindop; 6 George Williams (C); 7 Josh Drinkwater; 15 Joe Philbin; 9 Danny Walker; 10 Paul Vaughan; 13 Matty Nicholson; 12 Lachlan Fitzgibbon; 11 Ben Currie. Subs (all used): 16 Zane Musgrove; 28 Adam Holroyd; 32 Sam Powell; 34 Max Wood.
Tries: Josh Thewlis (9, 42, 55), Williams (37); **Goals:** Josh Thewlis 4/4.
HULL FC: 31 Jack Walker; 44 Tom Briscoe (D2); 43 Ed Chamberlain; 4 Liam Sutcliffe; 26 Lewis Martin; 19 Morgan Smith; 40 Jack Charles; 8 Herman Ese'ese; 9 Danny Houghton (C); 12 Ligi Sao; 17 Cameron Scott; 15 Jordan Lane; 14 Joe Cator. Subs (all used): 6 Jake Trueman; 10 Franklin Pele; 20 Jack Brown; 45 Yusuf Aydin.
Try: Briscoe (67); **Goals:** Charles 1/1.
Rugby Leaguer & League Express Men of the Match: *Wolves:* Josh Thewlis; *Hull FC:* Jack Walker.
Penalty count: 3-2; **Half-time:** 12-0;
Referee: Liam Moore; **Attendance:** 8,680.

Saturday 4th May 2024

HULL KR 40 ST HELENS 20

HULL KR: 2 Niall Evalds; 35 Joe Burgess; 1 Peta Hiku; 36 Jack Broadbent (D); 5 Ryan Hall; 7 Mikey Lewis; 27 Tyrone May; 8 Sauaso Sue; 9 Jez Litten; 16 Jai Whitbread; 11 Dean Hadley; 12 James Batchelor; 13 Elliot Minchella (C). Subs (all used): 14 Matt Parcell; 15 Sam Luckley; 17 Matty Storton; 20 Kelepi Tanginoa.
Tries: May (8), Lewis (17), Broadbent (32), Hiku (46), Litten (51), Hadley (71), R Hall (79); **Goals:** Lewis 6/7.
SAINTS: 1 Jack Welsby; 25 Tee Ritson; 23 Konrad Hurrell; 4 Mark Percival; 3 Waqa Blake; 6 Jonny Lomax (C); 7 Lewis Dodd; 11 Sione Mata'utia; 14 Moses Mbye; 10 Matty Lees; 19 Matt Whitley; 12 Joe Batchelor; 13 Morgan Knowles. Subs (all used): 9 Daryl Clark; 15 James Bell; 16 Curtis Sironen; 20 George Delaney.
Tries: Welsby (12), Blake (20), Hurrell (27, 63); **Goals:** Percival 2/4.
Sin bin: Knowles (15) - high tackle on Whitbread.
Rugby Leaguer & League Express Men of the Match: *Hull KR:* Jai Whitbread; *Saints:* Jack Welsby.
Penalty count: 4-1; **Half-time:** 16-14;
Referee: Chris Kendall; **Attendance:** 10,171.

LEIGH LEOPARDS 28 CASTLEFORD TIGERS 28
(after golden point extra-time)

LEOPARDS: 6 Matt Moylan; 24 Umyla Hanley; 3 Zak Hardaker; 4 Ricky Leutele; 5 Josh Charnley; 21 Ben McNamara; 7 Lachlan Lam (C); 8 Tom Amone; 33 Brad Dwyer; 17 Owen Trout; 11 Kai O'Donnell; 16 Frankie Halton; 12 Jack Hughes. Subs (all used): 9 Edwin Ipape; 15 Matt Davis; 20 Oliver Holmes; 30 Louis Brogan (D).
Tries: Moylan (27), Ipape (36), Charnley (39), Leutele (52), Lam (69); **Goals:** Moylan 4/5.
TIGERS: 34 Tex Hoy; 33 Louis Senior; 35 Corey Hall; 4 Sam Wood; 5 Innes Senior; 16 Rowan Milnes; 7 Jacob Miller; 8 Liam Watts; 9 Paul McShane (C); 13 Joe Westerman; 12 Alex Mellor; 11 Elie El-Zakhem; 29 George Hill. Subs (all used): 14 Liam Horne; 19 Sam Hall; 24 Cain Robb; 25 Brad Martin.
Tries: L Senior (11, 78), Hoy (17), Wood (62), I Senior (73); **Goals:** Milnes 4/5.
Rugby Leaguer & League Express Men of the Match: *Leopards:* Matt Moylan; *Tigers:* Tex Hoy.
Penalty count: 6-2; **Half-time:** 18-10;
Referee: James Vella; **Attendance:** 8,035.

ROUND 11

Thursday 9th May 2024

WARRINGTON WOLVES 20 HULL KR 8

WOLVES: 1 Matt Dufty; 2 Josh Thewlis; 3 Toby King; 14 Rodrick Tai; 5 Matty Ashton; 6 George Williams (C); 7 Josh Drinkwater; 8 James Harrison; 9 Danny Walker; 10 Paul Vaughan; 13 Matty Nicholson; 12 Lachlan Fitzgibbon; 11 Ben Currie. Subs (all used): 15 Joe Philbin; 16 Zane Musgrove; 17 Jordan Crowther; 32 Sam Powell.
Tries: King (8, 28), Ashton (12, pen);
Goals: Josh Thewlis 4/4.
HULL KR: 2 Niall Evalds; 35 Joe Burgess; 1 Peta Hiku; 36 Jack Broadbent; 5 Ryan Hall; 27 Tyrone May; 7 Mikey Lewis; 8 Sauaso Sue; 9 Jez Litten; 16 Jai Whitbread; 20 Kelepi Tanginoa; 12 James Batchelor (C); 11 Dean Hadley. Subs (all used): 10 George King; 14 Matt Parcell; 17 Matty Storton; 37 Jack Brown (D).
Tries: Broadbent (32), Lewis (51); **Goals:** Lewis 0/2.
Rugby Leaguer & League Express Men of the Match: *Wolves:* Toby King; *Hull KR:* Mikey Lewis.
Penalty count: 6-3; **Half-time:** 18-4;
Referee: James Vella; **Attendance:** 8,578.

Friday 10th May 2024

CASTLEFORD TIGERS 4 ST HELENS 60

TIGERS: 34 Tex Hoy; 33 Louis Senior; 35 Corey Hall; 4 Sam Wood; 5 Innes Senior; 16 Rowan Milnes; 7 Jacob Miller; 8 Liam Watts; 9 Paul McShane (C); 13 Joe Westerman; 12 Alex Mellor; 11 Elie El-Zakhem; 29 George Hill. Subs (all used): 14 Liam Horne; 15 George Griffin; 24 Cain Robb; 36 Sam Eseh (D). 18th man (used): 25 Brad Martin.
Try: L Senior (38); **Goals:** Milnes 0/1.
Dismissal: Horne (48) - dangerous challenge on Bell.
SAINTS: 1 Jack Welsby; 2 Tommy Makinson; 23 Konrad Hurrell; 4 Mark Percival; 3 Waqa Blake; 6 Jonny Lomax (C); 7 Lewis Dodd; 11 Sione Mata'utia; 9 Daryl Clark; 10 Matty Lees; 16 Curtis Sironen; 12 Joe Batchelor; 15 James Bell. Subs (all used): 14 Moses Mbye; 18 Jake Wingfield; 20 George Delaney; 31 Noah Stephens (D).
Tries: Mata'utia (4), Lomax (24), Welsby (42, 57), Percival (52), Blake (54, 72, 80), Bell (63, 68), Dodd (75);
Goals: Percival 8/12.
Dismissal: Makinson (14) - contact with the head of Hoy.
Rugby Leaguer & League Express Men of the Match: *Tigers:* Innes Senior; *Saints:* Jack Welsby.
Penalty count: 5-6; **Half-time:** 4-8;
Referee: Jack Smith; **Attendance:** 7,869.

LEIGH LEOPARDS 40 SALFORD RED DEVILS 12

LEOPARDS: 6 Matt Moylan; 24 Umyla Hanley; 3 Zak Hardaker; 4 Ricky Leutele; 5 Josh Charnley; 21 Ben McNamara; 7 Lachlan Lam (C); 8 Tom Amone; 9 Edwin Ipape; 10 Robbie Mulhern; 11 Kai O'Donnell; 16 Frankie Halton; 17 Owen Trout. Subs (all used): 12 Jack Hughes; 15 Matt Davis; 19 Ed Chamberlain; 33 Brad Dwyer.
Tries: Hanley (6, 34), Charnley (12, 43), Davis (47), Dwyer (58), Lam (67); **Goals:** Moylan 2/4, Hardaker 4/4.
RED DEVILS: 1 Ryan Brierley; 2 Ethan Ryan; 3 Nene Macdonald; 4 Tim Lafai; 5 Deon Cross; 14 Chris Atkin; 7 Marc Sneyd; 8 Brad Singleton; 6 Cade Cust; 17 Jack Ormondroyd; 11 Sam Stone; 12 Kallum Watkins (C); 13 Oliver Partington. Subs (all used): 9 Amir Bourouh; 10 King Vuniyayawa; 18 Ben Hellewell; 23 Chris Hankinson.
Tries: Brierley (19), Lafai (74); **Goals:** Sneyd 2/2.
Rugby Leaguer & League Express Men of the Match: *Leopards:* Brad Dwyer; *Red Devils:* Kallum Watkins.
Penalty count: 5-3; **Half-time:** 16-6;
Referee: Liam Moore; **Attendance:** 8,103.

Saturday 11th May 2024

HUDDERSFIELD GIANTS 6 WIGAN WARRIORS 48

GIANTS: 1 Jake Connor; 24 Sam Halsall; 3 Esan Marsters; 4 Kevin Naiqama; 20 Elliot Wallis; 6 Tui Lolohea; 7 Adam Clune; 17 Oliver Wilson; 9 Adam Milner; 15 Matty English; 16 Harry Rushton; 21 Leroy Cudjoe; 13 Luke Yates (C). Subs (all used): 10 Joe Greenwood; 12 Sam Hewitt; 14 Ashton Golding; 18 Sebastine Ikahihifo.
Try: Wallis (14); **Goals:** Connor 1/1.
Sin bin: Marsters (73) - trip on French.
WARRIORS: 1 Jai Field; 2 Abbas Miski; 3 Adam Keighran; 4 Jake Wardle; 5 Liam Marshall; 6 Bevan French; 7 Harry Smith; 16 Luke Thompson; 9 Brad O'Neill; 10 Liam Byrne; 21 Junior Nsemba; 12 Liam Farrell (C); 13 Kaide Ellis. Subs (all used): 8 Ethan Havard; 15 Patrick Mago; 17 Kruise Leeming; 19 Tyler Dupree.
Tries: Marshall (3, 42, 65), French (19, 62), Leeming (68), Miski (74, 78); **Goals:** Smith 8/9.
Sin bin: Byrne (1) - high tackle on English.
Rugby Leaguer & League Express Men of the Match: *Giants:* Esan Marsters; *Warriors:* Bevan French.
Penalty count: 4-5; **Half-time:** 6-12;
Referee: Aaron Moore; **Attendance:** 5,334.

CATALANS DRAGONS 26 LEEDS RHINOS 0

DRAGONS: 1 Arthur Mourgue; 2 Tom Davies; 3 Arthur Romano; 21 Matt Ikuvalu; 24 Tom Johnstone; 6 Jayden Nikorima; 27 Jordan Abdull; 16 Romain Navarrete; 9 Michael Mcllorum (C); 10 Julian Bousquet; 11 Tariq Sims; 15 Bayley Sironen; 8 Mike McMeeken. Subs (all used): 14 Alrix Da Costa; 17 Cesar Rouge; 20 Tevita Satae; 28 Franck Maria.
Tries: Davies (16), Johnstone (55), Mourgue (77), Da Costa (79); **Goals:** Mourgue 5/5.
RHINOS: 1 Lachlan Miller; 29 Alfie Edgell; 24 Luis Roberts; 12 Rhyse Martin; 5 Ash Handley; 7 Matt Frawley; 21 Jack Sinfield; 8 Mikolaj Oledzki; 14 Jarrod O'Connor; 17 Justin Sangare; 16 James McDonnell; 18 Mickael Goudemand; 13 Cameron Smith (C). Subs (all used): 9 Andy Ackers; 15 Sam Lisone; 23 Leon Ruan; 26 Corey Johnson.
Rugby Leaguer & League Express Men of the Match: *Dragons:* Mike McMeeken; *Rhinos:* Cameron Smith.
Penalty count: 5-4; **Half-time:** 8-0;
Referee: Tom Grant; **Attendance:** 9,546.

Sunday 12th May 2024

LONDON BRONCOS 34 HULL FC 18

BRONCOS: 1 Alex Walker; 2 Lee Kershaw; 21 Robbie Storey; 3 Jarred Bassett; 4 Hakim Miloudi; 20 Oliver Leyland; 7 James Meadows; 19 Rhys Kennedy; 34 Ugo Tison; 17 Sadiq Adebiyi; 11 Will Lovell (C); 12 Ethan Natoli; 15 Marcus Stock. Subs (all used): 8 Rob Butler; 10 Lewis Bienek; 29 Jacob Jones; 33 Harvey Makin.
Tries: Walker (24), Meadows (37), Storey (40), Bassett (55), Kershaw (61), O Leyland (68);
Goals: O Leyland 5/7.
HULL FC: 31 Jack Walker; 44 Tom Briscoe; 17 Cameron Scott; 4 Liam Sutcliffe; 26 Lewis Martin; 6 Jake Trueman; 40 Jack Charles; 8 Herman Ese'ese; 9 Danny Houghton (C); 45 Yusuf Aydin; 15 Jordan Lane; 12 Ligi Sao; 14 Joe Cator. Subs (all used): 10 Franklin Pele; 19 Morgan Smith; 27 Zach Jebson; 46 Tiaki Chan (D).
Tries: Ese'ese (20), Trueman (26), Aydin (47);
Goals: Charles 3/3.
Sin bin: Lane (54) - late challenge.
Rugby Leaguer & League Express Men of the Match: *Broncos:* Jarred Bassett; *Hull FC:* Danny Houghton.
Penalty count: 2-3; **Half-time:** 16-12;
Referee: Chris Kendall; **Attendance:** 3,225.

ROUND 12

Friday 24th May 2024

CASTLEFORD TIGERS 30 HULL FC 22

TIGERS: 34 Tex Hoy; 23 Jason Qareqare; 35 Corey Hall; 4 Sam Wood; 5 Innes Senior; 16 Rowan Milnes; 9 Paul McShane (C); 15 George Griffin; 14 Liam Horne; 19 Sam Hall; 12 Alex Mellor; 11 Elie El-Zakhem; 13 Joe Westerman. Subs: 8 Liam Watts; 18 Josh Hodson (not used); 21 Sylvester Namo; 29 George Hill.
Tries: Horne (7), Hoy (9), Milnes (31), Qareqare (50), C Hall (55); **Goals:** Milnes 5/5.
HULL FC: 37 Logan Moy; 44 Tom Briscoe; 17 Cameron Scott; 4 Liam Sutcliffe; 25 Harvey Barron; 6 Jake Trueman; 47 Ben Reynolds (D); 8 Herman Ese'ese; 9 Danny Houghton (C); 45 Yusuf Aydin; 15 Jordan Lane; 12 Ligi Sao; 13 Brad Fash. Subs (all used): 16 Jack Ashworth; 19 Morgan Smith; 27 Zach Jebson; 46 Tiaki Chan.
Tries: Barron (24), Sutcliffe (37), Chan (64), Trueman (74);
Goals: Reynolds 3/4.
Rugby Leaguer & League Express Men of the Match: *Tigers:* Rowan Milnes; *Hull FC:* Logan Moy.
Penalty count: 6-1; **Half-time:** 18-10;
Referee: Aaron Moore; **Attendance:** 8,269.

HUDDERSFIELD GIANTS 10 LEIGH LEOPARDS 16

GIANTS: 6 Tui Lolohea; 20 Elliot Wallis; 4 Kevin Naiqama; 3 Esan Marsters; 24 Sam Halsall; 23 Oliver Russell; 7 Adam Clune; 8 Chris Hill; 19 Thomas Deakin; 13 Luke Yates (C); 11 Jack Murchie; 12 Sam Hewitt; 21 Leroy Cudjoe. Subs (all used): 14 Ashton Golding; 16 Harry Rushton; 17 Oliver Wilson; 18 Sebastine Ikahihifo.
Tries: Hewitt (42), Naiqama (77); **Goals:** Russell 1/2.
Sin bin: Russell (28) - high tackle.
LEOPARDS: 6 Matt Moylan; 24 Umyla Hanley; 19 Ed Chamberlain; 4 Ricky Leutele; 5 Josh Charnley; 3 Zak Hardaker; 7 Lachlan Lam (C); 8 Tom Amone; 9 Edwin Ipape; 10 Robbie Mulhern; 11 Kai O'Donnell; 16 Frankie Halton; 17 Owen Trout. Subs (all used): 12 Jack Hughes; 14 Dan Norman; 33 Brad Dwyer; 34 Darnell McIntosh (D).
Tries: Charnley (11), Ipape (30); **Goals:** Moylan 4/4.
Sin bin: Chamberlain (35) - holding down; Halton (40) - late challenge; Dwyer (77) - trip.
Rugby Leaguer & League Express Men of the Match: *Giants:* Luke Yates; *Leopards:* Owen Trout.
Penalty count: 12-10; **Half-time:** 0-14;
Referee: James Vella; **Attendance:** 4,385.

ST HELENS 40 LEEDS RHINOS 10

SAINTS: 1 Jack Welsby; 2 Tommy Makinson; 23 Konrad Hurrell; 4 Mark Percival; 3 Waqa Blake; 6 Jonny Lomax (C); 7 Lewis Dodd; 11 Sione Mata'utia; 9 Daryl Clark; 10 Matty Lees; 16 Curtis Sironen; 12 Joe Batchelor; 15 James Bell. Subs (all used): 14 Moses Mbye; 20 George Delaney; 21 Ben Davies; 31 Noah Stephens.
Tries: Mata'utia (19), Mbye (38), Clark (44), Welsby (47, 71), Sironen (64), Makinson (68);
Goals: Percival 6/7.
RHINOS: 1 Lachlan Miller; 35 Matty Russell (D); 3 Harry Newman; 24 Luis Roberts; 5 Ash Handley; 6 Brodie Croft; 7 Matt Frawley; 8 Mikolaj Oledzki; 14 Jarrod O'Connor; 17 Justin Sangare; 16 James McDonnell; 12 Rhyse Martin; 13 Cameron Smith (C). Subs (all used): 9 Andy Ackers; 15 Sam Lisone; 18 Mickael Goudemand; 30 Tom Nicholson-Watton.
Tries: Handley (9), Roberts (58); **Goals:** Martin 1/2.
Rugby Leaguer & League Express Men of the Match: *Saints:* George Delaney; *Rhinos:* Ash Handley.
Penalty count: 6-3; **Half-time:** 12-6;
Referee: Liam Moore; **Attendance:** 11,367.

Saturday 25th May 2024

CATALANS DRAGONS 8 WARRINGTON WOLVES 16

DRAGONS: 1 Arthur Mourgue; 2 Tom Davies; 3 Arthur Romano; 21 Matt Ikuvalu; 24 Tom Johnstone; 27 Jordan Abdull; 7 Theo Fages; 16 Romain Navarrete; 14 Alrix Da Costa; 10 Julian Bousquet; 11 Tariq Sims; 15 Bayley Sironen; 13 Ben Garcia (C). Subs (all used): 6 Jayden Nikorima; 12 Paul Seguier; 20 Tevita Satae; 23 Jordan Dezaria.
Try: Davies (74); **Goals:** Mourgue 2/2.
Sin bin: Davies (19) - holding down.
WOLVES: 1 Matt Dufty; 2 Josh Thewlis; 3 Toby King; 14 Rodrick Tai; 5 Matty Ashton; 6 George Williams (C); 7 Josh Drinkwater; 8 James Harrison; 9 Danny Walker; 10 Paul Vaughan; 13 Matty Nicholson; 12 Lachlan Fitzgibbon; 11 Ben Currie. Subs: 15 Joe Philbin; 16 Zane Musgrove; 32 Sam Powell; 34 Max Wood (not used).
Tries: Williams (43), Ashton (69); **Goals:** Josh Thewlis 4/5.
Sin bin: Fitzgibbon (30) - high tackle.
Rugby Leaguer & League Express Men of the Match: *Dragons:* Ben Garcia; *Wolves:* George Williams.
Penalty count: 6-4; **Half-time:** 2-2;
Referee: Chris Kendall; **Attendance:** 9,440.

Sunday 26th May 2024

LONDON BRONCOS 14 HULL KR 64

BRONCOS: 1 Alex Walker; 2 Lee Kershaw; 21 Robbie Storey; 3 Jarred Bassett; 5 Iliess Macani; 20 Oliver Leyland; 4 Hakim Miloudi; 19 Rhys Kennedy; 34 Ugo Tison; 17 Sadiq Adebiyi; 11 Will Lovell (C); 12 Ethan Natoli; 15 Marcus Stock. Subs (all used): 8 Rob Butler; 9 Sam Davis; 10 Lewis Bienek; 29 Jacob Jones.
Tries: Walker (41), Macani (68), Bassett (76);
Goals: O Leyland 1/3.
HULL KR: 2 Niall Evalds; 36 Jack Broadbent; 1 Peta Hiku; 12 James Batchelor; 5 Ryan Hall; 27 Tyrone May; 7 Mikey Lewis; 8 Sauaso Sue; 14 Matt Parcell; 16 Jai Whitbread; 20 Kelepi Tanginoa; 11 Dean Hadley; 13 Elliot Minchella (C). Subs (all used): 10 George King; 15 Sam Luckley; 17 Matty Storton; 38 Danny Richardson (D).
Tries: Broadbent (6, 10), Hiku (12), Evalds (15, 37), Parcell (20), Hadley (32), Luckley (39, 48), Lewis (56, 72);
Goals: Lewis 9/10, Richardson 1/1.

Rugby Leaguer & League Express Men of the Match:
Broncos: Oliver Leyland; *Hull KR:* Niall Evalds.
Penalty count: 5-4; **Half-time:** 0-46;
Referee: Ben Thaler; **Attendance:** 3,750.

SALFORD RED DEVILS 6 WIGAN WARRIORS 26

RED DEVILS: 1 Ryan Brierley; 2 Ethan Ryan; 3 Nene Macdonald; 4 Tim Lafai; 5 Deon Cross; 14 Chris Atkin; 7 Marc Sneyd; 8 Brad Singleton; 16 Joe Shorrocks; 15 Shane Wright; 11 Sam Stone; 12 Kallum Watkins (C); 13 Oliver Partington. Subs (all used): 21 Matty Foster; 23 Chris Hankinson; 24 Joe Mellor; 27 Gil Dudson.
Try: Partington (47); **Goals:** Sneyd 1/1.
WARRIORS: 1 Jai Field; 2 Abbas Miski; 3 Adam Keighran; 4 Jake Wardle; 5 Liam Marshall; 6 Bevan French; 7 Harry Smith; 14 Mike Cooper; 9 Brad O'Neill; 16 Luke Thompson; 21 Junior Nsemba; 12 Liam Farrell (C); 8 Ethan Havard. Subs (all used): 15 Patrick Mago; 17 Kruise Leeming; 19 Tyler Dupree; 20 Harvie Hill.
Tries: Keighran (9), Nsemba (16), O'Neill (24), French (78);
Goals: Keighran 5/5.
Rugby Leaguer & League Express Men of the Match:
Red Devils: Joe Mellor; *Warriors:* Harry Smith.
Penalty count: 6-3; **Half-time:** 0-18;
Referee: Tom Grant; **Attendance:** 4,087.

ROUND 13

Friday 31st May 2024

HUDDERSFIELD GIANTS 24 HULL FC 18

GIANTS: 6 Tui Lolohea; 24 Sam Halsall; 3 Esan Marsters; 4 Kevin Naiqama; 5 Jake Bibby; 23 Oliver Russell; 7 Adam Clune; 8 Chris Hill; 19 Thomas Deakin; 13 Luke Yates (C); 12 Sam Hewitt; 16 Harry Rushton; 21 Leroy Cudjoe. Subs (all used): 1 Jake Connor; 14 Ashton Golding; 17 Oliver Wilson; 18 Sebastine Ikahihifo.
Tries: Jake Bibby (9, 55), Ikahihifo (26), Halsall (62);
Goals: Russell 4/6.
HULL FC: 37 Logan Moy; 25 Harvey Barron; 17 Cameron Scott; 4 Liam Sutcliffe; 44 Tom Briscoe; 6 Jake Trueman; 47 Ben Reynolds; 8 Herman Ese'ese; 9 Danny Houghton (C); 12 Ligi Sao; 15 Jordan Lane; 46 Tiaki Chan; 45 Yusuf Aydin. Subs (all used): 13 Brad Fash; 16 Jack Ashworth; 19 Morgan Smith; 23 Davy Litten.
Tries: Ese'ese (34), Moy (73), Scott (77);
Goals: Reynolds 3/3.
Rugby Leaguer & League Express Men of the Match:
Giants: Tui Lolohea; *Hull FC:* Herman Ese'ese.
Penalty count: 4-4; **Half-time:** 14-6;
Referee: Ben Thaler; **Attendance:** 4,102.

ST HELENS 24 CATALANS DRAGONS 12

SAINTS: 1 Jack Welsby (C); 2 Tommy Makinson; 23 Konrad Hurrell; 4 Mark Percival; 3 Waqa Blake; 14 Moses Mbye; 7 Lewis Dodd; 20 George Delaney; 9 Daryl Clark; 10 Matty Lees; 16 Curtis Sironen; 11 Sione Mata'utia; 15 James Bell. Subs (all used): 17 Agnatius Paasi; 21 Ben Davies; 22 Sam Royle; 31 Noah Stephens.
Tries: Hurrell (30), Mata'utia (42), Makinson (48), Lees (65); **Goals:** Percival 4/4.
DRAGONS: 17 Cesar Rouge; 2 Tom Davies; 21 Matt Ikuvalu; 4 Matthieu Laguerre; 24 Tom Johnstone; 27 Jordan Abdull; 7 Theo Fages; 16 Romain Navarrete; 1 Arthur Mourgue; 23 Jordan Dezaria; 11 Tariq Sims; 10 Julian Bousquet; 13 Ben Garcia (C). Subs (all used): 6 Jayden Nikorima; 20 Tevita Satae; 25 Loan Castano; 28 Franck Maria.
Tries: Johnstone (11), Bousquet (74); **Goals:** Mourgue 2/2.
Sin bin: Maria (34) - high tackle on Delaney.
Rugby Leaguer & League Express Men of the Match:
Saints: Jack Welsby; *Dragons:* Cesar Rouge.
Penalty count: 4-2; **Half-time:** 6-6;
Referee: Aaron Moore; **Attendance:** 11,088.

Saturday 1st June 2024

WARRINGTON WOLVES 18 WIGAN WARRIORS 19

WOLVES: 38 Cai Taylor-Wray (D); 33 Arron Lindop; 20 Connor Wrench; 14 Rodrick Tai; 31 Jake Thewlis (D); 4 Stefan Ratchford (C); 7 Josh Drinkwater; 19 Joe Bullock; 32 Sam Powell; 34 Max Wood; 28 Adam Holroyd; 36 Nolan Tupaea (D); 29 Tom Whitehead. Subs (all used): 13 Matty Nicholson; 16 Zane Musgrove; 25 Lucas Green; 40 Ben Hartill (D).
Tries: Lindop (16), Drinkwater (20), Ratchford (78);
Goals: Ratchford 3/4.
WARRIORS: 23 Ryan Hampshire; 28 Jacob Douglas (D); 3 Adam Keighran; 26 Zach Eckersley; 5 Liam Marshall; 6 Bevan French (C); 7 Harry Smith; 8 Ethan Havard; 9 Brad O'Neill; 10 Liam Byrne; 21 Junior Nsemba; 22 Sam Walters; 13 Kaide Ellis. Subs (all used): 15 Patrick Mago; 17 Kruise Leeming; 19 Tyler Dupree; 20 Harvie Hill.
Tries: Nsemba (23), Marshall (33), Leeming (35);
Goals: Keighran 3/3; **Field goal:** Smith (40).
Dismissal: Keighran (69) - high tackle on Lindop.
Rugby Leaguer & League Express Men of the Match:
Wolves: Josh Drinkwater; *Warriors:* Harry Smith.
Penalty count: 9-4; **Half-time:** 12-19;
Referee: Jack Smith; **Attendance:** 12,181.

HULL KR 12 LEIGH LEOPARDS 0

HULL KR: 2 Niall Evalds; 36 Jack Broadbent; 1 Peta Hiku; 3 Tom Opacic; 5 Ryan Hall; 7 Mikey Lewis; 27 Tyrone May; 8 Sauaso Sue; 9 Jez Litten; 16 Jai Whitbread; 11 Dean Hadley; 12 James Batchelor; 13 Elliot Minchella (C). Subs (all used): 10 George King; 14 Matt Parcell; 15 Sam Luckley; 20 Kelepi Tanginoa.
Tries: Opacic (25), Evalds (70); **Goals:** Lewis 2/2.
LEOPARDS: 3 Zak Hardaker; 24 Umyla Hanley; 4 Ricky Leutele; 19 Ed Chamberlain; 5 Josh Charnley; 6 Matt Moylan; 7 Lachlan Lam (C); 8 Tom Amone; 9 Edwin Ipape; 17 Owen Trout; 11 Kai O'Donnell; 16 Frankie Halton; 12 Jack Hughes. Subs (all used): 14 Dan Norman; 29 Lewis Baxter; 33 Brad Dwyer; 34 Darnell McIntosh.
Rugby Leaguer & League Express Men of the Match:
Hull KR: Kelepi Tanginoa; *Leopards:* Tom Amone.
Penalty count: 3-7; **Half-time:** 6-0;
Referee: Liam Moore; **Attendance:** 9,899.

LEEDS RHINOS 32 CASTLEFORD TIGERS 4

RHINOS: 1 Lachlan Miller; 29 Alfie Edgell; 3 Harry Newman; 4 Paul Momirovski; 5 Ash Handley; 6 Brodie Croft; 7 Matt Frawley; 8 Mikolaj Oledzki; 14 Jarrod O'Connor; 18 Mickael Goudemand; 16 James McDonnell; 12 Rhyse Martin; 13 Cameron Smith (C). Subs (all used): 15 Sam Lisone; 17 Justin Sangare; 26 Corey Johnson; 30 Tom Nicholson-Watton.
Tries: Handley (10), Croft (22), Frawley (42), Martin (45, 67); **Goals:** Martin 6/6.
TIGERS: 34 Tex Hoy; 23 Jason Qareqare; 35 Corey Hall; 4 Sam Wood; 5 Innes Senior; 16 Rowan Milnes; 7 Jacob Miller; 15 George Griffin; 14 Liam Horne; 19 Sam Hall; 12 Alex Mellor; 11 Elie El-Zakhem; 13 Joe Westerman (C). Subs (all used): 8 Liam Watts; 21 Sylvester Namo; 24 Cain Robb; 17 Nixon Putt.
Try: El-Zakhem (63); **Goals:** Milnes 0/1.
Rugby Leaguer & League Express Men of the Match:
Rhinos: Rhyse Martin; *Tigers:* Alex Mellor.
Penalty count: 5-6; **Half-time:** 14-0;
Referee: Chris Kendall; **Attendance:** 14,529.

Sunday 2nd June 2024

SALFORD RED DEVILS 34 LONDON BRONCOS 4

RED DEVILS: 23 Chris Hankinson; 2 Ethan Ryan; 3 Nene Macdonald; 4 Tim Lafai; 5 Deon Cross; 14 Chris Atkin; 7 Marc Sneyd; 8 Brad Singleton; 16 Joe Shorrocks; 15 Shane Wright; 11 Sam Stone; 12 Kallum Watkins (C); 13 Oliver Partington. Subs (all used): 21 Matty Foster; 24 Joe Mellor; 25 Nathan Connell (D); 27 Gil Dudson.
Tries: Stone (35), Cross (49), Macdonald (52), Lafai (67, 76), Wright (71); **Goals:** Sneyd 5/6.
BRONCOS: 1 Alex Walker; 2 Lee Kershaw; 21 Robbie Storey; 3 Jarred Bassett; 4 Hakim Miloudi; 20 Oliver Leyland; 7 James Meadows; 19 Rhys Kennedy; 9 Sam Davis; 10 Lewis Bienek; 11 Will Lovell (C); 17 Sadiq Adebiyi; 29 Jacob Jones. Subs (all used): 8 Rob Butler; 15 Marcus Stock; 16 Jordan Williams; 34 Ugo Tison.
Try: Miloudi (80); **Goals:** O Leyland 0/1.
Rugby Leaguer & League Express Men of the Match:
Red Devils: Marc Sneyd; *Broncos:* Hakim Miloudi.
Penalty count: 4-8; **Half-time:** 6-0;
Referee: Liam Rush; **Attendance:** 2,843.

ROUND 14

Friday 14th June 2024

CASTLEFORD TIGERS 8 WIGAN WARRIORS 10

TIGERS: 34 Tex Hoy; 23 Jason Qareqare; 35 Corey Hall; 4 Sam Wood; 5 Innes Senior; 16 Rowan Milnes; 7 Jacob Miller; 15 George Griffin; 14 Liam Horne; 8 Liam Watts (C); 12 Alex Mellor; 11 Elie El-Zakhem; 29 George Hill. Subs (all used): 17 Nixon Putt; 21 Sylvester Namo; 24 Cain Robb; 37 Matty English (D).
Try: Hoy (34); **Goals:** Milnes 2/3.
Sin bin: Robb (54) - high tackle on Miski.
WARRIORS: 6 Bevan French; 2 Abbas Miski; 26 Zach Eckersley; 4 Jake Wardle; 5 Liam Marshall; 23 Ryan Hampshire; 7 Harry Smith; 14 Mike Cooper; 9 Brad O'Neill; 16 Luke Thompson; 22 Sam Walters; 12 Liam Farrell (C); 13 Kaide Ellis. Subs (all used): 10 Liam Byrne; 15 Patrick Mago; 17 Kruise Leeming; 20 Harvie Hill.
Tries: Marshall (7, 60); **Goals:** Smith 1/3.
Rugby Leaguer & League Express Men of the Match:
Tigers: Cain Robb; *Warriors:* Bevan French.
Penalty count: 7-7; **Half-time:** 4-4;
Referee: Ben Thaler; **Attendance:** 6,965.

HULL KR 32 HUDDERSFIELD GIANTS 6

HULL KR: 2 Niall Evalds; 36 Jack Broadbent; 1 Peta Hiku; 3 Tom Opacic; 5 Ryan Hall; 7 Mikey Lewis; 27 Tyrone May; 8 Sauaso Sue; 9 Jez Litten; 16 Jai Whitbread; 11 Dean Hadley; 12 James Batchelor; 13 Elliot Minchella (C). Subs (all used): 14 Matt Parcell; 15 Sam Luckley; 17 Matty Storton; 20 Kelepi Tanginoa.
Tries: Hiku (32, 66), May (38), Parcell (44), R Hall (71, 77);
Goals: Lewis 4/6.
GIANTS: 6 Tui Lolohea; 24 Sam Halsall; 4 Kevin Naiqama; 3 Esan Marsters; 5 Jake Bibby; 23 Oliver Russell; 7 Adam Clune; 8 Chris Hill; 9 Adam Milner; 10 Joe Greenwood; 12 Sam Hewitt; 16 Harry Rushton; 13 Luke Yates (C). Subs (all used): 14 Ashton Golding; 17 Oliver Wilson; 18 Sebastine Ikahihifo; 33 Andre Savelio (D).
Try: Marsters (7); **Goals:** Russell 1/2.
Dismissal: Savelio (70) - dangerous challenge on Lewis.
Sin bin: Milner (25) - obstruction.
Rugby Leaguer & League Express Men of the Match:
Hull KR: Tyrone May; *Giants:* Tui Lolohea.
Penalty count: 9-6; **Half-time:** 10-6;
Referee: Tom Grant; **Attendance:** 9,304.

WARRINGTON WOLVES 14 SALFORD RED DEVILS 25

WOLVES: 1 Matt Dufty; 14 Rodrick Tai; 3 Toby King; 20 Connor Wrench; 5 Matty Ashton; 4 Stefan Ratchford (C); 7 Josh Drinkwater; 16 Zane Musgrove; 9 Danny Walker; 10 Paul Vaughan; 13 Matty Nicholson; 28 Adam Holroyd; 11 Ben Currie. Subs (all used): 8 James Harrison; 19 Joe Bullock; 32 Sam Powell; 34 Max Wood.
Tries: Tai (55, 79), Ashton (58);
Goals: Ratchford 0/1, Drinkwater 1/2.
RED DEVILS: 23 Chris Hankinson; 2 Ethan Ryan; 3 Nene Macdonald; 4 Tim Lafai; 5 Deon Cross; 14 Chris Atkin; 7 Marc Sneyd; 8 Brad Singleton; 24 Joe Mellor; 15 Shane Wright; 11 Sam Stone; 12 Kallum Watkins (C); 13 Oliver Partington. Subs (all used): 16 Joe Shorrocks; 27 Gil Dudson; 28 Harvey Wilson (D); 29 Loghan Lewis (D).
Tries: Macdonald (6), Cross (16, 63), Sneyd (23);
Goals: Sneyd 4/5; **Field goal:** Sneyd (40).
Rugby Leaguer & League Express Men of the Match:
Wolves: Matt Dufty; *Red Devils:* Marc Sneyd.
Penalty count: 1-4; **Half-time:** 0-19;
Referee: Aaron Moore; **Attendance:** 9,257.

Saturday 15th June 2024

HULL FC 18 LEEDS RHINOS 10

HULL FC: 37 Logan Moy; 44 Tom Briscoe; 3 Carlos Tuimavave; 4 Liam Sutcliffe; 26 Lewis Martin; 6 Jake Trueman; 47 Ben Reynolds; 8 Herman Ese'ese; 19 Morgan Smith; 12 Ligi Sao; 15 Jordan Lane; 17 Cameron Scott; 13 Brad Fash (C). Subs (all used): 16 Jack Ashworth; 28 Denive Balmforth; 45 Yusuf Aydin; 46 Tiaki Chan.
Tries: Martin (37), Balmforth (40), Scott (45);
Goals: Reynolds 3/3.
Sin bin: Briscoe (72) - professional foul.
RHINOS: 1 Lachlan Miller; 2 David Fusitu'a; 4 Paul Momirovski; 3 Harry Newman; 5 Ash Handley; 6 Brodie Croft; 7 Matt Frawley; 8 Mikolaj Oledzki; 14 Jarrod O'Connor; 18 Mickael Goudemand; 16 James McDonnell; 12 Rhyse Martin; 13 Cameron Smith (C). Subs (all used): 10 Tom Holroyd; 15 Sam Lisone; 17 Justin Sangare; 26 Corey Johnson.
Tries: Handley (56), Newman (77); **Goals:** Martin 1/2.
Rugby Leaguer & League Express Men of the Match:
Hull FC: Jordan Lane; *Rhinos:* Jarrod O'Connor.
Penalty count: 7-6; **Half-time:** 12-0;
Referee: Liam Moore; **Attendance:** 12,166.

CATALANS DRAGONS 2 LEIGH LEOPARDS 10

DRAGONS: 1 Arthur Mourgue; 2 Tom Davies; 3 Arthur Romano; 21 Matt Ikuvalu; 24 Tom Johnstone; 17 Cesar Rouge; 7 Theo Fages; 23 Jordan Dezaria; 9 Michael McIlorum; 10 Julian Bousquet; 15 Bayley Sironen; 12 Paul Seguier; 13 Ben Garcia (C). Subs (all used): 6 Jayden Nikorima; 14 Alrix Da Costa; 16 Romain Navarrete; 20 Tevita Satae.
Goals: Mourgue 1/1.
LEOPARDS: 6 Matt Moylan; 24 Umyla Hanley; 3 Zak Hardaker; 4 Ricky Leutele; 5 Josh Charnley; 1 Gareth O'Brien; 7 Lachlan Lam (C); 8 Tom Amone; 9 Edwin Ipape; 17 Owen Trout; 11 Kai O'Donnell; 16 Frankie Halton; 12 Jack Hughes. Subs (all used): 14 Dan Norman; 15 Matt Davis; 19 Ed Chamberlain; 33 Brad Dwyer.
Try: Amone (33); **Goals:** Moylan 3/3.
Rugby Leaguer & League Express Men of the Match:
Dragons: Michael McIlorum; *Leopards:* Tom Amone.
Penalty count: 6-5; **Half-time:** 2-8;
Referee: Jack Smith; **Attendance:** 9,480.

Sunday 16th June 2024

LONDON BRONCOS 6 ST HELENS 52

BRONCOS: 1 Alex Walker; 2 Lee Kershaw; 21 Robbie Storey; 3 Jarred Bassett; 4 Hakim Miloudi; 20 Oliver Leyland; 7 James Meadows; 19 Rhys Kennedy; 34 Ugo Tison; 10 Lewis Bienek; 11 Will Lovell (C); 12 Ethan Natoli; 29 Jacob Jones. Subs (all used): 15 Marcus Stock; 16 Jordan Williams; 17 Sadiq Adebiyi; 18 Emmanuel Waine.
Try: Kershaw (79); **Goals:** O Leyland 1/1.
SAINTS: 1 Jack Welsby (C); 2 Tommy Makinson; 23 Konrad Hurrell; 4 Mark Percival; 3 Waqa Blake; 14 Moses Mbye; 7 Lewis Dodd; 20 George Delaney; 9 Daryl Clark; 10 Matty Lees; 16 Curtis Sironen; 11 Sione Mata'utia; 15 James Bell. Subs (all used): 17 Agnatius Paasi; 21 Ben Davies; 22 Sam Royle; 31 Noah Stephens.
Tries: Blake (7, 15), Dodd (18), Mbye (25), Clark (45, 50, 53), Hurrell (70), Percival (75); **Goals:** Percival 8/9.
Rugby Leaguer & League Express Men of the Match: *Broncos:* Will Lovell; *Saints:* James Bell.
Penalty count: 5-5; **Half-time:** 0-24;
Referee: James Vella; **Attendance:** 4,600
(at Twickenham Stoop).

ROUND 15

Thursday 20th June 2024

CASTLEFORD TIGERS 12 HULL KR 13

TIGERS: 34 Tex Hoy; 23 Jason Qareqare; 35 Corey Hall; 4 Sam Wood; 5 Innes Senior; 16 Rowan Milnes; 7 Jacob Miller; 15 George Griffin; 14 Liam Horne; 13 Joe Westerman (C); 12 Alex Mellor; 11 Elie El-Zakhem; 29 George Hill. Subs (all used): 19 Sam Hall; 21 Sylvester Namo; 24 Cain Robb; 37 Matty English.
Tries: Wood (13), Milnes (60); **Goals:** Milnes 2/2.
HULL KR: 2 Niall Evalds; 36 Jack Broadbent; 1 Peta Hiku; 3 Tom Opacic; 5 Ryan Hall; 27 Tyrone May; 7 Mikey Lewis; 8 Sauaso Sue; 9 Jez Litten; 37 Jack Brown; 11 Dean Hadley; 20 Kelepi Tanginoa; 13 Elliot Minchella (C). Subs: 10 George King; 15 Sam Luckley; 17 Matty Storton; 38 Danny Richardson (not used).
Tries: Opacic (17), Minchella (20); **Goals:** Lewis 2/3;
Field goal: Litten (75).
Rugby Leaguer & League Express Men of the Match: *Tigers:* Cain Robb; *Hull KR:* Jez Litten.
Penalty count: 2-2; **Half-time:** 6-12;
Referee: Aaron Moore; **Attendance:** 7,897.

Friday 21st June 2024

LEEDS RHINOS 18 LEIGH LEOPARDS 10

RHINOS: 1 Lachlan Miller; 2 David Fusitu'a; 4 Paul Momirovski; 31 Ned McCormack; 29 Alfie Edgell; 6 Brodie Croft; 7 Matt Frawley; 8 Mikolaj Oledzki; 14 Jarrod O'Connor; 17 Justin Sangare; 16 James McDonnell; 12 Rhyse Martin; 13 Cameron Smith (C). Subs: 18 Mickael Goudemand; 26 Corey Johnson; 32 Ben Littlewood (not used); 36 Sam Eseh (D).
Tries: Croft (10, 27), Frawley (49); **Goals:** Martin 3/4.
LEOPARDS: 6 Matt Moylan; 24 Umyla Hanley; 3 Zak Hardaker; 4 Ricky Leutele; 5 Josh Charnley; 19 Ed Chamberlain; 7 Lachlan Lam (C); 8 Tom Amone; 15 Matt Davis; 17 Owen Trout; 11 Kai O'Donnell; 16 Frankie Halton; 12 Jack Hughes. Subs (all used): 9 Edwin Ipape; 14 Dan Norman; 33 Brad Dwyer; 35 Aaron Pene (D).
Tries: Moylan (57), Ipape (68); **Goals:** Moylan 1/2.
Rugby Leaguer & League Express Men of the Match: *Rhinos:* Brodie Croft; *Leopards:* Matt Moylan.
Penalty count: 5-3; **Half-time:** 12-0;
Referee: Chris Kendall; **Attendance:** 17,535.

WIGAN WARRIORS 36 LONDON BRONCOS 0

WARRIORS: 6 Bevan French; 2 Abbas Miski; 26 Zach Eckersley; 4 Jake Wardle; 5 Liam Marshall; 23 Ryan Hampshire; 30 Jack Farrimond; 15 Patrick Mago; 9 Brad O'Neill; 10 Liam Byrne; 21 Junior Nsemba; 12 Liam Farrell (C); 13 Kaide Ellis. Subs (all used): 8 Ethan Havard; 17 Kruise Leeming; 20 Harvie Hill; 22 Sam Walters.
Tries: Farrimond (3, 14), Marshall (23), Miski (37), Wardle (51, 56); **Goals:** Farrimond 6/6.
BRONCOS: 1 Alex Walker; 2 Lee Kershaw; 21 Robbie Storey; 3 Jarred Bassett; 4 Hakim Miloudi; 20 Oliver Leyland; 7 James Meadows; 10 Lewis Bienek; 24 Matthew Davies; 15 Marcus Stock; 11 Will Lovell (C); 17 Sadiq Adebiyi; 29 Jacob Jones. Subs (all used): 16 Jordan Williams; 18 Emmanuel Waine; 28 Jack Hughes; 34 Ugo Tison.
Sin bin: Waine (44) - dangerous contact on Leeming.
Rugby Leaguer & League Express Men of the Match: *Warriors:* Jack Farrimond; *Broncos:* Jarred Bassett.
Penalty count: 6-5; **Half-time:** 24-0;
Referee: Liam Rush; **Attendance:** 14,280.

Saturday 22nd June 2024

HULL FC 18 WARRINGTON WOLVES 24

HULL FC: 37 Logan Moy; 44 Tom Briscoe; 3 Carlos Tuimavave; 4 Liam Sutcliffe; 26 Lewis Martin; 6 Jake Trueman; 47 Ben Reynolds; 8 Herman Ese'ese; 19 Morgan Smith; 45 Yusuf Aydin; 17 Cameron Scott; 15 Jordan Lane; 12 Ligi Sao. Subs (all used): 13 Brad Fash (C); 16 Jack Ashworth; 21 Will Gardiner; 28 Denive Balmforth.
Tries: Balmforth (46), Sutcliffe (61), Briscoe (69);
Goals: Reynolds 3/3.
WOLVES: 1 Matt Dufty; 2 Josh Thewlis; 3 Toby King; 14 Rodrick Tai; 5 Matty Ashton; 6 George Williams (C); 7 Josh Drinkwater; 8 James Harrison; 9 Danny Walker; 10 Paul Vaughan; 13 Matty Nicholson; 28 Adam Holroyd; 11 Ben Currie. Subs (all used): 16 Zane Musgrove; 19 Joe Bullock; 32 Sam Powell; 34 Max Wood.
Tries: King (5), Dufty (34, 78), Walker (51);
Goals: Josh Thewlis 4/4.
Sin bin: Holroyd (31) - shoulder charge on Moy.
Rugby Leaguer & League Express Men of the Match: *Hull FC:* Herman Ese'ese; *Wolves:* Matt Dufty.
Penalty count: 3-2; **Half-time:** 0-12;
Referee: Ben Thaler; **Attendance:** 10,083.

CATALANS DRAGONS 22 HUDDERSFIELD GIANTS 18

DRAGONS: 1 Arthur Mourgue; 2 Tom Davies; 3 Arthur Romano; 21 Matt Ikuvalu; 24 Tom Johnstone; 27 Jordan Abdull; 7 Theo Fages; 16 Romain Navarrete; 9 Michael McIlorum; 10 Julian Bousquet; 11 Tariq Sims; 12 Paul Seguier; 13 Ben Garcia (C). Subs (all used): 6 Jayden Nikorima; 20 Tevita Satae; 23 Jordan Dezaria; 28 Franck Maria.
Tries: Davies (2), Fages (7), Romano (14), Johnstone (25);
Goals: Mourgue 3/4.
GIANTS: 6 Tui Lolohea; 24 Sam Halsall; 3 Esan Marsters; 4 Kevin Naiqama; 20 Elliot Wallis; 23 Oliver Russell; 7 Adam Clune; 8 Chris Hill; 9 Adam Milner; 10 Joe Greenwood; 12 Sam Hewitt; 16 Harry Rushton; 13 Luke Yates (C). Subs (all used): 14 Ashton Golding; 17 Oliver Wilson; 18 Sebastine Ikahihifo; 33 Andre Savelio.
Tries: Rushton (55), Golding (60), Yates (67);
Goals: Russell 3/3.
Rugby Leaguer & League Express Men of the Match: *Dragons:* Michael McIlorum; *Giants:* Oliver Russell.
Penalty count: 3-2; **Half-time:** 22-0;
Referee: Liam Moore; **Attendance:** 8,254.

Sunday 23rd June 2024

SALFORD RED DEVILS 20 ST HELENS 18

RED DEVILS: 23 Chris Hankinson; 2 Ethan Ryan; 3 Nene Macdonald; 11 Sam Stone; 5 Deon Cross; 14 Chris Atkin; 7 Marc Sneyd; 8 Brad Singleton; 24 Joe Mellor; 15 Shane Wright; 29 Loghan Lewis; 12 Kallum Watkins (C); 13 Oliver Partington. Subs: 10 King Vuniyayawa; 16 Joe Shorrocks; 27 Gil Dudson; 25 Nathan Connell (not used).
Tries: Cross (17, 32), Watkins (58), Hankinson (74);
Goals: Sneyd 2/5.
SAINTS: 1 Jack Welsby (C); 5 Jon Bennison; 23 Konrad Hurrell; 4 Mark Percival; 3 Waqa Blake; 14 Moses Mbye; 7 Lewis Dodd; 20 George Delaney; 9 Daryl Clark; 10 Matty Lees; 16 Curtis Sironen; 11 Sione Mata'utia; 15 James Bell. Subs (all used): 17 Agnatius Paasi; 21 Ben Davies; 22 Sam Royle; 31 Noah Stephens.
Tries: Bell (7), Sironen (54), Percival (68);
Goals: Percival 3/4.
Rugby Leaguer & League Express Men of the Match: *Red Devils:* Joe Mellor; *Saints:* Curtis Sironen.
Penalty count: 5-9; **Half-time:** 10-6;
Referee: Jack Smith; **Attendance:** 5,724.

ROUND 16

Friday 5th July 2024

ST HELENS 6 CASTLEFORD TIGERS 8

SAINTS: 1 Jack Welsby; 3 Waqa Blake; 21 Ben Davies; 4 Mark Percival; 25 Tee Ritson; 6 Jonny Lomax (C); 7 Lewis Dodd; 20 George Delaney; 14 Moses Mbye; 10 Matty Lees; 16 Curtis Sironen; 22 Sam Royle; 15 James Bell. Subs (all used): 17 Agnatius Paasi; 24 Jake Burns (D); 30 Jonny Vaughan (D); 31 Noah Stephens.
Try: Royle (38); **Goals:** Percival 1/2.
TIGERS: 34 Tex Hoy; 23 Jason Qareqare; 35 Corey Hall; 12 Alex Mellor; 5 Innes Senior; 16 Rowan Milnes; 7 Jacob Miller; 15 George Griffin; 14 Liam Horne; 20 Muizz Mustapha; 10 George Lawler; 11 Elie El-Zakhem; 13 Joe Westerman (C). Subs: 8 Liam Watts; 24 Cain Robb; 29 George Hill (not used); 37 Matty English.
Try: I Senior (56); **Goals:** Milnes 2/3.
Rugby Leaguer & League Express Men of the Match: *Saints:* Jack Welsby; *Tigers:* Rowan Milnes.
Penalty count: 7-6; **Half-time:** 4-0;
Referee: Tom Grant; **Attendance:** 9,808.

WARRINGTON WOLVES 48 HUDDERSFIELD GIANTS 0

WOLVES: 1 Matt Dufty; 14 Rodrick Tai; 20 Connor Wrench; 4 Stefan Ratchford (C); 3 Toby King; 6 George Williams; 7 Josh Drinkwater; 8 James Harrison; 9 Danny Walker; 10 Paul Vaughan; 13 Matty Nicholson; 12 Lachlan Fitzgibbon; 11 Ben Currie. Subs (all used): 28 Adam Holroyd; 16 Zane Musgrove; 29 Tom Whitehead; 32 Sam Powell.
Tries: Vaughan (2), King (15), Wrench (31), Drinkwater (43), Nicholson (53), Dufty (55), Ratchford (66), Tai (74);
Goals: Ratchford 8/8.
GIANTS: 1 Jake Connor; 30 Aidan McGowan (D); 24 Sam Halsall; 5 Jake Bibby; 20 Elliot Wallis; 6 Tui Lolohea; 7 Adam Clune; 18 Sebastine Ikahihifo; 9 Adam Milner; 10 Joe Greenwood; 16 Harry Rushton; 22 Harvey Livett; 13 Luke Yates (C). Subs (all used): 17 Oliver Wilson; 19 Thomas Deakin; 26 Hugo Salabio; 33 Andre Savelio. 18th man (used): 29 Jack Billington (D).
Rugby Leaguer & League Express Men of the Match: *Wolves:* Matt Dufty; *Giants:* Aidan McGowan.
Penalty count: 0-2; **Half-time:** 18-0;
Referee: Jack Smith; **Attendance:** 9,760.

WIGAN WARRIORS 24 LEIGH LEOPARDS 6

WARRIORS: 6 Bevan French; 2 Abbas Miski; 3 Adam Keighran; 4 Jake Wardle; 5 Liam Marshall; 30 Jack Farrimond; 7 Harry Smith; 14 Mike Cooper; 9 Brad O'Neill; 16 Luke Thompson; 21 Junior Nsemba; 12 Liam Farrell (C); 13 Kaide Ellis. Subs (all used): 8 Ethan Havard; 15 Patrick Mago; 19 Tyler Dupree; 22 Sam Walters.
Tries: French (21, 58), Marshall (56), Farrell (79);
Goals: Keighran 4/5.
Sin bin: O'Neill (38) - dangerous challenge on Mulhern.
LEOPARDS: 6 Matt Moylan; 24 Umyla Hanley; 3 Zak Hardaker; 4 Ricky Leutele; 5 Josh Charnley; 1 Gareth O'Brien; 7 Lachlan Lam; 8 Tom Amone; 9 Edwin Ipape; 10 Robbie Mulhern; 19 Ed Chamberlain; 11 Kai O'Donnell; 17 Owen Trout. Subs (all used): 12 Jack Hughes; 13 John Asiata (C); 33 Brad Dwyer; 35 Aaron Pene.
Try: Dwyer (53); **Goals:** Moylan 1/1.
Sin bin: Mulhern (20) - late challenge on Ellis.
Rugby Leaguer & League Express Men of the Match: *Warriors:* Brad O'Neill; *Leopards:* Robbie Mulhern.
Penalty count: 7-7; **Half-time:** 8-0;
Referee: Aaron Moore; **Attendance:** 16,053.

Saturday 6th July 2024

LEEDS RHINOS 17 LONDON BRONCOS 16
(after golden point extra-time)

RHINOS: 1 Lachlan Miller; 2 David Fusitu'a; 3 Harry Newman; 4 Paul Momirovski; 5 Ash Handley; 6 Brodie Croft; 7 Matt Frawley; 8 Mikolaj Oledzki; 14 Jarrod O'Connor; 18 Mickael Goudemand; 16 James McDonnell; 12 Rhyse Martin; 13 Cameron Smith (C). Subs (all used): 36 Sam Eseh; 17 Justin Sangare; 9 Andy Ackers; 15 Sam Lisone.
Tries: Handley (8), Momirovski (19), Martin (68);
Goals: Martin 2/3; **Field goal:** Croft (83).
BRONCOS: 23 Josh Rourke (D); 2 Lee Kershaw; 3 Jarred Bassett; 21 Robbie Storey; 5 Iliess Macani; 20 Oliver Leyland; 7 James Meadows; 19 Rhys Kennedy; 9 Sam Davis; 10 Lewis Bienek; 11 Will Lovell (C); 17 Sadiq Adebiyi; 29 Jacob Jones. Subs (all used): 34 Ugo Tison; 15 Marcus Stock; 16 Jordan Williams; 12 Ethan Natoli.
Tries: Rourke (5), Kennedy (29), Macani (32);
Goals: O Leyland 2/3.
Rugby Leaguer & League Express Men of the Match: *Rhinos:* Matt Frawley; *Broncos:* Josh Rourke.
Penalty count: 3-5; **Half-time:** 10-16;
Referee: Marcus Griffiths; **Attendance:** 12,958.

HULL KR 14 CATALANS DRAGONS 15
(after golden point extra-time)

HULL KR: 2 Niall Evalds; 35 Joe Burgess; 1 Peta Hiku; 36 Jack Broadbent; 5 Ryan Hall; 7 Mikey Lewis; 27 Tyrone May; 8 Sauaso Sue; 9 Jez Litten; 10 George King; 11 Dean Hadley; 20 Kelepi Tanginoa; 16 Jai Whitbread. Subs (all used): 13 Elliot Minchella (C); 14 Matt Parcell; 15 Sam Luckley; 17 Matty Storton.
Tries: Broadbent (44), Burgess (53); **Goals:** Lewis 3/3.
DRAGONS: 1 Arthur Mourgue; 2 Tom Davies; 21 Matt Ikuvalu; 3 Arthur Romano; 24 Tom Johnstone; 27 Jordan Abdull; 7 Theo Fages; 16 Romain Navarrete; 14 Alrix Da Costa; 10 Julian Bousquet; 11 Tariq Sims; 15 Bayley Sironen; 13 Ben Garcia (C). Subs (all used): 12 Paul Seguier; 17 Cesar Rouge; 20 Tevita Satae; 23 Jordan Dezaria.
Tries: Da Costa (5), Johnstone (36); **Goals:** Mourgue 3/3;
Field goal: Fages (87).
Rugby Leaguer & League Express Men of the Match: *Hull KR:* Joe Burgess; *Dragons:* Julian Bousquet.
Penalty count: 2-3; **Half-time:** 0-14;
Referee: Liam Moore; **Attendance:** 9,579.

Sunday 7th July 2024

SALFORD RED DEVILS 22 HULL FC 20

RED DEVILS: 1 Ryan Brierley; 2 Ethan Ryan; 12 Kallum Watkins (C); 23 Chris Hankinson; 5 Deon Cross; 14 Chris Atkin; 7 Marc Sneyd; 8 Brad Singleton; 24 Joe Mellor; 29 Loghan Lewis; 15 Shane Wright; 11 Sam Stone; 13 Oliver Partington. Subs (all used): 9 Amir Bourouh; 10 King Vuniyayawa; 16 Joe Shorrocks; 27 Gil Dudson.
Tries: Cross (27), Brierley (43), Hankinson (46);
Goals: Sneyd 5/6.
HULL FC: 37 Logan Moy; 44 Tom Briscoe; 3 Carlos Tuimavave; 4 Liam Sutcliffe; 26 Lewis Martin; 6 Jake Trueman; 47 Ben Reynolds; 8 Herman Ese'ese; 9 Danny Houghton (C); 45 Yusuf Aydin; 49 Will Kirby (D); 15 Jordan Lane; 12 Ligi Sao. Subs (all used): 13 Brad Fash; 21 Will Gardiner; 28 Denive Balmforth; 46 Tiaki Chan.
Tries: Reynolds (32), Balmforth (50), Lane (70), Martin (77); **Goals:** Reynolds 2/4.
Sin bin: Briscoe (40) - professional foul.
Rugby League & League Express Men of the Match:
Red Devils: Ryan Brierley; *Hull FC:* Jordan Lane.
Penalty count: 8-3; **Half-time:** 6-6;
Referee: Chris Kendall; **Attendance:** 3,910.

ROUND 17

Thursday 11th July 2024

WARRINGTON WOLVES 30 LEEDS RHINOS 18

WOLVES: 1 Matt Dufty; 33 Arron Lindop; 14 Rodrick Tai; 4 Stefan Ratchford (C); 5 Matty Ashton; 6 George Williams; 7 Josh Drinkwater; 8 James Harrison; 9 Danny Walker; 10 Paul Vaughan; 13 Matty Nicholson; 28 Adam Holroyd; 11 Ben Currie. Subs (all used): 16 Zane Musgrove; 17 Jordan Crowther; 29 Tom Whitehead; 32 Sam Powell.
Tries: Ashton (2), Dufty (4, 35), Tai (39), Whitehead (60);
Goals: Ratchford 5/5.
Sin bin: Williams (50) - high tackle on Ackers;
Ashton (74) - professional foul.
RHINOS: 1 Lachlan Miller; 2 David Fusitu'a; 4 Paul Momirovski; 31 Ned McCormack; 5 Ash Handley; 6 Brodie Croft; 21 Jack Sinfield; 8 Mikolaj Oledzki; 14 Jarrod O'Connor; 36 Sam Eseh; 16 James McDonnell; 12 Rhyse Martin; 13 Cameron Smith (C). Subs (all used): 9 Andy Ackers; 15 Sam Lisone; 18 Mickael Goudemand; 29 Alfie Edgell.
Tries: Fusitu'a (17), Miller (45), McCormack (51), Momirovski (75); **Goals:** Martin 1/4.
Rugby League & League Express Men of the Match:
Wolves: Matt Dufty; *Rhinos:* Sam Lisone.
Penalty count: 7-6; **Half-time:** 24-4;
Referee: Jack Smith; **Attendance:** 8,471.

Friday 12th July 2024

LONDON BRONCOS 20 CASTLEFORD TIGERS 34

BRONCOS: 23 Josh Rourke; 2 Lee Kershaw; 21 Robbie Storey; 3 Jarred Bassett; 5 Iliess Macani; 20 Oliver Leyland; 7 James Meadows; 19 Rhys Kennedy; 9 Sam Davis; 10 Lewis Bienek; 11 Will Lovell (C); 17 Sadiq Adebiyi; 29 Jacob Jones. Subs (all used): 8 Rob Butler; 12 Ethan Natoli; 15 Marcus Stock; 34 Ugo Tison.
Tries: Rourke (22), Lovell (37), Stock (60), Bienek (69);
Goals: O Leyland 2/4.
Sin bin: Kennedy (8) - dissent.
TIGERS: 34 Tex Hoy; 23 Jason Qareqare; 35 Corey Hall; 12 Alex Mellor; 5 Innes Senior; 16 Rowan Milnes; 7 Jacob Miller; 15 George Griffin; 14 Liam Horne; 20 Muizz Mustapha; 11 Elie El-Zakhem; 10 George Lawler; 13 Joe Westerman (C). Subs (all used): 8 Liam Watts; 24 Cain Robb; 30 Luis Johnson; 37 Matty English.
Tries: Hoy (3), I Senior (9, 32), Mellor (28, 53), Milnes (56);
Goals: Milnes 5/6.
Rugby League & League Express Men of the Match:
Broncos: Will Lovell; *Tigers:* Jacob Miller.
Penalty count: 6-5; **Half-time:** 8-22;
Referee: James Vella; **Attendance:** 2,050
(at Kuflink Stadium, Ebbsfleet).

WIGAN WARRIORS 16 ST HELENS 12

WARRIORS: 26 Zach Eckersley; 2 Abbas Miski; 3 Adam Keighran; 4 Jake Wardle; 5 Liam Marshall; 30 Jack Farrimond; 7 Harry Smith; 8 Ethan Havard; 16 Luke Thompson; 19 Tyler Dupree; 21 Junior Nsemba; 12 Liam Farrell (C); 13 Kaide Ellis. Subs (all used): 10 Liam Byrne; 15 Patrick Mago; 20 Harvie Hill; 22 Sam Walters.
Tries: Wardle (23), Keighran (62), Eckersley (68);
Goals: Smith 2/3.
SAINTS: 33 Harry Robertson (D); 25 Tee Ritson; 4 Mark Percival; 21 Ben Davies; 3 Waqa Blake; 1 Jack Welsby; 6 Jonny Lomax (C); 20 George Delaney; 9 Daryl Clark; 10 Matty Lees; 16 Curtis Sironen; 15 James Bell; 17 Agnatius Paasi. Subs: 22 Sam Royle (not used); 24 Jake Burns (not used); 30 Jonny Vaughan; 31 Noah Stephens.
Tries: Welsby (20), Blake (58); **Goals:** Percival 2/2.
Sin bin: Lees (1) - high tackle on Ellis.
Rugby League & League Express Men of the Match:
Warriors: Zach Eckersley; *Saints:* Harry Robertson.
Penalty count: 4-5; **Half-time:** 6-6;
Referee: Liam Moore; **Attendance:** 20,152.

Saturday 13th July 2024

HULL FC 10 HULL KR 24

HULL FC: 37 Logan Moy; 44 Tom Briscoe; 3 Carlos Tuimavave; 4 Liam Sutcliffe; 26 Lewis Martin; 6 Jake Trueman; 40 Jack Charles; 8 Herman Ese'ese; 19 Morgan Smith; 45 Yusuf Aydin; 15 Jordan Lane; 12 Ligi Sao; 21 Will Gardiner. Subs (all used): 13 Brad Fash (C); 23 Davy Litten; 28 Denive Balmforth; 46 Tiaki Chan.
Tries: Martin (56), Moy (58); **Goals:** Sutcliffe 1/2.
Sin bin: Fash (39) - fighting;
Balmforth (70) - late challenge on May.
HULL KR: 2 Niall Evalds; 35 Joe Burgess; 1 Peta Hiku; 4 Oliver Gildart; 5 Ryan Hall; 27 Tyrone May; 7 Mikey Lewis; 8 Sauaso Sue; 14 Matt Parcell; 11 Dean Hadley; 17 Matty Storton; 20 Kelepi Tanginoa; 13 Elliot Minchella (C). Subs (all used): 3 Tom Opacic; 9 Jez Litten; 16 Jai Whitbread; 37 Jack Brown.
Tries: Sue (4), Lewis (13), Storton (17), Minchella (79);
Goals: Lewis 4/4.
Sin bin: Minchella (39) - fighting;
Burgess (55) - professional foul.
Rugby League & League Express Men of the Match:
Hull FC: Davy Litten; *Hull KR:* Matt Parcell.
Penalty count: 6-10; **Half-time:** 0-18;
Referee: Chris Kendall; **Attendance:** 15,392.

LEIGH LEOPARDS 20 HUDDERSFIELD GIANTS 16

LEOPARDS: 6 Matt Moylan; 24 Umyla Hanley; 34 Darnell McIntosh; 4 Ricky Leutele; 3 Zak Hardaker; 1 Gareth O'Brien; 7 Lachlan Lam; 8 Tom Amone; 9 Edwin Ipape; 10 Robbie Mulhern; 11 Kai O'Donnell; 16 Frankie Halton; 17 Owen Trout. Subs (all used): 12 Jack Hughes; 13 John Asiata (C); 33 Brad Dwyer; 35 Aaron Pene.
Tries: McIntosh (27), O'Donnell (66), Hardaker (69);
Goals: Moylan 3/4, Hardaker 1/1.
Sin bin: Hughes (57) - retaliation.
GIANTS: 1 Jake Connor; 30 Aidan McGowan; 5 Jake Bibby; 24 Sam Halsall; 20 Elliot Wallis; 6 Tui Lolohea; 7 Adam Clune; 8 Chris Hill; 9 Adam Milner; 10 Joe Greenwood; 12 Sam Hewitt; 16 Harry Rushton; 13 Luke Yates (C). Subs (all used): 14 Ashton Golding; 17 Oliver Wilson; 25 Fenton Rogers; 33 Andre Savelio.
Tries: Wallis (7, 77, pen), Connor (48); **Goals:** Connor 2/4.
Dismissal: Savelio (58) - shoulder charge on Mulhern.
Sin bin: Hill (57) - high tackle on Dwyer.
Rugby League & League Express Men of the Match:
Leopards: Lachlan Lam; *Giants:* Luke Yates.
Penalty count: 8-8; **Half-time:** 6-4;
Referee: Tom Grant; **Attendance:** 7,160.

CATALANS DRAGONS 20 SALFORD RED DEVILS 0

DRAGONS: 1 Arthur Mourgue; 2 Tom Davies; 3 Arthur Romano; 21 Matt Ikuvalu; 5 Fouad Yaha; 17 Cesar Rouge; 7 Theo Fages; 16 Romain Navarrete; 9 Michael McIlorum; 10 Julian Bousquet; 11 Tariq Sims; 15 Bayley Sironen; 13 Ben Garcia (C). Subs (all used): 12 Paul Seguier; 14 Alrix Da Costa; 20 Tevita Satae; 23 Jordan Dezaria.
Tries: Rouge (5), Romano (11, 29); **Goals:** Mourgue 4/4.
RED DEVILS: 1 Ryan Brierley; 2 Ethan Ryan; 11 Sam Stone; 23 Chris Hankinson; 5 Deon Cross; 14 Chris Atkin; 7 Marc Sneyd; 8 Brad Singleton; 24 Joe Mellor; 29 Loghan Lewis; 15 Shane Wright; 12 Kallum Watkins (C); 13 Oliver Partington. Subs (all used): 9 Amir Bourouh; 10 King Vuniyayawa; 16 Joe Shorrocks; 27 Gil Dudson.
Rugby League & League Express Men of the Match:
Dragons: Theo Fages; *Red Devils:* Chris Atkin.
Penalty count: 6-1; **Half-time:** 18-0;
Referee: Aaron Moore; **Attendance:** 7,750.

ROUND 18

Friday 19th July 2024

HUDDERSFIELD GIANTS 16 SALFORD RED DEVILS 8

GIANTS: 1 Jake Connor; 30 Aidan McGowan; 4 Kevin Naiqama; 24 Sam Halsall; 20 Elliot Wallis; 6 Tui Lolohea; 7 Adam Clune; 8 Chris Hill; 9 Adam Milner; 15 Matty English; 21 Leroy Cudjoe (C); 5 Jake Bibby; 16 Harry Rushton. Subs (all used): 14 Ashton Golding; 23 Oliver Russell; 25 Fenton Rogers; 26 Hugo Salabio.
Tries: Halsall (51), Milner (79); **Goals:** Connor 4/5.
RED DEVILS: 1 Ryan Brierley; 2 Ethan Ryan; 3 Nene Macdonald; 23 Chris Hankinson; 5 Deon Cross; 6 Cade Cust; 7 Marc Sneyd; 8 Brad Singleton; 24 Joe Mellor; 13 Oliver Partington; 12 Kallum Watkins (C); 15 Shane Wright; 16 Joe Shorrocks. Subs (all used): 14 Chris Atkin; 27 Gil Dudson; 28 Harvey Wilson; 31 Joe Bullock (D).
Try: Mellor (37); **Goals:** Sneyd 2/2.
Sin bin: Singleton (67) - high tackle on English.
Rugby League & League Express Men of the Match:
Giants: Adam Milner; *Red Devils:* Chris Hankinson.
Penalty count: 7-4; **Half-time:** 2-6;
Referee: Jack Smith; **Attendance:** 4,119.

ST HELENS 10 WARRINGTON WOLVES 24

SAINTS: 33 Harry Robertson; 25 Tee Ritson; 30 Jonny Vaughan; 4 Mark Percival; 3 Waqa Blake; 1 Jack Welsby; 6 Jonny Lomax (C); 17 Agnatius Paasi; 9 Daryl Clark; 10 Matty Lees; 16 Curtis Sironen; 15 James Bell; 14 Moses Mbye. Subs (all used): 5 Jon Bennison; 7 Lewis Dodd; 22 Sam Royle; 31 Noah Stephens.
Tries: Paasi (45), Royle (67); **Goals:** Percival 1/2.
WOLVES: 1 Matt Dufty; 33 Arron Lindop; 14 Rodrick Tai; 4 Stefan Ratchford (C); 5 Matty Ashton; 6 George Williams; 7 Josh Drinkwater; 8 James Harrison; 32 Sam Powell; 10 Paul Vaughan; 13 Matty Nicholson; 28 Adam Holroyd; 11 Ben Currie. Subs (all used): 9 Danny Walker; 16 Zane Musgrove; 29 Tom Whitehead; 41 Luke Yates (D).
Tries: Ashton (10), Dufty (15), Holroyd (72), Nicholson (75);
Goals: Ratchford 2/3, Drinkwater 2/3.
Dismissal: Harrison (20) - high tackle on Stephens.
Sin bin: Nicholson (55) - obstruction.
Rugby League & League Express Men of the Match:
Saints: Noah Stephens; *Wolves:* George Williams.
Penalty count: 5-7; **Half-time:** 0-12;
Referee: Chris Kendall; **Attendance:** 13,135.

LEIGH LEOPARDS 36 LONDON BRONCOS 6

LEOPARDS: 3 Zak Hardaker; 34 Darnell McIntosh; 24 Umyla Hanley; 4 Ricky Leutele; 5 Josh Charnley; 1 Gareth O'Brien; 7 Lachlan Lam; 8 Tom Amone; 33 Brad Dwyer; 10 Robbie Mulhern; 11 Kai O'Donnell; 16 Frankie Halton; 13 John Asiata (C). Subs (all used): 17 Owen Trout; 12 Jack Hughes; 15 Matt Davis; 30 Louis Brogan.
Tries: McIntosh (3), Amone (10), Leutele (17), Davis (32), Charnley (49), Lam (63), Hughes (73); **Goals:** Hardaker 4/7.
BRONCOS: 23 Josh Rourke; 2 Lee Kershaw; 12 Ethan Natoli; 3 Jarred Bassett; 5 Iliess Macani; 20 Oliver Leyland; 34 Ugo Tison; 8 Rob Butler; 9 Sam Davis; 19 Rhys Kennedy; 11 Will Lovell (C); 17 Sadiq Adebiyi; 15 Marcus Stock. Subs (all used): 10 Lewis Bienek; 13 Dean Parata; 6 Jack Campagnolo; 18 Emmanuel Waine.
Try: Rourke (60); **Goals:** O Leyland 1/1.
Sin bin: Adebiyi (63) - late challenge on O'Brien.
Rugby League & League Express Men of the Match:
Leopards: Lachlan Lam; *Broncos:* Josh Rourke.
Penalty count: 6-8; **Half-time:** 22-0;
Referee: Liam Rush; **Attendance:** 6,677.

Saturday 20th July 2024

HULL FC 24 WIGAN WARRIORS 22

HULL FC: 31 Jack Walker; 44 Tom Briscoe; 23 Davy Litten; 4 Liam Sutcliffe; 26 Lewis Martin; 6 Jake Trueman; 40 Jack Charles; 8 Herman Ese'ese; 19 Morgan Smith; 12 Ligi Sao (C); 15 Jordan Lane; 43 Ed Chamberlain; 45 Yusuf Aydin. Subs (all used): 21 Will Gardiner; 28 Denive Balmforth; 30 Matty Laidlaw; 50 King Vuniyayawa (D).
Tries: Walker (5), Sutcliffe (20), Litten (32), Balmforth (43);
Goals: Charles 4/4.
Sin bin: Litten (72) - high tackle on Farrimond.
WARRIORS: 26 Zach Eckersley; 2 Abbas Miski; 3 Adam Keighran; 4 Jake Wardle; 5 Liam Marshall; 30 Jack Farrimond; 7 Harry Smith; 8 Ethan Havard; 9 Brad O'Neill; 16 Luke Thompson; 21 Junior Nsemba; 12 Liam Farrell (C); 13 Kaide Ellis. Subs (all used): 10 Liam Byrne; 15 Patrick Mago; 19 Tyler Dupree; 22 Sam Walters.
Tries: Marshall (16, 72), O'Neill (63), Eckersley (75);
Goals: Keighran 3/4.
Sin bin: Dupree (34) - dangerous challenge on Chamberlain.
Rugby League & League Express Men of the Match:
Hull FC: Jack Walker; *Warriors:* Brad O'Neill.
Penalty count: 4-1; **Half-time:** 18-4;
Referee: Aaron Moore; **Attendance:** 9,771.

LEEDS RHINOS 12 HULL KR 20

RHINOS: 1 Lachlan Miller; 2 David Fusitu'a; 4 Paul Momirovski; 3 Harry Newman; 5 Ash Handley; 6 Brodie Croft; 7 Matt Frawley; 8 Mikolaj Oledzki; 9 Andy Ackers; 36 Sam Eseh; 16 James McDonnell; 12 Rhyse Martin; 13 Cameron Smith (C). Subs: 14 Jarrod O'Connor; 15 Sam Lisone; 25 James Donaldson; 29 Alfie Edgell (not used).
Tries: Martin (5), Miller (69); **Goals:** Martin 2/3.
HULL KR: 36 Jack Broadbent; 35 Joe Burgess; 1 Peta Hiku; 4 Oliver Gildart; 5 Ryan Hall; 27 Tyrone May; 7 Mikey Lewis; 8 Sauaso Sue; 14 Matt Parcell; 11 Dean Hadley; 17

Matty Storton; 3 Tom Opacic; 13 Elliot Minchella (C). Subs (all used): 9 Jez Litten; 15 Sam Luckley; 16 Jai Whitbread; 20 Kelepi Tanginoa.
Tries: R Hall (45), Lewis (53), Whitbread (74), Litten (79); **Goals:** Lewis 2/4.
Rugby Leaguer & League Express Men of the Match: *Rhinos:* Matt Frawley; *Hull KR:* Jai Whitbread.
Penalty count: 7-2; **Half-time:** 6-0;
Referee: Liam Moore; **Attendance:** 14,555.

Sunday 21st July 2024

CASTLEFORD TIGERS 24 CATALANS DRAGONS 18

TIGERS: 34 Tex Hoy; 23 Jason Qareqare; 35 Corey Hall; 12 Alex Mellor; 5 Innes Senior; 16 Rowan Milnes; 7 Jacob Miller; 15 George Griffin; 14 Liam Horne; 20 Muizz Mustapha; 10 George Lawler; 11 Elie El-Zakhem; 13 Joe Westerman (C). Subs (all used): 8 Liam Watts; 21 Sylvester Namo; 24 Cain Robb; 30 Luis Johnson.
Tries: Horne (6, 24), Miller (14), Hoy (72); **Goals:** Milnes 4/4.
DRAGONS: 1 Arthur Mourgue; 2 Tom Davies; 3 Arthur Romano; 21 Matt Ikuvalu; 24 Tom Johnstone; 17 Cesar Rouge; 27 Jordan Abdull; 16 Romain Navarrete; 9 Michael McIlorum; 10 Julian Bousquet; 11 Tariq Sims; 12 Paul Seguier; 13 Ben Garcia (C). Subs (all used): 14 Alrix Da Costa; 20 Tevita Satae; 23 Jordan Dezaria; 30 Guillermo Aispuro-Bichet (D).
Tries: Johnstone (32), Ikuvalu (45), Mourgue (68);
Goals: Mourgue 3/3.
Rugby Leaguer & League Express Men of the Match: *Tigers:* Liam Horne; *Dragons:* Jordan Abdull.
Penalty count: 4-3; **Half-time:** 18-6;
Referee: Marcus Griffiths; **Attendance:** 7,331.

ROUND 19

Thursday 25th July 2024

HUDDERSFIELD GIANTS 6 LEEDS RHINOS 34

GIANTS: 1 Jake Connor; 20 Elliot Wallis; 24 Sam Halsall; 4 Kevin Naiqama; 30 Aidan McGowan; 6 Tui Lolohea; 7 Adam Clune; 8 Chris Hill; 9 Adam Milner; 15 Matty English; 5 Jake Bibby; 21 Leroy Cudjoe (C); 16 Harry Rushton. Subs (all used): 14 Ashton Golding; 23 Oliver Russell; 25 Fenton Rogers; 26 Hugo Salabio.
Try: McGowan (11); **Goals:** Connor 1/1.
Sin bin: Milner (76) - fighting.
RHINOS: 1 Lachlan Miller; 29 Alfie Edgell; 4 Paul Momirovski; 3 Harry Newman; 5 Ash Handley; 6 Brodie Croft; 7 Matt Frawley; 8 Mikolaj Oledzki; 9 Andy Ackers; 36 Sam Eseh; 16 James McDonnell; 12 Rhyse Martin; 13 Cameron Smith (C). Subs (all used): 11 James Bentley; 14 Jarrod O'Connor; 15 Sam Lisone; 25 James Donaldson.
Tries: Handley (2, 59), Newman (34), Frawley (37), Croft (67), Miller (74); **Goals:** Martin 5/6.
Sin bin: Lisone (76) - fighting.
Rugby Leaguer & League Express Men of the Match: *Giants:* Leroy Cudjoe; *Rhinos:* Rhyse Martin.
Penalty count: 6-1; **Half-time:** 6-18;
Referee: Marcus Griffiths; **Attendance:** 4,923.

Friday 26th July 2024

HULL KR 40 LONDON BRONCOS 16

HULL KR: 2 Niall Evalds; 35 Joe Burgess; 1 Peta Hiku; 4 Oliver Gildart; 5 Ryan Hall; 7 Mikey Lewis; 38 Danny Richardson; 8 Sauaso Sue; 9 Jez Litten; 16 Jai Whitbread; 17 Matty Storton; 12 James Batchelor (C); 11 Dean Hadley. Subs (all used): 14 Matt Parcell; 15 Sam Luckley; 20 Kelepi Tanginoa; 37 Jack Brown.
Tries: Sue (5), R Hall (12), Lewis (15, 66, 77), Parcell (56), Tanginoa (70); **Goals:** Richardson 6/7.
BRONCOS: 23 Josh Rourke; 4 Hakim Miloudi; 12 Ethan Natoli; 3 Jarred Bassett; 5 Iliess Macani; 20 Oliver Leyland; 6 Jack Campagnolo; 8 Rob Butler; 9 Sam Davis; 19 Rhys Kennedy; 11 Will Lovell (C); 17 Sadiq Adebiyi; 29 Jacob Jones. Subs (all used): 10 Lewis Bienek; 13 Dean Parata; 15 Marcus Stock; 34 Ugo Tison.
Tries: Bienek (38), Rourke (44), Macani (76);
Goals: O Leyland 2/3.
Rugby Leaguer & League Express Men of the Match: *Hull KR:* Mikey Lewis; *Broncos:* Josh Rourke.
Penalty count: 8-6; **Half-time:** 16-6;
Referee: Tom Grant; **Attendance:** 9,346.

LEIGH LEOPARDS 46 ST HELENS 4

LEOPARDS: 6 Matt Moylan; 5 Josh Charnley; 4 Ricky Leutele; 24 Umyla Hanley; 34 Darnell McIntosh; 1 Gareth O'Brien; 7 Lachlan Lam; 8 Tom Amone; 9 Edwin Ipape; 10 Robbie Mulhern; 11 Kai O'Donnell; 16 Frankie Halton; 13 John Asiata (C). Subs (all used): 12 Jack Hughes; 17 Owen Trout; 33 Brad Dwyer; 35 Aaron Pene. 18th man (used): 30 Louis Brogan.
Tries: Hanley (17), Amone (24), McIntosh (27), O'Donnell (39), Charnley (60, 80), Lam (65), Moylan (69);
Goals: McIntosh 7/9.

SAINTS: 33 Harry Robertson; 2 Tommy Makinson; 21 Ben Davies; 4 Mark Percival; 3 Waqa Blake; 1 Jack Welsby; 6 Jonny Lomax (C); 20 George Delaney; 9 Daryl Clark; 10 Matty Lees; 16 Curtis Sironen; 15 James Bell; 17 Agnatius Paasi. Subs (all used): 14 Moses Mbye; 19 Matt Whitley; 30 Jonny Vaughan; 31 Noah Stephens.
Try: Davies (47); **Goals:** Percival 0/1.
Sin bin: Percival (16) - late challenge on Moylan; Lomax (54) - late challenge on O'Brien.
Rugby Leaguer & League Express Men of the Match: *Leopards:* Lachlan Lam; *Saints:* Harry Robertson.
Penalty count: 5-1; **Half-time:** 24-0;
Referee: Aaron Moore; **Attendance:** 8,021.

WIGAN WARRIORS 4 WARRINGTON WOLVES 40

WARRIORS: 26 Zach Eckersley; 2 Abbas Miski; 12 Liam Farrell (C); 4 Jake Wardle; 5 Liam Marshall; 30 Jack Farrimond; 7 Harry Smith; 10 Liam Byrne; 9 Brad O'Neill; 16 Luke Thompson; 21 Junior Nsemba; 22 Sam Walters; 13 Kaide Ellis. Subs (all used): 8 Ethan Havard; 15 Patrick Mago; 19 Tyler Dupree; 20 Harvie Hill.
Try: Marshall (13); **Goals:** Smith 0/1.
WOLVES: 1 Matt Dufty; 2 Josh Thewlis; 14 Rodrick Tai; 33 Arron Lindop; 5 Matty Ashton; 6 George Williams (C); 7 Josh Drinkwater; 41 Luke Yates; 32 Sam Powell; 10 Paul Vaughan; 13 Matty Nicholson; 28 Adam Holroyd; 11 Ben Currie. Subs (all used): 9 Danny Walker; 16 Zane Musgrove; 17 Jordan Crowther; 34 Max Wood.
Tries: Lindop (2, 44), Holroyd (20), Ashton (32, 56), Josh Thewlis (66), Tai (80); **Goals:** Josh Thewlis 6/7.
Sin bin: Dufty (73) - dangerous challenge on Marshall.
Rugby Leaguer & League Express Men of the Match: *Warriors:* Liam Marshall; *Wolves:* George Williams.
Penalty count: 3-6; **Half-time:** 4-18;
Referee: Liam Moore; **Attendance:** 15,764.

Saturday 27th July 2024

SALFORD RED DEVILS 30 CASTLEFORD TIGERS 22

RED DEVILS: 1 Ryan Brierley; 2 Ethan Ryan; 3 Nene Macdonald; 4 Tim Lafai; 5 Deon Cross; 32 Jayden Nikorima (D); 7 Marc Sneyd; 8 Brad Singleton; 16 Joe Shorrocks; 31 Joe Bullock; 11 Sam Stone; 12 Kallum Watkins (C); 13 Oliver Partington. Subs (all used): 15 Shane Wright; 23 Chris Hankinson; 24 Joe Mellor; 29 Loghan Lewis.
Tries: Macdonald (25), Brierley (37), Ryan (60), Partington (66), Hankinson (69); **Goals:** Sneyd 5/5.
TIGERS: 34 Tex Hoy; 5 Innes Senior; 12 Alex Mellor; 35 Corey Hall; 23 Jason Qareqare; 16 Rowan Milnes; 7 Jacob Miller; 15 George Griffin; 14 Liam Horne; 20 Muizz Mustapha; 10 George Lawler; 11 Elie El-Zakhem; 13 Joe Westerman (C). Subs (all used): 19 Sam Hall; 21 Sylvester Namo; 24 Cain Robb; 30 Luis Johnson.
Tries: Qareqare (15, 49), El-Zakhem (56), Johnson (70);
Goals: Milnes 3/4.
Sin bin: Horne (33) - late challenge; Namo (65) - high tackle on Partington.
Rugby Leaguer & League Express Men of the Match: *Red Devils:* Nene Macdonald; *Tigers:* Elie El-Zakhem.
Penalty count: 3-5; **Half-time:** 12-6;
Referee: Chris Kendall; **Attendance:** 3,146.

CATALANS DRAGONS 24 HULL FC 16

DRAGONS: 29 Sam Tomkins; 2 Tom Davies; 3 Arthur Romano; 4 Matthieu Laguerre; 21 Matt Ikuvalu; 1 Arthur Mourgue; 7 Theo Fages; 16 Romain Navarrete; 9 Michael McIlorum; 10 Julian Bousquet; 11 Tariq Sims; 15 Bayley Sironen; 13 Ben Garcia (C). Subs (all used): 20 Tevita Satae; 23 Jordan Dezaria; 30 Guillermo Aispuro-Bichet; 33 Jarrod Wallace (D).
Tries: McIlorum (2), Tomkins (19), Garcia (54), Davies (71);
Goals: Mourgue 4/5.
Dismissal: Sims (9) - high tackle on Chamberlain.
HULL FC: 31 Jack Walker; 25 Harvey Barron; 3 Carlos Tuimavave; 4 Liam Sutcliffe; 26 Lewis Martin; 6 Jake Trueman; 40 Jack Charles; 8 Herman Ese'ese; 19 Morgan Smith; 12 Ligi Sao (C); 15 Jordan Lane; 43 Ed Chamberlain; 45 Yusuf Aydin. Subs (all used): 13 Brad Fash; 21 Will Gardiner; 28 Denive Balmforth; 50 King Vuniyayawa.
Tries: Tuimavave (11), Walker (43), Martin (75);
Goals: Charles 2/3.
Dismissal: Sao (16) - high tackle on Tomkins.
Rugby Leaguer & League Express Men of the Match: *Dragons:* Ben Garcia; *Hull FC:* Jack Walker.
Penalty count: 8-7; **Half-time:** 14-6;
Referee: Liam Rush; **Attendance:** 9,214.

ROUND 20

Thursday 1st August 2024

CASTLEFORD TIGERS 10 LEIGH LEOPARDS 20

TIGERS: 34 Tex Hoy; 31 Fletcher Rooney; 35 Corey Hall; 12 Alex Mellor; 5 Innes Senior; 16 Rowan Milnes; 7 Jacob Miller; 20 Muizz Mustapha; 10 George Lawler; 13 Joe Westerman (C); 30 Luis Johnson; 11 Elie El-Zakhem; 29 George Hill. Subs (all used): 8 Liam Watts; 21 Sylvester Namo; 24 Cain Robb; 32 Dan Hindmarsh.
Tries: Rooney (4), Westerman (63); **Goals:** Milnes 1/2.
Sin bin: Namo (78) - dangerous challenge.
LEOPARDS: 3 Zak Hardaker; 34 Darnell McIntosh; 24 Umyla Hanley; 4 Ricky Leutele; 5 Josh Charnley; 12 Jack Hughes; 7 Lachlan Lam; 17 Owen Trout; 9 Edwin Ipape; 10 Robbie Mulhern; 11 Kai O'Donnell; 16 Frankie Halton; 13 John Asiata (C). Subs (all used): 14 Dan Norman; 30 Louis Brogan; 33 Brad Dwyer; 35 Aaron Pene.
Tries: Hardaker (22), Charnley (31, 52), Ipape (46);
Goals: McIntosh 0/2, Hardaker 2/3.
Rugby Leaguer & League Express Men of the Match: *Tigers:* Joe Westerman; *Leopards:* Lachlan Lam.
Penalty count: 5-6; **Half-time:** 4-8;
Referee: Marcus Griffiths; **Attendance:** 7,247.

WIGAN WARRIORS 28 HUDDERSFIELD GIANTS 14

WARRIORS: 1 Jai Field; 2 Abbas Miski; 3 Adam Keighran; 4 Jake Wardle; 5 Liam Marshall; 23 Ryan Hampshire; 7 Harry Smith; 8 Ethan Havard; 17 Kruise Leeming; 16 Luke Thompson; 21 Junior Nsemba; 12 Liam Farrell (C); 13 Kaide Ellis. Subs (all used): 15 Patrick Mago; 19 Tyler Dupree; 22 Sam Walters; 26 Zach Eckersley.
Tries: Wardle (47), Hampshire (51), Field (64), Eckersley (75); **Goals:** Keighran 6/6.
GIANTS: 1 Jake Connor; 30 Aidan McGowan; 5 Jake Bibby; 4 Kevin Naiqama; 24 Sam Halsall; 6 Tui Lolohea; 23 Oliver Russell; 8 Chris Hill; 9 Adam Milner; 15 Matty English; 16 Harry Rushton; 12 Sam Hewitt; 21 Leroy Cudjoe (C). Subs (all used): 18 Sebastine Ikahihifo; 19 Thomas Deakin; 25 Fenton Rogers; 33 Andre Savelio.
Tries: Jake Bibby (16), Halsall (78); **Goals:** Connor 3/3.
Rugby Leaguer & League Express Men of the Match: *Warriors:* Jai Field; *Giants:* Harry Rushton.
Penalty count: 7-4; **Half-time:** 0-8;
Referee: Aaron Moore; **Attendance:** 11,660.

Friday 2nd August 2024

WARRINGTON WOLVES 4 HULL KR 22

WOLVES: 1 Matt Dufty; 2 Josh Thewlis; 14 Rodrick Tai; 33 Arron Lindop; 5 Matty Ashton; 6 George Williams (C); 7 Josh Drinkwater; 41 Luke Yates; 32 Sam Powell; 10 Paul Vaughan; 13 Matty Nicholson; 28 Adam Holroyd; 11 Ben Currie. Subs (all used): 9 Danny Walker; 16 Zane Musgrove; 17 Jordan Crowther; 42 John Bateman (D).
Try: Ashton (49); **Goals:** Josh Thewlis 0/1.
HULL KR: 2 Niall Evalds; 35 Joe Burgess; 1 Peta Hiku; 4 Oliver Gildart; 5 Ryan Hall; 27 Tyrone May; 7 Mikey Lewis; 8 Sauaso Sue; 14 Matt Parcell; 16 Jai Whitbread; 11 Dean Hadley; 12 James Batchelor; 13 Elliot Minchella (C). Subs (all used): 9 Jez Litten; 15 Sam Luckley; 20 Kelepi Tanginoa; 37 Jack Brown.
Tries: Sue (5), May (18), Lewis (57), Hiku (76);
Goals: Lewis 1/2, Litten 2/2.
Rugby Leaguer & League Express Men of the Match: *Wolves:* Luke Yates; *Hull KR:* Mikey Lewis.
Penalty count: 6-5; **Half-time:** 0-10;
Referee: Jack Smith; **Attendance:** 12,102.

Saturday 3rd August 2024

HULL FC 6 ST HELENS 46

HULL FC: 37 Logan Moy; 25 Harvey Barron; 3 Carlos Tuimavave; 44 Tom Briscoe; 26 Lewis Martin; 6 Jake Trueman; 31 Jack Walker; 45 Yusuf Aydin; 19 Morgan Smith; 13 Brad Fash (C); 15 Jordan Lane; 43 Ed Chamberlain; 21 Will Gardiner. Subs (all used): 28 Denive Balmforth; 30 Matty Laidlaw; 46 Tiaki Chan; 51 Leon Ruan (D). 18th man (used): 27 Zach Jebson.
Try: Walker (78); **Goals:** Lane 1/1.
Sin bin: Fash (60) - late challenge on Whitley.
SAINTS: 33 Harry Robertson; 2 Tommy Makinson; 21 Ben Davies; 3 Waqa Blake; 25 Tee Ritson; 14 Moses Mbye; 7 Lewis Dodd; 10 Matty Lees; 9 Daryl Clark; 17 Agnatius Paasi; 19 Matt Whitley; 16 Curtis Sironen; 13 Morgan Knowles (C). Subs (all used): 12 Joe Batchelor; 15 James Bell; 24 Jake Burns; 31 Noah Stephens.
Tries: Dodd (27, 42), Makinson (34), Clark (49), Whitley (61), Burns (65, 75), Paasi (71);
Goals: Makinson 7/8.
Rugby Leaguer & League Express Men of the Match: *Hull FC:* Jake Trueman; *Saints:* Daryl Clark.
Penalty count: 7-6; **Half-time:** 0-10;
Referee: Liam Moore; **Attendance:** 9,885.

SALFORD RED DEVILS 22 LEEDS RHINOS 16

RED DEVILS: 1 Ryan Brierley; 2 Ethan Ryan; 3 Nene Macdonald; 4 Tim Lafai; 5 Deon Cross; 32 Jayden Nikorima; 7 Marc Sneyd; 8 Brad Singleton; 16 Joe Shorrocks; 29 Loghan Lewis; 11 Sam Stone; 12 Kallum Watkins (C); 13 Oliver Partington. Subs (all used): 15 Shane Wright; 23 Chris Hankinson; 24 Joe Mellor; 31 Joe Bullock.
Tries: Watkins (20, 33), Mellor (54); **Goals:** Sneyd 5/5.
Sin bin: Lafai (3) - high tackle on Miller.
RHINOS: 1 Lachlan Miller; 29 Alfie Edgell; 3 Harry Newman; 4 Paul Momirovski; 5 Ash Handley; 6 Brodie Croft; 7 Matt Frawley; 8 Mikolaj Oledzki; 9 Andy Ackers; 17 Justin Sangare; 16 James McDonnell; 12 Rhyse Martin; 13 Cameron Smith (C). Subs (all used): 11 James Bentley; 14 Jarrod O'Connor; 15 Sam Lisone; 25 James Donaldson.
Tries: Frawley (4), Edgell (8), Croft (24); **Goals:** Martin 2/3.
Sin bin: Martin (14) - interference;
Bentley (65) - high tackle on Shorrocks.
Rugby Leaguer & League Express Men of the Match:
Red Devils: Kallum Watkins; *Rhinos:* Rhyse Martin.
Penalty count: 8-10; **Half-time:** 12-16;
Referee: Tom Grant; **Attendance:** 4,473.

Sunday 4th August 2024

LONDON BRONCOS 12 CATALANS DRAGONS 10

BRONCOS: 23 Josh Rourke; 2 Lee Kershaw; 3 Jarred Bassett; 12 Ethan Natoli; 4 Hakim Miloudi; 20 Oliver Leyland; 6 Jack Campagnolo; 15 Marcus Stock; 9 Sam Davis; 19 Rhys Kennedy; 11 Will Lovell (C); 17 Sadiq Adebiyi; 13 Dean Parata. Subs: 8 Rob Butler; 21 Robbie Storey (not used); 29 Jacob Jones; 34 Ugo Tison.
Tries: Jones (36), Bassett (60); **Goals:** O Leyland 2/2.
DRAGONS: 29 Sam Tomkins; 2 Tom Davies; 30 Guillermo Aispuro-Bichet; 4 Matthieu Laguerre; 5 Fouad Yaha; 7 Theo Fages; 1 Arthur Mourgue; 16 Romain Navarrete; 14 Alrix Da Costa; 10 Julian Bousquet; 12 Paul Seguier; 15 Bayley Sironen; 13 Ben Garcia (C). Subs (all used): 20 Tevita Satae; 23 Jordan Dezaria; 17 Cesar Rouge; 33 Jarrod Wallace.
Tries: Wallace (56), Yaha (71); **Goals:** Mourgue 1/2.
Rugby Leaguer & League Express Men of the Match:
Broncos: Oliver Leyland; *Dragons:* Sam Tomkins.
Penalty count: 9-7; **Half-time:** 6-0;
Referee: James Vella; **Attendance:** 1,900.

ROUND 2

Tuesday 6th August 2024

WIGAN WARRIORS 28 LEIGH LEOPARDS 6

WARRIORS: 26 Zach Eckersley; 2 Abbas Miski; 3 Adam Keighran; 4 Jake Wardle; 5 Liam Marshall; 23 Ryan Hampshire; 7 Harry Smith; 8 Ethan Havard; 17 Kruise Leeming; 16 Luke Thompson; 21 Junior Nsemba; 12 Liam Farrell (C); 13 Kaide Ellis. Subs (all used): 15 Patrick Mago; 19 Tyler Dupree; 20 Harvie Hill; 22 Sam Walters.
Tries: Nsemba (9), Wardle (16), Keighran (34), Mago (39), Hill (56); **Goals:** Keighran 4/5.
LEOPARDS: 6 Matt Moylan; 34 Darnell McIntosh; 24 Umyla Hanley; 4 Ricky Leutele; 5 Josh Charnley; 12 Jack Hughes; 7 Lachlan Lam; 17 Owen Trout; 9 Edwin Ipape; 10 Robbie Mulhern; 11 Kai O'Donnell; 16 Frankie Halton; 13 John Asiata (C). Subs (all used): 3 Zak Hardaker; 15 Matt Davis; 33 Brad Dwyer; 35 Aaron Pene.
Try: Lam (44); **Goals:** McIntosh 1/1.
Sin bin: Hughes (7) - high tackle on Leeming.
Rugby Leaguer & League Express Men of the Match:
Warriors: Kruise Leeming; *Leopards:* Kai O'Donnell.
Penalty count: 5-6; **Half-time:** 22-0;
Referee: Chris Kendall; **Attendance:** 13,249.

ROUND 21

Thursday 8th August 2024

ST HELENS 17 SALFORD RED DEVILS 16
(after golden point extra-time)

SAINTS: 33 Harry Robertson; 2 Tommy Makinson; 3 Waqa Blake; 4 Mark Percival; 25 Tee Ritson; 14 Moses Mbye; 7 Lewis Dodd; 10 Matty Lees; 9 Daryl Clark; 17 Agnatius Paasi; 19 Matt Whitley; 16 Curtis Sironen; 13 Morgan Knowles (C). Subs (all used): 8 Alex Walmsley; 12 Joe Batchelor; 15 James Bell; 24 Jake Burns.
Tries: Makinson (8), Blake (46), Batchelor (62);
Goals: Percival 2/3; **Field goal:** Mbye (85).
Sin bin: Knowles (68) - high tackle on Mellor;
Batchelor (69) - late challenge on Lewis.
RED DEVILS: 1 Ryan Brierley; 2 Ethan Ryan; 3 Nene Macdonald; 23 Chris Hankinson; 5 Deon Cross; 32 Jayden Nikorima; 7 Marc Sneyd; 8 Brad Singleton; 16 Joe Shorrocks; 31 Joe Bullock; 11 Sam Stone; 12 Kallum Watkins (C); 13 Oliver Partington. Subs (all used): 15 Shane Wright; 24 Joe Mellor; 27 Gil Dudson; 29 Loghan Lewis.
Tries: Hankinson (51), Macdonald (71); **Goals:** Sneyd 4/4.
Sin bin: Shorrocks (20) - professional foul;
Partington (69) - retaliation.
Rugby Leaguer & League Express Men of the Match:
Saints: Moses Mbye; *Red Devils:* Marc Sneyd.
Penalty count: 5-12; **Half-time:** 4-4;
Referee: Chris Kendall; **Attendance:** 11,050.

Friday 9th August 2024

HUDDERSFIELD GIANTS 22 CATALANS DRAGONS 23

GIANTS: 1 Jake Connor; 30 Aidan McGowan; 4 Kevin Naiqama; 5 Jake Bibby; 24 Sam Halsall; 6 Tui Lolohea; 23 Oliver Russell; 8 Chris Hill; 9 Adam Milner; 33 Andre Savelio; 12 Sam Hewitt; 16 Harry Rushton; 21 Leroy Cudjoe (C). Subs (all used): 18 Sebastine Ikahihifo; 19 Thomas Deakin; 22 Harvey Livett; 25 Fenton Rogers.
Tries: Jake Bibby (27), Naiqama (40), Hewitt (67), Lolohea (70); **Goals:** Connor 3/4.
DRAGONS: 29 Sam Tomkins; 2 Tom Davies; 3 Arthur Romano; 21 Matt Ikuvalu; 5 Fouad Yaha; 1 Arthur Mourgue; 7 Theo Fages; 23 Jordan Dezaria; 14 Alrix Da Costa; 16 Romain Navarrete; 13 Ben Garcia (C); 15 Bayley Sironen; 10 Julian Bousquet. Subs (all used): 20 Tevita Satae; 28 Franck Maria; 30 Guillermo Aispuro-Bichet; 33 Jarrod Wallace.
Tries: Sironen (3), Tomkins (8), Yaha (22), Romano (45), Ikuvalu (64); **Goals:** Mourgue 1/5; **Field goal:** Mourgue (76).
Sin bin: Bousquet (32) - high tackle;
Ikuvalu (77) - high tackle.
Rugby Leaguer & League Express Men of the Match:
Giants: Sebastine Ikahihifo; *Dragons:* Ben Garcia.
Penalty count: 8-3; **Half-time:** 10-14;
Referee: Tom Grant; **Attendance:** 3,330.

HULL KR 36 CASTLEFORD TIGERS 6

HULL KR: 2 Niall Evalds; 35 Joe Burgess; 1 Peta Hiku; 4 Oliver Gildart; 5 Ryan Hall; 7 Mikey Lewis; 27 Tyrone May; 8 Sauaso Sue; 14 Matt Parcell; 16 Jai Whitbread; 11 Dean Hadley; 12 James Batchelor; 13 Elliot Minchella (C). Subs (all used): 9 Jez Litten; 15 Sam Luckley; 17 Matty Storton; 20 Kelepi Tanginoa.
Tries: Hiku (8), Burgess (17, 64), Lewis (31), R Hall (37), Evalds (67), May (73); **Goals:** Lewis 4/8.
Sin bin: Sue (50) - dissent.
TIGERS: 34 Tex Hoy; 23 Jason Qareqare; 30 Luis Johnson; 12 Alex Mellor; 5 Innes Senior; 16 Rowan Milnes; 7 Jacob Miller; 20 Muizz Mustapha; 14 Liam Horne; 8 Liam Watts; 11 Elie El-Zakhem; 17 Nixon Putt; 13 Joe Westerman (C). Subs (all used): 21 Sylvester Namo; 24 Cain Robb; 29 George Hill; 32 Dan Hindmarsh.
Try: Mellor (5); **Goals:** Milnes 1/1.
Sin bin: Putt (42) - dangerous challenge on Hiku.
Rugby Leaguer & League Express Men of the Match:
Hull KR: Joe Burgess; *Tigers:* Liam Horne.
Penalty count: 6-7; **Half-time:** 18-6;
Referee: Liam Rush; **Attendance:** 9,585.

Saturday 10th August 2024

LEEDS RHINOS 30 WIGAN WARRIORS 4

RHINOS: 1 Lachlan Miller; 2 David Fusitu'a; 3 Harry Newman; 4 Paul Momirovski; 29 Alfie Edgell; 6 Brodie Croft; 7 Matt Frawley (C); 15 Sam Lisone; 9 Andy Ackers; 17 Justin Sangare; 16 James McDonnell; 12 Rhyse Martin; 14 Jarrod O'Connor. Subs (all used): 11 James Bentley; 18 Mickael Goudemand; 30 Tom Nicholson-Watton; 32 Ben Littlewood (D).
Tries: Newman (16), Miller (54), McDonnell (64), Martin (79); **Goals:** Martin 7/7.
WARRIORS: 1 Jai Field; 2 Abbas Miski; 3 Adam Keighran; 4 Jake Wardle; 5 Liam Marshall; 23 Ryan Hampshire; 7 Harry Smith; 8 Ethan Havard; 17 Kruise Leeming; 16 Luke Thompson; 21 Junior Nsemba; 12 Liam Farrell (C); 13 Kaide Ellis. Subs (all used): 10 Liam Byrne; 15 Patrick Mago; 22 Sam Walters; 26 Zach Eckersley.
Try: Marshall (72); **Goals:** Keighran 0/1.
Dismissal: Smith (78) - use of the elbow on Bentley.
Sin bin: Keighran (59) - high tackle.
Rugby Leaguer & League Express Men of the Match:
Rhinos: James Bentley; *Warriors:* Kaide Ellis.
Penalty count: 9-5; **Half-time:** 8-0;
Referee: Liam Moore; **Attendance:** 12,459.

Sunday 11th August 2024

LEIGH LEOPARDS 42 HULL FC 12

LEOPARDS: 3 Zak Hardaker; 34 Darnell McIntosh; 24 Umyla Hanley; 4 Ricky Leutele; 5 Josh Charnley; 12 Jack Hughes; 7 Lachlan Lam; 8 Tom Amone; 9 Edwin Ipape; 10 Robbie Mulhern; 11 Kai O'Donnell; 16 Frankie Halton; 13 John Asiata (C). Subs (all used): 15 Matt Davis; 17 Owen Trout; 33 Brad Dwyer; 35 Aaron Pene.
Tries: O'Donnell (18, 43, 68, 72), Halton (30), Hardaker (51, 79), McIntosh (62);
Goals: McIntosh 3/6, Hardaker 2/3.
Sin bin: McIntosh (37) - dangerous challenge;
Trout (58) - high tackle on Aydin.
HULL FC: 37 Logan Moy; 25 Harvey Barron; 3 Carlos Tuimavave (C); 44 Tom Briscoe; 26 Lewis Martin; 31 Jack Walker; 40 Jack Charles; 8 Herman Ese'ese; 19 Morgan Smith; 45 Yusuf Aydin; 48 Jed Cartwright (D); 51 Leon Ruan; 21 Will Gardiner. Subs (all used): 27 Zach Jebson; 28 Denive Balmforth; 46 Tiaki Chan; 52 Sam Eseh (D).
Tries: Moy (34), Barron (39); **Goals:** Charles 2/2.
Sin bin: Gardiner (17) - holding down.
Rugby Leaguer & League Express Men of the Match:
Leopards: Kai O'Donnell; *Hull FC:* Jack Walker.
Penalty count: 7-6; **Half-time:** 12-12;
Referee: Jack Smith; **Attendance:** 8,400.

LONDON BRONCOS 22 WARRINGTON WOLVES 36

BRONCOS: 23 Josh Rourke; 2 Lee Kershaw; 12 Ethan Natoli; 3 Jarred Bassett; 4 Hakim Miloudi; 20 Oliver Leyland; 6 Jack Campagnolo; 8 Rob Butler; 9 Sam Davis; 19 Rhys Kennedy; 11 Will Lovell (C); 17 Sadiq Adebiyi; 15 Marcus Stock. Subs (all used): 10 Lewis Bienek; 13 Dean Parata; 29 Jacob Jones; 34 Ugo Tison.
Tries: Rourke (17), Bienek (36), Davis (48), Tison (62);
Goals: O Leyland 3/4.
Sin bin: Kennedy (71) - high tackle.
WOLVES: 1 Matt Dufty (C); 33 Arron Lindop; 3 Toby King; 14 Rodrick Tai; 5 Matty Ashton; 32 Sam Powell; 7 Josh Drinkwater; 8 James Harrison; 9 Danny Walker; 10 Paul Vaughan; 42 John Bateman; 28 Adam Holroyd; 17 Jordan Crowther. Subs (all used): 15 Joe Philbin; 16 Zane Musgrove; 34 Max Wood; 38 Cai Taylor-Wray.
Tries: Tai (8), Ashton (14, 80), Vaughan (21), King (32), Holroyd (43); **Goals:** Drinkwater 6/7.
Rugby Leaguer & League Express Men of the Match:
Broncos: Josh Rourke; *Wolves:* Danny Walker.
Penalty count: 5-5; **Half-time:** 10-22;
Referee: Marcus Griffiths; **Attendance:** 2,150.

ROUND 22 - MAGIC WEEKEND

Saturday 17th August 2024

HULL FC 4 LONDON BRONCOS 29

HULL FC: 31 Jack Walker; 25 Harvey Barron; 3 Carlos Tuimavave; 44 Tom Briscoe; 26 Lewis Martin; 40 Jack Charles; 19 Morgan Smith; 8 Herman Ese'ese; 15 Jordan Lane (C); 12 Ligi Sao; 43 Ed Chamberlain; 48 Jed Cartwright; 45 Yusuf Aydin. Subs (all used): 13 Brad Fash; 27 Zach Jebson; 28 Denive Balmforth; 52 Sam Eseh.
Try: Martin (10); **Goals:** Charles 0/1.
Sin bin: Balmforth (80) - late challenge.
BRONCOS: 23 Josh Rourke; 2 Lee Kershaw; 3 Jarred Bassett; 12 Ethan Natoli; 4 Hakim Miloudi; 6 Jack Campagnolo; 20 Oliver Leyland; 19 Rhys Kennedy; 9 Sam Davis; 8 Rob Butler; 11 Will Lovell (C); 17 Sadiq Adebiyi; 15 Marcus Stock. Subs (all used): 18 Emmanuel Waine; 10 Lewis Bienek; 34 Ugo Tison; 29 Jacob Jones.
Tries: Rourke (7, 75), Campagnolo (25), O Leyland (77);
Goals: O Leyland 6/6; **Field goal:** O Leyland (71).
Rugby Leaguer & League Express Men of the Match:
Hull FC: Brad Fash; *Broncos:* Josh Rourke.
Penalty count: 5-9; **Half-time:** 4-12; **Referee:** Liam Rush.

ST HELENS 0 WIGAN WARRIORS 20

SAINTS: 33 Harry Robertson; 2 Tommy Makinson; 3 Waqa Blake; 12 Joe Batchelor; 25 Tee Ritson; 21 Ben Davies; 14 Moses Mbye; 20 George Delaney; 15 James Bell; 10 Matty Lees (C); 19 Matt Whitley; 16 Curtis Sironen; 17 Agnatius Paasi. Subs (all used): 8 Alex Walmsley; 24 Jake Burns; 30 Jonny Vaughan; 31 Noah Stephens.
WARRIORS: 1 Jai Field; 2 Abbas Miski; 26 Zach Eckersley; 4 Jake Wardle; 5 Liam Marshall; 30 Jack Farrimond; 3 Adam Keighran; 8 Ethan Havard; 17 Kruise Leeming; 16 Luke Thompson; 21 Junior Nsemba; 22 Sam Walters; 13 Kaide Ellis (C). Subs (all used): 10 Liam Byrne; 15 Patrick Mago; 19 Tyler Dupree; 27 Tom Forber.
Tries: Marshall (16), Farrimond (19), Walters (75);
Goals: Keighran 4/4.
Sin bin: Ellis (56) - high tackle on Batchelor.
Rugby Leaguer & League Express Men of the Match:
Saints: Harry Robertson; *Warriors:* Junior Nsemba.
Penalty count: 5-9; **Half-time:** 0-14; **Referee:** Jack Smith.

LEEDS RHINOS 6 WARRINGTON WOLVES 24

RHINOS: 1 Lachlan Miller; 2 David Fusitu'a; 4 Paul Momirovski; 3 Harry Newman; 5 Ash Handley; 21 Jack Sinfield; 7 Matt Frawley; 15 Sam Lisone; 9 Andy Ackers; 17 Justin Sangare; 16 James McDonnell; 12 Rhyse Martin; 13 Cameron Smith (C). Subs (all used): 11 James Bentley; 14 Jarrod O'Connor; 30 Tom Nicholson-Watton; 25 James Donaldson.
Try: Momirovski (71); **Goals:** Martin 1/1.
Sin bin: Fusitu'a (49) - professional foul;
Lisone (64) - fighting.

WOLVES: 1 Matt Dufty; 2 Josh Thewlis; 14 Rodrick Tai; 3 Toby King; 5 Matty Ashton; 6 George Williams (C); 7 Josh Drinkwater; 10 Paul Vaughan; 32 Sam Powell; 41 Luke Yates; 42 John Bateman; 13 Matty Nicholson; 11 Ben Currie. Subs (all used): 8 James Harrison; 9 Danny Walker; 17 Jordan Crowther; 16 Zane Musgrove.
Tries: Williams (37), Dufty (50, 55, 78);
Goals: Josh Thewlis 4/6.
Sin bin: Tai (64) - fighting.
Rugby Leaguer & League Express Men of the Match:
Rhinos: Rhyse Martin; *Wolves:* Matt Dufty.
Penalty count: 2-7; **Half-time:** 0-8; **Referee:** Chris Kendall.

Attendance: 30,810 *(at Elland Road, Leeds).*

Sunday 18th August 2024

LEIGH LEOPARDS 26 SALFORD RED DEVILS 0

LEOPARDS: 3 Zak Hardaker; 34 Darnell McIntosh; 24 Umyla Hanley; 4 Ricky Leutele; 22 Keanan Brand; 1 Gareth O'Brien; 7 Lachlan Lam; 8 Tom Amone; 9 Edwin Ipape; 10 Robbie Mulhern; 11 Kai O'Donnell; 16 Frankie Halton; 13 John Asiata (C). Subs (all used): 12 Jack Hughes; 17 Owen Trout; 33 Brad Dwyer; 35 Aaron Pene.
Tries: Ipape (6), Hanley (20), Hardaker (73), Leutele (77);
Goals: Hardaker 5/5.
RED DEVILS: 1 Ryan Brierley; 2 Ethan Ryan; 12 Kallum Watkins (C); 4 Tim Lafai; 5 Deon Cross; 32 Jayden Nikorima; 7 Marc Sneyd; 8 Brad Singleton; 24 Joe Mellor; 15 Shane Wright; 11 Sam Stone; 3 Nene Macdonald; 13 Oliver Partington. Subs (all used): 16 Joe Shorrocks; 23 Chris Hankinson; 29 Loghan Lewis; 31 Joe Bullock.
Sin bin: Ryan (13) - high tackle on Leutele;
Singleton (17) - high tackle on O'Brien.
Rugby Leaguer & League Express Men of the Match:
Leopards: Kai O'Donnell; *Red Devils:* Nene Macdonald.
Penalty count: 8-6; **Half-time:** 12-0; **Referee:** Liam Moore.

CATALANS DRAGONS 4 HULL KR 36

DRAGONS: 17 Cesar Rouge; 2 Tom Davies; 3 Arthur Romano; 34 Reimis Smith (D); 21 Matt Ikuvalu; 1 Arthur Mourgue; 7 Theo Fages; 23 Jordan Dezaria; 14 Alrix Da Costa; 16 Romain Navarrete; 13 Ben Garcia (C); 15 Bayley Sironen; 10 Julian Bousquet. Subs (all used): 12 Paul Seguier; 20 Tevita Satae; 28 Franck Maria; 33 Jarrod Wallace.
Try: Sironen (22); **Goals:** Mourgue 0/1.
HULL KR: 2 Niall Evalds; 35 Joe Burgess; 1 Peta Hiku; 4 Oliver Gildart; 5 Ryan Hall; 27 Tyrone May; 7 Mikey Lewis; 8 Sauaso Sue; 14 Matt Parcell; 16 Jai Whitbread; 11 Dean Hadley; 12 James Batchelor; 13 Elliot Minchella (C). Subs (all used): 9 Jez Litten; 15 Sam Luckley; 17 Matty Storton; 20 Kelepi Tanginoa.
Tries: Minchella (14, 41), Hiku (26), R Hall (38, 61), Tanginoa (51, 66), Evalds (75); **Goals:** Lewis 2/8.
Rugby Leaguer & League Express Men of the Match:
Dragons: Theo Fages; *Hull KR:* Elliot Minchella.
Penalty count: 3-7; **Half-time:** 4-12; **Referee:** Tom Grant.

CASTLEFORD TIGERS 12 HUDDERSFIELD GIANTS 20

TIGERS: 34 Tex Hoy; 23 Jason Qareqare; 35 Corey Hall; 28 Will Tate; 5 Innes Senior; 16 Rowan Milnes; 7 Jacob Miller; 20 Muizz Mustapha; 14 Liam Horne; 32 Dan Hindmarsh; 12 Alex Mellor; 11 Elie El-Zakhem; 13 Joe Westerman (C). Subs (all used): 8 Liam Watts; 21 Sylvester Namo; 25 Brad Martin; 29 George Hill.
Tries: Qareqare (59, 68); **Goals:** Milnes 2/2.
GIANTS: 1 Jake Connor; 5 Jake Bibby; 3 Esan Marsters; 4 Kevin Naiqama; 24 Sam Halsall; 6 Tui Lolohea; 23 Oliver Russell; 8 Chris Hill; 9 Adam Milner; 33 Andre Savelio; 16 Harry Rushton; 12 Sam Hewitt; 21 Leroy Cudjoe (C). Subs (all used): 15 Matty English; 18 Sebastine Ikahihifo; 25 Fenton Rogers; 27 Kieran Rush.
Tries: Halsall (4), Hewitt (13), Marsters (48);
Goals: Connor 4/4.
Sin bin: Lolohea (23) - high tackle on Miller;
Rogers (51) - high tackle on Namo.
Rugby Leaguer & League Express Men of the Match:
Tigers: Liam Horne; *Giants:* Jake Connor.
Penalty count: 6-3; **Half-time:** 0-12;
Referee: Aaron Moore.

Attendance: 22,293 *(at Elland Road, Leeds).*

ROUND 23

Friday 23rd August 2024

CASTLEFORD TIGERS 6 WARRINGTON WOLVES 28

TIGERS: 34 Tex Hoy; 23 Jason Qareqare; 1 Luke Hooley; 28 Will Tate; 5 Innes Senior; 38 Jenson Windley (D); 7 Jacob Miller; 8 Liam Watts; 14 Liam Horne; 13 Joe Westerman; 12 Alex Mellor; 11 Elie El-Zakhem; 29 George Hill. Subs (all used): 9 Paul McShane (C); 21 Sylvester Namo; 30 Luis Johnson; 32 Dan Hindmarsh.
Try: Hooley (53); **Goals:** Hooley 1/1.
WOLVES: 38 Cai Taylor-Wray; 2 Josh Thewlis; 3 Toby King; 14 Rodrick Tai; 5 Matty Ashton; 6 George Williams (C); 7 Josh Drinkwater; 41 Luke Yates; 32 Sam Powell; 10 Paul Vaughan; 13 Matty Nicholson; 42 John Bateman; 11 Ben Currie. Subs (all used): 8 James Harrison; 9 Danny Walker; 16 Zane Musgrove; 17 Jordan Crowther.
Tries: Taylor-Wray (24), Bateman (45), Nicholson (64), Ashton (73), Josh Thewlis (76); **Goals:** Josh Thewlis 4/6.
Sin bin: Yates (14) - high tackle on Watts.
Rugby Leaguer & League Express Men of the Match:
Tigers: Liam Watts; *Wolves:* Cai Taylor-Wray.
Penalty count: 7-7; **Half-time:** 0-8;
Referee: Tom Grant; **Attendance:** 7,449.

LEEDS RHINOS 18 CATALANS DRAGONS 6

RHINOS: 1 Lachlan Miller; 2 David Fusitu'a; 4 Paul Momirovski; 3 Harry Newman; 29 Alfie Edgell; 6 Brodie Croft; 7 Matt Frawley; 15 Sam Lisone; 9 Andy Ackers; 17 Justin Sangare; 12 Rhyse Martin; 16 James McDonnell; 13 Cameron Smith (C). Subs (all used): 11 James Bentley; 14 Jarrod O'Connor; 30 Tom Nicholson-Watton; 25 James Donaldson.
Tries: Fusitu'a (43), Frawley (54), Miller (66);
Goals: Martin 3/4.
DRAGONS: 17 Cesar Rouge; 2 Tom Davies; 3 Arthur Romano; 34 Reimis Smith; 5 Fouad Yaha; 1 Arthur Mourgue; 7 Theo Fages; 10 Julian Bousquet; 14 Alrix Da Costa; 16 Romain Navarrete; 12 Paul Seguier; 8 Mike McMeeken; 13 Ben Garcia (C). Subs (all used): 20 Tevita Satae; 23 Jordan Dezaria; 32 Yacine Ben Abdeslem (D); 4 Matthieu Laguerre.
Try: Romano (11); **Goals:** Mourgue 1/2.
Rugby Leaguer & League Express Men of the Match:
Rhinos: Jarrod O'Connor; *Dragons:* Tom Davies.
Penalty count: 5-3; **Half-time:** 0-6;
Referee: Liam Moore; **Attendance:** 13,050.

Saturday 24th August 2024

ST HELENS 6 HULL KR 42

SAINTS: 33 Harry Robertson; 2 Tommy Makinson; 3 Waqa Blake; 30 Jonny Vaughan; 25 Tee Ritson; 6 Jonny Lomax (C); 35 George Whitby (D); 20 George Delaney; 14 Moses Mbye; 10 Matty Lees; 19 Matt Whitley; 11 Sione Mata'utia; 12 Joe Batchelor. Subs (all used): 17 Agnatius Paasi; 22 Sam Royle; 24 Jake Burns; 31 Noah Stephens.
Try: Whitby (66); **Goals:** Whitby 1/1.
Dismissal: Makinson (75) - high tackle on May.
Sin bin: Blake (8) - high tackle on Broadbent.
HULL KR: 2 Niall Evalds; 35 Joe Burgess; 1 Peta Hiku; 36 Jack Broadbent; 5 Ryan Hall; 27 Tyrone May; 7 Mikey Lewis; 8 Sauaso Sue; 14 Matt Parcell; 16 Jai Whitbread; 11 Dean Hadley; 12 James Batchelor; 13 Elliot Minchella (C). Subs (all used): 9 Jez Litten; 15 Sam Luckley; 17 Matty Storton; 20 Kelepi Tanginoa.
Tries: Burgess (3, 19, 35, 70), Lewis (12), May (16), Tanginoa (48), Whitbread (76); **Goals:** Lewis 5/8.
Rugby Leaguer & League Express Men of the Match:
Saints: George Delaney; *Hull KR:* Joe Burgess.
Penalty count: 5-6; **Half-time:** 0-26;
Referee: Chris Kendall; **Attendance:** 13,588.

SALFORD RED DEVILS 60 HUDDERSFIELD GIANTS 10

RED DEVILS: 1 Ryan Brierley; 2 Ethan Ryan; 3 Nene Macdonald; 23 Chris Hankinson; 5 Deon Cross; 32 Jayden Nikorima; 7 Marc Sneyd; 8 Brad Singleton; 24 Joe Mellor; 29 Loghan Lewis; 15 Shane Wright; 12 Kallum Watkins (C); 14 Chris Atkin. Subs (all used): 9 Amir Bourouh; 16 Joe Shorrocks; 28 Harvey Wilson; 31 Joe Bullock.
Tries: Atkin (9), Brierley (13, 22, 65), Nikorima (36, 39), Ryan (43), Wilson (46), Macdonald (55), Sneyd (58);
Goals: Sneyd 10/11.
GIANTS: 1 Jake Connor; 30 Aidan McGowan; 5 Jake Bibby; 4 Kevin Naiqama; 24 Sam Halsall; 6 Tui Lolohea; 23 Oliver Russell; 33 Andre Savelio; 14 Ashton Golding; 8 Chris Hill; 16 Harry Rushton; 12 Sam Hewitt; 21 Leroy Cudjoe (C). Subs (all used): 15 Matty English; 18 Sebastine Ikahihifo; 25 Fenton Rogers; 27 Kieran Rush.
Tries: Hewitt (60), Rogers (73);
Goals: Lolohea 0/1, Russell 1/1.
Sin bin: Savelio (12) - high tackle; Russell (51) - high tackle.
Rugby Leaguer & League Express Men of the Match:
Red Devils: Ryan Brierley; *Giants:* Tui Lolohea.
Penalty count: 6-5; **Half-time:** 32-0;
Referee: Marcus Griffiths; **Attendance:** 3,319.

Sunday 25th August 2024

LONDON BRONCOS 12 LEIGH LEOPARDS 32

BRONCOS: 23 Josh Rourke; 2 Lee Kershaw; 12 Ethan Natoli; 3 Jarred Bassett; 5 Iliess Macani; 20 Oliver Leyland; 6 Jack Campagnolo; 8 Rob Butler; 9 Sam Davis; 19 Rhys Kennedy; 17 Sadiq Adebiyi; 11 Will Lovell (C); 15 Marcus Stock. Subs (all used): 4 Hakim Miloudi; 34 Ugo Tison; 10 Lewis Bienek; 29 Jacob Jones.
Tries: Davis (14), Rourke (45); **Goals:** O Leyland 2/2.
Sin bin: Butler (30) - late challenge.
LEOPARDS: 3 Zak Hardaker; 34 Darnell McIntosh; 24 Umyla Hanley; 4 Ricky Leutele; 22 Keanan Brand; 1 Gareth O'Brien; 7 Lachlan Lam; 8 Tom Amone; 9 Edwin Ipape; 35 Aaron Pene; 11 Kai O'Donnell; 16 Frankie Halton; 13 John Asiata (C). Subs (all used): 33 Brad Dwyer; 15 Matt Davis; 12 Jack Hughes; 17 Owen Trout.
Tries: McIntosh (17), Halton (29), Leutele (37), O'Donnell (67), O'Brien (73), Pene (80);
Goals: Hardaker 4/7.
Sin bin: Asiata (28) - high tackle.
Rugby Leaguer & League Express Men of the Match:
Broncos: Rhys Kennedy; *Leopards:* Gareth O'Brien.
Penalty count: 5-6; **Half-time:** 6-12;
Referee: Jack Smith; **Attendance:** 1,950.

WIGAN WARRIORS 22 HULL FC 4

WARRIORS: 1 Jai Field; 28 Jacob Douglas; 26 Zach Eckersley; 4 Jake Wardle; 5 Liam Marshall (C); 3 Adam Keighran; 30 Jack Farrimond; 8 Ethan Havard; 17 Kruise Leeming; 16 Luke Thompson; 21 Junior Nsemba; 22 Sam Walters; 15 Patrick Mago. Subs (all used): 10 Liam Byrne; 19 Tyler Dupree; 20 Harvie Hill; 27 Tom Forber.
Tries: Douglas (8), Eckersley (19), Nsemba (55), Farrimond (62); **Goals:** Keighran 3/4.
Sin bin: Mago (67) - late challenge on Ashworth.
HULL FC: 37 Logan Moy; 25 Harvey Barron; 3 Carlos Tuimavave; 44 Tom Briscoe; 26 Lewis Martin; 19 Morgan Smith; 40 Jack Charles; 8 Herman Ese'ese; 15 Jordan Lane (C); 21 Will Gardiner; 43 Ed Chamberlain; 48 Jed Cartwright; 45 Yusuf Aydin. Subs (all used): 13 Brad Fash; 16 Jack Ashworth; 27 Zach Jebson; 51 Leon Ruan.
Try: Cartwright (28); **Goals:** Charles 0/1.
Rugby Leaguer & League Express Men of the Match:
Warriors: Jai Field; *Hull FC:* Will Gardiner.
Penalty count: 5-3; **Half-time:** 10-4;
Referee: Aaron Moore; **Attendance:** 12,347.

ROUND 24

Friday 30th August 2024

HULL KR 32 SALFORD RED DEVILS 12

HULL KR: 2 Niall Evalds; 36 Jack Broadbent; 1 Peta Hiku; 3 Tom Opacic; 5 Ryan Hall; 27 Tyrone May; 7 Mikey Lewis; 8 Sauaso Sue; 14 Matt Parcell; 16 Jai Whitbread; 11 Dean Hadley; 17 Matty Storton; 13 Elliot Minchella (C). Subs (all used): 9 Jez Litten; 15 Sam Luckley; 20 Kelepi Tanginoa; 37 Jack Brown.
Tries: Broadbent (3, 38), Whitbread (24), Lewis (33), Opacic (44), Litten (64); **Goals:** Lewis 4/7.
RED DEVILS: 23 Chris Hankinson; 2 Ethan Ryan; 3 Nene Macdonald; 4 Tim Lafai; 5 Deon Cross; 32 Jayden Nikorima; 7 Marc Sneyd; 8 Brad Singleton; 24 Joe Mellor; 15 Shane Wright; 11 Sam Stone; 12 Kallum Watkins (C); 13 Oliver Partington. Subs (all used): 14 Chris Atkin; 16 Joe Shorrocks; 17 Jack Ormondroyd; 28 Harvey Wilson.
Tries: Mellor (8), Macdonald (76); **Goals:** Sneyd 2/2.
Rugby Leaguer & League Express Men of the Match:
Hull KR: Mikey Lewis; *Red Devils:* Shane Wright.
Penalty count: 6-4; **Half-time:** 20-6;
Referee: Jack Smith; **Attendance:** 9,694.

LEIGH LEOPARDS 16 WARRINGTON WOLVES 12

LEOPARDS: 6 Matt Moylan; 34 Darnell McIntosh; 24 Umyla Hanley; 4 Ricky Leutele; 5 Josh Charnley; 1 Gareth O'Brien; 7 Lachlan Lam (C); 17 Owen Trout; 9 Edwin Ipape; 10 Robbie Mulhern; 11 Kai O'Donnell; 16 Frankie Halton; 8 Tom Amone. Subs (all used): 3 Zak Hardaker; 12 Jack Hughes; 15 Matt Davis; 35 Aaron Pene.
Tries: Leutele (9), Halton (45), Charnley (53);
Goals: Moylan 2/4.
Sin bin: Hughes (58) - dangerous challenge.
WOLVES: 38 Cai Taylor-Wray; 2 Josh Thewlis; 14 Rodrick Tai; 3 Toby King; 5 Matty Ashton; 6 George Williams (C); 7 Josh Drinkwater; 10 Paul Vaughan; 32 Sam Powell; 41 Luke Yates; 42 John Bateman; 12 Lachlan Fitzgibbon; 11 Ben Currie. Subs (all used): 16 Zane Musgrove; 15 Joe Philbin; 9 Danny Walker; 17 Jordan Crowther.
Tries: Ashton (37), Powell (79); **Goals:** Josh Thewlis 2/2.
Dismissal: Vaughan (11) - shoulder charge on Trout.
Rugby Leaguer & League Express Men of the Match:
Leopards: Frankie Halton; *Wolves:* Matty Ashton.
Penalty count: 7-6; **Half-time:** 6-6;
Referee: Liam Moore; **Attendance:** 9,434.

Saturday 31st August 2024

HULL FC 20 CASTLEFORD TIGERS 39

HULL FC: 37 Logan Moy; 25 Harvey Barron; 3 Carlos Tuimavave; 44 Tom Briscoe; 26 Lewis Martin; 19 Morgan

Smith; 40 Jack Charles; 8 Herman Ese'ese; 9 Danny Houghton (C); 21 Will Gardiner; 15 Jordan Lane; 12 Ligi Sao; 45 Yusuf Aydin. Subs (all used): 16 Jack Ashworth; 28 Denive Balmforth; 51 Leon Ruan; 52 Sam Eseh.
Tries: Sao (10), Barron (35, 39), Tuimavave (49);
Goals: Charles 2/4.
Sin bin: Aydin (62) - high tackle on Mellor.
TIGERS: 34 Tex Hoy; 23 Jason Qareqare; 1 Luke Hooley; 28 Will Tate; 5 Innes Senior; 16 Rowan Milnes; 38 Jenson Windley; 8 Liam Watts; 14 Liam Horne; 13 Joe Westerman; 12 Alex Mellor; 11 Elie El-Zakhem; 29 George Hill. Subs (all used): 9 Paul McShane (C); 10 George Lawler; 20 Muizz Mustapha; 21 Sylvester Namo.
Tries: I Senior (4), Milnes (12), Windley (16), Hoy (25, 74), Namo (67); **Goals:** Milnes 7/7; **Field goal:** Milnes (70).
Sin bin: Namo (47) - late challenge on Charles; Horne (55) - high tackle on Briscoe.
Rugby Leaguer & League Express Men of the Match:
Hull FC: Herman Ese'ese; *Tigers:* Rowan Milnes.
Penalty count: 10-5; **Half-time:** 14-24;
Referee: Liam Rush; **Attendance:** 10,271.

CATALANS DRAGONS 18 WIGAN WARRIORS 26

DRAGONS: 17 Cesar Rouge; 2 Tom Davies; 3 Arthur Romano; 4 Matthieu Laguerre; 5 Fouad Yaha; 1 Arthur Mourgue; 7 Theo Fages; 16 Romain Navarrete; 14 Alrix Da Costa; 10 Julian Bousquet; 8 Mike McMeeken; 15 Bayley Sironen; 13 Ben Garcia (C). Subs (all used): 12 Paul Seguier; 20 Tevita Satae; 23 Jordan Dezaria; 30 Guillermo Aispuro-Bichet.
Tries: Yaha (14), Fages (19), Romano (78);
Goals: Mourgue 3/3.
WARRIORS: 1 Jai Field; 2 Abbas Miski; 26 Zach Eckersley; 4 Jake Wardle; 5 Liam Marshall; 6 Bevan French; 3 Adam Keighran; 8 Ethan Havard; 17 Kruise Leeming; 16 Luke Thompson; 21 Junior Nsemba; 22 Sam Walters; 13 Kaide Ellis (C). Subs (all used): 10 Liam Byrne; 15 Patrick Mago; 19 Tyler Dupree; 27 Tom Forber.
Tries: Field (9), Forber (37), Nsemba (43), Keighran (48);
Goals: Keighran 5/5.
Sin bin: Leeming (70) - repeated team offences.
Rugby Leaguer & League Express Men of the Match:
Dragons: Theo Fages; *Warriors:* Junior Nsemba.
Penalty count: 9-5; **Half-time:** 12-12;
Referee: Chris Kendall; **Attendance:** 11,038.

Sunday 1st September 2024

LONDON BRONCOS 20 LEEDS RHINOS 21
(after golden point extra-time)

BRONCOS: 23 Josh Rourke; 2 Lee Kershaw; 12 Ethan Natoli; 3 Jarred Bassett; 4 Hakim Miloudi; 20 Oliver Leyland; 6 Jack Campagnolo; 8 Rob Butler; 9 Sam Davis; 19 Rhys Kennedy; 17 Sadiq Adebiyi; 11 Will Lovell (C); 15 Marcus Stock. Subs (all used): 10 Lewis Bienek; 18 Emmanuel Waine; 29 Jacob Jones; 34 Ugo Tison.
Tries: Campagnolo (5), Waine (40), Kershaw (56), Natoli (75); **Goals:** O Leyland 2/4.
RHINOS: 1 Lachlan Miller; 2 David Fusitu'a; 4 Paul Momirovski; 3 Harry Newman; 29 Alfie Edgell; 6 Brodie Croft; 7 Matt Frawley; 15 Sam Lisone; 9 Andy Ackers; 17 Justin Sangare; 16 James McDonnell; 12 Rhyse Martin; 13 Cameron Smith (C). Subs (all used): 11 James Bentley; 14 Jarrod O'Connor; 25 James Donaldson; 30 Tom Nicholson-Watton.
Tries: Martin (10, 33, 63); **Goals:** Martin 4/4;
Field goal: Croft (89).
Rugby Leaguer & League Express Men of the Match:
Broncos: Lee Kershaw; *Rhinos:* Rhyse Martin.
Penalty count: 8-8; **Half-time:** 12-14;
Referee: Marcus Griffiths; **Attendance:** 4,403.

HUDDERSFIELD GIANTS 10 ST HELENS 18

GIANTS: 6 Tui Lolohea; 20 Elliot Wallis; 4 Kevin Naiqama; 3 Esan Marsters; 5 Jake Bibby; 23 Oliver Russell; 7 Adam Clune; 8 Chris Hill; 14 Ashton Golding; 10 Joe Greenwood; 12 Sam Hewitt; 16 Harry Rushton; 21 Leroy Cudjoe (C). Subs (all used): 18 Sebastine Ikahihifo; 22 Harvey Livett; 25 Fenton Rogers; 27 Kieran Rush.
Tries: Wallis (23), Jake Bibby (28); **Goals:** Russell 1/2.
Dismissal: Rogers (40) - high tackle on Ritson.
SAINTS: 33 Harry Robertson; 25 Tee Ritson; 11 Sione Mata'utia; 3 Waqa Blake; 5 Jon Bennison; 6 Jonny Lomax (C); 14 Moses Mbye; 8 Alex Walmsley; 24 Jake Burns; 10 Matty Lees; 19 Matt Whitley; 12 Joe Batchelor; 13 Morgan Knowles. Subs (all used): 17 Agnatius Paasi; 20 George Delaney; 30 Jonny Vaughan; 31 Noah Stephens.
Tries: Lomax (10), Mata'utia (50), Robertson (55);
Goals: Bennison 3/3.
Sin bin: Stephens (71) - delaying restart.
Rugby Leaguer & League Express Men of the Match:
Giants: Tui Lolohea; *Saints:* Moses Mbye.
Penalty count: 5-4; **Half-time:** 10-6;
Referee: Aaron Moore; **Attendance:** 3,877.

ROUND 25

Friday 6th September 2024

CASTLEFORD TIGERS 12 LEIGH LEOPARDS 34

TIGERS: 34 Tex Hoy; 23 Jason Qareqare; 1 Luke Hooley; 35 Corey Hall; 5 Innes Senior; 16 Rowan Milnes; 38 Jenson Windley; 8 Liam Watts; 9 Paul McShane (C); 13 Joe Westerman; 12 Alex Mellor; 11 Elie El-Zakhem; 29 George Hill. Subs (all used): 10 George Lawler; 20 Muizz Mustapha; 24 Cain Robb; 32 Dan Hindmarsh.
Tries: C Hall (33), Milnes (65); **Goals:** Milnes 2/2.
Sin bin: Windley (54) - late challenge on O'Brien.
LEOPARDS: 6 Matt Moylan; 5 Josh Charnley; 4 Ricky Leutele; 24 Umyla Hanley; 34 Darnell McIntosh; 1 Gareth O'Brien; 7 Lachlan Lam; 8 Tom Amone; 15 Matt Davis; 10 Robbie Mulhern; 11 Kai O'Donnell; 16 Frankie Halton; 13 John Asiata (C). Subs (all used): 17 Owen Trout; 35 Aaron Pene; 12 Jack Hughes; 33 Brad Dwyer.
Tries: O'Donnell (8), Charnley (14), Amone (35, 56), O'Brien (44), Leutele (58); **Goals:** Moylan 5/6.
Sin bin: Asiata (63) - late challenge on Westerman.
Rugby Leaguer & League Express Men of the Match:
Tigers: Tex Hoy; *Leopards:* Tom Amone.
Penalty count: 3-6; **Half-time:** 6-18;
Referee: Aaron Moore; **Attendance:** 9,053.

LEEDS RHINOS 68 HULL FC 6

RHINOS: 1 Lachlan Miller; 2 David Fusitu'a; 4 Paul Momirovski; 3 Harry Newman; 29 Alfie Edgell; 6 Brodie Croft; 7 Matt Frawley; 8 Mikolaj Oledzki; 9 Andy Ackers; 17 Justin Sangare; 16 James McDonnell; 12 Rhyse Martin; 13 Cameron Smith (C). Subs (all used): 11 James Bentley; 15 Sam Lisone; 25 James Donaldson; 14 Jarrod O'Connor.
Tries: Newman (10), Smith (22), Edgell (26, 42, 50, 56), Bentley (35, 78), Croft (38, 61);
Goals: Martin 13/13, Donaldson 1/1.
HULL FC: 37 Logan Moy; 25 Harvey Barron; 3 Carlos Tuimavave; 44 Tom Briscoe; 26 Lewis Martin; 40 Jack Charles; 31 Jack Walker; 8 Herman Ese'ese; 15 Jordan Lane (C); 52 Sam Eseh; 12 Ligi Sao; 48 Jed Cartwright; 45 Yusuf Aydin. Subs (all used): 13 Brad Fash; 28 Denive Balmforth; 16 Jack Ashworth; 27 Zach Jebson.
Try: Barron (54); **Goals:** Charles 1/1.
Sin bin: Cartwright (27) - late challenge on Croft, (78) - professional foul.
Rugby Leaguer & League Express Men of the Match:
Rhinos: Brodie Croft; *Hull FC:* Jordan Lane.
Penalty count: 7-2; **Half-time:** 32-0;
Referee: Tom Grant; **Attendance:** 14,105.

WIGAN WARRIORS 24 HULL KR 20

WARRIORS: 1 Jai Field; 2 Abbas Miski; 3 Adam Keighran; 4 Jake Wardle; 5 Liam Marshall; 6 Bevan French; 7 Harry Smith; 8 Ethan Havard; 17 Kruise Leeming; 16 Luke Thompson; 21 Junior Nsemba; 12 Liam Farrell (C); 13 Kaide Ellis. Subs: 10 Liam Byrne (not used); 15 Patrick Mago; 19 Tyler Dupree; 27 Tom Forber.
Tries: Miski (31), Nsemba (34), French (57), Marshall (63, 68); **Goals:** Keighran 2/5.
HULL KR: 36 Jack Broadbent; 35 Joe Burgess; 1 Peta Hiku; 4 Oliver Gildart; 5 Ryan Hall; 27 Tyrone May; 7 Mikey Lewis; 8 Sauaso Sue; 14 Matt Parcell; 16 Jai Whitbread; 11 Dean Hadley; 12 James Batchelor; 13 Elliot Minchella (C). Subs (all used): 9 Jez Litten; 15 Sam Luckley; 17 Matty Storton; 20 Kelepi Tanginoa.
Tries: Parcell (19), Lewis (24), Burgess (49);
Goals: Lewis 4/5.
Sin bin: Burgess (29) - holding down; Whitbread (60) - high tackle.
Rugby Leaguer & League Express Men of the Match:
Warriors: Junior Nsemba; *Hull KR:* Mikey Lewis.
Penalty count: 5-7; **Half-time:** 8-12;
Referee: Jack Smith; **Attendance:** 16,719.

Saturday 7th September 2024

WARRINGTON WOLVES 16 ST HELENS 2

WOLVES: 38 Cai Taylor-Wray; 2 Josh Thewlis; 14 Rodrick Tai; 3 Toby King; 5 Matty Ashton; 6 George Williams (C); 7 Josh Drinkwater; 41 Luke Yates; 32 Sam Powell; 16 Zane Musgrove; 42 John Bateman; 12 Lachlan Fitzgibbon; 11 Ben Currie. Subs (all used): 9 Danny Walker; 13 Matty Nicholson; 15 Joe Philbin; 17 Jordan Crowther.
Tries: Ashton (17), Crowther (37); **Goals:** Josh Thewlis 4/4.
Sin bin: Fitzgibbon (8) - high tackle on Ritson; Josh Thewlis (80) - professional foul.
SAINTS: 33 Harry Robertson; 25 Tee Ritson; 3 Waqa Blake; 11 Sione Mata'utia; 5 Jon Bennison; 6 Jonny Lomax (C); 14 Moses Mbye; 8 Alex Walmsley; 24 Jake Burns; 10 Matty Lees; 19 Matt Whitley; 12 Joe Batchelor; 13 Morgan Knowles. Subs (all used): 1 Jack Welsby; 17 Agnatius Paasi; 20 George Delaney; 30 Jonny Vaughan.
Goals: Bennison 1/1.
Sin bin: Lees (13) - late challenge on Drinkwater.
Rugby Leaguer & League Express Men of the Match:
Wolves: George Williams; *Saints:* George Delaney.
Penalty count: 9-9; **Half-time:** 12-2;
Referee: Chris Kendall; **Attendance:** 12,015.

SALFORD RED DEVILS 27 CATALANS DRAGONS 12

RED DEVILS: 1 Ryan Brierley; 2 Ethan Ryan; 3 Nene Macdonald; 4 Tim Lafai; 5 Deon Cross; 32 Jayden Nikorima; 7 Marc Sneyd; 8 Brad Singleton; 24 Joe Mellor; 27 Gil Dudson; 11 Sam Stone; 12 Kallum Watkins (C); 13 Oliver Partington. Subs (all used): 15 Shane Wright; 16 Joe Shorrocks; 23 Chris Hankinson; 31 Joe Bullock.
Tries: Nikorima (8), Mellor (38), Lafai (48), Cross (57);
Goals: Sneyd 5/6; **Field goal:** Sneyd (78).
DRAGONS: 1 Arthur Mourgue; 2 Tom Davies; 34 Reimis Smith; 4 Matthieu Laguerre; 5 Fouad Yaha; 17 Cesar Rouge; 7 Theo Fages; 16 Romain Navarrete; 14 Alrix Da Costa; 10 Julian Bousquet; 8 Mike McMeeken; 15 Bayley Sironen; 13 Ben Garcia (C). Subs (all used): 11 Tariq Sims; 23 Jordan Dezaria; 29 Sam Tomkins; 33 Jarrod Wallace.
Tries: Mourgue (21), Sironen (61); **Goals:** Mourgue 2/3.
Rugby Leaguer & League Express Men of the Match:
Red Devils: Marc Sneyd; *Dragons:* Arthur Mourgue.
Penalty count: 6-4; **Half-time:** 12-6;
Referee: Liam Moore; **Attendance:** 4,910.

Sunday 8th September 2024

HUDDERSFIELD GIANTS 22 LONDON BRONCOS 16

GIANTS: 6 Tui Lolohea; 30 Aidan McGowan; 3 Esan Marsters; 4 Kevin Naiqama; 5 Jake Bibby; 7 Adam Clune; 23 Oliver Russell; 8 Chris Hill; 19 Thomas Deakin; 10 Joe Greenwood; 22 Harvey Livett; 16 Harry Rushton; 21 Leroy Cudjoe (C). Subs (all used): 27 Kieran Rush; 18 Sebastine Ikahihifo; 15 Matty English; 17 Oliver Wilson.
Tries: Lolohea (28, 39), Rushton (76); **Goals:** Russell 5/6.
BRONCOS: 23 Josh Rourke; 2 Lee Kershaw; 12 Ethan Natoli; 3 Jarred Bassett; 4 Hakim Miloudi; 20 Oliver Leyland; 6 Jack Campagnolo; 8 Rob Butler; 9 Sam Davis; 19 Rhys Kennedy; 17 Sadiq Adebiyi; 11 Will Lovell (C); 15 Marcus Stock. Subs: 18 Emmanuel Waine; 34 Ugo Tison (not used); 10 Lewis Bienek; 29 Jacob Jones.
Tries: Stock (14), Miloudi (44), Adebiyi (52);
Goals: O Leyland 2/3.
Sin bin: Lovell (75) - late challenge on Russell.
Rugby Leaguer & League Express Men of the Match:
Giants: Tui Lolohea; *Broncos:* Oliver Leyland.
Penalty count: 7-5; **Half-time:** 14-6;
Referee: James Vella; **Attendance:** 3,439.

ROUND 26

Friday 13th September 2024

LEIGH LEOPARDS 0 HULL KR 24

LEOPARDS: 6 Matt Moylan; 34 Darnell McIntosh; 24 Umyla Hanley; 4 Ricky Leutele; 5 Josh Charnley; 1 Gareth O'Brien; 7 Lachlan Lam; 8 Tom Amone; 15 Matt Davis; 10 Robbie Mulhern; 11 Kai O'Donnell; 16 Frankie Halton; 13 John Asiata (C). Subs (all used): 17 Owen Trout; 12 Jack Hughes; 33 Brad Dwyer; 35 Aaron Pene.
HULL KR: 2 Niall Evalds; 35 Joe Burgess; 1 Peta Hiku; 4 Oliver Gildart; 5 Ryan Hall; 27 Tyrone May; 7 Mikey Lewis; 8 Sauaso Sue; 14 Matt Parcell; 11 Dean Hadley; 17 Matty Storton; 12 James Batchelor; 13 Elliot Minchella (C). Subs (all used): 3 Tom Opacic; 9 Jez Litten; 15 Sam Luckley; 37 Jack Brown.
Tries: R Hall (21), Lewis (29, 60), Sue (48);
Goals: Lewis 4/5.
Sin bin: Minchella (63) - high tackle on Moylan.
Rugby Leaguer & League Express Men of the Match:
Leopards: Ricky Leutele; *Hull KR:* Mikey Lewis.
Penalty count: 1-5; **Half-time:** 0-10;
Referee: Chris Kendall; **Attendance:** 8,412.

ST HELENS 40 CASTLEFORD TIGERS 4

SAINTS: 1 Jack Welsby; 2 Tommy Makinson; 11 Sione Mata'utia; 4 Mark Percival; 5 Jon Bennison; 6 Jonny Lomax (C); 7 Lewis Dodd; 8 Alex Walmsley; 24 Jake Burns; 10 Matty Lees; 19 Matt Whitley; 12 Joe Batchelor; 13 Morgan Knowles. Subs (all used): 9 Daryl Clark; 15 James Bell; 17 Agnatius Paasi; 20 George Delaney.
Tries: Burns (3), Bennison (9, 26, 62), Lomax (43), Paasi (55), Makinson (65), Delaney (79);
Goals: Bennison 3/7, Mata'utia 1/1.
TIGERS: 31 Fletcher Rooney; 23 Jason Qareqare; 1 Luke Hooley; 12 Alex Mellor; 5 Innes Senior; 16 Rowan Milnes; 7 Jacob Miller; 8 Liam Watts; 9 Paul McShane (C); 20 Muizz Mustapha; 10 George Lawler; 11 Elie El-Zakhem; 14 Liam Horne. Subs (all used): 25 Brad Martin; 32 Dan Hindmarsh; 38 Jenson Windley; 39 Akim Matvejev (D).
Try: Rooney (40); **Goals:** Milnes 0/1.

Rugby Leaguer & League Express Men of the Match:
Saints: Jon Bennison; *Tigers:* Rowan Milnes.
Penalty count: 5-8; **Half-time:** 14-4;
Referee: Jack Smith; **Attendance:** 12,058.

WIGAN WARRIORS 38 LEEDS RHINOS 0

WARRIORS: 1 Jai Field; 2 Abbas Miski; 3 Adam Keighran; 4 Jake Wardle; 5 Liam Marshall; 6 Bevan French; 7 Harry Smith; 8 Ethan Havard; 17 Kruise Leeming; 16 Luke Thompson; 21 Junior Nsemba; 12 Liam Farrell (C); 13 Kaide Ellis. Subs (all used): 10 Liam Byrne; 15 Patrick Mago; 19 Tyler Dupree; 27 Tom Forber.
Tries: Wardle (5), French (7, 79), Marshall (38), Ellis (45), Miski (61), Keighran (71); **Goals:** Keighran 5/7.
RHINOS: 29 Alfie Edgell; 2 David Fusitu'a; 4 Paul Momirovski; 3 Harry Newman; 33 Riley Lumb; 6 Brodie Croft; 7 Matt Frawley; 8 Mikolaj Oledzki; 9 Andy Ackers; 17 Justin Sangare; 16 James McDonnell; 12 Rhyse Martin; 13 Cameron Smith (C). Subs (all used): 11 James Bentley; 14 Jarrod O'Connor; 15 Sam Lisone; 25 James Donaldson.
Rugby Leaguer & League Express Men of the Match:
Warriors: Kaide Ellis; *Rhinos:* Riley Lumb.
Penalty count: 7-4; **Half-time:** 14-0;
Referee: Liam Moore; **Attendance:** 15,146.

Saturday 14th September 2024

HULL FC 4 SALFORD RED DEVILS 58

HULL FC: 37 Logan Moy; 25 Harvey Barron; 23 Davy Litten; 43 Ed Chamberlain; 26 Lewis Martin; 40 Jack Charles; 31 Jack Walker; 8 Herman Ese'ese; 19 Morgan Smith; 21 Will Gardiner; 15 Jordan Lane; 13 Brad Fash (C); 45 Yusuf Aydin. Subs (all used): 16 Jack Ashworth; 27 Zach Jebson; 28 Denive Balmforth; 46 Tiaki Chan.
Try: Jebson (66); **Goals:** Charles 0/1.
RED DEVILS: 1 Ryan Brierley; 2 Ethan Ryan; 3 Nene Macdonald; 4 Tim Lafai; 5 Dean Cross; 32 Jayden Nikorima; 7 Marc Sneyd; 8 Brad Singleton; 24 Joe Mellor; 27 Gil Dudson; 15 Shane Wright; 12 Kallum Watkins (C); 13 Oliver Partington. Subs (all used): 16 Joe Shorrocks; 23 Chris Hankinson; 29 Loghan Lewis; 31 Joe Bullock.
Tries: Lafai (5, 33, 62), Cross (9), Mellor (18, 76), Singleton (24), Macdonald (46), Wright (50), Watkins (55); **Goals:** Sneyd 9/10.
Rugby Leaguer & League Express Men of the Match:
Hull FC: Logan Moy; *Red Devils:* Tim Lafai.
Penalty count: 3-3; **Half-time:** 0-28;
Referee: Aaron Moore; **Attendance:** 9,274.

HUDDERSFIELD GIANTS 0 WARRINGTON WOLVES 66

GIANTS: 6 Tui Lolohea; 30 Aidan McGowan; 3 Esan Marsters; 34 Darius Carter (D); 20 Elliot Wallis; 7 Adam Clune (C); 23 Oliver Russell; 26 Hugo Salabio; 19 Thomas Deakin; 10 Joe Greenwood; 22 Harvey Livett; 5 Jake Bibby; 33 Andre Savelio. Subs (all used): 18 Sebastine Ikahihifo; 27 Kieran Rush; 28 Jack Bibby (D); 29 Jack Billington.
Sin bin: Billington (44) - high tackle on Josh Thewlis.
WOLVES: 38 Cai Taylor-Wray; 2 Josh Thewlis; 14 Rodrick Tai; 3 Toby King; 5 Matty Ashton; 6 George Williams (C); 7 Josh Drinkwater; 41 Luke Yates; 9 Danny Walker; 16 Zane Musgrove; 42 John Bateman; 13 Matty Nicholson; 11 Ben Currie. Subs (all used): 8 James Harrison; 15 Joe Philbin; 17 Jordan Crowther; 32 Sam Powell.
Tries: Ashton (6, 14, 63), Harrison (23), Williams (32), Nicholson (36, 72), Taylor-Wray (38, 65), Josh Thewlis (46), King (70), Tai (75); **Goals:** Josh Thewlis 9/12.
Rugby Leaguer & League Express Men of the Match:
Giants: Joe Greenwood; *Wolves:* George Williams.
Penalty count: 2-8; **Half-time:** 0-36;
Referee: Tom Grant; **Attendance:** 4,181.

CATALANS DRAGONS 12 LONDON BRONCOS 8

DRAGONS: 1 Arthur Mourgue; 2 Tom Davies; 3 Arthur Romano; 34 Reimis Smith; 5 Fouad Yaha; 27 Jordan Abdull; 29 Sam Tomkins; 16 Romain Navarrete; 13 Ben Garcia (C); 20 Tevita Satae; 11 Tariq Sims; 15 Bayley Sironen; 8 Mike McMeeken. Subs (all used): 10 Julian Bousquet; 17 Cesar Rouge; 23 Jordan Dezaria; 33 Jarrod Wallace.
Tries: Wallace (51), Romano (61); **Goals:** Mourgue 2/2.
Sin bin: Satae (68) - high tackle.
BRONCOS: 23 Josh Rourke; 2 Lee Kershaw; 12 Ethan Natoli; 3 Jarred Bassett; 4 Hakim Miloudi; 20 Oliver Leyland; 6 Jack Campagnolo; 8 Rob Butler; 9 Sam Davis; 19 Rhys Kennedy; 11 Will Lovell (C); 29 Jacob Jones; 15 Marcus Stock. Subs (all used): 10 Lewis Bienek; 17 Sadiq Adebiyi; 18 Emmanuel Waine; 34 Ugo Tison.
Try: Kershaw (32); **Goals:** O Leyland 2/2.
Rugby Leaguer & League Express Men of the Match:
Dragons: Ben Garcia; *Broncos:* Oliver Leyland.
Penalty count: 4-2; **Half-time:** 0-6;
Referee: Marcus Griffiths; **Attendance:** 8,855.

ROUND 27

Thursday 19th September 2024

HUDDERSFIELD GIANTS 34 CASTLEFORD TIGERS 10

GIANTS: 6 Tui Lolohea; 30 Aidan McGowan; 3 Esan Marsters; 22 Harvey Livett; 5 Jake Bibby; 7 Adam Clune; 23 Oliver Russell; 8 Chris Hill; 9 Adam Milner; 17 Oliver Wilson; 16 Harry Rushton; 12 Sam Hewitt; 21 Leroy Cudjoe (C). Subs (all used): 10 Joe Greenwood; 15 Matty English; 18 Sebastine Ikahihifo; 27 Kieran Rush.
Tries: Hewitt (18, 60), Rushton (21), McGowan (26), Lolohea (37), Clune (48); **Goals:** Russell 5/6.
TIGERS: 31 Fletcher Rooney; 23 Jason Qareqare; 1 Luke Hooley; 12 Alex Mellor; 5 Innes Senior; 16 Rowan Milnes; 7 Jacob Miller; 39 Akim Matvejev; 9 Paul McShane (C); 13 Joe Westerman; 11 Elie El-Zakhem; 10 George Lawler; 14 Liam Horne. Subs (all used): 8 Liam Watts; 20 Muizz Mustapha; 21 Sylvester Namo; 38 Jenson Windley.
Tries: Qareqare (55), Mellor (73); **Goals:** Milnes 1/2.
Rugby Leaguer & League Express Men of the Match:
Giants: Adam Clune; *Tigers:* Fletcher Rooney.
Penalty count: 2-4; **Half-time:** 22-0;
Referee: James Vella; **Attendance:** 4,138.

WIGAN WARRIORS 64 SALFORD RED DEVILS 0

WARRIORS: 1 Jai Field; 26 Zach Eckersley; 3 Adam Keighran; 4 Jake Wardle; 5 Liam Marshall; 6 Bevan French; 7 Harry Smith; 8 Ethan Havard; 17 Kruise Leeming; 16 Luke Thompson; 21 Junior Nsemba; 12 Liam Farrell (C); 13 Kaide Ellis. Subs (all used): 10 Liam Byrne; 15 Patrick Mago; 19 Tyler Dupree; 27 Tom Forber.
Tries: Marshall (6, 58), Field (10, 42, 72), French (18, 79), Eckersley (22), Wardle (27), Leeming (61, 69);
Goals: Keighran 10/11.
RED DEVILS: 14 Chris Atkin (C); 36 Ethan Fitzgerald (D); 34 Billy Glover (D); 33 Josh Wagstaffe (D); 25 Nathan Connell; 6 Cade Cust; 22 Kai Morgan; 17 Jack Ormondroyd; 9 Amir Bourouh; 19 Adam Sidlow; 18 Ben Hellewell; 38 Charlie McCurrie (D); 28 Harvey Wilson. Subs (all used): 30 Jamie Pye (D); 35 Charlie Glover (D); 37 Leunbou Bardyel-Wells (D); 39 Jack Gatcliffe (D).
Rugby Leaguer & League Express Men of the Match:
Warriors: Junior Nsemba; *Red Devils:* Jamie Pye.
Penalty count: 7-6; **Half-time:** 28-0;
Referee: Chris Kendall; **Attendance:** 15,589.

Friday 20th September 2024

HULL KR 26 LEEDS RHINOS 16

HULL KR: 36 Jack Broadbent; 35 Joe Burgess; 1 Peta Hiku; 3 Tom Opacic; 5 Ryan Hall; 27 Tyrone May; 7 Mikey Lewis; 8 Sauaso Sue; 14 Matt Parcell; 16 Jai Whitbread; 17 Matty Storton; 12 James Batchelor (C); 11 Dean Hadley. Subs (all used): 9 Jez Litten; 10 George King; 15 Sam Luckley; 37 Jack Brown.
Tries: Parcell (23), Hiku (37), Opacic (48), Sue (59), Burgess (69); **Goals:** Lewis 3/5.
RHINOS: 29 Alfie Edgell; 33 Riley Lumb; 4 Paul Momirovski; 3 Harry Newman; 24 Luis Roberts; 6 Brodie Croft; 7 Matt Frawley; 8 Mikolaj Oledzki; 9 Andy Ackers; 17 Justin Sangare; 16 James McDonnell; 12 Rhyse Martin; 13 Cameron Smith (C). Subs (all used): 11 James Bentley; 14 Jarrod O'Connor; 15 Sam Lisone; 25 James Donaldson.
Tries: Martin (17), Edgell (29), Ackers (79);
Goals: Martin 2/3.
Rugby Leaguer & League Express Men of the Match:
Hull KR: Matt Parcell; *Rhinos:* Brodie Croft.
Penalty count: 8-7; **Half-time:** 10-10;
Referee: Jack Smith; **Attendance:** 11,200.

LEIGH LEOPARDS 18 ST HELENS 12

LEOPARDS: 6 Matt Moylan; 34 Darnell McIntosh; 24 Umyla Hanley; 4 Ricky Leutele; 5 Josh Charnley; 1 Gareth O'Brien; 7 Lachlan Lam; 8 Tom Amone; 9 Edwin Ipape; 10 Robbie Mulhern; 11 Kai O'Donnell; 16 Frankie Halton; 13 John Asiata (C). Subs: 12 Jack Hughes; 17 Owen Trout; 33 Brad Dwyer (not used); 35 Aaron Pene.
Tries: Asiata (20), Leutele (38), Charnley (67);
Goals: Moylan 3/4.
Sin bin: Leutele (53) - high tackle on Welsby.
SAINTS: 1 Jack Welsby; 2 Tommy Makinson; 11 Sione Mata'utia; 4 Mark Percival; 5 Jon Bennison; 6 Jonny Lomax (C); 7 Lewis Dodd; 20 George Delaney; 24 Jake Burns; 10 Matty Lees; 19 Matt Whitley; 12 Joe Batchelor; 13 Morgan Knowles. Subs (all used): 9 Daryl Clark; 15 James Bell; 17 Agnatius Paasi; 31 Noah Stephens.
Tries: Makinson (59), Knowles (61); **Goals:** Bennison 2/2.
Rugby Leaguer & League Express Men of the Match:
Leopards: Edwin Ipape; *Saints:* Mark Percival.
Penalty count: 5-3; **Half-time:** 12-0;
Referee: Liam Moore; **Attendance:** 9,899.

WARRINGTON WOLVES 54 LONDON BRONCOS 0

WOLVES: 1 Matt Dufty; 2 Josh Thewlis; 33 Arron Lindop; 3 Toby King; 5 Matty Ashton; 6 George Williams (C); 7 Josh Drinkwater; 41 Luke Yates; 9 Danny Walker; 16 Zane Musgrove; 42 John Bateman; 13 Matty Nicholson; 11 Ben Currie. Subs (all used): 8 James Harrison; 17 Jordan Crowther; 32 Sam Powell; 34 Max Wood.
Tries: Ashton (9, 14, 36), Nicholson (22, 68), Lindop (39, 43), Harrison (49), Josh Thewlis (54), Currie (72); **Goals:** Josh Thewlis 7/10.
BRONCOS: 23 Josh Rourke; 2 Lee Kershaw; 12 Ethan Natoli; 3 Jarred Bassett; 4 Hakim Miloudi; 20 Oliver Leyland; 6 Jack Campagnolo; 8 Rob Butler; 29 Jacob Jones; 19 Rhys Kennedy; 11 Will Lovell (C); 17 Sadiq Adebiyi; 15 Marcus Stock. Subs (all used): 7 James Meadows; 10 Lewis Bienek; 18 Emmanuel Waine; 34 Ugo Tison.
Rugby Leaguer & League Express Men of the Match:
Wolves: Matt Dufty; *Broncos:* Jack Campagnolo.
Penalty count: 1-2; **Half-time:** 26-0;
Referee: Aaron Moore; **Attendance:** 10,192.

Saturday 21st September 2024

HULL FC 4 CATALANS DRAGONS 24

HULL FC: 37 Logan Moy; 25 Harvey Barron; 3 Carlos Tuimavave; 54 Ryan Westerman (D); 26 Lewis Martin; 19 Morgan Smith; 55 Callum Kemp (D); 8 Herman Ese'ese; 9 Danny Houghton (C); 21 Will Gardiner; 15 Jordan Lane; 48 Jed Cartwright; 45 Yusuf Aydin. Subs (all used): 16 Jack Ashworth; 27 Zach Jebson; 28 Denive Balmforth; 30 Matty Laidlaw.
Try: Martin (5); **Goals:** Lane 0/1.
DRAGONS: 29 Sam Tomkins; 2 Tom Davies; 34 Reimis Smith; 4 Matthieu Laguerre; 5 Fouad Yaha; 1 Arthur Mourgue; 7 Theo Fages; 16 Romain Navarrete; 14 Alrix Da Costa; 10 Julian Bousquet; 11 Tariq Sims; 15 Bayley Sironen; 13 Ben Garcia (C). Subs (all used): 17 Cesar Rouge; 20 Tevita Satae; 23 Jordan Dezaria; 33 Jarrod Wallace. 18th man (used): 12 Paul Seguier.
Tries: Satae (34), Laguerre (44), Mourgue (60), Davies (76);
Goals: Mourgue 4/5.
Rugby Leaguer & League Express Men of the Match:
Hull FC: Lewis Martin; *Dragons:* Arthur Mourgue.
Penalty count: 3-8; **Half-time:** 4-6;
Referee: Tom Grant; **Attendance:** 9,384.

THE ELIMINATORS

Friday 27th September 2024

SALFORD RED DEVILS 6 LEIGH LEOPARDS 14

RED DEVILS: 23 Chris Hankinson; 2 Ethan Ryan; 3 Nene Macdonald; 4 Tim Lafai; 5 Deon Cross; 32 Jayden Nikorima; 7 Marc Sneyd; 8 Brad Singleton; 24 Joe Mellor; 27 Gil Dudson; 11 Sam Stone; 12 Kallum Watkins (C); 13 Oliver Partington. Subs (all used): 1 Ryan Brierley; 15 Shane Wright; 16 Joe Shorrocks; 29 Loghan Lewis.
Try: Ryan (78); **Goals:** Sneyd 1/2.
LEOPARDS: 6 Matt Moylan; 34 Darnell McIntosh; 24 Umyla Hanley; 4 Ricky Leutele; 5 Josh Charnley; 1 Gareth O'Brien; 7 Lachlan Lam; 8 Tom Amone; 9 Edwin Ipape; 10 Robbie Mulhern; 16 Frankie Halton; 12 Jack Hughes; 13 John Asiata (C). Subs (all used): 3 Zak Hardaker; 17 Owen Trout; 33 Brad Dwyer; 35 Aaron Pene.
Tries: Charnley (53), O'Brien (59), Ipape (66);
Goals: Moylan 1/3.
Sin bin: Hughes (77) - obstruction.
Rugby Leaguer & League Express Men of the Match:
Red Devils: Nene Macdonald; *Leopards:* Edwin Ipape.
Penalty count: 7-10; **Half-time:** 2-0;
Referee: Jack Smith; **Attendance:** 10,867.

Saturday 28th September 2024

WARRINGTON WOLVES 23 ST HELENS 22
(after golden point extra-time)

WOLVES: 1 Matt Dufty; 2 Josh Thewlis; 14 Rodrick Tai; 3 Toby King; 5 Matty Ashton; 6 George Williams (C); 7 Josh Drinkwater; 41 Luke Yates; 9 Danny Walker; 16 Zane Musgrove; 42 John Bateman; 13 Matty Nicholson; 11 Ben Currie. Subs (all used): 8 James Harrison; 10 Paul Vaughan; 15 Joe Philbin; 32 Sam Powell.
Tries: King (2, 54), Ashton (36, 66);
Goals: Josh Thewlis 3/4; **Field goal:** Williams (84).
SAINTS: 1 Jack Welsby; 2 Tommy Makinson; 11 Sione Mata'utia; 4 Mark Percival; 5 Jon Bennison; 6 Jonny Lomax (C); 7 Lewis Dodd; 8 Alex Walmsley; 9 Daryl Clark; 10 Matty Lees; 19 Matt Whitley; 12 Joe Batchelor; 13 Morgan Knowles. Subs (all used): 15 James Bell; 17 Agnatius Paasi; 20 George Delaney; 24 Jake Burns.
Tries: Makinson (11, 32), Percival (24), Bennison (79);
Goals: Percival 3/4.

Super League XXIX - Round by Round

Wigan's Adam Keighran takes on Hull KR's Jack Broadbent and Dean Hadley during the Super League Grand Final

Rugby Leaguer & League Express Men of the Match:
Wolves: George Williams; *Saints:* Mark Percival.
Penalty count: 5-2; **Half-time:** 10-16;
Referee: Liam Moore; **Attendance:** 12,111.

SEMI-FINALS

Friday 4th October 2024

HULL KR 10 WARRINGTON WOLVES 8

HULL KR: 2 Niall Evalds; 35 Joe Burgess; 1 Peta Hiku; 36 Jack Broadbent; 5 Ryan Hall; 27 Tyrone May; 7 Mikey Lewis; 8 Sauaso Sue; 14 Matt Parcell (C); 11 Dean Hadley. Subs (all used): 9 Jez Litten; 15 Sam Luckley; 20 Kelepi Tanginoa; 37 Jack Brown.
Tries: Batchelor (17), Burgess (35); **Goals:** Lewis 1/2.
WOLVES: 1 Matt Dufty; 2 Josh Thewlis; 14 Rodrick Tai; 3 Toby King; 5 Matty Ashton; 6 George Williams (C); 7 Josh Drinkwater; 8 James Harrison; 9 Danny Walker; 41 Luke Yates; 13 Matty Nicholson; 42 John Bateman; 11 Ben Currie. Subs (all used): 10 Paul Vaughan; 15 Joe Philbin; 17 Jordan Crowther; 32 Sam Powell.
Tries: Ashton (45, 58); **Goals:** Josh Thewlis 0/2.
Rugby Leaguer & League Express Men of the Match:
Hull KR: Dean Hadley; *Wolves:* Matty Ashton.

Penalty count: 3-4; **Half-time:** 10-0;
Referee: Liam Moore; **Attendance:** 11,200.

Saturday 5th October 2024

WIGAN WARRIORS 38 LEIGH LEOPARDS 0

WARRIORS: 1 Jai Field; 2 Abbas Miski; 3 Adam Keighran; 4 Jake Wardle; 5 Liam Marshall; 6 Bevan French; 7 Harry Smith; 8 Ethan Havard; 17 Kruise Leeming; 16 Luke Thompson; 21 Junior Nsemba; 22 Sam Walters; 13 Kaide Ellis (C). Subs (all used): 10 Liam Byrne; 15 Patrick Mago; 19 Tyler Dupree; 27 Tom Forber.
Tries: Marshall (11, 38), Walters (19, 42), French (60), Field (77); **Goals:** Keighran 7/8.
Sin bin: Dupree (79) - dissent.
LEOPARDS: 6 Matt Moylan; 3 Zak Hardaker; 24 Umyla Hanley; 4 Ricky Leutele; 34 Darnell McIntosh; 1 Gareth O'Brien; 7 Lachlan Lam; 8 Tom Amone; 9 Edwin Ipape; 10 Robbie Mulhern; 12 Jack Hughes; 20 Oliver Holmes; 13 John Asiata (C). Subs (all used): 15 Matt Davis; 17 Owen Trout; 33 Brad Dwyer; 35 Aaron Pene.
Rugby Leaguer & League Express Men of the Match:
Warriors: Junior Nsemba; *Leopards:* Robbie Mulhern.
Penalty count: 4-4; **Half-time:** 18-0;
Referee: Chris Kendall; **Attendance:** 20,511.

GRAND FINAL

Saturday 12th October 2024

HULL KR 2 WIGAN WARRIORS 9

HULL KR: 2 Niall Evalds; 35 Joe Burgess; 1 Peta Hiku; 36 Jack Broadbent; 5 Ryan Hall; 27 Tyrone May; 7 Mikey Lewis; 8 Sauaso Sue; 14 Matt Parcell; 16 Jai Whitbread; 11 Dean Hadley; 12 James Batchelor; 13 Elliot Minchella (C). Subs (all used): 9 Jez Litten; 15 Sam Luckley; 17 Matty Storton; 20 Kelepi Tanginoa.
Goals: Lewis 1/1.
WARRIORS: 1 Jai Field; 2 Abbas Miski; 3 Adam Keighran; 4 Jake Wardle; 5 Liam Marshall; 6 Bevan French; 7 Harry Smith; 8 Ethan Havard; 17 Kruise Leeming; 16 Luke Thompson; 21 Junior Nsemba; 12 Liam Farrell (C); 13 Kaide Ellis. Subs (all used): 10 Liam Byrne; 15 Patrick Mago; 19 Tyler Dupree; 27 Tom Forber.
Try: French (22); **Goals:** Keighran 2/2;
Field goal: Smith (40).
Rugby Leaguer & League Express Men of the Match:
Hull KR: Elliot Minchella; *Warriors:* Bevan French.
Penalty count: 4-3; **Half-time:** 0-7;
Referee: Chris Kendall; **Attendance:** 68,173
(at Old Trafford, Manchester).

SUPER LEAGUE RECORDS *1996-2024*

PLAYER RECORDS

COMPETITION
Includes play-off games & Super League Super 8s (2015-2018)

TRIES
Ryan Hall (Hull KR/Leeds Rhinos)
(2007-2018, 2021-2024) 254

GOALS
Kevin Sinfield (Leeds Rhinos) (1997-2015) 1,566

FIELD GOALS
Lee Briers (Warrington Wolves/St Helens) (1997-2013) 70

POINTS
Kevin Sinfield (Leeds Rhinos) (1997-2015) 3,443

APPEARANCES
James Roby (St Helens) (2004-2023) 495

SEASON
Includes play-off games & Super League Super 8s (2015-2018)
(Play-offs in brackets)

TRIES
Denny Solomona (Castleford Tigers) (2016) 40 (-)

GOALS
Henry Paul (Bradford Bulls) (2001) 178 (13)

FIELD GOALS
Lee Briers (Warrington Wolves) (2002) 11 (-)

POINTS
Pat Richards (Wigan Warriors) (2010) 434 (46)

MATCH RECORDS
Includes play-off games & Super League Super 8s (2015-2018)

TRIES
Bevan French (Wigan Warriors) 7
(v Hull FC (h), 15/7/22)

GOALS
Henry Paul (Bradford Bulls) 14
(v Salford City Reds (h), 25/6/00)

FIELD GOALS
Lee Briers (Warrington Wolves) 5
(v Halifax Blue Sox (a), 25/5/02)

POINTS
Iestyn Harris (Leeds Rhinos) 42
(v Huddersfield Giants (h), 16/7/99)

TEAM RECORDS
Includes play-off games & Super League Super 8s (2015-2018)

HIGHEST SCORE
Bradford Bulls 96 Salford City Reds 16 (25/6/00)

WIDEST MARGIN
Leeds Rhinos 86 Huddersfield Giants 6 (16/7/99)
Bradford Bulls 96 Salford City Reds 16 (25/6/00)
Warrington Wolves 80 Wakefield Trinity Wildcats 0 (11/4/15)

ATTENDANCE RECORDS

GRAND FINAL
73,512 Leeds Rhinos v Wigan Warriors (10/10/15)

PLAY-OFFS
21,790 Wigan Warriors v St Helens (3/10/03)

REGULAR SEASON *(includes Super League Super 8s (2015-2018)*
31,555 Catalans Dragons v Wigan Warriors (18/5/19)
(at Camp Nou, Barcelona)

CHAMPIONSHIP 2024
Club by Club

Championship 2024 - Club by Club

BARROW RAIDERS

DATE	FIXTURE	RESULT	SCORERS	LGE	ATT
28/1/24	Workington (a) (1895CR1)	W8-30	t:Stack(2),Johnston,Clarke,Smith g:Shaw(5)	1st(G1)	901
4/2/24	Whitehaven (a) (1895CR2)	W12-18	t:Clarke,Costello,Greenwood g:Shaw(3)	1st(G1)	-
10/2/24	Oldham (h) (CCR3)	L10-22	t:Greenwood g:Shaw(3)	N/A	1,401
2/3/24	Wakefield (a) (1895CQF)	L30-12	t:Anderson-Moore(2) g:Shaw(2)	N/A	1,809
17/3/24	Widnes (a)	L44-8	t:Johnston g:Shaw(2)	14th	1,758
29/3/24	Whitehaven (a)	L23-22	t:Bulman,Forber,Stack,Shaw g:Shaw(3)	14th	-
7/4/24	York (h)	W15-14	t:Shaw,Clarke,Cresswell g:Shaw fg:B Walker	12th	1,692
14/4/24	Dewsbury (h)	W27-20	t:Wilkinson,Rothwell(2),Broadbent,Costello g:Shaw(3) fg:Johnston	7th	1,675
21/4/24	Doncaster (h)	L6-38	t:Gillam g:Shaw	9th	1,616
28/4/24	Sheffield (a)	L54-0		12th	1,103
5/5/24	Batley (h)	W24-14	t:Cresswell,Costello,Greenwood,Silva g:Shaw(4)	10th	1,976
18/5/24	Toulouse (a)	L38-16	t:Bulman,Broadbent,B Walker g:Johnston(2)	10th	2,313
26/5/24	Featherstone (h)	W25-12	t:Bulman(2),S Toal,Broadbent g:Johnston(4) fg:B Walker	8th	2,311
2/6/24	Bradford (a)	L36-24	t:Clarke,Shaw,Broadbent,Gillam g:Shaw(4)	11th	2,655
15/6/24	Halifax (h)	L28-38	t:Bulman,Cresswell(3),Costello g:Johnston(4)	13th	1,994
23/6/24	Swinton (a)	W10-24	t:Costello,Greenwood,Makin g:Johnston(6)	10th	945
30/6/24	Wakefield (h)	L0-36		12th	2,245
7/7/24	York (a)	L54-12	t:Stack,Bulman g:Johnston(2)	13th	1,792
14/7/24	Batley (a)	L22-2	g:Shaw	13th	-
21/7/24	Sheffield (h)	W8-6	t:Cresswell g:Shaw(2)	12th	1,552
28/7/24	Doncaster (a)	L37-30	t:Wood,Silva,Cresswell(2),Bulman g:Shaw(5)	13th	1,405
4/8/24	Bradford (h)	D24-24	t:Shaw,Broadbent,Bulman,Wood,Clarke g:Shaw(2)	11th	2,419
11/8/24	Halifax (a)	L38-12	t:S Toal,Cresswell g:B Walker(2)	11th	1,421
18/8/24	Dewsbury (a)	W24-31	t:B Walker,S Toal,Shaw,Wood g:Shaw(7) fg:B Walker	11th	940
25/8/24	Swinton (h)	W20-18	t:Smith(2),Stack g:Shaw(4)	10th	1,495
1/9/24	Featherstone (a)	L36-18	t:Johnston,Wood,Broadbent,S Toal g:Shaw	11th	1,345
7/9/24	Toulouse (h)	L24-36	t:Pye,B Walker,Shaw,Carter g:Shaw(4)	11th	1,709
15/9/24	Whitehaven (h)	W34-14	t:Bulman(2),Greenwood,Johnston,Broadbent g:Shaw(7)	11th	2,301
21/9/24	Wakefield (a)	L46-0		11th	5,011
29/9/24	Widnes (h)	L24-26	t:Cresswell,Clarke,Shaw,Broadbent g:Shaw(4)	11th	2,953

		APP		TRIES		GOALS		FG		PTS	
	D.O.B.	ALL	Ch	ALL	Ch	ALL	Ch	ALL	Ch	ALL	Ch
Max Anderson-Moore	9/12/01	2	1	2	0	0	0	0	0	8	0
Finley Beardsworth	16/1/04	1	1	0	0	0	0	0	0	0	0
Delaine Bedward-Gittens	28/6/01	3(5)	3(4)	0	0	0	0	0	0	0	0
Amir Bourouh	5/1/01	(1)	(1)	0	0	0	0	0	0	0	0
Luke Broadbent	17/12/02	25	22	8	8	0	0	0	0	32	32
Ryan Brown	15/5/05	8(3)	8(3)	0	0	0	0	0	0	0	0
Andrew Bulman	4/10/99	23	23	10	10	0	0	0	0	40	40
Greg Burke	12/2/93	4(8)	1(7)	0	0	0	0	0	0	0	0
Brett Carter	9/7/88	4(6)	3(6)	1	1	0	0	0	0	4	4
Max Clarke	1/1/00	14(2)	12(1)	6	4	0	0	0	0	24	16
Matty Costello	9/4/98	21	17	5	4	0	0	0	0	20	16
Luke Cresswell	5/5/95	30	26	10	10	0	0	0	0	40	40
Jacob Douglas	3/3/04	5	5	0	0	0	0	0	0	0	0
Finley Dutton-Rosconie	21/9/04	(1)	(1)	0	0	0	0	0	0	0	0
Charlie Emslie	30/10/00	6(5)	4(3)	0	0	0	0	0	0	0	0
Tom Forber	22/5/03	(7)	(7)	1	1	0	0	0	0	4	4
Ellis Gillam	6/10/97	17(5)	17(5)	2	2	0	0	0	0	8	8
James Greenwood	17/6/91	21(1)	18(1)	5	3	0	0	0	0	20	12
Adam Jackson	11/12/92	3	2	0	0	0	0	0	0	0	0
Ryan Johnston	16/3/98	22	18	4	3	18	18	1	1	53	49
Harvey Makin	17/11/03	1(8)	1(4)	1	1	0	0	0	0	4	4
Finn McMillan	9/12/05	3(1)	3	0	0	0	0	0	0	0	0
Mike Ogunwole	9/1/97	(3)	(1)	0	0	0	0	0	0	0	0
Jamie Pye	17/8/02	(6)	(6)	1	1	0	0	0	0	4	4
Kavan Rothwell	1/2/03	2(7)	2(7)	2	2	0	0	0	0	8	8
Ryan Shaw	27/2/92	24(2)	20(2)	7	7	68	55	0	0	164	138
Ramon Silva	7/11/01	21(1)	17(1)	2	2	0	0	0	0	8	8
Aaron Smith	12/10/96	9(11)	9(7)	3	2	0	0	0	0	12	8
Jarrad Stack	13/2/88	20	18	5	3	0	0	0	0	20	12
Reagan Sumner	23/2/04	1	1	0	0	0	0	0	0	0	0
Connor Terrill	3/7/01	(1)	(1)	0	0	0	0	0	0	0	0
Shane Toal	11/11/95	18	16	4	4	0	0	0	0	16	16
Brad Walker	30/1/98	28	25	3	3	2	2	3	3	19	19
Tom Walker	25/12/94	10(2)	9(12)	0	0	0	0	0	0	0	0
Tom Wilkinson	19/4/96	10(17)	6(17)	1	1	0	0	0	0	4	4
Josh Wood	15/11/95	23(7)	19(7)	4	4	0	0	0	0	16	16
Greg Worthington	17/7/90	11	11	0	0	0	0	0	0	0	0

'Ch' totals include Championship games only; 'All' totals also include Challenge Cup & 1895 Cup

Luke Cresswell

LEAGUE RECORD
P26-W9-D1-L16 (11th)
F458, A758, Diff-300, 19 points.

CHALLENGE CUP
Round Three

1895 CUP
Quarter Finalists

ATTENDANCES
Best - v Widnes (Ch - 2,953)
Worst - v Oldham (CC - 1,401)
Total (excluding Challenge Cup) - 25,938
Average (excluding Challenge Cup) - 1,995
(Down by 200 on 2023)

CLUB RECORDS
MATCH RECORDS Highest score: 138-0 v Nottingham City, 27/11/94 Highest score against: 0-90 v Leeds, 11/2/90 Record attendance: 21,651 v Salford, 15/4/38
Tries: 7 Theerapol Ritson v West Wales, 11/9/2021 Goals: 17 Darren Carter v Nottingham City, 27/11/94 Points: 42 Darren Carter v Nottingham City, 27/11/94
SEASON RECORDS Tries: 50 Jim Lewthwaite 1956-57 Goals: 135 Joe Ball 1956-57 Points: 323 Jamie Rooney 2010
CAREER RECORDS Tries: 352 Jim Lewthwaite 1943-57 Goals: 1,099 (inc 63fg) Darren Holt 1998-2002; 2004-2009; 2012
Points: 2,403 Darren Holt 1998-2002; 2004-2009; 2012 Appearances: 500 Jim Lewthwaite 1943-57

Championship 2024 - Club by Club

BATLEY BULLDOGS

DATE	FIXTURE	RESULT	SCORERS	LGE	ATT
4/2/24	Featherstone (h) (1895CR2)	W15-14	t:Cooper,Kear g:Woods(3) fg:Woods	2nd(G5)	784
11/2/24	Workington (h) (CCR3)	W48-18	t:Butterworth,Morton,Leak,Cooper,Walshaw,White,Flynn,Buchanan,Senior g:Woods(6)	N/A	-
18/2/24	Hunslet (a) (1895CR3)	W0-36	t:J Burton(3),White,Manning,Senior,Brown g:Woods(4)	1st(G5)	700
25/2/24	Rochdale (h) (CCR4)	W30-14	t:Senior,Cooper,J Burton,Flynn,Leak g:Woods(3),D Gibbons(2)	N/A	-
3/3/24	Sheffield (a) (1895CQF)	L26-10	t:White,Buchanan g:Woods	N/A	727
9/3/24	Widnes (a) (CCR5)	W14-18	t:Buchanan,D Gibbons,Cooper g:D Gibbons(3)	N/A	1,067
17/3/24	Featherstone (h)	L20-24	t:Flynn,J Burton,Morton g:Woods(4)	10th	1,961
23/3/24	Castleford (h) (CCR6)	L14-28	t:Manning,Moore g:D Gibbons(3)	N/A	2,015
29/3/24	Dewsbury (a)	L24-4	t:J Burton	13th	1,549
7/4/24	Halifax (a)	L18-10	t:Butterworth,J Burton g:Morton	14th	1,770
14/4/24	Whitehaven (a)	W12-25	t:Morton(2),Kear,Leak,Buchanan g:Butterworth,White fg:Woods	11th	596
21/4/24	Wakefield (h)	L14-34	t:Morton,Leak g:Woods(3)	12th	2,572
28/4/24	York (h)	W22-18	t:Walshaw,J Burton,Butterworth,Leak g:Woods(3)	9th	845
5/5/24	Barrow (a)	L24-14	t:Morton,Gledhill g:Woods(3)	11th	1,976
19/5/24	Doncaster (a)	L26-0		12th	1,236
26/5/24	Bradford (h)	W21-20	t:J Burton,White,Leak g:Woods(4) fg:Woods	12th	-
2/6/24	Sheffield (h)	W31-18	t:Hooley,Walshaw(2),Ward,Manning g:Woods(5) fg:Hooley	9th	983
16/6/24	Swinton (a)	W16-20	t:J Burton(2),Leak,Manning g:Woods(2)	7th	917
22/6/24	Toulouse (h)	L0-36		9th	-
30/6/24	Widnes (a)	W16-24	t:Walshaw,Morton,Senior(2) g:Woods(4)	7th	2,476
7/7/24	Wakefield (a)	L34-12	t:Morton,Moore g:Hooley(2)	9th	5,112
14/7/24	Barrow (h)	W22-2	t:J Burton,Buchanan,Hooley,Mitsias g:Woods(3)	8th	-
21/7/24	Dewsbury (h)	W29-22	t:Moore,White,J Burton(2),Hooley g:Woods(4) fg:Woods	7th	-
28/7/24	Halifax (h)	L16-22	t:J Burton,Woods g:Woods(2)	9th	-
4/8/24	Featherstone (a)	L24-16	t:Walshaw,J Burton,Manning g:Woods(2)	9th	1,544
11/8/24	Swinton (h)	W26-6	t:J Burton(2),Moore,Cooper,White g:Woods(3)	9th	-
16/8/24	Sheffield (a)	W14-24	t:Hooley(3),Kear g:Woods(4)	8th	877
25/8/24	York (a)	L37-6	t:Butterworth g:Woods	8th	2,003
1/9/24	Widnes (h)	L8-12	t:Flynn g:Woods(2)	8th	-
8/9/24	Doncaster (h)	L0-38		10th	-
15/9/24	Bradford (a)	L16-14	t:Walshaw,J Burton,Senior g:Woods	9th	3,212
22/9/24	Whitehaven (h)	W28-14	t:Moore,Manning,White,Buchanan,Flynn g:Woods(4)	9th	1,644
28/9/24	Toulouse (a)	L64-16	t:J Burton(2),Mitsias g:White(2)	10th	3,361

		APP		TRIES		GOALS		FG		PTS	
	D.O.B.	ALL	Ch	ALL	Ch	ALL	Ch	ALL	Ch	ALL	Ch
Luke Blake	10/8/89	9(1)	8(1)	0	0	0	0	0	0	0	0
James Brown	6/5/88	13(9)	12(6)	1	0	0	0	0	0	4	0
Kieran Buchanan	26/1/98	33	26	6	3	0	0	0	0	24	12
Joe Burton	15/3/02	32(1)	26	22	18	0	0	0	0	88	72
Oli Burton	15/3/02	1(20)	1(15)	0	0	0	0	0	0	0	0
Robbie Butterworth	7/6/02	20(1)	14(1)	4	3	1	1	0	0	18	14
Paul Chitakunye	28/1/03	(1)	(1)	0	0	0	0	0	0	0	0
Luke Cooper	28/7/94	29(3)	22(3)	5	1	0	0	0	0	20	4
Nyle Flynn	27/7/97	1(27)	1(21)	5	3	0	0	0	0	20	12
Dave Gibbons	27/11/01	4(1)	2	1	0	8	0	0	0	20	0
Joe Gibbons	5/12/02	(4)	(3)	0	0	0	0	0	0	0	0
Adam Gledhill	15/2/93	29(1)	22(1)	1	1	0	0	0	0	4	4
George Hill	29/7/04	(1)	(1)	0	0	0	0	0	0	0	0
Luke Hooley	1/8/98	12	12	6	6	2	2	1	1	29	29
Greg Johnson	20/2/90	1(1)	0	0	0	0	0	0	0	0	0
Ben Kaye	19/12/88	(3)	(3)	0	0	0	0	0	0	0	0
Elliot Kear	29/11/88	16(2)	13(2)	3	2	0	0	0	0	12	8
Samy Kibula	7/8/99	(6)	(6)	0	0	0	0	0	0	0	0
Alistair Leak	5/4/92	12(11)	7(9)	7	5	0	0	0	0	28	20
Dane Manning	15/4/89	31	24	6	4	0	0	0	0	24	16
John Mitsias	26/7/99	17(1)	14(1)	2	2	0	0	0	0	8	8
Brandon Moore	27/7/96	32	25	5	4	0	0	0	0	20	16
Dale Morton	31/10/90	24	19	8	7	1	1	0	0	34	30
Muizz Mustapha	3/4/00	1(1)	1(1)	0	0	0	0	0	0	0	0
Nixon Putt	3/3/95	4(2)	4(2)	0	0	0	0	0	0	0	0
George Senior	29/8/99	16(8)	12(6)	6	3	0	0	0	0	24	12
Lucas Walshaw	4/8/92	32	25	7	6	0	0	0	0	28	24
Michael Ward	10/2/91	1(24)	1(18)	1	1	0	0	0	0	4	4
Ben White	27/10/94	31	24	7	4	3	3	0	0	34	22
Josh Woods	13/12/97	28	23	1	1	71	54	4	3	150	115

'Ch' totals include Championship games only; 'All' totals also include Challenge Cup & 1895 Cup

Joe Burton

LEAGUE RECORD
P26-W11-D0-L15 (10th)
F422, A591, Diff-169, 22 points.

CHALLENGE CUP
Round Six

1895 CUP
Quarter Finalists

ATTENDANCES
Complete data not supplied during the season, or at time of publication

CLUB RECORDS
MATCH RECORDS Highest score: 100-4 v Gateshead, 17/3/2010 Highest score against: 9-78 v Wakefield, 26/8/67 Record attendance: 23,989 v Leeds, 14/3/25
Tries: 5 Joe Oakland v Bramley, 19/12/1908; Tommy Brannan v Swinton, 17/1/1920; Jim Wale v Bramley, 4/12/26; Jim Wale v Cottingham, 12/2/27; Tommy Oldroyd v Highfield, 6/3/76; Ben Feehan v Halifax, 10/8/2008; Jermaine McGillvary v Whitehaven, 24/5/2009
Goals: 16 Gareth Moore v Gateshead, 17/3/2010 Points: 40 Gareth Moore v Gateshead, 17/3/2010
SEASON RECORDS Tries: 30 Johnny Campbell 2010 Goals: 144 Barry Eaton 2004 Points: 308 Richard Price 1997
CAREER RECORDS Tries: 142 Craig Lingard 1998-2008 Goals: 463 Wharton 'Wattie' Davies 1897-1912 Points: 1,297 Wharton 'Wattie' Davies 1897-1912
Appearances: 421 Wharton 'Wattie' Davies 1897-1912

Championship 2024 - Club by Club

BRADFORD BULLS

DATE	FIXTURE	RESULT	SCORERS	LGE	ATT
4/2/24	Dewsbury (a) (1895CR2)	W4-40	t:Gill,Arundel,Scurr,Myers,Taufua(2),Souter,McGowan g:Lilley(4)	1st(G2)	1,009
11/2/24	North Wales (h) (CCR3)	W48-2	t:Doro,Arundel,McGowan,Appo,Butler,Flanagan(2),Gill g:Lilley(8)	N/A	-
18/2/24	Keighley (a) (1895CR3)	W18-26	t:Hallas,McGowan,Taufua,Lilley,Appo g:Lilley(3)	1st(G2)	3,729
25/2/24	Widnes (h) (CCR4)	L12-26	t:Gill,Jowitt g:Lilley(2)	N/A	-
3/3/24	Swinton (h) (1895CQF)	W21-12	t:Butler,Lilley,Gill g:Lilley(4) fg:Lilley	N/A	1,018
15/3/24	Wakefield (a)	L42-12	t:McGowan,Gill g:Lilley(2)	13th	7,221
29/3/24	Halifax (h)	W29-10	t:Myers,Souter,Wood,Fulton g:Lilley(6) fg:Lilley	10th	3,853
7/4/24	Featherstone (a)	W14-24	t:Carr(2),Gill,Butler g:Lilley(4)	5th	-
13/4/24	Toulouse (h)	W19-12	t:Gill(2),Fulton g:Lilley(3) fg:Lilley	4th	2,720
21/4/24	York (a)	L25-14	t:Gill,Peposhi,McGowan g:Lilley	5th	2,675
28/4/24	Widnes (h)	L13-14	t:Blackmore,Holmes g:Lilley(2) fg:Lilley	6th	3,029
5/5/24	Swinton (a)	W12-38	t:Fulton,Gill(2),Souter,Appo,Okoro,Myers g:Lilley(5)	5th	1,187
12/5/24	Wakefield (h) (1895CSF)	L14-40	t:Fulton,Gill g:Lilley(3)	N/A	5,340
19/5/24	Sheffield (h)	W28-10	t:Fulton(2),Okunbor,McGowan,Gill g:Lilley(4)	5th	2,234
26/5/24	Batley (a)	L21-20	t:Fulton(2),Holmes g:Lilley(4)	6th	-
2/6/24	Barrow (h)	W36-24	t:Butler,Okunbor,Fulton,Myers(2),Gill g:Lilley(6)	6th	2,655
16/6/24	Whitehaven (a)	W18-36	t:Souter,Gaskell,Taufua(2),Gill,Myers g:Lilley(6)	5th	-
23/6/24	Doncaster (h)	W38-4	t:Davies,Souter,Gill,Okunbor,Holmes,Appo,Lilley g:Lilley(5)	4th	2,909
30/6/24	Dewsbury (h)	W12-38	t:Lehmann,Fulton(2),Lilley,Holmes,Davies,Souter g:Lilley(5)	4th	2,151
6/7/24	Toulouse (a)	D12-12	t:Fulton,Lehmann g:Lilley(2)	4th	2,340
14/7/24	Wakefield (h)	L2-14	g:Lilley	4th	3,203
21/7/24	York (h)	W36-28	t:Lehmann,Myers,Gill(2),Davies,Doro,Fulton g:Lilley(4)	4th	3,025
28/7/24	Widnes (a)	L25-6	t:Lehmann g:Lilley	4th	3,065
4/8/24	Barrow (h)	D24-24	t:Holmes,Okunbor,Fulton,Appo,Gill g:Lilley(2)	5th	2,419
11/8/24	Whitehaven (h)	W58-0	t:Okunbor,Appo(2),Sammut,Doro,Myers,Makin(2),Pele,Taufua g:Lilley(9)	4th	2,502
18/8/24	Featherstone (h)	L21-22	t:Okunbor,Pele(2),Myers g:Lilley(2) fg:Lilley	4th	3,099
25/8/24	Doncaster (a)	W4-18	t:Lilley,Appo,Holmes g:Lilley(3)	3rd	1,758
30/8/24	Dewsbury (h)	W54-0	t:D Smith,Holmes,Pele(2),Ott,Scurr,Franco(2),Appo g:Lilley(9)	3rd	3,006
8/9/24	Sheffield (a)	W12-30	t:Hallas,Okunbor,Franco,Taufua(2) g:Lilley(5)	3rd	1,948
15/9/24	Batley (h)	W16-14	t:Taufua,Okunbor,Gill g:Lilley(2)	3rd	3,212
22/9/24	Halifax (h)	L14-10	t:Makin,Myers g:Lilley	3rd	3,285
29/9/24	Swinton (h)	W50-0	t:Lehmann(2),Holmes,Pele(3),Bayliss-Brow,Gill,Myers g:Lilley(6),Sammut	3rd	3,293
6/10/24	Featherstone (h) (E)	W25-12	t:Myers,Gill,Lilley,Appo g:Lilley(4) fg:Lilley	N/A	-
13/10/24	Toulouse (a) (SF)	L21-20	t:Lilley,Pele,Appo g:Lilley(4)	N/A	2,680

		APP		TRIES		GOALS		FG		PTS	
	D.O.B.	ALL	Ch	ALL	Ch	ALL	Ch	ALL	Ch	ALL	Ch
Keven Appo	9/1/99	12(20)	12(14)	11	9	0	0	0	0	44	36
Joe Arundel	22/8/91	11(1)	6	2	0	0	0	0	0	8	0
Jordan Baldwinson	10/11/94	4(2)	4(2)	0	0	0	0	0	0	0	0
Jacob Bateman	18/4/06	(1)	(1)	0	0	0	0	0	0	0	0
Logan Bayliss-Brow	29/8/99	10	10	1	1	0	0	0	0	4	4
Ben Blackmore	19/2/93	3	2	1	1	0	0	0	0	4	4
Keanan Brand	8/1/99	1	0	0	0	0	0	0	0	0	0
Chester Butler	10/3/95	11	6	4	2	0	0	0	0	16	8
Connor Carr	27/2/03	3	3	2	2	0	0	0	0	8	8
John Davies	8/1/97	22(5)	16(5)	3	3	0	0	0	0	12	12
Eribe Doro	26/3/01	22(1)	17(1)	3	2	0	0	0	0	12	8
Jacob Douglas	3/3/04	2	2	0	0	0	0	0	0	0	0
Zach Fishwick	9/3/05	(2)	(2)	0	0	0	0	0	0	0	0
George Flanagan	8/10/86	(6)	(1)	2	0	0	0	0	0	8	0
Romain Franco	5/6/98	4	4	3	3	0	0	0	0	12	12
Zac Fulton	14/8/01	26(1)	25(1)	14	13	0	0	0	0	56	52
Lee Gaskell	28/10/90	11	8	1	1	0	0	0	0	4	4
Kieran Gill	4/12/95	28	22	21	16	0	0	0	0	84	64
Lucas Green	11/9/04	(1)	(1)	0	0	0	0	0	0	0	0
Sam Hallas	18/10/96	21(3)	17(2)	2	1	0	0	0	0	8	4
Tom Holmes	2/3/96	23	22	8	8	0	0	0	0	32	32
Corey Johnson	16/11/00	1	0	0	0	0	0	0	0	0	0
Billy Jowitt	7/4/01	3	1	1	0	0	0	0	0	4	0
Michael Lawrence	12/4/90	15	11	0	0	0	0	0	0	0	0
Max Lehmann	1/2/00	12	12	6	6	0	0	0	0	24	24
Jordan Lilley	4/9/96	34	28	7	5	132	108	6	5	298	241
Harvey Makin	17/11/03	4(7)	4(7)	3	3	0	0	0	0	12	12
Nathan Mason	8/9/93	(3)	(3)	0	0	0	0	0	0	0	0
Aidan McGowan	12/3/02	17	11	6	3	0	0	0	0	24	12
Jayden Myers	13/4/03	27	21	12	11	0	0	0	0	48	44
Daniel Okoro	18/4/03	(11)	(5)	1	1	0	0	0	0	4	4
Jayden Okunbor	2/3/97	17	17	9	9	0	0	0	0	36	36
Tyran Ott	12/2/01	11(14)	11(13)	1	1	0	0	0	0	4	4
Franklin Pele	18/12/00	2(13)	2(13)	9	9	0	0	0	0	36	36
Eliot Peposhi	5/8/04	1(9)	1(7)	1	1	0	0	0	0	4	4
Fenton Rogers	4/8/03	7(5)	7(4)	0	0	0	0	0	0	0	0
Jarrod Sammut	25/2/87	7(1)	7(1)	1	1	1	1	0	0	6	6
Ebon Scurr	11/5/00	1(17)	(17)	2	1	0	0	0	0	8	4
Daniel Smith	20/3/93	11(4)	9(2)	1	1	0	0	0	0	4	4
Jack Smith	29/4/05	2	2	0	0	0	0	0	0	0	0
Mitch Souter	27/3/01	26(5)	21(5)	6	5	0	0	0	0	24	20
Jorge Taufua	23/10/91	22	16	9	6	0	0	0	0	36	24
Liam Tindall	27/9/01	4	4	0	0	0	0	0	0	0	0
Harvey Wilson	31/1/04	4(4)	3(4)	0	0	0	0	0	0	0	0
Max Wood	28/6/04	(1)	(1)	1	1	0	0	0	0	4	4

'Ch' totals include regular season & play-offs; 'All' totals also include Challenge Cup & 1895 Cup

Kieran Gill

LEAGUE RECORD
P26-W16-D2-L8 (3rd/Semi-Final)
F682, A387, Diff+295, 34 points.

CHALLENGE CUP
Round Four

1895 CUP
Semi-Finalists

ATTENDANCES
Complete data not supplied during the season, or at time of publication

CLUB RECORDS
MATCH RECORDS Highest score: 124-0 v West Wales, 6/5/2018 Highest score against: 6-84 v Wigan, 21/4/2014 Record attendance: 69,429 v Huddersfield, 14/3/53
Tries: 6 Eric Batten v Leeds, 15/9/45; Trevor Foster v Wakefield, 10/4/48; Steve McGowan v Barrow, 8/11/92; Lesley Vainikolo v Hull, 2/9/2005
Goals: 20 Dane Chisholm v West Wales, 6/5/2018 Points: 48 Dane Chisholm v West Wales, 6/5/2018
SEASON RECORDS Tries: 63 Jack McLean 1951-52 Goals: 213 (inc 5fg) Henry Paul 2001 Points: 457 Henry Paul 2001
CAREER RECORDS Tries: 261 Jack McLean 1950-56 Goals: 1,165 (inc 25fg) Paul Deacon 1998-2009 Points: 2,605 Paul Deacon 1998-2009
Appearances: 588 Keith Mumby 1973-90; 1992-93

Championship 2024 - Club by Club

DEWSBURY RAMS

DATE	FIXTURE	RESULT	SCORERS	LGE	ATT
28/1/24	Keighley (a) (1895CR1)	L35-6	t:Garside g:Sykes	3rd(G2)	839
4/2/24	Bradford (h) (1895CR2)	L4-40	t:Whiteley	3rd(G2)	1,009
11/2/24	York (h) (CCR3)	L8-14	t:Whiteley g:Turner(2)	N/A	824
17/3/24	Halifax (h)	L10-24	t:Whiteley,Hookem g:Turner	11th	1,449
29/3/24	Batley (h)	W24-4	t:Davies,Whiteley,Billington(2) g:Turner(4)	6th	1,549
7/4/24	Widnes (h)	L6-24	t:Beckett g:Sykes	8th	1,084
14/4/24	Barrow (a)	L27-20	t:Dawson,Hookem,Restall,Greensmith g:Sykes(2)	10th	1,675
21/4/24	Swinton (a)	L50-22	t:Davies,Restall,Graham,Corion g:Turner(3)	13th	894
28/4/24	Doncaster (a)	L38-12	t:Hookem,Graham g:Turner(2)	14th	1,296
4/5/24	Toulouse (h)	L21-38	t:Corion(2),Restall g:Turner(4) fg:Hookem	14th	995
19/5/24	Featherstone (h)	L12-46	t:Garside,Restall g:Turner(2)	14th	1,150
24/5/24	Sheffield (a)	L36-13	t:O'Connor,Billington g:Turner(2) fg:Turner	14th	971
31/5/24	Wakefield (a)	L56-0		14th	5,892
16/6/24	York (h)	L0-40		14th	927
23/6/24	Whitehaven (a)	L38-12	t:Billington,Davies g:Turner(2)	14th	-
30/6/24	Bradford (h)	L12-38	t:Restall,R Dixon g:Turner,Sykes	14th	2,151
7/7/24	Doncaster (h)	L16-20	t:O'Connor,Sykes g:Sykes,Hookem,O'Connor(2)	14th	853
14/7/24	Widnes (a)	L34-12	t:Carr(2) g:Turner(2)	14th	2,337
21/7/24	Batley (a)	L29-22	t:Carr(2),Restall,Butterworth g:Turner(3)	14th	-
27/7/24	Toulouse (a)	L58-6	t:R Dixon g:Turner	14th	2,155
4/8/24	Wakefield (h)	L16-42	t:Whiteley,Silk,Carr g:Turner(2)	14th	1,750
11/8/24	York (a)	L54-12	t:Whiteley,O'Connor g:Turner(2)	14th	1,936
18/8/24	Barrow (h)	L24-31	t:Whiteley(2),O'Connor(2) g:Turner(4)	14th	940
25/8/24	Whitehaven (h)	L10-18	t:O'Connor,Billington g:Sykes	14th	876
30/8/24	Bradford (a)	L54-0		14th	3,006
8/9/24	Halifax (a)	L34-6	t:Turner g:Turner	14th	1,647
15/9/24	Swinton (h)	L16-28	t:R Dixon,Tomlinson,Greensmith g:Sykes(2)	14th	922
21/9/24	Featherstone (a)	L50-12	t:Tomlinson,Greensmith g:Turner(2)	14th	-
29/9/24	Sheffield (h)	W28-8	t:Tomlinson,Butterworth,Greensmith(2),Carr g:Turner(4)	14th	1,007

		APP		TRIES		GOALS		FG		PTS	
	D.O.B.	ALL	Ch	ALL	Ch	ALL	Ch	ALL	Ch	ALL	Ch
Jimmy Beckett	29/8/99	20	17	1	1	0	0	0	0	4	4
Jack Bibby	14/10/01	3(9)	3(9)	0	0	0	0	0	0	0	0
Jack Billington	24/10/04	11(3)	11(3)	5	5	0	0	0	0	20	20
Jack Briggs	27/5/05	(8)	(8)	0	0	0	0	0	0	0	0
Reiss Butterworth	7/12/98	12(3)	12(3)	2	2	0	0	0	0	8	8
Lewis Carr	11/8/00	23	21	6	6	0	0	0	0	24	24
Louis Collinson	17/10/01	22(1)	19(1)	0	0	0	0	0	0	0	0
Harry Copley	29/9/01	(1)	(1)	0	0	0	0	0	0	0	0
Travis Corion	27/3/01	7	6	3	3	0	0	0	0	12	12
Curtis Davies	17/1/97	17(5)	14(5)	3	3	0	0	0	0	12	12
Bailey Dawson	18/5/03	10(7)	8(6)	1	1	0	0	0	0	4	4
Davey Dixon	31/5/97	2(2)	1(2)	0	0	0	0	0	0	0	0
Ronan Dixon	25/7/97	6(17)	5(15)	3	3	0	0	0	0	12	12
Dale Ferguson	13/4/88	7(4)	7(4)	0	0	0	0	0	0	0	0
Jamie Field	27/5/94	2(6)	2(4)	0	0	0	0	0	0	0	0
Matt Garside	1/10/90	18	17	2	1	0	0	0	0	8	4
Brad Graham	1/9/01	23	20	2	2	0	0	0	0	8	8
Ollie Greensmith	3/12/99	17	14	5	5	0	0	0	0	20	20
Joe Hird	8/2/03	(13)	(10)	0	0	0	0	0	0	0	0
Jacob Hookem	4/10/02	25(1)	23	3	3	1	1	1	1	15	15
Luke Mearns	9/6/04	1(3)	1(3)	0	0	0	0	0	0	0	0
Elliot Morris	4/1/96	14(8)	13(7)	0	0	0	0	0	0	0	0
Bailey O'Connor	29/5/02	22	19	6	6	2	2	0	0	28	28
Owen Restall	5/8/95	14	13	6	6	0	0	0	0	24	24
Kieran Rush	3/9/02	2(2)	2(2)	0	0	0	0	0	0	0	0
Joel Russell	7/12/00	(2)	(1)	0	0	0	0	0	0	0	0
Zeus Silk	23/10/97	4(5)	4(5)	1	1	0	0	0	0	4	4
Joe Summers	7/11/99	4(4)	4(4)	0	0	0	0	0	0	0	0
Paul Sykes	11/8/81	13(3)	12(2)	1	1	9	8	0	0	22	20
Keenen Tomlinson	22/5/97	5(4)	5(4)	3	3	0	0	0	0	12	12
Calum Turner	29/4/99	24	21	1	1	44	42	1	1	93	89
Jackson Walker	1/4/01	13(2)	12(2)	0	0	0	0	0	0	0	0
Marcus Walker	12/8/02	23	22	0	0	0	0	0	0	0	0
Perry Whiteley	22/2/93	13(2)	10(2)	8	6	0	0	0	0	32	24

'Ch' totals include Championship games only; 'All' totals also include Challenge Cup & 1895 Cup

Calum Turner

LEAGUE RECORD
P26-W2-D0-L24 (14th)
F344, A919, Diff-575, 4 points.

CHALLENGE CUP
Round Three

1895 CUP
3rd, Group 2

ATTENDANCES
Best - v Bradford (Ch - 2,151)
Worst - v York (CC - 824)
Total (excluding Challenge Cup) - 16,662
Average (excluding Challenge Cup) - 1,190
(Down by 21 on 2023, League One)

CLUB RECORDS	**Highest score:** 90-5 v Blackpool, 4/4/93 **Highest score against:** 0-82 v Widnes, 30/11/86
	Record attendance: 26,584 v Halifax, 30/10/1920 (Crown Flatt); 4,068 v Bradford, 6/4/2015 Tetley's/FLAIR Stadium)
MATCH RECORDS	**Tries:** 8 Dai Thomas v Liverpool, 13/4/1907
	Goals: 13 Greg Pearce v Blackpool Borough, 4/4/93; Francis Maloney v Hunslet, 25/3/2007 **Points:** 32 Les Holliday v Barrow, 11/9/94
SEASON RECORDS	**Tries:** 40 Dai Thomas 1906-07 **Goals:** 169 Barry Eaton 2000 **Points:** 394 Barry Eaton 2000
CAREER RECORDS	**Tries:** 144 Joe Lyman 1913-31 **Goals:** 863 Nigel Stephenson 1967-78; 1984-86 **Points:** 2,082 Nigel Stephenson 1967-78; 1984-86 **Appearances:** 454 Joe Lyman 1913-31

Championship 2024 - Club by Club

DONCASTER

DATE	FIXTURE	RESULT	SCORERS	LGE	ATT
28/1/24	Midlands Hurricanes (a) (1895CR1)	W4-40	t:Halliday(3),Robinson,Kenga,Pauli,Johnston g:Robinson(6)	1st(G7)	180
4/2/24	Sheffield (h) (1895CR2)	L18-22	t:Sutcliffe,Johnston,Lovodua g:Robinson(3)	1st(G7)	784
11/2/24	Widnes (a) (CCR3)	L50-16	t:Lovodua,Lyne,Halliday g:Robinson(2)	N/A	788
17/3/24	York (h)	W36-20	t:Halliday(2),Johnston,Pauli(2),Smeaton g:Robinson(6)	3rd	1,463
29/3/24	Sheffield (h)	L20-26	t:Guzdek,Robinson,Lovodua g:Robinson(4)	5th	1,719
7/4/24	Wakefield (h)	L6-42	t:Robinson g:Robinson	11th	2,520
14/4/24	Featherstone (h)	L4-46	t:Guzdek	13th	1,701
21/4/24	Barrow (a)	W6-38	t:Hey,Lovodua,Johnston,C Hall,Pauli,Lyne,Briscoe g:C Hall,Robinson(4)	8th	1,616
28/4/24	Dewsbury (h)	W38-12	t:Guzdek,Taulapapa,Knowles,Lovodua,Pauli,C Hall,Robinson g:Robinson(5)	7th	1,296
5/5/24	Widnes (a)	L16-14	t:Smeaton,C Hall g:C Hall(2),Robinson	7th	2,936
19/5/24	Batley (h)	W26-0	t:Boas,Tali,Faraimo(2),Ferres g:C Hall(2),Robinson	7th	1,236
26/5/24	Halifax (a)	L34-8	t:Faraimo,Briscoe	7th	1,479
2/6/24	Whitehaven (h)	D25-25	t:Briscoe(2),Pauli,Faraimo,McConnell g:Robinson(2) fg:Robinson	7th	1,740
15/6/24	Toulouse (a)	L52-0		8th	2,138
23/6/24	Bradford (a)	L38-4	t:Halliday	11th	2,909
29/6/24	Swinton (h) ●	W18-8	t:Lyne,Faraimo,Halliday g:Robinson(3)	8th	1,056
7/7/24	Dewsbury (a)	W16-20	t:Tali,Pauli,Guzdek g:Robinson(4)	7th	853
14/7/24	York (a)	L27-0		9th	1,902
20/7/24	Featherstone (a)	W12-24	t:Hey,Faraimo(2),Lyne g:Robinson(3),C Hall	8th	-
28/7/24	Barrow (a)	W37-30	t:Hey,Boas,Lyne(2),Lovodua(2),Faraimo g:Robinson(4) fg:C Hall	6th	1,405
4/8/24	Sheffield (a)	L22-20	t:Briscoe,Robinson,Guzdek,Faraimo g:Robinson(2)	7th	1,075
10/8/24	Toulouse (h)	W20-18	t:Guzdek,Tali,C Hall g:Robinson(4)	7th	1,121
18/8/24	Whitehaven (a)	L28-24	t:Lovodua,Pauli,Briscoe(2) g:Robinson(4)	9th	699
25/8/24	Bradford (h)	L4-18	t:Briscoe	9th	1,758
1/9/24	Halifax (h)	L16-17	t:Pauli,Lyne,Briscoe g:Robinson(2)	9th	1,443
8/9/24	Batley (a)	W0-38	t:Pauli(2),Faraimo(4),Smeaton g:Robinson(5)	8th	-
15/9/24	Widnes (h)	W30-14	t:Lyne,Robinson,Briscoe,Faraimo g:Robinson(7)	8th	1,360
22/9/24	Swinton (a)	W20-22	t:Pauli,McConnell(2),Briscoe g:Robinson(3)	8th	836
29/9/24	Wakefield (a)	L72-6	t:Tali g:C Hall	8th	5,233

● *Played at Millennium Stadium, Featherstone*

Craig Hall

	D.O.B.	APP ALL	APP Ch	TRIES ALL	TRIES Ch	GOALS ALL	GOALS Ch	FG ALL	FG Ch	PTS ALL	PTS Ch
Lewis Baxter	1/6/02	4(5)	4(5)	0	0	0	0	0	0	0	0
Watson Boas	8/11/94	19(6)	17(5)	2	2	0	0	0	0	8	8
Luke Briscoe	11/3/94	24	22	11	11	0	0	0	0	44	44
Greg Burns	25/3/95	12	11	0	0	0	0	0	0	0	0
Bureta Faraimo	16/7/90	17(1)	17(1)	14	14	0	0	0	0	56	56
Brett Ferres	17/4/86	15(5)	14(5)	1	1	0	0	0	0	4	4
Keelan Foster	26/1/00	4(7)	3(6)	0	0	0	0	0	0	0	0
Josh Guzdek	23/4/95	15(4)	13(4)	6	6	0	0	0	0	24	24
Craig Hall	21/2/88	21(3)	19(3)	4	4	7	7	1	1	31	31
Tom Halliday	2/2/97	11	8	8	4	0	0	0	0	32	16
Tyla Hepi	15/6/93	(11)	(9)	0	0	0	0	0	0	0	0
Brad Hey	4/9/94	23(6)	21(5)	3	3	0	0	0	0	12	12
Jeylan Hodgson	23/7/05	1	1	0	0	0	0	0	0	0	0
Alex Holdstock	16/6/01	1(10)	(9)	0	0	0	0	0	0	0	0
Ben Johnston	8/3/92	11(1)	9(1)	4	2	0	0	0	0	16	8
Jose Kenga	3/5/95	(5)	(4)	1	0	0	0	0	0	4	0
Brad Knowles	31/7/93	25	24	1	1	0	0	0	0	4	4
Joe Lovodua	18/3/98	14(9)	12(9)	8	6	0	0	0	0	32	24
Reece Lyne	2/12/92	21	19	8	7	0	0	0	0	32	28
Ilikaya Mafi	30/11/03	(9)	(8)	0	0	0	0	0	0	0	0
Suaia Matagi	23/3/88	26	23	0	0	0	0	0	0	0	0
Loui McConnell	21/11/99	18(5)	17(5)	3	3	0	0	0	0	12	12
Pauli Pauli	4/8/94	15(11)	15(9)	12	11	0	0	0	0	48	44
Connor Robinson	23/10/94	25(2)	22(2)	6	5	76	65	1	1	177	151
Leon Ruan	14/5/03	1	1	0	0	0	0	0	0	0	0
Sam Smeaton	26/10/88	11(7)	8(7)	3	3	0	0	0	0	12	12
Alex Sutcliffe	21/1/99	13(3)	10(3)	1	0	0	0	0	0	4	0
Jason Tali	7/7/87	15(1)	14	4	4	0	0	0	0	16	16
Misi Taulapapa	25/1/82	5(1)	4(1)	1	1	0	0	0	0	4	4
Jude Thompson	21/2/05	(1)	0	0	0	0	0	0	0	0	0
AJ Wallace	31/3/03	6(2)	6(2)	0	0	0	0	0	0	0	0
Nathan Wilde	29/12/99	4(1)	4(1)	0	0	0	0	0	0	0	0

'Ch' totals include Championship games only; 'All' totals also include Challenge Cup & 1895 Cup

LEAGUE RECORD
P26-W12-D1-L13 (8th)
F498, A619, Diff-121, 25 points.

CHALLENGE CUP
Round Three

1895 CUP
2nd, Group 7

ATTENDANCES
Best - v Wakefield (Ch - 2,520)
Worst - v Sheffield (1895C - 784)
Total (all home games included) - 20,602
Average (all home games included) - 1,472
(Up by 275 on 2023, League One)

CLUB RECORDS
MATCH RECORDS Highest score: 102-6 v West Wales, 15/7/2018 Highest score against: 4-90 v Widnes, 10/6/2007
Record attendance: 10,000 v Bradford, 16/2/52 *(York Road)*; 6,528 v Castleford, 12/4/2007 *(Keepmoat/Eco-Power Stadium)*
Tries: 6 Kane Epati v Oldham, 30/7/2006; Lee Waterman v Sharlston, 24/3/2012
Goals: 15 Liam Harris v West Wales, 15/7/2018 Points: 38 Liam Harris v West Wales, 15/7/2018
SEASON RECORDS Tries: 36 Lee Waterman 2012 Goals: 129 Jonny Woodcock 2002 Points: 306 Jonny Woodcock 2002
CAREER RECORDS Tries: 112 Mark Roache 1985-97 Goals: 850 David Noble 1976-77; 1980-89 Points: 1,751 David Noble 1976-77; 1980-89; 1992
Appearances: 327 Audley Pennant 1980-83; 1985-97

Championship 2024 - Club by Club

FEATHERSTONE ROVERS

DATE	FIXTURE	RESULT	SCORERS	LGE	ATT
28/1/24	Hunslet (a) (1895CR1)	W12-62	t:Gale(3),Reynolds,Jones(2),Minikin(2),Arnold,Aekins,Roberts g:Reynolds(5),Lacans(4)	1st(G5)	875
4/2/24	Batley (a) (1895CR2)	L15-14	t:Minikin,Gale,Wacokecoke g:Reynolds	1st(G5)	784
11/2/24	Thatto Heath (a) (CCR3)	W0-72	t:Day,Wacokecoke(2),Gale(2),Minikin,Reynolds,Lacans(3),Aekins,Addy,Jones g:Reynolds(6),Lacans,Hardcastle,Addy(2)	N/A	907
25/2/24	Keighley (a) (CCR4)	W14-58	t:Lacans,Jones(3),Day,Wacokecoke(2),Tomlinson,Addy(2) g:Lacans(9)	N/A	1,477
10/3/24	Wakefield (h) (CCR5)	W14-10 (aet)	t:Wynne(2),Gale g:Lacans	N/A	—
17/3/24	Batley (a)	W20-24	t:Day,Addy,Minikin,Aekins g:Gorman(4)	5th	1,961
23/3/24	Leigh (a) (CCR6)	L26-14	t:Wacokecoke(2),Gale g:Addy	N/A	4,287
29/3/24	Wakefield (h)	L12-20	t:Addy,Aekins g:Gorman(2)	8th	4,127
7/4/24	Bradford (h)	L14-24	t:Jones(2),Turner g:Gorman	9th	—
14/4/24	Doncaster (a)	W4-46	t:Jones(2),Gale,Reynolds,Aekins,Day(2),Bowes g:Reynolds(7)	5th	1,701
21/4/24	Widnes (h)	W32-24	t:Gale,England,Hall,Day,Wynne(2) g:Addy(4)	4th	2,200
28/4/24	Whitehaven (a)	W24-28	t:Wynne(2),Minikin,Addy(2) g:Gorman(4)	4th	521
5/5/24	Halifax (h)	W36-16	t:Wynne(4),Albert,Hardcastle g:Hooley(6)	4th	—
19/5/24	Dewsbury (a)	W12-46	t:Jones(2),Turner(2),Massey,Minikin(2),Bussey,England g:Addy(5)	4th	1,150
26/5/24	Barrow (a)	L25-12	t:Aekins,Turner g:Addy(2)	4th	2,311
2/6/24	Swinton (h)	L40-42	t:Jones(2),England,Day,Wynne,Minikin,Addy g:Addy(6)	4th	2,200
16/6/24	Sheffield (a)	L18-16	t:Jones,Gale,Turner g:Addy(2)	6th	1,444
23/6/24	York (h)	L24-34	t:Day,Aekins,Turner(2) g:Patton(4)	6th	1,564
29/6/24	Toulouse (a)	L20-0		6th	4,097
7/7/24	Whitehaven (h)	W66-0	t:Barley,Aekins,Hardcastle,Day(3),Patton,Gale,Wynne,Addy g:Patton(11)	6th	1,605
14/7/24	Halifax (a)	W6-14	t:Day,Barley g:Reynolds(3)	6th	1,760
20/7/24	Doncaster (h)	L12-24	t:Day,Wynne g:Reynolds(2)	6th	—
28/7/24	Wakefield (a)	L46-18	t:Day,Kamano,Minikin g:Reynolds(3)	7th	6,453
4/8/24	Batley (h)	W24-16	t:Wynne,Bussey,Reynolds,Beckett g:Reynolds(4)	6th	1,544
11/8/24	Widnes (a)	W0-8	t:Reynolds g:Reynolds(2)	6th	2,422
18/8/24	Bradford (a)	W21-22	t:Reynolds,Hardcastle,Springer g:Reynolds(5)	6th	3,099
24/8/24	Toulouse (h)	W22-10	t:Wynne(2),Hardcastle g:Reynolds(5)	6th	—
1/9/24	Barrow (h)	W36-18	t:Day,Reynolds,Jones(2),Beckett,Wynne g:Reynolds(6)	5th	1,345
8/9/24	Swinton (a)	L28-8	t:Minikin,Eden	6th	780
15/9/24	Sheffield (h)	L6-20	t:Wynne g:Reynolds	7th	1,246
21/9/24	Dewsbury (h)	W50-12	t:Aekins,Reynolds(2),Lacans,Beckett,Wynne(3),Jones g:Reynolds(7)	5th	—
29/9/24	York (a)	L16-6	t:Hardcastle g:Reynolds	6th	2,450
6/10/24	Bradford (a) (E)	L25-12	t:Hardcastle,Day g:Reynolds(2)	N/A	—

		APP		TRIES		GOALS		FG		PTS	
	D.O.B.	ALL	Ch	ALL	Ch	ALL	Ch	ALL	Ch	ALL	Ch
Danny Addy	15/1/91	29	23	9	6	22	19	0	0	80	62
Caleb Aekins	21/11/97	24	18	10	8	0	0	0	0	40	32
Wellington Albert	3/9/93	3(16)	2(15)	1	1	0	0	0	0	4	4
Jack Arnold	23/9/97	2(11)	2(10)	1	0	0	0	0	0	4	0
Yusuf Aydin	13/9/00	1(2)	1(2)	0	0	0	0	0	0	0	0
Connor Barley	16/9/04	8	8	2	2	0	0	0	0	8	8
Jimmy Beckett	29/8/99	9(1)	9(1)	3	3	0	0	0	0	12	12
Harry Bowes	7/9/01	16(9)	12(7)	1	1	0	0	0	0	4	4
Jack Brown	25/6/00	(1)	(1)	0	0	0	0	0	0	0	0
Jack Bussey	17/8/92	16(1)	15	2	2	0	0	0	0	8	8
Reiss Butterworth	7/12/98	(2)	(2)	0	0	0	0	0	0	0	0
Brad Day	23/9/94	29	23	16	14	0	0	0	0	64	56
Greg Eden	14/11/90	13(2)	13(2)	1	1	0	0	0	0	4	4
Brad England	20/11/94	11(8)	8(6)	3	3	0	0	0	0	12	12
Oliver Farrar	8/6/02	(1)	0	0	0	0	0	0	0	0	0
Zach Fishwick	9/3/05	(8)	(7)	0	0	0	0	0	0	0	0
Gareth Gale	5/6/93	27	21	12	4	0	0	0	0	48	16
Louix Gorman	25/4/05	6(1)	6(1)	0	0	11	11	0	0	22	22
Corey Hall	7/8/02	2	2	1	1	0	0	0	0	4	4
Josh Hardcastle	28/8/92	26(1)	20(1)	6	6	1	0	0	0	26	24
Charlie Harris	6/3/03	1	1	0	0	0	0	0	0	0	0
Luke Hooley	1/8/98	1	1	0	0	6	6	0	0	12	12
Maddox Jeffery	27/1/04	4	4	0	0	0	0	0	0	0	0
Luis Johnson	20/2/99	2	2	0	0	0	0	0	0	0	0
Connor Jones	26/1/96	26(5)	21(4)	18	12	0	0	0	0	72	48
Mo Kamano	22/3/01	9(11)	8(7)	1	1	0	0	0	0	4	4
Samy Kibula	7/8/99	1(2)	1(2)	0	0	0	0	0	0	0	0
Thomas Lacans	7/12/00	10	4	5	1	15	0	0	0	50	4
James Lockwood	21/3/86	9(1)	9(1)	0	0	0	0	0	0	0	0
Nathan Massey	11/7/89	6(1)	4	1	1	0	0	0	0	4	4
Greg Minikin	29/3/95	31	27	11	7	0	0	0	0	44	28
Ben Nakubuwai	15/3/96	15(3)	15(3)	0	0	0	0	0	0	0	0
Dec Patton	23/5/95	7(1)	7(1)	1	1	15	15	0	0	34	34
Ben Reynolds	15/1/94	16	13	9	7	60	48	0	0	156	124
Dean Roberts	19/8/96	(3)	(1)	1	0	0	0	0	0	4	0
Zeus Silk	23/10/97	2(1)	2(1)	0	0	0	0	0	0	0	0
Gadwin Springer	4/4/93	15(11)	9(11)	1	1	0	0	0	0	4	4
Jayden Tanner	25/7/00	1(1)	(1)	0	0	0	0	0	0	0	0
Leo Tennison	31/5/04	1(5)	1(5)	0	0	0	0	0	0	0	0
Keenen Tomlinson	22/5/97	2(7)	1(5)	1	0	0	0	0	0	4	0
Paul Turner	4/7/00	12(1)	12	7	7	0	0	0	0	28	28
Manoa Wacokecoke	3/7/04	10(1)	4(1)	7	0	0	0	0	0	28	0
AJ Wallace	31/3/03	2	2	0	0	0	0	0	0	0	0
Toby Warren	5/9/03	1(1)	1(1)	0	0	0	0	0	0	0	0
Connor Wynne	15/1/01	23(3)	19(2)	21	19	0	0	0	0	84	76
McKenzie Yei	3/6/97	(1)	0	0	0	0	0	0	0	0	0

'Ch' totals include regular season & play-offs; 'All' totals also include Challenge Cup & 1895 Cup

Connor Jones

LEAGUE RECORD
P26-W14-D0-L12 (6th/Eliminator)
F622, A500, Diff+122, 28 points.

CHALLENGE CUP
Round Six

1895 CUP
2nd, Group 5

ATTENDANCES
Complete data not supplied during the season, or at time of publication

CLUB RECORDS / MATCH RECORDS: Highest score: 96-0 v Castleford Lock Lane, 8/2/2004 Highest score against: 14-80 v Bradford, 3/4/2005 Record attendance: 17,531 v St Helens, 21/3/59 Tries: 6 Mike Smith v Doncaster, 13/4/68; Chris Bibb v Keighley, 17/9/89; Brad Dwyer v Rochdale, 1/7/2018; Gareth Gale v Newcastle, 26/6/2021 Goals: 13 Mark Knapper v Keighley, 17/9/89; Liam Finn v Hunslet Old Boys, 25/3/2012; Liam Finn v Swinton, 12/8/2012 Points: 40 Martin Pearson v Whitehaven, 26/11/95

SEASON RECORDS: Tries: 48 Paul Newlove 1992-93 Goals: 183 (inc 2fg) Liam Finn 2012 Points: 436 Liam Finn 2012

CAREER RECORDS: Tries: 162 Don Fox 1953-66 Goals: 1,210 Steve Quinn 1975-88 Points: 2,654 Steve Quinn 1975-88 Appearances: 440 Jim Denton 1921-34

Championship 2024 - Club by Club

HALIFAX PANTHERS

DATE	FIXTURE	RESULT	SCORERS	LGE	ATT
28/1/24	Oldham (a) (1895CR1)	L24-20	t:Eden(2),Woodburn-Hall,Tibbs g:Jouffret(2)	3rd(G4)	1,521
4/2/24	Rochdale (a) (1895CR2)	W12-52	t:Woodburn-Hall,Crooks(2),Eden,Tibbs,Kavanagh,Inman,Gee,Jouffret g:Jouffret(8)	1st(G4)	1,200
11/2/24	Whitehaven (h) (CCR3)	W32-4	t:Keyes(2),Jouffret,Crooks(2),Saltonstall g:Jouffret(4)	N/A	1,100
24/2/24	Hammersmith Hills Hoists (h) (CCR4)	W50-4	t:Tibbs,Crooks,Saltonstall(2),Jouffret(2),O'Brien,Inman,Lannon g:Jouffret(7)	N/A	900
10/3/24	York Acorn (h) (CCR5)	W62-6	t:Gee(3),Tibbs,Kavanagh,Keyes(2),Lannon,Jouffret,McComb(2) g:Jouffret(9)	N/A	785
17/3/24	Dewsbury (a)	W10-24	t:Jouffret(2),Keyes,Woodburn-Hall g:Jouffret(3),Widdop	4th	1,449
24/3/24	Catalans Dragons (h) (CCR6)	L4-40	t:Saltonstall	N/A	1,811
29/3/24	Bradford (a)	L29-10	t:Gee,Woodburn-Hall g:Jouffret	9th	3,853
7/4/24	Batley (h)	W18-10	t:Inman,Woodburn-Hall g:Jouffret(5)	4th	1,770
14/4/24	Widnes (a)	L40-14	t:Widdop,Jouffret,Kavanagh g:Jouffret	6th	2,558
21/4/24	Sheffield (h)	L0-46		10th	1,521
28/4/24	Swinton (h)	L12-28	t:Jouffret,Eden g:Jouffret(2)	11th	1,372
5/5/24	Featherstone (a)	L36-16	t:Eden,Widdop,Keyes g:Jouffret(2)	12th	
19/5/24	York (a)	L40-18	t:Tangata,Barber,McComb g:Widdop(3)	13th	1,693
26/5/24	Doncaster (h)	W34-8	t:Keyes(2),Widdop,McCormack,Larroyer g:Jouffret(7)	13th	1,479
1/6/24	Toulouse (h)	L24-38	t:Gee,Barber(2),Saltonstall g:Jouffret(4)	13th	1,347
15/6/24	Barrow (a)	W28-38	t:Tibbs,Keyes(2),Saltonstall(2),Woodburn-Hall,McComb g:Keyes,Jouffret(2),Widdop(2)	12th	1,994
23/6/24	Wakefield (a)	L46-24	t:Graham,Widdop,Woodburn-Hall,Gee g:Jouffret(4)	13th	6,138
30/6/24	Whitehaven (h) ●	W38-18	t:Keyes,Tibbs,Graham(2),Gee,Jouffret,Barber g:Jouffret(5)	11th	500
5/7/24	Sheffield (a)	L28-0		11th	1,023
14/7/24	Featherstone (h)	L6-14	t:Kavanagh g:Jouffret	11th	1,760
21/7/24	Widnes (h)	L20-24	t:Woodburn-Hall,Crooks,Jouffret,Saltonstall g:Jouffret(2)	13th	1,409
28/7/24	Batley (a)	W16-22	t:Barber(2),Graham,Keyes g:Jouffret(3)	11th	
4/8/24	York (h)	W38-18	t:Woodburn-Hall,Crooks,Graham(2),Keyes,Jouffret g:Jouffret(4),Keyes	10th	1,543
11/8/24	Barrow (h)	W38-12	t:Tibbs(2),Saltonstall,Woodburn-Hall,Keyes,Kavanagh,Graham g:Jouffret(5)	10th	1,421
18/8/24	Swinton (a)	L20-6	t:Widdop g:Jouffret	10th	1,037
25/8/24	Wakefield (h)	L6-48	t:Graham g:Jouffret	11th	2,500
1/9/24	Doncaster (a)	W16-17	t:Graham,Barber,Keyes g:Jouffret(2) fg:Woodburn-Hall	10th	1,443
8/9/24	Dewsbury (h)	W34-6	t:Barber,Woodburn-Hall,Widdop(2),Tibbs(2) g:Jouffret(5)	9th	1,647
14/9/24	Toulouse (a)	L38-18	t:Graham,Hursey(2),Tibbs g:Jouffret	10th	2,985
22/9/24	Bradford (h)	W14-10	t:Fairbank,Saltonstall g:Jouffret(3)	10th	3,285
29/9/24	Whitehaven (a)	L23-20	t:Woodburn-Hall(3),Graham g:Jouffret(2)	9th	876

● Played at DIY Kitchens Stadium, Wakefield

		APP		TRIES		GOALS		FG		PTS	
	D.O.B.	ALL	Ch	ALL	Ch	ALL	Ch	ALL	Ch	ALL	Ch
Ed Barber	26/4/90	13(4)	13(4)	8	8	0	0	0	0	32	32
Clement Boyer	27/1/94	4(10)	4(10)	0	0	0	0	0	0	0	0
Will Calcott	16/12/97	2	0	0	0	0	0	0	0	0	0
Sam Campbell	23/8/04	(1)	0	0	0	0	0	0	0	0	0
Ben Crooks	15/6/93	10	6	7	2	0	0	0	0	28	8
Connor Davies	17/1/97	23(4)	19(3)	0	0	0	0	0	0	0	0
Olly Davies	30/11/95	3(6)	2(4)	0	0	0	0	0	0	0	0
Brandon Douglas	17/8/97	2(2)	2(2)	0	0	0	0	0	0	0	0
Greg Eden	14/11/90	9	4	5	2	0	0	0	0	20	8
Jacob Fairbank	4/3/90	15(11)	13(8)	1	1	0	0	0	0	4	4
Keelan Foster	26/1/00	5(1)	5(1)	0	0	0	0	0	0	0	0
Matty Gee	12/12/94	23(1)	18(1)	8	4	0	0	0	0	32	16
Charlie Graham	14/5/00	16	16	11	11	0	0	0	0	44	44
Joe Hird	8/2/03	3(6)	3(6)	0	0	0	0	0	0	0	0
Kieran Hudson	13/6/00	1	1	0	0	0	0	0	0	0	0
Ben Hursey	19/11/02	4(5)	3(4)	2	2	0	0	0	0	8	8
Tom Inman	24/12/02	14(5)	11(2)	3	1	0	0	0	0	12	4
Corey Johnson	16/11/00	7(6)	7(6)	0	0	0	0	0	0	0	0
Louis Jouffret	24/8/95	32	26	13	8	96	66	0	0	244	164
Ben Kavanagh	4/3/88	24(2)	18(2)	5	3	0	0	0	0	20	12
Joe Keyes	17/9/95	27(2)	22(2)	15	11	2	2	0	0	64	48
Ryan Lannon	11/1/96	6(15)	3(12)	2	0	0	0	0	0	8	0
Kevin Larroyer	19/6/89	16(12)	14(9)	1	1	0	0	0	0	4	4
Ben Littlewood	20/1/05	(3)	(3)	0	0	0	0	0	0	0	0
Riley Lumb	18/12/04	1	1	0	0	0	0	0	0	0	0
Zack McComb	9/9/95	20(2)	14(2)	4	2	0	0	0	0	16	8
Ned McCormack	8/2/05	3	3	1	1	0	0	0	0	4	4
Kai Morgan	13/4/04	1(2)	1(2)	0	0	0	0	0	0	0	0
Dan Murray	21/3/96	1	0	0	0	0	0	0	0	0	0
Tom Nicholson-Watton	13/12/02	2	2	0	0	0	0	0	0	0	0
Adam O'Brien	11/7/93	11(6)	8(5)	1	0	0	0	0	0	4	0
Mathieu Pons	29/3/02	2	2	0	0	0	0	0	0	0	0
Leon Ruan	14/5/03	2	2	0	0	0	0	0	0	0	0
James Saltonstall	27/9/93	26	22	10	6	0	0	0	0	40	24
Jack Smith	29/4/05	3	3	0	0	0	0	0	0	0	0
Adam Tangata	17/3/91	18(13)	15(11)	1	1	0	0	0	0	4	4
Ben Tibbs	3/11/00	20(1)	15(1)	11	7	0	0	0	0	44	28
Gareth Widdop	12/3/89	17(7)	16(3)	7	7	6	6	0	0	40	40
James Woodburn-Hall	2/2/95	30	24	14	12	0	0	1	1	57	49

'Ch' totals include Championship games only; 'All' totals also include Challenge Cup & 1895 Cup

Louis Jouffret

LEAGUE RECORD
P26-W11-D0-L15 (9th)
F509, A650, Diff-141, 22 points.

CHALLENGE CUP
Round Six

1895 CUP
2nd, Group 4

ATTENDANCES
Best - v Bradford (Ch - 3,285)
Worst - v Whitehaven (Ch - 500)
Total (excluding Challenge Cup) - 21,554
Average (excluding Challenge Cup) - 1,658
(Down by 221 on 2023)

CLUB RECORDS
MATCH RECORDS Highest score: 94-4 v Myton, 25/3/2012 Highest score against: 6-88 v Hull KR, 23/4/2006
Record attendance: 29,153 v Wigan, 21/3/59 (Thrum Hall); 9,827 v Bradford, 12/3/2000 (The Shay)
Tries: 8 Keith Williams v Dewsbury, 9/11/57 Goals: 14 Bruce Burton v Hunslet, 27/8/72 Points: 34 Joe Keyes v Workington, 17/7/2022
SEASON RECORDS Tries: 48 Johnny Freeman 1956-57 Goals: 156 Graham Holroyd 2008 Points: 362 John Schuster 1994-95
CAREER RECORDS Tries: 290 Johnny Freeman 1954-67 Goals: 1,028 Ronnie James 1961-71 Points: 2,191 Ronnie James 1961-71 Appearances: 482 Stan Kielty 1946-58

Championship 2024 - Club by Club

SHEFFIELD EAGLES

DATE	FIXTURE	RESULT	SCORERS	LGE	ATT
4/2/24	Doncaster (a) (1895CR2)	W18-22	t:Gwaze,Roberts(2),Hodgson g:Aston(3)	2nd(G7)	784
10/2/24	Newcastle (h) (CCR3)	W88-12	t:I Farrell(3),Murphy(2),Marsh(2),Glover(3),Hansen(2),Halafihi(2),Clark g:Aston(5),I Farrell(9)	N/A	617
18/2/24	Midlands Hurricanes (a) (1895CR3)	W16-30	t:Marsh(2),Millar,Liu,Roberts,Johnson g:Aston(3)	1st(G7)	345
25/2/24	York (a) (CCR4)	W16-32	t:Marsh,Dawson-Jones,J Farrell,Battye,Jones-Bishop,Thackeray g:Aston(4)	N/A	1,280
3/3/24	Batley (h) (1895CQF)	W26-10	t:Jones-Bishop,J Farrell,Welham,Hansen g:Aston(5)	N/A	727
9/3/24	Swinton (a) (CCR5)	W12-14	t:Liu,Welham,Jones-Bishop g:Aston	N/A	412
15/3/24	Toulouse (h)	W24-22	t:Thackeray(2),Aston,Wood g:Aston(4)	6th	794
22/3/24	Wigan (a) (CCR6)	L44-18	t:Marsh,Dawson-Jones,Hodgson g:Aston(3)	N/A	5,733
29/3/24	Doncaster (a)	W20-26	t:Aston,Hansen,Glover,Welham,Dawson-Jones g:Aston(3)	3rd	1,719
7/4/24	Whitehaven (a)	W16-42	t:Thackeray,Liu,Aston,J Farrell,Marsh(2),Dawson-Jones g:Aston(7)	3rd	598
14/4/24	Swinton (a)	W4-22	t:Johnson(2),Welham,Hansen g:Aston(3)	3rd	786
21/4/24	Halifax (a)	W0-46	t:Murphy,Glover(2),Jones-Bishop(2),Halafihi,Marsh,Wood g:Aston(7)	2nd	1,521
28/4/24	Barrow (h)	W54-0	t:Battye,Hansen,J Farrell,Glover(2),Jones-Bishop,Wood,Liu,Dickinson g:Aston(7),Hansen(2)	2nd	1,103
3/5/24	Wakefield (h)	L10-36	t:Dawson-Jones,Welham g:Aston	2nd	1,998
12/5/24	York (a) (1895CSF)	W18-28	t:Dawson-Jones,Glover,Marsh(2) g:Aston(6)	N/A	1,309
19/5/24	Bradford (a)	L28-10	t:Dawson-Jones,Hansen g:Aston	3rd	2,234
24/5/24	Dewsbury (h)	W36-13	t:Welham(2),J Farrell,Marsh,Dawson-Jones(2),Bower(Aston(4)	2nd	971
2/6/24	Batley (a)	L31-18	t:Glover,J Farrell,Dawson-Jones g:Hansen(3)	3rd	983
8/6/24	Wakefield (1895CF) ●	L6-50	t:Thackeray g:Aston	N/A	N/A
16/6/24	Featherstone (h)	W18-16	t:Welham(2),Glover g:Aston(3)	2nd	1,444
23/6/24	Widnes (h)	W30-21	t:Welham(2),Bower,Glover,Halafihi g:Aston(5)	2nd	1,003
30/6/24	York (a)	W10-18	t:Welham,Thackeray,J Farrell g:Aston(3)	2nd	2,163
5/7/24	Halifax (h)	W28-0	t:Jones-Bishop(2),Liu,Dawson-Jones,Battye g:Aston(4)	2nd	1,023
14/7/24	Swinton (h)	L22-34	t:J Farrell,Dawson-Jones,I Farrell,Gwaze g:Aston(3)	2nd	1,063
21/7/24	Barrow (a)	L8-6	t:J Farrell g:Aston	3rd	1,552
28/7/24	Whitehaven (h)	W78-24	t:Dawson-Jones(3),Marsh(4),Welham,Foster(2),Jones-Bishop,Sene-Lefao,Gwaze g:Aston(13)	3rd	833
4/8/24	Doncaster (h)	W22-20	t:Dawson-Jones,Glover,Foster,Aston g:Aston(3)	3rd	1,075
9/8/24	Wakefield (a)	L42-6	t:Glover g:Aston	3rd	4,821
16/8/24	Batley (h)	L14-24	t:Jones-Bishop,Glover,Welham g:Aston	3rd	877
25/8/24	Widnes (a)	L35-20	t:Dawson-Jones(2),Sene-Lefao,Jones-Bishop g:Aston(2)	4th	2,486
31/8/24	Toulouse (a)	L32-12	t:Jones-Bishop,Liu g:Aston(2)	6th	2,079
8/9/24	Bradford (h)	L12-30	t:Foster,Marsh g:Aston(2)	7th	1,948
15/9/24	Featherstone (a)	W6-20	t:Jones-Bishop(2),Marsh g:Aston(4)	4th	1,246
20/9/24	York (h)	L24-26	t:Gwaze,Glover,Dawson-Jones,Dickinson g:Aston(4)	6th	952
29/9/24	Dewsbury (a)	L28-8	t:Jones-Bishop,Marsh	7th	1,007

● Played at Wembley Stadium

		APP		TRIES		GOALS		FG		PTS	
	D.O.B.	ALL	Ch	ALL	Ch	ALL	Ch	ALL	Ch	ALL	Ch
Cory Aston	1/3/95	34	25	4	4	119	88	0	0	254	192
Eddie Battye	24/7/91	34	26	3	2	0	0	0	0	12	8
Connor Bower	18/1/97	15(5)	12(4)	2	2	0	0	0	0	8	8
Blake Broadbent	11/12/98	(8)	(7)	0	0	0	0	0	0	0	0
Mitch Clark	13/3/93	6(20)	5(14)	1	0	0	0	0	0	4	0
Matty Dawson-Jones	2/10/90	33	24	19	16	0	0	0	0	76	64
Tyler Dickinson	18/8/96	28(1)	20(1)	2	2	0	0	0	0	8	8
Izaac Farrell	30/1/98	5(1)	3	4	1	9	0	0	0	34	4
Joel Farrell	15/3/94	23(5)	17(5)	9	7	0	0	0	0	36	28
Alex Foster	25/9/93	21(2)	16(1)	4	4	0	0	0	0	16	16
James Glover	2/12/93	30	22	16	12	0	0	0	0	64	48
Titus Gwaze	8/6/99	24(6)	16(6)	4	3	0	0	0	0	16	12
Vila Halafihi	24/1/94	30	22	4	2	0	0	0	0	16	8
Jack Hansen	12/1/97	16(6)	13(3)	7	4	5	0	0	0	38	26
Evan Hodgson	14/9/98	9(12)	9(10)	2	0	0	0	0	0	8	0
Ryan Johnson	3/8/00	4	2	3	2	0	0	0	0	12	8
Ben Jones-Bishop	24/8/88	29	23	15	12	0	0	0	0	60	48
Bayley Liu	3/8/96	11(9)	8(6)	7	5	0	0	0	0	28	20
Matty Marsh	21/4/95	29	22	19	11	0	0	0	0	76	44
Ryan Millar	12/5/94	9	6	1	0	0	0	0	0	4	0
Aaron Murphy	26/11/88	4(12)	2(7)	3	1	0	0	0	0	12	4
Lewis Peachey	25/3/01	1(2)	0	0	0	0	0	0	0	0	0
Oliver Roberts	24/12/94	2(18)	1(12)	3	0	0	0	0	0	12	0
Jesse Sene-Lefao	8/12/89	5(14)	5(12)	2	2	0	0	0	0	8	8
Anthony Thackeray	19/2/86	18	12	6	4	0	0	0	0	24	16
Kris Welham	10/3/87	30	23	13	11	0	0	0	0	52	44
Kyle Wood	18/6/89	5(19)	4(16)	3	3	0	0	0	0	12	12

'Ch' totals include Championship games only; 'All' totals also include Challenge Cup & 1895 Cup

Matty Marsh

LEAGUE RECORD
P26-W14-D0-L12 (7th)
F626, A526, Diff +100, 28 points.

CHALLENGE CUP
Round Six

1895 CUP
Runners-up

ATTENDANCES
Best - v Wakefield (Ch - 1,998)
Worst - v Newcastle (CC - 617)
Total (excluding Challenge Cup) - 15,811
Average (excluding Challenge Cup) - 1,129
(Down by 11 on 2023)

CLUB RECORDS
MATCH RECORDS Highest score: 112-6 v Leigh East, 7/4/2013 Highest score against: 0-88 v Hull, 2/3/2003
Record attendance: 10,603 v Bradford, 16/8/97 *(Don Valley Stadium)*; 1,998 v Wakefield, 3/5/2024 *(Olympic Legacy Park)*
Tries: 5 Daryl Powell v Mansfield, 2/1/89; Menzie Yere v Leigh East, 7/4/2013; Quentin Laulu-Togaga'e v Rochdale, 7/9/2014; Garry Lo v Rochdale, 4/6/2017
Goals: 14 Dominic Brambani v Leigh East, 7/4/2013 Points: 32 Roy Rafferty v Fulham, 21/9/86
SEASON RECORDS Tries: 46 Menzie Yere 2013 Goals: 169 *(inc 1fg)* Dominic Brambani 2013 Points: 361 Dominic Brambani 2013
CAREER RECORDS Tries: 196 Menzie Yere 2009-2020 Goals: 986 Mark Aston 1986-2004 Points: 2,142 Mark Aston 1986-2004 Appearances: 389 Mark Aston 1986-2004

Championship 2024 - Club by Club

SWINTON LIONS

DATE	FIXTURE	RESULT	SCORERS	LGE	ATT
28/1/24	North Wales (a) (1895CR1)	W12-40	t:Eaves,Abram(2),Roby,Chrimes,Patton,Cox g:Patton(6)	1st(G6)	520
4/2/24	Widnes (h) (1895CR2)	W18-6	t:Williams,Chrimes,Gibson g:Patton(3)	1st(G6)	1,006
11/2/24	West Hull (h) (CCR3)	W50-6	t:Abram(2),Badrock,Spencer-Tonks,Hammond,Lepori,Eaves,Stevens,Williams(2) g:Abram(5)	N/A	441
25/2/24	Oldham (h) (CCR4)	W28-12	t:Abram,Hatton,Hall,Spedding g:Patton(6)	N/A	746
3/3/24	Bradford (a) (1895CQF)	L21-12	t:Spedding,Abram g:Patton(2)	N/A	1,018
9/3/24	Sheffield (h) (CCR5)	L12-14	t:Bennion,Williams g:Patton(2)	N/A	412
17/3/24	Whitehaven (a)	L18-16	t:Badrock,Hatton g:Abram(4)	9th	653
29/3/24	Widnes (a)	L28-10	t:Badrock,Williams g:Patton	11th	2,751
6/4/24	Toulouse (a)	W14-20	t:Williams,Eaves,Gibson,Lepori g:Patton(2)	10th	3,542
14/4/24	Sheffield (h)	L4-22	t:Gibson	12th	786
21/4/24	Dewsbury (h)	W50-22	t:Cox,Hatton,Eaves,Ritson(2),Spencer-Tonks(2),Williams,Abram g:Patton(7)	7th	894
28/4/24	Halifax (a)	W12-28	t:Cox,Hatton,Abram,Vaughan,Gibson g:Patton(4)	5th	1,372
5/5/24	Bradford (h)	L12-38	t:Williams(2) g:Patton(2)	8th	1,187
19/5/24	Wakefield (a)	L46-22	t:Cox(2),Gibson,Purcell,Williams g:Davies	9th	5,268
26/5/24	York (h)	L22-30	t:Badrock(2),Spedding,Burns g:Abram(3)	10th	844
2/6/24	Featherstone (a)	W40-42	t:Hatton,Balmforth,Spedding,Gibson,Rodden,Cox,Badrock g:Patton(7)	8th	2,200
16/6/24	Batley (h)	L16-20	t:Hatton(2),Williams g:Patton(2)	10th	917
23/6/24	Barrow (h)	L10-24	t:Hatton,Cox g:Abram	12th	945
29/6/24	Doncaster (a) ●	L18-8	t:Purcell g:Abram(2)	13th	1,056
7/7/24	Widnes (h)	W24-12	t:Williams(2),Rodden,Hatton g:Abram(4)	10th	1,069
14/7/24	Sheffield (a)	W22-34	t:Rodden(2),Walker(2),Gibson,Spedding g:Abram(5)	10th	1,063
21/7/24	Whitehaven (h)	L20-22	t:Hatton(2),Hall g:Abram(4)	10th	859
28/7/24	York (a)	L34-4	t:Spedding	10th	2,125
3/8/24	Toulouse (h)	L4-48	t:Williams	12th	629
11/8/24	Batley (a)	L26-6	t:Stevens g:Stevens	12th	-
18/8/24	Halifax (h)	W20-6	t:Spedding,Williams,Hatton,Rodden g:Gibson(2)	12th	1,037
25/8/24	Barrow (a)	L20-18	t:Williams,Rodden,Spedding g:Abram(3)	13th	1,495
1/9/24	Wakefield (h)	L0-60		13th	1,048
8/9/24	Featherstone (h)	W28-8	t:Lepori(3),Hatton,Williams g:Abram(4)	12th	780
15/9/24	Dewsbury (a)	W16-28	t:Spedding,Hatton(3),Abram g:Abram(4)	12th	922
22/9/24	Doncaster (h)	L20-22	t:Lepori,Gibson,Ritson g:Stevens(4)	12th	836
29/9/24	Bradford (a)	L50-0		12th	3,293
13/10/24	Hunslet (h) (CP/RPO)	L20-22	t:Williams,Cox,Wood,Vaughan g:Abram(2)	N/A	885

● Played at Millennium Stadium, Featherstone

Dan Abram

	D.O.B.	APP ALL	APP Ch	TRIES ALL	TRIES Ch	GOALS ALL	GOALS Ch	FG ALL	FG Ch	PTS ALL	PTS Ch
Dan Abram	11/11/95	28(2)	21(2)	9	3	41	34	0	0	118	80
Andy Badrock	25/10/00	15(7)	14(3)	6	5	0	0	0	0	24	20
Brett Bailey	19/12/03	(1)	(1)	0	0	0	0	0	0	0	0
Denive Balmforth	1/10/03	1	1	1	1	0	0	0	0	4	4
Gavin Bennion	31/12/93	17	10	1	0	0	0	0	0	4	0
Louis Brogan	6/5/00	3	3	0	0	0	0	0	0	0	0
Jordan Brown	30/9/00	2(3)	2(3)	0	0	0	0	0	0	0	0
Jake Burns	23/6/00	3(1)	3(1)	1	1	0	0	0	0	4	4
Jordan Case	10/4/93	2(25)	2(20)	0	0	0	0	0	0	0	0
Matty Chrimes	2/11/97	9	4	2	0	0	0	0	0	8	0
Liam Cooper	5/10/96	2(15)	1(12)	0	0	0	0	0	0	0	0
Leon Cowen	31/10/04	5(6)	5(5)	0	0	0	0	0	0	0	0
Mitch Cox	15/11/93	28(2)	22(1)	8	6	0	0	0	0	32	24
Ben Davies	21/4/00	1	1	0	0	1	1	0	0	2	2
Josh Eaves	20/10/97	23(4)	16(4)	4	2	0	0	0	0	16	8
Matt Fletcher	15/2/00	1(4)	(1)	0	0	0	0	0	0	0	0
Matty Foster	25/6/01	2	2	0	0	0	0	0	0	0	0
Jacob Gannon	13/3/02	(1)	(1)	0	0	0	0	0	0	0	0
Jordy Gibson	11/6/92	29	22	8	7	2	2	0	0	36	32
Lucas Green	11/9/04	4	4	0	0	0	0	0	0	0	0
Lewis Hall	2/9/94	28	23	2	1	0	0	0	0	8	4
Brad Hammond	21/1/03	3(4)	2(4)	1	0	0	0	0	0	4	0
Ben Hartill	25/8/05	(4)	(4)	0	0	0	0	0	0	0	0
Jayden Hatton	23/9/99	29(1)	23(1)	16	15	0	0	0	0	64	60
Jack Houghton	10/1/97	9(10)	7(9)	0	0	0	0	0	0	0	0
Richard Lepori	22/10/91	15	14	6	5	0	0	0	0	24	20
Kai Morgan	13/4/04	1	1	0	0	0	0	0	0	0	0
Ciaran Nolan	23/6/05	(3)	(3)	0	0	0	0	0	0	0	0
Cole Oakley	25/10/00	1	0	0	0	0	0	0	0	0	0
Daniel Okoro	18/4/03	1	1	0	0	0	0	0	0	0	0
Dec Patton	23/5/95	14	9	1	0	44	25	0	0	92	50
Joe Purcell	22/8/99	5(1)	4	2	2	0	0	0	0	8	8
Tee Ritson	7/1/96	9	9	3	3	0	0	0	0	12	12
Will Roberts	24/2/05	2	2	0	0	0	0	0	0	0	0
George Roby	3/5/02	6(12)	6(6)	1	0	0	0	0	0	4	0
Gav Rodden	20/12/96	24(4)	18(4)	6	6	0	0	0	0	24	24
Sam Royle	12/2/00	(1)	(1)	0	0	0	0	0	0	0	0
Jake Spedding	26/9/96	25	20	9	7	0	0	0	0	36	28
Daniel Spencer-Tonks	18/1/95	3(5)	3(3)	3	2	0	0	0	0	12	8
Noah Stephens	3/10/04	1(1)	1(1)	0	0	0	0	0	0	0	0
Jack Stevens	1/11/02	11	9	2	1	5	5	0	0	18	14
Jonny Vaughan	12/2/04	8(2)	7(2)	2	1	0	0	0	0	8	4
Anthony Walker	28/12/91	2(10)	2(9)	2	2	0	0	0	0	8	8
Rhys Williams	8/12/89	33	26	18	13	0	0	0	0	72	52
Mikey Wood	18/4/96	24(2)	18(2)	1	0	0	0	0	0	4	0

'Ch' totals include Championship games only; 'All' totals also include Challenge Cup, 1895 Cup & Championship Promotion/Relegation play-off

LEAGUE RECORD
P26-W9-D0-L17 (12th)
F466, A678, Diff-212, 18 points.

CHALLENGE CUP
Round Five

1895 CUP
Quarter Finalists

ATTENDANCES
Best - v Bradford (Ch - 1,187)
Worst - v Sheffield (CC - 412)
Total (excluding Challenge Cup) - 13,722
Average (excluding Challenge Cup) - 915
(Down by 178 on 2023)

CLUB RECORDS
MATCH RECORDS Highest score: 96-4 v Oxford, 12/7/2015; 96-0 v West Wales, 30/1/2022 Highest score against: 0-112 v Warrington, 20/5/2011
Record attendance: 26,891 v Wigan, 12/2/64 (Station Road); 2,155 v Toulouse, 28/4/2018 (Heywood Road)
Tries: 6 Mark Riley v Prescot, 11/8/96 Goals: 15 Dan Abram v West Wales, 13/8/2022 Points: 48 Ian Mort v Oxford, 12/7/2015
SEASON RECORDS Tries: 42 John Stopford 1963-64 Goals: 154 Dan Abram 2022 Points: 352 Dan Abram 2022
CAREER RECORDS Tries: 197 Frank Evans 1921-31 Goals: 970 Ken Gowers 1954-73 Points: 2,105 Ken Gowers 1954-73 Appearances: 601 Ken Gowers 1954-73

Championship 2024 - Club by Club

TOULOUSE OLYMPIQUE

DATE	FIXTURE	RESULT	SCORERS	LGE	ATT
15/3/24	Sheffield (a)	L24-22	t:Armitage,Ulberg,Jussaume,Stefani g:Shorrocks(3)	8th	794
31/3/24	York (a)	W14-20	t:Stefani(2),Armitage g:Brochon(4)	7th	2,046
6/4/24	Swinton (h)	L14-20	t:Ulberg,Rennie,Shorrocks g:Shorrocks	7th	3,542
13/4/24	Bradford (a)	L19-12	t:Rennie,Ulberg g:Shorrocks(2)	9th	2,720
20/4/24	Whitehaven (h)	W40-4	t:Peyroux(2),Bretherton,Biscarro,Jussaume,Gahan,Rivett g:Shorrocks(6)	6th	2,055
27/4/24	Wakefield (a)	L28-12	t:Jussaume,Stefani g:Rivett(2)	8th	6,743
4/5/24	Dewsbury (a)	W21-38	t:Stefani(2),Jussaume,Ashall-Bott,Marion,Shorrocks,Diakhate g:Shorrocks(5)	6th	995
18/5/24	Barrow (h)	W38-16	t:Rennie(2),Stefani,Rivett(2),Roumanos,Marcon g:Shorrocks(5)	6th	2,313
25/5/24	Widnes (h)	W28-20	t:Marion,Ashall-Bott,Jussaume,Biscarro,Peyroux g:Shorrocks(4)	5th	2,130
1/6/24	Halifax (a)	W24-38	t:Shorrocks,Ulberg,Rivett,Gahan,Marcon,Peyroux g:Shorrocks(7)	5th	1,347
15/6/24	Doncaster (h)	W52-0	t:Belmas,Peyroux,Ulberg,Ashall-Bott,Stefani,Roumanos,Rivett,Marcon,Pelissier g:Shorrocks(8)	4th	2,138
22/6/24	Batley (a)	W0-36	t:Stefani(2),Peyroux(2),Jussaume,Rivett g:Shorrocks(6)	3rd	-
29/6/24	Featherstone (h)	W20-0	t:Rennie,Rivett,Marcon g:Shorrocks(4)	3rd	4,097
6/7/24	Bradford (h)	D12-12	t:Rennie,Ulberg g:Shorrocks,Rivett	3rd	2,340
13/7/24	Whitehaven (a)	W24-34	t:Peyroux(2),Biscarro,Rennie,Ulberg,Dall'asta g:Rivett(4)	3rd	331
20/7/24	Wakefield (h)	W32-4	t:Ashall-Bott(3),Ulberg(2),Rennie g:Brochon(4)	2nd	2,822
27/7/24	Dewsbury (h)	W58-6	t:Armitage(3),Jussaume,Marcon,Marion,Rivett,Ashall-Bott,Lima,Rodriguez g:Rivett(9)	2nd	2,155
3/8/24	Swinton (a)	W4-48	t:Ulberg(2),Rennie(2),Stefani,Lima(3),Marcon g:Rivett(2),Brochon(4)	2nd	629
10/8/24	Doncaster (a)	L20-18	t:Gahan,Peyroux,Rivett g:Shorrocks(3)	2nd	1,121
17/8/24	York (h)	L12-20	t:Marion,Ulberg g:Shorrocks(2)	2nd	2,181
24/8/24	Featherstone (a)	L22-10	t:Rennie,Stefani g:Shorrocks	2nd	-
31/8/24	Sheffield (h)	W32-12	t:Ulberg(3),Belmas,Ashall-Bott g:Shorrocks(6)	2nd	2,079
7/9/24	Barrow (a)	W24-36	t:Marcon,Ulberg(2),Rivett,Ashall-Bott,Laguerre g:Shorrocks(6)	2nd	1,709
14/9/24	Halifax (h)	W38-18	t:Armitage,Stefani(2),Laguerre,Rivett,Ulberg,Marion g:Shorrocks(2),Rivett(3)	2nd	2,985
21/9/24	Widnes (a)	W12-18	t:Biscarro,Pelissier,Armitage g:Rivett(3)	2nd	3,011
28/9/24	Batley (h)	W64-16	t:Ashall-Bott(2),Ulberg(2),Rivett,Stefani(2),Rennie,Laguerre,Armitage,Pelissier g:Shorrocks(9),Pelissier	2nd	3,361
13/10/24	Bradford (h) (SF)	W21-20	t:Laguerre,Ulberg,Armitage,Marion g:Shorrocks(2) fg:Pelissier	N/A	2,680
19/10/24	Wakefield (a) (GF)	L36-0		N/A	8,016

		APP		TRIES		GOALS		FG		PTS	
	D.O.B.	ALL	Ch	ALL	Ch	ALL	Ch	ALL	Ch	ALL	Ch
Sitaleki Akauola	7/4/92	(14)	(14)	0	0	0	0	0	0	0	0
Guy Armitage	29/11/91	10(7)	10(7)	9	9	0	0	0	0	36	36
Olly Ashall-Bott	24/11/97	20	20	11	11	0	0	0	0	44	44
Lambert Belmas	11/8/97	24	24	2	2	0	0	0	0	8	8
Dimitri Biscarro	11/7/01	1(17)	1(17)	4	4	0	0	0	0	16	16
Joe Bretherton	5/10/95	1(8)	1(8)	1	1	0	0	0	0	4	4
Robin Brochon	21/9/00	12(2)	12(2)	0	0	16	16	0	0	32	32
Joe Cator	15/6/98	(2)	(2)	0	0	0	0	0	0	0	0
Paolo Dall'asta	13/7/04	(3)	(3)	1	1	0	0	0	0	4	4
Damel Diakhate	28/3/01	(1)	(1)	1	1	0	0	0	0	4	4
Calum Gahan	23/4/97	26	26	3	3	0	0	0	0	12	12
Harrison Hansen	26/10/85	28	28	0	0	0	0	0	0	0	0
Mathieu Jussaume	17/5/99	21	21	7	7	0	0	0	0	28	28
Benjamin Laguerre	13/9/01	9(1)	9(1)	4	4	0	0	0	0	16	16
Pierre-Jean Lima	13/10/00	8(9)	8(9)	4	4	0	0	0	0	16	16
Paul Marcon	10/7/95	25	25	7	7	0	0	0	0	28	28
Anthony Marion	12/1/94	28	28	6	6	0	0	0	0	24	24
Eloi Pelissier	18/6/91	2(15)	2(15)	3	3	1	1	1	1	15	15
Dominique Peyroux	21/1/89	19(1)	19(1)	10	10	0	0	0	0	40	40
Reubenn Rennie	22/10/95	19(2)	19(2)	12	12	0	0	0	0	48	48
Greg Richards	12/7/95	(10)	(10)	0	0	0	0	0	0	0	0
Ryan Rivett	2/5/02	27	27	12	12	21	21	0	0	90	90
Baptiste Rodriguez	20/12/03	1(2)	1(2)	1	1	0	0	0	0	4	4
James Roumanos	10/8/99	4(18)	4(18)	2	2	0	0	0	0	8	8
Jake Shorrocks	26/10/95	22	22	3	3	83	83	0	0	178	178
Maxime Stefani	10/3/98	28	28	16	16	0	0	0	0	64	64
Paul Ulberg	14/11/95	27	27	21	21	0	0	0	0	84	84
Mac Walsh	23/12/03	2	2	0	0	0	0	0	0	0	0

'Ch' totals include regular season & play-offs

Paul Ulberg

LEAGUE RECORD
P26-W18-D1-L7
(2nd/Grand Final Runners-up)
F782, A384, Diff+398, 37 points.

CHALLENGE CUP
Not entered

1895 CUP
Not entered

ATTENDANCES
Best - v Featherstone (Ch - 4,097)
Worst - v Whitehaven (Ch - 2,055)
Total (all home games included) - 36,878
Average (all home games included) - 2,634
(Down by 740 on 2023)

CLUB RECORDS
MATCH RECORDS Highest score: 84-6 v Keighley, 18/6/2016. Highest score against: 10-90 v Featherstone, 3/7/2011. Record attendance: 9,235 v Featherstone, 10/10/2021. Tries: 6 Ilias Bergal v Rochdale, 13/7/2019. Goals: 12 Mark Kheirallah v Keighley, 18/6/2016; Jake Shorrocks v Whitehaven, 4/3/2023. Points: 40 Mark Kheirallah v Keighley, 18/6/2016
SEASON RECORDS Tries: 36 Kuni Minga 2016. Goals: 171 Mark Kheirallah 2016. Points: 466 Mark Kheirallah 2016
CAREER RECORDS Tries: 98 Mark Kheirallah 2016-2021. Goals: 650 (inc 1fg) Mark Kheirallah 2016-2021. Points: 1,691 Mark Kheirallah 2016-2021. Appearances: 205 Anthony Marion 2016-2019; 2021-2024

● Records only include seasons when the club competed in the British game (2009-2011 & 2016-2024)

Championship 2024 - Club by Club

WAKEFIELD TRINITY

DATE	FIXTURE	RESULT	SCORERS	LGE	ATT
4/2/24	York (a) (1895CR2)	W4-40	t:Gale,McGillvary,Griffin,Walmsley(3),Uele g:Jowitt(6)	2nd(G3)	2,817
10/2/24	Siddal (a) (CCR3)	W6-70	t:Pratt(2),Thornley,Griffin,Gale,Doyle,Atoni,Jowitt(2),Croft(2),Hood g:Jowitt(11)	N/A	900
18/2/24	Newcastle (a) (1895CR3) ●	W0-110	t:Lino(3),Franco(4),Pitts(2),Walmsley,Booth,Boothroyd(2),Cozza(2),Pratt,Smith,Atoni,Croft g:Jowitt(4),Lino(13)	1st(G3)	1,378
25/2/24	Hunslet ARLFC (h) (CCR4)	W78-6	t:Boothroyd,Gale(2),Hood,Ashurst,Walmsley(2),Pitts,Lawford(2),Griffin(2) g:Jowitt(13)	N/A	2,775
2/3/24	Barrow (h) (1895CQF)	W30-12	t:Atoni(2),Jowitt,Griffin,Smith g:Jowitt(5)	N/A	1,809
10/3/24	Featherstone (h) (CCR5)	L14-10 (aet)	t:Pratt,Franco g:Lino	N/A	
15/3/24	Bradford (h)	W42-12	t:Griffin(2),Hood,Pratt,Olpherts,Jowitt,Walmsley g:Jowitt(6),Lino	2nd	7,221
29/3/24	Featherstone (a)	W12-20	t:Walmsley(3) g:Jowitt(4)	2nd	4,127
7/4/24	Doncaster (a)	W6-42	t:Gale(3),Hood(2),Jowitt,Griffin,Lino g:Jowitt(5)	1st	2,520
14/4/24	York (a)	W6-50	t:Walmsley(4),Rodwell,Griffin,Cozza,Gale,Jowitt g:Jowitt(7)	1st	2,695
21/4/24	Batley (a)	W14-34	t:Jowitt(2),Uele,Ashurst,Croft,Thornley g:Jowitt(5)	1st	2,572
27/4/24	Toulouse (h)	W28-12	t:Walmsley(2),Griffin,Atoni,Jowitt g:Jowitt(4)	1st	6,743
3/5/24	Sheffield (a)	W10-36	t:Griffin,Gale,Jowitt,Pitts,Rodwell,Walmsley g:Jowitt(6)	1st	1,998
12/5/24	Bradford (a) (1895CSF)	W14-40	t:Rodwell,Ashurst(2),Hood,McGillvary,Atoni,Olpherts g:Jowitt(6)	N/A	5,340
19/5/24	Swinton (h)	W46-22	t:Bowden,McGillvary,Bain,Boothroyd,Atoni,Pitts,Rodwell,Kay g:Jowitt(7)	1st	5,268
26/5/24	Whitehaven (a)	W6-30	t:Pratt,Ashurst,Doyle,Rodwell,McGillvary g:Jowitt(5)	1st	1,572
31/5/24	Dewsbury (h)	W56-0	t:Lino,Olpherts,Gale,Walmsley,Rodwell,Booth,Bowden,Pitts,Uele,Atoni g:Lino(8)	1st	5,892
8/6/24	Sheffield (1895CF) ●●	W6-50	t:Walmsley,Gale,Doyle,Pratt(2),Griffin(2),McGillvary(2) g:Jowitt(7)	N/A	N/A
16/6/24	Widnes (a)	W18-20	t:Olpherts,Atoni,Pratt,Walmsley(2)	1st	4,056
23/6/24	Halifax (h)	W46-24	t:Olpherts(4),Pratt,Jowitt,Walmsley,Hood g:Jowitt(7)	1st	6,138
30/6/24	Barrow (a)	W0-36	t:Pratt,Olpherts(3),Pitts,Walmsley,Griffin g:Jowitt(2),Walmsley(2)	1st	2,245
7/7/24	Batley (h)	W34-12	t:Olpherts(2),Uele,Pratt,Kay,Griffin g:Jowitt(5)	1st	5,112
14/7/24	Bradford (a)	W2-14	t:Pratt g:Jowitt(5)	1st	3,203
20/7/24	Toulouse (a)	L32-4	t:Olpherts	1st	2,822
28/7/24	Featherstone (h)	W46-18	t:Bowden(2),McGillvary,Walmsley(2),Pratt,Croft,Olpherts g:Jowitt(7)	1st	6,453
4/8/24	Dewsbury (a)	W16-42	t:Jowitt(3),Smith,Rodwell,Olpherts,Pratt,Boothroyd g:Jowitt(5)	1st	1,750
9/8/24	Sheffield (h)	W42-6	t:Rodwell,Griffin,Olpherts(2),Thornley,Ashurst,Hood g:Jowitt(7)	1st	4,821
18/8/24	Widnes (h)	W36-12	t:Rodwell,Olpherts,Hood,McGillvary,Jowitt,Walmsley g:Jowitt(6)	1st	5,036
25/8/24	Halifax (a)	W6-48	t:Griffin,Hood(2),McGillvary,Jowitt,Doyle,Olpherts,Ashurst g:Jowitt(8)	1st	2,500
1/9/24	Swinton (a)	W0-60	t:Ashurst,Walmsley,Olpherts(2),Pitts,Rodwell(3),Vagana,Kay,Boothroyd g:Jowitt(8)	1st	1,048
8/9/24	Whitehaven (h)	W60-6	t:Rodwell(2),McGillvary(2),Booth,Cozza,Jowitt(2),Hood,Doyle g:Jowitt(10)	1st	5,096
15/9/24	York (h)	W20-4	t:Jowitt,Gale,McGillvary,Olpherts g:Jowitt(2)	1st	5,137
21/9/24	Barrow (h)	W46-0	t:Pitts,Rodwell,Jowitt(2),Pratt(3),Walmsley g:Jowitt(7)	1st	5,011
29/9/24	Doncaster (h)	W72-6	t:Jowitt(4),Olpherts,Lino,Thornley(2),Uele,McGillvary(2),Vagana,Atoni g:Jowitt(10)	1st	5,233
13/10/24	York (h) (SF)	W22-13	t:Jowitt,Gale,Olpherts,Thornley g:Jowitt(3)	N/A	5,946
19/10/24	Toulouse (h) (GF)	W36-0	t:Olpherts(2),Ashurst,McGillvary(2),Thornley,Pratt,Jowitt(3),McGillvary	N/A	8,016

● Played at Millennium Stadium, Featherstone
●● Played at Wembley Stadium

	D.O.B.	APP ALL	APP Ch	TRIES ALL	TRIES Ch	GOALS ALL	GOALS Ch	FG ALL	FG Ch	PTS ALL	PTS Ch
Matty Ashurst	1/11/89	30	23	9	6	0	0	0	0	36	24
Renouf Atoni	25/6/95	19(9)	12(8)	10	5	0	0	0	0	40	20
Luke Bain	4/10/00	5(7)	5(7)	1	1	0	0	0	0	4	4
Noah Booth	21/10/04	5(3)	5(1)	3	2	0	0	0	0	12	8
Toby Boothroyd	15/12/02	5(6)	3(5)	6	3	0	0	0	0	24	12
Josh Bowden	14/1/92	31	24	4	4	0	0	0	0	16	16
Mathieu Cozza	12/4/00	6(9)	4(7)	4	2	0	0	0	0	16	8
Jack Croft	21/12/00	14(4)	12(3)	5	2	0	0	0	0	20	8
Thomas Doyle	29/6/99	10(19)	9(15)	5	3	0	0	0	0	20	12
Romain Franco	5/6/98	5	1	5	0	0	0	0	0	20	0
Luke Gale	22/6/88	25	19	13	8	0	0	0	0	52	32
Josh Griffin	9/5/90	29	22	17	10	0	0	0	0	68	40
Liam Hood	6/1/92	25(4)	17(4)	12	9	0	0	0	0	48	36
Max Jowitt	6/5/97	35	27	26	23	198	146	0	0	500	384
Liam Kay	17/12/91	14(9)	13(8)	3	3	0	0	0	0	12	12
Myles Lawford	9/9/03	5	2	2	0	0	0	0	0	8	0
Ellis Lingard	22/10/06	(1)	(1)	0	0	0	0	0	0	0	0
Mason Lino	4/2/94	19	13	6	3	23	9	0	0	70	30
Jermaine McGillvary	16/5/88	17	13	16	12	1	1	0	0	66	50
Derrell Olpherts	7/1/92	28	27	27	26	0	0	0	0	108	104
Jay Pitts	9/12/89	30(2)	23(1)	10	6	0	0	0	0	40	24
Oliver Pratt	4/9/04	34	26	19	13	0	0	0	0	76	52
Ky Rodwell	21/6/99	13(12)	13(10)	15	14	0	0	0	0	60	56
Isaac Shaw	11/9/02	(6)	(6)	0	0	0	0	0	0	0	0
Harvey Smith	16/1/06	4(9)	4(5)	3	1	0	0	0	0	12	4
Rowan Stephenson	24/9/06	(1)	(1)	0	0	0	0	0	0	0	0
Iain Thornley	11/9/91	24	20	7	6	0	0	0	0	28	24
Caleb Uele	2/10/99	3(26)	2(19)	5	4	0	0	0	0	20	16
Isaiah Vagana	14/6/00	5(10)	4(7)	2	2	0	0	0	0	8	8
Lachlan Walmsley	12/6/98	28(4)	21(3)	27	20	2	2	0	0	112	84

'Ch' totals include regular season & play-offs; 'All' totals also include Challenge Cup & 1895 Cup

LEAGUE RECORD
P26-W25-D0-L1
(1st/Grand Final Winners, Champions)
F1010, A262, Diff+748, 50 points.

CHALLENGE CUP
Round Five

1895 CUP
Winners

ATTENDANCES
Best - v Toulouse (GF - 8,016)
Worst - v Barrow (1895C - 1,809)
Total (excluding Challenge Cup) - 88,932
Average (excluding Challenge Cup) - 5,558
(Up by 1,239 on 2023, Super League)

CLUB RECORDS
MATCH RECORDS Highest score: 110-0 v Newcastle, 18/2/2024 Highest score against: 0-86 v Castleford, 17/4/95 Record attendance: 30,676 v Huddersfield, 26/2/1921
Tries: 7 Fred Smith v Keighley, 25/4/59; Keith Slater v Hunslet, 6/2/71
Goals: 13 Mark Conway v Highfield, 27/10/92; Mason Lino v Newcastle, 18/2/2024; Max Jowitt v Hunslet ARLFC, 25/2/2024
Points: 38 Mason Lino v Newcastle, 18/2/2024
SEASON RECORDS Tries: 38 Fred Smith 1959-60; David Smith 1973-74 Goals: 198 Max Jowitt 2024 Points: 500 Max Jowitt 2024
CAREER RECORDS Tries: 272 Neil Fox 1956-74 Goals: 1,836 Neil Fox 1956-74 Points: 4,488 Neil Fox 1956-74 Appearances: 605 Harry Wilkinson 1930-49

Championship 2024 - Club by Club

WHITEHAVEN

DATE	FIXTURE	RESULT	SCORERS	LGE	ATT
4/2/24	Barrow (h) (1895CR2)	L12-18	t:Hanneghan,King g:Carter(2)	2nd(G1)	-
11/2/24	Halifax (a) (CCR3)	L32-4	t:Teare	N/A	1,100
18/2/24	Workington (a) (1895CR3)	W22-28	t:Maizen(2),Corkill,Romeo,Carter g:Carter(4)	2nd(G1)	1,476
17/3/24	Swinton (h)	W18-16	t:King,Newton,Corkill g:Carter(3)	7th	653
29/3/24	Barrow (a)	W23-22	t:Connell,Carter,King,Maizen g:Carter(3) fg:Carter	4th	-
7/4/24	Sheffield (h)	L16-42	t:Maizen,King,Carter g:Carter(2)	6th	598
14/4/24	Batley (h)	L12-25	t:Maizen,Bailey g:Carter(2)	8th	596
20/4/24	Toulouse (a)	L40-4	t:Evans	11th	2,055
28/4/24	Featherstone (h)	L24-28	t:Romeo(2),McCarron,Teare,Evans g:Carter(2)	10th	521
5/5/24	York (a)	W16-36	t:Gebbie,Graham,King,Corkill,Romeo,Hanneghan g:Carter(6)	9th	1,698
19/5/24	Widnes (a)	D28-28	t:Maizen(3),Hanneghan,Gebbie g:Hanneghan(4)	8th	2,741
26/5/24	Wakefield (h)	L6-30	t:Teare g:Carter	9th	1,572
2/6/24	Doncaster (a)	D25-25	t:Graham,Teare,Gebbie,King g:Carter(4) fg:Carter	10th	1,740
16/6/24	Bradford (h)	L18-36	t:Maizen,Holliday,Romeo g:Carter(3)	11th	-
23/6/24	Dewsbury (h)	W38-12	t:Boafo(2),Graham,High(2),Gebbie,King g:Carter(5)	8th	-
30/6/24	Halifax (a) ●	L38-18	t:Hanneghan(2),Corkill g:Carter(3)	10th	500
7/7/24	Featherstone (a)	L66-0		12th	1,605
13/7/24	Toulouse (h)	L24-34	t:Wallace,King,Teare,Maizen g:Hanneghan(4)	12th	331
21/7/24	Swinton (a)	W20-22	t:Hanneghan,Tchamambe,Carter,Evans g:Carter(3)	11th	859
28/7/24	Sheffield (a)	L78-24	t:Maizen,McCarron,Evans,Hanneghan g:Carter(4)	12th	833
4/8/24	Widnes (h)	L12-24	t:Gebbie,King g:Carter(2)	13th	855
11/8/24	Bradford (a)	L58-0		13th	2,502
18/8/24	Doncaster (h)	W28-24	t:Hanneghan,Campbell,Romeo(2),Maizen g:Hanneghan(4)	13th	699
25/8/24	Dewsbury (a)	W10-18	t:Hanneghan,McCarron,Walsh g:Hanneghan(3)	12th	876
1/9/24	York (h)	L0-40		12th	-
8/9/24	Wakefield (a)	L60-6	t:Gebbie g:Hanneghan	13th	5,096
15/9/24	Barrow (a)	L34-14	t:Gebbie(2),Hanneghan g:Hanneghan	13th	2,301
22/9/24	Batley (a)	L28-14	t:Gebbie,McCarron,Romeo g:Hanneghan	13th	1,644
29/9/24	Halifax (h)	W23-20	t:Evans,Corkill,Gebbie,Carter g:Carter(3) fg:Hanneghan	13th	876

● Played at DIY Kitchens Stadium, Wakefield

		APP		TRIES		GOALS		FG		PTS	
	D.O.B.	ALL	Ch	ALL	Ch	ALL	Ch	ALL	Ch	ALL	Ch
Sam Ackroyd	23/12/05	3(3)	3(3)	0	0	0	0	0	0	0	0
Ross Ainley	17/1/97	27	24	0	0	0	0	0	0	0	0
Dion Aiye	6/11/87	(4)	(1)	0	0	0	0	0	0	0	0
Luca Atkinson	18/9/02	1	1	0	0	0	0	0	0	0	0
Brett Bailey	19/12/03	(6)	(6)	1	1	0	0	0	0	4	4
Lewis Baxter	1/6/02	3	3	0	0	0	0	0	0	0	0
Gideon Boafo	10/2/99	2	2	2	2	0	0	0	0	8	8
McKenzie Buckley	3/12/03	(1)	(1)	0	0	0	0	0	0	0	0
Sam Campbell	23/8/04	(3)	(3)	1	1	0	0	0	0	4	4
Jake Carter	24/11/98	22(2)	19(2)	5	4	52	46	2	2	126	110
Lucas Castle	7/9/99	21(3)	19(3)	0	0	0	0	0	0	0	0
Nathan Connell	5/1/03	2(1)	2(1)	1	1	0	0	0	0	4	4
Rio Corkill	27/9/02	20(7)	18(6)	5	4	0	0	0	0	20	16
Dalton Desmond-Walker	25/4/93	(3)	(3)	0	0	0	0	0	0	0	0
Jamie Doran	8/12/94	9(5)	7(5)	0	0	0	0	0	0	0	0
Oscar Doran	17/10/04	6	4	0	0	0	0	0	0	0	0
Lennie Ellis	8/7/05	(4)	(4)	0	0	0	0	0	0	0	0
Will Evans	4/5/01	23(1)	21(1)	5	5	0	0	0	0	20	20
Edene Gebbie	6/5/95	17(1)	15(1)	10	10	0	0	0	0	40	40
Guy Graham	29/8/98	8(9)	7(7)	3	3	0	0	0	0	12	12
Lachlan Hanneghan	10/4/99	23(6)	22(4)	10	9	18	18	1	1	77	73
Bobby Hartley	9/11/05	2(1)	2(1)	0	0	0	0	0	0	0	0
Noah High	8/2/05	(8)	(8)	2	2	0	0	0	0	8	8
George Hill	29/7/04	(2)	(2)	0	0	0	0	0	0	0	0
Dan Hindmarsh	8/10/98	(5)	(5)	0	0	0	0	0	0	0	0
Connor Holliday	9/6/95	7	6	1	1	0	0	0	0	4	4
Ben Hursey	19/11/02	3	3	0	0	0	0	0	0	0	0
Jack Kellett	17/11/01	(1)	(1)	0	0	0	0	0	0	0	0
Ryan King	28/6/97	25(2)	22(2)	9	8	0	0	0	0	36	32
Evan Lawther	14/8/03	2(1)	0	0	0	0	0	0	0	0	0
Jake Maizen	4/1/97	20	18	12	10	0	0	0	0	48	40
Owen McCarron	2/3/99	25	23	4	4	0	0	0	0	16	16
James Newton	20/12/91	26(2)	24(1)	1	1	0	0	0	0	4	4
Callum Phillips	19/2/92	1(2)	0	0	0	0	0	0	0	0	0
Joey Romeo	28/9/99	25	22	8	7	0	0	0	0	32	28
Callum Shaw	25/7/05	8	8	0	0	0	0	0	0	0	0
Perry Singleton	5/1/94	(6)	(6)	0	0	0	0	0	0	0	0
Oliver Smart	17/5/06	1	1	0	0	0	0	0	0	0	0
Neil Tchamambe	14/2/05	2	2	1	1	0	0	0	0	4	4
Curtis Teare	13/2/99	28	25	5	4	0	0	0	0	20	16
AJ Wallace	31/3/03	2	2	1	1	0	0	0	0	4	4
Mac Walsh	23/12/03	7	7	1	1	0	0	0	0	4	4
Huw Worthington	28/10/94	6(14)	6(14)	0	0	0	0	0	0	0	0

'Ch' totals include Championship games only; 'All' totals also include Challenge Cup & 1895 Cup

Lachlan Hanneghan

LEAGUE RECORD
P26-W8-D2-L16 (13th)
F451, A854, Diff-403, 18 points.

CHALLENGE CUP
Round Three

1895 CUP
2nd, Group 1

ATTENDANCES
Complete data not supplied during the season, or at time of publication

CLUB RECORDS
MATCH RECORDS — Highest score: 86-6 v Highfield, 25/1/95 Highest score against: 8-106 v Wigan, 12/5/2008 Record attendance: 18,500 v Wakefield, 19/3/60
Tries: 6 Vince Gribbin v Doncaster, 18/11/84; Andrew Bulman v Wigan St Patricks, 10/3/2019
Goals: 13 Lee Anderson v Highfield, 25/1/95 Points: 32 Mick Nanyn v Batley, 22/8/2004
SEASON RECORDS — Tries: 34 Mike Pechey 1994-95 Goals: 141 John McKeown 1956-57 Points: 398 Mick Nanyn 2004
CAREER RECORDS — Tries: 239 Craig Calvert 2004-2017 Goals: 1,050 John McKeown 1948-61 Points: 2,133 John McKeown 1948-61 Appearances: 417 John McKeown 1948-61

Championship 2024 - Club by Club

WIDNES VIKINGS

DATE	FIXTURE	RESULT	SCORERS	LGE	ATT
4/2/24	Swinton (a) (1895CR2)	L18-6	t:Dixon g:Dixon	2nd(G6)	1,006
11/2/24	Doncaster (h) (CCR3)	W50-16	t:Dixon(2),Roby,Ince(2),Fleming(2),Lloyd,S Wilde,Edge g:Dixon(5)	N/A	788
18/2/24	North Wales (a) (1895CR3)	W14-30	t:Edge,Roby,Fozard,Butt,Lyons,Wood g:Edge,Gilmore(2)	2nd(G6)	1,088
25/2/24	Bradford (a) (CCR4)	W12-26	t:Lyons,Roby,S Wilde,Edge g:Gilmore(5)	N/A	-
9/3/24	Batley (h) (CCR5)	L14-18	t:Lyons,Gregson g:Gilmore(3)	N/A	1,067
17/3/24	Barrow (h)	W44-8	t:Butt(2),S Wilde,Lloyd,Langtree,Edge(2),Gilmore g:Gilmore(6)	1st	1,758
29/3/24	Swinton (h)	W28-10	t:Lloyd,Ince(2),Walker,Fozard g:Gilmore(4)	1st	2,751
7/4/24	Dewsbury (a)	W6-24	t:Johnstone,Langtree,Fozard(2) g:Gilmore(4)	2nd	1,084
14/4/24	Halifax (h)	W40-14	t:Lloyd(2),Fozard,Ince,Langtree,Owens(2) g:Gilmore(6)	2nd	2,558
21/4/24	Featherstone (a)	L32-24	t:Roberts,Ince(2),Owens g:Gilmore(4)	3rd	2,200
28/4/24	Bradford (a)	W13-14	t:Ince,Lyons g:Gilmore(2) fg:Gilmore(2)	3rd	3,029
5/5/24	Doncaster (h)	W16-14	t:Butt,Gilmore,S Wilde g:Gilmore(2)	3rd	2,936
19/5/24	Whitehaven (h)	D28-28	t:Butt,Johnstone,S Wilde,Fozard,Owens g:Gilmore(4)	2nd	2,741
25/5/24	Toulouse (a)	L28-20	t:Nisbet,Butt,Murray g:Gilmore(4)	3rd	2,130
2/6/24	York (a)	W18-22	t:Fozard,Dixon(2),Butt g:Gilmore(3)	2nd	2,163
16/6/24	Wakefield (h)	L18-20	t:Lyons,S Wilde,Lloyd g:Gilmore(3)	3rd	4,056
23/6/24	Sheffield (a)	L30-21	t:Roberts(2),Owens g:Gilmore(4) fg:Gilmore	5th	1,003
30/6/24	Batley (h)	L16-24	t:Butt,Owens,Fozard g:Gilmore(2)	5th	2,476
7/7/24	Swinton (a)	L24-12	t:Langtree,Gregson g:Gilmore(2)	5th	1,069
14/7/24	Dewsbury (h)	W34-12	t:S Wilde(2),Fozard(2),Lloyd,Butt g:Gilmore(5)	5th	2,337
21/7/24	Halifax (a)	W20-24	t:Brand,Roby,Gilmore,Ince g:Gilmore(4)	5th	1,409
28/7/24	Bradford (h)	W25-6	t:Ince(3),Butt,Roberts g:Gilmore fg:Gilmore	5th	3,065
4/8/24	Whitehaven (a)	W12-24	t:Ince(2),Lyons,Owens,Gilmore g:Gilmore(2)	4th	855
11/8/24	Featherstone (h)	L0-8		5th	2,422
18/8/24	Wakefield (a)	L36-12	t:Bardsley-Rowe,Sumner g:Gilmore(2)	5th	5,036
25/8/24	Sheffield (h)	W35-20	t:Lloyd,Grady(2),Ince,Butt,Fozard g:Gilmore(5) fg:Gilmore	5th	2,486
1/9/24	Batley (a)	W8-12	t:Lyons,Owens g:Gilmore(2)	4th	-
8/9/24	York (h)	L6-12	t:Butt g:Gilmore	4th	2,663
15/9/24	Doncaster (a)	L30-14	t:Gilmore,Ince g:Gilmore(3)	5th	1,360
21/9/24	Toulouse (h)	L12-18	t:Fleming,Ince g:Gilmore(2)	7th	3,011
29/9/24	Barrow (a)	W24-26	t:Owens(2),Lloyd,Lannon,Butt g:Gilmore(3)	5th	2,953
5/10/24	York (a) (E)	L27-10	t:Lloyd g:Gilmore(3)	N/A	2,010

		APP		TRIES		GOALS		FG		PTS	
	D.O.B.	ALL	Ch	ALL	Ch	ALL	Ch	ALL	Ch	ALL	Ch
Brett Bailey	19/12/03	(2)	(2)	0	0	0	0	0	0	0	0
Zac Bardsley-Rowe	8/10/04	10	10	1	1	0	0	0	0	4	4
Liam Bent	11/10/97	8(11)	7(10)	0	0	0	0	0	0	0	0
Keanan Brand	8/1/99	6	6	1	1	0	0	0	0	4	4
Louis Brogan	6/5/00	1(3)	1(3)	0	0	0	0	0	0	0	0
Ollie Brookes	19/6/01	4	3	0	0	0	0	0	0	0	0
Sam Brooks	29/9/93	3(16)	3(16)	0	0	0	0	0	0	0	0
Joe Bullock	27/11/92	(1)	0	0	0	0	0	0	0	0	0
Mike Butt	6/5/95	29(1)	25(1)	13	12	0	0	0	0	52	48
Kieran Dixon	22/8/92	6	4	5	2	6	0	0	0	32	8
Joe Edge	22/2/00	13	8	5	2	1	0	0	0	22	8
Callum Field	7/10/97	8(3)	5(3)	0	0	0	0	0	0	0	0
Matty Fleming	13/1/96	21	16	3	1	0	0	0	0	12	4
Matty Fozard	3/3/95	13(17)	9(16)	11	10	0	0	0	0	44	40
Tom Gilmore	2/2/94	31(1)	27	5	5	94	84	5	5	213	193
Shane Grady	13/12/89	3(3)	3(3)	2	2	0	0	0	0	8	8
Lucas Green	11/9/04	(8)	(8)	0	0	0	0	0	0	0	0
Nick Gregson	17/12/95	10(1)	7	2	1	0	0	0	0	8	4
Ryan Ince	16/9/96	24	20	17	15	0	0	0	0	68	60
Jordan Johnstone	24/5/97	21(7)	20(4)	2	2	0	0	0	0	8	8
Liam Kirk	26/3/97	19(9)	18(7)	0	0	0	0	0	0	0	0
Danny Langtree	18/2/91	5(5)	5(4)	4	4	0	0	0	0	16	16
Ryan Lannon	11/1/96	8(1)	8(1)	1	1	0	0	0	0	4	4
Rhodri Lloyd	22/7/93	28(1)	23(1)	10	9	0	0	0	0	40	36
Joe Lyons	16/10/97	31	26	7	4	0	0	0	0	28	16
Dan Murray	21/3/96	27(2)	25(2)	1	1	0	0	0	0	4	4
Tom Nisbet	8/10/99	4	4	1	1	0	0	0	0	4	4
Jack Owens	3/6/94	27	26	10	10	0	0	0	0	40	40
Martyn Reilly	5/1/96	(2)	(2)	0	0	0	0	0	0	0	0
Max Roberts	8/9/00	16(15)	14(12)	4	4	0	0	0	0	16	16
Lloyd Roby	3/1/99	9(4)	5(4)	4	1	0	0	0	0	16	4
Reagan Sumner	23/2/04	2	2	1	1	0	0	0	0	4	4
Will Tilleke	18/11/99	(2)	0	0	0	0	0	0	0	0	0
Anthony Walker	28/12/91	3(10)	1(8)	1	1	0	0	0	0	4	4
Tom Whitehead	7/11/02	1(1)	0	0	0	0	0	0	0	0	0
Nathan Wilde	29/12/99	2(1)	2(1)	0	0	0	0	0	0	0	0
Sam Wilde	8/9/95	22	17	8	6	0	0	0	0	32	24
Jordan Williams	4/6/97	1	1	0	0	0	0	0	0	0	0
Max Wood	28/6/04	(2)	(1)	1	0	0	0	0	0	4	0

'Ch' totals include regular season & play-offs; 'All' totals also include Challenge Cup & 1895 Cup

Tom Gilmore

LEAGUE RECORD
P26-W14-D1-L11 (5th/Eliminator)
F551, A475, Diff+76, 29 points.

CHALLENGE CUP
Round Five

1895 CUP
2nd, Group 6

ATTENDANCES
Best - v Wakefield (Ch - 4,056)
Worst - v Doncaster (CC - 788)
Total (excluding Challenge Cup) - 35,260
Average (excluding Challenge Cup) - 2,712
(Down by 210 on 2023)

CLUB RECORDS	
	Highest score: 90-4 v Doncaster, 10/6/2007; 90-0 v Coventry, 21/4/2018 **Highest score against:** 6-76 v Catalans Dragons, 31/3/2012
	Record attendance: 24,205 v St Helens, 16/2/61
MATCH RECORDS	**Tries:** 7 Phil Cantillon v York, 18/2/2001 **Goals:** 14 Mark Hewitt v Oldham, 25/7/99; Tim Hartley v Saddleworth, 7/3/2009
	Points: 38 Gavin Dodd v Doncaster, 10/6/2007
SEASON RECORDS	**Tries:** 58 Martin Offiah 1988-89 **Goals:** 161 Mick Nanyn 2007 **Points:** 434 Mick Nanyn 2007
CAREER RECORDS	**Tries:** 234 Mal Aspey 1964-80 **Goals:** 1,083 Ray Dutton 1966-78 **Points:** 2,195 Ray Dutton 1966-78 **Appearances:** 591 Keith Elwell 1970-86

Championship 2024 - Club by Club

YORK KNIGHTS

DATE	FIXTURE	RESULT	SCORERS	LGE	ATT
27/1/24	Newcastle (a) (1895CR1)	W10-114	t:Dagger(3),Bailey(4),Brown(2),Thompson(2),Williams,Field,Dee(2), Towse(3),Reynolds,Fitzsimmons,Harris g:Dagger(8),Harris(2),Williams(5)	1st(G3)	-
4/2/24	Wakefield (h) (1895CR2)	L4-40	t:Jubb	1st(G3)	2,817
11/2/24	Dewsbury (a) (CCR3)	W8-14	t:Field,Williams g:Pemberton(3)	N/A	824
25/2/24	Sheffield (h) (CCR4)	L16-32	t:Santi,Keinhorst,Dee g:Dagger(2)	N/A	1,280
3/3/24	Oldham (h) (1895CQF)	W46-12	t:Harrison,Harris,Dagger(2),Myler(2),Fitzsimmons,Towse g:Dagger(7)	N/A	1,048
17/3/24	Doncaster (a)	L36-20	t:Teanby,Towse,Daley,Lineham g:Williams(2)	12th	1,463
31/3/24	Toulouse (h)	L14-20	t:Brown,Bailey,Dee g:Harris	12th	2,046
7/4/24	Barrow (a)	L15-14	t:Jubb,Field,Severs g:Dagger	13th	1,692
14/4/24	Wakefield (h)	L6-50	t:Bailey g:Harrison	14th	2,695
21/4/24	Bradford (h)	W25-14	t:Keinhorst,Thompson,Harris(2) g:Harrison(4) fg:Harris	14th	2,675
28/4/24	Batley (a)	L22-18	t:Ta'ai,Thompson,Lineham g:Harrison(3)	13th	845
5/5/24	Whitehaven (h)	L16-36	t:Brown,Keinhorst,Lineham g:Dagger(2)	13th	1,698
12/5/24	Sheffield (h) (1895CSF)	L18-28	t:Severs,Lineham,Teanby g:Dagger(3)	N/A	1,309
19/5/24	Halifax (h)	W40-18	t:Towse,Ta'ai,Daley(2),Litten,Brown,Keinhorst g:Pemberton(6)	11th	1,693
26/5/24	Swinton (a)	W22-30	t:Dee,Daley(2),Brown,Pele g:Pemberton(5)	11th	844
2/6/24	Widnes (h)	L18-22	t:Fitzsimmons,Brown,Keinhorst g:Pemberton(3)	12th	2,163
16/6/24	Dewsbury (a)	W0-40	t:Ward,Hingano(2),Brown(2),Keinhorst,Thompson,Ta'ai g:Dagger(4)	9th	927
23/6/24	Featherstone (a)	W24-34	t:Teanby,Brown,Daley,Ta'ai,Hingano,Harris g:Dagger(5)	7th	1,564
30/6/24	Sheffield (h)	L10-18	t:Ward,Hingano g:Dagger	9th	2,163
7/7/24	Barrow (h)	W54-12	t:Brown(2),Cook,Ward,Bailey,Teanby,Field,Harris(2),Williams g:Dagger(7)	8th	1,792
14/7/24	Doncaster (h)	W27-0	t:Cook,Brown(2),Field g:Dagger(5) fg:Dagger	7th	1,902
21/7/24	Bradford (a)	L36-28	t:Ward,Bailey,Cook(2),Keinhorst g:Potter(4)	9th	3,025
28/7/24	Swinton (h)	W34-4	t:Daley,Williams(2),Keinhorst,Field,Cook g:Hingano(5)	8th	2,125
4/8/24	Halifax (a)	L38-18	t:Bailey,Ward,Gannon g:Hingano(3)	8th	1,543
11/8/24	Dewsbury (h)	W54-12	t:Law,Thompson,Brown(2),Cunningham,Towse,Keinhorst(2),Ward,Jubb g:Hingano(5),Keinhorst(2)	8th	1,936
17/8/24	Toulouse (a)	W12-20	t:Brown,Williams,Dagger g:Hingano,Dagger(3)	7th	2,181
25/8/24	Batley (h)	W37-6	t:Bailey,Cunningham,Law,Santi,Brown,Gannon g:Williams(6) fg:Williams	7th	2,003
1/9/24	Whitehaven (a)	W0-40	t:Williams(3),Law(2),Santi,Martin g:Williams(5),Jubb	7th	-
8/9/24	Widnes (a)	W6-12	t:Law g:Williams(4)	5th	2,663
15/9/24	Wakefield (a)	L20-4	t:Ward	6th	5,137
20/9/24	Sheffield (a)	W24-26	t:Hingano,Williams,Harris(2) g:Williams(5)	4th	952
29/9/24	Featherstone (h)	W16-6	t:Harris(2),Brown g:Williams(2)	4th	2,450
5/10/24	Widnes (h) (E)	W27-10	t:Lineham(3),Law,Dee g:Williams(3) fg:Harris	N/A	2,010
13/10/24	Wakefield (a) (SF)	L22-13	t:Field,Hingano g:Dagger(2) fg:Harris	N/A	5,946

		APP		TRIES		GOALS		FG		PTS	
	D.O.B.	ALL	Ch	ALL	Ch	ALL	Ch	ALL	Ch	ALL	Ch
Bailey Antrobus	18/2/00	1(3)	1(3)	0	0	0	0	0	0	0	0
Connor Bailey	10/10/00	34	28	10	6	0	0	0	0	40	24
Joe Brown	14/1/99	32	28	19	17	0	0	0	0	76	68
Francis Coggle	21/10/01	1	0	0	0	0	0	0	0	0	0
Sam Cook	1/8/93	6(1)	6(1)	5	5	0	0	0	0	20	20
James Cunningham	3/4/94	10(4)	9(4)	2	2	0	0	0	0	8	8
Will Dagger	21/2/99	13(1)	9(1)	6	1	50	30	1	1	125	65
Josh Daley	28/1/95	6(25)	4(23)	7	7	0	0	0	0	28	28
Jesse Dee	25/10/94	12(1)	8(1)	6	3	0	0	0	0	24	12
Alex Donaghy	22/9/01	1	0	0	0	0	0	0	0	0	0
Oli Field	3/9/02	25(1)	21(1)	7	5	0	0	0	0	28	20
Conor Fitzsimmons	7/5/98	11(14)	7(12)	3	1	0	0	0	0	12	4
Jacob Gannon	13/3/02	16	16	2	2	0	0	0	0	8	8
Liam Harris	20/4/97	19	14	11	9	3	1	3	3	53	41
Myles Harrison	11/8/03	9	6	1	0	8	8	0	0	20	16
Ata Hingano	11/3/97	25(3)	24(2)	6	6	14	14	0	0	52	52
Will Jubb	17/9/96	26	22	3	2	1	1	0	0	14	10
Jimmy Keinhorst	14/7/90	22	17	10	9	2	2	0	0	44	40
Joe Law	18/2/04	9	9	6	6	0	0	0	0	24	24
Tom Lineham	21/9/91	14	13	7	6	0	0	0	0	28	24
Davy Litten	3/5/03	2	2	1	1	0	0	0	0	4	4
Jack Martin	13/6/01	5(3)	5(3)	1	1	0	0	0	0	4	4
Ronan Michael	3/7/00	9(14)	9(13)	0	0	0	0	0	0	0	0
Richie Myler	21/5/90	3	1	2	0	0	0	0	0	8	0
Tom Nicholson-Watton	13/12/02	1(2)	1(2)	0	0	0	0	0	0	0	0
Franklin Pele	18/12/00	(2)	(2)	1	1	0	0	0	0	4	4
Taylor Pemberton	17/4/03	5(3)	4(1)	0	0	17	14	0	0	34	28
Jack Potter	12/6/04	2	2	0	0	4	4	0	0	8	8
Harry Price	8/11/03	(1)	0	0	0	0	0	0	0	0	0
Harvey Reynolds	2/2/04	4(8)	3(4)	1	0	0	0	0	0	4	0
Brenden Santi	5/8/93	8(16)	6(13)	3	2	0	0	0	0	12	8
Charlie Severs	1/10/03	5(1)	4(1)	2	1	0	0	0	0	8	4
Ukuma Ta'ai	17/1/87	20(1)	16	4	4	0	0	0	0	16	16
Jack Teanby	14/5/96	1(29)	(24)	4	3	0	0	0	0	16	12
Jordan Thompson	4/9/91	30	24	6	4	0	0	0	0	24	16
AJ Towse	19/8/03	13	8	7	3	0	0	0	0	28	12
Brad Ward	4/6/03	18	16	7	7	0	0	0	0	28	28
Nikau Williams	11/11/99	24(2)	21	10	8	32	27	1	1	105	87

'Ch' totals include regular season & play-offs; 'All' totals also include Challenge Cup & 1895 Cup

Joe Brown

LEAGUE RECORD
P26-W15-D0-L11 (4th/Semi-Final).
F655, A473, Diff+182, 30 points.

CHALLENGE CUP
Round Four

1895 CUP
Semi-Finalists

ATTENDANCES
Best - v Wakefield (1895C - 2,817)
Worst - v Oldham (1895C - 1,048)
Total (excluding Challenge Cup) - 34,525
Average (excluding Challenge Cup) - 2,031
(Up by 33 on 2023)

CLUB RECORDS			
MATCH RECORDS	Highest score: 144-0 v West Wales, 29/4/2018		Highest score against: 4-100 v Leigh, 21/8/2022
	Record attendance: 14,689 v Swinton, 10/2/34 (Clarence Street); 3,602 v Featherstone, 31/1/2022 (LNER Community Stadium)		
	Tries: 7 Brad Davis v Highfield, 17/9/95; Kieren Moss v West Wales, 29/4/2018		
	Goals: 21 Connor Robinson v West Wales, 11/8/2018 Points: 56 Chris Thorman v Northumbria University, 6/3/2011		
SEASON RECORDS	Tries: 35 John Crossley 1980-81 Goals: 186 (inc 4fg) Connor Robinson 2018 Points: 420 Connor Robinson 2018		
CAREER RECORDS	Tries: 167 Peter Foster 1955-67 Goals: 1,060 Vic Yorke 1954-67 Points: 2,159 Vic Yorke 1954-67 Appearances: 449 Willie Hargreaves 1952-65		

CHAMPIONSHIP 2024
Round by Round

Championship 2024 - Round by Round

ROUND 1

Friday 15th March 2024

SHEFFIELD EAGLES 24 TOULOUSE OLYMPIQUE 22

EAGLES: 14 Jack Hansen; 30 Ryan Millar; 3 Kris Welham; 4 James Glover; 5 Matty Dawson-Jones; 6 Cory Aston; 7 Anthony Thackeray; 8 Eddie Battye; 9 Vila Halafihi; 10 Tyler Dickinson; 26 Alex Foster; 23 Bayley Liu; 13 Titus Gwaze. Subs (all used): 15 Evan Hodgson; 18 Aaron Murphy; 22 Kyle Wood; 24 Oliver Roberts.
Tries: Thackeray (5, 39), Aston (35), Wood (60);
Goals: Aston 4/4.
OLYMPIQUE: 23 Robin Brochon; 2 Paul Ulberg; 4 Mathieu Jussaume; 18 Guy Armitage; 5 Paul Marcon; 6 Ryan Rivett; 7 Jake Shorrocks; 8 Lambert Belmas; 9 Calum Gahan; 10 Harrison Hansen; 11 Maxime Stefani; 12 Dominique Peyroux; 13 Anthony Marion. Subs (all used): 17 James Roumanos; 15 Sitaleki Akauola; 16 Joe Bretherton; 20 Greg Richards.
Tries: Armitage (1), Ulberg (20), Jussaume (24), Stefani (74); **Goals:** Shorrocks 3/4.
Rugby Leaguer & League Express Men of the Match: *Eagles:* James Glover; *Olympique:* Dominique Peyroux.
Penalty count: 5-7; **Half-time:** 18-16;
Referee: Michael Smaill; **Attendance:** 794.

WAKEFIELD TRINITY 42 BRADFORD BULLS 12

TRINITY: 1 Max Jowitt; 32 Derrell Olpherts; 22 Jack Croft; 3 Oliver Pratt; 5 Lachlan Walmsley; 6 Luke Gale; 7 Mason Lino; 8 Josh Bowden; 21 Thomas Doyle; 10 Renouf Atoni; 11 Matty Ashurst; 12 Josh Griffin; 13 Jay Pitts. Subs (all used): 9 Liam Hood; 15 Caleb Uele; 16 Mathieu Cozza; 19 Isaiah Vagana.
Tries: Griffin (5, 23), Hood (32), Pratt (40), Olpherts (54), Jowitt (65), Walmsley (78); **Goals:** Jowitt 6/7, Lino 1/1.
Sin bin: Jowitt (66) - retaliation.
BULLS: 24 Aidan McGowan; 21 Jayden Myers; 20 Billy Jowitt; 4 Kieran Gill; 5 Jorge Taufua; 6 Lee Gaskell; 7 Jordan Lilley; 13 Michael Lawrence; 18 Mitch Souter; 15 Daniel Smith; 28 Harvey Wilson; 12 Chester Butler; 19 Sam Hallas. Subs (all used): 9 George Flanagan; 16 Keven Appo; 23 Daniel Okoro; 27 Lucas Green.
Tries: McGowan (12), Gill (74); **Goals:** Lilley 2/3.
Sin bin: Taufua (5) - dangerous challenge on Griffin; Souter (66) - late challenge on Jowitt.
Rugby Leaguer & League Express Men of the Match: *Trinity:* Mason Lino; *Bulls:* Daniel Okoro.
Penalty count: 4-8; **Half-time:** 26-8;
Referee: Marcus Griffiths; **Attendance:** 7,221.

Sunday 17th March 2024

BATLEY BULLDOGS 20 FEATHERSTONE ROVERS 24

BULLDOGS: 1 Robbie Butterworth; 2 Dale Morton; 3 Kieran Buchanan; 4 George Senior; 18 Joe Burton; 6 Ben White; 7 Josh Woods; 15 Nyle Flynn; 9 Alistair Leak; 10 Luke Cooper; 11 Dane Manning; 12 Lucas Walshaw; 25 Brandon Moore. Subs (all used): 14 Oli Burton; 8 Adam Gledhill; 19 Joe Gibbons; 16 Michael Ward.
Tries: Flynn (8), J Burton (10), Morton (14);
Goals: Woods 4/4.
ROVERS: 29 Louix Gorman; 19 Manoa Wacokecoke; 3 Josh Hardcastle; 4 Greg Minikin; 5 Gareth Gale; 14 Harry Bowes; 1 Caleb Aekins; 8 Gadwin Springer; 9 Connor Jones; 18 Mo Kamano; 11 Brad Day; 17 Brad England; 13 Danny Addy. Subs: 2 Connor Wynne (not used); 15 Wellington Albert; 20 Keenen Tomlinson; 30 Yusuf Aydin.
Tries: Day (40), Addy (42), Minikin (66), Aekins (79);
Goals: Gorman 4/4.
Sin bin: Aydin (50) - high tackle on Manning.
Rugby Leaguer & League Express Men of the Match: *Bulldogs:* Josh Woods; *Rovers:* Danny Addy.
Penalty count: 10-3; **Half-time:** 18-6;
Referee: Scott Mikalauskas; **Attendance:** 1,961.

DEWSBURY RAMS 10 HALIFAX PANTHERS 24

RAMS: 4 Bailey O'Connor; 2 Perry Whiteley; 3 Ollie Greensmith; 22 Marcus Walker; 5 Lewis Carr; 9 Jacob Hookem; 7 Calum Turner; 8 Jimmy Beckett; 20 Curtis Davies; 29 Jack Bibby; 12 Matt Garside; 23 Bailey Dawson; 13 Louis Collinson. Subs (all used): 17 Jackson Walker; 27 Joe Hird; 28 Jack Billington; 31 Kieran Rush.
Tries: Whiteley (14), Hookem (52); **Goals:** Turner 1/2.
Sin bin: J Walker (56) - high tackle on Larroyer.
PANTHERS: 1 James Woodburn-Hall; 5 James Saltonstall; 3 Zack McComb; 17 Ben Tibbs; 2 Greg Eden; 6 Louis Jouffret; 7 Joe Keyes; 8 Adam Tangata; 20 Tom Inman; 31 Kevin Larroyer; 11 Ben Kavanagh; 12 Matty Gee; 19 Connor Davies. Subs (all used): 13 Jacob Fairbank; 15 Ryan Lannon; 21 Olly Davies; 23 Gareth Widdop.
Tries: Jouffret (22, 62), Keyes (58), Woodburn-Hall (80);
Goals: Jouffret 3/3, Widdop 1/1.
Sin bin: Fairbank (46) - kicking.
Rugby Leaguer & League Express Men of the Match: *Rams:* Joe Hird; *Panthers:* Louis Jouffret.
Penalty count: 9-13; **Half-time:** 4-6;
Referee: Kevin Moore; **Attendance:** 1,449.

DONCASTER 36 YORK KNIGHTS 20

DONCASTER: 19 Craig Hall; 2 Tom Halliday; 3 Brad Hey; 4 Reece Lyne; 5 Luke Briscoe; 6 Ben Johnston; 7 Connor Robinson; 20 Brad Knowles; 9 Greg Burns; 10 Suaia Matagi; 11 Sam Smeaton; 12 Alex Sutcliffe; 13 Loui McConnell. Subs (all used): 16 Pauli Pauli; 21 Tyla Hepi; 24 Watson Boas; 27 Brett Ferres.
Tries: Halliday (17, 46), Johnston (20), Pauli (41, 79), Smeaton (51); **Goals:** Robinson 6/7.
KNIGHTS: 2 Joe Brown; 34 Tom Lineham; 23 Myles Harrison; 4 Jimmy Keinhorst; 5 AJ Towse; 14 Nikau Williams; 6 Richie Myler; 8 Ukuma Ta'ai; 9 Will Jubb; 10 Conor Fitzsimmons; 11 Oli Field; 12 Connor Bailey; 35 Tom Nicholson-Watton. Subs (all used): 19 Josh Daley; 22 Ata Hingano; 17 Ronan Michael; 15 Jack Teanby.
Tries: Teanby (32), Towse (37), Daley (67), Lineham (72);
Goals: Williams 2/4.
Rugby Leaguer & League Express Men of the Match: *Doncaster:* Pauli Pauli; *Knights:* Jack Teanby.
Penalty count: 4-8; **Half-time:** 12-10;
Referee: Ryan Cox; **Attendance:** 1,463.

WHITEHAVEN 18 SWINTON LIONS 16

WHITEHAVEN: 2 Jake Maizen; 5 Curtis Teare; 21 Rio Corkill; 4 Will Evans; 3 Joey Romeo; 14 Jake Carter; 6 Jamie Doran; 8 Lucas Castle; 15 James Newton; 17 Ross Ainley; 20 Owen McCarron; 12 Connor Holliday; 11 Ryan King. Subs (all used): 7 Lachlan Hanneghan; 10 Guy Graham; 13 Dion Aiye; 26 Dalton Desmond-Walker.
Tries: King (36), Newton (48), Corkill (69);
Goals: Carter 3/3.
Sin bin: King (79) - fighting; Newton (79) - fighting.
LIONS: 1 Dan Abram; 2 Matty Chrimes; 21 Andy Badrock; 4 Jayden Hatton; 5 Rhys Williams; 18 Jack Stevens; 7 Jordy Gibson; 13 Mikey Wood; 14 Josh Eaves; 37 Noah Stephens; 11 Gav Rodden; 12 Mitch Cox; 16 Lewis Hall. Subs (all used): 9 George Roby; 15 Daniel Spencer-Tonks; 29 Jonny Vaughan; 17 Matt Fletcher.
Tries: Badrock (2), Hatton (21); **Goals:** Abram 4/4.
Sin bin: Roby (79) - fighting; Eaves (79) - fighting.
Rugby Leaguer & League Express Men of the Match: *Whitehaven:* Owen McCarron; *Lions:* Noah Stephens.
Penalty count: 12-5; **Half-time:** 6-14;
Referee: Brad Milligan; **Attendance:** 653.

WIDNES VIKINGS 44 BARROW RAIDERS 8

VIKINGS: 1 Jack Owens; 20 Mike Butt; 11 Rhodri Lloyd; 4 Joe Edge; 2 Ryan Ince; 6 Joe Lyons; 7 Tom Gilmore; 15 Liam Kirk; 9 Matty Fozard; 31 Dan Murray; 12 Danny Langtree; 19 Sam Wilde; 13 Nick Gregson. Subs (all used): 14 Jordan Johnstone; 16 Max Roberts; 17 Liam Bent; 22 Anthony Walker.
Tries: Butt (12, 69), S Wilde (16), Lloyd (25), Langtree (54), Edge (73, 78), Gilmore (80); **Goals:** Gilmore 6/8.
Sin bin: Ince (68) - retaliation.
RAIDERS: 1 Luke Cresswell; 2 Ryan Shaw; 3 Matty Costello; 16 Max Clarke; 4 Shane Toal; 6 Brad Walker; 7 Ryan Johnston; 22 Tom Walker; 9 Josh Wood; 20 Ramon Silva; 13 James Greenwood; 12 Jarrad Stack; 30 Harvey Makin. Subs (all used): 21 Aaron Smith; 15 Tom Wilkinson; 11 Charlie Emslie; 8 Greg Burke.
Try: Johnston (38); **Goals:** Shaw 2/2.
Dismissal: B Walker (59) - dissent.
Sin bin: Shaw (59) - obstruction; B Walker (59) - dissent; Stack (68) - high tackle on Ince.
Rugby Leaguer & League Express Men of the Match: *Vikings:* Tom Gilmore; *Raiders:* James Greenwood.
Penalty count: 13-10; **Half-time:** 16-8;
Referee: Cameron Worsley; **Attendance:** 1,758.

ROUND 2

Friday 29th March 2024

WIDNES VIKINGS 28 SWINTON LIONS 10

VIKINGS: 1 Jack Owens; 20 Mike Butt; 3 Matty Fleming; 4 Joe Edge; 2 Ryan Ince; 6 Joe Lyons; 7 Tom Gilmore; 15 Liam Kirk; 9 Matty Fozard; 31 Dan Murray; 11 Rhodri Lloyd; 19 Sam Wilde; 13 Nick Gregson. Subs (all used): 12 Danny Langtree; 14 Jordan Johnstone; 16 Max Roberts; 22 Anthony Walker.
Tries: Lloyd (11), Ince (25, 68), Walker (49), Fozard (80);
Goals: Gilmore 4/6.
Sin bin: Fleming (74) - obstruction.
LIONS: 1 Dan Abram; 2 Matty Chrimes; 4 Jayden Hatton; 21 Andy Badrock; 5 Rhys Williams; 6 Dec Patton; 7 Jordy Gibson; 24 Jordan Case; 14 Josh Eaves; 13 Mikey Wood; 11 Gav Rodden; 12 Mitch Cox; 34 Louis Brogan. Subs (all used): 9 George Roby; 33 Jacob Gannon; 31 Sam Royle; 37 Noah Stephens.
Tries: Badrock (2), Williams (45); **Goals:** Patton 1/3.
Rugby Leaguer & League Express Men of the Match: *Vikings:* Mike Butt; *Lions:* Dan Abram.
Penalty count: 9-9; **Half-time:** 10-6;
Referee: Michael Smaill; **Attendance:** 2,751.

DONCASTER 20 SHEFFIELD EAGLES 26

DONCASTER: 17 Josh Guzdek; 5 Luke Briscoe; 4 Reece Lyne; 3 Brad Hey; 2 Tom Halliday; 6 Ben Johnston; 7 Connor Robinson; 20 Brad Knowles; 9 Greg Burns; 10 Suaia Matagi; 30 Leon Ruan; 11 Sam Smeaton; 13 Loui McConnell. Subs (all used): 15 Joe Lovodua; 16 Pauli Pauli; 21 Tyla Hepi; 27 Brett Ferres.
Tries: Guzdek (22), Robinson (34), Lovodua (46);
Goals: Robinson 4/4.
EAGLES: 14 Jack Hansen; 2 Ben Jones-Bishop; 3 Kris Welham; 4 James Glover; 5 Matty Dawson-Jones; 6 Cory Aston; 7 Anthony Thackeray; 8 Eddie Battye; 9 Vila Halafihi; 10 Tyler Dickinson; 11 Connor Bower; 26 Alex Foster; 13 Titus Gwaze. Subs (all used): 12 Joel Farrell; 15 Evan Hodgson; 18 Aaron Murphy; 24 Oliver Roberts.
Tries: Aston (5), Hansen (15), Glover (40), Welham (61), Dawson-Jones (64); **Goals:** Aston 3/6.
Sin bin: Glover (72) - high tackle; Jones-Bishop (79) - dissent.
Rugby Leaguer & League Express Men of the Match: *Doncaster:* Connor Robinson; *Eagles:* Cory Aston.
Penalty count: 7-7; **Half-time:** 12-14;
Referee: Scott Mikalauskas; **Attendance:** 1,719.

WHITEHAVEN 23 BARROW RAIDERS 22

WHITEHAVEN: 24 Nathan Connell; 5 Curtis Teare; 21 Rio Corkill; 4 Will Evans; 2 Jake Maizen; 14 Jake Carter; 6 Jamie Doran; 8 Lucas Castle; 15 James Newton; 17 Ross Ainley; 20 Owen McCarron; 12 Connor Holliday; 11 Ryan King. Subs (all used): 7 Lachlan Hanneghan; 10 Guy Graham; 26 Dalton Desmond-Walker; 27 George Hill.
Tries: Connell (13), Carter (21), King (55), Maizen (59);
Goals: Carter 3/4; **Field goal:** Carter (75).
Sin bin: King (28) - late challenge on Stack.
RAIDERS: 1 Luke Cresswell; 5 Andrew Bulman; 3 Matty Costello; 4 Shane Toal; 2 Ryan Shaw; 6 Brad Walker; 7 Ryan Johnston; 22 Tom Walker; 9 Josh Wood; 20 Ramon Silva; 13 James Greenwood; 12 Jarrad Stack; 15 Tom Wilkinson. Subs (all used): 30 Tom Forber; 8 Greg Burke; 31 Kavan Rothwell; 11 Charlie Emslie.
Tries: Bulman (5), Forber (29), Stack (38), Shaw (43);
Goals: Shaw 3/4.
Rugby Leaguer & League Express Men of the Match: *Whitehaven:* Jake Carter; *Raiders:* Ramon Silva.
Penalty count: 6-7; **Half-time:** 12-18; **Referee:** Matty Lynn.

DEWSBURY RAMS 24 BATLEY BULLDOGS 4

RAMS: 4 Bailey O'Connor; 2 Perry Whiteley; 3 Ollie Greensmith; 22 Marcus Walker; 5 Lewis Carr; 9 Jacob Hookem; 7 Calum Turner; 8 Jimmy Beckett; 20 Curtis Davies; 29 Jack Bibby; 12 Matt Garside; 23 Bailey Dawson; 13 Louis Collinson. Subs (all used): 31 Kieran Rush; 28 Jack Billington; 10 Ronan Dixon; 27 Joe Hird.
Tries: Davies (14), Whiteley (53), Billington (58, 70);
Goals: Turner 4/5.
Sin bin: Rush (48) - fighting.
BULLDOGS: 5 Elliot Kear; 2 Dale Morton; 3 Kieran Buchanan; 4 George Senior; 18 Joe Burton; 6 Ben White; 20 Dave Gibbons; 8 Adam Gledhill; 9 Alistair Leak; 10 Luke Cooper; 11 Dane Manning; 12 Lucas Walshaw; 25 Brandon Moore. Subs (all used): 14 Oli Burton; 13 James Brown; 19 Joe Gibbons; 16 Michael Ward.
Try: J Burton (77); **Goals:** D Gibbons 0/1.
Sin bin: Manning (48) - fighting; Gledhill (70) - late challenge on Rush.
Rugby Leaguer & League Express Men of the Match: *Rams:* Jack Billington; *Bulldogs:* Elliot Kear.
Penalty count: 8-4; **Half-time:** 6-0;
Referee: Nick Bennett; **Attendance:** 1,549.

FEATHERSTONE ROVERS 12 WAKEFIELD TRINITY 20

ROVERS: 1 Caleb Aekins; 19 Manoa Wacokecoke; 29 Louix Gorman; 4 Greg Minikin; 5 Gareth Gale; 14 Harry Bowes; 28 Paul Turner; 8 Gadwin Springer; 9 Connor Jones; 18 Mo Kamano; 17 Brad England; 3 Josh Hardcastle; 13 Danny Addy. Subs (all used): 2 Connor Wynne; 15 Wellington Albert; 20 Keenen Tomlinson; 27 Zach Fishwick.
Tries: Addy (22), Aekins (55); **Goals:** Gorman 2/2.
Sin bin: England (59) - professional foul; Hardcastle (70) - high tackle on Jowitt.

Championship 2024 - Round by Round

TRINITY: 1 Max Jowitt; 32 Derrell Olpherts; 4 Iain Thornley; 3 Oliver Pratt; 5 Lachlan Walmsley; 6 Luke Gale; 7 Mason Lino; 8 Josh Bowden; 9 Liam Hood; 10 Renouf Atoni; 11 Matty Ashurst; 19 Isaiah Vagana; 13 Jay Pitts. Subs: 15 Caleb Uele; 18 Ky Rodwell; 21 Thomas Doyle; 22 Jack Croft (not used).
Tries: Walmsley (9, 14, 73); **Goals:** Jowitt 4/5.
Rugby Leaguer & League Express Men of the Match: *Rovers:* Caleb Aekins; *Trinity:* Max Jowitt.
Penalty count: 8-7; **Half-time:** 6-14;
Referee: Liam Rush; **Attendance:** 4,127.

BRADFORD BULLS 29 HALIFAX PANTHERS 10

BULLS: 24 Aidan McGowan; 21 Jayden Myers; 3 Joe Arundel; 4 Kieran Gill; 32 Connor Carr; 14 John Davies; 7 Jordan Lilley; 17 Eribe Doro; 18 Mitch Souter; 15 Daniel Smith; 29 Zac Fulton; 12 Chester Butler; 19 Sam Hallas. Subs (all used): 16 Keven Appo; 28 Harvey Wilson; 31 Tyran Ott; 33 Max Wood.
Tries: Myers (4), Souter (30), Wood (49), Fulton (77); **Goals:** Lilley 6/6; **Field goal:** Lilley (76).
PANTHERS: 1 James Woodburn-Hall; 5 James Saltonstall; 3 Zack McComb; 32 Jack Smith; 2 Greg Eden; 6 Louis Jouffret; 23 Gareth Widdop; 31 Kevin Larroyer; 20 Tom Inman; 33 Kieran Hudson; 11 Ben Kavanagh; 12 Matty Gee; 19 Connor Davies. Subs: 7 Joe Keyes (not used); 8 Adam Tangata; 15 Ryan Lannon; 21 Olly Davies.
Tries: Gee (21), Woodburn-Hall (26); **Goals:** Jouffret 1/2.
Rugby Leaguer & League Express Men of the Match: *Bulls:* Jordan Lilley; *Panthers:* Louis Jouffret.
Penalty count: 10-4; **Half-time:** 12-10;
Referee: Marcus Griffiths; **Attendance:** 3,853.

Sunday 31st March 2024

YORK KNIGHTS 14 TOULOUSE OLYMPIQUE 20

KNIGHTS: 23 Myles Harrison; 2 Joe Brown; 3 Jesse Dee; 4 Jimmy Keinhorst; 34 Tom Lineham; 22 Ata Hingano; 7 Liam Harris; 8 Ukuma Ta'ai; 19 Josh Daley; 17 Ronan Michael; 11 Oli Field; 33 Charlie Severs; 12 Connor Bailey. Subs (all used): 10 Conor Fitzsimmons; 15 Jack Teanby; 30 Harvey Reynolds; 35 Tom Nicholson-Watton.
Tries: Brown (72), Bailey (76), Dee (80); **Goals:** Harris 1/3.
OLYMPIQUE: 23 Robin Brochon; 2 Paul Ulberg; 18 Guy Armitage; 4 Mathieu Jussaume; 5 Paul Marcon; 6 Ryan Rivett; 7 Jake Shorrocks; 8 Lambert Belmas; 9 Calum Gahan; 10 Harrison Hansen; 11 Maxime Stefani; 12 Dominique Peyroux; 13 Anthony Marion. Subs (all used): 15 Sitaleki Akauola; 16 Joe Bretherton; 17 James Roumanos; 20 Greg Richards.
Tries: Stefani (7, 23), Armitage (37); **Goals:** Brochon 4/5.
Dismissals: Hansen (26) - high tackle on Harrison; Akauola (64) - use of the elbow on Michael.
Rugby Leaguer & League Express Men of the Match: *Knights:* Myles Harrison; *Olympique:* Guy Armitage.
Penalty count: 5-8; **Half-time:** 0-18;
Referee: Ben Thaler; **Attendance:** 2,046.

ROUND 3

Saturday 6th April 2024

TOULOUSE OLYMPIQUE 14 SWINTON LIONS 20

OLYMPIQUE: 23 Robin Brochon; 5 Paul Marcon; 4 Mathieu Jussaume; 18 Guy Armitage; 2 Paul Ulberg; 7 Jake Shorrocks; 6 Ryan Rivett; 8 Lambert Belmas; 14 Eloi Pelissier; 10 Harrison Hansen; 24 Pierre-Jean Lima; 11 Maxime Stefani; 13 Anthony Marion. Subs (all used): 3 Reubenn Rennie; 15 Sitaleki Akauola; 16 Joe Bretherton; 20 Greg Richards.
Tries: Ulberg (10), Rennie (70), Shorrocks (73); **Goals:** Shorrocks 1/3.
Sin bin: Belmas (32) - high tackle; Pelissier (77) - high tackle.
LIONS: 1 Dan Abram; 25 Richard Lepori; 3 Jake Spedding; 21 Andy Badrock; 5 Rhys Williams; 6 Dec Patton; 7 Jordy Gibson; 13 Mikey Wood; 14 Josh Eaves; 34 Louis Brogan; 11 Gav Rodden; 12 Mitch Cox; 16 Lewis Hall. Subs (all used): 4 Jayden Hatton; 8 Liam Cooper; 20 Jack Houghton; 24 Jordan Case.
Tries: Williams (5), Eaves (18), Gibson (32), Lepori (48); **Goals:** Patton 2/4.
Sin bin: Lepori (77) - dissent.
Rugby Leaguer & League Express Men of the Match: *Olympique:* Robin Brochon; *Lions:* Dec Patton.
Penalty count: 10-7; **Half-time:** 4-16;
Referee: Ryan Cox; **Attendance:** 3,542.

Sunday 7th April 2024

BARROW RAIDERS 15 YORK KNIGHTS 14

RAIDERS: 1 Luke Cresswell; 5 Andrew Bulman; 3 Matty Costello; 16 Max Clarke; 2 Ryan Shaw; 6 Brad Walker; 7 Ryan Johnston; 22 Tom Walker; 9 Josh Wood; 20 Ramon Silva; 13 James Greenwood; 12 Jarrad Stack; 15 Tom Wilkinson. Subs (all used): 10 Ellis Gillam; 11 Charlie Emslie; 30 Tom Forber; 31 Kavan Rothwell.
Tries: Shaw (36), Clarke (39), Cresswell (75); **Goals:** Shaw 1/3; **Field goal:** B Walker (79).
KNIGHTS: 1 Will Dagger; 2 Joe Brown; 3 Jesse Dee; 4 Jimmy Keinhorst; 34 Tom Lineham; 22 Ata Hingano; 7 Liam Harris; 8 Ukuma Ta'ai; 9 Will Jubb; 13 Jordan Thompson; 11 Oli Field; 33 Charlie Severs; 12 Connor Bailey. Subs (all used): 10 Conor Fitzsimmons; 15 Jack Teanby; 19 Josh Daley; 35 Tom Nicholson-Watton.
Tries: Jubb (18), Field (63), Severs (70); **Goals:** Dagger 1/3.
Rugby Leaguer & League Express Men of the Match: *Raiders:* Max Clarke; *Knights:* Ukuma Ta'ai.
Penalty count: 6-6; **Half-time:** 8-6;
Referee: Kevin Moore; **Attendance:** 1,692.

DEWSBURY RAMS 6 WIDNES VIKINGS 24

RAMS: 1 Owen Restall; 2 Perry Whiteley; 3 Ollie Greensmith; 22 Marcus Walker; 5 Lewis Carr; 9 Jacob Hookem; 6 Paul Sykes; 8 Jimmy Beckett; 20 Curtis Davies; 29 Jack Bibby; 23 Bailey Dawson; 12 Matt Garside; 13 Louis Collinson. Subs (all used): 10 Ronan Dixon; 16 Elliot Morris; 27 Joe Hird; 28 Jack Billington.
Try: Beckett (57); **Goals:** Sykes 1/1.
VIKINGS: 1 Jack Owens; 20 Mike Butt; 3 Matty Fleming; 4 Joe Edge; 2 Ryan Ince; 6 Joe Lyons; 7 Tom Gilmore; 15 Liam Kirk; 14 Jordan Johnstone; 31 Dan Murray; 12 Danny Langtree; 19 Sam Wilde; 13 Nick Gregson. Subs (all used): 9 Matty Fozard; 11 Rhodri Lloyd; 16 Max Roberts; 22 Anthony Walker.
Tries: Johnstone (18), Langtree (36), Fozard (42, 49); **Goals:** Gilmore 4/6.
Sin bin: Langtree (58) - dangerous challenge on Sykes.
Rugby Leaguer & League Express Men of the Match: *Rams:* Jimmy Beckett; *Vikings:* Max Roberts.
Penalty count: 7-7; **Half-time:** 0-12;
Referee: Matty Lynn; **Attendance:** 1,084.

DONCASTER 6 WAKEFIELD TRINITY 42

DONCASTER: 17 Josh Guzdek; 5 Luke Briscoe; 4 Reece Lyne; 23 Jason Tali; 2 Tom Halliday; 6 Ben Johnston; 7 Connor Robinson; 10 Suaia Matagi; 15 Joe Lovodua; 8 Keelan Foster; 16 Pauli Pauli; 3 Brad Hey; 20 Brad Knowles. Subs (all used): 11 Sam Smeaton; 14 Alex Holdstock; 21 Tyla Hepi; 24 Watson Boas.
Try: Robinson (44); **Goals:** Robinson 1/1.
TRINITY: 1 Max Jowitt; 32 Derrell Olpherts; 4 Iain Thornley; 3 Oliver Pratt; 5 Lachlan Walmsley; 6 Luke Gale; 7 Mason Lino; 8 Josh Bowden; 9 Liam Hood; 10 Renouf Atoni; 11 Matty Ashurst; 12 Josh Griffin; 16 Mathieu Cozza. Subs (all used): 15 Caleb Uele; 18 Ky Rodwell; 19 Isaiah Vagana; 21 Thomas Doyle.
Tries: Gale (7, 69, 80), Hood (17, 49), Jowitt (19), Griffin (40), Lino (77); **Goals:** Jowitt 5/8.
Sin bin: Olpherts (25) - high tackle.
Rugby Leaguer & League Express Men of the Match: *Doncaster:* Pauli Pauli; *Trinity:* Luke Gale.
Penalty count: 6-6; **Half-time:** 0-22;
Referee: Ben Thaler; **Attendance:** 2,520.

FEATHERSTONE ROVERS 14 BRADFORD BULLS 24

ROVERS: 1 Caleb Aekins; 19 Manoa Wacokecoke; 4 Greg Minikin; 29 Louix Gorman; 5 Gareth Gale; 14 Harry Bowes; 28 Paul Turner; 30 Yusuf Aydin; 9 Connor Jones; 18 Mo Kamano; 3 Josh Hardcastle; 31 AJ Wallace; 13 Danny Addy. Subs (all used): 17 Brad England; 15 Wellington Albert; 32 Leo Tennison; 20 Keenen Tomlinson.
Tries: Jones (37, 75), Turner (48); **Goals:** Gorman 1/3.
BULLS: 24 Aidan McGowan; 21 Jayden Myers; 3 Joe Arundel; 4 Kieran Gill; 32 Connor Carr; 14 John Davies; 7 Jordan Lilley; 17 Eribe Doro; 18 Mitch Souter; 15 Daniel Smith; 29 Zac Fulton; 12 Chester Butler; 19 Sam Hallas. Subs (all used): 31 Tyran Ott; 34 Fenton Rogers; 16 Keven Appo; 28 Harvey Wilson.
Tries: Carr (9, 57), Gill (23), Butler (63); **Goals:** Lilley 4/6.
Sin bin: Souter (32) - professional foul.
Rugby Leaguer & League Express Men of the Match: *Rovers:* Connor Jones; *Bulls:* Jordan Lilley.
Penalty count: 6-6; **Half-time:** 6-10;
Referee: Scott Mikalauskas.

HALIFAX PANTHERS 18 BATLEY BULLDOGS 10

PANTHERS: 1 James Woodburn-Hall; 5 James Saltonstall; 17 Ben Tibbs; 3 Zack McComb; 32 Jack Smith; 6 Louis Jouffret; 23 Gareth Widdop; 31 Kevin Larroyer; 20 Tom Inman; 13 Jacob Fairbank; 11 Ben Kavanagh; 12 Matty Gee; 19 Connor Davies. Subs (all used): 7 Joe Keyes; 8 Adam Tangata; 15 Ryan Lannon; 21 Olly Davies.
Tries: Inman (12), Woodburn-Hall (51); **Goals:** Jouffret 5/6.
BULLDOGS: 1 Robbie Butterworth; 2 Dale Morton; 24 John Mitsias; 3 Kieran Buchanan; 18 Joe Burton; 6 Ben White; 5 Elliot Kear; 8 Adam Gledhill; 9 Alistair Leak; 10 Luke Cooper; 11 Dane Manning; 12 Lucas Walshaw; 25 Brandon Moore. Subs (all used): 13 James Brown; 14 Oli Burton; 15 Nyle Flynn; 16 Michael Ward.
Tries: Butterworth (34), J Burton (78); **Goals:** Morton 1/2.
Rugby Leaguer & League Express Men of the Match: *Panthers:* Louis Jouffret; *Bulldogs:* Dale Morton.
Penalty count: 7-7; **Half-time:** 8-6;
Referee: Cameron Worsley; **Attendance:** 1,770.

WHITEHAVEN 16 SHEFFIELD EAGLES 42

WHITEHAVEN: 24 Nathan Connell; 5 Curtis Teare; 21 Rio Corkill; 4 Will Evans; 2 Jake Maizen; 6 Jamie Doran; 14 Jake Carter; 8 Lucas Castle; 15 James Newton; 17 Ross Ainley; 20 Owen McCarron; 12 Connor Holliday; 11 Ryan King. Subs (all used): 7 Lachlan Hanneghan; 10 Guy Graham; 26 Dalton Desmond-Walker; 27 George Hill.
Tries: Maizen (10), King (23), Carter (71); **Goals:** Carter 2/3.
EAGLES: 1 Matty Marsh; 2 Ben Jones-Bishop; 3 Kris Welham; 23 Bayley Liu; 5 Matty Dawson-Jones; 6 Cory Aston; 7 Anthony Thackeray; 8 Eddie Battye; 22 Kyle Wood; 24 Oliver Roberts; 11 Connor Bower; 26 Alex Foster; 13 Titus Gwaze. Subs (all used): 12 Joel Farrell; 15 Evan Hodgson; 17 Mitch Clark; 18 Aaron Murphy.
Tries: Thackeray (19), Liu (33), Aston (43), J Farrell (53), Marsh (56, 65), Dawson-Jones (60); **Goals:** Aston 7/7.
Rugby Leaguer & League Express Men of the Match: *Whitehaven:* Lucas Castle; *Eagles:* Cory Aston.
Penalty count: 7-4; **Half-time:** 10-12;
Referee: Marcus Griffiths; **Attendance:** 598.

ROUND 4

Saturday 13th April 2024

BRADFORD BULLS 19 TOULOUSE OLYMPIQUE 12

BULLS: 24 Aidan McGowan; 5 Jorge Taufua; 3 Joe Arundel; 4 Kieran Gill; 32 Connor Carr; 14 John Davies; 7 Jordan Lilley; 17 Eribe Doro; 16 Mitch Souter; 15 Daniel Smith; 29 Zac Fulton; 12 Chester Butler; 19 Sam Hallas. Subs (all used): 18 Keven Appo; 28 Harvey Wilson; 31 Tyran Ott; 34 Fenton Rogers.
Tries: Gill (24, 50), Fulton (28); **Goals:** Lilley 3/4; **Field goal:** Lilley (74).
OLYMPIQUE: 23 Robin Brochon; 2 Paul Ulberg; 4 Mathieu Jussaume; 3 Reubenn Rennie; 5 Paul Marcon; 6 Ryan Rivett; 7 Jake Shorrocks; 8 Lambert Belmas; 9 Calum Gahan; 10 Harrison Hansen; 13 Anthony Marion; 11 Maxime Stefani; 24 Pierre-Jean Lima. Subs (all used): 15 Sitaleki Akauola; 16 Joe Bretherton; 17 James Roumanos; 19 Benjamin Laguerre.
Tries: Rennie (2), Ulberg (60); **Goals:** Shorrocks 2/3.
Sin bin: Brochon (37) - high tackle on Carr.
Rugby Leaguer & League Express Men of the Match: *Bulls:* Jordan Lilley; *Olympique:* Calum Gahan.
Penalty count: 9-8; **Half-time:** 12-8;
Referee: James Vella; **Attendance:** 2,720.

Sunday 14th April 2024

BARROW RAIDERS 27 DEWSBURY RAMS 20

RAIDERS: 1 Luke Cresswell; 5 Andrew Bulman; 3 Matty Costello; 14 Luke Broadbent; 2 Ryan Shaw; 6 Brad Walker; 7 Ryan Johnston; 22 Tom Walker; 9 Josh Wood; 20 Roman Silva; 16 Max Clarke; 11 Charlie Emslie; 15 Tom Wilkinson. Subs (all used): 30 Tom Forber; 31 Kavan Rothwell; 10 Ellis Gillam; 8 Greg Burke.
Tries: Wilkinson (5), Rothwell (26, 32), Broadbent (27), Costello (36); **Goals:** Shaw 3/5; **Field goal:** Johnston (79).
RAMS: 1 Owen Restall; 5 Lewis Carr; 22 Marcus Walker; 3 Ollie Greensmith; 2 Perry Whiteley; 9 Jacob Hookem; 6 Paul Sykes; 8 Jimmy Beckett; 20 Curtis Davies; 10 Ronan Dixon; 23 Bailey Dawson; 28 Jack Billington; 13 Louis Collinson. Subs (all used): 29 Jack Bibby; 16 Elliot Morris; 27 Joe Hird; 25 Harry Copley.
Tries: Dawson (10), Hookem (51), Restall (56), Greensmith (67); **Goals:** Sykes 2/4.
Rugby Leaguer & League Express Men of the Match: *Raiders:* Charlie Emslie; *Rams:* Jacob Hookem.
Penalty count: 3-2; **Half-time:** 26-4;
Referee: Ryan Cox; **Attendance:** 1,675.

DONCASTER 4 FEATHERSTONE ROVERS 46

DONCASTER: 19 Craig Hall; 5 Luke Briscoe; 4 Reece Lyne; 3 Brad Hey; 17 Josh Guzdek; 6 Ben Johnston; 7 Connor Robinson; 20 Brad Knowles; 15 Joe Lovodua; 10 Suaia Matagi; 11 Sam Smeaton; 27 Brett Ferres; 16 Pauli Pauli. Subs (all used): 13 Loui McConnell; 14 Alex Holdstock; 21 Tyla Hepi; 24 Watson Boas.
Try: Guzdek (40); **Goals:** Robinson 0/1.
ROVERS: 1 Caleb Aekins; 2 Connor Wynne; 29 Corey Hall; 4 Greg Minikin; 5 Gareth Gale; 6 Ben Reynolds; 28 Paul Turner; 8 Gadwin Springer; 9 Connor Jones; 12 Jack

Championship 2024 - Round by Round

Bussey; 11 Brad Day; 17 Brad England; 13 Danny Addy. Subs (all used): 14 Harry Bowes; 18 Mo Kamano; 27 Zach Fishwick; 30 Yusuf Aydin.
Tries: Jones (10, 38), Gale (22), Reynolds (43), Aekins (47), Day (52, 59), Bowes (64); **Goals:** Addy 0/1, Reynolds 7/8.
Sin bin: Reynolds (4) - dissent.
Rugby Leaguer & League Express Men of the Match: *Doncaster:* Josh Guzdek; *Rovers:* Paul Turner.
Penalty count: 4-4; **Half-time:** 4-16;
Referee: Liam Rush; **Attendance:** 1,701.

SWINTON LIONS 4 SHEFFIELD EAGLES 22

LIONS: 1 Dan Abram; 25 Richard Lepori; 3 Jake Spedding; 4 Jayden Hatton; 5 Rhys Williams; 6 Dec Patton; 7 Jordy Gibson; 34 Louis Brogan; 14 Josh Eaves; 13 Mikey Wood; 11 Gav Rodden; 12 Mitch Cox; 16 Lewis Hall. Subs (all used): 20 Jack Houghton; 21 Andy Badrock; 24 Jordan Case; 35 Ben Hartill.
Try: Gibson (78); **Goals:** Patton 0/1.
Sin bin: Patton (15) - dissent.
EAGLES: 1 Matty Marsh; 3 Kris Welham; 23 Bayley Liu; 4 James Glover; 21 Ryan Johnson; 6 Cory Aston; 7 Anthony Thackeray; 8 Eddie Battye; 22 Kyle Wood; 10 Tyler Dickinson; 11 Connor Bower; 26 Alex Foster; 13 Titus Gwaze. Subs (all used): 12 Joel Farrell; 14 Jack Hansen; 18 Aaron Murphy; 24 Oliver Roberts.
Tries: Johnson (7, 70), Liu (35), Hansen (80);
Goals: Aston 3/5.
Rugby Leaguer & League Express Men of the Match: *Lions:* Jordy Gibson; *Eagles:* Anthony Thackeray.
Penalty count: 7-12; **Half-time:** 0-10;
Referee: Scott Mikalauskas; **Attendance:** 786.

WHITEHAVEN 12 BATLEY BULLDOGS 25

WHITEHAVEN: 2 Jake Maizen; 3 Joey Romeo; 5 Curtis Teare; 4 Will Evans; 22 Oscar Doran; 14 Jake Carter; 6 Jamie Doran; 8 Lucas Castle; 15 James Newton; 17 Ross Ainley; 20 Owen McCarron; 12 Connor Holliday; 11 Ryan King. Subs (all used): 7 Lachlan Hanneghan; 10 Guy Graham; 18 Perry Singleton; 28 Brett Bailey.
Tries: Maizen (38), Bailey (78); **Goals:** Carter 2/2.
BULLDOGS: 1 Robbie Butterworth; 2 Dale Morton; 5 Elliot Kear; 3 Kieran Buchanan; 18 Joe Burton; 6 Ben White; 7 Josh Woods; 8 Adam Gledhill; 9 Alistair Leak; 13 James Brown; 11 Dane Manning; 12 Lucas Walshaw; 25 Brandon Moore. Subs (all used): 14 Oli Burton; 15 Nyle Flynn; 10 Luke Cooper; 4 George Senior.
Tries: Morton (10, 61), Kear (14), Leak (22), Buchanan (74);
Goals: Butterworth 1/4, White 1/1; **Field goal:** Woods (67).
Rugby Leaguer & League Express Men of the Match: *Whitehaven:* Guy Graham; *Bulldogs:* Alistair Leak.
Penalty count: 8-5; **Half-time:** 6-14;
Referee: Michael Smaill; **Attendance:** 596.

WIDNES VIKINGS 40 HALIFAX PANTHERS 14

VIKINGS: 1 Jack Owens; 20 Mike Butt; 3 Matty Fleming; 4 Joe Edge; 2 Ryan Ince; 6 Joe Lyons; 7 Tom Gilmore; 15 Liam Kirk; 14 Jordan Johnstone; 31 Dan Murray; 11 Rhodri Lloyd; 19 Sam Wilde; 13 Nick Gregson. Subs (all used): 9 Matty Fozard; 12 Danny Langtree; 16 Max Roberts; 22 Anthony Walker.
Tries: Lloyd (31, 80), Fozard (44), Ince (47), Langtree (50), Owens (53, 70); **Goals:** Gilmore 6/8.
PANTHERS: 1 James Woodburn-Hall; 5 James Saltonstall; 17 Ben Tibbs; 32 Jack Smith; 3 Zack McComb; 6 Louis Jouffret; 23 Gareth Widdop; 31 Kevin Larroyer; 20 Tom Inman; 13 Jacob Fairbank; 11 Ben Kavanagh; 12 Matty Gee; 19 Connor Davies. Subs (all used): 8 Adam Tangata; 15 Ryan Lannon; 21 Olly Davies; 22 Ben Hursey.
Tries: Widdop (3), Jouffret (23), Kavanagh (37);
Goals: Jouffret 1/3.
Rugby Leaguer & League Express Men of the Match: *Vikings:* Jack Owens; *Panthers:* Tom Inman.
Penalty count: 8-2; **Half-time:** 4-14;
Referee: Ben Thaler; **Attendance:** 2,558.

YORK KNIGHTS 6 WAKEFIELD TRINITY 50

KNIGHTS: 2 Joe Brown; 5 AJ Towse; 23 Myles Harrison; 12 Connor Bailey; 34 Tom Lineham; 22 Ata Hingano; 19 Josh Daley; 8 Ukuma Ta'ai; 9 Will Jubb; 38 Jacob Gannon; 11 Oli Field; 30 Harvey Reynolds; 13 Jordan Thompson. Subs (all used): 10 Conor Fitzsimmons; 15 Jack Teanby; 17 Ronan Michael; 20 Taylor Pemberton.
Try: Bailey (39); **Goals:** Harrison 1/1.
TRINITY: 1 Max Jowitt; 32 Derrell Olpherts; 4 Iain Thornley; 22 Jack Croft; 5 Lachlan Walmsley; 6 Luke Gale; 7 Mason Lino; 8 Josh Bowden; 21 Thomas Doyle; 18 Ky Rodwell; 11 Matty Ashurst; 12 Josh Griffin; 16 Mathieu Cozza. Subs (all used): 14 Liam Kay; 15 Caleb Uele; 19 Isaiah Vagana; 26 Harvey Smith.
Tries: Walmsley (12, 16, 59, 75), Rodwell (19), Griffin (30), Cozza (35), Gale (62), Jowitt (70); **Goals:** Jowitt 7/9.
Rugby Leaguer & League Express Men of the Match: *Knights:* Ata Hingano; *Trinity:* Lachlan Walmsley.
Penalty count: 5-5; **Half-time:** 6-30;
Referee: Tom Grant; **Attendance:** 2,695.

ROUND 5

Saturday 20th April 2024

TOULOUSE OLYMPIQUE 40 WHITEHAVEN 4

OLYMPIQUE: 1 Olly Ashall-Bott; 5 Paul Marcon; 4 Mathieu Jussaume; 21 Mac Walsh; 2 Paul Ulberg; 7 Jake Shorrocks; 6 Ryan Rivett; 8 Lambert Belmas; 9 Calum Gahan; 10 Harrison Hansen; 12 Dominique Peyroux; 11 Maxime Stefani; 13 Anthony Marion. Subs (all used): 17 James Roumanos; 22 Dimitri Biscarro; 16 Joe Bretherton; 23 Robin Brochon.
Tries: Peyroux (9, 13), Bretherton (33), Biscarro (37), Jussaume (58), Gahan (66), Rivett (74);
Goals: Shorrocks 6/7.
WHITEHAVEN: 2 Jake Maizen; 22 Oscar Doran; 4 Will Evans; 5 Curtis Teare; 3 Joey Romeo; 14 Jake Carter; 7 Lachlan Hanneghan; 10 Guy Graham; 15 James Newton; 17 Ross Ainley; 20 Owen McCarron; 12 Connor Holliday; 11 Ryan King. Subs (all used): 28 Brett Bailey; 24 Nathan Connell; 21 Rio Corkill; 18 Perry Singleton.
Try: Evans (49); **Goals:** Carter 0/1.
Rugby Leaguer & League Express Men of the Match: *Olympique:* Anthony Marion; *Whitehaven:* Lachlan Hanneghan.
Penalty count: 6-4; **Half-time:** 22-0;
Referee: Kevin Moore; **Attendance:** 2,055.

Sunday 21st April 2024

BARROW RAIDERS 6 DONCASTER 38

RAIDERS: 1 Luke Cresswell; 5 Andrew Bulman; 3 Matty Costello; 14 Luke Broadbent; 2 Ryan Shaw; 6 Brad Walker; 7 Ryan Johnston; 22 Tom Walker; 9 Josh Wood; 20 Roman Silva; 13 James Greenwood; 16 Max Clarke; 11 Charlie Emslie. Subs (all used): 8 Greg Burke; 10 Ellis Gillam; 15 Tom Wilkinson; 30 Tom Forber.
Try: Gillam (34); **Goals:** Shaw 1/1.
Sin bin: Johnston (80) - late challenge.
DONCASTER: 19 Craig Hall; 5 Luke Briscoe; 4 Reece Lyne; 3 Brad Hey; 22 Misi Taulapapa; 6 Ben Johnston; 24 Watson Boas; 10 Suaia Matagi; 15 Joe Lovodua; 20 Brad Knowles; 16 Pauli Pauli; 27 Brett Ferres; 13 Loui McConnell. Subs (all used): 7 Connor Robinson; 8 Keelan Foster; 11 Sam Smeaton; 21 Tyla Hepi.
Tries: Hey (2), Lovodua (26), Johnston (56), C Hall (60), Pauli (71), Lyne (77), Briscoe (79);
Goals: C Hall 1/2, Robinson 4/5.
Rugby Leaguer & League Express Men of the Match: *Raiders:* Ellis Gillam; *Doncaster:* Craig Hall.
Penalty count: 1-5; **Half-time:** 6-10;
Referee: Matty Lynn; **Attendance:** 1,616.

BATLEY BULLDOGS 14 WAKEFIELD TRINITY 34

BULLDOGS: 1 Robbie Butterworth; 2 Dale Morton; 5 Elliot Kear; 3 Kieran Buchanan; 18 Joe Burton; 6 Ben White; 7 Josh Woods; 8 Adam Gledhill; 25 Brandon Moore; 10 Luke Cooper; 11 Dane Manning; 12 Lucas Walshaw; 13 James Brown. Subs (all used): 4 George Senior; 9 Alistair Leak; 15 Nyle Flynn; 16 Michael Ward.
Tries: Morton (21), Leak (31); **Goals:** Woods 3/4.
Sin bin: Gledhill (75) - late challenge on Walmsley.
TRINITY: 1 Max Jowitt; 32 Derrell Olpherts; 4 Iain Thornley; 22 Jack Croft; 5 Lachlan Walmsley; 24 Myles Lawford; 7 Mason Lino; 8 Josh Bowden; 9 Liam Hood; 10 Renouf Atoni; 11 Matty Ashurst; 12 Josh Griffin; 14 Liam Kay. Subs (all used): 16 Mathieu Cozza; 15 Caleb Uele; 18 Ky Rodwell; 21 Thomas Doyle.
Tries: Jowitt (3, 8), Uele (50), Ashurst (54), Croft (57), Thornley (70); **Goals:** Jowitt 5/7.
Rugby Leaguer & League Express Men of the Match: *Bulldogs:* Alistair Leak; *Trinity:* Renouf Atoni.
Penalty count: 5-5; **Half-time:** 12-12;
Referee: Cameron Worsley; **Attendance:** 2,572.

FEATHERSTONE ROVERS 32 WIDNES VIKINGS 24

ROVERS: 1 Caleb Aekins; 2 Connor Wynne; 4 Greg Minikin; 31 Corey Hall; 5 Gareth Gale; 14 Harry Bowes; 28 Paul Turner; 8 Gadwin Springer; 9 Connor Jones; 12 Jack Bussey; 11 Brad Day; 17 Brad England; 13 Danny Addy. Subs (all used): 25 Jayden Tanner; 18 Mo Kamano; 32 Leo Tennison; 29 Reiss Butterworth.
Tries: Gale (9), England (25), Hall (40), Day (43), Wynne (75, 78); **Goals:** Addy 4/6.
VIKINGS: 1 Jack Owens; 2 Ryan Ince; 16 Max Roberts; 11 Rhodri Lloyd; 20 Mike Butt; 6 Joe Lyons; 7 Tom Gilmore; 31 Dan Murray; 14 Jordan Johnstone; 15 Liam Kirk; 12 Danny Langtree; 19 Sam Wilde; 13 Nick Gregson. Subs (all used): 9 Matty Fozard; 22 Anthony Walker; 8 Callum Field; 10 Sam Brooks.
Tries: Roberts (37), Ince (50, 66), Owens (59);
Goals: Gilmore 4/4.
Rugby Leaguer & League Express Men of the Match: *Rovers:* Brad Day; *Vikings:* Ryan Ince.
Penalty count: 2-6; **Half-time:** 16-6;
Referee: Scott Mikalauskas; **Attendance:** 2,200.

HALIFAX PANTHERS 0 SHEFFIELD EAGLES 46

PANTHERS: 1 James Woodburn-Hall; 5 James Saltonstall; 17 Ben Tibbs; 3 Zack McComb; 33 Riley Lumb; 6 Louis Jouffret; 23 Gareth Widdop; 31 Kevin Larroyer; 20 Tom Inman; 8 Adam Tangata; 11 Ben Kavanagh; 21 Olly Davies; 12 Matty Gee. Subs (all used): 7 Joe Keyes; 13 Jacob Fairbank; 15 Ryan Lannon; 22 Ben Hursey.
EAGLES: 1 Matty Marsh; 2 Ben Jones-Bishop; 3 Kris Welham; 4 James Glover; 5 Matty Dawson-Jones; 6 Cory Aston; 7 Anthony Thackeray; 8 Eddie Battye; 9 Vila Halafihi; 10 Tyler Dickinson; 18 Aaron Murphy; 12 Joel Farrell; 13 Titus Gwaze. Subs (all used): 15 Evan Hodgson; 17 Mitch Clark; 22 Kyle Wood; 23 Bayley Liu.
Tries: Murphy (19), Glover (25, 79), Jones-Bishop (32, 37), Halafihi (45), Marsh (57), Wood (72); **Goals:** Aston 7/8.
Rugby Leaguer & League Express Men of the Match: *Panthers:* Riley Lumb; *Eagles:* Cory Aston.
Penalty count: 10-8; **Half-time:** 0-22;
Referee: Liam Rush; **Attendance:** 1,521.

SWINTON LIONS 50 DEWSBURY RAMS 22

LIONS: 1 Dan Abram; 32 Tee Ritson; 29 Jonny Vaughan; 4 Jayden Hatton; 5 Rhys Williams; 6 Dec Patton; 7 Jordy Gibson; 20 Jack Houghton; 14 Josh Eaves; 13 Mikey Wood; 11 Gav Rodden; 12 Mitch Cox; 16 Lewis Hall. Subs (all used): 35 Ben Hartill; 24 Jordan Case; 8 Liam Cooper; 15 Daniel Spencer-Tonks.
Tries: Cox (3), Hatton (26), Eaves (31), Ritson (33, 80), Spencer-Tonks (45, 78), Williams (61), Abram (66);
Goals: Patton 7/9.
RAMS: 1 Owen Restall; 19 Travis Corion; 22 Marcus Walker; 3 Ollie Greensmith; 5 Lewis Carr; 7 Calum Turner; 9 Jacob Hookem; 8 Jimmy Beckett; 20 Curtis Davies; 10 Ronan Dixon; 12 Matt Garside; 11 Brad Graham; 13 Louis Collinson. Subs (all used): 29 Jack Bibby; 27 Joe Hird; 6 Paul Sykes; 23 Bailey Dawson.
Tries: Davies (6), Restall (17), Graham (42), Corion (54);
Goals: Turner 3/4.
Sin bin: R Dixon (77) - high tackle on Hatton.
Rugby Leaguer & League Express Men of the Match: *Lions:* Dec Patton; *Rams:* Calum Turner.
Penalty count: 4-8; **Half-time:** 20-12;
Referee: Nick Bennett; **Attendance:** 894.

YORK KNIGHTS 25 BRADFORD BULLS 14

KNIGHTS: 23 Myles Harrison; 2 Joe Brown; 33 Charlie Severs; 4 Jimmy Keinhorst; 34 Tom Lineham; 20 Taylor Pemberton; 7 Liam Harris; 8 Ukuma Ta'ai; 9 Will Jubb; 10 Conor Fitzsimmons; 38 Jacob Gannon; 12 Connor Bailey; 13 Jordan Thompson. Subs (all used): 15 Jack Teanby; 17 Ronan Michael; 19 Josh Daley; 30 Harvey Reynolds.
Tries: Keinhorst (15), Thompson (34), Harris (43, 51);
Goals: Harrison 4/5; **Field goal:** Harris (57).
BULLS: 24 Aidan McGowan; 2 Ben Blackmore; 4 Kieran Gill; 3 Joe Arundel; 5 Jorge Taufua; 14 John Davies; 7 Jordan Lilley; 17 Eribe Doro; 18 Mitch Souter; 34 Fenton Rogers; 12 Chester Butler; 29 Zac Fulton; 19 Sam Hallas. Subs (all used): 16 Keven Appo; 28 Harvey Wilson; 30 Eliot Peposhi; 31 Tyran Ott.
Tries: Gill (12), Peposhi (69), McGowan (79);
Goals: Lilley 1/3.
Rugby Leaguer & League Express Men of the Match: *Knights:* Liam Harris; *Bulls:* Aidan McGowan.
Penalty count: 4-5; **Half-time:** 14-4;
Referee: Michael Smaill; **Attendance:** 2,675.

ROUND 6

Saturday 27th April 2024

WAKEFIELD TRINITY 28 TOULOUSE OLYMPIQUE 12

TRINITY: 1 Max Jowitt; 23 Romain Franco; 4 Iain Thornley; 3 Oliver Pratt; 5 Lachlan Walmsley; 6 Luke Gale; 7 Mason Lino; 8 Josh Bowden; 9 Liam Hood; 10 Renouf Atoni; 11 Matty Ashurst; 12 Josh Griffin; 13 Jay Pitts. Subs (all used): 14 Liam Kay; 15 Caleb Uele; 18 Ky Rodwell; 21 Thomas Doyle.
Tries: Walmsley (37, 63), Griffin (47), Atoni (69), Jowitt (78);
Goals: Jowitt 4/5.
OLYMPIQUE: 19 Benjamin Laguerre; 5 Paul Marcon; 4 Mathieu Jussaume; 3 Reubenn Rennie; 2 Paul Ulberg; 6 Ryan Rivett; 13 Anthony Marion; 8 Lambert Belmas; 9 Calum Gahan; 10 Harrison Hansen; 11 Maxime Stefani; 12 Dominique Peyroux; 16 Joe Bretherton. Subs (all used): 15 Sitaleki Akauola; 17 James Roumanos; 22 Dimitri Biscarro; 24 Pierre-Jean Lima.

Championship 2024 - Round by Round

Tries: Jussaume (55), Stefani (59); **Goals:** Rivett 2/3.
Sin bin: Peyroux (40) - high tackle on Jowitt.
Rugby Leaguer & League Express Men of the Match: *Trinity:* Max Jowitt; *Olympique:* Ryan Rivett.
Penalty count: 11-6; **Half-time:** 6-2;
Referee: Ben Thaler; **Attendance:** 6,743.

Sunday 28th April 2024

BATLEY BULLDOGS 22 YORK KNIGHTS 18

BULLDOGS: 1 Robbie Butterworth; 2 Dale Morton; 5 Elliot Kear; 3 Kieran Buchanan; 18 Joe Burton; 6 Ben White; 7 Josh Woods; 8 Adam Gledhill; 9 Alistair Leak; 10 Luke Cooper; 11 Dane Manning; 12 Lucas Walshaw; 25 Brandon Moore. Subs (all used): 14 Oli Burton; 15 Nyle Flynn; 16 Michael Ward; - Samy Kibula.
Tries: Walshaw (16), J Burton (29), Butterworth (47), Leak (54); **Goals:** Woods 3/4.
KNIGHTS: 23 Myles Harrison; 2 Joe Brown; 28 Brad Ward; 4 Jimmy Keinhorst; 34 Tom Lineham; 14 Nikau Williams; 7 Liam Harris; 8 Ukuma Ta'ai; 9 Will Jubb; 10 Conor Fitzsimmons; 12 Connor Bailey; 30 Harvey Reynolds; 13 Jordan Thompson. Subs (all used): 15 Jack Teanby; 17 Ronan Michael; 19 Josh Daley; 22 Ata Hingano.
Tries: Ta'ai (59), Thompson (63), Lineham (66);
Goals: Harrison 3/3.
Rugby Leaguer & League Express Men of the Match: *Bulldogs:* Samy Kibula; *Knights:* Ata Hingano.
Penalty count: 5-2; **Half-time:** 10-0;
Referee: Scott Mikalauskas; **Attendance:** 845.

BRADFORD BULLS 13 WIDNES VIKINGS 14

BULLS: 24 Aidan McGowan; 2 Ben Blackmore; 21 Jayden Myers; 4 Kieran Gill; 35 Jacob Douglas; 1 Tom Holmes; 7 Jordan Lilley; 17 Eribe Doro; 31 Tyran Ott; 34 Fenton Rogers; 3 Joe Arundel; 28 Harvey Wilson; 30 Eliot Peposhi. Subs (all used): 16 Keven Appo; 10 Ebon Scurr; 18 Mitch Souter; 23 Daniel Okoro.
Tries: Blackmore (36), Holmes (43); **Goals:** Lilley 2/3;
Field goal: Lilley (67).
VIKINGS: 1 Jack Owens; 20 Mike Butt; 11 Rhodri Lloyd; 4 Joe Edge; 2 Ryan Ince; 6 Joe Lyons; 7 Tom Gilmore; 15 Liam Kirk; 14 Jordan Johnstone; 31 Dan Murray; 12 Danny Langtree; 19 Sam Wilde; 8 Callum Field. Subs (all used): 9 Matty Fozard; 10 Sam Brooks; 16 Max Roberts; 17 Liam Bent.
Tries: Ince (15), Lyons (73); **Goals:** Gilmore 2/3;
Field goals: Gilmore (75, 78).
Rugby Leaguer & League Express Men of the Match: *Bulls:* Eribe Doro; *Vikings:* Callum Field.
Penalty count: 9-5; **Half-time:** 4-6;
Referee: Cameron Worsley; **Attendance:** 3,029.

DONCASTER 38 DEWSBURY RAMS 12

DONCASTER: 17 Josh Guzdek; 5 Luke Briscoe; 4 Reece Lyne; 3 Brad Hey; 22 Misi Taulapapa; 19 Craig Hall; 7 Connor Robinson; 20 Brad Knowles; 9 Greg Burns; 10 Suaia Matagi; 16 Pauli Pauli; 27 Brett Ferres; 13 Loui McConnell. Subs (all used): 8 Keelan Foster; 11 Sam Smeaton; 15 Joe Lovodua; 21 Tyla Hepi.
Tries: Guzdek (6), Taulapapa (22), Knowles (26), Lovodua (43), Pauli (49), C Hall (61), Robinson (79);
Goals: Robinson 5/7.
RAMS: 7 Calum Turner; 2 Perry Whiteley; 3 Ollie Greensmith; 22 Marcus Walker; 19 Travis Corion; 6 Paul Sykes; 9 Jacob Hookem; 8 Jimmy Beckett; 20 Curtis Davies; 17 Jackson Walker; 12 Matt Garside; 11 Brad Graham; 13 Louis Collinson. Subs (all used): 10 Ronan Dixon; 18 Davey Dixon; 23 Bailey Dawson; 27 Joe Hird.
Tries: Hookem (11), Graham (70); **Goals:** Turner 2/2.
Rugby Leaguer & League Express Men of the Match: *Doncaster:* Craig Hall; *Rams:* Calum Turner.
Penalty count: 3-2; **Half-time:** 16-6;
Referee: Matty Lynn; **Attendance:** 1,296.

HALIFAX PANTHERS 12 SWINTON LIONS 28

PANTHERS: 6 Louis Jouffret; 2 Greg Eden; 17 Ben Tibbs; 1 James Woodburn-Hall; 5 James Saltonstall; 23 Gareth Widdop; 7 Joe Keyes; 31 Kevin Larroyer; 20 Tom Inman; 8 Adam Tangata; 11 Ben Kavanagh; 12 Matty Gee; 3 Zack McComb. Subs (all used): 13 Jacob Fairbank; 15 Ryan Lannon; 18 Brandon Douglas; 26 Ed Barber.
Tries: Jouffret (43), Eden (67); **Goals:** Jouffret 2/2.
Sin bin: Larroyer (69) - use of the elbow on Eaves.
LIONS: 1 Dan Abram; 32 Tee Ritson; 29 Jonny Vaughan; 4 Jayden Hatton; 5 Rhys Williams; 6 Dec Patton; 7 Jordy Gibson; 34 Lucas Green; 14 Josh Eaves; 13 Mikey Wood; 37 Matty Foster; 12 Mitch Cox; 16 Lewis Hall. Subs (all used): 35 Ben Hartill; 8 Liam Cooper; 15 Daniel Spencer-Tonks; 21 Andy Badrock.
Tries: Cox (8), Hatton (20), Abram (27), Vaughan (39), Gibson (72); **Goals:** Patton 4/6.
Rugby Leaguer & League Express Men of the Match: *Panthers:* Zack McComb; *Lions:* Jordy Gibson.
Penalty count: 4-8; **Half-time:** 0-20;
Referee: Michael Smaill; **Attendance:** 1,372.

SHEFFIELD EAGLES 54 BARROW RAIDERS 0

EAGLES: 1 Matty Marsh; 2 Ben Jones-Bishop; 23 Bayley Liu; 4 James Glover; 5 Matty Dawson-Jones; 6 Cory Aston; 14 Jack Hansen; 8 Eddie Battye; 9 Vila Halafihi; 10 Tyler Dickinson; 26 Alex Foster; 12 Joel Farrell; 13 Titus Gwaze. Subs (all used): 15 Evan Hodgson; 17 Mitch Clark; 22 Kyle Wood; 27 Jesse Sene-Lefao.
Tries: Battye (20), Hansen (22), J Farrell (26), Glover (29, 66), Jones-Bishop (43), Wood (45), Liu (55), Dickinson (75); **Goals:** Aston 7/8, Hansen 2/2.
RAIDERS: 1 Luke Cresswell; 2 Ryan Shaw; 17 Brett Carter; 14 Luke Broadbent; 5 Andrew Bulman; 6 Brad Walker; 7 Ryan Johnston; 22 Tom Walker; 9 Josh Wood; 10 Ellis Gillam; 13 James Greenwood; 31 Finley Beardsworth; 15 Tom Wilkinson. Subs (all used): 30 Tom Forber; 33 Delaine Bedward-Gittens; 20 Ramon Silva; 8 Greg Burke.
Rugby Leaguer & League Express Men of the Match: *Eagles:* James Glover; *Raiders:* Ellis Gillam.
Penalty count: 8-1; **Half-time:** 24-0;
Referee: Kevin Moore; **Attendance:** 1,103.

WHITEHAVEN 24 FEATHERSTONE ROVERS 28

WHITEHAVEN: 2 Jake Maizen; 3 Joey Romeo; 5 Curtis Teare; 4 Will Evans; 1 Edene Gebbie; 14 Jake Carter; 7 Lachlan Hanneghan; 10 Guy Graham; 15 James Newton; 17 Ross Ainley; 20 Owen McCarron; 21 Rio Corkill; 11 Ryan King. Subs (all used): 6 Jamie Doran; 26 Huw Worthington; 27 Dan Hindmarsh; 28 Brett Bailey.
Tries: Romeo (10, 38), McCarron (22), Teare (64), Evans (77); **Goals:** Carter 2/5.
Sin bin: Gebbie (73) - shoulder charge.
ROVERS: 30 Louix Gorman; 2 Connor Wynne; 31 Connor Barley; 4 Greg Minikin; 5 Gareth Gale; 9 Connor Jones; 28 Paul Turner; 18 Mo Kamano; 14 Harry Bowes; 12 Jack Bussey; 11 Brad Day; 20 Keenen Tomlinson; 13 Danny Addy. Subs (all used): 29 Reiss Butterworth; 17 Brad England; 22 Dean Roberts; 15 Wellington Albert.
Tries: Wynne (5, 13), Minikin (17), Addy (27, 48);
Goals: Addy 0/1, Gorman 4/5.
Rugby Leaguer & League Express Men of the Match: *Whitehaven:* Lachlan Hanneghan; *Rovers:* Connor Jones.
Penalty count: 8-6; **Half-time:** 16-20;
Referee: Ryan Cox; **Attendance:** 521.

ROUND 7

Friday 3rd May 2024

SHEFFIELD EAGLES 10 WAKEFIELD TRINITY 36

EAGLES: 14 Jack Hansen; 2 Ben Jones-Bishop; 3 Kris Welham; 4 James Glover; 5 Matty Dawson-Jones; 6 Cory Aston; 7 Anthony Thackeray; 8 Eddie Battye; 9 Vila Halafihi; 10 Tyler Dickinson; 26 Alex Foster; 12 Joel Farrell; 13 Titus Gwaze. Subs (all used): 17 Mitch Clark; 18 Aaron Murphy; 24 Oliver Roberts; 27 Jesse Sene-Lefao.
Tries: Dawson-Jones (14), Welham (74); **Goals:** Aston 1/2.
TRINITY: 1 Max Jowitt; 32 Derrell Olpherts; 4 Iain Thornley; 3 Oliver Pratt; 5 Lachlan Walmsley; 6 Luke Gale; 7 Mason Lino; 8 Josh Bowden; 9 Liam Hood; 10 Renouf Atoni; 11 Matty Ashurst; 12 Josh Griffin; 13 Jay Pitts. Subs (all used): 14 Liam Kay; 15 Caleb Uele; 18 Ky Rodwell; 21 Thomas Doyle.
Tries: Griffin (2), Gale (26), Jowitt (37), Pitts (40), Rodwell (49), Walmsley (71); **Goals:** Jowitt 6/6.
Sin bin: Lino (68) - delaying restart.
Rugby Leaguer & League Express Men of the Match: *Eagles:* Jack Hansen; *Trinity:* Josh Griffin.
Penalty count: 8-7; **Half-time:** 6-24;
Referee: Ben Thaler; **Attendance:** 1,998.

Saturday 4th May 2024

DEWSBURY RAMS 21 TOULOUSE OLYMPIQUE 38

RAMS: 7 Calum Turner; 19 Travis Corion; 3 Ollie Greensmith; 11 Brad Graham; 1 Owen Restall; 6 Paul Sykes; 9 Jacob Hookem; 8 Jimmy Beckett; 20 Curtis Davies; 16 Elliot Morris; 28 Jack Billington; 12 Matt Garside; 13 Louis Collinson. Subs (all used): 17 Jackson Walker; 18 Davey Dixon; 23 Bailey Dawson; 27 Joe Hird.
Tries: Corion (12, 27), Restall (33); **Goals:** Turner 4/4;
Field goal: Hookem (40).
OLYMPIQUE: 1 Olly Ashall-Bott; 5 Paul Marcon; 4 Mathieu Jussaume; 3 Reubenn Rennie; 2 Paul Ulberg; 6 Ryan Rivett; 7 Jake Shorrocks; 8 Lambert Belmas; 9 Calum Gahan; 10 Harrison Hansen; 12 Dominique Peyroux; 11 Maxime Stefani; 13 Anthony Marion. Subs (all used): 14 Eloi Pelissier; 17 James Roumanos; 23 Robin Brochon; 25 Damel Diakhate.
Tries: Stefani (6, 43), Jussaume (20), Ashall-Bott (45), Marion (63), Shorrocks (70), Diakhate (75);
Goals: Shorrocks 5/7.
Rugby Leaguer & League Express Men of the Match: *Rams:* Curtis Davies; *Olympique:* Anthony Marion.
Penalty count: 4-15; **Half-time:** 19-10;
Referee: Brad Milligan; **Attendance:** 995.

Sunday 5th May 2024

BARROW RAIDERS 24 BATLEY BULLDOGS 14

RAIDERS: 1 Luke Cresswell; 5 Andrew Bulman; 4 Shane Toal; 14 Luke Broadbent; 2 Ryan Shaw; 6 Brad Walker; 3 Matty Costello; 10 Ellis Gillam; 9 Josh Wood; 20 Ramon Silva; 16 Max Clarke; 13 James Greenwood; 15 Tom Wilkinson. Subs (all used): 21 Aaron Smith; 31 Kavan Rothwell; 8 Greg Burke; 17 Brett Carter.
Tries: Cresswell (5), Costello (15), Greenwood (51), Silva (71); **Goals:** Shaw 4/4.
BULLDOGS: 1 Robbie Butterworth; 2 Dale Morton; 24 John Mitsias; 3 Kieran Buchanan; 18 Joe Burton; 5 Elliot Kear; 7 Josh Woods; 8 Adam Gledhill; 14 Oli Burton; 10 Luke Cooper; 11 Dane Manning; 12 Lucas Walshaw; 25 Brandon Moore. Subs (all used): 19 Joe Gibbons; 15 Nyle Flynn; 16 Michael Ward; 4 George Senior.
Tries: Morton (11), Gledhill (22); **Goals:** Woods 3/3.
Rugby Leaguer & League Express Men of the Match: *Raiders:* Brad Walker; *Bulldogs:* Adam Gledhill.
Penalty count: 2-5; **Half-time:** 12-14;
Referee: Kevin Moore; **Attendance:** 1,976.

FEATHERSTONE ROVERS 36 HALIFAX PANTHERS 16

ROVERS: 30 Luke Hooley; 2 Connor Wynne; 3 Josh Hardcastle; 4 Greg Minikin; 5 Gareth Gale; 13 Danny Addy; 28 Paul Turner; 18 Mo Kamano; 9 Connor Jones; 10 Nathan Massey; 11 Brad Day; 17 Brad England; 12 Jack Bussey. Subs: 14 Harry Bowes (not used); 15 Wellington Albert; 27 Zach Fishwick; 29 Louix Gorman.
Tries: Wynne (17, 65, 72, 76), Albert (33), Hardcastle (50);
Goals: Hooley 6/7.
Dismissal: Gale (61) - late challenge on Inman.
PANTHERS: 6 Louis Jouffret; 5 James Saltonstall; 1 James Woodburn-Hall; 17 Ben Tibbs; 2 Greg Eden; 7 Joe Keyes; 23 Gareth Widdop; 18 Brandon Douglas; 20 Tom Inman; 31 Kevin Larroyer; 19 Connor Davies; 12 Matty Gee; 3 Zack McComb. Subs (all used): 8 Adam Tangata; 13 Jacob Fairbank; 15 Ryan Lannon; 26 Ed Barber.
Tries: Eden (25), Widdop (39), Keyes (65);
Goals: Jouffret 2/3.
Rugby Leaguer & League Express Men of the Match: *Rovers:* Connor Wynne; *Panthers:* Joe Keyes.
Penalty count: 7-5; **Half-time:** 12-10;
Referee: Matty Lynn.

SWINTON LIONS 12 BRADFORD BULLS 38

LIONS: 1 Dan Abram; 25 Richard Lepori; 29 Jonny Vaughan; 4 Jayden Hatton; 5 Rhys Williams; 6 Dec Patton; 7 Jordy Gibson; 13 Mikey Wood; 14 Josh Eaves; 34 Lucas Green; 33 Matty Foster; 21 Andy Badrock; 16 Lewis Hall. Subs (all used): 8 Liam Cooper; 11 Gav Rodden; 20 Jack Houghton; 24 Jordan Case.
Tries: Williams (26, 69); **Goals:** Patton 2/2.
Sin bin: Rodden (57) - fighting; Patton (71) - dissent.
BULLS: 24 Aidan McGowan; 35 Jacob Douglas; 21 Jayden Myers; 4 Kieran Gill; 5 Jorge Taufua; 1 Tom Holmes; 7 Jordan Lilley; 34 Fenton Rogers; 18 Mitch Souter; 13 Michael Lawrence; 28 Harvey Wilson; 29 Zac Fulton; 17 Eribe Doro. Subs (all used): 10 Ebon Scurr; 16 Keven Appo; 23 Daniel Okoro; 31 Tyran Ott.
Tries: Fulton (14), Gill (20, 59), Souter (23), Appo (37), Okoro (44), Myers (72); **Goals:** Lilley 5/7.
Sin bin: Holmes (57) - fighting.
Rugby Leaguer & League Express Men of the Match: *Lions:* Jayden Hatton; *Bulls:* Jordan Lilley.
Penalty count: 7-7; **Half-time:** 6-24;
Referee: Liam Rush; **Attendance:** 1,187.

WIDNES VIKINGS 16 DONCASTER 14

VIKINGS: 1 Jack Owens; 20 Mike Butt; 25 Tom Nisbet; 4 Joe Edge; 2 Ryan Ince; 6 Joe Lyons; 7 Tom Gilmore; 15 Liam Kirk; 14 Jordan Johnstone; 31 Dan Murray; 11 Rhodri Lloyd; 19 Sam Wilde; 8 Callum Field. Subs (all used): 9 Matty Fozard; 10 Sam Brooks; 16 Max Roberts; 17 Liam Bent.
Tries: Butt (38), Gilmore (39), S Wilde (45);
Goals: Gilmore 2/3.
DONCASTER: 19 Craig Hall; 5 Luke Briscoe; 3 Brad Hey; 23 Jason Tali; 22 Misi Taulapapa; 6 Ben Johnston; 24 Watson Boas; 20 Brad Knowles; 9 Greg Burns; 10 Suaia Matagi; 16 Pauli Pauli; 27 Brett Ferres; 13 Loui McConnell. Subs (all used): 7 Connor Robinson; 11 Sam Smeaton; 15 Joe Lovodua; 21 Tyla Hepi.
Tries: Smeaton (19), C Hall (68);
Goals: C Hall 2/2, Robinson 1/1.

Championship 2024 - Round by Round

Rugby Leaguer & League Express Men of the Match: *Vikings:* Matty Fozard; *Doncaster:* Suaia Matagi.
Penalty count: 9-6; **Half-time:** 10-8;
Referee: Ryan Cox; **Attendance:** 2,936.

YORK KNIGHTS 16 WHITEHAVEN 36

KNIGHTS: 1 Will Dagger; 2 Joe Brown; 23 Myles Harrison; 4 Jimmy Keinhorst; 34 Tom Lineham; 14 Nikau Williams; 7 Liam Harris; 8 Ukuma Ta'ai; 9 Will Jubb; 13 Jordan Thompson; 30 Harvey Reynolds; 12 Connor Bailey; 22 Ata Hingano. Subs (all used): 10 Conor Fitzsimmons; 15 Jack Teanby; 19 Josh Daley; 17 Ronan Michael.
Tries: Brown (63), Keinhorst (68), Lineham (73);
Goals: Dagger 2/3.
Sin bin: Dagger (43) - dissent.
WHITEHAVEN: 2 Jake Maizen; 3 Joey Romeo; 5 Curtis Teare; 4 Will Evans; 1 Edene Gebbie; 14 Jake Carter; 7 Lachlan Hanneghan; 10 Guy Graham; 6 Jamie Doran; 17 Ross Ainley; 20 Owen McCarron; 21 Rio Corkill; 11 Ryan King. Subs: 22 Oscar Doran (not used); 28 Brett Bailey; 27 Dan Hindmarsh; 26 Huw Worthington.
Tries: Gebbie (5), Graham (15), King (27), Corkill (40), Romeo (43), Hanneghan (50); **Goals:** Carter 6/7.
Rugby Leaguer & League Express Men of the Match: *Knights:* Harvey Reynolds; *Whitehaven:* Will Evans.
Penalty count: 3-5; **Half-time:** 0-26;
Referee: Cameron Worsley; **Attendance:** 1,698.

ROUND 8

Saturday 18th May 2024

TOULOUSE OLYMPIQUE 38 BARROW RAIDERS 16

OLYMPIQUE: 1 Olly Ashall-Bott; 5 Paul Marcon; 4 Mathieu Jussaume; 3 Reubenn Rennie; 2 Paul Ulberg; 6 Ryan Rivett; 7 Jake Shorrocks; 8 Lambert Belmas; 9 Calum Gahan; 10 Harrison Hansen; 12 Dominique Peyroux; 11 Maxime Stefani; 13 Anthony Marion. Subs (all used): 14 Eloi Pelissier; 17 James Roumanos; 22 Dimitri Biscarro; 24 Pierre-Jean Lima.
Tries: Rennie (10, 36), Stefani (29), Rivett (33, 77), Roumanos (42), Marcon (65); **Goals:** Shorrocks 5/7.
Sin bin: Belmas (15) - dangerous challenge.
RAIDERS: 1 Luke Cresswell; 5 Andrew Bulman; 14 Luke Broadbent; 4 Shane Toal; 21 Jacob Douglas; 6 Brad Walker; 7 Ryan Johnston; 10 Ellis Gillam; 9 Josh Wood; 20 Ramon Silva; 3 Matty Costello; 25 Finn McMillan; 31 Ryan Brown. Subs (all used): 2 Ryan Shaw; 32 Mike Ogunwole; 30 Tom Forber; 33 Delaine Bedward-Gittens.
Tries: Bulman (17), Broadbent (19), B Walker (23);
Goals: Johnston 2/4.
Rugby Leaguer & League Express Men of the Match: *Olympique:* Jake Shorrocks; *Raiders:* Matty Costello.
Penalty count: 4-7; **Half-time:** 22-16;
Referee: Matty Lynn; **Attendance:** 2,313.

Sunday 19th May 2024

BRADFORD BULLS 28 SHEFFIELD EAGLES 10

BULLS: 1 Tom Holmes; 36 Liam Tindall; 37 Jayden Okunbor; 4 Kieran Gill; 24 Aidan McGowan; 31 Tyran Ott; 7 Jordan Lilley; 13 Michael Lawrence; 18 Mitch Souter; 34 Fenton Rogers; 14 John Davies; 29 Zac Fulton; 17 Eribe Doro. Subs (all used): 10 Ebon Scurr; 16 Keven Appo; 30 Eliot Peposhi; 38 Jacob Bateman.
Tries: Fulton (11, 33), Okunbor (22), McGowan (26), Gill (70); **Goals:** Lilley 4/6.
Sin bin: Davies (62) - persistent team offences.
EAGLES: 1 Matty Marsh; 2 Ben Jones-Bishop; 3 Kris Welham; 4 James Glover; 5 Matty Dawson-Jones; 6 Cory Aston; 7 Anthony Thackeray; 8 Eddie Battye; 22 Kyle Wood; 10 Tyler Dickinson; 26 Alex Foster; 27 Jesse Sene-Lefao; 13 Titus Gwaze. Subs (all used): 14 Jack Hansen; 15 Evan Hodgson; 24 Oliver Roberts; 17 Mitch Clark.
Tries: Dawson-Jones (15), Hansen (74); **Goals:** Aston 1/2.
Sin bin: Glover (58) - persistent team offences.
Rugby Leaguer & League Express Men of the Match: *Bulls:* Jayden Okunbor; *Eagles:* Matty Marsh.
Penalty count: 11-9; **Half-time:** 22-6;
Referee: James Vella; **Attendance:** 2,234.

DEWSBURY RAMS 12 FEATHERSTONE ROVERS 46

RAMS: 4 Bailey O'Connor; 19 Travis Corion; 3 Ollie Greensmith; 18 Davey Dixon; 1 Owen Restall; 7 Calum Turner; 9 Jacob Hookem; 8 Jimmy Beckett; 20 Curtis Davies; 16 Elliot Morris; 11 Brad Graham; 12 Matt Garside; 23 Bailey Dawson. Subs (all used): 6 Paul Sykes; 10 Ronan Dixon; 27 Joe Hird; 30 Dale Ferguson.
Tries: Garside (5), Restall (9); **Goals:** Turner 2/2.
Sin bin: Hookem (32) - professional foul.
ROVERS: 24 Charlie Harris; 19 Manoa Wacokecoke; 3 Josh Hardcastle; 4 Greg Minikin; 2 Connor Wynne; 13 Danny Addy; 28 Paul Turner; 15 Wellington Albert; 9 Connor Jones; 10 Nathan Massey; 11 Brad Day; 17 Brad England; 12 Jack Bussey. Subs (all used): 14 Harry Bowes; 18 Mo Kamano; 20 Keenen Tomlinson; 32 Leo Tennison.
Tries: Jones (20, 79), Turner (28, 63), Massey (34), Minikin (38, 54), Bussey (68), England (76);
Goals: Addy 5/9.
Rugby Leaguer & League Express Men of the Match: *Rams:* Owen Restall; *Rovers:* Jack Bussey.
Penalty count: 3-8; **Half-time:** 12-20;
Referee: Cameron Worsley; **Attendance:** 1,150.

DONCASTER 26 BATLEY BULLDOGS 0

DONCASTER: 19 Craig Hall; 5 Luke Briscoe; 3 Brad Hey; 23 Jason Tali; 30 Bureta Faraimo; 24 Watson Boas; 7 Connor Robinson; 20 Brad Knowles; 15 Joe Lovodua; 10 Suaia Matagi; 16 Pauli Pauli; 27 Brett Ferres; 13 Loui McConnell. Subs (all used): 14 Alex Holdstock; 17 Josh Guzdek; 18 Jose Kenga; 21 Tyla Hepi.
Tries: Boas (8), Tali (14), Faraimo (21, 79), Ferres (58);
Goals: C Hall 2/4, Robinson 1/1.
BULLDOGS: 1 Robbie Butterworth; 2 Dale Morton; 4 George Senior; 3 Kieran Buchanan; 18 Joe Burton; 20 Dave Gibbons; 7 Josh Woods; 8 Adam Gledhill; 9 Alistair Leak; 10 Luke Cooper; 11 Dane Manning; 12 Lucas Walshaw; 25 Brandon Moore. Subs (all used): 14 Oli Burton; 15 Nyle Flynn; 16 Michael Ward; 24 John Mitsias.
Rugby Leaguer & League Express Men of the Match: *Doncaster:* Luke Briscoe; *Bulldogs:* Joe Burton.
Penalty count: 4-5; **Half-time:** 16-0;
Referee: Michael Smaill; **Attendance:** 1,236.

WAKEFIELD TRINITY 46 SWINTON LIONS 22

TRINITY: 5 Lachlan Walmsley; 2 Jermaine McGillvary; 4 Iain Thornley; 3 Oliver Pratt; 32 Derrell Olpherts; 1 Max Jowitt; 24 Myles Lawford; 8 Josh Bowden; 21 Thomas Doyle; 10 Renouf Atoni; 20 Toby Boothroyd; 13 Jay Pitts; 14 Liam Kay. Subs (all used): 9 Liam Hood; 16 Mathieu Cozza; 17 Luke Bain; 18 Ky Rodwell.
Tries: Bowden (4), McGillvary (33), Bain (37), Boothroyd (52), Atoni (58), Pitts (70), Rodwell (74), Kay (78); **Goals:** Jowitt 7/8.
LIONS: 23 Joe Purcell; 32 Tee Ritson; 3 Jake Spedding; 28 Brad Hammond; 5 Rhys Williams; 18 Jack Stevens; 7 Jordy Gibson; 34 Lucas Green; 31 Jake Burns; 15 Daniel Spencer-Tonks; 29 Jonny Vaughan; 12 Mitch Cox; 35 Ben Davies. Subs (all used): 24 Jordan Case; 11 Gav Rodden; 1 Dan Abram; 13 Mikey Wood.
Tries: Cox (16, 25), Gibson (29), Purcell (43), Williams (49);
Goals: Davies 1/5.
Rugby Leaguer & League Express Men of the Match: *Trinity:* Liam Hood; *Lions:* Jack Stevens.
Penalty count: 8-3; **Half-time:** 16-12;
Referee: Ryan Cox; **Attendance:** 5,268.

WIDNES VIKINGS 28 WHITEHAVEN 28

VIKINGS: 1 Jack Owens; 20 Mike Butt; 25 Tom Nisbet; 4 Joe Edge; 5 Kieran Dixon; 6 Joe Lyons; 7 Tom Gilmore; 15 Liam Kirk; 14 Jordan Johnstone; 31 Dan Murray; 11 Rhodri Lloyd; 19 Sam Wilde; 8 Callum Field. Subs (all used): 9 Matty Fozard; 10 Sam Brooks; 16 Max Roberts; 17 Liam Bent.
Tries: Butt (18), Johnstone (31), S Wilde (35), Fozard (64), Owens (76); **Goals:** Gilmore 4/5.
WHITEHAVEN: 2 Jake Maizen; 3 Joey Romeo; 5 Curtis Teare; 4 Will Evans; 1 Edene Gebbie; 6 Jamie Doran; 7 Lachlan Hanneghan; 10 Guy Graham; 15 James Newton; 17 Ross Ainley; 20 Owen McCarron; 21 Rio Corkill; 11 Ryan King. Subs: 22 Oscar Doran (not used); 26 Huw Worthington; 27 Dan Hindmarsh; 28 Brett Bailey.
Tries: Maizen (13, 38, 43), Hanneghan (23), Gebbie (53);
Goals: Hanneghan 4/5.
Rugby Leaguer & League Express Men of the Match: *Vikings:* Matty Fozard; *Whitehaven:* Jake Maizen.
Penalty count: 6-3; **Half-time:** 16-18;
Referee: Kevin Moore; **Attendance:** 2,741.

YORK KNIGHTS 40 HALIFAX PANTHERS 18

KNIGHTS: 36 Davy Litten; 2 Joe Brown; 34 Tom Lineham; 4 Jimmy Keinhorst; 5 AJ Towse; 22 Ata Hingano; 20 Taylor Pemberton; 8 Ukuma Ta'ai; 9 Will Jubb; 16 Brenden Santi; 12 Connor Bailey; 3 Jesse Dee; 13 Jordan Thompson. Subs (all used): 10 Conor Fitzsimmons; 15 Jack Teanby; 19 Josh Daley; 39 Franklin Pele.
Tries: Towse (2), Ta'ai (17), Daley (22, 57), Litten (43), Brown (51), Keinhorst (79); **Goals:** Pemberton 6/7.
PANTHERS: 6 Louis Jouffret; 17 Ben Tibbs; 26 Ed Barber; 1 James Woodburn-Hall; 5 James Saltonstall; 23 Gareth Widdop; 7 Joe Keyes; 18 Brandon Douglas; 34 Corey Johnson; 31 Kevin Larroyer; 21 Olly Davies; 12 Matty Gee; 3 Zack McComb. Subs (all used): 8 Adam Tangata; 13 Jacob Fairbank; 15 Ryan Lannon; 22 Ben Hursey.
Tries: Tangata (39), Barber (66), McComb (70);
Goals: Widdop 3/3.
Rugby Leaguer & League Express Men of the Match: *Knights:* Connor Bailey; *Panthers:* Zack McComb.
Penalty count: 6-5; **Half-time:** 16-6;
Referee: Liam Rush; **Attendance:** 1,693.

ROUND 9

Friday 24th May 2024

SHEFFIELD EAGLES 36 DEWSBURY RAMS 13

EAGLES: 1 Matty Marsh; 30 Ryan Millar; 3 Kris Welham; 4 James Glover; 5 Matty Dawson-Jones; 6 Cory Aston; 14 Jack Hansen; 8 Eddie Battye; 9 Vila Halafihi; 17 Mitch Clark; 11 Connor Bower; 12 Joel Farrell; 15 Evan Hodgson. Subs (all used): 22 Kyle Wood; 23 Bayley Liu; 24 Oliver Roberts; 27 Jesse Sene-Lefao.
Tries: Welham (18, 30), J Farrell (50), Marsh (53), Dawson-Jones (60, 64), Bower (77); **Goals:** Aston 4/7.
Sin bin: Dawson-Jones (71) - delaying restart.
RAMS: 4 Bailey O'Connor; 1 Owen Restall; 22 Marcus Walker; 3 Ollie Greensmith; 19 Travis Corion; 7 Calum Turner; 9 Jacob Hookem; 8 Jimmy Beckett; 20 Curtis Davies; 10 Ronan Dixon; 28 Jack Billington; 12 Matt Garside; 13 Louis Collinson. Subs (all used): 16 Elliot Morris; 29 Jack Bibby; 30 Dale Ferguson; 31 Reiss Butterworth.
Tries: O'Connor (7), Billington (36); **Goals:** Turner 2/2;
Field goal: Turner (40).
Rugby Leaguer & League Express Men of the Match: *Eagles:* Joel Farrell; *Rams:* Jack Billington.
Penalty count: 5-5; **Half-time:** 12-13;
Referee: Ryan Cox; **Attendance:** 971.

Saturday 25th May 2024

TOULOUSE OLYMPIQUE 28 WIDNES VIKINGS 20

OLYMPIQUE: 1 Olly Ashall-Bott; 5 Paul Marcon; 4 Mathieu Jussaume; 3 Reubenn Rennie; 2 Paul Ulberg; 7 Jake Shorrocks; 6 Ryan Rivett; 8 Lambert Belmas; 9 Calum Gahan; 10 Harrison Hansen; 12 Dominique Peyroux; 11 Maxime Stefani; 13 Anthony Marion. Subs (all used): 14 Eloi Pelissier; 15 Sitaleki Akauola; 17 James Roumanos; 22 Dimitri Biscarro.
Tries: Marion (9), Ashall-Bott (17), Jussaume (39), Biscarro (50), Peyroux (62); **Goals:** Shorrocks 4/5.
Sin bin: Rennie (68) - high tackle.
VIKINGS: 1 Jack Owens; 20 Mike Butt; 25 Tom Nisbet; 4 Joe Edge; 5 Kieran Dixon; 6 Joe Lyons; 7 Tom Gilmore; 22 Anthony Walker; 9 Matty Fozard; 31 Dan Murray; 11 Rhodri Lloyd; 19 Sam Wilde; 14 Jordan Johnstone. Subs (all used): 10 Sam Brooks; 15 Liam Kirk; 16 Max Roberts; 17 Liam Bent.
Tries: Nisbet (5), Butt (29), Murray (75); **Goals:** Gilmore 4/4.
Rugby Leaguer & League Express Men of the Match: *Olympique:* Mathieu Jussaume; *Vikings:* Tom Nisbet.
Penalty count: 3-7; **Half-time:** 18-14;
Referee: Liam Rush; **Attendance:** 2,130.

Sunday 26th May 2024

BARROW RAIDERS 25 FEATHERSTONE ROVERS 12

RAIDERS: 1 Luke Cresswell; 5 Andrew Bulman; 4 Shane Toal; 14 Luke Broadbent; 21 Jacob Douglas; 6 Brad Walker; 7 Ryan Johnston; 20 Ramon Silva; 9 Josh Wood; 22 Tom Walker; 13 James Greenwood; 12 Jarrad Stack; 3 Matty Costello. Subs (all used): 30 Tom Forber; 31 Ryan Brown; 23 Harvey Makin; 15 Tom Wilkinson.
Tries: Bulman (39, 47), S Toal (59), Broadbent (63);
Goals: Johnston 4/4; **Field goal:** B Walker (68).
ROVERS: 1 Caleb Aekins; 5 Gareth Gale; 3 Josh Hardcastle; 4 Greg Minikin; 2 Connor Wynne; 14 Harry Bowes; 28 Paul Turner; 18 Mo Kamano; 9 Connor Jones; 12 Jack Bussey; 11 Brad Day; 17 Brad England; 13 Danny Addy. Subs (all used): 20 Keenen Tomlinson; 27 Zach Fishwick; 15 Wellington Albert; 19 Manoa Wacokecoke.
Tries: Aekins (18), Turner (53); **Goals:** Addy 2/2.
Rugby Leaguer & League Express Men of the Match: *Raiders:* Ryan Johnston; *Rovers:* Paul Turner.
Penalty count: 9-5; **Half-time:** 6-6;
Referee: Michael Smaill; **Attendance:** 2,311.

BATLEY BULLDOGS 21 BRADFORD BULLS 20

BULLDOGS: 27 Luke Hooley; 3 Kieran Buchanan; 24 John Mitsias; 4 George Senior; 18 Joe Burton; 6 Ben White; 7 Josh Woods; 8 Adam Gledhill; 25 Brandon Moore; 10 Luke Cooper; 11 Dane Manning; 12 Lucas Walshaw; 28 Nixon Putt. Subs (all used): 9 Alistair Leak; 29 Samy Kibula; 15 Nyle Flynn; 16 Michael Ward.
Tries: J Burton (20), White (23), Leak (70);
Goals: Woods 4/4; **Field goal:** Woods (79).

Championship 2024 - Round by Round

BULLS: 1 Tom Holmes; 36 Liam Tindall; 37 Jayden Okunbor; 4 Kieran Gill; 24 Aidan McGowan; 31 Tyran Ott; 7 Jordan Lilley; 34 Fenton Rogers; 18 Mitch Souter; 17 Eribe Doro; 3 Joe Arundel; 29 Zac Fulton; 14 John Davies. Subs (all used): 16 Keven Appo; 10 Ebon Scurr; 30 Eliot Peposhi; 8 Jordan Baldwinson.
Tries: Fulton (11, 14), Holmes (74); **Goals:** Lilley 4/5.
Rugby League & League Express Men of the Match: *Bulldogs:* Alistair Leak; *Bulls:* Zac Fulton.
Penalty count: 4-6; **Half-time:** 12-12;
Referee: Scott Mikalauskas.

HALIFAX PANTHERS 34 DONCASTER 8

PANTHERS: 23 Gareth Widdop; 5 James Saltonstall; 33 Ned McCormack; 3 Zack McComb; 32 Mathieu Pons; 6 Louis Jouffret; 7 Joe Keyes; 8 Adam Tangata; 34 Corey Johnson; 13 Jacob Fairbank; 35 Leon Ruan; 12 Matty Gee; 19 Connor Davies. Subs (all used): 22 Ben Hursey; 18 Brandon Douglas; 31 Kevin Larroyer; 15 Ryan Lannon.
Tries: Keyes (4, 14), Widdop (43), McCormack (63), Larroyer (73); **Goals:** Jouffret 7/7.
DONCASTER: 19 Craig Hall; 5 Luke Briscoe; 3 Brad Hey; 23 Jason Tali; 30 Bureta Faraimo; 6 Ben Johnston; 24 Watson Boas; 20 Brad Knowles; 15 Joe Lovodua; 10 Suaia Matagi; 12 Alex Sutcliffe; 16 Pauli Pauli; 13 Loui McConnell. Subs (all used): 14 Alex Holdstock; 17 Josh Guzdek; 18 Jose Kenga; 21 Tyla Hepi.
Tries: Faraimo (74), Briscoe (78); **Goals:** C Hall 0/2.
Rugby League & League Express Men of the Match: *Panthers:* Ned McCormack; *Doncaster:* Pauli Pauli.
Penalty count: 7-5; **Half-time:** 12-0;
Referee: Andy Sweet; **Attendance:** 1,479.

SWINTON LIONS 22 YORK KNIGHTS 30

LIONS: 1 Dan Abram; 32 Tee Ritson; 3 Jake Spedding; 4 Jayden Hatton; 5 Rhys Williams; 6 Dec Patton; 7 Jordy Gibson; 34 Lucas Green; 14 Josh Eaves; 15 Daniel Spencer-Tonks; 21 Andy Badrock; 11 Gav Rodden; 16 Lewis Hall. Subs: 31 Jake Burns; 24 Jordan Case; 8 Liam Cooper; 28 Brad Hammond (not used).
Tries: Badrock (3, 12), Spedding (15), Burns (32);
Goals: Abram 3/4.
Dismissal: Gibson (65) - shoulder charge on Dagger.
KNIGHTS: 36 Davy Litten; 2 Joe Brown; 12 Connor Bailey; 4 Jimmy Keinhorst; 5 AJ Towse; 22 Ata Hingano; 20 Tyler Pemberton; 8 Ukuma Ta'ai; 9 Will Jubb; 16 Brenden Santi; 3 Jesse Dee; 33 Charlie Severs; 13 Jordan Thompson. Subs (all used): 1 Will Dagger; 10 Conor Fitzsimmons; 19 Josh Daley; 39 Franklin Pele.
Tries: Dee (68), Daley (70, 74), Brown (75), Pele (79);
Goals: Pemberton 5/5.
Sin bin: Dagger (28) - professional foul.
Rugby League & League Express Men of the Match: *Lions:* Jayden Hatton; *Knights:* Josh Daley.
Penalty count: 6-6; **Half-time:** 22-0;
Referee: Matty Lynn; **Attendance:** 844.

WHITEHAVEN 6 WAKEFIELD TRINITY 30

WHITEHAVEN: 1 Edene Gebbie; 3 Joey Romeo; 5 Curtis Teare; 21 Rio Corkill; 22 Oscar Doran; 6 Jamie Doran; 7 Lachlan Hanneghan; 10 Guy Graham; 15 James Newton; 17 Ross Ainley; 20 Owen McCarron; 11 Ryan King; 26 Huw Worthington. Subs (all used): 14 Jake Carter; 8 Lucas Castle; 27 Dan Hindmarsh; 28 Brett Bailey.
Try: Teare (49); **Goals:** Carter 1/1.
TRINITY: 1 Max Jowitt; 2 Jermaine McGillvary; 30 Noah Booth; 3 Oliver Pratt; 32 Derrell Olpherts; 14 Liam Kay; 7 Mason Lino; 8 Josh Bowden; 21 Thomas Doyle; 10 Renouf Atoni; 11 Matty Ashurst; 18 Ky Rodwell; 13 Jay Pitts. Subs (all used): 15 Caleb Uele; 16 Mathieu Cozza; 17 Luke Bain; 26 Harvey Smith.
Tries: Pratt (20), Ashurst (29), Doyle (37), Rodwell (53), McGillvary (65); **Goals:** Jowitt 5/5.
Rugby League & League Express Men of the Match: *Whitehaven:* Jamie Doran; *Trinity:* Mason Lino.
Penalty count: 7-4; **Half-time:** 0-18;
Referee: Kevin Moore; **Attendance:** 1,572.

ROUND 10

Friday 31st May 2024

WAKEFIELD TRINITY 56 DEWSBURY RAMS 0

TRINITY: 30 Noah Booth; 32 Derrell Olpherts; 22 Jack Croft; 3 Oliver Pratt; 5 Lachlan Walmsley; 6 Luke Gale; 7 Mason Lino; 8 Josh Bowden; 9 Liam Hood; 15 Caleb Uele; 13 Jay Pitts; 16 Mathieu Cozza; 14 Liam Kay. Subs (all used): 10 Renouf Atoni; 17 Luke Bain; 18 Ky Rodwell; 21 Thomas Doyle.
Tries: Lino (13), Olpherts (23), Gale (38), Walmsley (46), Rodwell (55), Booth (63), Bowden (68), Pitts (72), Uele (75), Atoni (79); **Goals:** Lino 8/10.
RAMS: 4 Bailey O'Connor; 5 Lewis Carr; 22 Marcus Walker; 3 Ollie Greensmith; 19 Travis Corion; 6 Paul Sykes; 7 Calum Turner; 8 Jimmy Beckett; 33 Reiss Butterworth; 16 Elliot Morris; 28 Jack Billington; 11 Brad Graham; 13 Louis Collinson. Subs (all used): 20 Curtis Davies; 23 Bailey Dawson; 27 Joe Hird; 29 Jack Bibby.
Rugby League & League Express Men of the Match: *Trinity:* Mason Lino; *Rams:* Bailey O'Connor.
Penalty count: 5-7; **Half-time:** 16-0;
Referee: Matty Lynn; **Attendance:** 5,892.

Saturday 1st June 2024

HALIFAX PANTHERS 24 TOULOUSE OLYMPIQUE 38

PANTHERS: 23 Gareth Widdop; 5 James Saltonstall; 1 James Woodburn-Hall; 33 Ned McCormack; 27 Mathieu Pons; 6 Louis Jouffret; 7 Joe Keyes; 8 Adam Tangata; 19 Connor Davies; 13 Jacob Fairbank; 35 Leon Ruan; 12 Matty Gee; 3 Zack McComb. Subs (all used): 9 Adam O'Brien; 15 Ryan Lannon; 26 Ed Barber; 31 Kevin Larroyer.
Tries: Gee (45), Barber (52, 64), Saltonstall (67);
Goals: Jouffret 4/4.
OLYMPIQUE: 23 Robin Brochon; 5 Paul Marcon; 4 Mathieu Jussaume; 3 Reubenn Rennie; 2 Paul Ulberg; 6 Ryan Rivett; 7 Jake Shorrocks; 8 Lambert Belmas; 9 Calum Gahan; 10 Harrison Hansen; 12 Dominique Peyroux; 11 Maxime Stefani; 13 Anthony Marion. Subs (all used): 14 Eloi Pelissier; 17 James Roumanos; 22 Dimitri Biscarro; 24 Pierre-Jean Lima.
Tries: Shorrocks (2), Ulberg (13), Rivett (19), Gahan (23), Marcon (31), Peyroux (79); **Goals:** Shorrocks 7/7.
Rugby League & League Express Men of the Match: *Panthers:* Ed Barber; *Olympique:* Jake Shorrocks.
Penalty count: 9-7; **Half-time:** 0-30;
Referee: James Vella; **Attendance:** 1,347.

Sunday 2nd June 2024

BATLEY BULLDOGS 31 SHEFFIELD EAGLES 18

BULLDOGS: 27 Luke Hooley; 2 Dale Morton; 3 Kieran Buchanan; 4 George Senior; 18 Joe Burton; 6 Ben White; 7 Josh Woods; 8 Adam Gledhill; 25 Brandon Moore; 10 Luke Cooper; 11 Dane Manning; 12 Lucas Walshaw; - Muizz Mustapha. Subs (all used): 9 Alistair Leak; 15 Nyle Flynn; 16 Michael Ward; - George Hill.
Tries: Hooley (18), Walshaw (47, 68), Ward (55), Manning (80); **Goals:** Woods 5/7; **Field goal:** Hooley (72).
Sin bin: Manning (61) - fighting.
EAGLES: 1 Matty Marsh; 2 Ben Jones-Bishop; 23 Bayley Liu; 4 James Glover; 5 Matty Dawson-Jones; 14 Jack Hansen; 7 Anthony Thackeray; 8 Eddie Battye; 9 Vila Halafihi; 10 Tyler Dickinson; 11 Connor Bower; 12 Joel Farrell; 15 Evan Hodgson. Subs (all used): 17 Mitch Clark; 18 Aaron Murphy; 22 Kyle Wood; 27 Jesse Sene-Lefao.
Tries: Glover (3), J Farrell (24), Dawson-Jones (40);
Goals: Hansen 3/3.
Dismissal: Marsh (78) - high tackle.
Sin bin: Liu (61) - fighting.
Rugby League & League Express Men of the Match: *Bulldogs:* Lucas Walshaw; *Eagles:* Joel Farrell.
Penalty count: 7-6; **Half-time:** 4-18;
Referee: Cameron Worsley; **Attendance:** 983.

BRADFORD BULLS 36 BARROW RAIDERS 24

BULLS: 1 Tom Holmes; 37 Jayden Okunbor; 21 Jayden Myers; 4 Kieran Gill; 24 Aidan McGowan; 6 Lee Gaskell; 7 Jordan Lilley; 17 Eribe Doro; 18 Mitch Souter; 34 Fenton Rogers; 12 Chester Butler; 29 Zac Fulton; 16 Keven Appo. Subs (all used): 8 Jordan Baldwinson; 10 Ebon Scurr; 14 John Davies; 31 Tyran Ott.
Tries: Butler (6), Okunbor (12), Fulton (16), Myers (43, 51), Gill (64); **Goals:** Lilley 6/8.
Sin bin: Fulton (79) - retaliation.
RAIDERS: 1 Luke Cresswell; 5 Andrew Bulman; 14 Luke Broadbent; 4 Shane Toal; 2 Ryan Shaw; 6 Brad Walker; 18 Adam Jackson; 22 Tom Walker; 9 Josh Wood; 20 Ramon Silva; 16 Max Clarke; 12 Jarrad Stack; 3 Matty Costello. Subs (all used): 17 Brett Carter; 13 James Greenwood; 10 Ellis Gillam; 15 Tom Wilkinson.
Tries: Clarke (20), Shaw (21), Broadbent (58), Gillam (74);
Goals: Shaw 4/5.
Rugby League & League Express Men of the Match: *Bulls:* Keven Appo; *Raiders:* Ramon Silva.
Penalty count: 4-10; **Half-time:** 16-12;
Referee: Marcus Griffiths; **Attendance:** 2,655.

DONCASTER 25 WHITEHAVEN 25

DONCASTER: 19 Craig Hall; 5 Luke Briscoe; 3 Brad Hey; 23 Jason Tali; 30 Bureta Faraimo; 24 Watson Boas; 7 Connor Robinson; 8 Keelan Foster; 9 Greg Burns; 20 Brad Knowles; 27 Brett Ferres; 12 Alex Sutcliffe; 13 Loui McConnell. Subs (all used): 15 Joe Lovodua; 16 Pauli Pauli; 18 Jose Kenga; - Nathan Wilde.
Tries: Briscoe (37, 62), Pauli (41), Faraimo (48), McConnell (51); **Goals:** Robinson 2/5;
Field goal: Robinson (77).
WHITEHAVEN: 2 Jake Maizen; 1 Edene Gebbie; 3 Joey Romeo; 5 Curtis Teare; 22 Oscar Doran; 14 Jake Carter; 7 Lachlan Hanneghan; 17 Ross Ainley; 15 James Newton; 10 Guy Graham; 20 Owen McCarron; 23 Luca Atkinson; 11 Ryan King. Subs (all used): 6 Jamie Doran; 8 Lucas Castle; 21 Rio Corkill; 26 Huw Worthington.
Tries: Graham (6), Teare (24), Gebbie (39), King (55);
Goals: Carter 4/4; **Field goal:** Carter (78).
Sin bin: Castle (33) - high tackle on Briscoe.
Rugby Leaguer & League Express Men of the Match: *Doncaster:* Greg Burns; *Whitehaven:* Ryan King.
Penalty count: 5-5; **Half-time:** 4-18;
Referee: Ryan Cox; **Attendance:** 1,740.

FEATHERSTONE ROVERS 40 SWINTON LIONS 42

ROVERS: 1 Caleb Aekins; 2 Connor Wynne; 3 Josh Hardcastle; 4 Greg Minikin; 5 Gareth Gale; 13 Danny Addy; 26 Greg Eden; 32 Ben Nakubuwai; 9 Connor Jones; 10 Nathan Massey; 11 Brad Day; 17 Brad England; 12 Jack Bussey. Subs (all used): 14 Harry Bowes; 27 Zach Fishwick; 15 Wellington Albert; 30 Jack Brown.
Tries: Jones (8, 73), England (17), Day (29), Wynne (47), Minikin (50), Addy (55); **Goals:** Addy 6/7.
LIONS: 1 Dan Abram; 32 Tee Ritson; 3 Jake Spedding; 4 Jayden Hatton; 5 Rhys Williams; 6 Dec Patton; 7 Jordy Gibson; 33 Leon Cowen; 35 Denive Balmforth; 15 Daniel Spencer-Tonks; 21 Andy Badrock; 12 Mitch Cox; 16 Lewis Hall. Subs (all used): 14 Josh Eaves; 28 Brad Hammond; 11 Gav Rodden; 29 Jonny Vaughan.
Tries: Hatton (20), Balmforth (25), Spedding (33), Gibson (39), Rodden (61), Cox (63), Badrock (66);
Goals: Patton 7/8.
Rugby Leaguer & League Express Men of the Match: *Rovers:* Danny Addy; *Lions:* Dec Patton.
Penalty count: 6-3; **Half-time:** 18-22;
Referee: Scott Mikalauskas; **Attendance:** 2,200.

YORK KNIGHTS 18 WIDNES VIKINGS 22

KNIGHTS: 20 Taylor Pemberton; 2 Joe Brown; 11 Oli Field; 4 Jimmy Keinhorst; 28 Brad Ward; 22 Ata Hingano; 29 Jack Potter; 8 Ukuma Ta'ai; 9 Will Jubb; 10 Conor Fitzsimmons; 3 Jesse Dee; 12 Connor Bailey; 13 Jordan Thompson. Subs (all used): 15 Jack Teanby; 16 Brenden Santi; 19 Josh Daley; 33 Charlie Severs.
Tries: Fitzsimmons (16), Brown (36), Keinhorst (57);
Goals: Pemberton 3/4.
VIKINGS: 1 Jack Owens; 20 Mike Butt; 3 Matty Fleming; 16 Max Roberts; 5 Kieran Dixon; 6 Joe Lyons; 7 Tom Gilmore; 15 Liam Kirk; 9 Matty Fozard; 31 Dan Murray; 11 Rhodri Lloyd; 19 Sam Wilde; 14 Jordan Johnstone. Subs (all used): 17 Liam Bent; 22 Anthony Walker; 24 Lloyd Roby; 32 Brett Bailey.
Tries: Fozard (51), Dixon (64, 71), Butt (77);
Goals: Gilmore 3/4.
Rugby Leaguer & League Express Men of the Match: *Knights:* Jimmy Keinhorst; *Vikings:* Tom Gilmore.
Penalty count: 4-4; **Half-time:** 14-0;
Referee: Michael Smaill; **Attendance:** 2,163.

ROUND 11

Saturday 15th June 2024

BARROW RAIDERS 28 HALIFAX PANTHERS 38

RAIDERS: 1 Luke Cresswell; 5 Andrew Bulman; 3 Matty Costello; 14 Luke Broadbent; 30 Jacob Douglas; 18 Adam Jackson; 7 Ryan Johnston; 20 Ramon Silva; 9 Josh Wood; 22 Tom Walker; 13 James Greenwood; 12 Jarrad Stack; 31 Greg Worthington. Subs (all used): 2 Ryan Shaw; 10 Ellis Gillam; 15 Tom Wilkinson; 23 Harvey Makin.
Tries: Bulman (4), Cresswell (21, 26, 50), Costello (45);
Goals: Johnston 4/6.
PANTHERS: 1 James Woodburn-Hall; 5 James Saltonstall; 17 Ben Tibbs; 33 Ned McCormack; 28 Charlie Graham; 23 Gareth Widdop; 7 Joe Keyes; 8 Adam Tangata; 6 Louis Jouffret; 13 Jacob Fairbank; 11 Ben Kavanagh; 12 Matty Gee; 19 Connor Davies. Subs (all used): 3 Zack McComb; 9 Adam O'Brien; 15 Ryan Lannon; 29 Clement Boyer.
Tries: Tibbs (8), Keyes (15, 79), Saltonstall (54, 59), Woodburn-Hall (69), McComb (77);
Goals: Keyes 1/2, Jouffret 2/2, Widdop 2/3.
Sin bin: Widdop (49) - dissent.
Rugby Leaguer & League Express Men of the Match: *Raiders:* Luke Cresswell; *Panthers:* Joe Keyes.
Penalty count: 3-6; **Half-time:** 18-12;
Referee: Cameron Worsley; **Attendance:** 1,994.

TOULOUSE OLYMPIQUE 52 DONCASTER 0

OLYMPIQUE: 1 Olly Ashall-Bott; 2 Paul Ulberg; 3 Reubenn Rennie; 4 Mathieu Jussaume; 5 Paul Marcon; 6 Ryan Rivett;

Championship 2024 - Round by Round

7 Jake Shorrocks; 8 Lambert Belmas; 9 Calum Gahan; 10 Harrison Hansen; 11 Maxime Stefani; 12 Dominique Peyroux; 13 Anthony Marion. Subs (all used): 14 Eloi Pelissier; 17 James Roumanos; 22 Dimitri Biscarro; 24 Pierre-Jean Lima.
Tries: Belmas (12), Peyroux (24), Ulberg (34), Ashall-Bott (37), Stefani (49), Roumanos (54), Rivett (57), Marcon (66), Pelissier (75); **Goals:** Shorrocks 8/9.
DONCASTER: 17 Josh Guzdek; 2 Tom Halliday; 19 Craig Hall; 23 Jason Tali; 22 Misi Taulapapa; 6 Ben Johnston; 7 Connor Robinson; 8 Keelan Foster; 9 Greg Burns; 10 Suaia Matagi; 3 Brad Hey; 12 Alex Sutcliffe; 20 Brad Knowles. Subs (all used): 13 Loui McConnell; 15 Joe Lovodua; 16 Pauli Pauli; 18 Jose Kenga.
Rugby Leaguer & League Express Men of the Match: *Olympique:* Jake Shorrocks; *Doncaster:* Connor Robinson.
Penalty count: 6-4; **Half-time:** 24-0;
Referee: Marcus Griffiths; **Attendance:** 2,138.

Sunday 16th June 2024

DEWSBURY RAMS 0 YORK KNIGHTS 40

RAMS: 4 Bailey O'Connor; 5 Lewis Carr; 11 Brad Graham; 3 Ollie Greensmith; 1 Owen Restall; 7 Calum Turner; 31 Kieran Rush; 8 Jimmy Beckett; 20 Curtis Davies; 10 Ronan Dixon; 28 Jack Billington; 12 Matt Garside; 13 Louis Collinson. Subs (all used): 33 Reiss Butterworth; 29 Jack Bibby; 27 Joe Hird; 16 Elliot Morris.
KNIGHTS: 1 Will Dagger; 2 Joe Brown; 14 Nikau Williams; 4 Jimmy Keinhorst; 28 Brad Ward; 22 Ata Hingano; 7 Liam Harris; 8 Ukuma Ta'ai; 9 Will Jubb; 10 Conor Fitzsimmons; 12 Connor Bailey; 11 Oli Field; 13 Jordan Thompson. Subs (all used): 15 Jack Teanby; 16 Brenden Santi; 19 Josh Daley; 40 Sam Cook.
Tries: Ward (16), Hingano (20, 55), Brown (28, 37), Keinhorst (42), Thompson (75), Ta'ai (79);
Goals: Dagger 4/7, Harris 0/1.
Rugby Leaguer & League Express Men of the Match: *Rams:* Reiss Butterworth; *Knights:* Ata Hingano.
Penalty count: 4-5; **Half-time:** 0-18;
Referee: Kevin Moore; **Attendance:** 927.

SHEFFIELD EAGLES 18 FEATHERSTONE ROVERS 16

EAGLES: 2 Ben Jones-Bishop; 30 Ryan Millar; 3 Kris Welham; 4 James Glover; 5 Matty Dawson-Jones; 6 Cory Aston; 14 Jack Hansen; 8 Eddie Battye; 9 Vila Halafihi; 17 Mitch Clark; 26 Alex Foster; 27 Jesse Sene-Lefao; 15 Evan Hodgson. Subs (all used): 11 Connor Bower; 12 Joel Farrell; 13 Titus Gwaze; 22 Kyle Wood.
Tries: Welham (13, 78), Glover (30); **Goals:** Aston 3/3.
ROVERS: 1 Caleb Aekins; 5 Gareth Gale; 31 Connor Barley; 4 Greg Minikin; 26 Greg Eden; 28 Paul Turner; 13 Danny Addy; 8 Gadwin Springer; 9 Connor Jones; 15 Wellington Albert; 30 AJ Wallace; 33 Luis Johnson; 32 Ben Nakubuwai. Subs: 24 Charlie Harris (not used); 27 Zach Fishwick; 34 Leo Tennison; 17 Brad England.
Tries: Jones (20), Gale (52), Turner (65); **Goals:** Addy 2/3.
Rugby Leaguer & League Express Men of the Match: *Eagles:* Kris Welham; *Rovers:* Paul Turner.
Penalty count: 5-4; **Half-time:** 12-6;
Referee: Ryan Cox; **Attendance:** 1,444.

SWINTON LIONS 16 BATLEY BULLDOGS 20

LIONS: 1 Dan Abram; 32 Tee Ritson; 3 Jake Spedding; 4 Jayden Hatton; 5 Rhys Williams; 6 Dec Patton; 30 Will Roberts; 13 Mikey Wood; 14 Josh Eaves; 33 Leon Cowen; 21 Andy Badrock; 12 Mitch Cox; 16 Lewis Hall. Subs (all used): 31 Ciaran Nolan; 11 Gav Rodden; 20 Jack Houghton; 24 Jordan Case.
Tries: Hatton (4, 10), Williams (31); **Goals:** Patton 2/3.
BULLDOGS: 27 Luke Hooley; 3 Kieran Buchanan; 24 John Mitsias; 4 George Senior; 18 Joe Burton; 6 Ben White; 7 Josh Woods; 8 Adam Gledhill; 25 Brandon Moore; 10 Luke Cooper; 11 Dane Manning; 12 Lucas Walshaw; 13 James Brown. Subs (all used): 9 Alistair Leak; 15 Nyle Flynn; 16 Michael Ward; - Muizz Mustapha.
Tries: J Burton (14, 56), Leak (30), Manning (72);
Goals: Woods 2/4.
Rugby Leaguer & League Express Men of the Match: *Lions:* Jayden Hatton; *Bulldogs:* Josh Woods.
Penalty count: 7-6; **Half-time:** 16-10;
Referee: Michael Smaill; **Attendance:** 917.

WHITEHAVEN 18 BRADFORD BULLS 36

WHITEHAVEN: 2 Jake Maizen; 1 Edene Gebbie; 21 Rio Corkill; 5 Curtis Teare; 3 Joey Romeo; 14 Jake Carter; 7 Lachlan Hanneghan; 8 Lucas Castle; 15 James Newton; 17 Ross Ainley; 20 Owen McCarron; 12 Connor Holliday; 11 Ryan King. Subs (all used, only three named): 6 Jamie Doran; 26 Huw Worthington; 27 Dan Hindmarsh.
Tries: Maizen (12), Holliday (27), Romeo (71);
Goals: Carter 3/3.
Sin bin: Gebbie (53) - late challenge on Gill.
BULLS: 1 Tom Holmes; 5 Jorge Taufua; 4 Kieran Gill; 21 Jayden Myers; 37 Jayden Okunbor; 6 Lee Gaskell; 7 Jordan Lilley; 15 Daniel Smith; 18 Mitch Souter; 8 Jordan Baldwinson; 14 John Davies; 29 Zac Fulton; 16 Keven Appo. Subs (all used): 19 Sam Hallas; 34 Fenton Rogers; 10 Ebon Scurr; 31 Tyran Ott.
Tries: Souter (32), Gaskell (49), Taufua (53, 79), Gill (57), Myers (68); **Goals:** Lilley 6/7.
Sin bin: Rogers (64) - high tackle on Ainley.
Rugby Leaguer & League Express Men of the Match: *Whitehaven:* Connor Holliday; *Bulls:* Lee Gaskell.
Penalty count: 5-1; **Half-time:** 12-6; **Referee:** Matty Lynn.

WIDNES VIKINGS 18 WAKEFIELD TRINITY 20

VIKINGS: 1 Jack Owens; 20 Mike Butt; 25 Tom Nisbet; 3 Matty Fleming; 5 Kieran Dixon; 6 Joe Lyons; 7 Tom Gilmore; 15 Liam Kirk; 14 Jordan Johnstone; 31 Dan Murray; 11 Rhodri Lloyd; 19 Sam Wilde; 16 Max Roberts. Subs (all used): 9 Matty Fozard; 10 Sam Brooks; 22 Anthony Walker; 24 Lloyd Roby.
Tries: Lyons (14), S Wilde (69), Lloyd (78);
Goals: Gilmore 3/3.
TRINITY: 1 Max Jowitt; 32 Derrell Olpherts; 22 Jack Croft; 3 Oliver Pratt; 5 Lachlan Walmsley; 6 Luke Gale; 7 Mason Lino; 8 Josh Bowden; 21 Thomas Doyle; 15 Caleb Uele; 11 Matty Ashurst; 12 Josh Griffin; 13 Jay Pitts. Subs (all used): 9 Liam Hood; 10 Renouf Atoni; 14 Liam Kay; 17 Luke Bain.
Tries: Olpherts (22), Atoni (45), Pratt (50), Walmsley (54);
Goals: Jowitt 2/4.
Sin bin: Bain (37) - dissent.
Rugby Leaguer & League Express Men of the Match: *Vikings:* Jordan Johnstone; *Trinity:* Renouf Atoni.
Penalty count: 5-5; **Half-time:** 6-4;
Referee: Scott Mikalauskas; **Attendance:** 4,056.

ROUND 12

Saturday 22nd June 2024

BATLEY BULLDOGS 0 TOULOUSE OLYMPIQUE 36

BULLDOGS: 27 Luke Hooley; 2 Dale Morton; 24 John Mitsias; 4 George Senior; 18 Joe Burton; 6 Ben White; 7 Josh Woods; 8 Adam Gledhill; 25 Brandon Moore; 10 Luke Cooper; 11 Dane Manning; 3 Kieran Buchanan; 28 Nixon Putt. Subs (all used): 13 James Brown; 15 Nyle Flynn; 9 Alistair Leak; 16 Michael Ward.
Sin bin: Gledhill (71) - fighting; Manning (74) - high tackle.
OLYMPIQUE: 1 Olly Ashall-Bott; 5 Paul Marcon; 4 Mathieu Jussaume; 3 Reubenn Rennie; 2 Paul Ulberg; 6 Ryan Rivett; 7 Jake Shorrocks; 8 Lambert Belmas; 14 Eloi Pelissier; 10 Harrison Hansen; 12 Dominique Peyroux; 11 Maxime Stefani; 13 Anthony Marion. Subs (all used): 30 Baptiste Rodriguez; 17 James Roumanos; 22 Dimitri Biscarro; 18 Guy Armitage.
Tries: Stefani (8, 65), Peyroux (14, 20), Jussaume (36), Rivett (80); **Goals:** Shorrocks 6/6.
Sin bin: Belmas (71) - fighting.
Rugby Leaguer & League Express Men of the Match: *Bulldogs:* James Brown; *Olympique:* Olly Ashall-Bott.
Penalty count: 9-8; **Half-time:** 0-24;
Referee: James Vella.

Sunday 23rd June 2024

BRADFORD BULLS 38 DONCASTER 4

BULLS: 1 Tom Holmes; 37 Jayden Okunbor; 21 Jayden Myers; 4 Kieran Gill; 5 Jorge Taufua; 6 Lee Gaskell; 7 Jordan Lilley; 8 Jordan Baldwinson; 18 Mitch Souter; 34 Fenton Rogers; 14 John Davies; 29 Zac Fulton; 19 Sam Hallas. Subs (all used): 10 Ebon Scurr; 16 Keven Appo; 30 Eliot Peposhi; 31 Tyran Ott.
Tries: Davies (10), Souter (24), Gill (30), Okunbor (32), Holmes (36), Appo (47), Lilley (76); **Goals:** Lilley 5/7.
DONCASTER: 19 Craig Hall; 30 Bureta Faraimo; 3 Brad Hey; 23 Jason Tali; 2 Tom Halliday; 6 Ben Johnston; 7 Connor Robinson; 16 Pauli Pauli; 15 Joe Lovodua; 10 Suaia Matagi; 12 Alex Sutcliffe; 27 Brett Ferres; 20 Brad Knowles. Subs (all used): 8 Keelan Foster; 14 Alex Holdstock; 25 Ilikaya Mafi; 22 Misi Taulapapa.
Try: Halliday (52); **Goals:** Robinson 0/1.
Sin bin: Lovodua (56) - high tackle.
Rugby Leaguer & League Express Men of the Match: *Bulls:* Mitch Souter; *Doncaster:* Craig Hall.
Penalty count: 10-5; **Half-time:** 26-0;
Referee: Ryan Cox; **Attendance:** 2,909.

FEATHERSTONE ROVERS 24 YORK KNIGHTS 34

ROVERS: 1 Caleb Aekins; 5 Gareth Gale; 29 Louix Gorman; 4 Greg Minikin; 26 Greg Eden; 28 Paul Turner; 30 Dec Patton; 8 Gadwin Springer; 9 Connor Jones; 32 Ben Nakubuwai; 11 Brad Day; 33 Luis Johnson; 13 Danny Addy. Subs (all used): 14 Harry Bowes; 17 Brad England; 18 Mo Kamano; 27 Zach Fishwick.
Tries: Day (3), Aekins (7), Turner (19, 65); **Goals:** Patton 4/5.
KNIGHTS: 1 Will Dagger; 2 Joe Brown; 14 Nikau Williams; 4 Jimmy Keinhorst; 28 Brad Ward; 7 Liam Harris; 22 Ata Hingano; 8 Ukuma Ta'ai; 9 Will Jubb; 13 Jordan Thompson; 11 Oli Field; 12 Connor Bailey; 38 Jacob Gannon. Subs (all used): 10 Conor Fitzsimmons; 15 Jack Teanby; 16 Brenden Santi; 19 Josh Daley.
Tries: Teanby (26), Brown (45), Daley (55), Ta'ai (60), Hingano (72), Harris (80); **Goals:** Dagger 5/6.
Rugby Leaguer & League Express Men of the Match: *Rovers:* Gareth Gale; *Knights:* Ata Hingano.
Penalty count: 3-2; **Half-time:** 18-6;
Referee: Scott Mikalauskas; **Attendance:** 1,564.

SHEFFIELD EAGLES 30 WIDNES VIKINGS 21

EAGLES: 1 Matty Marsh; 2 Ben Jones-Bishop; 3 Kris Welham; 4 James Glover; 5 Matty Dawson-Jones; 6 Cory Aston; 14 Jack Hansen; 8 Eddie Battye; 9 Vila Halafihi; 17 Mitch Clark; 26 Alex Foster; 27 Jesse Sene-Lefao; 15 Evan Hodgson. Subs (all used): 11 Connor Bower; 12 Joel Farrell; 13 Titus Gwaze; 22 Kyle Wood.
Tries: Welham (26, 77), Bower (46), Glover (61), Halafihi (71); **Goals:** Aston 5/5.
Sin bin: Foster (29) - dangerous challenge on S Wilde.
VIKINGS: 1 Jack Owens; 20 Mike Butt; 3 Matty Fleming; 16 Max Roberts; 21 Ollie Brookes; 6 Joe Lyons; 7 Tom Gilmore; 15 Liam Kirk; 14 Jordan Johnstone; 31 Dan Murray; 11 Rhodri Lloyd; 19 Sam Wilde; 27 Louis Brogan. Subs (all used): 9 Matty Fozard; 10 Sam Brooks; 22 Anthony Walker; 12 Danny Langtree.
Tries: Roberts (9, 66), Owens (17); **Goals:** Gilmore 4/5;
Field goal: Gilmore (40).
Sin bin: Roberts (36) - late challenge;
Fleming (60) - late challenge.
Rugby Leaguer & League Express Men of the Match: *Eagles:* Kris Welham; *Vikings:* Jordan Johnstone.
Penalty count: 11-6; **Half-time:** 6-15;
Referee: Marcus Griffiths; **Attendance:** 1,003.

SWINTON LIONS 10 BARROW RAIDERS 24

LIONS: 2 Matty Chrimes; 32 Tee Ritson; 3 Jake Spedding; 4 Jayden Hatton; 5 Rhys Williams; 30 Will Roberts; 14 Josh Eaves; 24 Jordan Case; 1 Dan Abram; 13 Mikey Wood; 11 Gav Rodden; 12 Mitch Cox; 33 Leon Cowen. Subs (all used): 9 George Roby; 37 Brett Bailey; 20 Jack Houghton; 28 Brad Hammond.
Tries: Hatton (42), Cox (80); **Goals:** Abram 1/2.
Sin bin: Hatton (68) - dangerous challenge.
RAIDERS: 1 Luke Cresswell; 5 Andrew Bulman; 3 Matty Costello; 14 Luke Broadbent; 30 Jacob Douglas; 6 Brad Walker; 7 Ryan Johnston; 10 Ellis Gillam; 9 Josh Wood; 20 Ramon Silva; 13 James Greenwood; 12 Jarrad Stack; 31 Greg Worthington. Subs (all used): 19 Amir Bourouh; 22 Tom Walker; 15 Tom Wilkinson; 23 Harvey Makin.
Tries: Costello (7), Greenwood (35), Makin (38);
Goals: Johnston 6/7.
Rugby Leaguer & League Express Men of the Match: *Lions:* Dan Abram; *Raiders:* Ryan Johnston.
Penalty count: 6-9; **Half-time:** 0-20;
Referee: Kevin Moore; **Attendance:** 945.

WAKEFIELD TRINITY 46 HALIFAX PANTHERS 24

TRINITY: 5 Lachlan Walmsley; 2 Jermaine McGillvary; 22 Jack Croft; 3 Oliver Pratt; 32 Derrell Olpherts; 6 Luke Gale; 1 Max Jowitt; 8 Josh Bowden; 9 Liam Hood; 10 Renouf Atoni; 11 Matty Ashurst; 12 Josh Griffin; 13 Jay Pitts. Subs (all used): 14 Liam Kay; 15 Caleb Uele; 17 Luke Bain; 21 Thomas Doyle.
Tries: Olpherts (12, 18, 61, 64), Pratt (28), Jowitt (37), Walmsley (40), Hood (76); **Goals:** Jowitt 7/8.
PANTHERS: 1 James Woodburn-Hall; 5 James Saltonstall; 26 Ed Barber; 17 Ben Tibbs; 28 Charlie Graham; 6 Louis Jouffret; 7 Joe Keyes; 8 Adam Tangata; 9 Adam O'Brien; 13 Jacob Fairbank; 11 Ben Kavanagh; 12 Matty Gee; 19 Connor Davies. Subs (all used): 23 Gareth Widdop; 31 Kevin Larroyer; 29 Clement Boyer; 3 Zack McComb.
Tries: Graham (7), Widdop (50), Woodburn-Hall (53), Gee (71); **Goals:** Jouffret 4/4.
Rugby Leaguer & League Express Men of the Match: *Trinity:* Derrell Olpherts; *Panthers:* James Woodburn-Hall.
Penalty count: 5-3; **Half-time:** 28-6;
Referee: Matty Lynn; **Attendance:** 6,138.

WHITEHAVEN 38 DEWSBURY RAMS 12

WHITEHAVEN: 3 Joey Romeo; 1 Edene Gebbie; 4 Will Evans; 5 Curtis Teare; 25 Gideon Boafo; 14 Jake Carter; 7 Lachlan Hanneghan; 8 Lucas Castle; 15 James Newton; 17 Ross Ainley; 20 Owen McCarron; 21 Rio Corkill; 11 Ryan King. Subs (all used): 6 Jamie Doran; 26 Huw Worthington; 10 Guy Graham; 16 Noah High.
Tries: Boafo (7, 16), Graham (48), High (54, 66), Gebbie (60), King (71); **Goals:** Carter 5/7.

Championship 2024 - Round by Round

RAMS: 7 Calum Turner; 5 Lewis Carr; 22 Marcus Walker; 4 Bailey O'Connor; 1 Owen Restall; 31 Kieran Rush; 9 Jacob Hookem; 8 Jimmy Beckett; 33 Reiss Butterworth; 17 Jackson Walker; 11 Brad Graham; 28 Jack Billington; 13 Louis Collinson. Subs (all used): 20 Curtis Davies; 10 Ronan Dixon; 29 Jack Bibby; 23 Bailey Dawson.
Tries: Billington (26), Davies (37); **Goals:** Turner 2/2.
Sin bin: Turner (71) - dissent; Rush (73) - dissent.
Rugby Leaguer & League Express Men of the Match: *Whitehaven:* Huw Worthington; *Rams:* Reiss Butterworth.
Penalty count: 7-5; **Half-time:** 8-12;
Referee: Cameron Worsley.

ROUND 13

Saturday 29th June 2024

DONCASTER 18 SWINTON LIONS 8

DONCASTER: 17 Josh Guzdek; 30 Bureta Faraimo; 4 Reece Lyne; 23 Jason Tali; 2 Tom Halliday; 19 Craig Hall; 7 Connor Robinson; 20 Brad Knowles; 15 Joe Lovodua; 10 Suaia Matagi; 27 Brett Ferres; 16 Pauli Pauli; 31 Nathan Wilde. Subs (all used): 3 Brad Hey; 8 Keelan Foster; 24 Watson Boas; 25 Ilikaya Mafi.
Tries: Lyne (50), Faraimo (59), Halliday (72);
Goals: Robinson 3/4.
Sin bin: Ferres (15) - dangerous challenge; Pauli (16) - dangerous challenge.
LIONS: 23 Joe Purcell; 2 Matty Chrimes; 3 Jake Spedding; 4 Jayden Hatton; 5 Rhys Williams; 18 Jack Stevens; 1 Dan Abram; 13 Mikey Wood; 31 Jake Burns; 37 Anthony Walker; 29 Jonny Vaughan; 12 Mitch Cox; 16 Lewis Hall. Subs (all used): 9 George Roby; 21 Andy Badrock; 24 Jordan Case; 36 Jordan Brown.
Try: Purcell (17); **Goals:** Abram 2/2.
Rugby Leaguer & League Express Men of the Match: *Doncaster:* Connor Robinson; *Lions:* Joe Purcell.
Penalty count: 9-9; Half-time: 0-8;
Referee: Cameron Worsley; **Attendance:** 1,056 *(at Millennium Stadium, Featherstone).*

TOULOUSE OLYMPIQUE 20 FEATHERSTONE ROVERS 0

OLYMPIQUE: 1 Olly Ashall-Bott; 5 Paul Marcon; 3 Reubenn Rennie; 4 Mathieu Jussaume; 2 Paul Ulberg; 6 Ryan Rivett; 7 Jake Shorrocks; 8 Lambert Belmas; 9 Calum Gahan; 10 Harrison Hansen; 11 Maxime Stefani; 12 Dominique Peyroux; 13 Anthony Marion. Subs (all used): 14 Eloi Pelissier; 17 James Roumanos; 18 Guy Armitage; 22 Dimitri Biscarro.
Tries: Rennie (5), Rivett (11), Marcon (43);
Goals: Shorrocks 4/5.
Sin bin: Belmas (21) - high tackle on Patton; Marcon (76) - fighting.
ROVERS: 1 Caleb Aekins; 5 Gareth Gale; 28 Paul Turner; 4 Greg Minikin; 26 Greg Eden; 30 Dec Patton; 7 Thomas Lacans; 32 Ben Nakubuwai; 14 Harry Bowes; 18 Mo Kamano; 11 Brad Day; 3 Josh Hardcastle; 13 Danny Addy. Subs (all used): 9 Connor Jones; 8 Gadwin Springer; 17 Brad England; 2 Connor Wynne.
Sin bin: Addy (4) - dangerous challenge; Patton (76) - fighting.
Rugby Leaguer & League Express Men of the Match: *Olympique:* Calum Gahan; *Rovers:* Connor Jones.
Penalty count: 12-9; **Half-time:** 14-0;
Referee: Ryan Cox; **Attendance:** 4,097.

Sunday 30th June 2024

HALIFAX PANTHERS 38 WHITEHAVEN 18

PANTHERS: 1 James Woodburn-Hall; 3 Zack McComb; 26 Ed Barber; 17 Ben Tibbs; 28 Charlie Graham; 6 Louis Jouffret; 7 Joe Keyes; 8 Adam Tangata; 9 Adam O'Brien; 13 Jacob Fairbank; 11 Ben Kavanagh; 12 Matty Gee; 15 Ryan Lannon. Subs (all used): 19 Connor Davies; 23 Gareth Widdop; 29 Clement Boyer; 31 Kevin Larroyer.
Tries: Keyes (32), Tibbs (46), Graham (51, 55), Gee (59), Jouffret (64), Barber (77); **Goals:** Jouffret 5/7.
WHITEHAVEN: 2 Jake Maizen; 3 Joey Romeo; 4 Will Evans; 5 Curtis Teare; 25 Gideon Boafo; 14 Jake Carter; 7 Lachlan Hanneghan; 10 Guy Graham; 15 James Newton; 17 Ross Ainley; 20 Owen McCarron; 21 Rio Corkill; 11 Ryan King. Subs (all used): 6 Jamie Doran; 8 Lucas Castle; 16 Noah High; 26 Huw Worthington.
Tries: Hanneghan (13, 22), Corkill (79); **Goals:** Carter 3/4.
Rugby Leaguer & League Express Men of the Match: *Panthers:* Adam O'Brien; *Whitehaven:* Guy Graham.
Penalty count: 4-4; **Half-time:** 6-14;
Referee: Kevin Moore; **Attendance:** 500 *(at DIY Kitchens Stadium, Wakefield).*

BARROW RAIDERS 0 WAKEFIELD TRINITY 36

RAIDERS: 1 Luke Cresswell; 5 Andrew Bulman; 3 Matty Costello; 14 Luke Broadbent; 2 Ryan Shaw; 6 Brad Walker; 7 Ryan Johnston; 10 Ellis Gillam; 9 Josh Wood; 20 Ramon Silva; 13 James Greenwood; 12 Jarrad Stack; 31 Greg Worthington. Subs (all used): 21 Aaron Smith; 15 Tom Wilkinson; 16 Max Clarke; 22 Tom Walker.
TRINITY: 1 Max Jowitt; 2 Jermaine McGillvary; 22 Jack Croft; 3 Oliver Pratt; 32 Derrell Olpherts; 6 Luke Gale; 14 Liam Kay; 8 Josh Bowden; 9 Liam Hood; 10 Renouf Atoni; 11 Matty Ashurst; 12 Josh Griffin; 13 Jay Pitts. Subs (all used): 5 Lachlan Walmsley; 15 Caleb Uele; 26 Harvey Smith; 17 Luke Bain.
Tries: Pratt (5), Olpherts (15, 46, 56), Pitts (34), Walmsley (60), Griffin (68);
Goals: Jowitt 2/5, Walmsley 2/2.
Sin bin: Croft (25) - persistent offside; Bain (65) - high tackle; Walmsley (71) - high tackle.
Rugby Leaguer & League Express Men of the Match: *Raiders:* Ramon Silva; *Trinity:* Liam Kay.
Penalty count: 11-6; **Half-time:** 0-16;
Referee: Marcus Griffiths; **Attendance:** 2,245.

DEWSBURY RAMS 12 BRADFORD BULLS 38

RAMS: 7 Calum Turner; 5 Lewis Carr; 22 Marcus Walker; 4 Bailey O'Connor; 1 Owen Restall; 6 Paul Sykes; 9 Jacob Hookem; 8 Jimmy Beckett; 33 Reiss Butterworth; 17 Jackson Walker; 11 Brad Graham; 28 Jack Billington; 13 Louis Collinson. Subs (all used): 10 Ronan Dixon; 16 Elliot Morris; 20 Curtis Davies; 29 Jack Bibby.
Tries: Restall (27), R Dixon (79); **Goals:** Turner 1/1, Sykes 1/1.
BULLS: 24 Aidan McGowan; 5 Jorge Taufua; 4 Kieran Gill; 21 Jayden Myers; 39 Max Lehmann; 1 Tom Holmes; 7 Jordan Lilley; 16 Keven Appo; 18 Mitch Souter; 8 Jordan Baldwinson; 14 John Davies; 29 Zac Fulton; 19 Sam Hallas. Subs (all used): 10 Ebon Scurr; 30 Eliot Peposhi; 31 Tyran Ott; 38 Franklin Pele.
Tries: Lehmann (17), Fulton (20, 31), Lilley (52), Holmes (56), Davies (62), Souter (69); **Goals:** Lilley 5/7.
Sin bin: Pele (44) - high tackle on Beckett.
Rugby Leaguer & League Express Men of the Match: *Rams:* Calum Turner; *Bulls:* Tom Holmes.
Penalty count: 10-14; **Half-time:** 6-16;
Referee: Andy Sweet; **Attendance:** 2,151.

WIDNES VIKINGS 16 BATLEY BULLDOGS 24

VIKINGS: 1 Jack Owens; 20 Mike Butt; 3 Matty Fleming; 25 Keanan Brand; 21 Ollie Brookes; 24 Lloyd Roby; 7 Tom Gilmore; 15 Liam Kirk; 14 Jordan Johnstone; 31 Dan Murray; 11 Rhodri Lloyd; 19 Sam Wilde; 13 Nick Gregson. Subs (all used): 9 Matty Fozard; 12 Danny Langtree; 16 Max Roberts; 27 Louis Brogan.
Tries: Butt (10), Owens (14), Fozard (49);
Goals: Gilmore 2/3.
BULLDOGS: 27 Luke Hooley; 2 Dale Morton; 3 Kieran Buchanan; 4 George Senior; 18 Joe Burton; 6 Ben White; 7 Josh Woods; 13 James Brown; 25 Brandon Moore; 10 Luke Cooper; 11 Dane Manning; 12 Lucas Walshaw; 28 Nixon Putt. Subs: 14 Oli Burton; 16 Michael Ward; 24 John Mitsias (not used); 26 Samy Kibula.
Tries: Walshaw (2), Morton (20), Senior (53, 71);
Goals: Woods 4/4.
Sin bin: Putt (10) - high tackle on Murray.
Rugby Leaguer & League Express Men of the Match: *Vikings:* Jordan Johnstone; *Bulldogs:* Ben White.
Penalty count: 8-6; **Half-time:** 10-12;
Referee: Matty Lynn; **Attendance:** 2,476.

YORK KNIGHTS 10 SHEFFIELD EAGLES 18

KNIGHTS: 1 Will Dagger; 2 Joe Brown; 14 Nikau Williams; 4 Jimmy Keinhorst; 28 Brad Ward; 7 Liam Harris; 22 Ata Hingano; 16 Brenden Santi; 9 Will Jubb; 13 Jordan Thompson; 11 Oli Field; 12 Connor Bailey; 38 Jacob Gannon. Subs (all used): 10 Conor Fitzsimmons; 15 Jack Teanby; 17 Ronan Michael; 19 Josh Daley.
Tries: Ward (44), Hingano (73); **Goals:** Dagger 1/2.
EAGLES: 1 Matty Marsh; 2 Ben Jones-Bishop; 3 Kris Welham; 4 James Glover; 5 Matty Dawson-Jones; 6 Cory Aston; 7 Anthony Thackeray; 8 Eddie Battye; 9 Vila Halafihi; 17 Mitch Clark; 26 Alex Foster; 12 Joel Farrell; 15 Evan Hodgson. Subs (all used): 10 Tyler Dickinson; 11 Connor Bower; 13 Titus Gwaze; 22 Kyle Wood.
Tries: Welham (7), Thackeray (32), J Farrell (79);
Goals: Aston 3/3.
Rugby Leaguer & League Express Men of the Match: *Knights:* Jordan Thompson; *Eagles:* Joel Farrell.
Penalty count: 6-4; **Half-time:** 0-12;
Referee: Scott Mikalauskas; **Attendance:** 2,163.

ROUND 14

Friday 5th July 2024

SHEFFIELD EAGLES 28 HALIFAX PANTHERS 0

EAGLES: 1 Matty Marsh; 2 Ben Jones-Bishop; 3 Kris Welham; 23 Bayley Liu; 5 Matty Dawson-Jones; 6 Cory Aston; 7 Anthony Thackeray; 8 Eddie Battye; 9 Vila Halafihi; 10 Tyler Dickinson; 11 Connor Bower; 12 Joel Farrell; 13 Titus Gwaze. Subs (all used): 15 Evan Hodgson; 17 Mitch Clark; 22 Kyle Wood; 27 Jesse Sene-Lefao.
Tries: Jones-Bishop (23, 57), Liu (40), Dawson-Jones (49), Battye (61); **Goals:** Aston 4/6.
Sin bin: J Farrell (34) - fighting.
PANTHERS: 23 Gareth Widdop; 3 Zack McComb; 26 Ed Barber; 1 James Woodburn-Hall; 28 Charlie Graham; 6 Louis Jouffret; 7 Joe Keyes; 8 Adam Tangata; 9 Adam O'Brien; 13 Jacob Fairbank; 11 Ben Kavanagh; 12 Matty Gee; 15 Ryan Lannon. Subs (all used): 25 Corey Johnson; 31 Kevin Larroyer; 19 Connor Davies; 29 Clement Boyer.
Dismissal: McComb (55) - punching Sene-Lefao.
Sin bin: Kavanagh (34) - fighting.
Rugby Leaguer & League Express Men of the Match: *Eagles:* Cory Aston; *Panthers:* Adam O'Brien.
Penalty count: 8-6; **Half-time:** 10-0;
Referee: Cameron Worsley; **Attendance:** 1,023.

Saturday 6th July 2024

TOULOUSE OLYMPIQUE 12 BRADFORD BULLS 12

OLYMPIQUE: 1 Olly Ashall-Bott; 5 Paul Marcon; 3 Reubenn Rennie; 4 Mathieu Jussaume; 2 Paul Ulberg; 6 Ryan Rivett; 7 Jake Shorrocks; 8 Lambert Belmas; 9 Calum Gahan; 10 Harrison Hansen; 11 Maxime Stefani; 12 Dominique Peyroux; 13 Anthony Marion. Subs (all used): 14 Eloi Pelissier; 17 James Roumanos; 18 Guy Armitage; 22 Dimitri Biscarro.
Tries: Rennie (14), Ulberg (63);
Goals: Shorrocks 1/1, Rivett 1/1.
BULLS: 1 Tom Holmes; 37 Jayden Okunbor; 39 Max Lehmann; 4 Kieran Gill; 5 Jorge Taufua; 31 Tyran Ott; 7 Jordan Lilley; 40 Logan Bayliss-Brow; 18 Mitch Souter; 8 Jordan Baldwinson; 29 Zac Fulton; 14 John Davies; 17 Eribe Doro. Subs (all used): 38 Franklin Pele; 19 Sam Hallas; 10 Ebon Scurr; 34 Fenton Rogers.
Tries: Fulton (31), Lehmann (36); **Goals:** Lilley 2/2.
Sin bin: Taufua (6) - high tackle on Jussaume; Doro (54) - dangerous challenge on Shorrocks.
Rugby Leaguer & League Express Men of the Match: *Olympique:* Ryan Rivett; *Bulls:* Jordan Lilley.
Penalty count: 7-3; **Half-time:** 6-12;
Referee: James Vella; **Attendance:** 2,340.

Sunday 7th July 2024

DEWSBURY RAMS 16 DONCASTER 20

RAMS: 4 Bailey O'Connor; 5 Lewis Carr; 11 Brad Graham; 22 Marcus Walker; 1 Owen Restall; 6 Paul Sykes; 9 Jacob Hookem; 17 Jackson Walker; 33 Reiss Butterworth; 10 Ronan Dixon; 30 Dale Ferguson; 12 Matt Garside; 8 Jimmy Beckett. Subs (all used): 20 Curtis Davies; 29 Jack Bibby; 16 Elliot Morris; 13 Louis Collinson.
Tries: O'Connor (28), Sykes (36);
Goals: Sykes 1/1, Hookem 1/1, O'Connor 2/2.
DONCASTER: 17 Josh Guzdek; 2 Tom Halliday; 4 Reece Lyne; 23 Jason Tali; 30 Bureta Faraimo; 19 Craig Hall; 7 Connor Robinson; 20 Brad Knowles; 15 Joe Lovodua; 10 Suaia Matagi; 16 Pauli Pauli; 27 Brett Ferres; 31 Nathan Wilde. Subs (all used): 24 Watson Boas; 8 Keelan Foster; 13 Loui McConnell; 3 Brad Hey.
Tries: Tali (29), Pauli (44), Guzdek (60);
Goals: Robinson 4/5.
Rugby Leaguer & League Express Men of the Match: *Rams:* Dale Ferguson; *Doncaster:* Watson Boas.
Penalty count: 8-5; **Half-time:** 14-4;
Referee: Matty Lynn; **Attendance:** 853.

FEATHERSTONE ROVERS 66 WHITEHAVEN 0

ROVERS: 1 Caleb Aekins; 5 Gareth Gale; 31 Connor Barley; 4 Greg Minikin; 2 Connor Wynne; 28 Paul Turner; 30 Dec Patton; 34 Leo Tennison; 14 Harry Bowes; 8 Gadwin Springer; 11 Brad Day; 3 Josh Hardcastle; 13 Danny Addy. Subs (all used): 9 Connor Jones; 18 Mo Kamano; 32 Ben Nakubuwai; 33 Toby Warren.
Tries: Barley (14), Aekins (16, 68), Hardcastle (22), Day (24, 27, 59), Patton (42), Gale (74), Wynne (77), Addy (80); **Goals:** Patton 11/11.
Sin bin: Hardcastle (62) - late challenge.
WHITEHAVEN: 2 Jake Maizen; 3 Joey Romeo; 4 Will Evans; 21 Rio Corkill; 1 Edene Gebbie; 14 Jake Carter; 7 Lachlan Hanneghan; 8 Lucas Castle; 15 James Newton; 17 Ross Ainley; 20 Owen McCarron; 25 AJ Wallace; 11 Ryan King. Subs (all used): 10 Guy Graham; 16 Noah High; 24 Lennie Ellis; 26 Huw Worthington.
Sin bin: Gebbie (10) - dissent, (66) - high tackle.
Rugby Leaguer & League Express Men of the Match: *Rovers:* Dec Patton; *Whitehaven:* Ryan King.
Penalty count: 7-11; **Half-time:** 30-0;
Referee: Kevin Moore; **Attendance:** 1,605.

Championship 2024 - Round by Round

SWINTON LIONS 24 WIDNES VIKINGS 12

LIONS: 1 Dan Abram; 25 Richard Lepori; 3 Jake Spedding; 4 Jayden Hatton; 5 Rhys Williams; 16 Lewis Hall; 29 Kai Morgan; 31 Daniel Okoro; 9 George Roby; 20 Jack Houghton; 11 Gav Rodden; 21 Andy Badrock; 13 Mikey Wood. Subs (all used): 35 Ben Hartill; 12 Mitch Cox; 33 Leon Cowen; 24 Jordan Case.
Tries: Williams (46, 78), Rodden (53), Hatton (61);
Goals: Abram 4/6.
Sin bin: Roby (31) - use of the elbow.
VIKINGS: 1 Jack Owens; 20 Mike Butt; 25 Keanan Brand; 11 Rhodri Lloyd; 21 Ollie Brookes; 6 Joe Lyons; 7 Tom Gilmore; 15 Liam Kirk; 9 Matty Fozard; 31 Dan Murray; 19 Sam Wilde; 12 Danny Langtree; 13 Nick Gregson. Subs (all used): 14 Jordan Johnstone; 10 Sam Brooks; 17 Liam Bent; 27 Louis Brogan. 18th man (used): 24 Lloyd Roby.
Tries: Langtree (16), Gregson (20); **Goals:** Gilmore 2/2.
Sin bin: Brooks (71) - dangerous challenge.
Rugby Leaguer & League Express Men of the Match: *Lions:* Rhys Williams; *Vikings:* Tom Gilmore.
Penalty count: 5-6; **Half-time:** 0-12;
Referee: Liam Rush; **Attendance:** 1,069.

WAKEFIELD TRINITY 34 BATLEY BULLDOGS 12

TRINITY: 1 Max Jowitt; 5 Lachlan Walmsley; 4 Iain Thornley; 3 Oliver Pratt; 32 Derrell Olpherts; 6 Luke Gale; 14 Liam Kay; 18 Ky Rodwell; 26 Harvey Smith; 17 Luke Bain; 11 Matty Ashurst; 12 Josh Griffin; 13 Jay Pitts. Subs (all used): 15 Caleb Uele; 22 Jack Croft; 25 Isaac Shaw; 30 Noah Booth.
Tries: Olpherts (7, 75), Uele (46), Pratt (55), Kay (60), Griffin (80); **Goals:** Jowitt 5/6.
BULLDOGS: 1 Robbie Butterworth; 2 Dale Morton; 3 Kieran Buchanan; 4 George Senior; 18 Joe Burton; 6 Ben White; 27 Luke Hooley; 8 Adam Gledhill; 25 Brandon Moore; 10 Luke Cooper; 11 Dane Manning; 12 Lucas Walshaw; 13 James Brown. Subs (all used): 14 Oli Burton; 15 Nyle Flynn; 16 Michael Ward; - Samy Kibula.
Tries: Morton (29), Moore (36); **Goals:** Hooley 2/2.
Rugby Leaguer & League Express Men of the Match: *Trinity:* Max Jowitt; *Bulldogs:* Luke Hooley.
Penalty count: 3-6; **Half-time:** 6-12;
Referee: Scott Mikalauskas; **Attendance:** 5,112.

YORK KNIGHTS 54 BARROW RAIDERS 12

KNIGHTS: 1 Will Dagger; 2 Joe Brown; 14 Nikau Williams; 11 Oli Field; 28 Brad Ward; 22 Ata Hingano; 7 Liam Harris; 10 Conor Fitzsimmons; 40 Sam Cook; 13 Jordan Thompson; 38 Jacob Gannon; 12 Connor Bailey; 21 James Cunningham. Subs (all used): 15 Jack Teanby; 17 Ronan Michael; 19 Josh Daley; 30 Harvey Reynolds.
Tries: Brown (6, 11), Cook (18), Ward (27), Bailey (31), Teanby (35), Field (44), Harris (47, 63), Williams (76);
Goals: Dagger 7/11.
Sin bin: Brown (39) - professional foul.
RAIDERS: 1 Luke Cresswell; 5 Andrew Bulman; 3 Matty Costello; 14 Luke Broadbent; 30 Jacob Douglas; 6 Brad Walker; 7 Ryan Johnston; 10 Ellis Gillam; 9 Josh Wood; 20 Ramon Silva; 16 Max Clarke; 12 Jarrad Stack; 31 Greg Worthington. Subs (all used): 21 Aaron Smith; 23 Ryan Brown; 25 Harvey Makin; 26 Kavan Rothwell.
Tries: Stack (22), Bulman (70); **Goals:** Johnston 2/2.
Rugby Leaguer & League Express Men of the Match: *Knights:* Nikau Williams; *Raiders:* Jarrad Stack.
Penalty count: 5-4; **Half-time:** 32-6;
Referee: Ryan Cox; **Attendance:** 1,792.

ROUND 15

Saturday 13th July 2024

WHITEHAVEN 24 TOULOUSE OLYMPIQUE 34

WHITEHAVEN: 2 Jake Maizen; 3 Joey Romeo; 5 Curtis Teare; 4 Will Evans; 1 Edene Gebbie; 11 Ryan King; 7 Lachlan Hanneghan; 8 Lucas Castle; 15 James Newton; 17 Ross Ainley; 27 Lewis Baxter; 25 AJ Wallace; 26 Huw Worthington. Subs (all used): 24 Lennie Ellis; 10 Guy Graham; 16 Noah High; 18 Perry Singleton.
Tries: Wallace (14), King (26), Teare (30), Maizen (63);
Goals: Hanneghan 4/5.
Sin bin: Teare (65) - late challenge.
OLYMPIQUE: 1 Olly Ashall-Bott; 19 Benjamin Laguerre; 18 Guy Armitage; 3 Reubenn Rennie; 2 Paul Ulberg; 23 Robin Brochon; 6 Ryan Rivett; 8 Lambert Belmas; 9 Calum Gahan; 10 Harrison Hansen; 11 Maxime Stefani; 12 Dominique Peyroux; 13 Anthony Marion. Subs (all used): 26 Paolo Dall'asta; 20 Greg Richards; 22 Dimitri Biscarro; 24 Pierre-Jean Lima.
Tries: Peyroux (39, 53), Biscarro (43), Rennie (65), Ulberg (69), Dall'asta (73); **Goals:** Rivett 1/1, Brochon 4/6.
Sin bin: Ulberg (21) - retaliation, (57) - professional foul.
Rugby Leaguer & League Express Men of the Match: *Whitehaven:* AJ Wallace; *Olympique:* Calum Gahan.
Penalty count: 5-6; **Half-time:** 18-6;
Referee: Nick Bennett; **Attendance:** 331.

Sunday 14th July 2024

BATLEY BULLDOGS 22 BARROW RAIDERS 2

BULLDOGS: 27 Luke Hooley; 5 Elliot Kear; 24 John Mitsias; 4 George Senior; 18 Joe Burton; 6 Ben White; 7 Josh Woods; 8 Adam Gledhill; 25 Brandon Moore; 10 Luke Cooper; 3 Kieran Buchanan; 12 Lucas Walshaw; 13 James Brown. Subs (all used): 1 Robbie Butterworth; 14 Oli Burton; 15 Nyle Flynn; 26 Samy Kibula.
Tries: J Burton (16), Buchanan (47), Hooley (72), Mitsias (78); **Goals:** Woods 3/4.
RAIDERS: 1 Luke Cresswell; 5 Andrew Bulman; 3 Matty Costello; 14 Luke Broadbent; 2 Ryan Shaw; 6 Brad Walker; 7 Ryan Johnston; 10 Ellis Gillam; 9 Josh Wood; 20 Ramon Silva; 13 James Greenwood; 12 Jarrad Stack; 31 Greg Worthington. Subs (all used): 21 Aaron Smith; 15 Tom Wilkinson; 26 Kavan Rothwell; 17 Brett Carter.
Goals: Shaw 1/1.
Rugby Leaguer & League Express Men of the Match: *Bulldogs:* Luke Hooley; *Raiders:* Ryan Johnston.
Penalty count: 7-7; **Half-time:** 4-2;
Referee: Michael Smaill.

BRADFORD BULLS 2 WAKEFIELD TRINITY 14

BULLS: 1 Tom Holmes; 37 Jayden Okunbor; 39 Max Lehmann; 4 Kieran Gill; 5 Jorge Taufua; 31 Tyran Ott; 7 Jordan Lilley; 40 Logan Bayliss-Brow; 18 Mitch Souter; 17 Eribe Doro; 14 John Davies; 29 Zac Fulton; 19 Sam Hallas. Subs (all used): 10 Ebon Scurr; 16 Keven Appo; 30 Eliot Peposhi; 41 Nathan Mason.
Goals: Lilley 1/1.
Sin bin: Doro (60) - high tackle.
TRINITY: 1 Max Jowitt; 5 Lachlan Walmsley; 22 Jack Croft; 3 Oliver Pratt; 32 Derrell Olpherts; 6 Luke Gale; 14 Liam Kay; 18 Ky Rodwell; 21 Thomas Doyle; 11 Matty Ashurst; 4 Iain Thornley; 12 Josh Griffin; 13 Jay Pitts. Subs: 15 Caleb Uele; 25 Isaac Shaw; 26 Harvey Smith; 30 Noah Booth (not used).
Try: Pratt (28); **Goals:** Jowitt 5/5.
Rugby Leaguer & League Express Men of the Match: *Bulls:* Jayden Okunbor; *Trinity:* Thomas Doyle.
Penalty count: 8-12; **Half-time:** 2-8;
Referee: Marcus Griffiths; **Attendance:** 3,203.

HALIFAX PANTHERS 6 FEATHERSTONE ROVERS 14

PANTHERS: 1 James Woodburn-Hall; 3 Zack McComb; 26 Ed Barber; 4 Ben Crooks; 28 Charlie Graham; 6 Louis Jouffret; 7 Joe Keyes; 8 Adam Tangata; 25 Corey Johnson; 13 Jacob Fairbank; 11 Ben Kavanagh; 12 Matty Gee; 19 Connor Davies. Subs (all used): 15 Ryan Lannon; 20 Tom Inman; 29 Clement Boyer; 31 Kevin Larroyer.
Try: Kavanagh (44); **Goals:** Jouffret 1/1.
Sin bin: Fairbank (56) - dangerous contact on Wynne.
ROVERS: 26 Greg Eden; 5 Gareth Gale; 31 Connor Barley; 4 Greg Minikin; 2 Connor Wynne; 1 Caleb Aekins; 6 Ben Reynolds; 10 Nathan Massey; 9 Connor Jones; 18 Mo Kamano; 11 Brad Day; 3 Josh Hardcastle; 35 Zeus Silk. Subs: 14 Harry Bowes; 17 Brad England; 28 Paul Turner (not used); 32 Ben Nakubuwai.
Tries: Day (8), Barley (33); **Goals:** Reynolds 3/3.
Sin bin: England (51) - dangerous challenge.
Rugby Leaguer & League Express Men of the Match: *Panthers:* Louis Jouffret; *Rovers:* Connor Jones.
Penalty count: 10-10; **Half-time:** 0-14;
Referee: Liam Rush; **Attendance:** 1,760.

SHEFFIELD EAGLES 22 SWINTON LIONS 34

EAGLES: 1 Matty Marsh; 2 Ben Jones-Bishop; 3 Kris Welham; 23 Bayley Liu; 5 Matty Dawson-Jones; 6 Cory Aston; 19 Izaac Farrell; 8 Eddie Battye; 9 Vila Halafihi; 10 Tyler Dickinson; 11 Connor Bower; 12 Joel Farrell; 13 Titus Gwaze. Subs (all used): 15 Evan Hodgson; 18 Aaron Murphy; 22 Kyle Wood; 27 Jesse Sene-Lefao.
Tries: J Farrell (9), Dawson-Jones (56), I Farrell (64), Gwaze (79); **Goals:** Aston 3/4.
LIONS: 1 Dan Abram; 25 Richard Lepori; 3 Jake Spedding; 4 Jayden Hatton; 5 Rhys Williams; 16 Lewis Hall; 7 Jordy Gibson; 36 Jordan Brown; 9 George Roby; 20 Jack Houghton; 11 Gav Rodden; 21 Andy Badrock; 12 Mitch Cox. Subs (all used): 8 Liam Cooper; 24 Jordan Case; 26 Anthony Walker; 28 Brad Hammond.
Tries: Rodden (2, 26), Walker (40, 50), Gibson (77), Spedding (80); **Goals:** Abram 5/6.
Rugby Leaguer & League Express Men of the Match: *Eagles:* Joel Farrell; *Lions:* Gav Rodden.
Penalty count: 8-6; **Half-time:** 6-18;
Referee: Scott Mikalauskas *(replaced by Nick Bennett, 67)*;
Attendance: 1,063.

WIDNES VIKINGS 34 DEWSBURY RAMS 12

VIKINGS: 1 Jack Owens; 20 Mike Butt; 29 Zac Bardsley-Rowe; 25 Keanan Brand; 2 Ryan Ince; 6 Joe Lyons; 7 Tom Gilmore; 26 Jordan Williams; 14 Jordan Johnstone; 31 Dan Murray; 11 Rhodri Lloyd; 19 Sam Wilde; 16 Max Roberts. Subs (all used): 8 Callum Field; 9 Matty Fozard; 10 Sam Brooks; 27 Louis Brogan.
Tries: S Wilde (26, 77), Fozard (36, 78), Lloyd (49), Butt (63); **Goals:** Gilmore 5/6.
Sin bin: Brooks (58) - use of the elbow.
RAMS: 4 Bailey O'Connor; 5 Lewis Carr; 22 Marcus Walker; 11 Brad Graham; 1 Owen Restall; 7 Calum Turner; 9 Jacob Hookem; 8 Jimmy Beckett; 33 Reiss Butterworth; 16 Elliot Morris; 30 Dale Ferguson; 12 Matt Garside; 13 Louis Collinson. Subs (all used): 10 Ronan Dixon; 15 Joe Summers; 20 Curtis Davies; 29 Jack Bibby.
Tries: Carr (12, 44); **Goals:** Turner 2/2.
Sin bin: Garside (57) - high tackle on Gilmore.
Rugby Leaguer & League Express Men of the Match: *Vikings:* Matty Fozard; *Rams:* Reiss Butterworth.
Penalty count: 5-6; **Half-time:** 12-6;
Referee: Kevin Moore; **Attendance:** 2,337.

YORK KNIGHTS 27 DONCASTER 0

KNIGHTS: 1 Will Dagger; 2 Joe Brown; 14 Nikau Williams; 4 Jimmy Keinhorst; 28 Brad Ward; 22 Ata Hingano; 7 Liam Harris; 10 Conor Fitzsimmons; 40 Sam Cook; 13 Jordan Thompson; 38 Jacob Gannon; 12 Connor Bailey; 21 James Cunningham. Subs (all used): 11 Oli Field; 15 Jack Teanby; 17 Ronan Michael; 19 Josh Daley.
Tries: Cook (9), Brown (37, 73), Field (47);
Goals: Dagger 5/6; **Field goal:** Dagger (80).
DONCASTER: 17 Josh Guzdek; 5 Luke Briscoe; 4 Reece Lyne; 23 Jason Tali; 30 Bureta Faraimo; 24 Watson Boas; 7 Connor Robinson; 20 Brad Knowles; 15 Joe Lovodua; 10 Suaia Matagi; 3 Brad Hey; 27 Brett Ferres; 31 Nathan Wilde. Subs (all used): 8 Keelan Foster; 13 Loui McConnell; 19 Craig Hall; 25 Ilikaya Mafi.
Sin bin: Robinson (29) - high tackle on Dagger.
Rugby Leaguer & League Express Men of the Match: *Knights:* Ata Hingano; *Doncaster:* Brad Hey.
Penalty count: 6-4; **Half-time:** 12-0;
Referee: Cameron Worsley; **Attendance:** 1,902.

ROUND 16

Saturday 20th July 2024

TOULOUSE OLYMPIQUE 32 WAKEFIELD TRINITY 4

OLYMPIQUE: 1 Olly Ashall-Bott; 5 Paul Marcon; 4 Mathieu Jussaume; 3 Reubenn Rennie; 2 Paul Ulberg; 23 Robin Brochon; 6 Ryan Rivett; 17 James Roumanos; 9 Calum Gahan; 10 Harrison Hansen; 12 Dominique Peyroux; 11 Maxime Stefani; 13 Anthony Marion. Subs (all used): 26 Paolo Dall'asta; 20 Greg Richards; 24 Pierre-Jean Lima; 18 Guy Armitage.
Tries: Ashall-Bott (13, 26, 39), Ulberg (34, 75), Rennie (63);
Goals: Brochon 4/7.
TRINITY: 1 Max Jowitt; 5 Lachlan Walmsley; 4 Iain Thornley; 3 Oliver Pratt; 32 Derrell Olpherts; 14 Liam Kay; 6 Luke Gale; 8 Josh Bowden; 9 Liam Hood; 18 Ky Rodwell; 11 Matty Ashurst; 12 Josh Griffin; 13 Jay Pitts. Subs (all used): 21 Thomas Doyle; 15 Caleb Uele; 22 Jack Croft; 17 Luke Bain.
Try: Olpherts (45); **Goals:** Jowitt 0/1.
Sin bin: Croft (31) - dangerous challenge.
Rugby Leaguer & League Express Men of the Match: *Olympique:* Olly Ashall-Bott; *Trinity:* Caleb Uele.
Penalty count: 6-4; **Half-time:** 20-0;
Referee: Tom Grant; **Attendance:** 2,822.

FEATHERSTONE ROVERS 12 DONCASTER 24

ROVERS: 26 Greg Eden; 29 Louix Gorman; 31 Connor Barley; 4 Greg Minikin; 2 Connor Wynne; 6 Ben Reynolds; 1 Caleb Aekins; 32 Ben Nakubuwai; 14 Harry Bowes; 35 Zeus Silk; 11 Brad Day; 33 Toby Warren; 13 Danny Addy. Subs (all used): 9 Connor Jones; 8 Gadwin Springer; 18 Mo Kamano; 23 Jack Arnold.
Tries: Day (15), Wynne (80); **Goals:** Reynolds 2/2.
DONCASTER: 19 Craig Hall; 5 Luke Briscoe; 4 Reece Lyne; 3 Brad Hey; 30 Bureta Faraimo; 24 Watson Boas; 7 Connor Robinson; 20 Brad Knowles; 9 Greg Burns; 10 Suaia Matagi; 11 Sam Smeaton; 27 Brett Ferres; 31 Nathan Wilde. Subs (all used): 15 Joe Lovodua; 16 Pauli Pauli; 28 AJ Wallace; 13 Loui McConnell.
Tries: Hey (9), Faraimo (22, 46), Lyne (29);
Goals: Robinson 3/4, C Hall 1/1.
Rugby Leaguer & League Express Men of the Match: *Rovers:* Brad Day; *Doncaster:* Bureta Faraimo.
Penalty count: 4-6; **Half-time:** 6-16;
Referee: Michael Smaill.

Championship 2024 - Round by Round

Sunday 21st July 2024

BARROW RAIDERS 8 SHEFFIELD EAGLES 6

RAIDERS: 1 Luke Cresswell; 30 Reagan Sumner; 14 Luke Broadbent; 4 Shane Toal; 2 Ryan Shaw; 6 Brad Walker; 3 Matty Costello; 20 Ramon Silva; 21 Aaron Smith; 10 Ellis Gillam; 13 James Greenwood; 12 Jarrad Stack; 19 Greg Worthington. Subs (all used): 9 Josh Wood; 31 Kavan Rothwell; 32 Ryan Brown; 22 Tom Walker.
Try: Cresswell (22); **Goals:** Shaw 2/3.
EAGLES: 1 Matty Marsh; 2 Ben Jones-Bishop; 3 Kris Welham; 21 Ryan Johnson; 5 Matty Dawson-Jones; 6 Cory Aston; 14 Jack Hansen; 8 Eddie Battye; 9 Vila Halafihi; 10 Tyler Dickinson; 11 Connor Bower; 12 Joel Farrell; 13 Titus Gwaze. Subs (all used): 22 Kyle Wood; 16 Blake Broadbent; 27 Jesse Sene-Lefao; 26 Alex Foster.
Try: J Farrell (34); **Goals:** Aston 1/1.
Sin bin: Battye (44) - dissent.
Rugby Leaguer & League Express Men of the Match: *Raiders:* Ramon Silva; *Eagles:* Joel Farrell.
Penalty count: 5-7; **Half-time:** 6-6;
Referee: Brad Milligan; **Attendance:** 1,552.

BATLEY BULLDOGS 29 DEWSBURY RAMS 22

BULLDOGS: 27 Luke Hooley; 5 Elliot Kear; 24 John Mitsias; 4 George Senior; 18 Joe Burton; 6 Ben White; 7 Josh Woods; 8 Adam Gledhill; 25 Brandon Moore; 10 Luke Cooper; 3 Kieran Buchanan; 12 Lucas Walshaw; 13 James Brown. Subs (all used): 14 Oli Burton; 15 Nyle Flynn; 17 Luke Blake; 26 Samy Kibula.
Tries: Moore (8), White (28), J Burton (37, 66), Hooley (74); **Goals:** Woods 4/5; **Field goal:** Woods (40).
RAMS: 4 Bailey O'Connor; 5 Lewis Carr; 22 Marcus Walker; 11 Brad Graham; 1 Owen Restall; 7 Calum Turner; 9 Jacob Hookem; 8 Jimmy Beckett; 33 Reiss Butterworth; 17 Jackson Walker; 30 Dale Ferguson; 12 Matt Garside; 13 Louis Collinson. Subs (all used): 2 Perry Whiteley; 10 Ronan Dixon; 15 Joe Summers; 16 Elliot Morris.
Tries: Carr (12, 47), Restall (51), Butterworth (54); **Goals:** Turner 3/5.
Rugby Leaguer & League Express Men of the Match: *Bulldogs:* Joe Burton; *Rams:* Reiss Butterworth.
Penalty count: 7-3; **Half-time:** 19-6; **Referee:** Ryan Cox.

BRADFORD BULLS 36 YORK KNIGHTS 28

BULLS: 1 Tom Holmes; 39 Max Lehmann; 21 Jayden Myers; 4 Kieran Gill; 36 Liam Tindall; 31 Tyran Ott; 7 Jordan Lilley; 40 Logan Bayliss-Brow; 18 Mitch Souter; 17 Eribe Doro; 29 Zac Fulton; 14 John Davies; 19 Sam Hallas. Subs (all used): 16 Keven Appo; 30 Eliot Peposhi; 42 Franklin Pele; 43 Harvey Makin.
Tries: Lehmann (4), Myers (22), Gill (25, 33), Davies (45), Doro (61), Fulton (77); **Goals:** Lilley 4/7.
KNIGHTS: 14 Nikau Williams; 28 Brad Ward; 4 Jimmy Keinhorst; 11 Oli Field; 2 Joe Brown; 29 Jack Potter; 40 Sam Cook; 13 Jordan Thompson; 9 Will Jubb; 16 Brenden Santi; 12 Connor Bailey; 38 Jacob Gannon; 21 James Cunningham. Subs (all used): 10 Conor Fitzsimmons; 15 Jack Teanby; 17 Ronan Michael; 19 Josh Daley.
Tries: Ward (11), Bailey (15), Cook (66, 70), Keinhorst (75); **Goals:** Potter 4/5.
Sin bin: Williams (31) - high tackle on Myers.
Rugby Leaguer & League Express Men of the Match: *Bulls:* Mitch Souter; *Knights:* Sam Cook.
Penalty count: 10-6; **Half-time:** 18-10;
Referee: Matty Lynn; **Attendance:** 3,025.

HALIFAX PANTHERS 20 WIDNES VIKINGS 24

PANTHERS: 1 James Woodburn-Hall; 5 James Saltonstall; 26 Ed Barber; 4 Ben Crooks; 28 Charlie Graham; 6 Louis Jouffret; 7 Joe Keyes; 13 Jacob Fairbank; 25 Corey Johnson; 29 Clement Boyer; 15 Ryan Lannon; 11 Ben Kavanagh; 34 Tom Nicholson-Watton. Subs (all used): 20 Tom Inman; 8 Adam Tangata; 19 Connor Davies; 35 Ben Littlewood.
Tries: Woodburn-Hall (32), Crooks (38), Jouffret (50), Saltonstall (55); **Goals:** Jouffret 2/4.
VIKINGS: 24 Lloyd Roby; 20 Mike Butt; 29 Zac Bardsley-Rowe; 25 Keanan Brand; 2 Ryan Ince; 6 Joe Lyons; 7 Tom Gilmore; 8 Callum Field; 14 Jordan Johnstone; 31 Dan Murray; 11 Rhodri Lloyd; 19 Sam Wilde; 16 Max Roberts. Subs (all used): 9 Matty Fozard; 26 Lucas Green; 27 Max Wood; 32 Brett Bailey.
Tries: Brand (5), Roby (13), Gilmore (26), Ince (64); **Goals:** Gilmore 4/5.
Rugby Leaguer & League Express Men of the Match: *Panthers:* Jacob Fairbank; *Vikings:* Sam Wilde.
Penalty count: 9-4; **Half-time:** 10-18;
Referee: James Vella; **Attendance:** 1,409.

SWINTON LIONS 20 WHITEHAVEN 22

LIONS: 1 Dan Abram; 25 Richard Lepori; 3 Jake Spedding; 4 Jayden Hatton; 5 Rhys Williams; 16 Lewis Hall; 7 Jordy Gibson; 36 Jordan Brown; 9 George Roby; 20 Jack Houghton; 11 Gav Rodden; 21 Andy Badrock; 12 Mitch Cox. Subs (all used): 8 Liam Cooper; 24 Jordan Case; 26 Anthony Walker; 31 Ciaran Nolan.
Tries: Hatton (7, 60), Hall (22); **Goals:** Abram 4/4.
WHITEHAVEN: 2 Jake Maizen; 3 Joey Romeo; 4 Will Evans; 5 Curtis Teare; 25 Neil Tchamambe; 14 Jake Carter; 7 Lachlan Hanneghan; 8 Lucas Castle; 15 James Newton; 17 Ross Ainley; 20 Owen McCarron; 27 Lewis Baxter; 11 Ryan King. Subs (all used): 21 Rio Corkill; 24 Lennie Ellis; 16 Noah High; 26 Huw Worthington.
Tries: Hanneghan (32), Tchamambe (42), Carter (66), Evans (71); **Goals:** Carter 3/4.
Sin bin: King (75) - high tackle on Roby.
Rugby Leaguer & League Express Men of the Match: *Lions:* Jordy Gibson; *Whitehaven:* Lennie Ellis.
Penalty count: 6-7; **Half-time:** 14-6;
Referee: Cameron Worsley; **Attendance:** 859.

ROUND 17

Saturday 27th July 2024

TOULOUSE OLYMPIQUE 58 DEWSBURY RAMS 6

OLYMPIQUE: 1 Olly Ashall-Bott; 5 Paul Marcon; 4 Mathieu Jussaume; 18 Guy Armitage; 19 Benjamin Laguerre; 23 Robin Brochon; 6 Ryan Rivett; 17 James Roumanos; 9 Calum Gahan; 10 Harrison Hansen; 12 Dominique Peyroux; 11 Maxime Stefani; 13 Anthony Marion. Subs (all used): 26 Paolo Dall'asta; 20 Greg Richards; 24 Pierre-Jean Lima; 30 Baptiste Rodriguez.
Tries: Armitage (3, 18, 43), Jussaume (8), Marcon (15), Marion (23), Rivett (31), Ashall-Bott (41), Lima (49), Rodriguez (54); **Goals:** Rivett 9/10.
RAMS: 4 Bailey O'Connor; 5 Lewis Carr; 22 Marcus Walker; 11 Brad Graham; 1 Owen Restall; 7 Calum Turner; 9 Jacob Hookem; 8 Jimmy Beckett; 33 Reiss Butterworth; 17 Jackson Walker; 30 Dale Ferguson; 23 Bailey Dawson; 13 Louis Collinson. Subs (all used): 2 Perry Whiteley; 10 Ronan Dixon; 15 Joe Summers; - Jack Briggs.
Try: R Dixon (35); **Goals:** Turner 1/1.
Sin bin: J Walker (74) - high tackle.
Rugby Leaguer & League Express Men of the Match: *Olympique:* Ryan Rivett; *Rams:* Ronan Dixon.
Penalty count: 5-5; **Half-time:** 34-6;
Referee: Geoffrey Poumes; **Attendance:** 2,155.

Sunday 28th July 2024

BATLEY BULLDOGS 16 HALIFAX PANTHERS 22

BULLDOGS: 27 Luke Hooley; 5 Elliot Kear; 24 John Mitsias; 3 Kieran Buchanan; 18 Joe Burton; 6 Ben White; 7 Josh Woods; 17 Luke Blake; 25 Brandon Moore; 10 Luke Cooper; 11 Dane Manning; 12 Lucas Walshaw; 28 Nixon Putt. Subs (all used): 4 George Senior; 9 Alistair Leak; 15 Nyle Flynn; 16 Michael Ward.
Tries: J Burton (4, 74), Woods (19); **Goals:** Woods 2/3.
PANTHERS: 1 James Woodburn-Hall; 5 James Saltonstall; 26 Ed Barber; 4 Ben Crooks; 28 Charlie Graham; 6 Louis Jouffret; 7 Joe Keyes; 8 Adam Tangata; 20 Tom Inman; 29 Clement Boyer; 11 Ben Kavanagh; 19 Connor Davies; 34 Tom Nicholson-Watton. Subs (all used): 25 Corey Johnson; 30 Joe Hird; 31 Kevin Larroyer; 35 Ben Littlewood.
Tries: Barber (30, 48), Graham (39), Keyes (44); **Goals:** Jouffret 3/4.
Rugby Leaguer & League Express Men of the Match: *Bulldogs:* Josh Woods; *Panthers:* Ed Barber.
Penalty count: 10-1; **Half-time:** 10-12;
Referee: Matty Lynn.

DONCASTER 37 BARROW RAIDERS 30

DONCASTER: 19 Craig Hall; 5 Luke Briscoe; 4 Reece Lyne; 3 Brad Hey; 30 Bureta Faraimo; 24 Watson Boas; 7 Connor Robinson; 20 Brad Knowles; 9 Greg Burns; 10 Suaia Matagi; 11 Sam Smeaton; 27 Brett Ferres; 13 Loui McConnell. Subs (all used): 14 Alex Holdstock; 15 Joe Lovodua; 16 Pauli Pauli; 17 Josh Guzdek.
Tries: Hey (9), Boas (14), Lyne (40, 59), Lovodua (43, 74), Faraimo (77); **Goals:** Robinson 4/7; **Field goal:** C Hall (80).
RAIDERS: 1 Luke Cresswell; 5 Andrew Bulman; 14 Luke Broadbent; 4 Shane Toal; 2 Ryan Shaw; 3 Matty Costello; 6 Brad Walker; 20 Ramon Silva; 21 Aaron Smith; 10 Ellis Gillam; 16 Max Clarke; 13 James Greenwood; 15 Tom Wilkinson. Subs (all used): 9 Josh Wood; 17 Brett Carter; 22 Tom Walker; 33 Delaine Bedward-Gittens.
Tries: Wood (25), Silva (30), Cresswell (49, 68), Bulman (62); **Goals:** Shaw 5/5.
Rugby Leaguer & League Express Men of the Match: *Doncaster:* Brad Hey; *Raiders:* Luke Cresswell.
Penalty count: 2-4; **Half-time:** 16-12;
Referee: Brad Milligan; **Attendance:** 1,405.

SHEFFIELD EAGLES 78 WHITEHAVEN 24

EAGLES: 1 Matty Marsh; 2 Ben Jones-Bishop; 3 Kris Welham; 4 James Glover; 5 Matty Dawson-Jones; 6 Cory Aston; 14 Jack Hansen; 8 Eddie Battye; 9 Vila Halafihi; 10 Tyler Dickinson; 26 Alex Foster; 12 Joel Farrell; 15 Evan Hodgson. Subs (all used): 13 Titus Gwaze; 16 Blake Broadbent; 23 Bayley Liu; 27 Jesse Sene-Lefao.
Tries: Dawson-Jones (3, 14, 29), Marsh (8, 22, 46, 64), Welham (25), Foster (33, 60), Jones-Bishop (43), Sene-Lefao (58), Gwaze (69); **Goals:** Aston 13/13.
WHITEHAVEN: 2 Jake Maizen; 3 Joey Romeo; 4 Will Evans; 5 Curtis Teare; 25 Neil Tchamambe; 14 Jake Carter; 7 Lachlan Hanneghan; 8 Lucas Castle; 15 James Newton; 17 Ross Ainley; 20 Owen McCarron; 27 Lewis Baxter; 11 Ryan King. Subs (all used): 21 Rio Corkill; 24 Lennie Ellis; 16 Noah High; 26 Huw Worthington.
Tries: Maizen (17), McCarron (52), Evans (73), Hanneghan (76); **Goals:** Carter 4/4.
Rugby Leaguer & League Express Men of the Match: *Eagles:* Cory Aston; *Whitehaven:* Noah High.
Penalty count: 5-5; **Half-time:** 42-6;
Referee: Andy Sweet; **Attendance:** 833.

WAKEFIELD TRINITY 46 FEATHERSTONE ROVERS 18

TRINITY: 5 Lachlan Walmsley; 2 Jermaine McGillvary; 22 Jack Croft; 3 Oliver Pratt; 32 Derrell Olpherts; 6 Luke Gale; 1 Max Jowitt; 8 Josh Bowden; 9 Liam Hood; 17 Luke Bain; 11 Matty Ashurst; 12 Josh Griffin; 13 Jay Pitts. Subs (all used): 15 Caleb Uele; 20 Toby Boothroyd; 21 Thomas Doyle; 25 Isaac Shaw.
Tries: Bowden (10, 49), McGillvary (19), Walmsley (35, 60), Pratt (54), Croft (71), Olpherts (80); **Goals:** Jowitt 7/8.
ROVERS: 26 Greg Eden; 29 Maddox Jeffery; 4 Greg Minikin; 31 Connor Barley; 2 Connor Wynne; 6 Ben Reynolds; 1 Caleb Aekins; 8 Gadwin Springer; 14 Harry Bowes; 32 Ben Nakubuwai; 3 Josh Hardcastle; 11 Brad Day; 33 Samy Kibula. Subs (all used): 18 Mo Kamano; 23 Jack Arnold; 34 Leo Tennison; 35 Zeus Silk.
Tries: Day (39), Kamano (45), Minikin (78); **Goals:** Reynolds 3/3.
Rugby Leaguer & League Express Men of the Match: *Trinity:* Jay Pitts; *Rovers:* Greg Minikin.
Penalty count: 7-7; **Half-time:** 18-6;
Referee: James Vella; **Attendance:** 6,453.

WIDNES VIKINGS 25 BRADFORD BULLS 6

VIKINGS: 24 Lloyd Roby; 20 Mike Butt; 29 Zac Bardsley-Rowe; 1 Jack Owens; 2 Ryan Ince; 6 Joe Lyons; 7 Tom Gilmore; 15 Liam Kirk; 14 Jordan Johnstone; 31 Dan Murray; 11 Rhodri Lloyd; 19 Sam Wilde; 16 Max Roberts. Subs (all used): 9 Matty Fozard; 10 Sam Brooks; 17 Liam Bent; 26 Lucas Green.
Tries: Ince (30, 55, 59), Butt (64), Roberts (79); **Goals:** Gilmore 2/5; **Field goal:** Gilmore (73).
BULLS: 1 Tom Holmes; 39 Max Lehmann; 21 Jayden Myers; 4 Kieran Gill; 36 Liam Tindall; 31 Tyran Ott; 7 Jordan Lilley; 40 Logan Bayliss-Brow; 18 Mitch Souter; 42 Franklin Pele; 14 John Davies; 29 Zac Fulton; 19 Sam Hallas. Subs (all used): 16 Keven Appo; 23 Daniel Okoro; 43 Harvey Makin; 44 Zach Fishwick.
Try: Lehmann (21); **Goals:** Lilley 1/1.
Rugby Leaguer & League Express Men of the Match: *Vikings:* Ryan Ince; *Bulls:* Sam Hallas.
Penalty count: 6-3; **Half-time:** 4-6;
Referee: Ryan Cox; **Attendance:** 3,065.

YORK KNIGHTS 34 SWINTON LIONS 4

KNIGHTS: 14 Nikau Williams; 28 Brad Ward; 4 Jimmy Keinhorst; 11 Oli Field; 2 Joe Brown; 22 Ata Hingano; 40 Sam Cook; 13 Jordan Thompson; 19 Josh Daley; 16 Brenden Santi; 12 Connor Bailey; 38 Jacob Gannon; 17 Ronan Michael. Subs (all used): 10 Conor Fitzsimmons; 15 Jack Teanby; 21 James Cunningham; 30 Harvey Reynolds.
Tries: Daley (16), Williams (28, 56), Keinhorst (52), Field (58), Cook (67); **Goals:** Hingano 5/7, Brown 0/1.
Sin bin: Bailey (38) - high tackle.
LIONS: 23 Joe Purcell; 25 Richard Lepori; 3 Jake Spedding; 4 Jayden Hatton; 5 Rhys Williams; 16 Lewis Hall; 7 Jordy Gibson; 10 Gavin Bennion; 31 Jake Burns; 20 Jack Houghton; 11 Gav Rodden; 21 Andy Badrock; 12 Mitch Cox. Subs (all used): 9 George Roby; 36 Jordan Brown; 24 Jordan Case; 28 Brad Hammond.
Try: Spedding (78); **Goals:** Gibson 0/1.
Rugby Leaguer & League Express Men of the Match: *Knights:* Josh Daley; *Lions:* George Roby.
Penalty count: 8-12; **Half-time:** 12-0;
Referee: Kevin Moore; **Attendance:** 2,125.

ROUND 18

Saturday 3rd August 2024

SWINTON LIONS 4 TOULOUSE OLYMPIQUE 48

LIONS: 1 Dan Abram; 25 Richard Lepori; 3 Jake Spedding; 21 Andy Badrock; 5 Rhys Williams; 18 Jack Stevens; 7

Championship 2024 - Round by Round

Jordy Gibson; 10 Gavin Bennion; 14 Josh Eaves; 13 Mikey Wood; 11 Gav Rodden; 12 Mitch Cox; 16 Lewis Hall. Subs (all used): 9 George Roby; 24 Jordan Case; 20 Jack Houghton; 36 Jordan Brown.
Try: Williams (43); **Goals:** Abram 0/1.
Sin bin: Eaves (3) - delaying restart.
OLYMPIQUE: 1 Olly Ashall-Bott; 5 Paul Marcon; 4 Mathieu Jussaume; 3 Reubenn Rennie; 2 Paul Ulberg; 6 Ryan Rivett; 23 Robin Brochon; 17 James Roumanos; 9 Calum Gahan; 10 Harrison Hansen; 11 Maxime Stefani; 12 Dominique Peyroux; 13 Anthony Marion. Subs (all used): 20 Greg Richards; 22 Dimitri Biscarro; 24 Pierre-Jean Lima; 18 Guy Armitage.
Tries: Ulberg (10, 26), Rennie (15, 20), Stefani (54), Lima (58, 61, 74), Marcon (70);
Goals: Rivett 2/5, Brochon 4/4.
Rugby Leaguer & League Express Men of the Match:
Lions: Rhys Williams; *Olympique:* Anthony Marion.
Penalty count: 9-3; **Half-time:** 0-20;
Referee: Ryan Cox; **Attendance:** 629.

Sunday 4th August 2024

BARROW RAIDERS 24 BRADFORD BULLS 24

RAIDERS: 1 Luke Cresswell; 5 Andrew Bulman; 14 Luke Broadbent; 4 Shane Toal; 2 Ryan Shaw; 6 Brad Walker; 3 Matty Costello; 10 Ellis Gillam; 21 Aaron Smith; 32 Ryan Brown; 16 Max Clarke; 13 James Greenwood; 31 Kavan Rothwell. Subs (all used): 9 Josh Wood; 15 Tom Wilkinson; 22 Tom Walker; 36 Jamie Pye.
Tries: Shaw (27), Broadbent (31), Bulman (56), Wood (64), Clarke (78); **Goals:** Shaw 2/5.
BULLS: 1 Tom Holmes; 37 Jayden Okunbor; 39 Max Lehmann; 4 Kieran Gill; 46 Jack Smith; 45 Jarrod Sammut; 7 Jordan Lilley; 40 Logan Bayliss-Brow; 18 Mitch Souter; 42 Franklin Pele; 29 Zac Fulton; 14 John Davies; 19 Sam Hallas. Subs (all used): 16 Keven Appo; 44 Zach Fishwick; 23 Daniel Okoro; 31 Tyran Ott.
Tries: Holmes (6), Okunbor (17), Fulton (23), Appo (38), Gill (53); **Goals:** Lilley 2/5.
Rugby Leaguer & League Express Men of the Match:
Raiders: Josh Wood; *Bulls:* Jordan Lilley.
Penalty count: 6-3; **Half-time:** 8-18;
Referee: Michael Smaill; **Attendance:** 2,419.

DEWSBURY RAMS 16 WAKEFIELD TRINITY 42

RAMS: 4 Bailey O'Connor; 5 Lewis Carr; 11 Brad Graham; 22 Marcus Walker; 2 Perry Whiteley; 7 Calum Turner; 9 Jacob Hookem; 16 Elliot Morris; 33 Reiss Butterworth; 17 Jackson Walker; 15 Joe Summers; 23 Bailey Dawson; 13 Louis Collinson. Subs (all used): 10 Ronan Dixon; 32 Zeus Silk; 35 Jack Briggs; 37 Keenen Tomlinson.
Tries: Whiteley (6), Silk (44), Carr (79); **Goals:** Turner 2/3.
Sin bin: Morris (14) - late challenge on Bain.
TRINITY: 30 Noah Booth; 5 Lachlan Walmsley; 22 Jack Croft; 3 Oliver Pratt; 32 Derrell Olpherts; 1 Max Jowitt; 9 Liam Hood; 8 Josh Bowden; 26 Harvey Smith; 17 Luke Bain; 20 Toby Boothroyd; 12 Josh Griffin; 21 Thomas Doyle. Subs (all used): 13 Jay Pitts; 14 Liam Kay; 18 Ky Rodwell; 25 Isaac Shaw. 18th man (used): 33 Ellis Lingard.
Tries: Jowitt (10, 54, 76), Smith (15), Rodwell (21), Olpherts (27), Pratt (57), Boothroyd (63); **Goals:** Jowitt 5/8.
Rugby Leaguer & League Express Men of the Match:
Rams: Calum Turner; *Trinity:* Max Jowitt.
Penalty count: 7-7; **Half-time:** 6-22;
Referee: Denton Arnold; **Attendance:** 1,750.

FEATHERSTONE ROVERS 24 BATLEY BULLDOGS 16

ROVERS: 26 Greg Eden; 29 Maddox Jeffery; 4 Greg Minikin; 31 Connor Barley; 2 Connor Wynne; 6 Ben Reynolds; 1 Caleb Aekins; 32 Ben Nakubuwai; 13 Danny Addy; 36 James Lockwood; 11 Brad Day; 12 Jack Bussey; 37 Jimmy Beckett. Subs (all used): 14 Harry Bowes; 8 Gadwin Springer; 23 Jack Arnold; 3 Josh Hardcastle.
Tries: Wynne (9), Bussey (46), Reynolds (58), Beckett (76);
Goals: Reynolds 4/4.
BULLDOGS: 27 Luke Hooley; 2 Dale Morton; 24 John Mitsias; 3 Kieran Buchanan; 18 Joe Burton; 6 Ben White; 7 Josh Woods; 8 Adam Gledhill; 9 Alistair Leak; 10 Luke Cooper; 11 Dane Manning; 12 Lucas Walshaw; 17 Luke Blake. Subs (all used): 4 George Senior; 14 Oli Burton; 15 Nyle Flynn; 16 Michael Ward.
Tries: Walshaw (2), J Burton (24), Manning (39);
Goals: Woods 2/3.
Rugby Leaguer & League Express Men of the Match:
Rovers: Jimmy Beckett; *Bulldogs:* Dane Manning.
Penalty count: 5-4; **Half-time:** 6-16;
Referee: Cameron Worsley; **Attendance:** 1,544.

HALIFAX PANTHERS 38 YORK KNIGHTS 18

PANTHERS: 1 James Woodburn-Hall; 5 James Saltonstall; 26 Ed Barber; 4 Ben Crooks; 28 Charlie Graham; 6 Louis Jouffret; 7 Joe Keyes; 8 Adam Tangata; 20 Tom Inman; 29 Clement Boyer; 11 Ben Kavanagh; 19 Connor Davies; 30 Joe Hird. Subs (all used): 25 Corey Johnson; 31 Kevin Larroyer; 35 Ben Littlewood; 32 Kai Morgan.
Tries: Woodburn-Hall (17), Crooks (20), Graham (28, 54), Jouffret (40, 76), Keyes (71); **Goals:** Jouffret 4/5, Keyes 1/2.
KNIGHTS: 14 Nikau Williams; 28 Brad Ward; 4 Jimmy Keinhorst; 11 Oli Field; 2 Joe Brown; 22 Ata Hingano; 40 Sam Cook; 17 Ronan Michael; 19 Josh Daley; 16 Brenden Santi; 12 Connor Bailey; 38 Jacob Gannon; 13 Jordan Thompson. Subs (all used): 21 James Cunningham; 15 Jack Teanby; 10 Conor Fitzsimmons; 30 Harvey Reynolds.
Tries: Bailey (8), Ward (24), Gannon (62);
Goals: Hingano 3/4.
Rugby Leaguer & League Express Men of the Match:
Panthers: James Woodburn-Hall; *Knights:* Ata Hingano.
Penalty count: 6-4; **Half-time:** 22-14;
Referee: Liam Rush; **Attendance:** 1,543.

SHEFFIELD EAGLES 22 DONCASTER 20

EAGLES: 1 Matty Marsh; 2 Ben Jones-Bishop; 3 Kris Welham; 4 James Glover; 5 Matty Dawson-Jones; 6 Cory Aston; 14 Jack Hansen; 8 Eddie Battye; 9 Vila Halafihi; 10 Tyler Dickinson; 26 Alex Foster; 12 Joel Farrell; 15 Evan Hodgson. Subs (all used): 13 Titus Gwaze; 17 Mitch Clark; 23 Bayley Liu; 27 Jesse Sene-Lefao.
Tries: Dawson-Jones (6), Glover (22), Foster (32), Aston (37); **Goals:** Aston 3/4.
Sin bin:
Dawson-Jones (78) - dangerous challenge on Briscoe.
DONCASTER: 19 Craig Hall; 5 Luke Briscoe; 4 Reece Lyne; 3 Brad Hey; 30 Bureta Faraimo; 24 Watson Boas; 7 Connor Robinson; 20 Brad Knowles; 34 Jeylan Hodgson; 10 Suaia Matagi; 28 AJ Wallace; 27 Brett Ferres; 13 Loui McConnell. Subs (all used): 14 Alex Holdstock; 16 Pauli Pauli; 17 Josh Guzdek; 31 Lewis Baxter.
Tries: Briscoe (28), Robinson (52), Guzdek (59), Faraimo (70); **Goals:** Robinson 2/5.
Rugby Leaguer & League Express Men of the Match:
Eagles: Cory Aston; *Doncaster:* Connor Robinson.
Penalty count: 2-9; **Half-time:** 22-6;
Referee: Matty Lynn; **Attendance:** 1,075.

WHITEHAVEN 12 WIDNES VIKINGS 24

WHITEHAVEN: 2 Jake Maizen; 1 Edene Gebbie; 4 Will Evans; 22 Mac Walsh; 5 Curtis Teare; 14 Jake Carter; 7 Lachlan Hanneghan; 8 Lucas Castle; 15 James Newton; 17 Ross Ainley; 23 Ben Hursey; 21 Rio Corkill; 11 Ryan King. Subs (all used): 16 Noah High; 18 Perry Singleton; 25 Sam Campbell; 26 Huw Worthington.
Tries: Gebbie (1), King (11); **Goals:** Carter 2/2.
Sin bin: Gebbie (35) - dangerous challenge on Brand.
VIKINGS: 1 Jack Owens; 20 Mike Butt; 25 Keanan Brand; 29 Zac Bardsley-Rowe; 2 Ryan Ince; 6 Joe Lyons; 7 Tom Gilmore; 15 Liam Kirk; 14 Jordan Johnstone; 31 Dan Murray; 16 Max Roberts; 27 Ryan Lannon; 10 Sam Brooks. Subs (all used): 9 Matty Fozard; 17 Liam Bent; 26 Lucas Green; 28 Nathan Wilde.
Tries: Ince (34, 63), Lyons (37), Owens (43), Gilmore (54);
Goals: Gilmore 2/6.
Rugby Leaguer & League Express Men of the Match:
Whitehaven: Curtis Teare; *Vikings:* Ryan Lannon.
Penalty count: 5-7; **Half-time:** 12-12;
Referee: Andy Sweet; **Attendance:** 855.

ROUND 19

Friday 9th August 2024

WAKEFIELD TRINITY 42 SHEFFIELD EAGLES 6

TRINITY: 5 Lachlan Walmsley; 2 Jermaine McGillvary; 4 Iain Thornley; 3 Oliver Pratt; 32 Derrell Olpherts; 6 Luke Gale; 1 Max Jowitt; 18 Ky Rodwell; 9 Liam Hood; 17 Luke Bain; 11 Matty Ashurst; 12 Josh Griffin; 13 Jay Pitts. Subs (all used): 14 Liam Kay; 20 Toby Boothroyd; 21 Thomas Doyle; 25 Isaac Shaw.
Tries: Rodwell (16), Griffin (28), Olpherts (40, 72), Thornley (55), Ashurst (60), Hood (64); **Goals:** Jowitt 7/8.
Sin bin: Hood (45) - delaying restart.
EAGLES: 1 Matty Marsh; 2 Ben Jones-Bishop; 3 Kris Welham; 4 James Glover; 5 Matty Dawson-Jones; 6 Cory Aston; 14 Jack Hansen; 8 Eddie Battye; 9 Vila Halafihi; 17 Mitch Clark; 11 Connor Bower; 27 Jesse Sene-Lefao; 13 Titus Gwaze. Subs (all used): 15 Evan Hodgson; 16 Blake Broadbent; 23 Bayley Liu; 24 Oliver Roberts.
Try: Glover (51); **Goals:** Aston 1/1.
Rugby Leaguer & League Express Men of the Match:
Trinity: Max Jowitt; *Eagles:* Titus Gwaze.
Penalty count: 6-4; **Half-time:** 18-0;
Referee: Aaron Moore; **Attendance:** 4,821.

Saturday 10th August 2024

DONCASTER 20 TOULOUSE OLYMPIQUE 18

DONCASTER: 17 Josh Guzdek; 5 Luke Briscoe; 3 Brad Hey; 23 Jason Tali; 30 Bureta Faraimo; 24 Watson Boas; 7 Connor Robinson; 31 Lewis Baxter; 15 Joe Lovodua; 20 Brad Knowles; 11 Sam Smeaton; 28 AJ Wallace; 13 Loui McConnell. Subs (all used): 12 Alex Sutcliffe; 16 Pauli Pauli; 19 Craig Hall; 25 Ilikaya Mafi.
Tries: Guzdek (5), Tali (39), C Hall (80);
Goals: Robinson 4/5.
OLYMPIQUE: 1 Olly Ashall-Bott; 5 Paul Marcon; 4 Mathieu Jussaume; 3 Reubenn Rennie; 2 Paul Ulberg; 6 Ryan Rivett; 7 Jake Shorrocks; 17 James Roumanos; 9 Calum Gahan; 10 Harrison Hansen; 11 Maxime Stefani; 12 Dominique Peyroux; 13 Anthony Marion. Subs (all used): 20 Greg Richards; 22 Dimitri Biscarro; 15 Sitaleki Akauola; 18 Guy Armitage.
Tries: Gahan (14), Peyroux (35), Rivett (77);
Goals: Shorrocks 3/3.
Rugby Leaguer & League Express Men of the Match:
Doncaster: Connor Robinson; *Olympique:* Calum Gahan.
Penalty count: 8-4; **Half-time:** 10-12;
Referee: Michael Smaill; **Attendance:** 1,121.

Sunday 11th August 2024

BATLEY BULLDOGS 26 SWINTON LIONS 6

BULLDOGS: 1 Robbie Butterworth; 2 Dale Morton; 24 John Mitsias; 3 Kieran Buchanan; 18 Joe Burton; 6 Ben White; 7 Josh Woods; 8 Adam Gledhill; 25 Brandon Moore; 10 Luke Cooper; 11 Dane Manning; 12 Lucas Walshaw; 17 Luke Blake. Subs (all used): 9 Alistair Leak; 13 James Brown; 15 Nyle Flynn; 20 Ben Kaye.
Tries: J Burton (2, 33), Moore (21), Cooper (69), White (80);
Goals: Woods 3/6.
LIONS: 23 Joe Purcell; 25 Richard Lepori; 4 Jayden Hatton; 21 Andy Badrock; 5 Rhys Williams; 18 Jack Stevens; 7 Jordy Gibson; 26 Anthony Walker; 9 George Roby; 10 Gavin Bennion; 11 Gav Rodden; 29 Jonny Vaughan; 16 Lewis Hall. Subs (all used): 14 Josh Eaves; 33 Leon Cowen; 20 Jack Houghton; 13 Mikey Wood.
Try: Stevens (49); **Goals:** Stevens 1/1.
Rugby Leaguer & League Express Men of the Match:
Bulldogs: Lucas Walshaw; *Lions:* Jayden Hatton.
Penalty count: 4-4; **Half-time:** 14-0;
Referee: James Vella.

BRADFORD BULLS 58 WHITEHAVEN 0

BULLS: 1 Tom Holmes; 37 Jayden Okunbor; 21 Jayden Myers; 39 Max Lehmann; 5 Jorge Taufua; 45 Jarrod Sammut; 7 Jordan Lilley; 40 Logan Bayliss-Brow; 31 Tyran Ott; 13 Michael Lawrence; 29 Zac Fulton; 16 Keven Appo; 19 Sam Hallas. Subs (all used): 17 Eribe Doro; 18 Mitch Souter; 42 Franklin Pele; 43 Harvey Makin.
Tries: Okunbor (3), Appo (15, 75), Sammut (20), Doro (28), Myers (33), Makin (40, 46), Pele (50), Taufua (66);
Goals: Lilley 9/10.
Sin bin: Pele (59) - late challenge on King.
WHITEHAVEN: 1 Edene Gebbie; 24 Callum Shaw; 4 Will Evans; 22 Mac Walsh; 5 Curtis Teare; 2 Jake Maizen; 7 Lachlan Hanneghan; 8 Lucas Castle; 15 James Newton; 17 Ross Ainley; 20 Owen McCarron; 23 Ben Hursey; 11 Ryan King. Subs (all used, only three named): 21 Rio Corkill; 25 Sam Campbell; 26 Huw Worthington.
Sin bin: Campbell (79) - dangerous challenge.
Rugby Leaguer & League Express Men of the Match:
Bulls: Eribe Doro; *Whitehaven:* Huw Worthington.
Penalty count: 5-7; **Half-time:** 34-0;
Referee: Cameron Worsley; **Attendance:** 2,502.

HALIFAX PANTHERS 38 BARROW RAIDERS 12

PANTHERS: 1 James Woodburn-Hall; 5 James Saltonstall; 17 Ben Tibbs; 4 Ben Crooks; 28 Charlie Graham; 6 Louis Jouffret; 7 Joe Keyes; 8 Adam Tangata; 20 Tom Inman; 34 Keelan Foster; 11 Ben Kavanagh; 19 Connor Davies; 25 Corey Johnson. Subs (all used): 9 Adam O'Brien; 31 Kevin Larroyer; 30 Joe Hird; 29 Clement Boyer.
Tries: Tibbs (8, 41), Saltonstall (13), Woodburn-Hall (20), Keyes (60), Kavanagh (73), Graham (79);
Goals: Jouffret 5/8.
RAIDERS: 1 Luke Cresswell; 5 Andrew Bulman; 14 Luke Broadbent; 16 Max Clarke; 4 Shane Toal; 6 Brad Walker; 9 Josh Wood; 10 Ellis Gillam; 21 Aaron Smith; 33 Delaine Bedward-Gittens; 13 James Greenwood; 25 Finn McMillan; 32 Ryan Brown. Subs (all used): 17 Brett Carter; 15 Tom Wilkinson; 22 Tom Walker; 36 Jamie Pye.
Tries: S Toal (29), Cresswell (33); **Goals:** B Walker 2/2.
Dismissal: Bedward-Gittens (44) - fighting.
Sin bin: Carter (44) - fighting.
Rugby Leaguer & League Express Men of the Match:
Panthers: Joe Keyes; *Raiders:* Shane Toal.
Penalty count: 1-5; **Half-time:** 14-12;
Referee: Ryan Cox; **Attendance:** 1,421.

WIDNES VIKINGS 0 FEATHERSTONE ROVERS 8

VIKINGS: 1 Jack Owens; 20 Mike Butt; 3 Matty Fleming; 25 Keanan Brand; 2 Ryan Ince; 6 Joe Lyons; 7 Tom Gilmore; 15 Liam Kirk; 14 Jordan Johnstone; 31 Dan Murray;

Championship 2024 - Round by Round

16 Max Roberts; 27 Ryan Lannon; 28 Nathan Wilde. Subs (all used): 10 Sam Brooks; 17 Liam Bent; 24 Lloyd Roby; 26 Lucas Green.
ROVERS: 26 Greg Eden; 29 Maddox Jeffery; 4 Greg Minikin; 9 Connor Jones; 3 Josh Hardcastle; 13 Danny Addy; 6 Ben Reynolds; 32 Ben Nakubuwai; 14 Harry Bowes; 36 James Lockwood; 11 Brad Day; 12 Jack Bussey; 37 Jimmy Beckett. Subs: 8 Gadwin Springer; 15 Wellington Albert; 23 Jack Arnold; 33 Samy Kibula (not used).
Try: Reynolds (38); **Goals:** Reynolds 2/2.
Sin bin:
Springer (25) - high tackle on Fleming, (79) - late challenge.
Rugby Leaguer & League Express Men of the Match:
Vikings: Dan Murray; *Rovers:* Ben Reynolds.
Penalty count: 9-5; **Half-time:** 0-6;
Referee: Matty Lynn; **Attendance:** 2,422.

YORK KNIGHTS 54 DEWSBURY RAMS 12

KNIGHTS: 2 Joe Brown; 28 Brad Ward; 4 Jimmy Keinhorst; 41 Joe Law; 5 AJ Towse; 22 Ata Hingano; 14 Nikau Williams; 17 Ronan Michael; 9 Will Jubb; 42 Jack Martin; 12 Connor Bailey; 38 Jacob Gannon; 13 Jordan Thompson. Subs (all used): 15 Jack Teanby; 16 Brenden Santi; 21 James Cunningham; 25 Bailey Antrobus.
Tries: Law (3), Thompson (14), Brown (20, 54), Cunningham (34), Towse (39), Keinhorst (49, 80), Ward (71), Jubb (78); **Goals:** Hingano 5/8, Keinhorst 2/2.
RAMS: 4 Bailey O'Connor; 5 Lewis Carr; 11 Brad Graham; 22 Marcus Walker; 2 Perry Whiteley; 7 Calum Turner; 9 Jacob Hookem; 16 Elliot Morris; 33 Reiss Butterworth; 32 Zeus Silk; 12 Matt Garside; 15 Joe Summers; 23 Bailey Dawson. Subs (all used): 10 Ronan Dixon; 35 Jack Briggs; 36 Luke Mearns; 37 Keenen Tomlinson.
Tries: Whiteley (8), O'Connor (74); **Goals:** Turner 2/2.
Rugby Leaguer & League Express Men of the Match:
Knights: Jimmy Keinhorst; *Rams:* Perry Whiteley.
Penalty count: 5-5; **Half-time:** 24-6;
Referee: Warren Turley; **Attendance:** 1,936.

ROUND 20

Friday 16th August 2024

SHEFFIELD EAGLES 14 BATLEY BULLDOGS 24

EAGLES: 1 Matty Marsh; 2 Ben Jones-Bishop; 3 Kris Welham; 4 James Glover; 30 Ryan Millar; 6 Cory Aston; 19 Izaac Farrell; 8 Eddie Battye; 9 Vila Halafihi; 10 Tyler Dickinson; 26 Alex Foster; 12 Joel Farrell; 13 Titus Gwaze. Subs (all used): 17 Mitch Clark; 22 Kyle Wood; 24 Oliver Roberts; 27 Jesse Sene-Lefao.
Tries: Jones-Bishop (26), Glover (52), Welham (62);
Goals: Aston 1/3.
BULLDOGS: 27 Luke Hooley; 5 Elliot Kear; 24 John Mitsias; 3 Kieran Buchanan; 18 Joe Burton; 6 Ben White; 7 Josh Woods; 8 Adam Gledhill; 25 Brandon Moore; 10 Luke Cooper; 11 Dane Manning; 12 Lucas Walshaw; 17 Luke Blake. Subs: 1 Robbie Butterworth (not used); 9 Alistair Leak; 13 James Brown; 15 Nyle Flynn.
Tries: Hooley (9, 21, 59), Kear (15); **Goals:** Woods 4/5.
Rugby Leaguer & League Express Men of the Match:
Eagles: Kris Welham; *Bulldogs:* Luke Hooley.
Penalty count: 2-5; **Half-time:** 4-18;
Referee: James Vella; **Attendance:** 877.

Saturday 17th August 2024

TOULOUSE OLYMPIQUE 12 YORK KNIGHTS 20

OLYMPIQUE: 23 Robin Brochon; 5 Paul Marcon; 4 Mathieu Jussaume; 3 Reubenn Rennie; 2 Paul Ulberg; 7 Jake Shorrocks; 6 Ryan Rivett; 8 Lambert Belmas; 9 Calum Gahan; 10 Harrison Hansen; 12 Dominique Peyroux; 11 Maxime Stefani; 13 Anthony Marion. Subs (all used): 24 Pierre-Jean Lima; 17 James Roumanos; 15 Sitaleki Akauola; 18 Guy Armitage.
Tries: Marion (6), Ulberg (69); **Goals:** Shorrocks 2/2.
KNIGHTS: 1 Will Dagger; 28 Brad Ward; 11 Oli Field; 41 Joe Law; 2 Joe Brown; 22 Ata Hingano; 14 Nikau Williams; 17 Ronan Michael; 9 Will Jubb; 13 Jordan Thompson; 12 Connor Bailey; 38 Jacob Gannon; 21 James Cunningham. Subs (all used): 10 Conor Fitzsimmons; 15 Jack Teanby; 16 Brenden Santi; 19 Josh Daley.
Tries: Brown (20), Williams (27), Dagger (65);
Goals: Hingano 1/1, Dagger 3/3.
Sin bin: Thompson (53) - dangerous challenge on Marion.
Rugby Leaguer & League Express Men of the Match:
Olympique: Calum Gahan; *Knights:* Nikau Williams.
Penalty count: 11-2; **Half-time:** 6-14;
Referee: Aaron Moore; **Attendance:** 2,181.

Sunday 18th August 2024

BRADFORD BULLS 21 FEATHERSTONE ROVERS 22

BULLS: 1 Tom Holmes; 37 Jayden Okunbor; 21 Jayden Myers; 39 Max Lehmann; 5 Jorge Taufua; 45 Jarrod Sammut; 7 Jordan Lilley; 40 Logan Bayliss-Brow; 31 Tyran Ott; 13 Michael Lawrence; 29 Zac Fulton; 16 Keven Appo; 17 Eribe Doro. Subs (all used): 42 Franklin Pele; 14 John Davies; 18 Mitch Souter; 43 Harvey Makin.
Tries: Okunbor (20), Pele (31, 37), Myers (60);
Goals: Lilley 2/4; **Field goal:** Lilley (72).
Sin bin: Taufua (74) - fighting.
ROVERS: 26 Greg Eden; 2 Connor Wynne; 3 Josh Hardcastle; 4 Greg Minikin; 5 Gareth Gale; 6 Ben Reynolds; 13 Danny Addy; 32 Ben Nakubuwai; 9 Connor Jones; 36 James Lockwood; 12 Jack Bussey; 11 Brad Day; 37 Jimmy Beckett. Subs (all used): 8 Gadwin Springer; 15 Wellington Albert; 23 Jack Arnold; 33 Samy Kibula.
Tries: Reynolds (2), Hardcastle (12), Springer (50);
Goals: Reynolds 5/5.
Sin bin: Bussey (60) - trip.
Rugby Leaguer & League Express Men of the Match:
Bulls: Eribe Doro; *Rovers:* Ben Reynolds.
Penalty count: 6-4; **Half-time:** 14-12;
Referee: Cameron Worsley; **Attendance:** 3,099.

DEWSBURY RAMS 24 BARROW RAIDERS 31

RAMS: 4 Bailey O'Connor; 5 Lewis Carr; 11 Brad Graham; 22 Marcus Walker; 2 Perry Whiteley; 7 Calum Turner; 9 Jacob Hookem; 16 Elliot Morris; 20 Curtis Davies; 17 Jackson Walker; 28 Jack Billington; 12 Matt Garside; 15 Joe Summers. Subs (all used): 23 Bailey Dawson; 35 Jack Briggs; 32 Zeus Silk; 37 Keenen Tomlinson.
Tries: Whiteley (4, 36), O'Connor (62, 65);
Goals: Turner 4/5.
RAIDERS: 1 Luke Cresswell; 5 Andrew Bulman; 4 Shane Toal; 14 Luke Broadbent; 2 Ryan Shaw; 6 Brad Walker; 9 Josh Wood; 10 Ellis Gillam; 21 Aaron Smith; 8 Greg Burke; 13 James Greenwood; 12 Jarrad Stack; 32 Ryan Brown. Subs (all used): 15 Tom Wilkinson; 22 Tom Walker; 17 Brett Carter; 36 Jamie Pye.
Tries: B Walker (14), S Toal (39), Shaw (55), Wood (80);
Goals: Shaw 7/7; **Field goal:** B Walker (77).
Rugby Leaguer & League Express Men of the Match:
Rams: Bailey O'Connor; *Raiders:* Josh Wood.
Penalty count: 8-10; **Half-time:** 12-14;
Referee: Andy Sweet; **Attendance:** 940.

SWINTON LIONS 20 HALIFAX PANTHERS 6

LIONS: 25 Richard Lepori; 3 Jake Spedding; 21 Andy Badrock; 4 Jayden Hatton; 5 Rhys Williams; 16 Lewis Hall; 7 Jordy Gibson; 10 Gavin Bennion; 9 George Roby; 20 Jack Houghton; 11 Gav Rodden; 12 Mitch Cox; 33 Leon Cowen. Subs (all used): 14 Josh Eaves; 24 Jordan Case; 26 Anthony Walker; 8 Liam Cooper.
Tries: Spedding (11), Williams (21), Hatton (64), Rodden (71); **Goals:** Gibson 2/4.
PANTHERS: 23 Gareth Widdop; 5 James Saltonstall; 17 Ben Tibbs; 4 Ben Crooks; 28 Charlie Graham; 6 Louis Jouffret; 7 Joe Keyes; 8 Adam Tangata; 20 Tom Inman; 34 Keelan Foster; 11 Ben Kavanagh; 19 Connor Davies; 25 Corey Johnson. Subs (all used): 9 Adam O'Brien; 13 Jacob Fairbank; 30 Joe Hird; 29 Clement Boyer.
Try: Widdop (74); **Goals:** Jouffret 1/1.
Rugby Leaguer & League Express Men of the Match:
Lions: Jordy Gibson; *Panthers:* Connor Davies.
Penalty count: 3-10; **Half-time:** 10-0;
Referee: Scott Mikalauskas; **Attendance:** 1,037.

WAKEFIELD TRINITY 36 WIDNES VIKINGS 12

TRINITY: 5 Lachlan Walmsley; 2 Jermaine McGillvary; 4 Iain Thornley; 3 Oliver Pratt; 32 Derrell Olpherts; 1 Max Jowitt; 14 Liam Kay; 18 Ky Rodwell; 9 Liam Hood; 17 Luke Bain; 11 Matty Ashurst; 12 Josh Griffin; 13 Jay Pitts. Subs (all used): 20 Toby Boothroyd; 21 Thomas Doyle; 25 Isaac Shaw; 26 Harvey Smith.
Tries: Rodwell (15), Olpherts (40), Hood (45), McGillvary (58), Jowitt (71), Walmsley (75);
Goals: Jowitt 6/8.
VIKINGS: 1 Jack Owens; 2 Ryan Ince; 3 Matty Fleming; 29 Zac Bardsley-Rowe; 25 Reagan Sumner; 6 Joe Lyons; 7 Tom Gilmore; 31 Dan Murray; 14 Jordan Johnstone; 17 Liam Bent; 16 Max Roberts; 27 Ryan Lannon; 28 Nathan Wilde. Subs (all used): 32 Shane Grady; 26 Lucas Green; 15 Liam Kirk; 10 Sam Brooks.
Tries: Bardsley-Rowe (25), Sumner (49);
Goals: Gilmore 2/3.
Rugby Leaguer & League Express Men of the Match:
Trinity: Max Jowitt; *Vikings:* Jack Owens.
Penalty count: 7-2; **Half-time:** 10-6;
Referee: Marcus Griffiths; **Attendance:** 5,036.

WHITEHAVEN 28 DONCASTER 24

WHITEHAVEN: 3 Joey Romeo; 24 Callum Shaw; 21 Rio Corkill; 5 Curtis Teare; 22 Mac Walsh; 2 Jake Maizen; 7 Lachlan Hanneghan; 8 Lucas Castle; 15 James Newton; 17 Ross Ainley; 23 Ben Hursey; 20 Owen McCarron; 11 Ryan King. Subs (all used, only three named): 25 Sam Campbell; 26 Huw Worthington; 18 Perry Singleton.
Tries: Hanneghan (9), Campbell (27), Romeo (43, 64), Maizen (80); **Goals:** Hanneghan 4/6.
DONCASTER: 17 Josh Guzdek; 5 Luke Briscoe; 4 Reece Lyne; 23 Jason Tali; 30 Bureta Faraimo; 24 Watson Boas; 7 Connor Robinson; 31 Lewis Baxter; 15 Joe Lovodua; 20 Brad Knowles; 28 AJ Wallace; 27 Brett Ferres; 13 Loui McConnell. Subs (all used): 3 Brad Hey; 12 Alex Sutcliffe; 16 Pauli Pauli; 25 Ilikaya Mafi.
Tries: Lovodua (5), Pauli (33), Briscoe (36, 53);
Goals: Robinson 4/4.
Rugby Leaguer & League Express Men of the Match:
Whitehaven: Ross Ainley; *Doncaster:* Loui McConnell.
Penalty count: 6-5; **Half-time:** 14-18;
Referee: Brad Milligan; **Attendance:** 699.

ROUND 21

Saturday 24th August 2024

FEATHERSTONE ROVERS 22 TOULOUSE OLYMPIQUE 10

ROVERS: 26 Greg Eden; 5 Gareth Gale; 3 Josh Hardcastle; 4 Greg Minikin; 2 Connor Wynne; 6 Ben Reynolds; 30 Dec Patton; 32 Ben Nakubuwai; 9 Connor Jones; 36 James Lockwood; 11 Brad Day; 37 Jimmy Beckett; 13 Danny Addy. Subs: 8 Gadwin Springer; 14 Harry Bowes (not used); 15 Wellington Albert; 23 Jack Arnold.
Tries: Wynne (22, 64), Hardcastle (77);
Goals: Reynolds 5/5.
Sin bin: Wynne (79) - retaliation.
OLYMPIQUE: 1 Olly Ashall-Bott; 2 Paul Ulberg; 3 Reubenn Rennie; 4 Mathieu Jussaume; 5 Paul Marcon; 7 Jake Shorrocks; 23 Robin Brochon; 8 Lambert Belmas; 9 Calum Gahan; 22 Dimitri Biscarro; 11 Maxime Stefani; 10 Harrison Hansen; 13 Anthony Marion. Subs (all used): 14 Eloi Pelissier; 15 Sitaleki Akauola; 17 James Roumanos; 20 Greg Richards.
Tries: Rennie (40), Stefani (72); **Goals:** Shorrocks 1/2.
Sin bin: Rennie (79) - dangerous challenge.
Rugby Leaguer & League Express Men of the Match:
Rovers: Ben Reynolds; *Olympique:* Paul Ulberg.
Penalty count: 6-7; **Half-time:** 8-4; **Referee:** James Vella.

Sunday 25th August 2024

BARROW RAIDERS 20 SWINTON LIONS 18

RAIDERS: 1 Luke Cresswell; 5 Andrew Bulman; 4 Shane Toal; 14 Luke Broadbent; 2 Ryan Shaw; 6 Brad Walker; 7 Ryan Johnston; 10 Ellis Gillam; 21 Aaron Smith; 20 Ramon Silva; 31 Kavan Rothwell; 12 Jarrad Stack; 19 Greg Worthington. Subs (all used): 9 Josh Wood; 8 Greg Burke; 22 Tom Walker; 15 Tom Wilkinson.
Tries: Smith (7, 14), Stack (68); **Goals:** Shaw 4/6.
LIONS: 1 Dan Abram; 25 Richard Lepori; 3 Jake Spedding; 4 Jayden Hatton; 5 Rhys Williams; 16 Lewis Hall; 7 Jordy Gibson; 10 Gavin Bennion; 9 George Roby; 20 Jack Houghton; 11 Gav Rodden; 12 Mitch Cox; 13 Mikey Wood. Subs (all used): 14 Josh Eaves; 24 Jordan Case; 37 Anthony Walker; 8 Liam Cooper.
Tries: Williams (33), Rodden (45), Spedding (49);
Goals: Abram 3/5.
Sin bin: Roby (72) - late challenge on B Walker.
Rugby Leaguer & League Express Men of the Match:
Raiders: Aaron Smith; *Lions:* Gavin Bennion.
Penalty count: 11-8; **Half-time:** 12-8;
Referee: Kevin Moore; **Attendance:** 1,495.

DEWSBURY RAMS 10 WHITEHAVEN 18

RAMS: 4 Bailey O'Connor; 5 Lewis Carr; 11 Brad Graham; 37 Keenen Tomlinson; 2 Perry Whiteley; 6 Paul Sykes; 9 Jacob Hookem; 16 Elliot Morris; 20 Curtis Davies; 17 Jackson Walker; 28 Jack Billington; 12 Matt Garside; 15 Joe Summers. Subs (all used): 32 Zeus Silk; 30 Dale Ferguson; 35 Jack Briggs; 26 Jamie Field.
Tries: O'Connor (52), Billington (72); **Goals:** Sykes 1/2.
Dismissal: Ferguson (38) - high tackle on Shaw.
WHITEHAVEN: 3 Joey Romeo; 24 Callum Shaw; 21 Rio Corkill; 5 Curtis Teare; 22 Mac Walsh; 9 Sam Ackroyd; 7 Lachlan Hanneghan; 8 Lucas Castle; 15 James Newton; 17 Ross Ainley; 11 Ryan King; 20 Owen McCarron; 26 Huw Worthington. Sub (used, only one named): 4 Will Evans.
Tries: Hanneghan (21), McCarron (24), Walsh (35);
Goals: Hanneghan 3/4.
Rugby Leaguer & League Express Men of the Match:
Rams: Bailey O'Connor; *Whitehaven:* Lachlan Hanneghan.
Penalty count: 4-6; **Half-time:** 0-16;
Referee: Warren Turley; **Attendance:** 876.

Championship 2024 - Round by Round

DONCASTER 4 BRADFORD BULLS 18

DONCASTER: 17 Josh Guzdek; 5 Luke Briscoe; 4 Reece Lyne; 3 Brad Hey; 30 Bureta Faraimo; 24 Watson Boas; 7 Connor Robinson; 20 Brad Knowles; 15 Joe Lovodua; 10 Suaia Matagi; 16 Pauli Pauli; 12 Alex Sutcliffe; 13 Loui McConnell. Subs (all used): 19 Craig Hall; 25 Ilikaya Mafi; 27 Brett Ferres; 31 Lewis Baxter.
Try: Briscoe (25); **Goals:** Robinson 0/1.
BULLS: 1 Tom Holmes; 37 Jayden Okunbor; 21 Jayden Myers; 39 Max Lehmann; 5 Jorge Taufua; 45 Jarrod Sammut; 7 Jordan Lilley; 40 Logan Bayliss-Brow; 18 Mitch Souter; 13 Michael Lawrence; 29 Zac Fulton; 16 Keven Appo; 17 Eribe Doro. Subs (all used): 14 John Davies; 31 Tyran Ott; 42 Franklin Pele; 43 Harvey Makin.
Tries: Lilley (65), Appo (72), Holmes (75); **Goals:** Lilley 3/3.
Rugby Leaguer & League Express Men of the Match:
Doncaster: Pauli Pauli; *Bulls:* Eribe Doro.
Penalty count: 5-8; **Half-time:** 4-0;
Referee: Matty Lynn; **Attendance:** 1,758.

HALIFAX PANTHERS 6 WAKEFIELD TRINITY 48

PANTHERS: 1 James Woodburn-Hall; 5 James Saltonstall; 17 Ben Tibbs; 23 Gareth Widdop; 28 Charlie Graham; 6 Louis Jouffret; 7 Joe Keyes; 31 Kevin Larroyer; 9 Adam O'Brien; 34 Keelan Foster; 11 Ben Kavanagh; 19 Connor Davies; 13 Jacob Fairbank. Subs (all used): 8 Adam Tangata; 26 Ed Barber; 30 Joe Hird; 32 Kai Morgan.
Try: Graham (46); **Goals:** Jouffret 1/1.
TRINITY: 5 Lachlan Walmsley; 2 Jermaine McGillvary; 4 Iain Thornley; 3 Oliver Pratt; 32 Derrell Olpherts; 1 Max Jowitt; 14 Liam Kay; 8 Josh Bowden; 9 Liam Hood; 18 Ky Rodwell; 11 Matty Ashurst; 12 Josh Griffin; 13 Jay Pitts. Subs (all used): 10 Renouf Atoni; 16 Mathieu Cozza; 20 Toby Boothroyd; 21 Thomas Doyle.
Tries: Griffin (4), Hood (17, 71), McGillvary (25), Jowitt (37), Doyle (61), Olpherts (65), Ashurst (74);
Goals: Jowitt 8/8.
Sin bin: Ashurst (44) - dissent.
Rugby Leaguer & League Express Men of the Match:
Panthers: Louis Jouffret; *Trinity:* Lachlan Walmsley.
Penalty count: 5-7; **Half-time:** 0-24;
Referee: Liam Rush; **Attendance:** 2,500.

WIDNES VIKINGS 35 SHEFFIELD EAGLES 20

VIKINGS: 24 Lloyd Roby; 20 Mike Butt; 1 Jack Owens; 3 Matty Fleming; 2 Ryan Ince; 6 Joe Lyons; 7 Tom Gilmore; 17 Liam Bent; 14 Jordan Johnstone; 31 Dan Murray; 11 Rhodri Lloyd; 32 Shane Grady; 16 Max Roberts. Subs (all used): 9 Matty Fozard; 10 Sam Brooks; 15 Liam Kirk; 26 Lucas Green.
Tries: Lloyd (6), Grady (23, 34), Ince (43), Butt (65), Fozard (68); **Goals:** Gilmore 5/6; **Field goal:** Gilmore (40).
EAGLES: 1 Matty Marsh; 2 Ben Jones-Bishop; 3 Kris Welham; 4 James Glover; 5 Matty Dawson-Jones; 6 Cory Aston; 19 Izaac Farrell; 8 Eddie Battye; 9 Vila Halafihi; 10 Tyler Dickinson; 26 Alex Foster; 12 Joel Farrell; 15 Evan Hodgson. Subs (all used): 11 Connor Bower; 13 Titus Gwaze; 22 Kyle Wood; 27 Jesse Sene-Lefao.
Tries: Dawson-Jones (47, 53), Sene-Lefao (51), Jones-Bishop (77); **Goals:** Aston 2/4.
Rugby Leaguer & League Express Men of the Match:
Vikings: Shane Grady; *Eagles:* Tyler Dickinson.
Penalty count: 7-6; **Half-time:** 19-0;
Referee: Scott Mikalauskas; **Attendance:** 2,486.

YORK KNIGHTS 37 BATLEY BULLDOGS 6

KNIGHTS: 2 Joe Brown; 28 Brad Ward; 41 Joe Law; 11 Oli Field; 5 AJ Towse; 22 Ata Hingano; 14 Nikau Williams; 17 Ronan Michael; 9 Will Jubb; 13 Jordan Thompson; 12 Connor Bailey; 38 Jacob Gannon; 21 James Cunningham. Subs (all used): 15 Jack Teanby; 16 Brenden Santi; 19 Josh Daley; 42 Jack Martin.
Tries: Bailey (7), Cunningham (10), Law (23), Santi (49), Brown (66), Gannon (70); **Goals:** Williams 6/7;
Field goal: Williams (74).
BULLDOGS: 1 Robbie Butterworth; 5 Elliot Kear; 24 John Mitsias; 3 Kieran Buchanan; 18 Joe Burton; 6 Ben White; 7 Josh Woods; 13 James Brown; 25 Brandon Moore; 10 Luke Cooper; 11 Dane Manning; 12 Lucas Walshaw; 17 Luke Blake. Subs (all used): 9 Alistair Leak; 15 Nyle Flynn; 20 Ben Kaye; 28 Nixon Putt.
Try: Butterworth (17); **Goals:** Woods 1/1.
Rugby Leaguer & League Express Men of the Match:
Knights: Nikau Williams; *Bulldogs:* Lucas Walshaw.
Penalty count: 5-7; **Half-time:** 18-6;
Referee: Ryan Cox; **Attendance:** 2,003.

ROUND 22

Friday 30th August 2024

BRADFORD BULLS 54 DEWSBURY RAMS 0

BULLS: 1 Tom Holmes; 37 Jayden Okunbor; 21 Jayden Myers; 47 Romain Franco; 46 Jack Smith; 6 Lee Gaskell; 7 Jordan Lilley; 43 Harvey Makin; 31 Tyran Ott; 15 Daniel Smith; 14 John Davies; 16 Keven Appo; 19 Sam Hallas. Subs (all used): 10 Ebon Scurr; 29 Zac Fulton; 42 Franklin Pele; 41 Nathan Mason.
Tries: D Smith (15), Holmes (35), Pele (47, 58), Ott (53), Scurr (68), Franco (70, 72), Appo (80); **Goals:** Lilley 9/9.
RAMS: 7 Calum Turner; 5 Lewis Carr; 11 Brad Graham; 22 Marcus Walker; 2 Perry Whiteley; 6 Paul Sykes; 9 Jacob Hookem; 16 Elliot Morris; 20 Curtis Davies; 17 Jackson Walker; 28 Jack Billington; 12 Matt Garside; 32 Zeus Silk. Subs (all used): 10 Ronan Dixon; 26 Jamie Field; 30 Dale Ferguson; 37 Keenen Tomlinson.
Sin bin: Sykes (65) - dissent.
Rugby Leaguer & League Express Men of the Match:
Bulls: Franklin Pele; *Rams:* Elliot Morris.
Penalty count: 8-3; **Half-time:** 12-0;
Referee: Ryan Cox; **Attendance:** 3,006.

Saturday 31st August 2024

TOULOUSE OLYMPIQUE 32 SHEFFIELD EAGLES 12

OLYMPIQUE: 1 Olly Ashall-Bott; 5 Paul Marcon; 4 Mathieu Jussaume; 3 Reubenn Rennie; 2 Paul Ulberg; 7 Jake Shorrocks; 6 Ryan Rivett; 8 Lambert Belmas; 9 Calum Gahan; 10 Harrison Hansen; 24 Pierre-Jean Lima; 11 Maxime Stefani; 13 Anthony Marion. Subs (all used): 14 Eloi Pelissier; 17 James Roumanos; 15 Sitaleki Akauola; 25 Joe Cator.
Tries: Ulberg (17, 35, 60), Belmas (50), Ashall-Bott (77);
Goals: Shorrocks 6/6.
EAGLES: 2 Ben Jones-Bishop; 30 Ryan Millar; 23 Bayley Liu; 4 James Glover; 5 Matty Dawson-Jones; 6 Cory Aston; 1 Matty Marsh; 8 Eddie Battye; 9 Vila Halafihi; 10 Tyler Dickinson; 26 Alex Foster; 12 Joel Farrell; 11 Connor Bower. Subs (all used): 15 Evan Hodgson; 27 Jesse Sene-Lefao; 16 Blake Broadbent; 17 Mitch Clark.
Tries: Jones-Bishop (25), Liu (30); **Goals:** Aston 2/2.
Rugby Leaguer & League Express Men of the Match:
Olympique: Paul Ulberg; *Eagles:* Joel Farrell.
Penalty count: 7-8; **Half-time:** 14-12;
Referee: Matty Lynn; **Attendance:** 2,079.

Sunday 1st September 2024

BATLEY BULLDOGS 8 WIDNES VIKINGS 12

BULLDOGS: 1 Robbie Butterworth; 2 Dale Morton; 24 John Mitsias; 3 Kieran Buchanan; 18 Joe Burton; 6 Ben White; 7 Josh Woods; 8 Adam Gledhill; 25 Brandon Moore; 10 Luke Cooper; 11 Dane Manning; 12 Lucas Walshaw; 17 Luke Blake. Subs (all used): 14 Oli Burton; 15 Nyle Flynn; 13 James Brown; 28 Nixon Putt.
Try: Flynn (65); **Goals:** Woods 2/2.
VIKINGS: 1 Jack Owens; 20 Mike Butt; 29 Zac Bardsley-Rowe; 3 Matty Fleming; 2 Ryan Ince; 6 Joe Lyons; 7 Tom Gilmore; 17 Liam Bent; 14 Jordan Johnstone; 31 Dan Murray; 11 Rhodri Lloyd; 27 Ryan Lannon; 16 Max Roberts. Subs (all used): 9 Matty Fozard; 10 Sam Brooks; 15 Liam Kirk; 26 Lucas Green.
Tries: Lyons (36), Owens (60); **Goals:** Gilmore 2/2.
Rugby Leaguer & League Express Men of the Match:
Bulldogs: Josh Woods; *Vikings:* Mike Butt.
Penalty count: 6-7; **Half-time:** 2-6;
Referee: Cameron Worsley.

DONCASTER 16 HALIFAX PANTHERS 17

DONCASTER: 19 Craig Hall; 5 Luke Briscoe; 4 Reece Lyne; 3 Brad Hey; 30 Bureta Faraimo; 24 Watson Boas; 7 Connor Robinson; 20 Brad Knowles; 9 Greg Burns; 10 Suaia Matagi; 11 Sam Smeaton; 16 Pauli Pauli; 13 Loui McConnell. Subs (all used): 12 Alex Sutcliffe; 15 Joe Lovodua; 28 AJ Wallace; 31 Lewis Baxter.
Tries: Pauli (55), Lyne (73), Briscoe (77);
Goals: Robinson 2/3.
Sin bin: Knowles (20) - repeated team offences.
PANTHERS: 1 James Woodburn-Hall; 5 James Saltonstall; 23 Gareth Widdop; 26 Ed Barber; 28 Charlie Graham; 6 Louis Jouffret; 7 Joe Keyes; 31 Kevin Larroyer; 9 Adam O'Brien; 29 Clement Boyer; 11 Ben Kavanagh; 19 Connor Davies; 13 Jacob Fairbank. Subs (all used): 8 Adam Tangata; 12 Matty Gee; 25 Corey Johnson; 30 Joe Hird.
Tries: Graham (10), Barber (38), Keyes (66);
Goals: Jouffret 2/3; **Field goal:** Woodburn-Hall (79).
Rugby Leaguer & League Express Men of the Match:
Doncaster: Pauli Pauli; *Panthers:* Joe Keyes.
Penalty count: 6-8; **Half-time:** 0-10;
Referee: James Vella; **Attendance:** 1,443.

FEATHERSTONE ROVERS 36 BARROW RAIDERS 18

ROVERS: 6 Ben Reynolds; 5 Gareth Gale; 3 Josh Hardcastle; 4 Greg Minikin; 2 Connor Wynne; 13 Danny Addy; 30 Dec Patton; 32 Ben Nakubuwai; 14 Harry Bowes; 36 James Lockwood; 11 Brad Day; 37 Jimmy Beckett; 23 Jack Arnold. Subs (all used): 9 Connor Jones; 8 Gadwin Springer; 15 Wellington Albert; 33 Samy Kibula.
Tries: Day (9), Reynolds (22), Jones (38, 70), Beckett (46), Wynne (58); **Goals:** Reynolds 6/6.
Sin bin: Addy (77) - fighting; Bowes (80) - fighting.
RAIDERS: 1 Luke Cresswell; 5 Andrew Bulman; 4 Shane Toal; 14 Luke Broadbent; 2 Ryan Shaw; 6 Brad Walker; 7 Ryan Johnston; 10 Ellis Gillam; 21 Aaron Smith; 32 Ryan Brown; 13 James Greenwood; 12 Jarrad Stack; 19 Greg Worthington. Subs (all used): 9 Josh Wood; 15 Tom Wilkinson; 22 Tom Walker; 36 Jamie Pye.
Tries: Johnston (19), Wood (51), Broadbent (62), S Toal (76); **Goals:** Shaw 1/4.
Sin bin: Wood (80) - fighting.
Rugby Leaguer & League Express Men of the Match:
Rovers: Ben Reynolds; *Raiders:* Luke Broadbent.
Penalty count: 6-9; **Half-time:** 18-4;
Referee: Scott Mikalauskas; **Attendance:** 1,345.

SWINTON LIONS 0 WAKEFIELD TRINITY 60

LIONS: 1 Dan Abram; 3 Jake Spedding; 28 Brad Hammond; 4 Jayden Hatton; 5 Rhys Williams; 16 Lewis Hall; 7 Jordy Gibson; 10 Gavin Bennion; 14 Josh Eaves; 13 Mikey Wood; 8 Liam Cooper; 12 Mitch Cox; 33 Leon Cowen. Subs (all used): 31 Ciaran Nolan; 24 Jordan Case; 26 Anthony Walker; 20 Jack Houghton.
TRINITY: 5 Lachlan Walmsley; 22 Jack Croft; 4 Iain Thornley; 3 Oliver Pratt; 32 Derrell Olpherts; 1 Max Jowitt; 14 Liam Kay; 18 Ky Rodwell; 9 Liam Hood; 8 Josh Bowden; 11 Matty Ashurst; 20 Toby Boothroyd; 13 Jay Pitts. Subs (all used): 10 Renouf Atoni; 16 Mathieu Cozza; 19 Isaiah Vagana; 21 Thomas Doyle.
Tries: Ashurst (4), Walmsley (8), Olpherts (16, 62), Pitts (21), Rodwell (27, 75, 78), Vagana (30), Kay (38), Boothroyd (70); **Goals:** Jowitt 8/11.
Rugby Leaguer & League Express Men of the Match:
Lions: Leon Cowen; *Trinity:* Matty Ashurst.
Penalty count: 7-5; **Half-time:** 0-38;
Referee: Michael Smaill; **Attendance:** 1,048.

WHITEHAVEN 0 YORK KNIGHTS 40

WHITEHAVEN: 3 Joey Romeo; 24 Callum Shaw; 4 Will Evans; 5 Curtis Teare; 22 Mac Walsh; 9 Sam Ackroyd; 7 Lachlan Hanneghan; 8 Lucas Castle; 15 James Newton; 17 Ross Ainley; 21 Rio Corkill; 20 Owen McCarron; 26 Huw Worthington. Subs (all used): 14 Jake Carter; 18 Perry Singleton; 11 Ryan King; 1 Edene Gebbie.
KNIGHTS: 2 Joe Brown; 5 AJ Towse; 11 Oli Field; 41 Joe Law; 28 Brad Ward; 14 Nikau Williams; 22 Ata Hingano; 17 Ronan Michael; 9 Will Jubb; 42 Jack Martin; 12 Connor Bailey; 38 Jacob Gannon; 21 James Cunningham. Subs (all used): 15 Jack Teanby; 16 Brenden Santi; 19 Josh Daley; 25 Bailey Antrobus.
Tries: Williams (4, 38, 79), Law (30, 34), Santi (42), Martin (72); **Goals:** Williams 5/8, Jubb 1/1.
Rugby Leaguer & League Express Men of the Match:
Whitehaven: Huw Worthington; *Knights:* Ata Hingano.
Penalty count: 8-8; **Half-time:** 0-20;
Referee: Kevin Moore.

ROUND 23

Saturday 7th September 2024

BARROW RAIDERS 24 TOULOUSE OLYMPIQUE 36

RAIDERS: 1 Luke Cresswell; 5 Andrew Bulman; 17 Brett Carter; 14 Luke Broadbent; 2 Ryan Shaw; 6 Brad Walker; 7 Ryan Johnston; 10 Ellis Gillam; 21 Aaron Smith; 33 Delaine Bedward-Gittens; 11 Charlie Emslie; 12 Jarrad Stack; 19 Greg Worthington. Subs (all used): 9 Josh Wood; 15 Tom Wilkinson; 22 Tom Walker; 36 Jamie Pye.
Tries: Pye (45), B Walker (61), Shaw (69), Carter (79);
Goals: Shaw 4/4.
OLYMPIQUE: 1 Olly Ashall-Bott; 19 Benjamin Laguerre; 5 Paul Marcon; 3 Reubenn Rennie; 2 Paul Ulberg; 6 Ryan Rivett; 7 Jake Shorrocks; 8 Lambert Belmas; 9 Calum Gahan; 10 Harrison Hansen; 11 Maxime Stefani; 24 Pierre-Jean-Lima; 13 Anthony Marion. Subs (all used): 14 Eloi Pelissier; 15 Sitaleki Akauola; 20 Greg Richards; 22 Dimitri Biscarro.
Tries: Marcon (2), Ulberg (22, 39), Rivett (36), Ashall-Bott (57), Laguerre (76); **Goals:** Shorrocks 6/7.
Rugby Leaguer & League Express Men of the Match:
Raiders: Ellis Gillam; *Olympique:* Olly Ashall-Bott.
Penalty count: 7-4; **Half-time:** 0-22;
Referee: Matty Lynn; **Attendance:** 1,709.

Sunday 8th September 2024

BATLEY BULLDOGS 0 DONCASTER 38

BULLDOGS: 1 Robbie Butterworth; 2 Dale Morton; 4 George Senior; 3 Kieran Buchanan; 18 Joe Burton; 6 Ben White; 7 Josh Woods; 8 Adam Gledhill; 25 Brandon Moore; 10 Luke Cooper; 11 Dane Manning; 12 Lucas Walshaw; 13 James Brown. Subs (all used): 14 Oli Burton; 15 Nyle Flynn; 16 Michael Ward; 5 Elliot Kear.

Championship 2024 - Round by Round

DONCASTER: 19 Craig Hall; 5 Luke Briscoe; 4 Reece Lyne; 3 Brad Hey; 30 Bureta Faraimo; 24 Watson Boas; 7 Connor Robinson; 20 Brad Knowles; 9 Greg Burns; 10 Suaia Matagi; 12 Alex Sutcliffe; 16 Pauli Pauli; 13 Loui McConnell. Subs (all used): 11 Sam Smeaton; 15 Joe Lovodua; 27 Brett Ferres; 31 Lewis Baxter.
Tries: Pauli (10, 45), Faraimo (22, 38, 50, 77), Smeaton (65); **Goals:** Robinson 5/7.
Sin bin: Matagi (27) - high tackle.
Rugby Leaguer & League Express Men of the Match:
Bulldogs: Josh Woods; *Doncaster:* Bureta Faraimo.
Penalty count: 7-4; **Half-time:** 0-16; **Referee:** Kevin Moore.

HALIFAX PANTHERS 34 DEWSBURY RAMS 6

PANTHERS: 1 James Woodburn-Hall; 5 James Saltonstall; 23 Gareth Widdop; 17 Ben Tibbs; 28 Charlie Graham; 6 Louis Jouffret; 7 Joe Keyes; 31 Kevin Larroyer; 9 Adam O'Brien; 34 Keelan Foster; 26 Ed Barber; 12 Matty Gee; 30 Joe Hird. Subs (all used): 25 Corey Johnson; 29 Clement Boyer; 8 Adam Tangata; 13 Jacob Fairbank.
Tries: Barber (24), Woodburn-Hall (31), Widdop (43, 58), Tibbs (55, 73); **Goals:** Jouffret 5/6.
RAMS: 7 Calum Turner; 5 Lewis Carr; 22 Marcus Walker; 11 Brad Graham; 37 Keenen Tomlinson; 6 Paul Sykes; 9 Jacob Hookem; 17 Jackson Walker; 20 Curtis Davies; 16 Elliot Morris; 28 Jack Billington; 12 Matt Garside; 32 Zeus Silk. Subs (all used): 33 Reiss Butterworth; 26 Jamie Field; 10 Ronan Dixon; 35 Jack Briggs.
Try: Turner (62); **Goals:** Turner 1/1.
Rugby Leaguer & League Express Men of the Match:
Panthers: Ed Barber; *Rams:* Reiss Butterworth.
Penalty count: 5-4; **Half-time:** 10-0;
Referee: Ben Thaler; **Attendance:** 1,647.

SHEFFIELD EAGLES 12 BRADFORD BULLS 30

EAGLES: 2 Ben Jones-Bishop; 30 Ryan Millar; 3 Kris Welham; 4 James Glover; 5 Matty Dawson-Jones; 6 Cory Aston; 1 Matty Marsh; 8 Eddie Battye; 9 Vila Halafihi; 10 Tyler Dickinson; 26 Alex Foster; 27 Jesse Sene-Lefao; 13 Titus Gwaze. Subs (all used): 16 Blake Broadbent; 17 Mitch Clark; 22 Kyle Wood; 24 Oliver Roberts.
Tries: Foster (36), Marsh (69); **Goals:** Aston 2/2.
Sin bin: Sene-Lefao (60) - repeated team offences.
BULLS: 1 Tom Holmes; 37 Jayden Okunbor; 21 Jayden Myers; 47 Romain Franco; 5 Jorge Taufua; 6 Lee Gaskell; 7 Jordan Lilley; 13 Michael Lawrence; 31 Tyran Ott; 17 Eribe Doro; 29 Zac Fulton; 16 Keven Appo; 19 Sam Hallas. Subs (all used): 10 Ebon Scurr; 14 John Davies; 42 Franklin Pele; 15 Daniel Smith.
Tries: Hallas (10), Okunbor (18), Franco (62), Taufua (75, 77); **Goals:** Lilley 5/6.
Sin bin: Myers (47) - dangerous challenge.
Rugby Leaguer & League Express Men of the Match:
Eagles: Matty Marsh; *Bulls:* Franklin Pele.
Penalty count: 6-13; **Half-time:** 6-12;
Referee: Cameron Worsley; **Attendance:** 1,948.

SWINTON LIONS 28 FEATHERSTONE ROVERS 8

LIONS: 1 Dan Abram; 25 Richard Lepori; 3 Jake Spedding; 4 Jayden Hatton; 5 Rhys Williams; 18 Jack Stevens; 7 Jordy Gibson; 10 Gavin Bennion; 14 Josh Eaves; 13 Mikey Wood; 11 Gav Rodden; 12 Mitch Cox; 16 Lewis Hall. Subs (all used): 8 Liam Cooper; 20 Jack Houghton; 24 Jordan Case; 26 Anthony Walker.
Tries: Lepori (16, 60, 67), Hatton (26), Williams (46); **Goals:** Abram 4/6.
Sin bin: Abram (29) - delaying restart.
ROVERS: 26 Greg Eden; 31 Connor Barley; 4 Greg Minikin; 3 Josh Hardcastle; 29 Maddox Jeffery; 13 Danny Addy; 30 Dec Patton; 36 James Lockwood; 9 Connor Jones; 32 Ben Nakubuwai; 11 Brad Day; 12 Jack Bussey; 37 Jimmy Beckett. Subs (all used): 8 Gadwin Springer; 14 Harry Bowes; 15 Wellington Albert; 23 Jack Arnold.
Tries: Minikin (4), Eden (65); **Goals:** Patton 0/2.
Rugby Leaguer & League Express Men of the Match:
Lions: Richard Lepori; *Rovers:* Greg Eden.
Penalty count: 6-5; **Half-time:** 12-4;
Referee: Scott Mikalauskas; **Attendance:** 780.

WAKEFIELD TRINITY 60 WHITEHAVEN 6

TRINITY: 30 Noah Booth; 2 Jermaine McGillvary; 4 Iain Thornley; 3 Oliver Pratt; 32 Derrell Olpherts; 14 Liam Kay; 1 Max Jowitt; 18 Ky Rodwell; 21 Thomas Doyle; 8 Josh Bowden; 19 Isaiah Vagana; 12 Josh Griffin; 16 Mathieu Cozza. Subs (all used): 9 Liam Hood; 10 Renouf Atoni; 20 Toby Boothroyd; 22 Jack Croft.
Tries: Rodwell (19, 66), McGillvary (24, 48), Booth (33), Cozza (37), Jowitt (40, 45), Hood (62), Doyle (72);
Goals: Jowitt 10/10.
WHITEHAVEN: 3 Joey Romeo; 24 Callum Shaw; 4 Will Evans; 22 Mac Walsh; 1 Edene Gebbie; 14 Jake Carter; 7 Lachlan Hanneghan; 8 Lucas Castle; 9 Sam Ackroyd; 17 Ross Ainley; 21 Rio Corkill; 5 Curtis Teare; 20 Owen

Halifax's Gareth Widdop goes past Dewsbury's Marcus Walker

McCarron. Subs (both used, only two named): 15 James Newton; 26 Huw Worthington.
Try: Gebbie (77); **Goals:** Hanneghan 1/1.
Sin bin: Hanneghan (44) - delaying restart.
Rugby Leaguer & League Express Men of the Match:
Trinity: Noah Booth; *Whitehaven:* Lachlan Hanneghan.
Penalty count: 2-5; **Half-time:** 30-0;
Referee: Ryan Cox; **Attendance:** 5,096.

WIDNES VIKINGS 6 YORK KNIGHTS 12

VIKINGS: 1 Jack Owens; 20 Mike Butt; 29 Zac Bardsley-Rowe; 3 Matty Fleming; 2 Ryan Ince; 6 Joe Lyons; 7 Tom Gilmore; 17 Liam Bent; 14 Jordan Johnstone; 31 Dan Murray; 11 Rhodri Lloyd; 32 Shane Grady; 27 Ryan Lannon. Subs (all used): 9 Matty Fozard; 10 Sam Brooks; 15 Liam Kirk; 16 Max Roberts.
Try: Butt (54); **Goals:** Gilmore 1/2.
KNIGHTS: 2 Joe Brown; 5 AJ Towse; 11 Oli Field; 41 Joe Law; 28 Brad Ward; 14 Nikau Williams; 22 Ata Hingano; 25 Bailey Antrobus; 9 Will Jubb; 42 Jack Martin; 12 Connor Bailey; 38 Jacob Gannon; 21 James Cunningham. Subs (all used): 15 Jack Teanby; 16 Brenden Santi; 17 Ronan Michael; 19 Josh Daley.
Try: Law (15); **Goals:** Williams 4/4.
Dismissal: Gannon (65) - fighting.
Rugby Leaguer & League Express Men of the Match:
Vikings: Sam Brooks; *Knights:* Ata Hingano.
Penalty count: 5-9; **Half-time:** 0-10;
Referee: Liam Rush; **Attendance:** 2,663.

ROUND 24

Saturday 14th September 2024

TOULOUSE OLYMPIQUE 38 HALIFAX PANTHERS 18

OLYMPIQUE: 1 Olly Ashall-Bott; 19 Benjamin Laguerre; 5 Paul Marcon; 18 Guy Armitage; 2 Paul Ulberg; 7 Jake Shorrocks; 6 Ryan Rivett; 8 Lambert Belmas; 9 Calum Gahan; 10 Harrison Hansen; 24 Pierre-Jean Lima; 11 Maxime Stefani; 13 Anthony Marion. Subs (all used): 14 Eloi Pelissier; 25 Joe Cator; 15 Sitaleki Akauola; 22 Dimitri Biscarro.
Tries: Armitage (6), Stefani (13, 21), Laguerre (24), Rivett (60), Ulberg (72), Marion (74);
Goals: Shorrocks 2/4, Rivett 3/3.
PANTHERS: 6 Louis Jouffret; 1 James Woodburn-Hall; 26 Ed Barber; 17 Ben Tibbs; 28 Charlie Graham; 32 Kai Morgan; 7 Joe Keyes; 34 Keelan Foster; 9 Adam O'Brien; 31 Kevin Larroyer; 22 Ben Hursey; 19 Connor Davies; 35 Joe Hird. Subs (all used): 25 Corey Johnson; 8 Adam Tangata; 29 Clement Boyer; 13 Jacob Fairbank.
Tries: Graham (17), Hursey (34, 65), Tibbs (45);
Goals: Jouffret 1/4.
Rugby Leaguer & League Express Men of the Match:
Olympique: Olly Ashall-Bott; *Panthers:* Ben Hursey.
Penalty count: 6-8; **Half-time:** 20-10;
Referee: Aaryn Belafonte; **Attendance:** 2,985.

Sunday 15th September 2024

BARROW RAIDERS 34 WHITEHAVEN 14

RAIDERS: 1 Luke Cresswell; 5 Andrew Bulman; 14 Luke Broadbent; 4 Shane Toal; 2 Ryan Shaw; 6 Brad Walker; 7 Ryan Johnston; 10 Ellis Gillam; 9 Josh Wood; 32 Ryan Brown; 12 Jarrad Stack; 13 James Greenwood; 19 Greg Worthington. Subs (all used): 21 Aaron Smith; 15 Tom Wilkinson; 22 Tom Walker; 36 Jamie Pye.
Tries: Bulman (10, 49), Greenwood (25), Johnston (62), Broadbent (79); **Goals:** Shaw 7/7.
Dismissal: Worthington (73) - fighting.
WHITEHAVEN: 3 Joey Romeo; 24 Callum Shaw; 4 Will Evans; 22 Mac Walsh; 1 Edene Gebbie; 14 Jake Carter; 7 Lachlan Hanneghan; 8 Lucas Castle; 15 James Newton; 17 Ross Ainley; 5 Curtis Teare; 20 Owen McCarron; 26 Huw Worthington. Subs (all used): 9 Sam Ackroyd; 21 Rio Corkill; 27 Bobby Hartley; 16 Noah High.
Tries: Gebbie (5, 65), Hanneghan (16);
Goals: Hanneghan 1/3.
Dismissal: McCarron (73) - fighting.
Sin bin: Ackroyd (43) - dissent.
Rugby Leaguer & League Express Men of the Match:
Raiders: Luke Cresswell; *Whitehaven:* Lachlan Hanneghan.
Penalty count: 10-3; **Half-time:** 14-10;
Referee: Scott Mikalauskas; **Attendance:** 2,301.

Championship 2024 - Round by Round

BRADFORD BULLS 16 BATLEY BULLDOGS 14

BULLS: 1 Tom Holmes; 37 Jayden Okunbor; 21 Jayden Myers; 47 Romain Franco; 5 Jorge Taufua; 6 Lee Gaskell; 7 Jordan Lilley; 13 Michael Lawrence; 18 Mitch Souter; 43 Harvey Makin; 29 Zac Fulton; 16 Keven Appo; 19 Sam Hallas. Subs (all used): 10 Ebon Scurr; 15 Daniel Smith; 42 Franklin Pele; 45 Jarrod Sammut.
Tries: Taufua (10), Okunbor (37, 51); **Goals:** Lilley 2/3.
BULLDOGS: 1 Robbie Butterworth; 2 Dale Morton; 5 Elliot Kear; 3 Kieran Buchanan; 18 Joe Burton; 6 Ben White; 7 Josh Woods; 8 Adam Gledhill; 25 Brandon Moore; 13 James Brown; 11 Dane Manning; 12 Lucas Walshaw; 17 Luke Blake. Subs (all used): 4 George Senior; 14 Oli Burton; 16 Michael Ward; 20 Ben Kaye.
Tries: Walshaw (16), J Burton (33), Senior (76);
Goals: Woods 1/3.
Rugby Leaguer & League Express Men of the Match:
Bulls: Jordan Lilley; *Bulldogs:* Lucas Walshaw.
Penalty count: 5-4; **Half-time:** 12-10;
Referee: Ryan Cox; Attendance: 3,212.

DEWSBURY RAMS 16 SWINTON LIONS 28

RAMS: 4 Bailey O'Connor; 5 Lewis Carr; 22 Marcus Walker; 3 Ollie Greensmith; 37 Keenen Tomlinson; 6 Paul Sykes; 9 Jacob Hookem; 16 Elliot Morris; 33 Reiss Butterworth; 17 Jackson Walker; 11 Brad Graham; 30 Dale Ferguson; 13 Louis Collinson. Subs (all used): 36 Luke Mearns; 26 Jamie Field; 10 Ronan Dixon; 32 Zeus Silk.
Tries: R Dixon (24), Tomlinson (31), Greensmith (59);
Goals: Sykes 2/3.
Sin bin: R Dixon (30) - retaliation, (41) - late challenge on Gibson; O'Connor (36) - holding down.
LIONS: 1 Dan Abram; 25 Richard Lepori; 3 Jake Spedding; 4 Jayden Hatton; 5 Rhys Williams; 18 Jack Stevens; 7 Jordy Gibson; 10 Gavin Bennion; 14 Josh Eaves; 13 Mikey Wood; 11 Gav Rodden; 12 Mitch Cox; 16 Lewis Hall. Subs (all used): 33 Leon Cowen; 26 Anthony Walker; 24 Jordan Case; 8 Liam Cooper.
Tries: Spedding (14), Hatton (17, 46, 49), Abram (22);
Goals: Abram 4/6.
Dismissal: Rodden (30) - use of the head;
Lepori (58) - use of the head.
Rugby Leaguer & League Express Men of the Match:
Rams: Jacob Hookem; *Lions:* Jordy Gibson.
Penalty count: 6-5; **Half-time:** 12-20;
Referee: Ben Thaler; **Attendance:** 922.

DONCASTER 30 WIDNES VIKINGS 14

DONCASTER: 19 Craig Hall; 5 Luke Briscoe; 4 Reece Lyne; 3 Brad Hey; 30 Bureta Faraimo; 24 Watson Boas; 7 Connor Robinson; 20 Brad Knowles; 9 Greg Burns; 10 Suaia Matagi; 12 Alex Sutcliffe; 16 Pauli Pauli; 28 AJ Wallace. Subs (all used): 6 Ben Johnston; 11 Sam Smeaton; 27 Brett Ferres; 31 Lewis Baxter.
Tries: Lyne (4), Robinson (19), Briscoe (46), Faraimo (78);
Goals: Robinson 7/7.
VIKINGS: 24 Lloyd Roby; 20 Mike Butt; 3 Matty Fleming; 1 Jack Owens; 2 Ryan Ince; 6 Joe Lyons; 7 Tom Gilmore; 15 Liam Kirk; 9 Matty Fozard; 31 Dan Murray; 11 Rhodri Lloyd; 32 Shane Grady; 17 Liam Bent. Subs (all used): 10 Sam Brooks; 16 Max Roberts; 26 Lucas Green; 27 Ryan Lannon.
Tries: Gilmore (55), Ince (72); **Goals:** Gilmore 3/3.
Sin bin: Fleming (67) - high tackle on Briscoe.
Rugby Leaguer & League Express Men of the Match:
Doncaster: Reece Lyne; *Vikings:* Matty Fozard.
Penalty count: 8-7; **Half-time:** 14-2;
Referee: Michael Smaill; **Attendance:** 1,360.

FEATHERSTONE ROVERS 6 SHEFFIELD EAGLES 20

ROVERS: 26 Greg Eden; 5 Gareth Gale; 3 Josh Hardcastle; 4 Greg Minikin; 2 Connor Wynne; 6 Ben Reynolds; 30 Dec Patton; 32 Ben Nakubuwai; 9 Connor Jones; 36 James Lockwood; 12 Jack Bussey; 37 Jimmy Beckett; 13 Danny Addy. Subs: 8 Gadwin Springer; 14 Harry Bowes (not used); 15 Wellington Albert; 23 Jack Arnold.
Try: Wynne (15); **Goals:** Reynolds 1/1.
EAGLES: 1 Matty Marsh; 2 Ben Jones-Bishop; 3 Kris Welham; 4 James Glover; 5 Matty Dawson-Jones; 6 Cory Aston; 14 Jack Hansen; 8 Eddie Battye; 9 Vila Halafihi; 10 Tyler Dickinson; 11 Connor Bower; 12 Joel Farrell; 13 Titus Gwaze. Subs (all used): 16 Blake Broadbent; 17 Mitch Clark; 22 Kyle Wood; 24 Oliver Roberts.
Tries: Jones-Bishop (11, 67), Marsh (37); **Goals:** Aston 4/5.
Sin bin: Broadbent (49) - dangerous challenge.
Rugby Leaguer & League Express Men of the Match:
Rovers: James Lockwood; *Eagles:* Titus Gwaze.
Penalty count: 8-6; **Half-time:** 6-12;
Referee: Cameron Worsley; **Attendance:** 1,246.

WAKEFIELD TRINITY 20 YORK KNIGHTS 4

TRINITY: 1 Max Jowitt; 2 Jermaine McGillvary; 4 Iain Thornley; 3 Oliver Pratt; 32 Derrell Olpherts; 6 Luke Gale; 14 Liam Kay; 8 Josh Bowden; 21 Thomas Doyle; 10 Renouf Atoni; 11 Matty Ashurst; 12 Josh Griffin; 13 Jay Pitts. Subs (all used): 5 Lachlan Walmsley; 15 Caleb Uele; 18 Ky Rodwell; 19 Isaiah Vagana.
Tries: Jowitt (8), Gale (11), McGillvary (34), Olpherts (77);
Goals: Jowitt 2/4.
KNIGHTS: 2 Joe Brown; 34 Tom Lineham; 11 Oli Field; 41 Joe Law; 28 Brad Ward; 14 Nikau Williams; 22 Ata Hingano; 17 Ronan Michael; 9 Will Jubb; 42 Jack Martin; 12 Connor Bailey; 38 Jacob Gannon; 13 Jordan Thompson. Subs (all used): 15 Jack Teanby; 16 Brenden Santi; 19 Josh Daley; 25 Bailey Antrobus.
Try: Ward (19); **Goals:** Williams 0/1.
Rugby Leaguer & League Express Men of the Match:
Trinity: Jermaine McGillvary; *Knights:* Ata Hingano.
Penalty count: 6-1; **Half-time:** 16-4;
Referee: James Vella; **Attendance:** 5,137.

ROUND 25

Friday 20th September 2024

SHEFFIELD EAGLES 24 YORK KNIGHTS 26

EAGLES: 1 Matty Marsh; 2 Ben Jones-Bishop; 3 Kris Welham; 4 James Glover; 5 Matty Dawson-Jones; 6 Cory Aston; 7 Anthony Thackeray; 8 Eddie Battye; 9 Vila Halafihi; 10 Tyler Dickinson; 11 Connor Bower; 12 Joel Farrell; 13 Titus Gwaze. Subs (all used): 16 Blake Broadbent; 17 Mitch Clark; 22 Kyle Wood; 24 Oliver Roberts.
Tries: Gwaze (3), Glover (37), Dawson-Jones (72), Dickinson (76); **Goals:** Aston 4/4.
KNIGHTS: 14 Nikau Williams; 2 Joe Brown; 11 Oli Field; 41 Joe Law; 34 Tom Lineham; 22 Ata Hingano; 7 Liam Harris; 17 Ronan Michael; 9 Will Jubb; 8 Ukuma Ta'ai; 12 Connor Bailey; 38 Jacob Gannon; 13 Jordan Thompson. Subs (all used): 3 Jesse Dee; 16 Brenden Santi; 19 Josh Daley; 42 Jack Martin.
Tries: Hingano (7), Williams (25), Harris (31, 59);
Goals: Williams 5/5.
Rugby Leaguer & League Express Men of the Match:
Eagles: Joel Farrell; *Knights:* Ata Hingano.
Penalty count: 4-7; **Half-time:** 12-18;
Referee: Liam Rush; **Attendance:** 952.

Saturday 21st September 2024

FEATHERSTONE ROVERS 50 DEWSBURY RAMS 12

ROVERS: 1 Caleb Aekins; 2 Connor Wynne; 3 Josh Hardcastle; 4 Greg Minikin; 5 Gareth Gale; 6 Ben Reynolds; 7 Thomas Lacans; 23 Jack Arnold; 9 Connor Jones; 32 Ben Nakubuwai; 11 Brad Day; 12 Jack Bussey; 13 Danny Addy. Subs (all used): 8 Gadwin Springer; 26 Greg Eden; 36 James Lockwood; 37 Jimmy Beckett.
Tries: Aekins (7), Reynolds (12, 30), Lacans (40), Beckett (43), Wynne (49, 59, 80), Jones (68);
Goals: Reynolds 7/9.
Sin bin: Addy (78) - late challenge;
Arnold (80) - late challenge.
RAMS: 7 Calum Turner; 22 Marcus Walker; 4 Bailey O'Connor; 3 Ollie Greensmith; 37 Keenen Tomlinson; 6 Paul Sykes; 9 Jacob Hookem; 16 Elliot Morris; 33 Reiss Butterworth; 26 Jamie Field; 30 Dale Ferguson; 11 Brad Graham; 13 Louis Collinson. Subs (all used): 10 Ronan Dixon; 32 Zeus Silk; 35 Jack Briggs; 36 Luke Mearns.
Tries: Tomlinson (22), Greensmith (79); **Goals:** Turner 2/2.
Rugby Leaguer & League Express Men of the Match:
Rovers: Connor Wynne; *Rams:* Ollie Greensmith.
Penalty count: 5-7; **Half-time:** 22-6;
Referee: Michael Smaill.

WAKEFIELD TRINITY 46 BARROW RAIDERS 0

TRINITY: 5 Lachlan Walmsley; 32 Derrell Olpherts; 4 Iain Thornley; 22 Jack Croft; 3 Oliver Pratt; 30 Noah Booth; 1 Max Jowitt; 8 Josh Bowden; 26 Harvey Smith; 18 Ky Rodwell; 19 Isaiah Vagana; 12 Josh Griffin; 13 Jay Pitts. Subs (all used): 10 Renouf Atoni; 15 Caleb Uele; 16 Mathieu Cozza; 34 Rowan Stephenson.
Tries: Pitts (4), Rodwell (8), Jowitt (15, 63), Pratt (22, 48, 58), Walmsley (69); **Goals:** Jowitt 7/8.
RAIDERS: 1 Luke Cresswell; 17 Brett Carter; 16 Max Clarke; 4 Shane Toal; 2 Ryan Shaw; 6 Brad Walker; 30 Max Anderson-Moore; 33 Delaine Bedward-Gittens; 21 Aaron Smith; 32 Ryan Brown; 25 Finn McMillan; 12 Jarrad Stack; 19 Greg Worthington. Subs (all used): 9 Josh Wood; 15 Tom Wilkinson; 31 Finley Dutton-Rosconie; 35 Connor Terrill.
Rugby Leaguer & League Express Men of the Match:
Trinity: Oliver Pratt; *Raiders:* Delaine Bedward-Gittens.
Penalty count: 1-7; **Half-time:** 24-0;
Referee: Warren Turley; **Attendance:** 5,011.

WIDNES VIKINGS 12 TOULOUSE OLYMPIQUE 18

VIKINGS: 1 Jack Owens; 25 Reagan Sumner; 29 Zac Bardsley-Rowe; 3 Matty Fleming; 2 Ryan Ince; 6 Joe Lyons; 7 Tom Gilmore; 10 Sam Brooks; 9 Matty Fozard; 17 Liam Bent; 11 Rhodri Lloyd; 16 Max Roberts; 27 Ryan Lannon. Subs (all used): 15 Liam Kirk; 20 Mike Butt; 31 Dan Murray; 32 Shane Grady.
Tries: Fleming (3), Ince (30); **Goals:** Gilmore 2/3.
Sin bin: Butt (69) - obstruction.
OLYMPIQUE: 23 Robin Brochon; 2 Paul Ulberg; 18 Guy Armitage; 21 Mac Walsh; 19 Benjamin Laguerre; 6 Ryan Rivett; 13 Anthony Marion; 8 Lambert Belmas; 9 Calum Gahan; 10 Harrison Hansen; 11 Maxime Stefani; 24 Pierre-Jean Lima; 30 Baptiste Rodriguez. Subs (all used): 14 Eloi Pelissier; 15 Sitaleki Akauola; 16 Joe Bretherton; 22 Dimitri Biscarro.
Tries: Biscarro (50), Pelissier (64), Armitage (75);
Goals: Rivett 3/4.
Rugby Leaguer & League Express Men of the Match:
Vikings: Jack Owens; *Olympique:* Eloi Pelissier.
Penalty count: 9-5; **Half-time:** 12-0;
Referee: Kevin Moore; **Attendance:** 3,011.

Sunday 22nd September 2024

BATLEY BULLDOGS 28 WHITEHAVEN 14

BULLDOGS: 27 Luke Hooley; 2 Dale Morton; 5 Elliot Kear; 3 Kieran Buchanan; 18 Joe Burton; 6 Ben White; 7 Josh Woods; 8 Adam Gledhill; 25 Brandon Moore; 13 James Brown; 11 Dane Manning; 12 Lucas Walshaw; 17 Luke Blake. Subs (all used): 14 Oli Burton; 15 Nyle Flynn; 16 Michael Ward; 10 Luke Cooper.
Tries: Moore (22), Manning (30), White (36), Buchanan (46), Flynn (66); **Goals:** Woods 4/6.
Sin bin: Brown (68) - dangerous contact;
Hooley (73) - high tackle.
WHITEHAVEN: 3 Joey Romeo; 1 Edene Gebbie; 4 Will Evans; 5 Curtis Teare; 24 Callum Shaw; 14 Jake Carter; 7 Lachlan Hanneghan; 8 Lucas Castle; 15 James Newton; 26 Huw Worthington; 20 Owen McCarron; 21 Rio Corkill; 27 Bobby Hartley. Subs (both used, only two named): 9 Sam Ackroyd; 11 Ryan King.
Tries: Gebbie (13), McCarron (52), Romeo (58);
Goals: Hanneghan 1/3.
Sin bin: King (48) - dangerous challenge.
Rugby Leaguer & League Express Men of the Match:
Bulldogs: Josh Woods; *Whitehaven:* Bobby Hartley.
Penalty count: 8-6; **Half-time:** 16-6;
Referee: Cameron Worsley; **Attendance:** 1,644.

HALIFAX PANTHERS 14 BRADFORD BULLS 10

PANTHERS: 1 James Woodburn-Hall; 5 James Saltonstall; 23 Gareth Widdop; 26 Ed Barber; 28 Charlie Graham; 6 Louis Jouffret; 7 Joe Keyes; 31 Kevin Larroyer; 25 Corey Johnson; 13 Jacob Fairbank; 22 Ben Hursey; 19 Connor Davies; 12 Matty Gee. Subs (all used): 9 Adam O'Brien; 8 Adam Tangata; 29 Clement Boyer; 11 Ben Kavanagh.
Tries: Fairbank (12), Saltonstall (61); **Goals:** Jouffret 3/5.
Dismissal: Barber (80) - fighting.
Sin bin: Tangata (80) - fighting.
BULLS: 1 Tom Holmes; 37 Jayden Okunbor; 21 Jayden Myers; 4 Kieran Gill; 39 Max Lehmann; 6 Lee Gaskell; 7 Jordan Lilley; 43 Harvey Makin; 18 Mitch Souter; 40 Logan Bayliss-Brow; 16 Keven Appo; 29 Zac Fulton; 13 Michael Lawrence. Subs (all used): 31 Tyran Ott; 42 Franklin Pele; 10 Ebon Scurr; 14 John Davies.
Tries: Makin (18), Myers (24); **Goals:** Lilley 1/2.
Sin bin: Souter (57) - professional foul, (80) - fighting.
Rugby Leaguer & League Express Men of the Match:
Panthers: Matty Gee; *Bulls:* Lee Gaskell.
Penalty count: 5-10; **Half-time:** 8-10;
Referee: Matty Lynn; **Attendance:** 3,285.

SWINTON LIONS 20 DONCASTER 22

LIONS: 25 Richard Lepori; 32 Tee Ritson; 3 Jake Spedding; 4 Jayden Hatton; 5 Rhys Williams; 18 Jack Stevens; 7 Jordy Gibson; 13 Mikey Wood; 14 Josh Eaves; 10 Gavin Bennion; 11 Gav Rodden; 12 Mitch Cox; 16 Lewis Hall. Subs (all used): 1 Dan Abram; 26 Anthony Walker; 24 Jordan Case; 33 Leon Cowen.
Tries: Lepori (8), Gibson (36), Ritson (59);
Goals: Stevens 4/5.
Sin bin: Rodden (62) - holding down.
DONCASTER: 17 Josh Guzdek; 5 Luke Briscoe; 4 Reece Lyne; 23 Jason Tali; 30 Bureta Faraimo; 24 Watson Boas; 7 Connor Robinson; 31 Lewis Baxter; 13 Loui McConnell; 10 Suaia Matagi; 12 Alex Sutcliffe; 16 Pauli Pauli; 28 AJ Wallace. Subs (all used): 3 Brad Hey; 14 Alex Holdstock; 11 Sam Smeaton; 25 Ilikaya Mafi.
Tries: Pauli (4), McConnell (15, 67), Briscoe (22);
Goals: Robinson 3/5.
Rugby Leaguer & League Express Men of the Match:
Lions: Lewis Hall; *Doncaster:* Loui McConnell.
Penalty count: 3-8; **Half-time:** 14-16;
Referee: Scott Mikalauskas; **Attendance:** 836.

Championship 2024 - Round by Round

ROUND 26

Saturday 28th September 2024

TOULOUSE OLYMPIQUE 64 BATLEY BULLDOGS 16

OLYMPIQUE: 1 Olly Ashall-Bott; 19 Benjamin Laguerre; 18 Guy Armitage; 3 Reubenn Rennie; 2 Paul Ulberg; 7 Jake Shorrocks; 6 Ryan Rivett; 8 Lambert Belmas; 9 Calum Gahan; 10 Harrison Hansen; 24 Pierre-Jean Lima; 11 Maxime Stefani; 13 Anthony Marion. Subs (all used): 14 Eloi Pelissier; 16 Joe Bretherton; 15 Sitaleki Akauola; 22 Dimitri Biscarro.
Tries: Ashall-Bott (8, 62), Ulberg (13, 54), Rivett (19), Stefani (40, 73), Rennie (60), Laguerre (70), Armitage (78), Pelissier (80); **Goals:** Shorrocks 9/10, Pelissier 1/1.
BULLDOGS: 1 Robbie Butterworth; 2 Dale Morton; 24 John Mitsias; 3 Kieran Buchanan; 18 Joe Burton; 6 Ben White; 7 Josh Woods; 8 Adam Gledhill; 25 Brandon Moore; 16 Michael Ward; 11 Dane Manning; 12 Lucas Walshaw; 13 James Brown. Subs (all used, only three named): 10 Luke Cooper; 22 Paul Chitakunye; 5 Elliot Kear.
Tries: J Burton (24, 49), Mitsias (44); **Goals:** White 2/3.
Sin bin: Buchanan (80) - delaying restart.
Rugby Leaguer & League Express Men of the Match:
Olympique: Olly Ashall-Bott; *Bulldogs:* Robbie Butterworth.
Penalty count: 2-2; **Half-time:** 24-6;
Referee: Geoffrey Poumes; **Attendance:** 3,361.

Bradford's Franklin Pele charges at Swinton's Mitch Cox and Jack Stevens

Sunday 29th September 2024

BARROW RAIDERS 24 WIDNES VIKINGS 26

RAIDERS: 1 Luke Cresswell; 5 Andrew Bulman; 14 Luke Broadbent; 4 Shane Toal; 2 Ryan Shaw; 6 Brad Walker; 7 Ryan Johnston; 10 Ellis Gillam; 9 Josh Wood; 32 Ryan Brown; 16 Max Clarke; 12 Jarrad Stack; 11 Charlie Emslie. Subs (all used): 21 Aaron Smith; 15 Tom Wilkinson; 22 Tom Walker; 33 Delaine Bedward-Gittens.
Tries: Cresswell (7), Clarke (50), Shaw (63), Broadbent (71); **Goals:** Shaw 4/5.
Sin bin: T Walker (25) - trip on Lloyd.
VIKINGS: 1 Jack Owens; 20 Mike Butt; 29 Zac Bardsley-Rowe; 3 Matty Fleming; 2 Ryan Ince; 6 Joe Lyons; 7 Tom Gilmore; 15 Liam Kirk; 9 Matty Fozard; 10 Sam Brooks; 11 Rhodri Lloyd; 16 Max Roberts; 27 Ryan Lannon. Subs (all used): 8 Callum Field; 30 Martyn Reilly; 31 Dan Murray; 32 Shane Grady.
Tries: Owens (22, 58), Lloyd (25), Lannon (38), Butt (67); **Goals:** Gilmore 3/6.
Rugby Leaguer & League Express Men of the Match:
Raiders: Luke Cresswell; *Vikings:* Tom Gilmore.
Penalty count: 8-5; **Half-time:** 8-16;
Referee: Liam Rush; **Attendance:** 2,953.

BRADFORD BULLS 50 SWINTON LIONS 0

BULLS: 1 Tom Holmes; 21 Jayden Myers; 47 Romain Franco; 4 Kieran Gill; 39 Max Lehmann; 45 Jarrod Sammut; 7 Jordan Lilley; 15 Daniel Smith; 18 Mitch Souter; 40 Logan Bayliss-Brow; 14 John Davies; 29 Zac Fulton; 43 Harvey Makin. Subs (all used): 10 Ebon Scurr; 31 Tyran Ott; 41 Nathan Mason; 42 Franklin Pele.
Tries: Lehmann (8, 35), Holmes (16), Pele (31, 48, 75), Bayliss-Brow (39), Gill (45), Myers (59); **Goals:** Lilley 6/8, Sammut 1/1.
LIONS: 1 Dan Abram; 32 Tee Ritson; 3 Jake Spedding; 4 Jayden Hatton; 5 Rhys Williams; 18 Jack Stevens; 7 Jordy Gibson; 13 Mikey Wood; 14 Josh Eaves; 10 Gavin Bennion; 29 Jonny Vaughan; 12 Mitch Cox; 16 Lewis Hall. Subs (all used): 24 Jordan Case; 26 Anthony Walker; 33 Leon Cowen; 8 Liam Cooper.
Rugby Leaguer & League Express Men of the Match:
Bulls: Tom Holmes; *Lions:* Mitch Cox.
Penalty count: 8-5; **Half-time:** 28-0;
Referee: Michael Smaill; **Attendance:** 3,293.

DEWSBURY RAMS 28 SHEFFIELD EAGLES 8

RAMS: 4 Bailey O'Connor; 5 Lewis Carr; 22 Marcus Walker; 3 Ollie Greensmith; 37 Keenen Tomlinson; 7 Calum Turner; 33 Reiss Butterworth; 16 Elliot Morris; 36 Luke Mearns; 26 Jamie Field; 30 Dale Ferguson; 32 Zeus Silk; 13 Louis Collinson. Subs (all used, only three named): 24 Joel Russell; 35 Jack Briggs; 15 Joe Summers.
Tries: Tomlinson (12), Butterworth (18), Greensmith (39, 54), Carr (74); **Goals:** Turner 4/6.
Sin bin: O'Connor (29) - dangerous challenge; Field (50) - late challenge.
EAGLES: 1 Matty Marsh; 2 Ben Jones-Bishop; 3 Kris Welham; 4 James Glover; 5 Matty Dawson-Jones; 6 Cory Aston; 7 Anthony Thackeray; 8 Eddie Battye; 22 Kyle Wood; 10 Tyler Dickinson; 18 Aaron Murphy; 12 Joel Farrell; 15 Evan Hodgson. Subs (all used): 14 Jack Hansen; 17 Mitch Clark; 23 Bayley Liu; 24 Oliver Roberts.
Tries: Jones-Bishop (32), Marsh (65); **Goals:** Aston 0/2.
Sin bin: J Farrell (29) - retaliation.

WAKEFIELD TRINITY 72 DONCASTER 6

TRINITY: 1 Max Jowitt; 2 Jermaine McGillvary; 4 Iain Thornley; 3 Oliver Pratt; 32 Derrell Olpherts; 6 Luke Gale; 7 Mason Lino; 8 Josh Bowden; 26 Harvey Smith; 18 Ky Rodwell; 11 Matty Ashurst; 12 Josh Griffin; 13 Jay Pitts. Subs (all used): 10 Renouf Atoni; 14 Liam Kay; 15 Caleb Uele; 19 Isaiah Vagana.
Tries: Jowitt (4, 36, 46, 68), Olpherts (8), Lino (24), Thornley (34, 57), Uele (44), McGillvary (62, 80), Vagana (65), Atoni (72); **Goals:** Jowitt 10/13.
DONCASTER: 17 Josh Guzdek; 5 Luke Briscoe; 4 Reece Lyne; 23 Jason Tali; 2 Tom Halliday; 19 Craig Hall; 24 Watson Boas; 31 Lewis Baxter; 13 Loui McConnell; 10 Suaia Matagi; 12 Alex Sutcliffe; 11 Sam Smeaton; 28 AJ Wallace. Subs (all used): 3 Brad Hey; 14 Alex Holdstock; 25 Ilikaya Mafi; 30 Bureta Faraimo.
Try: Tali (19); **Goals:** C Hall 1/1.
Rugby Leaguer & League Express Men of the Match:
Trinity: Max Jowitt; *Doncaster:* Craig Hall.
Penalty count: 5-3; **Half-time:** 24-6;
Referee: Ben Thaler; **Attendance:** 5,233.

WHITEHAVEN 23 HALIFAX PANTHERS 20

WHITEHAVEN: 3 Joey Romeo; 24 Callum Shaw; 4 Will Evans; 16 Oliver Smart; 1 Edene Gebbie; 14 Jake Carter; 7 Lachlan Hanneghan; 8 Lucas Castle; 15 James Newton; 27 Bobby Hartley; 5 Curtis Teare; 21 Rio Corkill; 11 Ryan King. Subs (all used, only three named): 9 Sam Ackroyd; 10 Jack Kellett; 23 McKenzie Buckley.
Tries: Evans (27), Corkill (31), Gebbie (37), Carter (47); **Goals:** Carter 3/4; **Field goal:** Hanneghan (75).
PANTHERS: 1 James Woodburn-Hall; 5 James Saltonstall; 3 Zack McComb; 26 Ed Barber; 28 Charlie Graham; 6 Louis Jouffret; 7 Joe Keyes; 8 Adam Tangata; 9 Adam O'Brien; 31 Kevin Larroyer; 19 Connor Davies; 22 Ben Hursey; 12 Matty Gee. Subs (all used): 35 Joe Hird; 34 Keelan Foster; 11 Ben Kavanagh; 17 Ben Tibbs.
Tries: Woodburn-Hall (4, 12, 61), Graham (16); **Goals:** Jouffret 2/4.
Dismissal: Gee (77) - high tackle.

Rugby Leaguer & League Express Men of the Match:
Rams: Reiss Butterworth; *Eagles:* Matty Marsh.
Penalty count: 7-6; **Half-time:** 16-4;
Referee: Kevin Moore; **Attendance:** 1,007.

Rugby Leaguer & League Express Men of the Match:
Whitehaven: Jack Kellett; *Panthers:* James Woodburn-Hall.
Penalty count: 7-3; **Half-time:** 16-16;
Referee: James Vella; **Attendance:** 876.

YORK KNIGHTS 16 FEATHERSTONE ROVERS 6

KNIGHTS: 14 Nikau Williams; 2 Joe Brown; 11 Oli Field; 41 Joe Law; 34 Tom Lineham; 22 Ata Hingano; 7 Liam Harris; 42 Jack Martin; 9 Will Jubb; 8 Ukuma Ta'ai; 12 Connor Bailey; 3 Jesse Dee; 13 Jordan Thompson. Subs (all used): 16 Brendan Santi; 17 Ronan Michael; 19 Josh Daley; 21 James Cunningham.
Tries: Harris (18, 73), Brown (36); **Goals:** Williams 2/3.
ROVERS: 1 Caleb Aekins; 5 Gareth Gale; 3 Josh Hardcastle; 4 Greg Minikin; 2 Connor Wynne; 6 Ben Reynolds; 7 Thomas Lacans; 36 James Lockwood; 9 Connor Jones; 32 Ben Nakubuwai; 11 Brad Day; 12 Jack Bussey; 37 Jimmy Beckett. Subs (all used): 8 Gadwin Springer; 15 Wellington Albert; 23 Jack Arnold; 26 Greg Eden.
Try: Hardcastle (5); **Goals:** Reynolds 1/1.
Rugby Leaguer & League Express Men of the Match:
Knights: Liam Harris; *Rovers:* Connor Jones.
Penalty count: 4-5; **Half-time:** 10-6;
Referee: Aaron Moore; **Attendance:** 2,450.

THE ELIMINATORS

Saturday 5th October 2024

YORK KNIGHTS 27 WIDNES VIKINGS 10

KNIGHTS: 14 Nikau Williams; 2 Joe Brown; 11 Oli Field; 41 Joe Law; 34 Tom Lineham; 22 Ata Hingano; 7 Liam Harris; 13 Jordan Thompson; 40 Sam Cook; 8 Ukuma Ta'ai; 3 Jesse Dee; 12 Connor Bailey; 21 James Cunningham. Subs (all used): 16 Brendan Santi; 17 Ronan Michael; 19 Josh Daley; 15 Jack Teanby.
Tries: Lineham (8, 48, 65), Law (28), Dee (61); **Goals:** Williams 3/5; **Field goal:** Harris (57).
VIKINGS: 1 Jack Owens; 20 Mike Butt; 29 Zac Bardsley-Rowe; 3 Matty Fleming; 2 Ryan Ince; 6 Joe Lyons; 7 Tom Gilmore; 17 Liam Bent; 9 Matty Fozard; 31 Dan Murray; 11 Rhodri Lloyd; 27 Ryan Lannon; 8 Callum Field. Subs (all used): 14 Jordan Johnstone; 15 Liam Kirk; 16 Max Roberts; 30 Martyn Reilly.
Try: Lloyd (38); **Goals:** Gilmore 3/3.

Championship 2024 - Round by Round

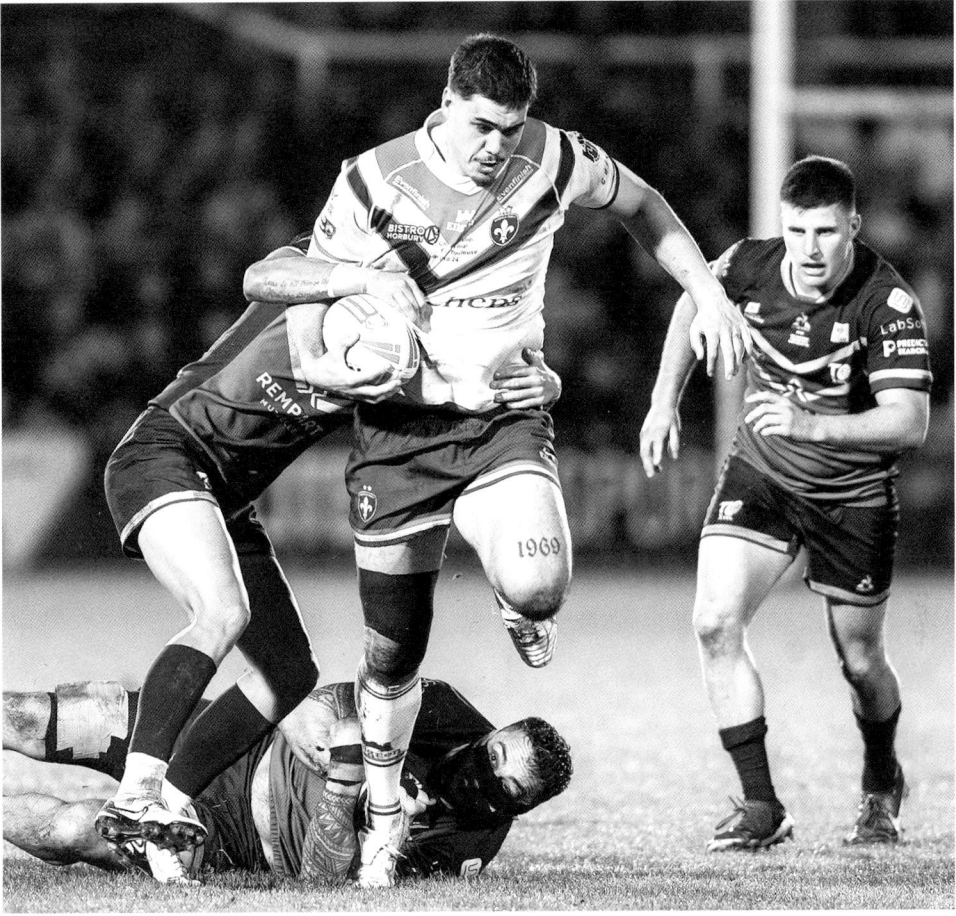

Wakefield's Caleb Uele takes on the Toulouse defence during the Championship Grand Final

Rugby Leaguer & League Express Men of the Match: *Knights:* Tom Lineham; *Vikings:* Rhodri Lloyd.
Penalty count: 3-5; **Half-time:** 10-10;
Referee: James Vella; **Attendance:** 2,010.

Sunday 6th October 2024

BRADFORD BULLS 25 FEATHERSTONE ROVERS 12

BULLS: 1 Tom Holmes; 37 Jayden Okunbor; 21 Jayden Myers; 4 Kieran Gill; 5 Jorge Taufua; 45 Jarrod Sammut; 7 Jordan Lilley; 13 Michael Lawrence; 19 Sam Hallas; 17 Eribe Doro; 29 Zac Fulton; 16 Keven Appo; 15 Daniel Smith. Subs (all used): 10 Ebon Scurr; 42 Franklin Pele; 43 Harvey Makin; 18 Mitch Souter.
Tries: Myers (2), Gill (50), Lilley (57), Appo (64);
Goals: Lilley 4/5; **Field goal:** Lilley (35).
ROVERS: 1 Caleb Aekins; 2 Connor Wynne; 3 Josh Hardcastle; 4 Greg Minikin; 5 Gareth Gale; 6 Ben Reynolds; 7 Thomas Lacans; 8 Gadwin Springer; 9 Connor Jones; 36 James Lockwood; 11 Brad Day; 12 Jack Bussey; 37 Jimmy Beckett. Subs (all used): 15 Wellington Albert; 23 Jack Arnold; 30 Dec Patton; 32 Ben Nakubuwai.
Tries: Hardcastle (75), Day (77); **Goals:** Reynolds 2/2.
Rugby Leaguer & League Express Men of the Match: *Bulls:* Ebon Scurr; *Rovers:* Brad Day.
Penalty count: 5-6; **Half-time:** 7-0; **Referee:** Aaron Moore.

SEMI-FINALS

Sunday 13th October 2024

WAKEFIELD TRINITY 22 YORK KNIGHTS 13

TRINITY: 1 Max Jowitt; 2 Jermaine McGillvary; 4 Iain Thornley; 3 Oliver Pratt; 32 Derrell Olpherts; 6 Luke Gale; 7 Mason Lino; 8 Josh Bowden; 9 Liam Hood; 18 Ky Rodwell; 11 Matty Ashurst; 12 Josh Griffin; 13 Jay Pitts. Subs (all used): 10 Renouf Atoni; 15 Caleb Uele; 19 Isaiah Vagana; 21 Thomas Doyle.
Tries: Jowitt (9), Gale (49), Olpherts (65), Thornley (75);
Goals: Jowitt 3/4.
KNIGHTS: 1 Will Dagger; 2 Joe Brown; 11 Oli Field; 14 Nikau Williams; 34 Tom Lineham; 22 Ata Hingano; 7 Liam Harris; 13 Jordan Thompson; 9 Will Jubb; 8 Ukuma Ta'ai; 3 Jesse Dee; 12 Connor Bailey; 21 James Cunningham. Subs (all used): 16 Brenden Santi; 17 Ronan Michael; 19 Josh Daley; 42 Jack Martin.
Tries: Field (15), Hingano (59); **Goals:** Dagger 2/2;
Field goal: Harris (40).
Rugby Leaguer & League Express Men of the Match: *Trinity:* Caleb Uele; *Knights:* Ata Hingano.
Penalty count: 4-1; **Half-time:** 6-7;
Referee: Aaron Moore; **Attendance:** 5,946.

TOULOUSE OLYMPIQUE 21 BRADFORD BULLS 20

OLYMPIQUE: 1 Olly Ashall-Bott; 2 Paul Ulberg; 18 Guy Armitage; 5 Paul Marcon; 19 Benjamin Laguerre; 6 Ryan Rivett; 7 Jake Shorrocks; 8 Lambert Belmas; 9 Calum Gahan; 10 Harrison Hansen; 11 Maxime Stefani; 24 Pierre-Jean Lima; 13 Anthony Marion. Subs (all used): 12 Dominique Peyroux; 14 Eloi Pelissier; 16 Joe Bretherton; 17 James Roumanos.
Tries: Laguerre (2), Ulberg (9), Armitage (61), Marion (69);
Goals: Shorrocks 2/4; **Field goal:** Pelissier (75).
BULLS: 39 Max Lehmann; 37 Jayden Okunbor; 21 Jayden Myers; 4 Kieran Gill; 5 Jorge Taufua; 45 Jarrod Sammut; 7 Jordan Lilley; 13 Michael Lawrence; 19 Sam Hallas; 17 Eribe Doro; 29 Zac Fulton; 16 Keven Appo; 15 Daniel Smith. Subs (all used): 10 Ebon Scurr; 42 Franklin Pele; 43 Harvey Makin; 18 Mitch Souter.
Tries: Lilley (22), Pele (34), Appo (77); **Goals:** Lilley 4/4.
Sin bin: Gill (27) - high tackle;
Myers (58) - dangerous challenge.
Rugby Leaguer & League Express Men of the Match: *Olympique:* Jake Shorrocks; *Bulls:* Jordan Lilley.
Penalty count: 3-4; **Half-time:** 8-12;
Referee: Tom Grant; **Attendance:** 2,680.

GRAND FINAL

Saturday 19th October 2024

WAKEFIELD TRINITY 36 TOULOUSE OLYMPIQUE 0

TRINITY: 1 Max Jowitt; 2 Jermaine McGillvary; 4 Iain Thornley; 3 Oliver Pratt; 32 Derrell Olpherts; 6 Luke Gale; 7 Mason Lino; 8 Josh Bowden; 9 Liam Hood; 10 Renouf Atoni; 11 Matty Ashurst; 19 Isaiah Vagana; 13 Jay Pitts. Subs (all used): 5 Lachlan Walmsley; 15 Caleb Uele; 18 Ky Rodwell; 21 Thomas Doyle.
Tries: Olpherts (16, 69), Ashurst (26), McGillvary (33, 76), Thornley (38), Pratt (58);
Goals: Jowitt 3/5, Gale 0/1, McGillvary 1/1.
OLYMPIQUE: 1 Olly Ashall-Bott; 2 Paul Ulberg; 18 Guy Armitage; 5 Paul Marcon; 19 Benjamin Laguerre; 6 Ryan Rivett; 7 Jake Shorrocks; 8 Lambert Belmas; 9 Calum Gahan; 10 Harrison Hansen; 11 Maxime Stefani; 12 Dominique Peyroux; 13 Anthony Marion. Subs (all used): 3 Reubenn Rennie; 14 Eloi Pelissier; 17 James Roumanos; 22 Dimitri Biscarro.
Rugby Leaguer & League Express Men of the Match: *Trinity:* Max Jowitt; *Olympique:* Paul Ulberg.
Penalty count: 6-3; **Half-time:** 22-0;
Referee: Aaron Moore; **Attendance:** 8,016.

LEAGUE ONE 2024
Club by Club

___

League One 2024 - Club by Club

CORNWALL

DATE	FIXTURE	RESULT	SCORERS	LGE	ATT
10/2/24	York Acorn (h) (CCR3)	L10-18	t:Dimech,Rusling g:Rusling	N/A	-
17/3/24	Keighley (a)	L56-12	t:Mitchell,Aaronson g:Brown(2)	9th	971
24/3/24	North Wales (h) ●	L16-40	t:Aaronson,Cullen,Brown g:Brown(2)	7th	300
14/4/24	Oldham (a)	L46-10	t:Aaronson,Ashton g:Brown	8th	1,136
21/4/24	Midlands Hurricanes (h)	L6-72	t:Nichol g:Brown	8th	456
28/4/24	Workington (a)	L52-18	t:Black,Conroy,Brown g:Brown(3)	8th	599
5/5/24	Rochdale (a)	L56-24	t:Nichol,Conroy,Brown(2) g:Brown(4)	8th	891
12/5/24	Midlands Hurricanes (a)	W22-24	t:Ashton,Conroy,Weetman,Brown g:Brown(4)	8th	271
19/5/24	Oldham (h)	L0-42		8th	-
26/5/24	Hunslet (a)	L42-16	t:Nichol,Conroy,Black g:Brown(2)	8th	296
2/6/24	Newcastle (h)	W30-6	t:Weetman,Black,Brown(2),Boots g:Brown(5)	8th	-
16/6/24	Rochdale (h)	L14-38	t:Nichol,Brown(2) g:Brown	8th	-
23/6/24	Keighley (h)	L0-26		8th	-
30/6/24	North Wales (h)	L10-16	t:Brown,Trerise g:Brown	8th	-
21/7/24	Workington (h)	L8-30	t:Brown,Abbott	8th	-
28/7/24	Newcastle (a) ●●	W34-44	t:Cullen(2),Aaronson,Conroy(2),Black(2),Abbott g:Brown(6)	8th	329
4/8/24	Rochdale (a)	L46-32	t:Black,Aaronson(2),Weetman,Bateman,Brown g:Brown(4)	8th	427
10/8/24	Hunslet (h)	L26-33	t:Abbott(2),Small(2),Cullen g:Brown(3)	8th	-
18/8/24	Midlands Hurricanes (h)	L6-18	t:Brown g:Brown	8th	-
25/8/24	Oldham (a)	L72-0		8th	1,421
1/9/24	North Wales (a)	L40-10	t:Aaronson,Rusling g:Brown	8th	755

● *Played at Truro College*
●● *Played at Gateshead International Stadium*

Jake Lloyd

	D.O.B.	APP ALL	APP L1	TRIES ALL	TRIES L1	GOALS ALL	GOALS L1	FG ALL	FG L1	PTS ALL	PTS L1
Harry Aaronson	28/3/98	20	19	7	7	0	0	0	0	28	28
Callum Abbott	29/12/98	5	5	4	4	0	0	0	0	16	16
Tom Ashton	20/6/92	16	15	2	2	0	0	0	0	8	8
Christian Bannister	22/1/04	(8)	(8)	0	0	0	0	0	0	0	0
Jacob Bateman	18/4/06	3(2)	3(2)	1	1	0	0	0	0	4	4
Bailey Black	18/7/02	16	16	6	6	0	0	0	0	24	24
AJ Boardman	11/11/89	1(3)	1(3)	0	0	0	0	0	0	0	0
Harry Boots	15/12/96	12	11	1	1	0	0	0	0	4	4
Cameron Brown	8/4/00	20	19	13	13	41	41	0	0	134	134
Sam Campbell	23/8/04	(4)	(4)	0	0	0	0	0	0	0	0
Tomo Clark	14/8/05	(3)	(3)	0	0	0	0	0	0	0	0
Luke Collins	7/12/97	19(1)	18(1)	0	0	0	0	0	0	0	0
Nathan Conroy	6/3/95	4(14)	4(14)	6	6	0	0	0	0	24	24
Nathan Cullen	24/11/02	16	15	4	4	0	0	0	0	16	16
Kaine Dimech	23/11/95	13(4)	13(3)	1	0	0	0	0	0	4	0
Jamie Gill	8/9/05	1(4)	1(4)	0	0	0	0	0	0	0	0
Harry Gray	22/2/04	(1)	(1)	0	0	0	0	0	0	0	0
Josh Hartshorne	6/11/95	2	1	0	0	0	0	0	0	0	0
Jake Lloyd	2/11/97	6(13)	6(12)	0	0	0	0	0	0	0	0
Kyle Marvin	23/4/00	2	2	0	0	0	0	0	0	0	0
Waldimar Matahwa	27/9/04	1	1	0	0	0	0	0	0	0	0
George Mitchell	22/5/97	7(1)	7(1)	1	1	0	0	0	0	4	4
Courage Mkuhlani	29/10/03	(2)	(2)	0	0	0	0	0	0	0	0
Coby Nichol	16/4/03	19	18	4	4	0	0	0	0	16	16
Liam O'Callaghan	24/9/94	(4)	(4)	0	0	0	0	0	0	0	0
Morgan Punchard	26/1/99	11	10	0	0	0	0	0	0	0	0
Josh Rhodes	22/2/04	3(6)	3(6)	0	0	0	0	0	0	0	0
Matt Ross	2/9/92	13(2)	13(1)	0	0	0	0	0	0	0	0
Adam Rusling	25/5/03	11	10	2	1	1	0	0	0	10	4
Darcy Simpson	17/9/02	20	19	0	0	0	0	0	0	0	0
Aaron Small	28/10/91	12	12	2	2	0	0	0	0	8	8
Decarlo Trerise	27/12/94	(10)	(9)	1	1	0	0	0	0	4	4
David Weetman	24/5/98	19(2)	18(2)	3	3	0	0	0	0	12	12
Liam Whitton	14/7/01	1	0	0	0	0	0	0	0	0	0

'L1' totals include League One games only; 'All' totals also include Challenge Cup

LEAGUE RECORD
P20-W3-D0-L17 (8th)
F306, A787, Diff-481, 6 points.

CHALLENGE CUP
Round Three

1895 CUP
Not entered

ATTENDANCES
Complete data not supplied during the season, or at time of publication

CLUB RECORDS — **Highest score:** 44-34 v Newcastle, 28/7/2024 **Highest score against:** 78-10 v Dewsbury, 16/4/2023
Record attendance: 1,473 v Midlands Hurricanes, 10/4/2022
MATCH RECORDS — **Tries:** 2 (12 players) **Goals:** 6 Adam Rusling v North Wales, 30/7/2023; Cameron Brown v Newcastle, 28/7/2024
Points: 16 Adam Rusling v North Wales, 30/7/2023; Cameron Brown v Rochdale, 5/5/2024
SEASON RECORDS — **Tries:** 14 Cameron Brown 2023 **Goals:** 41 Cameron Brown 2024 **Points:** 134 Cameron Brown 2024
CAREER RECORDS — **Tries:** 27 Cameron Brown 2023-2024 **Goals:** 47 Cameron Brown 2023-2024 **Points:** 202 Cameron Brown 2023-2024
Appearances: 49 Harry Aaronson 2022-2024

League One 2024 - Club by Club

HUNSLET

DATE	FIXTURE	RESULT	SCORERS	LGE	ATT
28/1/24	Featherstone (h) (1895CR1)	L12-62	t:Render,Goddard g:Beharrell(2)	3rd(G5)	875
11/2/24	Keighley (h) (CCR3)	L14-22	t:Ferreira,Beharrell,Render g:Beharrell	N/A	817
18/2/24	Batley (h) (1895CR3)	L0-36		3rd(G5)	700
17/3/24	Newcastle (h)	W48-12	t:Render(2),Goddard(3),Ferreira(2),Berry,Jordan-Roberts g:Beharrell(6)	3rd	402
24/3/24	Rochdale (a)	W24-26	t:Ferreira(2),Williams,Darley,Hallas g:Beharrell(3)	2nd	448
29/3/24	Keighley (h)	L14-42	t:Jordan-Roberts,Goddard g:Beharrell(3)	4th	618
7/4/24	Oldham (h)	L0-62		5th	725
14/4/24	Midlands Hurricanes (a) ●	W26-30	t:Goddard,Watson,Jordan-Roberts,Berry,Ferreira g:Beharrell(5)	4th	302
21/4/24	Workington (h)	L18-30	t:Levy,Berry,Ferreira g:Beharrell(3)	6th	410
28/4/24	North Wales (h)	W22-14	t:Beharrell,Hallas,Scurr,Render g:Beharrell(3)	4th	396
5/5/24	Keighley (a)	W18-26	t:Ferreira(4),Law g:Beharrell(3)	3rd	1,389
26/5/24	Cornwall (h)	W42-16	t:O'Hanlon(2),Jordan-Roberts,Ferreira,Adams(2),Render g:Beharrell(7)	4th	296
2/6/24	Workington (a)	W22-24	t:Jordan-Roberts,Fletcher,Ferreira,Watson g:Beharrell(4)	3rd	1,486
16/6/24	Midlands Hurricanes (h)	W25-18	t:Berry,Render,Watson,Flanagan g:Beharrell(4) fg:Beharrell	3rd	504
23/6/24	Rochdale (h)	L18-48	t:Flanagan,Beharrell,Knowles g:Beharrell(3)	4th	402
30/6/24	Oldham (a)	L30-6	t:Law g:Flanagan	4th	1,126
14/7/24	Newcastle (a) ●●	W16-42	t:Render,Watson,Paga,Ferreira(2),Goddard,Carr(2) g:Beharrell(5)	3rd	-
21/7/24	North Wales (a)	W16-46	t:Render(3),Booth,Berry,Law(2),Carr g:Beharrell(5),Knowles(2)	3rd	488
28/7/24	Workington (h)	L24-32	t:Ferreira(2),O'Hanlon,Carr g:Beharrell(4)	3rd	572
10/8/24	Cornwall (a)	W26-33	t:Render(2),Flanagan(2),Berry,Knowles g:Beharrell(4) fg:Beharrell	3rd	-
18/8/24	North Wales (h)	W28-20	t:Ferreira,Syme,Wood,Watson,Turner g:Beharrell(4)	3rd	556
25/8/24	Keighley (a)	L40-22	t:Turner,Render,Flanagan,Ferreira g:Beharrell(3)	4th	1,642
31/8/24	Midlands Hurricanes (h)	W22-28	t:Whitmore(2),Jordan-Roberts(2),Render g:Beharrell(4)	4th	420
15/9/24	Rochdale (a) (QPO)	L30-18	t:Ferreira,Goddard,Render(2) g:Beharrell	N/A	826
22/9/24	Midlands Hurricanes (h) (ESF)	W18-14	t:Ferreira,Delaney,Render g:Beharrell(3)	N/A	474
29/9/24	Rochdale (a) (FE)	W26-46	t:Ferreira(2),Berry,Turner,Render(2),Ferreira,Wood g:Beharrell(7)	N/A	428
6/10/24	Keighley (a) (POF)	W6-20	t:Wood,Turner,Render g:Beharrell(4)	N/A	1,037
13/10/24	Swinton (a) (CP/RPO)	W20-22	t:Turner,Berry,Flanagan,Render g:Beharrell(3)	N/A	885

● Played at Olympic Legacy Park, Sheffield   ●● Played at Crow Trees, Blaydon

Jack Render

		APP		TRIES		GOALS		FG		PTS	
	D.O.B.	ALL	L1	ALL	L1	ALL	L1	ALL	L1	ALL	L1
Will Adams	29/8/02	4	3	2	2	0	0	0	0	8	8
Matty Beharrell	29/3/94	27	23	3	2	94	88	2	2	202	186
Cam Berry	7/8/01	(27)	(23)	8	7	0	0	0	0	32	28
Noah Booth	21/10/04	1	1	1	1	0	0	0	0	4	4
Liam Carr	10/11/02	3(8)	2(7)	4	4	0	0	0	0	16	16
Nathan Carter	30/9/01	1	0	0	0	0	0	0	0	0	0
Matty Chrimes	2/11/97	1	1	0	0	0	0	0	0	0	0
Jack Coventry	5/3/94	(12)	(10)	0	0	0	0	0	0	0	0
Spencer Darley	25/9/98	(5)	(3)	1	1	0	0	0	0	4	4
Thomas Delaney	16/10/04	1	1	1	1	0	0	0	0	4	4
Toby Everett	22/12/95	6(2)	3(2)	0	0	0	0	0	0	0	0
Jude Ferreira	15/10/01	28	24	22	21	0	0	0	0	88	84
George Flanagan	24/12/04	13	12	8	7	1	1	0	0	34	30
Matt Fletcher	15/2/00	12(3)	11(3)	1	1	0	0	0	0	4	4
Billy Gaylor	30/4/97	6(3)	3(3)	0	0	0	0	0	0	0	0
Alfie Goddard	16/3/00	18	14	8	7	0	0	0	0	32	28
Harvey Hallas	14/11/97	25(3)	22(2)	2	2	0	0	0	0	8	8
Josh Jordan-Roberts	26/8/98	22	20	7	7	0	0	0	0	28	28
Michael Knowles	2/5/87	23(1)	22	2	2	2	2	0	0	12	12
Donald Kudangirana	23/5/95	1	1	0	0	0	0	0	0	0	0
Joe Law	18/2/04	8	8	4	4	0	0	0	0	16	16
Myles Lawford	9/9/03	2	2	0	0	0	0	0	0	0	0
Aaron Levy	19/12/95	17	15	1	1	0	0	0	0	4	4
Jack Mallinson	21/10/01	1	1	0	0	0	0	0	0	0	0
Dan McGrath	2/12/01	1	0	0	0	0	0	0	0	0	0
Luke Mearns	9/6/04	1	0	0	0	0	0	0	0	0	0
Ethan O'Hanlon	19/5/01	1(25)	1(23)	3	3	0	0	0	0	12	12
Cole Oakley	25/10/00	1(1)	1(1)	0	0	0	0	0	0	0	0
Iwan Orr	17/5/02	1	0	0	0	0	0	0	0	0	0
Jordan Paga	23/5/01	5(2)	5(2)	1	1	0	0	0	0	4	4
Luke Punton	1/11/00	1	1	0	0	0	0	0	0	0	0
Jack Render	4/7/99	25	22	22	19	0	0	0	0	88	76
Aidan Scully	16/5/92	1	1	0	0	0	0	0	0	0	0
Mackenzie Scurr	3/6/03	7	7	1	1	0	0	0	0	4	4
Isaac Shaw	11/9/02	(4)	(4)	0	0	0	0	0	0	0	0
Daniel Spencer-Tonks	18/1/95	(2)	(2)	0	0	0	0	0	0	0	0
Jordan Syme	14/11/96	26(2)	22(1)	1	1	0	0	0	0	4	4
Keenen Tomlinson	22/5/97	2(1)	2(1)	0	0	0	0	0	0	0	0
Mackenzie Turner	30/1/03	8	7	5	4	0	0	0	0	20	16
Jimmy Watson	9/9/91	24	21	5	5	0	0	0	0	20	20
Ross Whitmore	9/2/00	25(1)	22(1)	2	2	0	0	0	0	8	8
Brandan Wilkinson	7/9/97	(1)	0	0	0	0	0	0	0	0	0
Harry Williams	29/5/99	8	5	1	1	0	0	0	0	4	4
Ethan Wood	4/4/05	6(1)	5(1)	3	3	0	0	0	0	12	12
Lewis Wray	6/5/98	1(7)	1(5)	0	0	0	0	0	0	0	0

'L1' totals include regular season & play-offs; 'All' totals also include Challenge Cup, 1895 Cup & Championship Promotion/Relegation play-off

LEAGUE RECORD
P20-W13-D0-L7
(4th/Play-off Final Winners)
F522, A534, Diff-12, 26 points.

CHALLENGE CUP
Round Three

1895 CUP
3rd, Group 5

ATTENDANCES
Best - v Featherstone (1895C - 875)
Worst - v Cornwall (L1 - 296)
Total (excluding Challenge Cup) - 6,930
Average (excluding Challenge Cup) - 533
(Down by 75 on 2023)

CLUB RECORDS
MATCH RECORDS Highest score: 86-0 v West Wales, 27/5/2018; 86-6 v West Wales, 4/8/2018 Highest score against: 0-82 v Bradford, 2/3/2003
Record attendance: 24,700 v Wigan, 15/3/1924 (Parkside); 2,454 v Wakefield, 13/4/98 (South Leeds Stadium)
Tries: 7 George Dennis v Bradford, 20/1/34 Goals: 13 Joe Sanderson v West Wales, 27/5/2018; Joe Sanderson v West Wales, 4/8/2018
Points: 30 Simon Wilson v Highfield, 21/1/96; Joe Sanderson v West Wales, 27/5/2018
SEASON RECORDS Tries: 34 Alan Snowden 1956-57 Goals: 181 Billy Langton 1958-59 Points: 380 Billy Langton 1958-59
CAREER RECORDS Tries: 154 Fred Williamson 1943-55 Goals: 1,044 Billy Langton 1955-66 Points: 2,202 Billy Langton 1955-66 Appearances: 579 Geoff Gunney 1951-73

League One 2024 - Club by Club

KEIGHLEY COUGARS

DATE	FIXTURE	RESULT	SCORERS	LGE	ATT
28/1/24	Dewsbury (h) (1895CR1)	W35-6	t:Dean,Pickersgill,Lanskey,Graham(2),Brown g:Miller(5) fg:Miller	1st(G2)	839
11/2/24	Hunslet (a) (CCR3)	W14-22	t:Graham,Thomas,Robson(2),Ryder g:Thomas	N/A	817
18/2/24	Bradford (h) (1895CR3)	L18-26	t:Lanskey,Graham,Ioane g:Miller(3)	2nd(G2)	3,729
25/2/24	Featherstone (h) (CCR4)	L14-58	t:Downey,Pickersgill g:Miller(2),Thomas	N/A	1,477
17/3/24	Cornwall (h)	W56-12	t:Robson(3),Walkley,Parker,Thomas,Ryder,Pickersgill(2),Bishop g:Miller(8)	1st	971
24/3/24	Workington (h)	W58-16	t:Ioane(2),Robson,Miller,Parker,Pickersgill(2),Sa'u(2),Thomas g:Miller(9)	1st	916
29/3/24	Hunslet (a)	W14-42	t:Ioane,Bishop,Walkley(2),Robson,Brown,Sa'u g:Miller(5)	1st	618
14/4/24	North Wales (h)	W22-6	t:Bishop,Walkley(2),Hatton g:Miller(3)	2nd	1,096
21/4/24	Newcastle (a)	W6-82	t:Robson(2),Brown,Dean(2),Lynam,Walkley(3),Ryder(2),Schofield(2),Bailey g:Miller(13)	1st	461
28/4/24	Rochdale (a)	W30-42	t:Walkley(2),Sa'u(3),Robson,Ryder g:Miller(7)	1st	734
5/5/24	Hunslet (h)	L18-26	t:Robson,Walkley(2),Sa'u g:Miller	2nd	1,389
19/5/24	North Wales (a)	W10-30	t:Pickersgill,Walkley(2),Thomas,Flanagan g:Miller(5)	2nd	462
26/5/24	Oldham (h)	W28-18	t:Farrell,Graham,Flanagan,Sa'u(2) g:Miller(4)	1st	1,852
2/6/24	Midlands Hurricanes (a)	W18-25	t:Hatton,Lambourne,Farrell,Walkley g:Miller(4) fg:Miller	1st	463
23/6/24	Cornwall (a)	W0-26	t:Ryder,Blackmore,Sa'u,Robson(2) g:Miller	2nd	-
30/6/24	Workington (a)	W18-37	t:Sa'u(2),Robson,Thomas(2),Lanskey g:Miller(6) fg:Miller	2nd	793
7/7/24	Rochdale (h)	D20-20	t:Walkley,Ioane(2) g:Miller(4)	1st	1,608
21/7/24	Oldham (a)	L44-6	t:Schofield g:Parker	2nd	2,572
28/7/24	Midlands Hurricanes (h)	W36-12	t:Ioane,Pickersgill(2),Sa'u,Flanagan,Robson g:Thomas(6)	2nd	1,056
4/8/24	Newcastle (h)	W72-12	t:Nuu(2),McEwan-Peters(4),Schofield,Thomas(2),Ryder,Walkley,Flanagan,Parker g:Thomas(5),Miller(5)	2nd	968
11/8/24	North Wales (a) ●	W16-24	t:Miller,Ryder,Bishop,Flanagan g:Miller(4)	2nd	401
18/8/24	Oldham (h)	L12-20	t:Pickersgill,Robson g:Miller(2)	2nd	2,174
25/8/24	Hunslet (h)	W40-22	t:Robson(2),Ryder,Walkley(2),Ioane,Thomas,Miller(6)	2nd	1,642
1/9/24	Rochdale (a)	L32-18	t:Lynam,Walkley,Flanagan g:Miller(3)	2nd	1,474
22/9/24	Rochdale (h) (QSF)	W26-22	t:Lanskey,Lynam,Miller,Ioane g:Miller(5)	N/A	1,037
6/10/24	Hunslet (h) (POF)	L6-20	t:Flanagan g:Miller	N/A	1,037

● Played at Hare Lane, Chester

Billy Walkley

		APP		TRIES		GOALS		FG		PTS	
	D.O.B.	ALL	L1	ALL	L1	ALL	L1	ALL	L1	ALL	L1
Matthew Bailey	1/12/91	(1)	(1)	1	1	0	0	0	0	4	4
Alex Bishop	18/1/94	6(8)	6(8)	4	4	0	0	0	0	16	16
Ben Blackmore	19/2/93	8	8	1	1	0	0	0	0	4	4
Aaron Brown	27/7/92	21(3)	17(3)	3	2	0	0	0	0	12	8
Nathan Conroy	6/3/95	(1)		0	0	0	0	0	0	0	0
Ben Dean	29/12/03	7(2)	6(1)	3	2	0	0	0	0	12	8
Codey Downey	25/11/03	1	1	1	1	0	0	0	0	4	4
Brad England	20/11/94	(4)	(4)	0	0	0	0	0	0	0	0
Izaac Farrell	30/1/98	2	2	2	2	0	0	0	0	8	8
George Flanagan	8/10/86	4(11)	4(11)	7	7	0	0	0	0	28	28
Charlie Graham	14/5/00	10	6	5	1	0	0	0	0	20	4
Lewis Hatton	14/1/97	3(13)	3(11)	2	2	0	0	0	0	8	8
Mark Ioane	3/12/90	15(11)	11(11)	9	8	0	0	0	0	36	32
Kyle Kesik	3/6/89	15(4)	15(1)	0	0	0	0	0	0	0	0
Max Lambourne	17/1/04	1	1	1	1	0	0	0	0	4	4
Lachlan Lanskey	29/5/97	18	14	4	2	0	0	0	0	16	8
Josh Lynam	16/2/93	7(3)	7(1)	3	3	0	0	0	0	12	12
Will Maher	4/11/95	24	20	0	0	0	0	0	0	0	0
Lloyd McEwan-Peters	25/10/05	2	2	4	4	0	0	0	0	16	16
Jack Miller	28/11/94	24(1)	20(1)	3	3	106	96	3	2	227	206
Junior Nuu	12/2/94	6(1)	6(1)	2	2	0	0	0	0	8	8
Dan Parker	11/3/93	15(9)	11(9)	3	3	1	1	0	0	14	14
Brandon Pickersgill	29/3/97	19	15	10	8	0	0	0	0	40	32
Mitch Revell	15/10/98	12(6)	12(6)	0	0	0	0	0	0	0	0
Ellis Robson	14/9/98	25	21	19	17	0	0	0	0	76	68
Adam Ryder	20/10/89	24	20	10	9	0	0	0	0	40	36
Junior Sa'u	18/4/87	21	18	13	13	0	0	0	0	52	52
Jordan Schofield	23/9/00	2(20)	2(16)	4	4	0	0	0	0	16	16
Ben Stead	13/10/92	(3)	0	0	0	0	0	0	0	0	0
Oscar Thomas	3/1/94	20(3)	17(3)	9	8	13	11	0	0	62	54
Billy Walkley	13/6/04	26	22	20	20	0	0	0	0	80	80

'L1' totals include regular season & play-offs; 'All' totals also include Challenge Cup & 1895 Cup

LEAGUE RECORD
P20-W15-D1-L4
(2nd/Play-off Final Runners-up)
F694, A352, Diff+342, 31 points.

CHALLENGE CUP
Round Four

1895 CUP
2nd, Group 2

ATTENDANCES
Best - v Bradford (1895C - 3,729)
Worst - v Dewsbury (1895C - 839)
Total (excluding Challenge Cup) - 20,314
Average (excluding Challenge Cup) - 1,451
(Down by 511 on 2023, Championship)

CLUB RECORDS
MATCH RECORDS Highest score: 112-6 v West Wales, 15/9/2018 Highest score against: 2-92 v Leigh, 30/4/86 Record attendance: 14,500 v Halifax, 3/3/51
Tries: 6 Jason Critchley v Widnes, 18/8/96
Goals: 15 John Wasyliw v Nottingham City, 1/11/92; Martyn Wood v Lancashire Lynx, 1/5/2000 Points: 36 John Wasyliw v Nottingham City, 1/11/92
SEASON RECORDS Tries: 45 Nick Pinkney 1994-95 Goals: 187 John Wasyliw 1992-93 Points: 490 John Wasyliw 1992-93
CAREER RECORDS Tries: 155 Sam Stacey 1904-20 Goals: 967 Brian Jefferson 1965-77 Points: 2,116 Brian Jefferson 1965-77
Appearances: 372 Hartley Tempest 1902-15; David McGoun 1925-38

League One 2024 - Club by Club

MIDLANDS HURRICANES

DATE	FIXTURE	RESULT	SCORERS	LGE	ATT
28/1/24	Doncaster (h) (1895CR1)	L4-40	t:Kirkbright	3rd(G7)	180
11/2/24	Rochdale (a) (CCR3)	L24-20	t:Clavering,Wilkinson,Barcoe g:Hewitt(4)	N/A	411
18/2/24	Sheffield (h) (1895CR3)	L16-30	t:Nakoronivalu,Varo,Oakes g:Hewitt(2)	3rd(G7)	345
17/3/24	Rochdale (h)	L28-38	t:Bass,Barcoe,Nakoronivalu,Wilkinson(2),Billsborough(3),Hewitt	6th	465
24/3/24	Newcastle (h)	W70-16	t:Barcoe(2),Oakes,Billsborough,Wilkinson(3),Moran,Bass,Horner,M Welham,Kirby g:Hewitt(11)	3rd	377
31/3/24	North Wales (a)	L20-14	t:M Welham,Billsborough,Kirkbright g:Hewitt	5th	707
14/4/24	Hunslet (h) ●	L26-30	t:Barcoe,Horner,M Welham,Sweeting g:Hewitt(5)	7th	302
21/4/24	Cornwall (a)	W6-72	t:Wilkinson(2),Sweeting,Oakes(2),McLelland,Johnson(2),M Welham,Willis,Horner,L Welham g:Sweeting(12)	7th	456
27/4/24	Oldham (h)	L16-44	t:McLelland,Peachey,Johnson g:Sweeting(2)	7th	367
5/5/24	Workington (a)	W16-26	t:Johnson,Sweeting,McLelland,Wilkinson g:Sweeting(5)	6th	678
12/5/24	Cornwall (h)	L22-24	t:L Welham,Sweeting,Bass,Peachey g:Sweeting(3)	6th	271
19/5/24	Newcastle (h)	W66-4	t:L Welham(4),Horner(2),McLelland,Peachey(2),Bass(2),Barcoe g:Sweeting,Hewitt(8)	5th	302
26/5/24	North Wales (h)	W18-10	t:Hewitt,Chrimes,Johnson g:Hewitt(3)	5th	527
2/6/24	Keighley (h)	L18-25	t:Chrimes(2),L Welham g:Hewitt(3)	5th	463
16/6/24	Hunslet (a)	L25-18	t:L Welham(2),M Welham g:Hewitt(3)	5th	504
30/6/24	Newcastle (a) ●●	W10-44	t:M Welham(2),Wilkinson(2),Horner,Dixon,Peachey,Windley g:Hewitt(6)	5th	
7/7/24	North Wales (h)	W18-32	t:M Welham,Horner(2),Johnson(2),Chrimes g:Hewitt(3),Chrimes	5th	552
21/7/24	Rochdale (a)	L14-10	t:McLelland,L Welham g:Chrimes	5th	676
28/7/24	Keighley (a)	L36-12	t:Horner,Millar g:Sweeting(2)	6th	1,056
4/8/24	Oldham (a)	L32-0		6th	1,582
11/8/24	Workington (h)	W34-22	t:Kirby,Higham,Sweeting,Bass,Chrimes g:Sweeting(7)	5th	677
18/8/24	Cornwall (a)	W6-18	t:Peachey,Wilkinson,Horner g:Medforth(3)	5th	-
31/8/24	Hunslet (h)	L22-28	t:Willis,Johnson,Medforth,Chrimes g:Sweeting(3)	5th	420
15/9/24	Workington (h) (EPO)	W24-22	t:Hewitt,Kirby,Chrimes g:Sweeting(6)	N/A	323
22/9/24	Hunslet (a) (ESF)	L18-14	t:Clavering,Barcoe g:Sweeting(3)	N/A	474

● Played at Olympic Legacy Park, Sheffield
●● Played at Gateshead International Stadium

Jason Bass

	D.O.B.	APP ALL	APP L1	TRIES ALL	TRIES L1	GOALS ALL	GOALS L1	FG ALL	FG L1	PTS ALL	PTS L1
Kye Armstrong	12/9/04	(2)	(2)	0	0	0	0	0	0	0	0
Danny Barcoe	5/7/00	17(6)	15(6)	7	6	0	0	0	0	28	24
Jason Bass	10/5/96	19	18	6	6	0	0	0	0	24	24
Finley Beardsworth	16/1/04	(1)	(1)	0	0	0	0	0	0	0	0
Brad Billsborough	4/8/98	5(1)	3(1)	2	2	3	3	0	0	14	14
Sam Bowring	1/7/91	5(6)	5(3)	0	0	0	0	0	0	0	0
Blake Broadbent	11/12/98	8(2)	8(2)	0	0	0	0	0	0	0	0
Ryan Brown	15/5/05	(3)	(3)	0	0	0	0	0	0	0	0
Matty Chrimes	2/11/97	11	11	7	7	2	2	0	0	32	32
Brad Clavering	14/3/98	12(2)	10(2)	2	1	0	0	0	0	8	4
Chris Cullimore	13/2/93	8(12)	7(11)	0	0	0	0	0	0	0	0
Davey Dixon	31/5/97	4	4	1	1	0	0	0	0	4	4
Marcus Green	27/3/03	7(14)	5(13)	0	0	0	0	0	0	0	0
Dave Hewitt	4/11/95	15	12	2	2	50	44	0	0	108	96
Harry Higham	1/11/05	1	1	1	1	0	0	0	0	4	4
Ellis Hobson	30/11/03	13(2)	13	0	0	0	0	0	0	0	0
Todd Horner	19/3/04	24	21	10	10	0	0	0	0	40	40
Ryan Johnson	3/8/00	14	14	8	8	0	0	0	0	32	32
Jose Kenga	3/5/95	1(4)	1(4)	0	0	0	0	0	0	0	0
Jon Luke Kirby	23/9/98	23	20	3	3	0	0	0	0	12	12
Max Kirkbright	18/5/03	3(1)	1(1)	2	1	0	0	0	0	8	4
Owen Maull	7/2/04	1(3)	(2)	0	0	0	0	0	0	0	0
Callum McLelland	16/9/99	15	14	5	5	0	0	0	0	20	20
Sully Medforth	26/1/05	3	3	1	1	3	3	0	0	10	10
Ryan Millar	12/5/94	2	2	1	1	0	0	0	0	4	4
Kieran Moran	2/11/96	1(13)	(12)	1	1	0	0	0	0	4	4
Inoke Nakoronivalu	29/10/96	5	4	2	1	0	0	0	0	8	4
Ross Oakes	12/10/96	13	11	4	3	0	0	0	0	16	12
Lewis Peachey	25/3/01	5(14)	5(14)	6	6	0	0	0	0	24	24
Peceli Suguvanua	15/8/90	(3)	(2)	0	0	0	0	0	0	0	0
Jake Sweeting	15/12/99	13	13	5	5	44	44	0	0	108	108
Joe Varo	4/3/99	4	3	1	0	0	0	0	0	4	0
Liam Welham	11/1/88	18	16	10	10	0	0	0	0	40	40
Matt Welham	1/2/93	17	14	8	8	0	0	0	0	32	32
Tom Wilkinson	3/10/02	24	21	12	11	0	0	0	0	48	44
Aaron Willis	11/12/03	14(7)	11(7)	2	2	0	0	0	0	8	8
Elliot Windley	9/7/99	(4)	(2)	1	1	0	0	0	0	4	4

'L1' totals include regular season & play-offs; 'All' totals also include Challenge Cup & 1895 Cup

LEAGUE RECORD
P20-W9-D0-L11
(5th/Elimination Semi-Final)
F566, A424, Diff+142, 18 points.

CHALLENGE CUP
Round Three

1895 CUP
3rd, Group 7

ATTENDANCES
Best - v Workington (L1 - 677)
Worst - v Doncaster (1895C - 180)
Total (all home games included) - 5,019
Average (all home games included) - 386
(Up by 19 on 2023)

CLUB RECORDS
MATCH RECORDS Highest score: 72-6 v Cornwall, 21/4/2024 Highest score against: 6-98 v Keighley, 6/5/2018
Record attendance: 1,465 v Bradford, 30/6/2018 (Butts Park Arena); 453 v Cornwall, 19/2/2023 (Alexander Stadium)
Tries: 4 Liam Welham v Newcastle, 19/5/2024 Goals: 12 Jake Sweeting v Cornwall, 21/4/2024 Points: 28 Jake Sweeting v Cornwall, 21/4/2024
SEASON RECORDS Tries: 17 Elliot Hall 2019 Goals: 61 Ben Stead 2018 Points: 141 Dan Coates 2021
CAREER RECORDS Tries: 58 Hayden Freeman 2016-2023 Goals: 163 (inc 1fg) Ben Stead 2018; 2022-2023 Points: 365 Ben Stead 2018; 2022-2023
Appearances: 115 Hayden Freeman 2016-2023

League One 2024 - Club by Club

NEWCASTLE THUNDER

DATE	FIXTURE	RESULT	SCORERS	LGE	ATT
27/1/24	York (h) (1895CR1)	L10-114	t:White,Snowden g:Hepple	3rd(G3)	-
10/2/24	Sheffield (a) (CCR3)	L88-12	t:Birch,Newbound g:Hepple(2)	N/A	617
18/2/24	Wakefield (h) (1895CR3) ●	L0-110		3rd(G3)	1,378
17/3/24	Hunslet (a)	L48-12	t:Lowery,Ward g:Potter(2)	7th	402
24/3/24	Midlands Hurricanes (a)	L70-16	t:Birch,Lowery,Bibby g:Potter(2)	9th	377
30/3/24	Workington (h)	L18-48	t:Ward,Donaghy,Jeremy g:Potter(3)	9th	412
7/4/24	North Wales (a)	L58-18	t:Siddle,Price,Lowery g:Potter(3)	9th	306
14/4/24	Rochdale (a)	L68-4	t:Birch	9th	379
21/4/24	Keighley (h)	L6-82	t:Lawther g:Hepple	9th	461
5/5/24	Oldham (a)	L74-0		9th	1,303
19/5/24	Midlands Hurricanes (a)	L66-4	t:Burns	9th	302
26/5/24	Rochdale (h) ●●	L18-24	t:Burns,Lawther,Lowery g:Hepple(3)	9th	326
2/6/24	Cornwall (a)	L30-6	t:Lawther g:Harman	9th	-
16/6/24	Oldham (h) ●●	L6-60	t:Price g:Harman	9th	-
23/6/24	North Wales (h) ●●●	L4-42	t:Croston	9th	-
30/6/24	Midlands Hurricanes (h) ●●	L10-44	t:Lawther,Donaghy g:Harman	9th	-
7/7/24	Workington (a)	L0-44		9th	-
14/7/24	Hunslet (h) ●●	L16-42	t:Donaghy,Lawther,Shaw g:Donaghy(2)	9th	329
28/7/24	Cornwall (h) ●●	L34-44	t:Shaw,Price,Hepple,Lawther(2),Croston g:Donaghy(5)	9th	968
4/8/24	Keighley (a)	L72-12	t:Rushworth,Donaghy g:Donaghy(2)	9th	1,006
11/8/24	Oldham (a)	L84-0		9th	220
17/8/24	Rochdale (h) ●●	L6-78	t:Jeremy g:Donaghy	9th	631
25/8/24	Workington (a)	L46-0		9th	-

● _Played at Millennium Stadium, Featherstone_ ●● _Played at Gateshead International Stadium_ ●●● _Played at Crow Trees, Blaydon_

Alex Donaghy

	D.O.B.	APP ALL	L1	TRIES ALL	L1	GOALS ALL	L1	FG ALL	L1	PTS ALL	L1
Jake Anderson	21/11/02	10(1)	10(1)	0	0	0	0	0	0	0	0
Will Bate	6/12/89	4(14)	1(14)	0	0	0	0	0	0	0	0
Olly Bibby	26/9/03	13(2)	13	1	1	0	0	0	0	4	4
George Birch	24/3/05	11	9	3	2	0	0	0	0	12	8
Joe Bradley	14/12/04	3	0	0	0	0	0	0	0	0	0
Leo Bradley	13/7/06	7	4	0	0	0	0	0	0	0	0
Paddy Burns	15/3/98	14	11	2	2	0	0	0	0	8	8
Lennon Bursell	19/1/05	5	5	0	0	0	0	0	0	0	0
Francis Coggle	21/10/01	1	1	0	0	0	0	0	0	0	0
Sean Croston	1/11/99	13	13	2	2	0	0	0	0	8	8
Alfie Dean	14/9/04	3	3	0	0	0	0	0	0	0	0
Alex Donaghy	22/9/01	18	18	4	4	10	10	0	0	36	36
Jamie Field	27/5/94	2	2	0	0	0	0	0	0	0	0
Oli Field	3/9/02	1	1	0	0	0	0	0	0	0	0
Joe Gibbons	5/12/02	1	1	0	0	0	0	0	0	0	0
Tobias Gibson	24/12/04	8(11)	8(8)	0	0	0	0	0	0	0	0
Lloyd Hall	26/5/05	(2)	(1)	0	0	0	0	0	0	0	0
Matthew Handy	22/7/05	4(1)	3(1)	0	0	0	0	0	0	0	0
Mike Hansen	15/1/01	3	3	0	0	0	0	0	0	0	0
Aaron Harlow-Stephenson	5/6/98	4(4)	1(4)	0	0	3	3	0	0	6	6
Mackenzie Harman	7/12/04	6	6	0	0	7	4	0	0	18	12
Tyler Hepple	28/10/02	13(7)	10(7)	1	1	7	4	0	0	18	12
Dan Hindmarsh	8/10/98	(1)	(1)	0	0	0	0	0	0	0	0
Robin Hugues	6/12/99	1(2)	1(2)	0	0	0	0	0	0	0	0
Luke Jeremy	20/5/03	16	15	2	2	0	0	0	0	8	8
Evan Lawther	14/8/03	10	10	7	7	0	0	0	0	28	28
Jaiden Linford	2/8/05	1	1	0	0	0	0	0	0	0	0
Will Lintin	11/8/04	3(1)	3(1)	0	0	0	0	0	0	0	0
Harry Lowery	19/10/04	18(2)	15(2)	4	4	0	0	0	0	16	16
Ilikaya Mafi	30/11/03	(1)	(1)	0	0	0	0	0	0	0	0
Toby Mallinson	21/12/04	3	3	0	0	0	0	0	0	0	0
Sylvester Namo	26/8/00	(1)	(1)	0	0	0	0	0	0	0	0
Nathan Newbound	17/8/00	9(3)	6(3)	1	1	0	0	0	0	4	4
Nathan Ohimor	17/5/05	(1)	0	0	0	0	0	0	0	0	0
Jason Payne	20/1/88	1(4)	1(4)	0	0	0	0	0	0	0	0
Taylor Pemberton	17/4/03	6	6	0	0	0	0	0	0	0	0
Austin Phillips	18/5/91	(2)	(2)	0	0	0	0	0	0	0	0
Jack Potter	12/6/04	6	6	0	0	10	10	0	0	20	20
Harry Price	8/11/03	19	19	3	3	0	0	0	0	12	12
Nixon Putt	3/3/95	1	1	0	0	0	0	0	0	0	0
Owen Reed	25/8/99	1(1)	1(1)	0	0	0	0	0	0	0	0
Jacob Rennison	13/3/05	1	0	0	0	0	0	0	0	0	0
Harvey Reynolds	2/2/04	1(1)	1(1)	0	0	0	0	0	0	0	0
Nathan Rushworth	16/10/02	13(5)	12(5)	1	1	0	0	0	0	4	4
Joel Russell	7/12/00	6(3)	6(3)	0	0	0	0	0	0	0	0
Peter Ryan	25/2/95	(1)	0	0	0	0	0	0	0	0	0
Elliott Shaw	12/2/03	6	6	2	2	0	0	0	0	8	8
Tom Siddle	9/11/04	17(2)	15(1)	1	1	0	0	0	0	4	4
Oliver Simpson	16/3/04	(2)	(2)	0	0	0	0	0	0	0	0
Jack Skelton	23/4/04	(11)	(8)	0	0	0	0	0	0	0	0
James Snowden	21/1/05	1	0	1	0	0	0	0	0	4	0
Josh Stoker	26/7/92	3(5)	3(5)	0	0	0	0	0	0	0	0
AJ Towse	19/8/03	2	2	0	0	0	0	0	0	0	0
Brad Ward	4/6/03	4	4	2	2	0	0	0	0	8	8
Dan White	26/4/01	6(1)	3(1)	1	0	0	0	0	0	4	0

'L1' totals include League One games only; 'All' totals also include Challenge Cup & 1895 Cup

LEAGUE RECORD
P20-W0-D0-L20 (9th)
F190, A1124, Diff-934, 0 points.

CHALLENGE CUP
Round Three

1895 CUP
3rd, Group 3

ATTENDANCES
Complete data not supplied during the season, or at time of publication

CLUB RECORDS
MATCH RECORDS Highest score: 98-6 v West Wales, 23/9/2018 Highest score against: 0-132 v Blackpool Panthers, 16/5/2010
Record attendance: 6,631 v Bradford, 16/5/99 _(Gateshead International Stadium)_; 4,137 v Bradford, 18/5/2018 _(Kingston Park)_
Tries: 5 Andy Walker v London Skolars, 22/6/2003 Goals: 12 Rhys Clarke v Coventry, 18/8/2019 Points: 28 Benn Hardcastle v Oxford, 18/6/2017
SEASON RECORDS Tries: 28 Kieran Gill 2019 Goals: 129 _(inc 1fg)_ Dan Russell 2008 Points: 293 Dan Russell 2008
CAREER RECORDS Tries: 74 Kevin Neighbour 2001-2006; 2008-2010 Goals: 283 _(inc 8fg)_ Benn Hardcastle 2013-2017 Points: 682 Benn Hardcastle 2013-2017
Appearances: 234 Joe Brown 2005-2006; 2010-2021

League One 2024 - Club by Club

NORTH WALES CRUSADERS

DATE	FIXTURE	RESULT	SCORERS	LGE	ATT
28/1/24	Swinton (h) (1895CR1)	L12-40	t:Ah Van,B Evans g:Abel(2)	3rd(G6)	520
11/2/24	Bradford (a) (CCR3)	L48-2	g:Abel	N/A	-
18/2/24	Widnes (h) (1895CR3)	L14-30	t:Reid,Ah Van g:Abel	3rd(G6)	1,088
24/3/24	Cornwall (a) ●	W16-40	t:Taylor,Hughes(2),Barratt,Forster(2),Coates g:Abel(6)	5th	300
31/3/24	Midlands Hurricanes (h)	W20-14	t:Ah Van(2),Ellis,Forster g:Abel(2)	3rd	707
7/4/24	Newcastle (h)	W58-18	t:Reid(2),Holmes(2),Ah Van,Costello,Fletcher,Nzoungou,Forster,Ellis g:Coates(7)	3rd	306
14/4/24	Keighley (a)	L22-6	t:Barratt g:Abel	3rd	1,096
21/4/24	Rochdale (h)	L36-37	t:Coates,Ah Van,Forster(2),Baldwin,Burns g:Abel(6)	3rd	511
28/4/24	Hunslet (a)	L22-14	t:Taylor,Whitehead g:Abel(3)	5th	396
19/5/24	Keighley (h)	L10-30	t:Reid,Taylor g:Coates	7th	462
26/5/24	Midlands Hurricanes (a)	L18-10	t:Ah Van,Reid g:Lane	7th	527
1/6/24	Oldham (a)	L24-25	t:B Evans,Ah Van,Taylor,Davies g:Lane(4)	7th	756
16/6/24	Workington (h)	W34-32	t:Holmes,Costello,Taylor,Cooper,B Evans,Barratt g:Lane(5)	6th	459
23/6/24	Newcastle (a) ●●	W4-42	t:Lane(2),B Evans,Massam(3),Taylor,Costello g:Lane(5)	6th	-
30/6/24	Cornwall (a)	W10-16	t:Davies,Ah Van,Barratt g:Ah Van(2)	6th	-
7/7/24	Midlands Hurricanes (h)	L18-32	t:Barratt,Nash,Carr g:Lane(2),Coates	6th	552
14/7/24	Oldham (a)	L32-6	t:Barratt g:Coates	6th	1,270
21/7/24	Hunslet (h)	L16-46	t:Massam(2),Lane g:Lane,Moss	7th	488
4/8/24	Workington (a)	W24-28	t:B Evans,Ah Van,Barratt(2),Lane g:Moss(4)	7th	857
11/8/24	Keighley (h) ●●●	L16-24	t:Unsworth,Lane g:Lane(4)	7th	401
18/8/24	Hunslet (a)	L28-20	t:Lane,Barratt,Taylor g:Lane(4)	7th	556
25/8/24	Rochdale (a)	L28-10	t:Hughes,Taylor g:Moss	7th	657
1/9/24	Cornwall (h)	W40-10	t:L Evans,Forster,Ellis(2),Reid,Barratt,Moss g:Moss(6)	7th	755

● Played at Truro College ●● Played at Crow Trees, Blaydon ●●● Played at Hare Lane, Chester

		APP		TRIES		GOALS		FG		PTS	
	D.O.B.	ALL	L1	ALL	L1	ALL	L1	ALL	L1	ALL	L1
Owain Abel	21/11/00	8	5	0	0	22	18	0	0	44	36
Patrick Ah Van	17/3/88	21	18	11	8	2	2	0	0	48	36
Brett Bailey	19/12/03	(1)	(1)	0	0	0	0	0	0	0	0
Kenny Baker	1/3/92	(2)	(2)	0	0	0	0	0	0	0	0
Joe Baldwin	16/4/05	10(10)	9(9)	1	1	0	0	0	0	4	4
Zac Bardsley-Rowe	8/10/04	1	0	0	0	0	0	0	0	0	0
Chris Barratt	7/2/93	23	20	10	10	0	0	0	0	40	40
Liam Bent	11/10/97	1	0	0	0	0	0	0	0	0	0
Jake Bloxham	1/9/04	(1)	(1)	0	0	0	0	0	0	0	0
Jake Burns	23/6/00	4(1)	4(1)	1	1	0	0	0	0	4	4
Reece Bushell	18/9/03	4(1)	2(1)	0	0	0	0	0	0	0	0
Jorge Cabral	23/8/97	1	1	0	0	0	0	0	0	0	0
Callum Cameron	31/10/00	(2)		0	0	0	0	0	0	0	0
Adam Carr	24/12/99	2(12)	2(10)	1	1	0	0	0	0	4	4
Dan Coates	30/8/99	16	16	2	2	10	10	0	0	28	28
Liam Cooper	5/10/96	1(2)	1(2)	1	1	0	0	0	0	4	4
Shaun Costello	8/9/98	9(14)	7(13)	3	3	0	0	0	0	12	12
Olly Davies	30/11/95	10(2)	10(2)	2	2	0	0	0	0	8	8
Alex Deery	24/2/02	1	0	0	0	0	0	0	0	0	0
Ryan Ellis	29/6/01	11(2)	8(2)	4	4	0	0	0	0	16	16
Louis Else	30/3/00	5(7)	5(7)	0	0	0	0	0	0	0	0
Ben Evans	30/10/92	14(3)	11(3)	5	4	0	0	0	0	20	16
Lloyd Evans	12/2/97	1	1	1	1	0	0	0	0	4	4
Matt Fletcher	15/2/00	2	2	1	1	0	0	0	0	4	4
Carl Forster	4/6/92	9(9)	8(9)	8	8	0	0	0	0	32	32
Lucas Green	11/9/04	(2)	(1)	0	0	0	0	0	0	0	0
Jack Holmes	15/1/94	18(4)	15(4)	3	3	0	0	0	0	12	12
Toby Hughes	22/8/03	20	17	3	3	0	0	0	0	12	12
Jamie Jenkins	28/11/04	(1)	(1)	0	0	0	0	0	0	0	0
Ben Lane	2/9/03	10	10	6	6	26	26	0	0	76	76
Rob Massam	29/11/87	3	3	5	5	0	0	0	0	20	20
Daniel Moss	23/11/02	5	5	1	1	12	12	0	0	28	28
Paul Nash	16/4/00	2(5)	2(4)	1	1	0	0	0	0	4	4
Levy Nzoungou	22/1/98	(4)		1		0	0	0	0	4	
Cole Oakley	25/10/00	16(1)	16(1)	0	0	0	0	0	0	0	0
Pat Rainford	24/11/96	7(2)	5(1)	0	0	0	0	0	0	0	0
Matt Reid	16/9/92	15	12	6	5	0	0	0	0	24	20
Kallem Rodgers	16/12/02	1	1	0	0	0	0	0	0	0	0
Dayon Sambou	14/4/05	2	2	0	0	0	0	0	0	0	0
Alfie Sinclair	29/10/04	1(1)	1(1)	0	0	0	0	0	0	0	0
Ewan Smith	25/8/05	2	2	0	0	0	0	0	0	0	0
Jono Smith	12/11/88	(2)	(1)	0	0	0	0	0	0	0	0
Kieran Taylor	8/10/00	23	20	8	8	0	0	0	0	32	32
Jake Thewlis	24/5/05	7	7	0	0	0	0	0	0	0	0
Matt Unsworth	29/7/96	12(1)	10(1)	1	1	0	0	0	0	4	4
Tom Whitehead	7/11/02	1	1	1	1	0	0	0	0	4	4

'L1' totals include League One games only; 'All' totals also include Challenge Cup & 1895 Cup

Ben Lane

LEAGUE RECORD
P20-W8-D0-L12 (7th)
F464, A472, Diff-8, 16 points.

CHALLENGE CUP
Round Three

1895 CUP
3rd, Group 6

ATTENDANCES
Best - v Widnes (1895C - 1,088)
Worst - v Newcastle (L1 - 306)
Total (all home games included) - 7,005
Average (all home games included) - 584
(Up by 179 on 2023)

CLUB RECORDS
MATCH RECORDS Highest score: 84-4 v West Wales, 1/5/2022 Highest score against: 4-98 v Wigan, 15/4/2012
Record attendance: 1,562 v South Wales, 1/9/2013 (Racecourse Ground); 1,088 v Widnes, 18/2/2024 (Stadiwm Eirias)
Tries: 5 Rob Massam v Rochdale, 30/6/2013; Jono Smith v Hemel, 16/5/2015 Goals: 12 Tommy Johnson v West Hull, 16/7/2022
Points: 30 Tommy Johnson v West Hull, 6/4/2013
SEASON RECORDS Tries: 29 Rob Massam 2015 Goals: 110 Tommy Johnson 2022 Points: 276 Tommy Johnson 2022
CAREER RECORDS Tries: 183 Rob Massam 2012-2016; 2019-2024 Goals: 740 Tommy Johnson 2012-2018; 2020-2022 Points: 1,800 Tommy Johnson 2012-2018; 2020-2022
Appearances: 209 Tommy Johnson 2012-2018; 2020-2022

League One 2024 - Club by Club

OLDHAM

DATE	FIXTURE	RESULT	SCORERS	LGE	ATT
28/1/24	Halifax (h) (1895CR1)	W24-20	t:Agoro(2),O'Keefe,J Turner g:Ellis(4)	1st(G4)	1,521
10/2/24	Barrow (a) (CCR3)	W10-22	t:O'Keefe(2),Wildie,Lawton g:Ellis(3)	N/A	1,401
18/2/24	Rochdale (h) (1895CR3)	W38-12	t:J Turner,Craven,Jack Johnson,Lawton,Astley,T Chapelhow,Agoro g:Ellis(5)	1st(G4)	1,662
25/2/24	Swinton (a) (CCR4)	L28-12	t:Craven,T Chapelhow g:Ellis(2)	N/A	746
3/3/24	York (a) (1895CQF)	L46-12	t:Astley,Farnworth g:Ellis(2)	N/A	1,048
17/3/24	Workington (a)	W10-48	t:Farnworth,Wildie,O'Keefe,J Turner,Wardle(2),Hirst,Astley g:Ellis(8)	2nd	685
31/3/24	Rochdale (h)	W54-6	t:Ellis,O'Keefe(2),J Turner(2),T Chapelhow,Farnworth,Agoro,Lawton(2) g:Ellis(7)	2nd	2,041
7/4/24	Hunslet (a)	W0-62	t:C Tyrer(6),Lawton,Laulu-Togaga'e,Morgan,Astley g:Ellis(4),Craven(3),C Tyrer(2)	1st	725
14/4/24	Cornwall (h)	W46-10	t:J Turner,C Tyrer(4),Craven,Laulu-Togaga'e(2),M Turner g:Craven(2),C Tyrer(3)	1st	1,136
27/4/24	Midlands Hurricanes (a)	W16-44	t:Agoro(2),Laulu-Togaga'e(2),Hirst,Craven,C Tyrer,Kopczak g:Ellis(4),C Tyrer(2)	2nd	367
5/5/24	Newcastle (h)	W74-0	t:Craven,Laulu-Togaga'e(2),Lawton(4),C Tyrer(2),J Chapelhow,Agoro,J Turner,Astley g:Ellis(11)	1st	1,303
19/5/24	Cornwall (a)	W0-42	t:C Tyrer(2),Gallagher,Agoro(2),Astley,J Turner,Lawton(2) g:Astley(3)	1st	-
26/5/24	Keighley (a)	L28-18	t:J Turner,Laulu-Togaga'e,C Tyrer g:Ellis(3)	2nd	1,852
1/6/24	North Wales (a)	W24-25	t:Jack Johnson,Laulu-Togaga'e,Astley,Aldridge,Craven g:Craven(2) fg:Craven	2nd	756
16/6/24	Newcastle (a) ●	W6-60	t:Moran(3),J Chapelhow,Craven(2),Roebuck,C Tyrer(2),M Turner,Kopczak g:Astley(8)	1st	-
23/6/24	Workington (a)	W4-28	t:O'Keefe(2),Craven,Roebuck,Astley,C Tyrer g:C Tyrer(2)	1st	706
30/6/24	Hunslet (h)	W30-6	t:Laulu-Togaga'e(2),Craven,Aldridge,Astley g:C Tyrer(3)	1st	1,126
14/7/24	North Wales (h)	W32-6	t:O'Keefe,Dixon(2),Agoro(2),Gallagher g:Dixon(4)	1st	1,270
21/7/24	Keighley (h)	W44-6	t:Agoro(2),J Turner,Gallagher,Craven,Jack Johnson(2) g:Dixon(8)	1st	2,572
28/7/24	Rochdale (a)	W10-14	t:Dixon,Jack Johnson,Laulu-Togaga'e g:Dixon	1st	2,178
4/8/24	Midlands Hurricanes (h)	W32-0	t:J Turner,Laulu-Togaga'e,Agoro,Astley,Dixon,Wildie g:Dixon(4)	1st	1,582
11/8/24	Newcastle (h)	W84-0	t:Sambou(2),C Tyrer(5),Dixon(3),T Chapelhow,J Turner,Aldridge,Kopczak,Laulu-Togaga'e g:Dixon(12)	1st	1,006
18/8/24	Keighley (a)	W12-20	t:Agoro(2),Laulu-Togaga'e,Hirst g:Dixon(2)	1st	2,174
25/8/24	Cornwall (h)	W72-0	t:O'Keefe(4),Sidlow,Astley,J Turner(2),Kopczak,C Tyrer(2),Josh Johnson,Sambou(2) g:Ellis(8)	1st	1,421
1/9/24	Workington (h)	W56-0	t:Dixon,Lawton,Wildie,J Turner(2),Laulu-Togaga'e,Craven,Astley,Wardle g:Dixon(8)	1st	2,681

● Played at Gateshead International Stadium

		APP		TRIES		GOALS		FG		PTS	
	D.O.B.	ALL	L1	ALL	L1	ALL	L1	ALL	L1	ALL	L1
Mo Agoro	29/1/93	15	11	16	13	0	0	0	0	64	52
Bailey Aldridge	15/4/04	3(15)	2(12)	3	3	0	0	0	0	12	12
Logan Astley	18/5/03	17(3)	12(3)	13	11	11	11	0	0	74	66
Jay Chapelhow	21/9/95	20(1)	15(1)	2	2	0	0	0	0	8	8
Ted Chapelhow	21/9/95	6(18)	6(13)	4	2	0	0	0	0	16	8
Danny Craven	21/11/91	22	17	11	9	7	7	1	1	59	51
Riley Dean	10/8/01	4	4	0	0	0	0	0	0	0	0
Kieran Dixon	22/8/92	7	7	9	9	39	39	0	0	114	114
Jamie Ellis	4/10/89	14	9	1	1	61	45	0	0	126	94
Owen Farnworth	11/2/99	20(4)	18(1)	3	2	0	0	0	0	12	8
Brad Gallagher	28/2/00	9(2)	9(2)	3	3	0	0	0	0	12	12
George Hirst	27/5/01	8(7)	8(7)	3	3	0	0	0	0	12	12
Jack Johnson	25/4/96	16(1)	12	5	4	0	0	0	0	20	16
Josh Johnson	25/7/94	(16)	(14)	1	1	0	0	0	0	4	4
Craig Kopczak	20/12/86	9(11)	6(10)	4	4	0	0	0	0	16	16
Phoenix Laulu-Togaga'e	16/4/03	17(1)	17(1)	15	15	0	0	0	0	60	60
Adam Lawton	13/6/93	14(3)	9(3)	12	10	0	0	0	0	48	40
Pat Moran	2/4/98	9(5)	9(1)	3	3	0	0	0	0	12	12
Kian Morgan	11/5/00	5	5	1	1	0	0	0	0	4	4
Ben O'Keefe	23/5/02	12	7	13	10	0	0	0	0	52	40
Jordan Paga	23/5/01	(5)	(4)	0	0	0	0	0	0	0	0
Nathan Roebuck	2/10/99	3	3	2	2	0	0	0	0	8	8
Jumah Sambou	21/1/01	2	2	4	4	0	0	0	0	16	16
Adam Sidlow	25/10/87	2(5)	2(5)	1	1	0	0	0	0	4	4
Elijah Taylor	27/2/90	16(1)	12(1)	0	0	0	0	0	0	0	0
Jordan Turner	9/1/89	21	16	16	14	0	0	0	0	64	56
Mackenzie Turner	30/1/03	5	4	2	2	0	0	0	0	8	8
Cian Tyrer	3/2/01	13	12	29	29	12	12	0	0	140	140
Joe Wardle	22/9/91	13(1)	8(1)	3	3	0	0	0	0	12	12
Matty Wildie	25/10/90	23(1)	18(1)	4	3	0	0	0	0	16	12

'L1' totals include League One games only; 'All' totals also include Challenge Cup & 1895 Cup

Cian Tyrer

LEAGUE RECORD
P20-W19-D0-L1 (1st/Champions)
F885, A144, Diff+741, 38 points.

CHALLENGE CUP
Round Four

1895 CUP
Quarter Finalists

ATTENDANCES
Best - v Workington (L1 - 2,681)
Worst - v Newcastle (L1 - 1,006)
Total (all home games included) - 19,321
Average (all home games included) - 1,610
(Up by 873 on 2023)

CLUB RECORDS

MATCH RECORDS Highest score: 102-6 v West Wales, 8/7/2018 Highest score against: 0-84 v Widnes, 25/7/99
Record attendance: 28,000 v Huddersfield, 24/2/1912 *(Watersheddings)*; 2,681 v Workington, 1/9/2024 *(Boundary Park, current spell)*
Tries: 7 James Miller v Barry, 31/10/1908 Goals: 14 Bernard Ganley v Liverpool City, 4/4/59; Martyn Ridyard v West Wales, 10/4/2022
Points: 36 Kieran Dixon v Newcastle, 11/8/2024

SEASON RECORDS Tries: 49 Reg Farrar 1921-22 Goals: 200 Bernard Ganley 1957-58 Points: 412 Bernard Ganley 1957-58
CAREER RECORDS Tries: 174 Alan Davies 1950-61 Goals: 1,358 Bernard Ganley 1951-61 Points: 2,761 Bernard Ganley 1951-61 Appearances: 627 Joe Ferguson 1899-1923

League One 2024 - Club by Club

ROCHDALE HORNETS

DATE	FIXTURE	RESULT	SCORERS	LGE	ATT
4/2/24	Halifax (h) (1895CR2)	L12-52	t:Killan,Nixon g:Ridyard(2)	3rd(G4)	1,200
11/2/24	Midlands Hurricanes (h) (CCR3)	W24-20	t:Nixon(3),Hartley g:Ridyard(4)	N/A	411
18/2/24	Oldham (a) (1895CR3)	L38-12	t:Andrade,Baker g:Rudd(2)	3rd(G4)	1,662
25/2/24	Batley (a) (CCR4)	L30-14	t:Brierley(2),Nixon g:Ridyard	N/A	-
17/3/24	Midlands Hurricanes (a)	W28-38	t:Brierley,McNally(2),Openshaw(2),Straugheir,Hartley g:Ridyard(4),Rudd	4th	465
24/3/24	Hunslet (h)	L24-26	t:Else(2),Hartley(2),M Flanagan g:Rudd(2)	6th	448
31/3/24	Oldham (h)	L54-6	t:Harrop g:M Flanagan	6th	2,041
7/4/24	Workington (a)	L32-22	t:Brierley,Hartley,Andrade,Ratcliffe g:M Flanagan(3)	7th	614
14/4/24	Newcastle (h)	W68-4	t:Blackmore(3),Else(3),Forber(2),Hartley,Ratcliffe,Killan g:Ridyard(10)	5th	379
21/4/24	North Wales (a)	W36-37	t:Harrop(2),Hartley,Forber,Dayes,Juma g:Ridyard(6) fg:Ridyard	4th	511
28/4/24	Keighley (h)	L30-42	t:Forber(3),Openshaw,Harrop g:Ridyard(5)	6th	734
5/5/24	Cornwall (h)	W56-24	t:Harrop,Forber(2),Straugheir,Brierley(3),Brennan,Else,McNally g:Ridyard(8)	4th	891
19/5/24	Workington (h)	W56-12	t:Darbyshire(2),Nelmes(2),Straugheir(2),Brookes,McNally,Forster,Else g:Ridyard(8)	3rd	797
26/5/24	Newcastle (a) ●	W18-24	t:Roden,Forber(2),Ridyard g:Ridyard(4)	3rd	326
16/6/24	Cornwall (a)	W14-38	t:Nixon(2),Roden,Spencer-Tonks,Forber(3) g:Ridyard(5)	4th	-
23/6/24	Hunslet (a)	W18-48	t:Nixon,Straugheir,McNally(2),Else,Andrade(2),Openshaw g:Ridyard(8)	3rd	402
7/7/24	Keighley (a)	D20-20	t:Straugheir,Nixon,Whittel g:Ridyard(4)	3rd	1,608
14/7/24	Workington (a)	L14-12	t:Andrade,Spencer-Tonks g:M Flanagan(2)	4th	573
21/7/24	Midlands Hurricanes (h)	W14-10	t:Andrade(2) g:Harman(3)	4th	676
28/7/24	Oldham (h)	L10-14	t:Forber(2) g:W Roberts	4th	2,178
4/8/24	Cornwall (a)	W46-32	t:Forster,Taulapapa,Else,Forber,Roden,Harrop,Dayes,Andrade g:Harman(7)	3rd	427
17/8/24	Newcastle (a) ●	W6-78	t:Else(3),Forber(2),Straugheir,Taulapapa,Ratchford(3),Harman,Harrop,Andrade,McNally g:Harman(11)		
25/8/24	North Wales (h)	W28-10	t:Forster,Killan,Harrop,McNally(4) g:Harman(4)	4th	220
1/9/24	Keighley (h)	W32-18	t:Forber,D Roberts,Taulapapa,Harrop,Andrade,Else g:Harman(4)	3rd	657
15/9/24	Hunslet (h) (QPO)	W30-18	t:Juma,Else(2),Andrade,Forber,Harrop g:Harman(3)	N/A	1,474
22/9/24	Keighley (a) (QSF)	L26-22	t:D Roberts,Andrade,Forber,Harrop g:Harman(3)	N/A	826
29/9/24	Hunslet (h) (FE)	L26-46	t:Darbyshire,Forber(2),Andrade,Taulapapa g:Harman(3)	N/A	1,037
					428

● Played at Gateshead International Stadium

		APP		TRIES		GOALS		FG		PTS	
	D.O.B.	ALL	L1	ALL	L1	ALL	L1	ALL	L1	ALL	L1
Jordan Andrade	24/1/92	(27)	(23)	13	12	0	0	0	0	52	48
Kenny Baker	1/3/92	2(1)	0	1	0	0	0	0	0	4	0
Jordan Baldwinson	10/11/94	(1)	(1)	0	0	0	0	0	0	0	0
Liam Bent	11/10/97	2	2	0	0	0	0	0	0	0	0
Ben Blackmore	19/2/93	1	1	3	3	0	0	0	0	12	12
AJ Boardman	11/11/89	1	0	0	0	0	0	0	0	0	0
Toby Brannan	27/11/02	6(3)	4(3)	0	0	0	0	0	0	0	0
Brad Brennan	18/1/93	(7)	(5)	1	1	0	0	0	0	4	4
Tommy Brierley	8/9/96	9	5	7	5	0	0	0	0	28	20
Ollie Brookes	19/6/01	2	2	1	1	0	0	0	0	4	4
Joe Coope-Franklin	19/11/01	1	0	0	0	0	0	0	0	0	0
Jack Darbyshire	5/11/03	10	10	3	3	0	0	0	0	12	12
Jaden Dayes	19/5/04	4(4)	4(3)	2	2	0	0	0	0	8	8
Lewis Else	30/3/00	23	19	15	15	0	0	0	0	60	60
George Flanagan	8/10/86	2	2	0	0	0	0	0	0	0	0
Max Flanagan	20/6/01	8(1)	6	0	1	6	6	0	0	16	16
Luke Forber	6/7/98	19	18	23	23	0	0	0	0	92	92
Ben Forster	27/12/00	25(1)	22	3	3	0	0	0	0	12	12
Mackenzie Harman	7/12/04	8	8	1	1	38	38	0	0	80	80
Myles Harrop	21/10/98	22	19	11	11	0	0	0	0	44	44
Joe Hartley	2/5/98	10	8	8	7	0	0	0	0	32	28
Lewis Hollidge	29/3/00	1	1	0	0	0	0	0	0	0	0
Callum Hughes	28/2/95	1	0	0	0	0	0	0	0	0	0
Kyle Huish	11/9/02	1	0	0	0	0	0	0	0	0	0
Lameck Juma	6/12/90	11(1)	10(1)	2	2	0	0	0	0	8	8
Ben Killan	13/5/03	8(12)	7(9)	3	2	0	0	0	0	12	8
Gregg McNally	2/1/91	21	19	9	9	0	0	0	0	36	36
Deane Meadows	11/5/94	11(11)	7(11)	0	0	0	0	0	0	0	0
Kai Morgan	13/4/04	1	1	0	0	0	0	0	0	0	0
Luke Nelmes	7/6/93	23	19	2	2	0	0	0	0	8	8
Dan Nixon	27/7/02	11	8	9	4	0	0	0	0	36	16
Jonny Openshaw	6/5/02	1(12)	1(12)	4	4	0	0	0	0	16	16
Tom Ratchford	10/10/04	1(4)	1(4)	3	3	0	0	0	0	12	12
Connor Ratcliffe	22/5/96	7	6	2	2	0	0	0	0	8	8
Martyn Ridyard	25/7/86	14	11	1	1	69	62	1	1	143	129
Dean Roberts	19/8/96	4(8)	4(8)	2	2	0	0	0	0	8	8
Will Roberts	24/2/05	2	2	0	0	1	1	0	0	2	2
Lloyd Roby	3/1/99	2	2	0	0	0	0	0	0	0	0
Aiden Roden	4/6/00	18(1)	16(1)	3	3	0	0	0	0	12	12
Matty Rudd	31/8/01	5(4)	3(4)	0	5	3	0	0	0	10	6
Daniel Spencer-Tonks	18/1/95	5(5)	5(5)	2	2	0	0	0	0	8	8
Duane Straugheir	29/9/89	22	20	7	7	0	0	0	0	28	28
Misi Taulapapa	25/1/82	9	9	4	4	0	0	0	0	16	16
Emmerson Whittel	13/9/94	17(2)	17(2)	1	1	0	0	0	0	4	4
Matty Wilkinson	13/6/96	1	0	0	0	0	0	0	0	0	0

'L1' totals include regular season & play-offs; 'All' totals also include Challenge Cup & 1895 Cup

Lewis Else

LEAGUE RECORD
P20-W13-D1-L6 (3rd/Final Eliminator)
F687, A432, Diff+255, 27 points.

CHALLENGE CUP
Round Four

1895 CUP
3rd, Group 4

ATTENDANCES
Best - v Oldham (L1 - 2,178)
Worst - v Newcastle (L1 - 379)
Total (excluding Challenge Cup) - 11,115
Average (excluding Challenge Cup) - 855
(Up by 270 on 2023)

CLUB RECORDS Highest score: 120-4 v Illingworth, 13/3/2005 Highest score against: 0-106 v Castleford, 9/9/2007
Record attendance: 26,664 v Oldham, 25/3/1922 (Athletic Grounds); 8,061 v Oldham, 26/12/89 (Spotland)
MATCH RECORDS Tries: 5 Jack Corsi v Barrow, 31/12/1921; Jack Corsi v Broughton Moor, 25/2/1922; Jack Williams v St Helens, 4/4/33; Norman Brelsford v Whitehaven, 3/9/73; Marlon Billy v York, 8/4/2001 Goals: 18 Lee Birdseye v Illingworth, 13/3/2005 Points: 44 Lee Birdseye v Illingworth, 13/3/2005
SEASON RECORDS Tries: 31 Marlon Billy 2001 Goals: 150 Martin Strett 1994-95 Points: 350 Mick Nanyn 2003
CAREER RECORDS Tries: 103 Jack Williams 1931-37 Goals: 741 Walter Gowers 1922-36
Points: 1,497 Walter Gowers 1922-36; Paul Crook 2010-2016 Appearances: 456 Walter Gowers 1922-36

League One 2024 - Club by Club

WORKINGTON TOWN

DATE	FIXTURE	RESULT	SCORERS	LGE	ATT
28/1/24	Barrow (h) (1895CR1)	L8-30	t:Eccleston,C Taylor	3rd(G1)	901
11/2/24	Batley (a) (CCR3)	L48-18	t:Reid,C Taylor,Bradley g:Walker(3)	N/A	-
18/2/24	Whitehaven (h) (1895CR3)	L22-28	t:Scholey,Eccleston,Sammut,Henson g:Forber(3)	3rd(G1)	1,476
17/3/24	Oldham (h)	L10-48	t:Burns,Bradley g:Walker	8th	685
24/3/24	Keighley (a)	L58-16	t:Key(2),Henson g:Forber(2)	8th	916
30/3/24	Newcastle (a)	W18-48	t:Thomson,Mossop,B Taylor(3),Henson,C Tyrer,C Taylor,McNicholas g:Walker(6)	7th	412
7/4/24	Rochdale (h)	W32-22	t:Burns,Hutton(2),Bradley,B Taylor,Henson g:Walker(4)	4th	614
21/4/24	Hunslet (a)	W18-30	t:Scholey(2),Reid,Walker,Key g:Walker(5)	5th	410
28/4/24	Cornwall (h)	W52-18	t:Henson(2),Sammut(3),Walton,Burns,Stephenson,Hutton g:Forber(8)	3rd	599
5/5/24	Midlands Hurricanes (h)	L16-26	t:Bickerdike,Tongia,Sammut g:Walker(2)	5th	678
19/5/24	Rochdale (a)	L56-12	t:Bradley,Galea g:Forber(2)	6th	797
2/6/24	Hunslet (h)	L22-24	t:Bickerdike,Bradley,Forber,Mossop g:Forber(3)	6th	1,486
16/6/24	North Wales (a)	L34-32	t:Brierley,Key,Walton,Archer,Burns g:Walker(6)	7th	459
23/6/24	Oldham (h)	L4-28	t:Lepori	7th	706
30/6/24	Keighley (a)	L18-37	t:Walton,Brierley,Forber g:Forber(3)	7th	793
7/7/24	Newcastle (a) ●	W0-44	t:Brierley,Henson,Galea(2),Brennan(2),Forber,Hartley g:Forber(6)	7th	-
14/7/24	Rochdale (h)	W14-12	t:Mossop,Hadfield,Burns g:Forber	6th	573
21/7/24	Cornwall (a)	W8-30	t:Stephenson,Key,Galea,Bradley,Reid g:Forber(5)	5th	572
28/7/24	Hunslet (a)	W24-32	t:Galea,Brierley,Forber,Reid,C Taylor g:Forber(6)	5th	857
4/8/24	North Wales (h)	L24-28	t:Stephenson,Key,Bradley,Southward g:Forber(4)	6th	677
11/8/24	Midlands Hurricanes (a)	L34-22	t:Hartley(2),Galea,Henson g:Forber(3)	6th	631
25/8/24	Newcastle (h)	W46-0	t:Henson(2),Brennan(2),Brierley,C Taylor,Galea,Bradley,Stephenson g:Forber(5)	6th	2,681
1/9/24	Oldham (a)	L56-0		6th	-
15/9/24	Midlands Hurricanes (a) (EPO)	L24-22	t:Burns(2),Brennan,Bickerdike g:Forber(3)	N/A	323

● Played at Gateshead International Stadium

	D.O.B.	APP ALL	APP L1	TRIES ALL	TRIES L1	GOALS ALL	GOALS L1	FG ALL	FG L1	PTS ALL	PTS L1
Ellis Archer	21/4/04	2(2)	2(2)	1	1	0	0	0	0	4	4
Ethan Bickerdike	15/2/01	10(2)	8(2)	3	3	0	0	0	0	12	12
Jake Bradley	29/4/01	21	18	8	7	0	0	0	0	32	28
Brad Brennan	18/1/93	2(8)	2(8)	5	5	0	0	0	0	20	20
Tommy Brierley	8/9/96	10	10	5	5	0	0	0	0	20	20
Jordan Burns	2/9/95	18	16	7	7	0	0	0	0	28	28
Luke Charlton	29/3/95	(4)	(3)	0	0	0	0	0	0	0	0
Sean Croston	1/11/99	2(1)	1(1)	0	0	0	0	0	0	0	0
Dave Eccleston	12/9/96	3	0	2	0	0	0	0	0	8	0
Carl Forber	17/3/85	20	18	4	4	54	51	0	0	124	118
Zarrin Galea	12/12/00	15	15	7	7	0	0	0	0	28	28
Henry Hadfield	17/10/95	6	6	1	1	0	0	0	0	4	4
Brad Hammond	21/1/03	(1)	(1)	0	0	0	0	0	0	0	0
Joe Hartley	2/5/98	6	6	3	3	0	0	0	0	12	12
Matty Henson	31/10/94	22	20	10	9	0	0	0	0	40	36
Jonny Hutton	12/9/98	8	5	3	3	0	0	0	0	12	12
JJ Key	1/10/95	12(11)	12(8)	6	6	0	0	0	0	24	24
Richard Lepori	22/10/91	4	4	1	1	0	0	0	0	4	4
Jake Lightowler	22/2/99	2(4)	2(3)	0	0	0	0	0	0	0	0
Blain Marwood	23/1/98	1(4)	1(2)	0	0	0	0	0	0	0	0
Liam McNicholas	14/1/97	12	12	1	1	0	0	0	0	4	4
Kian McPherson	23/6/02	(1)	(1)	0	0	0	0	0	0	0	0
Jason Mossop	12/9/85	12	11	3	3	0	0	0	0	12	12
Mike Ogunwole	9/1/97	(1)	(1)	0	0	0	0	0	0	0	0
Joe Purcell	22/8/99	1	1	0	0	0	0	0	0	0	0
Grant Reid	20/4/98	(19)	(18)	4	3	0	0	0	0	16	12
Jarrod Sammut	15/2/87	10(1)	8	5	4	0	0	0	0	20	16
Connor Saunders	31/5/97	7(9)	4(9)	0	0	0	0	0	0	0	0
Stevie Scholey	7/1/96	12(1)	10(1)	3	2	0	0	0	0	12	8
Billy Southward	8/5/98	6	6	1	1	0	0	0	0	4	4
Malik Steele	1/1/01	4	1	0	0	0	0	0	0	0	0
Jack Stephenson	4/9/01	15(1)	14	4	4	0	0	0	0	16	16
Lasarusa Tabu	8/8/89	(3)	(3)	0	0	0	0	0	0	0	0
Brad Taylor	5/10/97	3	3	4	4	0	0	0	0	16	16
Chris Taylor	25/10/93	23	20	5	3	0	0	0	0	20	12
Jordan Thomson	23/1/93	16(3)	13(3)	1	1	0	0	0	0	4	4
Pone Tongia	22/5/99	2(8)	2(8)	1	1	0	0	0	0	4	4
Cian Tyrer	3/2/01	2	2	1	1	0	0	0	0	4	4
Kieran Tyrer	24/10/02	1	1	0	0	0	0	0	0	0	0
Ciaran Walker	29/5/03	13(1)	11(1)	1	1	27	24	0	0	58	52
Tyler Walton	20/12/00	9(11)	8(9)	3	3	0	0	0	0	12	12

'L1' totals include regular season & play-offs; 'All' totals also include Challenge Cup & 1895 Cup

Matty Henson

LEAGUE RECORD
P20-W9-D0-L11
(6th/Elimination Play-off)
F504, A549, Diff-45, 18 points.

CHALLENGE CUP
Round Three

1895 CUP
3rd, Group 1

ATTENDANCES
Best - v Hunslet (L1 - 1,486)
Worst - v Rochdale (L1 - 573)
Total (all home games included) - 9,999
Average (all home games included) - 833
(Up by 30 on 2023)

CLUB RECORDS
MATCH RECORDS: Highest score: 94-4 v Leigh, 26/2/95 Highest score against: 0-92 v Bradford, 14/2/99 Record attendance: 17,741 v Wigan, 3/3/65
Tries: 7 Ike Southward v Blackpool, 17/9/55 Goals: 14 Darren Holt v Gateshead, 12/6/2011
Points: 42 Dean Marwood v Highfield, 1/11/92; Dean Marwood v Leigh, 26/2/95
SEASON RECORDS: Tries: 49 Johnny Lawrenson 1951-52 Goals: 186 Lyn Hopkins 1981-82 Points: 438 Lyn Hopkins 1981-82
CAREER RECORDS: Tries: 274 Ike Southward 1952-68 Goals: 991 (inc 5fg) Carl Forber 2007-2009; 2012-2024 Points: 2,265 Carl Forber 2007-2009; 2012-2024
Appearances: 419 Paul Charlton 1961-69; 1975-80

LEAGUE ONE 2024
Round by Round

ROUND 1

Sunday 17th March 2024

HUNSLET 48 NEWCASTLE THUNDER 12

HUNSLET: 1 Jimmy Watson; 5 Alfie Goddard; 32 Will Adams; 4 Jude Ferreira; 31 Jack Render; 6 Harry Williams; 7 Matty Beharrell; 8 Harvey Hallas; 15 Ross Whitmore; 10 Toby Everett; 11 Josh Jordan-Roberts; 12 Aaron Levy; 16 Jordan Syme. Subs (all used): 9 Billy Gaylor; 18 Cam Berry; 19 Spencer Darley; 26 Ethan O'Hanlon.
Tries: Render (13, 24), Goddard (20, 35, 53), Ferreira (56, 76), Berry (62), Jordan-Roberts (63); **Goals:** Beharrell 6/9.
Sin bin: Goddard (80) - high tackle on Coggle.
THUNDER: 1 Luke Jeremy; 2 Francis Coggle; 3 Dan White; 4 Tom Siddle; 5 Brad Ward; 6 Olly Bibby; 7 Jack Potter; 15 Harry Price; 9 Tyler Hepple; 10 Harry Lowery; 11 Paddy Burns; 12 Nixon Putt; 13 Nathan Newbound. Subs (all used): 14 Will Bate; 17 Sylvester Namo; 8 Dan Hindmarsh; 16 Aaron Harlow-Stephenson.
Tries: Lowery (8), Ward (45); **Goals:** Potter 2/2.
Sin bin: Coggle (80) - retaliation.
Rugby Leaguer & League Express Men of the Match: *Hunslet:* Jordan Syme; *Thunder:* Brad Ward.
Penalty count: 11-2; **Half-time:** 18-6;
Referee: Luke Bland; **Attendance:** 402.

KEIGHLEY COUGARS 56 CORNWALL 12

COUGARS: 1 Brandon Pickersgill; 3 Adam Ryder; 2 Charlie Graham; 4 Junior Sa'u; 5 Billy Walkley; 17 Oscar Thomas; 7 Jack Miller; 20 Will Maher; 15 Aaron Brown; 10 Mark Ioane; 11 Ellis Robson; 12 Lachlan Lanskey; 13 Dan Parker. Subs (all used): 14 Alex Bishop; 9 Kyle Kesik; 8 Lewis Hatton; 18 Jordan Schofield.
Tries: Robson (4, 15, 50), Walkley (7), Parker (13), Thomas (32), Ryder (46), Pickersgill (53, 80), Bishop (65); **Goals:** Miller 8/10.
CORNWALL: 3 Coby Nichol; 5 Harry Aaronson; 12 Darcy Simpson; 4 Tom Ashton; 2 George Mitchell; 6 Cameron Brown; 7 Adam Rusling; 18 Matt Ross; 9 Luke Collins; 10 Harry Boots; 11 Nathan Cullen; 13 David Weetman; 15 Kaine Dimech. Subs (all used): 19 Liam O'Callaghan; 16 Decarlo Trerise; 20 Christian Bannister; 22 Jake Lloyd.
Tries: Mitchell (19), Aaronson (60); **Goals:** Brown 2/2.
Sin bin: Brown (29) - dissent.
Rugby Leaguer & League Express Men of the Match: *Cougars:* Brandon Pickersgill; *Cornwall:* Coby Nichol.
Penalty count: 11-7; **Half-time:** 26-6;
Referee: Andy Sweet; **Attendance:** 971.

MIDLANDS HURRICANES 28 ROCHDALE HORNETS 38

HURRICANES: 1 Todd Horner; 25 Inoke Nakoronivalu; 3 Matt Welham; 4 Ross Oakes; 5 Jason Bass; 14 Brad Billsborough; 7 Dave Hewitt; 8 Jon Luke Kirby; 9 Danny Barcoe; 24 Marcus Green; 11 Tom Wilkinson; 15 Aaron Willis; 13 Brad Clavering. Subs (all used): 27 Peceli Suguvanua; 29 Lewis Peachey; 17 Kieran Moran; 19 Chris Cullimore.
Tries: Bass (24), Barcoe (27), Nakoronivalu (38), Wilkinson (53, 78); **Goals:** Billsborough 3/4, Hewitt 1/1.
HORNETS: 1 Gregg McNally; 2 Dan Nixon; 4 Joe Hartley; 3 Myles Harrop; 5 Tommy Brierley; 6 Martyn Ridyard; 7 Lewis Else; 10 Luke Nelmes; 25 Matty Rudd; 20 Toby Brannan; 11 Ben Forster; 12 Duane Straugheir; 18 Deane Meadows. Subs (all used): 30 Jonny Openshaw; 16 Jordan Andrade; 28 Brad Brennan; 17 Ben Killan.
Tries: Brierley (5), McNally (15, 18), Openshaw (32, 68), Straugheir (60), Hartley (72); **Goals:** Ridyard 4/5, Rudd 1/2.
Rugby Leaguer & League Express Men of the Match: *Hurricanes:* Danny Barcoe; *Hornets:* Jonny Openshaw.
Penalty count: 3-4; **Half-time:** 16-22;
Referee: Matty Lynn; **Attendance:** 465.

WORKINGTON TOWN 10 OLDHAM 48

TOWN: 28 Jarrod Sammut; 27 Richard Lepori; 3 Chris Taylor; 1 Jordan Burns; 24 Jonny Hutton; 6 Ciaran Walker; 7 Carl Forber; 8 Jordan Thomson; 9 Matty Henson; 21 Jake Lightowler; 12 Jake Bradley; 25 Sean Croston; 22 Tyler Walton. Subs (all used): 14 Blain Marwood; 17 Grant Reid; 13 JJ Key; 18 Brad Hammond.
Tries: Burns (45), Bradley (52); **Goals:** Walker 1/2.
OLDHAM: 6 Danny Craven; 24 Ben O'Keefe; 3 Jordan Turner; 4 Kian Morgan; 5 Mo Agoro; 1 Logan Astley; 7 Jamie Ellis; 16 Owen Farnworth; 9 Matty Wildie; 18 Jay Chapelhow; 11 Joe Wardle; 12 Adam Lawton; 22 Ted Chapelhow. Subs (all used): 14 Jordan Paga; 15 Josh Johnson; 20 George Hirst; 26 Brad Gallagher.
Tries: Farnworth (4), Wildie (9), O'Keefe (17), J Turner (20), Wardle (30, 43), Hirst (58), Astley (71); **Goals:** Ellis 8/8.
Rugby Leaguer & League Express Men of the Match: *Town:* Ciaran Walker; *Oldham:* Logan Astley.
Penalty count: 8-8; **Half-time:** 0-30;
Referee: Nick Bennett; **Attendance:** 685.

ROUND 2

Sunday 24th March 2024

MIDLANDS HURRICANES 70 NEWCASTLE THUNDER 16

HURRICANES: 1 Todd Horner; 25 Inoke Nakoronivalu; 3 Matt Welham; 4 Ross Oakes; 5 Jason Bass; 14 Brad Billsborough; 7 Dave Hewitt; 8 Jon Luke Kirby; 9 Danny Barcoe; 24 Marcus Green; 11 Tom Wilkinson; 15 Aaron Willis; 13 Brad Clavering. Subs (all used): 27 Peceli Suguvanua; 17 Kieran Moran; 19 Chris Cullimore; 20 Owen Maull.
Tries: Barcoe (3, 30), Oakes (16), Billsborough (21), Wilkinson (33, 70, 78), Moran (48), Bass (51), Horner (57), M Welham (66), Kirby (75); **Goals:** Hewitt 11/12.
THUNDER: 1 Alex Donaghy; 2 Luke Jeremy; 3 George Birch; 4 Alfie Dean; 5 Brad Ward; 6 Olly Bibby; 7 Jack Potter; 8 Harry Price; 9 Taylor Pemberton; 10 Tobias Gibson; 11 Harvey Reynolds; 12 Nathan Rushworth; 13 Harry Lowery. Subs (all used): 14 Tom Siddle; 15 Lloyd Hall; 16 Jack Skelton; 17 Aaron Harlow-Stephenson.
Tries: Birch (9), Lowery (26), Bibby (38); **Goals:** Potter 2/3.
Sin bin: Gibson (12) - dangerous challenge on Bass.
Rugby Leaguer & League Express Men of the Match: *Hurricanes:* Tom Wilkinson; *Thunder:* George Birch.
Penalty count: 11-11; **Half-time:** 30-16;
Referee: Andy Sweet; **Attendance:** 377.

CORNWALL 16 NORTH WALES CRUSADERS 40

CORNWALL: 3 Coby Nichol; 5 Harry Aaronson; 12 Darcy Simpson; 4 Tom Ashton; 2 George Mitchell; 6 Cameron Brown; 14 Morgan Punchard; 18 Matt Ross; 9 Luke Collins; 10 Harry Boots; 11 Nathan Cullen; 13 David Weetman; 15 Kaine Dimech. Subs (all used): 19 Liam O'Callaghan; 22 Jake Lloyd; 16 Decarlo Trerise; 20 Christian Bannister.
Tries: Aaronson (48), Cullen (70), Brown (80); **Goals:** Brown 2/3.
CRUSADERS: 1 Owain Abel; 16 Jack Holmes; 3 Kieran Taylor; 4 Matt Reid; 5 Patrick Ah Van; 6 Dan Coates; 7 Toby Hughes; 15 Shaun Costello; 9 Pat Rainford; 10 Chris Barratt; 11 Ryan Ellis; 12 Matt Unsworth; 22 Adam Carr. Subs (all used): 19 Joe Baldwin; 13 Carl Forster; 23 Louis Else; 21 Levy Nzoungou.
Tries: Taylor (7), Hughes (18, 67), Barratt (22), Forster (32, 56), Coates (51); **Goals:** Abel 6/7.
Sin bin: Rainford (72) - high tackle on Aaronson.
Rugby Leaguer & League Express Men of the Match: *Cornwall:* Nathan Cullen; *Crusaders:* Chris Barratt.
Penalty count: 5-4; **Half-time:** 0-22;
Referee: Aaryn Belafonte; **Attendance:** 300 *(at Truro College).*

KEIGHLEY COUGARS 58 WORKINGTON TOWN 16

COUGARS: 1 Brandon Pickersgill; 3 Adam Ryder; 2 Charlie Graham; 4 Junior Sa'u; 5 Billy Walkley; 17 Oscar Thomas; 7 Jack Miller; 20 Will Maher; 9 Kyle Kesik; 10 Mark Ioane; 11 Ellis Robson; 12 Lachlan Lanskey; 15 Aaron Brown. Subs (all used): 14 Alex Bishop; 13 Dan Parker; 8 Lewis Hatton; 18 Jordan Schofield.
Tries: Ioane (7, 70), Robson (10), Miller (17), Parker (25), Pickersgill (35, 79), Sa'u (40, 58), Thomas (56); **Goals:** Miller 9/10.
Sin bin: Brown (65) - late challenge.
TOWN: 19 Joe Purcell; 27 Richard Lepori; 3 Chris Taylor; 4 Jason Mossop; 6 Cian Tyrer; 28 Jarrod Sammut; 7 Carl Forber; 22 Tyler Walton; 9 Matty Henson; 13 JJ Key; 11 Malik Steele; 15 Liam McNicholas; 12 Jake Bradley. Subs (all used): 17 Grant Reid; 14 Blain Marwood; 25 Sean Croston; 26 Luke Charlton.
Tries: Key (31, 50), Henson (64); **Goals:** Forber 2/3.
Sin bin: C Taylor (54) - high tackle.
Rugby Leaguer & League Express Men of the Match: *Cougars:* Oscar Thomas; *Town:* JJ Key.
Penalty count: 14-8; **Half-time:** 36-6;
Referee: Matty Lynn; **Attendance:** 916.

ROCHDALE HORNETS 24 HUNSLET 26

HORNETS: 1 Gregg McNally; 2 Dan Nixon; 4 Joe Hartley; 3 Myles Harrop; 5 Tommy Brierley; 26 Max Flanagan; 7 Lewis Else; 20 Toby Brannan; 25 Matty Rudd; 10 Luke Nelmes; 11 Ben Forster; 18 Deane Meadows; 12 Duane Straugheir. Subs (all used): 30 Jonny Openshaw; 16 Jordan Andrade; 28 Brad Brennan; 17 Ben Killan.
Tries: Else (3, 76), Hartley (15, 69), M Flanagan (66); **Goals:** Rudd 2/5.
HUNSLET: 1 Jimmy Watson; 5 Alfie Goddard; 32 Will Adams; 4 Jude Ferreira; 31 Jack Render; 6 Harry Williams; 7 Matty Beharrell; 8 Harvey Hallas; 9 Billy Gaylor; 10 Toby Everett; 11 Josh Jordan-Roberts; 12 Aaron Levy; 16 Jordan Syme. Subs (all used): 18 Cam Berry; 15 Ross Whitmore; 19 Spencer Darley; 26 Ethan O'Hanlon.
Tries: Ferreira (22, 55), Williams (29), Darley (33), Hallas (73); **Goals:** Beharrell 3/5.
Rugby Leaguer & League Express Men of the Match: *Hornets:* Lewis Else; *Hunslet:* Jude Ferreira.
Penalty count: 5-6; **Half-time:** 10-14;
Referee: Nick Bennett; **Attendance:** 448.

ROUND 3

Friday 29th March 2024

HUNSLET 14 KEIGHLEY COUGARS 42

HUNSLET: 1 Jimmy Watson; 5 Alfie Goddard; 25 Aidan Scully; 4 Jude Ferreira; 31 Jack Render; 6 Harry Williams; 7 Matty Beharrell; 8 Harvey Hallas; 15 Ross Whitmore; 13 Michael Knowles; 11 Josh Jordan-Roberts; 12 Aaron Levy; 16 Jordan Syme. Subs (all used): 18 Cam Berry; 19 Spencer Darley; 26 Ethan O'Hanlon; 40 Cole Oakley.
Tries: Jordan-Roberts (3), Goddard (54);
Goals: Beharrell 3/3.
Sin bin: Ferreira (69) - delaying restart.
COUGARS: 1 Brandon Pickersgill; 3 Adam Ryder; 2 Charlie Graham; 4 Junior Sa'u; 5 Billy Walkley; 17 Oscar Thomas; 7 Jack Miller; 20 Will Maher; 9 Kyle Kesik; 10 Mark Ioane; 11 Ellis Robson; 12 Lachlan Lanskey; 15 Aaron Brown. Subs (all used): 14 Alex Bishop; 13 Dan Parker; 8 Lewis Hatton; 18 Jordan Schofield.
Tries: Ioane (22), Bishop (31), Walkley (35, 39), Robson (49, 75), Brown (64), Sa'u (73); **Goals:** Miller 5/8.
Rugby Leaguer & League Express Men of the Match: *Hunslet:* Josh Jordan-Roberts; *Cougars:* Alex Bishop.
Penalty count: 7-15; **Half-time:** 8-20;
Referee: Kevin Moore; **Attendance:** 618.

Saturday 30th March 2024

NEWCASTLE THUNDER 18 WORKINGTON TOWN 48

THUNDER: 1 Alex Donaghy; 2 Luke Jeremy; 3 George Birch; 4 Alfie Dean; 5 Brad Ward; 6 Olly Bibby; 7 Jack Potter; 8 Harry Price; 9 Taylor Pemberton; 10 Harry Lowery; 11 Nathan Rushworth; 12 Dan White; 13 Nathan Newbound. Subs (all used): 14 Will Bate; 15 Jake Anderson; 16 Tobias Gibson; 17 Jack Skelton.
Tries: Ward (15), Donaghy (22), Jeremy (34);
Goals: Potter 3/3.
Dismissal: Skelton (75) - dangerous challenge.
TOWN: 27 Richard Lepori; 18 Brad Taylor; 3 Chris Taylor; 4 Jason Mossop; 14 Cian Tyrer; 28 Jarrod Sammut; 7 Carl Forber; 8 Jordan Thomson; 9 Matty Henson; 10 Stevie Scholey; 12 Jake Bradley; 15 Liam McNicholas; 6 Ciaran Walker. Subs (all used): 13 JJ Key; 22 Tyler Walton; 21 Jake Lightowler; 17 Grant Reid.
Tries: Thomson (5), Mossop (11), B Taylor (50, 56, 79), Henson (62), C Tyrer (69), C Taylor (74), McNicholas (77);
Goals: Walker 6/8, Sammut 0/1.
Rugby Leaguer & League Express Men of the Match: *Thunder:* Jack Potter; *Town:* Jake Bradley.
Penalty count: 7-2; **Half-time:** 18-12;
Referee: Luke Bland; **Attendance:** 412.

Sunday 31st March 2024

NORTH WALES CRUSADERS 20 MIDLANDS HURRICANES 14

CRUSADERS: 1 Owain Abel; 16 Jack Holmes; 3 Kieran Taylor; 4 Matt Reid; 5 Patrick Ah Van; 6 Dan Coates; 7 Toby Hughes; 8 Ben Evans; 9 Pat Rainford; 10 Chris Barratt; 11 Ryan Ellis; 12 Matt Unsworth; 15 Shaun Costello. Subs (all used): 25 Jake Burns; 13 Carl Forster; 23 Louis Else; 22 Adam Carr.
Tries: Ah Van (7, 62), Ellis (26), Forster (49); **Goals:** Abel 2/4.
HURRICANES: 1 Todd Horner; 25 Inoke Nakoronivalu; 3 Matt Welham; 4 Ross Oakes; 5 Jason Bass; 14 Brad Billsborough; 7 Dave Hewitt; 24 Marcus Green; 9 Danny Barcoe; 30 Blake Broadbent; 11 Tom Wilkinson; 15 Aaron Willis; 13 Brad Clavering. Subs (all used): 19 Chris Cullimore; 2 Max Kirkbright; 29 Lewis Peachey; 17 Kieran Moran.
Tries: M Welham (22), Billsborough (33), Kirkbright (78);
Goals: Hewitt 1/3.
Rugby Leaguer & League Express Men of the Match: *Crusaders:* Patrick Ah Van; *Hurricanes:* Dave Hewitt.
Penalty count: 6-8; **Half-time:** 10-10;
Referee: Ryan Cox; **Attendance:** 707.

OLDHAM 54 ROCHDALE HORNETS 6

OLDHAM: 1 Logan Astley; 5 Mo Agoro; 3 Jordan Turner; 4 Kian Morgan; 24 Ben O'Keefe; 6 Danny Craven; 7 Jamie Ellis; 16 Owen Farnworth; 9 Matty Wildie; 8 Craig Kopczak; 11 Joe Wardle; 12 Adam Lawton; 18 Jay Chapelhow. Subs (all used): 14 Jordan Paga; 15 Josh Johnson; 20 George Hirst; 22 Ted Chapelhow.
Tries: Ellis (6), O'Keefe (19, 54), J Turner (23, 30), T Chapelhow (57), Farnworth (67), Agoro (69), Lawton (72, 80); **Goals:** Ellis 7/10.
Sin bin: Kopczak (36) - professional foul.

HORNETS: 26 Max Flanagan; 2 Dan Nixon; 4 Joe Hartley; 3 Myles Harrop; 5 Tommy Brierley; 32 Lewis Hollidge; 7 Lewis Else; 20 Toby Brannan; 30 Jonny Openshaw; 10 Luke Nelmes; 11 Ben Forster; 19 Connor Ratcliffe; 12 Duane Straugheir. Subs (all used): 16 Jordan Andrade; 22 Emmerson Whittel; 23 Lameck Juma; 28 Brad Brennan.
Try: Harrop (9); **Goals:** M Flanagan 1/1.
Rugby Leaguer & League Express Men of the Match: *Oldham:* Jordan Turner; *Hornets:* Myles Harrop.
Penalty count: 11-7; **Half-time:** 20-6;
Referee: Andy Sweet; **Attendance:** 2,041.

ROUND 4

Sunday 7th April 2024

NORTH WALES CRUSADERS 58 NEWCASTLE THUNDER 18

CRUSADERS: 16 Jack Holmes; 2 Kallem Rodgers; 3 Kieran Taylor; 4 Matt Reid; 5 Patrick Ah Van; 6 Dan Coates; 7 Toby Hughes; 23 Louis Else; 19 Joe Baldwin; 10 Chris Barratt; 11 Ryan Ellis; 17 Matt Fletcher; 15 Shaun Costello. Subs (all used): 13 Carl Forster; 14 Paul Nash; 21 Levy Nzoungou; 22 Adam Carr.
Tries: Reid (1, 12), Holmes (8, 40), Ah Van (14), Costello (18), Fletcher (28), Nzoungou (31), Forster (56, 73), Ellis (78);
Goals: Coates 7/11.
THUNDER: 1 Alex Donaghy; 2 Luke Jeremy; 3 George Birch; 4 Tom Siddle; 5 Brad Ward; 6 Olly Bibby; 7 Jack Potter; 8 Harry Price; 9 Taylor Pemberton; 10 Harry Lowery; 11 Tyler Hepple; 12 Jake Anderson; 13 Nathan Rushworth. Subs (all used): 14 Will Bate; 15 Harvey Reynolds; 16 Nathan Newbound; 17 Tobias Gibson.
Tries: Siddle (48), Price (67), Lowery (80);
Goals: Potter 3/3.
Sin bin: Price (1) - delaying restart.
Rugby Leaguer & League Express Men of the Match: *Crusaders:* Dan Coates; *Thunder:* Harry Lowery.
Penalty count: 7-6; **Half-time:** 42-0;
Referee: Andy Sweet; **Attendance:** 306.

HUNSLET 0 OLDHAM 62

HUNSLET: 1 Jimmy Watson; 5 Alfie Goddard; 40 Cole Oakley; 4 Jude Ferreira; 29 Donald Kudangirana; 6 Harry Williams; 9 Billy Gaylor; 8 Harvey Hallas; 15 Ross Whitmore; 13 Michael Knowles; 11 Josh Jordan-Roberts; 12 Aaron Levy; 16 Jordan Syme. Subs (all used): 10 Toby Everett; 18 Cam Berry; 26 Ethan O'Hanlon; 41 Daniel Spencer-Tonks.
OLDHAM: 1 Logan Astley; 27 Cian Tyrer; 4 Kian Morgan; 3 Jordan Turner; 21 Mackenzie Turner; 6 Danny Craven; 7 Jamie Ellis; 16 Owen Farnworth; 9 Matty Wildie; 8 Craig Kopczak; 11 Joe Wardle; 12 Adam Lawton; 18 Jay Chapelhow. Subs (all used): 15 Josh Johnson; 22 Ted Chapelhow; 20 George Hirst; 30 Phoenix Laulu-Togaga'e.
Tries: C Tyrer (2, 7, 23, 36, 46, 48), Lawton (52), Laulu-Togaga'e (57), Morgan (66), Astley (72, 74);
Goals: Ellis 4/5, Craven 3/4, C Tyrer 2/2.
Rugby Leaguer & League Express Men of the Match: *Hunslet:* Jimmy Watson; *Oldham:* Cian Tyrer.
Penalty count: 8-9; **Half-time:** 0-24;
Referee: Brad Milligan; **Attendance:** 725.

WORKINGTON TOWN 32 ROCHDALE HORNETS 22

TOWN: 1 Jordan Burns; 2 Brad Taylor; 3 Chris Taylor; 4 Jason Mossop; 24 Jonny Hutton; 7 Ciaran Walker; 28 Jarrod Sammut; 10 Jordan Thomson; 9 Matty Henson; 11 Stevie Scholey; 20 Jack Stephenson; 12 Jake Bradley; 27 Liam McNicholas. Subs (all used): 13 JJ Key; 14 Jake Lightowler; 22 Tyler Walton; 26 Connor Saunders.
Tries: Burns (1), Hutton (11, 68), Bradley (16), B Taylor (23), Henson (50); **Goals:** Walker 4/6.
HORNETS: 26 Max Flanagan; 5 Tommy Brierley; 4 Joe Hartley; 3 Myles Harrop; 2 Dan Nixon; 14 Lloyd Roby; 7 Kai Morgan; 20 Toby Brannan; 25 Matty Rudd; 10 Luke Nelmes; 11 Ben Forster; 19 Connor Ratcliffe; 12 Duane Straugheir. Subs (all used): 16 Jordan Andrade; 22 Emmerson Whittel; 28 Brad Brennan; 30 Jonny Openshaw.
Tries: Brierley (30), Hartley (46), Andrade (75), Ratcliffe (79); **Goals:** M Flanagan 3/4.
Rugby Leaguer & League Express Men of the Match: *Town:* Jordan Burns; *Hornets:* Jordan Andrade.
Penalty count: 5-5; **Half-time:** 22-4;
Referee: Nick Bennett; **Attendance:** 614.

ROUND 5

Sunday 14th April 2024

OLDHAM 46 CORNWALL 10

OLDHAM: 30 Phoenix Laulu-Togaga'e; 21 Mackenzie Turner; 4 Kian Morgan; 3 Jordan Turner; 27 Cian Tyrer; 6 Danny Craven; 1 Logan Astley; 8 Craig Kopczak; 25 Bailey Aldridge; 16 Owen Farnworth; 26 Brad Gallagher; 12 Adam Lawton; 18 Jay Chapelhow. Subs (all used): 13 Elijah Taylor; 14 Jordan Paga; 15 Josh Johnson; 22 Ted Chapelhow.
Tries: J Turner (4), C Tyrer (19, 35, 50, 66), Craven (24), Laulu-Togaga'e (38, 69), M Turner (62);
Goals: Craven 2/4, C Tyrer 3/5.
CORNWALL: 6 Cameron Brown; 5 Harry Aaronson; 3 Coby Nichol; 4 Tom Ashton; 2 George Mitchell; 14 Morgan Punchard; 27 Bailey Black; 18 Matt Ross; 9 Luke Collins; 10 Harry Boots; 11 Nathan Cullen; 12 Darcy Simpson; 13 David Weetman. Subs (all used): 15 Kaine Dimech; 16 Decarlo Trerise; 22 Jake Lloyd; 26 Nathan Conroy.
Tries: Aaronson (15), Ashton (42); **Goals:** Brown 1/2.
Rugby Leaguer & League Express Men of the Match: *Oldham:* Cian Tyrer; *Cornwall:* Cameron Brown.
Penalty count: 9-8; **Half-time:** 26-4;
Referee: Tara Jones; **Attendance:** 1,136.

MIDLANDS HURRICANES 26 HUNSLET 30

HURRICANES: 1 Todd Horner; 2 Max Kirkbright; 3 Matt Welham; 4 Ross Oakes; 5 Jason Bass; 6 Jake Sweeting; 7 Dave Hewitt; 8 Jon Luke Kirby; 9 Danny Barcoe; 24 Marcus Green; 11 Tom Wilkinson; 12 Liam Welham; 30 Blake Broadbent. Subs (all used): 18 Elliot Windley; 15 Aaron Willis; 29 Lewis Peachey; 17 Kieran Moran.
Tries: Barcoe (8), Horner (13), M Welham (15), Sweeting (35); **Goals:** Hewitt 5/5.
Sin bin: Green (28) - high tackle;
Wilkinson (78) - high tackle.
HUNSLET: 1 Jimmy Watson; 35 Mackenzie Scurr; 5 Alfie Goddard; 4 Jude Ferreira; 31 Jack Render; 6 Harry Williams; 7 Matty Beharrell; 8 Harvey Hallas; 15 Ross Whitmore; 13 Michael Knowles; 11 Josh Jordan-Roberts; 12 Aaron Levy; 16 Jordan Syme. Subs (all used): 18 Cam Berry; 10 Toby Everett; 41 Daniel Spencer-Tonks; 26 Ethan O'Hanlon.
Tries: Goddard (20), Watson (26), Jordan-Roberts (32), Berry (68), Ferreira (71); **Goals:** Beharrell 5/5.
Rugby Leaguer & League Express Men of the Match: *Hurricanes:* Jake Sweeting; *Hunslet:* Daniel Spencer-Tonks.
Penalty count: 6-7; **Half-time:** 26-18;
Referee: Kevin Moore; **Attendance:** 302
(at Olympic Legacy Park, Sheffield).

KEIGHLEY COUGARS 22 NORTH WALES CRUSADERS 6

COUGARS: 1 Brandon Pickersgill; 3 Adam Ryder; 2 Charlie Graham; 4 Junior Sa'u; 5 Billy Walkley; 17 Oscar Thomas; 7 Jack Miller; 20 Will Maher; 9 Kyle Kesik; 10 Mark Ioane; 11 Ellis Robson; 12 Lachlan Lanskey; 15 Aaron Brown. Subs (all used): 8 Lewis Hatton; 13 Dan Parker; 14 Alex Bishop; 18 Jordan Schofield.
Tries: Bishop (26), Walkley (45, 49), Hatton (61);
Goals: Miller 3/4.
CRUSADERS: 1 Owain Abel; 16 Jack Holmes; 3 Kieran Taylor; 24 Cole Oakley; 5 Patrick Ah Van; 6 Dan Coates; 7 Toby Hughes; 15 Shaun Costello; 25 Jake Burns; 10 Chris Barratt; 11 Ryan Ellis; 12 Matt Unsworth; 17 Matt Fletcher. Subs (all used): 13 Carl Forster; 20 Lucas Green; 19 Joe Baldwin; 23 Louis Else.
Try: Barratt (13); **Goals:** Abel 1/1.
Rugby Leaguer & League Express Men of the Match: *Cougars:* Alex Bishop; *Crusaders:* Owain Abel.
Penalty count: 8-7; **Half-time:** 6-6;
Referee: Matty Lynn; **Attendance:** 1,096.

ROCHDALE HORNETS 68 NEWCASTLE THUNDER 4

HORNETS: 32 Lloyd Roby; 27 Ben Blackmore; 22 Lameck Juma; 4 Joe Hartley; 21 Luke Forber; 6 Martyn Ridyard; 7 Lewis Else; 8 Liam Bent; 12 George Flanagan; 17 Ben Killan; 11 Ben Forster; 19 Connor Ratcliffe; 23 Emmerson Whittel. Subs (all used): 30 Jonny Openshaw; 18 Deane Meadows; 16 Jordan Andrade; 24 Jaden Dayes.
Tries: Blackmore (2, 28, 34), Else (4, 9, 57), Forber (17, 43), Hartley (20, 64), Ratcliffe (50), Killan (75);
Goals: Ridyard 10/12.
THUNDER: 1 Alex Donaghy; 2 George Birch; 3 Alfie Dean; 4 Tom Siddle; 5 Luke Jeremy; 6 Jaiden Linford; 7 Jack Potter; 8 Harry Price; 9 Tyler Hepple; 10 Harry Lowery; 11 Nathan Rushworth; 12 Jake Anderson; 13 Nathan Newbound. Subs (all used): 14 Will Bate; 15 Tobias Gibson; 16 Aaron Harlow-Stephenson; 17 Oliver Simpson.
Try: Birch (39); **Goals:** Potter 0/1.
Sin bin: Simpson (43) - high tackle.
Rugby Leaguer & League Express Men of the Match: *Hornets:* Lewis Else; *Thunder:* Will Bate.
Penalty count: 10-4; **Half-time:** 38-4;
Referee: Aaryn Belafonte; **Attendance:** 379.

ROUND 6

Sunday 21st April 2024

NORTH WALES CRUSADERS 36 ROCHDALE HORNETS 37

CRUSADERS: 1 Owain Abel; 16 Jack Holmes; 3 Kieran Taylor; 24 Cole Oakley; 5 Patrick Ah Van; 6 Dan Coates; 7 Toby Hughes; 13 Carl Forster; 25 Jake Burns; 10 Chris Barratt; 11 Ryan Ellis; 12 Matt Unsworth; 22 Adam Carr. Subs (all used): 15 Shaun Costello; 19 Joe Baldwin; 23 Louis Else; 27 Jono Smith.
Tries: Coates (21), Ah Van (27), Forster (32, 68), Baldwin (57), Burns (71); **Goals:** Abel 6/7.
HORNETS: 26 Max Flanagan; 22 Lameck Juma; 3 Myles Harrop; 4 Joe Hartley; 21 Luke Forber; 6 Martyn Ridyard; 7 Lewis Else; 8 Liam Bent; 32 George Flanagan; 17 Ben Killan; 11 Ben Forster; 19 Connor Ratcliffe; 23 Emmerson Whittel. Subs (all used): 9 Aiden Roden; 16 Jordan Andrade; 18 Deane Meadows; 24 Jaden Dayes.
Tries: Harrop (12, 50), Hartley (24), Forber (37), Dayes (58), Juma (75); **Goals:** Ridyard 6/6; **Field goal:** Ridyard (40).
Rugby Leaguer & League Express Men of the Match: *Crusaders:* Owain Abel; *Hornets:* Martyn Ridyard.
Penalty count: 4-4; **Half-time:** 18-19;
Referee: Aaryn Belafonte; **Attendance:** 511.

CORNWALL 6 MIDLANDS HURRICANES 72

CORNWALL: 6 Cameron Brown; 25 Kyle Marvin; 3 Coby Nichol; 4 Tom Ashton; 5 Harry Aaronson; 27 Bailey Black; 7 Adam Rusling; 15 Kaine Dimech; 28 Nathan Conroy; 18 Matt Ross; 13 David Weetman; 12 Darcy Simpson; 22 Jake Lloyd. Subs (all used): 8 Josh Rhodes; 9 Luke Collins; 19 Liam O'Callaghan; 20 Christian Bannister.
Try: Nichol (73); **Goals:** Brown 1/1.
HURRICANES: 1 Todd Horner; 22 Ryan Johnson; 3 Matt Welham; 4 Ross Oakes; 5 Jason Bass; 6 Jake Sweeting; 23 Callum McLelland; 8 Jon Luke Kirby; 9 Danny Barcoe; 16 Ellis Hobson; 11 Tom Wilkinson; 12 Liam Welham; 30 Blake Broadbent. Subs (all used): 15 Aaron Willis; 19 Chris Cullimore; 24 Marcus Green; 29 Lewis Peachey.
Tries: Wilkinson (3, 47), Sweeting (6), Oakes (14, 37), McLelland (20), Johnson (29, 79), M Welham (44), Willis (54), Horner (56), L Welham (60);
Goals: Sweeting 12/12.
Rugby Leaguer & League Express Men of the Match: *Cornwall:* Josh Rhodes; *Hurricanes:* Jake Sweeting.
Penalty count: 1-8; **Half-time:** 0-36;
Referee: Adam Williams; **Attendance:** 456.

HUNSLET 18 WORKINGTON TOWN 30

HUNSLET: 1 Jimmy Watson; 2 Matty Chrimes; 5 Alfie Goddard; 4 Jude Ferreira; 31 Jack Render; 14 Jack Mallinson; 7 Matty Beharrell; 8 Harvey Hallas; 9 Billy Gaylor; 10 Toby Everett; 11 Josh Jordan-Roberts; 12 Aaron Levy; 13 Michael Knowles. Subs (all used): 16 Jordan Syme; 18 Cam Berry; 22 Liam Carr; 26 Ethan O'Hanlon.
Tries: Levy (26), Berry (33), Ferreira (36);
Goals: Beharrell 3/3.
TOWN: 1 Jordan Burns; 29 Brad Taylor; 3 Chris Taylor; 4 Jason Mossop; 24 Jonny Hutton; 6 Ciaran Walker; 28 Jarrod Sammut; 8 Jordan Thomson; 9 Matty Henson; 10 Stevie Scholey; 18 Liam McNicholas; 12 Jake Bradley; 16 Jack Stephenson. Subs (all used): 13 JJ Key; 17 Grant Reid; 19 Connor Saunders; 21 Jake Lightowler.
Tries: Scholey (12, 21), Reid (59), Walker (62), Key (66);
Goals: Walker 5/5.
Rugby Leaguer & League Express Men of the Match: *Hunslet:* Matty Beharrell; *Town:* Ciaran Walker.
Penalty count: 6-7; **Half-time:** 18-12;
Referee: Luke Bland; **Attendance:** 410.

NEWCASTLE THUNDER 6 KEIGHLEY COUGARS 82

THUNDER: 1 Alex Donaghy; 2 George Birch; 3 Evan Lawther; 4 Tom Siddle; 5 Luke Jeremy; 6 Tyler Hepple; 7 Olly Bibby; 8 Aaron Harlow-Stephenson; 9 Owen Reed; 10 Harry Lowery; 11 Nathan Rushworth; 12 Jake Anderson; 13 Tobias Gibson. Subs (all used): 14 Will Bate; 15 Nathan Newbound; 16 Dan White; 17 Oliver Simpson.
Try: Lawther (48); **Goals:** Hepple 1/1.
COUGARS: 1 Brandon Pickersgill; 3 Adam Ryder; 24 Junior Nuu; 4 Junior Sa'u; 5 Billy Walkley; 21 Ben Dean; 7 Jack Miller; 8 Lewis Hatton; 9 Kyle Kesik; 10 Mark Ioane; 11 Ellis Robson; 16 Josh Lynam; 15 Aaron Brown. Subs (all used): 17 Oscar Thomas; 18 Jordan Schofield; 30 Mitch Revell; 23 Matthew Bailey.
Tries: Robson (5, 31), Brown (14), Dean (18, 36), Lynam (22), Walkley (26, 63, 71), Ryder (39, 55), Schofield (45, 51), Bailey (67); **Goals:** Miller 13/14.
Rugby Leaguer & League Express Men of the Match: *Thunder:* Evan Lawther; *Cougars:* Jack Miller.
Penalty count: 7-7; **Half-time:** 0-46;
Referee: Sam Houghton; **Attendance:** 461.

ROUND 7

Saturday 27th April 2024

MIDLANDS HURRICANES 16 OLDHAM 44

HURRICANES: 1 Todd Horner; 22 Ryan Johnson; 4 Ross Oakes; 3 Matt Welham; 5 Jason Bass; 6 Jake Sweeting; 23 Callum McLelland; 8 Jon Luke Kirby; 9 Danny Barcoe; 30 Blake Broadbent; 12 Liam Welham; 11 Tom Wilkinson; 16 Ellis Hobson. Subs (all used): 15 Aaron Willis; 19 Chris Cullimore; 29 Lewis Peachey; - Ryan Brown.
Tries: McLelland (11), Peachey (39), Johnson (49);
Goals: Sweeting 2/3.
Dismissal: M Welham (27) - late challenge on Craven.
OLDHAM: 30 Phoenix Laulu-Togaga'e; 5 Mo Agoro; 11 Joe Wardle; 3 Jordan Turner; 27 Cian Tyrer; 6 Danny Craven; 7 Jamie Ellis; 8 Craig Kopczak; 9 Matty Wildie; 18 Jay Chapelhow; 26 Brad Gallagher; 12 Adam Lawton; 13 Elijah Taylor. Subs (all used): 1 Logan Astley; 16 Owen Farnworth; 20 George Hirst; 22 Ted Chapelhow.
Tries: Agoro (7, 30), Laulu-Togaga'e (24, 54), Hirst (67), Craven (73), C Tyrer (76), Kopczak (79);
Goals: Ellis 4/7, C Tyrer 2/2.
Rugby Leaguer & League Express Men of the Match: *Hurricanes:* Ryan Johnson; *Oldham:* Danny Craven.
Penalty count: 6-8; **Half-time:** 12-14;
Referee: Tara Jones; **Attendance:** 367.

Sunday 28th April 2024

WORKINGTON TOWN 52 CORNWALL 18

TOWN: 1 Jordan Burns; 5 Ethan Bickerdike; 3 Chris Taylor; 4 Jason Mossop; 24 Jonny Hutton; 28 Jarrod Sammut; 7 Carl Forber; 8 Jordan Thomson; 9 Matty Henson; 21 Jake Lightowler; 12 Jake Bradley; 15 Liam McNicholas; 16 Jack Stephenson. Subs (all used): 13 JJ Key; 17 Grant Reid; 20 Ellis Archer; 22 Tyler Walton.
Tries: Henson (18, 35), Sammut (24, 45, 62), Walton (41), Burns (43), Stephenson (59), Hutton (74);
Goals: Forber 8/9.
Sin bin: Lightowler (6) - high tackle on Ashton.
CORNWALL: 6 Cameron Brown; 3 Coby Nichol; 21 Aaron Small; 4 Tom Ashton; 5 Harry Aaronson; 14 Morgan Punchard; 27 Bailey Black; 18 Matt Ross; 9 Luke Collins; 15 Kaine Dimech; 13 David Weetman; 12 Darcy Simpson; 22 Jake Lloyd. Subs (all used): 8 Josh Rhodes; 19 Liam O'Callaghan; 20 Christian Bannister; 25 Nathan Conroy.
Tries: Black (6), Conroy (57), Brown (79); **Goals:** Brown 3/3.
Sin bin: Nichol (16) - professional foul, (63) - late challenge.
Rugby Leaguer & League Express Men of the Match: *Town:* Jarrod Sammut; *Cornwall:* David Weetman.
Penalty count: 6-6; **Half-time:** 18-6;
Referee: Andy Sweet; **Attendance:** 599.

HUNSLET 22 NORTH WALES CRUSADERS 14

HUNSLET: 1 Jimmy Watson; 3 Mackenzie Scurr; 28 Joe Law; 4 Jude Ferreira; 31 Jack Render; 23 Myles Lawford; 7 Matty Beharrell; 8 Harvey Hallas; 15 Ross Whitmore; 13 Michael Knowles; 11 Josh Jordan-Roberts; 12 Aaron Levy; 16 Jordan Syme. Subs (all used): 9 Billy Gaylor; 18 Cam Berry; 20 Isaac Shaw; 26 Ethan O'Hanlon.
Tries: Beharrell (27), Hallas (59), Scurr (74), Render (79);
Goals: Beharrell 3/4.
CRUSADERS: 1 Owain Abel; 16 Jack Holmes; 3 Kieran Taylor; 2 Jake Thewlis; 5 Patrick Ah Van; 26 Reece Bushell; 7 Toby Hughes; 13 Carl Forster; 25 Jake Burns; 10 Chris Barratt; 11 Ryan Ellis; 24 Cole Oakley; 17 Tom Whitehead. Subs (all used): 23 Louis Else; 15 Shaun Costello; 19 Joe Baldwin; 22 Adam Carr.
Tries: Taylor (1), Whitehead (15); **Goals:** Abel 3/3.
Rugby Leaguer & League Express Men of the Match: *Hunslet:* Mackenzie Scurr; *Crusaders:* Owain Abel.
Penalty count: 2-2; **Half-time:** 6-12;
Referee: Nick Bennett; **Attendance:** 396.

ROCHDALE HORNETS 30 KEIGHLEY COUGARS 42

HORNETS: 1 Gregg McNally; 22 Lameck Juma; 3 Myles Harrop; 4 Joe Hartley; 21 Luke Forber; 6 Martyn Ridyard; 7 Lewis Else; 24 Jaden Dayes; 9 Aidan Roden; 10 Luke Nelmes; 11 Ben Forster; 12 Duane Straugheir; 23 Emmerson Whittel. Subs (all used): 30 Jonny Openshaw; 17 Ben Killan; 16 Jordan Andrade; 18 Deane Meadows.
Tries: Forber (15, 23, 56), Openshaw (58), Harrop (68);
Goals: Ridyard 5/5.
COUGARS: 1 Brandon Pickersgill; 3 Adam Ryder; 24 Junior Nuu; 4 Junior Sa'u; 5 Billy Walkley; 21 Ben Dean; 7 Jack Miller; 20 Will Maher; 9 Kyle Kesik; 10 Mark Ioane; 11 Ellis Robson; 30 Mitch Revell; 13 Dan Parker. Subs (all used): 14 Alex Bishop; 17 Oscar Thomas; 8 Lewis Hatton; 18 Jordan Schofield.
Tries: Walkley (6, 40), Sa'u (11, 18, 46), Robson (38), Ryder (80); **Goals:** Miller 7/7.
Rugby Leaguer & League Express Men of the Match: *Hornets:* Lewis Else; *Cougars:* Junior Sa'u.
Penalty count: 3-6; **Half-time:** 12-30;
Referee: Brad Milligan; **Attendance:** 734.

ROUND 8

Sunday 5th May 2024

KEIGHLEY COUGARS 18 HUNSLET 26

COUGARS: 1 Brandon Pickersgill; 3 Adam Ryder; 24 Junior Nuu; 4 Junior Sa'u; 5 Billy Walkley; 14 Alex Bishop; 7 Jack Miller; 20 Will Maher; 9 Kyle Kesik; 10 Mark Ioane; 11 Ellis Robson; 30 Mitch Revell; 15 Aaron Brown. Subs (all used): 8 Lewis Hatton; 13 Dan Parker; 17 Oscar Thomas; 18 Jordan Schofield.
Tries: Robson (26), Walkley (33, 55), Sa'u (36);
Goals: Miller 1/4.
HUNSLET: 1 Jimmy Watson; 3 Mackenzie Scurr; 4 Jude Ferreira; 28 Joe Law; 31 Jack Render; 23 Myles Lawford; 7 Matty Beharrell; 13 Michael Knowles; 15 Ross Whitmore; 8 Harvey Hallas; 11 Josh Jordan-Roberts; 12 Aaron Levy; 16 Jordan Syme. Subs (all used): 9 Billy Gaylor; 18 Cam Berry; 20 Isaac Shaw; 26 Ethan O'Hanlon.
Tries: Ferreira (14, 24, 64, 74), Law (51);
Goals: Beharrell 3/5.
Rugby Leaguer & League Express Men of the Match: *Cougars:* Junior Sa'u; *Hunslet:* Jude Ferreira.
Penalty count: 6-6; **Half-time:** 14-8;
Referee: Nick Bennett; **Attendance:** 1,389.

OLDHAM 74 NEWCASTLE THUNDER 0

OLDHAM: 30 Phoenix Laulu-Togaga'e; 5 Mo Agoro; 23 Jack Johnson; 3 Jordan Turner; 27 Cian Tyrer; 6 Danny Craven; 7 Jamie Ellis; 16 Owen Farnworth; 9 Matty Wildie; 22 Ted Chapelhow; 26 Brad Gallagher; 12 Adam Lawton; 13 Elijah Taylor. Subs (all used): 18 Jay Chapelhow; 20 George Hirst; 8 Craig Kopczak; 1 Logan Astley.
Tries: Craven (2), Laulu-Togaga'e (6, 62), Lawton (11, 33, 57, 80), C Tyrer (22, 42), J Chapelhow (36), Agoro (40), J Turner (47), Astley (74); **Goals:** Ellis 11/13.
THUNDER: 1 Alex Donaghy; 2 Leo Bradley; 3 Tom Siddle; 4 Dan White; 5 AJ Towse; 6 Jack Potter; 7 Olly Bibby; 8 Harry Price; 9 Taylor Pemberton; 10 Harry Lowery; 11 Nathan Rushworth; 12 Jake Anderson; 13 Tyler Hepple. Subs (all used): 14 Owen Reed; 15 Ilikaya Mafi; 16 Will Bate; 17 Aaron Harlow-Stephenson.
Rugby Leaguer & League Express Men of the Match: *Oldham:* Danny Craven; *Thunder:* Taylor Pemberton.
Penalty count: 4-5; **Half-time:** 40-0;
Referee: Adam Williams; **Attendance:** 1,303.

ROCHDALE HORNETS 56 CORNWALL 24

HORNETS: 1 Gregg McNally; 5 Tommy Brierley; 3 Myles Harrop; 19 Connor Ratcliffe; 21 Luke Forber; 6 Martyn Ridyard; 7 Lewis Else; 10 Luke Nelmes; 9 Aiden Roden; 24 Jaden Dayes; 11 Ben Forster; 12 Duane Straugheir; 18 Deane Meadows. Subs (all used): 30 Jonny Openshaw; 16 Jordan Andrade; 17 Ben Killan; 28 Brad Brennan.
Tries: Harrop (12), Forber (32, 52), Straugheir (35), Brierley (38, 61, 64), Brennan (42), Else (45), McNally (56);
Goals: Ridyard 8/10.
Sin bin: Roden (19) - high tackle.
CORNWALL: 6 Cameron Brown; 3 Coby Nichol; 21 Aaron Small; 11 Nathan Cullen; 5 Harry Aaronson; 14 Morgan Punchard; 27 Bailey Black; 15 Kaine Dimech; 9 Luke Collins; 10 Harry Boots; 13 David Weetman; 12 Darcy Simpson; 22 Jake Lloyd. Subs (all used): 24 Nathan Conroy; 20 Courage Mkuhlani; 16 Decarlo Trerise; 8 Josh Rhodes.
Tries: Nichol (20), Conroy (43), Brown (58, 69);
Goals: Brown 4/4.
Dismissal: Punchard (31) - punching.
Rugby Leaguer & League Express Men of the Match: *Hornets:* Martyn Ridyard; *Cornwall:* Cameron Brown.
Penalty count: 8-9; **Half-time:** 20-6;
Referee: Luke Bland; **Attendance:** 891.

WORKINGTON TOWN 16 MIDLANDS HURRICANES 26

TOWN: 1 Jordan Burns; 5 Ethan Bickerdike; 3 Chris Taylor; 4 Jason Mossop; - Zarrin Galea; 6 Ciaran Walker; 28 Jarrod Sammut; 8 Jordan Thomson; 9 Matty Henson; 10 Stevie Scholey; 18 Liam McNicholas; 12 Jake Bradley; 22 Tyler Walton. Subs (all used): 13 JJ Key; - Pone Tongia; - Lasarusa Tabu; 19 Connor Saunders.
Tries: Bickerdike (17), Tongia (34), Sammut (68);
Goals: Walker 2/3.
Dismissal: Walker (74) - punching L Welham.
Sin bin: Scholey (66) - fighting, (80) - fighting.
HURRICANES: 1 Todd Horner; 5 Jason Bass; 3 Matt Welham; 4 Ross Oakes; 22 Ryan Johnson; 6 Jake Sweeting; 23 Callum McLelland; 8 Jon Luke Kirby; 9 Danny Barcoe; 30 Blake Broadbent; 11 Tom Wilkinson; 12 Liam Welham; 16 Ellis Hobson. Subs (all used): 14 Brad Billsborough; 15 Aaron Willis; 29 Lewis Peachey; - Ryan Brown.
Tries: Johnson (8), Sweeting (27), McLelland (55), Wilkinson (58); **Goals:** Sweeting 5/7.
Sin bin: Brown (64) - punching; L Welham (66) - fighting.
Rugby Leaguer & League Express Men of the Match: *Town:* Zarrin Galea; *Hurricanes:* Callum McLelland.
Penalty count: 7-3; **Half-time:** 10-12;
Referee: Aaryn Belafonte; **Attendance:** 678.

ROUND 16

Sunday 12th May 2024

MIDLANDS HURRICANES 22 CORNWALL 24

HURRICANES: 1 Todd Horner; 22 Ryan Johnson; 26 Joe Varo; 4 Ross Oakes; 5 Jason Bass; 6 Jake Sweeting; 23 Callum McLelland; 8 Jon Luke Kirby; 9 Danny Barcoe; 30 Blake Broadbent; 11 Tom Wilkinson; 12 Liam Welham; 16 Ellis Hobson. Subs (all used): 19 Chris Cullimore; 15 Aaron Willis; - Ryan Brown; 29 Lewis Peachey.
Tries: L Welham (19), Sweeting (23), Bass (30), Peachey (62); **Goals:** Sweeting 3/5.
Sin bin: Broadbent (74) - late challenge on Punchard.
CORNWALL: 6 Cameron Brown; 3 Coby Nichol; 21 Aaron Small; 4 Tom Ashton; 5 Harry Aaronson; 14 Morgan Punchard; 27 Bailey Black; 8 Josh Hartshorne; 9 Luke Collins; 19 Josh Rhodes; 11 Nathan Cullen; 12 Darcy Simpson; 13 David Weetman. Subs (all used): 25 Nathan Conroy; 10 AJ Boardman; 16 Decarlo Trerise; 22 Jake Lloyd.
Tries: Ashton (6), Conroy (49), Weetman (76), Brown (78);
Goals: Brown 4/4.
Rugby Leaguer & League Express Men of the Match: *Hurricanes:* Danny Barcoe; *Cornwall:* Jake Lloyd.
Penalty count: 9-8; **Half-time:** 16-6;
Referee: Andy Sweet; **Attendance:** 271.

ROUND 9

Sunday 19th May 2024

CORNWALL 0 OLDHAM 42

CORNWALL: 7 Adam Rusling; 3 Coby Nichol; 21 Aaron Small; 25 Kyle Marvin; 2 George Mitchell; 28 Nathan Conroy; 27 Bailey Black; 8 Josh Rhodes; 9 Luke Collins; 10 Harry Boots; 11 Nathan Cullen; 12 Darcy Simpson; 22 Jake Lloyd. Subs (all used): 19 AJ Boardman; 13 David Weetman; 18 Courage Mkuhlani; 20 Christian Bannister.
Dismissal: Collins (71) - fighting.
Sin bin: Cullen (71) - fighting.
OLDHAM: 30 Phoenix Laulu-Togaga'e; 5 Mo Agoro; 23 Jack Johnson; 3 Jordan Turner; 27 Cian Tyrer; 6 Danny Craven; 1 Logan Astley; 16 Owen Farnworth; 9 Matty Wildie; 18 Jay Chapelhow; 26 Brad Gallagher; 12 Adam Lawton; 13 Elijah Taylor. Subs (all used): 25 Bailey Aldridge; 22 Ted Chapelhow; 20 George Hirst; 15 Josh Johnson.
Tries: C Tyrer (22, 79), Gallagher (27), Agoro (37, 56), Astley (52), J Turner (59), Lawton (62, 65);
Goals: C Tyrer 0/2, Craven 0/1, Astley 3/6.
Sin bin: Agoro (71) - fighting.
Rugby Leaguer & League Express Men of the Match: *Cornwall:* Harry Boots; *Oldham:* Adam Lawton.
Penalty count: 4-2; **Half-time:** 0-12;
Referee: Denton Arnold.

MIDLANDS HURRICANES 66
NEWCASTLE THUNDER 4

HURRICANES: 6 Jake Sweeting; - Ryan Millar; 5 Jason Bass; 1 Todd Horner; 26 Joe Varo; 7 Dave Hewitt; 23 Callum McLelland; 8 Jon Luke Kirby; 9 Danny Barcoe; 29 Lewis Peachey; 11 Tom Wilkinson; 12 Liam Welham; 16 Ellis Hobson. Subs (all used): 19 Chris Cullimore; 24 Marcus Green; 15 Aaron Willis; 17 Kieran Moran.
Tries: L Welham (15, 43, 46, 56), Horner (19, 39), McLelland (36), Peachey (53, 65), Bass (72, 76), Barcoe (80); **Goals:** Sweeting 1/2, Hewitt 8/10.
THUNDER: 1 Alex Donaghy; 2 Leo Bradley; 3 Sean Croston; 4 Evan Lawther; 5 George Birch; 6 Olly Bibby; 7 Tom Siddle; 8 Harry Price; 9 Tyler Hepple; 10 Harry Lowery; 11 Paddy Burns; 12 Jake Anderson; 13 Nathan Newbound. Subs (all used): 14 Will Lintin; 15 Tobias Gibson; 16 Nathan Rushworth; 17 Will Bate.
Try: Burns (69); **Goals:** Hepple 0/1.
Rugby Leaguer & League Express Men of the Match: *Hurricanes:* Liam Welham; *Thunder:* Paddy Burns.
Penalty count: 6-3; **Half-time:** 22-0;
Referee: Brad Milligan; **Attendance:** 302.

NORTH WALES CRUSADERS 10
KEIGHLEY COUGARS 30

CRUSADERS: 25 Ben Lane; 16 Jack Holmes; 2 Dayon Sambou; 4 Matt Reid; 5 Patrick Ah Van; 6 Dan Coates;

7 Toby Hughes; 13 Carl Forster; 14 Paul Nash; 10 Chris Barratt; 3 Kieran Taylor; 24 Cole Oakley; 23 Louis Else. Subs (all used): 8 Ben Evans; 11 Ryan Ellis; 15 Shaun Costello; 19 Joe Baldwin.
Tries: Reid (6), Taylor (45); **Goals:** Coates 1/2.
COUGARS: 1 Brandon Pickersgill; 2 Charlie Graham; 3 Adam Ryder; 11 Ellis Robson; 5 Billy Walkley; 17 Oscar Thomas; 7 Jack Miller; 20 Will Maher; 9 Kyle Kesik; 10 Mark Ioane; 16 Josh Lynam; 12 Lachlan Lanskey; 15 Aaron Brown. Subs (all used): 31 George Flanagan; 8 Lewis Hatton; 18 Jordan Schofield; 30 Mitch Revell.
Tries: Pickersgill (21), Walkley (30, 62), Thomas (55), Flanagan (74); **Goals:** Miller 5/5.
Rugby Leaguer & League Express Men of the Match:
Crusaders: Chris Barratt; *Cougars:* George Flanagan.
Penalty count: 5-8; **Half-time:** 4-12;
Referee: Nick Bennett; **Attendance:** 462.

ROCHDALE HORNETS 56 WORKINGTON TOWN 12

HORNETS: 1 Gregg McNally; 31 Ollie Brookes; 22 Lameck Juma; 32 Jack Darbyshire; 21 Luke Forber; 6 Martyn Ridyard; 7 Lewis Else; 24 Jaden Dayes; 9 Aiden Roden; 10 Luke Nelmes; 11 Ben Forster; 12 Duane Straugheir; 18 Deane Meadows. Subs (all used): 30 Jonny Openshaw; 16 Jordan Andrade; 13 Jordan Baldwinson; 20 Toby Brannan.
Tries: Darbyshire (2, 6), Nelmes (24, 28), Straugheir (33, 35), Brookes (44), McNally (59), Forster (66), Else (72); **Goals:** Ridyard 8/11.
TOWN: 1 Kieran Tyrer; 5 Ethan Bickerdike; 3 Chris Taylor; 4 Jason Mossop; 27 Zarrin Galea; 28 Jarrod Sammut; 7 Carl Forber; 10 Stevie Scholey; 19 Connor Saunders; 8 Jordan Thomson; 12 Jake Bradley; 18 Liam McNicholas; 16 Jack Stephenson. Subs (all used): 13 JJ Key; 17 Grant Reid; 30 Lasarusa Tabu; 29 Pone Tongia.
Tries: Bradley (17), Galea (63); **Goals:** Forber 2/2.
Sin bin: Tongia (41) - dangerous contact.
Rugby Leaguer & League Express Men of the Match:
Hornets: Luke Nelmes; *Town:* Carl Forber.
Penalty count: 7-5; **Half-time:** 34-6;
Referee: Andy Sweet; **Attendance:** 797.

ROUND 10

Sunday 26th May 2024

HUNSLET 42 CORNWALL 16

HUNSLET: 1 Jimmy Watson; 3 Mackenzie Scurr; 32 Will Adams; 4 Jude Ferreira; 31 Jack Render; 6 Luke Punton; 7 Matty Beharrell; 8 Harvey Hallas; 15 Ross Whitmore; 13 Michael Knowles; 11 Josh Jordan-Roberts; 12 Aaron Levy; 16 Jordan Syme. Subs (all used): 18 Cam Berry; 20 Matt Fletcher; 26 Ethan O'Hanlon; 30 Jack Coventry.
Tries: O'Hanlon (40, 60), Jordan-Roberts (51), Ferreira (63), Adams (73, 78), Render (80); **Goals:** Beharrell 7/7.
CORNWALL: 6 Cameron Brown; 3 Coby Nichol; 21 Aaron Small; 19 AJ Boardman; 5 Harry Aaronson; 27 Bailey Black; 7 Adam Rusling; 8 Josh Rhodes; 9 Luke Collins; 10 Harry Boots; 11 Nathan Cullen; 12 Darcy Simpson; 13 David Weetman. Subs (all used): 24 Nathan Conroy; 22 Jake Lloyd; 18 Matt Ross; 25 Sam Campbell.
Tries: Nichol (16), Conroy (48), Black (66);
Goals: Brown 2/3.
Sin bin: Brown (69) - high tackle on Watson.
Rugby Leaguer & League Express Men of the Match:
Hunslet: Josh Jordan-Roberts; *Cornwall:* Adam Rusling.
Penalty count: 12-5; **Half-time:** 6-4;
Referee: Tara Jones; **Attendance:** 296.

MIDLANDS HURRICANES 18
NORTH WALES CRUSADERS 10

HURRICANES: 22 Ryan Johnson; - Matty Chrimes; 3 Matt Welham; 12 Liam Welham; 5 Jason Bass; 23 Callum McLelland; 7 Dave Hewitt; 8 Jon Luke Kirby; 19 Chris Cullimore; 29 Lewis Peachey; 11 Tom Wilkinson; 15 Aaron Willis; 16 Ellis Hobson. Subs (all used): 9 Danny Barcoe; 24 Marcus Green; 20 Owen Maull; 17 Kieran Moran.
Tries: Hewitt (26), Chrimes (47), Johnson (55);
Goals: Hewitt 3/4.
CRUSADERS: 25 Ben Lane; 2 Dayon Sambou; 3 Kieran Taylor; 4 Matt Reid; 5 Patrick Ah Van; 6 Dan Coates; 7 Toby Hughes; 13 Carl Forster; 14 Paul Nash; 10 Chris Barratt; 11 Ryan Ellis; 24 Cole Oakley; 15 Shaun Costello. Subs (all used): 12 Matt Unsworth; 23 Louis Else; 19 Joe Baldwin; 8 Ben Evans.
Tries: Ah Van (18), Reid (36); **Goals:** Coates 0/1, Lane 1/2.
Rugby Leaguer & League Express Men of the Match:
Hurricanes: Dave Hewitt; *Crusaders:* Ryan Ellis.
Penalty count: 7-7; **Half-time:** 6-10;
Referee: Adam Williams; **Attendance:** 527.

KEIGHLEY COUGARS 28 OLDHAM 18

COUGARS: 1 Brandon Pickersgill; 2 Charlie Graham; 4 Junior Sa'u; 11 Ellis Robson; 5 Billy Walkley; 32 Izaac Farrell; 7 Jack Miller; 20 Will Maher; 9 Kyle Kesik; 10 Mark Ioane; 13 Dan Parker; 12 Lachlan Lanskey; 15 Aaron Brown. Subs (all used): 31 George Flanagan; 18 Jordan Schofield; 8 Lewis Hatton; 30 Mitch Revell.
Tries: Farrell (7), Graham (28), Flanagan (33), Sa'u (57, 65);
Goals: Miller 4/5.
OLDHAM: 30 Phoenix Laulu-Togaga'e; 21 Mackenzie Turner; 23 Jack Johnson; 3 Jordan Turner; 27 Cian Tyrer; 6 Danny Craven; 7 Jamie Ellis; 16 Owen Farnworth; 9 Matty Wildie; 18 Jay Chapelhow; 26 Brad Gallagher; 12 Adam Lawton; 13 Elijah Taylor. Subs (all used): 22 Ted Chapelhow; 8 Craig Kopczak; 20 George Hirst; 15 Josh Johnson.
Tries: J Turner (51), Laulu-Togaga'e (75), C Tyrer (79);
Goals: Ellis 3/3.
Rugby Leaguer & League Express Men of the Match:
Cougars: Jack Miller; *Oldham:* Adam Lawton.
Penalty count: 7-4; **Half-time:** 18-0;
Referee: Nick Bennett; **Attendance:** 1,852.

NEWCASTLE THUNDER 18 ROCHDALE HORNETS 24

THUNDER: 1 Alex Donaghy; 5 George Birch; 21 Evan Lawther; 4 Oli Field; 3 Sean Croston; 7 Mackenzie Harman; 6 Olly Bibby; 10 Harry Lowery; 25 Will Lintin; 8 Harry Price; 12 Lennon Bursell; 11 Paddy Burns; 13 Nathan Newbound. Subs (all used): 17 Will Bate; 9 Tyler Hepple; 15 Tobias Gibson; 18 Nathan Rushworth.
Tries: Burns (40), Lawther (58), Lowery (63);
Goals: Hepple 3/3.
HORNETS: 1 Gregg McNally; 31 Ollie Brookes; 4 Joe Hartley; 32 Jack Darbyshire; 21 Luke Forber; 6 Martyn Ridyard; 7 Lewis Else; 24 Jaden Dayes; 9 Aiden Roden; 10 Luke Nelmes; 18 Deane Meadows; 19 Connor Ratcliffe; 23 Emmerson Whittel. Subs (all used): 30 Jonny Openshaw; 20 Toby Brannan; 16 Jordan Andrade; 17 Ben Killan.
Tries: Roden (4), Forber (11, 18), Ridyard (51);
Goals: Ridyard 4/5.
Rugby Leaguer & League Express Men of the Match:
Thunder: Evan Lawther; *Hornets:* Luke Forber.
Penalty count: 3-3; **Half-time:** 6-16;
Referee: Denton Arnold; **Attendance:** 326
(at Gateshead International Stadium).

ROUND 11

Saturday 1st June 2024

NORTH WALES CRUSADERS 24 OLDHAM 25

CRUSADERS: 25 Ben Lane; 16 Jack Holmes; 3 Kieran Taylor; 24 Cole Oakley; 5 Patrick Ah Van; 6 Dan Coates; 7 Toby Hughes; 8 Ben Evans; 2 Jake Burns; 10 Chris Barratt; 12 Matt Unsworth; 17 Olly Davies; 23 Louis Else. Subs (all used): 9 Pat Rainford; 11 Ryan Ellis; 15 Shaun Costello; 22 Adam Carr.
Tries: B Evans (10), Ah Van (15), Taylor (41), Davies (51);
Goals: Lane 4/4.
OLDHAM: 30 Phoenix Laulu-Togaga'e; 23 Jack Johnson; 4 Kian Morgan; 24 Ben O'Keefe; 27 Cian Tyrer; 6 Danny Craven; 1 Logan Astley; 16 Owen Farnworth; 9 Matty Wildie; 18 Jay Chapelhow; 26 Brad Gallagher; 13 Elijah Taylor; 20 George Hirst. Subs (all used): 8 Craig Kopczak; 14 Jordan Paga; 15 Josh Johnson; 25 Bailey Aldridge.
Tries: Jack Johnson (28), Laulu-Togaga'e (39), Astley (64), Aldridge (72), Craven (77);
Goals: Craven 2/5; **Field goal:** Craven (80).
Sin bin: Kopczak (44) - high tackle.
Rugby Leaguer & League Express Men of the Match:
Crusaders: Dan Coates; *Oldham:* Danny Craven.
Penalty count: 5-10; **Half-time:** 12-8;
Referee: Andy Sweet; **Attendance:** 756.

Sunday 2nd June 2024

CORNWALL 30 NEWCASTLE THUNDER 6

CORNWALL: 6 Cameron Brown; 3 Coby Nichol; 21 Aaron Small; 4 Tom Ashton; 5 Harry Aaronson; 27 Bailey Black; 7 Adam Rusling; 18 Matt Ross; 9 Luke Collins; 10 Harry Boots; 11 Nathan Cullen; 12 Darcy Simpson; 13 David Weetman. Subs (all used): 8 Josh Rhodes; 19 AJ Boardman; 24 Nathan Conroy; 25 Sam Campbell.
Tries: Weetman (25), Black (41), Brown (53, 60), Boots (69); **Goals:** Brown 5/5.
THUNDER: 1 Alex Donaghy; 2 Sean Croston; 3 Jake Anderson; 4 Evan Lawther; 5 George Birch; 6 Mackenzie Harman; 7 Olly Bibby; 8 Harry Price; 9 Will Lintin; 10 Harry Lowery; 11 Paddy Burns; 12 Lennon Bursell; 13 Nathan Newbound. Subs (all used): 14 Will Bate; 15 Nathan Rushworth; 16 Tobias Gibson; 17 Tyler Hepple.
Try: Lawther (10); **Goals:** Harman 1/1.
Rugby Leaguer & League Express Men of the Match:
Cornwall: Nathan Conroy; *Thunder:* Harry Lowery.
Penalty count: 4-5; **Half-time:** 6-6;
Referee: Alan Millington.

MIDLANDS HURRICANES 18 KEIGHLEY COUGARS 25

HURRICANES: 1 Todd Horner; 22 Ryan Johnson; 3 Matt Welham; 12 Liam Welham; - Matty Chrimes; 23 Callum McLelland; 7 Dave Hewitt; 8 Jon Luke Kirby; 9 Danny Barcoe; 30 Blake Broadbent; 11 Tom Wilkinson; 15 Aaron Willis; 16 Ellis Hobson. Subs (all used): 19 Chris Cullimore; 24 Marcus Green; 17 Kieran Moran; 10 Sam Bowring.
Tries: Chrimes (3, 48), L Welham (70); **Goals:** Hewitt 3/3.
Sin bin: Kirby (18) - late challenge on Farrell.
COUGARS: 17 Oscar Thomas; 27 Max Lambourne; 11 Ellis Robson; 4 Junior Sa'u; 5 Billy Walkley; 32 Izaac Farrell; 7 Jack Miller; 20 Will Maher; 9 Kyle Kesik; 10 Mark Ioane; 13 Dan Parker; 12 Lachlan Lanskey; 15 Aaron Brown. Subs (all used): 31 George Flanagan; 8 Lewis Hatton; 18 Jordan Schofield; 30 Mitch Revell.
Tries: Hatton (20), Lambourne (28), Farrell (52), Walkley (62); **Goals:** Miller 4/4; **Field goal:** Miller (40).
Rugby Leaguer & League Express Men of the Match:
Hurricanes: Marcus Green; *Cougars:* Jack Miller.
Penalty count: 7-7; **Half-time:** 6-13;
Referee: Kevin Moore; **Attendance:** 463.

WORKINGTON TOWN 22 HUNSLET 24

TOWN: 1 Jordan Burns; 5 Ethan Bickerdike; 3 Chris Taylor; 4 Jason Mossop; 27 Zarrin Galea; 20 Ellis Archer; 7 Carl Forber; 13 JJ Key; 9 Matty Henson; 10 Stevie Scholey; 12 Jake Bradley; 18 Liam McNicholas; 16 Jack Stephenson. Subs (all used): 31 Pone Tongia; 30 Lasarusa Tabu; 22 Tyler Walton; 8 Jordan Thomson.
Tries: Bickerdike (5), Bradley (39), Forber (49), Mossop (61);
Goals: Forber 3/4.
Sin bin: Bradley (19) - dangerous challenge; Burns (39) - fighting.
HUNSLET: 1 Jimmy Watson; 5 Alfie Goddard; 23 Joe Law; 4 Jude Ferreira; 31 Jack Render; 13 Michael Knowles; 7 Matty Beharrell; 8 Harvey Hallas; 15 Ross Whitmore; 20 Matt Fletcher; 11 Josh Jordan-Roberts; - Keenen Tomlinson; 16 Jordan Syme. Subs (all used): 18 Cam Berry; 26 Ethan O'Hanlon; 28 Ethan Wood; 30 Jack Coventry.
Tries: Jordan-Roberts (13), Fletcher (20), Ferreira (25), Watson (30); **Goals:** Beharrell 4/4.
Sin bin: Fletcher (39) - fighting.
Rugby Leaguer & League Express Men of the Match:
Town: JJ Key; *Hunslet:* Matty Beharrell.
Penalty count: 1-4; **Half-time:** 10-24;
Referee: Nick Bennett; **Attendance:** 1,486.

ROUND 12

Sunday 16th June 2024

NORTH WALES CRUSADERS 34
WORKINGTON TOWN 32

CRUSADERS: 25 Ben Lane; 16 Jack Holmes; 3 Kieran Taylor; 4 Matt Reid; 5 Patrick Ah Van; 6 Dan Coates; 7 Toby Hughes; 8 Ben Evans; 9 Pat Rainford; 10 Chris Barratt; 24 Cole Oakley; 17 Olly Davies; 23 Louis Else. Subs (all used): 15 Shaun Costello; 19 Joe Baldwin; 22 Adam Carr; 11 Liam Cooper.
Tries: Holmes (18), Costello (38), Taylor (40), Cooper (42), B Evans (77), Barratt (79); **Goals:** Lane 5/7.
Sin bin: Oakley (29) - high tackle on Scholey.
TOWN: 1 Jordan Burns; 5 Ethan Bickerdike; 20 Ellis Archer; 27 Zarrin Galea; 25 Tommy Brierley; 6 Ciaran Walker; 7 Carl Forber; 13 JJ Key; 14 Blain Marwood; 8 Jordan Thomson; 16 Jack Stephenson; 29 Pone Tongia; 9 Matty Henson. Subs (all used): 10 Stevie Scholey; 17 Grant Reid; 22 Tyler Walton; 26 Luke Charlton.
Tries: Brierley (13), Key (27), Walton (45), Archer (57), Burns (71); **Goals:** Walker 6/7.
Rugby Leaguer & League Express Men of the Match:
Crusaders: Chris Barratt; *Town:* Ciaran Walker.
Penalty count: 6-7; **Half-time:** 14-14;
Referee: Denton Arnold; **Attendance:** 459.

CORNWALL 14 ROCHDALE HORNETS 38

CORNWALL: 6 Cameron Brown; 3 Coby Nichol; 21 Aaron Small; 2 George Mitchell; 5 Harry Aaronson; 27 Bailey Black; 7 Adam Rusling; 18 Matt Ross; 9 Luke Collins; 10 Harry Boots; 11 Nathan Cullen; 12 Darcy Simpson; 13 David Weetman. Subs (all used): 8 Josh Rhodes; 15 Kaine Dimech; 24 Nathan Conroy; 25 Sam Campbell.
Tries: Nichol (6), Brown (37, 49); **Goals:** Brown 1/3.
Dismissal: Small (79) - use of the head.
Sin bin: Nichol (22) - use of the elbow.
HORNETS: 1 Gregg McNally; 2 Dan Nixon; 18 Deane Meadows; 32 Jack Darbyshire; 21 Luke Forber; 6 Martyn Ridyard; 7 Lewis Else; 17 Ben Killan; 9 Aidan Roden; 10 Luke Nelmes; 11 Ben Forster; 12 Duane Straugheir; 23 Emerson Whittel. Subs (all used): 30 Jonny Openshaw; 20 Dean Roberts; 16 Jordan Andrade; 8 Daniel Spencer-Tonks.

Tries: Nixon (18, 42), Roden (22), Spencer-Tonks (27), Forber (39, 68, 72); **Goals:** Ridyard 5/8.
Sin bin: Nelmes (11) - use of the head.
Rugby Leaguer & League Express Men of the Match: *Cornwall:* Bailey Black; *Hornets:* Luke Forber.
Penalty count: 3-7; **Half-time:** 10-20;
Referee: Carl Hughes.

HUNSLET 25 MIDLANDS HURRICANES 18

HUNSLET: 1 Jimmy Watson; 2 Mackenzie Scurr; 28 Joe Law; 4 Jude Ferreira; 31 Jack Render; 23 George Flanagan; 7 Matty Beharrell; 8 Harvey Hallas; 15 Ross Whitmore; 32 Matt Fletcher; 11 Josh Jordan-Roberts; 13 Michael Knowles; 16 Jordan Syme. Subs (all used): 18 Cam Berry; 20 Isaac Shaw; 26 Ethan O'Hanlon; 30 Jack Coventry.
Tries: Berry (34), Render (40), Watson (51), Flanagan (68); **Goals:** Beharrell 4/4; **Field goal:** Beharrell (69).
Sin bin: Watson (23) - late challenge on Horner.
HURRICANES: 1 Todd Horner; 5 Jason Bass; 3 Matt Welham; 4 Ross Oakes; 22 Davey Dixon; 23 Callum McLelland; 7 Dave Hewitt; 8 Jon Luke Kirby; 9 Danny Barcoe; 29 Lewis Peachey; 11 Tom Wilkinson; 12 Liam Welham; 16 Ellis Hobson. Subs (all used): 13 Brad Clavering; 19 Chris Cullimore; 24 Marcus Green; 30 Blake Broadbent.
Tries: L Welham (28, 30), M Welham (76);
Goals: Hewitt 3/4.
Rugby Leaguer & League Express Men of the Match: *Hunslet:* Matty Beharrell; *Hurricanes:* Marcus Green.
Penalty count: 3-6; **Half-time:** 12-10;
Referee: Brad Milligan; **Attendance:** 504.

NEWCASTLE THUNDER 6 OLDHAM 60

THUNDER: 1 Luke Jeremy; 5 George Birch; 4 Evan Lawther; 3 Tom Siddle; 2 Sean Croston; 6 Olly Bibby; 7 Mackenzie Harman; 8 Jamie Field; 9 Will Lintin; 10 Harry Price; 11 Lennon Bursell; 12 Jake Anderson; 13 Harry Lowery. Subs (all used): 14 Joel Russell; 15 Tyler Hepple; 16 Nathan Newbound; 17 Nathan Rushworth.
Try: Price (73); **Goals:** Harman 1/1.
OLDHAM: 30 Phoenix Laulu-Togaga'e; 21 Mackenzie Turner; 34 Nathan Roebuck; 23 Jack Johnson; 27 Cian Tyrer; 6 Danny Craven; 1 Logan Astley; 16 Owen Farnworth; 9 Matty Wildie; 18 Jay Chapelhow; 20 George Hirst; 13 Elijah Taylor; 10 Pat Moran. Subs (all used): 25 Bailey Aldridge; 22 Ted Chapelhow; 15 Josh Johnson; 8 Craig Kopczak.
Tries: Moran (4, 13, 25), J Chapelhow (17), Craven (29, 45), Roebuck (40), C Tyrer (43, 80), M Turner (53), Kopczak (56);
Goals: Astley 8/10, Craven 0/1.
Rugby Leaguer & League Express Men of the Match: *Thunder:* Mackenzie Harman; *Oldham:* Logan Astley.
Penalty count: 6-9; **Half-time:** 0-36;
Referee: Andy Sweet.
(at Gateshead International Stadium).

ROUND 13

Sunday 23rd June 2024

CORNWALL 0 KEIGHLEY COUGARS 26

CORNWALL: 6 Cameron Brown; 3 Coby Nichol; 21 Aaron Small; 2 George Mitchell; 5 Harry Aaronson; 24 Nathan Conroy; 27 Bailey Black; 18 Matt Ross; 9 Luke Collins; 10 Harry Boots; 11 Nathan Cullen; 12 Darcy Simpson; 13 David Weetman. Subs (all used): 8 Josh Rhodes; 25 Sam Campbell; 22 Jake Lloyd; 15 Kaine Dimech.
Sin bin: Brown (48) - delaying restart; Small (74) - fighting.
COUGARS: 17 Oscar Thomas; 34 Ben Blackmore; 3 Adam Ryder; 4 Junior Sa'u; 5 Billy Walkley; 14 Alex Bishop; 7 Jack Miller; 20 Will Maher; 9 Kyle Kesik; 30 Mitch Revell; 11 Ellis Robson; 12 Lachlan Lanskey; 13 Dan Parker. Subs (all used): 21 Ben Dean; 31 George Flanagan; 8 Lewis Hatton; 10 Mark Ioane.
Tries: Ryder (1, 18), Blackmore (8), Sa'u (26), Robson (50, 68); **Goals:** Miller 1/5, Thomas 0/1.
Sin bin: Bishop (74) - fighting.
Rugby Leaguer & League Express Men of the Match: *Cornwall:* Bailey Black; *Cougars:* Adam Ryder.
Penalty count: 5-10; **Half-time:** 0-18;
Referee: Adam Williams.

HUNSLET 18 ROCHDALE HORNETS 48

HUNSLET: 1 Jimmy Watson; 2 Mackenzie Scurr; 28 Joe Law; 4 Jude Ferreira; 31 Jack Render; 6 George Flanagan; 7 Matty Beharrell; 8 Harvey Hallas; 15 Ross Whitmore; 32 Matt Fletcher; 11 Josh Jordan-Roberts; 13 Michael Knowles; 16 Jordan Syme. Subs (all used): 18 Cam Berry; 20 Isaac Shaw; 26 Ethan O'Hanlon; 30 Jack Coventry.
Tries: Flanagan (16), Beharrell (30), Knowles (47);
Goals: Beharrell 3/3.
Dismissal: Fletcher (69) - fighting.
Sin bin: Watson (52) - holding down.
HORNETS: 1 Gregg McNally; 2 Dan Nixon; 32 Jack Darbyshire; 3 Myles Harrop; 21 Luke Forber; 6 Martyn Ridyard; 7 Lewis Else; 20 Dean Roberts; 9 Aiden Roden; 10 Luke Nelmes; 11 Ben Forster; 12 Duane Straugheir; 23 Emmerson Whittel. Subs (all used): 30 Jonny Openshaw; 16 Jordan Andrade; 8 Daniel Spencer-Tonks; 18 Deane Meadows.
Tries: Nixon (12), Straugheir (22), McNally (29, 75), Else (37), Andrade (54, 61), Openshaw (55);
Goals: Ridyard 8/8.
Dismissal: Nelmes (69) - fighting.
Rugby Leaguer & League Express Men of the Match: *Hunslet:* Matty Beharrell; *Hornets:* Lewis Else.
Penalty count: 5-7; **Half-time:** 12-24;
Referee: Warren Turley; **Attendance:** 402.

NEWCASTLE THUNDER 4 NORTH WALES CRUSADERS 42

THUNDER: 1 Alex Donaghy; 2 Sean Croston; 3 Jake Anderson; 4 Evan Lawther; 5 Luke Jeremy; 6 Taylor Pemberton; 7 Mackenzie Harman; 8 Harry Price; 9 Joel Russell; 10 Jamie Field; 11 Paddy Burns; 12 Lennon Bursell; 13 Nathan Rushworth. Subs (all used): 14 Will Bate; 15 Tobias Gibson; 16 Jason Payne; 17 Tyler Hepple.
Try: Croston (79); **Goals:** Harman 0/1.
CRUSADERS: 25 Ben Lane; 16 Jack Holmes; 3 Kieran Taylor; 4 Matt Reid; 18 Rob Massam; 6 Dan Coates; 26 Reece Bushell; 8 Ben Evans; 9 Pat Rainford; 10 Chris Barratt; 24 Cole Oakley; 17 Olly Davies; 23 Louis Else. Subs (all used): 15 Shaun Costello; 19 Joe Baldwin; 22 Adam Carr; 11 Liam Cooper.
Tries: Lane (6, 77), B Evans (10), Massam (18, 68, 73), Taylor (31), Costello (50); **Goals:** Lane 5/8.
Rugby Leaguer & League Express Men of the Match: *Thunder:* Sean Croston; *Crusaders:* Rob Massam.
Penalty count: 7-8; **Half-time:** 0-20;
Referee: Brad Milligan. *(at Crow Trees, Blaydon).*

WORKINGTON TOWN 4 OLDHAM 28

TOWN: 27 Zarrin Galea; - Richard Lepori; 3 Chris Taylor; 5 Ethan Bickerdike; - Tommy Brierley; 6 Ciaran Walker; 7 Carl Forber; 13 JJ Key; 19 Connor Saunders; 10 Stevie Scholey; 16 Jack Stephenson; 12 Jake Bradley; 9 Matty Henson. Subs (all used): - Brad Brennan; 17 Grant Reid; 31 Pone Tongia; 22 Tyler Walton.
Try: Lepori (77); **Goals:** Walker 0/1.
OLDHAM: 30 Phoenix Laulu-Togaga'e; 23 Jack Johnson; 34 Nathan Roebuck; 24 Ben O'Keefe; 27 Cian Tyrer; 6 Danny Craven; 1 Logan Astley; 16 Owen Farnworth; 9 Matty Wildie; 18 Jay Chapelhow; 20 George Hirst; 13 Elijah Taylor; 10 Pat Moran. Subs (all used): 25 Bailey Aldridge; 11 Joe Wardle; 22 Ted Chapelhow; 8 Craig Kopczak.
Tries: O'Keefe (18, 70), Craven (36), Roebuck (55), Astley (63), C Tyrer (65); **Goals:** Astley 0/2, C Tyrer 2/4.
Rugby Leaguer & League Express Men of the Match: *Town:* Richard Lepori; *Oldham:* Danny Craven.
Penalty count: 3-4; **Half-time:** 0-8;
Referee: Nick Bennett; **Attendance:** 706.

ROUND 14

Sunday 30th June 2024

CORNWALL 10 NORTH WALES CRUSADERS 16

CORNWALL: 6 Cameron Brown; 23 Callum Abbott; 3 Coby Nichol; 4 Tom Ashton; 5 Harry Aaronson; 14 Morgan Punchard; 27 Bailey Black; 18 Matt Ross; 9 Luke Collins; 15 Kaine Dimech; 11 Nathan Cullen; 12 Darcy Simpson; 13 David Weetman. Subs (all used): 16 Decarlo Trerise; 22 Jake Lloyd; 28 Nathan Conroy; 30 Tomo Clark.
Tries: Brown (6), Trerise (21); **Goals:** Brown 1/2.
Sin bin: Cullen (35) - dangerous challenge.
CRUSADERS: 16 Jack Holmes; 2 Jorge Cabral; 3 Kieran Taylor; 24 Cole Oakley; 5 Patrick Ah Van; 6 Dan Coates; 7 Toby Hughes; 8 Ben Evans; 9 Pat Rainford; 10 Chris Barratt; 17 Olly Davies; 12 Matt Unsworth; 18 Liam Bent. Subs (all used): 13 Carl Forster; 15 Shaun Costello; 19 Joe Baldwin; 23 Louis Else.
Tries: Davies (39), Ah Van (45), Barratt (54);
Goals: Coates 0/1, Ah Van 2/3.
Rugby Leaguer & League Express Men of the Match: *Cornwall:* Bailey Black; *Crusaders:* Carl Forster.
Penalty count: 4-7; **Half-time:** 10-4;
Referee: Alan Billington.

NEWCASTLE THUNDER 10 MIDLANDS HURRICANES 44

THUNDER: 1 Alex Donaghy; 2 Luke Jeremy; 3 Evan Lawther; 4 Jake Anderson; 5 Sean Croston; 6 Tom Siddle; 7 Mackenzie Harman; 8 Harry Price; 9 Joel Russell; 10 Josh Stoker; 11 Lennon Bursell; 12 Paddy Burns; 13 Nathan Rushworth. Subs (all used): 14 Jack Skelton; 15 Robin Hugues; 16 Jason Payne; 17 Tyler Hepple.
Tries: Lawther (8), Donaghy (22); **Goals:** Harman 1/2.
HURRICANES: 1 Todd Horner; - Ryan Johnson; 3 Matt Welham; 12 Liam Welham; 22 Davey Dixon; 23 Callum McLelland; 7 Dave Hewitt; 8 Jon Luke Kirby; 9 Danny Barcoe; 30 Blake Broadbent; 11 Tom Wilkinson; 16 Ellis Hobson; 13 Brad Clavering. Subs (all used): 17 Kieran Moran; 18 Elliot Windley; 24 Marcus Green; 29 Lewis Peachey.
Tries: M Welham (1, 39), Wilkinson (4, 46), Horner (15), Dixon (31), Peachey (66), Windley (77); **Goals:** Hewitt 6/8.
Rugby Leaguer & League Express Men of the Match: *Thunder:* Alex Donaghy; *Hurricanes:* Tom Wilkinson.
Penalty count: 5-8; **Half-time:** 10-26;
Referee: Nick Bennett.
(at Gateshead International Stadium).

OLDHAM 30 HUNSLET 6

OLDHAM: 30 Phoenix Laulu-Togaga'e; 23 Jack Johnson; 34 Nathan Roebuck; 24 Ben O'Keefe; 27 Cian Tyrer; 6 Danny Craven; 1 Logan Astley; 16 Owen Farnworth; 9 Matty Wildie; 18 Jay Chapelhow; 20 George Hirst; 13 Elijah Taylor; 10 Pat Moran. Subs (all used): 22 Ted Chapelhow; 15 Josh Johnson; 8 Craig Kopczak; 25 Bailey Aldridge.
Tries: Laulu-Togaga'e (3), C Tyrer (7, 58, 75), Aldridge (53), Astley (64); **Goals:** C Tyrer 3/6.
Sin bin: Craven (49) - dissent.
HUNSLET: 1 Jimmy Watson; 5 Alfie Goddard; 28 Joe Law; 4 Jude Ferreira; 2 Mackenzie Scurr; 23 George Flanagan; 7 Matty Beharrell; 8 Harvey Hallas; 15 Ross Whitmore; 32 Matt Fletcher; 11 Josh Jordan-Roberts; 12 Aaron Levy; 13 Michael Knowles. Subs (all used): 16 Jordan Syme; 18 Cam Berry; 26 Ethan O'Hanlon; 30 Jack Coventry.
Try: Law (49); **Goals:** Flanagan 1/1.
Rugby Leaguer & League Express Men of the Match: *Oldham:* Logan Astley; *Hunslet:* Michael Knowles.
Penalty count: 4-6; **Half-time:** 10-0;
Referee: Brad Milligan; **Attendance:** 1,126.

WORKINGTON TOWN 18 KEIGHLEY COUGARS 37

TOWN: 1 Jordan Burns; 25 Tommy Brierley; 3 Chris Taylor; 27 Zarrin Galea; - Joe Hartley; 7 Carl Forber; 6 Ciaran Walker; 13 JJ Key; 19 Connor Saunders; 10 Stevie Scholey; 12 Jake Bradley; 31 Pone Tongia; 9 Matty Henson. Subs (all used): 30 Brad Brennan; 17 Grant Reid; 22 Tyler Walton; 11 Mike Ogunwole.
Tries: Walton (50), Brierley (68), Forber (76);
Goals: Forber 3/3.
COUGARS: 17 Oscar Thomas; 34 Ben Blackmore; 3 Adam Ryder; 4 Junior Sa'u; 5 Billy Walkley; 14 Alex Bishop; 7 Jack Miller; 20 Will Maher; 9 Kyle Kesik; 30 Mitch Revell; 11 Ellis Robson; 12 Lachlan Lanskey; 15 Aaron Brown. Subs (all used): 31 George Flanagan; 13 Dan Parker; 10 Mark Ioane; 18 Jordan Schofield.
Tries: Sa'u (8, 44), Robson (17), Thomas (28, 35), Lanskey (79); **Goals:** Miller 6/6; **Field goal:** Miller (39).
Rugby Leaguer & League Express Men of the Match: *Town:* Brad Brennan; *Cougars:* Junior Sa'u.
Penalty count: 5-4; **Half-time:** 0-25;
Referee: Denton Arnold; **Attendance:** 793.

ROUND 15

Sunday 7th July 2024

NEWCASTLE THUNDER 0 WORKINGTON TOWN 44

THUNDER: 6 Alex Donaghy; 1 Luke Jeremy; 21 Evan Lawther; 22 Jake Anderson; 25 Sean Croston; 4 Tom Siddle; 28 Mackenzie Harman; 31 Josh Stoker; 24 Joel Russell; 15 Harry Price; 12 Nathan Rushworth; 18 Paddy Burns; 14 Will Bate. Subs (all used): 32 Robin Hugues; 9 Tyler Hepple; - Tobias Gibson; 10 Harry Lowery.
TOWN: 27 Zarrin Galea; 25 Tommy Brierley; 3 Chris Taylor; 4 Jason Mossop; - Joe Hartley; 1 Jordan Burns; 7 Carl Forber; 13 JJ Key; 9 Matty Henson; 10 Stevie Scholey; 15 Liam McNicholas; 12 Jake Bradley; 19 Tyler Walton. Subs (all used): 30 Brad Brennan; 17 Grant Reid; 18 Connor Saunders; 8 Jordan Thomson.
Tries: Brierley (2), Henson (11), Galea (25, 72), Brennan (39, 56), Forber (48), Hartley (65);
Goals: Forber 6/8.
Rugby Leaguer & League Express Men of the Match: *Thunder:* Jake Anderson; *Town:* Zarrin Galea.
Penalty count: 3-5; **Half-time:** 0-22;
Referee: Michael Smaill.
(at Gateshead International Stadium).

NORTH WALES CRUSADERS 18 MIDLANDS HURRICANES 32

CRUSADERS: 25 Ben Lane; 16 Jack Holmes; 3 Kieran Taylor; 2 Jake Thewlis; 5 Patrick Ah Van; 7 Toby Hughes; 6 Dan Coates; 15 Shaun Costello; 19 Joe Baldwin; 10 Chris Barratt; 24 Cole Oakley; 17 Olly Davies; 11 Liam Cooper. Subs (all used): 22 Adam Carr; 21 Brett Bailey; 13 Carl Forster; 14 Paul Nash.

Tries: Barratt (25), Nash (58), Carr (67);
Goals: Lane 2/2, Coates 1/1.
Dismissal: Taylor (39) - late challenge on McLelland.
Sin bin: Coates (32) - dangerous challenge on Bass.
HURRICANES: 1 Todd Horner; 5 Jason Bass; 3 Matt Welham; - Ryan Johnson; 32 Matty Chrimes; 23 Callum McLelland; 7 Dave Hewitt; 8 Jon Luke Kirby; 19 Chris Cullimore; 29 Lewis Peachey; 11 Tom Wilkinson; 12 Liam Welham; 16 Ellis Hobson. Subs (all used): 9 Danny Barcoe; 13 Brad Clavering; 30 Blake Broadbent; 24 Marcus Green.
Tries: M Welham (35), Horner (37, 43), Johnson (39, 76), Chrimes (62); **Goals:** Hewitt 3/5, Chrimes 1/1.
Rugby Leaguer & League Express Men of the Match:
Crusaders: Liam Cooper; *Hurricanes:* Callum McLelland.
Penalty count: 6-5; **Half-time:** 6-16;
Referee: Geoffrey Poumes; **Attendance:** 552.

KEIGHLEY COUGARS 20 ROCHDALE HORNETS 20

COUGARS: 17 Oscar Thomas; 34 Ben Blackmore; 3 Adam Ryder; 4 Junior Sa'u; 5 Billy Walkley; 14 Alex Bishop; 7 Jack Miller; 20 Will Maher; 9 Kyle Kesik; 30 Mitch Revell; 11 Ellis Robson; 12 Lachlan Lanskey; 15 Aaron Brown. Subs (all used): 31 George Flanagan; 18 Jordan Schofield; 13 Dan Parker; 10 Mark Ioane.
Tries: Walkley (31), Ioane (49, 58); **Goals:** Miller 4/4.
Sin bin: Kesik (10) - high tackle on Nelmes.
HORNETS: 1 Gregg McNally; 2 Dan Nixon; 32 Jack Darbyshire; 3 Myles Harrop; 21 Luke Forber; 6 Martyn Ridyard; 7 Lewis Else; 20 Dean Roberts; 9 Aiden Roden; 10 Luke Nelmes; 11 Ben Forster; 12 Duane Straugheir; 23 Emmerson Whittel. Subs (all used): 30 Jonny Openshaw; 16 Jordan Andrade; 8 Daniel Spencer-Tonks; 18 Deane Meadows.
Tries: Straugheir (4), Nixon (8), Whittel (61);
Goals: Ridyard 4/5.
Rugby Leaguer & League Express Men of the Match:
Cougars: Mark Ioane; *Hornets:* Martyn Ridyard.
Penalty count: 8-7; **Half-time:** 6-12;
Referee: Warren Turley; **Attendance:** 1,608.

ROUND 16

Sunday 14th July 2024

NEWCASTLE THUNDER 16 HUNSLET 42

THUNDER: 1 Alex Donaghy; 2 Luke Jeremy; 3 Evan Lawther; 4 Sean Croston; 5 AJ Towse; 6 Tom Siddle; 7 Elliott Shaw; 8 Robin Hugues; 9 Joel Russell; 10 Harry Price; 11 Nathan Rushworth; 12 Jason Payne; 13 Tobias Gibson. Subs (all used): 14 Will Bate; 15 Josh Stoker; 16 Jack Skelton; 17 Harry Lowery.
Tries: Donaghy (17), Lawther (25), Shaw (57);
Goals: Donaghy 2/3.
HUNSLET: 23 George Flanagan; 1 Jimmy Watson; 5 Alfie Goddard; 4 Jude Ferreira; 31 Jack Render; 6 Jordan Paga; 7 Matty Beharrell; 8 Harvey Hallas; 15 Ross Whitmore; 13 Michael Knowles; 11 Josh Jordan-Roberts; 12 Aaron Levy; 16 Jordan Syme. Subs (all used): 18 Cam Berry; 22 Liam Carr; 26 Ethan O'Hanlon; 38 Keenen Tomlinson.
Tries: Render (2), Watson (9), Paga (37), Ferreira (40, 65), Goddard (47), Carr (71, 80); **Goals:** Beharrell 5/8.
Rugby Leaguer & League Express Men of the Match:
Thunder: Alex Donaghy; *Hunslet:* Jude Ferreira.
Penalty count: 7-7; **Half-time:** 10-20;
Referee: Andy Sweet. *(at Crow Trees, Blaydon).*

OLDHAM 32 NORTH WALES CRUSADERS 6

OLDHAM: 30 Phoenix Laulu-Togaga'e; 5 Mo Agoro; 24 Ben O'Keefe; 3 Jordan Turner; 29 Kieran Dixon; 1 Logan Astley; 9 Matty Wildie; 16 Owen Farnworth; 13 Elijah Taylor; 18 Jay Chapelhow; 20 George Hirst; 11 Joe Wardle; 8 Craig Kopczak. Subs (all used): 22 Ted Chapelhow; 15 Josh Johnson; 25 Bailey Aldridge; 26 Brad Gallagher.
Tries: O'Keefe (17), Dixon (37, 40), Agoro (53, 69), Gallagher (58); **Goals:** Dixon 4/6.
Dismissal: Josh Johnson (80) - headbutt.
CRUSADERS: 16 Jack Holmes; 5 Patrick Ah Van; 3 Kieran Taylor; 23 Ewan Smith; 2 Jake Thewlis; 6 Dan Coates; 7 Daniel Moss; 15 Shaun Costello; 19 Joe Baldwin; 10 Chris Barratt; 24 Cole Oakley; 17 Olly Davies; 13 Carl Forster. Subs (all used): 22 Adam Carr; 8 Ben Evans; 27 Kenny Baker; 26 Reece Bushell.
Try: Barratt (77); **Goals:** Coates 1/1.
Rugby Leaguer & League Express Men of the Match:
Oldham: Ben O'Keefe; *Crusaders:* Chris Barratt.
Penalty count: 7-8; **Half-time:** 16-0;
Referee: Ryan Cox; **Attendance:** 1,270.

WORKINGTON TOWN 14 ROCHDALE HORNETS 12

TOWN: 27 Zarrin Galea; 25 Henry Hadfield; 3 Chris Taylor; 4 Jason Mossop; - Billy Southward; 1 Jordan Burns; 7 Carl Forber; 13 JJ Key; 9 Matty Henson; 10 Stevie Scholey; 15 Liam McNicholas; 12 Jake Bradley; 19 Tyler Walton. Subs (all used): 29 Pone Tongia; 18 Connor Saunders; 8 Jordan Thomson; 17 Grant Reid.
Tries: Mossop (43), Hadfield (51), Burns (66);
Goals: Forber 1/3.
Sin bin: Thomson (56) - high tackle.
HORNETS: 1 Gregg McNally; 2 Dan Nixon; 32 Jack Darbyshire; 3 Myles Harrop; 21 Luke Forber; 6 Martyn Ridyard; 26 Max Flanagan; 20 Dean Roberts; 9 Aiden Roden; 17 Ben Killan; 11 Ben Forster; 12 Duane Straugheir; 23 Emmerson Whittel. Subs (all used): 30 Jonny Openshaw; 8 Daniel Spencer-Tonks; 16 Jordan Andrade; 18 Deane Meadows.
Tries: Andrade (32), Spencer-Tonks (76);
Goals: M Flanagan 2/2.
Rugby Leaguer & League Express Men of the Match:
Town: Zarrin Galea; *Hornets:* Max Flanagan.
Penalty count: 2-3; **Half-time:** 0-6;
Referee: Matty Lynn; **Attendance:** 573.

ROUND 17

Sunday 21st July 2024

CORNWALL 8 WORKINGTON TOWN 30

CORNWALL: 6 Cameron Brown; 23 Callum Abbott; 3 Coby Nichol; 4 Tom Ashton; 5 Harry Aaronson; 14 Morgan Punchard; 27 Bailey Black; 10 Harry Boots; 9 Luke Collins; 15 Kaine Dimech; 13 David Weetman; 12 Darcy Simpson; 22 Jake Lloyd. Subs (all used): 16 Decarlo Trerise; 20 Christian Bannister; 19 Tomo Clark; 24 Nathan Conroy.
Tries: Brown (16), Abbott (55); **Goals:** Brown 0/3.
TOWN: 27 Zarrin Galea; 18 Henry Hadfield; 3 Chris Taylor; 4 Jason Mossop; 14 Billy Southward; 1 Jordan Burns; 7 Carl Forber; 13 JJ Key; 9 Matty Henson; 22 Tyler Walton; 12 Jake Bradley; 15 Liam McNicholas; 16 Jack Stephenson. Subs (all used): 31 Pone Tongia; 30 Brad Brennan; 19 Connor Saunders; 17 Grant Reid.
Tries: Stephenson (14), Key (23), Galea (32), Bradley (50), Reid (67); **Goals:** Forber 5/5.
Sin bin: Walton (75) - use of the elbow.
Rugby Leaguer & League Express Men of the Match:
Cornwall: Luke Collins; *Town:* Zarrin Galea.
Penalty count: 6-10; **Half-time:** 4-18;
Referee: Adam Williams.

NORTH WALES CRUSADERS 16 HUNSLET 46

CRUSADERS: 25 Ben Lane; 18 Rob Massam; 3 Kieran Taylor; 23 Ewan Smith; 2 Jake Thewlis; 6 Dan Coates; 7 Daniel Moss; 8 Ben Evans; 19 Joe Baldwin; 10 Chris Barratt; 24 Cole Oakley; 17 Olly Davies; 13 Carl Forster. Subs (all used): 15 Shaun Costello; 16 Jack Holmes; 22 Adam Carr; 27 Kenny Baker.
Tries: Massam (6, 28), Lane (78); **Goals:** Lane 1/4, Moss 1/1.
Sin bin: Davies (57) - late challenge.
HUNSLET: 1 Jimmy Watson; 2 Noah Booth; 28 Joe Law; 4 Jude Ferreira; 31 Jack Render; 6 Jordan Paga; 7 Matty Beharrell; 8 Harvey Hallas; 15 Ross Whitmore; 13 Michael Knowles; 11 Josh Jordan-Roberts; 12 Aaron Levy; 16 Jordan Syme. Subs (all used): 18 Cam Berry; 22 Liam Carr; 26 Ethan O'Hanlon; 30 Jack Coventry.
Tries: Render (14, 47, 63), Booth (31), Berry (46), Law (57, 67), Carr (72); **Goals:** Beharrell 5/6, Knowles 2/2.
Rugby Leaguer & League Express Men of the Match:
Crusaders: Rob Massam; *Hunslet:* Matty Beharrell.
Penalty count: 5-8; **Half-time:** 10-12;
Referee: Aaryn Belafonte; **Attendance:** 488.

OLDHAM 44 KEIGHLEY COUGARS 6

OLDHAM: 30 Phoenix Laulu-Togaga'e; 5 Mo Agoro; 23 Jack Johnson; 3 Jordan Turner; 29 Kieran Dixon; 6 Danny Craven; 38 Riley Dean; 16 Owen Farnworth; 9 Matty Wildie; 18 Jay Chapelhow; 11 Joe Wardle; 26 Brad Gallagher; 10 Pat Moran. Subs (all used): 22 Ted Chapelhow; 15 Josh Johnson; 25 Bailey Aldridge; 33 Adam Sidlow.
Tries: Agoro (6, 55), J Turner (19), Gallagher (36), Craven (66), Jack Johnson (76, 79); **Goals:** Dixon 8/9.
COUGARS: 1 Brandon Pickersgill; 34 Ben Blackmore; 3 Adam Ryder; 4 Junior Sa'u; 5 Billy Walkley; 14 Alex Bishop; 7 Jack Miller; 20 Will Maher; 31 George Flanagan; 30 Mitch Revell; 11 Ellis Robson; 12 Lachlan Lanskey; 15 Aaron Brown. Subs (all used): 18 Jordan Schofield; 13 Dan Parker; 10 Mark Ioane; 35 Brad England.
Try: Schofield (63); **Goals:** Parker 1/1.
Rugby Leaguer & League Express Men of the Match:
Oldham: Danny Craven; *Cougars:* Adam Ryder.
Penalty count: 11-7; **Half-time:** 20-0;
Referee: Kevin Moore; **Attendance:** 2,572.

ROCHDALE HORNETS 14 MIDLANDS HURRICANES 10

HORNETS: 1 Gregg McNally; 2 Misi Taulapapa; 27 Jack Darbyshire; 3 Myles Harrop; 22 Lameck Juma; 31 Will Roberts; 5 Mackenzie Harman; 17 Ben Killan; 9 Aiden Roden; 10 Luke Nelmes; 11 Ben Forster; 12 Duane Straugheir; 23 Emmerson Whittel. Subs (all used): 25 Matty Rudd; 20 Dean Roberts; 16 Jordan Andrade; 18 Deane Meadows.
Tries: Andrade (47, 50); **Goals:** Harman 3/3.
HURRICANES: 1 Todd Horner; - Matty Chrimes; 3 Matt Welham; 4 Ross Oakes; 5 Jason Bass; 23 Callum McLelland; 6 Jake Sweeting; 24 Marcus Green; 19 Chris Cullimore; 29 Lewis Peachey; 11 Tom Wilkinson; 12 Liam Welham; 16 Ellis Hobson. Subs (all used): 15 Aaron Willis; 9 Danny Barcoe; 17 Kieran Moran; 10 Sam Bowring.
Tries: McLelland (17), L Welham (73); **Goals:** Chrimes 1/2.
Rugby Leaguer & League Express Men of the Match:
Hornets: Jordan Andrade; *Hurricanes:* Callum McLelland.
Penalty count: 7-7; **Half-time:** 0-6;
Referee: Andy Sweet; **Attendance:** 676.

ROUND 18

Sunday 28th July 2024

NEWCASTLE THUNDER 34 CORNWALL 44

THUNDER: 1 Alex Donaghy; 2 Sean Croston; 3 Tom Siddle; 4 Evan Lawther; 5 Luke Jeremy; 18 Josh Stoker; 7 Elliott Shaw; 8 Tobias Gibson; 9 Joel Russell; 10 Harry Price; 11 Joe Gibbons; 12 Paddy Burns; 13 Harry Lowery. Subs (all used): 14 Tyler Hepple; 15 Nathan Rushworth; 16 Jack Skelton; 17 Jason Payne.
Tries: Shaw (9), Price (27), Hepple (39), Lawther (56, 60), Croston (74); **Goals:** Donaghy 5/6.
CORNWALL: 6 Cameron Brown; 23 Callum Abbott; 3 Coby Nichol; 4 Tom Ashton; 5 Harry Aaronson; 14 Morgan Punchard; 27 Bailey Black; 18 Matt Ross; 9 Luke Collins; 15 Kaine Dimech; 11 Nathan Cullen; 12 Darcy Simpson; 13 David Weetman. Subs (all used): 20 Christian Bannister; 19 Tomo Clark; 24 Nathan Conroy; 22 Jake Lloyd.
Tries: Cullen (4, 14), Aaronson (19), Conroy (33, 49), Black (36, 70), Abbott (45); **Goals:** Brown 6/8.
Rugby Leaguer & League Express Men of the Match:
Thunder: Evan Lawther; *Cornwall:* Bailey Black.
Penalty count: 3-4; **Half-time:** 18-26;
Referee: Aaryn Belafonte; **Attendance:** 329
(at Gateshead International Stadium).

HUNSLET 24 WORKINGTON TOWN 32

HUNSLET: 1 Jimmy Watson; 5 Alfie Goddard; 28 Joe Law; 4 Jude Ferreira; 31 Jack Render; 6 Jordan Paga; 7 Matty Beharrell; 8 Harvey Hallas; 15 Ross Whitmore; 13 Michael Knowles; 11 Josh Jordan-Roberts; 20 Keenen Tomlinson; 16 Jordan Syme. Subs (all used): 18 Cam Berry; 22 Liam Carr; 26 Ethan O'Hanlon; 32 Matt Fletcher.
Tries: Ferreira (13, 74), O'Hanlon (42), Carr (57);
Goals: Beharrell 4/4.
TOWN: 27 Zarrin Galea; 18 Henry Hadfield; 3 Chris Taylor; 25 Tommy Brierley; 14 Billy Southward; 1 Jordan Burns; 7 Carl Forber; 13 JJ Key; 9 Matty Henson; 22 Tyler Walton; 12 Jake Bradley; 15 Liam McNicholas; 16 Jack Stephenson. Subs (all used): 20 Ellis Archer; 30 Brad Brennan; 17 Grant Reid; 31 Pone Tongia.
Tries: Galea (18), Brierley (23), Forber (30), Reid (35), C Taylor (50); **Goals:** Forber 6/7.
Rugby Leaguer & League Express Men of the Match:
Hunslet: Matty Beharrell; *Town:* Carl Forber.
Penalty count: 5-7; **Half-time:** 6-22;
Referee: Warren Turley; **Attendance:** 572.

KEIGHLEY COUGARS 36 MIDLANDS HURRICANES 12

COUGARS: 1 Brandon Pickersgill; 34 Ben Blackmore; 3 Adam Ryder; 4 Junior Sa'u; 5 Billy Walkley; 17 Oscar Thomas; 21 Ben Dean; 20 Will Maher; 15 Aaron Brown; 10 Mark Ioane; 11 Ellis Robson; 12 Lachlan Lanskey; 13 Dan Parker. Subs (all used): 24 Junior Nuu; 16 Josh Lynam; 31 George Flanagan; 30 Mitch Revell.
Tries: Ioane (8), Pickersgill (12, 59), Sa'u (28), Flanagan (69), Robson (76); **Goals:** Thomas 6/6.
HURRICANES: 3 Matt Welham; - Matty Chrimes; 1 Todd Horner; 4 Ross Oakes; - Ryan Millar; 6 Jake Sweeting; 23 Callum McLelland; 8 Jon Luke Kirby; 9 Danny Barcoe; 13 Brad Clavering; 22 Ryan Johnson; 16 Ellis Hobson; 12 Liam Welham. Subs (all used): 19 Chris Cullimore; - Kye Armstrong; 10 Sam Bowring; 24 Marcus Green.
Tries: Horner (4), Millar (18); **Goals:** Sweeting 2/2.
Rugby Leaguer & League Express Men of the Match:
Cougars: Oscar Thomas; *Hurricanes:* Danny Barcoe.
Penalty count: 4-3; **Half-time:** 18-12;
Referee: Adam Williams; **Attendance:** 1,056.

ROCHDALE HORNETS 10 OLDHAM 14

HORNETS: 1 Gregg McNally; 22 Lameck Juma; 27 Misi Taulapapa; 3 Myles Harrop; 21 Luke Forber; 31 Will Roberts; 7 Lewis Else; 17 Ben Killan; 9 Aiden Roden; 10 Luke Nelmes; 11 Ben Forster; 12 Duane Straugheir; 23 Emmerson Whittel. Subs (all used): 25 Matty Rudd; 20 Dean Roberts; 16 Jordan Andrade; 18 Deane Meadows.
Tries: Forber (26, 32); **Goals:** W Roberts 1/2.

OLDHAM: 30 Phoenix Laulu-Togaga'e; 5 Mo Agoro; 23 Jack Johnson; 3 Jordan Turner; 29 Kieran Dixon; 6 Danny Craven; 38 Riley Dean; 16 Owen Farnworth; 9 Matty Wildie; 18 Jay Chapelhow; 13 Elijah Taylor; 26 Brad Gallagher; 10 Pat Moran. Subs (all used): 25 Bailey Aldridge; 22 Ted Chapelhow; 15 Josh Johnson; 33 Adam Sidlow.
Tries: Dixon (9), Jack Johnson (15), Laulu-Togaga'e (68);
Goals: Dixon 1/3.
Sin bin: Dixon (25) - obstruction.
Rugby Leaguer & League Express Men of the Match:
Hornets: Lewis Else; *Oldham:* Phoenix Laulu-Togaga'e.
Penalty count: 6-5; **Half-time:** 10-8;
Referee: Denton Arnold; **Attendance:** 2,178.

ROUND 19

Sunday 4th August 2024

KEIGHLEY COUGARS 72 NEWCASTLE THUNDER 12

COUGARS: 1 Brandon Pickersgill; 36 Lloyd McEwan-Peters; 3 Adam Ryder; 24 Junior Nuu; 5 Billy Walkley; 17 Oscar Thomas; 21 Ben Dean; 20 Will Maher; 15 Aaron Brown; 8 Lewis Hatton; 16 Josh Lynam; 13 Dan Parker; 18 Jordan Schofield. Subs (all used): 31 George Flanagan; 10 Mark Ioane; 30 Mitch Revell; 7 Jack Miller.
Tries: Nuu (5, 79), McEwan-Peters (9, 33, 70, 76), Schofield (18), Thomas (39, 74), Ryder (49), Walkley (52), Flanagan (60), Parker (66);
Goals: Thomas 5/6, Miller 5/7.
THUNDER: 1 Alex Donaghy; 5 Leo Bradley; 4 Sean Croston; 3 Tom Siddle; 2 Luke Jeremy; 6 Mike Hansen; 7 Elliott Shaw; 13 Tobias Gibson; 17 Tyler Hepple; 8 Harry Price; 11 Nathan Rushworth; 12 Matthew Handy; 10 Harry Lowery. Subs (all used): 14 Joel Russell; 9 Josh Stoker; 16 Jason Payne; 15 Will Bate.
Tries: Rushworth (29), Donaghy (80); **Goals:** Donaghy 2/2.
Rugby Leaguer & League Express Men of the Match:
Cougars: Lloyd McEwan-Peters; *Thunder:* Alex Donaghy.
Penalty count: 3-1; **Half-time:** 28-6;
Referee: Nick Bennett; **Attendance:** 968.

OLDHAM 32 MIDLANDS HURRICANES 0

OLDHAM: 30 Phoenix Laulu-Togaga'e; 5 Mo Agoro; 23 Jack Johnson; 3 Jordan Turner; 29 Kieran Dixon; 1 Logan Astley; 38 Riley Dean; 16 Owen Farnworth; 9 Matty Wildie; 18 Jay Chapelhow; 26 Brad Gallagher; 10 Pat Moran; 8 Craig Kopczak. Subs (all used): 12 Adam Lawton; 22 Ted Chapelhow; 25 Bailey Aldridge; 33 Adam Sidlow.
Tries: J Turner (8), Laulu-Togaga'e (15), Agoro (27), Astley (35), Dixon (48), Wildie (58); **Goals:** Dixon 4/6.
HURRICANES: 1 Todd Horner; 25 Inoke Nakoronivalu; 31 Davey Dixon; 22 Ryan Johnson; 32 Matty Chrimes; 6 Jake Sweeting; 14 Sully Medforth; 8 Jon Luke Kirby; 9 Danny Barcoe; 10 Sam Bowring; 11 Tom Wilkinson; 15 Aaron Willis; 13 Brad Clavering. Subs (all used): 29 Lewis Peachey; 17 Kieran Moran; - Jose Kenga; - Kye Armstrong.
Rugby Leaguer & League Express Men of the Match:
Oldham: Matty Wildie; *Hurricanes:* Jake Sweeting.
Penalty count: 8-4; **Half-time:** 22-0;
Referee: Warren Turley; **Attendance:** 1,582.

ROCHDALE HORNETS 46 CORNWALL 32

HORNETS: 1 Gregg McNally; 22 Lameck Juma; 27 Misi Taulapapa; 3 Myles Harrop; 21 Luke Forber; 7 Lewis Else; 31 Mackenzie Harman; 8 Daniel Spencer-Tonks; 9 Aiden Roden; 19 Dean Roberts; 11 Ben Forster; 12 Duane Straugheir; 23 Emmerson Whittel. Subs (all used): 16 Jordan Andrade; 20 Toby Brannan; 24 Jaden Dayes; 25 Matty Rudd.
Tries: Forster (6), Taulapapa (11), Else (20), Forber (25), Roden (38), Harrop (43), Dayes (46), Andrade (50);
Goals: Harman 7/8.
CORNWALL: 6 Cameron Brown; 23 Callum Abbott; 21 Aaron Small; 4 Tom Ashton; 5 Harry Aaronson; 14 Morgan Punchard; 27 Bailey Black; 18 Matt Ross; 9 Luke Collins; 15 Kaine Dimech; 11 Nathan Cullen; 12 Darcy Simpson; 13 David Weetman. Subs (all used): 8 Jacob Bateman; 17 Jamie Gill; 22 Jake Lloyd; 24 Nathan Conroy.
Tries: Black (39), Aaronson (53, 75), Weetman (58), Bateman (67), Brown (77); **Goals:** Brown 4/6.
Rugby Leaguer & League Express Men of the Match:
Hornets: Lameck Juma; *Cornwall:* Jacob Bateman.
Penalty count: 4-3; **Half-time:** 28-6;
Referee: Brad Milligan; **Attendance:** 427.

WORKINGTON TOWN 24 NORTH WALES CRUSADERS 28

TOWN: 27 Zarrin Galea; 34 Henry Hadfield; 3 Chris Taylor; 21 Tommy Brierley; 33 Billy Southward; 1 Jordan Burns; 7 Carl Forber; 13 JJ Key; 9 Matty Henson; 8 Jordan Thomson; 15 Jack Stephenson; 12 Jake Bradley; 22 Tyler Walton. Subs (all used): 30 Brad Brennan; 29 Pone Tongia; 16 Grant Reid; 6 Ciaran Walker.
Tries: Stephenson (5), Key (16), Bradley (22), Southward (27); **Goals:** Forber 4/5.
Dismissal: Burns (39) - use of the elbow.
Sin bin: Brennan (47) - late challenge.
CRUSADERS: 25 Ben Lane; 2 Jake Thewlis; 3 Kieran Taylor; 4 Matt Reid; 5 Patrick Ah Van; 6 Daniel Moss; 7 Toby Hughes; 8 Ben Evans; 19 Joe Baldwin; 10 Chris Barratt; 12 Matt Unsworth; 17 Olly Davies; 27 Alfie Sinclair. (Subs all used): 15 Shaun Costello; 16 Jack Holmes; 24 Cole Oakley; 13 Carl Forster.
Tries: B Evans (19), Ah Van (33), Barratt (60, 65), Lane (76);
Goals: Moss 4/5.
Rugby Leaguer & League Express Men of the Match:
Town: Carl Forber; *Crusaders:* Carl Forster.
Penalty count: 6-10; **Half-time:** 22-12;
Referee: Luke Bland; **Attendance:** 857.

ROUND 20

Saturday 10th August 2024

CORNWALL 26 HUNSLET 33

CORNWALL: 6 Cameron Brown; 23 Callum Abbott; 21 Aaron Small; 4 Tom Ashton; 5 Harry Aaronson; 27 Bailey Black; 7 Adam Rusling; 15 Kaine Dimech; 9 Luke Collins; 18 Matt Ross; 11 Nathan Cullen; 13 David Weetman; 17 Jacob Bateman. Subs (all used): 22 Jake Lloyd; 16 Decarlo Trerise; 24 Nathan Conroy; 8 Jamie Gill.
Tries: Abbott (11, 72), Small (33, 41), Cullen (67);
Goals: Brown 3/5.
Sin bin: Collins (23) - late challenge, (38) - dangerous challenge.
HUNSLET: 23 George Flanagan; 28 Mackenzie Turner; 1 Jimmy Watson; 4 Jude Ferreira; 31 Jack Render; 6 Jordan Paga; 7 Matty Beharrell; 8 Harvey Hallas; 15 Ross Whitmore; 26 Ethan O'Hanlon; 16 Jordan Syme; 13 Michael Knowles; 32 Matt Fletcher. Subs: 18 Cam Berry; 22 Liam Carr; 30 Jack Coventry; - Josh Rhodes (not used).
Tries: Render (9, 18), Flanagan (27, 49), Berry (48), Knowles (79); **Goals:** Beharrell 4/6;
Field goal: Beharrell (79).
Sin bin: Fletcher (56) - high tackle on Brown.
Rugby Leaguer & League Express Men of the Match:
Cornwall: Cameron Brown; *Hunslet:* Matty Beharrell.
Penalty count: 6-5; **Half-time:** 10-14;
Referee: Sam Jenkinson.

Sunday 11th August 2024

MIDLANDS HURRICANES 34 WORKINGTON TOWN 22

HURRICANES: 31 Davey Dixon; 32 Matty Chrimes; 22 Harry Higham; 1 Todd Horner; 5 Jason Bass; 6 Jake Sweeting; 23 Callum McLelland; 8 Jon Luke Kirby; 19 Chris Cullimore; 10 Sam Bowring; 11 Tom Wilkinson; 15 Aaron Willis; 13 Brad Clavering. Subs (all used): 9 Danny Barcoe; 24 Marcus Green; - Jose Kenga; 29 Lewis Peachey.
Tries: Kirby (4), Higham (9), Sweeting (30), Bass (46), Chrimes (72); **Goals:** Sweeting 7/7.
TOWN: 27 Zarrin Galea; 18 Henry Hadfield; 3 Chris Taylor; 2 Joe Hartley; 14 Billy Southward; 1 Jordan Burns; 7 Carl Forber; 13 JJ Key; 19 Connor Saunders; 8 Jordan Thomson; 16 Jack Stephenson; 25 Tommy Brierley; 9 Matty Henson. Subs (all used): 5 Ethan Bickerdike; 30 Brad Brennan; 17 Grant Reid; 23 Kian McPherson.
Tries: Hartley (16, 56), Galea (42), Henson (68);
Goals: Forber 3/4.
Rugby Leaguer & League Express Men of the Match:
Hurricanes: Jake Sweeting; *Town:* Joe Hartley.
Penalty count: 4-2; **Half-time:** 20-6;
Referee: Denton Arnold; **Attendance:** 677.

NORTH WALES CRUSADERS 16 KEIGHLEY COUGARS 24

CRUSADERS: 25 Ben Lane; 5 Patrick Ah Van; 3 Kieran Taylor; 4 Matt Reid; 18 Rob Massam; 7 Toby Hughes; 6 Dan Coates; 8 Ben Evans; 19 Joe Baldwin; 10 Chris Barratt; 24 Cole Oakley; 12 Matt Unsworth; 17 Olly Davies. Subs (all used): 16 Jack Holmes; 15 Shaun Costello; - Jake Bloxham; 13 Carl Forster.
Tries: Unsworth (42), Lane (49); **Goals:** Lane 4/4.
COUGARS: 1 Brandon Pickersgill; 34 Ben Blackmore; 3 Adam Ryder; 24 Junior Nuu; 5 Billy Walkley; 17 Oscar Thomas; 7 Jack Miller; 8 Lewis Hatton; 31 George Flanagan; 30 Mitch Revell; 13 Dan Parker; 11 Ellis Robson; 18 Jordan Schofield. Subs (all used): 14 Alex Bishop; 35 Brad England; 15 Aaron Brown; 10 Mark Ioane.
Tries: Miller (13), Ryder (32), Bishop (38), Flanagan (74);
Goals: Miller 4/6.
Sin bin: England (40) - interference, (60) - high tackle.
Rugby Leaguer & League Express Men of the Match:
Crusaders: Ben Lane; *Cougars:* Jack Miller.
Penalty count: 4-4; **Half-time:** 2-16;
Referee: Nick Bennett; **Attendance:** 401.
(at Hare Lane, Chester).

OLDHAM 84 NEWCASTLE THUNDER 0

OLDHAM: 30 Phoenix Laulu-Togaga'e; 27 Cian Tyrer; 19 Jumah Sambou; 3 Jordan Turner; 29 Kieran Dixon; 6 Danny Craven; 7 Jamie Ellis; 16 Owen Farnworth; 9 Matty Wildie; 22 Ted Chapelhow; 20 George Hirst; 11 Joe Wardle; 10 Pat Moran. Subs (all used): 25 Bailey Aldridge; 33 Adam Sidlow; 12 Adam Lawton; 8 Craig Kopczak.
Tries: Sambou (3, 43), C Tyrer (10, 23, 46, 72, 76), Dixon (13, 63, 68), T Chapelhow (27), J Turner (29), Aldridge (49), Kopczak (52), Laulu-Togaga'e (79);
Goals: Dixon 12/15.
THUNDER: 1 Alex Donaghy; 5 Leo Bradley; 4 Tom Siddle; 3 Matthew Handy; 2 Sean Croston; 6 Olly Bibby; 7 Elliott Shaw; 13 Tobias Gibson; 17 Tyler Hepple; 8 Harry Price; 12 Nathan Rushworth; 11 Paddy Burns; 10 Harry Lowery. Subs (all used): 14 Joel Russell; - Josh Stoker; 15 Jack Skelton; 16 Will Bate.
Rugby Leaguer & League Express Men of the Match:
Oldham: Jumah Sambou; *Thunder:* Nathan Rushworth.
Penalty count: 6-2; **Half-time:** 32-0;
Referee: Brad Milligan; **Attendance:** 1,006.

ROUND 21

Saturday 17th August 2024

NEWCASTLE THUNDER 6 ROCHDALE HORNETS 78

THUNDER: 1 Alex Donaghy; 2 Sean Croston; 3 Mike Hansen; 4 Tom Siddle; 5 Luke Jeremy; 6 Olly Bibby; 7 Elliott Shaw; 8 Harry Price; 9 Taylor Pemberton; 10 Tyler Hepple; 11 Paddy Burns; 12 Matthew Handy; 13 Tobias Gibson. Subs (all used): 14 Will Bate; 15 Jack Skelton; 16 Josh Stoker; 17 Austin Phillips.
Try: Jeremy (60); **Goals:** Donaghy 1/1.
HORNETS: 1 Gregg McNally; 5 Misi Taulapapa; 27 Jack Darbyshire; 3 Myles Harrop; 21 Luke Forber; 31 Mackenzie Harman; 7 Lewis Else; 8 Daniel Spencer-Tonks; 9 Aiden Roden; 10 Luke Nelmes; 11 Ben Forster; 12 Duane Straugheir; 23 Emmerson Whittel. Subs (all used): 30 Tom Ratchford; - Dean Roberts; 16 Jordan Andrade; 18 Deane Meadows.
Tries: Else (6, 17, 64), Forber (14, 74), Straugheir (20), Taulapapa (23), Ratchford (28, 35, 50), Harman (46), Harrop (54), Andrade (67), McNally (71);
Goals: Harman 11/14.
Rugby Leaguer & League Express Men of the Match:
Thunder: Alex Donaghy; *Hornets:* Lewis Else.
Penalty count: 1-4; **Half-time:** 0-38;
Referee: Carl Hughes; **Attendance:** 220
(at Gateshead International Stadium).

Sunday 18th August 2024

CORNWALL 6 MIDLANDS HURRICANES 18

CORNWALL: 6 Cameron Brown; 3 Coby Nichol; 21 Aaron Small; 4 Tom Ashton; 5 Harry Aaronson; 27 Bailey Black; 7 Adam Rusling; 10 Harry Boots; 9 Luke Collins; 15 Kaine Dimech; 13 David Weetman; 12 Darcy Simpson; 8 Jacob Bateman. Subs (all used): 16 Decarlo Trerise; 17 Jamie Gill; 22 Jake Lloyd; 24 Nathan Conroy.
Try: Brown (25); **Goals:** Brown 1/1.
HURRICANES: 32 Matty Chrimes; 5 Jason Bass; 22 Ryan Johnson; 1 Todd Horner; 26 Joe Varo; 14 Sully Medforth; 23 Callum McLelland; 8 Jon Luke Kirby; 9 Danny Barcoe; 10 Sam Bowring; 11 Tom Wilkinson; 15 Aaron Willis; 13 Brad Clavering. Subs (all used): 19 Chris Cullimore; 36 Jose Kenga; 29 Lewis Peachey; 24 Marcus Green.
Tries: Peachey (47), Wilkinson (56), Horner (63);
Goals: Medforth 3/4.
Rugby Leaguer & League Express Men of the Match:
Cornwall: David Weetman; *Hurricanes:* Sully Medforth.
Penalty count: 5-6; **Half-time:** 6-0;
Referee: Sam Houghton.

HUNSLET 28 NORTH WALES CRUSADERS 20

HUNSLET: 39 George Flanagan; 28 Mackenzie Turner; 1 Jimmy Watson; 4 Jude Ferreira; 31 Jack Render; 13 Michael Knowles; 7 Matty Beharrell; 8 Harvey Hallas; 15 Ross Whitmore; 32 Matt Fletcher; 11 Josh Jordan-Roberts; 23 Ethan Wood; 16 Jordan Syme. Subs (all used): 18 Cam Berry; 22 Liam Carr; 26 Ethan O'Hanlon; 30 Jack Coventry.
Tries: Ferreira (38), Syme (55), Wood (59), Watson (70), Turner (76); **Goals:** Beharrell 4/5.
CRUSADERS: 25 Ben Lane; 5 Patrick Ah Van; 3 Kieran Taylor; 4 Matt Reid; 2 Jake Thewlis; 6 Dan Coates; 7 Toby Hughes; 8 Ben Evans; 19 Joe Baldwin; 10 Chris Barratt; 24 Cole Oakley; 12 Matt Unsworth; 17 Olly Davies. Subs (all used): 15 Shaun Costello; 16 Jack Holmes; 27 Alfie Sinclair; 13 Carl Forster.
Tries: Lane (7), Barratt (23), Taylor (28); **Goals:** Lane 4/4.
Rugby Leaguer & League Express Men of the Match:
Hunslet: Matty Beharrell; *Crusaders:* Ben Lane.
Penalty count: 5-5; **Half-time:** 6-18;
Referee: Luke Bland; **Attendance:** 556.

KEIGHLEY COUGARS 12 OLDHAM 20

COUGARS: 1 Brandon Pickersgill; 36 Lloyd McEwan-Peters; 3 Adam Ryder; 4 Junior Sa'u; 5 Billy Walkley; 17 Oscar Thomas; 7 Jack Miller; 20 Will Maher; 31 George Flanagan; 30 Mitch Revell; 11 Ellis Robson; 13 Dan Parker; 9 Kyle Kesik. Subs (all used): 14 Alex Bishop; 15 Aaron Brown; 10 Mark Ioane; 18 Jordan Schofield.
Tries: Pickersgill (34), Robson (74); **Goals:** Miller 2/2.
Sin bin: Robson (57) - late challenge.
OLDHAM: 30 Phoenix Laulu-Togaga'e; 5 Mo Agoro; 23 Jack Johnson; 3 Jordan Turner; 29 Kieran Dixon; 6 Danny Craven; 7 Jamie Ellis; 16 Owen Farnworth; 9 Matty Wildie; 22 Ted Chapelhow; 13 Elijah Taylor; 20 George Hirst; 10 Pat Moran. Subs (all used): 25 Bailey Aldridge; 8 Craig Kopczak; 33 Adam Sidlow; 12 Adam Lawton.
Tries: Agoro (7, 15), Laulu-Togaga'e (19), Hirst (61);
Goals: Dixon 2/4.
Sin bin: Farnworth (66) - dangerous challenge.
Rugby Leaguer & League Express Men of the Match:
Cougars: Brandon Pickersgill;
Oldham: Phoenix Laulu-Togaga'e.
Penalty count: 7-4; **Half-time:** 6-14;
Referee: Matty Lynn; **Attendance:** 2,174.

ROUND 22

Sunday 25th August 2024

OLDHAM 72 CORNWALL 0

OLDHAM: 30 Phoenix Laulu-Togaga'e; 19 Jumah Sambou; 24 Ben O'Keefe; 3 Jordan Turner; 27 Cian Tyrer; 1 Logan Astley; 7 Jamie Ellis; 16 Owen Farnworth; 25 Bailey Aldridge; 22 Ted Chapelhow; 20 George Hirst; 13 Elijah Taylor; 33 Adam Sidlow. Subs (all used): 9 Matty Wildie; 10 Pat Moran; 8 Craig Kopczak; 15 Josh Johnson.
Tries: O'Keefe (6, 27, 50, 57), Sidlow (15), Astley (19), J Turner (32, 66), Kopczak (39), C Tyrer (44, 60), Josh Johnson (54), Sambou (63, 77); **Goals:** Ellis 8/14.
CORNWALL: 6 Cameron Brown; 23 Waldimar Matahwa; 3 Coby Nichol; 4 Tom Ashton; 5 Harry Aaronson; 14 Morgan Punchard; 7 Adam Rusling; 15 Kaine Dimech; 24 Nathan Conroy; 17 Jamie Gill; 8 Jacob Bateman; 12 Darcy Simpson; 22 Jake Lloyd. Subs (all used): 2 George Mitchell; 13 David Weetman; 20 Christian Bannister; 21 Harry Gray.
Rugby Leaguer & League Express Men of the Match:
Oldham: Ben O'Keefe; *Cornwall:* Coby Nichol.
Penalty count: 11-4; **Half-time:** 36-0;
Referee: Aaryn Belafonte; **Attendance:** 1,421.

KEIGHLEY COUGARS 40 HUNSLET 22

COUGARS: 1 Brandon Pickersgill; 34 Ben Blackmore; 3 Adam Ryder; 4 Junior Sa'u; 5 Billy Walkley; 17 Oscar Thomas; 7 Jack Miller; 20 Will Maher; 31 George Flanagan Sr; 30 Mitch Revell; 11 Ellis Robson; 16 Josh Lynam; 15 Aaron Brown. Subs (all used): 14 Alex Bishop; 10 Mark Ioane; 13 Dan Parker; 18 Jordan Schofield.
Tries: Robson (12, 80), Ryder (18), Walkley (34, 69), Ioane (40), Thomas (76); **Goals:** Miller 6/8.
Dismissal: Blackmore (26) - late challenge on Flanagan Jr.
Sin bin: Thomas (61) - interference.
HUNSLET: 6 George Flanagan Jr; 28 Mackenzie Turner; 1 Jimmy Watson; 4 Jude Ferreira; 31 Jack Render; 13 Michael Knowles; 7 Matty Beharrell; 8 Harvey Hallas; 15 Ross Whitmore; 32 Matt Fletcher; 11 Josh Jordan-Roberts; 23 Ethan Wood; 16 Jordan Syme. Subs (all used): 18 Cam Berry; 17 Lewis Wray; 26 Ethan O'Hanlon; 30 Jack Coventry.
Tries: Turner (5), Render (16), Flanagan Jr (71), Ferreira (74);
Goals: Beharrell 3/4.
Sin bin: Flanagan Jr (26) - retaliation.
Rugby Leaguer & League Express Men of the Match:
Cougars: Oscar Thomas; *Hunslet:* George Flanagan Jr.
Penalty count: 8-9; **Half-time:** 22-10;
Referee: Andy Sweet; **Attendance:** 1,642.

ROCHDALE HORNETS 28
NORTH WALES CRUSADERS 10

HORNETS: 1 Gregg McNally; 22 Lameck Juma; 5 Misi Taulapapa; 3 Myles Harrop; 21 Luke Forber; 31 Mackenzie Harman; 7 Lewis Else; 8 Daniel Spencer-Tonks; 9 Aiden Roden; 10 Luke Nelmes; 11 Ben Forster; 12 Duane Straugheir; 23 Emmerson Whittel. Subs (all used): 16 Jordan Andrade; 17 Ben Killan; 18 Deane Meadows; 25 Matty Rudd.
Tries: Forster (9), Killan (35), Harrop (46), McNally (58, 71);
Goals: Harman 4/5.
Sin bin: Nelmes (28) - dangerous contact.
CRUSADERS: 16 Jack Holmes; 5 Patrick Ah Van; 3 Kieran Taylor; 4 Matt Reid; 2 Jake Thewlis; 6 Toby Hughes; 7 Daniel Moss; 8 Ben Evans; 19 Joe Baldwin; 10 Chris Barratt; 24 Cole Oakley; 12 Matt Unsworth; 13 Carl Forster. Subs (all used): 14 Paul Nash; 15 Shaun Costello; 17 Olly Davies; 22 Adam Carr.
Tries: Hughes (18), Taylor (73); **Goals:** Moss 1/2.
Rugby Leaguer & League Express Men of the Match:
Hornets: Myles Harrop; *Crusaders:* Cole Oakley.
Penalty count: 8-9; **Half-time:** 12-4;
Referee: Brad Milligan; **Attendance:** 657.

WORKINGTON TOWN 46 NEWCASTLE THUNDER 0

TOWN: 1 Jordan Burns; 5 Ethan Bickerdike; 3 Chris Taylor; 2 Joe Hartley; 27 Zarrin Galea; 6 Ciaran Walker; 7 Carl Forber; 8 Jordan Thomson; 9 Matty Henson; 30 Brad Brennan; 25 Tommy Brierley; 12 Jake Bradley; 16 Jack Stephenson. Subs (all used): 26 Luke Charlton; 17 Grant Reid; 19 Connor Saunders; 22 Tyler Walton.
Tries: Henson (4, 61), Brennan (7, 73), Brierley (11), C Taylor (15), Galea (23), Bradley (26), Stephenson (78);
Goals: Forber 5/9.
THUNDER: 1 Alex Donaghy; 2 Sean Croston; 3 Mike Hansen; 4 Tom Siddle; 5 Luke Jeremy; 6 Olly Bibby; 7 Elliott Shaw; 8 Harry Price; 9 Joel Russell; 10 Harry Lowery; 11 Tobias Gibson; 12 Paddy Burns; 13 Tyler Hepple. Subs (all used): 14 Matthew Handy; 15 Jack Skelton; 16 Josh Stoker; 17 Austin Phillips.
Rugby Leaguer & League Express Men of the Match:
Town: Brad Brennan; *Thunder:* Paddy Burns.
Penalty count: 7-3; **Half-time:** 28-0;
Referee: Sam Jenkinson; **Attendance:** 631.

ROUND 23

Saturday 31st August 2024

MIDLANDS HURRICANES 22 HUNSLET 28

HURRICANES: 1 Todd Horner; 32 Matty Chrimes; 12 Liam Welham; 22 Ryan Johnson; 5 Jason Bass; 6 Jake Sweeting; 14 Sully Medforth; 8 Jon Luke Kirby; 19 Chris Cullimore; 36 Jose Kenga; 11 Tom Wilkinson; 15 Aaron Willis; 16 Ellis Hobson. Subs (all used): 17 Kieran Moran; 24 Marcus Green; 29 Lewis Peachey; - Finley Beardsworth.
Tries: Willis (7), Johnson (47), Medforth (55), Chrimes (58);
Goals: Sweeting 3/4.
HUNSLET: 39 George Flanagan; 42 Mackenzie Turner; 1 Jimmy Watson; 31 Jack Render; 4 Jude Ferreira; 40 Jordan Paga; 7 Matty Beharrell; 8 Harvey Hallas; 15 Ross Whitmore; 37 Matt Fletcher; 11 Josh Jordan-Roberts; 16 Jordan Syme; 13 Michael Knowles. Subs (all used): 17 Lewis Wray; 18 Cam Berry; 26 Ethan O'Hanlon; 30 Jack Coventry.
Tries: Whitmore (15, 22), Jordan-Roberts (25, 74), Render (52); **Goals:** Beharrell 4/5.
Rugby Leaguer & League Express Men of the Match:
Hurricanes: Matty Chrimes; *Hunslet:* Josh Jordan-Roberts.
Penalty count: 3-6; **Half-time:** 6-18;
Referee: Brad Milligan; **Attendance:** 420.

Sunday 1st September 2024

NORTH WALES CRUSADERS 40 CORNWALL 10

CRUSADERS: 16 Jack Holmes; 5 Patrick Ah Van; 3 Kieran Taylor; 4 Matt Reid; 2 Lloyd Evans; 7 Toby Hughes; 6 Daniel Moss; 8 Ben Evans; 19 Joe Baldwin; 10 Chris Barratt; 24 Cole Oakley; 11 Ryan Ellis; 13 Carl Forster. Subs (all used): 14 Paul Nash; 15 Shaun Costello; 17 Olly Davies; - Jamie Jenkins.
Tries: L Evans (9), Forster (17), Ellis (21, 62), Reid (24), Barratt (49), Moss (52); **Goals:** Moss 6/7.
CORNWALL: 3 Coby Nichol; 2 George Mitchell; 21 Aaron Small; 4 Tom Ashton; 5 Harry Aaronson; 6 Cameron Brown; 7 Adam Rusling; 15 Kaine Dimech; 9 Luke Collins; 18 Matt Ross; 11 Nathan Cullen; 12 Darcy Simpson; 13 David Weetman. Subs (all used): 8 Jacob Bateman; 17 Jamie Gill; 22 Jake Lloyd; 24 Nathan Conroy.
Tries: Aaronson (14), Rusling (42); **Goals:** Brown 1/2.
Rugby Leaguer & League Express Men of the Match:
Crusaders: Carl Forster; *Cornwall:* Adam Rusling.
Penalty count: 7-6; **Half-time:** 22-4;
Referee: Adam Williams; **Attendance:** 755.

OLDHAM 56 WORKINGTON TOWN 0

OLDHAM: 30 Phoenix Laulu-Togaga'e; 5 Mo Agoro; 23 Jack Johnson; 3 Jordan Turner; 29 Kieran Dixon; 6 Danny Craven; 38 Riley Dean; 33 Adam Sidlow; 9 Matty Wildie; 22 Ted Chapelhow; 11 Joe Wardle; 12 Adam Lawton; 10 Pat Moran. Subs (all used): 1 Logan Astley; 8 Craig Kopczak; 15 Josh Johnson; 25 Bailey Aldridge.
Tries: Dixon (11, 52), Lawton (27), Wildie (33), J Turner (36, 60), Laulu-Togaga'e (38), Craven (48), Astley (74), Wardle (77); **Goals:** Dixon 8/10.
TOWN: 27 Zarrin Galea; 18 Henry Hadfield; 3 Chris Taylor; 21 Joe Hartley; 14 Billy Southward; 6 Ciaran Walker; 7 Carl Forber; 8 Jordan Thomson; 9 Matty Henson; 23 Brad Brennan; 25 Tommy Brierley; 12 Jake Bradley; 16 Jack Stephenson. Subs (all used): 5 Ethan Bickerdike; 13 JJ Key; 17 Grant Reid; 19 Connor Saunders.
Rugby Leaguer & League Express Men of the Match:
Oldham: Danny Craven; *Town:* Ciaran Walker.
Penalty count: 4-4; **Half-time:** 28-0;
Referee: Warren Turley; **Attendance:** 2,681.

ROCHDALE HORNETS 32 KEIGHLEY COUGARS 18

HORNETS: 1 Gregg McNally; 22 Lameck Juma; 2 Misi Taulapapa; 3 Myles Harrop; 21 Luke Forber; 31 Mackenzie Harman; 7 Lewis Else; 8 Daniel Spencer-Tonks; 9 Aiden Roden; 10 Luke Nelmes; 11 Ben Forster; 12 Duane Straugheir; 23 Emmerson Whittel. Subs (all used): 16 Jordan Andrade; 17 Ben Killan; 20 Dean Roberts; 30 Tom Ratchford.
Tries: Forber (23), D Roberts (37), Taulapapa (40), Harrop (41), Andrade (44), Else (75); **Goals:** Harman 4/6.
COUGARS: 17 Oscar Thomas; 34 Ben Blackmore; 3 Adam Ryder; 24 Junior Nuu; 5 Billy Walkley; 14 Alex Bishop; 7 Jack Miller; 20 Will Maher; 9 Kyle Kesik; 30 Mitch Revell; 11 Ellis Robson; 16 Josh Lynam; 15 Aaron Brown. Subs (all used): 10 Mark Ioane; 13 Dan Parker; 18 Jordan Schofield; 31 George Flanagan.
Tries: Lynam (27), Walkley (52), Flanagan (65);
Goals: Miller 3/3.
Rugby Leaguer & League Express Men of the Match:
Hornets: Lewis Else; *Cougars:* Josh Lynam.
Penalty count: 7-5; **Half-time:** 16-6;
Referee: Denton Arnold; **Attendance:** 1,474.

QUALIFYING PLAY-OFF

Sunday 15th September 2024

ROCHDALE HORNETS 30 HUNSLET 18

HORNETS: 1 Gregg McNally; 22 Lameck Juma; 5 Misi Taulapapa; 3 Myles Harrop; 21 Luke Forber; 31 Mackenzie Harman; 7 Lewis Else; 8 Daniel Spencer-Tonks; 9 Aiden Roden; 10 Luke Nelmes; 11 Ben Forster; 12 Duane Straugheir; 13 Emmerson Whittel. Subs (all used): 16 Jordan Andrade; 17 Ben Killan; 30 Tom Ratchford; 34 Dean Roberts.
Tries: Juma (13), Else (29, 72), Andrade (34), Forber (37), Harrop (45); **Goals:** Harman 3/6.
Dismissal: Nelmes (80) - high tackle.
Sin bin: Taulapapa (80) - fighting.
HUNSLET: 1 Jimmy Watson; 28 Mackenzie Turner; 5 Alfie Goddard; 4 Jude Ferreira; 31 Jack Render; 23 George Flanagan; 7 Matty Beharrell; 8 Harvey Hallas; 15 Ross Whitmore; 32 Matt Fletcher; 11 Josh Jordan-Roberts; 16 Jordan Syme; 13 Michael Knowles. Subs (all used): 6 Jordan Paga; 17 Lewis Wray; 18 Cam Berry; 26 Ethan O'Hanlon.
Tries: Ferreira (5), Goddard (8), Render (18, 58);
Goals: Beharrell 1/4.
Sin bin: Flanagan (80) - fighting.
Rugby Leaguer & League Express Men of the Match:
Hornets: Myles Harrop; *Hunslet:* George Flanagan.
Penalty count: 9-8; **Half-time:** 20-14;
Referee: Kevin Moore; **Attendance:** 826.

ELIMINATION PLAY-OFF

Sunday 15th September 2024

MIDLANDS HURRICANES 24 WORKINGTON TOWN 22

HURRICANES: 1 Todd Horner; 22 Ryan Johnson; 5 Jason Bass; 15 Aaron Willis; 32 Matty Chrimes; 6 Jake Sweeting; 7 Dave Hewitt; 8 Jon Luke Kirby; 19 Chris Cullimore; 10 Sam Bowring; 11 Tom Wilkinson; 12 Liam Welham; 13 Brad Clavering. Subs (all used): 9 Danny Barcoe; 24 Marcus Green; 36 Jose Kenga; 29 Lewis Peachey.
Tries: Hewitt (7), Kirby (29), Chrimes (70);
Goals: Sweeting 6/7.
TOWN: 1 Jordan Burns; 24 Jonny Hutton; 3 Chris Taylor; 18 Joe Hartley; 27 Zarrin Galea; 6 Ciaran Walker; 7 Carl Forber; 13 JJ Key; 9 Matty Henson; 8 Jordan Thomson; 5 Ethan Bickerdike; 25 Tommy Brierley; 16 Jack Stephenson. Subs (all used): 30 Brad Brennan; 17 Grant Reid; 19 Connor Saunders; 22 Tyler Walton.
Tries: Burns (2, 51), Brennan (32), Bickerdike (41);
Goals: Forber 3/4.
Rugby Leaguer & League Express Men of the Match:
Hurricanes: Jake Sweeting; *Town:* Jordan Burns.
Penalty count: 7-4; **Half-time:** 18-12;
Referee: Matty Lynn; **Attendance:** 323.

QUALIFYING SEMI-FINAL

Sunday 22nd September 2024

KEIGHLEY COUGARS 26 ROCHDALE HORNETS 22

COUGARS: 17 Oscar Thomas; 5 Billy Walkley; 3 Adam Ryder; 11 Ellis Robson; 4 Junior Sa'u; 21 Ben Dean; 7 Jack Miller; 20 Will Maher; 9 Kyle Kesik; 30 Mitch Revell; 12 Lachlan Lanskey; 16 Josh Lynam; 13 Dan Parker. Subs (all used): 10 Mark Ioane; 15 Aaron Brown; 31 George Flanagan; 35 Brad England.

League One 2024 - Round by Round

Hunslet's Ethan Wood beats Keighley's Dan Parker to score during the League One Play-off Final

Tries: Lanskey (4), Lynam (11), Miller (26), Ioane (38); **Goals:** Miller 5/6.
Sin bin: Maher (76) - high tackle.
HORNETS: 1 Gregg McNally; 5 Misi Taulapapa; 22 Jack Darbyshire; 3 Myles Harrop; 21 Luke Forber; 31 Mackenzie Harman; 7 Lewis Else; 18 Deane Meadows; 9 Aiden Roden; 10 Luke Nelmes; 11 Ben Forster; 12 Duane Straugheir; 23 Emmerson Whittel. Subs (all used): 30 Tom Ratchford; 34 Dean Roberts; 16 Jordan Andrade; 17 Ben Killan.
Tries: D Roberts (33), Andrade (50), Forber (65), Harrop (76); **Goals:** Harman 3/4.
Dismissal: Roden (72) - dangerous challenge on Walkley.
Rugby Leaguer & League Express Men of the Match: *Cougars:* Jack Miller; *Hornets:* Gregg McNally.
Penalty count: 5-9; **Half-time:** 22-6;
Referee: Ben Thaler; **Attendance:** 1,037.

ELIMINATION SEMI-FINAL

Sunday 22nd September 2024

HUNSLET 18 MIDLANDS HURRICANES 14

HUNSLET: 23 George Flanagan; 2 Thomas Delaney; 5 Alfie Goddard; 4 Jude Ferreira; 31 Jack Render; 13 Michael Knowles; 7 Matty Beharrell; 8 Harvey Hallas; 15 Ross Whitmore; 17 Lewis Wray; 28 Ethan Wood; 12 Aaron Levy; 16 Jordan Syme. Subs (all used): 6 Jordan Paga; 22 Liam Carr; 26 Ethan O'Hanlon; 32 Matt Fletcher.
Tries: Ferreira (22), Delaney (32), Render (77); **Goals:** Beharrell 3/4.
Sin bin: Flanagan (48) - dissent.
HURRICANES: 1 Todd Horner; 32 Matty Chrimes; 12 Liam Welham; 22 Ryan Johnson; 5 Jason Bass; 6 Jake Sweeting; 7 Dave Hewitt; 8 Jon Luke Kirby; 19 Chris Cullimore; 10 Sam Bowring; 15 Aaron Willis; 11 Tom Wilkinson; 13 Brad Clavering. Subs (all used): 9 Danny Barcoe; 24 Marcus Green; 29 Lewis Peachey; 17 Kieran Moran.
Tries: Clavering (11), Barcoe (48); **Goals:** Sweeting 3/3.
Rugby Leaguer & League Express Men of the Match: *Hunslet:* Matty Beharrell; *Hurricanes:* Brad Clavering.
Penalty count: 7-5; **Half-time:** 12-6;
Referee: Ryan Cox; **Attendance:** 474.

FINAL ELIMINATOR

Sunday 29th September 2024

ROCHDALE HORNETS 26 HUNSLET 46

HORNETS: 1 Gregg McNally; 2 Misi Taulapapa; 22 Jack Darbyshire; 3 Myles Harrop; 21 Luke Forber; 26 Max Flanagan; 31 Mackenzie Harman; 17 Ben Killan; 30 Tom Ratchford; 10 Luke Nelmes; 11 Ben Forster; 12 Duane Straugheir; 23 Emmerson Whittel. Subs (all used): 8 Daniel Spencer-Tonks; 16 Jordan Andrade; 18 Deane Meadows; 34 Dean Roberts.
Tries: Darbyshire (4), Forber (23, 68), Andrade (37), Taulapapa (62); **Goals:** Harman 3/5.
HUNSLET: 23 George Flanagan; 28 Mackenzie Turner; 5 Alfie Goddard; 4 Jude Ferreira; 31 Jack Render; 13 Michael Knowles; 7 Matty Beharrell; 22 Liam Carr; 15 Ross Whitmore; 32 Matt Fletcher; 12 Aaron Levy; 20 Ethan Wood; 16 Jordan Syme. Subs (all used): 8 Harvey Hallas; 17 Lewis Wray; 18 Cam Berry; 26 Ethan O'Hanlon.
Tries: Flanagan (10, 76), Berry (28), Turner (39), Render (43, 46), Ferreira (52), Wood (59);
Goals: Beharrell 7/8.
Rugby Leaguer & League Express Men of the Match: *Hornets:* Ben Forster; *Hunslet:* George Flanagan.
Penalty count: 4-7; **Half-time:** 18-18;
Referee: Scott Mikalauskas; **Attendance:** 428.

PLAY-OFF FINAL

Sunday 6th October 2024

KEIGHLEY COUGARS 6 HUNSLET 20

COUGARS: 17 Oscar Thomas; 5 Billy Walkley; 3 Adam Ryder; 11 Ellis Robson; 4 Junior Sa'u; 21 Ben Dean; 7 Jack Miller; 20 Will Maher; 15 Aaron Brown; 30 Mitch Revell; 12 Lachlan Lanskey; 16 Josh Lynam; 13 Dan Parker. Subs (all used): 31 George Flanagan Sr; 10 Mark Ioane; 8 Lewis Hatton; 35 Brad England.
Try: Flanagan Sr (56); **Goals:** Miller 1/1.
Dismissal: Hatton (72) - dissent.
Sin bin: Flanagan Sr (36) - late challenge.
HUNSLET: 23 George Flanagan Jr; 28 Mackenzie Turner; 5 Alfie Goddard; 4 Jude Ferreira; 31 Jack Render; 13 Michael Knowles; 7 Matty Beharrell; 22 Liam Carr; 15 Ross Whitmore; 32 Matt Fletcher; 20 Ethan Wood; 12 Aaron Levy; 16 Jordan Syme. Subs (all used): 18 Cam Berry; 8 Harvey Hallas; 17 Lewis Wray; 26 Ethan O'Hanlon.
Tries: Wood (14), Turner (31), Render (67);
Goals: Beharrell 4/7.
Rugby Leaguer & League Express Men of the Match: *Cougars:* Jack Miller; *Hunslet:* Matty Beharrell.
Penalty count: 6-10; **Half-time:** 0-12;
Referee: Cameron Worsley; **Attendance:** 1,037.

CHALLENGE CUP 2024
Round by Round

ROUND 1

Saturday 13th January 2024
Clock Face Miners 22 Heworth 20
Doncaster Toll Bar 22 Ashton Bears 20
Fryston Warriors 13 British Army 10
Hammersmith Hills Hoists 56 Medway Dragons 6
Lowca 22 Edinburgh Eagles 28
Oulton Raiders 22 West Bowling 34
Royal Air Force 22 Royal Navy 28
South Wales Jets 4 Stanningley 40
Wests Warriors 28 Newsome Panthers 4
Sunday 14th January 2024
Orrell St James 20 Haresfinch 4

ROUND 2

Saturday 27th January 2024
Clock Face Miners 4 Siddal 38
Doncaster Toll Bar 18 West Hull 40
Fryston Warriors 0 Hunslet ARLFC 66
Hammersmith Hills Hoists 32 West Bowling 10
Hull Dockers 0 Wath Brow Hornets 38
Leigh Miners Rangers 18 Stanningley 19
Lock Lane 72 Edinburgh Eagles 0
Wests Warriors 28 Rochdale Mayfield 22
Sunday 28th January 2024
Orrell St James 12 York Acorn 22
Royal Navy 24 Thatto Heath Crusaders 32

ROUND 3

Saturday 10th February 2024

BARROW RAIDERS 10 OLDHAM 22

RAIDERS: 1 Luke Cresswell; 2 Ryan Shaw; 3 Matty Costello; 17 Brett Carter; 14 Luke Broadbent; 18 Adam Jackson; 7 Ryan Johnston; 8 Greg Burke; 9 Josh Wood; 20 Ramon Silva; 13 James Greenwood; 11 Charlie Emslie; 15 Tom Wilkinson. Subs (all used): 21 Aaron Smith; 31 Harvey Makin; 30 Finn McMillan; 32 Mike Ogunwole.
Try: Greenwood (15); **Goals:** Shaw 3/3.
Dismissal: Broadbent (80) - fighting.
OLDHAM: 1 Logan Astley; 5 Mo Agoro; 24 Ben O'Keefe; 3 Jordan Turner; 23 Jack Johnson; 6 Danny Craven; 7 Jamie Ellis; 8 Craig Kopczak; 9 Matty Wildie; 13 Elijah Taylor; 18 Jay Chapelhow; 12 Adam Lawton; 11 Joe Wardle. Subs (all used): 25 Bailey Aldridge; 10 Pat Moran; 22 Ted Chapelhow; 16 Owen Farnworth.
Tries: O'Keefe (18, 73), Wildie (50), Lawton (60);
Goals: Ellis 3/4.
Dismissal: O'Keefe (80) - fighting.
Rugby Leaguer & League Express Men of the Match:
Raiders: Ryan Johnston; *Oldham:* Adam Lawton.
Penalty count: 9-8; **Half-time:** 10-4;
Referee: Marcus Griffiths; **Attendance:** 1,401.

CORNWALL 10 YORK ACORN 18

CORNWALL: 6 Cameron Brown; 1 Liam Whitton; 3 Coby Nichol; 4 Tom Ashton; 5 Harry Aaronson; 14 Morgan Punchard; 7 Adam Rusling; 8 Josh Hartshorne; 9 Luke Collins; 10 Harry Boots; 11 Nathan Cullen; 12 Darcy Simpson; 13 David Weetman. Subs (all used): 22 Jake Lloyd; 15 Kaine Dimech; 16 Decarlo Trerise; 18 Matt Ross.
Tries: Dimech (33), Rusling (52); **Goals:** Rusling 1/2.
Dismissal: Hartshorne (60) - fighting.
Sin bin: Whitton (25) - fighting; Nichol (77) - high tackle.
ACORN: 1 Matt Chilton; 2 Clayton Shepherdson; 3 Josh Parker; 14 Jordan Potter; 5 Ben Tenge; 6 Antony Chilton; 7 Nathan Hammerton; 18 Eddie Prescott; 9 Alfie Crawford; 10 Chris Rushworth; 11 George Hunt; 13 Jordan Myers; 16 Josh Lord. Subs (all used): 20 Nathan Conroy; 21 Davey Burns; 19 Jack Byrnes; 15 Joe Porter.
Tries: Byrnes (12, 66), Crawford (35); **Goals:** A Chilton 3/4.
Sin bin: M Chilton (6) - professional foul;
Burns (25) - late challenge on Rusling.
Rugby Leaguer & League Express Men of the Match:
Cornwall: David Weetman; *Acorn:* Antony Chilton.
Penalty count: 9-13; **Half-time:** 6-12;
Referee: Kristoff Young.

SHEFFIELD EAGLES 88 NEWCASTLE THUNDER 12

EAGLES: 1 Matty Marsh; 30 Ryan Millar; 21 Ryan Johnson; 4 James Glover; 5 Matty Dawson-Jones; 6 Cory Aston; 19 Izaac Farrell; 8 Eddie Battye; 9 Vila Halafihi; 10 Tyler Dickinson; 23 Bayley Liu; 11 Connor Bower; 18 Aaron Murphy. Subs (all used): 14 Jack Hansen; 16 Blake Broadbent; 17 Mitch Clark; 20 Lewis Peachey.
Tries: I Farrell (15, 38, 60), Murphy (18, 70), Marsh (19, 45), Glover (36, 40, 68), Hansen (48, 57), Halafihi (50, 76), Clark (66); **Goals:** Aston 5/6, I Farrell 9/9.
THUNDER: 1 Joe Bradley; 5 Leo Bradley; 4 George Birch; 15 Tom Siddle; 18 Jacob Rennison; 23 Tyler Hepple; 7 Toby Mallinson; 8 Aaron Harlow-Stephenson; 9 Will Bate; 10 Henry Lowery; 12 Paddy Burns; 58 Dan White; 13 Nathan Newbound. Subs (all used): 57 Nathan Ohimor; 24 Tobias Gibson; 17 Jack Skelton; 14 Olly Bibby.
Tries: Birch (24), Newbound (32); **Goals:** Hepple 2/2.
Rugby Leaguer & League Express Men of the Match:
Eagles: Matty Marsh; *Thunder:* Tyler Hepple.
Penalty count: 9-5; **Half-time:** 34-12;
Referee: Denton Arnold; **Attendance:** 617.

SIDDAL 6 WAKEFIELD TRINITY 70

SIDDAL: 1 Lewis Hosty; 2 Dom Booth; 3 Sam Walsh; 4 Henry Turner; 5 Oli Lewis; 6 Jake Hancock; 7 Christian Ackroyd; 8 Josh Milnes; 9 Jamie Greenwood; 10 Canaan Smithies; 11 Conner MacCallum; 12 Danny Williams; 13 Keenan Ramsden. Subs (all used): 14 Dan May; 16 Adam Horner; 17 Harvey Williams; 18 Dan Rushworth.
Try: Lewis (14); **Goals:** Hosty 1/2.
Dismissal: Lewis (29) - fighting.
TRINITY: 1 Max Jowitt; 2 Jermaine McGillvary; 4 Iain Thornley; 3 Oliver Pratt; 5 Lachlan Walmsley; 7 Mason Lino; 6 Luke Gale; 16 Mathieu Cozza; 9 Liam Hood; 10 Renouf Atoni; 11 Matty Ashurst; 12 Josh Griffin; 13 Jay Pitts. Subs (all used): 15 Caleb Uele; 19 Isaiah Vagana; 21 Thomas Doyle; 22 Jack Croft.
Tries: Pratt (8, 62), Thornley (32), Griffin (43), Gale (46), Doyle (51), Atoni (56), Jowitt (59, 79), Croft (66, 73), Hood (76); **Goals:** Jowitt 11/12.
Dismissal: Lino (29) - fighting.
Rugby Leaguer & League Express Men of the Match:
Siddal: Conner MacCallum; *Trinity:* Caleb Uele.
Penalty count: 4-7; **Half-time:** 6-12;
Referee: Luke Bland; **Attendance:** 900.

Hammersmith Hills Hoists 22 Wests Warriors 12
Lock Lane 6 Hunslet ARLFC 46
Stanningley 4 Wath Brow Hornets 30

Sunday 11th February 2024

BATLEY BULLDOGS 48 WORKINGTON TOWN 18

BULLDOGS: 1 Robbie Butterworth; 2 Dale Morton; 3 Kieran Buchanan; 4 George Senior; 21 Greg Johnson; 6 Ben White; 7 Josh Woods; 8 Adam Gledhill; 9 Alistair Leak; 10 Luke Cooper; 11 Dane Manning; 12 Lucas Walshaw; 25 Brandon Moore. Subs (all used): 14 Oli Burton; 15 Nyle Flynn; 18 Joe Burton; 16 Michael Ward.
Tries: Butterworth (3), Morton (12), Leak (17), Cooper (22), Walshaw (26), White (32), Flynn (39), Buchanan (58), Senior (75); **Goals:** Woods 6/9.
TOWN: 5 Ethan Bickerdike; 2 Dave Eccleston; 3 Chris Taylor; 25 Sean Croston; 24 Jonny Hutton; 6 Ciaran Walker; 28 Jarrod Sammut; 8 Jordan Thomson; 19 Connor Saunders; 22 Tyler Walton; 11 Malik Steele; 12 Jake Bradley; 9 Matty Henson. Subs (all used): 13 JJ Key; 14 Blain Marwood; 16 Jack Stephenson; 17 Grant Reid.
Tries: Reid (43), C Taylor (47), Bradley (68);
Goals: Walker 3/3.
Sin bin: Sammut (63) - late challenge.
Rugby Leaguer & League Express Men of the Match:
Bulldogs: Brandon Moore; *Town:* Ciaran Walker.
Penalty count: 7-4; **Half-time:** 40-0;
Referee: Kevin Moore.

DEWSBURY RAMS 8 YORK KNIGHTS 14

RAMS: 4 Bailey O'Connor; 2 Perry Whiteley; 3 Ollie Greensmith; 22 Marcus Walker; 5 Lewis Carr; 9 Jacob Hookem; 7 Calum Turner; 8 Jimmy Beckett; 20 Curtis Davies; 17 Jackson Walker; 11 Brad Graham; 23 Bailey Dawson; 13 Louis Collinson. Subs (all used): 10 Ronan Dixon; 24 Joel Russell; 26 Jamie Field; 27 Joe Hird.
Try: Whiteley (27); **Goals:** Turner 2/3.
KNIGHTS: 26 Alex Donaghy; 31 Francis Coggle; 23 Myles Harrison; 12 Connor Bailey; 28 Brad Ward; 14 Nikau Williams; 20 Taylor Pemberton; 8 Ukuma Ta'ai; 9 Will Jubb; 15 Jack Teanby; 11 Oli Field; 30 Harvey Reynolds; 13 Jordan Thompson. Subs (all used): 10 Conor Fitzsimmons; 16 Brenden Santi; 19 Josh Daley; 27 Harry Price.
Tries: Field (63), Williams (78); **Goals:** Pemberton 3/3.
Rugby Leaguer & League Express Men of the Match:
Rams: Lewis Carr; *Knights:* Jordan Thompson.
Penalty count: 7-7; **Half-time:** 8-2;
Referee: Michael Smaill; **Attendance:** 824.

BRADFORD BULLS 48 NORTH WALES CRUSADERS 2

BULLS: 24 Aidan McGowan; 21 Jayden Myers; 3 Joe Arundel; 4 Kieran Gill; 5 Jorge Taufua; 6 Lee Gaskell; 7 Jordan Lilley; 17 Eribe Doro; 16 Mitch Souter; 15 Daniel Smith; 12 Chester Butler; 14 John Davies; 19 Sam Hallas. Subs (all used): 9 George Flanagan; 18 Keven Appo; 23 Daniel Okoro; 30 Eliot Peposhi.
Tries: Doro (23), Arundel (28), McGowan (38), Appo (49), Butler (64), Flanagan (67, 78), Gill (72); **Goals:** Lilley 8/8.
CRUSADERS: 1 Owain Abel; 16 Jack Holmes; 3 Kieran Taylor; 4 Matt Reid; 5 Patrick Ah Van; 7 Toby Hughes; 26 Reece Bushell; 8 Ben Evans; 9 Pat Rainford; 10 Chris Barratt; 11 Ryan Ellis; 12 Matt Unsworth; 15 Shaun Costello. Subs (all used): 19 Joe Baldwin; 17 Callum Cameron; 21 Levy Nzoungou; 22 Adam Carr.
Goals: Abel 1/1.
Sin bin: Baldwin (48) - high tackle.
Rugby Leaguer & League Express Men of the Match:
Bulls: Keven Appo; *Crusaders:* Owain Abel.
Penalty count: 11-7; **Half-time:** 18-2;
Referee: Brad Milligan.

HALIFAX PANTHERS 32 WHITEHAVEN 4

PANTHERS: 1 James Woodburn-Hall; 5 James Saltonstall; 3 Zack McComb; 4 Ben Crooks; 2 Greg Eden; 6 Louis Jouffret; 7 Joe Keyes; 8 Adam Tangata; 9 Adam O'Brien; 16 Will Calcott; 11 Ben Kavanagh; 12 Matty Gee; 19 Connor Davies. Subs (all used): 13 Jacob Fairbank; 15 Ryan Lannon; 20 Tom Inman; 23 Gareth Widdop.
Tries: Keyes (3, 20), Jouffret (6), Crooks (13, 75), Saltonstall (78); **Goals:** Jouffret 4/6.
WHITEHAVEN: 1 Edene Gebbie; 22 Oscar Doran; 2 Jake Maizen; 3 Joey Romeo; 5 Curtis Teare; 14 Jake Carter; 6 Jamie Doran; 17 Ross Ainley; 9 Callum Phillips; 10 Guy Graham; 20 Owen McCarron; 21 Rio Corkill; 11 Ryan King. Subs (all used): 13 Dion Aiye; 7 Lachlan Hanneghan; 15 James Newton; 23 Evan Lawther.
Try: Teare (30); **Goals:** Carter 0/1.
Sin bin: King (68) - fighting.
Rugby Leaguer & League Express Men of the Match:
Panthers: Joe Keyes; *Whitehaven:* Owen McCarron.
Penalty count: 6-8; **Half-time:** 22-4;
Referee: Cameron Worsley; **Attendance:** 1,100.

HUNSLET 14 KEIGHLEY COUGARS 22

HUNSLET: 1 Jimmy Watson; 5 Alfie Goddard; 32 Will Adams; 4 Jude Ferreira; 31 Jack Render; 6 Harry Williams; 7 Matty Beharrell; 8 Harvey Hallas; 15 Ross Whitmore; 10 Toby Everett; 16 Jordan Syme; 12 Aaron Levy; 9 Billy Gaylor. Subs (all used): 18 Cam Berry; 19 Spencer Darley; 22 Liam Carr; 30 Jack Coventry.
Tries: Ferreira (15), Beharrell (21), Render (78);
Goals: Beharrell 1/3.
Dismissal: Everett (74) - dangerous challenge.
COUGARS: 1 Brandon Pickersgill; 2 Charlie Graham; 3 Adam Ryder; 4 Junior Sa'u; 5 Billy Walkley; 17 Oscar Thomas; 7 Jack Miller; 20 Will Maher; 15 Aaron Brown; 10 Mark Ioane; 11 Ellis Robson; 12 Lachlan Lanskey; 13 Dan Parker. Subs (all used): 19 Ben Stead; 9 Kyle Kesik; 18 Jordan Schofield; 8 Lewis Hatton.
Tries: Graham (27), Thomas (39), Robson (43, 60), Ryder (70); **Goals:** Miller 0/3, Thomas 1/2.
Rugby Leaguer & League Express Men of the Match:
Hunslet: Matty Beharrell; *Cougars:* Junior Sa'u.
Penalty count: 10-9; **Half-time:** 10-8;
Referee: Andy Sweet; **Attendance:** 817.

ROCHDALE HORNETS 24 MIDLANDS HURRICANES 20

HORNETS: 26 Max Flanagan; 5 Tommy Brierley; 4 Joe Hartley; 3 Myles Harrop; 2 Dan Nixon; 6 Martyn Ridyard; 7 Lewis Else; 8 Kenny Baker; 9 Aiden Roden; 10 Luke Nelmes; 11 Ben Forster; 12 Duane Straugheir; 18 Deane Meadows. Subs (all used): 14 Matty Wilkinson; 16 Jordan Andrade; 17 Ben Killan; 28 Brad Brennan.
Tries: Nixon (14, 27, 63), Hartley (47); **Goals:** Ridyard 4/4.
HURRICANES: 1 Todd Horner; 2 Max Kirkbright; 12 Liam Welham; 4 Ross Oakes; 3 Matt Welham; 23 Callum McLelland; 7 Dave Hewitt; 8 Jon Luke Kirby; 9 Danny Barcoe; 24 Marcus Green; 11 Tom Wilkinson; 15 Aaron Willis; 13 Brad Clavering. Subs (all used): 10 Sam Bowring; 16 Ellis Hobson; 17 Kieran Moran; 18 Elliot Windley.
Tries: Clavering (9), Wilkinson (18), Barcoe (30);
Goals: Hewitt 4/4.
Rugby Leaguer & League Express Men of the Match:
Hornets: Matty Wilkinson; *Hurricanes:* Callum McLelland.
Penalty count: 11-10; **Half-time:** 12-20;
Referee: Matty Lynn; **Attendance:** 411.

SWINTON LIONS 50 WEST HULL 6

LIONS: 1 Dan Abram; 25 Richard Lepori; 28 Brad Hammond; 21 Andy Badrock; 5 Rhys Williams; 18 Jack Stevens; 7 Jordy Gibson; 13 Mikey Wood; 14 Josh Eaves; 10 Gavin Bennion; 11 Gav Rodden; 22 Cole Oakley; 17 Matt Fletcher. Subs (all used): 8 Liam Cooper; 12 Mitch Cox; 15 Daniel Spencer-Tonks; 23 Joe Purcell.
Tries: Abram (5, 44), Badrock (20), Spencer-Tonks (37), Hammond (51), Lepori (59), Eaves (61), Stevens (65), Williams (71, 80); **Goals:** Abram 5/10.

WEST HULL: 1 Mason Palmer; 2 Keiran Masike; 3 AJ Chambers; 4 Leon Stewart; 5 Jay Hampshire; 6 Josh Wood; 7 Elliott Jones; 14 Zeus Silk; 9 Nathan Powley; 18 Oscar Ellerington; 20 Ryan Wilson; 12 Benn Arbon; 13 Ryan Steen. Subs (all used): 10 Robbie Jones; 15 Ben Bradshaw; 16 Kieran Welburn; 17 Scott Howlett.
Try: Wilson (34); **Goals:** Wilson 1/1.
Rugby Leaguer & League Express Men of the Match: *Lions:* Dan Abram; *West Hull:* Ryan Wilson.
Penalty count: 10-8; **Half-time:** 18-6;
Referee: Tara Jones; **Attendance:** 441.

**THATTO HEATH CRUSADERS 0
FEATHERSTONE ROVERS 72**

CRUSADERS: 1 Dan McGahan; 2 Ellis Keppel; 3 Adam Saunders; 4 Dave Pike; 5 Jake Dickinson; 6 Sean Kenny; 7 Ryan Houghton; 8 Max Dudley; 9 Lewis Foster; 10 Louis Paul; 11 Jamie Holroyd; 12 Connor Dwyer; 13 Jamie Tracey. Subs (all used): 14 Connor Dutton; 15 Sam Haynes; 16 Lewis Stewart; 17 Paul Hunt.
Sin bin: Tracey (30) - high tackle.
ROVERS: 1 Caleb Aekins; 19 Manoa Wacokecoke; 3 Josh Hardcastle; 4 Greg Minikin; 5 Gareth Gale; 6 Ben Reynolds; 7 Thomas Lacans; 8 Gadwin Springer; 14 Harry Bowes; 10 Nathan Massey; 11 Brad Day; 17 Brad England; 13 Danny Addy. Subs (all used): 9 Connor Jones; 18 Mo Kamano; 20 Keenen Tomlinson; 22 Dean Roberts.
Tries: Day (3), Wacokecoke (10, 51), Gale (17, 70), Minikin (24), Reynolds (32), Lacans (36, 38, 73), Aekins (59), Addy (68), Jones (78);
Goals: Reynolds 6/6, Lacans 1/1, Bowes 0/1, Hardcastle 1/2, Minikin 0/1, Addy 2/2.
Dismissal: Roberts (79) - dissent.
Rugby Leaguer & League Express Men of the Match: *Crusaders:* Lewis Foster; *Rovers:* Danny Addy.
Penalty count: 4-12; **Half-time:** 0-42;
Referee: Sam Houghton; **Attendance:** 907.

WIDNES VIKINGS 50 DONCASTER 16

VIKINGS: 5 Kieran Dixon; 2 Ryan Ince; 4 Joe Edge; 3 Matty Fleming; 20 Mike Butt; 6 Joe Lyons; 24 Lloyd Roby; 15 Liam Kirk; 9 Matty Fozard; 17 Liam Bent; 11 Rhodri Lloyd; 19 Sam Wilde; 16 Max Roberts. Subs (all used): 7 Tom Gilmore; 13 Nick Gregson; 22 Anthony Walker; 23 Will Tilleke.
Tries: Dixon (12, 73), Roby (18), Ince (34, 43), Fleming (37, 57), Lloyd (66), S Wilde (70), Edge (77);
Goals: Dixon 5/10.
DONCASTER: 17 Josh Guzdek; 22 Misi Taulapapa; 4 Reece Lyne; 19 Craig Hall; 2 Tom Halliday; 24 Watson Boas; 7 Connor Robinson; 8 Keelan Foster; 9 Greg Burns; 10 Suaia Matagi; 11 Sam Smeaton; 12 Alex Sutcliffe; 15 Joe Lovodua. Subs (all used): 21 Tyla Hepi; 3 Brad Hey; 25 Ilikaya Mafi; 26 Jude Thompson.
Tries: Lovodua (2), Lyne (46), Halliday (60);
Goals: Robinson 2/3.
Sin bin: Lovodua (56) - high tackle.
Rugby Leaguer & League Express Men of the Match: *Vikings:* Lloyd Roby; *Doncaster:* Watson Boas.
Penalty count: 11-6; **Half-time:** 20-6;
Referee: Liam Rush; **Attendance:** 788.

ROUND 4

Saturday 24th February 2024

**HALIFAX PANTHERS 50
HAMMERSMITH HILLS HOISTS 4**

PANTHERS: 1 James Woodburn-Hall; 5 James Saltonstall; 17 Ben Tibbs; 4 Ben Crooks; 3 Zack McComb; 6 Louis Jouffret; 23 Gareth Widdop; 16 Will Calcott; 20 Tom Inman; 31 Kevin Larroyer; 11 Ben Kavanagh; 22 Ben Hursey; 21 Olly Davies. Subs (all used): 9 Adam O'Brien; 13 Jacob Fairbank; 15 Ryan Lannon; 24 Sam Campbell.
Tries: Tibbs (8), Crooks (15), Saltonstall (23, 28), Jouffret (40, 70), O'Brien (53), Inman (64), Lannon (78);
Goals: Jouffret 7/9.
HILLS HOISTS: 1 Joel Strasser; 2 Tevita Ruhen; 3 Charlie Beatty; 4 Tom West; 5 Mark Elbourne; 6 Jack Ryan; 7 Luke Morrissey; 8 Harry Wecker; 9 Tom Condon; 10 Jake McLoughlin; 11 Rhys Dixon; 12 Chris Ball; 13 Brody Baker. Subs (all used): 14 Charlie Tyler; 16 Blaise Lomax; 17 Ricc Caligiuri; 19 Ross Peltier.
Try: Beatty (70); **Goals:** Morrissey 0/1.
Sin bin: Caligiuri (52) - high tackle.
Rugby Leaguer & League Express Men of the Match: *Panthers:* Louis Jouffret; *Hills Hoists:* Jack Ryan.
Penalty count: 7-5; **Half-time:** 26-0;
Referee: Brad Milligan; **Attendance:** 900.

York Acorn 32 Wath Brow Hornets 28

Sunday 25th February 2024

BRADFORD BULLS 12 WIDNES VIKINGS 26

BULLS: 24 Aidan McGowan; 21 Jayden Myers; 3 Joe Arundel; 4 Kieran Gill; 5 Jorge Taufua; 20 Billy Jowitt; 7 Jordan Lilley; 17 Eribe Doro; 16 Mitch Souter; 13 Michael Lawrence; 12 Chester Butler; 14 John Davies; 19 Sam Hallas. Subs (all used): 9 George Flanagan; 18 Keven Appo; 15 Daniel Smith; 23 Daniel Okoro.
Tries: Gill (15), Jowitt (58); **Goals:** Lilley 2/2.
VIKINGS: 24 Lloyd Roby; 20 Mike Butt; 3 Matty Fleming; 4 Joe Edge; 2 Ryan Ince; 6 Joe Lyons; 7 Tom Gilmore; 8 Callum Field; 9 Matty Fozard; 31 Dan Murray; 11 Rhodri Lloyd; 19 Sam Wilde; 13 Nick Gregson. Subs (all used): 14 Jordan Johnstone; 17 Liam Bent; 16 Max Roberts; 22 Anthony Walker.
Tries: Lyons (31), Roby (45), S Wilde (65), Edge (78);
Goals: Gilmore 5/5.
Sin bin: Lloyd (17) - high tackle on Davies; Roby (47) - dangerous challenge on McGowan.
Rugby Leaguer & League Express Men of the Match: *Bulls:* John Davies; *Vikings:* Tom Gilmore.
Penalty count: 8-11; **Half-time:** 6-8; **Referee:** Ben Thaler.

BATLEY BULLDOGS 30 ROCHDALE HORNETS 14

BULLDOGS: 1 Robbie Butterworth; 24 John Mitsias; 3 Kieran Buchanan; 4 George Senior; 18 Joe Burton; 6 Ben White; 7 Josh Woods; 8 Adam Gledhill; 25 Brandon Moore; 10 Luke Cooper; 11 Dane Manning; 12 Lucas Walshaw; 17 Luke Blake. Subs (all used): 9 Alistair Leak; 15 Nyle Flynn; 13 James Brown; 20 Dave Gibbons.
Tries: Senior (22), Cooper (26), J Burton (36), Flynn (55), Leak (71); **Goals:** Woods 3/3, D Gibbons 2/2.
HORNETS: 1 Gregg McNally; 5 Tommy Brierley; 22 Lameck Juma; 3 Myles Harrop; 2 Dan Nixon; 6 Martyn Ridyard; 7 Lewis Else; 10 Luke Nelmes; 25 Matty Rudd; 20 Toby Brannan; 11 Ben Forster; 12 Duane Straugheir; 18 Deane Meadows. Subs (all used): 26 Max Flanagan; 16 Jordan Andrade; 28 Brad Brennan; 17 Ben Killan.
Tries: Brierley (13, 39), Nixon (64); **Goals:** Ridyard 1/3.
Rugby Leaguer & League Express Men of the Match: *Bulldogs:* Nyle Flynn; *Hornets:* Lewis Else.
Penalty count: 6-10; **Half-time:** 18-10;
Referee: Michael Smaill.

WAKEFIELD TRINITY 78 HUNSLET ARLFC 6

TRINITY: 1 Max Jowitt; 22 Jack Croft; 23 Romain Franco; 3 Oliver Pratt; 5 Lachlan Walmsley; 24 Myles Lawford; 6 Luke Gale; 8 Josh Bowden; 9 Liam Hood; 15 Caleb Uele; 12 Josh Griffin; 20 Toby Boothroyd; 11 Matty Ashurst. Subs (all used): 10 Renouf Atoni; 13 Jay Pitts; 19 Isaiah Vagana; 26 Harvey Smith.
Tries: Boothroyd (3), Gale (11, 69), Hood (19), Ashurst (22), Walmsley (27, 60), Pitts (32, 43), Lawford (37, 40), Griffin (51, 77); **Goals:** Jowitt 13/13.
HUNSLET ARLFC: 1 Craig McShane; 2 Will Cohen; 3 Josh McLelland; 4 Michael Waite; 5 Tyler Dargan; 6 Jordan Gale; 7 Danny Rowse; 8 Elliot Morgan; 9 Andy Hullock; 10 Jamie Fields; 11 Liam Thompson; 12 Harry Dodd; 13 Ben Shulver. Subs (all used): 14 Matty Scott; 15 Brad Wheeler; 16 Craig Miles; 17 Kieran Webster.
Try: Dargan (7); **Goals:** Gale 1/1.
Rugby Leaguer & League Express Men of the Match: *Trinity:* Max Jowitt; *Hunslet ARLFC:* Craig McShane.
Penalty count: 8-6; **Half-time:** 48-6;
Referee: Matty Lynn; **Attendance:** 2,775.

YORK KNIGHTS 16 SHEFFIELD EAGLES 32

KNIGHTS: 1 Will Dagger; 2 Joe Brown; 3 Jesse Dee; 4 Jimmy Keinhorst; 5 AJ Towse; 6 Richie Myler; 7 Liam Harris; 16 Brenden Santi; 19 Josh Daley; 10 Conor Fitzsimmons; 11 Oli Field; 12 Connor Bailey; 13 Jordan Thompson. Subs (all used): 8 Ukuma Ta'ai; 14 Nikau Williams; 15 Jack Teanby; 30 Harvey Reynolds.
Tries: Santi (6), Keinhorst (31), Dee (69);
Goals: Dagger 2/2, Harris 0/1.
Dismissal: Dagger (36) - headbutt.
Sin bin: Thompson (16) - late challenge, (38) - holding down; Dee (18) - late challenge.
EAGLES: 1 Matty Marsh; 2 Ben Jones-Bishop; 3 Kris Welham; 4 James Glover; 5 Matty Dawson-Jones; 6 Cory Aston; 7 Anthony Thackeray; 8 Eddie Battye; 9 Vila Halafihi; 10 Tyler Dickinson; 26 Alex Foster; 12 Joel Farrell; 13 Titus Gwaze. Subs (all used): 17 Mitch Clark; 18 Aaron Murphy; 23 Bayley Liu; 24 Oliver Roberts.
Tries: Marsh (13), Dawson-Jones (17), J Farrell (39), Battye (50), Jones-Bishop (56), Thackeray (79);
Goals: Aston 4/6.
Sin bin: Welham (30) - holding down.
Rugby Leaguer & League Express Men of the Match: *Knights:* Liam Harris; *Eagles:* Matty Marsh.
Penalty count: 13-15; **Half-time:** 12-16;
Referee: Liam Rush; **Attendance:** 1,280.

KEIGHLEY COUGARS 14 FEATHERSTONE ROVERS 58

COUGARS: 1 Brandon Pickersgill; 22 Codey Downey; 3 Adam Ryder; 2 Charlie Graham; 5 Billy Walkley; 17 Oscar Thomas; 7 Jack Miller; 20 Will Maher; 15 Aaron Brown; 10 Mark Ioane; 11 Ellis Robson; 12 Lachlan Lanskey; 13 Dan Parker. Subs (all used): 21 Ben Dean; 29 Nathan Conroy; 16 Josh Lynam; 18 Jordan Schofield.
Tries: Downey (53), Pickersgill (80);
Goals: Miller 2/2, Thomas 1/1.
ROVERS: 1 Caleb Aekins; 19 Manoa Wacokecoke; 3 Josh Hardcastle; 2 Connor Wynne; 5 Gareth Gale; 14 Harry Bowes; 7 Thomas Lacans; 8 Gadwin Springer; 9 Connor Jones; 25 Jayden Tanner; 11 Brad Day; 17 Brad England; 13 Danny Addy. Subs (all used): 21 Oliver Farrar; 18 Mo Kamano; 20 Keenen Tomlinson; 12 Jack Bussey.
Tries: Lacans (18), Jones (28, 35, 57), Day (32), Wacokecoke (42, 68), Tomlinson (45), Addy (49, 65);
Goals: Lacans 9/10.
Rugby Leaguer & League Express Men of the Match: *Cougars:* Adam Ryder; *Rovers:* Connor Jones.
Penalty count: 5-6; **Half-time:** 2-24;
Referee: Scott Mikalauskas; **Attendance:** 1,477.

SWINTON LIONS 28 OLDHAM 12

LIONS: 1 Dan Abram; 2 Matty Chrimes; 3 Jake Spedding; 4 Jayden Hatton; 5 Rhys Williams; 6 Dec Patton; 7 Jordy Gibson; 13 Mikey Wood; 14 Josh Eaves; 10 Gavin Bennion; 11 Gav Rodden; 12 Mitch Cox; 16 Lewis Hall. Subs (all used): 9 George Roby; 15 Daniel Spencer-Tonks; 21 Andy Badrock; 24 Jordan Case.
Tries: Abram (2), Hatton (13), Hall (57), Spedding (61);
Goals: Patton 6/6.
OLDHAM: 1 Logan Astley; 5 Mo Agoro; 24 Ben O'Keefe; 3 Jordan Turner; 23 Jack Johnson; 6 Danny Craven; 7 Jamie Ellis; 16 Owen Farnworth; 9 Matty Wildie; 18 Jay Chapelhow; 11 Joe Wardle; 12 Adam Lawton; 13 Elijah Taylor. Subs (all used): 8 Craig Kopczak; 10 Pat Moran; 15 Josh Johnson; 22 Ted Chapelhow.
Tries: Craven (38), T Chapelhow (70); **Goals:** Ellis 2/2.
Sin bin: T Chapelhow (70) - pushing.
Rugby Leaguer & League Express Men of the Match: *Lions:* Dan Abram; *Oldham:* Danny Craven.
Penalty count: 7-14; **Half-time:** 14-6;
Referee: Cameron Worsley; **Attendance:** 746.

ROUND 5

Saturday 9th March 2024

SWINTON LIONS 12 SHEFFIELD EAGLES 14

LIONS: 1 Dan Abram; 2 Matty Chrimes; 3 Jake Spedding; 4 Jayden Hatton; 5 Rhys Williams; 6 Dec Patton; 7 Jordy Gibson; 13 Mikey Wood; 14 Josh Eaves; 10 Gavin Bennion; 11 Gav Rodden; 12 Mitch Cox; 16 Lewis Hall. Subs (all used): 9 George Roby; 17 Matt Fletcher; 21 Andy Badrock; 24 Jordan Case.
Tries: Bennion (8), Williams (76); **Goals:** Patton 2/2.
Sin bin: Fletcher (54) - late challenge.
EAGLES: 1 Matty Marsh; 2 Ben Jones-Bishop; 3 Kris Welham; 4 James Glover; 5 Matty Dawson-Jones; 6 Cory Aston; 7 Anthony Thackeray; 8 Eddie Battye; 9 Vila Halafihi; 10 Tyler Dickinson; 26 Alex Foster; 23 Bayley Liu; 13 Titus Gwaze. Subs (all used): 14 Jack Hansen; 24 Oliver Roberts; 18 Aaron Murphy; 17 Mitch Clark.
Tries: Liu (16), Welham (45), Jones-Bishop (55);
Goals: Aston 1/3.
Rugby Leaguer & League Express Men of the Match: *Lions:* Lewis Hall; *Eagles:* Anthony Thackeray.
Penalty count: 7-13; **Half-time:** 6-4;
Referee: Marcus Griffiths; **Attendance:** 412.

WIDNES VIKINGS 14 BATLEY BULLDOGS 18

VIKINGS: 1 Jack Owens; 21 Ollie Brookes; 3 Matty Fleming; 4 Joe Edge; 2 Ryan Ince; 6 Joe Lyons; 7 Tom Gilmore; 8 Callum Field; 9 Matty Fozard; 31 Dan Murray; 11 Rhodri Lloyd; 19 Sam Wilde; 13 Nick Gregson. Subs (all used): 12 Danny Langtree; 14 Jordan Johnstone; 15 Liam Kirk; 16 Max Roberts.
Tries: Lyons (16), Gregson (78); **Goals:** Gilmore 3/3.
BULLDOGS: 5 Elliot Kear; 2 Dale Morton; 3 Kieran Buchanan; 24 John Mitsias; 18 Joe Burton; 6 Ben White; 20 Dave Gibbons; 8 Adam Gledhill; 25 Brandon Moore; 10 Luke Cooper; 11 Dane Manning; 12 Lucas Walshaw; 13 James Brown. Subs (all used): 4 George Senior; 9 Alistair Leak; 15 Nyle Flynn; 16 Michael Ward.
Tries: Buchanan (65), D Gibbons (71), Cooper (76);
Goals: D Gibbons 3/3.
Rugby Leaguer & League Express Men of the Match: *Vikings:* Rhodri Lloyd; *Bulldogs:* Ben White.
Penalty count: 8-6; **Half-time:** 8-0;
Referee: Liam Rush; **Attendance:** 1,067.

Challenge Cup 2024 - Round by Round

Wakefield's Thomas Doyle closed down by Featherstone's Gadwin Springer and Danny Addy

ROUND 6

Sunday 10th March 2024

FEATHERSTONE ROVERS 14 WAKEFIELD TRINITY 10
(after golden point extra-time)

ROVERS: 1 Caleb Aekins; 19 Manoa Wacokecoke; 3 Josh Hardcastle; 2 Connor Wynne; 5 Gareth Gale; 14 Harry Bowes; 7 Thomas Lacans; 8 Gadwin Springer; 9 Connor Jones; 12 Jack Bussey; 11 Brad Day; 17 Brad England; 13 Danny Addy. Subs: 15 Wellington Albert; 18 Mo Kamano; 20 Keenen Tomlinson (not used); 27 Zach Fishwick.
Tries: Wynne (32, 38), Gale (85); **Goals:** Lacans 1/2.
Sin bin: England (24) - fighting.
TRINITY: 1 Max Jowitt; 23 Romain Franco; 12 Josh Griffin; 3 Oliver Pratt; 5 Lachlan Walmsley; 6 Luke Gale; 7 Mason Lino; 8 Josh Bowden; 9 Liam Hood; 10 Renouf Atoni; 11 Matty Ashurst; 13 Jay Pitts; 21 Thomas Doyle. Subs: 15 Caleb Uele; 19 Isaiah Vagana; 26 Harvey Smith; 30 Noah Booth (not used).
Tries: Pratt (48), Franco (58); **Goals:** Jowitt 0/2, Lino 1/1.
Sin bin: Atoni (24) - fighting.
Rugby Leaguer & League Express Men of the Match: *Rovers:* Gadwin Springer; *Trinity:* Oliver Pratt.
Penalty count: 6-7; **Half-time:** 10-0; **Referee:** Ben Thaler.

HALIFAX PANTHERS 62 YORK ACORN 6

PANTHERS: 1 James Woodburn-Hall; 5 James Saltonstall; 3 Zack McComb; 17 Ben Tibbs; 2 Greg Eden; 6 Louis Jouffret; 7 Joe Keyes; 8 Adam Tangata; 20 Tom Inman; 15 Ryan Lannon; 11 Ben Kavanagh; 12 Matty Gee; 19 Connor Davies. Subs (all used): 21 Olly Davies; 22 Ben Hursey; 23 Gareth Widdop; 31 Kevin Larroyer.
Tries: Gee (18, 44, 54), Tibbs (23), Kavanagh (31), Keyes (37, 70), Lannon (63), Jouffret (65), McComb (72, 75); **Goals:** Jouffret 9/11.
ACORN: 1 Matt Chilton; 2 Ben Tenge; 3 Josh Parker; 4 Jordan Potter; 5 Clayton Shepherdson; 6 Antony Chilton; 7 Nathan Conroy; 18 Eddie Prescott; 9 Alfie Crawford; 19 Jack Byrnes; 11 George Hunt; 12 Jordan Myers; 13 Lewis Lord. Subs (all used): 8 Davey Burns; 14 Chris Rushworth; 15 Joe Porter; 20 Nathan Hammerton.
Try: A Chilton (78); **Goals:** A Chilton 1/1.
Sin bin: Prescott (17) - high tackle.
Rugby Leaguer & League Express Men of the Match: *Panthers:* Louis Jouffret; *Acorn:* Lewis Lord.
Penalty count: 7-4; **Half-time:** 22-0; **Referee:** Kevin Moore; **Attendance:** 785.

Friday 22nd March 2024

HULL KR 40 SALFORD RED DEVILS 0

HULL KR: 2 Niall Evalds; 35 Joe Burgess; 1 Peta Hiku; 4 Oliver Gildart; 5 Ryan Hall; 27 Tyrone May; 9 Jez Litten; 8 Sauaso Sue; 14 Matt Parcell; 16 Jai Whitbread; 11 Dean Hadley; 12 James Batchelor; 13 Elliot Minchella (C). Subs (all used): 3 Tom Opacic; 15 Sam Luckley; 17 Matty Storton; 20 Kelepi Tanginoa.
Tries: R Hall (7, 22), Burgess (29), Tanginoa (35), Hiku (50), Storton (57), Evalds (77);
Goals: Litten 5/7, Batchelor 1/1.
RED DEVILS: 1 Ryan Brierley; 2 Ethan Ryan; 3 Nene Macdonald; 4 Tim Lafai; 5 Dean Cross; 6 Cade Cust; 7 Marc Sneyd; 27 Gil Dudson; 9 Amir Bourouh; 17 Jack Ormondroyd; 11 Sam Stone; 12 Kallum Watkins (C); 16 Joe Shorrocks. Subs (all used): 10 King Vuniyayawa; 13 Oliver Partington; 14 Chris Atkin; 15 Shane Wright.
Rugby Leaguer & League Express Men of the Match: *Hull KR:* Jez Litten; *Red Devils:* King Vuniyayawa.
Penalty count: 5-3; **Half-time:** 24-0;
Referee: Liam Moore; **Attendance:** 5,636.

LEEDS RHINOS 6 ST HELENS 20

RHINOS: 1 Lachlan Miller; 4 Paul Momirovski; 3 Harry Newman; 12 Rhyse Martin; 5 Ash Handley; 6 Brodie Croft; 7 Matt Frawley; 17 Justin Sangare; 9 Andy Ackers; 8 Mikolaj Oledzki; 11 James Bentley; 16 James McDonnell; 13 Cameron Smith (C). Subs: 10 Tom Holroyd; 14 Jarrod O'Connor; 15 Sam Lisone; 24 Luis Roberts (not used).
Try: Newman (27); **Goals:** Martin 1/1.
Sin bin: Holroyd (58) - fighting.
SAINTS: 1 Jack Welsby; 5 Jon Bennison; 23 Konrad Hurrell; 11 Sione Mata'utia; 3 Waqa Blake; 6 Jonny Lomax (C); 14 Moses Mbye; 8 Alex Walmsley; 9 Daryl Clark; 10 Matty Lees; 16 Curtis Sironen; 19 Matt Whitley; 13 Morgan Knowles. Subs (all used): 12 Joe Batchelor; 15 James Bell; 18 Jake Wingfield; 20 George Delaney.
Tries: Clark (39), Bennison (59), Walmsley (68);
Goals: Lomax 4/6.
Sin bin: Clark (58) - fighting.
Rugby Leaguer & League Express Men of the Match: *Rhinos:* Rhyse Martin; *Saints:* Moses Mbye.
Penalty count: 6-10; **Half-time:** 6-10;
Referee: Chris Kendall; **Attendance:** 7,108.

WIGAN WARRIORS 44 SHEFFIELD EAGLES 18

WARRIORS: 23 Ryan Hampshire; 2 Abbas Miski; 3 Adam Keighran; 4 Jake Wardle; 5 Liam Marshall; 6 Bevan French; 7 Harry Smith; 16 Luke Thompson; 9 Brad O'Neill; 10 Liam Byrne; 21 Junior Nsemba; 12 Liam Farrell (C); 13 Kaide Ellis. Subs (all used): 15 Patrick Mago; 17 Kruise Leeming; 19 Tyler Dupree; 20 Harvie Hill.
Tries: French (16, 49, 57), Marshall (23, 77), Wardle (41), Leeming (69), Mago (75); **Goals:** Smith 6/9.
EAGLES: 1 Matty Marsh; 30 Ryan Millar; 3 Kris Welham; 4 James Glover; 5 Matty Dawson-Jones; 6 Cory Aston; 14 Jack Hansen; 8 Eddie Battye; 9 Vila Halafihi; 10 Tyler Dickinson; 18 Aaron Murphy; 11 Connor Bower; 13 Titus Gwaze. Subs (all used): 15 Evan Hodgson; 19 Izaac Farrell; 20 Lewis Peachey; 24 Oliver Roberts.
Tries: Marsh (28), Dawson-Jones (36), Hodgson (62);
Goals: Aston 3/3.
Sin bin: Roberts (39) - holding down.
Rugby Leaguer & League Express Men of the Match: *Warriors:* Ryan Hampshire; *Eagles:* Matty Marsh.
Penalty count: 5-10; **Half-time:** 12-12;
Referee: James Vella; **Attendance:** 5,733.

Saturday 23rd March 2024

HUDDERSFIELD GIANTS 50 HULL FC 6

GIANTS: 1 Jake Connor; 2 Adam Swift; 3 Esan Marsters; 4 Kevin Naiqama; 24 Sam Halsall; 6 Tui Lolohea; 7 Adam Clune; 15 Matty English; 9 Adam Milner; 17 Oliver Wilson; 11 Jack Murchie; 22 Harvey Livett; 21 Leroy Cudjoe (C). Subs (all used): 10 Joe Greenwood; 14 Ashton Golding; 16 Harry Rushton; 18 Sebastine Ikahihifo.
Tries: Halsall (3, 26, 62), Naiqama (12, 75), Swift (33, 52, 67, 78), Livett (74);
Goals: Connor 2/4, Lolohea 3/6.
HULL FC: 1 Tex Hoy; 26 Lewis Martin; 5 Darnell McIntosh; 4 Liam Sutcliffe; 2 Liam Tindall; 40 Jack Charles; 19 Morgan Smith; 8 Herman Ese'ese; 7 Fa'amanu Brown; 12 Ligi Sao; 17 Cameron Scott; 24 Nick Staveley; 15 Jordan Lane. Subs (all used): 9 Danny Houghton (C); 11 Jayden Okunbor; 20 Jack Brown; 21 Will Gardiner.
Try: Lane (17); **Goals:** Charles 1/1.
Sin bin: Sao (31) - late challenge on Clune.
Rugby Leaguer & League Express Men of the Match: *Giants:* Jake Connor; *Hull FC:* Herman Ese'ese.
Penalty count: 2-2; **Half-time:** 20-6;
Referee: Aaron Moore; **Attendance:** 1,673.

Challenge Cup 2024 - Round by Round

Hull KR's Dean Hadley tries to break free from Leigh's Tom Amone and Kai O'Donnell

LEIGH LEOPARDS 26 FEATHERSTONE ROVERS 14

LEOPARDS: 22 Keanan Brand; 24 Umyla Hanley; 3 Zak Hardaker; 4 Ricky Leutele; 5 Josh Charnley; 6 Matt Moylan; 21 Ben McNamara; 14 Dan Norman; 15 Matt Davis; 10 Robbie Mulhern (C); 11 Kai O'Donnell; 16 Frankie Halton; 12 Jack Hughes. Subs (all used): 7 Lachlan Lam; 17 Owen Trout; 18 Ben Nakubuwai; 20 Oliver Holmes.
Tries: Hanley (3, 29, 36), Charnley (49), Moylan (51);
Goals: Moylan 3/6.
ROVERS: 1 Caleb Aekins; 19 Manoa Wacokecoke; 3 Josh Hardcastle; 4 Greg Minikin; 5 Gareth Gale; 14 Harry Bowes; 7 Thomas Lacans; 8 Gadwin Springer; 9 Connor Jones; 15 Wellington Albert; 11 Brad Day; 20 Keenen Tomlinson; 13 Danny Addy. Subs (all used): 2 Connor Wynne; 16 McKenzie Yei; 17 Brad England; 28 Paul Turner.
Tries: Wacokecoke (19, 45), Gale (71);
Goals: Lacans 0/1, Addy 1/1, Wynne 0/1.
Sin bin: Yei (35) - dangerous challenge on Trout.
Rugby Leaguer & League Express Men of the Match:
Leopards: Lachlan Lam; *Rovers:* Brad Day.
Penalty count: 9-6; **Half-time:** 14-4;
Referee: Jack Smith; **Attendance:** 4,287.

BATLEY BULLDOGS 14 CASTLEFORD TIGERS 28

BULLDOGS: 1 Robbie Butterworth; 2 Dale Morton; 3 Kieran Buchanan; 24 John Mitsias; 18 Joe Burton; 6 Ben White; 20 Dave Gibbons; 8 Adam Gledhill; 9 Alistair Leak; 10 Luke Cooper; 11 Dane Manning; 12 Lucas Walshaw; 25 Brandon Moore. Subs (all used): 4 George Senior; 14 Oli Burton; 16 Michael Ward; 19 Joe Gibbons.
Tries: Manning (9), Moore (31); **Goals:** D Gibbons 3/3.
TIGERS: 3 Jack Broadbent; 2 Josh Simm; 18 Josh Hodson (D); 12 Alex Mellor; 5 Innes Senior; 16 Rowan Milnes; 7 Jacob Miller; 19 Sam Hall; 9 Paul McShane (C); 13 Joe Westerman; 30 Luis Johnson; 25 Brad Martin; 14 Liam Horne. Subs (all used): 1 Luke Hooley; 8 Liam Watts; 24 Cain Robb; 27 Albert Vete.
Tries: Simm (23), Milnes (26), I Senior (40, 71), McShane (43), Miller (64); **Goals:** Milnes 0/1, McShane 2/5.
Sin bin: Mellor (56) - late challenge on D Gibbons.
Rugby Leaguer & League Express Men of the Match:
Bulldogs: Dane Manning; *Tigers:* Paul McShane.
Penalty count: 7-5; **Half-time:** 14-14;
Referee: Marcus Griffiths; **Attendance:** 2,015.

WARRINGTON WOLVES 42 LONDON BRONCOS 0

WOLVES: 1 Matt Dufty; 2 Josh Thewlis; 3 Toby King; 14 Rodrick Tai (D); 5 Matty Ashton; 4 Stefan Ratchford (C); 18 Leon Hayes; 8 James Harrison; 9 Danny Walker; 10 Paul Vaughan; 28 Adam Holroyd; 15 Joe Philbin; 17 Jordan Crowther. Subs: 13 Matty Nicholson; 16 Zane Musgrove; 19 Joe Bullock (not used); 32 Sam Powell.

Tries: Josh Thewlis (1, 48), Crowther (18), Tai (25), King (31), Ashton (38, 53, 65), Nicholson (73);
Goals: Ratchford 3/7, Josh Thewlis 0/2.
BRONCOS: 1 Alex Walker; 22 Gideon Boafo (D2); 3 Jarred Bassett; 4 Hakim Miloudi; 2 Lee Kershaw; 20 Oliver Leyland; 7 James Meadows; 19 Rhys Kennedy; 9 Sam Davis; 16 Jordan Williams; 21 Robbie Storey; 15 Marcus Stock; 13 Dean Parata (C). Subs (all used): 8 Rob Butler; 26 Jensen Monk; 28 Jack Hughes (D); 32 Joe Stocks (D).
Rugby Leaguer & League Express Men of the Match:
Wolves: Matt Dufty; *Broncos:* Oliver Leyland.
Penalty count: 5-4; **Half-time:** 24-0;
Referee: Tom Grant; **Attendance:** 3,416.

Sunday 24th March 2024

HALIFAX PANTHERS 4 CATALANS DRAGONS 40

PANTHERS: 1 James Woodburn-Hall; 5 James Saltonstall; 3 Zack McComb; 17 Ben Tibbs; 2 Greg Eden; 6 Louis Jouffret; 7 Joe Keyes; 31 Kevin Larroyer; 20 Tom Inman; 13 Jacob Fairbank; 11 Ben Kavanagh; 12 Matty Gee; 19 Connor Davies. Subs (all used): 23 Gareth Widdop; 8 Adam Tangata; 15 Ryan Lannon; 21 Olly Davies.
Try: Saltonstall (80); **Goals:** Widdop 0/1.
DRAGONS: 17 Cesar Rouge; 2 Tom Davies; 21 Matt Ikuvalu; 4 Matthieu Laguerre; 5 Fouad Yaha; 27 Jordan Abdull; 7 Theo Fages; 16 Romain Navarrete; 9 Michael Mcllorum; 10 Julian Bousquet; 8 Mike McMeeken; 12 Paul Seguier; 13 Ben Garcia (C). Subs (all used): 3 Arthur Romano; 14 Alrix Da Costa; 20 Tevita Satae; 23 Jordan Dezaria.
Tries: Davies (1, 6, 14), Seguier (32), Romano (42), Rouge (61), Satae (65); **Goals:** Abdull 6/7.
Rugby Leaguer & League Express Men of the Match:
Panthers: Jacob Fairbank; *Dragons:* Matt Ikuvalu.
Penalty count: 7-7; **Half-time:** 0-24;
Referee: Liam Rush; **Attendance:** 1,811.

QUARTER FINALS

Saturday 13th April 2024

HULL KR 26 LEIGH LEOPARDS 14

HULL KR: 2 Niall Evalds; 35 Joe Burgess; 1 Peta Hiku; 3 Tom Opacic; 5 Ryan Hall; 27 Tyrone May; 7 Mikey Lewis; 8 Sauaso Sue; 9 Jez Litten; 16 Jai Whitbread; 11 Dean Hadley; 12 James Batchelor; 13 Elliot Minchella (C). Subs: 14 Matt Parcell; 17 Matty Storton; 20 Kelepi Tanginoa; 30 Leo Tennison (not used).
Tries: Burgess (8, 46), Tanginoa (52), Evalds (71), Minchella (80); **Goals:** Lewis 3/5.

LEOPARDS: 6 Matt Moylan; 24 Umyla Hanley; 3 Zak Hardaker; 4 Ricky Leutele; 5 Josh Charnley; 21 Ben McNamara; 7 Lachlan Lam (C); 8 Tom Amone; 33 Brad Dwyer; 17 Owen Trout; 11 Kai O'Donnell; 16 Frankie Halton; 12 Jack Hughes. Subs: 14 Dan Norman; 15 Matt Davis; 18 Ben Nakubuwai; 19 Ed Chamberlain (not used).
Tries: O'Donnell (13), Hanley (56); **Goals:** Moylan 3/3.
Rugby Leaguer & League Express Men of the Match:
Hull KR: Tyrone May; *Leopards:* Tom Amone.
Penalty count: 4-4; **Half-time:** 4-8;
Referee: Chris Kendall; **Attendance:** 7,363.

CATALANS DRAGONS 6 HUDDERSFIELD GIANTS 34

DRAGONS: 1 Arthur Mourgue; 2 Tom Davies; 3 Arthur Romano; 4 Matthieu Laguerre; 21 Matt Ikuvalu; 6 Jayden Nikorima; 7 Theo Fages; 8 Mike McMeeken; 14 Alrix Da Costa; 16 Romain Navarrete; 11 Tariq Sims; 12 Paul Seguier; 13 Ben Garcia (C). Subs (all used): 10 Julian Bousquet; 15 Bayley Sironen; 17 Cesar Rouge; 20 Tevita Satae.
Try: Ikuvalu (54); **Goals:** Mourgue 1/1.
Sin bin: Romano (67) - fighting.
GIANTS: 1 Jake Connor; 2 Adam Swift; 3 Esan Marsters; 4 Kevin Naiqama; 20 Elliot Wallis; 6 Tui Lolohea; 7 Adam Clune; 15 Matty English; 9 Adam Milner; 10 Joe Greenwood; 11 Jack Murchie; 21 Leroy Cudjoe; 13 Luke Yates (C). Subs (all used): 14 Ashton Golding; 16 Harry Rushton; 18 Sebastine Ikahihifo; 26 Hugo Salabio.
Tries: Connor (15), Milner (23), Swift (27), Ikahihifo (41), Marsters (48), Naiqama (69); **Goals:** Connor 5/7.
Sin bin: Wallis (67) - fighting.
Rugby Leaguer & League Express Men of the Match:
Dragons: Theo Fages; *Giants:* Jake Connor.
Penalty count: 7-3; **Half-time:** 0-16;
Referee: Aaron Moore; **Attendance:** 5,892.

Sunday 14th April 2024

CASTLEFORD TIGERS 6 WIGAN WARRIORS 60

TIGERS: 3 Jack Broadbent; 18 Josh Hodson; 22 Charbel Tasipale; 4 Sam Wood; 5 Innes Senior; 6 Danny Richardson; 7 Jacob Miller; 30 Luis Johnson; 14 Liam Horne; 26 Samy Kibula; 12 Alex Mellor; 11 Elie El-Zakhem; 13 Joe Westerman (C). Subs (all used): 21 Sylvester Namo; 24 Cain Robb; 25 Brad Martin; 32 Dan Hindmarsh (D).
Try: I Senior (30); **Goals:** Richardson 1/1.
WARRIORS: 1 Jai Field; 2 Abbas Miski; 3 Adam Keighran; 4 Jake Wardle; 5 Liam Marshall; 6 Bevan French; 7 Harry Smith; 16 Luke Thompson; 9 Brad O'Neill; 19 Tyler Dupree; 11 Willie Isa; 12 Liam Farrell (C); 13 Kaide Ellis. Subs (all used): 15 Patrick Mago; 17 Kruise Leeming; 20 Harvie Hill; 21 Junior Nsemba.

Challenge Cup 2024 - Round by Round

Wigan's Bevan French takes on Warrington's Toby King and Josh Drinkwater during the Challenge Cup Final

Tries: Marshall (4, 19, 50, 57), O'Neill (8), French (14), Keighran (24), Miski (45, 69), Leeming (48), Wardle (65), Dupree (78); **Goals:** Smith 6/12.
Rugby Leaguer & League Express Men of the Match: *Tigers:* Liam Horne; *Warriors:* Liam Marshall.
Penalty count: 3-7; **Half-time:** 6-28;
Referee: Liam Moore; **Attendance:** 4,097.

ST HELENS 8 WARRINGTON WOLVES 31

SAINTS: 1 Jack Welsby; 2 Tommy Makinson; 23 Konrad Hurrell; 3 Waqa Blake; 5 Jon Bennison; 6 Jonny Lomax (C); 7 Lewis Dodd; 8 Alex Walmsley; 9 Daryl Clark; 20 George Delaney; 16 Curtis Sironen; 12 Joe Batchelor; 13 Morgan Knowles. Subs (all used): 11 Sione Mata'utia; 14 Moses Mbye; 15 James Bell; 19 Matt Whitley.
Try: Hurrell (26); **Goals:** Bennison 2/2.
WOLVES: 1 Matt Dufty; 2 Josh Thewlis; 3 Toby King; 20 Connor Wrench; 5 Matty Ashton; 6 George Williams (C); 18 Leon Hayes; 8 James Harrison; 9 Danny Walker; 15 Joe Philbin; 13 Matty Nicholson; 12 Lachlan Fitzgibbon; 17 Jordan Crowther. Subs (all used): 19 Joe Bullock; 28 Adam Holroyd; 32 Sam Powell; 34 Max Wood.
Tries: Josh Thewlis (10), Ashton (56), Wrench (61), Harrison (69), Williams (71); **Goals:** Josh Thewlis 5/6;
Field goal: Williams (39).
Rugby Leaguer & League Express Men of the Match: *Saints:* Konrad Hurrell; *Wolves:* George Williams.
Penalty count: 3-5; **Half-time:** 6-7;
Referee: Jack Smith; **Attendance:** 11,280.

SEMI-FINALS

Saturday 18th May 2024

HULL KR 6 WIGAN WARRIORS 38

HULL KR: 2 Niall Evalds; 35 Joe Burgess; 1 Peta Hiku; 3 Tom Opacic; 5 Ryan Hall; 27 Tyrone May; 7 Mikey Lewis; 8 Sauaso Sue; 9 Jez Litten; 16 Jai Whitbread; 11 Dean Hadley; 12 James Batchelor; 13 Elliot Minchella (C). Subs (all used): 10 George King; 14 Matt Parcell; 15 Sam Luckley; 20 Kelepi Tanginoa.
Try: Burgess (51); **Goals:** Lewis 1/1.
Sin bin: Opacic (64) - fighting.
WARRIORS: 1 Jai Field; 2 Abbas Miski; 3 Adam Keighran; 4 Jake Wardle; 5 Liam Marshall; 6 Bevan French; 7 Harry Smith; 8 Ethan Havard; 9 Brad O'Neill; 16 Luke Thompson; 21 Junior Nsemba; 12 Liam Farrell (C); 13 Kaide Ellis. Subs (all used): 15 Patrick Mago; 17 Kruise Leeming; 19 Tyler Dupree; 22 Sam Walters (D).
Tries: Wardle (4, 66), Miski (15, 34), Nsemba (29), Smith (37), Dupree (53); **Goals:** Smith 2/5, Keighran 3/3.
Sin bin: Keighran (64) - fighting.
Rugby Leaguer & League Express Men of the Match: *Hull KR:* Mikey Lewis; *Warriors:* Jake Wardle.
Penalty count: 8-5; **Half-time:** 0-24;
Referee: Chris Kendall; **Attendance:** 11,163
(at Eco-Power Stadium, Doncaster).

Sunday 19th May 2024

HUDDERSFIELD GIANTS 10 WARRINGTON WOLVES 46

GIANTS: 1 Jake Connor; 2 Adam Swift; 3 Esan Marsters; 4 Kevin Naiqama; 20 Elliot Wallis; 6 Tui Lolohea; 7 Adam Clune; 17 Oliver Wilson; 9 Adam Milner; 15 Matty English; 11 Jack Murchie; 21 Leroy Cudjoe; 13 Luke Yates (C). Subs (all used): 14 Ashton Golding; 16 Harry Rushton; 18 Sebastine Ikahihifo; 26 Hugo Salabio.
Tries: Swift (25), Naiqama (62); **Goals:** Connor 1/2.
Sin bin: Connor (68) - interference.
WOLVES: 1 Matt Dufty; 2 Josh Thewlis; 3 Toby King; 14 Rodrick Tai; 5 Matty Ashton; 6 George Williams (C); 7 Josh Drinkwater; 8 James Harrison; 9 Danny Walker; 10 Paul Vaughan; 13 Matty Nicholson; 12 Lachlan Fitzgibbon; 11 Ben Currie. Subs (all used): 15 Joe Philbin; 16 Zane Musgrove; 17 Jordan Crowther; 32 Sam Powell.
Tries: Drinkwater (7), Ashton (9), Walker (18), Williams (34), Dufty (48, 53), Powell (76), Tai (78);
Goals: Josh Thewlis 7/10.
Rugby Leaguer & League Express Men of the Match: *Giants:* Tui Lolohea; *Wolves:* George Williams.
Penalty count: 1-4; **Half-time:** 4-22;
Referee: Liam Moore; **Attendance:** 9,253
(at Totally Wicked Stadium, St Helens).

FINAL

Saturday 8th June 2024

WARRINGTON WOLVES 8 WIGAN WARRIORS 18

WOLVES: 1 Matt Dufty; 2 Josh Thewlis; 3 Toby King; 14 Rodrick Tai; 5 Matty Ashton; 6 George Williams (C); 7 Josh Drinkwater; 8 James Harrison; 9 Danny Walker; 10 Paul Vaughan; 13 Matty Nicholson; 12 Lachlan Fitzgibbon; 11 Ben Currie. Subs (all used): 16 Zane Musgrove; 17 Jordan Crowther; 19 Joe Bullock; 32 Sam Powell.
Try: Dufty (64); **Goals:** Josh Thewlis 2/2.
Sin bin: Dufty (4) - high tackle on Marshall.
WARRIORS: 1 Jai Field; 2 Abbas Miski; 26 Zach Eckersley; 4 Jake Wardle; 5 Liam Marshall; 6 Bevan French; 7 Harry Smith; 16 Luke Thompson; 9 Brad O'Neill; 14 Mike Cooper; 21 Junior Nsemba; 12 Liam Farrell (C); 13 Kaide Ellis. Subs (all used): 8 Ethan Havard; 10 Liam Byrne; 15 Patrick Mago; 17 Kruise Leeming.
Tries: Eckersley (17), French (23), Farrell (57);
Goals: Smith 3/3.
Sin bin: Cooper (2) - high tackle on Josh Thewlis.
Rugby Leaguer & League Express Men of the Match: *Wolves:* Sam Powell; *Warriors:* Bevan French.
Penalty count: 9-4; **Half-time:** 2-12;
Referee: Chris Kendall; **Attendance:** 64,845
(at Wembley Stadium).

1895 CUP 2024
Round by Round

1895 Cup 2024 - Round by Round

ROUND 1

Saturday 27th January 2024

GROUP 3

NEWCASTLE THUNDER 10 YORK KNIGHTS 114

THUNDER: 1 Joe Bradley; 18 Leo Bradley; 3 George Birch; 40 Dan White; 5 James Snowden; 23 Tyler Hepple; 7 Toby Mallinson; 10 Harry Lowery; 9 Will Bate; 8 Aaron Harlow-Stephenson; 12 Paddy Burns; 11 Nathan Rushworth; 13 Nathan Newbound. Subs (all used): 14 Tom Siddle; 15 Jack Skelton; 17 Tobias Gibson; 24 Peter Ryan.
Tries: White (3), Snowden (80); **Goals:** Hepple 1/2.
KNIGHTS: 1 Will Dagger; 2 Joe Brown; 3 Jesse Dee; 4 Jimmy Keinhorst; 5 AJ Towse; 14 Nikau Williams; 7 Liam Harris; 13 Jordan Thompson; 9 Will Jubb; 10 Conor Fitzsimmons; 11 Oli Field; 12 Connor Bailey; 21 James Cunningham. Subs (all used): 15 Jack Teanby; 16 Brenden Santi; 22 Ata Hingano; 30 Harvey Reynolds.
Tries: Dagger (10, 40, 57), Bailey (13, 62, 69, 78), Brown (18, 23), Thompson (26, 71), Williams (28), Field (38), Dee (45, 51), Towse (54, 60, 76), Reynolds (65), Fitzsimmons (74), Harris (80);
Goals: Dagger 8/11, Harris 2/4, Williams 5/6.
Rugby Leaguer & League Express Men of the Match: *Thunder:* Tyler Hepple; *Knights:* Will Dagger.
Penalty count: 2-7; **Half-time:** 6-46;
Referee: Brad Milligan.

Sunday 28th January 2024

GROUP 1

WORKINGTON TOWN 8 BARROW RAIDERS 30

TOWN: 1 Jordan Burns; 2 Dave Eccleston; 3 Chris Taylor; 4 Jason Mossop; 24 Jonny Hutton; 6 Ciaran Walker; 7 Carl Forber; 10 Stevie Scholey; 19 Connor Saunders; 8 Jordan Thomson; 12 Jake Bradley; 11 Malik Steele; 16 Jack Stephenson. Subs (all used): 13 JJ Key; 21 Jake Lightowler; 28 Jarrod Sammut; 22 Tyler Walton.
Tries: Eccleston (71), C Taylor (80); **Goals:** Walker 0/2.
RAIDERS: 1 Luke Cresswell; 2 Ryan Shaw; 3 Matty Costello; 4 Shane Toal; 14 Luke Broadbent; 6 Brad Walker; 7 Ryan Johnston; 8 Greg Burke; 9 Josh Wood; 20 Ramon Silva; 13 James Greenwood; 12 Jarrad Stack; 15 Tom Wilkinson. Subs (all used): 21 Aaron Smith; 16 Max Clarke; 11 Charlie Emslie; 30 Harvey Makin.
Tries: Stack (10, 42), Johnston (23), Clarke (50), Smith (58);
Goals: Shaw 5/6.
Rugby Leaguer & League Express Men of the Match: *Town:* Ciaran Walker; *Raiders:* Jarrad Stack.
Penalty count: 7-10; **Half-time:** 0-12;
Referee: Andy Sweet; **Attendance:** 901.

GROUP 2

KEIGHLEY COUGARS 35 DEWSBURY RAMS 6

COUGARS: 1 Brandon Pickersgill; 2 Charlie Graham; 3 Adam Ryder; 4 Junior Sa'u; 5 Billy Walkley; 21 Ben Dean; 7 Jack Miller; 20 Will Maher; 15 Aaron Brown; 10 Mark Ioane; 11 Ellis Robson; 12 Lachlan Lanskey; 13 Dan Parker. Subs (all used): 19 Ben Stead; 9 Kyle Kesik; 8 Lewis Hatton; 18 Jordan Schofield.
Tries: Dean (14), Pickersgill (26), Lanskey (32), Graham (55, 67), Brown (75); **Goals:** Miller 5/6;
Field goal: Miller (40).
RAMS: 1 Owen Restall; 2 Perry Whiteley; 3 Ollie Greensmith; 4 Bailey O'Connor; 19 Travis Corion; 6 Paul Sykes; 7 Calum Turner; 8 Jimmy Beckett; 20 Curtis Davies; 16 Elliot Morris; 11 Brad Graham; 12 Matt Garside; 13 Louis Collinson. Subs (all used): 10 Ronan Dixon; 27 Joe Hird; 9 Jacob Hookem; 23 Bailey Dawson.
Try: Garside (8); **Goals:** Sykes 1/1.
Sin bin: Sykes (66) - high tackle.
Rugby Leaguer & League Express Men of the Match: *Cougars:* Jack Miller; *Rams:* Ollie Greensmith.
Penalty count: 2-7; **Half-time:** 17-6;
Referee: Kevin Moore; **Attendance:** 839.

GROUP 4

OLDHAM 24 HALIFAX PANTHERS 20

OLDHAM: 1 Logan Astley; 5 Mo Agoro; 24 Ben O'Keefe; 3 Jordan Turner; 23 Jack Johnson; 6 Danny Craven; 7 Jamie Ellis; 8 Craig Kopczak; 9 Matty Wildie; 18 Jay Chapelhow; 11 Joe Wardle; 12 Adam Lawton; 13 Elijah Taylor. Subs (all used): 10 Pat Moran; 16 Owen Farnworth; 22 Ted Chapelhow; 25 Bailey Aldridge.
Tries: Agoro (13, 39), O'Keefe (45), J Turner (57);
Goals: Ellis 4/5.
PANTHERS: 1 James Woodburn-Hall; 3 Zack McComb; 17 Ben Tibbs; 4 Ben Crooks; 2 Greg Eden; 6 Louis Jouffret; 7 Joe Keyes; 10 Dan Murray; 9 Adam O'Brien; 15 Ryan Lannon; 11 Ben Kavanagh; 12 Matty Gee; 13 Jacob Fairbank. Subs (all used): 8 Adam Tangata; 19 Connor Davies; 20 Tom Inman; 31 Kevin Larroyer.
Tries: Eden (33, 48), Woodburn-Hall (54), Tibbs (78);
Goals: Keyes 0/3, Jouffret 2/2.
Rugby Leaguer & League Express Men of the Match: *Oldham:* Mo Agoro; *Panthers:* Greg Eden.
Penalty count: 2-3; **Half-time:** 12-4;
Referee: Michael Smaill; **Attendance:** 1,521.

GROUP 5

HUNSLET 12 FEATHERSTONE ROVERS 62

HUNSLET: 23 Iwan Orr; 1 Jimmy Watson; 5 Alfie Goddard; 4 Jude Ferreira; 31 Jack Render; 6 Harry Williams; 7 Matty Beharrell; 8 Harvey Hallas; 9 Billy Gaylor; 10 Toby Everett; 11 Josh Jordan-Roberts; 12 Aaron Levy; 16 Jordan Syme. Subs (all used): 18 Cam Berry; 13 Michael Knowles; 17 Lewis Wray; 26 Ethan O'Hanlon.
Tries: Render (15), Goddard (65); **Goals:** Beharrell 2/2.
Sin bin: Render (38) - dissent; Knowles (53) - high tackle.
ROVERS: 1 Caleb Aekins; 19 Manoa Wacokecoke; 2 Connor Wynne; 4 Greg Minikin; 5 Gareth Gale; 6 Ben Reynolds; 7 Thomas Lacans; 8 Gadwin Springer; 9 Connor Jones; 18 Mo Kamano; 11 Brad Day; 3 Josh Hardcastle; 13 Danny Addy. Subs (all used): 14 Harry Bowes; 10 Nathan Massey; 22 Dean Roberts; 23 Jack Arnold.
Tries: Gale (9, 75, 80), Reynolds (12), Jones (30, 38), Minikin (31, 40), Arnold (60), Aekins (72), Roberts (78);
Goals: Reynolds 5/6, Lacans 4/5.
Rugby Leaguer & League Express Men of the Match: *Hunslet:* Iwan Orr; *Rovers:* Ben Reynolds.
Penalty count: 6-4; **Half-time:** 6-34;
Referee: Ryan Cox; **Attendance:** 875.

GROUP 6

NORTH WALES CRUSADERS 12 SWINTON LIONS 40

CRUSADERS: 1 Owain Abel; 16 Jack Holmes; 3 Kieran Taylor; 4 Matt Reid; 5 Patrick Ah Van; 7 Toby Hughes; 26 Reece Bushell; 8 Ben Evans; 19 Joe Baldwin; 10 Chris Barratt; 11 Ryan Ellis; 12 Matt Unsworth; 13 Carl Forster. Subs (all used): 9 Pat Rainford; 15 Shaun Costello; 27 Jono Smith; 22 Adam Carr.
Tries: Ah Van (67), B Evans (78); **Goals:** Abel 2/2.
Dismissal: Smith (28) - dissent.
Sin bin: Forster (26) - trip.
LIONS: 1 Dan Abram; 2 Matty Chrimes; 3 Jake Spedding; 4 Jayden Hatton; 5 Rhys Williams; 6 Dec Patton; 7 Jordy Gibson; 10 Gavin Bennion; 14 Josh Eaves; 13 Mikey Wood; 11 Gav Rodden; 12 Mitch Cox; 16 Lewis Hall. Subs (all used): 9 George Roby; 20 Jack Houghton; 24 Jordan Case; 17 Matt Fletcher.
Tries: Eaves (4), Abram (15, 75), Roby (28), Chrimes (33), Patton (54), Cox (59); **Goals:** Patton 6/7.
Rugby Leaguer & League Express Men of the Match: *Crusaders:* Owain Abel; *Lions:* Dec Patton.
Penalty count: 9-6; **Half-time:** 0-24;
Referee: Scott Mikalauskas; **Attendance:** 520.

GROUP 7

MIDLANDS HURRICANES 4 DONCASTER 40

HURRICANES: 1 Todd Horner; 2 Max Kirkbright; 3 Matt Welham; 12 Liam Welham; 5 Jason Bass; 7 Dave Hewitt; 14 Brad Billsborough; 8 Jon Luke Kirby; 9 Danny Barcoe; 11 Tom Wilkinson; 13 Brad Clavering; 15 Aaron Willis; 17 Kieran Moran. Subs (all used): 10 Sam Bowring; 19 Chris Cullimore; 20 Owen Maull; 24 Marcus Green.
Try: Kirkbright (69); **Goals:** Hewitt 0/1.
DONCASTER: 19 Craig Hall; 5 Luke Briscoe; 3 Brad Hey; 4 Reece Lyne; 2 Tom Halliday; 6 Ben Johnston; 7 Connor Robinson; 10 Suaia Matagi; 24 Watson Boas; 20 Brad Knowles; 11 Sam Smeaton; 12 Alex Sutcliffe; 13 Loui McConnell. Subs (all used): 14 Alex Holdstock; 16 Pauli Pauli; 18 Jose Kenga; 23 Jason Tali.
Tries: Halliday (33, 54, 80), Robinson (37), Kenga (46), Pauli (58), Johnston (75); **Goals:** Robinson 6/8.
Sin bin: Pauli (62) - late challenge.
Rugby Leaguer & League Express Men of the Match: *Hurricanes:* Danny Barcoe; *Doncaster:* Tom Halliday.
Penalty count: 11-13; **Half-time:** 0-10;
Referee: Luke Bland; **Attendance:** 180.

ROUND 2

Sunday 4th February 2024

GROUP 1

WHITEHAVEN 12 BARROW RAIDERS 18

WHITEHAVEN: 3 Joey Romeo; 22 Oscar Doran; 4 Will Evans; 21 Rio Corkill; 5 Curtis Teare; 6 Jamie Doran; 14 Jake Carter; 8 Lucas Castle; 15 James Newton; 17 Ross Ainley; 23 Evan Lawther; 12 Connor Holliday; 11 Ryan King. Subs (all used): 7 Lachlan Hanneghan; 9 Callum Phillips; 10 Guy Graham; 13 Dion Aiye.
Tries: Hanneghan (42), King (58); **Goals:** Carter 2/2.
RAIDERS: 1 Luke Cresswell; 2 Ryan Shaw; 3 Matty Costello; 16 Max Clarke; 14 Luke Broadbent; 6 Brad Walker; 7 Ryan Johnston; 8 Greg Burke; 9 Josh Wood; 20 Ramon Silva; 13 James Greenwood; 12 Jarrad Stack; 15 Tom Wilkinson. Subs (all used): 21 Aaron Smith; 11 Charlie Emslie; 31 Harvey Makin; 32 Mike Ogunwole.
Tries: Clarke (23), Costello (67), Greenwood (74);
Goals: Shaw 3/4.
Rugby Leaguer & League Express Men of the Match: *Whitehaven:* Guy Graham; *Raiders:* Ramon Silva.
Penalty count: 9-8; **Half-time:** 0-4;
Referee: Brad Milligan.

GROUP 2

DEWSBURY RAMS 4 BRADFORD BULLS 40

RAMS: 4 Bailey O'Connor; 2 Perry Whiteley; 3 Ollie Greensmith; 18 Davey Dixon; 5 Lewis Carr; 9 Jacob Hookem; 7 Calum Turner; 8 Jimmy Beckett; 20 Curtis Davies; 10 Ronan Dixon; 11 Brad Graham; 23 Bailey Dawson; 13 Louis Collinson. Subs (all used): 6 Paul Sykes; 16 Elliot Morris; 26 Jamie Field; 27 Joe Hird.
Try: Whiteley (29); **Goals:** Turner 0/1.
Sin bin: R Dixon (12) - high tackle on Blackmore.
BULLS: 24 Aidan McGowan; 2 Ben Blackmore; 21 Jayden Myers; 4 Kieran Gill; 5 Jorge Taufua; 6 Lee Gaskell; 7 Jordan Lilley; 17 Eribe Doro; 18 Mitch Souter; 10 Ebon Scurr; 14 John Davies; 12 Chester Butler; 19 Sam Hallas. Subs (all used): 3 Joe Arundel; 9 George Flanagan; 16 Keven Appo; 23 Daniel Okoro. 18th man (used): 30 Eliot Peposhi.
Tries: Gill (3), Arundel (13), Scurr (20), Myers (23), Taufua (34, 47), Souter (37), McGowan (56);
Goals: Lilley 4/8.
Sin bin: Flanagan (61) - fighting.
Rugby Leaguer & League Express Men of the Match: *Rams:* Calum Turner; *Bulls:* Jorge Taufua.
Penalty count: 3-4; **Half-time:** 4-32;
Referee: Andy Sweet; **Attendance:** 1,009.

GROUP 3

YORK KNIGHTS 4 WAKEFIELD TRINITY 40

KNIGHTS: 2 Joe Brown; 23 Myles Harrison; 3 Jesse Dee; 4 Jimmy Keinhorst; 5 AJ Towse; 14 Nikau Williams; 7 Liam Harris; 8 Ukuma Ta'ai; 9 Will Jubb; 10 Conor Fitzsimmons; 11 Oli Field; 12 Connor Bailey; 13 Jordan Thompson. Subs (all used): 15 Jack Teanby; 16 Brenden Santi; 20 Taylor Pemberton; 30 Harvey Reynolds.
Try: Jubb (70); **Goals:** Williams 0/1.
TRINITY: 1 Max Jowitt; 2 Jermaine McGillvary; 3 Oliver Pratt; 4 Iain Thornley; 5 Lachlan Walmsley; 6 Luke Gale; 7 Mason Lino; 8 Josh Bowden; 9 Liam Hood; 10 Renouf Atoni; 11 Matty Ashurst; 12 Josh Griffin; 13 Jay Pitts. Subs (all used): 15 Caleb Uele; 16 Mathieu Cozza; 20 Toby Boothroyd; 21 Thomas Doyle.
Tries: Gale (4), McGillvary (9), Griffin (12), Walmsley (23, 53, 79), Uele (45); **Goals:** Jowitt 6/7.
Rugby Leaguer & League Express Men of the Match: *Knights:* Jimmy Keinhorst; *Trinity:* Lachlan Walmsley.
Penalty count: 4-5; **Half-time:** 0-24;
Referee: Scott Mikalauskas; **Attendance:** 2,817.

GROUP 4

ROCHDALE HORNETS 12 HALIFAX PANTHERS 52

HORNETS: 1 Gregg McNally; 2 Dan Nixon; 21 Luke Forber; 4 Joe Hartley; 5 Tommy Brierley; 6 Martyn Ridyard; 7 Lewis Else; 8 Kenny Baker; 9 Aiden Roden; 10 Luke Nelmes; 19 Connor Ratcliffe; 18 Deane Meadows; 13 AJ Boardman. Subs (all used): 14 Matty Wilkinson; 17 Ben Killan; 11 Ben Forster; 16 Jordan Andrade.
Tries: Killan (56), Nixon (59); **Goals:** Ridyard 2/2.
PANTHERS: 1 James Woodburn-Hall; 17 Ben Tibbs; 3 Zack McComb; 4 Ben Crooks; 2 Greg Eden; 6 Louis Jouffret; 7 Joe Keyes; 8 Adam Tangata; 9 Adam O'Brien; 15 Ryan Lannon; 11 Ben Kavanagh; 12 Matty Gee; 19 Connor Davies. Subs (all used): 20 Tom Inman; 13 Jacob Fairbank; 31 Kevin Larroyer; 23 Gareth Widdop.
Tries: Woodburn-Hall (3), Crooks (8, 18), Eden (30), Tibbs (49), Kavanagh (68), Inman (75), Gee (77), Jouffret (80); **Goals:** Jouffret 8/9.
Rugby Leaguer & League Express Men of the Match: *Hornets:* Luke Forber; *Panthers:* Ben Crooks.
Penalty count: 4-6; **Half-time:** 0-22;
Referee: Ryan Cox; **Attendance:** 1,200.

1895 Cup 2024 - Round by Round

GROUP 5

BATLEY BULLDOGS 15 FEATHERSTONE ROVERS 14

BULLDOGS: 1 Robbie Butterworth; 2 Dale Morton; 3 Kieran Buchanan; 18 Joe Burton; 5 Elliot Kear; 6 Ben White; 7 Josh Woods; 8 Adam Gledhill; 9 Alistair Leak; 10 Luke Cooper; 11 Dane Manning; 12 Lucas Walshaw; 25 Brandon Moore. Subs (all used): 14 Oli Burton; 15 Nyle Flynn; 16 Michael Ward; 21 Greg Johnson.
Tries: Cooper (8), Kear (20); **Goals:** Woods 3/5;
Field goal: Woods (75).
ROVERS: 1 Caleb Aekins; 19 Manoa Wacokecoke; 2 Connor Wynne; 4 Greg Minikin; 5 Gareth Gale; 6 Ben Reynolds; 7 Thomas Lacans; 8 Gadwin Springer; 9 Connor Jones; 10 Nathan Massey; 11 Brad Day; 3 Josh Hardcastle; 13 Danny Addy. Subs: 14 Harry Bowes; 22 Dean Roberts (not used); 18 Mo Kamano; 17 Brad England.
Tries: Minikin (5), Gale (55), Wacokecoke (58);
Goals: Reynolds 1/3.
Sin bin: Addy (17) - late challenge; Minikin (78) - high tackle.
Rugby Leaguer & League Express Men of the Match:
Bulldogs: Josh Woods; *Rovers:* Ben Reynolds.
Penalty count: 8-11; **Half-time:** 12-6;
Referee: Cameron Worsley; **Attendance:** 784.

GROUP 6

SWINTON LIONS 18 WIDNES VIKINGS 6

LIONS: 1 Dan Abram; 2 Matty Chrimes; 3 Jake Spedding; 4 Jayden Hatton; 5 Rhys Williams; 6 Dec Patton; 7 Jordy Gibson; 10 Gavin Bennion; 14 Josh Eaves; 20 Jack Houghton; 11 Gav Rodden; 12 Mitch Cox; 16 Lewis Hall. Subs (all used): 9 George Roby; 8 Liam Cooper; 21 Andy Badrock; 24 Jordan Case.
Tries: Williams (9), Chrimes (55), Gibson (63);
Goals: Patton 3/4.
Sin bin: Roby (30) - use of the knees; Eaves (70) - fighting.
VIKINGS: 24 Lloyd Roby; 20 Mike Butt; 3 Matty Fleming; 4 Joe Edge; 5 Kieran Dixon; 6 Joe Lyons; 7 Tom Gilmore; 22 Anthony Walker; 14 Jordan Johnstone; 8 Callum Field; 11 Rhodri Lloyd; 19 Sam Wilde; 13 Nick Gregson. Subs (all used): 9 Matty Fozard; 15 Liam Kirk; 16 Max Roberts; 28 Tom Whitehead.
Try: Dixon (40); **Goals:** Dixon 1/2.
Sin bin: Johnstone (70) - fighting.
Rugby Leaguer & League Express Men of the Match:
Lions: Dec Patton; *Vikings:* Tom Gilmore.
Penalty count: 6-12; **Half-time:** 4-4;
Referee: Michael Smaill; **Attendance:** 1,006.

GROUP 7

DONCASTER 18 SHEFFIELD EAGLES 22

DONCASTER: 17 Josh Guzdek; 5 Luke Briscoe; 3 Brad Hey; 23 Jason Tali; 2 Tom Halliday; 7 Connor Robinson; 4 Alex Holdstock; 15 Joe Lovodua; 10 Suaia Matagi; 11 Sam Smeaton; 12 Alex Sutcliffe; 27 Brett Ferres. Subs (all used): 8 Keelan Foster; 16 Pauli Pauli; 21 Tyla Hepi; 24 Watson Boas.
Tries: Sutcliffe (34), Johnston (59), Lovodua (62);
Goals: Robinson 3/3.
Sin bin: Smeaton (18) - high tackle.
EAGLES: 14 Jack Hansen; 2 Ben Jones-Bishop; 3 Kris Welham; 4 James Glover; 5 Matty Dawson-Jones; 6 Cory Aston; 7 Anthony Thackeray; 8 Eddie Battye; 9 Vila Halafihi; 17 Mitch Clark; 26 Alex Foster; 12 Joel Farrell; 13 Titus Gwaze. Subs (all used): 22 Kyle Wood; 24 Oliver Roberts; 23 Bayley Liu; 15 Evan Hodgson.
Tries: Gwaze (27), Roberts (42, 55), Hodgson (44);
Goals: Aston 3/5.
Sin bin: Hodgson (33) - high tackle.
Rugby Leaguer & League Express Men of the Match:
Doncaster: Ben Johnston; *Eagles:* Titus Gwaze.
Penalty count: 11-12; **Half-time:** 6-8;
Referee: Kevin Moore; **Attendance:** 784.

ROUND 3

Sunday 18th February 2024

GROUP 1

WORKINGTON TOWN 22 WHITEHAVEN 28

TOWN: 1 Jordan Burns; 2 Dave Eccleston; 3 Chris Taylor; 5 Ethan Bickerdike; 24 Jonny Hutton; 7 Carl Forber; 28 Jarrod Sammut; 10 Stevie Scholey; 19 Connor Saunders; 8 Jordan Thomson; 11 Malik Steele; 12 Jake Bradley; 9 Harry Henson. Subs (all used): 13 JJ Key; 14 Blain Marwood; 22 Tyler Walton; 26 Luke Charlton.
Tries: Scholey (5), Eccleston (12), Sammut (23), Henson (44); **Goals:** Forber 3/4.
WHITEHAVEN: 1 Edene Gebbie; 2 Jake Maizen; 4 Will Evans; 5 Curtis Teare; 3 Joey Romeo; 14 Jake Carter; 7 Lachlan Hanneghan; 8 Lucas Castle; 15 James Newton; 17 Ross Ainley; 20 Owen McCarron; 23 Evan Lawther; 11 Ryan King. Subs (all used): 9 Callum Phillips; 10 Guy Graham; 13 Dion Aiye; 21 Rio Corkill.
Tries: Maizen (21, 35), Corkill (49), Romeo (54), Carter (59);
Goals: Carter 4/5.
Rugby Leaguer & League Express Men of the Match:
Town: Jonny Hutton; *Whitehaven:* Jake Carter.
Penalty count: 6-3; **Half-time:** 16-12;
Referee: Ryan Cox; **Attendance:** 1,476.

GROUP 2

KEIGHLEY COUGARS 18 BRADFORD BULLS 26

COUGARS: 1 Brandon Pickersgill; 2 Charlie Graham; 3 Adam Ryder, 5 Billy Walkley; 17 Oscar Thomas; 7 Jack Miller; 20 Will Maher; 15 Aaron Brown; 10 Mark Ioane; 11 Ellis Robson; 12 Lachlan Lanskey; 13 Dan Parker. Subs (all used): 9 Kyle Kesik; 16 Josh Lynam; 18 Jordan Schofield; 19 Ben Stead.
Tries: Lanskey (30), Graham (65), Ioane (70);
Goals: Miller 3/3.
BULLS: 24 Aidan McGowan; 21 Jayden Myers; 3 Joe Arundel; 4 Kieran Gill; 5 Jorge Taufua; 20 Billy Jowitt; 7 Jordan Lilley; 17 Eribe Doro; 16 Mitch Souter; 13 Michael Lawrence; 12 Chester Butler; 14 John Davies; 19 Sam Hallas. Subs (all used): 9 George Flanagan; 18 Keven Appo; 23 Daniel Okoro; 15 Daniel Smith.
Tries: Hallas (10), McGowan (36), Taufua (39), Lilley (44), Appo (46); **Goals:** Lilley 3/5.
Rugby Leaguer & League Express Men of the Match:
Cougars: Mark Ioane; *Bulls:* Aidan McGowan.
Penalty count: 11-6; **Half-time:** 6-16;
Referee: Cameron Worsley; **Attendance:** 3,729.

GROUP 3

NEWCASTLE THUNDER 0 WAKEFIELD TRINITY 110

THUNDER: 1 Joe Bradley; 5 Leo Bradley; 4 Matthew Handy; 40 Tom Siddle; 2 Luke Jeremy; 23 Tyler Hepple; 7 Toby Mallinson; 8 Harry Lowery; 9 Will Bate; 10 Aaron Harlow-Stephenson; 12 Paddy Burns; 59 Dan White; 13 Nathan Newbound. Subs (all used): 24 Tobias Gibson; 17 Jack Skelton; 14 Olly Bibby; 58 Lloyd Hall.
TRINITY: 1 Max Jowitt; 5 Lachlan Walmsley; 22 Jack Croft; 3 Oliver Pratt; 23 Romain Franco; 24 Myles Lawford; 7 Mason Lino; 8 Josh Bowden; 9 Liam Hood; 10 Renouf Atoni; 20 Toby Boothroyd; 13 Jay Pitts; 16 Mathieu Cozza. Subs: 26 Harvey Smith; 15 Caleb Uele; 11 Matty Ashurst (not used); 30 Noah Booth.
Tries: Lino (1, 27, 37), Franco (6, 9, 49, 64), Pitts (14, 23), Walmsley (25), Booth (30), Boothroyd (33, 60), Cozza (39, 53), Pratt (42), Smith (45), Atoni (56), Croft (78); **Goals:** Jowitt 4/5, Lino 13/14.
Rugby Leaguer & League Express Men of the Match:
Thunder: Tyler Hepple; *Trinity:* Mason Lino.
Penalty count: 1-6; **Half-time:** 0-64;
Referee: Aaryn Belafonte; **Attendance:** 1,378
(at Millennium Stadium, Featherstone).

GROUP 4

OLDHAM 38 ROCHDALE HORNETS 12

OLDHAM: 1 Logan Astley; 5 Mo Agoro; 24 Ben O'Keefe; 3 Jordan Turner, 23 Jack Johnson; 6 Danny Craven; 7 Jamie Ellis; 8 Craig Kopczak; 9 Matty Wildie; 18 Jay Chapelhow; 11 Joe Wardle; 12 Adam Lawton; 13 Elijah Taylor. Subs (all used): 22 Ted Chapelhow; 10 Pat Moran; 16 Owen Farnworth; 25 Bailey Aldridge.
Tries: J Turner (7), Craven (11), Jack Johnson (22), Lawton (26), Astley (33), T Chapelhow (45), Agoro (56);
Goals: Ellis 5/7.
Sin bin: Lawton (68) - late challenge.
HORNETS: 26 Max Flanagan; 23 Callum Hughes; 3 Myles Harrop; 27 Joe Coope-Franklin; 5 Tommy Brierley; 7 Lewis Else; 25 Matty Rudd; 17 Ben Kilian; 22 Kyle Huish; 10 Luke Nelmes; 11 Ben Forster; 18 Deane Meadows; 20 Toby Brannan. Subs (all used): 14 Matty Wilkinson; 24 Jaden Dayes; 8 Kenny Baker; 16 Jordan Andrade.
Tries: Andrade (42), Baker (53); **Goals:** Rudd 2/2.
Rugby Leaguer & League Express Men of the Match:
Oldham: Jordan Turner; *Hornets:* Lewis Else.
Penalty count: 10-7; **Half-time:** 26-0;
Referee: Kevin Moore; **Attendance:** 1,662.

GROUP 5

HUNSLET 0 BATLEY BULLDOGS 36

HUNSLET: 1 Jimmy Watson; 2 Dan McGrath; 27 Nathan Carter; 4 Jude Ferreira; 5 Alfie Goddard; 6 Harry Williams; 7 Matty Beharrell; 8 Harvey Hallas; 15 Ross Whitmore; 10 Toby Everett; 16 Jordan Syme; 33 Luke Mearns; 9 Billy Gaylor. Subs (all used): 18 Cam Berry; 19 Spencer Darley; 21 Brandan Wilkinson; 30 Jack Coventry.
BULLDOGS: 1 Robbie Butterworth; 2 Dale Morton; 3 Kieran Buchanan; 4 George Senior; 18 Joe Burton; 6 Ben White; 7 Josh Woods; 8 Adam Gledhill; 9 Alistair Leak; 10 Luke Cooper; 11 Dane Manning; 12 Lucas Walshaw; 25 Brandon Moore. Subs (all used): 13 James Brown; 14 Oli Burton; 15 Nyle Flynn; 16 Michael Ward.
Tries: J Burton (12, 31, 64), White (17), Manning (47), Senior (50), Brown (61); **Goals:** Woods 4/7.
Rugby Leaguer & League Express Men of the Match:
Hunslet: Matty Beharrell; *Bulldogs:* Robbie Butterworth.
Penalty count: 4-2; **Half-time:** 0-14;
Referee: Scott Mikalauskas; **Attendance:** 700.

GROUP 6

NORTH WALES CRUSADERS 14 WIDNES VIKINGS 30

CRUSADERS: 1 Owain Abel; 5 Patrick Ah Van; 4 Matt Reid; 23 Zac Bardsley-Rowe; 16 Jack Holmes; 19 Alex Deery; 7 Toby Hughes; 8 Ben Evans; 9 Pat Rainford; 10 Chris Barratt; 3 Kieran Taylor; 11 Ryan Ellis; 15 Shaun Costello. Subs (all used): 14 Paul Nash; 17 Callum Cameron; 21 Lucas Green; 21 Levy Nzoungou.
Tries: Reid (1), Ah Van (6, 56); **Goals:** Abel 1/3.
VIKINGS: 24 Lloyd Roby; 2 Ryan Ince; 3 Matty Fleming; 4 Joe Edge; 20 Mike Butt; 6 Joe Lyons; 7 Tom Gilmore; 22 Anthony Walker; 9 Matty Fozard; 16 Max Roberts; 11 Rhodri Lloyd; 19 Sam Wilde; 28 Tom Whitehead. Subs (all used): 14 Jordan Johnstone; 23 Will Tilleke; 27 Joe Bullock; 31 Max Wood.
Tries: Edge (18), Roby (22), Fozard (25), Butt (37), Lyons (46), Wood (70); **Goals:** Edge 1/4, Gilmore 2/2.
Rugby Leaguer & League Express Men of the Match:
Crusaders: Lucas Green; *Vikings:* Joe Bullock.
Penalty count: 10-8; **Half-time:** 10-18;
Referee: Matty Lynn; **Attendance:** 1,088.

GROUP 7

MIDLANDS HURRICANES 16 SHEFFIELD EAGLES 30

HURRICANES: 1 Todd Horner; 25 Inoke Nakoronivalu; 4 Ross Oakes; 3 Matt Welham; 26 Joe Varo; 14 Brad Billsborough; 7 Dave Hewitt; 8 John Ray Kirby; 19 Chris Cullimore; 24 Marcus Green; 15 Aaron Willis; 11 Tom Wilkinson; 20 Owen Maull. Subs (all used): 10 Sam Bowring; 16 Ellis Hobson; 18 Elliot Windley; 27 Peceli Suguvanua.
Tries: Nakoronivalu (60), Varo (63), Oakes (75);
Goals: Hewitt 2/3.
Sin bin: M Welham (24) - fighting.
EAGLES: 1 Matty Marsh; 30 Ryan Millar; 21 Ryan Johnson; 23 Bayley Liu; 5 Matty Dawson-Jones; 6 Cory Aston; 19 Izaac Farrell; 20 Lewis Peachey; 22 Kyle Wood; 10 Tyler Dickinson; 24 Oliver Roberts; 12 Joel Farrell; 13 Titus Gwaze. Subs (all used): 11 Connor Bower; 17 Mitch Clark; 18 Aaron Murphy; 26 Alex Foster.
Tries: Marsh (4, 78), Millar (11), Liu (31), Roberts (48), Johnson (52); **Goals:** Aston 3/6.
Sin bin: J Farrell (24) - fighting.
Rugby Leaguer & League Express Men of the Match:
Hurricanes: Dave Hewitt; *Eagles:* Matty Marsh.
Penalty count: 7-7; **Half-time:** 0-14;
Referee: Michael Smaill; **Attendance:** 345.

GROUP 1

	P	W	D	L	F	A	D	Pts
Barrow Raiders	2	2	0	0	48	20	28	4
Whitehaven	2	1	0	1	40	40	0	2
Workington Town	2	0	0	2	30	58	-28	0

GROUP 2

	P	W	D	L	F	A	D	Pts
Bradford Bulls	2	2	0	0	66	22	44	4
Keighley Cougars	2	1	0	1	53	32	21	2
Dewsbury Rams	2	0	0	2	10	75	-65	0

GROUP 3

	P	W	D	L	F	A	D	Pts
Wakefield Trinity	2	2	0	0	150	4	146	4
York Knights	2	1	0	1	118	50	68	2
Newcastle Thunder	2	0	0	2	10	224	-214	0

GROUP 4

	P	W	D	L	F	A	D	Pts
Oldham	2	2	0	0	62	32	30	4
Halifax Panthers	2	1	0	1	72	36	36	2
Rochdale Hornets	2	0	0	2	24	90	-66	0

1895 Cup 2024 - Round by Round

GROUP 5

	P	W	D	L	F	A	D	Pts
Batley Bulldogs	2	2	0	0	51	14	37	4
Featherstone Rovers	2	1	0	1	76	27	49	2
Hunslet	2	0	0	2	12	98	-86	0

GROUP 6

	P	W	D	L	F	A	D	Pts
Swinton Lions	2	2	0	0	58	18	40	4
Widnes Vikings	2	1	0	1	36	32	4	2
North Wales Crusaders	2	0	0	2	26	70	-44	0

GROUP 7

	P	W	D	L	F	A	D	Pts
Sheffield Eagles	2	2	0	0	52	34	18	4
Doncaster	2	1	0	1	58	26	32	2
Midlands Hurricanes	2	0	0	2	20	70	-50	0

QUARTER FINALS

Saturday 2nd March 2024

WAKEFIELD TRINITY 30 BARROW RAIDERS 12

TRINITY: 1 Max Jowitt; 23 Romain Franco; 12 Josh Griffin; 3 Oliver Pratt; 5 Lachlan Walmsley; 24 Myles Lawford; 6 Luke Gale; 8 Josh Bowden; 9 Liam Hood; 10 Renouf Atoni; 11 Matty Ashurst; 19 Isaiah Vagana; 13 Jay Pitts. Subs (all used): 15 Caleb Uele; 16 Mathieu Cozza; 26 Harvey Smith; 30 Noah Booth.
Tries: Atoni (2, 68), Jowitt (5), Griffin (35), Smith (78); **Goals:** Jowitt 5/5.
RAIDERS: 1 Luke Cresswell; 2 Ryan Shaw; 3 Matty Costello; 4 Shane Toal; 30 Max Anderson-Moore; 6 Brad Walker; 7 Ryan Johnston; 22 Tom Walker; 9 Josh Wood; 20 Ramon Silva; 16 Max Clarke; 11 Charlie Emslie; 15 Tom Wilkinson. Subs (all used): 8 Greg Burke; 21 Aaron Smith; 31 Harvey Makin; 33 Delaine Bedward-Gittens.
Tries: Anderson-Moore (53, 73); **Goals:** Shaw 2/2.
Rugby Leaguer & League Express Men of the Match: *Trinity:* Renouf Atoni; *Raiders:* Max Clarke.
Penalty count: 6-8; **Half-time:** 18-0;
Referee: Liam Rush; **Attendance:** 1,809.

Sunday 3rd March 2024

BRADFORD BULLS 21 SWINTON LIONS 12

BULLS: 24 Aidan McGowan; 21 Jayden Myers; 26 Keanan Brand; 4 Kieran Gill; 5 Jorge Taufua; 6 Lee Gaskell; 7 Jordan Lilley; 13 Michael Lawrence; 25 Corey Johnson; 15 Daniel Smith; 12 Chester Butler; 3 Joe Arundel; 14 John Davies. Subs (all used): 9 George Flanagan; 16 Keven Appo; 19 Sam Hallas; 23 Daniel Okoro.
Tries: Butler (6), Lilley (54), Gill (78); **Goals:** Lilley 4/4; **Field goal:** Lilley (33).
Sin bin: Arundel (28) - professional foul.
LIONS: 1 Dan Abram; 2 Matty Chrimes; 3 Jake Spedding; 4 Jayden Hatton; 5 Rhys Williams; 6 Dec Patton; 7 Jordy Gibson; 13 Mikey Wood; 14 Josh Eaves; 10 Gavin Bennion; 11 Gav Rodden; 12 Mitch Cox; 16 Lewis Hall. Subs (all used): 9 George Roby; 8 Liam Cooper; 17 Matt Fletcher; 21 Andy Badrock.
Tries: Spedding (36), Abram (70); **Goals:** Patton 2/2.
Rugby Leaguer & League Express Men of the Match: *Bulls:* Jordan Lilley; *Lions:* Jordy Gibson.
Penalty count: 7-11; **Half-time:** 9-6;
Referee: Scott Mikalauskas; **Attendance:** 1,018.

SHEFFIELD EAGLES 26 BATLEY BULLDOGS 10

EAGLES: 1 Matty Marsh; 2 Ben Jones-Bishop; 3 Kris Welham; 4 James Glover; 5 Matty Dawson-Jones; 6 Cory Aston; 7 Anthony Thackeray; 8 Eddie Battye; 9 Vila Halafihi; 10 Tyler Dickinson; 26 Alex Foster; 12 Joel Farrell; 13 Titus Gwaze. Subs (all used): 14 Jack Hansen; 17 Mitch Clark; 23 Bayley Liu; 24 Oliver Roberts.
Tries: Jones-Bishop (5), J Farrell (17), Welham (54), Hansen (75); **Goals:** Aston 5/5.
BULLDOGS: 1 Robbie Butterworth; 5 Elliot Kear; 3 Kieran Buchanan; 4 George Senior; 18 Joe Burton; 6 Ben White; 7 Josh Woods; 8 Adam Gledhill; 9 Alistair Leak; 10 Luke Cooper; 11 Dane Manning; 12 Lucas Walshaw; 25 Brandon Moore. Subs (all used): 13 James Brown; 15 Nyle Flynn; 16 Michael Ward; 14 Oli Burton.
Tries: White (30), Buchanan (65); **Goals:** Woods 1/2.
Rugby Leaguer & League Express Men of the Match: *Eagles:* Titus Gwaze; *Bulldogs:* Kieran Buchanan.
Penalty count: 5-5; **Half-time:** 12-6;
Referee: Marcus Griffiths; **Attendance:** 727.

Wakefield's Mason Lino, Renouf Atoni and Thomas Doyle wrap up Sheffield's Jesse Sene-Lefao during the 1895 Cup Final

YORK KNIGHTS 46 OLDHAM 12

KNIGHTS: 1 Will Dagger; 28 Brad Ward; 23 Myles Harrison; 4 Jimmy Keinhorst; 5 AJ Towse; 6 Richie Myler; 7 Liam Harris; 8 Ukuma Ta'ai; 9 Will Jubb; 10 Conor Fitzsimmons; 3 Jesse Dee; 12 Connor Bailey; 13 Jordan Thompson. Subs: 14 Nikau Williams; 15 Jack Teanby; 19 Josh Daley; 30 Harvey Reynolds (not used).
Tries: Harrison (6), Harris (13), Dagger (16, 25), Myler (28, 37), Fitzsimmons (55), Towse (74);
Goals: Dagger 7/8.
OLDHAM: 1 Logan Astley; 27 Cian Tyrer; 24 Ben O'Keefe; 3 Jordan Turner; 21 Mackenzie Turner; 6 Danny Craven; 7 Jamie Ellis; 16 Owen Farnworth; 25 Bailey Aldridge; 18 Jay Chapelhow; 12 Adam Lawton; 11 Joe Wardle; 9 Matty Wildie. Subs (all used): 14 Jordan Paga; 15 Josh Johnson; 22 Ted Chapelhow; 23 Jack Johnson.
Tries: Astley (32), Farnworth (67); **Goals:** Ellis 2/2.
Rugby Leaguer & League Express Men of the Match: *Knights:* Richie Myler; *Oldham:* Cian Tyrer.
Penalty count: 7-4; **Half-time:** 34-6;
Referee: Ben Thaler; **Attendance:** 1,048.

SEMI-FINALS

Sunday 12th May 2024

BRADFORD BULLS 14 WAKEFIELD TRINITY 40

BULLS: 24 Aidan McGowan; 21 Jayden Myers; 3 Joe Arundel; 4 Kieran Gill; 5 Jorge Taufua; 1 Tom Holmes; 7 Jordan Lilley; 19 Eribe Doro; 18 Mitch Souter; 13 Michael Lawrence; 28 Harvey Wilson; 29 Zac Fulton; 14 John Davies. Subs (all used): 16 Keven Appo; 23 Daniel Okoro; 31 Tyran Ott; 34 Fenton Rogers.
Tries: Fulton (9), Gill (67); **Goals:** Lilley 3/3.
TRINITY: 1 Max Jowitt; 2 Jermaine McGillvary; 3 Oliver Pratt; 4 Iain Thornley; 32 Derrell Olpherts; 14 Liam Kay; 7 Mason Lino; 8 Josh Bowden; 9 Liam Hood; 10 Renouf Atoni; 11 Matty Ashurst; 12 Josh Griffin; 13 Jay Pitts. Subs (all used): 5 Lachlan Walmsley; 15 Caleb Uele; 18 Ky Rodwell; 21 Thomas Doyle.
Tries: Rodwell (34), Ashurst (43, 56), Hood (44), McGillvary (63), Atoni (67), Olpherts (76); **Goals:** Jowitt 6/7.
Rugby Leaguer & League Express Men of the Match: *Bulls:* Eribe Doro; *Trinity:* Mason Lino.
Penalty count: 6-6; **Half-time:** 8-6;
Referee: Liam Rush; **Attendance:** 5,340.

YORK KNIGHTS 18 SHEFFIELD EAGLES 28

KNIGHTS: 1 Will Dagger; 2 Joe Brown; 34 Tom Lineham; 4 Jimmy Keinhorst; 5 AJ Towse; 22 Ata Hingano; 7 Liam Harris; 8 Ukuma Ta'ai; 19 Josh Daley; 16 Brenden Santi; 33 Charlie Severs; 12 Connor Bailey; 13 Jordan Thompson. Subs (all used): 10 Conor Fitzsimmons; 15 Jack Teanby; 17 Ronan Michael; 20 Taylor Pemberton.
Tries: Severs (22), Lineham (38), Teanby (55);
Goals: Dagger 3/3.
EAGLES: 1 Matty Marsh; 2 Ben Jones-Bishop; 3 Kris Welham; 4 James Glover; 5 Matty Dawson-Jones; 6 Cory Aston; 7 Anthony Thackeray; 8 Eddie Battye; 9 Vila Halafihi; 10 Tyler Dickinson; 26 Alex Foster; 12 Joel Farrell; 13 Titus Gwaze. Subs (all used): 18 Aaron Murphy; 22 Kyle Wood; 24 Oliver Roberts; 27 Jesse Sene-Lefao.
Tries: Dawson-Jones (2), Glover (7), Marsh (14, 49);
Goals: Aston 6/7.
Rugby Leaguer & League Express Men of the Match: *Knights:* Ata Hingano; *Eagles:* Matty Marsh.
Penalty count: 9-12; **Half-time:** 12-16;
Referee: Scott Mikalauskas; **Attendance:** 1,309.

FINAL

Saturday 8th June 2024

SHEFFIELD EAGLES 6 WAKEFIELD TRINITY 50

EAGLES: 14 Jack Hansen; 2 Ben Jones-Bishop; 3 Kris Welham; 4 James Glover; 5 Matty Dawson-Jones; 6 Cory Aston; 7 Anthony Thackeray; 8 Eddie Battye; 9 Vila Halafihi; 10 Tyler Dickinson; 11 Connor Bower; 12 Joel Farrell; 13 Titus Gwaze. Subs (all used): 22 Kyle Wood; 27 Jesse Sene-Lefao; 18 Aaron Murphy; 17 Mitch Clark.
Try: Thackeray (16); **Goals:** Aston 1/1.
TRINITY: 1 Max Jowitt; 2 Jermaine McGillvary; 4 Iain Thornley; 3 Oliver Pratt; 5 Lachlan Walmsley; 6 Luke Gale; 7 Mason Lino; 8 Josh Bowden; 9 Liam Hood; 10 Renouf Atoni; 11 Matty Ashurst; 12 Josh Griffin; 13 Jay Pitts. Subs (all used): 14 Liam Kay; 15 Caleb Uele; 18 Ky Rodwell; 21 Thomas Doyle.
Tries: Walmsley (24), Gale (27), Doyle (40), Pratt (43, 53), Griffin (47, 65), McGillvary (62, 74); **Goals:** Jowitt 7/9.
Rugby Leaguer & League Express Men of the Match: *Eagles:* Anthony Thackeray; *Trinity:* Luke Gale.
Penalty count: 6-3; **Half-time:** 6-18;
Referee: Tom Grant. *(at Wembley Stadium).*

WOMEN'S SUPER LEAGUE 2024
Club by Club

BARROW RAIDERS

DATE	FIXTURE	RESULT	SCORERS	LGE
16/3/24	Cardiff (a) (CCR1)	L22-16	t:Cottier,Stirzaker,E Hutchinson g:Litherland(2)	3rd(G2)
24/3/24	Wigan (h) (CCR2)	L18-20	t:Larkin,Temple(2),Rush g:Litherland	3rd(G2)
7/4/24	Salford (a) (CCR3)	W0-46	t:Dobson,C Hutchinson,Temple(3),E Hutchinson,Lindsay,Norman,Friend,Rush g:Litherland(3)	3rd(G2)
19/4/24	Wigan (a)	L18-4	t:Larkin	7th
27/4/24	York (h)	L8-28	t:E Hutchinson(2)	6th
12/5/24	Warrington (a)	L10-6	t:Temple g:Litherland	6th
26/5/24	Featherstone (h)	W22-10	t:Larkin,Lindsay,Temple g:Litherland(5)	6th
1/6/24	Leeds (a)	L68-0		6th
15/6/24	Wigan (h)	L6-46	t:Morley g:Litherland	6th
7/7/24	York (a)	L44-0		7th
12/7/24	Huddersfield (a)	W14-26	t:Morley, E Hutchinson,Temple(2),C Hutchinson g:Litherland(3)	6th
21/7/24	Leeds (h)	L10-28	t:Norman,Temple g:Litherland	7th
4/8/24	St Helens (h)	L6-64	t:Norman g:Litherland	7th
10/8/24	Warrington (h)	W32-14	t:Norman(2),Fisher,Temple(2),Stirzaker g:Litherland(4)	5th
1/9/24	Featherstone (a)	W16-28	t:Temple(2),Cottier,Stewart,Stirzaker g:Stewart(4)	5th
8/9/24	Huddersfield (h)	W24-4	t:E Hutchinson(3),Norman,Temple g:Stewart(2)	5th
13/9/24	St Helens (a)	L68-0		5th

	APP		TRIES		GOALS		FG		PTS	
	ALL	SL	ALL	SL	ALL	SL	ALL	SL	ALL	SL
Chloe Capstick	1	0	0	0	0	0	0	0	0	0
Leah Clough	12(2)	10(2)	0	0	0	0	0	0	0	0
Leah Cottier	9(7)	6(7)	2	1	0	0	0	0	8	4
Mia Dobson	17	14	1	0	0	0	0	0	4	0
Demi Fisher	15	13	1	1	0	0	0	0	4	4
Kelly Friend	1(15)	1(12)	1	0	0	0	0	0	4	0
Fran Harley	1	1	0	0	0	0	0	0	0	0
Claire Hutchinson	17	14	2	1	0	0	0	0	8	4
Emma Hutchinson	14	11	8	6	0	0	0	0	32	24
Michelle Larkin	13	10	3	2	0	0	0	0	12	8
Beth Lindsay	11(4)	11(3)	2	1	0	0	0	0	8	4
Jodie Litherland	17	14	0	0	22	16	0	0	44	32
Laura Mellen	1(8)	(7)	0	0	0	0	0	0	0	0
Jodie Morley	17	14	2	2	0	0	0	0	8	8
Maddie Neale	1(2)	1(2)	0	0	0	0	0	0	0	0
Sam Norman	16	13	6	5	0	0	0	0	24	20
Shannon Parker	(2)	(1)	0	0	0	0	0	0	0	0
Alice Rush	7(3)	6(1)	2	0	0	0	0	0	8	0
Hannah Sherlock	(6)	(4)	0	0	0	0	0	0	0	0
Kerrie-Ann Smith	10(4)	8(4)	0	0	0	0	0	0	0	0
Nicole Stewart	2(6)	2(6)	1	1	6	6	0	0	16	16
Emily Stirzaker	17	14	3	2	0	0	0	0	12	8
Amy Sunderland	1	1	0	0	0	0	0	0	0	0
Venessa Temple	17	14	15	10	0	0	0	0	60	40
Charlotte Todhunter	4(2)	4(1)	0	0	0	0	0	0	0	0

'SL' totals include Super League games only; 'All' totals also include Challenge Cup

Emma Hutchinson

LEAGUE RECORD
P14-W5-D0-L9
(5th)
F172, A432, Diff-260
10 points.

CHALLENGE CUP
3rd, Group 2

Women's Super League 2024 - Club by Club

FEATHERSTONE ROVERS

DATE	FIXTURE	RESULT	SCORERS	LGE
24/3/24	Sheffield (h) (CCR2)	W38-6	t:Mannion,Lamb,Churm(2),Watt,Evans,Billington g:Smith,Bryer(4)	2nd(G1)
6/4/24	York (a) (CCR3)	L80-6	t:Smith g:Bryer	2nd(G1)
14/4/24	York (a) (CCQF)	L70-0		N/A
21/4/24	Warrington (a)	L34-28	t:Courtney(2),Kennedy,Grace,Copley g:Bryer(4)	6th
28/4/24	Wigan (a)	L54-12	t:Kennedy,Grace g:Bryer(2)	7th
11/5/24	St Helens (h)	L4-58	t:Carr	7th
26/5/24	Barrow (a)	L22-10	t:Watt,Prescott g:Smith	7th
1/6/24	Huddersfield (h)	L10-30	t:Billington,Lamb g:Bryer	8th
15/6/24	Warrington (h)	L10-16	t:Johnson,Lamb g:Bryer	8th
6/7/24	Wigan (h)	L0-50		8th
14/7/24	York (a)	L62-0		8th
21/7/24	Huddersfield (a)	L44-8	t:Smith,Evans	8th
4/8/24	Leeds (h)	L6-68	t:Blackburn g:Bryer	8th
10/8/24	St Helens (a)	L56-6	t:Churm g:Waters	8th
1/9/24	Barrow (h)	L16-28	t:Churm,Evans,Bryer g:Bryer(2)	8th
8/9/24	Leeds (a)	L52-12	t:Grace,Copley g:Bryer(2)	8th
15/9/24	York (h)	L6-32	t:Lamb g:Bryer	8th
6/10/24	Leigh (P/RPO) ●	L16-34	t:Churm,Courtney,Billington g:Bryer(2)	N/A

● *Played at Totally Wicked Stadium, St Helens*

	APP		TRIES		GOALS		FG		PTS	
	ALL	SL	ALL	SL	ALL	SL	ALL	SL	ALL	SL
Chloe Billington	16	12	3	1	0	0	0	0	12	4
Charley Blackburn	17	13	1	1	0	0	0	0	4	4
Tally Bryer	14(1)	11	1	1	21	14	0	0	46	32
Natalie Carr	11	8	1	1	0	0	0	0	4	4
Brogan Churm	15	11	5	2	0	0	0	0	20	8
Fran Copley	14	12	2	2	0	0	0	0	8	8
Alyssa Courtney	2(13)	2(10)	3	2	0	0	0	0	12	8
Shavon Craven	6(2)	6(1)	0	0	0	0	0	0	0	0
Kacey Davies	6	3	0	0	0	0	0	0	0	0
Kirsty Duffield	1(4)	1(4)	0	0	0	0	0	0	0	0
Katie Evans	9(6)	8(4)	3	2	0	0	0	0	12	8
Olivia Grace	15	11	3	3	0	0	0	0	12	12
Gabrielle Harrison	9(6)	8(3)	0	0	0	0	0	0	0	0
Emillie Holmes	(10)	(9)	0	0	0	0	0	0	0	0
Ella Johnson	8(6)	5(5)	1	1	0	0	0	0	4	4
Brogan Kennedy	4(8)	3(6)	2	2	0	0	0	0	8	8
Ellie Lamb	13	10	4	3	0	0	0	0	16	4
Bettie Lambert	1	1	0	0	0	0	0	0	0	0
Deanna Limbert	3(2)	3(2)	0	0	0	0	0	0	0	0
Sophia Liu	(1)	(1)	0	0	0	0	0	0	0	0
Shanelle Mannion	9	6	1	0	0	0	0	0	4	0
Ashlea Prescott	11(3)	8(3)	1	1	0	0	0	0	4	4
Brooke Price	5	4	0	0	0	0	0	0	0	0
Maddison Rainey	1	1	0	0	0	0	0	0	0	0
Lacey Sefton-Appleyard	1	1	0	0	0	0	0	0	0	0
Chloe Smith	4(6)	3(4)	2	1	2	1	0	0	12	6
Georgia Taylor	(1)	(1)	0	0	0	0	0	0	0	0
Zoe Teece	1(2)	1(2)	0	0	0	0	0	0	0	0
Ellie Wainhouse	2	2	0	0	1	1	0	0	2	2
Danielle Waters	18	14	0	0	1	0	0	0	2	0
Hannah Watt	18	14	2	1	0	0	0	0	8	4

'SL' totals include Super League games only; 'All' totals also include Challenge Cup and Promotion/Relegation play-off

Chloe Billington

LEAGUE RECORD
P14-W0-D0-L14
(8th)
F128, A606, Diff-478
0 points.

CHALLENGE CUP
Quarter Finalists

Women's Super League 2024 - Club by Club

HUDDERSFIELD GIANTS

DATE	FIXTURE	RESULT	SCORERS	LGE
16/3/24	Hull KR (h) (CCR1)	W74-0	t:Grady(2),Brown(2),Oates,Da Silva(3),Oldroyd(2),Naidole,Harrap(2),Townend g:Townend(9)	1st(G4)
24/3/24	Leigh (a) (CCR2)	W6-36	t:Brown(5),Da Silva(2) g:Townend(2),Thompson(2)	2nd(G4)
7/4/24	Leeds (a) (CCR3)	L54-10	t:Brown(2) g:Townend	2nd(G4)
13/4/24	St Helens (a) (CCQF)	L74-0		N/A
19/4/24	Leeds (a)	L66-4	t:Brown	8th
28/4/24	St Helens (a)	L60-0		8th
11/5/24	Wigan (h)	L0-102		8th
26/5/24	York (h)	L12-50	t:Hobbs,Goddard g:Townend(2)	8th
1/6/24	Featherstone (a)	W10-30	t:Dadds,Naidole(2),Brown,Townend,Iceton g:Townend(3)	7th
16/6/24	Leeds (h)	L4-42	t:Brown	7th
7/7/24	Warrington (a)	W10-32	t:Naidole(2),Brown,Iceton(2) g:Thompson(4)	6th
14/7/24	Barrow (h)	L14-26	t:Brown(2),Iceton g:Thompson	6th
21/7/24	Featherstone (h)	W44-8	t:Townend(2),Brown(3),Iceton,Webster,Hulme g:Townend(6)	5th
4/8/24	Wigan (a)	L70-0		5th
11/8/24	York (a)	L48-10	t:Brown,Fairbank g:Thompson	6th
1/9/24	St Helens (h)	L8-40	t:Brown,Iceton	6th
8/9/24	Barrow (a)	L24-4	t:Iceton	6th
15/9/24	Warrington (h)	W36-0	t:Brown(3),Naidole(2),Hulme,Townend g:Thompson(2),Townend(2)	6th

	APP		TRIES		GOALS		FG		PTS	
	ALL	SL	ALL	SL	ALL	SL	ALL	SL	ALL	SL
Beth Armstrong	(3)	(1)	0	0	0	0	0	0	0	0
Grace Arrowsmith	1	1	0	0	0	0	0	0	0	0
Amy Bennett	9(1)	5(1)	0	0	0	0	0	0	0	0
Amelia Brown	16	12	25	16	0	0	0	0	100	64
Ana Da Silva	18	14	5	0	0	0	0	0	20	0
Jess Dadds	2	2	1	1	0	0	0	0	4	4
Chloe Fairbank	1(7)	(6)	1	1	0	0	0	0	4	4
Katy Fisher	12	10	0	0	0	0	0	0	0	0
Hannah Goddard	6	6	1	1	0	0	0	0	4	4
Becky Grady	7(2)	4(2)	2	0	0	0	0	0	8	0
Kacy Haley	14	11	0	0	0	0	0	0	0	0
Georgia Hampshaw	8(8)	5(8)	0	0	0	0	0	0	0	0
Jess Harrap	14(1)	10(1)	2	0	0	0	0	0	8	0
Eloise Hayward	(1)	(1)	0	0	0	0	0	0	0	0
Gracie Hobbs	4(9)	4(8)	1	1	0	0	0	0	4	4
Sam Hulme	17	13	2	2	0	0	0	0	8	8
Mollie Iceton	9	9	7	7	0	0	0	0	28	28
Em Johnston	(1)	0	0	0	0	0	0	0	0	0
Dani McGifford	2	2	0	0	0	0	0	0	0	0
Tara Moxon	2	2	0	0	0	0	0	0	0	0
Lois Naidole	10(2)	8(2)	7	6	0	0	0	0	28	24
Bethan Oates	14	10	1	0	0	0	0	0	4	0
Ellie Oldroyd	3(3)	2(1)	2	0	0	0	0	0	8	0
Megan Preston	7(7)	7(5)	0	0	0	0	0	0	0	0
Grace Ramsden	(5)	(2)	0	0	0	0	0	0	0	0
Leah Schofield	(2)	(2)	0	0	0	0	0	0	0	0
Ellie Thompson	9(4)	9(3)	0	0	10	8	0	0	20	16
Frankie Townend	16(2)	12(2)	5	4	26	14	0	0	72	44
Ruby Tyson	1(6)	1(6)	0	0	0	0	0	0	0	0
Allana Waller	7(1)	5	0	0	0	0	0	0	0	0
Lauren Waller	1(2)	(1)	0	0	0	0	0	0	0	0
Paige Webster	6(3)	4(3)	1	1	0	0	0	0	4	4
Freya Whitehead	(1)	(1)	0	0	0	0	0	0	0	0
Emma Wilkinson	18	14	0	0	0	0	0	0	0	0

'SL' totals include Super League games only; 'All' totals also include Challenge Cup

Amelia Brown

LEAGUE RECORD
P14-W4-D0-L10
(6th)
F204, A556, Diff-352
8 points.

CHALLENGE CUP
Quarter Finalists

Women's Super League 2024 - Club by Club

LEEDS RHINOS

DATE	FIXTURE	RESULT	SCORERS	LGE
17/3/24	Leigh (a) (CCR1)	W4-52	t:Robinson,Hornby(2),Casey,Dainton,Murray,Whitehead,Hoyle,Enright,Moxon g:Enright(6)	2nd(G4)
24/3/24	Hull KR (a) (CCR2)	W0-90	t:Field,Dainton,Hoyle(2),Murray,Hornby,Casey(2),Enright(3),Cudjoe,Watson,Sykes,Northrop,Moxon g:Enright(12),Whitehead	1st(G4)
7/4/24	Huddersfield (h) (CCR3)	W54-10	t:Northrop,Hornby,Murray,Hardcastle,Moxon(3),Hoyle,Dainton(2),Whitehead g:Enright(5)	1st(G4)
13/4/24	Warrington (h) (CCQF)	W70-10	t:Field,Hardcastle(2),Enright(4),Robinson(2),Cousins(2),Bennett,Dainton,Moxon g:Enright(7)	N/A
19/4/24	Huddersfield (h)	W66-4	t:Hornby(3),Beevers(2),Cousins(3),Murray(3),Enright,Robinson g:Enright(7)	1st
27/4/24	Warrington (h)	W68-0	t:Beevers,Cousins,Northrop(3),Murray,Enright(2),Hardcastle(2),Moxon,Hoyle,Greening g:Enright(8)	1st
12/5/24	York (a)	W10-16	t:Hoyle,Beevers g:Enright(4)	2nd
19/5/24	Wigan (CCSF) ●	W34-20	t: Enright(2),Beevers,Hornby,Butcher,Murray,Bennett g:Enright(3)	N/A
24/5/24	St Helens (a)	L12-6	t:Bennett g:Bennett	2nd
1/6/24	Barrow (h)	W68-0	t:Murray(2),Cousins,Donnelly,Northrop(5),Casey,Sykes,Short,Macmillan g:Bennett(3),Whitehead(5)	2nd
8/6/24	St Helens (CCF) ●●	L0-22		N/A
16/6/24	Huddersfield (a)	W4-42	t:Donnelly,Hardcastle,Hornby,Northrop(2),Robinson,Watson,Hoyle g:Bennett(4),Butcher	1st
6/7/24	St Helens (h)	L6-16	t:Cousins g:Enright	2nd
14/7/24	Warrington (a)	W4-50	t:Beeves(4),Hardcastle(3),Cousins,Hoyle,Bruce g:Bennett(3),Whitehead(2)	1st
21/7/24	Barrow (a)	W10-28	t:Hardcastle,Whitehead(4),Cousins g:Bennett(2)	1st
4/8/24	Featherstone (a)	W6-68	t:Whitehead(3),Stead(2),Dainton(2),Cousins,Short,Sykes,Walker(2),Bennett g:Bennett(5),Walker(3)	2nd
9/8/24	Wigan (h)	W28-8	t:Dainton(2),Stead,Sykes,Hoyle(2) g:Bennett(2)	2nd
1/9/24	York (a)	L6-32	t:Cousins g:Bennett	3rd
8/9/24	Featherstone (h)	W52-12	t:Whitehead(2),Northrop,Hardcastle(2),Bennett,Stead,Walker,Butcher,Short g:Walker(3),Bennett(3)	2nd
13/9/24	Wigan (a)	W4-24	t:Casey,Bennett,Robinson(2),Hardcastle g:Bennett,Whitehead	2nd
22/9/24	York (h) (SF)	L10-12	t:Stead,Murray g:Bennett	N/A

● Played at Totally Wicked Stadium, St Helens
●● Played at Wembley Stadium

	APP		TRIES		GOALS		FG		PTS	
	ALL	SL	ALL	SL	ALL	SL	ALL	SL	ALL	SL
Caitlin Beevers	10	8	9	8	0	0	0	0	36	32
Keara Bennett	14(3)	12(2)	6	4	26	26	0	0	76	68
Tilly Jae Brown	(1)	(1)	0	0	0	0	0	0	0	0
Ruby Bruce	1(5)	1(5)	1	1	0	0	0	0	4	4
Hanna Butcher	21	15	2	1	1	1	0	0	10	6
Caitlin Casey	19(1)	13(1)	5	2	0	0	0	0	20	8
Evie Cousins	17	14	12	10	0	0	0	0	48	40
Jasmine Cudjoe	5(1)	2	1	0	0	0	0	0	4	0
Bethan Dainton	14(1)	9	9	4	0	0	0	0	36	16
Ella Donnelly	5(16)	5(10)	2	2	0	0	0	0	8	8
Ruby Enright	10	4	13	3	53	20	0	0	158	52
Grace Field	8(4)	4(2)	2	0	0	0	0	0	8	0
Kaiya Glynn	(9)	(7)	0	0	0	0	0	0	0	0
Jenna Greening	6(5)	6(4)	1	1	0	0	0	0	4	4
Amy Hardcastle	18	14	13	10	0	0	0	0	52	40
Zoe Hornby	4(6)	2(3)	9	4	0	0	0	0	36	16
Shona Hoyle	15(1)	10(1)	10	6	0	0	0	0	40	24
Beth Lockwood	(2)	(2)	0	0	0	0	0	0	0	0
Beth Macmillan	3(3)	(3)	1	1	0	0	0	0	4	4
Tara Moxon	5(2)	2(1)	7	1	0	0	0	0	28	4
Lucy Murray	19	13	11	7	0	0	0	0	44	28
Izzy Northrop	17(3)	11(3)	13	11	0	0	0	0	52	44
Sophie Robinson	16(4)	13(2)	7	4	0	0	0	0	28	16
Grace Short	3(5)	3(5)	3	3	0	0	0	0	12	12
Ebony Stead	6	6	5	5	0	0	0	0	20	20
Bella Sykes	15(2)	12(1)	4	3	0	0	0	0	16	12
Ruby Walker	1(3)	1(3)	3	3	6	6	0	0	24	24
Elychia Watson	2(4)	2(2)	2	1	0	0	0	0	8	4
Liv Whitehead	19	13	11	9	9	8	0	0	62	52

'SL' totals include regular season & play-offs; 'All' totals also include Challenge Cup

Lucy Murray

LEAGUE RECORD
P14-W11-D0-L3
(2nd/Semi-Final)
F528, A122, Diff+406
22 points.

CHALLENGE CUP
Runners-up

Women's Super League 2024 - Club by Club

ST HELENS

DATE	FIXTURE	RESULT	SCORERS	LGE
16/3/24	London (h) (CCR1)	W64-0	t:Rudge(3),Crowl,Gaskin,Hook(3),Birchall,Harris,Roberts,Travis g:Taylor(5),Gaskin(3)	1st(G3)
23/3/24	Bradford (a) (CCR2)	W0-48	(walkover)	1st(G3)
7/4/24	Warrington (a) (CCR3)	W6-58	t:Salihi(3),D Stott,Hook(2),Woosey(2),Jones,E Stott,Gaskin g:Taylor(7)	1st(G3)
13/4/24	Huddersfield (h) (CCQF)	W74-0	t:Burke(3),Bridge,Woosey,Williams(2),Travis,Whitfield,Mottershead,D Stott(2),Crowl,Jones g:Taylor(9)	N/A
21/4/24	York (a)	L20-16	t:Mottershead,Burke,Woosey g:Taylor(2)	5th
28/4/24	Huddersfield (h)	W60-0	t:E Stott(2),Burke(4),McColm(2),Hook,Sutherland,Jones,Mottershead g:Gaskin(6)	4th
11/5/24	Featherstone (a)	W4-58	t:Gaskin,E Stott,Whitfield,Cunningham,D Stott,Hook(2),Salihi,Burke,M Williams g:Gaskin(7)	3rd
18/5/24	York (CCSF) ●	W32-2	t:Burke,D Stott,Rudge,Hook(2),Sutherland g:Gaskin(4)	N/A
24/5/24	Leeds (h)	W12-6	t:Gaskin g:Gaskin(4)	3rd
31/5/24	Wigan (h)	W24-8	t:McColm(2),Whitfield,Salihi(2) g:Gaskin(2)	3rd
8/6/24	Leeds (CCF) ●●	W0-22	t:Gaskin,Hook,McColm,Crowl g:Gaskin(3)	N/A
6/7/24	Leeds (a)	W6-16	t:Jones,Gaskin,Harris g:Gaskin,Harris	4th
12/7/24	Wigan (a)	W12-16	t:Woosey(2),Whitfield g:Gaskin(2)	4th
20/7/24	Warrington (h)	W82-0	t:Woosey(3),Jones(2),Cunningham(2),McGifford(3),Birchall,McDonald,Travis,Harris,Mottershead g:Gaskin (11)	3rd
31/7/24	York (h)	W10-6	t:Burke(2) g:Gaskin	1st
4/8/24	Barrow (a)	W6-64	t:Cunningham,Burke,M Williams(2),Harris,Gaskin(2),Travis,Woosey(3),Whitfield g:Gaskin(8)	1st
10/8/24	Featherstone (h)	W56-6	t:Birchall,McGifford(3),Cunningham,Burke(4),Mottershead(2) g:Gaskin(4),Taylor(2)	1st
1/9/24	Huddersfield (a)	W8-40	t:Burke(4),McGifford(3),M Williams g:Taylor(4)	1st
7/9/24	Warrington (a)	W0-98	t:Burke(4),Gaskin,Travis(3),Salihi(2),McGifford,Cunningham,E Stott(3),Jones,M Williams,Sutherland g:Gaskin(13)	1st
13/9/24	Barrow (h)	W68-0	t:Hook(2),Burke(3),Travis(3),Mottershead,M Williams(2),Harris,Jones g:Gaskin(6),Harris(2)	1st
22/9/24	Wigan (h) (SF)	W18-4	t:Rudge,Burke(2),Woosey g:Gaskin	N/A
6/10/24	York (h) (GF)	L8-18	t:Burke g:Gaskin(2)	N/A

● Played at Eco-Power Stadium, Doncaster
●● Played at Wembley Stadium

	APP		TRIES		GOALS		FG		PTS	
	ALL	SL	ALL	SL	ALL	SL	ALL	SL	ALL	SL
Grace Arrowsmith	1	1	0	0	0	0	0	0	0	0
Pip Birchall	1(10)	1(8)	3	2	0	0	0	0	12	8
Alyx Bridge	2(1)	(1)	1	0	0	0	0	0	4	0
Leah Burke	16	12	32	28	0	0	0	0	128	112
Chantelle Crowl	20	15	3	0	0	0	0	0	12	0
Jodie Cunningham	19	14	6	6	0	0	0	0	24	24
Faye Gaskin	20	15	9	6	78	68	0	0	192	160
Zoe Harris	16(1)	14	5	4	3	3	0	0	26	22
Phoebe Hook	13	8	13	5	0	0	0	0	52	20
Tara Jones	19(2)	14(2)	8	6	0	0	0	0	32	24
Luci McColm	10	8	5	4	0	0	0	0	20	16
Erin McDonald	(4)	(4)	1	1	0	0	0	0	4	4
Dani McGifford	4	4	10	10	0	0	0	0	40	40
Katie Mottershead	2(19)	2(14)	7	6	0	0	0	0	28	24
Hannah Roberts	1	0	1	0	0	0	0	0	4	0
Rebecca Rotheram	4(1)	3	0	0	0	0	0	0	0	0
Emily Rudge	16	12	5	1	0	0	0	0	20	4
Beri Salihi	19	14	8	5	0	0	0	0	32	20
Darcy Stott	5(14)	2(12)	5	1	0	0	0	0	20	4
Erin Stott	20	15	7	6	0	0	0	0	28	24
Georgia Sutherland	(8)	(5)	3	2	0	0	0	0	12	8
Amy Taylor	7(1)	4(1)	0	0	29	8	0	0	58	16
Paige Travis	19	15	10	8	0	0	0	0	40	32
Vicky Whitfield	17(1)	15	5	4	0	0	0	0	20	16
Megan Williams	7(6)	7(5)	7	7	0	0	0	0	28	28
Naomi Williams	2(16)	2(12)	2	0	0	0	0	0	8	0
Rachael Woosey	13	11	13	10	0	0	0	0	52	40

'SL' totals include regular season & play-offs; 'All' totals also include Challenge Cup

Leah Burke

LEAGUE RECORD
P14-W13-D0-L1
(1st/Grand Final Runners-up)
F620, A88, Diff+532
26 points.

CHALLENGE CUP
Winners

Women's Super League 2024 - Club by Club

WARRINGTON WOLVES

DATE	FIXTURE	RESULT	SCORERS	LGE
16/3/24	Bradford (a) (CCR1)	W4-52	Simpson(2),Bound(2),Burnett,Barnett,Ellison,Westwood,Johnston(2),Dennis g:Magraw(4)	2nd(G3)
24/3/24	London (a) (CCR2)	W6-24	Simpson(2),Ellison,Burnett,Johnston g:Magraw(2)	2nd(G3)
7/4/24	St Helens (h) (CCR3)	L6-58	Donougher g:Magraw	2nd(G3)
13/4/24	Leeds (a) (CCQF)	L70-10	Burnett,Bound g:Magraw	N/A
21/4/24	Featherstone (h)	W34-28	Bell,Nixon,Coates,Johnston(2),Dennis,Barnett g:Magraw(3)	3rd
27/4/24	Leeds (a)	L68-0		5th
12/5/24	Barrow (h)	W10-6	t:Bound,Johnston g:Magraw	5th
25/5/24	Wigan (h)	L4-40	t:Simpson	5th
2/6/24	York (a)	L44-4	t:Magraw	5th
15/6/24	Featherstone (a)	W10-16	t:Burnett,Baggaley,Simpson g:Magraw	5th
7/7/24	Huddersfield (h)	L10-32	t:Simpson,Baggaley g:Magraw	5th
14/7/24	Leeds (h)	L4-50	t:Turner	5th
20/7/24	St Helens (a)	L82-0		6th
4/8/24	York (h)	L61-0		6th
10/8/24	Barrow (a)	L32-14	t:Johnston(2),Barnett g:Doria	7th
1/9/24	Wigan (a)	L82-0		7th
7/9/24	St Helens (h)	L0-98		7th
15/9/24	Huddersfield (a)	L36-0		7th

	APP ALL	APP SL	TRIES ALL	TRIES SL	GOALS ALL	GOALS SL	FG ALL	FG SL	PTS ALL	PTS SL
Emily Baggaley	9	9	2	2	0	0	0	0	8	8
Nicole Barnett	15	11	3	2	0	0	0	0	12	8
Millie Bell	14	11	1	1	0	0	0	0	4	4
Talicia Blythe	(1)	(1)	0	0	0	0	0	0	0	0
Georgia Bogg	2(3)	2(3)	0	0	0	0	0	0	0	0
Dani Bound	6	2	4	1	0	0	0	0	16	4
Grace Burnett	17	13	4	1	0	0	0	0	16	4
Albany-D Coates	13	12	1	1	0	0	0	0	4	4
Megan Condliffe	4(14)	2(12)	0	0	0	0	0	0	0	0
Lilly Day	(1)	(1)	0	0	0	0	0	0	0	0
Anna Dennis	7	5	2	1	0	0	0	0	8	4
Stevie Donougher	1	0	1	0	0	0	0	0	4	0
Sinead Doria	2	2	0	0	1	1	0	0	2	2
Emily Downs	9	6	0	0	0	0	0	0	0	0
Lauren Ellison	9	6	2	0	0	0	0	0	8	0
Louise Fellingham	8(3)	8(3)	0	0	0	0	0	0	0	0
Olivia Hill	1(4)	1(3)	0	0	0	0	0	0	0	0
Ellie Hunt-Pain	1	1	0	0	0	0	0	0	0	0
Ellie Jelves	8(4)	8(4)	0	0	0	0	0	0	0	0
Lucy Johnson	(9)	(9)	0	0	0	0	0	0	0	0
Abi Johnston	16	12	8	5	0	0	0	0	32	20
Abby Latchford	11	9	0	0	0	0	0	0	0	0
Charlie Magraw	15	11	1	1	15	7	0	0	34	18
Tina Millan	1(3)	0	0	0	0	0	0	0	0	0
Chelsea Newton	1(1)	1(1)	0	0	0	0	0	0	0	0
Rebecca Nixon	11	9	1	1	0	0	0	0	4	4
Hannah Roberts	2	2	0	0	0	0	0	0	0	0
Imogen Roberts	(1)	(1)	0	0	0	0	0	0	0	0
Kim Seddon	(4)	(2)	0	0	0	0	0	0	0	0
Sammi Simpson	13	9	7	3	0	0	0	0	28	12
Sarina Tamou	(1)	0	0	0	0	0	0	0	0	0
Emily Tandy	(2)	(1)	0	0	0	0	0	0	0	0
Helena Turner	9(6)	8(5)	1	1	0	0	0	0	4	4
Olivia Webb	1(3)	1(2)	0	0	0	0	0	0	0	0
Georgia Westwood	1(1)	0	1	0	0	0	0	0	4	0
Katie May Williams	18	14	0	0	0	0	0	0	0	0
Jasmine Wilson	4(10)	4(7)	0	0	0	0	0	0	0	0
Grace Wray	5	3	0	0	0	0	0	0	0	0

Katie May Williams

'SL' totals include Super League games only; 'All' totals also include Challenge Cup

LEAGUE RECORD
P14-W3-D0-L11
(7th)
F96, A669, Diff-573
6 points.

CHALLENGE CUP
Quarter Finalists

Women's Super League 2024 - Club by Club

WIGAN WARRIORS

DATE	FIXTURE	RESULT	SCORERS	LGE
17/3/24	Salford (a) (CCR1)	W0-68	t:Derbyshire(3),Fisher,Coleman,Singleton,Davies(2),E Hunter,Speakman, M Jones,Rowe(2) g:Knowles(8)	1st(G2)
24/3/24	Barrow (a) (CCR2)	W18-20	t:Derbyshire(2),Hilton,Rowe g:Rowe(2)	2nd(G2)
7/4/24	Cardiff (h) (CCR3)	W44-4	t:Rowe,Derbyshire,Harborow,E Hunter,Davies(2),Fisher(2) g:Knowles(6)	1st(G2)
13/4/24	Cardiff (h) (CCQF)	W44-4	t:Coleman(2),Davies,Hilton(2),Casey,Miller,Banks,Rowe g:Knowles(4)	N/A
19/4/24	Barrow (h)	W18-4	t:Davies(2),Rowe,Hilton g:Knowles	2nd
28/4/24	Featherstone (h)	W54-12	t:Banks,Coleman(2),Rowe(3),Davies(2),Derbyshire g:Knowles(9)	2nd
11/5/24	Huddersfield (a)	W0-102	t:Thompson(2),Davies(3),Coleman(5),Banks,Molyneux(2),Casey,Welsford,Foubister, Hilton,Rowe g:Knowles(15)	1st
19/5/24	Leeds (CCSF) ●	L34-20	t:Molyneux,Banks,Gregory-Haselden g:Knowles(4)	N/A
25/5/24	Warrington (a)	W4-40	t:Thompson,Rowe,Coleman,Derbyshire,Davies(2),Hayes g:Knowles(6)	1st
31/5/24	St Helens (a)	L24-8	t:Coleman g:Knowles(2)	2nd
15/6/24	Barrow (a)	W6-46	t:Davies(5),Banks,Singleton,Hilton,Casey g:Rowe(5)	2nd
6/7/24	Featherstone (a)	W0-50	t:E Hunter,Wilson(2),Thompson,Banks(2),Foubister,Casey,Davies g:Rowe(7)	1st
12/7/24	St Helens (h)	L12-16	t:Derbyshire,E Hunter g:Rowe(2)	2nd
21/7/24	York (a)	W10-18	t:E Hunter(2),Derbyshire,Foubister g:Rowe	2nd
4/8/24	Huddersfield (h)	W70-0	t:Casey,Davies(2),Hilton,Coleman,Banks(2),Foubister(2),R Hunter,Derbyshire(2) g:Rowe(11)	3rd
9/8/24	Leeds (a)	L28-8	t:Davies,Wilson	3rd
1/9/24	Warrington (h)	W82-0	t:M Jones,Davies(3),Rowe(2),Derbyshire,Banks(3),E Hunter(2),R Hunter(2),C Jones g:Rowe(11)	2nd
8/9/24	York (h)	L12-16	t:M Jones,Banks g:Rowe(2)	4th
13/9/24	Leeds (h)	L4-24	t:Davies	4th
22/9/24	St Helens (a) (SF)	L18-4	t:Foubister	N/A

● Played at Totally Wicked Stadium, St Helens

	APP		TRIES		GOALS		FG		PTS	
	ALL	SL	ALL	SL	ALL	SL	ALL	SL	ALL	SL
Grace Banks	14(1)	13	13	11	0	0	0	0	52	44
Rease Casey	12(1)	10	5	4	0	0	0	0	20	16
Mary Coleman	20	15	13	10	0	0	0	0	52	40
Ellie Costello	(1)	0	0	0	0	0	0	0	0	0
Anna Davies	20	15	27	22	0	0	0	0	108	88
Ellise Derbyshire	20	15	13	7	0	0	0	0	52	28
Sinead Doria	4	0	0	0	0	0	0	0	0	0
Emma Dwyer	1	0	0	0	0	0	0	0	0	0
Brogan Evans	(2)	0	0	0	0	0	0	0	0	09
Alice Fisher	15	11	3	0	0	0	0	0	12	0
Jenna Foubister	8(2)	8(1)	6	6	0	0	0	0	24	24
Jade Gregory-Haselden	(19)	(15)	1	0	0	0	0	0	4	0
Olivia Harborow	(5)	(2)	1	0	0	0	0	0	4	0
Bethany Hayes	(7)	(6)	1	1	0	0	0	0	4	4
Kaitlin Hilton	11(7)	6(7)	7	4	0	0	0	0	28	16
Eva Hunter	10(1)	7(1)	8	6	0	0	0	0	32	24
Ruby Hunter	(5)	(5)	3	3	0	0	0	0	12	12
Lucy Johnson	1	0	0	0	0	0	0	0	0	0
Cerys Jones	2(17)	2(13)	1	1	0	0	0	0	4	4
Molly Jones	9	8	3	2	0	0	0	0	12	8
Emma Knowles	12	7	0	0	56	33	0	0	112	66
Carys Marsh	5(4)	5(4)	0	0	0	0	0	0	0	0
Cailey Miller	5	2	1	0	0	0	0	0	4	0
Vicky Molyneux	10(1)	9(1)	3	2	0	0	0	0	12	8
Jodie Morris	(1)	0	0	0	0	0	0	0	0	0
Isabel Rowe	20	15	13	8	40	39	0	0	132	110
Abbie Singleton	6(5)	3(4)	2	1	0	0	0	0	8	4
Holly Speakman	20	15	1	0	0	0	0	0	4	0
Rachel Thompson	20	15	4	4	0	0	0	0	16	16
Emma Welsford	4	3	1	1	0	0	0	0	4	4
Georgia Wilson	11	11	3	3	0	0	0	0	12	12

'SL' totals include regular season & play-offs; 'All' totals also include Challenge Cup

Anna Davies

LEAGUE RECORD
P14-W9-D0-L5
(4th/Semi-Final)
F524, A144, Diff+380
18 points.

CHALLENGE CUP
Semi-Finalists

Women's Super League 2024 - Club by Club

YORK VALKYRIE

DATE	FIXTURE	RESULT	SCORERS	LGE
17/3/24	Sheffield (a) (CCR1)	W10-74	t:Andrade(3),Gentles(2),Stanley(2),Izumi,Stimpson,Marshall,Partington(2),Bell g:Stanley(11)	1st(G1)
8/4/24	Featherstone (h) (CCR3)	W80-6	t:Renouf,Partington(2),Stimpson,Rihari,Kershaw(2),Eastwood,Gentles,Stanley(2),Roberts(2),Marshall,Fitzpatrick g:Stanley(10)	1st(G1)
14/4/24	Featherstone (h) (CCQF)	W70-0	t:L Wood,Roberts,Partington(2),Owen(2),Kershaw,Sharp,Renouf,Hetherington(2),Stanley,Marshall g:Stanley(9)	N/A
21/4/24	St Helens (h)	W20-16	t:Roberts(2),Kershaw,Renouf g:Stanley(2)	4th
27/4/24	Barrow (a)	W8-28	t:Kershaw(4),Andrade g:Stanley(4)	3rd
12/5/24	Leeds (a)	L10-16	t:Partington,Owen g:Stanley	4th
18/5/24	St Helens (CCSF) ●	L32-2	g:Marshall	N/A
26/5/24	Huddersfield (a)	W12-50	t:Kershaw(3),Partington(2),Roberts,Brennan(2),Sharp,Lambert g:Roberts(5)	4th
2/6/24	Warrington (h)	W44-4	t:Owen,Partington(3),Lambert,Stimpson,L Wood,Komaitai(2) g:Brennan(3),Hendry	4th
7/7/24	Barrow (h)	W44-0	t:Gale,Andrade,Kershaw(3),Hetherington,Partington,L Wood g:Stanley(6)	3rd
14/7/24	Featherstone (h)	W62-0	t:Stanley,L Wood,Andrade(3),Izumi,Kershaw(2),Partington(2),Pakulis g:Stanley(9)	3rd
21/7/24	Wigan (h)	L10-18	t:Partington(2) g:Stanley	4th
31/7/24	St Helens (a)	L10-6	t:Wilton g:Stanley	4th
4/8/24	Warrington (a)	W0-61	t:Kershaw(3),Wilton,Andrade,Partington(4),Hetherington,Stanley,Roberts g:Stanley(6) fg:Stanley	4th
11/8/24	Huddersfield (h)	W48-10	t:Partington(2),L Wood,Stanley(2),Roberts,Pakulis,Kershaw,Renouf g:Stanley(6)	4th
1/9/24	Leeds (a)	W6-32	t:Pakulis,L Wood,Marshall,Owen,Andrade g:Stanley(6)	3rd
8/9/24	Wigan (a)	W12-16	t:Parker,Brennan g:Brennan(4)	3rd
15/9/24	Featherstone (a)	W6-32	t:Pakulis(2),Renouf,Marshall,Brennan,Exley g:Brennan, Marshall(3)	N/A
22/9/24	Leeds (a) (SF)	W10-12	t:Gentles,Andrade g:Marshall(2)	N/A
6/10/24	St Helens (a) (GF)	W8-18	t:Owen,Partington,Gentles g:Brennan,Marshall(2)	

● Played at Eco-Power Stadium, Doncaster

	APP		TRIES		GOALS		FG		PTS	
	ALL	SL	ALL	SL	ALL	SL	ALL	SL	ALL	SL
Savannah Andrade	20	16	11	8	0	0	0	0	44	32
Jas Bell	17(2)	14(1)	1	0	0	0	0	0	4	0
Izzy Brennan	4(4)	4(4)	4	4	9	9	0	0	34	34
Lucy Eastwood	12(4)	8(4)	1	0	0	0	0	0	4	0
Lauren Exley	(3)	(3)	1	1	0	0	0	0	4	4
Kira Fitzpatrick	(1)	0	1	0	0	0	0	0	4	0
Liv Gale	6(1)	6	1	1	0	0	0	0	4	4
Kelsey Gentles	1(11)	(9)	5	2	0	0	0	0	20	8
Ellie Hendry	(2)	(2)	0	0	1	1	0	0	2	2
Georgie Hetherington	15(1)	12(1)	4	2	0	0	0	0	16	8
Eva Izumi	8(1)	6(1)	2	1	0	0	0	0	8	4
Sian Judd	1	1	0	0	0	0	0	0	0	0
Emma Kershaw	17	13	20	17	0	0	0	0	80	68
Manuqalo Komaitai	3	3	2	2	0	0	0	0	8	8
Bettie Lambert	2(2)	2(1)	2	2	0	0	0	0	8	8
Rhiannion Marshall	2(9)	(7)	5	2	8	7	0	0	36	22
Lacey Owen	14(1)	11(1)	6	4	0	0	0	0	24	16
Megan Pakulis	11	11	5	5	0	0	0	0	20	20
Lisa Parker	7(2)	7(2)	1	1	0	0	0	0	4	4
Eboni Partington	20	16	24	18	0	0	0	0	96	72
Mahault Pommier	2(2)	2(2)	0	0	0	0	0	0	0	0
Tamzin Renouf	12(1)	8(1)	5	3	0	0	0	0	20	12
Sade Rihari	17	13	1	0	0	0	0	0	4	0
Carrie Roberts	10(1)	8	8	5	5	5	0	0	42	30
Daisy Sanderson	1(4)	1(1)	0	0	0	0	0	0	0	0
Evie Sexton	2(1)	2(1)	0	0	0	0	0	0	0	0
Jess Sharp	6(10)	5(8)	2	1	0	0	0	0	8	4
Tara Jane Stanley	13	10	9	4	72	42	1	1	181	101
Alex Stimpson	6(4)	3(3)	3	1	0	0	0	0	12	4
Georgia Taylor	4(3)	4(2)	0	0	0	0	0	0	0	0
Remi Wilton	8(2)	7(2)	2	2	0	0	0	0	8	8
Agnes Wood	(3)	(3)	0	0	0	0	0	0	0	0
Liv Wood	19	15	6	5	0	0	0	0	24	20

'SL' totals include regular season & play-offs; 'All' totals also include Challenge Cup

Eboni Partington

LEAGUE RECORD
P14-W11-D0-L3
(3rd/Grand Final Winners, Champions)
F463, A118, Diff+345
22 points.

CHALLENGE CUP
Semi-Finalists

WOMEN'S SUPER LEAGUE 2024
Round by Round

Women's Super League 2024 - Round by Round

ROUND 1

Friday 19th April 2024

LEEDS RHINOS 66 HUDDERSFIELD GIANTS 4

RHINOS: 1 Ruby Enright; 21 Evie Cousins; 4 Amy Hardcastle; 3 Caitlin Beevers; 18 Liv Whitehead; 6 Hanna Butcher; 7 Caitlin Casey; 8 Zoe Hornby; 15 Jasmine Cudjoe; 10 Izzy Northrop; 11 Shona Hoyle; 17 Lucy Murray; 13 Bethan Dainton. Subs (all used): 25 Ella Donnelly; 9 Keara Bennett; 2 Sophie Robinson; 20 Kaiya Glynn.
Tries: Hornby (2, 65, 68), Beevers (8, 24), Cousins (12, 32, 62), Murray (28, 34, 47), Enright (44), Robinson (56); **Goals:** Enright 7/13.
GIANTS: 1 Amy Bennett; 15 Rebekah Grady; 3 Ana Da Silva; 24 Ellie Thompson; 5 Amelia Brown; 6 Frankie Townend; 7 Sam Hulme; 10 Ellie Oldroyd; 9 Bethan Oates; 16 Emma Wilkinson; 11 Jess Harrap; 20 Georgia Hampshaw; 13 Katy Fisher. Subs (all used): 19 Beth Armstrong; 17 Megan Preston; 18 Grace Ramsden; 25 Chloe Fairbank.
Try: Brown (16); **Goals:** Townend 0/1.
Half-time: 36-4.

WIGAN WARRIORS 18 BARROW RAIDERS 4

WARRIORS: 1 Grace Banks; 2 Cailey Miller; 23 Kaitlin Hilton; 3 Anna Davies; 5 Ellise Derbyshire; 32 Isabel Rowe; 7 Emma Knowles; 10 Holly Speakman; 9 Abbie Singleton; 8 Alice Fisher; 35 Rease Casey; 12 Mary Coleman; 14 Rachel Thompson. Subs (all used): 26 Cerys Jones; 21 Jade Gregory-Haselden; 28 Olivia Harborow; 27 Bethany Hayes.
Tries: Davies (43, 49), Rowe (47), Hilton (60);
Goals: Knowles 1/4
RAIDERS: 5 Sam Norman; 2 Emma Hutchinson; 4 Claire Hutchinson; 1 Michelle Larkin; 24 Alice Rush; 6 Demi Fisher; 7 Jodie Litherland; 14 Mia Dobson; 9 Beth Lindsay; 10 Jodie Morley; 3 Leah Clough; 12 Vanessa Temple; 11 Emily Stirzaker. Subs (all used): 15 Leah Cottier; 16 Hannah Sherlock; 17 Charlotte Todhunter; 23 Shannon Parker.
Try: Larkin (72); **Goals:** Sherlock 0/1.
Half-time: 0-0.

Sunday 21st April 2024

WARRINGTON WOLVES 34 FEATHERSTONE ROVERS 28

WOLVES: 1 Anna Dennis; 2 Abi Johnston; 3 Nicole Barnett; 33 Albany-D Coates; 5 Rebecca Nixon; 6 Millie Bell; 7 Charlie Magraw; 16 Megan Condliffe; 14 Jasmine Wilson; 10 Grace Burnett; 11 Katie May Williams; 12 Sammi Simpson; 20 Helena Turner. Subs: 9 Dani Bound (not used); 24 Olivia Hill; 26 Ellie Jelves; 23 Kim Seddon.
Tries: Bell (5), Nixon (16), Coates (22), Johnston (44, 47), Dennis (62), N Barnett (80); **Goals:** Magraw 3/7.
ROVERS: 1 Danielle Waters; 2 Ellie Lamb; 3 Fran Copley; 4 Ella Johnson; 22 Natalie Carr; 6 Tally Bryer; 7 Olivia Grace; 8 Shanelle Mannion; 9 Charley Blackburn; 11 Hannah Watt; 23 Ellie Wainhouse; 14 Kacey Davies; 13 Chloe Billington. Subs (all used) 15 Chloe Smith; 18 Alyssa Courtney; 20 Brogan Kennedy; 31 Emillie Holmes.
Tries: Courtney (27, 66), Kennedy (33), Grace (68), Copley (70); **Goals:** Bryer 4/5.
Sin bin: Watt (35) - leading with the elbow.
Half-time: 14-12.

YORK VALKYRIE 20 ST HELENS 16

VALKYRIE: 1 Tara Jane Stanley; 2 Eboni Partington; 3 Tamzin Renouf; 26 Carrie Roberts; 4 Emma Kershaw; 6 Sade Rihari ;7 Liv Gale; 8 Liv Wood; 5 Georgie Hetherington; 20 Alex Stimpson; 11 Lacey Owen; 12 Savannah Andrade; 10 Jas Bell. Subs (all used): 13 Rhiannion Marshall; 15 Kelsey Gentles; 19 Jess Sharp; 21 Lucy Eastwood.
Tries: Roberts (18, 78), Kershaw (22), Renouf (36);
Goals: Stanley 2/5.
SAINTS: 1 Beri Salihi; 20 Phoebe Hook; 30 Rachael Woosey; 4 Erin Stott; 5 Leah Burke; 21 Amy Taylor; 7 Faye Gaskin; 8 Vicky Whitfield; 9 Tara Jones; 10 Chantelle Crowl; 11 Paige Travis; 12 Emily Rudge; 13 Jodie Cunningham. Subs (all used): 14 Naomi Williams; 16 Darcy Stott; 19 Katie Mottershead; 24 Georgia Sutherland.
Tries: Mottershead (48), Burke (60), Woosey (74);
Goals: Taylor 2/3.
Half-time: 12-0.

ROUND 2

Saturday 27th April 2024

BARROW RAIDERS 8 YORK VALKYRIE 28

RAIDERS: 5 Sam Norman; 2 Emma Hutchinson; 4 Claire Hutchinson; 1 Michelle Larkin; 17 Charlotte Todhunter; 6 Demi Fisher; 7 Jodie Litherland; 14 Mia Dobson; 9 Beth Lindsay; 10 Jodie Morley; 15 Leah Cottier; 12 Vanessa Temple; 11 Emily Stirzaker. Subs (all used): 8 Kelly Friend; 13 Kerrie-Ann Smith; 16 Hannah Sherlock; 24 Alice Rush.
Tries: E Hutchinson (69, 71); **Goals:** Lindsay 0/2.
Sin bin: Temple (63) - fighting.
VALKYRIE: 1 Tara Jane Stanley; 2 Eboni Partington; 3 Tamzin Renouf; 22 Eva Izumi; 4 Emma Kershaw; 6 Sade Rihari; 7 Liv Gale; 8 Liv Wood; 21 Lucy Eastwood; 18 Jess Sharp; 16 Daisy Sanderson; 12 Savannah Andrade; 10 Jas Bell. Subs (all used): 11 Lacey Owen; 15 Kelsey Gentles; 24 Ellie Hendry; 28 Remi Wilton.
Tries: Kershaw (11, 32, 36, 39), Andrade (29);
Goals: Stanley 4/5.
Sin bin: Owen (63) - fighting.
Half-time: 0-28.

LEEDS RHINOS 68 WARRINGTON WOLVES 0

RHINOS: 1 Ruby Enright; 21 Evie Cousins; 4 Amy Hardcastle; 3 Caitlin Beevers; 2 Sophie Robinson; 6 Hanna Butcher; 7 Caitlin Casey; 10 Izzy Northrop; 15 Jasmine Cudjoe; 19 Grace Field; 11 Shona Hoyle; 17 Lucy Murray; 25 Ella Donnelly. Subs (all used): 14 Tara Moxon; 23 Elychia Watson; 20 Kaiya Glynn; 22 Jenna Greening.
Tries: Beevers (3), Cousins (11), Northrop (12, 32, 78), Murray (17), Enright (26, 57), Hardcastle (36, 48), Moxon (54), Hoyle (64), Greening (68); **Goals:** Enright 8/13.
WOLVES: 1 Anna Dennis; 2 Abi Johnston; 3 Nicole Barnett; 19 Grace Wray; 21 Lauren Ellison; 6 Millie Bell; 7 Charlie Magraw; 34 Ellie Hunt-Pain; 14 Jasmine Wilson; 16 Megan Condliffe; 11 Katie May Williams; 12 Sammi Simpson; 24 Olivia Hill. Subs (all used): 27 Emily Tandy; 25 Olivia Webb; 26 Ellie Jelves; 23 Kim Seddon.
Sin bin: Seddon (70) - dangerous tackle.
Half-time: 36-0.

Sunday 28th April 2024

ST HELENS 60 HUDDERSFIELD GIANTS 0

SAINTS: 1 Beri Salihi; 20 Phoebe Hook; 4 Erin Stott; 3 Luci McColm; 5 Leah Burke; 6 Zoe Harris; 7 Faye Gaskin; 8 Vicky Whitfield; 19 Katie Mottershead; 16 Darcy Stott; 11 Paige Travis; 22 Megan Williams; 14 Naomi Williams. Subs (all used): 9 Tara Jones; 17 Pip Birchall; 24 Georgia Sutherland; 28 Erin McDonald.
Tries: E Stott (4, 78), Burke (10, 22, 51, 62), McColm (13, 28), Hook (33), Sutherland (39), Jones (55), Mottershead (72);
Goals: Gaskin 6/12.
GIANTS: 1 Amy Bennett; 15 Becky Grady; 3 Ana Da Silva; 22 Allana Waller; 5 Amelia Brown; 6 Frankie Townend; 7 Sam Hulme; 10 Ellie Oldroyd; 9 Bethan Oates; 16 Emma Wilkinson; 11 Jess Harrap; 20 Georgia Hampshaw; 13 Katy Fisher. Subs (all used): 18 Grace Ramsden; 21 Lauren Waller; 25 Chloe Fairbank; 27 Gracie Hobbs.
Try: Brown (43); **Goals:** Townend 1/1.
Half-time: 38-0.

WIGAN WARRIORS 54 FEATHERSTONE ROVERS 12

WARRIORS: 1 Grace Banks; 2 Cailey Miller; 23 Kaitlin Hilton; 3 Anna Davies; 5 Ellise Derbyshire; 32 Isabel Rowe; 7 Emma Knowles; 10 Holly Speakman; 9 Abbie Singleton; 8 Alice Fisher; 35 Rease Casey; 12 Mary Coleman; 14 Rachel Thompson. Subs (all used): 21 Jade Gregory-Haselden; 26 Cerys Jones; 27 Bethany Hayes; 28 Olivia Harborow.
Tries: Banks (15), Coleman (19, 77), Rowe (24, 28, 72), Davies (36, 58), Derbyshire (50); **Goals:** Knowles 9/9.
ROVERS: 1 Danielle Waters; 2 Ellie Lamb; 13 Chloe Billington; 4 Ella Johnson; 5 Brooke Price; 6 Tally Bryer; 7 Olivia Grace; 8 Shanelle Mannion; 9 Charley Blackburn; 16 Gabrielle Harrison; 11 Hannah Watt; 23 Ellie Wainhouse; 10 Brogan Churm. Subs (all used): 17 Kirsty Duffield; 18 Alyssa Courtney; 20 Brogan Kennedy; 26 Katie Evans.
Tries: Kennedy (40), Grace (54); **Goals:** Bryer 2/2.
Half-time: 30-6.

ROUND 3

Saturday 11th May 2024

FEATHERSTONE ROVERS 4 ST HELENS 58

ROVERS: 3 Fran Copley; 22 Natalie Carr; 13 Chloe Billington; 19 Ashlea Prescott; - Bettie Lambert; 15 Chloe Smith; 7 Olivia Grace; 8 Shanelle Mannion; 9 Charley Blackburn; 10 Brogan Churm; 11 Hannah Watt; 14 Kacey Davies; 1 Danielle Waters. Subs (all used): 18 Alyssa Courtney; 16 Gabrielle Harrison; 26 Katie Evans; - Georgia Taylor.
Try: Carr (60); **Goals:** Smith 0/1.
Sin bin: Mannion (76) - fighting.
SAINTS: 1 Beri Salihi; 20 Phoebe Hook; 4 Erin Stott; 3 Luci McColm; 5 Leah Burke; 6 Zoe Harris; 7 Faye Gaskin; 8 Vicky Whitfield; 9 Tara Jones; 10 Chantelle Crowl; 11 Paige Travis; 22 Megan Williams; 13 Jodie Cunningham. Subs (all used): 14 Naomi Williams; 16 Darcy Stott; 19 Katie Mottershead; 24 Georgia Sutherland.
Tries: Gaskin (5), E Stott (12), Whitfield (18), Cunningham (27), D Stott (30), Hook (34, 38), Salihi (43), Burke (50, 70), M Williams (54); **Goals:** Gaskin 7/11.
Half-time: 0-40.

HUDDERSFIELD GIANTS 0 WIGAN WARRIORS 102

GIANTS: 1 Amy Bennett; 2 Hannah Goddard; 3 Ana Da Silva; 29 Grace Arrowsmith; 30 Dani McGifford; 6 Frankie Townend; 7 Sam Hulme; 8 Paige Webster; 9 Bethan Oates; 16 Emma Wilkinson; 11 Jess Harrap; 12 Kacy Haley; 13 Katy Fisher. Subs (all used): 20 Georgia Hampshaw; 24 Ellie Thompson; 26 Ruby Tyson; 27 Gracie Hobbs.
WARRIORS: 1 Grace Banks; 34 Emma Welsford; 23 Kaitlin Hilton; 3 Anna Davies; 5 Ellise Derbyshire; 32 Isabel Rowe; 7 Emma Knowles; 10 Holly Speakman; 9 Abbie Singleton; 8 Alice Fisher; 35 Rease Casey; 12 Mary Coleman; 14 Rachel Thompson. Subs (all used): 13 Vicky Molyneux; 21 Jade Gregory-Haselden; 26 Cerys Jones; 37 Jenna Foubister.
Tries: Thompson (6, 22), Davies (8, 11, 43), Coleman (14, 39, 48, 52, 78), Banks (31), Molyneux (36, 45), Casey (55), Welsford (59), Foubister (64), Hilton (67), Rowe (71); **Goals:** Knowles 15/18.
Half-time: 0-48.

Sunday 12th May 2024

WARRINGTON WOLVES 10 BARROW RAIDERS 6

WOLVES: 1 Anna Dennis; 2 Abi Johnston; 3 Nicole Barnett; 33 Albany-D Coates; 5 Rebecca Nixon; 6 Millie Bell; 7 Charlie Magraw; 8 Abby Latchford; 9 Dani Bound; 10 Grace Burnett; 11 Katie May Williams; 12 Sammi Simpson; 20 Helena Turner. Subs (all used): 14 Jasmine Wilson; 16 Megan Condliffe; 17 Louise Fellingham; 34 Lucy Johnson.
Tries: Bound (21), Johnston (61); **Goals:** Magraw 1/2.
RAIDERS: 5 Sam Norman; 2 Emma Hutchinson; 4 Claire Hutchinson; 1 Michelle Larkin; 24 Alice Rush; 6 Demi Fisher; 7 Jodie Litherland; 14 Mia Dobson; 9 Beth Lindsay; 10 Jodie Morley; 15 Leah Cottier; 12 Vanessa Temple; 11 Emily Stirzaker. Subs: 8 Kelly Friend; 13 Kerrie-Ann Smith; 16 Hannah Sherlock; 17 Charlotte Todhunter (not used).
Try: Temple (58); **Goals:** Litherland 1/1.
Half-time: 6-0.

YORK VALKYRIE 10 LEEDS RHINOS 16

VALKYRIE: 1 Tara Jane Stanley; 2 Eboni Partington; 3 Tamzin Renouf; 26 Carrie Roberts; 4 Emma Kershaw; 6 Sade Rihari; 7 Liv Gale; 8 Liv Wood; 5 Georgie Hetherington; 20 Alex Stimpson; 11 Lacey Owen; 12 Savannah Andrade; 10 Jas Bell. Subs: 13 Rhiannion Marshall; 18 Jess Sharp; 28 Remi Wilton; 29 Izzy Brennan (not used).
Tries: Partington (13), Owen (74); **Goals:** Stanley 1/2.
RHINOS: 1 Ruby Enright; 2 Liv Whitehead; 3 Caitlin Beevers; 4 Amy Hardcastle; 21 Evie Cousins; 6 Hanna Butcher; 7 Caitlin Casey; 19 Grace Field; 9 Keara Bennett; 8 Izzy Northrop; 11 Shona Hoyle; 17 Lucy Murray; 13 Bethan Dainton. Subs (all used): 2 Sophie Robinson; 8 Zoe Hornby; 12 Bella Sykes; 25 Ella Donnelly.
Tries: Hoyle (26), Beevers (57); **Goals:** Enright 4/4.
Half-time: 6-8.

ROUND 4

Friday 24th May 2024

ST HELENS 12 LEEDS RHINOS 6

SAINTS: 1 Beri Salihi; 20 Phoebe Hook; 4 Erin Stott; 3 Luci McColm; 5 Leah Burke; 6 Zoe Harris; 7 Faye Gaskin; 8 Vicky Whitfield; 9 Tara Jones; 10 Chantelle Crowl; 11 Paige Travis; 12 Emily Rudge; 13 Jodie Cunningham. Subs (all used): 14 Naomi Williams; 16 Darcy Stott; 17 Pip Birchall; 19 Katie Mottershead.
Try: Gaskin (34); **Goals:** Gaskin 4/4.
RHINOS: 18 Liv Whitehead; 21 Evie Cousins; 4 Amy Hardcastle; 3 Caitlin Beevers; 2 Sophie Robinson; 6 Hanna Butcher; 7 Caitlin Casey; 19 Grace Field; 9 Keara Bennett; 10 Izzy Northrop; 12 Bella Sykes; 17 Lucy Murray; 25 Ella Donnelly. Subs: 8 Zoe Hornby; 14 Tara Moxon (not used); 16 Beth Lockwood; 22 Jenna Greening.
Try: Bennett (55); **Goals:** Bennett 1/1.
Half-time: 10-0.

Saturday 25th May 2024

WARRINGTON WOLVES 4 WIGAN WARRIORS 40

WOLVES: 1 Anna Dennis; 2 Abi Johnston; 3 Nicole Barnett; 12 Sammi Simpson; 5 Rebecca Nixon; 6 Millie Bell; 7 Charlie Magraw; 8 Abby Latchford; 9 Dani Bound; 10 Grace Burnett; 11 Katie May Williams; 35 Emily Baggaley; 13 Emily Downs. Subs (all used): 14 Jasmine Wilson; 20 Helena Turner; 16 Megan Condliffe; 34 Lucy Johnson.
Try: Simpson (58); **Goals:** Magraw 0/1.

Women's Super League 2024 - Round by Round

WARRIORS: 39 Georgia Wilson; 34 Emma Welsford; 23 Kaitlin Hilton; 3 Anna Davies; 5 Ellise Derbyshire; 32 Isabel Rowe; 7 Emma Knowles; 10 Holly Speakman; 35 Rease Casey; 8 Alice Fisher; 13 Victoria Molyneux; 12 Mary Coleman; 14 Rachel Thompson. Subs (all used): 9 Abbie Singleton; 21 Jade Gregory-Haselden; 26 Cerys Jones; 27 Bethany Hayes.
Tries: Thompson (6), Rowe (9), Coleman (19), Derbyshire (42), Davies (45, 79), Hayes (67);
Goals: Knowles 6/7.
Half-time: 0-18.

Sunday 26th May 2024

BARROW RAIDERS 22 FEATHERSTONE ROVERS 10

RAIDERS: 5 Sam Norman; 2 Emma Hutchinson; 4 Claire Hutchinson; 1 Michelle Larkin; 24 Alice Rush; 6 Demi Fisher; 7 Jodie Litherland; 14 Mia Dobson; 9 Beth Lindsay; 10 Jodie Morley; 11 Emily Stirzaker; 12 Vanessa Temple; 13 Kerrie-Ann Smith. Subs (all used): 8 Kelly Friend; 3 Leah Clough; 15 Leah Cottier; 16 Hannah Sherlock.
Tries: Larkin (10), Lindsay (33), Temple (66);
Goals: Litherland 5/5.
ROVERS: 3 Fran Copley; 22 Natalie Carr; 13 Chloe Billington; 19 Ashlea Prescott; 5 Brooke Price; 15 Chloe Smith; 7 Olivia Grace; 8 Shanelle Mannion; 9 Charley Blackburn; 10 Brogan Churm; 11 Hannah Watt; 26 Katie Evans; 1 Danielle Waters. Subs (all used): 16 Gabrielle Harrison; 17 Kirsty Duffield; 28 Shavon Craven; 4 Ella Johnson.
Tries: Watt (4), Prescott (23); **Goals:** Smith 1/2.
Sin bin: Waters (63) - high tackle.
Half-time: 14-10.

HUDDERSFIELD GIANTS 12 YORK VALKYRIE 50

GIANTS: 30 Dani McGifford; 2 Hannah Goddard; 3 Ana Da Silva; 27 Gracie Hobbs; 22 Allana Waller; 6 Frankie Townend; 26 Ruby Tyson; 8 Paige Webster; 9 Bethan Oates; 16 Emma Wilkinson; 11 Jess Harrap; 12 Kacy Haley; 13 Katy Fisher. Subs (all used): Lois Naidole; 17 Megan Preston; 20 Georgia Hampshaw; 24 Ellie Thompson.
Tries: Hobbs (52), Goddard (76); **Goals:** Townend 2/2.
VALKYRIE: 30 Sian Judd; 4 Emma Kershaw; 23 Manuqalo Komaitai; 26 Carrie Roberts; 2 Eboni Partington; 6 Sade Rihari; 21 Lucy Eastwood; 18 Jess Sharp; 28 Remi Wilton; 20 Alex Stimpson; 11 Lacey Owen; 12 Savannah Andrade; 8 Liv Wood. Subs (all used) 14 Georgia Taylor; 19 Bettie Lambert; 29 Izzy Brennan; 31 Agnes Wood.
Tries: Kershaw (12, 30, 43), Partington (20, 48), Roberts (25), Brennan (33, 70), Sharp (39), Lambert (57);
Goals: Roberts 5/9.
Half-time: 0-32.

ROUND 5

Friday 31st May 2024

ST HELENS 24 WIGAN WARRIORS 8

SAINTS: 1 Beri Salihi; 20 Phoebe Hook; 4 Erin Stott; 3 Luci McColm; 2 Rebecca Rotheram; 6 Zoe Harris; 7 Faye Gaskin; 8 Vicky Whitfield; 9 Tara Jones; 10 Chantelle Crowl; 11 Paige Travis; 12 Emily Rudge; 14 Naomi Williams. Subs (all used): 17 Pip Birchall; 19 Katie Mottershead; 21 Amy Taylor; 24 Georgia Sutherland.
Tries: McColm (36, 50), Whitfield (65), Salihi (77, 79);
Goals: Gaskin 2/6.
WARRIORS: 39 Georgia Wilson; 34 Emma Welsford; 23 Kaitlin Hilton; 3 Anna Davies; 5 Ellise Derbyshire; 32 Isabel Rowe; 7 Emma Knowles; 10 Holly Speakman; 35 Rease Casey; 8 Alice Fisher; 13 Vicky Molyneux; 12 Mary Coleman; 14 Rachel Thompson. Subs (all used): 9 Abbie Singleton; 21 Jade Gregory-Haselden; 26 Cerys Jones; 27 Bethany Hayes.
Try: Coleman (15); **Goals:** Knowles 2/2.
Half-time: 4-8.

Saturday 1st June 2024

FEATHERSTONE ROVERS 10 HUDDERSFIELD GIANTS 30

ROVERS: 3 Fran Copley; 2 Ellie Lamb; 22 Natalie Carr; 19 Ashlea Prescott; 5 Brooke Price; 6 Tally Bryer; 7 Olivia Grace; 8 Shanelle Mannion; 9 Charley Blackburn; 10 Brogan Churm; 13 Chloe Billington; 11 Hannah Watt; 1 Danielle Waters. Subs (all used): 4 Ella Johnson; 16 Gabrielle Harrison; 20 Brogan Kennedy; 26 Katie Evans.
Tries: Billington (45), Lamb (53); **Goals:** Bryer 1/2.
Sin bin: Price (63) - foul play.
GIANTS: 28 Jess Dadds; 31 Mollie Iceton; 3 Ana Da Silva; 4 Lois Naidole; 5 Amelia Brown; 6 Frankie Townend; 7 Sam Hulme; 8 Paige Webster; 9 Bethan Oates; 16 Emma Wilkinson; 11 Jess Harrap; 12 Kacy Haley; 13 Katy Fisher. Subs (all used): 17 Megan Preston; 20 Georgia Hampshaw; 24 Ellie Thompson; 27 Gracie Hobbs.
Tries: Dadds (5), Naidole (13, 68), Brown (15), Townend (35), Iceton (65); **Goals:** Townend 3/6.
Half-time: 0-22.

LEEDS RHINOS 68 BARROW RAIDERS 0

RHINOS: 18 Liv Whitehead; 14 Tara Moxon; 3 Sophie Robinson; 4 Amy Hardcastle; 21 Evie Cousins; 6 Hanna Butcher; 7 Caitlin Casey; 12 Bella Sykes; 9 Keara Bennett; 10 Izzy Northrop; 23 Elychia Watson; 17 Lucy Murray; 25 Ella Donnelly. Subs (all used) 16 Beth Lockwood; 22 Jenna Greening; 24 Beth Macmillan; 31 Grace Short.
Tries: Murray (1, 27), Cousins (5), Donnelly (7), Northrop (13, 23, 52, 74, 80), Casey (40), Sykes (56), Short (61), Macmillan (67);
Goals: Bennett 3/6, Whitehead 5/7.
RAIDERS: 5 Sam Norman; 2 Emma Hutchinson; 4 Claire Hutchinson; 11 Emily Stirzaker; 24 Alice Rush; 6 Demi Fisher; 7 Jodie Litherland; 14 Mia Dobson; 9 Beth Lindsay; 10 Jodie Morley; 3 Leah Clough; 12 Vanessa Temple; 13 Kerrie-Ann Smith. Subs: 8 Kelly Friend; 15 Leah Cottier; 20 Laura Mellen; 17 Charlotte Todhunter (not used).
Half-time: 34-0.

Sunday 2nd June 2024

YORK VALKYRIE 44 WARRINGTON WOLVES 4

VALKYRIE: 4 Emma Kershaw; 19 Bettie Lambert; 11 Lacey Owen; 23 Manuqalo Komaitai; 2 Eboni Partington; 6 Sade Rihari; 21 Lucy Eastwood; 18 Jess Sharp; 28 Remi Wilton; 8 Liv Wood; 14 Georgia Taylor; 12 Savannah Andrade; 10 Jas Bell. Subs (all used): 16 Daisy Sanderson; 20 Alex Stimpson; 24 Ellie Hendry; 29 Izzy Brennan.
Tries: Owen (4), Partington (16, 24, 31), Lambert (40), Stimpson (45), L Wood (65), Komaitai (71, 76);
Goals: Bell 0/2, Brennan 3/6, Hendry 1/1.
WOLVES: 5 Rebecca Nixon; 2 Abi Johnston; 3 Nicole Barnett; 12 Sammi Simpson; 33 Albany-D Coates; 6 Millie Bell; 7 Charlie Magraw; 8 Abby Latchford; 14 Jasmine Wilson; 10 Grace Burnett; 11 Katie May Williams; 35 Emily Baggaley; 20 Helena Turner. Subs (all used): 17 Louise Fellingham; 16 Megan Condliffe; 26 Ellie Jelves; 34 Lucy Johnson.
Try: Magraw (14); **Goals:** Magraw 0/1.
Half-time: 22-4.

ROUND 6

Saturday 15th June 2024

BARROW RAIDERS 6 WIGAN WARRIORS 46

RAIDERS: 5 Sam Norman; 2 Emma Hutchinson; 4 Claire Hutchinson; 24 Alice Rush; 17 Charlotte Todhunter; 6 Demi Fisher; 7 Jodie Literland; 14 Mia Dobson; 9 Beth Lindsay; 10 Jodie Morley; 3 Leah Clough; 12 Vanessa Temple; 11 Emily Stirzaker. Subs (all used): 8 Kelly Friend; 15 Leah Cottier; 20 Laura Mellen; 22 Maddie Neale.
Try: Morley (58); **Goals:** Litherland 1/1.
WARRIORS: 1 Grace Banks; 3 Anna Davies; 39 Georgia Wilson; 4 Molly Jones; 5 Ellise Derbyshire; 32 Isabel Rowe; 7 Emma Knowles; 10 Holly Speakman; 35 Rease Casey; 8 Alice Fisher; 26 Cerys Jones; 12 Mary Coleman; 14 Rachel Thompson. Subs (all used): 9 Abbie Singleton; 17 Bethany Hayes; 21 Jade Gregory-Haselden; 23 Kaitlin Hilton.
Tries: Davies (16, 32, 40, 67, 71) Banks (18), Singleton (42), Hilton (63), Casey (76); **Goals:** Rowe 5/9.
Half-time: 0-22.

FEATHERSTONE ROVERS 10 WARRINGTON WOLVES 16

ROVERS: 3 Fran Copley; 2 Ellie Lamb; 13 Chloe Billington; 4 Ella Johnson; 5 Brooke Price; 6 Tally Bryer; 7 Olivia Grace; 8 Shanelle Mannion; 9 Charley Blackburn; 16 Gabrielle Harrison; 14 Kacey Davies; 11 Hannah Watt; 1 Danielle Waters. Subs (all used): 15 Chloe Smith; 18 Alyssa Courtney; 20 Brogan Kennedy; 31 Emillie Holmes.
Tries: Johnson (8), Lamb (29); **Goals:** Bryer 1/2.
WOLVES: 7 Charlie Magraw; 33 Albany-D Coates; 3 Nicole Barnett; 12 Sammi Simpson; 21 Lauren Ellison; 6 Millie Bell; 17 Louise Fellingham; 8 Abby Latchford; 14 Jasmine Wilson; 10 Grace Burnett; 11 Katie May Williams; 35 Emily Baggaley; 13 Emily Downs. Subs (all used): 16 Megan Condliffe; 20 Helena Turner; 26 Ellie Jelves; 34 Lucy Johnson.
Tries: Burnett (18), Baggaley (50), Simpson (68);
Goals: Magraw 2/3.
Half-time: 10-4.

Sunday 16th June 2024

HUDDERSFIELD GIANTS 4 LEEDS RHINOS 42

GIANTS: 28 Jess Dadds; 31 Mollie Iceton; 3 Ana Da Silva; 4 Lois Naidole; 5 Amelia Brown; 6 Frankie Townend; 7 Sam Hulme; 11 Jess Harrap; 9 Bethan Oates; 16 Emma Wilkinson; 12 Kacy Haley; 13 Katy Fisher; 24 Ellie Thompson. Subs (all used): 10 Ellie Oldroyd; 17 Meg Preston; 20 Georgia Hampshaw; 27 Gracie Hobbs.
Try: Brown (29); **Goals:** Townend 0/1.

RHINOS: 18 Liv Whitehead; 2 Sophie Robinson; 4 Amy Hardcastle; 3 Caitlin Beevers; 14 Tara Moxon; 6 Hanna Butcher; 22 Jenna Greening; 8 Zoe Hornby; 9 Keara Bennett; 25 Ella Donnelly; 17 Lucy Murray; 11 Shona Hoyle; 12 Bella Sykes. Subs (all used): 10 Izzy Northrop; 23 Elychia Watson; 24 Beth Macmillan; 31 Grace Short.
Tries: Donnelly (5), Hardcastle (7), Hornby (17), Northrop (27, 76), Robinson (33), Watson (57), Hoyle (58);
Goals: Bennett 4/7, Butcher 1/1.
Half-time: 4-26.

ROUND 7

Saturday 6th July 2024

FEATHERSTONE ROVERS 0 WIGAN WARRIORS 50

ROVERS: 3 Fran Copley; 2 Ellie Lamb; 19 Ashlea Prescott; 4 Ella Johnson; 22 Natalie Carr; 6 Tally Bryer; 7 Olivia Grace; 16 Gabrielle Harrison; 9 Charley Blackburn; 10 Brogan Churm; 11 Hannah Watt; 13 Chloe Billington; 1 Danielle Waters. Subs (all used): 15 Chloe Smith; 18 Alyssa Courtney; 26 Katie Evans; 31 Emillie Holmes.
WARRIORS: 1 Grace Banks; 3 Anna Davies; 14 Rachel Thompson; 39 Georgia Wilson; 5 Ellise Derbyshire; 32 Isabel Rowe; 37 Jenna Foubister; 10 Holly Speakman; 35 Rease Casey; 8 Alice Fisher; 11 Eva Hunter; 13 Vicky Molyneux; 12 Mary Coleman. Subs (all used): 21 Jade Gregory-Haselden; 23 Kaitlin Hilton; 26 Cerys Jones; 33 Carys Marsh.
Tries: E Hunter (5), Wilson (14, 60), Thompson (21), Banks (28, 72), Foubister (47), Casey (65), Davies (79);
Goals: Rowe 7/9.
Half-time: 0-22.

LEEDS RHINOS 6 ST HELENS 16

RHINOS: 1 Ruby Enright; 21 Evie Cousins; 4 Amy Hardcastle; 3 Caitlin Beevers; 2 Sophie Robinson; 6 Hanna Butcher; 7 Caitlin Casey; 10 Izzy Northrop; 9 Keara Bennett; 12 Bella Sykes; 17 Lucy Murray; 11 Shona Hoyle; 13 Bethan Dainton. Subs: 8 Zoe Hornby; 18 Liv Whitehead (not used); 22 Jenna Greening; 25 Ella Donnelly.
Try: Cousins (75); **Goals:** Enright 1/2.
SAINTS: 1 Beri Salihi; 2 Rebecca Rotheram; 3 Luci McColm; 4 Erin Stott; 30 Rachael Woosey; 6 Zoe Harris; 7 Faye Gaskin; 8 Vicky Whitfield; 9 Tara Jones; 10 Chantelle Crowl; 11 Paige Travis; 12 Emily Rudge; 13 Jodie Cunningham. Subs (all used): 14 Naomi Williams; 16 Darcy Stott; 19 Katie Mottershead; 22 Megan Williams.
Tries: Jones (11), Gaskin (66), Harris (79);
Goals: Gaskin 1/2, Harris 1/1.
Half-time: 2-4.

Sunday 7th July 2024

WARRINGTON WOLVES 10 HUDDERSFIELD GIANTS 32

WOLVES: 7 Charlie Magraw; 2 Abi Johnston; 33 Albany-D Coates; 12 Sammi Simpson; 21 Lauren Ellison; 6 Millie Bell; 17 Louise Fellingham; 8 Abby Latchford; 26 Ellie Jelves; 10 Grace Burnett; 11 Katie May Williams; 35 Emily Baggaley; 13 Emily Downs. Subs (all used): 14 Jasmine Wilson; 16 Megan Condliffe; 20 Helena Turner; 34 Lucy Johnson.
Tries: Simpson (7), Baggaley (48); **Goals:** Magraw 1/2.
GIANTS: 1 Amy Bennett; 31 Mollie Iceton; 3 Ana Da Silva; 4 Lois Naidole; 5 Amelia Brown; 6 Frankie Townend; 7 Sam Hulme; 11 Jess Harrap; 9 Bethan Oates; 16 Emma Wilkinson; 12 Kacy Haley; 13 Katy Fisher; 24 Ellie Thompson. Subs (all used): 8 Paige Webster; 17 Megan Preston; 20 Georgia Hampshaw; 25 Chloe Fairbank.
Tries: Naidole (20, 60), Brown (52, 75), Iceton (58, 62);
Goals: Thompson 4/4, Townend 0/1.
Half-time: 4-6.

YORK VALKYRIE 44 BARROW RAIDERS 0

VALKYRIE: 1 Tara Jane Stanley; 2 Eboni Partington; 34 Evie Sexton; 14 Georgia Taylor; 4 Emma Kershaw; 6 Sade Rihari; 28 Remi Wilton; 8 Liv Wood; 5 Georgie Hetherington; 10 Jas Bell; 7 Liv Gale; 12 Savannah Andrade; 33 Megan Pakulis. Subs (all used) 18 Jess Sharp; 20 Alex Stimpson; 21 Lucy Eastwood; 22 Eva Izumi.
Tries: Gale (13), Andrade (19), Kershaw (25, 67, 74), Hetherington (28), Partington (47), L Wood (58);
Goals: Stanley 6/9.
RAIDERS: 5 Sam Norman; 2 Emma Hutchinson; 4 Claire Hutchinson; 24 Alice Rush; 1 Michelle Larkin; 6 Demi Fisher; 7 Jodie Litherland; 14 Mia Dobson; 9 Beth Lindsay; 10 Jodie Morley; 3 Leah Clough; 12 Vanessa Temple; 11 Emily Stirzaker. Subs: 8 Kelly Friend; 13 Kerrie-Ann Smith; 15 Leah Cottier (not used); 32 Nicole Stewart.
Half-time: 20-0.

Women's Super League 2024 - Round by Round

ROUND 8

Friday 12th July 2024

WIGAN WARRIORS 12 ST HELENS 16

WARRIORS: 1 Grace Banks; 3 Anna Davies; 39 Georgia Wilson; 4 Molly Jones; 5 Ellise Derbyshire; 32 Isabel Rowe; 37 Jenna Foubister; 10 Holly Speakman; 35 Rease Casey; 8 Alice Fisher; 12 Mary Coleman; 13 Vicky Molyneux; 14 Rachel Thompson. Subs (all used): 11 Eva Hunter; 21 Jade Gregory-Haselden; 26 Cerys Jones; 33 Carys Marsh.
Tries: Derbyshire (50), E Hunter (79); **Goals:** Rowe 2/2.
SAINTS: 1 Beri Salihi; 4 Erin Stott; 3 Luci McColm; 11 Paige Travis; 30 Rachael Woosey; 6 Zoe Harris; 7 Faye Gaskin; 8 Vicky Whitfield; 9 Tara Jones; 10 Chantelle Crowl; 22 Megan Williams; 12 Emily Rudge; 13 Jodie Cunningham. Subs (all used): 14 Naomi Williams; 16 Katie Mottershead; 17 Pip Birchall; 19 Darcy Stott.
Tries: Woosey (8, 23), Whitfield (72); **Goals:** Gaskin 2/3.
Half-time: 0-10.

Sunday 14th July 2024

HUDDERSFIELD GIANTS 14 BARROW RAIDERS 26

GIANTS: 1 Amy Bennett; 31 Mollie Iceton; 3 Ana Da Silve; 4 Lois Naidole; 5 Amelia Brown; 6 Frankie Townend; 7 Sam Hulme; 11 Jess Harrap; 17 Megan Preston; 16 Emma Wilkinson; 12 Kacy Haley; 13 Katy Fisher; 24 Ellie Thompson. Subs (all used): 8 Paige Webster; 20 Georgia Hampshaw; 26 Ruby Tyson; 27 Gracie Hobbs.
Tries: Brown (30, 61), Iceton (42); **Goals:** Thompson 1/3.
RAIDERS: 12 Vanessa Temple; 2 Emma Hutchinson; 4 Claire Hutchinson; 1 Michelle Larkin; 5 Sam Norman; 6 Demi Fisher; 7 Jodie Litherland; 14 Mia Dobson; 9 Beth Lindsay; 10 Jodie Morley; 3 Leah Clough; 11 Emily Stirzaker; 13 Kerrie-Ann Smith. Subs (all used): 8 Kelly Friend; 15 Leah Cottier; 20 Laura Mellen; 32 Nicole Stewart.
Tries: Morley (6), E Hutchinson (23), Temple (38, 46), C Hutchinson (65);
Goals: Litherland 3/3, Stewart 0/1, Lindsay 0/1.
Half-time: 4-18.

WARRINGTON WOLVES 4 LEEDS RHINOS 50

WOLVES: 19 Grace Wray; 2 Abi Johnston; - Hannah Roberts; 33 Albany-D Coates; 5 Rebecca Nixon; 17 Louise Fellingham; 7 Charlie Magraw; 8 Abby Latchford; 26 Ellie Jelves; 10 Grace Burnett; 11 Katie May Williams; 13 Emily Downs; 20 Helena Turner. Subs (all used) 14 Jasmine Wilson; 16 Megan Condliffe; 29 Georgia Bogg; 34 Lucy Johnson.
Try: Turner (74); **Goals:** Magraw 0/1.
RHINOS: 18 Liv Whitehead; 21 Evie Cousins; 4 Amy Hardcastle; 3 Caitlin Beevers; 2 Sophie Robinson; 6 Hanna Butcher; 7 Caitlin Casey; 12 Bella Sykes; 9 Keara Bennett; 11 Shona Hoyle; 22 Jenna Greening; 23 Elychia Watson; 13 Bethan Dainton. Subs (all used): 25 Ella Donnelly; 30 Tilly Jae Brown; 31 Grace Short; 33 Ruby Bruce.
Tries: Beevers (5, 41, 52, 56), Hardcastle (7, 65, 80), Cousins (19), Hoyle (25), Bruce (28);
Goals: Bennett 3/4, Whitehead 2/6.
Half-time: 0-26.

YORK VALKYRIE 62 FEATHERSTONE ROVERS 0

VALKYRIE: 1 Tara Jane Stanley; 2 Eboni Partington; 34 Evie Sexton; 22 Eva Izumi; 4 Emma Kershaw; 6 Sade Rihari; 21 Lucy Eastwood; 8 Liv Wood; 5 Georgie Hetherington; 10 Jas Bell; 7 Liv Gale; 12 Savannah Andrade; 33 Megan Pakulis. Subs (all used): 14 Georgia Taylor; 18 Jess Sharp; 29 Izzy Brennan; 35 Mahault Pommier.
Tries: Stanley (4), L Wood (8), Andrade (17, 34, 50), Izumi (40), Kershaw (43, 58), Partington (54, 69), Pakulis (63); **Goals:** Stanley 9/11.
ROVERS: 3 Fran Copley; 2 Ellie Lamb; 13 Chloe Billington; 1 Danielle Waters; 28 Shavon Craven; 6 Tally Bryer; 7 Olivia Grace; 16 Gabrielle Harrison; 18 Alyssa Courtney; 10 Brogan Churm; 11 Hannah Watt; 26 Katie Evans; 9 Charley Blackburn. Subs (all used): 15 Chloe Smith; 19 Ashlea Prescott; 20 Brogan Kennedy; 33 Zoe Teece.
Half-time: 28-0.

ROUND 9

Saturday 20th July 2024

ST HELENS 82 WARRINGTON WOLVES 0

SAINTS: 6 Zoe Harris; 30 Rachael Woosey; 4 Erin Stott; 13 Jodie Cunningham; 25 Dani McGifford; 21 Amy Taylor; 7 Faye Gaskin; 8 Vicky Whitfield; 9 Tara Jones; 16 Darcy Stott; 11 Paige Travis; 12 Emily Rudge; 10 Chantelle Crowl. Subs (all used): 17 Pip Birchall; 19 Katie Mottershead; 22 Megan Williams; 28 Erin McDonald.
Tries: Woosey (3, 44, 70), Jones (10, 12), Cunningham (17, 38), McGifford (20, 28, 50), Birchall (34), McDonald (41), Travis (48), Harris (53), Mottershead (60); **Goals:** Gaskin 11/15.
WOLVES: 19 Grace Wray; 2 Abi Johnston; - Hannah Roberts; 33 Albany D-Coates; 5 Rebecca Nixon; 17 Louise Fellingham; 7 Charlie Magraw; 8 Abby Latchford; 26 Ellie Jelves; 18 Grace Burnett; 11 Katie May Williams; 35 Emily Baggaley; 20 Helena Turner. Subs (all used): 14 Jasmine Wilson; 16 Megan Condliffe; 29 Georgia Bogg; 34 Lucy Johnson.
Half-time: 42-0.

Sunday 21st July 2024

BARROW RAIDERS 10 LEEDS RHINOS 28

RAIDERS: 12 Vanessa Temple; 17 Charlotte Todhunter; 4 Claire Hutchinson; 2 Emma Hutchinson; 5 Sam Norman; 6 Demi Fisher; 7 Jodie Litherland; 14 Mia Dobson; 9 Beth Lindsay; 10 Jodie Morley; 3 Leah Clough; 11 Emily Stirzaker; 13 Kerrie-Ann Smith. Subs (all used): 8 Kelly Friend; 15 Leah Cottier; 20 Laura Mellen; 32 Nicole Stewart.
Tries: Norman (9), Temple (55); **Goals:** Litherland 1/2.
RHINOS: 21 Evie Cousins; 18 Liv Whitehead; 4 Amy Hardcastle; 3 Caitlin Beevers; 2 Sophie Robinson; 6 Hanna Butcher; 7 Caitlin Casey; 11 Shona Hoyle; 9 Keara Bennett; 10 Izzy Northrop; 17 Lucy Murray; 22 Jenna Greening; 12 Bella Sykes. Subs (all used): 25 Ella Donnelly; 24 Beth Macmillan; 31 Grace Short; 33 Ruby Bruce.
Tries: Hardcastle (1), Whitehead (11, 20, 22, 28), Cousins (74); **Goals:** Bennett 2/6.
Half-time: 4-22.

HUDDERSFIELD GIANTS 44 FEATHERSTONE ROVERS 8

GIANTS: 5 Amelia Brown; 31 Mollie Iceton; 3 Ana Da Silva; 4 Lois Naidole; 22 Allana Waller; 6 Frankie Townend; 7 Sam Hulme; 11 Jess Harrap; 17 Meg Preston; 16 Emma Wilkinson; 20 Georgia Hampshaw; 12 Kacy Haley; 13 Katy Fisher. Subs (all used): 8 Paige Webster; 25 Chloe Fairbank; 26 Ruby Tyson; 27 Gracie Hobbs.
Tries: Townend (13, 70), Brown (18, 65, 75), Iceton (24), Webster (43), Hulme (73); **Goals:** Townend 6/8.
ROVERS: 3 Fran Copley; 28 Shavon Craven; 1 Danielle Waters; 13 Chloe Billington; 22 Natalie Carr; 6 Tally Bryer; 15 Chloe Smith; 16 Gabrielle Harrison; 18 Alyssa Courtney; 10 Brogan Churm; 11 Hannah Watt; 26 Katie Evans; 9 Charley Blackburn. Subs (all used): 19 Ash Prescott; 31 Emillie Holmes; 33 Zoe Teece; 37 Deanna Limbert.
Tries: Smith (50), Evans (80); **Goals:** Bryer 0/2.
Half-time: 18-0.

YORK VALKYRIE 10 WIGAN WARRIORS 18

VALKYRIE: 1 Tara Jane Stanley; 2 Eboni Partington; 7 Liv Gale; 22 Eva Izumi; 4 Emma Kershaw; 6 Sade Rihari; 35 Mahault Pommier; 8 Liv Wood; 5 Georgie Hetherington; 18 Jess Sharp; 11 Lacey Owen; 12 Savannah Andrade; 33 Megan Pakulis. Subs (all used): 10 Jas Bell; 21 Lucy Eastwood; 34 Evie Sexton; 36 Lisa Parker.
Tries: Partington (21, 78); **Goals:** Stanley 1/2.
WARRIORS: 1 Grace Banks; 3 Anna Davies; 39 Georgia Wilson; 4 Molly Jones; 5 Ellise Derbyshire; 32 Isabel Rowe; 37 Jenna Foubister; 10 Holly Speakman; 35 Rease Casey; 12 Mary Coleman; 11 Eva Hunter; 13 Vicky Molyneux; 14 Rachel Thompson. Subs: 21 Jade Gregory-Haselden; 26 Cerys Jones; 27 Bethany Hayes (not used); 33 Carys Marsh.
Tries: E Hunter (3, 30), Derbyshire (15), Foubister (43);
Goals: Rowe 1/4.
Half-time: 6-14.

ROUND 6

Wednesday 31st July 2024

ST HELENS 10 YORK VALKYRIE 6

SAINTS: 1 Beri Salihi; 30 Rachael Woosey; 4 Erin Stott; 3 Luci McColm; 5 Leah Burke; 6 Zoe Harris; 7 Faye Gaskin; 8 Vicky Whitfield; 9 Tara Jones; 10 Chantelle Crowl; 11 Paige Travis; 12 Emily Rudge; 13 Jodie Cunningham. Subs (all used): 14 Naomi Williams; 16 Darcy Stott; 17 Pip Birchall; 19 Katie Mottershead.
Tries: Burke (12, 15); **Goals:** Gaskin 1/3.
VALKYRIE: 1 Tara Jane Stanley; 4 Emma Kershaw; 26 Carrie Roberts; 11 Lacey Owen; 2 Eboni Partington; 28 Remi Wilton; 21 Lucy Eastwood; 18 Jess Sharp; 5 Georgie Hetherington; 10 Jas Bell; 14 Georgia Taylor; 12 Savannah Andrade; 33 Megan Pakulis. Subs: 15 Kelsey Gentles; 31 Agnes Wood; 35 Mahault Pommier (not used); 36 Lisa Parker.
Try Wilton (32); **Goals:** Stanley 1/1.
Half-time: 10-6.

ROUND 10

Sunday 4th August 2024

BARROW RAIDERS 6 ST HELENS 64

RAIDERS: 12 Vanessa Temple; 17 Charlotte Todhunter; 4 Claire Hutchinson; 11 Emily Stirzaker; 5 Sam Norman; 6 Demi Fisher; 7 Jodie Litherland; 14 Mia Dobson; 15 Leah Cottier; 10 Jodie Morley; 3 Leah Clough; 8 Kelly Friend; 13 Kerrie-Ann Smith. Subs: 9 Beth Lindsay; 19 Amy Sunderland (not used); 20 Laura Mellen; 32 Nicole Stewart.
Try: Norman (61); **Goals:** Litherland 1/2.
SAINTS: 1 Beri Salihi; 30 Rachael Woosey; 4 Erin Stott; 3 Luci McColm; 5 Leah Burke; 6 Zoe Harris; 7 Faye Gaskin; 8 Vicky Whitfield; 9 Tara Jones; 10 Chantelle Crowl; 11 Paige Travis; 22 Megan Williams; 13 Jodie Cunningham. Subs (all used): 14 Naomi Williams; 16 Darcy Stott; 17 Pip Birchall; 19 Katie Mottershead.
Tries: Cunningham (1), Burke (7), M Williams (16, 54), Harris (19), Gaskin (23, 47), Travis (25), Woosey (31, 43, 69), Whitfield (77); **Goals:** Gaskin 8/12.
Half-time: 2-38.

FEATHERSTONE ROVERS 6 LEEDS RHINOS 68

ROVERS: 2 Ellie Lamb; 28 Shavon Craven; 3 Fran Copley; 4 Ella Johnson; 22 Natalie Carr; 1 Danielle Waters; 6 Tally Bryer; 16 Gabrielle Harrison; 9 Charley Blackburn; 37 Deanna Limbert; 11 Hannah Watt; 26 Katie Evans; 33 Zoe Teece. Subs (all used): 18 Alyssa Courtney; 19 Ashlea Prescott; 20 Brogan Kennedy; 31 Emillie Holmes.
Try: Blackburn (18); **Goals:** Bryer 1/1.
RHINOS: 21 Evie Cousins; 18 Liv Whitehead; 22 Jenna Greening; 2 Sophie Robinson; 34 Ebony Stead; 6 Hanna Butcher; 7 Caitlin Casey; 10 Izzy Northrop; 9 Keara Bennett; 12 Bella Sykes; 17 Lucy Murray; 31 Grace Short; 13 Bethan Dainton. Subs (all used): 18 Grace Field; 20 Kaiya Glynn; 25 Ella Donnelly; 35 Ruby Walker.
Tries: Whitehead (3, 30, 49), Stead (7, 14), Dainton (10, 71), Cousins (24), Short (33), Sykes (52), Walker (58, 68), Bennett (79);
Goals: Bennett 5/8, Walker 3/5.
Half-time: 6-38.

WARRINGTON WOLVES 0 YORK VALKYRIE 61

WOLVES: 3 Nicole Barnett; 2 Abi Johnston; 29 Georgia Bogg; 33 Albany-D Coates; 21 Lauren Ellison; 18 Sinead Doria; 17 Louise Fellingham; 8 Abby Latchford; 26 Ellie Jelves; 10 Grace Burnett; 11 Katie May Williams; 35 Emily Baggaley; 13 Emily Downs. Subs (all used): 14 Jasmine Wilson; 16 Megan Condliffe; 20 Helena Turner; 34 Lucy Johnson.
VALKYRIE: 1 Tara Jane Stanley; 2 Eboni Partington; 36 Lisa Parker; 26 Carrie Roberts; 4 Emma Kershaw; 28 Remi Wilton; 21 Lucy Eastwood; 8 Liv Wood; 5 Georgie Hetherington; 10 Jas Bell; 11 Lacey Owen; 12 Savannah Andrade; 33 Megan Pakulis. Subs (all used): 15 Kelsey Gentles; 18 Jess Sharp; 31 Agnes Wood; 35 Mahault Pommier.
Tries: Kershaw (1, 39, 62), Wilton (4), Andrade (12), Partington (23, 43, 51, 76), Hetherington (55), Stanley (66), Roberts (79); **Goals:** Stanley 6/12;
Field goal: Stanley (80).
Half-time: 0-26.

WIGAN WARRIORS 70 HUDDERSFIELD GIANTS 0

WARRIORS: 1 Grace Banks; 3 Anna Davies; 14 Rachel Thompson; 23 Kaitlin Hilton; 5 Ellise Derbyshire; 32 Isabel Rowe; 37 Jenna Foubister; 10 Holly Speakman; 35 Rease Casey; 8 Alice Fisher; 11 Eva Hunter; 12 Mary Coleman; 26 Cerys Jones. Subs (all used): 21 Jade Gregory-Haselden; 27 Bethany Hayes; 33 Carys Marsh; 40 Ruby Hunter.
Tries: Casey (3), Davies (10, 46), Hilton (18), Coleman (22), Banks (28, 38), Foubister (33, 51), R Hunter (43), Derbyshire (47, 79); **Goals:** Rowe 11/12.
GIANTS: 5 Amelia Brown; 2 Hannah Goddard; 3 Ana Da Silva; 29 Tara Moxon; 22 Allana Waller; 15 Becky Grady; 7 Sam Hulme; 12 Kacy Haley; 17 Megan Preston; 16 Emma Wilkinson; 4 Lois Naidole; 13 Katy Fisher; 24 Ellie Thompson. Subs (all used): 6 Frankie Townend; 20 Georgia Hampshaw; 26 Ruby Tyson; 27 Gracie Hobbs.
Half-time: 40-0.

ROUND 11

Friday 9th August 2024

LEEDS RHINOS 28 WIGAN WARRIORS 8

RHINOS: 21 Evie Cousins; 34 Ebony Stead; 2 Sophie Robinson; 4 Amy Hardcastle; 18 Liv Whitehead; 6 Hanna Butcher; 7 Caitlin Casey; 12 Bella Sykes; 9 Keara Bennett; 10 Izzy Northrop; 17 Lucy Murray; 22 Jenna Greening; 13 Bethan Dainton. Subs (all used): 11 Shona Hoyle; 19 Grace Field; 25 Ella Donnelly; 31 Grace Short.

Women's Super League 2024 - Round by Round

Tries: Dainton (19, 22), Stead (48), Sykes (60), Hoyle (72, 79); **Goals:** Bennett 2/4, Whitehead 0/2.
WARRIORS: 1 Grace Banks; 3 Anna Davies; 39 Georgia Wilson; 4 Molly Jones; 5 Ellise Derbyshire; 32 Isabel Rowe; 37 Jenna Foubister; 10 Holly Speakman; 33 Carys Marsh; 8 Alice Fisher; 11 Eva Hunter; 12 Mary Coleman; 14 Rachel Thompson. Subs (all used): 9 Abbie Singleton; 21 Jade Greory-Haselden; 23 Kaitlin Hilton; 26 Cerys Jones.
Tries: Davies (28), Wilson (45); **Goals:** Rowe 0/1.
Half-time: 10-4.

Saturday 10th August 2024

BARROW RAIDERS 32 WARRINGTON WOLVES 14

RAIDERS: 12 Vanessa Temple; 19 Amy Sunderland; 4 Claire Hutchinson; 1 Michelle Larkin; 5 Sam Norman; 6 Demi Fisher; 7 Jodie Litherland; 14 Mia Dobson; 9 Beth Lindsay; 10 Jodie Morley; 3 Leah Clough; 11 Emily Stirzaker; 13 Kerrie-Ann Smith. Subs (all used): 8 Kelly Friend; 15 Leah Cottier; 20 Laura Mellen; 32 Nicole Stewart.
Tries: Norman (11, 24), Fisher (20), Temple (53, 73), Stirzaker (77); **Goals:** Litherland 4/6.
WOLVES: 3 Nicole Barnett; 2 Abi Johnston; 17 Louise Fellingham; 33 Albany-D Coates; 21 Lauren Ellison; 6 Millie Bell; 18 Sinead Doria; 8 Abby Latchford; 26 Ellie Jelves; 10 Grace Burnett; 11 Katie May Williams; 35 Emily Baggaley; 13 Emily Downs. Subs (all used): 14 Jasmine Wilson; 16 Megan Condliffe; 20 Helena Turner; 34 Lucy Johnson.
Tries: Johnston (4, 36) Barnett (40); **Goals:** Doria 1/3.
Half-time: 16-14.

ST HELENS 56 FEATHERSTONE ROVERS 6

SAINTS: 2 Rebecca Rotheram; 30 Rachael Woosey; 29 Grace Arrowsmith; 5 Leah Burke; 25 Dani McGifford; 21 Amy Taylor; 7 Faye Gaskin; 10 Chantelle Crowl; 19 Katie Mottershead; 17 Pip Birchall; 12 Emily Rudge; 22 Megan Williams; 13 Jodie Cunningham. Subs (all used): 9 Tara Jones; 14 Naomi Williams; 18 Alyx Bridge; 28 Erin McDonald.
Tries: Birchall (2), McGifford (16, 25, 30), Cunningham (39), Burke (58, 61, 73, 79), Mottershead (65, 69); **Goals:** Gaskin 4/6, Taylor 2/5.
ROVERS: 11 Hannah Watt; 19 Ashlea Prescott; - Lacey Sefton-Appleyard; 26 Katie Evans; 28 Shavon Craven; 1 Danielle Waters; 10 Brogan Churm; 17 Kirsty Duffield; 9 Charley Blackburn; 37 Deanna Limbert; 16 Gabrielle Harrison; 30 Maddison Rainey; 20 Brogan Kennedy. Subs (all used, only three named): 18 Alyssa Courtney; 31 Emillie Holmes; - Sophia Liu.
Try: Churm (21); **Goals:** Waters 1/1.
Half-time: 28-6.

Sunday 11th August 2024

YORK VALKYRIE 48 HUDDERSFIELD GIANTS 10

VALKYRIE: 1 Tara Jane Stanley; 2 Eboni Partington; 36 Lisa Parker; 26 Carrie Roberts; 4 Emma Kershaw; 35 Mahault Pommier; 21 Lucy Eastwood; 8 Liv Wood; 5 Georgie Hetherington; 10 Jas Bell; 14 Georgia Taylor; 12 Savannah Andrade; 33 Megan Pakulis. Subs (all used): 3 Tamzin Renouf; 15 Kelsey Gentles; 18 Jess Sharp; 32 Lauren Exley.
Tries: Partington (11, 63), L Wood (14), Stanley (19, 30), Roberts (38), Pakulis (41), Kershaw (50), Renouf (57);
Goals: Stanley 6/9.
GIANTS: 5 Amelia Brown; 31 Mollie Iceton; 3 Ana Da Silva; 29 Tara Moxon; 2 Hannah Goddard; 6 Frankie Townend; 7 Sam Hulme; 8 Paige Webster; 17 Megan Preston; 16 Emma Wilkinson; 4 Lois Naidole; 27 Gracie Hobbs; 24 Ellie Thompson. Subs (all used): 15 Becky Grady; 19 Leah Schofield; 25 Chloe Fairbank; 30 Freya Whitehead.
Tries: Brown (25), Fairbank (77); **Goals:** Thompson 1/2.
Half-time: 26-4.

ROUND 12

Sunday 1st September 2024

FEATHERSTONE ROVERS 16 BARROW RAIDERS 28

ROVERS: 1 Danielle Waters; 2 Ellie Lamb; 3 Fran Copley; 19 Ashlea Prescott; 22 Natalie Carr; 6 Tally Bryer; 7 Liv Grace; 20 Brogan Kennedy; 9 Charley Blackburn; 11 Hannah Watt; 13 Chloe Billington; 26 Katie Evans; 10 Brogan Churm. Subs (all used): 4 Ella Johnson; 17 Kirsty Duffield; 18 Alyssa Courtney; 31 Emillie Holmes.
Tries: Churm (64), Evans (74), Bryer (77); **Goals:** Bryer 2/3.
RAIDERS: 12 Vanessa Temple; 1 Michelle Larkin; 4 Claire Hutchinson; 15 Leah Cottier; 5 Sam Norman; 6 Demi Fisher; 7 Jodie Litherland; 14 Mia Dobson; 9 Beth Lindsay; 10 Jodie Morley; 3 Leah Clough; 11 Emily Stirzaker; 32 Nicole Stewart. Subs: 8 Kelly Friend; 13 Kerrie-Ann Smith; 20 Laura Mellen (not used); 22 Maddie Neale.
Tries: Temple (10, 52), Cottier (16), Stewart (27), Stirzaker (70); **Goals:** Stewart 4/5.
Half-time: 0-18.

HUDDERSFIELD GIANTS 8 ST HELENS 40

GIANTS: 5 Amelia Brown, 31 Mollie Iceton, 3 Ana Da Silva, 24 Ellie Thompson, 2 Hannah Goddard, 15 Becky Grady, 7 Sam Hulme, 16 Emma Wilkinson, 17 Megan Preston, 27 Gracie Hobbs, 20 Georgia Hampshaw, 12 Kacy Haley, 9 Bethan Oates. Subs (all used): 6 Frankie Townend, 19 Leah Schofield, 25 Chloe Fairbank, 26 Ruby Tyson.
Tries: Brown (32), Iceton (55); **Goals:** Townend 0/2.
SAINTS: 1 Beri Salihi, 25 Dani McGifford, 4 Erin Stott, 30 Rachael Woosey, 5 Leah Burke, 6 Zoe Harris, 21 Amy Taylor, 8 Vicky Whitfield, 9 Tara Jones, 10 Chantelle Crowl, 22 Megan Williams, 11 Paige Travis, 13 Jodie Cunningham. Subs (all used): 14 Naomi Williams, 16 Darcy Stott, 19 Katie Mottershead, 28 Erin McDonald.
Tries: Burke (2, 16, 24, 28), McGifford (10, 49, 77), M Williams (63); **Goals:** Taylor 4/8.
Half-time: 4-24.

LEEDS RHINOS 6 YORK VALKYRIE 32

RHINOS: 21 Evie Cousins; 34 Ebony Stead; 2 Sophie Robinson; 4 Amy Hardcastle; 18 Liv Whitehead; 6 Hanna Butcher; 7 Caitlin Casey; 12 Bella Sykes; 9 Keara Bennett; 19 Grace Field; 17 Lucy Murray; 31 Grace Short; 13 Bethan Dainton. Subs (all used): 10 Izzy Northrop; 20 Kaiya Glynn; 25 Ella Donnelly; 33 Ruby Bruce.
Try: Cousins (28); **Goals:** Bennett 1/1.
VALKYRIE: 1 Tara Jane Stanley; 4 Emma Kershaw; 22 Eva Izumi; 36 Lisa Parker; 2 Eboni Partington; 6 Sade Rihari; 3 Tamzin Renouf; 8 Liv Wood; 5 Georgie Hetherington; 10 Jas Bell; 11 Lacey Owen; 12 Savannah Andrade; 33 Megan Pakulis. Subs (all used): 13 Rhiannion Marshall; 15 Kelsey Gentles; 21 Lucy Eastwood; 29 Izzy Brennan.
Tries: Pakulis (9), L Wood (20), Marshall (38), Owen (45), Andrade (57); **Goals:** Stanley 6/7.
Half-time: 6-22.

WIGAN WARRIORS 82 WARRINGTON WOLVES 0

WARRIORS: 1 Grace Banks; 3 Anna Davies; 39 Georgia Wilson; 4 Molly Jones; 5 Ellise Derbyshire; 32 Isabel Rowe; 7 Emma Knowles; 10 Holly Speakman; 33 Carys Marsh; 12 Mary Coleman; 11 Eva Hunter; 13 Vicky Molyneux; 14 Rachel Thompson. Subs (all used): 21 Jade Gregory-Hasleden; 23 Kaitlin Hilton; 26 Cerys Jones; 40 Ruby Hunter.
Tries: M Jones (4), Davies (8, 38, 45), Rowe (15, 49), Derbyshire (24), Banks (20, 27, 60), E Hunter (32, 77), R Hunter (41, 72), C Jones (57); **Goals:** Rowe 11/15.
WOLVES: 3 Nicole Barnett; 21 Lauren Ellison; 33 Albany-D Coates; 36 Chelsea Newton; 5 Rebecca Nixon; 6 Millie Bell; 17 Louise Fellingham; 20 Helena Turner; 25 Olivia Webb; 10 Grace Burnett; 11 Katie May Williams; 29 Georgia Bogg; 26 Ellie Jelves. Subs (all used): 16 Megan Condliffe; 24 Olivia Hill; - Talicia Blythe; - Imogen Roberts.
Half-time: 42-0.

ROUND 13

Saturday 7th September 2024

WARRINGTON WOLVES 0 ST HELENS 98

WOLVES: 5 Rebecca Nixon; 2 Abi Johnston; 17 Louise Fellingham; 4 Nicole Barnett; 33 Albany-D Coates; 6 Millie Bell; 7 Charlie Magraw; 20 Helena Turner; 26 Ellie Jelves; 18 Grace Burnett; 11 Katie May Williams; 35 Emily Baggaley; 12 Sammi Simpson. Subs (all used): 16 Megan Condliffe; 24 Olivia Hill; 25 Olivia Webb; 29 Georgia Bogg.
SAINTS: 1 Beri Salihi; 25 Dani McGifford; 4 Erin Stott; 30 Rachael Woosey; 5 Leah Burke; 6 Zoe Harris; 7 Faye Gaskin; 8 Vicky Whitfield; 9 Tara Jones; 10 Chantelle Crowl; 11 Paige Travis; 12 Emily Rudge; 13 Jodie Cunningham. Subs (all used): 16 Darcy Stott; 19 Katie Mottershead; 22 Megan Williams; 24 Georgia Sutherland.
Tries: Burke (3, 11, 38, 52), Gaskin (14), Travis (17, 30, 41), Salihi (20, 67), McGifford (24), Cunningham (46), E Stott (58, 63, 80), Jones (68), M Williams (73), Sutherland (78); **Goals:** Gaskin 13/18.
Half-time: 0-42.

Sunday 8th September 2024

BARROW RAIDERS 24 HUDDERSFIELD GIANTS 4

RAIDERS: 12 Vanessa Temple; 2 Emma Hutchinson; 4 Claire Hutchinson; 1 Michelle Larkin; 5 Sam Norman; 6 Demi Fisher; 7 Jodie Litherland; 14 Mia Dobson; 15 Leah Cottier; 10 Jodie Morley; 3 Leah Clough; 11 Emily Stirzaker; 13 Kerrie-Ann Smith. Subs: 8 Kelly Friend; 9 Beth Lindsay; 20 Laura Mellen (not used); 32 Nicole Stewart.
Tries: E Hutchinson (30, 65, 80), Norman (52), Temple (57);
Goals: Stewart 2/3.

GIANTS: 5 Amelia Brown; 31 Mollie Iceton; 3 Ana Da Silva; 24 Ellie Thompson; 2 Hannah Goddard; 6 Frankie Townend; 7 Sam Hulme; 16 Emma Wilkinson; 17 Megan Preston; 27 Gracie Hobbs; 20 Georgia Hampshaw; 12 Kacy Haley; 9 Bethan Oates. Subs (all used): 4 Lois Naidole; 11 Jess Harrap; 15 Becky Grady; 26 Ruby Tyson.
Try: Iceton (15); **Goals:** Thompson 0/1.
Half-time: 6-4.

LEEDS RHINOS 52 FEATHERSTONE ROVERS 12

RHINOS: 34 Ebony Stead; 18 Liv Whitehead; 2 Sophie Robinson; 4 Amy Hardcastle; 21 Evie Cousins; 6 Hanna Butcher; 35 Ruby Walker; 11 Shona Hoyle; 33 Ruby Bruce; 10 Izzy Northrop; 31 Grace Short; Jenna Greening; 12 Bella Sykes. Subs (all used): 7 Caitlin Casey; 9 Keara Bennett; 20 Kaiya Glynn; 25 Ella Donnelly.
Tries: Whitehead (3, 61), Northrop (12), Hardcastle (34, 51), Bennett (43), Stead (46), Walker (49), Butcher (58), Short (79);
Goals: Walker 3/5, Bennett 3/5.
ROVERS: 1 Danielle Waters; 2 Ellie Lamb; 3 Fran Copley; 19 Ashlea Prescott; 28 Shavon Craven; 10 Brogan Churm; 6 Tally Bryer; 20 Brogan Kennedy; 7 Olivia Grace; 11 Hannah Watt; 13 Chloe Billington; 26 Katie Evans; 9 Charley Blackburn. Subs (all used): 4 Ella Johnson; 18 Alyssa Courtney; 31 Emillie Holmes; 37 Deanna Limbert.
Tries: Grace (21), Copley (37); **Goals:** Bryer 2/2.
Half-time: 18-12.

WIGAN WARRIORS 12 YORK VALKYRIE 16

WARRIORS: 1 Grace Banks; 3 Anna Davies; 39 Georgia Wilson; 4 Molly Jones; 5 Ellise Derbyshire; 32 Isabel Rowe; 37 Jenna Foubister; 10 Holly Speakman; 33 Carys Marsh; 12 Mary Coleman; 11 Eva Hunter; 13 Vicky Molyneux; 14 Rachel Thompson. Subs (all used): 21 Jade Gregory-Haselden; 23 Kaitlin Hilton; 26 Cerys Jones; 40 Ruby Hunter.
Tries: M Jones (1), Banks (78); **Goals:** Rowe 2/2.
Sin bin: E Hunter (64) - dangerous challenge.
VALKYRIE: 5 Georgie Hetherington; 2 Eboni Partington; 36 Lisa Parker; 22 Eva Izumi; 4 Emma Kershaw; 6 Sade Rihari; 3 Tamzin Renouf; 8 Liv Wood; 29 Izzy Brennan; 10 Jas Bell; 11 Lacey Owen; 12 Savannah Andrade; 33 Megan Pakulis. Subs: 13 Rhiannion Marshall; 15 Kelsey Gentles; 18 Jess Sharp; 28 Remi Wilton (not used).
Tries: Parker (10), Brennan (16); **Goals:** Brennan 4/5.
Half-time: 6-12.

ROUND 14

Friday 13th September 2024

ST HELENS 68 BARROW RAIDERS 0

SAINTS: 1 Beri Salihi; 20 Phoebe Hook; 4 Erin Stott; 22 Megan Williams; 5 Leah Burke; 6 Zoe Harris; 7 Faye Gaskin; 8 Vicky Whitfield; 9 Tara Jones; 10 Chantelle Crowl; 12 Emily Rudge; 11 Paige Travis; 13 Jodie Cunningham. Subs (all used): 14 Naomi Williams; 16 Darcy Stott; 17 Pip Birchall; 19 Katie Mottershead.
Tries: Hook (3, 29), Burke (15, 35, 58), Travis (20, 38, 43), Mottershead (46), M Williams (60, 63), Harris (66), Jones (79); **Goals:** Gaskin 6/9, Harris 2/4.
RAIDERS: 12 Vanessa Temple; 2 Emma Hutchinson; 4 Claire Hutchinson; 22 Maddie Neale; 1 Michelle Larkin; 13 Kerrie-Ann Smith; 7 Jodie Litherland; 14 Mia Dobson; 15 Leah Cottier; 10 Jodie Morley; 21 Fran Harley; 11 Emily Stirzaker; 32 Nicole Stewart. Subs (all used): 3 Leah Clough; 8 Kelly Friend; 9 Beth Lindsay; 20 Laura Mellen.
Half-time: 30-0.

WIGAN WARRIORS 4 LEEDS RHINOS 24

WARRIORS: 1 Grace Banks; 3 Anna Davies; 39 Georgia Wilson; 4 Molly Jones; 5 Ellise Derbyshire; 32 Isabel Rowe; 37 Jenna Foubister; 10 Holly Speakman; 33 Carys Marsh; 12 Mary Coleman; 11 Eva Hunter; 13 Vicky Molyneux; 14 Rachel Thompson. Subs (all used): 21 Jade Gregory-Haselden; 23 Kaitlin Hilton; 26 Cerys Jones; 40 Ruby Hunter.
Try: Davies (15); **Goals:** Rowe 0/1.
RHINOS: 34 Ebony Stead; 21 Evie Cousins; 4 Amy Hardcastle; 2 Sophie Robinson; 18 Liv Whitehead; 6 Hanna Butcher; 7 Caitlin Casey; 12 Bella Sykes; 9 Keara Bennett; 25 Ella Donnelly; 17 Lucy Murray; 11 Shona Hoyle; 13 Bethan Dainton. Subs (all used): 10 Izzy Northrop; 20 Kaiya Glynn; 33 Ruby Bruce; 35 Ruby Walker.
Tries: Casey (9), Bennett (25), Robinson (39, 65), Hardcastle (56); **Goals:** Bennett 1/3, Whitehead 1/2.
Half time: 4-14.

Sunday 15th September 2024

FEATHERSTONE ROVERS 6 YORK VALKYRIE 32

ROVERS: 1 Danielle Waters; 2 Ellie Lamb; 3 Fran Copley; 19 Ashlea Prescott; 28 Shavon Craven; 10 Brogan Churm;

Women's Super League 2024 - Round by Round

York's Georgie Hetherington halted by St Helens' Emily Rudge during the Super League Grand Final

6 Tally Bryer; 37 Deanna Limbert; 7 Olivia Grace; 16 Gabrielle Harrison; 11 Hannah Watt; 26 Katie Evans; 13 Chloe Billington. Subs (all used): 4 Ella Johnson; 17 Kirsty Duffield; 18 Alyssa Courtney; 31 Emillie Holmes.
Try: Lamb (70); **Goals:** Bryer 1/1.
VALKYRIE: 21 Lucy Eastwood; 19 Bettie Lambert; 22 Eva Izumi; 36 Lisa Parker; 2 Eboni Partington; 6 Sade Rihari; 3 Tamzin Renouf; 10 Jas Bell; 28 Remi Wilton; 29 Izzy Brennan; 12 Savannah Andrade; 8 Liv Wood; 33 Megan Pakulis. Subs (all used): 5 Georgie Hetherington; 13 Rhiannion Marshall; 20 Alex Stimpson; 32 Lauren Exley.
Tries: Pakulis (3, 13), Renouf (28), Marshall (40), Brennan (47), Exley (66); **Goals:** Brennan 1/3, Marshall 3/3.
Sin bin: Izumi (23) - high tackle.
Half-time: 0-22.

HUDDERSFIELD GIANTS 36 WARRINGTON WOLVES 0

GIANTS: 5 Amelia Brown; 31 Mollie Iceton; 3 Ana Da Silva; 4 Lois Naidole; 22 Allana Waller; 6 Frankie Townend; 7 Sam Hulme; 16 Emma Wilkinson; 17 Megan Preston; 11 Jess Harrap; 24 Ellie Thompson; 12 Kacy Haley; 9 Bethan Oates. Subs (all used): 1 Amy Bennett; 20 Georgia Hampshaw; 27 Gracie Hobbs; 32 Eloise Hayward.
Tries: Brown (20, 46, 70), Naidole (28, 40), Hulme (35), Townend (56); **Goals:** Thompson 2/5, Townend 2/2.
WOLVES: 1 Anna Dennis; 2 Abi Johnston; 3 Nicole Barnett; 33 Albany D-Coates; 5 Rebecca Nixon; 6 Millie Bell; 7 Charlie Magraw; 10 Grace Burnett; 26 Ellie Jelves; 20 Helena Turner; 11 Katie May Williams; 35 Emily Baggaley; 25 Sammi Simpson. Subs (all used): 9 Dani Bound; 16 Megan Condliffe; 17 Louise Fellingham; - Lilly Day.
Half-time: 18-0.

SEMI-FINALS

Sunday 22nd September 2024

LEEDS RHINOS 10 YORK VALKYRIE 12

RHINOS: 34 Ebony Stead; 21 Evie Cousins; 4 Amy Hardcastle; 2 Sophie Robinson; 18 Liv Whitehead; 6 Hanna Butcher (C); 7 Caitlin Casey; 12 Bella Sykes; 9 Keara Bennett; 10 Izzy Northrop; 11 Shona Hoyle; 17 Lucy Murray; 13 Bethan Dainton. Subs (all used): 20 Kaiya Glynn; 25 Ella Donnelly; 23 Ruby Bruce; 35 Ruby Walker.
Tries: Stead (68), Murray (77); **Goals:** Bennett 1/2.

VALKYRIE: 5 Georgie Hetherington; 28 Remi Wilton; 26 Carrie Roberts; 36 Lisa Parker; 2 Eboni Partington; 6 Sade Rihari (C); 3 Tamzin Renouf; 10 Jas Bell; 8 Liv Wood; 29 Izzy Brennan; 11 Lacey Owen; 12 Savannah Andrade; 33 Megan Pakulis. Subs (all used): 13 Rhiannion Marshall; 15 Kelsey Gentles; 18 Jess Sharp; 32 Lauren Exley.
Tries: Gentles (20), Andrade (42); **Goals:** Marshall 2/2.
Sin bin: Renouf (74) - late tackle.
Rugby Leaguer & League Express
Women of the Match:
Rhinos: Ebony Stead; *Valkyrie:* Georgie Hetherington.
Penalty count: 4-5; **Half-time:** 0-6;
Referee: Aaryn Belafonte; **Attendance:** 954.

ST HELENS 18 WIGAN WARRIORS 4

SAINTS: 1 Beri Salihi; 20 Phoebe Hook; 4 Erin Stott; 30 Rachael Woosey; 5 Leah Burke; 6 Zoe Harris; 7 Faye Gaskin; 8 Vicky Whitfield; 9 Tara Jones; 10 Chantelle Crowl; 12 Emily Rudge; 11 Paige Travis; 13 Jodie Cunningham (C). Subs (all used): 14 Naomi Williams; 16 Darcy Stott; 19 Katie Mottershead; 22 Megan Williams.
Tries: Rudge (14), Burke (42, 72), Woosey (46);
Goals: Gaskin 1/3.
WARRIORS: 1 Grace Banks; 3 Anna Davies; 39 Georgia Wilson; 4 Molly Jones; 5 Ellise Derbyshire; 32 Isabel Rowe; 37 Jenna Foubister; 10 Holly Speakman; 33 Carys Marsh; 8 Alice Fisher; 12 Mary Coleman; 13 Vicky Molyneux (C); 14 Rachel Thompson. Subs (all used): 21 Jade Gregory-Haselden; 23 Kaitlin Hilton; 26 Cerys Jones; 34 Ruby Hunter.
Try: Foubister (18); **Goals:** Rowe 0/1.
Rugby Leaguer & League Express
Women of the Match:
Saints: Zoe Harris; *Warriors:* Isabel Rowe.
Penalty count: 3-4; **Half-time:** 6-4;
Referee: Luke Bland; **Attendance:** 1,193.

PROMOTION/RELEGATION PLAY-OFF

Sunday 6th October 2024

FEATHERSTONE ROVERS 16 LEIGH LEOPARDS 34

ROVERS: 1 Danielle Waters; 2 Ellie Lamb; 13 Chloe Billington; 3 Fran Copley; 22 Natalie Carr; 6 Tally Bryer; 7 Olivia Grace; 17 Gabrielle Harrison; 9 Charley Blackburn; 20 Brogan Kennedy; 11 Hannah Watt; 26 Katie Evans; 10 Brogan Churm (C). Subs (all used): 4 Ella Johnson; 18 Alyssa Courtney; 28 Shavon Craven; 31 Emillie Holmes.
Tries: Churm (57), Courtney (61), Billington (71);
Goals: Bryer 2/3.
LEOPARDS: 1 Hattie Dogus; 2 Toryn Blackwood; 4 Gabi Leigh; 22 Mollie Young; 32 Becky Greenfield; 6 Rhianna Burke; 7 Leah Morris; 20 Eleanor Dainty; 9 Kate Howard; 10 Mairead Quinn (C); 12 Charlotte Melvin; 16 Storm Cobain; 18 Grace Hill. Subs (all used): 8 Keira McCosh; 13 Claire Collins; 17 Claire Mullaney; 34 Lucy Johnson.
Tries: Leigh (3), Dogus (15), Young (24, 75), Cobain (34), Greenfield (50), Blackwood (67); **Goals:** Melvin 3/7.
Rugby Leaguer & League Express
Women of the Match:
Rovers: Alyssa Courtney; *Leopards:* Leah Morris.
Penalty count: 4-7; **Half-time:** 0-22;
Referee: Luke Bland; **Attendance:** 4,813.
(at Totally Wicked Stadium, St Helens).

GRAND FINAL

Sunday 6th October 2024

ST HELENS 8 YORK VALKYRIE 18

SAINTS: 1 Beri Salihi; 20 Phoebe Hook; 4 Erin Stott; 30 Rachael Woosey; 5 Leah Burke; 6 Zoe Harris; 7 Faye Gaskin; 8 Vicky Whitfield; 9 Tara Jones; 10 Chantelle Crowl; 11 Paige Travis; 12 Emily Rudge; 13 Jodie Cunningham (C). Subs (all used): 14 Naomi Williams; 19 Katie Mottershead; 16 Darcy Stott; 22 Megan Williams.
Try: Burke (11); **Goals:** Gaskin 2/3.
VALKYRIE: 5 Georgie Hetherington; 26 Carrie Roberts; 23 Manuqalo Komaitai; 36 Lisa Parker; 2 Eboni Partington; 6 Sade Rihari (C); 3 Tamzin Renouf; 8 Liv Wood; 29 Izzy Brennan; 10 Jas Bell; 11 Lacey Owen; 12 Savannah Andrade; 33 Megan Pakulis. Subs: 13 Rhiannion Marshall; 15 Kelsey Gentles; 18 Jess Sharp (not used); 28 Remi Wilton (not used).
Tries: Owen (14), Partington (44), Gentles (55);
Goals: Brennan 1/2, Marshall 2/2.
Rugby Leaguer & League Express
Women of the Match:
Saints: Paige Travis; *Valkyrie:* Georgie Hetherington.
Penalty count: 3-5; **Half-time:** 8-6;
Referee: Liam Rush; **Attendance:** 4,813.

WOMEN'S CHALLENGE CUP 2024
Round by Round

Women's Challenge Cup 2024 - Round by Round

GROUP 1

Sheffield Eagles 10 York Valkyrie 74
Featherstone Rovers 38 Sheffield Eagles 6
York Valkyrie 80 Featherstone Rovers 6

	P	W	D	L	F	A	D	Pts
York Valkyrie	2	2	0	0	154	16	138	4
Featherstone Rovers	2	1	0	1	44	86	-42	2
Sheffield Eagles	2	0	0	2	16	112	-96	0

GROUP 2

Cardiff Demons 22 Barrow Raiders 16
Salford Red Devils 0 Wigan Warriors 68
Barrow Raiders 18 Wigan Warriors 20
Cardiff Demons 58 Salford Red Devils 0
Salford Red Devils 0 Barrow Raiders 46
Wigan Warriors 44 Cardiff Demons 4

	P	W	D	L	F	A	D	Pts
Wigan Warriors	3	3	0	0	132	22	110	6
Cardiff Demons	3	2	0	1	84	50	34	4
Barrow Raiders	3	1	0	2	70	42	28	2
Salford Red Devils	3	0	0	3	0	172	-172	0

GROUP 3

Bradford Bulls 4 Warrington Wolves 52
St Helens 64 London Broncos 0
Bradford Bulls 0 St Helens 48 *(match forfeited by Bradford)*
London Broncos 6 Warrington Wolves 24
London Broncos 48 Bradford Bulls 0
Warrington Wolves 6 St Helens 58

	P	W	D	L	F	A	D	Pts
St Helens	3	3	0	0	170	6	164	6
Warrington Wolves	3	2	0	1	82	68	14	4
London Broncos	3	1	0	2	54	88	-34	2
Bradford Bulls	3	0	0	3	4	148	-144	0

GROUP 4

Huddersfield Giants 74 Hull KR 0
Leigh Leopards 4 Leeds Rhinos 52
Hull KR 0 Leeds Rhinos 90
Leigh Leopards 6 Huddersfield Giants 36
Hull KR 0 Leigh Leopards 46
Leeds Rhinos 54 Huddersfield Giants 10

	P	W	D	L	F	A	D	Pts
Leeds Rhinos	3	3	0	0	196	14	182	6
Huddersfield Giants	3	2	0	1	120	60	60	4
Leigh Leopards	3	1	0	2	56	88	-32	2
Hull KR	3	0	0	3	0	210	-210	0

QUARTER FINALS

Saturday 13th April 2024

LEEDS RHINOS 70 WARRINGTON WOLVES 10

RHINOS: 1 Ruby Enright; 21 Evie Cousins; 2 Sophie Robinson; 4 Amy Hardcastle; 18 Liv Whitehead; 6 Hanna Butcher; 7 Caitlin Casey; 19 Grace Field; 15 Jasmine Cudjoe; 10 Izzy Northrop; 17 Lucy Murray; 11 Shona Hoyle; 13 Bethan Dainton. Subs (all used): 9 Keara Bennett; 14 Tara Moxon; 20 Kaiya Glynn; 25 Ella Donnelly.
Tries: Field (2), Hardcastle (10, 77), Enright (20, 46, 71, 79), Robinson (22, 62), Cousins (29, 54), Bennett (34), Dainton (65), Moxon (74); **Goals:** Enright 7/14.
WOLVES: 5 Rebecca Nixon; 2 Abi Johnston; 3 Nicole Barnett; 20 Helena Turner; 21 Lauren Ellison; 6 Millie Bell; 7 Charlie Magraw; 22 Tina Millan; 9 Dani Bound; 10 Grace Burnett; 11 Katie May Williams; 12 Sammi Simpson; 13 Emily Downs. Subs (all used): 14 Jasmine Wilson; 16 Megan Condliffe; 23 Kim Seddon; 24 Olivia Hill.
Tries: Burnett (18), Bound (27); **Goals:** Magraw 1/2.
Half-time: 28-10.

ST HELENS 74 HUDDERSFIELD GIANTS 0

SAINTS: 1 Beri Salihi; 5 Leah Burke; 30 Rachael Woosey; 4 Erin Stott; 20 Phoebe Hook; 21 Amy Taylor; 7 Faye Gaskin; 10 Chantelle Crowl; 9 Tara Jones; 16 Darcy Stott; 18 Alyx Bridge; 11 Paige Travis; 13 Jodie Cunningham. Subs (all used): 8 Vicky Whitfield; 14 Naomi Williams; 19 Katie Mottershead; 24 Georgia Sutherland.
Tries: Burke (6, 30, 45), Woosey (35), Williams (42, 72), Travis (49), Whitfield (58), Mottershead (60), D Stott (65, 75), Crowl (78), Jones (80); **Goals:** Taylor 9/14.

Leeds' Grace Field tackles St Helens' Chantelle Crowl in the Challenge Cup Final

GIANTS: 1 Amy Bennett; 21 Lauren Waller; 3 Ana Da Silva; 22 Allana Waller; 5 Amelia Brown; 6 Frankie Townend; 7 Sam Hulme; 20 Georgia Hampshaw; 9 Bethan Oates; 16 Emma Wilkinson; 11 Jess Harrap; 12 Kacy Haley; 25 Chloe Fairbank. Subs (all used): 17 Meg Preston; 18 Grace Ramsden; 19 Beth Armstrong; 27 Gracie Hobbs.
Half-time: 20-0.

WIGAN WARRIORS 44 CARDIFF DEMONS 4

WARRIORS: 32 Isabel Rowe; 2 Cailey Miller; 3 Anna Davies; 23 Kaitlyn Hilton; 5 Ellise Derbyshire; 6 Sinead Doria; 7 Emma Knowles; 10 Holly Speakman; 9 Abbie Singleton; 8 Alice Fisher; 35 Rease Casey; 12 Mary Coleman; 14 Rachel Thompson. Subs (all used): 1 Grace Banks; 21 Jade Gregory-Haselden; 26 Cerys Jones; 28 Olivia Harborow.
Tries: Coleman (6, 70), Davies (13), Hilton (21, 49), Casey (29), Miller (42), Banks (60), Rowe (63); **Goals:** Knowles 4/9.
DEMONS: - Brittony Price; 2 Eleri Michael; 25 Chelcey Greasley; 3 Kaitlin Hubbert; 5 Zoe Heeley; 6 Shaunni Davies; 7 Rhi Parker; 16 Katie Carr; 9 Jasmine Gibbons; 8 Sara Jones; 11 Bridget Jones; 12 Charlie Mundy; 22 Amy Price. Subs (all used): 10 Lauren Aitken; 15 Ffion Jenkins; 21 Ffion Jones; 26 Kim Boaler.
Try: Michael (35); **Goals:** Davies 0/1.
Half-time: 20-4.

Sunday 14th April 2024

YORK VALKYRIE 70 FEATHERSTONE ROVERS 0

VALKYRIE: 1 Tara Jane Stanley; 2 Eboni Partington; 3 Tamzin Renouf; 26 Carrie Roberts; 4 Emma Kershaw; 6 Sade Rihari; 21 Lucy Eastwood; 8 Liv Wood; 5 Georgie Hetherington; 20 Alex Stimpson; 11 Lacey Owen; 12 Savannah Andrade; 13 Rhiannon Marshall. Subs (all used): 7 Liv Gale; 10 Jas Bell; 16 Daisy Sanderson; 18 Jess Sharp.
Tries: L Wood (2), Roberts (8), Partington (15, 21), Owen (25, 65), Kershaw (29), Sharp (35), Renouf (38), Hetherington (42, 69), Stanley (75), Marshall (78); **Goals:** Stanley 9/13.
ROVERS: 1 Danielle Waters; 2 Ellie Lamb; 19 Ashlea Prescott; 4 Ella Johnson; 2 Natalie Carr; 6 Tally Bryer; 7 Olivia Grace; 8 Shanelle Mannion; 9 Charley Blackburn; 10 Brogan Churm; 11 Hannah Watt; 14 Kacey Davies; 13 Chloe Billington. Subs (all used): 15 Chloe Smith; 16 Gabrielle Harrison; 18 Alyssa Courtney; 20 Brogan Kennedy.
Half-time: 44-0.

SEMI-FINALS

Saturday 18th May 2024

ST HELENS 32 YORK VALKYRIE 2

SAINTS: 1 Beri Salihi; 20 Phoebe Hook; 4 Erin Stott; 3 Luci McColm; 5 Leah Burke; 6 Zoe Harris; 7 Faye Gaskin; 8 Vicky Whitfield; 9 Tara Jones; 10 Chantelle Crowl; 11 Paige Travis; 12 Emily Rudge; 13 Jodie Cunningham (C). Subs (all used): 14 Naomi Williams; 16 Darcy Stott; 19 Katie Mottershead; 24 Georgia Sutherland.
Tries: Burke (30), D Stott (42), Rudge (55), Hook (63, 75), Sutherland (78); **Goals:** Gaskin 4/7.
VALKYRIE: 5 Georgie Hetherington; 4 Emma Kershaw; 26 Carrie Roberts; 3 Tamzin Renouf; 2 Eboni Partington; 6 Sade Rihari (C); 21 Lucy Eastwood; 8 Liv Wood; 28 Remi Wilton; 20 Alex Stimpson; 11 Lacey Owen; 12 Savannah Andrade; 10 Jas Bell. Subs (all used): 13 Rhiannion Marshall; 15 Kelsey Gentles; 16 Daisy Sanderson; 18 Jess Sharp.
Goals: Marshall 1/1.
Rugby Leaguer & League Express Women of the Match:
Saints: Jodie Cunningham; *Valkyrie:* Georgie Hetherington.
Penalty count: 7-6; **Half-time:** 6-0;
Referee: Aaryn Belafonte; **Attendance:** 11,163
(at Eco-Power Stadium, Doncaster)

Sunday 19th May 2024

LEEDS RHINOS 34 WIGAN WARRIORS 20

RHINOS: 1 Ruby Enright; 21 Evie Cousins; 4 Amy Hardcastle; 3 Caitlin Beevers; 18 Liv Whitehead; 6 Hanna Butcher (C); 7 Caitlin Casey; 19 Grace Field; 9 Keara Bennett; 10 Izzy Northrop; 17 Lucy Murray; 12 Bella Sykes; 13 Bethan Dainton. Subs (all used): 2 Sophie Robinson; 8 Zoe Hornby; 22 Jenna Greening; 25 Ella Donnelly.
Tries: Enright (2, 50), Beevers (21), Hornby (37), Butcher (45), Murray (54), Bennett (72); **Goals:** Enright 3/7.
WARRIORS: 1 Grace Banks; 34 Emma Welsford; 23 Kaitlin Hilton; 3 Anna Davies; 5 Ellise Derbyshire; 32 Isabel Rowe; 7 Emma Knowles; 10 Holly Speakman; 35 Rease Casey; 8 Alice Fisher; 13 Vicky Molyneux (C); 12 Mary Coleman; 14 Rachel Thompson. Subs (all used): 9 Abbie Singleton; 21 Jade Gregory-Haselden; 26 Cerys Jones; 37 Jenna Foubister.
Tries: Molyneux (11), Banks (32), Gregory-Haselden (42); **Goals:** Knowles 4/4.
Rugby Leaguer & League Express Women of the Match:
Rhinos: Ruby Enright; *Warriors:* Mary Coleman.
Penalty count: 4-5; **Half-time:** 14-14;
Referee: Adam Williams; **Attendance:** 9,253
(at Totally Wicked Stadium, St Helens).

FINAL

Saturday 8th June 2024

LEEDS RHINOS 0 ST HELENS 22

RHINOS: 1 Ruby Enright; 21 Evie Cousins; 4 Amy Hardcastle; 3 Caitlin Beevers; 18 Liv Whitehead; 6 Hanna Butcher (C); 7 Caitlin Casey; 19 Grace Field; 9 Keara Bennett; 10 Izzy Northrop; 17 Lucy Murray; 11 Shona Hoyle; 12 Bella Sykes; 13 Bethan Dainton; 25 Ella Donnelly.
SAINTS: 1 Beri Salihi; 20 Phoebe Hook; 4 Erin Stott; 3 Luci McColm; 5 Leah Burke; 6 Zoe Harris; 7 Faye Gaskin; 8 Vicky Whitfield; 9 Tara Jones; 10 Chantelle Crowl; 11 Paige Travis; 12 Emily Rudge; 13 Jodie Cunningham (C). Subs (all used): 14 Naomi Williams; 16 Darcy Stott; 19 Katie Mottershead; 24 Georgia Sutherland.
Tries: Gaskin (25), Hook (30), McColm (45), Crowl (70); **Goals:** Gaskin 3/4.
Rugby Leaguer & League Express Women of the Match:
Rhinos: Lucy Murray; *Saints:* Faye Gaskin.
Penalty count: 1-4; **Half-time:** 0-10;
Referee: Aaron Moore; **Attendance:** 64,845
(at Wembley Stadium).

2024 SEASON
Stats round-up

2024 Season - Stats round-up

LEADING SCORERS

CHAMPIONSHIP (Regular season & play-offs)

TRIES

1	Derrell Olpherts	Wakefield Trinity	26
2	Max Jowitt	Wakefield Trinity	23
3	Paul Ulberg	Toulouse Olympique	21
4	Lachlan Walmsley	Wakefield Trinity	20
5	Connor Wynne	Featherstone Rovers	19
6	Joe Burton	Batley Bulldogs	18
7	Joe Brown	York Knights	17
8	Kieran Gill	Bradford Bulls	16
	Matty Dawson-Jones	Sheffield Eagles	16
	Maxime Stefani	Toulouse Olympique	16

GOALS

1	Max Jowitt	Wakefield Trinity	146
2	Jordan Lilley	Bradford Bulls	108
3	Cory Aston	Sheffield Eagles	88
4	Tom Gilmore	Widnes Vikings	84
5	Jake Shorrocks	Toulouse Olympique	83
6	Louis Jouffret	Halifax Panthers	66
7	Connor Robinson	Doncaster	65
8	Ryan Shaw	Barrow Raiders	55
9	Josh Woods	Batley Bulldogs	54
10	Ben Reynolds	Featherstone Rovers	48

POINTS

#	Player	Team	T	G	FG	Pts
1	Max Jowitt	Wakefield Trinity	23	146	0	384
2	Jordan Lilley	Bradford Bulls	5	108	5	241
3	Tom Gilmore	Widnes Vikings	5	84	5	193
4	Cory Aston	Sheffield Eagles	4	88	0	192
5	Jake Shorrocks	Toulouse Olympique	3	83	0	178
6	Louis Jouffret	Halifax Panthers	8	66	0	164
7	Connor Robinson	Doncaster	5	65	1	151
8	Ryan Shaw	Barrow Raiders	7	55	0	138
9	Ben Reynolds	Featherstone Rovers	7	48	0	124
10	Josh Woods	Batley Bulldogs	1	54	3	115

LEAGUE ONE (Regular season & play-offs)

TRIES

1	Cian Tyrer	Oldham/Workington Town	30
2	Luke Forber	Rochdale Hornets	23
3	Jude Ferreira	Hunslet	21
4	Billy Walkley	Keighley Cougars	20
5	Jack Render	Hunslet	19
6	Ellis Robson	Keighley Cougars	17
7	Phoenix Laulu-Togaga'e	Oldham	15
	Lewis Else	Rochdale Hornets	15
9	Jordan Turner	Oldham	14
10	Cameron Brown	Cornwall	13
	Junior Sa'u	Keighley Cougars	13
	Mo Agoro	Oldham	13

GOALS

1	Jack Miller	Keighley Cougars	96
2	Matty Beharrell	Hunslet	88
3	Martyn Ridyard	Rochdale Hornets	62
4	Carl Forber	Workington Town	51
5	Jamie Ellis	Oldham	45
6	Dave Hewitt	Midlands Hurricanes	44
	Jake Sweeting	Midlands Hurricanes	44
8	Cameron Brown	Cornwall	41
	Mackenzie Harman	Rochdale Hornets/Newcastle Thunder	41
10	Kieran Dixon	Oldham	39

POINTS

#	Player	Team	T	G	FG	Pts
1	Jack Miller	Keighley Cougars	3	96	2	206
2	Matty Beharrell	Hunslet	2	88	2	186
3	Cian Tyrer	Oldham/Workington Town	30	12	0	144
4	Cameron Brown	Cornwall	13	41	0	134
5	Martyn Ridyard	Rochdale Hornets	1	62	1	129
6	Carl Forber	Workington Town	4	51	0	118
7	Kieran Dixon	Oldham	9	39	0	114
8	Jake Sweeting	Midlands Hurricanes	5	44	0	108
9	Dave Hewitt	Midlands Hurricanes	2	44	0	96
10	Jamie Ellis	Oldham	1	45	0	94

1895 CUP

TRIES

1	Lachlan Walmsley	Wakefield Trinity	5
	Will Dagger	York Knights	5
3	Gareth Gale	Featherstone Rovers	4
	Matty Marsh	Sheffield Eagles	4
	Renouf Atoni	Wakefield Trinity	4
	Romain Franco	Wakefield Trinity	4
	Josh Griffin	Wakefield Trinity	4
	Jermaine McGillvary	Wakefield Trinity	4
	Connor Bailey	York Knights	4
	AJ Towse	York Knights	4

GOALS

1	Max Jowitt	Wakefield Trinity	28
2	Cory Aston	Sheffield Eagles	18
	Will Dagger	York Knights	18
4	Jordan Lilley	Bradford Bulls	14
5	Mason Lino	Wakefield Trinity	13

POINTS

#	Player	Team	T	G	FG	Pts
1	Max Jowitt	Wakefield Trinity	1	28	0	60
2	Will Dagger	York Knights	5	18	0	56
3	Mason Lino	Wakefield Trinity	3	13	0	38
4	Jordan Lilley	Bradford Bulls	2	14	1	37
5	Cory Aston	Sheffield Eagles	0	18	0	36

2024 Season - Stats round-up

LEADING SCORERS

SUPER LEAGUE *(Regular season & play-offs)*

TRIES

1	Liam Marshall	Wigan Warriors	29
2	Matty Ashton	Warrington Wolves	27
3	Mikey Lewis	Hull KR	19
4	Josh Charnley	Leigh Leopards	18
	Bevan French	Wigan Warriors	18
6	Matt Dufty	Warrington Wolves	17
7	Peta Hiku	Hull KR	15
8	Innes Senior	Castleford Tigers	14
	Joe Burgess	Hull KR	14
	Ryan Hall	Hull KR	14
	Ash Handley	Leeds Rhinos	14
	Tommy Makinson	St Helens	14

GOALS

1	Marc Sneyd	Salford Red Devils	98
2	Rhyse Martin	Leeds Rhinos	87
3	Adam Keighran	Wigan Warriors	79
4	Mikey Lewis	Hull KR	72
	Arthur Mourgue	Catalans Dragons	72
6	Josh Thewlis	Warrington Wolves	68
7	Mark Percival	St Helens	58
8	Rowan Milnes	Castleford Tigers	51
	Matt Moylan	Leigh Leopards	51
10	Oliver Leyland	London Broncos	40

GOALS PERCENTAGE

			G	Att	%
1	Marc Sneyd	Salford Red Devils	98	111	88.28
2	Stefan Ratchford	Warrington Wolves	39	45	86.66
3	Adam Keighran	Wigan Warriors	79	93	84.94
4	Rhyse Martin	Leeds Rhinos	87	104	83.65
5	Ben Reynolds	Hull FC/Hull KR	15	18	83.33
6	Danny Richardson	Hull KR/Castleford Tigers	17	21	80.95
7	Arthur Mourgue	Catalans Dragons	72	89	80.89
8	Rowan Milnes	Castleford Tigers	51	66	77.27
9	Josh Thewlis	Warrington Wolves	68	90	75.55
10	Jon Bennison	St Helens	12	16	75.00

(10 minimum attempts to qualify)

POINTS

			T	G	FG	Pts
1	Mikey Lewis	Hull KR	19	72	0	220
2	Rhyse Martin	Leeds Rhinos	10	87	0	214
3	Marc Sneyd	Salford Red Devils	3	98	4	212
4	Adam Keighran	Wigan Warriors	8	79	0	190
5	Josh Thewlis	Warrington Wolves	12	68	0	184
6	Arthur Mourgue	Catalans Dragons	7	72	1	173
7	Mark Percival	St Helens	6	58	0	140
8	Rowan Milnes	Castleford Tigers	7	51	1	131
9	Matt Moylan	Leigh Leopards	5	51	0	122
10	Liam Marshall	Wigan Warriors	29	0	0	116

CHALLENGE CUP

TRIES

1	Manoa Wacokecoke	Featherstone Rovers	6
	Adam Swift	Huddersfield Giants	6
	Liam Marshall	Wigan Warriors	6
4	Matty Ashton	Warrington Wolves	5
	Bevan French	Wigan Warriors	5

GOALS

1	Max Jowitt	Wakefield Trinity	24
2	Louis Jouffret	Halifax Panthers	20
3	Harry Smith	Wigan Warriors	17
4	Josh Thewlis	Warrington Wolves	14
5	Cory Aston	Sheffield Eagles	13

POINTS

			T	G	FG	Pts
1	Louis Jouffret	Halifax Panthers	4	20	0	56
	Max Jowitt	Wakefield Trinity	2	24	0	56
3	Josh Thewlis	Warrington Wolves	3	14	0	40
4	Thomas Lacans	Featherstone Rovers	4	11	0	38
	Harry Smith	Wigan Warriors	1	17	0	38

NRL PREMIERSHIP *(Regular season & play-offs)*

TRIES

1	Alofiana Khan-Pereira	Gold Coast Titans	24
2	Kyle Feldt	North Queensland Cowboys	23
3	Daniel Tupou	Sydney Roosters	21
4	Dom Young	Sydney Roosters	20
5	Ronaldo Mulitalo	Cronulla Sharks	18
	Tommy Talau	Manly Sea Eagles	18
7	Deine Mariner	Brisbane Broncos	17
	Sione Katoa	Cronulla Sharks	17
	Tom Trbojevic	Manly Sea Eagles	17
	Maika Sivo	Parramatta Eels	17
	Sunia Turuva	Penrith Panthers	17
	James Tedesco	Sydney Roosters	17

GOALS

1	Nick Meaney	Melbourne Storm	106
2	Valentine Holmes	North Queensland Cowboys	101
3	Sam Walker	Sydney Roosters	88
4	Jamayne Isaako	Dolphins	87
5	Reuben Garrick	Manly Sea Eagles	81
6	Matt Burton	Canterbury Bulldogs	74
7	Zac Lomax	St George Illawarra Dragons	63
8	Nicho Hynes	Cronulla Sharks	61
9	Nathan Cleary	Penrith Panthers	50
10	Kalyn Ponga	Newcastle Knights	46

POINTS

			T	G	FG	Pts
1	Valentine Holmes	North Queensland Cowboys	16	101	0	266
2	Nick Meaney	Melbourne Storm	5	106	0	232
3	Jamayne Isaako	Dolphins	12	87	1	223
4	Sam Walker	Sydney Roosters	7	88	0	204
5	Reuben Garrick	Manly Sea Eagles	10	81	0	202
6	Matt Burton	Canterbury Bulldogs	9	74	3	187
7	Zac Lomax	St George Illawarra Dragons	15	63	0	186
8	Nicho Hynes	Cronulla Sharks	2	61	1	131
9	Nathan Cleary	Penrith Panthers	4	50	2	118
10	Clinton Gutherson	Parramatta Eels	9	38	0	112

2024 Season - Stats round-up

LEADING SCORERS

Liam Marshall

ALL COMPETITIONS

TRIES

1	Liam Marshall	Wigan Warriors	35
2	Matty Ashton	Warrington Wolves	32
3	Cian Tyrer	Oldham/Workington Town	30
4	Derrell Olpherts	Wakefield Trinity	27
	Lachlan Walmsley	Wakefield Trinity	27
6	Max Jowitt	Wakefield Trinity	26
7	Bevan French	Wigan Warriors	23
	Luke Forber	Rochdale Hornets	23
9	Joe Burton	Batley Bulldogs	22
	Jude Ferreira	Hunslet	22
	Jack Render	Hunslet	22

GOALS

1	Max Jowitt	Wakefield Trinity	198
2	Jordan Lilley	Bradford Bulls	132
3	Cory Aston	Sheffield Eagles	119
4	Jack Miller	Keighley Cougars	106
5	Marc Sneyd	Salford Red Devils	98
6	Louis Jouffret	Halifax Panthers	96
7	Tom Gilmore	Widnes Vikings	94
	Matty Beharrell	Hunslet	94
9	Rhyse Martin	Leeds Rhinos	88
10	Jake Shorrocks	Toulouse Olympique	83

POINTS

			T	G	FG	Pts
1	Max Jowitt	Wakefield Trinity	26	198	0	500
2	Jordan Lilley	Bradford Bulls	7	132	6	298
3	Cory Aston	Sheffield Eagles	4	119	0	254
4	Louis Jouffret	Halifax Panthers	13	96	0	244
5	Mikey Lewis	Hull KR	19	76	0	228
6	Jack Miller	Keighley Cougars	3	106	3	227
7	Josh Thewlis	Warrington Wolves	15	82	0	224
8	Rhyse Martin	Leeds Rhinos	10	88	0	216
9	Tom Gilmore	Widnes Vikings	5	94	5	213
10	Marc Sneyd	Salford Red Devils	3	98	4	212

FIELD GOALS

1	Jordan Lilley	Bradford Bulls	6
2	Tom Gilmore	Widnes Vikings	5
3	Marc Sneyd	Salford Red Devils	4
	Josh Woods	Batley Bulldogs	4
5	Liam Harris	York Knights	3
	Jack Miller	Keighley Cougars	3
	Brad Walker	Barrow Raiders	3

WOMEN'S SUPER LEAGUE *(Regular season & play-offs)*

TRIES

1	Leah Burke	St Helens	28
2	Anna Davies	Wigan Warriors	22
3	Eboni Partington	York Valkyrie	18
4	Emma Kershaw	York Valkyrie	17
5	Amelia Brown	Huddersfield Giants	16

GOALS

1	Faye Gaskin	St Helens	68
2	Tara Jane Stanley	York Valkyrie	42
3	Isabel Rowe	Wigan Warriors	39
4	Emma Knowles	Wigan Warriors	33
5	Keara Bennett	Leeds Rhinos	26

POINTS

			T	G	FG	Pts
1	Faye Gaskin	St Helens	6	68	0	160
2	Leah Burke	St Helens	28	0	0	112
3	Isabel Rowe	Wigan Warriors	8	39	0	110
4	Tara Jane Stanley	York Valkyrie	4	42	1	101
5	Anna Davies	Wigan Warriors	22	0	0	88

WOMEN'S CHALLENGE CUP

TRIES

1	Ruby Enright	Leeds Rhinos	10
2	Amelia Brown	Huddersfield Giants	9
3	Phoebe Hook	St Helens	8
4	Zoe Heeley	Cardiff Demons	6
	Tara Moxon	Leeds Rhinos	6
	Ellise Derbyshire	Wigan Warriors	6
	Eboni Partington	York Valkyrie	6

GOALS

1	Ruby Enright	Leeds Rhinos	33
2	Tara Jane Stanley	York Valkyrie	30
3	Emma Knowles	Wigan Warriors	23
4	Amy Taylor	St Helens	21
5	Frankie Townend	Huddersfield Giants	12

POINTS

			T	G	FG	Pts
1	Ruby Enright	Leeds Rhinos	10	33	0	106
2	Tara Jane Stanley	York Valkyrie	5	30	0	80
3	Emma Knowles	Wigan Warriors	0	23	0	46
4	Amy Taylor	St Helens	0	21	0	42
5	Amelia Brown	Huddersfield Giants	9	0	0	36

2024 Season - Stats round-up

FINAL TABLES

SUPER LEAGUE

	P	W	D	L	F	A	D	Pts
Wigan Warriors	27	22	0	5	723	338	385	44
Hull KR	27	21	0	6	719	326	393	42
Warrington Wolves	27	20	0	7	740	319	421	40
Salford Red Devils	27	16	0	11	550	547	3	32
Leigh Leopards	27	15	1	11	566	398	168	31
St Helens	27	15	0	12	596	388	208	30
Catalans Dragons	27	15	0	12	474	427	47	30
Leeds Rhinos	27	14	0	13	530	488	42	28
Huddersfield Giants	27	10	0	17	468	660	-192	20
Castleford Tigers	27	7	1	19	425	735	-310	15
Hull FC	27	3	0	24	328	894	-566	6
London Broncos	27	3	0	24	317	916	-599	6

WOMEN'S SUPER LEAGUE

	P	W	D	L	F	A	D	Pts
St Helens	14	13	0	1	620	88	532	26
Leeds Rhinos	14	11	0	3	528	122	406	22
York Valkyrie	14	11	0	3	463	118	345	22
Wigan Warriors	14	9	0	5	524	144	380	18
Barrow Raiders	14	5	0	9	172	432	-260	10
Huddersfield Giants	14	4	0	10	204	556	-352	8
Warrington Wolves	14	3	0	11	96	669	-573	6
Featherstone Rovers	14	0	0	14	128	606	-478	0

CHAMPIONSHIP

	P	W	D	L	F	A	D	Pts
Wakefield Trinity	26	25	0	1	1010	262	748	50
Toulouse Olympique	26	18	1	7	782	384	398	37
Bradford Bulls	26	16	2	8	682	387	295	34
York Knights	26	15	0	11	655	473	182	30
Widnes Vikings	26	14	1	11	551	475	76	29
Featherstone Rovers	26	14	0	12	622	500	122	28
Sheffield Eagles	26	14	0	12	626	526	100	28
Doncaster	26	12	1	13	498	619	-121	25
Halifax Panthers	26	11	0	15	509	650	-141	22
Batley Bulldogs	26	11	0	15	422	591	-169	22
Barrow Raiders	26	9	1	16	458	758	-300	19
Swinton Lions	26	9	0	17	466	678	-212	18
Whitehaven	26	8	2	16	451	854	-403	18
Dewsbury Rams	26	2	0	24	344	919	-575	4

LEAGUE ONE

	P	W	D	L	F	A	D	Pts
Oldham	20	19	0	1	885	144	741	38
Keighley Cougars	20	15	1	4	694	352	342	31
Rochdale Hornets	20	13	1	6	687	432	255	27
Hunslet	20	13	0	7	522	534	-12	26
Midlands Hurricanes	20	9	0	11	566	424	142	18
Workington Town	20	9	0	11	504	549	-45	18
North Wales Crusaders	20	8	0	12	464	472	-8	16
Cornwall	20	3	0	17	306	787	-481	6
Newcastle Thunder	20	0	0	20	190	1124	-934	0

WHEELCHAIR SUPER LEAGUE

	P	W	D	L	F	A	D	Pts
Leeds Rhinos	8	8	0	0	398	300	98	16
Halifax Panthers	8	4	1	3	428	346	82	9
London Roosters	8	3	0	5	324	316	8	6
Wigan Warriors	8	3	0	5	280	316	-36	6
Hull FC	8	1	1	6	230	382	-152	3

NRL PREMIERSHIP

	P	W	D	L	B	F	A	Pts
Melbourne Storm	24	19	0	5	3	692	449	44
Penrith Panthers	24	17	0	7	3	580	394	40
Sydney Roosters	24	16	0	8	3	738	463	38
Cronulla Sharks	24	16	0	8	3	653	431	38
North Queensland Cowboys	24	15	0	9	3	657	568	36
Canterbury Bulldogs	24	14	0	10	3	529	433	34
Manly Sea Eagles	24	13	1	10	3	634	521	33
Newcastle Knights	24	12	0	12	3	470	510	30
Canberra Raiders	24	12	0	12	3	474	601	30
Dolphins	24	11	0	13	3	577	578	28
St George Illawarra Dragons	24	11	0	13	3	508	634	28
Brisbane Broncos	24	10	0	14	3	537	607	26
New Zealand Warriors	24	9	1	14	3	512	574	25
Gold Coast Titans	24	8	0	16	3	488	656	22
Parramatta Eels	24	7	0	17	3	561	716	20
South Sydney Rabbitohs	24	7	0	17	3	494	682	20
Wests Tigers	24	6	0	18	3	463	750	18

ATTENDANCES

SUPER LEAGUE CLUBS - AVERAGES

	2024 Avg	2023 Avg	Diff
Wigan Warriors	15,310	13,616	+1,694
Leeds Rhinos	14,035	13,805	+230
St Helens	12,237	12,856	-619
Hull FC	11,282	12,355	-1,073
Warrington Wolves	10,210	10,894	-684
Hull KR	10,041	8,808	+1,233
Catalans Dragons	9,174	9,239	-65
Leigh Leopards	8,337	7,254	+1,083
Castleford Tigers	7,940	7,186	+754
Salford Red Devils	5,090	5,293	-203
Huddersfield Giants	4,531	5,244	-713
London Broncos	3,178	1,019	+2,159
		(Championship)	
2024 Average	9,280		
2023 Average		9,239	
Difference	+41		